W9-CEZ-040

THE HEATH INTRODUCTION TO DRAMA

THE HEATH INTRODUCTION TO
⟿ DRAMA

Third Edition

with a Preface on Drama and Introductory Notes by

Jordan Y. Miller
University of Rhode Island

D. C. HEATH AND COMPANY

Lexington, Massachusetts / Toronto

Cover Illustration: Mary Cassatt, *At the Opera*, Charles
Henry Hayden Fund, Courtesy, Museum of Fine
Arts, Boston.

Published simultaneously in Canada.

Printed in the United States of America.

International Standard Book Number: 0–669–14812–1

Library of Congress Catalog Card Number: 87–80582

ACKNOWLEDGMENTS

⌒ CONTENTS

⌇ FOREWORD

As in the past, the *Preface—On Drama,* introductory notes, and *Select Bibliography* are the work of Jordan Y. Miller. In this third edition Professor Miller has also written extensive explanatory footnotes for one of the new plays, Congreve's *The Way of the World.* Also new are Brecht's *The Good Woman of Setzuan* and Shaw's complete *Preface to Major Barbara.*

In response to many requests, reference line numbers have been added to *Oedipus Rex, Lysistrata, Hamlet,* and *The Misanthrope.* For this and other helpful suggestions, we are grateful to many devoted users of *The Heath Introduction to Drama.* Special thanks are owed the following teachers for their questionnaire responses: Janice Anderson, Scott Community College; Merle Fifield, Ball State University; Thomas Gay, Youngstown State University; Thomas Holbrook, Youngstown State University; James Hunt, University of Illinois; Maude M. Jennings, Ball State University; William Lindblad, Ball State University; and T. Patrick Lynch, S.J., St. Peter's College.

"And now to patient judgments we appeal"

H. HOLTON JOHNSON, SENIOR EDITOR

D. C. Heath and Company

THE HEATH INTRODUCTION TO DRAMA

✑ PREFACE—ON DRAMA

Concerning the Drama, the Theatre, and the Play

To Perform Is to Entertain

Ever since Og returned to the cave and, for the benefit of Zog and his friends, elaborated on the size of the saber-tooth tiger that got away, the human animal has delighted in putting on a show. While we may not possess Og's complete script, we do know from such surviving evidence as Europe's cave paintings and various artifacts of primitive masks, wigs, and costumes that men and women since prehistory have possessed a keen sense of the beauties and emotional stimulation of man and beast in motion. The essence of theatre has been with us in tribal dance or religious ecstasy from far back in human time, whether we have shaken the rattle and sung the songs ourselves, or have witnessed the proceedings in awed fear or happy delight in the give and take which is the fundamental nature of the art.

Everything that follows in this volume is a direct descendant of the show that Og probably put on for Zog. The fact that, in a comparative instant of history, we have developed the ability to put it all down in the scratchings we call written language and have come to possess thereby what we call a "body of dramatic literature" does

1

not alter the basic primitive formula. Every major culture has, at one time or another, possessed a highly developed tradition of theatre. The survival of this tradition in the form of the written word, in considerable quantity in Western culture, less so in others, has provided unique insights into those cultures available in no other form of art.

The reading of "dramatic literature" is a dismally poor alternative to the theatrical experience itself. There is no way to substitute for the interrelationship that exists between those who *do* and those who *watch*. The only reason Og told Zog about that tiger was to create a reaction in his listener that he hoped would approach his own emotion. The drama, that is, the story, be it literal truth or fantastic embellishment as Og may have related it, simultaneously demands that the interpreter bring it to life as theatre and that the audience react appreciatively. In that manner the full impact of the art has been manifested. But for all practical purposes we have no alternative to reading the written words, strictly second best as that choice may be. Doing so can be made most rewarding by a constant awareness of the Og-Zog relationship. Every written piece in this book was designed first and foremost for *performance*.

Furthermore, every work contained here is a great piece of *entertainment*. Whatever sophisticated social or religious theme, whatever erudite subject, propagandistic motive, or moral didacticism that may be apparent in any single play does not alter the fact that to witness a theatrical performance in a Greek amphitheatre holding 15,000 spectators or in a tiny converted night club with room for fewer than 200 is to be entertained. This does not imply mere passing amusement, an aspect of theatre valid enough in its own right. It does, however, imply that we who watch expect to experience some form of emotional pleasure. We can be excited, mystified, intrigued, challenged, frightened, or horrified, and we can be driven to tears or laughter, concurrently, consecutively, or entirely independently, but one thing is sure: we will have enjoyed the experience that has been offered to us, for we have, in short, been entertained.

How It Is Said

The drama, the theatre, and the play are so closely related in their broad connotations as to be, on occasion, interchangeable. For our purposes here, however, they will be separately identified in order to establish a sharper distinction among their meanings. Each element demands a different appreciation, and each performs a distinct function. We shall restrict the term *drama* to the written form, the creation of the *dramatist,*[1] who starts on square one with a clean sheet of paper and typewriter—or these days probably word processor—at the ready. But unlike the creative artistry of other writers, it does not end on the paper. Once the pages are filled, the novelist, the poet, or the essayist has, to all intents and purposes, concluded his effort. The dramatist, on the other hand, has just begun his ordeal. Before it's all over there looms ahead the intervention of all elements of *theatre* and the transformation of the entire effort into the production of the *play*. The trip will not be smooth.

Regardless of the eventual metamorphosis in the theatre, what appears in performance is essentially the artistic creation of the dramatist, who comes up with the *idea* in the first place. The source of the idea may be religion and its faith and morals, whence all Western drama originated, or it may be a sociological problem, a philosophical question, a political viewpoint, or, indeed, almost anything that strikes the artist's fancy. Closely related to idea is *theme,* the fabric that holds the idea together. Idea and theme can sometimes be very close to the same thing, but generally speaking the development of an idea is planned along specific thematic lines such as the family, the state, and various human relationships, or the more abstract concepts of cowardice and heroism, good and evil, right and wrong.

The *type* of the drama remains the prerogative of the dramatist, and this choice now begins to place him in a somewhat different creative area from other writers. For the novelist or short story writer there are choices as well, whether to be serious or comic, to create pure fiction, re-create history, and so on. The poet, too, chooses whether to write a lyric, a sonnet, a narrative epic, or something in between. But the dramatist is creating for that special medium, the theatre, and while he is not necessarily prevented from developing along any lines he may wish, he is restrained by certain limitations of the medium and its long traditions which, as we shall see, convey specialized artistic meaning to such terms as tragedy or comedy and which, of course, assume a number of physical restrictions. Then, when the dramatist makes his choice of *style,* the manner in which his creation is to be staged, he finds himself with far more problems than his other literary colleagues. While they, of course, may ma-

---

[1] If you prefer the term *playwright*—maker of plays—well and good, although we're going to regard the *play* as the entire finished product put on before an audience.

nipulate their language to suggest anything from literal transcription of contemporary speech to the most imaginative stream-of-consciousness, or may choose to describe the most vivid photographic detail or expand into the realms of utter fantasy, the dramatist must conceive of his style far beyond the printed page and into the live and visible arena of the stage where not only what is said but how it is delivered to and visualized by the audience in both sight and sound become primary considerations. As in the choice of *type*, so in the choice of *style* the dramatist must face the realities of his medium and be prepared to function within the strict limitations it presents.

What Is to Be Said

As Aristotle pointed out some 2300 years ago in writing that first great piece of dramatic criticism, *The Poetics*, in the fourth century B.C., the most important element of tragedy (to him all serious drama was tragedy) is the *fable*, or more colloquially, the *story*. Some people call it plot, but whatever you want to call it there can be little argument with Aristotle that what goes on and the way it happens is the single most important consideration for the dramatist in putting across his idea and his theme. This fable, says Aristotle, has to have a beginning, a middle, and an end. Ridiculously self-evident as this statement may seem, Aristotle is emphasizing a basic dramatic tenet which insists that the dramatist begin his creation at a clearly defined point, proceed in a logical fashion to develop it, and arrive at a conclusion which follows equally logically upon what has happened. The many convolutions into which a novelist may enter in the course of telling his tale in whatever length he pleases are not the privilege of the dramatist, upon whom is imposed an absolute limit that other literary artists never have to worry about: *time*.

The conventional Western dramatist, following the traditions that have existed since the ancient Greeks, must hold the telling of his story to the constraints of a very few hours of time upon the stage. Further, within that time, he must do it all at once. Those who watch cannot put his story down, pick it up tomorrow, and go back to Chapter One to remind themselves of what has happened. Moreover, there is a limit to the physical endurance of the audience who must sit or stand, or even crouch, within that entire length of time. The dramatist places heavy demands of concentration upon his audience, but it, in turn, puts strict demands on him. If he must repeat too much to make a point, he will quickly bore and lose the audience. If he leaps too many gaps and assumes an ability to comprehend beyond normal capacity, he will leave his audience muddled, confused, and disappointed. Within the strict confines of time the dramatist must arrive at what he has to say in a linear progression that keeps his audience constantly with him, and that's all that Aristotle was really saying.

Who Says It

The consideration which comes next, regarded as second in importance by Aristotle as well, is *character*. It is interesting that a more literal translation of the word is *indicant*—the one who indicates what is going on. Who relates the story? Who goes through the action? The limitations placed upon the dramatist continue to be unique in literature, for he must carefully consider not only the restrictions of physical space in which his characters move but also the ever-present time factor. The dramatist must be careful not to clutter the stage with crowds and complicated action which can become an impossible logistics problem. The alarums and excursions of Shakespeare's battle scenes, properly handled, are far more effective with a handful of participants than any try at verisimilitude could ever be. But probably more important to the dramatist is how many principal characters, the ones on whom the audience's interest centers, can be accommodated within the time allotted for proper identification and establishment of relationships.

Unlike the novelist, who can take any amount of time to inform his solitary reader about who is who (plus that constant advantage of checking Chapter One), the dramatist must do everything relatively quickly, and he must do it clearly. The audience left at final curtain trying to figure out who all those people were and what they were doing will depart unsatisfied, and the play will fail. Everyone knows from reading Shakespeare how closely one must keep track of the many dukes, lords, and ladies who come and go with such rapidity, but one also notices that it doesn't take Shakespeare long to make clear who's getting the focus of attention. The dramatist does have one distinct advantage over the novelist, for he has the privilege of instant visibility. Once a character has made his entrance and established who or what he is, he is going to be recognized promptly the next time around.

Because of the visual element and the fact that his story is being told by live bodies, moving and speaking, the dramatist must maintain a constant awareness of the physical appearance and capabilities of his characters. How will they look together? What variations are desirable and possible? Is there need for some kind of characteristic that costume or makeup can't convey, such as a dwarf or a very young child? Will the character need to fly, like Peter Pan? Will there perhaps be an animal, like Harvey, the giant rabbit, who *never* appears,[2] or like the birds in Aristophanes' ancient Greek comedy of that name, who do? Within the closely limited time will the characters age? or get younger? or become something else, in the frog-into-prince or Beauty-and-the-Beast tradition? Will the audience accept it, or be turned off? The novelist can do anything he wants in this regard, but the dramatist must plan with extreme care what every single character, living and breathing on a stage, will be, whether human, divine, supernatural, or four-legged.

The Method of Saying It

Everything now comes down to the end-all and be-all of what we are pursuing in the study of dramatic literature, the *dialogue*. Aristotle says that what is said (*thought*) and how it is said (*diction*) are next in importance after character, and they obviously combine in what we call dialogue. Without it, we would have nothing, and dramatic literature would not exist.

Dialogue isn't, literally, everything, for there are exceedingly fine plays in our literature in which the importance of theme, plot, or character transcend pedestrian writing. The total artistic creation, however, does rely ultimately on the strength of the dialogue which, even when less than grand, must carry everything along. The dramatist who creates it must have that innate, undefinable consciousness of what will work on stage; he must have a *sense of theatre* or he will be in trouble. This sense is virtually impossible to define, and many a writer of successful fiction has found he does not have it. Such was the case of the American writer, Henry James, one of the great novelists of all time, who was fascinated by the theatre and tried play after play, only to fail so badly as to be hooted off the stage. He did not realize that he possessed no sense of theatre in relating his story through dialogue alone. Instead of holding his audience, as he held his readers, he succeeded only in being boring, turgid, and deadly dull. Ironically, many of the stories he wrote, placed in the hands of good dramatists, became critical successes and popular theatre pieces.

---

2 In the very early tryout days of Mary Chase's phenomenally successful farce in 1944 Harvey, who gave the play its title, was fully visible, but an actor in a six-foot rabbit suit could not make the fantasy work and the idea was dropped.

The dramatist must be aware of what he is doing and how he is doing it through the single medium of making his characters speak all the time. From opening curtain to final exit everything that goes on must be revealed through what people say to each other. During some periods of theatre history audiences relied on dialogue to convey almost everything, including the scenery and the time of day, as when Horatio in the opening of *Hamlet* tells the spectators, standing in broad daylight, that dawn is breaking. But more importantly, dialogue exists as the only means by which characters may develop and establish relationships. In all manner of speeches from long poetic soliloquies to contemporary gutter language, the only way we can learn what characters think of themselves and each other is the way they talk.

Dialogue presents a paradox in the theatre. Because it keeps up incessantly throughout the drama, it becomes essentially unreal. On the other hand, even in blank verse or heroic couplets, the dialogue must still *appear* real. The fact that nobody really talks that way is totally irrelevant. It must *seem* that they talk that way, no matter how they say it. The quality of the dialogue, the words that the dramatist puts on paper for his characters to say and for us to read, is what makes the difference between the merely *literate* drama and true *dramatic literature.* All drama is, of course, literate, but it is the exceptional drama that survives as great literature. The Greeks and the Elizabethans wrote mostly in verse, and today we write almost entirely in prose (which at times can be highly poetic), but however it is written, effective dialogue must have a sense of the rhythms and patterns of speech that are appropriate to the speaker and the particular dramatic situation in which he is placed. Characters in the great dramas do not just talk; they speak a highly literate dramatic dialogue. It holds the audience, it tells the story, it reveals the character, and it exposes the theme and idea. The quality of what everybody says to everybody else is what finally comes through as the essence of great dramatic literature.

Where It Is Said

Unless, in the manner of Browning or Shelley or one or two others, the dramatist wants to end it all here and publish a "closet" drama, meant only to be read, there is still a long road before him. The drama, as written, contains within it the dramatic situations conceived by the dramatist, including everything we've talked about so far, but however brilliant the concept it will go nowhere until it is put in motion. What happens from here on out is *theatre,* the visual and the audible within the three-dimensional physical structure that holds the performance. Now the time arrives when the dramatist needs every bit of faith in himself, because he will witness the awful truth of what takes place when his vision comes to life. Although it may please and delight, the far greater chance is for shock and dismay, and there is probably no dramatist who ever lived who at one time or another has not suffered the horrifying trauma of one who witnesses the sacrificial slaughter of a loved one. There were, at one time, those who wrote, produced, and acted, and even owned the theatre together with the company that played in it, so they could hold the drama they created reasonably close to their initial concepts. In the contemporary theatre this kind of impresario has all but disappeared, and a great army of individuals charged with putting on the production subject the dramatist's work to their wills and their skills in order to place it in front of the audience for which it was originally designed.

We are now in the realm of *spectacle,* the theatrical consideration which Aristotle places far down the list, for he was correctly aware, even in his time, that the dramatist who focussed primarily on the showy aspects was bound to write inferior pieces. Moreover, the decor, including setting and costumes, the whole picture which we lump together with lighting under the term *mise-en-scène,* is meant not to dominate the drama but to serve it.

The prime mover among the many who will eventually place their stamp upon the drama in the playhouse, producing that "spectacle," is the *director.* He alone has the final say on what appears. Unheard of until this century, the director has achieved such prominence in the modern theatre that he may receive billing and pay equal to, and perhaps even above, the dramatist or the star. The final production is his. He may succeed in driving the audience out of the theatre, the play out the window, and the dramatist off the roof by the time it is all over, but what he says goes. Under his guidance all others function. In order to provide the appropriate area in which the characters move, he approves the setting, conceived by the scene designer, who can be a highly accomplished professional artist in his own right, and built by the stage technician and his crew. So that everybody is fully visible (or invisible, if so demanded), the director must approve the lighting, designed and supervised by another skilled artist whose conceptions are carried out by the electrician and *his* crew. Costumes, created by yet another artist (who can be and frequently is the scene designer as well), and constructed by still another crew, must also receive the director's approval. And so with sound or any other special effects. Everybody and everything must function flawlessly together, all under the eye and ear of the director.

In addition to all those aspects of the spectacle, there happens to be a very important element that remains the director's primary responsibility and *raison d'être*. He must choose the actors, and he must move them around the stage to project as best he can everything that the dramatist has to say. If the writer is living and available, the director may consult him or even have him present from day one to opening night. More than one dramatist has been forced to watch the characters he created, interpreted by the actors chosen by and under the guidance of the director, become something quite apart from his first conception. Lighting, setting, sound, even costumes, are one thing, but the living and thinking actors, under a living and thinking director, observed by the living and thinking dramatist who thought everything up can be quite another. If the writer witnesses precisely what he had in mind, he's lucky. If he runs screaming into the street, denying all, he isn't. It's all a part of the game of theatre, and the dramatist knows, whatever the pleasures and pains, that he must play it if he is to survive at all.

Who Hears It Said

Unlike all other art forms, the drama demands a very special participant for its full effect and enjoyment: the *audience*. It is the group of people out front which finally turns everything that has been accomplished up to now into the mutual experience of the *play*. No artist outside the theatre is concerned with pleasing numbers of people simultaneously. Outside of the theatre the admiration of a work of art is a very personal thing, experienced on a one-to-one basis. The painter, the composer, or almost any artist you can name, other than the dramatist, conceives of his audience, broad-based and numerous as he may hope for, as encountering and reacting to his work as a single individual, unrelated to the crowd around him. To enjoy a great symphony or to admire the beauties of the graceful intricacies of ballet does not depend upon whether or not others are watching at the same time. In no other art form is there anything comparable to the instantaneous and continuing action and reaction between the performers and the spectators who form a unit, a living entity, that reacts entirely independently from the separate psyches which make up the individual human components. The sense of mass participation in spectator sports, where the individual identity becomes melded into and altered by the "mob" psychology, is well known, but in art only the theatre expects and receives that same participation.

The psychology of the theatre, functioning on this basis of simultaneous mass experience, does not differentiate among the sizes of the audiences so much as it does the capacity of the area that holds them. The proper response comes best when the house, however large or small, is full, or at least seems to be. The spark that flies all the way between stage and gallery will ignite effectively only if everyone's there. The play, to work, needs audience response. If there's nobody there, the actors know it; the spark doesn't fly back, and the house turns into an echo chamber. Besides, if you're sitting out there alone, with rows of empty seats between you and the rest of the crowd, it's not easy to catch the spark and throw it back.

The poet Samuel Taylor Coleridge was a drama and theatre critic who explained in very simple terms what actually happens in the theatre. Watching a play, he said, involves a tacit agreement between actors and audience to enter into a *willing suspension of disbelief*. It works in both directions. On the part of the actor it involves a sincere belief in the role, a belief that must be conveyed to the audience. John Smith believes in Hamlet, but he knows, all the same, that he himself is *not* Hamlet. But he does not disbelieve that he is Hamlet, either, knowing that the belief in the role is a vital part of the illusion that he, John Smith, really is Hamlet after all. The audience, while it must believe in what is going on in front of it, knows full well, on the other hand, that Hamlet is, in reality, merely John Smith. Still, it puts that reality aside and *refuses to disbelieve* that it is watching Hamlet and not John Smith. The audience knows that John Smith will get up and walk away after the curtain comes down; it also knows that Hamlet won't. In Coleridge's terms one neither denies what is happening nor truly believes what is happening. One remains suspended, accepting as truth neither illusion nor reality. In the enjoyment of the performance, it's just a matter of agreeing not *not* to believe.

In order for the suspension of disbelief to function properly, a balance must exist between performer and spectator in a kind of two-way stretch. Pulling one way is *empathy;* pulling the other is the maintenance of *aesthetic distance*.

Empathy means emotional identification, a "going out to" the characters by the audience. Although none of us will have met a fraction of the problems of an Oedipus or a Hamlet, we know that each is suffering physical and emotional pain in the same manner as all humankind. Thus we identify as fellow human beings, regardless of the circumstances, so long as our sympathies and understanding, our ultimate belief in the characters and the incidents portrayed, are kept within reasonable bounds. Failure of empathy can be the fault of the dramatist, whose characters appear too gross, too repulsive, extravagant, or ridiculous. It can be the fault of the director, whose control over what is said and done may be so unimaginative, exaggerated, or dull that the audience refuses to accept the theatrical validity of what it sees. Or it can be the fault of the actors who just don't "come across" and who fail to convince. The audience must constantly believe in what it sees. The whole thing must be convincingly plausible, even if it's set on Mars. The audience, in short, must be kept interested and sympathetic.

Against this force is the equal and opposite reaction, *aesthetic distance*. While moving constantly toward the stage in emotional, that is, empathic belief, the audience must simultaneously pull back in the realization that what it witnesses is art, not life. However vivid the stage picture, the audience must never lose that sense of remaining outside, at a distance. Excessive violence, for instance, can alter the balance very quickly. If the audience feels that the actor— not the character, but the actor—is really suffering so that the difference between illusion and reality is indistinguishable, aesthetic distance can be lost. If the situation on stage is unclear and the audience cannot distinguish between a planned event, something written into the play, or an accidental event, resulting, say, from an actor's lapsed memory, empathy and aesthetic distance both suffer. Children and animals are notorious destroyers of the empathy-aesthetic distance balance. Will they behave? Does the child know its lines? Or, on the other side: How well-trained they are! How brilliantly they perform! The animal is judged against its human counterpart, and the child against the adult. The illusion, laboriously established, can easily disintegrate.

It's relatively easy to put on a show. It's not all that difficult to mount a good play, but it's very nearly impossible to write, stage, and perform a piece of dramatic and theatrical art that will survive as genuinely great literature. The hurdles are nigh insurmountable, but when they are successfully leaped, there emerges an *Oedipus Rex* or a *Hamlet*. There's an irony behind many of the greatest works of dramatic art. We read them and we go to see them performed, and we praise them for their durability, their insights, their poetry, their stories, their universality. It's hard, sometimes, to remember how many were originally written and performed only for the moment, with survival in an enduring body of dramatic literature very likely never considered. The ancient Greeks staged their plays as part of a religious festival and, once performed, the dramas were normally never revived. Shakespeare was in the business for the money, and he had to keep hopping to help provide his acting company with good playable scripts. If somebody had not safely stored that manuscript of Sophocles in some ancient vault, we might never have known of Oedipus. If Ben Jonson, seeing the First Folio through the press, had not been determined to keep the memory of his friend Shakespeare alive, we would have missed about half of that marvelous collection. Instantaneous, ephemeral, existing only for the time it takes to watch, a hybrid of all the arts, a bastard art claimed as nobody's child but everybody's responsibility, the greatest *drama* survives through its language on a printed page, but it must not be permanently entombed there. Somewhat like the butterfly, encased within its cocoon, the drama is ready for the performer's art, for the *theatre,* emerging from its chrysalis to display its fragile beauty in that single exciting moment of becoming a *play,* before it once more disappears.

Concerning the Form, the Type, and the Style

Literature other than that created for the stage has no particular bounds imposed upon it with regard to the way it is put together or the way it treats its subject matter. The dramatist, however, even beyond the matters of time and space, has further restrictions imposed upon him to a far greater degree than other writers. Dramatic art by no means lays exclusive claim to what we are going to discuss in the next several pages, but if one hears of a piece of literature that is an "expressionistic comedy," a "naturalistic tragedy," or a "romantic melodrama" it is almost certain that reference is being made only to a play. Furthermore, the drama is constructed and shaped within fairly close limits controlled by factors relating almost wholly to drama and theatre alone.

The Way It's Put Together

If the fable, or the story, is the soul of drama as Aristotle maintains, the heart is the *agon,* or *argument.* Aristotle defines a tragedy as the imitation of an action, and he meant just that—action. A tragedy was not mere narration, which he assigned to the epic poem. Further, recognizing the element of time, he set forth a number of conditions that should be met in the development of that action as it involved the incidents and the character relationships. To sum it up, though he may not have said it in precisely these words, it is the *conflict* surrounding the argument which becomes the very pulse of drama. The two sides of the conflict, the pros and cons of the agon, center around the *protagonistic* forces and the *antagonistic* forces. The *protagonist* may be one person or many, and the *antagonist* may be a person, a group, a thing, or a force—supernatural, natural, or divine.

The manner by which the argument is developed becomes the structure or the *form* of the play, involving how the beginning, middle, and end of which Aristotle speaks are put together. First of all there has to be a starting point, known as the *point of attack,* at which moment the dramatist leads his audience into the picture. He can start at the beginning of things, in an *accretive plot,* with the essentials cumulatively revealed as they actually occur, thus permitting both the audience and the characters to discover what's going on at the same time. This is the method Shakespeare uses in *Hamlet.* Or he can start at the middle of things, or even very near the end, in a *climactic plot,* with the forward progress of the story gradually revealing the essentials that have already transpired. This is the method Sophocles uses in *Oedipus.*

No matter where the point of attack takes place, the first thing the dramatist has to do is to establish what is going on and who is involved, which he does through the technique of *exposition,* the exposing of the facts. This can involve a variety of approaches, from the maid and visitor routine of characters telling each other, and thus telling the audience, what the basic situation is, much as Chekhov uses in *The Cherry Orchard,* to the direct and immediate involvement in fast developing action that Shakespeare employs in the opening of *Hamlet.* Exposition must be revealed clearly and slowly enough for the audience to retain the necessary information in order to relate it to subsequent scenes, and dramatic exposition can continue well into the play, through several scenes, as the past is revealed, the present explained, and characters introduced and assimilated. Then, once everything is sufficiently established, the conflict heads toward its climax and eventual resolution, and the dramatist cannot return to any further exposition without confusing the audience and muddying up what he has already said.

Almost at once, having established where things stand, the dramatist proceeds with the *complications* that provide the conflict with its depth and breadth. These proceed through the *rising action,* a literal building of interest through suspense, emotional reaction, deepening mystery, and so on. It is the time for plottings and counterplottings, intrigues and conspiracies, accumulation of incidents and development of character. Revelations from the past, forebodings and foreshadowings of the future begin carrying the conflict toward the play's high point, its *climax*. Here everything is pulled together. The protagonist and antagonist have established their sides of the agon and have, in one way or another, met head on. This is the point toward which everything has aimed, and the confrontation of protagonist and antagonist results in a climactic showdown, serious or comic, which is termed the *obligatory scene*, the one that everybody knows must happen. It is, in other words, a turning point, after which nothing new can be added. Any high point in the story hereafter becomes *anticlimactic*, and is in serious danger of losing any dramatic effect it may have. There may be a lot of the play left, or it may all terminate very quickly, but once reached, the climax is a point of no return. It can be but a moment, as when Oedipus finally learns the truth of who and what he is, very late in the play, or it can be a series of events, as in *Hamlet*, somewhat past the middle, from the mousetrap play scene to the killing of Polonius.

Following the climax everything heads downward in *falling action*, the period when the action unravels. Now we can see how it all comes out, for there is no more building toward a suspenseful moment in the manner of the rising action. Things fall into place, and the play heads toward the conclusion, or *denouement*, or, as the Greeks put it, particularly as it pertains to tragedy, the *catastrophe*. Then it's all over, the bodies are removed, the lovers embrace, and everybody goes home.

A great number of plays follow the exposition-to-denouement routine in almost perfect balance, capable of being graphically illustrated, scene by scene, act by act, in a uniformly parabolic curve. Such plays have been given the label "well-made," and because the structure rather than the theme or idea or character became the most important aspect, emphasizing mass popular entertainment rather than good dramatic literature, the term "well-made" has long been one of critical disfavor. But all great plays are essentially "well-made," as you will discover in the brilliant structure of plays as diverse as *Oedipus, Hamlet,* or *A Doll's House*. It is what the dramatist does with his story, how he develops the conflict of that fable, how well defined his protagonist and antagonist, that make the real difference. That parabola may be perfectly formed or completely erratic in its rise and fall. That is not what really matters. Mix everything up, change things around, invent new ways of displaying them, be as "well-made" or experimental as you please, but by the time the last curtain comes down, the dramatist must have established his conflict, developed both sides of his argument, and reached a reasonable conclusion—all involving the elements we have discussed here, for the basic structure, the form of the play, whatever else, remains a whole made out of these very fundamental parts.

What Kind of Play It Is

Polonius gives Hamlet a pretty good catalogue of the variety of entertainment provided by the strolling players who happen by Elsinore:

> The best actors in the world, either for tragedy, comedy, history, pastoral, pastoral-comical, historical-pastoral, tragical-historical, tragical-comical-historical-pastoral, scene individable, or poem unlimited. Seneca cannot be too heavy, nor Plautus too light. For the law of writ and the liberty, these are the only men.

Apparently the performers of that day could, upon occasion, do just about everything.

What Polonius was describing, of course, was a variety of dramatic *types,* or individual kinds of plays. Whether or not all the multiple combinations he cites would be recognizable definitions today remains a question, but Polonius touched upon the full spectrum of his own time from the most serious classical to the lightest contemporary approach. He well knew that there could be extensive intermingling of the serious and comic and he recognized the difficulty of pigeonholing any single play, but he was equally aware that what he said conveyed meaning to the Prince in terms of the dramatic types that lay within the players' repertoire.

Tragedy and *comedy* were common terms in fifth-century Greece, as we know from Aristotle. They remain today as the most all-inclusive identifications of type, though there are important variations. The Elizabethans, as Polonius states, were familiar with *historical* plays as in the Richard and Henry sequences of Shakespeare, but the term "tragedy" was used almost universally to mean a serious treatment of the subject. Throughout the Renaissance the *pastoral* was a major form, dealing, as in Shakespeare's *As You Like It* with shepherds, shepherdesses, and the pure country life. But pastorals are essentially comedies and, as a distinct type, have not survived.

On the serious side in today's definitions of type are the three broadly general terms of *tragedy, melodrama,* and *drama,* sometimes called a *"straight play,"* or, in more precise critical terms, the *"middle genre"* or *drame.* On the lighter side are *comedy* and *farce.* Recognizing, like Polonius, that nothing falls easily into one place, we can still fairly easily put the bulk of dramatic art into one of these five broad definitions.[3]

Dramatic tragedy is not what nearly everybody will say it is—a sad play with an unhappy ending. The root of tragedy has nothing at all to do with death or sadness, for it comes down to us from the Greek *tragos*, or goat, plus *aeidein*, to sing, or, simply put, "song of the goat." The goat was sacred to Dionysus, god of wine and fertility in whose name were held the early festivals of song and dance out of which the drama grew. The whole concept of tragedy as we shall now define it is a product of Greek civilization and remains virtually unknown outside the West, for it is founded upon a very special view which the Greeks held concerning mankind and its relationship to the gods. The Greek gods were not animals or freakish creatures. They were human beings in perfect form, immortal to be sure, but subject to every passion of love, hate, jealousy, rage, and sensual delight endured by men and women on earth. The Greeks admired the human body, male and female, and in the great classic age which concerns us here painted and sculpted it undraped, to be revealed, not hidden. Not only did they marvel at its physical beauty, but at the accomplishments it could achieve. There was, in fact, such admiration for the human creature that the Greeks created their gods in the image of themselves, beautiful, handsome, radiant, powerful. Developing naturally from this concept was the realization that Zeus, the king of gods, could be stricken with helpless infatuation for a nubile earthling, and that Hera, his wife, the goddess queen, could be violently jealous. The gods did not necessarily act with common sense and good judgment, any more than their human counterparts, but when they did act, it was along human lines which could be readily understood if not entirely appreciated by ordinary mortals. And the gods were not completely independent, for they were subject to the final act of the Fates, the three sisters who spun out the thread of life, drew it to its full length, and cut it, an event the gods could not alter.

Bearing this in mind, we can fairly easily see how the idea of tragedy developed. It is an assertion of the fundamental greatness of man. It demonstrates the individual's ability to rise to heights of human dignity in the face of an antagonistic force which he himself knows will finally destroy him. The protagonist of the tragedy may commit the most heinous deeds, knowingly or unknowingly, but because the gods are as they are, capable of carrying grudges and

---

[3] The *tragi-comedy*, a serious play approaching tragedy but with a "happy" ending, is sometimes identified as a sixth type.

taking offense in the same manner as their mortal counterparts, he may suffer from outrageous curses upon himself and his family unto several generations. The point of tragedy is that the protagonist, male or female, when faced with the inevitability of the fact that the forces arrayed against him are to cause his literal or figurative death, can rise to the occasion and assert his magnificence as a human being, defying those forces and, in the end, bringing them to bay or destroying them with himself. For the tragic protagonist there is no possibility of escape. He is doomed, and we watch in awe as, finally, in full recognition of his inevitable fate, he proceeds toward that doom. Thereafter comes a balance of forces, a tranquility, a laying to rest, and an absolute finality. Nothing comes afterwards. The end is complete. What the protagonist has done in the process of the struggle and in facing the actual or symbolic death is what counts. Without hope of rescue or relief, absolutely alone against the forces that he knows will destroy him, the tragic protagonist, whatever foul deeds he may have committed or whatever human foolishness he may have displayed, rises to the ultimate in strength, courage, and defiance, demonstrating the potential godlike quality that lies within mankind, but which only legendary figures in tragedy can ever approach.

Tragedy is not saddening and depressing in the ordinary sense of a fatal accident or some destructive human or natural catastrophe. Tragedy is positive and optimistic in its view of the heights the human being can reach. There is considerable distinction, as well, between the tragic protagonist and the martyr. The martyr suffers and dies for a particular cause, but the death of a martyr, unlike that of the tragic protagonist, implies that something comes after, making the suffering and death worth the pain. Those who survive are expected to carry on in the name of whatever cause may have driven the martyr to his fate. Things begin, they do not end, as in tragedy, with the death of the central figure. A martyr, asserting his cause, may consciously seek death. The tragic protagonist, on the contrary, has every reason to live, and he makes a heroic struggle to survive in the face of the overwhelming odds against him. So long as he survives, there is no tragedy. Only in death does the tragic grandeur emerge. The death of the tragic protagonist is, however, a kind of passion, not necessarily religious, for that would enter into the area of martyrdom, but there is a certain kinship in the great sacrifice involved. At the moment of his destruction the tragic protagonist has proven the best there is in mankind, far beyond what's in most of us, but still very very human, and his death is a profound loss to humanity. If the protagonist could accomplish that much in death, what might he have accomplished in life? But that's the irony of tragedy. Proof of human greatness, in the tragic sense, comes only in death, and mankind has sacrificed something it can ill afford to lose. A genuine sacrifice is the offering of a highly valued, even priceless, possession for the benefit of the gods and the demonstration of one's faith. In the case of tragedy, however, this sacrifice is not offered in the usual sense. The protagonist, displaying his greatness, actually approaches the god-like, and his sacrifice is a kind of reverse act, an offering not for the benefit of the gods but for the benefit of mankind—a proof of ultimate human worthiness.

Such tears as may be shed at the final catastrophe are not tears of sadness, but of compassion. There can be profound emotional involvement, but there remains the fundamental optimism that must be present at the end of the best of tragedy. We have witnessed how near the gods a man can be. Aristotle gets involved in this whole matter of emotion when he speaks briefly of the *catharsis,* or *purgation* as sometimes translated, and the arousal in the audience of *pity* and *terror,* or *fear.* What he seems to be saying is that when one views a tragedy he is moved by a compassionate pity toward the protagonist for what he endures, and it is not a sentimental pity, nor merely a "pitiful" reaction. Similarly, one experiences an emotional reaction akin to terror from a realization of the magnitude of the forces and their power in bringing down the struggling protagonist. By the end, when tranquility has been restored, the audience has gone through a kind of cleansing, a kind of spiritual purgation, in the realization of how great the human creature can be upon occasion.

What kind of person is the "ideal" tragic protagonist? Aristotle goes into some detail, and his general description applies amazingly well even now. Certainly the protagonist is human and cannot be a god. He must also be of a certain noble stature. Originally this meant royalty or similar "nobility," whose deaths could make empires tremble and kingdoms crumble. The ordinary man in the street held virtually no interest. Today, of course, if we are to assert that tragedy can exist there must still be contained within the protagonist that element of human greatness involving stature beyond the ordinary. The tragic protagonist may, in today's drama, be a little man, but he is not in any sense a little person.

The tragic protagonist cannot be evil or villainous by nature, a person whose death the audience welcomes as justified. Neither can the protagonist be all good, for then his death becomes truly pitiable and shocking, displeasing to those who watch. What makes him consistently and recognizably human is the fact that he suffers, as Hamlet says, from "some vicious mole of nature" in him which can and will destroy. In other words, for all his potential, the protagonist must have within him the *tragic flaw,* the making of his own destruction. To the Greeks *hubris,* or excessive pride, more often than not could drive the tragic protagonist to his fate. But whether you call it pride, arrogance, vanity, or whatever, within the human psyche must rest the seeds of doom. In the end, the protagonist must finally recognize what he is and what is happening. He neither cringes nor flees. He turns and shouts his defiance, much as Macbeth in his final moments, who welcomes his advancing adversary with, "Lay on, Macduff/ And damn'd be him that first cries, 'Hold, enough!' "

Throughout tragedy runs the constant thread of *irony.* The variations are almost endless, but the force of tragic irony contributes substantially to the final impact of the tragic experience. Irony can involve the audience, aware of what is going to happen, or aware of why it is happening from a knowledge of the past, while the protagonist remains in ignorance. It can involve the twists and turns of fate when the harder the protagonist seeks to avoid the catastrophe, the faster it arrives. It can involve human procrastination or unthinking impulsiveness, as in the refusal of Hamlet to kill the king when he has the chance, or in his killing Polonius whom he takes to be the king while knowing full well it cannot possibly be the king.

The dramatist who thinks he has created tragedy, but ends up with merely a "sad" play with an "unhappy" ending, is not writing tragedy at all. If the catastrophe brings only sorrow, lacking awe; if it brings pathos instead of majesty, depression instead of elevation; or if the dramatist moralizes upon the fate of his protagonist and speaks of "justice," he is not entertaining the tragic view.

Melodrama, like tragedy, has come to mean something quite different from its original semantic roots. A combination of *melo,* music, plus *drama,* it means "a play with music." The term originated some time during the eighteenth century when the popular theatre of the day, offering entertainment outside the limited number of duly licensed theatres in London or the aristocratic, more "classical" theatres in Paris, made extensive use of background and incidental music. The subject matter of these theatrical diversions was full of blood and thunder with lots of broad and exciting action. By the end of the eighteenth century, when melodrama as a theatrical type emerged both in England and France, a great many of these characteristics were inherited, together with the most significant tradition of innocent maidens persecuted by villains and saved by handsome heroes.

The difference between a tragedy which, like *Oedipus* or *Hamlet,* may rely upon the sensational events and excitement of what we now call melodrama, and a true melodrama lies in the degree of emphasis. Action in a tragedy is an integral part of the progression toward a final catastrophe, while melodrama creates action for its own sake. Characters in tragedy are well developed, more "rounded out"; those in melodrama are flat and instantly recognizable so that the action and the fast developing plot can move along unencumbered. The end of a tragedy is unrelated to justice and retribution as such; melodrama punishes the bad and rewards the good. Melodrama anticipates that things will all work out in the end, thus creating hope. Tragedy, as we know, provides its central figure with no hope and no way out.

The non-tragic, non-melodramatic, non-comic play known as the *middle genre,* the *"straight" drama,* or the *drame,* is a product of literary realism. It achieves its hold on its audience by means of its treatment of men and women who may be king or commoner, rich or poor, in terms of their essential everyday humanity, encountering neither Hamlet's slings and arrows of outrageous fortune nor the arbitrary sensations of a contrived melodrama, but facing the challenges of daily existence in the milieu of a familiar and easily recognizable society, reasonably contemporary to that in which the audience itself exists. It avoids the extravagances of tragedy or melodrama at either end, and can present its protagonist as one who may, upon occasion, refuse to shout and who may, if he feels like it, run, hide, whimper, or beg. Such characters and the action that they encounter are no less attractive as dramatic figures than their tragic or melodramatic counterparts. In fact, the logic and the rationale of what they are and what they experience may win audiences far more easily and send them home far more satisfied, for they will have seen before them individuals far closer to what they are themselves.

Aristotle had little to say about *comedy,* at least in *The Poetics,* and if he said much at all it has been lost. His main observation holds true, for he said that tragedy shows men as greater than they are, while comedy shows them as less than they are. One thing is certain, Aristotle or not: comedy keeps reminding us how unlike the gods we are, all of our noblest urges notwithstanding.

The popular idea is that comedy is "funny," and that it has a "happy ending." In general, yes. But a comedy can have death and suffering of all kinds. The main thing that distinguishes it from serious drama is the *detached point of view.* Any comic situation carried through to its logical conclusion would probably end in disaster, but comedy forces us to keep our distance, compelling us to recognize that the pain is not damaging nor the disaster permanent. Comedy does not let those who watch become emotionally involved. The moment that we do so, the comedy has ended.

Comedy continually emphasizes the inferior, second-rate nature of most of us, pulling us down from the heights with a reminder of our vulnerability and the foolishness of our posturing. It does this by tripping us up with the sudden reversal, the unexpected twist, the ludicrous juxtaposition and gross exaggeration. Comedy makes us fall flat on our face, and although we who hit the ground with a thud may not like it and may fail to see the joke, those watching see it as ridiculous, and they refuse to feel the pain. It is in this action-reaction combination that comedy treads a very narrow emotional line. Things that have made people laugh may not have changed through history, but artistic taste in dramatic comedy has altered. Physical defects, race, or mental instability no longer work as comic devices among sophisticated audiences in the manner they once did. We do not hire hunchbacks to be our jesters any more, nor go to the insane asylum of a Sunday afternoon to watch the inmates perform, as the Elizabethans would do at Bethlehem (Bedlam) Hospital. Still with us, however, basically unaltered and effective as ever, is the sex joke in its infinity of variations, along with the pratfall, the pie-in-the-face routine, the wisecrack and the witty epigram.

The extremes of comedy are generally identified as "high" and "low." *High comedy* in its best form, defined from time to time as *social comedy, comedy of manners,* or *drawing room comedy,* is intellectual in its appeal, relying heavily upon sex, sophistication, and brilliant wit. High comedy is mostly dramatic, rather than theatrical, with very little action. It is static, given to words more than deeds. Most of the characters are fairly well rounded, and they are aware of the fact that they are playing an elaborate game in a comic world. The game, however, is taken very seriously, and the rules by which it operates bring laughter through the reversal of normally expected values. At the other end is *farce,* which includes many of the same qualities of melodrama, but the result is meant for fun and laughter, in toto and without exception. Farce is considered "low" comedy, but that does not mean inferiority. High comedy has a fairly narrow intellectual appeal, while low comedy, in farce, has a broad and anti-intellectual appeal. Incident piles on incident; the jokes, the sight gags and wisecracks come thick and fast. Farce is theatrical, and its premise is that of a wacky world without much sense, inhabited by a lot of zany people, where logic and reason have no known function. The more a sane rationale is sought by characters within a farce, the more it is likely to escape and, hence, the more the laughter. Farce, like melodrama, is visceral. The "belly laugh" means just that.

The large in-between area, neither "high" nor "low," is inhabited by "straight" comedy or, as much of it can also be defined, the *comedy of sensibility.* Those who inhabit this middle genre of comedy are, like their counterparts in the "straight" drama or *drame*, comparatively unsophisticated people who can, in the course of events, experience death and suffering as well as fun and games. Plot development depends mostly on its emphasis on character behavior and attitude, avoiding the vulgarities of farce as well as the intellectual appeal of high comedy. This broad range of the comic shows the fundamental charm of average, plodding, ordinary people, but the characters maintain their comic character, permitting the audience no opportunity for lingering sentimentality, even if the pain and suffering get a little close to home. As Henri Bergson has said in his famous essay on laughter, when we laugh, especially in this type of comedy, we put affection aside and silence our pity. The heart, he said, must undergo "a momentary anesthesia."

The Manner in Which It's Done

Style was not much of a concern in drama and theatre until well within the last hundred years. In fact, the meaning of the term as we use it today would have conveyed little sense to a dramatist or an actor of ancient Greece or Elizabethan England. *Style* refers to the *manner* and *method* in which a drama is originally conceived and written and in which it is produced on stage. There are dramatic as well as theatrical styles, each typical of a given period in history, each complementing the other. The drama of one era, such as the Greek, or the Elizabethan, or the Restoration, was designed for production in a specific kind of theatre building, and the building itself was designed to accommodate the drama it received. Until roughly the last century, the style of drama and the style of theatre worked in harmony to present the audience with a style of play relatively unaltered in form for periods of 75 to 100 years or more. Regardless of subject, theme, character, or incident, the general style of what we call Shakespearean (or Elizabethan), for instance, remained consistent in costuming, staging, theatre structure and dramaturgy from the opening of the first commercial theatre, the familiar open-air Globe-like structure patterned after Elizabethan innyards, in 1576 until all theatres were closed by the Puritans in 1642. Likewise, from the time of the reopening of the theatres by Charles II in 1660, the style that we have come to call Restoration and Eighteenth Century remained relatively constant in dramatic form and structure, in subject matter and theme, and, of course, in the increasingly large indoor opera-house type of theatre with its horseshoe galleries and sloping stage. Today all this has changed, as style is no longer so rigidly associated with a particular time and place but involves an almost limitless variety of methods of writing and staging, unrestricted by custom or theatre structure.

It would, of course, be possible to spend a considerable amount of time in discussing this stylistic evolution through a couple of thousand years, but for our purposes we will restrict ourselves to four fairly broad basic styles which are now associated with the writing of drama and its production in the theatre. While these are clearly arbitrary, they have significant meanings and connotations in today's theatre, even though the variations, combinations, and overlappings are everywhere apparent.

Classic

The *classic style* is carefully structured in its dramaturgy in the manner of Greek tragedy which, like all ancient Greek art, followed clean structural lines conceived, like the Parthenon and other classic temples, primarily for the aesthetic effect. In keeping with the traditions of classic Greek drama, the classic style restricts its subject matter to a single story, avoiding side issues and sub-plots, devoted mainly to heroic legendary or historical myths and tales. Behavior on stage is decorous and lacks overt physical violence, nearly all of which takes place offstage, though to be sure the physical and mental agonies, such as suffered by an Oedipus, are in full view. Action is held in the main to a single place and a single time. Dialogue is elevated in tone, highly poetic, carefully planned in long set speeches alternating with passages of quick exchange of lines between the major characters. Staging itself is uncluttered, with the whole production, writing included, suggesting the smoothness of polished marble, the grace of fluted columns, the dignity of the Acropolis, the magnificence of a sculptured god or goddess. The dramatist who entertains the *classic* view is interested in the relationship of his larger-than-life characters to the gods (or God, or Fate, or Nature, or the Universe) as well as to each other, and he frequently raises profound philosophical questions about human behavior and the forces that control it. Though not necessarily synonymous, the classic and tragic views work very closely together.

Romantic

The *romantic style* chooses its emphasis quite differently. Because the romanticist sees man as essentially good, unaffected by curses from malevolent gods and untainted by original sin, he finds that the rigid uniformity of subject matter, theme, and decor of the classic style is overly restrictive and innovatively stifling. Instead of the artificialities and the stately decorum of the classic view, the romantic outlook calls for originality, freedom to innovate and to move about in time and space, and to entertain high adventure and multiple plotlines. This means, especially in staging, a lot of color, spectacle, exciting adventure, and derring-do. It means the free appeal directly to the emotions, so apparent in melodrama, the dramatic style most obviously an exponent of the romantic.

Central to the philosophy of the romantic is the idea that many of man's problems are caused by the veneer imposed upon him by "civilization," thus hiding his true nature. Strip it away and underneath will be revealed not the horrors of a soul doomed by primal curse or original sin to eternal damnation but the source of human kindness and goodness. "Natural man" to the romanticist is pure and uncontaminated. Hence, the romanticist looks to nature itself, to the woods, fields, streams, to the winds, rains, storms and sunshine for the understanding of mankind. In addition, because, in retrospect, the past invariably seems to have been a time of "better days," the romanticist is historically oriented, recalling the times when men were men and challenges were met with honor and dignity.[4] The romantic attitude involves delight in playing upon the senses, emphasizing sentiment, nostalgia, and the emotionalism of undying love and eternal devotion. At heart, there is eternal optimism.

At the opposite extreme, in a kind of contradiction, obsessed as he is with the goodness of things, the romanticist maintains an equal fascination with the powers of evil and the mysteries of death. The hold upon the mind of evil deeds and Satanic acts is ever gripping; there is far more dramatic appeal in the Hellish than in the Heavenly. What is death? Whence comes it? Can it be overcome? What exists on the other side of the grave? The romantic seeks to know, and he revels in the fantastic, the supernatural, the magical, and the exotic, setting his tales in secluded vales, on treacherous shores, atop craggy mountains, or in far distant and mysterious lands.

---

[4] The romanticist often cannot resist altering history, preferring as he does the ideal of what ought to have been, rather than what actually happened. The German romanticist Friedrich Schiller wrote a version of the Joan of Arc story in 1801 and sent his heroine to her death in battle. His 1800 version of Mary of Scotland brings Mary and Elizabeth together in a key confrontation that never took place. We are still affected in the same manner today. The 1970 movie version of the same story brought the two queens together twice.

Realism and Naturalism

The classicist writes of royalty and nobility, viewing them with awe and a certain fearful respect. The romanticist becomes involved with his sentiments and his emotions in his treatment of men and nature, preferring the ideal, trusting in nature and natural goodness. The literary artist drawn to the realities of life and death, in the ordinary individual man and woman as part and product of their surroundings, their civilization, their society, quite apart from moral aspects of sin and retribution and punishing gods, displays interest in one of the stylistic Siamese twins of *realism* and *naturalism*. The metaphorical joining of these two terms is not without good reason. Trying to separate them reveals so many overlappings and duplications that contemporary critics use them almost interchangeably. They are, however, separate entities in enough ways to make them exist individually, if not entirely independently.

Realism, then, as we apply it to the drama, takes mankind pretty much as it is in the society in which it operates, with that society in turn presented as a product of the men and women in it. The subject matter thus becomes a transcription of reality, placing on stage individuals and their surroundings through language and action as they would be found in real life, performing against the background of a fully articulated illusionistic stage setting. Within the theatre the characters become isolated from the audience behind the proscenium arch where, through the brilliance of electric lighting, the one great invention which forever changed the basic concepts of staging and provided controlled illumination never before available to the theatrical producer, they address each other as if in complete privacy. Asides, soliloquies, and declamatory speeches, the hallmarks of nearly all drama of the past, disappear. The characters become those with whom the audience has a close personal identity. The realist, writing of what transpires in the actual world, presents his characters for what they are as the product of their own society, unromanticized and unsentimentalized. The realist strips nothing away, presenting what he sees as in the eye of the camera. The characters he creates are made into rounded, three-dimensional individuals, neither wholly good nor wholly evil, but wholly human, appearing strong or fragile, heroic or fearful as the situation demands.

The dialogue of realism is keyed to the idiom of the time. Poetry gives way to the cadences of ordinary speech. Action flows naturally upon previous action, avoiding all arbitrary twists of plot merely for the effect they may create. Realistic drama recognizes that the events portrayed did not begin with the rise, nor do they end with the fall of the curtain. Of course the realist must be selective about what he places upon the stage, for he is creating art, however "real" the illusion he creates. This presents one of the major challenges for the realistic dramatist, for he must learn how to balance the illusion of reality with the creativity of art. Recognizing the impossibility of placing reality literally on stage, the dramatist must determine how to convey the sense of reality, through art, while still keeping it "artless." How does one contrive "reality"? The coincidences and accidents which make up reality will appear as contrivances artificially introduced for effect if the dramatist is not careful. Life may lead an individual up one blind alley after another, but too many of them in a realistic play will make an audience restless, dissatisfied at having been fooled too many times. The dramatic realist knows that art is art and life is life. Each can only suggest, not become, the other. What the dramatist writes and places on the stage must remain reasonably real, for it is only realis*tic*; it cannot be *reality*. It must be, in fact, a highly contrived art which consistently must mask its contrivances. It must eliminate the imaginative play of the mind, while compelling the audience to imagine that the illusion is real. It is art that is not art; it is reality that is not reality.

The emphasis of *naturalism* is somewhat different. It makes use of the same subject matter, but regards the characters it treats in a more objective or even scientific sense. To the naturalistic writer characters are subjects for close analysis, a kind of artistic dissection. The naturalist is interested in the fundamental nature of man, what makes him function not so much as a character in society but as a creature in the natural world. According to the naturalist's perspective, society has imposed upon the individual a certain pattern of behavior made up of the customs and taboos of "civilization." If that veneer is removed, man stands revealed in his animalistic primitiveness, interested primarily in the three urges of natural gratification: eating, evacuation, and sex. Because the naturalist dwells upon these things and, unlike the realist, is not particularly selective, preferring to reveal all, he has often been accused of being a mere sensationalist, a seeker of horrors. His defense rests upon the need to remove society's veneer in order to get to the analysis itself and to probe the forces of nature that have made man what he is. As a result, life, as seen by the naturalist, tends to become a jungle. Sex becomes an animal battle, often to the death. The naturalist writer avoids the subjective emotional involvement of the romanticist, sees little to be gained from lessons of the past. He regards the future with pessimism, as opposed to his realist counterpart who is really neither a pessimist nor an optimist. The eternal "progress" toward a better world seen by the romanticist is not a part of man's nature to the naturalist, who sees very little possibility of becoming better.

Recognizing that the forces of nature which work on mankind, making him a direct product of his natural environment, can be devastating, the naturalist can offer no particular solutions. He is uncertain as to whether or not there are any. The realist, in treating the social problems of his day, often takes a stand, advocates a cause, perhaps even offers a solution. Still, a lot of the difference between the artistic realist and the artistic naturalist comes down to a degree of emphasis. Henrik Ibsen, regarded as the first great dramatic realist, once explained the difference between himself and Emile Zola, widely recognized as one of the greatest naturalists at the end of the nineteenth century. In words to this effect Ibsen is supposed to have said, "When I go down into the sewer I go to clean it out. When Zola goes down, he takes a bath."

Stylization—Expressionism, Impressionism, Absurdism

Realism (we shall use the single term from now on) has become the commonly accepted definition of the style of "modern" drama, which means from the time of Ibsen in the 1870s and 1880s until the present, and any departure in writing or staging has come to be known as *stylization.* Stylization works in two directions, involving the staging of contemporary plays and revivals of plays from the past. A contemporary subject treated dramatically or theatrically in non-realistic fashion, as discussed below, is regarded as "stylized." On the other hand, the staging of a Shakespearean play in nineteenth-century Edwardian costume and setting, as was recently done with *Much Ado About Nothing,* or the portrayal of a Hamlet or Macbeth in strictly modern costume is also "stylized." Our interest here, however, is in the departures from realism which modern theatre techniques in sound and lighting have made possible, opening up a wide variety of inventive possibilities for the dramatist.

Foremost among the forms of stylization is *expressionism.* First acknowledged in a 1902 drama by the Swedish ultra-realist, August Strindberg, entitled *The Dream Play,* this style placed upon the stage a graphic picture of a nightmare in which time, place, and characters interchanged, blended, and disappeared in the fashion of a long dream. It was the theatrical *expression* of a very subjective viewpoint of life. That is what the expressionist does. He takes reality and expresses it as he sees it, not as life is, but as it seems. If the artist finds man to be a cipher in the monolith of big business he can call him, as Elmer Rice did in his expressionistic play *The Adding*

Machine of 1924, Mr. Zero, and his friends Mr. and Mrs. One, Two, and Three. If a man or woman seems indistinguishable from the machines he or she operates, make them speak and move as mechanical automatons. If they seem to make no sense in what they say and do in daily living, make their voices monotonous, sing-song, metallic, or staccato. Give them gibberish to say. Display them in a world that is being closed in, if escape is hopeless, by constricting scenery. If you are an expressionist, *express* your views and display them with the fullest extent of dramatic and theatrical distortion, exaggeration, or caricature.

Expressionism is socially oriented in its philosophy, critical in serious as well as comic vein, concerned with the present that man has created for himself, and fearful of the future which may or may not arrive. It is a thoroughly pessimistic view in one perspective, but realizing that mankind has done all this to himself, expressionism has an air of hope that things might be corrected before it is too late. Like the naturalist, however, the expressionist doesn't have much faith in what the past can teach, and the present bodes ill for the questionable future.

Expressionism as an independent style was popular for only two or three decades at the beginning of this century, but its effects have remained a permanent legacy in the theatre. Today, the "style" of a play can range from the starkest literal realism in setting, characters, and dialogue, to the most highly imaginative expression of the author's innermost thoughts and attitudes. The expressionist opened up the use of the stage, including even the theatre auditorium itself as an acting area, and imposed no limits whatever on dramatic or theatrical technique. The result is that the "offshoots" (or, at least, the parallel developments) of styles like *impressionism* and *absurdism* are equally at home in the modern theatre. The *impressionist* with his view of life from a particular vantage point, through the haze of physical or psychical distance, can make use of sights and sounds, dialogue and actions not wholly real, not wholly unreal, to create not a distorted "expression," but a highly personal "impression," and he can find an audience. The *absurdist* can view his world as a ridiculous dark joke, with life as a pointless existentialist exercise, a baffling endurance contest with unknown disinterested forces, an absurdity on the face of it, and he can send his characters through a thoroughly stylized world to make his point. And all because the expressionist, making use of the miracle controls of electric lighting and eventually of mobile stages—revolving, elevator, or what not—and electronic sound, went on his own independent and imaginative way while the realist sought to present life as it really is. But both were doing the same thing. Each created a style, each based that style on the same premises about humanity and its place in society. The outward, literal, objective presentation is *realism*. The inward, imaginative, subjective presentation is *expressionism*. Independently and collectively they have brought the contemporary drama and the contemporary theatre a lot of excitement and intellectual stimulation.

The retelling of Og's exploits before the cave fire was a type of dramatic experience which had its own form and style, created in the mind, presented with embellishments of sight and sound, ending in a presentation before an audience. There was a *drama*, there was *theatre*, and there was a *play*. Things haven't changed much since. They've just become more complicated.

Everything you will read in this volume has proven its worth, deserving by one means or another to be known as great literature—a special literature for a special kind of experience. Each drama that you read will affect you differently, as it did every man or woman who came to watch or the critic who came to judge since the first one was displayed two and a half thousand years ago. These dramas represent artistic accomplishments that rank among the finest creations of the human mind. But they were meant first and foremost to entertain. They must be approached as sources of aesthetic pleasure, for which reason they were created in the first place.

So read.

Enjoy.

Jordan Y. Miller

✑ OEDIPUS REX
(C. 430 B.C.)

SOPHOCLES (496–406 B.C.)

The tale of the House of Thebes is one of the two great Greek myths of families cursed by the gods. The other, the House of Atreus, forms the subject of three plays by Aeschylus (c. 513–c. 456 B.C.) written in 458. Known collectively as *The Oresteia,* this only surviving trilogy involves the blood feud within the family of King Agamemnon, hero of the Trojan War, his wife and murderer, Clytemnestra, and their avenging children, Electra and Orestes. The cycle of plays by Sophocles concerning King Oedipus and his family exists in three separate works, the *Oedipus Rex,* first in sequence but second to be written, *Oedipus at Colonus* (c. 406) his last play, and *Antigone* (c. 446). Together with Aeschylus' *Seven Against Thebes* (467) they provide the full story of this tremendously exciting and powerfully moving legend.

The Greek gods seldom acted without provocation, but when they brought their wrath upon a mortal it could be devastating through several generations. So it is with the House of Thebes. Somewhere in the dim past the founder of the city, King Kadmos, somehow offended the gods; the reason remains obscure. A curse fell upon his seed, bringing its greatest destruction to the family of the fourth generation, King Oedipus. This play is the story of his tragic final hours.

Oedipus Rex, favored by critics ever since Aristotle, is probably the greatest tragedy ever written. The central figure of the King, powerful, respected, impetuous, given to emotional extravagances and violent outbursts, subject to the fatal flaw of pride, emerges as

31

the finest example of the classic tragic protagonist. Doomed even before his birth to commit the most heinous and repulsive of crimes, this giant figure still arouses the emotions. His terrifying experiences demand compassionate understanding from the audience as he struggles to make the discoveries that will tell him the truth while rushing him headlong into his frightful destruction. Of exceeding noble stature, but fatefully human, he rises in his final symbolic death to the heights which give tragedy its deepest meaning.

As a play the *Oedipus* is brilliantly structured, one of the enduringly great examples of effective dramatic art. From the opening exchange between the King and the suppliants to the horrifying climax, the dramatist has complete control of his action and the development of his characters. Each central figure is fully realized, prompted by recognizable human motives. Each scene rises successively toward the inevitable catastrophe, piling up the evidence, compelling the participants, even the frightened Iokastê on whom the truth dawns early, to reject its terrible implications, arriving at the almost unbearable but inevitable revelation. In the true classic sense the play proceeds relentlessly in uncluttered fashion, its lines as severe and orderly as a Greek temple. The ironies multiply; the trap around the doomed protagonist steadily closes. Knowing all the while the fate that must come, still we cringe, hold our breath, and find ourselves gripped by the mounting tensions. The powerful effect of the poetic language, even in translation, is moving as it carries the dialogue along with dignity and steady pace.

Sophocles survives in but seven plays as the "middle" of the three great Greek tragedians with Aeschylus and Euripides (c. 485–c. 407 B.C.). The plays of Aeschylus frequently sought out the deeper meanings behind men's struggles with primal forces and their search for reason and rational behavior. Euripides often reduced his legendary figures to realistic, almost everyday proportions. Sophocles expressed his great concern for men and women struggling to find their individual identities and to establish an understandable relationship with impersonal gods and disinterested fate. His major protagonists are worthy heroic figures, and his tragedy is the best we have.

Oedipus Rex

SOPHOCLES

An English version by Dudley Fitts and Robert Fitzgerald

CHARACTERS

OEDIPUS, *King of Thebes, supposed son of Polybos and Meropê,*
King and Queen of Corinth
IOKASTÊ, *wife of Oedipus and widow of the late King Laïos*
KREON, *brother of Iokastê, a prince of Thebes*
TEIRESIAS, *a blind seer who serves Apollo*
PRIEST
MESSENGER, *from Corinth*
SHEPHERD, *former servant of Laïos*
SECOND MESSENGER, *from the palace*
CHORUS OF THEBAN ELDERS
CHORAGOS, *leader of the Chorus*
ANTIGONÊ *and* ISMENÊ, *young daughters of Oedipus and*
Iokastê. They appear in the Exodos but do not speak.
SUPPLIANTS, GUARDS, SERVANTS

THE SCENE. *Before the palace of* OEDIPUS, *King of Thebes. A central*
door and two lateral doors open onto a platform which runs the length of
the façade. On the platform, right and left, are altars; and three steps lead
down into the "orchestra" or chorus-ground. At the beginning of the action
these steps are crowded by suppliants who have brought branches and
chaplets of olive leaves and who sit in various attitudes of despair. OEDIPUS
enters.

PROLOGUE

OEDIPUS   My children, generations of the living
In the line of Kadmos,[1] nursed at his ancient hearth:
Why have you strewn yourselves before these altars
5   In supplication, with your boughs and garlands?

---

[1] *Kadmos* founder of Thebes

33

The breath of incense rises from the city
With a sound of prayer and lamentation.
                                        Children,
I would not have you speak through messengers,
5   And therefore I have come myself to hear you—
I, Oedipus, who bear the famous name.
(*To a* PRIEST) You, there, since you are eldest in the company,
Speak for them all, tell me what preys upon you,
Whether you come in dread, or crave some blessing:
10 Tell me, and never doubt that I will help you
In every way I can; I should be heartless
Were I not moved to find you suppliant here.
    PRIEST   Great Oedipus, O powerful king of Thebes!
You see how all the ages of our people
15 Cling to your altar steps: here are boys
Who can barely stand alone, and here are priests
By weight of age, as I am a priest of God,
And young men chosen from those yet unmarried;
As for the others, all that multitude,
20 They wait with olive chaplets in the squares,
At the two shrines of Pallas, and where Apollo
Speaks in the glowing embers.
                              Your own eyes
Must tell you: Thebes is tossed on a murdering sea
25 And can not lift her head from the death surge.
A rust consumes the buds and fruits of the earth;
The herds are sick; children die unborn,
And labor is vain. The god of plague and pyre
Raids like detestable lightning through the city,
30 And all the house of Kadmos is laid waste,
All emptied, and all darkened: Death alone
Battens upon the misery of Thebes.

You are not one of the immortal gods, we know;
Yet we have come to you to make our prayer
35 As to the man surest in mortal ways
And wisest in the ways of God. You saved us
From the Sphinx, that flinty singer, and the tribute
We paid to her so long; yet you were never
Better informed than we, nor could we teach you:
40 A god's touch, it seems, enabled you to help us.

Therefore, O mighty power, we turn to you:
Find us our safety, find us a remedy,

Whether by counsel of the gods or of men.
A king of wisdom tested in the past
Can act in a time of troubles, and act well.
Noblest of men, restore
5   Life to your city! Think how all men call you
Liberator for your boldness long ago;
Ah, when your years of kingship are remembered,
Let them not say *We rose, but later fell*—
Keep the State from going down in the storm!
10   Once, years ago, with happy augury,
You brought us fortune; be the same again!
No man questions your power to rule the land:
But rule over men, not over a dead city!
Ships are only hulls, high walls are nothing,
15   When no life moves in the empty passageways.
    OEDIPUS   Poor children! You may be sure I know
All that you longed for in your coming here.
I know that you are deathly sick; and yet,
Sick as you are, not one is as sick as I.
20   Each of you suffers in himself alone
His anguish, not another's; but my spirit
Groans for the city, for myself, for you.

I was not sleeping, you are not waking me.
No, I have been in tears for a long while
25   And in my restless thought walked many ways.
In all my search I found one remedy,
And I have adopted it: I have sent Kreon,
Son of Menoikeus, brother of the queen,
To Delphi, Apollo's place of revelation,
30   To learn there, if he can,
What act or pledge of mine may save the city.
I have counted the days, and now, this very day,
I am troubled, for he has overstayed his time.
What is he doing? He has been gone too long.
35   Yet whenever he comes back, I should do ill
Not to take any action the god orders.
    PRIEST   It is a timely promise. At this instant
They tell me Kreon is here.
    OEDIPUS   O Lord Apollo!
40   May his news be fair as his face is radiant!
    PRIEST   Good news, I gather! he is crowned with bay,
The chaplet is thick with berries.

OEDIPUS   We shall soon know;
He is near enough to hear us now.

(*Enter* KREON.)

                             O prince:
5   Brother: son of Menoikeus:
What answer do you bring us from the god?
KREON   A strong one. I can tell you, great afflictions
Will turn out well, if they are taken well.
OEDIPUS   What was the oracle? These vague words
10   Leave me still hanging between hope and fear.
KREON   Is it your pleasure to hear me with all these
Gathered around us? I am prepared to speak,
But should we not go in?
OEDIPUS   Speak to them all,
15   It is for them I suffer, more than for myself.
KREON   Then I will tell you what I heard at Delphi.
In plain words
The god commands us to expel from the land of Thebes
An old defilement we are sheltering.
20   It is a deathly thing, beyond cure;
We must not let it feed upon us longer.
OEDIPUS   What defilement? How shall we rid ourselves of it?
KREON   By exile or death, blood for blood. It was
Murder that brought the plague-wind on the city.
25   OEDIPUS   Murder of whom? Surely the god has named him?
KREON   My lord: Laïos once ruled this land,
Before you came to govern us.
OEDIPUS   I know;
I learned of him from others; I never saw him.
30   KREON   He was murdered; and Apollo commands us now
To take revenge upon whoever killed him.
OEDIPUS   Upon whom? Where are they? Where shall we find a clue
To solve that crime, after so many years?
KREON   Here in this land, he said. Search reveals
35   Things that escape an inattentive man.
OEDIPUS   Tell me: Was Laïos murdered in his house,
Or in the fields, or in some foreign country?
KREON   He said he planned to make a pilgrimage.
He did not come home again.
40   OEDIPUS   And was there no one,
No witness, no companion, to tell what happened?
KREON   They were all killed but one, and he got away

So frightened that he could remember one thing only.

OEDIPUS   What was the one thing? One may be the key
To everything, if we resolve to use it.

KREON   He said that a band of highwaymen attacked them,
5   Outnumbered them, and overwhelmed the king.

OEDIPUS   Strange, that a highwayman should be so daring—
Unless some faction here bribed him to do it.

KREON   We thought of that. But after Laïos' death
New troubles arose and we had no avenger.

10   OEDIPUS   What troubles could prevent your hunting down
the killers?

KREON   The riddling Sphinx's song
Made us deaf to all mysteries but her own.

OEDIPUS   Then once more I must bring what is dark to light.
15   It is most fitting that Apollo shows,
As you do, this compunction for the dead.
You shall see how I stand by you, as I should,
Avenging this country and the god as well,
And not as though it were for some distant friend,
20   But for my own sake, to be rid of evil.
Whoever killed King Laïos might—who knows?—
Lay violent hands even on me—and soon.
I act for the murdered king in my own interest.

Come, then, my children: leave the altar steps,
25   Lift up your olive boughs!
                        One of you go
And summon the people of Kadmos to gather here.
I will do all that I can; you may tell them that.

(*Exit a* PAGE.)

30   So, with the help of God,
We shall be saved—or else indeed we are lost.

PRIEST   Let us rise, children. It was for this we came,
And now the king has promised it.
Phoibos[1] has sent us an oracle; may he descend
35   Himself to save us and drive out the plague.

(*Exeunt* OEDIPUS *and* KREON *into the palace by the central door. The*
PRIEST *and the* SUPPLIANTS *disperse R and L. After a short pause the*
CHORUS *enters the* orchestra.)

---

[1] *Phoibos* Apollo

PÁRODOS [1]

Strophe 1

CHORUS What is God singing in his profound
Delphi of gold and shadow?

5 What oracle for Thebes, the sunwhipped city?
Fear unjoints me, the roots of my heart tremble.
Now I remember, O Healer, your power, and wonder:
Will you send doom like a sudden cloud, or weave it
Like nightfall of the past?

10 Speak to me, tell me, O
Child of golden Hope, immortal Voice.

Antistrophe 1

Let me pray to Athenê, the immortal daughter of Zeus,
And to Artemis her sister

15 Who keeps her famous throne in the market ring,
And to Apollo, archer from distant heaven—
O gods, descend! Like three streams leap against
The fires of our grief, the fires of darkness;
Be swift to bring us rest!

20 As in the old time from the brilliant house
Of air you stepped to save us, come again!

Strophe 2

Now our afflictions have no end,
Now all our stricken host lies down

25 And no man fights off death with his mind;
The noble plowland bears no grain,
And groaning mothers can not bear—
See, how our lives like birds take wing,

---

1 *Párodos* the song or ode chanted by the chorus on its entry. It is accompanied by dancing and music played on a flute. The chorus in this play represents elders of the city of Thebes. Chorus members remain on stage (on a level lower than the principal actors) for the remainder of the play. The choral odes and dances serve to separate one scene from another (there was no curtain in Greek theater) as well as to comment on the action, reinforce the emotion, and interpret the situation. The chorus also performs dance movements during certain portions of the scenes themselves. *Strophe* and *antistrophe* are terms denoting the movement and counter-movement of the chorus from one side of its playing area to the other. When the chorus participates in dialogue with the other characters, its lines are spoken by the Choragos, its leader.

Like sparks that fly when a fire soars,
To the shore of the god of evening.

Antistrophe 2

The plague burns on, it is pitiless,
5 Though pallid children laden with death
Lie unwept in the stony ways,
And old gray women by every path
Flock to the strand about the altars
There to strike their breasts and cry
10 Worship of Phoibos in wailing prayers:
Be kind, God's golden child!

Strophe 3

There are no swords in this attack by fire,
No shields, but we are ringed with cries.
15 Send the besieger plunging from our homes
Into the vast sea-room of the Atlantic
Or into the waves that foam eastward of Thrace—
For the day ravages what the night spares—
Destroy our enemy, lord of the thunder!
20 Let him be riven by lightning from heaven!

Antistrophe 3

Phoibos Apollo, stretch the sun's bowstring,
That golden cord, until it sing for us,
Flashing arrows in heaven!
25   Artemis, Huntress,
Race with flaring lights upon our mountains!
O scarlet god, O golden-banded brow,
O Theban Bacchos in a storm of Maenads,

(*Enter* OEDIPUS, *C.*)

30 Whirl upon Death, that all the Undying hate!
Come with blinding torches, come in joy!

SCENE I

OEDIPUS   Is this your prayer? It may be answered. Come,
Listen to me, act as the crisis demands,
35 And you shall have relief from all these evils.

Until now I was a stranger to this tale,
As I had been a stranger to the crime.

Could I track down the murderer without a clue?
But now, friends,
As one who became a citizen after the murder,
I make this proclamation to all Thebans:
5   If any man knows by whose hand Laïos, son of Labdakos,
Met his death, I direct that man to tell me everything,
No matter what he fears for having so long withheld it.
Let it stand as promised that no further trouble
Will come to him, but he may leave the land in safety.

10 Moreover: If anyone knows the murderer to be foreign,
Let him not keep silent: he shall have his reward from me.
However, if he does conceal it; if any man
Fearing for his friend or for himself disobeys this edict,
Hear what I propose to do:

15 I solemnly forbid the people of this country,
Where power and throne are mine, ever to receive that man
Or speak to him, no matter who he is, or let him
Join in sacrifice, lustration, or in prayer.
I decree that he be driven from every house,
20 Being, as he is, corruption itself to us: the Delphic
Voice of Apollo has pronounced this revelation.
Thus I associate myself with the oracle
And take the side of the murdered king.

As for the criminal, I pray to God—
25 Whether it be a lurking thief, or one of a number—
I pray that that man's life be consumed in evil and wretchedness.
And as for me, this curse applies no less
If it should turn out that the culprit is my guest here,
Sharing my hearth.
30   You have heard the penalty.
I lay it on you now to attend to this
For my sake, for Apollo's, for the sick
Sterile city that heaven has abandoned.
Suppose the oracle had given you no command:
35 Should this defilement go uncleansed for ever?
You should have found the murderer: your king,
A noble king, had been destroyed!
                          Now I,
Having the power that he held before me,
40 Having his bed, begetting children there
Upon his wife, as he would have, had he lived—
Their son would have been my children's brother,

If Laïos had had luck in fatherhood!
(And now his bad fortune has struck him down) —
I say I take the son's part, just as though
I were his son, to press the fight for him
5   And see it won! I'll find the hand that brought
Death to Labdakos' and Polydoros' child,
Heir of Kadmos' and Agenor's line.[1]
And as for those who fail me,
May the gods deny them the fruit of the earth,
10   Fruit of the womb, and may they rot utterly!
Let them be wretched as we are wretched, and worse!

For you, for loyal Thebans, and for all
Who find my actions right, I pray the favor
Of justice, and of all the immortal gods.
15   CHORAGOS   Since I am under oath, my lord, I swear
I did not do the murder, I can not name
The murderer. Phoibos ordained the search;
Why did he not say who the culprit was?
OEDIPUS   An honest question. But no man in the world
20   Can make the gods do more than the gods will.
CHORAGOS   There is an alternative, I think—
OEDIPUS   Tell me.
Any or all, you must not fail to tell me.
CHORAGOS   A lord clairvoyant to the lord Apollo,
25   As we all know, is the skilled Teiresias.
One might learn much about this from him, Oedipus.
OEDIPUS   I am not wasting time:
Kreon spoke of this, and I have sent for him—
Twice, in fact; it is strange that he is not here.
30   CHORAGOS   The other matter—that old report—seems useless.
OEDIPUS   What was that? I am interested in all reports.
CHORAGOS   The king was said to have been killed by highwaymen.
OEDIPUS   I know. But we have no witnesses to that.
CHORAGOS   If the killer can feel a particle of dread,
35   Your curse will bring him out of hiding!
OEDIPUS   No.
The man who dared that act will fear no curse.

(*Enter the blind seer* TEIRESIAS, *led by a* PAGE.)

CHORAGOS   But there is one man who may detect the criminal.

---

[1] *Labdakos, Polydoros, Kadmos,* and *Agenor* father, grandfather, great-grandfather, and great-great-grandfather of Laïos

This is Teiresias, this is the holy prophet
In whom, alone of all men, truth was born.
OEDIPUS   Teiresias: seer: student of mysteries,
Of all that's taught and all that no man tells,
5   Secrets of Heaven and secrets of the earth:
Blind though you are, you know the city lies
Sick with plague; and from this plague, my lord,
We find that you alone can guard or save us.

Possibly you did not hear the messengers?
10   Apollo, when we sent to him,
Sent us back word that this great pestilence
Would lift, but only if we established clearly
The identity of those who murdered Laïos.
They must be killed or exiled.
15   Can you use
Birdflight[1] or any art of divination
To purify yourself, and Thebes, and me
From this contagion? We are in your hands.
There is no fairer duty
20   Than that of helping others in distress.
TEIRESIAS   How dreadful knowledge of the truth can be
When there's no help in truth! I knew this well,
But did not act on it: else I should not have come.
OEDIPUS   What is troubling you? Why are your eyes so cold?
25   TEIRESIAS   Let me go home. Bear your own fate, and I'll
Bear mine. It is better so: trust what I say.
OEDIPUS   What you say is ungracious and unhelpful
To your native country. Do not refuse to speak.
TEIRESIAS   When it comes to speech, your own is neither temperate
30   Nor opportune. I wish to be more prudent.
OEDIPUS   In God's name, we all beg you—
TEIRESIAS   You are all ignorant.
No; I will never tell you what I know.
Now it is my misery; then, it would be yours.
35   OEDIPUS   What! You do know something, and will not tell us?
You would betray us all and wreck the State?
TEIRESIAS   I do not intend to torture myself, or you.
Why persist in asking? You will not persuade me.
OEDIPUS   What a wicked old man you are! You'd try a stone's
40   Patience! Out with it! Have you no feeling at all?

_____

1 *Birdflight* Prophets predicted the future or divined the unknown by observing the flight of birds.

TEIRESIAS   You call me unfeeling. If you could only see
The nature of your own feelings . . .
OEDIPUS   Why,
Who would not feel as I do? Who could endure
5   Your arrogance toward the city?
TEIRESIAS   What does it matter?
Whether I speak or not, it is bound to come.
OEDIPUS   Then, if "it" is bound to come, you are bound to tell me.
TEIRESIAS   No, I will not go on. Rage as you please.
10   OEDIPUS   Rage? Why not!
                                And I'll tell you what I think:
You planned it, you had it done, you all but
Killed him with your own hands: if you had eyes,
I'd say the crime was yours, and yours alone.
15   TEIRESIAS   So? I charge you, then,
Abide by the proclamation you have made:
From this day forth
Never speak again to these men or to me;
You yourself are the pollution of this country.
20   OEDIPUS   You dare say that! Can you possibly think you have
Some way of going free, after such insolence?
TEIRESIAS   I have gone free. It is the truth sustains me.
OEDIPUS   Who taught you shamelessness? It was not your craft.
TEIRESIAS   You did. You made me speak. I did not want to.
25   OEDIPUS   Speak what? Let me hear it again more clearly.
TEIRESIAS   Was it not clear before? Are you tempting me?
OEDIPUS   I did not understand it. Say it again.
TEIRESIAS   I say that you are the murderer whom you seek.
OEDIPUS   Now twice you have spat out infamy. You'll pay for it!
30   TEIRESIAS   Would you care for more? Do you wish to be
really angry?
OEDIPUS   Say what you will. Whatever you say is worthless.
TEIRESIAS   I say you live in hideous shame with those
Most dear to you. You can not see the evil.
35   OEDIPUS   Can you go on babbling like this for ever?
TEIRESIAS   I can, if there is power in truth.
OEDIPUS   There is:
But not for you, not for you,
You sightless, witless, senseless, mad old man!
40   TEIRESIAS   You are the madman. There is no one here
Who will not curse you soon, as you curse me.
OEDIPUS   You child of total night! I would not touch you;
Neither would any man who sees the sun.
TEIRESIAS   True: it is not from you my fate will come.

That lies within Apollo's competence,
As it is his concern.
OEDIPUS.   Tell me, who made
These fine discoveries? Kreon? or someone else?
5 TEIRESIAS   Kreon is no threat. You weave your own doom.
OEDIPUS   Wealth, power, craft of statesmanship!
Kingly position, everywhere admired!
What savage envy is stored up against these,
If Kreon, whom I trusted, Kreon my friend,
10 For this great office which the city once
Put in my hands unsought—if for this power
Kreon desires in secret to destroy me!

He has bought this decrepit fortune-teller, this
Collector of dirty pennies, this prophet fraud—
15 Why, he is no more clairvoyant than I am!
                                        Tell us:
Has your mystic mummery ever approached the truth?
When that hellcat the Sphinx was performing here,
What help were you to these people?
Her magic was not for the first man who came along:
20 It demanded a real exorcist. Your birds—
What good were they? or the gods, for the matter of that?
But I came by,
Oedipus, the simple man, who knows nothing—
I thought it out for myself, no birds helped me!
25 And this is the man you think you can destroy,
That you may be close to Kreon when he's king!
Well, you and your friend Kreon, it seems to me,
Will suffer most. If you were not an old man,
You would have paid already for your plot.
30 CHORAGOS   We can not see that his words or yours
Have been spoken except in anger, Oedipus,
And of anger we have no need. How to accomplish
The god's will best: that is what most concerns us.
TEIRESIAS   You are a king. But where argument's concerned
35 I am your man, as much a king as you.
I am not your servant, but Apollo's.
I have no need of Kreon or Kreon's name.

Listen to me. You mock my blindness, do you?
But I say that you, with both your eyes, are blind:
40 You can not see the wretchedness of your life,
Nor in whose house you live, no, nor with whom.
Who are your father and mother? Can you tell me?

You do not even know the blind wrongs
That you have done them, on earth and in the world below.
But the double lash of your parents' curse will whip you
Out of this land some day, with only night
5   Upon your precious eyes.
Your cries then—where will they not be heard?
What fastness of Kithairon[1] will not echo them?
And that bridal-descant of yours—you'll know it then,
The song they sang when you came here to Thebes
10 And found your misguided berthing.
All this, and more, that you can not guess at now,
Will bring you to yourself among your children.

Be angry, then. Curse Kreon. Curse my words.
I tell you, no man that walks upon the earth
15 Shall be rooted out more horribly than you.
OEDIPUS   Am I to bear this from him?—Damnation
Take you! Out of this place! Out of my sight!
TEIRESIAS   I would not have come at all if you had not asked me.
OEDIPUS   Could I have told that you'd talk nonsense, that
20 You'd come here to make a fool of yourself, and of me?
TEIRESIAS   A fool? Your parents thought me sane enough.
OEDIPUS   My parents again!—Wait: who were my parents?
TEIRESIAS   This day will give you a father, and break your heart.
OEDIPUS   Your infantile riddles! Your damned abracadabra!
25 TEIRESIAS   You were a great man once at solving riddles.
OEDIPUS   Mock me with that if you like; you will find it true.
TEIRESIAS   It was true enough. It brought about your ruin.
OEDIPUS   But if it saved this town?
TEIRESIAS *(to the* PAGE)   Boy, give me your hand.
30 OEDIPUS   Yes, boy; lead him away.
                              —While you are here
We can do nothing. Go; leave us in peace.
TEIRESIAS   I will go when I have said what I have to say.
How can you hurt me? And I tell you again:
35 The man you have been looking for all this time,
The damned man, the murderer of Laïos,
That man is in Thebes. To your mind he is foreign-born,
But it will soon be shown that he is a Theban,
A revelation that will fail to please.
40   A blind man,

_____

1 *Kithairon* the mountain where Oedipus was taken to be exposed as an
infant

Who has his eyes now; a penniless man, who is rich now;
And he will go tapping the strange earth with his staff.
To the children with whom he lives now he will be
Brother and father—the very same; to her
5   Who bore him, son and husband—the very same
Who came to his father's bed, wet with his father's blood.

Enough. Go think that over.
If later you find error in what I have said,
You may say that I have no skill in prophecy.

10   (*Exit* TEIRESIAS, *led by his* PAGE. OEDIPUS *goes into the palace.*)

ODE I

Strophe 1

CHORUS   The Delphic stone of prophecies
Remembers ancient regicide
15   And a still bloody hand.
That killer's hour of flight has come.
He must be stronger than riderless
Coursers of untiring wind,
For the son[1] of Zeus armed with his father's thunder
20   Leaps in lightning after him;
And the Furies hold his track, the sad Furies.

Antistrophe 1

Holy Parnassos'[2] peak of snow
Flashes and blinds that secret man,
25   That all shall hunt him down:
Though he may roam the forest shade
Like a bull gone wild from pasture
To rage through glooms of stone.
Doom comes down on him; flight will not avail him;
30   For the world's heart calls him desolate,
And the immortal voices follow, for ever follow.

Strophe 2

But now a wilder thing is heard
From the old man skilled at hearing Fate in the wing-beat
35   of a bird.

---

1 *son* Apollo
2 *Parnassos* mountain sacred to Apollo

Bewildered as a blown bird, my soul hovers and can not find
Foothold in this debate, or any reason or rest of mind.
But no man ever brought—none can bring
Proof of strife between Thebes' royal house,
5 Labdakos' line, and the son of Polybos;
And never until now has any man brought word
Of Laïos' dark death staining Oedipus the King.

Antistrophe 2

Divine Zeus and Apollo hold
10 Perfect intelligence alone of all tales ever told;
And well though this diviner works, he works in his own night;
No man can judge that rough unknown or trust in second sight,
For wisdom changes hands among the wise.
Shall I believe my great lord criminal
15 At a raging word that a blind old man let fall?
I saw him, when the carrion woman[1] faced him of old,
Prove his heroic mind. These evil words are lies.

SCENE II

KREON Men of Thebes:
20 I am told that heavy accusations
Have been brought against me by King Oedipus.

I am not the kind of man to bear this tamely.

If in these present difficulties
He holds me accountable for any harm to him
25 Through anything I have said or done—why, then,
I do not value life in this dishonor.
It is not as though this rumor touched upon
Some private indiscretion. The matter is grave.
The fact is that I am being called disloyal
30 To the State, to my fellow citizens, to my friends.
CHORAGOS He may have spoken in anger, not from his mind.
KREON But did you not hear him say I was the one
Who seduced the old prophet into lying?
CHORAGOS The thing was said; I do not know how seriously.
35 KREON But you were watching him! Were his eyes steady?
Did he look like a man in his right mind?
CHORAGOS   I do not know.

---

[1] *woman* the Sphinx

I can not judge the behavior of great men.
But here is the king himself.

(*Enter* OEDIPUS.)

OEDIPUS   So you dared come back.

5   Why? How brazen of you to come to my house,
You murderer!
                    Do you think I do not know
That you plotted to kill me, plotted to steal my throne?
Tell me, in God's name: am I coward, a fool,

10   That you should dream you could accomplish this?
A fool who could not see your slippery game?
A coward, not to fight back when I saw it?
You are the fool, Kreon, are you not? hoping
Without support or friends to get a throne?

15   Thrones may be won or bought: you could do neither.
KREON   Now listen to me. You have talked; let me talk, too.
You can not judge unless you know the facts.
OEDIPUS   You speak well: there is one fact; but I find it hard
To learn from the deadliest enemy I have.

20   KREON   That above all I must dispute with you.
OEDIPUS   That above all I will not hear you deny.
KREON   If you think there is anything good in being stubborn
Against all reason, then I say you are wrong.
OEDIPUS   If you think a man can sin against his own kind

25   And not be punished for it, I say you are mad.
KREON   I agree. But tell me: What have I done to you?
OEDIPUS   You advised me to send for that wizard, did you not?
KREON   I did. I should do it again.
OEDIPUS   Very well. Now tell me:

30   How long has it been since Laïos—
KREON   What of Laïos?
OEDIPUS   Since he vanished in that onset by the road?
KREON   It was long ago, a long time.
OEDIPUS   And this prophet,

35   Was he practicing here then?
KREON   He was; and with honor, as now.
OEDIPUS   Did he speak of me at that time?
KREON   He never did,
At least, not when I was present.

40   OEDIPUS   But . . . the enquiry?
I suppose you held one?
KREON   We did, but we learned nothing.

OEDIPUS   Why did the prophet not speak against me then?
KREON   I do not know; and I am the kind of man
Who holds his tongue when he has no facts to go on.
OEDIPUS   There's one fact that you know, and you could tell it.
5   KREON   What fact is that? If I know it, you shall have it.
OEDIPUS   If he were not involved with you, he could not say
That it was I who murdered Laïos.
KREON   If he says that, you are the one that knows it!—
But now it is my turn to question you.
10   OEDIPUS   Put your questions. I am no murderer.
KREON   First, then: You married my sister?
OEDIPUS   I married your sister.
KREON   And you rule the kingdom equally with her?
OEDIPUS   Everything that she wants she has from me.
15   KREON   And I am the third, equal to both of you?
OEDIPUS   That is why I call you a bad friend.
KREON   No. Reason it out, as I have done.
Think of this first: Would any sane man prefer
Power, with all a king's anxieties,
20   To that same power and the grace of sleep?
Certainly not I.
I have never longed for the king's power—only his rights.
Would any wise man differ from me in this?
As matters stand, I have my way in everything
25   With your consent, and no responsibilities.
If I were king, I should be a slave to policy.

How could I desire a scepter more
Than what is now mine—untroubled influence?
No, I have not gone mad; I need no honors,
30   Except those with the perquisites I have now.
I am welcome everywhere; every man salutes me,
And those who want your favor seek my ear,
Since I know how to manage what they ask.
Should I exchange this ease for that anxiety?
35   Besides, no sober mind is treasonable.
I hate anarchy
And never would deal with any man who likes it.
Test what I have said. Go to the priestess
At Delphi, ask if I quoted her correctly.
40   And as for this other thing: if I am found
Guilty of treason with Teiresias,
Then sentence me to death. You have my word

It is a sentence I should cast my vote for—
But not without evidence!
      You do wrong
When you take good men for bad, bad men for good.
5 A true friend thrown aside—why, life itself
Is not more precious!
       In time you will know this well:
For time, and time alone, will show the just man,
Though scoundrels are discovered in a day.
10 CHORAGOS This is well said, and a prudent man would ponder it.
Judgments too quickly formed are dangerous.
OEDIPUS But is he not quick in his duplicity?
And shall I not be quick to parry him?
Would you have me stand still, hold my peace, and let
15 This man win everything, through my inaction?
KREON And you want—what is it, then? To banish me?
OEDIPUS No, not exile. It is your death I want,
So that all the world may see what treason means.
KREON You will persist, then? You will not believe me?
20 OEDIPUS How can I believe you?
KREON   Then you are a fool.
OEDIPUS To save myself?
KREON   In justice, think of me.
OEDIPUS You are evil incarnate.
25 KREON   But suppose that you are wrong?
OEDIPUS Still I must rule.
KREON   But not if you rule badly.
OEDIPUS O city, city!
KREON   It is my city, too!
30 CHORAGOS Now, my lords, be still. I see the queen,
Iokastê, coming from her palace chambers;
And it is time she came, for the sake of you both.
This dreadful quarrel can be resolved through her.

(*Enter* IOKASTÊ.)

35 IOKASTÊ Poor foolish men, what wicked din is this?
With Thebes sick to death, is it not shameful
That you should rake some private quarrel up?
(*To* OEDIPUS) Come into the house.
        —And you, Kreon, go now:
40 Let us have no more of this tumult over nothing.
KREON Nothing? No, sister: what your husband plans for me
Is one of two great evils: exile or death.

OEDIPUS   He is right.
                              Why, woman I have caught him squarely
        Plotting against my life.
        KREON   No! Let me die
5   Accurst if ever I have wished you harm!
        IOKASTÊ   Ah, believe it, Oedipus!
        In the name of the gods, respect this oath of his
        For my sake, for the sake of these people here!

Strophe 1

10   CHORAGOS   Open your mind to her, my lord. Be ruled by her, I beg
                you!
        OEDIPUS   What would you have me do?
        CHORAGOS   Respect Kreon's word. He has never spoken like a fool,
        And now he has sworn an oath.
15   OEDIPUS   You know what you ask?
        CHORAGOS   I do.
        OEDIPUS   Speak on, then.
        CHORAGOS   A friend so sworn should not be baited so,
        In blind malice, and without final proof.
20   OEDIPUS   You are aware, I hope, that what you say
        Means death for me, or exile at the least.

Strophe 2

        CHORAGOS   No, I swear by Helios, first in Heaven!
        May I die friendless and accurst,
25   The worst of deaths, if ever I meant that!
                It is the withering fields
                    That hurt my sick heart:
                Must we bear all these ills,
                    And now your bad blood as well?
30   OEDIPUS   Then let him go. And let me die, if I must,
        Or be driven by him in shame from the land of Thebes.
        It is your unhappiness, and not his talk,
        That touches me.
                              As for him—
35   Wherever he goes, hatred will follow him.
        KREON   Ugly in yielding, as you were ugly in rage!
        Natures like yours chiefly torment themselves.
        OEDIPUS   Can you not go? Can you not leave me?
        KREON   I can.
40   You do not know me; but the city knows me,
        And in its eyes I am just, if not in yours.

(*Exit* KREON.)

Antistrophe 1

CHORAGOS   Lady Iokastê, did you not ask the King to go to
his chambers?
5   IOKASTÊ   First tell me what has happened.
CHORAGOS   There was suspicion without evidence; yet it rankled
As even false charges will.
IOKASTÊ   On both sides?
CHORAGOS   On both.
10   IOKASTÊ   But what was said?
CHORAGOS.   Oh let it rest, let it be done with!
Have we not suffered enough?
OEDIPUS   You see to what your decency has brought you:
You have made difficulties where my heart saw none.

15   ### Antistrophe 2

CHORAGOS   Oedipus, it is not once only I have told you—
You must know I should count myself unwise
To the point of madness, should I now forsake you—
You, under whose hand,
20   In the storm of another time,
Our dear land sailed out free.
But now stand fast at the helm!
IOKASTÊ   In God's name, Oedipus, inform your wife as well:
Why are you so set in this hard anger?
25   OEDIPUS   I will tell you, for none of these men deserves
My confidence as you do. It is Kreon's work,
His treachery, his plotting against me.
IOKASTÊ   Go on, if you can make this clear to me.
OEDIPUS   He charges me with the murder of Laïos.
30   IOKASTÊ   Has he some knowledge? Or does he speak from hearsay?
OEDIPUS   He would not commit himself to such a charge,
But he has brought in that damnable soothsayer
To tell his story.
IOKASTÊ   Set your mind at rest.
35   If it is a question of soothsayers, I tell you
That you will find no man whose craft gives knowledge
Of the unknowable.
Here is my proof:
An oracle was reported to Laïos once
40   (I will not say from Phoibos himself, but from
His appointed ministers, at any rate)

That his doom would be death at the hands of his own son—
His son, born of his flesh and of mine!

Now, you remember the story: Laïos was killed
By marauding strangers where three highways meet;
5   But his child had not been three days in this world
Before the king had pierced the baby's ankles
And left him to die on a lonely mountainside.

Thus, Apollo never caused that child
To kill his father, and it was not Laïos' fate
10 To die at the hands of his son, as he had feared.
This is what prophets and prophecies are worth!
Have no dread of them.
                    It is God himself
Who can show us what he wills, in his own way.

15 OEDIPUS   How strange a shadowy memory crossed my mind,
Just now while you were speaking; it chilled my heart.
IOKASTÊ   What do you mean? What memory do you speak of?
OEDIPUS   If I understand you, Laïos was killed
At a place where three roads meet.
20 IOKASTÊ   So it was said;
We have no later story.
OEDIPUS   Where did it happen?
IOKASTÊ   Phokis, it is called: at a place where the Theban Way
Divides into the roads toward Delphi and Daulia.
25 OEDIPUS   When?
IOKASTÊ   We had the news not long before you came
And proved the right to your succession here.
OEDIPUS   Ah, what net has God been weaving for me?
IOKASTÊ   Oedipus! Why does this trouble you?
30 OEDIPUS   Do not ask me yet.
First, tell me how Laïos looked, and tell me
How old he was.
IOKASTÊ   He was tall, his hair just touched
With white; his form was not unlike your own.
35 OEDIPUS   I think that I myself may be accurst
By my own ignorant edict.
IOKASTÊ   You speak strangely.
It makes me tremble to look at you, my king.
OEDIPUS   I am not sure that the blind man can not see.
40 But I should know better if you were to tell me—
IOKASTÊ   Anything—though I dread to hear you ask it.

OEDIPUS　Was the king lightly escorted, or did he ride
With a large company, as a ruler should?
IOKASTÊ　There were five men with him in all: one was a herald.
And a single chariot, which he was driving.
5　OEDIPUS　Alas, that makes it plain enough!
　　　　　　　　　　　　　　　　But who—
Who told you how it happened?
IOKASTÊ　　　　　　　　　　A household servant,
The only one to escape.
10　OEDIPUS　　　　　　　　And is he still
A servant of ours?
IOKASTÊ　No; for when he came back at last
And found you enthroned in the place of the dead king,
He came to me, touched my hand with his, and begged
15　That I would send him away to the frontier district
Where only the shepherds go—
As far away from the city as I could send him.
I granted his prayer; for although the man was a slave,
He had earned more than this favor at my hands.
20　OEDIPUS　Can he be called back quickly?
IOKASTÊ　　　　　　　　　　　　Easily.
But why?
OEDIPUS　I have taken too much upon myself
Without enquiry; therefore I wish to consult him.
25　IOKASTÊ　Then he shall come.
　　　　　　　　　　But am I not one also
To whom you might confide these fears of yours?
OEDIPUS　That is your right; it will not be denied you,
Now least of all; for I have reached a pitch
30　Of wild foreboding. Is there anyone
To whom I should sooner speak?

Polybos of Corinth is my father.
My mother is a Dorian: Meropê.
I grew up chief among the men of Corinth
35　Until a strange thing happened—
Not worth my passion, it may be, but strange.
At a feast, a drunken man maundering in his cups
Cries out that I am not my father's son! [1]

---

[1] *not my father's son* Oedipus perhaps interprets this as an allegation that
he is a bastard, the son of Meropê but not of Polybos. The implication, at
any rate, is that he is not of royal birth, not the legitimate heir to the
throne of Corinth.

I contained myself that night, though I felt anger
And a sinking heart. The next day I visited
My father and mother, and questioned them. They stormed,
Calling it all the slanderous rant of a fool;
5   And this relieved me. Yet the suspicion
Remained always aching in my mind;
I knew there was talk; I could not rest;
And finally, saying nothing to my parents,
I went to the shrine at Delphi.

10   The god dismissed my question without reply;
He spoke of other things.
                      Some were clear,
Full of wretchedness, dreadful, unbearable:
As, that I should lie with my own mother, breed
15   Children from whom all men would turn their eyes;
And that I should be my father's murderer.

I heard all this, and fled. And from that day
Corinth to me was only in the stars
Descending in that quarter of the sky,
20   As I wandered farther and farther on my way
To a land where I should never see the evil
Sung by the oracle. And I came to this country
Where, so you say, King Laïos was killed.

I will tell you all that happened there, my lady.

25   There were three highways
Coming together at a place I passed;
And there a herald came towards me, and a chariot
Drawn by horses, with a man such as you describe
Seated in it. The groom leading the horses
30   Forced me off the road at his lord's command;
But as this charioteer lurched over towards me
I struck him in my rage. The old man saw me
And brought his double goad down upon my head
As I came abreast.
35   He was paid back, and more!
Swinging my club in this right hand I knocked him
Out of his car, and he rolled on the ground.
                          I killed him.

I killed them all.
40   Now if that stranger and Laïos were—kin,
Where is a man more miserable than I?
More hated by the gods? Citizen and alien alike

Must never shelter me or speak to me—
I must be shunned by all.
                              And I myself
Pronounced this malediction upon myself!

5   Think of it: I have touched you with these hands,
These hands that killed your husband. What defilement!

Am I all evil, then? It must be so,
Since I must flee from Thebes, yet never again
See my own countrymen, my own country,
10 For fear of joining my mother in marriage
And killing Polybos, my father.
                                        Ah,
If I was created so, born to this fate,
Who could deny the savagery of God?

15 O holy majesty of heavenly powers!
May I never see that day! Never!
Rather let me vanish from the race of men
Than know the abomination destined me!

CHORAGOS We too, my lord, have felt dismay at this.
20 But there is hope: you have yet to hear the shepherd.

OEDIPUS Indeed, I fear no other hope is left me.

IOKASTÊ What do you hope from him when he comes?

OEDIPUS   This much:
If his account of the murder tallies with yours,
25 Then I am cleared.

IOKASTÊ   What was it that I said
Of such importance?

OEDIPUS   Why, "marauders," you said,
Killed the king, according to this man's story.
30 If he maintains that still, if there were several,
Clearly the guilt is not mine: I was alone.
But if he says one man, singlehanded, did it,
Then the evidence all points to me.

IOKASTÊ You may be sure that he said there were several;
35 And can he call back that story now? He can not.
The whole city heard it as plainly as I.
But suppose he alters some detail of it:
He can not ever show that Laïos' death
Fulfilled the oracle: for Apollo said
40 My child was doomed to kill him; and my child—
Poor baby!—it was my child that died first.

No. From now on, where oracles are concerned,
I would not waste a second thought on any.
OEDIPUS   You may be right.
                                But come: let someone go
5   For the shepherd at once. This matter must be settled.
IOKASTÊ   I will send for him.
I would not wish to cross you in anything,
And surely not in this.—Let us go in.

(*Exeunt into the palace.*)

10   ODE II

Strophe 1

CHORUS   Let me be reverent in the ways of right,
    Lowly the paths I journey on;
    Let all my words and actions keep
15   The laws of the pure universe
    From highest Heaven handed down.
    For Heaven is their bright nurse,
    Those generations of the realms of light;
    Ah, never of mortal kind were they begot,
20   Nor are they slaves of memory, lost in sleep:
    Their Father is greater than Time, and ages not.

Antistrophe 1

    The tyrant is a child of Pride
    Who drinks from his great sickening cup
25   Recklessness and vanity,
    Until from his high crest headlong
    He plummets to the dust of hope.
    That strong man is not strong.
    But let no fair ambition be denied;
30   May God protect the wrestler for the State
    In government, in comely policy,
    Who will fear God, and on His ordinance wait.

Strophe 2

    Haughtiness and the high hand of disdain
35   Tempt and outrage God's holy law;
    And any mortal who dares hold
    No immortal Power in awe
    Will be caught up in a net of pain:

The price for which his levity is sold.
Let each man take due earnings, then,
And keep his hands from holy things,
And from blasphemy stand apart—
5   Else the crackling blast of heaven
Blows on his head, and on his desperate heart.
Though fools will honor impious men,
In their cities no tragic poet sings.

Antistrophe 2

10   Shall we lose faith in Delphi's obscurities,
We who have heard the world's core
Discredited, and the sacred wood
Of Zeus at Elis praised no more?
The deeds and the strange prophecies
15   Must make a pattern yet to be understood.
Zeus, if indeed you are lord of all,
Throned in light over night and day,
Mirror this in your endless mind:
Our masters call the oracle
20   Words on the wind, and the Delphic vision blind!
Their hearts no longer know Apollo,
And reverence for the gods has died away.

SCENE III

(*Enter* IOKASTÊ.)

25   IOKASTÊ   Princes of Thebes, it has occurred to me
To visit the altars of the gods, bearing
These branches as a suppliant, and this incense.
Our king is not himself: his noble soul
Is overwrought with fantasies of dread,
30   Else he would consider
The new prophecies in the light of the old.
He will listen to any voice that speaks disaster,
And my advice goes for nothing.

(*She approaches the altar, R.*)

35   To you, then, Apollo,
Lycéan lord, since you are nearest, I turn in prayer.
Receive these offerings, and grant us deliverance
From defilement. Our hearts are heavy with fear

When we see our leader distracted, as helpless sailors
Are terrified by the confusion of their helmsman.

(*Enter* MESSENGER.)

MESSENGER   Friends, no doubt you can direct me:
5   Where shall I find the house of Oedipus,
Or, better still, where is the king himself?
CHORAGOS   It is this very place, stranger; he is inside.
This is his wife and mother of his children.
MESSENGER   I wish her happiness in a happy house,
10   Blest in all the fulfillment of her marriage.
IOKASTÊ   I wish as much for you: your courtesy
Deserves a like good fortune. But now, tell me:
Why have you come? What have you to say to us?
MESSENGER   Good news, my lady, for your house and your husband.
15 IOKASTÊ   What news? Who sent you here?
MESSENGER   I am from Corinth.
The news I bring ought to mean joy for you,
Though it may be you will find some grief in it.
IOKASTÊ   What is it? How can it touch us in both ways?
20 MESSENGER   The word is that the people of the Isthmus
Intend to call Oedipus to be their king.
IOKASTÊ   But old King Polybos—is he not reigning still?
MESSENGER   No. Death holds him in his sepulchre.
IOKASTÊ   What are you saying? Polybos is dead?
25 MESSENGER   If I am not telling the truth, may I die myself.
IOKASTÊ (*to a* MAIDSERVANT)   Go in, go quickly; tell this to
your master.

O riddlers of God's will, where are you now!
This was the man whom Oedipus, long ago,
30   Feared so, fled so, in dread of destroying him—
But it was another fate by which he died.

(*Enter* OEDIPUS, *C.*)

OEDIPUS   Dearest Iokastê, why have you sent for me?
IOKASTÊ   Listen to what this man says, and then tell me
35   What has become of the solemn prophecies.
OEDIPUS   Who is this man? What is his news for me?
IOKASTÊ   He has come from Corinth to announce your
father's death!
OEDIPUS   Is it true, stranger? Tell me in your own words.
40 MESSENGER   I can not say it more clearly: the king is dead.

OEDIPUS   Was it by treason? Or by an attack of illness?
MESSENGER   A little thing brings old men to their rest.
OEDIPUS   It was sickness, then?
MESSENGER   Yes, and his many years.
5   OEDIPUS   Ah!
Why should a man respect the Pythian hearth,[1] or
Give heed to the birds that jangle above his head?
They prophesied that I should kill Polybos,
Kill my own father; but he is dead and buried,
10   And I am here—I never touched him, never,
Unless he died of grief for my departure,
And thus, in a sense, through me. No. Polybos
Has packed the oracles off with him underground.
They are empty words.
15   IOKASTÊ   Had I not told you so?
OEDIPUS   You had; it was my faint heart that betrayed me.
IOKASTÊ   From now on never think of those things again.
OEDIPUS   And yet—must I not fear my mother's bed?
IOKASTÊ   Why should anyone in this world be afraid,
20   Since Fate rules us and nothing can be foreseen?
A man should live only for the present day.

Have no more fear of sleeping with your mother:
How many men, in dreams, have lain with their mothers!
No reasonable man is troubled by such things.
25   OEDIPUS   That is true; only—
If only my mother were not still alive!
But she is alive. I can not help my dread.
IOKASTÊ   Yet this news of your father's death is wonderful.
OEDIPUS   Wonderful. But I fear the living woman.
30   MESSENGER   Tell me, who is this woman that you fear?
OEDIPUS   It is Meropê, man; the wife of King Polybos.
MESSENGER   Meropê? Why should you be afraid of her?
OEDIPUS   An oracle of the gods, a dreadful saying.
MESSENGER   Can you tell me about it or are you sworn to silence?
35   OEDIPUS   I can tell you, and I will.
Apollo said through his prophet that I was the man
Who should marry his own mother, shed his father's blood
With his own hands. And so, for all these years
I have kept clear of Corinth, and no harm has come—
40   Though it would have been sweet to see my parents again.

---

[1] *Pythian hearth* Delphi

MESSENGER   And is this the fear that drove you out of Corinth?
OEDIPUS   Would you have me kill my father?
MESSENGER   As for that
   You must be reassured by the news I gave you.
5 OEDIPUS   If you could reassure me, I would reward you.
MESSENGER   I had that in mind, I will confess: I thought
   I could count on you when you returned to Corinth.
OEDIPUS   No: I will never go near my parents again.
MESSENGER   Ah, son, you still do not know what you are doing—
10 OEDIPUS   What do you mean? In the name of God tell me!
MESSENGER   —if these are your reasons for not going home.
OEDIPUS   I tell you, I fear the oracle may come true.
MESSENGER   And guilt may come upon you through your parents?
OEDIPUS   That is the dread that is always in my heart.
15 MESSENGER   Can you not see that all your fears are groundless?
OEDIPUS   Groundless? Am I not my parents' son?
MESSENGER   Polybos was not your father.
OEDIPUS   Not my father?
MESSENGER   No more your father than the man speaking to you.
20 OEDIPUS   But you are nothing to me!
MESSENGER   Neither was he.
OEDIPUS   Then why did he call me son?
MESSENGER   I will tell you:
   Long ago he had you from my hands, as a gift.
25 OEDIPUS   Then how could he love me so, if I was not his?
MESSENGER   He had no children, and his heart turned to you.
OEDIPUS   What of you? Did you buy me? Did you find me by
   chance?
MESSENGER   . I came upon you in the woody vales of Kithairon.
30 OEDIPUS   And what were you doing there?
MESSENGER   Tending my flocks.
OEDIPUS   A wandering shepherd?
MESSENGER   But your savior, son, that day.
OEDIPUS   From what did you save me?
35 MESSENGER   Your ankles should tell you that.
OEDIPUS   Ah, stranger, why do you speak of that childhood pain?
MESSENGER   I pulled the skewer that pinned your feet together.
OEDIPUS   I have had the mark as long as I can remember.
MESSENGER   That was why you were given the name you bear.
40 OEDIPUS   God! Was it my father or my mother who did it?
   Tell me!
MESSENGER   I do not know. The man who gave you to me
   Can tell you better than I.
OEDIPUS   It was not you that found me, but another?

MESSENGER   It was another shepherd gave you to me.

OEDIPUS   Who was he? Can you tell me who he was?

MESSENGER   I think he was said to be one of Laïos' people.

OEDIPUS   You mean the Laïos who was king here years ago?

5   MESSENGER   Yes; King Laïos; and the man was one of his
herdsmen.

OEDIPUS   Is he still alive? Can I see him?

MESSENGER   These men here
Know best about such things.

10   OEDIPUS   Does anyone here
Know this shepherd that he is talking about?
Have you seen him in the fields, or in the town?
If you have, tell me. It is time things were made plain.

CHORAGOS   I think the man he means is that same shepherd

15   You have already asked to see. Iokastê perhaps
Could tell you something.

OEDIPUS   Do you know anything
About him, Lady? Is he the man we have summoned?
Is that the man this shepherd means?

20   IOKASTÊ   Why think of him?
Forget this herdsman. Forget it all.
This talk is a waste of time.

OEDIPUS   How can you say that,
When the clues to my true birth are in my hands?

25   IOKASTÊ   For God's love, let us have no more questioning!
Is your life nothing to you?
My own is pain enough for me to bear.

OEDIPUS   You need not worry. Suppose my mother a slave,
And born of slaves: no baseness can touch you.

30   IOKASTÊ   Listen to me, I beg you: do not do this thing!

OEDIPUS   I will not listen; the truth must be made known.

IOKASTÊ   Everything that I say is for your own good!

OEDIPUS   My own good
Snaps my patience, then! I want none of it.

35   IOKASTÊ   You are fatally wrong! May you never learn who you are!

OEDIPUS   Go, one of you, and bring the shepherd here.
Let us leave this woman to brag of her royal name.

IOKASTÊ   Ah, miserable!
That is the only word I have for you now.

40   That is the only word I can ever have.

(*Exit into the palace.*)

CHORAGOS   Why has she left us, Oedipus? Why has she gone

In such a passion of sorrow? I fear this silence:
Something dreadful may come of it.
OEDIPUS   Let it come!
However base my birth, I must know about it.
5   The Queen, like a woman, is perhaps ashamed
To think of my low origin. But I
Am a child of Luck; I can not be dishonered.
Luck is my mother; the passing months, my brothers,
Have seen me rich and poor.
10   If this is so,
How could I wish that I were someone else?
How could I not be glad to know my birth?

ODE III

Strophe

15   CHORUS   If ever the coming time were known
To my heart's pondering,
Kithairon, now by Heaven I see the torches
At the festival of the next full moon,
And see the dance, and hear the choir sing
20   A grace to your gentle shade:
Mountain where Oedipus was found,
O mountain guard of a noble race!
May the god [1] who heals us lend his aid,
And let that glory come to pass
25   For our king's cradling-ground.

Antistrophe

Of the nymphs that flower beyond the years,
Who bore you,[2] royal child,
To Pan of the hills or the timberline Apollo,
30   Cold in delight where the upland clears,
Or Hermês for whom Kyllenê's heights are piled?
Or flushed as evening cloud,
Great Dionysos, roamer of mountains,
He—was it he who found you there,

---

[1] *god* Apollo
[2] *Who bore you* The chorus is suggesting that perhaps Oedipus is the son
of one of the immortal nymphs and of a god—Pan, Apollo, Hermes, or
Dionysos. The "sweet god-ravisher" (below) is the presumed mother.

And caught you up in his own proud
Arms from the sweet god-ravisher
Who laughed by the Muses' fountains?

SCENE IV

5 OEDIPUS Sirs: though I do not know the man,
I think I see him coming, this shepherd we want:
He is old, like our friend here, and the men
Bringing him seem to be servants of my house.
But you can tell, if you have ever seen him.

10 (*Enter* SHEPHERD *escorted by* SERVANTS.)

CHORAGOS I know him, he was Laïos' man. You can trust him.
OEDIPUS Tell me first, you from Corinth: is this the shepherd
We were discussing?
MESSENGER This is the very man.
15 OEDIPUS (*to* SHEPHERD) Come here. No, look at me. You
must answer
Everything I ask.—You belonged to Laïos?
SHEPHERD Yes: born his slave, brought up in his house.
OEDIPUS Tell me: what kind of work did you do for him?
20 SHEPHERD I was a shepherd of his, most of my life.
OEDIPUS Where mainly did you go for pasturage?
SHEPHERD Sometimes Kithairon, sometimes the hills near-by.
OEDIPUS Do you remember ever seeing this man out there?
SHEPHERD What would he be doing there? This man?
25 OEDIPUS This man standing here. Have you ever seen him before?
SHEPHERD No. At least, not to my recollection.
MESSENGER And that is not strange, my lord. But I'll refresh
His memory: he must remember when we two
Spent three whole seasons together, March to September,
30 On Kithairon or thereabouts. He had two flocks;
I had one. Each autumn I'd drive mine home
And he would go back with his to Laïos' sheepfold.—
Is this not true, just as I have described it?
SHEPHERD True, yes; but it was all so long ago.
35 MESSENGER Well, then: do you remember, back in those days,
That you gave me a baby boy to bring up as my own?
SHEPHERD What if I did? What are you trying to say?
MESSENGER King Oedipus was once that little child.
SHEPHERD Damn you, hold your tongue!
40 OEDIPUS   No more of that!
It is your tongue needs watching, not this man's.

SHEPHERD   My king, my master, what is it I have done wrong?
OEDIPUS   You have not answered his question about the boy.
SHEPHERD   He does not know . . . He is only making trouble . . .
OEDIPUS   Come, speak plainly, or it will go hard with you.
5   SHEPHERD   In God's name, do not torture an old man!
OEDIPUS   Come here, one of you; bind his arms behind him.
SHEPHERD   Unhappy king! What more do you wish to learn?
OEDIPUS   Did you give this man the child he speaks of?
SHEPHERD   I did.
10   And I would to God I had died that very day.
OEDIPUS   You will die now unless you speak the truth.
SHEPHERD   Yet if I speak the truth, I am worse than dead.
OEDIPUS (*to* ATTENDANT)   He intends to draw it out, apparently—
SHEPHERD   No! I have told you already that I gave him the boy.
15   OEDIPUS   Where did you get him? From your house? From
        somewhere else?
SHEPHERD   Not from mine, no. A man gave him to me.
OEDIPUS   Is that man here? Whose house did he belong to?
SHEPHERD   For God's love, my king, do not ask me any more!
20   OEDIPUS   You are a dead man if I have to ask you again.
SHEPHERD   Then . . . Then the child was from the palace of Laïos.
OEDIPUS   A slave child? or a child of his own line?
SHEPHERD   Ah, I am on the brink of dreadful speech!
OEDIPUS   And I of dreadful hearing. Yet I must hear.
25   SHEPHERD   If you must be told, then . . .
                                        They said it was Laïos' child;
    But it is your wife who can tell you about that.
OEDIPUS   My wife!—Did she give it to you?
SHEPHERD   My lord, she did.
30   OEDIPUS   Do you know why?
SHEPHERD   I was told to get rid of it.
OEDIPUS   Oh heartless mother!
SHEPHERD   But in dread of prophecies . . .
OEDIPUS   Tell me.
35   SHEPHERD   It was said that the boy would kill his own father.
OEDIPUS   Then why did you give him over to this old man?
SHEPHERD   I pitied the baby, my king,
    And I thought that this man would take him far away
    To his own country.
40   He saved him—but for what a fate!
    For if you are what this man says you are,
    No man living is more wretched than Oedipus.
OEDIPUS   Ah God!
    It was true!

All the prophecies!
—Now,
O Light, may I look on you for the last time!
I, Oedipus,
5   Oedipus, damned in his birth, in his marriage damned,
Damned in the blood he shed with his own hand!

(*He rushes into the palace.*)

ODE IV

Strophe 1

10   CHORUS   Alas for the seed of men.
What measure shall I give these generations
That breathe on the void and are void
And exist and do not exist?
Who bears more weight of joy
15   Than mass of sunlight shifting in images,
Or who shall make his thought stay on
That down time drifts away?
Your splendor is all fallen.
O naked brow of wrath and tears,
20   O change of Oedipus!
I who saw your days call no man blest—
Your great days like ghosts gone.

Antistrophe 1

That mind was a strong bow.
25   Deep, how deep you drew it then, hard archer,
At a dim fearful range,
And brought dear glory down!
You overcame the stranger[1]—
The virgin with her hooking lion claws—
30   And though death sang, stood like a tower
To make pale Thebes take heart.
Fortress against our sorrow!
True king, giver of laws,
Majestic Oedipus!
35   No prince in Thebes had ever such renown,
No prince won such grace of power.

---

[1] *stranger* the Sphinx

Strophe 2

And now of all men ever known
Most pitiful is this man's story:
His fortunes are most changed, his state
5   Fallen to a low slave's
Ground under bitter fate.
O Oedipus, most royal one!
The great door[1] that expelled you to the light
Gave at night—ah, gave night to your glory:
10   As to the father, to the fathering son.
All understood too late.
How could that queen whom Laïos won,
The garden that he harrowed at his height,
Be silent when that act was done?

15 ## Antistrophe 2

But all eyes fail before time's eye,
All actions come to justice there.
Though never willed, though far down the deep past,
Your bed, your dread sirings,
20   Are brought to book at last.
Child by Laïos doomed to die,
Then doomed to lose that fortunate little death,
Would God you never took breath in this air
That with my wailing lips I take to cry:
25   For I weep the world's outcast.
I was blind, and now I can tell why:
Asleep, for you had given ease of breath
To Thebes, while the false years went by.

EXODOS [2]

30   (*Enter, from the palace,* SECOND MESSENGER.)

SECOND MESSENGER   Elders of Thebes, most honored in this land,
What horrors are yours to see and hear, what weight
Of sorrow to be endured, if, true to your birth,
You venerate the line of Labdakos!
35   I think neither Istros nor Phasis, those great rivers,
Could purify this place of all the evil

---

[1] *door* Iokastê's womb
[2] *Exodos* final scene

It shelters now, or soon must bring to light—
Evil not done unconsciously, but willed.

The greatest griefs are those we cause ourselves.
CHORAGOS   Surely, friend, we have grief enough already;
5   What new sorrow do you mean?
SECOND MESSENGER   The queen is dead.
CHORAGOS   O miserable queen! But at whose hand?
SECOND MESSENGER   Her own.
The full horror of what happened you can not know,
10   For you did not see it; but I, who did, will tell you
As clearly as I can how she met her death.

When she had left us,
In passionate silence, passing through the court,
She ran to her apartment in the house,
15   Her hair clutched by the fingers of both hands.
She closed the doors behind her; then, by that bed
Where long ago the fatal son was conceived—
That son who should bring about his father's death—
We heard her call upon Laïos, dead so many years,
20   And heard her wail for the double fruit of her marriage,
A husband by her husband, children by her child.

Exactly how she died I do not know:
For Oedipus burst in moaning and would not let us
Keep vigil to the end: it was by him
25   As he stormed about the room that our eyes were caught.
From one to another of us he went, begging a sword,
Hunting the wife who was not his wife, the mother
Whose womb had carried his own children and himself.
I do not know: it was none of us aided him,
30   But surely one of the gods was in control!
For with a dreadful cry
He hurled his weight, as though wrenched out of himself,
At the twin doors: the bolts gave, and he rushed in.
And there we saw her hanging, her body swaying
35   From the cruel cord she had noosed about her neck.
A great sob broke from him, heartbreaking to hear,
As he loosed the rope and lowered her to the ground.

I would blot out from my mind what happened next!
For the king ripped from her gown the golden brooches
40   That were her ornament, and raised them, and plunged
    them down

Straight into his own eyeballs, crying, "No more,
No more shall you look on the misery about me,
The horrors of my own doing! Too long you have known
The faces of those whom I should never have seen,
5   Too long been blind to those for whom I was searching!
From this hour, go in darkness!" And as he spoke,
He struck at his eyes—not once, but many times;
And the blood spattered his beard,
Bursting from his ruined sockets like red hail.

10   So from the unhappiness of two this evil has sprung,
A curse on the man and woman alike. The old
Happiness of the house of Labdakos
Was happiness enough: where is it today?
It is all wailing and ruin, disgrace, death—all
15   The misery of mankind that has a name—
And it is wholly and for ever theirs.
    CHORAGOS   Is he in agony still? Is there no rest for him?
    SECOND MESSENGER   He is calling for someone to open the
        doors wide
20   So that all the children of Kadmos may look upon
His father's murderer, his mother's—no,
I can not say it!
                And then he will leave Thebes,
Self-exiled, in order that the curse
25   Which he himself pronounced may depart from the house.
He is weak, and there is none to lead him,
So terrible is his suffering.
                    But you will see:
Look, the doors are opening; in a moment
30   You will see a thing that would crush a heart of stone.

    (*The central door is opened;* OEDIPUS, *blinded, is led in.*)

    CHORAGOS   Dreadful indeed for men to see.
Never have my own eyes
Looked on a sight so full of fear.

35   Oedipus!
What madness came upon you, what daemon
Leaped on your life with heavier
Punishment than a mortal man can bear?
No: I can not even
40   Look at you, poor ruined one.
And I would speak, question, ponder,

If I were able. No.
You make me shudder.
OEDIPUS   God. God.
Is there a sorrow greater?
5   Where shall I find harbor in this world?
My voice is hurled far on a dark wind.
What has God done to me?
CHORAGOS   Too terrible to think of, or to see.

Strophe 1

10   OEDIPUS   O cloud of night,
Never to be turned away: night coming on,
I can not tell how: night like a shroud!
My fair winds brought me here.
O God. Again
15   The pain of the spikes where I had sight,
The flooding pain
Of memory, never to be gouged out.
CHORAGOS   This is not strange.
You suffer it all twice over, remorse in pain,
20   Pain in remorse.

Antistrophe 1

OEDIPUS   Ah dear friend
Are you faithful even yet, you alone?
Are you still standing near me, will you stay here,
25   Patient, to care for the blind?
The blind man!
Yet even blind I know who it is attends me,
By the voice's tone—
Though my new darkness hide the comforter.
30   CHORAGOS   Oh fearful act!
What god was it drove you to rake black
Night across your eyes?

Strophe 2

OEDIPUS   Apollo. Apollo. Dear
35   Children, the god was Apollo.
He brought my sick, sick fate upon me.
But the blinding hand was my own!
How could I bear to see
When all my sight was horror everywhere?
40   CHORAGOS   Everywhere; that is true.

OEDIPUS   And now what is left?
Images? Love? A greeting even,
Sweet to the senses? Is there anything?
Ah, no, friends: lead me away.
5   Lead me away from Thebes.
                                        Lead the great wreck
And hell of Oedipus, whom the gods hate.
CHORAGOS   Your misery, you are not blind to that.
Would God you had never found it out!

10   **Antistrophe 2**

OEDIPUS   Death take the man who unbound
My feet on that hillside
And delivered me from death to life! What life?
If only I had died,
15   This weight of monstrous doom
Could not have dragged me and my darlings down.
CHORAGOS   I would have wished the same.
OEDIPUS   Oh never to have come here
With my father's blood upon me! Never
20   To have been the man they call his mother's husband!
Oh accurst! Oh child of evil,
To have entered that wretched bed—
                                        the selfsame one!
More primal than sin itself, this fell to me.
25   CHORAGOS   I do not know what words to offer you.
You were better dead than alive and blind.

OEDIPUS   Do not counsel me any more. This punishment
That I have laid upon myself is just.
If I had eyes,
30   I do not know how I could bear the sight
Of my father, when I came to the house of Death,
Or my mother: for I have sinned against them both
So vilely that I could not make my peace
By strangling my own life.
35   Or do you think my children,
Born as they were born, would be sweet to my eyes?
Ah never, never! Nor this town with its high walls,
Nor the holy images of the gods.
                                        For I,
40   Thrice miserable!—Oedipus, noblest of all the line
Of Kadmos, have condemned myself to enjoy

These things no more, by my own malediction
Expelling that man whom the gods declared
To be a defilement in the house of Laïos.
After exposing the rankness of my own guilt,
5   How could I look men frankly in the eyes?
No, I swear it,
If I could have stifled my hearing at its source,
I would have done it and made all this body
A tight cell of misery, blank to light and sound:
10   So I should have been safe in my dark mind
Beyond external evil.
                   Ah Kithairon!
Why did you shelter me? When I was cast upon you,
Why did I not die? Then I should never
15   Have shown the world my execrable birth.

Ah Polybos! Corinth, city that I believed
The ancient seat of my ancestors: how fair
I seemed, your child! And all the while this evil
Was cancerous within me!
20   For I am sick
In my own being, sick in my origin.

O three roads, dark ravine, woodland and way
Where three roads met: you, drinking my father's blood,
My own blood, spilled by my own hand: can you remember
25   The unspeakable things I did there, and the things
I went on from there to do?
                 O marriage, marriage!
That act that engendered me, and again the act
Performed by the son in the same bed—
30   Ah, the net
Of incest, mingling fathers, brothers, sons,
With brides, wives, mothers: the last evil
That can be known by men: no tongue can say
How evil!
35   No. For the love of God, conceal me
Somewhere far from Thebes; or kill me; or hurl me
Into the sea, away from men's eyes for ever.

Come, lead me. You need not fear to touch me.
Of all men, I alone can bear this guilt.

40   (*Enter* KREON.)

CHORAGOS   Kreon is here now. As to what you ask,
He may decide the course to take. He only
Is left to protect the city in your place.
OEDIPUS   Alas, how can I speak to him? What right have I
5   To beg his courtesy whom I have deeply wronged?
KREON   I have not come to mock you, Oedipus,
Or to reproach you, either. (*To* ATTENDANTS)
                              —You, standing there:
If you have lost all respect for man's dignity,
10   At least respect the flame of Lord Helios:
Do not allow this pollution to show itself
Openly here, an affront to the earth
And Heaven's rain and the light of day. No, take him
Into the house as quickly as you can.
15   For it is proper
That only the close kindred see his grief.
OEDIPUS   I pray you in God's name, since your courtesy
Ignores my dark expectation, visiting
With mercy this man of all men most execrable:
20   Give me what I ask—for your good, not for mine.
KREON   And what is it that you turn to me begging for?
OEDIPUS   Drive me out of this country as quickly as may be
To a place where no human voice can ever greet me.
KREON   I should have done that before now—only,
25   God's will had not been wholly revealed to me.
OEDIPUS   But his command is plain: the parricide
Must be destroyed. I am that evil man.
KREON   That is the sense of it, yes; but as things are,
We had best discover clearly what is to be done.
30   OEDIPUS   You would learn more about a man like me?
KREON   You are ready now to listen to the god.
OEDIPUS   I will listen. But it is to you
That I must turn for help. I beg you, hear me.

The woman in there—
35   Give her whatever funeral you think proper:
She is your sister.
                    —But let me go, Kreon!
Let me purge my father's Thebes of the pollution
Of my living here, and go out to the wild hills,
40   To Kithairon, that has won such fame with me,
The tomb my mother and father appointed for me,
And let me die there, as they willed I should.

And yet I know
Death will not ever come to me through sickness
Or in any natural way: I have been preserved
For some unthinkable fate. But let that be.

5 As for my sons, you need not care for them.
They are men, they will find some way to live.
But my poor daughters, who have shared my table,
Who never before have been parted from their father—
Take care of them, Kreon; do this for me.

10 And will you let me touch them with my hands
A last time, and let us weep together?
Be kind, my lord,
Great prince, be kind!
                    Could I but touch them,
15 They would be mine again, as when I had my eyes.

(*Enter* ANTIGONÊ *and* ISMENÊ, *attended.*)

Ah, God!
Is it my dearest children I hear weeping?
Has Kreon pitied me and sent my daughters?
20 KREON Yes, Oedipus: I knew that they were dear to you
In the old days, and know you must love them still.
OEDIPUS May God bless you for this—and be a friendlier
Guardian to you than he has been to me!

Children, where are you?
25 Come quickly to my hands: they are your brother's—
Hands that have brought your father's once clear eyes
To this way of seeing—
                    Ah dearest ones,
I had neither sight nor knowledge then, your father
30 By the woman who was the source of his own life!
And I weep for you—having no strength to see you—,
I weep for you when I think of the bitterness
That men will visit upon you all your lives.
What homes, what festivals can you attend
35 Without being forced to depart again in tears?
And when you come to marriageable age,
Where is the man, my daughters, who would dare
Risk the bane that lies on all my children?
Is there any evil wanting? Your father killed
40 His father; sowed the womb of her who bore him;
Engendered you at the fount of his own existence!

That is what they will say of you.
                                Then, whom
Can you ever marry? There are no bridegrooms for you,
And your lives must wither away in sterile dreaming.

5   O Kreon, son of Menoikeus!
You are the only father my daughters have,
Since we, their parents, are both of us gone for ever.
They are your own blood: you will not let them
Fall into beggary and loneliness;
10   You will keep them from the miseries that are mine!
Take pity on them; see, they are only children,
Friendless except for you. Promise me this,
Great prince, and give me your hand in token of it.

(KREON *clasps his right hand.*)

15   Children:
I could say much, if you could understand me,
But as it is, I have only this prayer for you:
Live where you can, be as happy as you can—
Happier, please God, than God has made your father.
20   KREON   Enough. You have wept enough. Now go within.
OEDIPUS   I must; but it is hard.
KREON   Time eases all things.
OEDIPUS   You know my mind, then?
KREON   Say what you desire.
25   OEDIPUS   Send me from Thebes!
KREON   God grant that I may!
OEDIPUS   But since God hates me . . .
KREON   No, he will grant your wish.
OEDIPUS   You promise?
30   KREON   I can not speak beyond my knowledge.
OEDIPUS   Then lead me in.
KREON   Come now, and leave your children.
OEDIPUS   No! Do not take them from me!
KREON   Think no longer
35   That you are in command here, but rather think
How, when you were, you served your own destruction.

(*Exeunt into the house all but the* CHORUS; *the* CHORAGOS *chants directly to the audience.*)

CHORAGOS   Men of Thebes: look upon Oedipus.

40   This is the king who solved the famous riddle
And towered up, most powerful of men.

No mortal eyes but looked on him with envy,
Yet in the end ruin swept over him.

Let every man in mankind's frailty
Consider his last day; and let none
5   Presume on his good fortune until he find
Life, at his death, a memory without pain.

⌒ LYSISTRATA
(411 B.C.)

ARISTOPHANES (c. 450–387 B.C.)

"Old" Greek comedy, represented only by the eleven surviving plays of Aristophanes, is a combination of farce, strip-tease burlesque, music hall routine, fantasy, and serious literary and political satire. It is, in fact, a unique form which did not extend beyond its brief era in history, but it is one of the most delightfully original and entertaining of all comic drama. The *Lysistrata* is the most eminently producible and the most easily appreciated today, with a plot line and variety of characters that appeal to contemporary audiences. Furthermore, its satire on the idiocies of war and the incompetent bumblers who conduct it is universal and immediately comprehensible.

Tragedies were presented in the mornings at the Festival of Dionysus, while afternoons were apparently reserved for comedy. They, too, followed a fairly rigid structural form, including set choral passages and dancing, and a unique section known as the *parabasis* during which the author presented directly to the audience his own personal views about a variety of things. The most characteristic aspect of Old Comedy, however, was its broadly licentious nature, evident, as in the Lysistrata, in the overt sexual and scatological passages and in the traditional costume. The uniform characteristic of male figures (all characters were taken by men, as in tragedy) was the huge leather sex organ, the *phallus,* worn just beneath the extremely short tunic and in full view at all times.

We should not associate the phallic aspect of Greek comedy with decadence or debilitating immoral social behavior. The Dionysiac Festival was a time of revelry, and Dionysus was god not only of the vine, hence wine, but also of fertility and, by extension, plain ordinary sex. The ancient Greek, who accepted the performance of athletic events by nude participants (though witnessed only by men) and admired the beauties of the male and female undraped body, entertained a healthy respect for sex as a perfectly natural function, susceptible, as in all civilizations, to a lot of very funny dirty jokes. Once a year the performance of these comedies at the Dionysiac was regarded as an appropriate outlet for a very natural urge. The Greek husband may have kept his wife virtually secluded in his house as an individual with few civil rights, but he was not above thoroughly enjoying in public the rambunctious obscenities of Aristophanic comedy.

The *Lysistrata* is emphatically not in itself a "dirty" play. It is, even more than fairly liberal modern translations indicate, a hilariously obscene play, but it is certainly not pornographic. True, the central theme of the sex strike extends the jokes longer and more fully than in any other of Aristophanes' plays, but the wide-open nature of his exploration of the women's use of their ultimate weapon is tremendously funny and wholly free from any sniggering peep-show quality. Moreover, in demonstrating the difficulties which Lysistrata herself encounters in organizing her battle plan and holding her troops in line, Aristophanes makes very clear that sex is not just one-sided and male-dominated. His women, every bit as much as men, openly desire and thoroughly enjoy the experience. While the play does present sex as a source for pointed social and political comment, there is no gainsaying that Aristophanes is also providing, fully intentionally, some of the best comic sex sequences in Western drama.

Lysistrata should be read and experienced in production as what it is meant to be: a brilliant satire on sex itself and on the relative position of supposedly dominating men and submissive women turned topsy-turvy in a society gone mad, and as a superb condemnation of the stupidities of the politicians and bureaucrats who have lived in every historical age and who don't know how to stop the troubles they have let themselves in for. Athens experienced its Vietnam in the Peloponnesian war against which Aristophanes rages in many of his plays. When it ended, Athens of the Golden Age had been permanently destroyed. If he couldn't stop the foolishness in any other way, Aristophanes must have hoped that, through the *Lysistrata,* he could at least laugh it to death.

Lysistrata

ARISTOPHANES

An English version by Dudley Fitts

CHARACTERS

LYSISTRATA ⎫
KALONIKE ⎬ *Athenian women*
MYRRHINE ⎭
LAMPITO, *a Spartan woman*
CHORUS
MAGISTRATE
KINESIAS, *husband of Myrrhine*
SPARTAN HERALD
SPARTAN AMBASSADOR
A SENTRY
ATHENIAN DRUNKARD

The supernumeraries include the BABY SON *of Kinesias;* STRATYLLIS, *a member of the hemichorus of Old Women; various individual speakers, both Spartan and Athenian.*

Until the exodos, *the* CHORUS *is divided into two hemichori: the first, of Old Men; the second, of Old Women. Each of these has its* CHORAGOS. *In the exodos, the hemichori return as Athenians and Spartans.*

Athens. First, a public square; later, beneath the walls of the Acropolis; later, a courtyard within the Acropolis. Time: early in 411 B.C.

Athens; a public square; early morning; LYSISTRATA *sola.*

PROLOGUE

LYSISTRATA   If someone had invited them to a festival—
    Bacchus's, say, or Pan's, or Aphrodite's, or
    that Genetyllis business[1]—, you couldn't get through the streets,
5   what with the drums and the dancing. But now,
    not a woman in sight!
                     Except—oh, yes!

---

[1] *Bacchus, Pan, Aphrodite, Genetyllis* references to cults of love and wine

(*Enter* KALONIKE)

Here's one, at last. Good
morning, Kalonike.

KALONIKE   Good morning, Lysistrata.

5   Darling,
don't frown so! You'll ruin your face!

LYSISTRATA   Never mind my face.
Kalonike,
the way we women behave! Really, I don't blame the men
10 for what they say about us.

KALONIKE   No; I imagine they're right.

LYSISTRATA For example: I call a meeting
to think out a most important matter—and what happens?
The women all stay in bed!

15 KALONIKE   Oh, they'll be along.
It's hard to get away, you know: a husband, a cook,
a child . . . Home life can be *so* demanding!

LYSISTRATA What I have in mind is even more demanding.

KALONIKE Tell me: what is it?

20 LYSISTRATA   Something big.

KALONIKE   Goodness! *How* big?

LYSISTRATA Big enough for all of us.

KALONIKE   But we're not all here!

LYSISTRATA We would be, if *that's* what was up!

25   No, Kalonike,
this is something I've been turning over for nights;
and, I may say, sleepless nights.

KALONIKE   Can't be so hard, then,
if you've spent so much time on it.

30 LYSISTRATA   Hard or not,
it comes to this: Only we women can save Greece!

KALONIKE Only we women? Poor Greece!

LYSISTRATA   Just the same,
it's up to us. First, we must liquidate
35 the Peloponnesians—

KALONIKE   Fun, fun!

LYSISTRATA   —and then the Boeotians.

KALONIKE Oh! But not those heavenly eels! [1]

LYSISTRATA   You needn't worry.

40 Athens shall have her sea food. —But here's the point:
If we can get the women from those places

---

[1] *eels* Boeotia was famous for its sea food, especially its eels.

to join us women here, why, we can save
all Greece!

KALONIKE   But dearest Lysistrata!
How can women do a thing so austere, so
5   political? We belong at home. Our only armor's
our transparent saffron dresses and
our pretty little shoes!

LYSISTRATA   That's it exactly.
Those transparent saffron dresses, those little shoes—
10   well, there we are!

KALONIKE   Oh?

LYSISTRATA   Not a single man would lift
his spear—

KALONIKE   I'll get my dress from the dyer's tomorrow!
15   LYSISTRATA   —or need a shield—

KALONIKE   The sweetest little negligée—

LYSISTRATA   —or bring out his sword.

KALONIKE   I know where I can buy
the dreamiest sandals!

20   LYSISTRATA   Well, so you see. Now, shouldn't
the women have come?

KALONIKE   Come? they should have *flown*!

LYSISTRATA   Athenians are always late.
                                    But imagine!
25   There's no one here from the South Shore.

KALONIKE   They go to work early,
I can swear to that.

LYSISTRATA   And nobody from Acharnai.
They should have been here hours ago!

30   KALONIKE   Well, you'll get
that awful Theagenes woman: she's been having
her fortune told at Hecate's shrine.[1]
                                    But look!
Someone at last! Can you see who they are?

35   (*Enter* MYRRHINE *and other women*)

LYSISTRATA   People from the suburbs.

KALONIKE   Yes! The entire
membership of the Suburban League!

---

[1] *Hecate's shrine* Theagenes was notoriously superstitious; his practice of
never leaving home without consulting Hecate is here transferred to his
wife.

MYRRHINE   Sorry to be late, Lysistrata.
                                    Oh, come,
   don't scowl so! Say something!
   LYSISTRATA   My dear Myrrhine,
5   what is there to say? After all,
   you've been pretty casual about the whole thing.
   MYRRHINE   Couldn't find
   my girdle in the dark, that's all.
                                    But what *is*
10   "the whole thing"?
   LYSISTRATA   Wait for the rest of them.
   KALONIKE   I suppose so. But, look!
   Here's Lampito!

   (*Enter* LAMPITO *with women from Sparta*)

15   LYSISTRATA   Darling Lampito,
   how pretty you are today! What a nice color!
   Goodness, you look as though you could strangle a bull!
   LAMPITO   Ah think Ah could! It's the work-out
   in the gym every day; and, of co'se that dance of ahs
20   where y' kick yo' own tail.[1]
   LYSISTRATA   What lovely breasts!
   LAMPITO   Lawdy, when y' touch me lahk that,
   Ah feel lahk a heifer at the altar!
   LYSISTRATA   And this young lady?
25   Where is she from?
   LAMPITO   Boeotia. Social-Register type.
   LYSISTRATA   Good morning, Boeotian. You're as pretty as
      green grass.
   KALONIKE   And if you look,
30   you'll find that the lawn has just been cut.
   LYSISTRATA   And this lady?
   LAMPITO   From Corinth. But a good woman.
   LYSISTRATA   Well, in Corinth
   anything's possible.
35   LAMPITO   But let's get to work. Which one of you
   called this meeting, and why?
   LYSISTRATA   *I* did.
   LAMPITO   Well, then:
   what's up?

---

[1] *tail* Among the physical exercises practised by Greek girls was the strenuous *bibasis*, a dance in which the dancer kicked her buttocks with her heels. (Lampito and other Spartans speak with a distinctly "southern" Greek accent; hence the translator's choice of an American southern drawl for comic effect.)

MYRRHINE Yes, what *is* "the whole thing," after all?
LYSISTRATA I'll tell you. —But first, one question.
MYRRHINE Ask away!
LYSISTRATA It's your husbands. Fathers of your children. Doesn't it
5 bother you
that they're always off with the Army? I'll stake my life,
not one of you has a man in the house this minute!
KALONIKE Mine's been in Thrace the last five months, keeping an
eye
10 on that General.[1]
MYRRHINE Mine's been in Pylos for seven.
LAMPITO And mahn,
whenever he gets a *dis*charge, he goes raht back
with that li'l ole speah of his, and enlists again!
15 LYSISTRATA And not the ghost of a lover to be found!
From the very day the war began—
those Milesians!
I could skin them alive!
—I've not seen so much, even,
20 as one of those devices they call Widow's Delight.
But there! What's important is: I've found a way
to end the war, are you with me?
MYRRHINE I should *say* so!
Even if I have to pawn my best dress and
25 drink up the proceeds.[2]
KALONIKE Me, too! Even if they split me
right up the middle, like a flounder.
LAMPITO Ah'm shorely with you.
Ah'd crawl up Taygetos[3] on mah knees
30 if that'd bring peace.
LYSISTRATA Then here it is.
Women! Sisters!
If we really want our men to make an armistice,
we must be ready to give up—
35 MYRRHINE Give up what?
Quick, tell us!
LYSISTRATA But *will* you?
MYRRHINE We will, even if it kills us.

---

[1] *General* a certain Eukrates about whom nothing is known
[2] *drink up the proceeds* Athenian women were frequently satirized for heavy
drinking.
[3] *Taygetos* a rugged mountain range in the Peloponnesus

LYSISTRATA Then we must give up sleeping with our men. (*Long silence*)
Oh? So now you're sorry? Won't look at me?
Doubtful? Pale? All teary-eyed?
5 But come: be frank with me,
as I've certainly been with you. Will you do it?
MYRRHINE I couldn't. No.
Let the war go on.
KALONIKE Nor I. Let the war go on.
10 LYSISTRATA You, you little flounder,
ready to be split up the middle?
KALONIKE Lysistrata, no!
I'd walk through fire for you—you *know* I would!—, but don't
ask us to give up *that*! Why, there's nothing like it!
15 LYSISTRATA And you?
BOEOTIAN No. I must say *I'd* rather walk through fire.
LYSISTRATA You little salamanders!
No wonder poets write tragedies about women.
All we want's a quick tumble!
20 But you from Sparta:
if you stand by me, we may win yet! Will you?
It means so much!
LAMPITO Ah sweah, it means *too* much!
By the Two Goddesses,[1] it does! Asking a girl
25 to sleep—Heaven knows how long!—in a great big bed
with nobody there but herself! But Ah'll stay with you!
Peace comes first!
LYSISTRATA Spoken like a true Spartan!
KALONIKE But, if—
30 oh dear!
—if we give up what you tell us to,
will there *be* any peace?
LYSISTRATA Why, mercy, of course there will!
We'll just sit snug in our very thinnest gowns,
35 perfumed and powdered from top to bottom, and those men
simply won't stand still! And when we say No,
they'll go out of their minds! And there's your peace.
You can take my word for it.
LAMPITO Ah seem to remember
40 that Colonel Menelaus threw his sword away
when he saw Helen's breast all bare.

---

[1] *Two Goddesses* Demeter and Persephone; a woman's oath

KALONIKE But, goodness me!
What if they just get up and leave us?
LYSISTRATA Well,
we'd have to fall back on ourselves, of course.
5   But they won't.
KALONIKE What if they drag us into the bedroom?
LYSISTRATA Hang on to the door.
KALONIKE What if they slap us?
LYSISTRATA If they do, you'd better give in.
10 But be sulky about it. Do I have to teach you how?
You know there's no fun for men when they have to force you.
There are millions of ways of getting them to see reason.
Don't you worry: a man
doesn't like it unless the girl co-operates.
15 KALONIKE I suppose so. Oh, all right! We'll go along!
LAMPITO Ah imagine us Spahtans can arrange a peace. But you
Athenians! Why, you're just war-mongerers!
LYSISTRATA Leave that to me.
I know how to make them listen.
20 LAMPITO Ah don't see how.
After all, they've got their boats; and there's lots of money
piled up in the Acropolis.
LYSISTRATA The Acropolis? Darling,
we're taking over the Acropolis today!
25 That's the older women's job. All the rest of us
are going to the Citadel to sacrifice—you understand me?
And once there, we're in for good!
LAMPITO Whee! Up the rebels!
Ah can see you're a good strat*ee*gist.
30 LYSISTRATA Well, then, Lampito,
let's take the oath.
LAMPITO Say it. We'll sweah.
LYSISTRATA This is it.
—But Lord! Where's our Inner Guard? Never mind.
35 —You see this
shield? Put it down there. Now bring me the victim's entrails.
KALONIKE But the oath?
LYSISTRATA You remember how in Aeschylus' *Seven*[1]
they killed a sheep and swore on a shield? Well, then?
40 KALONIKE But I don't see how you can swear for peace on a shield.
LYSISTRATA What else do you suggest?

---

[1] *The Seven Against Thebes*

KALONIKE Why not a white horse?
We could swear by that.
LYSISTRATA And where will you get a white horse?
KALONIKE I never thought of that. *What* can we do?
5 MYRRHINE I have it!
Let's set this big black wine-bowl on the ground
and pour in a gallon or so of Thasian,[1] and swear
not to add one drop of water.
LAMPITO Ah lahk *that* oath!
10 LYSISTRATA Bring the bowl and the wine-jug.
KALONIKE Oh, what a simply *huge* one!
LYSISTRATA Set it down; and, women, place your hands on the gift-
offering.

O Goddess of Persuasion! And thou, O Loving-cup!
15 Look upon this our sacrifice, and
be gracious!

KALONIKE It spills out like blood. How red and pretty it is!
LAMPITO And Ah must say it smells good.
MYRRHINE Let me swear first!
20 KALONIKE No, by Aphrodite, let's toss for it!
LYSISTRATA Lampito: all of you women: come, touch the bowl,
and repeat after me:
I WILL HAVE NOTHING TO DO WITH MY HUSBAND
OR MY LOVER
25 KALONIKE *I will have nothing to do with my husband or my lover*
LYSISTRATA THOUGH HE COME TO ME IN PITIABLE
CONDITION
KALONIKE *Though he come to me in pitiable condition*
(Oh, Lysistrata! This is killing me!)
30 LYSISTRATA I WILL STAY IN MY HOUSE UNTOUCHABLE
KALONIKE *I will stay in my house untouchable*
LYSISTRATA IN MY THINNEST SAFFRON SILK
KALONIKE *In my thinnest saffron silk*
LYSISTRATA AND MAKE HIM LONG FOR ME.
35 KALONIKE *And make him long for me.*
LYSISTRATA I WILL NOT GIVE MYSELF
KALONIKE *I will not give myself*
LYSISTRATA AND IF HE CONSTRAINS ME

---

[1] *Thasian* a popular wine from Thasos

KALONIKE *And if he constrains me*
LYSISTRATA I WILL BE AS COLD AS ICE AND NEVER MOVE
KALONIKE *I will be as cold as ice and never move*
5 LYSISTRATA I WILL NOT LIFT MY SLIPPERS TOWARD THE CEILING
KALONIKE *I will not lift my slippers toward the ceiling*
LYSISTRATA OR CROUCH ON ALL FOURS LIKE THE LIONESS IN THE CARVING
10 KALONIKE *Or crouch on all fours like the lioness in the carving*
LYSISTRATA AND IF I KEEP THIS OATH LET ME DRINK FROM THIS BOWL
KALONIKE *And if I keep this oath let me drink from this bowl*
LYSISTRATA IF NOT, LET MY OWN BOWL BE FILLED
15 WITH WATER.
KALONIKE *If not, let my own bowl be filled with water.*
LYSISTRATA You have all sworn?
MYRRHINE We have.
LYSISTRATA Then thus
20 I sacrifice the victim. (*Drinks largely*)
KALONIKE Save some for us!
Here's to you, darling, and to you, and to you! It's all
for us women. (*Loud cries off-stage*)
LAMPITO What's all *that* whoozy-goozy?
25 LYSISTRATA Just what I told you.
The older women have taken the Acropolis. Now you, Lampito,
rush back to Sparta. We'll take care of things here. And
be sure you get organized!
The rest of you girls,
30 up to the Citadel: and mind you push in the bolts.
KALONIKE But the men? Won't they be after us?
LYSISTRATA Just you leave
the men to me. There's not fire enough in the world
to make me open *my* door.
35 KALONIKE I hope so, by Aphrodite!
At any rate,
let's remember the League's reputation for hanging on!

(*Exeunt*)

PÁRODOS

40 *The hillside just under the Acropolis*

(*Enter* CHORUS OF OLD MEN *with burning torches and braziers; much puffing and coughing*)

MALE CHORAGOS   Easy, Drakes, old friend! Don't skin your shoulders
with those damnable big olive-branches. What a job!

Strophe 1

OLD MEN   Forward, forward, comrades! Whew!
5   The things that old age does to you!
   Neighbor Strymodoros, would you have thought it?
      We've caught it—
                  And from women, too!
   Women that used to board with us, bed with us—
10   Now, by the gods, they've got ahead of us,
   Taken the Acropolis (Heaven knows why!),
   Profaned the sacred statuar-y,
                  And barred the doors,
                  The aggravating whores!
15 MALE CHORAGOS   Come, Philourgos, quick, pile your brushwood
   next to the wall there.
                  These traitors to Athens and to us,
   we'll fry each last one of them! And the very first
   will be old Lykon's wife.[1]

20 **Antistrophe 1**

OLD MEN   By Demeter I swear it—(ouch!),
   I'll not perform the Kleomenes-crouch!
   How he looked—and a good soldier, too—
      When out he flew,
25   that filthy pouch
   Of a body of his all stinking and shaggy,
   Bare as an eel, except for the bag he
   Covered his rear with. Lord, what a mess!
   Never a bath in six years, I'd guess!
30   Unhappy Sparta,
                  With such a martyr![2]
   MALE CHORAGOS   What a siege, friends! Seventeen ranks strong
   we stood at the Gate, and never a chance for a nap.
   And all because of women, whom the gods hate
35   (and so does Euripides).
                  It's enough to make a veteran
   turn in his medals from Marathon!

---

[1] *Lykon's wife* Rhodia, a famous belle of the day
[2] *martyr* Kleomenes, a King of Sparta, had captured the Acropolis but had
   been forced to give it up.

Strophe 2

OLD MEN Forward, men! Just up the hillside,
And we're there!
Keep to the path! A yoke of oxen
5 Wouldn't care
To haul this lumber. Mind the fire,
Or it'll die before we're higher!
Puff! Puff!
This smoke will strangle me, sure enough!

10 **Antistrophe 2**

Holy Heracles, I'm blinded,
Sure as fate!
It's Lemnos-fire[1] we've been toting;
And isn't it great
15 To be singed by this infernal flame?
(Laches, remember the Goddess: for shame!)
Woof! Woof!
A few steps more, and we're under the roof!
MALE CHORAGOS It catches! It's blazing!
20 Down with your loads!
We'll sizzle 'em now,
By all the gods!
Vine-branches here, quick!
Light 'em up,
25 And in through the gate with 'em!
If that doesn't stop
Their nonsense—well,
We'll smoke 'em to Hell.
Ker*shoo*!
30 (What we really need
Is a grad-u-ate,
Top of his class,
From Samos Military State.[2]
Achoo!)
35 Come, do
Your duty, you!
Pour out your braziers,

---

[1] *Lemnos-fire* volcanic; Mount Moschylus on the island of Lemnos was the site of Vulcan's forge.
[2] *Samos Military State* At this time Samos was the headquarters of Athenian military activities.

Embers ablaze!
But first, Gentlemen, allow me to raise
The paean:
   Lady
5 *Victory, now*
 Assist thine adherents
 Here below!
Down with women!
Up with men!
10 *Io triumphe!* [1]
OLD MEN Amen!

(*Enter* CHORUS OF OLD WOMEN *on the walls of the Acropolis, carrying jars of water to extinguish the fire set by the* CHORUS OF OLD MEN.)

FEMALE CHORAGOS Fire, fire!
15 Quickly, quickly, women, if we're to save ourselves!

Strophe

OLD WOMEN Nikodike, run!
 Or Kalyke's done
 To a turn, and poor Kratylla's
20 Smoked like a ham.
    Damn
 These men and their wars,
 Their hateful ways!
 I nearly died before I got to the place
25 Where we fill our jars:
  Slaves pushing and jostling—
  Such a hustling
 I never saw in all my days!

Antistrophe

30 But here's water at last.
 Sisters, make haste
 And slosh it down on them,
 The silly old wrecks!
    Sex
35 Almighty! What they want's
 A hot bath? Send it down!
 And thou, Athena of Athens town,
 Assist us in drowning their wheezy taunts!

---

[1] *Io triumphe* a ritual cry of triumph

O Trito-born! [1] Helmet of Gold!
Help us to cripple their backs, the old
Fools with their semi-incendiary brawn!

(*The* OLD MEN *capture a woman,* STRATYLLIS)

5   STRATYLLIS   Let me go! Let me go!
FEMALE CHORAGOS   You walking corpses,
have you no shame?
MALE CHORAGOS   I wouldn't have believed it!
An army of women in the Acropolis!
10   FEMALE CHORAGOS   So we scare you, do we? Grandpa, you've seen
only our pickets yet!
MALE CHORAGOS   Hey, Phaidrias!
Help me with the necks of these jabbering hens!
FEMALE CHORAGOS   Down with your pots, girls! We'll need
15   both hands
if these antiques attack us.
MALE CHORAGOS   Want your face kicked in?
FEMALE CHORAGOS   Want to try my teeth?
MALE CHORAGOS   Look out! I've got a stick!
20   FEMALE CHORAGOS   You lay a half-inch of your stick on Stratyllis,
and you'll never stick again!
MALE CHORAGOS   Fall apart!
FEMALE CHORAGOS   I'll chew your guts!
MALE CHORAGOS   Euripides! Master!
25   How well you knew women!
FEMALE CHORAGOS   Listen to him! Rhodippe,
up with the pots!
MALE CHORAGOS   Demolition of God,
what good are your pots?
30   FEMALE CHORAGOS   You refugee from the tomb,
what good is your fire?
MALE CHORAGOS   Good enough to make a pyre
to barbecue you!
FEMALE CHORAGOS   We'll squizzle your kindling!
35   MALE CHORAGOS   You think so?
FEMALE CHORAGOS   Yah! Just hang around a while!
MALE CHORAGOS   Want a touch of my torch?
FEMALE CHORAGOS   Your torch needs a bath.
MALE CHORAGOS   How about you?

---

[1] *Trito-born* Athena; according to some versions of her story, she was born
at Lake Tritonis in Libya.

FEMALE CHORAGOS   Soap for a senile bridegroom!
MALE CHORAGOS   Senile? Hold your trap!
FEMALE CHORAGOS   Just *you* try to hold it!
MALE CHORAGOS   The yammer of women!
5   FEMALE CHORAGOS   The yatter of men!
But you'll never sit in the jury-box again.
MALE CHORAGOS   Gentlemen, I beg you, burn off that woman's hair!
FEMALE CHORAGOS   Let it come down! (*They empty their pots on
the men*)
10   MALE CHORAGOS   What a way to drown!
FEMALE CHORAGOS   Hot, hey?
MALE CHORAGOS   Say,
enough!
FEMALE CHORAGOS   Dandruff
15   needs watering. I'll make you
nice and fresh.
MALE CHORAGOS   For God's sake, you
sluts, hold off!

SCENE I

20   (*Enter a* MAGISTRATE *accompanied by four constables*)

MAGISTRATE   These degenerate women! What a racket of little
drums,
what a yapping for Adonis on every house-top!
It's like the time in the Assembly when I was listening
25   to a speech—out of order, as usual—by that fool
Demostratos,[1] all about troops for Sicily,
that kind of nonsense—
and there was his wife
trotting around in circles howling
30   *Alas for Adonis!*—
and Demostratos insisting
we must draft every last Zakynthian that can walk—
and his wife up there on the roof,
drunk as an owl, yowling
35   *Oh weep for Adonis!*—
and that damned ox Demostratos
mooing away through the rumpus. That's what we get
for putting up with this wretched woman-business!

---

[1] *Demostratos* a well known demagogue; the speech alludes to the festival in honor of Adonis which four years earlier had coincided with the decision to undertake the disastrous Sicilian expedition. It was believed that the women's madness in lamenting Adonis had influenced the decision.

MALE CHORAGOS Sir, you haven't heard the half of it. They laughed
at us!
Insulted us! They took pitchers of water
and nearly drowned us! We're still wringing out our clothes,
5 for all the world like unhousebroken brats.
MAGISTRATE And a good thing, by Poseidon!
Whose fault is it if these women-folk of ours
get out of hand? We coddle them,
we teach them to be wasteful and loose. You'll see a husband
10 go into a jeweler's. "Look," he'll say,
"jeweler," he'll say, "you remember that gold choker
"you made for my wife? Well, she went to a dance last night
"and broke the clasp. Now, I've got to go to Salamis,
"and can't be bothered. Run over to my house tonight,
15 "will you, and see if you can put it together for her."
Or another one
goes to a cobbler—a good strong workman, too,
with an awl that was never meant for child's play. "Here,"
he'll tell him, "one of my wife's shoes is pinching
20 "her little toe. Could you come up about noon
"and stretch it out for her?"
                                     Well, what do you expect?
Look at me, for example. I'm a Public Officer,
and it's one of my duties to pay off the sailors.
25 And where's the money? Up there in the Acropolis!
And those blasted women slam the door in my face!
But what are we waiting for?
                              —Look here, constable,
stop sniffing around for a tavern, and get us
30 some crowbars. We'll force their gates! As a matter of fact,
I'll do a little forcing myself.

(*Enter* LYSISTRATA, *above, with* MYRRHINE, KALONIKE, *and the*
BOEOTIAN)

LYSISTRATA   No need of forcing.
35 Here I am, of my own accord. And all this talk
about locked doors—! We don't need locked doors,
but just the least bit of common sense.
MAGISTRATE Is that so, ma'am!
                              —Where's my constable?
40   —Constable,
arrest that woman, and tie her hands behind her.
LYSISTRATA If he touches me, I swear by Artemis
there'll be one scamp dropped from the public pay-roll tomorrow!

MAGISTRATE Well, constable? You're not afraid, I suppose? Grab her,
two of you, around the middle!

KALONIKE No, by Pandrosos! [1]

5 Lay a hand on her, and I'll jump on you so hard
your guts will come out the back door!

MAGISTRATE That's what *you* think!
Where's the sergeant?—Here, you: tie up that trollop first,
the one with the pretty talk!

10 MYRRHINE By the Moon-Goddess! [2]
Just you try it, and you'd better call a surgeon!

MAGISTRATE Another one!
Officer, seize that woman!
I swear

15 I'll put an end to this riot!

BOEOTIAN By the Taurian, [3]
one inch closer and you won't have a hair on your head!

MAGISTRATE Lord, what a mess! And my constables seem to have
left me.

20 But—women get the best of us? By God, no!
—Scythians! [4]
Close ranks and forward march!

LYSISTRATA "Forward," indeed!
By the Two Goddesses, what's the sense in *that*?

25 They're up against four companies of women
armed from top to bottom.

MAGISTRATE Forward, my Scythians!

LYSISTRATA Forward, yourselves, dear comrades!
You grainlettucebeanseedmarket girls!

30 You garlicandonionbreadbakery girls!
Give it to 'em! Knock 'em down! Scratch 'em!
Tell 'em what you think of 'em! (*General mêlée; the Scythians
yield*)
—Ah, that's enough!

35 Sound a retreat; good soldiers don't rob the dead!

MAGISTRATE A nice day *this* has been for the police!

LYSISTRATA Well, there you are.—Did you really think we women

---

1 *Pandrosos* one of the daughters of the founder of Athens; a woman's oath
2 *Moon-Goddess* Artemis
3 *Taurian* again Artemis, who was worshipped at Taurica Chersonesos
4 *Scythians* Athens' finest archers

would be driven like slaves? Maybe now you'll admit
that a woman knows something about glory.
MAGISTRATE   Glory enough.
especially glory in bottles! Dear Lord Apollo!
5   MALE CHORAGOS   Your Honor, there's no use talking to them. Words
mean nothing whatever to wild animals like these.
Think of the sousing they gave us! and the water
was not, I believe, of the purest.
FEMALE CHORAGOS   You shouldn't have come after us. And if you
10   try it again,
you'll be one eye short!—Although, as a matter of fact,
what I like best is just to stay at home and read,
like a sweet little bride: never hurting a soul, no,
never going out. But if you *must* shake hornets' nests,
15   look out for the hornets!

Strophe

OLD MEN   Good God, what can we do?
        What are we coming to?
These women! Who could bear it? But, for that matter, who
20   Will find
        What they had in mind
        When they seized Cranaos' city
        And held it (more's the pity!)
Against us men of Athens, and our police force, too?

25   MALE CHORAGOS   We might question them, I suppose. But I warn
        you, sir,
don't believe anything you hear! It would be un-Athenian
not to get to the bottom of this plot.
MAGISTRATE   Very well.
30   My first question is this: Why, so help you God,
did you bar the gates of the Acropolis?
LYSISTRATA   Why?
To keep the money, of course. No money, no war.
MAGISTRATE   You think that money's the cause of war?
35   LYSISTRATA   I do.
Money brought about the Peisandros business[1]

---

[1] *Peisandros* a politician who, even as Aristophanes was completing this play,
was bringing about the revolution of the Four Hundred, which overthrew
Athenian democracy

and all the other attacks on the State. Well and good!
They'll not get another cent here!
MAGISTRATE   And what will you do?
LYSISTRATA   What a question! From now on, we intend
5   to control the Treasury.
MAGISTRATE   Control the Treasury!
LYSISTRATA   Why not? Does that seem strange? After all,
we control our household budgets.
MAGISTRATE   But that's different!
10   LYSISTRATA   "Different"? What do you mean?
MAGISTRATE   I mean simply this:
it's the Treasury that pays for National Defense.
LYSISTRATA   Unnecessary. We propose to abolish war!
MAGISTRATE   Good God.—And National Security?
15   LYSISTRATA   Leave that to us.
MAGISTRATE   You?
LYSISTRATA   Us.
MAGISTRATE   We're done for, then!
LYSISTRATA   Never mind.
20   We women will save you in spite of yourselves.
MAGISTRATE   What nonsense!
LYSISTRATA   If you like. But you must accept it, like it or not.
MAGISTRATE   Why, this is downright subversion!
LYSISTRATA   Maybe it is.
25   But we're going to save you, Judge.
MAGISTRATE   I don't *want* to be saved!
LYSISTRATA   Tut. The death-wish. All the more reason.
MAGISTRATE   But the idea
of women bothering themselves about peace and war!
30   LYSISTRATA   Will you listen to me?
MAGISTRATE   Yes. But be brief, or I'll—
LYSISTRATA   This is no time for stupid threats.
MAGISTRATE   By the gods,
I'm losing my mind!
35   AN OLD WOMAN   That's nice. If you do, remember
you've less to lose than *we* have.
MAGISTRATE   Quiet, you old buzzard!
Now, Lysistrata: tell me what you're thinking.
LYSISTRATA   Glad to.
40   Ever since this war began
we women have been watching you men, agreeing with you,
keeping our thoughts to ourselves. That doesn't mean
we were happy: we weren't, for we saw how things were going;

but we'd listen to you at dinner
arguing this way and that.
                              —Oh you, and your big
Top Secrets!—
5   And then we'd grin like little patriots
(though goodness knows we didn't feel like grinning) and ask you:
"Dear, did the Armistice come up in Assembly today?"
And you'd say, "None of your business! Pipe down!," you'd say.
And so we would.
10 AN OLD WOMAN   *I* wouldn't have, by God!
    MAGISTRATE   You'd have taken a beating, then!
                                      —Please go on.
    LYSISTRATA   Well, we'd be quiet. But then, you know, all at once
    you men would think up something worse than ever.
15 Even *I* could see it was fatal. And, "Darling," I'd say,
    "have you gone completely mad?" And my husband would look at
      me
    and say, "Wife, you've got your weaving to attend to.
    "Mind your tongue, if you don't want a slap. 'War's
20 "'a man's affair!'"[1]
    MAGISTRATE   Good words, and well pronounced!
    LYSISTRATA   You're a fool if you think so.
                                   It was hard enough
    to put up with all this banquet-hall strategy.
25 But then we'd hear you out in the public square:
    "Nobody left for the draft-quota here in Athens?"
    you'd say; and, "No," someone else would say, "not a man!"
    And so we women decided to rescue Greece.
    You might as well listen to us now: you'll have to, later.
30 MAGISTRATE   *You* rescue Greece? Absurd!
    LYSISTRATA   You're the absurd one!
    MAGISTRATE   You expect me to take orders from a woman?
    LYSISTRATA   Heavens, if that's what's bothering you, take my veil,
    here, and my girdle, and my market-basket. Go home
35 to your weaving and your cooking! I tell you, "War's
    a woman's affair!"
    FEMALE CHORAGOS   Down with your pitchers, comrades,
    but keep them close at hand. It's time for a rally!

---

[1] *War's a man's affair* quoted from Hector's farewell to Andromache, *Iliad,*
VI, 492

Antistrophe

OLD WOMEN   Dance, girls, dance for peace!
             Who cares if our knees
       Wobble and creak? Shall we not dance for such allies as these?
       Their wit! their grace! their beauty!
5   It's a municipal duty
       To dance them luck and happiness who risk their all for Greece!

FEMALE CHORAGOS   Women, remember your grandmothers! Re-
       member, you were born
       among brambles and nettles! Dance for victory!
10 LYSISTRATA   O Eros, god of delight! O Aphrodite! Cyprian!
       Drench us now with the savor of love!
       Let these men, getting wind of us, dream such joy
       that they'll tail us through all the provinces of Hellas!
   MAGISTRATE   And if we do?
15 LYSISTRATA   Well, for one thing, we shan't have to
       watch you
       going to market, a spear in one hand, and heavens knows
       what in the other.
   FEMALE CHORAGOS   Nicely said, by Aphrodite!
20 LYSISTRATA   As things stand now, you're neither men nor women.
       Armor clanking with kitchen pans and pots—
       you sound like a pack of Corybantes! [1]
   MAGISTRATE   A man must do what a man must do.
   LYSISTRATA   So I'm told.
25   But to see a General, complete with Gorgon-shield,
       jingling along the dock to buy a couple of herrings!
   FEMALE CHORAGOS   *I* saw a Captain the other day—lovely fellow he
       was,
       nice curly hair—sitting on his horse; and—can you believe it?—
30   he'd just bought some soup, and was pouring it into his helmet!
       And there was a soldier from Thrace
       swishing his lance like something out of Euripides,
       and the poor fruit-store woman got so scared
       that she ran away and let him have his figs free!
35 MAGISTRATE   All this is beside the point.
                                       Will you be so kind
       as to tell me how you mean to save Greece?
   LYSISTRATA   Of course!
       Nothing could be simpler.[2]

---

[1] *Corybantes* wild and frenzied dancers; attendants of the goddess Cybele
[2] This extended *agon* (argument) between Lysistrata and The Magistrate is the closest
the play comes to presenting the traditional *parabasis* (see p. 77).

MAGISTRATE   I assure you, I'm all ears.
LYSISTRATA   Do you know anything about weaving?
Say the yarn gets tangled: we thread it
this way and that through the skein, up and down,
5   until it's free. And it's like that with war.
We'll send our envoys
up and down, this way and that, all over Greece,
until it's finished.
MAGISTRATE   Yarn? Thread? Skein?
10   Are you out of your mind? I tell you,
war is a serious business.
LYSISTRATA   So serious
that I'd like to go on talking about weaving.
MAGISTRATE   All right. Go ahead.
15   LYSISTRATA   The first thing we have to do
is to wash our yarn, get the dirt out of it.
You see? Isn't there too much dirt here in Athens?
You must wash those men away.
                                Then our spoiled wool—
20   that's like your job-hunters, out for a life
of no work and big pay. Back to the basket,
citizens or not, allies or not,
or friendly immigrants!
                              And your colonies?
25   Hanks of wool lost in various places. Pull them
together, weave them into one great whole,
and our voters are clothed for ever.
MAGISTRATE   It would take a woman
to reduce state questions to a matter of carding and weaving!
30   LYSISTRATA   You fool! Who were the mothers whose sons sailed off
to fight for Athens in Sicily?
MAGISTRATE   Enough!
I beg you, do not call back those memories.
LYSISTRATA   And then,
35   instead of the love that every woman needs,
we have only our single beds, where we can dream
of our husbands off with the Army.
                              Bad enough for wives!
But what about our girls, getting older every day,
40   and older, and no kisses?
MAGISTRATE   Men get older, too.
LYSISTRATA   Not in the same sense.
                        A soldier's discharged,
and he may be bald and toothless, yet he'll find

a pretty young thing to go to bed with.
> But a woman!

Her beauty is gone with the first grey hair.
She can spend her time
5   consulting the oracles and the fortune-tellers,
but they'll never send her a husband.

MAGISTRATE   Still, if a man can rise to the occasion—

LYSISTRATA (*Furiously*)   Rise? Rise, yourself!
Go invest in a coffin!
10   > You've money enough.
> > I'll bake you

a cake for the Underworld.[1]
> And here's your funeral

wreath! (*She pours water upon him*)

15   MYRRHINE   > And here's another! (*More water*)

KALONIKE   > > And here's

my contribution! (*More water*)

LYSISTRATA   What are you waiting for?
All aboard Styx Ferry![2]
20   > Charon's calling for you!

It's sailing-time: don't disrupt the schedule!

MAGISTRATE   The insolence of women! And to me!
No, by God, I'll go back to court and show
the rest of the Bench the things that might happen to them!

25   (*Exit* MAGISTRATE)

LYSISTRATA   Really, I suppose we should have laid out his corpse
on the doorstep, in the usual way.
> But never mind!

We'll give him the rites of the dead tomorrow morning!

30   (*Exit* LYSISTRATA *with* MYRRHINE *and* KALONIKE)

CHORAL EPISODE

Strophe 1

OLD MEN   Sons of Liberty, strip off your clothes for action! Men
arise!
35   Shall we stand here limp and useless while old Cleisthenes'[3] allies

---

[1] *Underworld* a honey cake was usually placed in the hand of the dead to be given to Cerberus, the three-headed dog guarding the gates of Hades

[2] *Styx Ferry* the Styx was the river over which Charon ferried the souls of the dead

[3] *Cleisthenes* an Athenian of notorious bisexual tendencies

Prod a herd of furious grandmas to attempt to bring to pass
A female restoration of the Reign of Hippias? [1]
    Forbid it, gods misogynist!
    Return our Treasury, at least!
5   We must clothe ourselves and feed ourselves to face these civic
    rages,
    And who can do a single thing if they cut off our wages?
MALE CHORAGOS   Gentlemen, we are disgraced forever if we allow
    these madwomen to jabber about spears and shields
10 and make friends with the Spartans. What's a Spartan? a wild
    wolf's a safer companion any day! No; their plan's
    to bring back Dictatorship; and we won't stand for that!
    From now on, let's go armed, each one of us
    a new Aristogeiton!
15   And to begin with,
    I propose to poke a number of teeth
    down the gullet of that harridan over there.

Antistrophe 1

OLD WOMEN   Hold your tongues, you senile bravoes, or I swear,
20 when you get home
    Your own mothers wouldn't know you! Strip for action, ladies,
    come!
    I bore the holy vessels in my eighth year,[2] and at ten
    I was pounding out the barley for Athena Goddess,[3] then
25   They elected me Little Bear
                    For Artemis at Brauron Fair,[4]
    I'd been made a Basket-Carrier[5] by the time I came of age:
    So trust me to advise you in this feminist rampage!
FEMALE CHORAGOS   As a woman, I pay my taxes to the State,
30 though I pay them in baby boys. What do you contribute,
    you impotent horrors? Nothing but waste:

---

1 *Hippias* last of the Athenian tyrants. He had ruled with his brother Hipparchos until the latter's death at the hands of the patriots Aristogeiton
and Harmonius; Hippias was killed later at Marathon
2 *eighth year* four girls of high birth between the ages of seven and eleven
were appointed to service in the Temple of Athena in the Acropolis
3 *Athena Goddess* at ten a girl of aristocratic family was eligible to be Mill-
maid and to grind the sacred grain of Athena
4 *Brauron Fair* Brauron was a town on the coast of Attica where a ceremony
to Artemis was celebrated in which a little girl impersonated a bear
5 *Basket-Carrier* girls carried baskets containing precious objects sacred to
Athena

our treasury, the so-called Glory of the Persian Wars,
gone! rifled! parceled out for privilege! And you
have the insolence to control public policy,
leading us all to disaster!
5   No, don't answer back
unless you want the heel of my slipper
slap against that ugly jaw of yours!

Strophe 2

OLD MEN   What impudence!
10   What malevolence!
           Comrades, make haste,
All those of you who still are sensitive below the waist!
           Off with your clothes, men!
           Nobody knows when
15   We'll put them back on.
             Remember Leipsydrion! [1]
           We may be old,
           But let's be bold!
MALE CHORAGOS   Give them an inch, and we're done for! We'll have
20   them
launching boats next and planning naval strategy.
Or perhaps they fancy themselves as cavalry!
That's fair enough: women know how to ride,
they're good in the saddle. Just think of Mikon's paintings,[2]
25   all those Amazons wrestling with men! No, it's time
to bridle these wild mares!

Antistrophe 2

OLD WOMEN   Hold on, or
           You *are* done for,
30   By the Two Goddesses above!
Strip, strip, my women: we've got the veterans on the move!
           Tangle with me, Gramps,
           And you'll have cramps
            For the rest of your days!
35   No more beans! No more cheese!

---

[1] *Leipsydrion* after the patriots had killed Hipparchos, they fled and fortified
themselves in Leipsydrion; after a heroic defense they were forced to surrender
[2] *Mikon's paintings* Mikon was one of the many painters who dealt with the
invasion of Attica by the Amazons, a fabulous race of warrior-women

My two legs
Will scramble your eggs!
FEMALE CHORAGOS   If Lampito stands by me, and that elegant
Theban girl, Ismenia—what good are *you*?

5   Pass your laws!
Laws upon laws, you decrepit legislators!
At the worst you're just a nuisance, rationing Boeotian eels
on the Feast of Hecate, making our girls go without!
That was statesmanship! And we'll have to put up with it
10   until some patriot slits your silly old gizzards!

(*Exeunt omnes*)

SCENE II

The scene shifts to a court within the Acropolis
(*Re-enter* LYSISTRATA)

15   FEMALE CHORAGOS   But Lysistrata! Leader! Why such a grim face?
LYSISTRATA   Oh the behavior of these idiotic women!
There's something about the female temperament
that I can't bear!
FEMALE CHORAGOS   What in the world do you mean?
20   LYSISTRATA   Exactly what I say.
FEMALE CHORAGOS   What dreadful thing has happened?
Come, tell us: we're all your friends.
LYSISTRATA   It isn't easy
to say it; yet, God knows, we can't hush it up.
25   FEMALE CHORAGOS   Well, then? Out with it!
LYSISTRATA   To put it bluntly,
we're desperate for men.
  FEMALE CHORAGOS   Almighty God!
LYSISTRATA   Why bring God into it?—No, it's just as I say.
30   I can't manage them any longer: they've gone man-crazy,
they're all trying to get out.
                              Why, look:
one of them was sneaking out the back door
over there by Pan's cave,[1] another
35   was sliding down the walls with rope and tackle;
another was climbing aboard a sparrow,[2] ready to take off
for the nearest brothel—I dragged *her* back by the hair!
They're all finding some reason to leave.
                              Look there!

---

[1] *Pan's cave* a grotto on the north side of the Acropolis
[2] *sparrow* a bird sacred to Aphrodite; it had been harnessed to the chariot
of the goddess

There goes another one.
　　　　　　　　—Just a minute, you!
Where are you off to so fast?

5 FIRST WOMAN　　　　　　　I've got to get home!
I've a lot of Milesian wool, and the worms are spoiling it.
LYSISTRATA　Oh bother you and your worms! Get back inside!
FIRST WOMAN　I'll be back right away, I swear I will!
I just want to get it stretched out on my bed.
LYSISTRATA　You'll do no such thing. You'll stay right here.
10 FIRST WOMAN　　　　　　　　　　　　And my wool?
You want it ruined?
LYSISTRATA　　　　　Yes, for all I care.
SECOND WOMAN　Oh dear! My lovely new flax from Amorgos—[1]
I left it at home, all uncarded!
15 LYSISTRATA　　　　　　　　　Another one!
And all she wants is someone to card her flax.
Get back in there!
SECOND WOMAN　　　But I swear by the Moon-Goddess,
the minute I get it done, I'll be back!
20 LYSISTRATA　　　　　　　　　　I say No!
If you, why not all the other women as well?
THIRD WOMAN　O Lady Eileithyia! [2] Radiant goddess! Thou
intercessor for women in childbirth! Stay, I pray thee,
oh stay this parturition! Shall I pollute
25 a sacred spot?
LYSISTRATA　　　And what's the matter with *you*?
THIRD WOMAN　I'm having a baby—any minute now!
LYSISTRATA　But you weren't pregnant yesterday.
THIRD WOMAN　　　　　　　　Well, I am today!
30 Let me go home for a midwife, Lysistrata:
there's not much time.
LYSISTRATA　　　　　I never heard such nonsense.
What's that bulging under your cloak?
THIRD WOMAN　　　　　　　A little baby boy.
35 LYSISTRATA　It certainly isn't. But it's something hollow,
like a basin or— Why, it's the helmet of Athena!
And you said you were having a baby!
THIRD WOMAN　　　　　　Well, I am! So there!
LYSISTRATA　Then why the helmet?

---

[1] *Amorgos* an island in the Aegean famed for its flax
[2] *Lady Eileithyia* the goddess invoked by women at childbirth; it was unlawful to bear
children on the Acropolis because it was holy ground

THIRD WOMAN I was afraid that my pains
might begin here in the Acropolis; and I wanted
to drop my chick into it, just as the dear doves do.
LYSISTRATA Lies! Evasions!—But at least one thing's clear:
5   you can't leave the place before your purification.
THIRD WOMAN But I can't stay here in the Acropolis! Last night I
dreamed
of a snake.[1]
FIRST WOMAN And those horrible owls,[2] the noise they make!
10 I can't get a bit of sleep; I'm just about dead.
LYSISTRATA You useless girls, that's enough: Let's have no more
lying.
Of course you want your men. But don't you imagine
that they want you just as much? I'll give you my word,
15 their nights must be pretty hard.
Just stick it out!
A little patience, that's all, and our battle's won.
I have heard an Oracle. Should you like to hear it?
FIRST WOMAN An Oracle? Yes, tell us!
20 LYSISTRATA Quiet, then.—Here
is what it said:
IF EVER THE SWALLOWS, ESCHEWING HOOPOE-BIRDS,
SHALL CONSPIRE TOGETHER TO DENY THEM ALL
ACCESS,
25 THEIR GRIEF IS FOREVER OVER.
These are the words
from the Shrine itself.
AYE, AND ZEUS WILL REDRESS
THEIR WRONGS, AND SET THE LOWER ABOVE THE
30 HIGHER.
FIRST WOMAN Does that mean we'll be on top?
LYSISTRATA BUT IF THEY RETIRE,
EACH SWALLOW HER OWN WAY, FROM THIS HOLY
PLACE,
35 LET THE WORLD PROCLAIM NO BIRD OF SORRIER
GRACE
THAN THE SWALLOW.
FIRST WOMAN I swear, *that* Oracle makes sense!
LYSISTRATA Now, then, by all the gods,

---

1 *snake* the sacred snake of the Acropolis; it was never seen but was believed
to guard the holy ground
2 *owls* birds sacred to Athena

let's show that we're bigger than these annoyances.
Back to your places! Let's not disgrace the Oracle.

(*Exeunt* LYSISTRATA *and the dissident women; the* CHORUSES *renew their conflict*)

5 CHORAL EPISODE

Strophe

OLD MEN   I know a little story that I learned way back in school
Goes like this:
Once upon a time there was a young man—and no fool—
10   Named Melanion;[1] and his
One aversi-on was marriage. He loathed the very thought!
So he ran off to the hills, and in a special grot
Raised a dog, and spent his days
Hunting rabbits. And it says
15   That he never never never did come home.
It might be called a refuge *from* the womb.
All right,
   all right,
      all right!
20   We're as pure as young Melanion, and we hate the very sight
Of you sluts!
A MAN   How about a kiss, old woman?
A WOMAN   Here's an onion in your eye!
A MAN   A kick in the guts, then?
25   A WOMAN   Try, old bristle-tail, just try!
A MAN   Yet they say Myronides[2]
On hands and knees
Looked just as shaggy fore and aft as I!

Antistrophe

30   OLD WOMEN   Well, *I* know a little story, and it's just as good as yours.
Goes like this:
Once there was a man named Timon[3]—a rough diamond, of
   course,
And that whiskery face of his
35   Looked like murder in the shrubbery. By God, he was a son
Of the Furies, let me tell you! And what did he do but run
From the world and all its ways,

---

1 *Melanion* the suitor of Atalanta, who hated men. The Chorus of Old Men have made him a hater of women
2 *Myronides* a famous Athenenian general
3 *Timon* a famous Athenian misanthrope

Cursing mankind! And it says
That his choicest execrations as of then
Were leveled almost wholly at *old* men.
All right,
5   all right,
               all right!
But there's one thing about Timon: he could always stand the sight
Of us "sluts"!
A WOMAN   How about a crack in the jaw, Pop?
10 A MAN   I can take it, Ma—no fear!
A WOMAN   How about a kick in the face?
A MAN   You'd show your venerable rear.
A WOMAN   I may be old;
But I've been told
15 That I've nothing to worry about down there!

SCENE III

(*Re-enter* LYSISTRATA)

LYSISTRATA   Oh, quick, girls, quick! Come here!
FEMALE CHORAGOS   What is it?
20 LYSISTRATA   A man!
A man simply bulging with love!
                    O Cyprian Queen,
O Paphian, O Cythereian! Hear us and aid us!
FEMALE CHORAGOS   Where is this enemy?
25 LYSISTRATA   Over there, by Demeter's shrine.
FEMALE CHORAGOS   Damned if he isn't. But who *is* he?
MYRRHINE   My husband.
Kinesias.
LYSISTRATA   Oh then, get busy! Tease him! Undermine him!
30 Wreck him! Give him everything—kissing, tickling, nudging,
whatever you generally torture him with—: give him everything
except what we swore on the wine we would not give.
MYRRHINE   Trust me!
LYSISTRATA   I do. But I'll help you get him started.
35 The rest of you women, stay back.

(*Enter* KINESIAS)

KINESIAS   Oh God! Oh my God!
I'm stiff for lack of exercise. All I can do to stand up!
LYSISTRATA   Halt! Who are you, approaching our lines?
40 KINESIAS   Me? I.
LYSISTRATA   A man?
KINESIAS   You have eyes, haven't you?
LYSISTRATA   Go away.

KINESIAS Who says so?

LYSISTRATA Officer of the Day.

KINESIAS Officer, I beg you, by all the gods at once, bring Myrrhine out!

5 LYSISTRATA Myrrhine? And who, my good sir, are you?

KINESIAS Kinesias. Last name's Pennison. Her husband.

LYSISTRATA Oh, of course. I beg your pardon. We're glad to see you.
We've heard so much about you. Dearest Myrrhine
10 is always talking about "Kinesias"—never nibbles an egg
or an apple without saying
"Here's to Kinesias!"

KINESIAS Do you really mean it?

LYSISTRATA I do.
15 When we're discussing men, she always says,
"Well, after all, there's nobody like Kinesias!"

KINESIAS Good God.—Well, then, please send her down here.

LYSISTRATA And what do *I* get out of it?

KINESIAS A standing promise.

20 LYSISTRATA I'll take it up with her.

(*Exit* LYSISTRATA)

KINESIAS But be quick about it!
Lord, what's life without a wife? Can't eat. Can't sleep.
Every time I go home, the place is so empty, so
25 insufferably sad! Love's killing me! Oh,
hurry!

(*Enter* MANES, *a slave, with Kinesias' baby; the voice of* MYRRHINE *is heard off-stage*)

MYRRHINE But of course I love him! Adore him!—but no,
30 he hates love. No. I won't go down.

(*Enter* MYRRHINE, *above*)

KINESIAS Myrrhine!
Darlingest little Myrrhine! Come down quick!

MYRRHINE Certainly not.

35 . KINESIAS Not? But why, Myrrhine?

MYRRHINE Why? You don't need me.

KINESIAS Need you? My God, *look* at me!

MYRRHINE So long! (*Turns to go*)

KINESIAS Myrrhine, Myrrhine, Myrrhine!
40 If not for my sake, for our child! (*Pinches* BABY)
—All right, you: pipe up!

BABY   Mummie! Mummie! Mummie!

KINESIAS   You hear that?
Pitiful, I call it. Six days now
with never a bath; no food; enough to break your heart!

5   MYRRHINE   My darlingest child! What a father *you* acquired!

KINESIAS   At least come down for his sake!

MYRRHINE   I suppose I must.
Oh, this mother business! [1]

(*Exit*)

10   KINESIAS   How pretty she is! And younger!
She's so much nicer when she's bothered!

(MYRRHINE *enters, below*)

MYRRHINE   Dearest child,
you're as sweet as your father's horrid. Give me a kiss.

15   KINESIAS   Now you see how wrong it was to get involved
in this scheming League of women. All this agony
for nothing!

MYRRHINE   Keep your hands to yourself!

KINESIAS   But our house

20   going to rack and ruin?

MYRRHINE   *I* don't care.

KINESIAS   And your knitting
all torn to pieces by the chickens? Don't you care?

MYRRHINE   Not at all.

25   KINESIAS   And our vows to Aphrodite?
Oh, *won't* you come back?

MYRRHINE   No.—At least, not until you men
make a treaty to end the war.

KINESIAS   Why, if that's all you want,

30   by God, we'll make your treaty!

MYRRHINE   Oh? Very well.
When you've done that, I'll come home. But meanwhile,
I've sworn an oath.

KINESIAS   Don't worry.—Now, let's have fun.

35   MYRRHINE   No! Stop it! I said no!
                              —Although, of course,
I *do* love you.

---

[1] *Oh, this mother business!* a line that parodies Euripides' *Iphigenia at Aulis*, 917

KINESIAS   I know you do. Darling Myrrhine:
come, shall we?
MYRRHINE   Are you out of your mind? In front of the child?
KINESIAS   Take him home, Manes.

5   (*Exit* MANES *with baby*)

There. He's gone.
Come on!
There's nothing to stop us now.
MYRRHINE   You devil! But where?
10   KINESIAS   In Pan's cave. What could be snugger than that?
MYRRHINE   But my purification before I go back to the Citadel?
KINESIAS   There's always the Klepsydra.[1]
MYRRHINE   And my oath?
KINESIAS   Leave the oath to me.
15   After all, I'm the man.
MYRRHINE   Well . . . if you say so!
I'll go find a bed.
KINESIAS   Oh, bother a bed! The ground's good enough for me!
MYRRHINE   No. You're a bad man, but you deserve something
20   better than dirt.

(*Exit* MYRRHINE)

KINESIAS   What a love she is! And how thoughtful!

(*Re-enter* MYRRHINE)

MYRRHINE   Here's your bed.
25   Now let me get my clothes off.
But, good horrors!
We haven't a mattress!
KINESIAS   Oh, forget the mattress!
MYRRHINE   No.
30   Just lying on blankets? Too sordid!
KINESIAS   Give me a kiss.
MYRRHINE   Just a second.

(*Exit* MYRRHINE)

KINESIAS   I swear, I'll explode!

35   (*Re-enter* MYRRHINE)

[1] *Klepsydra* a sacred spring near Pan's cave

MYRRHINE Here's your mattress.
Go to bed now. I'll just take my dress off.
But look—
where's our pillow?
5 KINESIAS I don't need a pillow!
MYRRHINE Well, *I* do.

(*Exit* MYRRHINE)

KINESIAS I don't suppose even Heracles
would stand for this!

10 (*Re-enter* MYRRHINE)

MYRRHINE There we are. Ups-a-daisy!
KINESIAS So we are. Well, come to bed.
MYRRHINE But I wonder:
is everything ready now?
15 KINESIAS I can swear to that. Come, darling!
MYRRHINE Just getting out of my girdle.
But remember, now,
what you promised about the treaty!
KINESIAS I'll remember.
20 MYRRHINE But no coverlet!
KINESIAS Damn it, I'll be
your coverlet!
MYRRHINE Be right back.

(*Exit* MYRRHINE)

25 KINESIAS This girl and her coverlets
will be the death of me.

(*Re-enter* MYRRHINE)

MYRRHINE Here we are. Up you go!
KINESIAS Up? I've been up for ages!
30 MYRRHINE Some perfume?
KINESIAS No, by Apollo!
MYRRHINE Yes, by Aphrodite!
I don't care whether you want it or not.

(*Exit* MYRRHINE)

35 KINESIAS For love's sake, hurry!

(*Re-enter* MYRRHINE)

MYRRHINE Here, in your hand. Rub it right in.

KINESIAS Never cared for perfume.
And this is particularly strong. Still, here goes!
MYRRHINE What a nitwit I am! I brought you the Rhodian bottle! [1]
KINESIAS Forget it.
5 MYRRHINE No trouble at all. You just wait here.

(*Exit* MYRRHINE)

KINESIAS God damn the man who invented perfume!

(*Re-enter* MYRRHINE)

MYRRHINE At last! The right bottle!
10 KINESIAS I've got the rightest
bottle of all, and it's right here waiting for you.
Darling, forget everything else. Do come to bed!
MYRRHINE Just let me get my shoes off.
—And, by the way,
15 you'll vote for the treaty?
KINESIAS I'll think about it.

(MYRRHINE *runs away*)

There! That's done it! Off she runs,
with never a thought for the way I'm feeling. I must
20 have *some*one, or I'll go mad! Myrrhine
has just about ruined me.
And you, strutting little soldier:
what about you? There's nothing for it, I guess,
but an expedition to old Dog-fox's[2] bordello.
25 OLD MEN She's left you in a sorry state:
You have my sympathy.
What upright citizen could bear
Your pain? I swear, not I!
Just the look of you, with never a woman
30 To come to your aid! It isn't human!
KINESIAS The agony!
MALE CHORAGOS Well, why not?
She has you on the spot!
FEMALE CHORAGOS A lovelier girl never breathed, you old sot!
35 KINESIAS A lovelier girl? Zeus! Zeus!
Produce a hurricane

---

[1] *Rhodian bottle* i.e. from Rhodes
[2] *Dog-fox* nickname for a famous procurer

To hoist these lovely girls aloft
And drop them down again
Bump on our lances! Then they'd know
What they do that makes men suffer so.

5   (*Exit* KINESIAS)

SCENE IV

(*Enter a* SPARTAN HERALD)

HERALD   Gentlemen, Ah beg you will be so kind
as to direct me to the Central Committee.
10   Ah have a communication.

(*Re-enter* MAGISTRATE)

MAGISTRATE   Are you a man,
or a fertility symbol?
HERALD   Ah refuse to answer that question!
15   Ah'm a certified herald from Spahta, and Ah've come
to talk about an ahmistice.
MAGISTRATE   Then why
that spear under your cloak?
HERALD   Ah have no speah!
20   MAGISTRATE   You don't walk naturally, with your tunic
poked out so. You have a tumor, maybe,
or a hernia?
HERALD   No, by Castor! [1]
MAGISTRATE   Well,
25   something's wrong, I can see that. And I don't like it.
HERALD   Colonel, Ah resent this.
MAGISTRATE   So I see. But what *is* it?
HERALD   A scroll
with a message from Spahta.
30   MAGISTRATE   Oh. I've heard about these scrolls.
Well, then, man, speak out: How are things in Sparta?
HERALD   Hard, Colonel, hard! We're at a standstill.
Can't seem to think of anything but women.
MAGISTRATE   How curious! Tell me, do you Spartans think
35   that maybe Pan's to blame?
HERALD   Pan? No. Lampito and her little naked friends.
They won't let a man come near them.
MAGISTRATE   How are you handling it?

---

[1] *Castor* one of Sparta's protective spirits

HERALD   Losing our minds,
if you want to know, and walking around hunched over
like men carrying candles in a gale.
The women have sworn they'll have nothing to do with us
5   until we get a treaty.
MAGISTRATE   Yes, I know.
It's a general uprising, sir, in all parts of Greece.
But as for the answer—
                              Sir: go back to Sparta
10 and have them send us your Armistice Commission.
I'll arrange things in Athens.
                              And I may say
that my standing is good enough to make them listen.
HERALD   A man after mah own heart! Sir, Ah thank you!

15 (*Exit* HERALD)

CHORAL EPISODE

Strophe

OLD MEN   Oh these women! Where will you find
                A slavering beast that's more unkind?
20   Where a hotter fire?
                Give me a panther, any day!
                He's not so merciless as they,
                    And panthers don't conspire!

Antistrophe

25 OLD WOMEN   We may be hard, you silly old ass,
                But who brought you to this stupid pass?
                    You're the ones to blame.
                Fighting with us, your oldest friends,
                Simply to serve your selfish ends—
30   Really, you have no shame!
MALE CHORAGOS   No, I'm through with women for ever! [1]
FEMALE CHORAGOS   If you say so.
Still, you might put some clothes on. You look too absurd
standing around naked. Come, get into this cloak.
35 MALE CHORAGOS   Thank you; you're right. I merely took it off
because I was in such a temper.
FEMALE CHORAGOS   That's much better
Now you resemble a man again.
                              Why have you been so horrid?

---
[1] Parodies lines in Euripides' *Hippolytus*

And look: there's some sort of insect in your eye!
Shall I take it out?
MALE CHORAGOS   An insect, is it? So that's
what's been bothering me! Lord, yes: take it out!
5   FEMALE CHORAGOS   You might be more polite.
                                        —But, heavens!
What an enormous gnat!
MALE CHORAGOS   You've saved my life.
That gnat was drilling an artesian well
10   in my left eye.
FEMALE CHORAGOS   Let me wipe
those tears away!—And now: one little kiss?
MALE CHORAGOS   Over my dead body!
FEMALE CHORAGOS   You're so difficult!
15   MALE CHORAGOS   These impossible women! How they do get around
us!
The poet was right: Can't live with them, or without them!
But let's be friends.
And to celebrate, you might lead off with an Ode.

20   **Strophe**

OLD WOMEN   Let it never be said
That my tongue is malicious:
Both by word and by deed
I would set an example that's noble and gracious.
25   We've had sorrow and care
Till we're sick of the tune.
Is there anyone here
Who would like a small loan?
My purse is crammed,
30   As you'll soon find;
And you needn't pay me back if the Peace gets signed!
I've invited to lunch
Some Karystian rips—[1]
An esurient bunch,
35   But I've ordered a menu to water their lips!
I can still make soup
And slaughter a pig.
You're all coming, I hope?
But a bath first, I beg!

---

[1] *Karystian rips* the Karystians were allies of Athens at this time, but were
disdained for their primitive manners and loose morals

Walk right up
As though you owned the place,
And you'll get the front door slammed to in your face!

SCENE V

5 (*Enter* SPARTAN AMBASSADOR, *with entourage*)

MALE CHORAGOS The Commission has arrived from Sparta.
How oddly
they're walking!
Gentlemen, welcome to Athens!
10 How is life in Laconia?
AMBASSADOR Need we discuss that?
Simply use your eyes.
OLD MEN The poor man's right:
What a sight!
15 AMBASSADOR Words fail me.
But come, gentlemen, call in your Commissioners,
and let's get down to a Peace.
MALE CHORAGOS The state we're in! Can't bear
a stitch below the waist. It's a kind of pelvic
20 paralysis.
AN ATHENIAN Won't somebody call Lysistrata?
She has the answer.
A SPARTAN Yes, there, look at him.
Same thing.
25 Seh, do y'all feel a certain strain
early in the morning?
ATHENIAN I do, sir. It's worse than a strain.
A few more days, and there's nothing for us but Cleisthenes,
that broken blossom!
30 MALE CHORAGOS But you'd better get dressed again.
You know these prudes who go around Athens with chisels,
looking for prominent statues.[1]
ATHENIAN Sir, you are right.
SPARTAN He certainly is! Ah'll put mah own clothes back on.

35 (*Enter* ATHENIAN COMMISSIONERS)

AN ATHENIAN They're no better off than we are!
—Greetings, Laconians!
SPARTAN (*To one of his own group*) Colonel, we got dressed just
in time.

---

1 *prominent statues* i.e. statues with prominent male sexual organs, or *phalloi*

Ah sweah,
if they'd seen us the way we were, there'd have been a new war
between the states.
ATHENIAN　Call the meeting to order.
5　　　　　　　　　　　　　　　　Now, Laconians,
what's your proposal?
AMBASSADOR　　　　　We'd lahk to consider peace.
ATHENIAN　Good. That's on our minds, too.
　　　　　　　　　　　　　　　　　—Summon Lysistrata.
10　We'll never get anywhere without her.
AMBASSADOR　　　　　　　　Lysistrata?
Summon Lysis-*any*body! [1] Only, summon!
MALE CHORAGOS　　　　　　No need to summon:
here she is, herself.

15　(*Enter* LYSISTRATA)

　　　　　　　　　　　Lysistrata! Lion of women!
This is your hour to be
hard and yielding, outspoken and sly, austere and
gentle. You see here
20　the best brains of Hellas (confused, I admit,
by your devious charming) met as one man
to turn the future over to you.
LYSISTRATA　　　　　　That's fair enough,
unless you men take it into your heads
25　to turn to each other instead of to me. But I'd know
soon enough if you did!
　　　　　　　　　　—Where is that goddess of Peace?
Go, some of you: bring her here.

(*Exeunt two* SERVANTS)

30　　　　　　　　　　　　　And now,
summon the Spartan Commission. Treat them courteously:
our husbands have been lax in that respect.
Take them by the hand, women,
or by anything else, if they seem unwilling.
35　　　　　　　　　　　　—Spartans:
you stand here. Athenians: on this side. Now listen to me.

(*Re-enter* SERVANTS, *staggering under the weight of a more than life-size statue of a naked woman: this is* PEACE)

---

[1] *Lysis-anybody* Lysistrata's name means "dissolver of armies"

I'm only a woman, I know; but I've a mind,
and I can distinguish between sense and foolishness.
I owe the first to my father; the rest
to the local politicians.[1] So much for that.

5   Now, then.
What I have to say concerns both sides in this war.
We are all Greeks.
Must I remind you of Thermopylae? of Olympia?
of Delphi? names deep in all our hearts?

10   And yet you men go raiding through the country,
Greek killing Greek, storming down Greek cities—
and all the time the Barbarian across the sea
is waiting for his chance.—That's my first point.

AN ATHENIAN   Lord! I can hardly contain myself!

15 LYSISTRATA   And you Spartans:
Was it so long ago that Pericleides
came here to beg our help? [2] I can see him still,
his white face, his sombre gown. And what did he want?
An army from Athens! Messenia

20   was at your heels, and the sea-god splitting your shores.
Well, Kimon and his men,
four thousand infantry, marched out of here to save you.
What thanks do we get? You come back to murder us.

ATHENIAN   Can't trust a Spartan, Lysistrata!

25 A SPARTAN   Ah admit it.
When Ah look at those legs, Ah sweah Ah can't trust mahself!

LYSISTRATA   And you, men of Athens:
you might remember that bad time when we were down,
and an army came from Sparta

30   and sent Hippias and the Thessalians
whimpering back to the hills. That was Sparta,
and only Sparta; without Sparta, we'd now be
cringing helots, not walking about like free men!

    (*From this point, the male responses are less to* LYSISTRATA *than to the*
35   *statue of* PEACE)

A SPARTAN   An eloquent speech!

AN ATHENIAN   An elegant construction!

---

[1] The preceding four lines are probably quoted from Euripides' *Melanippe the Wise*

[2] *help* in 464 B.C. during a revolt in Sparta, when an earthquake had just severely damaged the city

LYSISTRATA Why are we fighting each other? Why not make peace?
AMBASSADOR Spahta is ready, ma'am,
   so long as we get that place back.
LYSISTRATA   Place? What place?
5 AMBASSADOR Ah refer to Pylos.[1]
MAGISTRATE   Not while I'm alive, by God!
LYSISTRATA You'd better give in.
MAGISTRATE   But—what were we fighting about?
LYSISTRATA Lots of places left.
10 MAGISTRATE   All right. Well, then:
   Hog Island first, and that gulf behind there, and the land between
   the Legs of Megara.
AMBASSADOR   Mah government objects.
LYSISTRATA Over-ruled. Why fuss about a pair of legs?

15   (*General assent; the statue of* PEACE *is removed*)

AN ATHENIAN Let's take off our clothes and plow our fields.
A SPARTAN Ah'll fertilize mahn first, by the Heavenly Twins!
LYSISTRATA And so you shall,
   once we have peace. If you are serious,
20 go, both of you, and talk with your allies.
ATHENIAN Too much talk already. We'll stand together!
   We've only one end in view. All that we want
   is our women: and I speak for our allies.
AMBASSADOR Mah government concurs.
25 ATHENIAN   So does Karystos.
LYSISTRATA Good.—But before you come inside
   to join your wives at supper, you must perform
   the usual lustration. Then we'll open
   our baskets for you, and all that we have is yours.
30 But you must promise upright good behavior
   from this day on. Then each man home with his woman!
ATHENIAN Let's get it over with!
SPARTAN   Lead on: Ah follow!
ATHENIAN Quick as a cat can wink!

35   (*Exeunt all but the* CHORUSES)

Antistrophe

OLD WOMEN Embroideries and
            Twinkling ornaments and

---

[1] *Pylos* A lost Spartan possession; for the moment political and sexual desires
become confused

Pretty dresses—I hand
Them all over to you, and with never a qualm.
They'll be nice for your daughters
On festival days
5 When the girls bring the Goddess
The ritual prize.
Come in, one and all:
Take what you will.
I've nothing here so tightly corked that you can't make it spill!
10 You may search my house,
But you'll not find
The least thing of use,
Unless your two eyes are keener than mine.
Your numberless brats
15 Are half starved? and your slaves?
Courage, grandpa! I've lots
Of grain left, and big loaves.
I'll fill your guts,
I'll go the whole hog;
20 But if you come too close to me, remember: 'ware the dog!

(*Exeunt* CHORUSES)

EXODOS

(*An* ATHENIAN DRUNKARD *approaches the gate and is halted by a* SENTRY)

25 DRUNKARD   Open. The. Door.
SENTRY   Now, friend, just shove along!
So you want to sit down! If it weren't such an old joke,
I'd tickle your tail with this torch. Just the sort of thing
that this kind of audience appreciates.
30 DRUNKARD   I. Stay. Right. Here.
SENTRY   Oh, all right. But you'll see some funny sights!
DRUNKARD   Bring. Them. On.
SENTRY   No, what am I thinking of?
The gentlemen from Sparta are just coming back from supper.
35 Get out of here, or I'll scalp you!

(*Exit* DRUNKARD)

(*The general company re-enters; the two* CHORUSES *now represent* SPARTANS *and* ATHENIANS)

MAGISTRATE   I must say,
40 I've never tasted a better meal. And those Laconians!
They're gentlemen, by the Lord! Just goes to show:

a drink to the wise is sufficient. And why not?
A sober man's an ass.
Men of Athens, mark my words: the only efficient
Ambassador's a drunk Ambassador. Is that clear?
5   Look: we go to Sparta,
and when we get there we're dead sober. The result?
Everyone cackling at everyone else. They make speeches;
and even if we understand, we get it all wrong
when we file our reports in Athens. But today—!
10   Everybody's happy. Couldn't tell the difference
between *Drink to Me Only* and
the *Star Spangled Athens.*
                    What's a few lies,
washed down in good strong drink?

15   (*Re-enter* DRUNKARD)

SENTRY   God almighty,
he's back again!
DRUNKARD   I. Resume. My. Place.
A SPARTAN (*To an* ATHENIAN)   I beg you, seh,
20   take your instrument in your hand and play for us.
Ah'm told
you understand the in*tri*cacies of the floot?
Ah'd lahk to execute a song and dance
in honor of Athens,
25   and, of course, of Spahta.

(*The following song is a solo—an aria—accompanied by the flute. The*
CHORUS OF SPARTANS *begins a slow dance*)

DRUNKARD   Toot. On. Your. Flute.
SPARTAN CHORAGOS   Mnemosyne,[1]
30   Inspire once more the Grecian Muse
To sing of glory glory glory without end.
Sing Artemesion's shore,[2]
Where Athens fluttered the Persian fleet—
Alalai,[3] that great
35   Victory! Sing Leonidas and his men,
Those wild boars, sweat and blood

---

[1] *Mnemosyne* goddess of memory and mother of the Muses
[2] *Artemesion's shore* where in 480 B.C. the Athenian fleet successfully engaged the Persians, while Leonidas and his Spartans were making their famous stand at Thermopylae
[3] *Alalai* a war cry

Down in a red drench. Then, then
The barbarians broke, though they had stood
A myriad strong before!
O Artemis,
5 Virgin Goddess, whose darts
Flash in our forests: approve
This pact of peace, and join our hearts,
From this day on, in love.
Huntress, descend!
10 LYSISTRATA All that will come in time.
But now, Laconians,
take home your wives. Athenians, take yours.
Each man be kind to his woman; and you, women,
be equally kind. Never again, pray God,
15 shall we lose our way in such madness.
—And now
let's dance our joy! (*From this point the dance becomes general*)
CHORUS OF ATHENIANS Dance!
Dance!
20 Dance, you Graces!
Artemis, dance!
Dance, Phoebus, Lord of dancing!
Dance, Dionysus, in a scurry of Maenads!
Dance, Zeus Thunderer!
25 Dance, Lady Hera,
Queen of the sky!
Dance, dance, all you gods!
Dance for the dearest, the bringer of peace,
Deathless Aphrodite!
30 LYSISTRATA Now let us have another song from Sparta.
CHORUS OF SPARTANS From Taygetos' skyey summit,
Laconian Muse, come down!
Sing the glories of Apollo,
Regent of Amyclae Town.
35 Sing of Leda's Twins,
Those gallant sons,
On the banks of Eurotas—
Alalai Evohe! [1]
Here's to our girls
40 With their tangling curls,
Legs a-wriggle,

---

[1] *Alalai Evohe!* now an orgiastic war cry. The play now ends with an erotic dance and
the mandatory sexual union, in this case of the warring parties.

Bellies a-jiggle,
A riot of hair,
A fury of feet,
Evohe! Evohai! Evohe!
5   as they pass
Dancing,
            dancing,
                    dancing,
                         to greet
10   Athena of the House of Brass! [1]

---

[1] *House of Brass* a famous temple on the acropolis of Sparta

HAMLET
(1600)

WILLIAM SHAKESPEARE (1564–1616)

The hyperbole may be too strong in defining *Hamlet* as the greatest play ever written, but it is a superlative drama and a magnificent piece of theatre. It is virtually impossible to perform a thoroughly bad *Hamlet*. The play has so much to offer, is so "actor proof," that no matter how ineffective a particular interpretation may be or however inept the staging, so much comes through that the magnificence of its artistry transcends even the most botched and bowdlerized version.

There has probably been more serious scholarship and more pompous blather written about who, what, and why Hamlet is what he is than about any other person, living, dead, or imagined. Millions of words in thousands of documents have explained, analyzed, and dissected this most fascinating of dramatic characters. That a dramatist like William Shakespeare, who may or may not have been educated beyond the most elementary schooling, who was basically a theatre producer and actor grinding out pieces for his company's repertoire, could have created within the framework of some few hours upon the stage an individual so alive in the consciences and minds of generations ever since is one of the great tributes to human artistic genius.

At the heart of things, *Hamlet* is a rip-roaring Elizabethan revenge melodrama. Dark doings behind dismal castle walls, conspiracies, bloody ghosts crying vengeance, an innocent maiden, a faithless wife, a usurping king, treacherous friends, swordplay and derring-do.

They are all here in profusion, and the play moves from first to last through a series of events that scarcely permit one to catch his breath. More than that, the story, Aristotle's soul, is perfectly plotted. The opening sequences on the parapets slam the audience into the thick of things from the first lines. Scenes of fervent activity followed by calm; then quick and exciting action, then sober introspection. Brutality and tenderness, a seamy court intrigue, a deadly cat-and-mouse game, a gentle family caught helplessly in the middle—all this and more combine in a totally absorbing tale of noble acts and infamous skulduggery. The characters are revealed in thoroughly convincing depth and breadth, their actions humanly reasonable and comprehensible. And all told in some of the most magnificent dramatic poetry ever written.

More than that, of course, *Hamlet* is a superb psychological study. Into the unfathomable and increasingly horrible affairs in Elsinore is thrown the young prince, still at the university, unprepared for the deeds he must do, aware of his unquestioned obligation to do them. The tax upon his strength, his mind, his personal philosophy of life is tremendous and eventually overwhelming. The constant peaks and valleys of the trauma through which he moves are fascinating to observe.

An important part of the development of Hamlet as a character is Shakespeare's skilled use of the soliloquy, that familiar theatrical device which all but disappeared with the development of modern "realistic" dramaturgy. But the soliloquy, however artificial or contrived it may seem, properly written and properly delivered, is no more "unrealistic" than the ubiquitous "voice-over" of today's film and television drama— a modern convention of which the soliloquy is a legitimate forbear. In fact, Laurence Olivier made excellent use of the soliloquy–voice-over combination in his film version of *Hamlet.*

The soliloquy permits the dramatist to reveal the character's most intimate thoughts, which can help explain what has happened, what is churning about in his or her mind at present, or even what motivation exists for things to come. In *Hamlet* the soliloquy provides the audience with a fascinating portrayal of Hamlet's psychological progress from a confused, frustrated, and seemingly helpless witness of deeds from which he shrinks in revulsion to the positive, determined avenger. Starting with the initial self-pitying summation of his problems with "O that this too too sullied flesh would melt" (I.ii.8.p.138), Hamlet next proceeds to berate himself in "O, what a rogue and peasant slave am I!" (II.ii.32.p.174), while turning his brain about as he hits upon the trap wherein he'll "catch the conscience of the king." Following quickly is "To be or not to be" (III.i.17.p.178) with Hamlet's look into his own deep concern for his soul, soon to be contrasted to "Tis the very witching time of night" when he could "drink hot blood" (III.ii.13.p.193). And then, with the final soliloquy, "How all occasions do inform against me" (IV.iv.25.p.210), he drives himself into his final determination to act with "My thoughts be bloody or be nothing worth," after which Shakespeare finds no further need for the soliloquy as Hamlet now has revealed the full circle of his development and goes forward to his vengeance, and his doom, with very little further introspection.

It is difficult to fault Hamlet for what might be regarded as his frequent eccentric behavior. With "wild and whirling words" he baffles Horatio after the encounter with the ghost; he is crude to Ophelia in her closet, and insults her in the nunnery scene; he is contemptuous of Rosencrantz and Guildenstern, and he ridicules Polonius in the fishmonger scene. His assault upon his mother in her bedroom after the mousetrap scene is particularly vicious, and his slaying of the stupidly intrusive Polonius is an act of totally unreasoning violence. But Hamlet, as a sensitive, thinking individual, is a man struggling to maintain his own mental balance in the face of murder, incest, and faithlessness which would severely tax the self-control of the strongest human will.

But finally, *Hamlet* is a tragedy. The prince is doomed, driven by forces beyond his control into the ultimate catastrophe. He wishes to avoid it, seeks to postpone it, becomes increasingly aware that it must come and that he must himself bring it about. Hamlet is no coward, but he blames himself for being one. He is not a procrastinator by nature, yet he fatally procrastinates. He is a thinker who weighs his thoughts and deeds, yet he acts with foolish impetuosity and unthinking cruelty. He commands our passion and our understanding. He is a potentially great man, capable of being a great king, but he must face the task the fates have ordained for him, ultimately realizing that escape is impossible, disaster inevitable. Who cannot weep, not for sentiment, but for the tremendous loss, the sacrifice endured, when, as Horatio tells us, "Now cracks a noble heart." As old Hamlet's perturbed spirit has been laid to rest, so we wish, with Horatio, for young Hamlet, that flights of angels sing him to his rest.

Hamlet, Prince of Denmark

SHAKESPEARE

CHARACTERS

CLAUDIUS, *King of Denmark*
HAMLET, *son to the late, and nephew to the present, King*
POLONIUS, *Lord Chamberlain*
HORATIO, *friend to Hamlet*
LAERTES, *son to Polonius*
VOLTEMAND
CORNELIUS
ROSENCRANTZ
GUILDENSTERN } *courtiers*
OSRIC
A GENTLEMAN
A PRIEST
MARCELLUS
BERNARDO } *officers*
FRANCISCO, *a soldier*
REYNALDO, *servant to Polonius*
PLAYERS
TWO CLOWNS, *gravediggers*
FORTINBRAS, *Prince of Norway*
A NORWEGIAN CAPTAIN
ENGLISH AMBASSADORS
GERTRUDE, *Queen of Denmark, mother to Hamlet*
OPHELIA, *daughter to Polonius*
GHOST OF HAMLET'S FATHER
LORDS, LADIES, OFFICERS, SOLDIERS, SAILORS, MESSENGERS,
    ATTENDANTS

ACT I

Scene I

Elsinore Castle: a sentry-post

(*Enter* BERNARDO *and* FRANCISCO, *two sentinels*)

5   BERNARDO   Who's there?
FRANCISCO   Nay, answer me. Stand and unfold yourself.
BERNARDO   Long live the king!
FRANCISCO   Bernardo?
BERNARDO   He.
10   FRANCISCO   You come most carefully upon your hour.
BERNARDO   'Tis now struck twelve. Get thee to bed, Francisco.
FRANCISCO   For this relief much thanks. 'Tis bitter cold,
And I am sick at heart.
BERNARDO   Have you had quiet guard?
15   FRANCISCO   Not a mouse stirring.
BERNARDO   Well, good night.
If you do meet Horatio and Marcellus,
The rivals[1] of my watch, bid them make haste.

(*Enter* HORATIO *and* MARCELLUS)

20   FRANCISCO   I think I hear them. Stand, ho! Who is there?
HORATIO   Friends to this ground.
MARCELLUS   And liegemen to the Dane.[2]
FRANCISCO   Give you good night.
MARCELLUS   O, farewell, honest soldier.
25   Who hath relieved you?
FRANCISCO   Bernardo hath my place.
Give you good night.

(*Exit* FRANCISCO)

MARCELLUS   Holla, Bernardo!
30   BERNARDO   Say—
What, is Horatio there?
HORATIO   A piece of him.
BERNARDO   Welcome, Horatio. Welcome, good Marcellus.
HORATIO   What, has this thing appeared again to-night?
35   BERNARDO   I have seen nothing.
MARCELLUS   Horatio says 'tis but our fantasy,
And will not let belief take hold of him

---

[1] *rivals* sharers   [2] *Dane* King of Denmark

Touching this dreaded sight twice seen of us.
Therefore I have entreated him along
With us to watch the minutes of this night,
That, if again this apparition come,
5   He may approve[3] our eyes and speak to it.
HORATIO   Tush, tush, 'twill not appear.
BERNARDO   Sit down awhile,
And let us once again assail your ears,
That are so fortified against our story,
10   What we two nights have seen.
HORATIO   Well, sit we down,
And let us hear Bernardo speak of this.
BERNARDO   Last night of all,
When yond same star that's westward from the pole[4]
15   Had made his course t' illume that part of heaven
Where now it burns, Marcellus and myself,
The bell then beating one—

(*Enter* GHOST)

MARCELLUS   Peace, break thee off. Look where it comes again.
20   BERNARDO   In the same figure like the king that's dead.
MARCELLUS   Thou art a scholar; speak to it, Horatio.
BERNARDO   Looks 'a not like the king? Mark it, Horatio.
HORATIO   Most like. It harrows me with fear and wonder.
BERNARDO   It would be spoke to.
25   MARCELLUS   Speak to it, Horatio.
HORATIO   What art thou that usurp'st this time of night
Together with that fair and warlike form
In which the majesty of buried Denmark[5]
Did sometimes[6] march? By heaven I charge thee, speak.
30   MARCELLUS   It is offended.
BERNARDO   See, it stalks away.
HORATIO   Stay. Speak, speak. I charge thee, speak.

(*Exit* GHOST)

MARCELLUS   'Tis gone and will not answer.
35   BERNARDO   How now, Horatio? You tremble and look pale.
Is not this something more than fantasy?
What think you on't?
HORATIO   Before my God, I might not this believe

---

[3] *approve* confirm   [4] *pole* polestar   [5] *buried Denmark* the buried King of
Denmark   [6] *sometimes* formerly

Without the sensible and true avouch
Of mine own eyes.
MARCELLUS   Is it not like the king?
HORATIO   As thou art to thyself.
5   Such was the very armor he had on
When he th' ambitious Norway[7] combated.
So frowned he once when, in an angry parle,[8]
He smote the sledded Polacks on the ice.
'Tis strange.
10 MARCELLUS   Thus twice before, and jump[9] at this dead hour,
With martial stalk hath he gone by our watch.
HORATIO   In what particular thought to work I know not;
But, in the gross and scope[10] of my opinion,
This bodes some strange eruption to our state.
15 MARCELLUS   Good now, sit down, and tell me he that knows,
Why this same strict and most observant watch
So nightly toils the subject[11] of the land,
And why such daily cast of brazen cannon
And foreign mart[12] for implements of war,
20 Why such impress[13] of shipwrights, whose sore task
Does not divide the Sunday from the week.
What might be toward [14] that this sweaty haste
Doth make the night joint-laborer with the day?
Who is't that can inform me?
25 HORATIO   That can I.
At least the whisper goes so. Our last king,
Whose image even but now appeared to us,
Was as you know by Fortinbras of Norway,
Thereto pricked on by a most emulate[15] pride,
30 Dared to the combat; in which our valiant Hamlet
(For so this side of our known world esteemed him)
Did slay this Fortinbras; who, by a sealed compact
Well ratified by law and heraldry,[16]
Did forfeit, with his life, all those his lands
35 Which he stood seized [17] of to the conqueror;
Against the which a moiety competent[18]
Was gagèd [19] by our king, which had returned
To the inheritance of Fortinbras

---

7 *Norway* King of Norway   8 *parle* parley   9 *jump* just, exactly   10 *gross and scope* gross scope, general view   11 *toils* makes toil; *subject* subjects   12 *mart* trading   13 *impress* conscription   14 *toward* in preparation   15 *emulate* jealously rivalling   16 *law and heraldry* law of heralds regulating combat   17 *seized* possessed   18 *moiety competent* sufficient portion   19 *gagèd* engaged, staked

Had he been vanquisher, as, by the same comart[20]
And carriage[21] of the article designed,
His fell to Hamlet. Now, sir, young Fortinbras,
Of unimprovèd [22] mettle hot and full,
5   Hath in the skirts of Norway here and there
Sharked [23] up a list of lawless resolutes[24]
For food and diet to some enterprise
That hath a stomach[25] in't; which is no other,
As it doth well appear unto our state,
10   But to recover of us by strong hand
And terms compulsatory those foresaid lands
So by his father lost; and this, I take it,
Is the main motive of our preparations,
The source of this our watch, and the chief head [26]
15   Of this posthaste and romage[27] in the land.
    BERNARDO   I think it be no other but e'en so.
    ·Well may it sort[28] that this portentous figure
Comes armèd through our watch so like the king
That was and is the question of these wars.
20   HORATIO   A mote[29] it is to trouble the mind's eye.
In the most high and palmy state of Rome,
A little ere the mightiest Julius fell,
The graves stood tenantless and the sheeted [30] dead
Did squeak and gibber in the Roman streets;
25   As stars with trains of fire and dews of blood,
Disasters[31] in the sun; and the moist star[32]
Upon whose influence Neptune's empire stands
Was sick almost to doomsday with eclipse.
And even the like precurse[33] of feared events,
30   As harbingers[34] preceding still [35] the fates
And prologue to the omen[36] coming on,
Have heaven and earth together demonstrated
Unto our climatures[37] and countrymen.

    (*Enter* GHOST)

35   But soft, behold, lo where it comes again!

---

[20] *comart* joint bargain   [21] *carriage* purport   [22] *unimprovèd* unused
[23] *Sharked* snatched indiscriminately as the shark takes prey   [24] *resolutes*
desperadoes   [25] *stomach* show of venturesomeness   [26] *head* fountainhead,
source   [27] *romage* intense activity   [28] *sort* suit   [29] *mote* speck of dust
[30] *sheeted* in shrouds   [31] *Disasters* ominous signs   [32] *moist star* moon   [33] *precurse* foreshadowing   [34] *harbingers* forerunners   [35] *still* constantly   [36] *omen*
calamity   [37] *climatures* regions

I'll cross it,[38] though it blast me.—Stay, illusion.

(*He spreads his arms*)

If thou hast any sound or use of voice,
Speak to me.
5   If there be any good thing to be done
That may to thee do ease and grace to me,
Speak to me.
If thou art privy to thy country's fate,
Which happily[39] foreknowing may avoid,
10   O, speak!
Or if thou hast uphoarded in thy life
Extorted treasure in the womb of earth,
For which, they say, you spirits oft walk in death,

(*The cock crows*)

15   Speak of it. Stay and speak. Stop it, Marcellus.
MARCELLUS   Shall I strike at it with my partisan?[40]
HORATIO   Do, if it will not stand.
BERNARDO   'Tis here.
HORATIO   'Tis here.

20   (*Exit* GHOST)

MARCELLUS   'Tis gone.
We do it wrong, being so majestical,
To offer it the show of violence,
For it is as the air invulnerable,
25   And our vain blows malicious mockery.
BERNARDO   It was about to speak when the cock crew.
HORATIO   And then it started, like a guilty thing
Upon a fearful summons. I have heard
The cock, that is the trumpet to the morn,
30   Doth with his lofty and shrill-sounding throat
Awake the god of day, and at his warning,
Whether in sea or fire, in earth or air,
Th' extravagant[41] and erring[42] spirit hies
To his confine; and of the truth herein
35   This present object made probation.[43]

---

[38] *cross it* cross its path   [39] *happily* haply, perchance   [40] *partisan* pike   [41] *extravagant* wandering beyond bounds   [42] *erring* wandering   [43] *probation* proof

MARCELLUS   It faded on the crowing of the cock.
Some say that ever 'gainst[44] that season comes
Wherein our Saviour's birth is celebrated,
This bird of dawning singeth all night long,
5   And then, they say, no spirit dare stir abroad,
The nights are wholesome, then no planets strike,[45]
No fairy takes,[46] nor witch hath power to charm.
So hallowed and so gracious is that time.
HORATIO   So have I heard and do in part believe it.
10   But look, the morn in russet mantle clad
Walks o'er the dew of yon high eastward hill.
Break we our watch up, and by my advice
Let us impart what we have seen to-night
Unto young Hamlet, for upon my life
15   This spirit, dumb to us, will speak to him.
Do you consent we shall acquaint him with it,
As needful in our loves, fitting our duty?
MARCELLUS   Let's do't, I pray, and I this morning know
Where we shall find him most conveniently.

20   (*Exeunt*)

Act I, Scene II

Elsinore Castle: a room of state

Flourish. Enter CLAUDIUS, *King of Denmark,* GERTRUDE *the Queen,* COUN-
CILLORS, POLONIUS *and his son* LAERTES, HAMLET, *cum aliis*[1] [*including*
25   VOLTEMAND *and* CORNELIUS]

KING   Though yet of Hamlet our dear brother's death
The memory be green, and that it us befitted
To bear our hearts in grief, and our whole kingdom
To be contracted in one brow of woe,
30   Yet so far hath discretion fought with nature
That we with wisest sorrow think on him
Together with remembrance of ourselves.
Therefore our sometime sister, now our queen,
Th' imperial jointress[2] to this warlike state,
35   Have we, as 'twere with a defeated joy,
With an auspicious and a dropping eye,

---

[44] *'gainst* just before   [45] *strike* work evil by influence   [46] *takes* bewitches
[1] *cum aliis* with others   [2] *jointress* a woman who has a jointure, or joint ten-
ancy of an estate

With mirth in funeral and with dirge in marriage,
In equal scale weighing delight and dole,
Taken to wife. Nor have we herein barred [3]
Your better wisdoms, which have freely gone
5   With this affair along. For all, our thanks.
Now follows, that you know, young Fortinbras,
Holding a weak supposal of our worth,
Or thinking by our late dear brother's death
Our state to be disjoint and out of frame,
10 Colleaguèd [4] with this dream of his advantage,
He hath not failed to pester us with message
Importing the surrender of those lands
Lost by his father, with all bands of law,
To our most valiant brother. So much for him.
15 Now for ourself and for this time of meeting.
Thus much the business is: we have here writ
To Norway, uncle of young Fortinbras—
Who, impotent and bedrid, scarcely hears
Of this his nephew's purpose—to suppress
20 His further gait[5] herein, in that the levies,
The lists, and full proportions[6] are all made
Out of his subject; and we here dispatch
You, good Cornelius, and you, Voltemand,
For bearers of this greeting to old Norway,
25 Giving to you no further personal power
To business with the king, more than the scope
Of these delated [7] articles allow.
Farewell, and let your haste commend your duty.
    CORNELIUS, VOLTEMAND   In that, and all things, will we show our
30   duty.
    KING   We doubt it nothing. Heartily farewell.

(*Exeunt* VOLTEMAND *and* CORNELIUS)

And now, Laertes, what's the news with you?
You told us of some suit. What is't, Laertes?
35 You cannot speak of reason to the Dane[8]
And lose your voice.[9] What wouldst thou beg, Laertes,
That shall not be my offer, not thy asking?
The head is not more native[10] to the heart,

---

[3] *barred* excluded   [4] *Colleaguèd* united   [5] *gait* going   [6] *proportions* amounts
of forces and supplies   [7] *delated* detailed   [8] *Dane* King of Denmark   [9] *lose
your voice* speak in vain   [10] *native* joined by nature

The hand more instrumental [11] to the mouth,
Than is the throne of Denmark to thy father.
What wouldst thou have, Laertes?
LAERTES   My dread lord,
5   Your leave and favor to return to France,
From whence though willingly I came to Denmark
To show my duty in your coronation,
Yet now I must confess, that duty done,
My thoughts and wishes bend again toward France
10   And bow them to your gracious leave and pardon.
KING   Have you your father's leave? What says Polonius?
POLONIUS   He hath, my lord, wrung from me my slow leave
By laborsome petition, and at last
Upon his will I sealed my hard consent.
15   I do beseech you give him leave to go.
KING   Take thy fair hour, Laertes. Time be thine,
And thy best graces spend it at thy will.
But now, my cousin[12] Hamlet, and my son—
HAMLET (*aside*)   A little more than kin,[13] and less than kind! [14]
20   KING   How is it that the clouds still hang on you?
HAMLET   Not so, my lord. I am too much in the sun.[15]
QUEEN   Good Hamlet, cast thy nighted color off,
And let thine eye look like a friend on Denmark.
Do not for ever with thy vailèd [16] lids
25   Seek for thy noble father in the dust.
Thou know'st 'tis common. All that lives must die,
Passing through nature to eternity.
HAMLET   Ay, madam, it is common.
QUEEN   If it be,
30   Why seems it so particular with thee?
HAMLET   Seems, madam? Nay, it is. I know not "seems."
'Tis not alone my inky cloak, good mother,
Nor customary suits of solemn black,
Nor windy suspiration of forced breath,
35   No, nor the fruitful [17] river in the eye,
Nor the dejected havior of the visage,
Together with all forms, moods, shapes of grief,

---

[11] *instrumental* serviceable   [12] *cousin* kinsman more distant than parent, child, brother, or sister   [13] *kin* related as nephew   [14] *kind* kindly in feeling, as by kind, or nature, a son would be to his father   [15] *sun* sunshine of the king's undesired favor (with the punning additional meaning of "place of a son")   [16] *vailèd* downcast   [17] *fruitful* copious

That can denote me truly. These indeed seem,
For they are actions that a man might play,
But I have that within which passeth show—
These but the trappings and the suits of woe.

5   KING   'Tis sweet and commendable in your nature, Hamlet,
To give these mourning duties to your father,
But you must know your father lost a father,
That father lost, lost his, and the survivor bound
In filial obligation for some term

10   To do obsequious[18] sorrow. But to persever[19]
In obstinate condolement is a course
Of impious stubbornness. 'Tis unmanly grief.
It shows a will most incorrect to heaven,
A heart unfortified, a mind impatient,

15   An understanding simple and unschooled.
For what we know must be and is as common
As any the most vulgar thing to sense,
Why should we in our peevish opposition
Take it to heart? Fie, 'tis a fault to heaven,

20   A fault against the dead, a fault to nature,
To reason most absurd, whose common theme
Is death of fathers, and who still hath cried,
From the first corse till he that died to-day,
"This must be so." We pray you throw to earth

25   This unprevailing woe, and think of us
As a father, for let the world take note
You are the most immediate to our throne,
And with no less nobility of love
Than that which dearest father bears his son

30   Do I impart toward you. For your intent
In going back to school in Wittenberg,
It is most retrograde[20] to our desire,
And we beseech you, bend you to remain
Here in the cheer and comfort of our eye,

35   Our chiefest courtier, cousin, and our son.
  QUEEN   Let not thy mother lose her prayers, Hamlet.
I pray thee stay with us, go not to Wittenberg.
  HAMLET   I shall in all my best obey you, madam.
  KING   Why, 'tis a loving and a fair reply.

40   Be as ourself in Denmark. Madam, come.

---

[18] *obsequious* proper to obsequies or funerals   [19] *persever* persevere (accented on the second syllable, as always in Shakespeare)   [20] *retrograde* contrary

This gentle and unforced accord of Hamlet
Sits smiling to my heart, in grace whereof
No jocund health that Denmark drinks to-day
But the great cannon to the clouds shall tell,
5 And the king's rouse[21] the heaven shall bruit[22] again,
Respeaking earthly thunder. Come away.

(*Flourish. Exeunt all but* HAMLET)

HAMLET   O that this too too sullied flesh would melt,
Thaw, and resolve itself into a dew,
10 Or that the Everlasting had not fixed
His canon[23] gainst self-slaughter. O God, God,
How weary, stale, flat, and unprofitable
Seem to me all the uses of this world!
Fie on't, ah, fie, 'tis an unweeded garden
15 That grows to seed. Things rank and gross in nature
Possess it merely.[24] That it should come to this,
But two months dead, nay, not so much, not two,
So excellent a king, that was to this
Hyperion[25] to a satyr, so loving to my mother
20 That he might not beteem[26] the winds of heaven
Visit her face too roughly. Heaven and earth,
Must I remember? Why, she would hang on him
As if increase of appetite had grown
By what it fed on, and yet within a month—
25 Let me not think on't; frailty, thy name is woman—
A little month, or ere those shoes were old
With which she followed my poor father's body
Like Niobe,[27] all tears, why she, even she—
O God, a beast that wants discourse[28] of reason
30 Would have mourned longer—married with my uncle,
My father's brother, but no more like my father
Than I to Hercules. Within a month,
Ere yet the salt of most unrighteous tears
Had left the flushing in her gallèd [29] eyes,
35 She married. O, most wicked speed, to post
With such dexterity to incestuous sheets!

---

[21] *rouse* toast drunk in wine   [22] *bruit* echo   [23] *canon* law   [24] *merely* completely   [25] *Hyperion* the sun god   [26] *beteem* allow   [27] *Niobe* the proud mother who boasted of having more children than Leto and was punished when they were slain by Apollo and Artemis, children of Leto; the grieving Niobe was changed by Zeus into a stone, which continually dropped tears   [28] *discourse* logical power or process   [29] *gallèd* irritated

It is not nor it cannot come to good.
But break my heart, for I must hold my tongue.

(*Enter* HORATIO, MARCELLUS, *and* BERNARDO)

HORATIO   Hail to your lordship!
5   HAMLET   I am glad to see you well.
Horatio—or I do forget myself.
HORATIO   The same, my lord, and your poor servant ever.
HAMLET   Sir, my good friend, I'll change[30] that name with you.
And what make[31] you from Wittenberg, Horatio?
10   Marcellus?
MARCELLUS   My good lord!
HAMLET   I am very glad to see you. (*to* BERNARDO) Good even, sir.
But what, in faith, make you from Wittenberg?
HORATIO   A truant disposition, good my lord.
15   HAMLET   I would not hear your enemy say so,
Nor shall you do my ear that violence
To make it truster of your own report
Against yourself. I know you are no truant.
But what is your affair in Elsinore?
20   We'll teach you to drink deep ere you depart.
HORATIO   My lord, I came to see your father's funeral.
HAMLET   I prithee do not mock me, fellow student.
I think it was to see my mother's wedding.
HORATIO   Indeed, my lord, it followed hard upon.
25   HAMLET   Thrift, thrift, Horatio. The funeral baked meats
Did coldly furnish forth the marriage tables.
Would I had met my dearest[32] foe in heaven
Or ever I had seen that day, Horatio!
My father—methinks I see my father.
30   HORATIO   Where, my lord?
HAMLET   In my mind's eye, Horatio.
HORATIO   I saw him once. 'A was a goodly king.
HAMLET   'A was a man, take him for all in all,
I shall not look upon his like again.
35   HORATIO   My lord, I think I saw him yesternight.
HAMLET   Saw? who?
HORATIO   My lord, the king your father.
HAMLET   The king my father?
HORATIO   Season your admiration[33] for a while

---

[30] *change* exchange   [31] *make* do   [32] *dearest* direst, bitterest   [33] *Season your admiration* control your wonder

With an attent ear till I may deliver
Upon the witness of these gentlemen
This marvel to you.
HAMLET   For God's love let me hear!
5   HORATIO   Two nights together had these gentlemen,
Marcellus and Bernardo, on their watch
In the dead waste and middle of the night
Been thus encountered. A figure like your father,
Armèd at point[34] exactly, cap-a-pe,[35]
10   Appears before them and with solemn march
Goes slow and stately by them. Thrice he walked
By their oppressed and fear-surprisèd eyes
Within his truncheon's[36] length, whilst they, distilled
Almost to jelly with the act of fear,
15   Stand dumb and speak not to him. This to me
In dreadful secrecy impart they did,
And I with them the third night kept the watch,
Where, as they had delivered, both in time,
Form of the thing, each word made true and good,
20   The apparition comes. I knew your father.
These hands are not more like.
HAMLET   But where was this?
MARCELLUS   My lord, upon the platform where we watched.
HAMLET   Did you not speak to it?
25   HORATIO   My lord, I did,
But answer made it none. Yet once methought
It lifted up it[37] head and did address
Itself to motion like as it would speak.
But even then the morning cock crew loud,
30   And at the sound it shrunk in haste away
And vanished from our sight.
HAMLET   'Tis very strange.
HORATIO   As I do live, my honored lord, 'tis true,
And we did think it writ down in our duty
35   To let you know of it.
HAMLET   Indeed, indeed, sirs, but this troubles me.
Hold you the watch to-night?
ALL   We do, my lord.
HAMLET   Armed, say you?
40   ALL   Armed, my lord.

---

[34] *at point* completely   [35] *cap-a pe* from head to foot   [36] *truncheon* military
commander's baton   [37] *it* its

HAMLET   From top to toe?
ALL   My lord, from head to foot.
HAMLET   Then saw you not his face?
HORATIO   O, yes, my lord. He wore his beaver[38] up.
5 HAMLET   What, looked he frowningly?
HORATIO   A countenance more in sorrow than in anger.
HAMLET   Pale or red?
HORATIO   Nay, very pale.
HAMLET   And fixed his eyes upon you?
10 HORATIO   Most constantly.
HAMLET   I would I had been there.
HORATIO   It would have much amazed you.
HAMLET   Very like, very like. Stayed it long?
HORATIO   While one with moderate haste might tell [39] a hundred.
15 BOTH   Longer, longer.
HORATIO   Not when I saw't.
HAMLET   His beard was grizzled,[40] no?
HORATIO   It was as I have seen it in his life,
A sable silvered.[41]
20 HAMLET   I will watch to-night.
Perchance 'twill walk again.
HORATIO   I warr'nt it will.
HAMLET   If it assume my noble father's person,
I'll speak to it though hell itself should gape
25 And bid me hold my peace. I pray you all,
If you have hitherto concealed this sight,
Let it be tenable[42] in your silence still,
And whatsomever else shall hap to-night,
Give it an understanding but no tongue.
30 I will requite your loves. So fare you well.
Upon the platform, 'twixt eleven and twelve
I'll visit you.
ALL   Our duty to your honor.
HAMLET   Your loves, as mine to you. Farewell.

35 (*Exeunt all but* HAMLET)

My father's spirit—in arms? All is not well.
I doubt[43] some foul play. Would the night were come!

---

[38] *beaver* visor or movable faceguard of the helmet   [39] *tell* count   [40] *grizzled*
grey   [41] *sable silvered* black mixed with white   [42] *tenable* held firmly
[43] *doubt* suspect, fear

Till then sit still, my soul. Foul deeds will rise,
Though all the earth o'erwhelm them, to men's eyes.

(*Exit*)

Act I, Scene III

5   *Elsinore Castle: the chambers of* POLONIUS

(*Enter* LAERTES *and* OPHELIA, *his sister*)

LAERTES   My necessaries are embarked. Farewell.
And, sister, as the winds give benefit
And convoy[1] is assistant, do not sleep,
10   But let me hear from you.
OPHELIA   Do you doubt that?
LAERTES   For Hamlet, and the trifling of his favor,
Hold it a fashion and a toy in blood,
A violet in the youth of primy[2] nature,
15   Forward, not permanent, sweet, not lasting,
The perfume and suppliance[3] of a minute,
No more.
OPHELIA   No more but so?
LAERTES   Think it no more.
20   For nature crescent[4] does not grow alone
In thews and bulk, but as this temple[5] waxes
The inward service of the mind and soul
Grows wide withal. Perhaps he loves you now,
And now no soil nor cautel [6] doth besmirch
25   The virtue of his will,[7] but you must fear,
His greatness weighed,[8] his will is not his own.
(For he himself is subject to his birth.)
He may not, as unvalued persons do,
Carve for himself, for on his choice depends
30   The safety and health of this whole state,
And therefore must his choice be circumscribed
Unto the voice and yielding[9] of that body
Whereof he is the head. Then if he says he loves you,
It fits your wisdom so far to believe it
35   As he in his particular act and place

---

[1] *convoy* means of transport   [2] *primy* of the springtime   [3] *perfume and suppliance* filling sweetness   [4] *crescent* growing   [5] *this temple* the body
[6] *cautel* deceit   [7] *will* desire   [8] *greatness weighed* high position considered
[9] *yielding* assent

May give his saying deed, which is no further
Than the main voice of Denmark goes withal.
Then weigh what loss your honor may sustain
If with too credent[10] ear you list his songs,
5   Or lose your heart, or your chaste treasure open
To his unmastered importunity.
Fear it, Ophelia, fear it, my dear sister,
And keep you in the rear of your affection,[11]
Out of the shot and danger of desire.
10   The chariest maid is prodigal enough
If she unmask her beauty to the moon.
Virtue itself scapes not calumnious strokes.
The canker[12] galls[13] the infants of the spring
Too oft before their buttons[14] be disclosed,
15   And in the morn and liquid dew of youth
Contagious blastments[15] are most imminent.
Be wary then; best safety lies in fear.
Youth to itself rebels, though none else near.
OPHELIA   I shall the effect of this good lesson keep
20   As watchman to my heart, but, good my brother,
Do not as some ungracious pastors do,
Show me the steep and thorny way to heaven,
Whiles like a puffed and reckless libertine
Himself the primrose path of dalliance treads
25   And recks[16] not his own rede.[17]

(*Enter* POLONIUS)

LAERTES   O, fear me not.
I stay too long. But here my father comes.
A double blessing is a double grace;
30   Occasion smiles upon a second leave.
POLONIUS   Yet here, Laertes? Aboard, aboard, for shame!
The wind sits in the shoulder of your sail,
And you are stayed for. There—my blessing with thee,
And these few precepts in thy memory
35   Look thou character.[18] Give thy thoughts no tongue,
Nor any unproportioned[19] thought his act.

---

[10] *credent* credulous   [11] *affection* feelings, which rashly lead forward into
dangers   [12] *canker* rose worm   [13] *galls* injures   [14] *buttons* buds   [15] *blastments* blights   [16] *recks* regards   [17]*rede* counsel   [18] *character* inscribe
[19] *unproportioned* unadjusted to what is right

Be thou familiar, but by no means vulgar.
Those friends thou hast, and their adoption tried,
Grapple them unto thy soul with hoops of steel,
But do not dull thy palm with entertainment
5   Of each new-hatched, unfledged courage.[20] Beware
Of entrance to a quarrel; but being in,
Bear't that th' opposèd may beware of thee.
Give every man thine ear, but few thy voice;
Take each man's censure,[21] but reserve thy judgment.
10   Costly thy habit as thy purse can buy,
But not expressed in fancy; rich, not gaudy,
For the apparel oft proclaims the man,
And they in France of the best rank and station
Are of a most select and generous chief [22] in that.
15   Neither a borrower nor a lender be,
For loan oft loses both itself and friend,
And borrowing dulleth edge of husbandry.[23]
This above all, to thine own self be true,
And it must follow as the night the day
20   Thou canst not then be false to any man.
Farewell. My blessing season[24] this in thee!
LAERTES   Most humbly do I take my leave, my lord.
POLONIUS   The time invites you. Go, your servants tend.[25]
LAERTES   Farewell, Ophelia, and remember well
25   What I have said to you.
OPHELIA   'Tis in my memory locked,
And you yourself shall keep the key of it.
LAERTES   Farewell.

(*Exit* LAERTES)

30   POLONIUS   What is't, Ophelia, he hath said to you?
OPHELIA   So please you, something touching the Lord Hamlet.
POLONIUS   Marry,[26] well bethought.
'Tis told me he hath very oft of late
Given private time to you, and you yourself
35   Have of your audience been most free and bounteous.
If it be so—as so 'tis put on me,
And that in way of caution—I must tell you

---

[20] *courage* man of spirit, young blood   [21] *censure* judgment   [22] *chief* eminence   [23] *husbandry* thriftiness   [24] *season* ripen and make fruitful   [25] *tend* wait   [26] *Marry* by Mary

You do not understand yourself so clearly
As it behooves my daughter and your honor.
What is between you? Give me up the truth.
OPHELIA   He hath, my lord, of late made many tenders[27]
5   Of his affection to me.
POLONIUS   Affection? Pooh! You speak like a green girl,
Unsifted [28] in such perilous circumstance.
Do you believe his tenders, as you call them?
OPHELIA   I do not know, my lord, what I should think.
10   POLONIUS   Marry, I will teach you. Think yourself a baby
That you have ta'en these tenders[29] for true pay
Which are not sterling. Tender yourself more dearly,
Or (not to crack the wind of [30] the poor phrase,
Running it thus) you'll tender me a fool.
15   OPHELIA   My lord, he hath importuned me with love
In honorable fashion.
POLONIUS   Ay, fashion you may call it. Go to, go to.[31]
OPHELIA   And hath given countenance to his speech, my lord,
With almost all the holy vows of heaven.
20   POLONIUS   Ay, springes[32] to catch woodcocks.[33] I do know,
When the blood burns, how prodigal the soul
Lends the tongue vows. These blazes, daughter,
Giving more light than heat, extinct in both
Even in their promise, as it is a-making,
25   You must not take for fire. From this time
Be something scanter of your maiden presence.
Set your entreatments[34] at a higher rate
Than a command to parley.[35] For Lord Hamlet,
Believe so much in him that he is young,
30   And with a larger tether may he walk
Than may be given you. In few, Ophelia,
Do not believe his vows, for they are brokers,[36]
Not of that dye which their investments[37] show,

---

[27] *tenders* offers   [28] *Unsifted* untested   [29] *tenders . . . Tender . . . tender* offers . . . hold in regard . . . present (a word play going through three meanings, the last use of the word yielding further complexity with its valid implications that she will show herself to him as a fool, will show him to the world as a fool, and may go so far as to present him with a baby, which would be a fool because "fool" was an Elizabethan term of endearment especially applicable to an infant as a "little innocent")   [30] *crack . . . of* make wheeze like a horse driven too hard   [31] *Go to* go away, go on (expressing impatience)   [32] *springes* snares   [33] *woodcocks* birds believed foolish   [34] *entreatments* military negotiations for surrender   [35] *parley* confer with a besieger   [36] *brokers* middlemen, panders   [37] *investments* clothes

But mere implorators of unholy suits,
Breathing like sanctified and pious bawds,
The better to beguile. This is for all:
I would not, in plain terms, from this time forth
5   Have you so slander[38] any moment[39] leisure
As to give words or talk with the Lord Hamlet.
Look to't, I charge you. Come your ways.
OPHELIA   I shall obey, my lord.

(Exeunt)

10 **Act I, Scene IV**

The sentry-post

(Enter HAMLET, HORATIO, *and* MARCELLUS*)*

HAMLET   The air bites shrewdly[1]; it is very cold.
HORATIO   It is a nipping and an eager[2] air.
15 HAMLET   What hour now?
HORATIO   I think it lacks of twelve.
MARCELLUS   No, it is struck.
HORATIO   Indeed? I heard it not. It then draws near the season
Wherein the spirit held his wont to walk.

20   *(A flourish of trumpets, and two pieces goes off)*

What does this mean, my lord?
HAMLET   The king doth wake to-night and takes his rouse,[3]
Keeps wassail, and the swaggering upspring[4] reels,
And as he drains his draughts of Rhenish[5] down
25   The kettledrum and trumpet thus bray out
The triumph[6] of his pledge.
HORATIO   Is it a custom?
HAMLET   Ay, marry, is't,
But to my mind, though I am native here
30   And to the manner born, it is a custom
More honored in the breach than the observance.[7]
This heavy-headed revel east and west
Makes us traduced and taxed of [8] other nations.
They clepe[9] us drunkards and with swinish phrase

---

[38] *slander* use disgracefully [39] *moment* momentary
[1] *shrewdly* wickedly [2] *eager* sharp [3] *rouse* carousal [4] *upspring* a German
dance [5] *Rhenish* Rhine wine [6] *triumph* achievement, feat (in downing a
cup of wine at one draught) [7] *More ... observance* better broken than observed [8] *taxed of* censured by [9] *clepe* call

Soil our addition,[10] and indeed it takes
From our achievements, though performed at height,
The pith and marrow of our attribute.[11]
So oft it chances in particular men
5   That (for some vicious mole[12] of nature in them,
As in their birth, wherein they are not guilty,
Since nature cannot choose his[13] origin)
By the o'ergrowth of some complexion,[14]
Oft breaking down the pales[15] and forts of reason,
10   Or by some habit that too much o'erleavens[16]
The form of plausive[17] manners—that (these men
Carrying, I say, the stamp of one defect,
Being nature's livery,[18] or fortune's star)[19]
Their virtues else, be they as pure as grace,
15   As infinite as man may undergo,
Shall in the general censure take corruption
From that particular fault. The dram of evil
Doth all the noble substance of a doubt,
To his own scandal.

20   (*Enter* GHOST)

HORATIO   Look, my lord, it comes.
HAMLET   Angels and ministers of grace defend us!
Be thou a spirit of health[20] or goblin[21] damned,
Bring with thee airs from heaven or blasts from hell,
25   Be thy intents wicked or charitable,
Thou com'st in such a questionable shape
That I will speak to thee. I'll call thee Hamlet,
King, father, royal Dane. O, answer me!
Let me not burst in ignorance, but tell
30   Why thy canonized [22] bones, hearsèd in death,
Have burst their cerements,[23] why the sepulchre
Wherein we saw thee quietly interred
Hath oped his ponderous and marble jaws
To cast thee up again. What may this mean

---

[10] *addition* reputation, title added as a distinction   [11] *attribute* reputation, what is attributed   [12] *mole* blemish, flaw   [13] *his* its   [14] *complexion* part of the make-up, combination of humors   [15] *pales* barriers, fences   [16] *o'erleavens* works change throughout, as yeast ferments dough   [17] *plausive* pleasing   [18] *livery* characteristic equipment or provision   [19] *star* make-up as formed by stellar influence   [20] *of health* sound, good   [21] *goblin* fiend   [22] *canonized* buried with the established rites of the Church   [23] *cerements* waxed grave-cloths

That thou, dead corse, again in complete steel,
Revisits thus the glimpses of the moon,
Making night hideous, and we fools of nature[24]
So horridly to shake our disposition
5   With thoughts beyond the reaches of our souls?
Say, why is this? wherefore? what should we do?

(GHOST *beckons*)

HORATIO   It beckons you to go away with it,
As if it some impartment did desire
10   To you alone.
MARCELLUS   Look with what courteous action
It waves you to a more removèd ground.
But do not go with it.
HORATIO   No, by no means.
15 HAMLET   It will not speak. Then will I follow it.
HORATIO   Do not, my lord.
HAMLET   Why, what should be the fear?
I do not set my life at a pin's fee,
And for my soul, what can it do to that,
20   Being a thing immortal as itself?
It waves me forth again. I'll follow it.
HORATIO   What if it tempt you toward the flood, my lord,
Or to the dreadful summit of the cliff
That beetles[25] o'er his base into the sea,
25   And there assume some other horrible form,
Which might deprive[26] your sovereignty of reason[27]
And draw you into madness? Think of it.
The very place puts toys[28] of desperation,
Without more motive, into every brain
30   That looks so many fathoms to the sea
And hears it roar beneath.
HAMLET   It waves me still.
Go on. I'll follow thee.
MARCELLUS   You shall not go, my lord.
35 HAMLET   Hold off your hands.
HORATIO   Be ruled. You shall not go.
HAMLET   My fate cries out
And makes each petty artere[29] in this body

---

[24] *fools of nature* men made conscious of natural limitations by a supernatural manifestation   [25] *beetles* juts out   [26] *deprive* take away   [27] *sovereignty of reason* state of being ruled by reason   [28] *toys* fancies   [29] *artere* artery

As hardy as the Nemean lion's [30] nerve.[31]
Still am I called. Unhand me, gentlemen.
By heaven, I'll make a ghost of him that lets[32] me!
I say, away! Go on. I'll follow thee.

5   (*Exit* GHOST, *and* HAMLET)

HORATIO   He waxes desperate with imagination.
MARCELLUS   Let's follow. 'Tis not fit thus to obey him.
HORATIO   Have after. To what issue will this come?
MARCELLUS   Something is rotten in the state of Denmark.
10   HORATIO   Heaven will direct it.
MARCELLUS   Nay, let's follow him.

     (*Exeunt*)

Act I, Scene V

Another part of the fortifications

15   (*Enter* GHOST *and* HAMLET)

HAMLET   Whither wilt thou lead me? Speak. I'll go no further.
GHOST   Mark me.
HAMLET   I will.
GHOST   My hour is almost come,
20   When I to sulph'rous and tormenting flames[1]
     Must render up myself.
HAMLET   Alas, poor ghost!
GHOST   Pity me not, but lend thy serious hearing
     To what I shall unfold.
25   HAMLET   Speak. I am bound to hear.
GHOST   So art thou to revenge, when thou shalt hear.
HAMLET   What?
GHOST   I am thy father's spirit,
     Doomed for a certain term to walk the night,
30   And for the day confined to fast[2] in fires,
     Till the foul crimes done in my days of nature
     Are burnt and purged away. But that I am forbid
     To tell the secrets of my prison house,
     I could a tale unfold whose lightest word
35   Would harrow up thy soul, freeze thy young blood,

---

[30] *Nemean lion* a lion slain by Hercules in the performance of one of his twelve labors [31] *nerve* sinew [32] *lets* hinders
[1] *flames* sufferings in purgatory (not hell) [2] *fast* do penance

Make thy two eyes like stars start from their spheres,[3]
Thy knotted and combinèd locks to part,
And each particular hair to stand an[4] end
Like quills upon the fretful porpentine.[5]
5   But this eternal blazon[6] must not be
To ears of flesh and blood. List, list, O, list!
If thou didst ever thy dear father love—
HAMLET O God!
GHOST Revenge his foul and most unnatural murder.
10 HAMLET Murder?
GHOST Murder most foul, as in the best it is,
But this most foul, strange, and unnatural.
HAMLET Haste me to know't, that I, with wings as swift
As meditation[7] or the thoughts of love,
15 May sweep to my revenge.
GHOST   I find thee apt,
And duller shouldst thou be than the fat weed
That roots itself in ease on Lethe[8] wharf,
Wouldst thou not stir in this. Now, Hamlet, hear.
20 'Tis given out that, sleeping in my orchard,
A serpent stung me. So the whole ear of Denmark
Is by a forgèd process[9] of my death
Rankly abused. But know, thou noble youth,
The serpent that did sting thy father's life
25 Now wears his crown.
HAMLET   O my prophetic soul!
My uncle?
GHOST Ay, that incestuous, that adulterate[10] beast,
With witchcraft of his wit, with traitorous gifts—
30 O wicked wit and gifts, that have the power
So to seduce!—won to this shameful lust
The will of my most seeming-virtuous queen.
O Hamlet, what a falling-off was there,
From me, whose love was of that dignity
35 That it went hand in hand even with the vow
I made to her in marriage, and to decline

---

[3] *spheres* transparent revolving shells in each of which, according to the Ptolemaic astronomy, a planet or other heavenly body was placed   [4] *an* on   [5] *porpentine* porcupine   [6] *eternal blazon* revelation of eternity   [7] *meditation* thought   [8] *Lethe* the river in Hades which brings forgetfulness of past life to a spirit who drinks of it   [9] *forgèd process* falsified official report   [10] *adulterate* adulterous

Upon a wretch whose natural gifts were poor
To those of mine!
But virtue, as it never will be moved,
Though lewdness court it in a shape of heaven,[11]
5   So lust, though to a radiant angel linked,
Will sate itself in a celestial bed
And prey on garbage.
But soft, methinks I scent the morning air.
Brief let me be. Sleeping within my orchard,
10   My custom always of the afternoon,
Upon my secure[12] hour thy uncle stole
With juice of cursed hebona[13] in a vial,
And in the porches of my ears did pour
The leperous distilment, whose effect
15   Holds such an enmity with blood of man
That swift as quicksilver it courses through
The natural gates and alleys of the body,
And with a sudden vigor it doth posset[14]
And curd, like eager[15] droppings into milk,
20   The thin and wholesome blood. So did it mine,
And a most instant tetter[16] barked [17] about
Most lazar-like[18] with vile and loathsome crust
All my smooth body.
Thus was I sleeping by a brother's hand
25   Of life, of crown, of queen at once dispatched,
Cut off even in the blossoms of my sin,
Unhouseled,[19] disappointed,[20] unaneled,[21]
No reck'ning made, but sent to my account
With all my imperfections on my head.
30   O, horrible! O, horrible! most horrible!
If thou hast nature in thee, bear it not.
Let not the royal bed of Denmark be
A couch for luxury[22] and damnèd incest.
But howsomever thou pursues this act,
35   Taint not thy mind, nor let thy soul contrive
Against thy mother aught. Leave her to heaven
And to those thorns that in her bosom lodge

---

[11] *shape of heaven* angelic disguise   [12] *secure* carefree, unsuspecting   [13] *hebona* some poisonous plant   [14] *posset* curdle   [15] *eager* sour   [16] *tetter* eruption   [17] *barked* covered as with a bark   [18] *lazar-like* leper-like   [19] *Unhouseled* without the Sacrament   [20] *disappointed* unprepared spiritually   [21] *unaneled* without extreme unction   [22] *luxury* lust

To prick and sting her. Fare thee well at once.
The glowworm shows the matin[23] to be near
And gins to pale his uneffectual fire.
Adieu, adieu, adieu. Remember me.

5 (*Exit*)

HAMLET O all you host of heaven! O earth! What else?
And shall I couple hell? O fie! Hold, hold, my heart,
And you, my sinews, grow not instant old,
But bear me stiffly up. Remember thee?
10 Ay, thou poor ghost, while memory holds a seat
In this distracted globe.[24] Remember thee?
Yea, from the table[25] of my memory
I'll wipe away all trivial fond records,
All saws[26] of books, all forms,[27] all pressures[28] past
15 That youth and observation copied there,
And thy commandment all alone shall live
Within the book and volume of my brain,
Unmixed with baser matter. Yes, by heaven!
O most pernicious woman!
20 O villain, villain, smiling, damnèd villain!
My tables—meet it is I set it down
That one may smile, and smile, and be a villain.
At least I am sure it may be so in Denmark.

(*Writes*)

25 So, uncle, there you are. Now to my word:
It is "Adieu, adieu, remember me."
I have sworn't.

(*Enter* HORATIO *and* MARCELLUS)

HORATIO My lord, my lord!
30 MARCELLUS   Lord Hamlet!
HORATIO   Heavens secure him!
HAMLET So be it!
MARCELLUS Illo, ho, ho,[29] my lord!
HAMLET Hillo, ho, ho, boy! Come, bird, come.
35 MARCELLUS How is't, my noble lord?
HORATIO   What news, my lord?

---

[23] *matin* morning [24] *globe* head [25] *table* writing tablet, record book
[26] *saws* wise sayings [27] *forms* mental images, concepts [28] *pressures* impressions [29] *Illo, ho, ho* cry of the falconer to summon his hawk

HAMLET O, wonderful!

HORATIO Good my lord, tell it.

HAMLET   No, you will reveal it.

HORATIO Not I, my lord, by heaven.

5 MARCELLUS   Nor I, my lord.

HAMLET How say you then? Would heart of man once think it?
But you'll be secret?

BOTH   Ay, by heaven, my lord.

HAMLET There's never a villain dwelling in all Denmark

10 But he's an arrant knave.

HORATIO There needs no ghost, my lord, come from the grave
To tell us this.

HAMLET   Why, right, you are in the right,
And so, without more circumstance[30] at all,

15 I hold it fit that we shake hands and part:
You, as your business and desires shall point you,
For every man hath business and desire
Such as it is, and for my own poor part,
Look you, I'll go pray.

20 HORATIO These are but wild and whirling words, my lord.

HAMLET I am sorry they offend you, heartily;
Yes, faith, heartily.

HORATIO   There's no offense, my lord.

HAMLET Yes, by Saint Patrick, but there is, Horatio,

25 And much offense too. Touching this vision here,
It is an honest[31] ghost, that let me tell you.
For your desire to know what is between us,
O'ermaster't as you may. And now, good friends,
As you are friends, scholars, and soldiers,

30 Give me one poor request.

HORATIO What is't, my lord? We will.

HAMLET Never make known what you have seen to-night.

BOTH My lord, we will not.

HAMLET   Nay, but swear't.

35 HORATIO   In faith,
My lord, not I.

MARCELLUS   Nor I, my lord—in faith.

HAMLET Upon my sword.[32]

MARCELLUS   We have sworn, my lord, already.

---

[30] *circumstance* ceremony   [31] *honest* genuine (not a disguised demon)
[32] *sword* i.e. upon the cross formed by the sword hilt

HAMLET   Indeed, upon my sword, indeed.

(GHOST *cries under the stage*)

GHOST   Swear.

HAMLET   Ha, ha, boy, say'st thou so? Art thou there, truepenny? [33]

5   Come on. You hear this fellow in the cellarage.
Consent to swear.

HORATIO   Propose the oath, my lord.

HAMLET   Never to speak of this that you have seen,
Swear by my sword.

10   GHOST (*beneath*)   Swear.

HAMLET   Hic et ubique? [34] Then we'll shift our ground.
Come hither, gentlemen,
And lay your hands again upon my sword.
Swear by my sword

15   Never to speak of this that you have heard.

GHOST (*beneath*)   Swear by his sword.

HAMLET   Well said, old mole! Canst work i' th' earth so fast?
A worthy pioner! [35] Once more remove, good friends.

HORATIO   O day and night, but this is wondrous strange!

20   HAMLET   And therefore as a stranger give it welcome.
There are more things in heaven and earth, Horatio,
Than are dreamt of in your philosophy.[36]
But come:
Here as before, never, so help you mercy,

25   How strange or odd some'er I bear myself
(As I perchance hereafter shall think meet
To put an antic[37] disposition on),
That you, at such times seeing me, never shall,
With arms encumb'red [38] thus, or this head-shake,

30   Or by pronouncing of some doubtful phrase,
As "Well, well, we know," or "We could, an if [39] we would,"
Or "If we list to speak," or "There be, an if they might,"
Or such ambiguous giving out, to note
That you know aught of me—this do swear,

35   So grace and mercy at your most need help you.

GHOST (*beneath*)   Swear.

(*They swear*)

---

[33] *truepenny* honest old fellow   [34] *Hic et ubique* here and everywhere   [35] *pioner* pioneer, miner   [36] *your philosophy* this philosophy one hears about   [37] *antic* grotesque, mad   [38] *encumb'red* folded   [39] *an if* if

HAMLET   Rest, rest, perturbèd spirit! So, gentlemen,
With all my love I do commend [40] me to you,
And what so poor a man as Hamlet is
May do t' express his love and friending to you,
5   God willing, shall not lack. Let us go in together,
And still [41] your fingers on your lips, I pray.
The time is out of joint. O cursèd spite
That ever I was born to set it right!
Nay, come, let's go together.

10   (*Exeunt*)

ACT II

Scene I

The chambers of POLONIUS

(*Enter old* POLONIUS, *with his man* [REYNALDO])

15   POLONIUS   Give him this money and these notes, Reynaldo.
REYNALDO   I will, my lord.
POLONIUS   You shall do marvellous wisely, good Reynaldo,
Before you visit him, to make inquire
Of his behavior.
20   REYNALDO   My lord, I did intend it.
POLONIUS   Marry, well said, very well said. Look you, sir,
Enquire me first what Danskers[1] are in Paris,
And how, and who, what means,[2] and where they keep,[3]
What company, at what expense; and finding
25   By this encompassment[4] and drift of question
That they do know my son, come you more nearer
Than your particular demands[5] will touch it.
Take you as 'twere some distant knowledge of him,
As thus, "I know his father and his friends,
30   And in part him"—do you mark this, Reynaldo?
REYNALDO   Ay, very well, my lord.
POLONIUS   "And in part him, but," you may say, "not well,
But if't be he I mean, he's very wild
Addicted so and so." And there put on him
35   What forgeries[6] you please; marry, none so rank

---

[40] *commend* entrust   [41] *still* always
[1] *Danskers* Danes   [2] *what means* what their wealth   [3] *keep* dwell   [4] *encompassment* circling about   [5] *particular demands* definite questions   [6] *forgeries* invented wrongdoings

As may dishonor him—take heed of that—
But, sir, such wanton, wild, and usual slips
As are companions noted and most known
To youth and liberty.

5 REYNALDO As gaming, my lord.
POLONIUS Ay, or drinking, fencing, swearing, quarrelling,
Drabbing.[7] You may go so far.
REYNALDO My lord, that would dishonor him.
POLONIUS Faith, no, as you may season[8] it in the charge.
10 You must not put another scandal on him,
That he is open to incontinency.[9]
That's not my meaning. But breathe his faults so quaintly[10]
That they may seem the taints of liberty,
The flash and outbreak of a fiery mind,
15 A savageness in unreclaimèd [11] blood,
Of general assault.[12]
REYNALDO But, my good lord—
POLONIUS Wherefore should you do this?
REYNALDO Ay, my lord,
20 I would know that.
POLONIUS Marry, sir, here's my drift,
And I believe it is a fetch of warrant.[13]
You laying these slight sullies on my son
As 'twere a thing a little soiled i' th' working,
25 Mark you,
Your party in converse, him you would sound,
Having ever[14] seen in the prenominate[15] crimes
The youth you breathe of guilty, be assured
He closes with you[16] in this consequence:[17]
30 "Good sir," or so, or "friend," or "gentleman"—
According to the phrase or the addition[18]
Of man and country—
REYNALDO Very good, my lord.
POLONIUS And then, sir, does 'a this—'a does—
35 What was I about to say? By the mass, I was about to say some-
thing! Where did I leave?

---

[7] *Drabbing* whoring   [8] *season* soften   [9] *incontinency* extreme sensuality
[10] *quaintly* expertly, gracefully   [11] *unreclaimèd* untamed   [12] *Of general assault* assailing all young men   [13] *fetch of warrant* allowable trick   [14] *Having
ever* if he has ever   [15] *prenominate* aforementioned   [16] *closes with you* follows your lead to a conclusion   [17] *consequence* following way   [18] *addition*
title

REYNALDO   At "closes in the consequence," at "friend or so," and "gentleman."
POLONIUS   At "closes in the consequence"—Ay, marry!
He closes thus: "I know the gentleman;
5   I saw him yesterday, or t' other day,
Or then, or then, with such or such, and, as you say,
There was 'a gaming, there o'ertook[19] in's rouse,[20]
There falling[21] out at tennis"; or perchance,
"I saw him enter such a house of sale,"
10   Videlicet,[22] a brothel, or so forth.
See you now—
Your bait of falsehood takes this carp of truth,
And thus do we of wisdom and of reach,[23]
With windlasses[24] and with assays of bias,[25]
15   By indirections find directions[26] out.
So, by my former lecture and advice,
Shall you my son. You have me, have you not?
REYNALDO   My lord, I have.
POLONIUS   God bye ye,[27] fare ye well.
20   REYNALDO   Good my lord.
POLONIUS   Observe his inclination in yourself.
REYNALDO   I shall, my lord.
POLONIUS   And let him ply his music.
REYNALDO   Well, my lord.
25   POLONIUS   Farewell.

(*Exit* REYNALDO)

(*Enter* OPHELIA)

                    How now, Ophelia, what's the matter?
OPHELIA   O my lord, my lord, I have been so affrighted!
30   POLONIUS   With what, i' th' name of God?
OPHELIA   My lord, as I was sewing in my closet,[28]
Lord Hamlet, with his doublet[29] all unbraced,[30]
No hat upon his head, his stockings fouled,
Ungartered, and down-gyvèd [31] to his ankle,
35   Pale as his shirt, his knees knocking each other,

---

19 *o'ertook* overcome with drunkenness   20 *rouse* carousal   21 *falling out* quarrelling   22 *Videlicet* namely   23 *reach* far-reaching comprehension   24 *windlasses* roundabout courses   25 *assays of bias* devious attacks   26 *directions* ways of procedure   27 *God bye ye* God be with you, good-bye   28 *closet* private living-room   29 *doublet* jacket   30 *unbraced* unlaced   31 *down-gyvèd* fallen down like gyves or fetters on a prisoner's legs

And with a look so piteous in purport
As if he had been loosèd out of hell
To speak of horrors—he comes before me.
POLONIUS   Mad for thy love?

5   OPHELIA   My lord, I do not know,
But truly I do fear it.
POLONIUS   What said he?
OPHELIA   He took me by the wrist and held me hard.
Then goes he to the length of all his arm,

10   And with his other hand thus o'er his brow
He falls to such perusal of my face
As 'a would draw it. Long stayed he so.
At last, a little shaking of mine arm
And thrice his head thus waving up and down,

15   He raised a sigh so piteous and profound
As it did seem to shatter all his bulk
And end his being. That done, he lets me go,
And with his head over his shoulder turned
He seemed to find his way without his eyes,

20   For out o' doors he went without their helps
And to the last bended their light on me.
POLONIUS   Come, go with me. I will go seek the king.
This is the very ecstasy[32] of love,
Whose violent property[33] fordoes[34] itself

25   And leads the will to desperate undertakings
As oft as any passion under heaven
That does afflict our natures. I am sorry.
What, have you given him any hard words of late?
OPHELIA   No, my good lord; but as you did command

30   I did repel his letters and denied
His access to me.
POLONIUS   That hath made him mad.
I am sorry that with better heed and judgment
I had not quoted[35] him. I feared he did but trifle

35   And meant to wrack thee; but beshrew[36] my jealousy.
By heaven, it is as proper to our age
To cast beyond ourselves[37] in our opinions
As it is common for the younger sort
To lack discretion. Come, go we to the king.

---

[32] *ecstasy* madness   [33] *property* quality   [34] *fordoes* destroys   [35] *quoted* observed   [36] *beshrew* curse   [37] *cast beyond ourselves* find by calculation more significance in something than we ought to

This must be known, which, being kept close,[38] might move[39]
More grief to hide than hate to utter love.[40]
Come.

(Exeunt)

5   **Act II, Scene II**

A chamber in the castle

(Flourish. Enter KING *and* QUEEN, ROSENCRANTZ, *and* GUILDENSTERN
[*with others*])

KING   Welcome, dear Rosencrantz and Guildenstern.
10   Moreover that[1] we much did long to see you,
The need we have to use you did provoke
Our hasty sending. Something have you heard
Of Hamlet's transformation—so call it,
Sith[2] nor th' exterior nor the inward man
15   Resembles that it was. What it should be,
More than his father's death, that thus hath put him
So much from th' understanding of himself,
I cannot dream of. I entreat you both
That, being of so young days brought up with him,
20   And sith so neighbored to his youth and havior,[3]
That you vouchsafe your rest here in our court
Some little time, so by your companies
To draw him on to pleasures, and to gather
So much as from occasion you may glean,
25   Whether aught to us unknown afflicts him thus,
That opened[4] lies within our remedy.
QUEEN   Good gentlemen, he hath much talked of you,
And sure I am two men there are not living
To whom he more adheres.[5] If it will please you
30   To show us so much gentry[6] and good will
As to expend your time with us awhile
For the supply and profit of our hope,
Your visitation shall receive such thanks
As fits a king's remembrance.

---

[38] *close* secret   [39] *move* cause   [40] *to hide . . . love* by such hiding of love than
there would be hate moved by a revelation of it (a violently condensed
putting of the case which is a triumph of special statement for Polonius)
[1] *Moreover that* besides the fact that   [2] *Sith* since   [3] *youth and havior*
youthful ways of life   [4] *opened* revealed   [5] *more adheres* is more attached
[6] *gentry* courtesy

ROSENCRANTZ   Both your majesties
Might, by the sovereign power you have of us,
Put your dread pleasures more into command
Than to entreaty.
5   GUILDENSTERN   But we both obey,
And here give up ourselves in the full bent[7]
To lay our service freely at your feet,
To be commanded.
KING   Thanks, Rosencrantz and gentle Guildenstern.
10   QUEEN   Thanks, Guildenstern and gentle Rosencrantz.
And I beseech you instantly to visit
My too much changèd son.—Go, some of you,
And bring these gentlemen where Hamlet is.
GUILDENSTERN   Heavens make our presence and our practices
15   Pleasant and helpful to him!
QUEEN   Ay, amen!

(*Exeunt* ROSENCRANTZ *and* GUILDENSTERN [*with some* ATTENDANTS])

(*Enter* POLONIUS)

POLONIUS   Th' ambassadors from Norway, my good lord,
20   Are joyfully returned.
KING   Thou still [8] hast been the father of good news.
POLONIUS   Have I, my lord? Assure you, my good liege,
I hold my duty as I hold my soul,
Both to my God and to my gracious king,
25   And I do think—or else this brain of mine
Hunts not the trail of policy so sure
As it hath used to do—that I have found
The very cause of Hamlet's lunacy.
KING   O, speak of that! That do I long to hear.
30   POLONIUS   Give first admittance to th' ambassadors.
My news shall be the fruit[9] to that great feast.
KING   Thyself do grace[10] to them and bring them in.

(*Exit* POLONIUS)

He tells me, my dear Gertrude, he hath found
35   The head and source of all your son's distemper.
QUEEN   I doubt[11] it is no other but the main,
His father's death and our o'erhasty marriage.

---

[7] *in the full bent* at the limit of bending (of a bow), to full capacity   [8] *still* always   [9] *fruit* dessert   [10] *grace* honor   [11] *doubt* suspect

KING Well, we shall sift him.

(*Enter* AMBASSADORS [VOLTEMAND *and* CORNELIUS, *with* POLONIUS])

Welcome, my good friends.
Say, Voltemand, what from our brother Norway?

5   VOLTEMAND Most fair return of greetings and desires.
Upon our first,[12] he sent out to suppress
His nephew's levies, which to him appeared
To be a preparation 'gainst the Polack,
But better looked into, he truly found

10   It was against your highness, whereat grieved,
That so his sickness, age, and impotence
Was falsely borne in hand,[13] sends out arrests
On Fortinbras; which he in brief obeys,
Receives rebuke from Norway, and in fine[14]

15   Makes vow before his uncle never more
To give th' assay[15] of arms against your majesty.
Whereon old Norway, overcome with joy,
Gives him threescore thousand crowns in annual fee
And his commission to employ those soldiers,

20   So levied as before, against the Polack,
With an entreaty, herein further shown,

(*Gives a paper*)

That it might please you to give quiet pass
Through your dominions for this enterprise,

25   On such regards[16] of safety and allowance
As therein are set down.

KING   It likes us well;
And at our more considered time[17] we'll read,
Answer, and think upon this business.

30   Meantime we thank you for your well-took labor.
Go to your rest; at night we'll feast together.
Most welcome home!

(*Exeunt* AMBASSADORS)

POLONIUS   This business is well ended.

35   My liege and madam, to expostulate[18]
What majesty should be, what duty is,

---

[12] *our first* our first words about the matter   [13] *borne in hand* deceived   [14] *in fine* in the end   [15] *assay* trial   [16] *regards* terms   [17] *considered time* convenient time for consideration   [18] *expostulate* discuss

Why day is day, night night, and time is time,
Were nothing but to waste night, day, and time.
Therefore, since brevity is the soul of wit,[19]
And tediousness the limbs and outward flourishes,
5   I will be brief. Your noble son is mad.
Mad call I it, for, to define true madness,
What is't but to be nothing else but mad?
But let that go.
    QUEEN   More matter, with less art.
10 POLONIUS   Madam, I swear I use no art at all.
That he is mad, 'tis true: 'tis true 'tis pity,
And pity 'tis 'tis true—a foolish figure.[20]
But farewell it, for I will use no art.
Mad let us grant him then, and now remains
15 That we find out the cause of this effect—
Or rather say, the cause of this defect,
For this effect defective comes by cause.
Thus it remains, and the remainder thus.
Perpend.[21]
20 I have a daughter (have while she is mine),
Who in her duty and obedience, mark,
Hath given me this. Now gather, and surmise.

(Reads the letter)

"To the celestial, and my soul's idol, the most beautified
25 Ophelia,"—
That's an ill phrase, a vile phrase; "beautified" is a vile phrase.
    But you shall hear. Thus:

(Reads)

"In her excellent white bosom, these, &c."
30 QUEEN   Came this from Hamlet to her?
    POLONIUS   Good madam, stay awhile. I will be faithful.

(Reads)

      "Doubt thou the stars are fire;
        Doubt that the sun doth move;
35   Doubt[22] truth to be a liar;
        But never doubt I love.
O dear Ophelia, I am ill at these numbers.[23] I have not art to

---

[19] *wit* understanding   [20] *figure* figure in rhetoric   [21] *Perpend* ponder
[22] *Doubt* suspect   [23] *numbers* verses

reckon my groans, but that I love thee best, O most best, believe it.
Adieu.
     Thine evermore, most dear lady,
       whilst this machine^{24} is to^{25} him, Hamlet."

5   This in obedience hath my daughter shown me,
And more above^{26} hath his solicitings,
As they fell out by time, by means, and place,
All given to mine ear.
KING   But how hath she
10 Received his love?
POLONIUS   What do you think of me?
KING   As of a man faithful and honorable.
POLONIUS   I would fain prove so. But what might you think,
When I had seen this hot love on the wing
15 (As I perceived it, I must tell you that,
Before my daughter told me), what might you,
Or my dear majesty your queen here, think,
If I had played the desk or table book,^{27}
Or given my heart a winking,^{28} mute and dumb,
20 Or looked upon this love with idle sight?
What might you think? No, I went round ^{29} to work
And my young mistress thus I did bespeak:
"Lord Hamlet is a prince, out of thy star.^{30}
This must not be." And then I prescripts^{31} gave her,
25 That she should lock herself from his resort,
Admit no messengers, receive no tokens.
Which done, she took the fruits of my advice,
And he, repellèd, a short tale to make,
Fell into a sadness, then into a fast,
30 Thence to a watch,^{32} thence into a weakness,
Thence to a lightness,^{33} and, by this declension,
Into the madness wherein now he raves,
And all we mourn for.
KING   Do you think 'tis this?
35 QUEEN   It may be, very like.
POLONIUS   Hath there been such a time—I would fain know that—

---

24 *machine* body   25 *to* attached to   26 *above* besides   27 *desk or table book*
i.e. silent receiver   28 *winking* closing of the eyes   29 *round* roundly, plainly
30 *star* condition determined by stellar influence   31 *prescripts* instructions
32 *watch* sleepless state   33 *lightness* lightheadedness

That I have positively said " 'Tis so,"
When it proved otherwise?
KING   Not that I know.
POLONIUS (*pointing to his head and shoulder*)
5   Take this from this, if this be otherwise.
If circumstances lead me, I will find
Where truth is hid, though it were hid indeed
Within the center.[34]
KING   How may we try it further?
10 POLONIUS   You know sometimes he walks four hours together
Here in the lobby.
QUEEN   So he does indeed.
POLONIUS   At such a time I'll loose my daughter to him.
Be you and I behind an arras[35] then.
15   Mark the encounter. If he love her not,
And be not from his reason fallen thereon,[36]
Let me be no assistant for a state
But keep a farm and carters.
KING   We will try it.

20   (*Enter* HAMLET [*reading on a book*])

QUEEN   But look where sadly the poor wretch comes reading.
POLONIUS   Away, I do beseech you both, away.

(*Exit* KING *and* QUEEN [*with* ATTENDANTS])

I'll board [37] him presently.[38] O, give me leave.
25   How does my good Lord Hamlet?
HAMLET   Well, God-a-mercy.[39]
POLONIUS   Do you know me, my lord?
HAMLET   Excellent well. You are a fishmonger.[40]
POLONIUS   Not I, my lord.
30 HAMLET   Then I would you were so honest a man.
POLONIUS   Honest, my lord?
HAMLET   Ay, sir. To be honest, as this world goes, is to be one man
picked out of ten thousand.
POLONIUS   That's very true, my lord.

---

[34] *center* center of the earth and also of the Ptolemaic universe   [35] *arras*
hanging tapestry   [36] *thereon* on that account   [37] *board* accost   [38] *presently*
at once   [39] *God-a-mercy* thank you (literally, "God have mercy!")   [40] *fishmonger* seller of harlots, procurer (a cant term used here with a glance at
the fishing Polonius is doing when he offers Ophelia as bait)

HAMLET   For if the sun breed maggots in a dead dog, being a good kissing carrion[41]—Have you a daughter?

POLONIUS   I have, my lord.

HAMLET   Let her not walk i' th' sun. Conception is a blessing, but
5   as your daughter may conceive, friend, look to't.

POLONIUS   (*aside*)   How say you by that? Still harping on my daughter. Yet he knew me not at first. 'A said I was a fishmonger. 'A is far gone, far gone. And truly in my youth I suffered much extremity for love, very near this. I'll speak to him again.—What do
10   you read, my lord?

HAMLET   Words, words, words.

POLONIUS   What is the matter, my lord?

HAMLET   Between who? [42]

POLONIUS   I mean the matter that you read, my lord.

15   HAMLET   Slanders, sir, for the satirical rogue says here that old men have grey beards, that their faces are wrinkled, their eyes purging thick amber and plum-tree gum, and that they have a plentiful lack of wit, together with most weak hams. All which, sir, though I most powerfully and potently believe, yet I hold it not honesty
20   to have it thus set down, for you yourself, sir, should be old as I am if, like a crab, you could go backward.

POLONIUS   (*aside*)   Though this be madness, yet there is method in't. —Will you walk out of the air, my lord?

HAMLET   Into my grave?

25   POLONIUS   Indeed, that's out of the air. (*aside*) How pregnant[43] sometimes his replies are! a happiness[44] that often madness hits on, which reason and sanity could not so prosperously be delivered of. I will leave him and suddenly contrive the means of meeting between him and my daughter.—My honorable lord, I will most
30   humbly take my leave of you.

HAMLET   You cannot, sir, take from me anything that I will more willingly part withal [45]—except my life, except my life, except my life.

(*Enter* GUILDENSTERN *and* ROSENCRANTZ)

35   POLONIUS   Fare you well, my lord.

HAMLET   These tedious old fools!

POLONIUS   You go to seek the Lord Hamlet. There he is.

---

[41] *good kissing carrion* good bit of flesh for kissing   [42] *Between who* matter for a quarrel between what persons (Hamlet's willful misunderstanding) [43] *pregnant* full of meaning   [44] *happiness* aptness of expression   [45] *withal* with

ROSENCRANTZ (*to* POLONIUS) God save you, sir!

(*Exit* POLONIUS)

GUILDENSTERN My honored lord!

ROSENCRANTZ My most dear lord!

5 HAMLET My excellent good friends! How dost thou, Guildenstern?
Ah, Rosencrantz! Good lads, how do ye both?

ROSENCRANTZ As the indifferent[46] children of the earth.

GUILDENSTERN Happy in that we are not over-happy.
On Fortune's cap we are not the very button.

10 HAMLET Nor the soles of her shoe?

ROSENCRANTZ Neither, my lord.

HAMLET Then you live about her waist, or in the middle of her
favors?

GUILDENSTERN Faith, her privates[47] we.

15 HAMLET In the secret parts of Fortune? O, most true! she is a
strumpet. What news?

ROSENCRANTZ None, my lord, but that the world's grown honest.

HAMLET Then is doomsday near. But your news is not true. (Let
me question more in particular.) What have you, my good friends,

20 deserved at the hands of Fortune that she sends you to prison
hither?

GUILDENSTERN Prison, my lord?

HAMLET Denmark 's a prison.

ROSENCRANTZ Then is the world one.

25 HAMLET A goodly one; in which there are many confines,[48]
wards,[49] and dungeons, Denmark being one o' th' worst.

ROSENCRANTZ We think not so, my lord.

HAMLET Why, then 'tis none to you, for there is nothing either
good or bad but thinking makes it so. To me it is a prison.

30 ROSENCRANTZ Why, then your ambition makes it one. 'Tis too narrow for your mind.

HAMLET O God, I could be hounded in a nutshell and count myself
a king of infinite space, were it not that I have bad dreams.

GUILDENSTERN Which dreams indeed are ambition, for the very

35 substance of the ambitious is merely the shadow of a dream.

HAMLET A dream itself is but a shadow.

ROSENCRANTZ Truly, and I hold ambition of so airy and light a
quality that it is but a shadow's shadow.

---

[46] *indifferent* average [47] *privates* ordinary men in private, not public, life
(with obvious play upon the sexual term "private parts") [48] *confines* places
of imprisonment [49] *wards* cells

HAMLET Then are our beggars bodies,[50] and our monarchs and outstretched [51] heroes the beggars' shadows. Shall we to th' court?
for, by my fay,[52] I cannot reason.
BOTH We'll wait upon[53] you.

5 HAMLET No such matter. I will not sort you with the rest of my
servants, for, to speak to you like an honest man, I am most dreadfully attended. But in the beaten way of friendship, what make[54]
you at Elsinore?
ROSENCRANTZ To visit you, my lord; no other occasion.

10 HAMLET Beggar that I am, I am even poor in thanks, but I thank
you; and sure, dear friends, my thanks are too dear a halfpenny.[55]
Were you not sent for? Is it your own inclining? Is it a free visitation? Come, come, deal justly with me. Come, come. Nay, speak.
GUILDENSTERN What should we say, my lord?

15 HAMLET Why, anything—but to th' purpose. You were sent for,
and there is a kind of confession in your looks, which your modes-
ties have not craft enough to color. I know the good king and
queen have sent for you.
ROSENCRANTZ To what end, my lord?

20 HAMLET That you must teach me. But let me conjure you by the
rights of our fellowship, by the consonancy[56] of our youth, by the
obligation of our ever-preserved love, and by what more dear a
better proposer[57] can charge you withal,[58] be even[59] and direct
with me whether you were sent for or no.

25 ROSENCRANTZ (*aside to* GUILDENSTERN) What say you?
HAMLET (*aside*) Nay then, I have an eye of you.—If you love me,
hold not off.
GUILDENSTERN My lord, we were sent for.
HAMLET I will tell you why. So shall my anticipation prevent[60]

30 your discovery,[61] and your secrecy to the king and queen moult no
feather.[62] I have of late—but wherefore I know not—lost all my
mirth, forgone all custom of exercises; and indeed, it goes so heavily with my disposition that this goodly frame the earth seems to
me a sterile promontory; this most excellent canopy, the air, look

35 you, this brave o'erhanging firmament,[63] this majestical roof

---

[50] *bodies* solid substances, not shadows (because beggars lack ambition)
[51] *outstretched* elongated as shadows (with a corollary implication of far-
reaching with respect to the ambitions that make both heroes and monarchs
into shadows) [52] *fay* faith [53] *wait upon* attend [54] *make* do [55] *a halfpenny* at a halfpenny [56] *consonancy* accord (in sameness of age) [57] *proposer* propounder [58] *withal* with [59] *even* straight [60] *prevent* forestall
[61] *discovery* disclosure [62] *moult no feather* be left whole [63] *firmament* sky

fretted [64] with golden fire—why, it appeareth nothing to me but a foul and pestilent congregation of vapors. What a piece of work is a man, how noble in reason, how infinite in faculties; in form and moving how express[65] and admirable, in action how like an
5   angel, in apprehension how like a god: the beauty of the world, the paragon of animals! And yet to me what is this quintessence[66] of dust? Man delights not me—nor woman neither, though by your smiling you seem to say so.

ROSENCRANTZ My lord, there was no such stuff in my thoughts.

10 HAMLET Why did ye laugh then, when I said "Man delights not me"?

ROSENCRANTZ To think, my lord, if you delight not in man, what lenten[67] entertainment the players shall receive from you. We coted [68] them on the way, and hither are they coming to offer you
15 service.

HAMLET He that plays the king shall be welcome—his majesty shall have tribute of me—, the adventurous knight shall use his foil and target,[69] the lover shall not sigh gratis, the humorous man[70] shall end his part in peace, the clown shall make those laugh whose
20 lungs are tickle o' th' sere,[71] and the lady shall say her mind freely, or the blank verse shall halt[72] for't. What players are they?

ROSENCRANTZ Even those you were wont to take such delight in, the tragedians of the city.

HAMLET How chances it they travel? Their residence,[73] both in
25 reputation and profit, was better both ways.

ROSENCRANTZ I think their inhibition[74] comes by the means of the late innovation.[75]

HAMLET Do they hold the same estimation they did when I was in the city? Are they so followed?

30 ROSENCRANTZ No indeed, are they not.

HAMLET How comes it? Do they grow rusty?

ROSENCRANTZ Nay, their endeavor keeps in the wonted pace, but there is, sir, an eyrie[76] of children, little eyases,[77] that cry out on

---

[64] *fretted* decorated with fretwork [65] *express* well framed [66] *quintessence* fifth or last and finest essence (an alchemical term) [67] *lenten* scanty [68] *coted* overtook [69] *foil and target* sword and shield [70] *humorous man* eccentric character dominated by one of the humours [71] *tickle o' th' sere* hair-triggered for the discharge of laughter ("sere": part of a gunlock) [72] *halt* go lame [73] *residence* residing at the capital [74] *inhibition* impediment to acting in residence (formal prohibition?) [75] *innovation* new fashion of having companies of boy actors play on the "private" stage (?), political upheaval (?) [76] *eyrie* nest [77] *eyases* nestling hawks

the top of question[78] and are most tyranically clapped for't. These are now the fashion, and so berattle[79] the common stages[80] (so they call them) that many wearing rapiers are afraid of goose-quills[81] and dare scarce come thither.

5 HAMLET What, are they children? Who maintains 'em? How are they escoted?[82] Will they pursue the quality[83] no longer than they can sing?[84] Will they not say afterwards, if they should grow themselves to common players (as it is most like, if their means are no better), their writers do them wrong to make them exclaim
10 against their own succession?

ROSENCRANTZ Faith, there has been much to do on both sides, and the nation holds it no sin to tarre[85] them to controversy. There was, for a while, no money bid for argument[86] unless the poet and the player went to cuffs in the question.

15 HAMLET Is't possible?

GUILDENSTERN O, there has been much throwing about of brains.

HAMLET Do the boys carry it away?

ROSENCRANTZ Ay, that they do, my lord—Hercules and his load[87] too.

20 HAMLET It is not very strange, for my uncle is King of Denmark, and those that would make mows[88] at him while my father lived give twenty, forty, fifty, a hundred ducats apiece for his picture in little. 'Sblood,[89] there is something in this more than natural, if philosophy could find it out.

25 *A flourish*

GUILDENSTERN There are the players.

HAMLET Gentlemen, you are welcome to Elsinore. Your hands, come then. Th' appurtenance of welcome is fashion and cere-mony. Let me comply with you in this garb,[90] lest my extent[91] to
30 the players (which I tell you must show fairly outwards) should more appear like entertainment than yours. You are welcome. But my uncle-father and aunt-mother are deceived.

---

[78] *on the top of question* above others on matter of dispute   [79] *berattle* be-rate   [80] *common stages* "public" theatres of the "common" players, who were organized in companies mainly composed of adult actors (allusion being made to the "War of the Theatres" in Shakespeare's London)   [81] *goosequills* pens (of satirists who made out that the London public stage showed low taste)   [82] *escoted* supported   [83] *quality* profession of acting   [84] *sing* i.e. with unchanged voices   [85] *tarre* incite   [86] *argument* matter of a play   [87] *load* i.e. the whole word (with a topical reference to the sign of the Globe Theatre, a representation of Hercules bearing the world on his shoulders)   [88] *mows* grimaces   [89] *'Sblood* by God's blood   [90] *garb* fashion   [91] *extent* showing of welcome

GUILDENSTERN In what, my dear lord?

HAMLET I am but mad north-north-west. When the wind is southerly I know a hawk from a handsaw.[92]

(*Enter* POLONIUS)

5 POLONIUS Well be with you, gentlemen.

HAMLET Hark you, Guildenstern—and you too—at each ear a hearer. That great baby you see there is not yet out of his swaddling clouts.[93]

ROSENCRANTZ Happily[94] he is the second time come to them, for 10 they say an old man is twice a child.

HAMLET I will prophesy he comes to tell me of the players. Mark it.—You say right, sir; a Monday morning, 'twas then indeed.

POLONIUS My lord, I have news to tell you.

HAMLET My lord, I have news to tell you. When Roscius[95] was an 15 actor in Rome—

POLONIUS The actors are come hither, my lord.

HAMLET Buzz, buzz.

POLONIUS Upon my honor—

HAMLET Then came each actor on his ass—

20 POLONIUS The best actors in the world, either for tragedy, comedy, history, pastoral, pastoral-comical, historical-pastoral, tragical-historical, tragical-comical-historical-pastoral; scene individable,[96] or poem unlimited.[97] Seneca[98] cannot be too heavy, nor Plautus[99] too light. For the law of writ[100] and the liberty,[101] these are the 25 only men.

HAMLET O Jephthah,[102] judge of Israel, what a treasure hadst thou!

POLONIUS What treasure had he, my lord?

HAMLET Why,

30   "One fair daughter, and no more,
        The which he lovèd passing[103] well."

---

[92] *hawk* mattock or pickaxe (also called "hack"; here used apparently with a play on "hawk": a bird); *handsaw* carpenter's tool (apparently with a play on some corrupt form of "hernshaw"; heron, a bird often hunted with the hawk) [93] *clouts* clothes [94] *Happily* haply, perhaps [95] *Roscius* the greatest of Roman comic actors [96] *scene individable* drama observing the unities [97] *poem unlimited* drama not observing the unities [98] *Seneca* Roman writer of tragedies [99] *Plautus* Roman writer of comedies [100] *law of writ* orthodoxy determined by critical rules of the drama [101] *liberty* freedom from such orthodoxy [102] *Jephthah* the compelled sacrificer of a dearly beloved daughter (Judges xi) [103] *passing* surpassingly (verses are from a ballad on Jephthah)

POLONIUS (*aside*) Still on my daughter.

HAMLET Am I not i' th' right, old Jephthah?

POLONIUS If you call me Jephthah, my lord, I have a daughter that I love passing well.

5 HAMLET Nay, that follows not.

POLONIUS What follows then, my lord?

HAMLET Why,
    "As by lot, God wot,"
and then, you know,
10   "It came to pass, as most like it was."
The first row^{104} of the pious chanson^{105} will show you more, for look where my abridgment^{106} comes.

(*Enter the* PLAYERS)

You are welcome, masters, welcome, all.—I am glad to see thee
15 well.—Welcome, good friends.—O, old friend, why, thy face is valanced ^{107} since I saw thee last. Com'st thou to beard me in Denmark?—What, my young lady^{108} and mistress? By'r Lady, your ladyship is nearer to heaven than when I saw you last by the altitude of a chopine.^{109} Pray God your voice, like a piece of un-
20 current^{110} gold, be not cracked within the ring.^{111}—Masters, you are all welcome. We'll e'en to't like French falconers, fly at anything we see. We'll have a speech straight. Come, give us a taste of your quality. Come, a passionate speech.

PLAYER What speech, my good lord?

25 HAMLET I heard thee speak me a speech once, but it was never acted, or if it was, not above once, for the play, I remember, pleased not the million; 'twas caviary^{112} to the general,^{113} but it was (as I received it, and others, whose judgments in such matters cried in the top of ^{114} mine) an excellent play, well digested in the
30 scenes, set down with as much modesty as cunning. I remember one said there were no sallets^{115} in the lines to make the matter savory, nor no matter in the phrase that might indict the author of affectation, but called it an honest method, as wholesome as sweet, and by very much more handsome than fine. One speech

---

^{104} *row* stanza ^{105} *chanson* song ^{106} *my abridgment* that which shortens my talk ^{107} *valanced* fringed (with a beard) ^{108} *young lady* boy who plays women's parts ^{109} *chopine* women's thick-soled shoe ^{110} *uncurrent* not legal tender ^{111} *within the ring* from the edge through the line circling the design on the coin (with a play on "ring": a sound) ^{112} *caviary* caviare ^{113} *general* multitude ^{114} *in the top of* more authoritatively than ^{115} *sallets* salads, highly seasoned passages in't I chiefly loved. 'Twas Aeneas' tale to Dido, and thereabout of it especially where he speaks of Priam's[116] slaughter. If it live in your memory, begin at this line—let me see, let me see: "The rugged Pyrrhus, like th' Hyrcanian beast[117]—"

5 'Tis not so; it begins with Pyrrhus:
"The rugged Pyrrhus, he whose sable[118] arms,
Black as his purpose, did the night resemble
When he lay couchèd in the ominous[119] horse,[120]
Hath now this dread and black complexion smeared
10 With heraldry more dismal.[121] Head to foot
Now is he total gules,[122] horridly tricked [123]
With blood of fathers, mothers, daughters, sons,
Baked and impasted with the parching[124] streets,
That lend a tyrannous and a damnèd light
15 To their lord's murder. Roasted in wrath and fire,
And thus o'ersizèd [125] with coagulate[126] gore,
With eyes like carbuncles, the hellish Pyrrhus
Old grandsire Priam seeks."
So, proceed you.

20 POLONIUS Fore God, my lord, well spoken, with good accent and good discretion.

PLAYER   "Anon he finds him,
Striking too short at Greeks. His antique sword,
Rebellious to his arms, lies where it falls,
25 Repugnant to command. Unequal matched,
Pyrrhus at Priam drives, in rage strikes wide,
But with the whiff and wind of his fell [127] sword
Th' unnervèd father falls. Then senseless[128] Ilium,
Seeming to feel this blow, with flaming top
30 Stoops to his[129] base, and with a hideous crash
Takes prisoner Pyrrhus' ear. For lo! his sword,
Which was declining on the milky head
Of reverend Priam, seemed i' th' air to stick.
So as a painted [130] tyrant Pyrrhus stood,

---

116 *Priam's slaughter* i.e. at the fall of Troy (Aeneid II, 506 ff.)   117 *Hyrcanian beast* tiger   118 *sable* black   119 *ominous* fateful   120 *horse* the wooden horse by which the Greeks gained entrance to Troy   121 *dismal* ill-omened   122 *gules* red (heraldic term)   123 *tricked* decorated in color (heraldic term)   124 *parching* i.e. because Troy was burning   125 *o'ersizèd* covered as with size, a glutinous material used for filling pores of plaster, etc.   126 *coagulate* clotted   127 *fell* cruel   128 *senseless* without feeling   129 *his* its   130 *painted* pictured

And like a neutral to his will and matter[131]
Did nothing.
But as we often see, against[132] some storm,
A silence in the heavens, the rack[133] stand still,
5   The bold winds speechless, and the orb below
As hush as death, anon the dreadful thunder
Doth rend the region,[134] so after Pyrrhus' pause,
Aroused vengeance sets him new awork,
And never did the Cyclops'[135] hammers fall
10   On Mars' armor, forged for proof eterne,[136]
With less remorse than Pyrrhus' bleeding sword
Now falls on Priam.
Out, out, thou strumpet Fortune! All you gods,
In general synod take away her power,
15   Break all the spokes and fellies[137] from her wheel,
And bowl the round nave[138] down the hill of heaven,
As low as to the fiends."
POLONIUS   This is too long.
HAMLET   It shall to the barber's, with your beard.—Prithee say on.
20   He's for a jig[139] or a tale of bawdry, or he sleeps. Say on; come to
Hecuba.
PLAYER   "But who (ah woe!) had seen the mobled[140] queen—"
HAMLET   "The mobled queen"?
POLONIUS   That's good. "Mobled queen" is good.
25   PLAYER   "Run barefoot up and down, threat'ning the flames
With bisson rheum;[141] a clout[142] upon that head
Where late the diadem stood, and for a robe,
About her lank and all o'erteemed[143] loins,
A blanket in the alarm of fear caught up—
30   Who this had seen, with tongue in venom steeped
'Gainst Fortune's state[144] would treason have pronounced.
But if the gods themselves did see her then,
When she saw Pyrrhus make malicious sport
In mincing with his sword her husband's limbs,
35   The instant burst of clamor that she made

---

131 *will and matter* purpose and its realization (between which he stands motionless)   132 *against* just before   133 *rack* clouds   134 *region* sky   135 *Cyclops* giant workmen who made armor in the smithy of Vulcan   136 *proof eterne* eternal protection   137 *fellies* segments of the rim   138 *nave* hub   139 *jig* short comic piece with singing and dancing often presented after a play   140 *mobled* muffled   141 *bisson rheum* blinding tears   142 *clout* cloth   143 *o'erteemed* overproductive of children   144 *state* government of worldly events

(Unless things mortal move them not at all)
Would have made milch[145] the burning eyes[146] of heaven
And passion in the gods."

POLONIUS Look, whe'r[147] he has not turned his color, and has tears
5 in's eyes. Prithee no more.

HAMLET 'Tis well. I'll have thee speak out the rest of this soon.—
Good my lord, will you see the players well bestowed?[148] Do you
hear? Let them be well used, for they are the abstract and brief
chronicles of the time. After your death you were better have a
10 bad epitaph than their ill report while you live.

POLONIUS My lord, I will use them according to their desert.

HAMLET God's bodkin,[149] man, much better! Use every man after
his desert, and who shall scape whipping? Use them after your
own honor and dignity. The less they deserve, the more merit is
15 in your bounty. Take them in.

POLONIUS Come, sirs.

HAMLET Follow him, friends. We'll hear a play tomorrow. (*aside
to* PLAYER) Dost thou hear me, old friend? Can you play "The
Murder of Gonzago"?

20 PLAYER Ay, my lord.

HAMLET We'll ha't to-morrow night. You could for a need study a
speech of some dozen or sixteen lines which I would set down and
insert in't, could you not?

PLAYER Ay, my lord.

25 HAMLET Very well. Follow that lord, and look you mock him not.
—My good friends, I'll leave you till night. You are welcome to
Elsinore.

(*Exeunt* POLONIUS *and* PLAYERS)

ROSENCRANTZ Good my lord.

30 (*Exeunt* ROSENCRANTZ *and* GUILDENSTERN)

HAMLET Ay, so, God bye to you.—Now I am alone.
O, what a rogue and peasant slave am I!
Is it not monstrous that this player here,
But in a fiction, in a dream of passion,
35 Could force his soul so to his own conceit[150]
That from her working all his visage wanned,
Tears in his eyes, distraction in his aspect.

---

[145] *milch* tearful (milk-giving) [146] *eyes* i.e. stars [147] *whe'r* whether [148] *bestowed* lodged [149] *God's bodkin* by God's little body [150] *conceit* conception, idea

A broken voice, and his whole function[151] suiting
With forms to his conceit? And all for nothing,
For Hecuba!
What's Hecuba to him, or he to Hecuba,
5   That he should weep for her? What would he do
Had he the motive and the cue for passion
That I have? He would drown the stage with tears
And cleave the general ear with horrid speech,
Make mad the guilty and appal the free,
10   Confound the ignorant, and amaze indeed
The very faculties of eyes and ears.
Yet I,
A dull and muddy-mettled [152] rascal, peak[153]
Like John-a-dreams,[154] unpregnant[155] of my cause,
15   And can say nothing. No, not for a king,
Upon whose property and most dear life
A damned defeat was made. Am I a coward?
Who calls me villain? breaks my pate across?
Plucks off my beard and blows it in my face?
20   Tweaks me by the nose? gives me the lie i' th' throat
As deep as to the lungs? Who does me this?
Ha, 'swounds,[156] I should take it, for it cannot be
But I am pigeon-livered [157] and lack gall
To make oppression bitter, or ere this
25   I should ha' fatted all the region kites[158]
With this slave's offal.[159] Bloody, bawdy villain!
Remorseless, treacherous, lecherous, kindless[160] villain!
O, vengeance!
Why, what an ass am I! This is most brave,
30   That I, the son of a dear father murdered,
Prompted to my revenge by heaven and hell,
Must like a whore unpack my heart with words
And fall a-cursing like a very drab,
A stallion! [161] Fie upon't, foh! About, my brains.
35   Hum—
I have heard that guilty creatures sitting at a play
Have by the very cunning of the scene

---

[151] *function* action of bodily powers   [152] *muddy-mettled* dull-spirited [153] *peak* mope   [154] *John-a-dreams* a sleepy dawdler   [155] *unpregnant* barren of realization   [156] *'swounds* by God's wounds   [157] *pigeon-livered* of dove-like gentleness   [158] *region kites* kites of the air   [159] *offal* guts   [160] *kindless* unnatural   [161] *stallion* prostitute (male or female)

Been struck so to the soul that presently[162]
They have proclaimed their malefactions.
For murder, though it have no tongue, will speak
With most miraculous organ. I'll have these players
5   Play something like the murder of my father
Before mine uncle. I'll observe his looks.
I'll tent[163] him to the quick. If 'a do blench,[164]
I know my course. The spirit that I have seen
May be a devil, and the devil hath power
10   T' assume a pleasing shape, yea, and perhaps
Out of my weakness and my melancholy,
As he is very potent with such spirits,
Abuses[165] me to damn me. I'll have grounds
More relative[166] than this. The play 's the thing
15   Wherein I'll catch the conscience of the king.

    (*Exit*)

ACT III

Scene I

A chamber in the castle

20   (*Enter* KING, QUEEN, POLONIUS, OPHELIA, ROSENCRANTZ, GUILDEN-
STERN, LORDS)

KING   And can you by no drift of conference[1]
Get from him why he puts on this confusion,
Grating so harshly all his days of quiet
25   With turbulent and dangerous lunacy?
ROSENCRANTZ   He does confess he feels himself distracted,
But from what cause 'a will by no means speak.
GUILDENSTERN   Nor do we find him forward to be sounded,
But with a crafty madness keeps aloof
30   When we would bring him on to some confession
Of his true state.
QUEEN   Did he receive you well?
ROSENCRANTZ   Most like a gentleman.
GUILDENSTERN   But with much forcing of his disposition.
35   ROSENCRANTZ   Niggard of question, but of our demands
Most free in his reply.

---

[162] *presently* immediately   [163] *tent* probe   [164] *blench* flinch   [165] *Abuses* deludes   [166] *relative* pertinent
[1] *drift of conference* direction of conversation

QUEEN   Did you assay[2] him
To any pastime?
ROSENCRANTZ   Madam, it so fell out that certain players
We o'erraught[3] on the way. Of these we told him,
5   And there did seem in him a kind of joy
To hear of it. They are here about the court,
And, as I think, they have already order
This night to play before him.
POLONIUS   'Tis most true,
10   And he beseeched me to entreat your majesties
To hear and see the matter.
KING   With all my heart, and it doth much content me
To hear him so inclined.
Good gentlemen, give him a further edge[4]
15   And drive his purpose into these delights.
ROSENCRANTZ   We shall, my lord.

    (*Exeunt* ROSENCRANTZ *and* GUILDENSTERN)

KING   Sweet Gertrude, leave us too,
For we have closely[5] sent for Hamlet hither,
20   That he, as 'twere by accident, may here
Affront[6] Ophelia.
Her father and myself (lawful espials[7])
Will so bestow ourselves that, seeing unseen,
We may of their encounter frankly judge
25   And gather by him, as he is behaved,
If't be th' affliction of his love or no
That thus he suffers for.
QUEEN   I shall obey you.—
And for your part, Ophelia, I do wish
30   That your good beauties be the happy cause
Of Hamlet's wildness. So shall I hope your virtues
Will bring him to his wonted way again,
To both your honors.
OPHELIA   Madam, I wish it may.

35   (*Exit* QUEEN)

POLONIUS   Ophelia, walk you here.—Gracious, so please you,
We will bestow ourselves.—

---

[2] *assay* try to win   [3] *o'erraught* overtook   [4] *edge* keenness of desire   [5] *closely* privately   [6] *Affront* come face to face with   [7] *espials* spies

(*To* OPHELIA)
                                        Read on this book,
That show of such an exercise[8] may color[9]
Your loneliness. We are oft to blame in this,

5   'Tis too much proved, that with devotion's visage
And pious action we do sugar o'er
The devil himself.
KING (*aside*)   O, 'tis too true.
How smart a lash that speech doth give my conscience!

10 The harlot's cheek, beautied with plast'ring art,
Is not more ugly to[10] the thing that helps it
Than is my deed to my most painted word.
O heavy burthen!
POLONIUS   I hear him coming. Let's withdraw, my lord.

15 (*Exeunt* KING *and* POLONIUS)

(*Enter* HAMLET)

HAMLET   To be, or not to be—that is the question:
Whether 'tis nobler in the mind to suffer
The slings and arrows of outrageous fortune

20 Or to take arms against a sea of troubles
And by opposing end them. To die, to sleep—
No more—and by a sleep to say we end
The heartache, and the thousand natural shocks
That flesh is heir to. 'Tis a consummation

25 Devoutly to be wished. To die, to sleep—
To sleep—perchance to dream: ay, there's the rub,[11]
For in that sleep of death what dreams may come
When we have shuffled off [12] this mortal coil,[13]
Must give us pause. There's the respect[14]

30 That makes calamity of so long life.[15]
For who would bear the whips and scorns of time,
Th' oppressor's wrong, the proud man's contumely
The pangs of despised love, the law's delay,
The insolence of office, and the spurns

35 That patient merit of th' unworthy takes,
When he himself might his quietus[16] make

---

[8] *exercise* religious exercise (the book being obviously one of devotion)
[9] *color* give an appearance of naturalness to   [10] *to* compared to   [11] *rub* obstacle (literally, obstruction encountered by a bowler's ball)   [12] *shuffled off* cast off as an encumbrance   [13] *coil* to-do, turmoil   [14] *respect* consideration
[15] *of so long life* so long-lived   [16] *quietus* settlement (literally, release from debt)

With a bare bodkin? [17] Who would fardels[18] bear,
To grunt and sweat under a weary life,
But that the dread of something after death,
The undiscovered country, from whose bourn[19]
5 No traveller returns, puzzles the will,
And makes us rather bear those ills we have
Than fly to others that we know not of?
Thus conscience does make cowards of us all,
And thus the native hue of resolution
10 Is sicklied o'er with the pale cast of thought,
And enterprises of great pitch[20] and moment
With this regard [21] their currents turn awry
And lose the name of action.—Soft you now,
The fair Ophelia!—Nymph, in thy orisons[22]
15 Be all my sins remembered.
OPHELIA   Good my lord,
How does your honor for this many a day?
HAMLET   I humbly thank you, well, well, well.
OPHELIA   My lord, I have remembrances of yours
20 That I have longèd long to re-deliver.
I pray you, now receive them.
HAMLET   No, not I,
I never gave you aught.
OPHELIA   My honored lord, you know right well you did,
25 And with them words of so sweet breath composed
As made the things more rich. Their perfume lost,
Take these again, for to the noble mind
Rich gifts wax poor when givers prove unkind.
There, my lord.
30 HAMLET   Ha, ha! Are you honest? [23]
OPHELIA   My lord?
HAMLET   Are you fair?
OPHELIA   What means your lordship?
HAMLET   That if you be honest and fair, your honesty should admit
35 no discourse to your beauty.
OPHELIA   Could beauty, my lord, have better commerce[24] than
with honesty?
HAMLET   Ay, truly; for the power of beauty will sooner transform

---

[17] *bodkin* dagger   [18] *fardels* burdens   [19] *bourn* confine, region   [20] *pitch*
height (of a soaring falcon's flight)   [21] *regard* consideration   [22] *orisons*
prayers (because of the book of devotion she reads)   [23] *honest* chaste
[24] *commerce* intercourse

honesty from what it is to a bawd than the force of honesty can translate beauty into his likeness. This was sometime a paradox,[25] but now the time gives it proof. I did love you once.

OPHELIA Indeed, my lord, you made me believe so.

5 HAMLET You should not have believed me, for virtue cannot so inoculate[26] our old stock but we shall relish[27] of it. I loved you not.

OPHELIA I was the more deceived.

HAMLET Get thee to a nunnery. Why wouldst thou be a breeder
10 of sinners? I am myself indifferent honest,[28] but yet I could accuse me of such things that it were better my mother had not borne me: I am very proud, revengeful, ambitious, with more offenses at my beck than I have thoughts to put them in, imagination to give them shape, or time to act them in. What should
15 such fellows as I do crawling between earth and heaven? We are arrant knaves all; believe none of us. Go thy ways to a nunnery. Where's your father?

OPHELIA At home, my lord.

HAMLET Let the doors be shut upon him, that he may play the
20 fool nowhere but in's own house. Farewell.

OPHELIA O, help him, you sweet heavens!

HAMLET If thou dost marry, I'll give thee this plague for thy dowry: be thou as chaste as ice, as pure as snow, thou shalt not escape calumny. Get thee to a nunnery. Go, farewell. Or if thou
25 wilt needs marry, marry a fool, for wise men know well enough what monsters[29] you make of them. To a nunnery, go, and quickly too. Farewell.

OPHELIA O heavenly powers, restore him!

HAMLET I have heard of your paintings too, well enough. God
30 hath given you one face, and you make yourselves another. You jig, you amble, and you lisp; you nickname God's creatures and make your wantonness[30] your ignorance.[31] Go to, I'll no more on't; it hath made me mad. I say we will have no more marriage. Those that are married already—all but one—shall live. The rest
35 shall keep as they are. To a nunnery, go.

(*Exit*)

OPHELIA O, what a noble mind is here o'erthrown!

---

[25] *paradox* idea contrary to common opinion [26] *inoculate* graft [27] *relish* have a flavor (because of original sin) [28] *indifferent honest* moderately respectable [29] *monsters* i.e. unnatural combinations of wisdom and uxorious folly [30] *wantonness* affectation [31] *your ignorance* a matter for which you offer the excuse that you don't know any better

The courtier's, soldier's, scholar's, eye, tongue, sword,
Th' expectancy and rose[32] of the fair state,
The glass[33] of fashion and the mould of form,
Th' observed of all observers, quite, quite down!
5 And I, of ladies most deject and wretched,
That sucked the honey of his music vows,
Now see that noble and most sovereign reason
Like sweet bells jangled, out of time and harsh,
That unmatched form and feature of blown youth
10 Blasted with ecstasy.[34] O, woe is me
T' have seen what I have seen, see what I see!

(*Enter* KING *and* POLONIUS)

KING   Love? his affections[35] do not that way tend,
Nor what he spake, though it lacked form a little,
15 Was not like madness. There's something in his soul
O'er which his melancholy sits on brood,
And I do doubt[36] the hatch and the disclose
Will be some danger; which for to prevent,
I have in quick determination
20 Thus set it down: he shall with speed to England
For the demand of our neglected tribute.
Haply the seas, and countries different,
With variable objects, shall expel
This something-settled [37] matter in his heart,
25 Whereon his brains still beating puts him thus
From fashion of himself. What think you on't?
POLONIUS   It shall do well. But yet do I believe
The origin and commencement of his grief
Sprung from neglected love.—How now, Ophelia?
30 You need not tell us what Lord Hamlet said.
We heard it all.—My lord, do as you please,
But if you hold it fit, after the play
Let his queen mother all alone entreat him
To show his grief. Let her be round [38] with him,
35 And I'll be placed, so please you, in the ear
Of all their conference. If she find him not,
To England send him, or confine him where
Your wisdom best shall think.

---

[32] *expectancy and rose* fair hope   [33] *glass* mirror   [34] *ecstasy* madness   [35] *affections* emotions   [36] *doubt* fear   [37] *something-settled* somewhat settled   [38] *round* plain-spoken

KING It shall be so.
Madness in great ones must not unwatched go.

(*Exeunt*)

Act III, Scene II

5 *The hall of the castle*

(*Enter* HAMLET *and three of the* PLAYERS)

HAMLET Speak the speech, I pray you, as I pronounced it to you, trippingly[1] on the tongue. But if you mouth it, as many of our players do, I had as lief the town crier spoke my lines. Nor do
10 not saw the air too much with your hand, thus, but use all gently, for in the very torrent, tempest, and (as I may say) whirlwind of your passion, you must acquire and beget a temperance that may give it smoothness. O, it offends me to the soul to hear a robustious[2] periwig-pated [3] fellow tear a passion to tatters, to very rags,
15 to split the ears of the groundlings,[4] who for the most part are capable of nothing but inexplicable dumb shows[5] and noise. I would have such a fellow whipped for o'erdoing Termagant.[6] It out-herods Herod.[7] Pray you avoid it.

PLAYER I warrant your honor.

20 HAMLET Be not too tame neither, but let your own discretion be your tutor. Suit the action to the word, the word to the action, with this special observance, that you o'erstep not the modesty of nature. For anything so overdone is from[8] the purpose of playing, whose end, both at the first and now, was and is, to hold, as
25 'twere, the mirror up to nature, to show virtue her own feature, scorn her own image, and the very age and body of the time his form and pressure.[9] Now this overdone, or come tardy off,[10] though it make the unskillful laugh, cannot but make the judicious grieve, the censure of the which one[11] must in your allow-
30 ance o'erweigh a whole theatre of others. O, there be players that I have seen play, and heard others praise, and that highly (not to

---

[1] *trippingly* easily [2] *robustious* boisterous [3] *periwig-pated* wig-wearing (after the custom of actors) [4] *groundlings* spectators who paid least and stood on the ground in the pit or yard of the theatre [5] *dumb shows* brief actions without words, forecasting dramatic matter to follow (the play presented later in this scene giving an old-fashioned example) [6] *Termagant* a Saracen "god" in medieval romance and drama [7] *Herod* the raging tyrant of old Biblical plays [8] *from* apart from [9] *pressure* impressed or printed character [10] *come tardy off* brought off slowly and badly [11] *the censure of the which one* the judgment of even one of whom

speak it profanely), that neither having th' accent of Christians, nor the gait of Christian, pagan, nor man, have so strutted and bellowed that I have thought some of Nature's journeymen[12] had made men, and not made them well, they imitated humanity so
5   abominably.

PLAYER   I hope we have reformed that indifferently[13] with us, sir.

HAMLET   O, reform it altogether! And let those that play your clowns speak no more than is set down for them, for there be of them[14] that will themselves laugh, to set on some quantity of
10   barren spectators to laugh too, though in the mean time some necessary question of the play be then to be considered. That's villainous and shows a most pitiful ambition in the fool that uses it. Go make you ready.

(*Exeunt* PLAYERS)

15   (*Enter* POLONIUS, GUILDENSTERN, *and* ROSENCRANTZ)

How now, my lord? Will the king hear this piece of work?

POLONIUS   And the queen too, and that presently.[15]

HAMLET   Bid the players make haste.

(*Exit* POLONIUS)

20   Will you two help to hasten them?

ROSENCRANTZ   Ay, my lord.

(*Exeunt they two*)

HAMLET   What, ho, Horatio!

(*Enter* HORATIO)

25   HORATIO   Here, sweet lord, at your service.

HAMLET   Horatio, thou art e'en as just a man
As e'er my conversation coped withal.[16]

HORATIO   O, my dear lord—

HAMLET   Nay, do not think I flatter.
30   For what advancement may I hope from thee,
That no revenue hast but thy good spirits
To feed and clothe thee? Why should the poor be flattered?
No, let the candied tongue lick absurd pomp,
And crook the pregnant[17] hinges of the knee

---

12 *journeymen* workmen not yet masters of their trade   13 *indifferently* fairly well   14 *of them* some of them   15 *presently* at once   16 *conversation coped withal* intercourse with men encountered   17 *pregnant* quick to move

Where thrift[18] may follow fawning. Dost thou hear?
Since my dear soul was mistress of her choice
And could of men distinguish her election,
S' hath sealed [19] thee for herself, for thou hast been
5 As one in suff'ring all that suffers nothing,
A man that Fortune's buffets and rewards
Hast ta'en with equal thanks; and blest are those
Whose blood [20] and judgment are so well commeddled [21]
That they are not a pipe for Fortune's finger
10 To sound what stop she please. Give me that man
That is not passion's slave, and I will wear him
In my heart's core, ay, in my heart of heart,
As I do thee. Something too much of this—
There is a play to-night before the king.
15 One scene of it comes near the circumstance
Which I have told thee, of my father's death.
I prithee, when thou seest that act afoot,
Even with the very comment of thy soul [22]
Observe my uncle. If his occulted [23] guilt
20 Do not itself unkennel in one speech,
It is a damnèd ghost[24] that we have seen,
And my imaginations are as foul
As Vulcan's stithy.[25] Give him heedful note,
For I mine eyes will rivet to his face,
25 And after we will both our judgments join
In censure of [26] his seeming.
HORATIO   Well, my lord.
If 'a steal aught the while this play is playing,
And scape detecting, I will pay the theft.

30 (*Enter* TRUMPETS *and* KETTLEDRUMS, KING, QUEEN, POLONIUS, OPHE-
LIA, [ROSENCRANTZ, GUILDENSTERN, *and other* LORDS *attendant*])

HAMLET   They are coming to the play. I must be idle.[27]
Get you a place.
KING   How fares our cousin[28] Hamlet?
35 HAMLET   Excellent, i' faith, of the chameleon's dish.[29] I eat the air,
promise-crammed. You cannot feed capons so.

---

[18] *thrift* profit   [19] *sealed* marked   [20] *blood* passion   [21] *commeddled* mixed
together   [22] *the very ... soul* thy deepest sagacity   [23] *occulted* hidden
[24] *damnèd ghost* evil spirit, devil   [25] *stithy* smithy   [26] *censure of* sentence
upon   [27] *be idle* be foolish, act the madman   [28] *cousin* nephew   [29] *chameleon's dish* i.e. air (which was believed the chameleon's food; Hamlet willfully takes *fares* in the sense of "feeds")

KING I have nothing with this answer, Hamlet. These words are not mine.[30]

HAMLET No, nor mine now. (*to Polonius*) My lord, you played once i' th' university, you say?

5   POLONIUS That did I, my lord, and was accounted a good actor.

HAMLET What did you enact?

POLONIUS I did enact Julius Caesar. I was killed i' th' Capitol; Brutus killed me.

HAMLET It was a brute part of him to kill so capital a calf there.

10   Be the players ready?

ROSENCRANTZ Ay, my lord. They stay upon your patience.[31]

QUEEN Come hither, my dear Hamlet, sit by me.

HAMLET No, good mother. Here's metal more attractive.

POLONIUS (*to the King*) O ho! do you mark that?

15   HAMLET Lady, shall I lie in your lap?

He lies at OPHELIA'S *feet*

OPHELIA No, my lord.

HAMLET I mean, my head upon your lap?

OPHELIA Ay, my lord.

20   HAMLET Do you think I meant country matters?[32]

OPHELIA I think nothing, my lord.

HAMLET That's a fair thought to lie between maids' legs.

OPHELIA What is, my lord?

HAMLET Nothing.

25   OPHELIA You are merry, my lord.

HAMLET Who, I?

OPHELIA Ay, my lord.

HAMLET O God, your only jig-maker![33] What should a man do but be merry? For look you how cheerfully my mother looks, and

30   my father died within's two hours.

OPHELIA Nay, 'tis twice two months, my lord.

HAMLET So long? Nay then, let the devil wear black, for I'll have a suit of sables.[34] O heavens! die two months ago, and not forgotten yet? Then there's hope a great man's memory may out-

35   live his life half a year. But, by'r Lady, 'a must build churches then, or else shall 'a suffer not thinking on, with the hobby-

---

[30] *not mine* not for me as the asker of my question [31] *stay upon your patience* await your indulgence [32] *country matters* rustic goings-on, barnyard mating (with a play upon a sexual term) [33] *jig-maker* writer of jigs [34] *sables* black furs (luxurious garb, not for mourning)

horse,[35] whose epitaph is "For O, for O, the hobby-horse is forgot!"

The trumpets sound. Dumb show follows:
Enter a KING *and a* QUEEN [*very lovingly*], *the* QUEEN *embracing him, and*
5 *he her.* [*She kneels; and makes show of protestation unto him.*] *He takes her up, and declines his head upon her neck. He lies him down upon a bank of flowers. She, seeing him asleep, leaves him. Anon come in another man: takes off his crown, kisses it, pours poison in the sleeper's ears, and leaves him. The* QUEEN *returns, finds the* KING *dead, makes passionate*
10 *action. The poisoner, with some three or four, come in again, seem to condole with her. The dead body is carried away. The poisoner woos the* QUEEN *with gifts; she seems harsh awhile, but in the end accepts love.*

(*Exeunt*)

OPHELIA   What means this, my lord?
15 HAMLET   Marry, this is miching mallecho;[36] it means mischief.
OPHELIA   Belike this show imports the argument of the play.

(*Enter* PROLOGUE)

HAMLET   We shall know by this fellow. The players cannot keep counsel; they'll tell all.
20 OPHELIA   Will 'a tell us what this show meant?
HAMLET   Ay, or any show that you'll show him. Be not you ashamed to show, he'll not shame to tell you what it means.
OPHELIA   You are naught, you are naught.[37] I'll mark the play.
PROLOGUE   For us and for our tragedy,
25   Here stooping to your clemency,
           We beg your hearing patiently.

(*Exit*)

HAMLET   Is this a prologue, or the posy[38] of a ring? [39]
OPHELIA   'Tis brief, my lord.
30 HAMLET   As woman's love.

(*Enter* [*two* PLAYERS *as*] KING *and* QUEEN)

[P.] KING   Full thirty times hath Phoebus' cart[40] gone round
Neptune's salt wash and Tellus' [41] orbèd ground,
And thirty dozen moons with borrowed [42] sheen

---

[35] *hobby-horse* traditional figure strapped round the waist of a performer in May games and morris dances   [36] *miching mallecho* sneaking iniquity   [37] *naught* indecent   [38] *posy* brief motto in rhyme ("poesy")   [39] *ring* finger ring   [40] *Phoebus' cart* the sun's chariot   [41] *Tellus* Roman goddess of the earth   [42] *borrowed* i.e. taken from the sun

About the world have times twelve thirties been,
Since love our hearts, and Hymen[43] did our hands,
Unite commutual [44] in most sacred bands.
[P.] QUEEN   So many journeys may the sun and moon
5   Make us again count o'er ere love be done!
But woe is me, you are so sick of late,
So far from cheer and from your former state,
That I distrust you.[45] Yet, though I distrust,
Discomfort you, my lord, it nothing must.
10   For women fear too much, even as they love,
And women's fear and love hold quantity,[46]
In neither aught, or in extremity.
Now what my love is, proof hath made you know,
And as my love is sized, my fear is so.
15   Where love is great, the littlest doubts are fear;
Where little fears grow great, great love grows there.
[P.] KING   Faith, I must leave thee, love, and shortly too;
My operant powers[47] their functions leave to do.
And thou shalt live in this fair world behind,
20   Honored, beloved, and haply one as kind
For husband shalt thou—
[P.] QUEEN   O, confound the rest!
Such love must needs be treason in my breast.
In second husband let me be accurst!
25   None wed the second but who killed the first.
HAMLET (*aside*)   That's wormwood.[48]
[P.] QUEEN   The instances[49] that second marriage move
Are base respects of thrift, but none of love.
A second time I kill my husband dead
30   When second husband kisses me in bed.
[P.] KING   I do believe you think what now you speak,
But what we do determine oft we break.
Purpose is but the slave to[50] memory,
Of violent birth, but poor validity,[51]
35   Which now like fruit unripe sticks on the tree,
But fall unshaken when they mellow be.
Most necessary 'tis that we forget
To pay ourselves what to ourselves is debt.

---

[43] *Hymen* Greek god of marriage   [44] *commutual* mutually   [45] *distrust you*
fear for you   [46] *quantity* proportion   [47] *operant powers* active bodily forces
[48] *wormwood* a bitter herb   [49] *instances* motives   [50] *slave to* i.e. dependent
upon for life   [51] *validity* strength

What to ourselves in passion we propose,
The passion ending, doth the purpose lose.
The violence of either grief or joy
Their own enactures[52] with themselves destroy.
5   Where joy most revels, grief doth most lament;
Grief joys, joy grieves, on slender accident.
This world is not for aye, nor 'tis not strange
That even our loves should with our fortunes change,
For 'tis a question left us yet to prove,
10   Whether love lead fortune, or else fortune love.
The great man down, you mark his favorite flies,
The poor advanced makes friends of enemies;
And hitherto doth love on fortune tend,
For who not needs shall never lack a friend,
15   And who in want a hollow friend doth try,
Directly seasons him[53] his enemy.
But, orderly to end where I begun,
Our wills and fates do so contrary run
That our devices still [54] are overthrown;
20   Our thoughts are ours, their ends none of our own.
So think thou wilt no second husband wed,
But die thy thoughts when thy first lord is dead.
     [P.] QUEEN   Nor earth to me give food, nor heaven light,
Sport and repose lock from me day and night,
25   To desperation turn my trust and hope,
An anchor's[55] cheer in prison be my scope,
Each opposite that blanks[56] the face of joy
Meet what I would have well, and it destroy,
Both here and hence[57] pursue me lasting strife,
30   If, once a widow, ever I be wife!
     HAMLET   If she should break it now!
     [P.] KING   'Tis deeply sworn. Sweet, leave me here awhile.
My spirits grow dull, and fain I would beguile
The tedious day with sleep.
35   [P.] QUEEN   Sleep rock thy brain,

     (*He sleeps*)

And never come mischance between us twain!

     (*Exit*)

---

[52] *enactures* fulfillments   [53] *seasons him* ripens him into   [54] *still* always
[55] *anchor's* hermit's   [56] *blanks* blanches, makes pale   [57] *hence* in the next
world.

HAMLET Madam, how like you this play?

QUEEN The lady doth protest too much, methinks.

HAMLET O, but she'll keep her word.

KING Have you heard the argument?[58] Is there no offense in't?

5   HAMLET No, no, they do but jest, poison in jest; no offense i' th' world.

KING What do you call the play?

HAMLET "The Mousetrap." Marry, how? Tropically.[59] This play is the image of a murder done in Vienna. Gonzago is the duke's

10 name; his wife, Baptista. You shall see anon. 'Tis a knavish piece of work, but what o' that? Your majesty, and we that have free[60] souls, it touches us not. Let the galled [61] jade[62] winch;[63] our withers[64] are unwrung.

(*Enter* LUCIANUS)

15 This is one Lucianus, nephew to the king.

OPHELIA You are as good as a chorus,[65] my lord.

HAMLET I could interpret between you and your love, if I could see the puppets[66] dallying.

OPHELIA You are keen, my lord, you are keen.

20 HAMLET It would cost you a groaning to take off my edge.

OPHELIA Still better, and worse.

HAMLET So you must take your husbands.—Begin, murderer. Leave thy damnable faces and begin. Come, the croaking raven doth bellow for revenge.

25 LUCIANUS Thoughts black, hands apt, drugs fit, and time agreeing, Confederate season,[67] else no creature seeing, Thou mixture rank, of midnight weeds collected, With Hecate's[68] ban[69] thrice blasted, thrice infected, Thy natural magic and dire property

30 On wholesome life usurps immediately.

(*Pours the poison in his ears*)

HAMLET 'A poisons him i' th' garden for his estate. His name's Gonzago. The story is extant, and written in very choice Italian. You shall see anon how the murderer gets the love of Gonzago's

35 wife.

---

[58] *argument* plot summary   [59] *Tropically* in the way of a trope or figure (with a play on "trapically")   [60] *free* guiltless   [61] *galled* sore-backed   [62] *jade* horse   [63] *winch* wince   [64] *withers* shoulders   [65] *chorus* one in a play who explains the action   [66] *puppets* i.e. you and your lover as in a puppet show   [67] *Confederate season* the occasion being my ally   [68] *Hecate* goddess of witchcraft and black magic   [69] *ban* curse

OPHELIA The king rises.
HAMLET What, frighted with false fire? [70]
QUEEN How fares my lord?
POLONIUS Give o'er the play.
5 KING Give me some light. Away!
POLONIUS Lights, lights, lights!

(*Exeunt all but* HAMLET *and* HORATIO)

HAMLET Why, let the strucken deer go weep,
          The hart ungallèd play.
10   For some must watch, while some must sleep;
          Thus runs the world away.
      Would not this, sir, and a forest of feathers[71]—if the rest of my
      fortunes turn Turk[72] with me—with two Provincial roses[73] on my
      razed [74] shoes, get me a fellowship in a cry[75] of players, sir?
15 HORATIO Half a share.
HAMLET A whole one, I.
          For thou dost know, O Damon dear,
          This realm dismantled was
          Of Jove himself; and now reigns here
20   A very, very—peacock.
HORATIO You might have rhymed.
HAMLET O good Horatio, I'll take the ghost's word for a thousand
      pound. Didst perceive?
HORATIO Very well, my lord.
25 HAMLET Upon the talk of the poisoning?
HORATIO I did very well note him.
HAMLET Aha! Come, some music! Come, the recorders! [76]
          For if the king like not the comedy,
          Why then, belike he likes it not, perdy.[77]
30 Come, some music!

(*Enter* ROSENCRANTZ *and* GUILDENSTERN)

GUILDENSTERN Good my lord, vouchsafe me a word with you.
HAMLET Sir, a whole history.
GUILDENSTERN The king, sir—
35 HAMLET Ay, sir, what of him?

---

[70] *false fire* a firing of a gun charged with powder but no shot, a blank-discharge [71] *feathers* plumes for actors' costumes [72] *turn Turk* turn renegade, like a Christian turning Mohammedan [73] *Provincial roses* ribbon rosettes [74] *razed* decorated with cut patterns [75] *cry* pack [76] *recorders* musical instruments of the flute class [77] *perdy* by God (*"par dieu"*)

GUILDENSTERN   Is in his retirement marvellous distempered.[78]
HAMLET   With drink, sir?
GUILDENSTERN   No, my lord, with choler.[79]
HAMLET   Your wisdom should show itself more richer to signify this
5   to the doctor, for for me to put him to his purgation would perhaps plunge him into more choler.
GUILDENSTERN   Good my lord, put your discourse into some
frame,[80] and start not so wildly from my affair.
HAMLET   I am tame, sir; pronounce.
10   GUILDENSTERN   The queen, your mother, in most great affliction of
spirit hath sent me to you.
HAMLET   You are welcome.
GUILDENSTERN   Nay, good my lord, this courtesy is not of the right
breed. If it shall please you to make me a wholesome answer, I
15   will do your mother's commandment. If not, your pardon and my
return shall be the end of my business.
HAMLET   Sir, I cannot.
ROSENCRANTZ   What, my lord?
HAMLET   Make you a wholesome answer; my wit's diseased. But,
20   sir, such answer as I can make, you shall command, or rather, as
you say, my mother. Therefore no more, but to the matter. My
mother, you say—
ROSENCRANTZ   Then thus she says: your behavior hath struck her
into amazement and admiration.[81]
25   HAMLET   O wonderful son, that can so stonish a mother! But is
there no sequel at the heels of this mother's admiration? Impart.
ROSENCRANTZ   She desires to speak with you in her closet[82] ere you
go to bed.
HAMLET   We shall obey, were she ten times our mother. Have you
30   any further trade with us?
ROSENCRANTZ   My lord, you once did love me.
HAMLET   And do still, by these pickers and stealers.[83]
ROSENCRANTZ   Good my lord, what is your cause of distemper?
You do surely bar the door upon your own liberty, if you deny
35   your griefs to your friend.
HAMLET   Sir, I lack advancement.
ROSENCRANTZ   How can that be, when you have the voice of the
king himself for your succession in Denmark?

---

[78] *distempered* out of temper, vexed (twisted by Hamlet into "deranged")
[79] *choler* anger (twisted by Hamlet into "biliousness")   [80] *frame* logical order
[81] *admiration* wonder   [82] *closet* private room   [83] *pickers and stealers* i.e.
hands

HAMLET   Ay, sir, but "while the grass grows" [84] the proverb is something musty.

(*Enter the* PLAYER *with recorders*)

O, the recorders. Let me see one. To withdraw[85] with you—why
5 do you go about to recover the wind [86] of me, as if you would drive me into a toil? [87]

GUILDENSTERN   O my lord, if my duty be too bold, my love is too unmannerly.[88]

HAMLET   I do not well understand that. Will you play upon this
10 pipe?

GUILDENSTERN   My lord, I cannot.

HAMLET   I pray you.

GUILDENSTERN   Believe me, I cannot.

HAMLET   I do beseech you.

15 GUILDENSTERN   I know no touch of it, my lord.

HAMLET   It is as easy as lying. Govern these ventages[89] with your fingers and thumb, give it breath with your mouth, and it will discourse most eloquent music. Look you, these are the stops.

GUILDENSTERN   But these cannot I command to any utt'rance of
20 harmony. I have not the skill.

HAMLET   Why, look you now, how unworthy a thing you make of me! You would play upon me, you would seem to know my stops, you would pluck out the heart of my mystery, you would sound me from my lowest note to the top of my compass; and there is
25 much music, excellent voice, in this little organ, yet cannot you make it speak. 'Sblood, do you think I am easier to be played on than a pipe? Call me what instrument you will, though you can fret[90] me, you cannot play upon me.

(*Enter* POLONIUS)

30 God bless you, sir!

POLONIUS   My lord, the queen would speak with you, and presently.[91]

HAMLET   Do you see yonder cloud that's almost in shape of a camel?

35 POLONIUS   By th' mass and 'tis, like a camel indeed.

---

[84] *while the grass grows* (a proverb, ending: "the horse starves")   [85] *withdraw* step aside   [86] *recover the wind* come up to windward like a hunter   [87] *toil* snare   [88] *is too unmannerly* leads me beyond the restraint of good manners   [89] *ventages* holes, vents   [90] *fret* irritate (with a play on the fret-fingering of certain stringed musical instruments)   [91] *presently* at once

HAMLET   Methinks it is like a weasel.
POLONIUS   It is backed like a weasel.
HAMLET   Or like a whale.
POLONIUS   Very like a whale.
5   HAMLET   Then I will come to my mother by and by.[92] (*aside*)
They fool me to the top of my bent.—I will come by and by.
POLONIUS   I will say so.

(*Exit*)

HAMLET   "By and by" is easily said. Leave me, friends.

10   (*Exeunt all but* HAMLET)

'Tis now the very witching time of night,
When churchyards yawn, and hell itself breathes out
Contagion to this world. Now could I drink hot blood
And do such bitter business as the day
15   Would quake to look on. Soft, now to my mother.
O heart, lose not thy nature; let not ever
The soul of Nero[93] enter this firm bosom.
Let me be cruel, not unnatural;
I will speak daggers to her, but use none.
20   My tongue and soul in this be hypocrites:
How in my words somever she be shent,[94]
To give them seals[95] never, my soul, consent!

(*Exit*)

Act III, Scene III

25   *A chamber in the castle*

(*Enter* KING, ROSENCRANTZ, *and* GUILDENSTERN)

KING   I like him not, nor stands it safe with us
To let his madness range. Therefore prepare you.
I your commission will forthwith dispatch,
30   And he to England shall along with you.
The terms[1] of our estate[2] may not endure
Hazard so near's as doth hourly grow
Out of his brows.[3]

---

[92] *by and by* immediately   [93] *Nero* murderer of his mother   [94] *shent* reproved
[95] *seals* authentications in actions
[1] *terms* circumstances   [2] *estate* royal position   [3] *brows* effronteries (apparently with an implication of knitted brows)

GUILDENSTERN   We will ourselves provide.
Most holy and religious fear it is
To keep those many many bodies safe
That live and feed upon your majesty.

5   ROSENCRANTZ   The single and peculiar[4] life is bound
With all the strength and armor of the mind
To keep itself from noyance,[5] but much more
That spirit upon whose weal depends and rests
The lives of many. The cess[6] of majesty

10   Dies not alone, but like a gulf [7]doth draw
What's near it with it; or 'tis a massy wheel
Fixed on the summit of the highest mount,
To whose huge spokes ten thousand lesser things
Are mortised and adjoined, which when it falls,

15   Each small annexment, petty consequence,
Attends[8] the boist'rous ruin. Never alone
Did the king sigh, but with a general groan.

KING   Arm[9] you, I pray you, to this speedy voyage,
For we will fetters put upon this fear,

20   Which now goes too free-footed.

ROSENCRANTZ   We will haste us.

(*Exeunt* GENTLEMEN)

(*Enter* POLONIUS)

POLONIUS   My lord, he's going to his mother's closet.

25   Behind the arras I'll convey myself
To hear the process.[10] I'll warrant she'll tax him home,[11]
And, as you said, and wisely was it said,
'Tis meet that some more audience than a mother,
Since nature makes them partial, should o'erhear

30   The speech, of vantage.[12] Fare you well, my liege.
I'll call upon you ere you go to bed
And tell you what I know.

KING   Thanks, dear my lord.

(*Exit* POLONIUS)

35   O, my offense is rank, it smells to heaven;
It hath the primal eldest curse[13] upon't,

---

[4] *peculiar* individual   [5] *noyance* harm   [6] *cess* cessation, decease   [7] *gulf* whirlpool   [8] *Attends* joins in (like a royal attendant)   [9] *Arm* prepare   [10] *process* proceedings   [11] *tax him home* thrust home in reprimanding him   [12] *of vantage* from an advantageous position   [13] *primal eldest curse* that of Cain, who also murdered a brother

A brother's murder. Pray can I not,
Though inclination be as sharp as will.
My stronger guilt defeats my strong intent,
And like a man to double business bound
5   I stand in pause where I shall first begin,
And both neglect. What if this cursèd hand
Were thicker than itself with brother's blood,
Is there not rain enough in the sweet heavens
To wash it white as snow? Whereto serves mercy
10   But to confront the visage of offense? [14]
And what's in prayer but this twofold force,
To be forestallèd ere we come to fall,
Or pardoned being down? Then I'll look up.
My fault is past. But, O, what form of prayer
15   Can serve my turn? "Forgive me my foul murder"?
That cannot be, since I am still possessed
Of those effects[15] for which I did the murder,
My crown, mine own ambition, and my queen.
May one be pardoned and retain th' offense?
20   In the corrupted currents of this world
Offense's gilded [16] hand may shove by justice,
And oft 'tis seen the wicked prize itself
Buys out the law. But 'tis not so above.
There is no shuffling;[17] there the action[18] lies
25   In his true nature, and we ourselves compelled,
Even to the teeth and forehead [19] of our faults,
To give in evidence. What then? What rests?
Try what repentance can. What can it not?
Yet what can it when one cannot repent?
30   O wretched state! O bosom black as death!
O limèd [20] soul, that struggling to be free
Art more engaged! [21] Help, angels! Make assay.[22]
Bow, stubborn knees, and, heart with strings of steel,
Be soft as sinews of the new-born babe.
35   All may be well.

He kneels

(*Enter* HAMLET)

---

[14] *offense* sin   [15] *effects* things acquired   [16] *gilded* gold-laden   [17] *shuffling* sharp practice, double-dealing   [18] *action* legal proceeding (in heaven's court) [19] *teeth and forehead* face-to-face recognition   [20] *limèd* caught in birdlime, a gluey material spread as a bird-snare   [21] *engaged* embedded   [22] *assay* an attempt

HAMLET   Now might I do it pat,[23] now 'a is a-praying,
And now I'll do't. And so 'a goes to heaven,
And so am I revenged. That would be scanned.
A villain kills my father, and for that
5   I, his sole son, do this same villain send
To heaven.
Why, this is hire and salary, not revenge.
'A took my father grossly,[24] full of bread,[25]
With all his crimes broad blown,[26] as flush[27] as May;
10   And how his audit[28] stands, who knows save heaven?
But in our circumstance and course of thought,
'Tis heavy with him; and am I then revenged,
To take him in the purging of his soul,
When he is fit and seasoned for his passage?
15   No.
Up, sword, and know thou a more horrid hent.[29]
When he is drunk asleep, or in his rage,
Or in th' incestuous pleasure of his bed,
At game a-swearing, or about some act
20   That has no relish[30] of salvation in't—
Then trip him, that his heels may kick at heaven,
And that his soul may be as damned and black
As hell, whereto it goes. My mother stays.
This physic but prolongs thy sickly days.

25   (*Exit*)

KING (*rises*)   My words fly up, my thoughts remain below.
Words without thoughts never to heaven go.

(*Exit*)

Act III, Scene IV

30   *The private chamber of the* QUEEN

(*Enter* [QUEEN] GERTRUDE *and* POLONIUS)

POLONIUS   'A will come straight. Look you lay[1] home to him.
Tell him his pranks have been too broad [2] to bear with,
And that your grace hath screened and stood between

---

[23] *pat* opportunely   [24] *grossly* in a state of gross unpreparedness   [25] *bread*
i.e. worldly sense gratification   [26] *broad blown* fully blossomed   [27] *flush* vigorous   [28] *audit* account   [29] *more horrid hent* grasping by me on a more horrid occasion   [30] *relish* flavor
[1] *lay* thrust   [2] *broad* unrestrained

Much heat and him. I'll silence me even here.
Pray you be round [3] with him.
[HAMLET (*within*)   Mother, mother, mother!]
QUEEN   I'll warrant you; fear me not. Withdraw; I hear him
5   coming.

(POLONIUS *hides behind the arras*)

(*Enter* HAMLET)

HAMLET   Now, mother, what's the matter?
QUEEN   Hamlet, thou hast thy father much offended.
10   HAMLET   Mother, you have my father much offended.
QUEEN   Come, come, you answer with an idle[4] tongue.
HAMLET   Go, go, you question with a wicked tongue.
QUEEN   Why, how now, Hamlet?
HAMLET   What's the matter now?
15   QUEEN   Have you forgot me?
HAMLET   No, by the rood,[5] not so!
You are the queen, your husband's brother's wife,
And (would it were not so) you are my mother.
QUEEN   Nay, then I'll set those to you that can speak.
20   HAMLET   Come, come, and sit you down. You shall not budge.
You go not till I set you up a glass
Where you may see the inmost part of you.
QUEEN   What wilt thou do? Thou wilt not murder me?
Help, ho!
25   POLONIUS (*behind*)   What, ho! help!
HAMLET (*draws*)   How now? a rat? Dead for a ducat, dead!

(*Makes a pass through the arras and kills* POLONIUS)

POLONIUS (*behind*)   O, I am slain!
QUEEN   O me, what hast thou done?
30   HAMLET   Nay, I know not. Is it the king?
QUEEN   O, what a rash and bloody deed is this!
HAMLET   A bloody deed—almost as bad, good mother,
As kill a king, and marry with his brother.
QUEEN   As kill a king?
35   HAMLET   Ay, lady, it was my word.

(*Lifts up the arras and sees* POLONIUS)

Thou wretched, rash, intruding fool, farewell!

---

[3] *round* plain-spoken   [4] *idle* foolish   [5] *rood* cross

I took thee for thy better. Take thy fortune.
Thou find'st to be too busy is some danger.—
Leave wringing of your hands. Peace, sit you down
And let me wring your heart, for so I shall
5   If it be made of penetrable stuff,
If damnèd custom[6] have not brazed [7] it so
That it is proof [8] and bulwark against sense.[9]
QUEEN   What have I done that thou dar'st wag thy tongue
In noise so rude against me?
10 HAMLET   Such an act
That blurs the grace and blush of modesty,
Calls virtue hypocrite, takes off the rose
From the fair forehead of an innocent love,
And sets a blister[10] there, makes marriage vows
15 As false as dicers' oaths. O, such a deed
As from the body of contraction[11] plucks
The very soul, and sweet religion[12] makes
A rhapsody of words! Heaven's face does glow,
And this solidity and compound mass,[13]
20 With heated visage, as against[14] the doom,[15]
Is thought-sick at the act.

QUEEN   Ay me, what act,
That roars so loud and thunders in the index? [16]
HAMLET   Look here upon this picture, and on this,
25 The counterfeit presentment[17] of two brothers.
See what a grace was seated on this brow:
Hyperion's[18] curls, the front[19] of Jove himself,
An eye like Mars, to threaten and command,
A station[20] like the herald Mercury
30 New lighted on a heaven-kissing hill—
A combination and a form indeed
Where every god did seem to set his seal
To give the world assurance of a man.
This was your husband. Look you now what follows.
35 Here is your husband, like a mildewed ear
Blasting his wholesome brother. Have you eyes?

---

6 *custom* habit   7 *brazed* hardened like brass   8 *proof* armor   9 *sense* feeling   10 *blister* brand (of degradation)   11 *contraction* the marriage contract   12 *religion* i.e. sacred marriage vows   13 *compound mass* the earth as compounded of the four elements   14 *against* in expectation of   15 *doom* Day of Judgment   16 *index* table of contents preceding the body of a book   17 *counterfeit presentment* portrayed representation   18 *Hyperion* the sun god   19 *front* forehead   20 *station* attitude in standing

Could you on this fair mountain leave to feed,
And batten[21] on this moor? Ha! have you eyes?
You cannot call it love, for at your age
The heyday[22] in the blood is tame, it's humble,
5   And waits upon[23] the judgment, and what judgment
Would step from this to this? Sense[24] sure you have,
Else could you not have motion,[25] but sure that sense
Is apoplexed,[26] for madness would not err,
Nor sense to ecstasy[27] was ne'er so thralled
10   But it reserved some quantity of choice
To serve in such a difference. What devil was't
That thus hath cozened [28] you at hoodman-blind? [29]
Eyes without feeling, feeling without sight,
Ears without hands or eyes, smelling sans[30] all,
15   Or but a sickly part of one true sense
Could not so mope.[31]
O shame, where is thy blush? Rebellious hell,
If thou canst mutine[32] in a matron's bones,
To flaming youth let virtue be as wax
20   And melt in her own fire. Proclaim no shame
When the compulsive[33] ardor gives the charge,[34]
Since frost itself as actively doth burn,
And reason panders will.[35]
QUEEN   O Hamlet, speak no more.
25   Thou turn'st mine eyes into my very soul,
And there I see such black and grainèd [36] spots
As will not leave their tinct.[37]
HAMLET   Nay, but to live
In the rank sweat of an enseamèd [38] bed,
30   Stewed in corruption, honeying and making love
Over the nasty sty—
QUEEN   O, speak to me no more.
These words like daggers enter in mine ears.
No more, sweet Hamlet.
35   HAMLET   A murderer and a villain,
A slave that is not twentieth part the tithe[39]

---

21 *batten* feed greedily   22 *heyday* excitement of passion   23 *waits upon* yields to   24 *Sense* feeling   25 *motion* desire, impulse   26 *apoplexed* paralyzed 27 *ecstasy* madness   28 *cozened* cheated   29 *hoodman-blind* blindman's buff 30 *sans* without   31 *mope* be stupid   32 *mutine* mutiny   33 *compulsive* compelling   34 *gives the charge* delivers the attack   35 *panders will* acts as procurer for desire   36 *grainèd* dyed in grain   37 *tinct* color   38 *enseamèd* grease-laden   39 *tithe* tenth part

Of your precedent lord, a vice[40] of kings,
A cutpurse[41] of the empire and the rule,
That from a shelf the precious diadem stole
And put it in his pocket—
5 QUEEN   No more.

(*Enter [the]* GHOST *[in his nightgown[42]]*)

HAMLET   A king of shreds and patches—
Save me and hover o'er me with your wings,
You heavenly guards? What would your gracious figure?
10 QUEEN Alas, he's mad.
HAMLET   Do you not come your tardy son to chide,
That, lapsed in time and passion,[43] lets go by
Th' important acting of your dread command?
O, say!
15 GHOST Do not forget. This visitation
Is but to whet thy almost blunted purpose.
But look, amazement on thy mother sits.
O, step between her and her fighting soul!
Conceit[44] in weakest bodies strongest works.
20 Speak to her, Hamlet.
HAMLET   How is it with you, lady?
QUEEN   Alas, how is't with you,
That you do bend your eye on vacancy,
And with th' incorporal [45] air do hold discourse?
25 Forth at your eyes your spirits wildly peep,
And as the sleeping soldiers in th' alarm
Your bedded hairs like life in excrements[46]
Start up and stand an[47] end. O gentle son,
Upon the heat and flame of thy distemper[48]
30 Sprinkle cool patience. Whereon do you look?
HAMLET   On him, on him! Look you, how pale he glares!
His form and cause conjoined, preaching to stones,
Would make them capable.[49]—Do not look upon me,
Lest with his piteous action you convert
35 My stern effects.[50] Then what I have to do
Will want true color—tears perchance for blood.

---

[40] *vice* clownish rogue (like the Vice of the morality plays)   [41] *cutpurse* skulking thief   [42] *nightgown* dressing gown   [43] *lapsed . . . passion* having let the moment slip and passion cool   [44] *Conceit* imagination   [45] *incorporal* bodiless   [46] *excrements* outgrowths   [47] *an* on   [48] *distemper* mental disorder   [49] *capable* susceptible   [50] *effects* manifestations of emotion and purpose

QUEEN To whom do you speak this?
HAMLET Do you see nothing there?
QUEEN Nothing at all; yet all that is I see.
HAMLET Nor did you nothing hear?
5 QUEEN No, nothing but ourselves.
HAMLET Why, look you there! Look how it steals away!
My father, in his habit as he lived!
Look where he goes even now out at the portal!

(*Exit* GHOST)

10 QUEEN This is the very coinage of your brain.
This bodiless creation ecstasy[51]
Is very cunning in.
HAMLET Ecstasy?
My pulse as yours doth temperately keep time
15 And makes as healthful music. It is not madness
That I have uttered. Bring me to the test,
And I the matter will reword, which madness
Would gambol [52] from. Mother, for love of grace,
Lay not that flattering unction[53] to your soul,
20 That not your trespass but my madness speaks.
It will but skin and film the ulcerous place
Whiles rank corruption, mining[54] all within,
Infects unseen. Confess yourself to heaven,
Repent what's past, avoid what is to come,
25 And do not spread the compost[55] on the weeds
To make them ranker. Forgive me this my virtue.
For in the fatness[56] of these pursy[57] times
Virtue itself of vice must pardon beg,
Yea, curb[58] and woo for leave to do him good.
30 QUEEN O Hamlet, thou hast cleft my heart in twain.
HAMLET O, throw away the worser part of it,
And live the purer with the other half.
Good night—but go not to my uncle's bed.
Assume a virtue, if you have it not.
35 That monster custom, who all sense doth eat,
Of habits devil, is angel yet in this,
That to the use of actions fair and good

---

[51] *ecstasy* madness [52] *gambol* shy (like a startled horse) [53] *unction* ointment [54] *mining* undermining [55] *compost* fertilizing mixture [56] *fatness* gross slackness [57] *pursy* corpulent [58] *curb* bow to

He likewise gives a frock or livery[59]
That aptly is put on. Refrain to-night,
And that shall lend a kind of easiness
To the next abstinence; the next more easy;
5   For use[60] almost can change the stamp[61] of nature,
And either [. . .] [62] the devil, or throw him out
With wondrous potency. Once more, good night,
And when you are desirous to be blest,
I'll blessing beg of you.—For this same lord,
10   I do repent; but heaven hath pleased it so,
To punish me with this, and this with me,
That I must be their scourge and minister.
I will bestow[63] him and will answer well
The death I gave him. So again, good night.
15   I must be cruel only to be kind.
Thus bad begins, and worse remains behind.[64]
One word more, good lady.

QUEEN   What shall I do?

HAMLET   Not this, by no means, that I bid you do:
20   Let the bloat[65] king tempt you again to bed,
Pinch wanton on your cheek, call you his mouse,
And let him, for a pair of reechy[66] kisses,
Or paddling in your neck with his damned fingers,
Make you to ravel all this matter out,[67]
25   That I essentially am not in madness,
But mad in craft. 'Twere good you let him know,
For who that's but a queen, fair, sober, wise,
Would from a paddock,[68] from a bat, a gib,[69]
Such dear concernings[70] hide? Who would do so?
30   No, in despite of sense and secrecy,
Unpeg the basket on the house's top,
Let the birds fly, and like the famous ape,[71]
To try conclusions,[72] in the basket creep
And break your own neck down.

35   QUEEN   Be thou assured, if words be made of breath,
And breath of life, I have no life to breathe

---

[59] *livery* characteristic dress (accompanying the suggestion of "garb" in *habits*)   [60] *use* habit   [61] *stamp* impression, form   [62] A word is apparently omitted here   [63] *bestow* stow, hide   [64] *behind* to come   [65] *bloat* bloated with sense gratification   [66] *reechy* filthy   [67] *ravel . . . out* disentangle   [68] *paddock* toad   [69] *gib* tomcat   [70] *dear concernings* matters of great personal significance   [71] *famous ape* (one in a story now unknown)   [72] *conclusions* experiments

What thou hast said to me.
HAMLET I must to England; you know that?
QUEEN   Alack,
I had forgot. 'Tis so concluded on.
5 HAMLET There's letters sealed, and my two schoolfellows,
Whom I will trust as I will adders fanged,
They bear the mandate;[73] they must sweep my way
And marshal me to knavery. Let it work.
For 'tis the sport to have the enginer[74]
10 Hoist[75] with his own petar,[76] and 't shall go hard
But I will delve one yard below their mines
And blow them at the moon. O, 'tis most sweet
When in one line two crafts directly meet.
This man shall set me packing.[77]
15 I'll lug the guts into the neighbor room.
Mother, good night. Indeed, this counsellor
Is now most still, most secret, and most grave,
Who was in life a foolish prating knave.
Come, sir, to draw toward an end with you.
20 Good night, mother.

(*Exit the* QUEEN. *Then exit* HAMLET, *tugging in* POLONIUS)

ACT IV

Scene I

A chamber in the castle

25 (*Enter* KING *and* QUEEN, *with* ROSENCRANTZ *and* GUILDENSTERN)

KING There's matter in these sighs. These profound heaves
You must translate; 'tis fit we understand them.
Where is your son?
QUEEN Bestow this place on us a little while.

30 (*Exeunt* ROSENCRANTZ *and* GUILDENSTERN)

Ah, mine own lord, what have I seen to-night!
KING What, Gertrude? How does Hamlet?

---

[73] *mandate* order [74] *enginer* engineer, constructor of military engines or
works [75] *Hoist* blown up [76] *petar* petard, bomb or mine [77] *packing* travelling in a hurry (with a play upon his "packing" or shouldering of Polonius'
body and also upon his "packing" in the sense of "plotting" or "contriving")

QUEEN   Mad as the sea and wind when both contend
Which is the mightier. In his lawless fit,
Behind the arras hearing something stir,
Whips out his rapier, cries, "A rat, a rat!"
5 And in this brainish apprehension[1] kills
The unseen good old man.
KING   O heavy deed!
It had been so with us, had we been there.
His liberty is full of threats to all,
10 To you yourself, to us, to every one.
Alas, how shall this bloody deed be answered?
It will be laid to us, whose providence[2]
Should have kept short, restrained, and out of haunt[3]
This mad young man. But so much was our love
15 We would not understand what was most fit,
But, like the owner of a foul disease,
To keep it from divulging,[4] let it feed
Even on the pith of life. Where is he gone?
QUEEN   To draw apart the body he hath killed;
20 O'er whom his very madness, like some ore[5]
Among a mineral [6] of metals base,
Shows itself pure. 'A weeps for what is done.
KING   O Gertrude, come away!
The sun no sooner shall the mountains touch
25 But we will ship him hence, and this vile deed
We must with all our majesty and skill
Both countenance and excuse. Ho, Guildenstern!

(*Enter* ROSENCRANTZ *and* GUILDENSTERN)

Friends both, go join you with some further aid.
30 Hamlet in madness hath Polonius slain,
And from his mother's closet hath he dragged him.
Go seek him out; speak fair, and bring the body
Into the chapel. I pray you haste in this.

(*Exeunt* ROSENCRANTZ *and* GUILDENSTERN)

35 Come, Gertrude, we'll call up our wisest friends
And let them know both what we mean to do
And what's untimely done [. . .] [7]

---

[1] *brainish apprehension* headstrong conception   [2] *providence* foresight
[3] *haunt* association with others   [4] *divulging* becoming known   [5] *ore* vein of
gold   [6] *mineral* mine   [7] Incomplete line; Capell suggests "So, haply, slander"

Whose whisper o'er the world's diameter,
As level [8] as the cannon to his blank[9]
Transports his poisoned shot, may miss our name
And hit the woundless air. O, come away!
5   My soul is full of discord and dismay.

(*Exeunt*)

Act IV, Scene II

A passage in the castle

(*Enter* HAMLET)

10   HAMLET Safely stowed.
GENTLEMEN (*within*) Hamlet! Lord Hamlet!
HAMLET But soft, what noise? Who calls on Hamlet? O, here they
come.

(*Enter* ROSENCRANTZ, GUILDENSTERN, *and others*)

15   ROSENCRANTZ What have you done, my lord, with the dead body?
HAMLET Compounded it with dust, whereto 'tis kin.
ROSENCRANTZ Tell us where 'tis, that we may take it thence
And bear it to the chapel.
HAMLET Do not believe it.
20   ROSENCRANTZ Believe what?
HAMLET That I can keep your counsel and not mine own. Besides,
to be demanded of a sponge, what replication[1] should be made
by the son of a king?
ROSENCRANTZ Take you me for a sponge, my lord?
25   HAMLET Ay, sir, that soaks up the king's countenance,[2] his rewards, his authorities. But such officers do the king best service in
the end. He keeps them, like an ape, in the corner of his jaw, first
mouthed, to be last swallowed. When he needs what you have
gleaned, it is but squeezing you and, sponge, you shall be dry
30   again.
ROSENCRANTZ I understand you not, my lord.
HAMLET I am glad of it. A knavish speech sleeps in[3] a foolish ear.
ROSENCRANTZ My lord, you must tell us where the body is and go
with us to the king.
35   HAMLET The body is with the king, but the king is not with the
body. The king is a thing—

---

[8] *As level* with as direct aim [9] *blank* mark, central white spot on a target
[1] *replication* reply [2] *countenance* favor [3] *sleeps in* means nothing to

GUILDENSTERN A thing, my lord?
HAMLET   Of nothing.[4] Bring me to him. Hide fox, and all after.[5]

(*Exeunt*)

Act IV, Scene III

5   *A chamber in the castle*

(*Enter* KING, *and two or three*)

KING   I have sent to seek him and to find the body.
How dangerous is it that this man goes loose!
Yet must not we put the strong law on him;
10   He's loved of the distracted [1] multitude,
Who like not in their judgment, but their eyes,
And where 'tis so, th' offender's scourge[2] is weighed,
But never the offense. To bear all smooth and even,
This sudden sending him away must seem
15   Deliberate pause.[3] Diseases desperate grown
By desperate appliance are relieved,
Or not at all.

(*Enter* ROSENCRANTZ, GUILDENSTERN, *and all the rest*)

How now? What hath befallen?
20   ROSENCRANTZ   Where the dead body is bestowed, my lord,
We cannot get from him.
KING   But where is he?
ROSENCRANTZ   Without, my lord; guarded, to know your pleasure.
KING   Bring him before us.
25   ROSENCRANTZ   Ho! Bring in the lord.

(*They enter* [*with* HAMLET])

KING   Now, Hamlet, where's Polonius?
HAMLET   At supper.
KING   At supper? Where?
30   HAMLET   Not where he eats, but where 'a is eaten. A certain convocation of politic worms[4] are e'en at him. Your worm is your

---

4 *Of nothing* (cf. Prayer Book, Psalm cxliv, 4, "Man is like a thing of naught:
his time passeth away like a shadow")   5 *Hide . . . after* (apparently well-
known words from some game of hide-and-seek)
1 *distracted* confused   2 *scourge* punishment   3 *Deliberate pause* something
done with much deliberation   4 *politic worms* political and craftily scheming
worms (such as Polonius might well attract)

only emperor for diet.[5] We fat all creatures else to fat us, and we fat ourselves for maggots. Your fat king and your lean beggar is but variable service[6]—two dishes, but to one table. That's the end.

KING   Alas, alas!

5   HAMLET   A man may fish with the worm that hath eat of a king, and eat of the fish that hath fed of that worm.

KING   What dost thou mean by this?

HAMLET   Nothing but to show you how a king may go a progress[7] through the guts of a beggar.

10   KING   Where is Polonius?

HAMLET   In heaven. Send thither to see. If your messenger find him not there, seek him i' th' other place yourself. But if indeed you find him not within this month, you shall nose him as you go up the stairs into the lobby.

15   KING   (*to* ATTENDANTS)   Go seek him there.

HAMLET   'A will stay till you come.

(*Exeunt* ATTENDANTS)

KING   Hamlet, this deed, for thine especial safety,
Which we do tender[8] as we dearly[9] grieve
20   For that which thou hast done, must send thee hence
With fiery quickness. Therefore prepare thyself.
The bark is ready and the wind at help,
Th' associates tend,[10] and everything is bent[11]
For England.

25   HAMLET   For England?

KING   Ay, Hamlet.

HAMLET   Good.

KING   So is it, if thou knew'st our purposes.

HAMLET   I see a cherub[12] that sees them. But come, for England!
30   Farewell, dear mother.

KING   Thy loving father, Hamlet.

HAMLET   My mother—father and mother is man and wife, man and wife is one flesh, and so, my mother. Come, for England!

(*Exit*)

---

[5] *diet* food and drink (perhaps with a play upon a famous "convocation," the Diet of Worms opened by the Emperor Charles V on January 28, 1521, before which Luther appeared)   [6] *variable service* different servings of one food   [7] *progress* royal journey of state   [8] *tender* hold dear   [9] *dearly* intensely   [10] *tend* wait   [11] *bent* set in readiness (like a bent bow)   [12] *cherub* one of the cherubim (angels with a distinctive quality of knowledge)

KING Follow him at foot;[13] tempt him with speed aboard.
Delay it not; I'll have him hence to-night.
Away! for everything is sealed and done
That else leans on[14] th' affair. Pray you make haste.

5   (*Exeunt all but the* KING)

And, England,[15] if my love thou hold'st at aught—
As my great power thereof may give thee sense,
Since yet thy cicatrice looks raw and red
After the Danish sword, and thy free awe[16]
10   Pays homage to us—thou mayst not coldly set[17]
Our sovereign process,[18] which imports at full
By letters congruing[19] to that effect
The present[20] death of Hamlet. Do it, England,
For like the hectic[21] in my blood he rages,
15   And thou must cure me. Till I know 'tis done,
Howe'er my haps,[22] my joys were ne'er begun.

(*Exit*)

Act IV, Scene IV

A coastal highway

20   (*Enter* FORTINBRAS *with his* ARMY *over the stage*)

FORTINBRAS Go, captain, from me greet the Danish king.
Tell him that by his license Fortinbras
Craves the conveyance[1] of a promised march
Over his kingdom. You know the rendezvous.
25   If that his majesty would aught with us,
We shall express our duty in his eye;[2]
And let him know so.
CAPTAIN   I will do't, my lord.
FORTINBRAS Go softly[3] on.

30   (*Exeunt all but the* CAPTAIN)

(*Enter* HAMLET, ROSENCRANTZ, GUILDENSTERN, *and others*)

HAMLET Good sir, whose powers[4] are these?

---

[13] *at foot* at heel, close   [14] *leans on* is connected with   [15] *England* King of
England   [16] *free awe* voluntary show of respect   [17] *set* esteem   [18] *process*
formal command   [19] *congruing* agreeing   [20] *present* instant   [21] *hectic* a
continuous fever   [22] *haps* fortunes
[1] *conveyance* escort   [2] *eye* presence   [3] *softly* slowly   [4] *powers* forces

CAPTAIN They are of Norway, sir.
HAMLET How purposed, sir, I pray you?
CAPTAIN Against some part of Poland.
HAMLET Who commands them, sir?
5 CAPTAIN The nephew to old Norway, Fortinbras.
HAMLET Goes it against the main[5] of Poland, sir,
Or for some frontier?
CAPTAIN Truly to speak, and with no addition,[6]
We go to gain a little patch of ground
10 That hath in it no profit but the name.
To pay[7] five ducats, five, I would not farm it,
Nor will it yield to Norway or the Pole
A ranker[8] rate, should it be sold in fee.[9]
HAMLET Why, then the Polack never will defend it.
15 CAPTAIN Yes, it is already garrisoned.
HAMLET Two thousand souls and twenty thousand ducats
Will not debate the question of this straw.
This is th' imposthume[10] of much wealth and peace,
That inward breaks, and shows no cause without
20 Why the man dies. I humbly thank you, sir.
CAPTAIN God bye you, sir.

(Exit)

ROSENCRANTZ Will't please you go, my lord?
HAMLET I'll be with you straight. Go a little before.

25 *(Exeunt all but* HAMLET*)*

How all occasions do inform[11] against me
And spur my dull revenge! What is a man,
If his chief good and market of [12] his time
Be but to sleep and feed? A beast, no more.
30 Sure he that made us with such large discourse,[13]
Looking before and after, gave us not
That capability and godlike reason
To fust[14] in us unused. Now, whether it be
Bestial oblivion,[15] or some craven scruple
35 Of thinking too precisely on th' event—[16]

---

[5] *main* main body   [6] *addition* exaggeration   [7] *To pay* i.e. for a yearly rental of   [8] *ranker* more abundant   [9] *in fee* outright   [10] *imposthume* abscess   [11] *inform* take shape   [12] *market of* compensation for   [13] *discourse* power of thought   [14] *fust* grow mouldy   [15] *oblivion* forgetfulness   [16] *event* outcome

A thought which, quartered, hath but one part wisdom
And ever three parts coward—I do not know
Why yet I live to say, "This thing 's to do,"
Sith I have cause, and will, and strength, and means
5   To do't. Examples gross[17] as earth exhort me.
Witness this army of such mass and charge,[18]
Led by a delicate and tender prince,
Whose spirit, with divine ambition puffed,
Makes mouths[19] at the invisible event,
10   Exposing what is mortal and unsure
To all that fortune, death, and danger dare,
Even for an eggshell. Rightly to be great
Is not to stir without great argument,
But greatly to find quarrel in a straw[20]
15   When honor 's at the stake. How stand I then,
That have a father killed, a mother stained,
Excitements of my reason and my blood,
And let all sleep, while to my shame I see
The imminent death of twenty thousand men
20   That for a fantasy[21] and trick[22] of fame
Go to their graves like beds, fight for a plot
Whereon the numbers cannot try the cause,[23]
Which is not tomb enough and continent[24]
To hide the slain? O, from this time forth,
25   My thoughts be bloody, or be nothing worth!

(*Exit*)

Act IV, Scene V

A chamber in the castle

(*Enter* Horatio, [Queen] Gertrude, *and a* Gentleman)

30   QUEEN   I will not speak with her.
GENTLEMAN   She is importunate, indeed distract.[1]
Her mood will needs be pitied.
QUEEN   What would she have?
GENTLEMAN   She speaks much of her father, says she hears

---

[17] *gross* large and evident   [18] *charge* expense   [19] *Makes mouths* makes faces scornfully   [20] *greatly ... straw* to recognize the great argument even in some small matter   [21] *fantasy* fanciful image   [22] *trick* toy   [23] *try the cause* find space in which to settle the issue by battle   [24] *continent* receptacle
[1] *distract* insane

There's tricks[2] i' th' world, and hems, and beats her heart,
Spurns enviously[3] at straws,[4] speaks things in doubt
That carry but half sense. Her speech is nothing,
Yet the unshapèd use[5] of it doth move
5   The hearers to collection;[6] they aim[7] at it,
And botch[8] the words up fit to their own thoughts,
Which, as her winks and nods and gestures yield them,
Indeed would make one think there might be thought,
Though nothing sure, yet much unhappily.
10 HORATIO   'Twere good she were spoken with, for she may strew
Dangerous conjectures in ill-breeding minds.
QUEEN   Let her come in.

(*Exit* GENTLEMAN)

(*Aside*)

15 To my sick soul (as sin's true nature is)
Each toy[9] seems prologue to some great amiss.[10]
So full of artless[11] jealousy[12] is guilt
It spills[13] itself in fearing to be spilt.

(*Enter* OPHELIA [*distracted*])

20 OPHELIA   Where is the beauteous majesty of Denmark?
QUEEN   How now, Ophelia?
OPHELIA   (*She sings.*)
How should I your true-love know
From another one?
25 By his cockle hat[14] and staff
And his sandal shoon.[15]
QUEEN   Alas, sweet lady, what imports this song?
OPHELIA   Say you? Nay, pray you mark.

Song

30 He is dead and gone, lady,
He is dead and gone;
At his head a grass-green turf,
At his heels a stone.
O, ho!

---

[2] *tricks* deceits   [3] *Spurns enviously* kicks spitefully, takes offense   [4] *straws* trifles   [5] *unshapèd use* disordered manner   [6] *collection* attempts at shaping meaning   [7] *aim* guess   [8] *botch* patch   [9] *toy* trifle   [10] *amiss* calamity   [11] *artless* unskillfully managed   [12] *jealousy* suspicion   [13] *spills* destroys   [14] *cockle hat* hat bearing a cockle shell, worn by a pilgrim who had been to the shrine of St James of Compostela   [15] *shoon* shoes

QUEEN Nay, but Ophelia—
OPHELIA Pray you mark.
(*Sings*) White his shroud as the mountain snow—

(*Enter* KING)

5 QUEEN Alas, look here, my lord.
OPHELIA

Song

Larded [16] all with sweet flowers;
Which bewept to the grave did not go
10 With true-love showers.
KING How do you, pretty lady?
OPHELIA Well, God dild [17] you! They say the owl [18] was a baker's daughter. Lord, we know what we are, but know not what we may be. God be at your table!
15 KING Conceit[19] upon her father.
OPHELIA Pray let's have no words of this, but when they ask you what it means, say you this:

Song

To-morrow is Saint Valentine's day.
20 All in the morning betime,[20]
And I a maid at your window,
To be your Valentine.
Then up he rose and donned his clo'es
And dupped [21] the chamber door,
25 Let in the maid, that out a maid
Never departed more.
KING Pretty Ophelia!
OPHELIA Indeed, la, without an oath, I'll make an end on't:
(*Sings*) By Gis[22] and by Saint Charity,
30 Alack, and fie for shame!
Young men will do't if they come to't.
By Cock,[23] they are to blame.
Quoth she, "Before you tumbled me,
You promised me to wed."

---

[16] *Larded* garnished [17] *dild* yield, repay [18] *the owl* an owl into which, according to a folk-tale, a baker's daughter was transformed because of her failure to show whole-hearted generosity when Christ asked for bread in the baker's shop [19] *Conceit* thought [20] *betime* early [21] *dupped* opened [22] *Gis* Jesus [23] *Cock* God (with a perversion of the name not uncommon in oaths)

He answers:
> "So would I 'a' done, by yonder sun,
> And thou hadst not come to my bed."

KING   How long hath she been thus?

5   OPHELIA   I hope all will be well. We must be patient, but I cannot choose but weep to think they would lay him i' th' cold ground. My brother shall know of it; and so I thank you for your good counsel. Come, my coach! Good night, ladies, good night. Sweet ladies, good night, good night.

10   (*Exit*)

KING   Follow her close; give her good watch, I pray you.

(*Exit* HORATIO)

O, this is the poison of deep grief; it springs
All from her father's death—and now behold!
15   O Gertrude, Gertrude,
When sorrows come, they come not single spies,
But in battalions: first, her father slain;
Next, your son gone, and he most violent author
Of his own just remove; the people muddied,[24]
20   Thick and unwholesome in their thoughts and whispers
For good Polonius' death, and we have done but greenly[25]
In hugger-mugger[26] to inter him; poor Ophelia
Divided from herself and her fair judgment,
Without the which we are pictures or mere beasts;
25   Last, and as much containing as all these,
Her brother is in secret come from France,
Feeds on his wonder, keeps himself in clouds,[27]
And wants[28] not buzzers[29] to infect his ear
With pestilent speeches of his father's death,
30   Wherein necessity, of matter beggared,[30]
Will nothing stick[31] our person to arraign[32]
In ear and ear. O my dear Gertrude, this,
Like to a murd'ring piece,[33] in many places
Gives me superfluous death.

35   *A noise within*

---

[24] *muddied* stirred up and confused   [25] *greenly* foolishly   [26] *hugger-mugger* secrecy and disorder   [27] *clouds* obscurity   [28] *wants* lacks   [29] *buzzers* whispering tale-bearers   [30] *of matter beggared* unprovided with facts   [31] *nothing stick* in no way hesitate   [32] *arraign* accuse   [33] *murd'ring piece* cannon loaded with shot meant to scatter

(*Enter a* MESSENGER)

QUEEN Alack, what noise is this?

KING Attend, where are my Switzers?[34] Let them guard the door. What is the matter?

5 MESSENGER Save yourself, my lord.
The ocean, overpeering of [35] his list,[36]
Eats not the flats with more impiteous[37] haste
Than young Laertes, in a riotous head,[38]
O'erbears your officers. The rabble call him lord,
10 And, as the world were now but to begin,
Antiquity forgot, custom not known,
The ratifiers and props of every word,[39]
They cry, "Choose we! Laertes shall be king!"
Caps, hands, and tongues applaud it to the clouds,
15 "Laertes shall be king! Laertes king!"

A noise within

QUEEN How cheerfully on the false trail they cry!
O, this is counter,[40] you false Danish dogs!

KING The doors are broke.

20 (*Enter* LAERTES *with others*)

LAERTES Where is this king?—Sirs, stand you all without.

ALL No, let's come in.

LAERTES I pray you give me leave.

ALL We will, we will.

25 LAERTES I thank you. Keep the door.

(*Exeunt his* FOLLOWERS)

O thou vile king,
Give me my father.

QUEEN Calmly, good Laertes.

30 LAERTES That drop of blood that's calm proclaims me bastard,
Cries cuckold to my father, brands the harlot
Even here between the chaste unsmirchèd brows
Of my true mother.

KING What is the cause, Laertes,
35 That thy rebellion looks so giant-like?
Let him go, Gertrude. Do not fear[41] our person.

---

34 *Switzers* hired Swiss guards   35 *overpeering of* rising to look over and pass beyond   36 *list* boundary   37 *impiteous* pitiless   38 *head* armed force   39 *word* promise   40 *counter* hunting backward on the trail   41 *fear* fear for

There's such divinity doth hedge a king
That treason can but peep to[42] what it would,
Acts little of his will. Tell me, Laertes,
Why thou art thus incensed. Let him go, Gertrude.
5   Speak, man.
LAERTES   Where is my father?
KING   Dead.
QUEEN   But not by him.
KING   Let him demand his fill.
10   LAERTES   How came he dead? I'll not be juggled with.
To hell allegiance, vows to the blackest devil,
Conscience and grace to the profoundest pit!
I dare damnation. To this point I stand,
That both the worlds[43] I give to negligence,[44]
15   Let come what comes, only I'll be revenged
Most throughly[45] for my father.
KING   Who shall stay you?
LAERTES   My will, not all the world's.
And for my means, I'll husband them so well
20   They shall go far with little.
KING   Good Laertes,
If you desire to know the certainty
Of your dear father, is't writ in your revenge
That swoopstake[46] you will draw both friend and foe,
25   Winner and loser?
LAERTES   None but his enemies.
KING   Will you know them then?
LAERTES   To his good friends thus wide I'll ope my arms
And like the kind life-rend'ring[47] pelican
30   Repast them with my blood.
KING   Why, now you speak
Like a good child and a true gentleman.
That I am guiltless of your father's death,
And am most sensibly[48] in grief for it,
35   It shall as level [49] to your judgment 'pear
As day does to your eye.
      A noise within: "Let her come in!"

---

[42] *peep to* i.e. through the barrier   [43] *both the worlds* whatever may result in this world or the next   [44] *give to negligence* disregard   [45] *throughly* thoroughly   [46] *swoopstake* sweepstake, taking all stakes on the gambling table   [47] *life-rend'ring* life-yielding (because the mother pelican supposedly took blood from her breast with her bill to feed her young)   [48] *sensibly* feelingly   [49] *level* plain

LAERTES How now? What noise is that?

(*Enter* OPHELIA)

O heat, dry up my brains; tears seven times salt
Burn out the sense and virtue of mine eye!
5 By heaven, thy madness shall be paid by weight
Till our scale turn the beam.[50] O rose of May,
Dear maid, kind sister, sweet Ophelia!
O heavens, is't possible a young maid's wits
Should be as mortal as an old man's life?
10 Nature is fine[51] in love, and where 'tis fine,
It sends some precious instance[52] of itself
After the thing it loves.

OPHELIA

Song

15 They bore him barefaced on the bier
    Hey non nony, nony, hey nony
    And in his grave rained many a tear—
Fare you well, my dove!

LAERTES Hadst thou thy wits, and didst persuade revenge,
20 It could not move thus.

OPHELIA You must sing "A-down a-down, and you call him
a-down-a." O, how the wheel [53] becomes it! It is the false stew-
ard, that stole his master's daughter.

LAERTES This nothing 's more than matter.[54]

25 OPHELIA There's rosemary, that's for remembrance. Pray you, love,
remember. And there is pansies, that's for thoughts.

LAERTES A document[55] in madness, thoughts and remembrance
fitted.

OPHELIA There's fennel [56] for you, and columbines.[57] There's rue[58]
30 for you, and here's some for me. We may call it herb of grace o'
Sundays. O, you must wear your rue with a difference. There's
a daisy.[59] I would give you some violets,[60] but they withered all
when my father died. They say 'a made a good end.
(*Sings*) For bonny sweet Robin is all my joy.

35 LAERTES Thought and affliction, passion, hell itself,
She turns to favor[61] and to prettiness.

---

[50] *beam* bar of a balance   [51] *fine* refined to purity   [52] *instance* token   [53] *wheel*
burden, refrain   [54] *more than matter* more meaningful than sane speech
[55] *document* lesson   [56] *fennel* symbol of flattery   [57] *columbines* symbol of
thanklessness   [58] *rue* symbol of repentance   [59] *daisy* symbol of dissembling
[60] *violets* symbol of faithfulness   [61] *favor* charm

OPHELIA

Song

And will 'a not come again?
And will 'a not come again?
5   No, no, he is dead;
Go to thy deathbed;
He never will come again.
His beard was as white as snow,
All flaxen was his poll.[62]
10   He is gone, he is gone,
And we cast away moan.
God 'a' mercy on his soul!
And of [63] all Christian souls, I pray God. God bye you.

(*Exit*)

15 LAERTES   Do you see this, O God?
KING   Laertes, I must commune with your grief,
Or you deny me right. Go but apart,
Make choice of whom your wisest friends you will,
And they shall hear and judge 'twixt you and me.
20 If by direct or by collateral [64] hand
They find us touched,[65] we will our kingdom give,
Our crown, our life, and all that we call ours,
To you in satisfaction; but if not,
Be you content to lend your patience to us,
25 And we shall jointly labor with your soul
To give it due content.
LAERTES   Let this be so.
His means of death, his obscure funeral—
No trophy,[66] sword, nor hatchment[67] o'er his bones,
30 No noble rite nor formal ostentation[68]—
Cry to be heard, as 'twere from heaven to earth,
That[69] I must call't in question.
KING   So you shall;
And where th' offense is, let the great axe fall.
35 I pray you go with me.

(*Exeunt*)

---

[62] *poll* head   [63] *of* on   [64] *collateral* indirect   [65] *touched* i.e. with the crime
[66] *trophy* memorial   [67] *hatchment* coat of arms   [68] *ostentation* ceremony
[69] *That* so that

Act IV, Scene VI

A chamber in the castle

(*Enter* HORATIO *and others*)

HORATIO What are they that would speak with me?
5 GENTLEMAN Seafaring men, sir. They say they have letters for you.
HORATIO Let them come in.

(*Exit* ATTENDANT)

I do not know from what part of the world
I should be greeted, if not from Lord Hamlet.

10 (*Enter* SAILORS)

SAILOR God bless you, sir.
HORATIO Let him bless thee too.
SAILOR 'A shall, sir, an't please him. There's a letter for you, sir—
it came from th' ambassador that was bound for England—if
15 your name be Horatio, as I am let to know it is.
HORATIO (*reads the letter*) "Horatio, when thou shalt have overlooked [1] this, give these fellows some means[2] to the king. They
have letters for him. Ere we were two days old at sea, a pirate of
very warlike appointment[3] gave us chase. Finding ourselves too
20 slow of sail, we put on a compelled valor, and in the grapple I
boarded them. On the instant they got clear of our ship; so I
alone became their prisoner. They have dealt with me like thieves
of mercy,[4] but they knew what they did: I am to do a good turn
for them. Let the king have the letters I have sent, and repair
25 thou to me with as much speed as thou wouldest fly death. I have
words to speak in thine ear will make thee dumb; yet are they
much too light for the bore[5] of the matter. These good fellows
will bring thee where I am. Rosencrantz and Guildenstern hold
their course for England. Of them I have much to tell thee.
30 Farewell.
                            He that thou knowest thine, Hamlet."
Come, I will give you way for these your letters,
And do't the speedier that you may direct me
To him from whom you brought them.

35 (*Exeunt*)

---

1 *overlooked* surveyed, scanned 2 *means* i.e. of access 3 *appointment* equipment 4 *thieves of mercy* merciful thieves 5 *bore* caliber (as of a gun)

Act IV, Scene VII

A chamber in the castle

(*Enter* KING *and* LAERTES)

KING Now must your conscience my acquittance seal,
5   And you must put me in your heart for friend,
       Sith you have heard, and with a knowing ear,
       That he which hath your noble father slain
       Pursued my life.
       LAERTES   It well appears. But tell me
10   Why you proceeded not against these feats[1]
       So crimeful and so capital [2] in nature,
       As by your safety, wisdom, all things else,
       You mainly[3] were stirred up.
       KING   O, for two special reasons,
15   Which may to you perhaps seem much unsinewed,
       But yet to me they're strong. The queen his mother
       Lives almost by his looks, and for myself—
       My virtue or my plague, be it either which—
       She is so conjunctive[4] to my life and soul
20   That, as the star moves not but in his sphere,
       I could not but by her. The other motive
       Why to a public count[5] I might not go
       Is the great love the general gender[6] bear him,
       Who, dipping all his faults in their affection,
25   Would, like the spring that turneth wood to stone,
       Convert his gyves[7] to graces; so that my arrows,
       Too slightly timbered for so loud a wind,
       Would have reverted to my bow again,
       And not where I had aimed them.
30   LAERTES And so have I a noble father lost,
       A sister driven into desp'rate terms,[8]
       Whose worth, if praises may go back again,[9]
       Stood challenger on mount[10] of all the age
       For her perfections. But my revenge will come.
35   KING Break not your sleeps for that. You must not think
       That we are made of stuff so flat and dull
       That we can let our beard be shook with danger,

---

[1] *feats* deeds [2] *capital* punishable by death [3] *mainly* powerfully [4] *conjunctive* closely united [5] *count* trial, accounting [6] *general gender* common people [7] *gyves* fetters [8] *terms* circumstances [9] *back again* i.e. to her better circumstances [10] *on mount* on a height

And think it pastime. You shortly shall hear more.
I loved your father, and we love ourself,
And that, I hope, will teach you to imagine—

(*Enter a* MESSENGER *with letters*)

5   How now? What news?
MESSENGER   Letters, my lord, from Hamlet:
These to your majesty, this to the queen.
KING   From Hamlet? Who brought them?
MESSENGER   Sailors, my lord, they say; I saw them not.
10   They were given me by Claudio; he received them
Of him that brought them.
KING   Laertes, you shall hear them.—
Leave us.

(*Exit* MESSENGER)

15   (*Reads*) "High and mighty, you shall know I am set naked [11]
on your kingdom. To-morrow shall I beg leave to see your kingly
eyes; when I shall (first asking your pardon thereunto) recount
the occasion of my sudden and more strange return.   Hamlet."
What should this mean? Are all the rest come back?
20   Or is it some abuse,[12] and no such thing?
LAERTES   Know you the hand?
KING   'Tis Hamlet's character.[13] "Naked"!
And in a postscript here, he says "alone."
Can you devise[14] me?
25   LAERTES   I am lost in it, my lord. But let him come.
It warms the very sickness in my heart
That I shall live and tell him to his teeth,
"Thus diddest thou."
KING   If it be so, Laertes,
30   (As how should it be so? how otherwise?)
Will you be ruled by me?
LAERTES   Ay, my lord,
So you will not o'errule me to a peace.
KING   To thine own peace. If he be now returned,
35   As checking at[15] his voyage, and that he means
No more to undertake it, I will work him

---

[11] *naked* destitute   [12] *abuse* imposture   [13] *character* handwriting   [14] *devise* explain to   [15] *checking at* turning aside from (like a falcon turning from its quarry for other prey)

To an exploit now ripe in my device,
Under the which he shall not choose but fall;
And for his death no wind of blame shall breathe,
But even his mother shall uncharge the practice[16]
5   And call it accident.
    LAERTES   My lord, I will be ruled;
    The rather if you could devise it so
    That I might be the organ.[17]
    KING   It falls right.
10 You have been talked of since your travel much,
    And that in Hamlet's hearing, for a quality
    Wherein they say you shine. Your sum of parts
    Did not together pluck such envy from him
    As did that one, and that, in my regard,
15 Of the unworthiest siege.[18]
    LAERTES   What part is that, my lord?
    KING   A very riband [19] in the cap of youth,
    Yet needful too, for youth no less becomes
    The light and careless livery[20] that it wears
20 Than settled age his sables[21] and his weeds,[22]
    Importing health[23] and graveness. Two months since
    Here was a gentleman of Normandy.
    I have seen myself, and served against, the French,
    And they can well [24] on horseback, but this gallant
25 Had witchcraft in't. He grew unto his seat,
    And to such wondrous doing brought his horse
    As had he been incorpsed [25] and demi-natured [26]
    With the brave beast. So far he topped [27] my thought[28]
    That I, in forgery[29] of shapes and tricks,
30 Come short of what he did.
    LAERTES   A Norman was't?
    KING   A Norman.
    LAERTES   Upon my life, Lamord.
    KING   The very same.
35 LAERTES   I know him well. He is the brooch[30] indeed

---

[16] *uncharge the practice* acquit the stratagem of being a plot   [17] *organ* instrument   [18] *siege* seat, rank   [19] *riband* decoration   [20] *livery* distinctive attire   [21] *sables* dignified robes richly furred with sable   [22] *weeds* distinctive garments   [23] *health* welfare, prosperity   [24] *can well* can perform well   [25] *incorpsed* made one body   [26] *demi-natured* made sharer of nature half and half (as man shares with horse in the centaur)   [27] *topped* excelled   [28] *thought* imagination of possibilities   [29] *forgery* invention   [30] *brooch* ornament

And gem of all the nation.
KING   He made confession[31] of you,
And gave you such a masterly report
For art and exercise in your defense,
5   And for your rapier most especial,
That he cried out 'twould be a sight indeed
If one could match you. The scrimers[32] of their nation
He swore had neither motion, guard, nor eye,
If you opposed them. Sir, this report of his
10   Did Hamlet so envenom with his envy
That he could nothing do but wish and beg
Your sudden coming o'er to play with you.
Now, out of this—
LAERTES   What out of this, my lord?
15   KING   Laertes, was your father dear to you?
Or are you like the painting of a sorrow,
A face without a heart?
LAERTES   Why ask you this?
KING   Not that I think you did not love your father,
20   But that I know love is begun by time,
And that I see, in passages of proof,[33]
Time qualifies[34] the spark and fire of it.
There lives within the very flame of love
A kind of wick or snuff [35] that will abate it,
25   And nothing is at a like goodness still,[36]
For goodness, growing to a plurisy,[37]
Dies in his own too-much. That we would do
We should do when we would, for this "would" changes,
And hath abatements and delays as many
30   As there are tongues, are hands, are accidents,
And then this "should" is like a spendthrift sigh,
That hurts[38] by easing. But to the quick[39] o' th' ulcer—
Hamlet comes back; what would you undertake
To show yourself your father's son in deed
35   More than in words?
LAERTES   To cut his throat i' th' church!

---

[31] *made confession* admitted the rival accomplishments   [32] *scrimers* fencers
[33] *passages of proof* incidents of experience   [34] *qualifies* weakens   [35] *snuff*
unconsumed portion of the burned wick   [36] *still* always   [37] *plurisy* excess
[38] *hurts* i.e. shortens life by drawing blood from the heart (as was believed)
[39] *quick* sensitive flesh

KING   No place indeed should murder sanctuarize;[40]
Revenge should have no bounds. But, good Laertes,
Will you do this? Keep close within your chamber.
Hamlet returned shall know you are come home.
5   We'll put on[41] those shall praise your excellence
And set a double varnish on the fame
The Frenchman gave you, bring you in fine[42] together
And wager on your heads. He, being remiss,[43]
Most generous, and free from all contriving,
10   Will not peruse[44] the foils, so that with ease,
Or with a little shuffling, you may choose
A sword unbated,[45] and, in a pass of practice,[46]
Requite him for your father.
LAERTES   I will do't,
15   And for that purpose I'll anoint my sword.
I bought an unction[47] of a mountebank,[48]
So mortal that, but dip a knife in it,
Where it draws blood no cataplasm[49] so rare,
Collected from all simples[50] that have virtue
20   Under the moon, can save the thing from death
That is but scratched withal.[51] I'll touch my point
With this contagion, that, if I gall [52] him slightly,
It may be death.
KING   Let's further think of this,
25   Weigh what convenience both of time and means
May fit us to our shape.[53] If this should fail,
And that our drift[54] look[55] through our bad performance,
'Twere better not assayed. Therefore this project
Should have a back or second, that might hold
30   If this did blast in proof.[56] Soft, let me see.
We'll make a solemn wager on your cunnings—
I ha't!
When in your motion you are hot and dry—
As make your bouts more violent to that end—
35   And that he calls for drink, I'll have preferred [57] him
A chalice for the nonce,[58] whereon but sipping,

---

40 *sanctuarize* protect from punishment, give sanctuary to   41 *put on* instigate
42 *in fine* finally   43 *remiss* negligent   44 *peruse* scan   45 *unbated* not blunted
46 *pass of practice* thrust made effective by trickery   47 *unction* ointment
48 *mountebank* quack-doctor   49 *cataplasm* poultice   50 *simples* herbs   51 *withal*
with it   52 *gall* scratch   53 *shape* plan   54 *drift* intention   55 *look* show
56 *blast in proof* burst during trial (like a faulty cannon)   57 *preferred* offered
58 *nonce* occasion

If he by chance escape your venomed stuck,[59]
Our purpose may hold there.—But stay, what noise?

(*Enter* QUEEN)

QUEEN   One woe doth tread upon another's heel,
5   So fast they follow. Your sister 's drowned, Laertes.
LAERTES   Drowned! O, where?
QUEEN   There is a willow grows askant[60] the brook,
That shows his hoar[61] leaves in the glassy stream.
Therewith fantastic garlands did she make
10   Of crowflowers, nettles, daisies, and long purples,
That liberal [62] shepherds give a grosser name,
But our cold maids do dead men's fingers call them.
There on the pendent boughs her crownet[63] weeds
Clamb'ring to hang, an envious sliver broke,
15   When down her weedy trophies and herself
Fell in the weeping brook. Her clothes spread wide,
And mermaid-like awhile they bore her up,
Which time she chanted snatches of old lauds,[64]
As one incapable of [65] her own distress,
20   Or like a creature native and indued [66]
Unto that element. But long it could not be
Till that her garments, heavy with their drink,
Pulled the poor wretch from her melodious lay
To muddy death.
25   LAERTES   Alas, then she is drowned?
QUEEN   Drowned, drowned.
LAERTES   Too much of water hast thou, poor Ophelia,
And therefore I forbid my tears; but yet
It is our trick;[67] nature her custom holds,
30   Let shame say what it will. When these are gone,
The woman[68] will be out. Adieu, my lord.
I have a speech o' fire, that fain would blaze
But that this folly drowns it.

(*Exit*)

35   KING   Let's follow, Gertrude.
How much I had to do to calm his rage!

---

[59] *stuck* thrust   [60] *askant* alongside   [61] *hoar* grey   [62] *liberal* free-spoken,
licentious   [63] *crownet* coronet   [64] *lauds* hymns   [65] *incapable of* insensible
to   [66] *indued* endowed   [67] *trick* way (i.e. to shed tears when sorrowful)
[68] *woman* unmanly part of nature.

Now fear I this will give it start again;
Therefore let's follow.

(*Exeunt*)

ACT V

5 **Scene I**

A churchyard

(*Enter two* CLOWNS[1])

CLOWN Is she to be buried in Christian burial [2] when she willfully seeks her own salvation?

10 OTHER I tell thee she is. Therefore make her grave straight.[3] The crowner[4] hath sate on her, and finds it Christian burial.

CLOWN How can that be, unless she drowned herself in her own defense?

OTHER Why, 'tis found so.

15 CLOWN It must be *se offendendo*;[5] it cannot be else. For here lies the point: if I drown myself wittingly, it argues an act, and an act hath three branches—it is to act, to do, and to perform. Argal,[6] she drowned herself wittingly.

OTHER Nay, but hear you, Goodman Delver.[7]

20 CLOWN Give me leave. Here lies the water—good. Here stands the man—good. If the man go to this water and drown himself, it is, will he nill he,[8] he goes, mark you that. But if the water come to him and drown him, he drowns not himself. Argal, he that is not guilty of his own death shortens not his own life.

25 OTHER But is this law?

CLOWN Ay marry, is't—crowner's quest[9] law.

OTHER Will you ha' the truth on't? If this had not been a gentle-woman, she should have been buried out o' Christian burial.

CLOWN Why, there thou say'st.[10] And the more pity that great folk

30 should have count'nance[11] in this world to drown or hang themselves more than their even-Christen.[12] Come, my spade. There

---

[1] *Clowns* rustics [2] *in Christian burial* in consecrated ground with the prescribed service of the Church (a burial denied to suicides) [3] *straight* straightway, at once [4] *crowner* coroner [5] *se offendendo* a clownish transformation of "*se defendendo*," "in self-defense" [6] *Argal* for "*ergo*," "therefore" [7] *Delver* Digger [8] *will he nill he* willy-nilly [9] *quest* inquest [10] *thou say'st* you have it right [11] *count'nance* privilege [12] *even-Christen* fellow Christian

is no ancient gentlemen but gard'ners, ditchers, and grave-makers.
They hold up Adam's profession.

OTHER   Was he a gentleman?

CLOWN   'A was the first that ever bore arms.

5   OTHER   Why, he had none.[13]

CLOWN   What, art a heathen? How dost thou understand the
Scripture? The Scripture says Adam digged. Could he dig without arms? I'll put another question to thee. If thou answerest me
not to the purpose, confess thyself—

10   OTHER   Go to.

CLOWN   What is he that builds stronger than either the mason, the
shipwright, or the carpenter?

OTHER   The gallows-maker, for that frame outlives a thousand
tenants.

15   CLOWN   I like thy wit well, in good faith. The gallows does well.
But how does it well? It does well to those that do ill. Now thou
dost ill to say the gallows is built stronger than the church. Argal,
the gallows may do well to thee. To't again, come.

OTHER   Who builds stronger than a mason, a shipwright, or a car-
20   penter?

CLOWN   Ay, tell me that, and unyoke.[14]

OTHER   Marry, now I can tell.

CLOWN   To't.

OTHER   Mass,[15] I cannot tell.

25   CLOWN   Cudgel thy brains no more about it, for your dull ass will
not mend his pace with beating. And when you are asked this
question next, say "a grave-maker." The houses he makes last till
doomsday. Go, get thee in, and fetch me a stoup[16] of liquor.

(*Exit* OTHER CLOWN)

30   (*Enter* HAMLET *and* HORATIO [*as* CLOWN *digs and sings*])

Song

In youth when I did love, did love,
  Methought it was very sweet
To contract—O—the time for—a—my behove,[17]
35   O, methought there—a—was nothing—a—meet.

HAMLET   Has this fellow no feeling of his business, that 'a sings at
grave-making?

---

[13] *had none* i.e. had no gentleman's coat of arms   [14] *unyoke* i.e. unharness
your powers of thought after a good day's work   [15] *Mass* by the Mass   [16] *stoup*
large mug   [17] *behove* behoof, benefit

HORATIO Custom hath made it in him a property[18] of easiness.[19]
HAMLET 'Tis e'en so. The hand of little employment hath the daintier sense.[20]
CLOWN

5 **Song**

But age with his stealing steps
Hath clawed me in his clutch,
And hath shipped me intil [21] the land,
As if I had never been such.

10 (*Throws up a skull*)

HAMLET That skull had a tongue in it, and could sing once. How the knave jowls[22] it to the ground, as if 'twere Cain's jawbone, that did the first murder! This might be the pate of a politician,[23] which this ass now o'erreaches;[24] one that would circumvent
15 God, might it not?
HORATIO It might, my lord.
HAMLET Or of a courtier, which could say "Good morrow, sweet lord! How dost thou, sweet lord?" This might be my Lord Such-a-one, that praised my Lord Such-a-one's horse when 'a meant to
20 beg it, might it not?
HORATIO Ay, my lord.
HAMLET Why, e'en so, and now my Lady Worm's, chapless,[25] and knocked about the mazzard [26] with a sexton's spade. Here's fine revolution, an we had the trick to see't. Did these bones cost no
25 more the breeding but to play at loggets[27] with 'em? Mine ache to think on't.
CLOWN

Song

A pickaxe and a spade, a spade,
30 For and [28] a shrouding sheet;
O, a pit of clay for to be made
For such a guest is meet.

(*Throws up another skull*)

---

[18] *property* peculiarity [19] *easiness* easy acceptability [20] *daintier sense* more delicate feeling (because the hand is less calloused) [21] *intil* into [22] *jowls* hurls [23] *politician* crafty schemer [24] *o'erreaches* gets the better of (with a play upon the literal meaning) [25] *chapless* lacking the lower chap or jaw [26] *mazzard* head [27] *loggets* small pieces of wood thrown in a game [28] *For and* and

HAMLET There's another. Why may not that be the skull of a lawyer? Where be his quiddities[29] now, his quillities,[30] his cases, his tenures,[31] and his tricks? Why does he suffer this mad knave now to knock him about the sconce[32] with a dirty shovel, and will not tell him of his action of battery? Hum! This fellow might be in's time a great buyer of land, with his statutes, his recognizances,[33] his fines,[34] his double vouchers,[35] his recoveries. Is this the fine[36] of his fines, and the recovery of his recoveries, to have his fine pate full of fine dirt? Will his vouchers vouch him no more of his purchases, and double ones too, than the length and breadth of a pair of indentures?[37] The very conveyances[38] of his lands will scarcely lie in this box, and must th' inheritor himself have no more, ha?

HORATIO Not a jot more, my lord.

HAMLET Is not parchment made of sheepskins?

HORATIO Ay, my lord, and of calveskins too.

HAMLET They are sheep and calves which seek out assurance in that. I will speak to this fellow. Whose grave 's this, sirrah?

CLOWN Mine, sir.

(*Sings*) O, a pit of clay for to be made
For such a guest is meet.

HAMLET I think it be thine indeed, for thou liest in't.

CLOWN You lie out on't, sir, and therefore 'tis not yours. For my part, I do not lie in't, yet it is mine.

HAMLET Thou dost lie in't, to be in't and say it is thine. 'Tis for the dead, not for the quick;[39] therefore thou liest.

CLOWN 'Tis a quick lie, sir; 'twill away again from me to you.

HAMLET What man dost thou dig it for?

CLOWN For no man, sir.

HAMLET What woman then?

CLOWN For none neither.

HAMLET Who is to be buried in't?

CLOWN One that was a woman, sir; but, rest her soul, she's dead.

HAMLET How absolute[40] the knave is! We must speak by the

---

[29] *quiddities* subtleties (from scholastic *"quidditas,"* meaning the distinctive nature of anything) [30] *quillities* nice distinctions [31] *tenures* holdings of property [32] *sconce* head [33] *statutes, recognizances* legal documents or bonds acknowledging debt [34] *fines, recoveries* modes of converting estate tail into fee simple [35] *vouchers* persons vouched or called on to warrant a title [36] *fine* end (introducing a word play involving four meanings of "fine") [37] *pair of indentures* deed or legal agreement in duplicate [38] *conveyances* deeds [39] *quick* living [40] *absolute* positive

card,[41] or equivocation[42] will undo us. By the Lord, Horatio, this three years I have taken note of it, the age is grown so picked [43] that the toe of the peasant comes so near the heel of the courtier he galls[44] his kibe.[45]—How long hast thou been a grave-maker?

5 CLOWN   Of all the days i' th' year, I came to't that day that our last king Hamlet overcame Fortinbras.

HAMLET   How long is that since?

CLOWN   Cannot you tell that? Every fool can tell that. It was the very day that young Hamlet was born—he that is mad, and sent

10 into England.

HAMLET   Ay, marry, why was he sent into England?

CLOWN   Why, because 'a was mad. 'A shall recover his wits there; or, if 'a do not, 'tis no great matter there.

HAMLET   Why?

15 CLOWN   'Twill not be seen in him there. There the men are as mad as he.

HAMLET   How came he mad?

CLOWN   Very strangely, they say.

HAMLET   How strangely?

20 CLOWN   Faith, e'en with losing his wits.

HAMLET   Upon what ground?

CLOWN   Why, here in Denmark. I have been sexton here, man and boy, thirty years.

HAMLET   How long will a man lie i' th' earth ere he rot?

25 CLOWN   Faith, if 'a be not rotten before 'a die (as we have many pocky[46] corses now-a-days that will scarce hold the laying in), 'a will last you some eight year or nine year. A tanner will last you nine year.

HAMLET   Why he more than another?

30 CLOWN   Why, sir, his hide is so tanned with his trade that 'a will keep out water a great while, and your water is a sore decayer of your whoreson dead body. Here's a skull now hath lien you i' th' earth three-and-twenty years.

HAMLET   Whose was it?

35 CLOWN   A whoreson mad fellow's it was. Whose do you think it was?

HAMLET   Nay, I know not.

---

[41] *by the card* by the card on which the points of the mariner's compass are marked, absolutely to the point   [42] *equivocation* ambiguity   [43] *picked* refined, spruce   [44] *galls* chafes   [45] *kibe* chilblain   [46] *pocky* rotten (literally, corrupted by pox, or syphilis)

CLOWN A pestilence on him for a mad rogue! 'A poured a flagon of Rhenish[47] on my head once. This same skull, sir, was—sir— Yorick's skull, the king's jester.

HAMLET This?

5 CLOWN E'en that.

HAMLET Let me see. (*Takes the skull.*) Alas, poor Yorick! I knew him, Horatio, a fellow of infinite jest, of most excellent fancy. He hath borne me on his back a thousand times. And now how abhorred in my imagination it is! My gorge rises at it. Here hung
10 those lips that I have kissed I know not how oft. Where be your gibes now? Your gambols, your songs, your flashes of merriment that were wont to set the table on a roar? Not one now to mock your own grinning? Quite chapfall'n? [48] Now get you to my lady's chamber, and tell her, let her paint an inch thick, to this favor[49]
15 she must come. Make her laugh at that. Prithee, Horatio, tell me one thing.

HORATIO What's that, my lord?

HAMLET Dost thou think Alexander looked o' this fashion i' th' earth?

20 HORATIO E'en so.

HAMLET And smelt so? Pah!

(*Puts down the skull*)

HORATIO E'en so, my lord.

HAMLET To what base uses we may return, Horatio! Why may
25 not imagination trace the noble dust of Alexander till 'a find it stopping a bunghole?

HORATIO 'Twere to consider too curiously,[50] to consider so.

HAMLET No, faith, not a jot, but to follow him thither with modesty[51] enough, and likelihood to lead it; as thus: Alexander died,
30 Alexander was buried, Alexander returneth to dust; the dust is earth; of earth we make loam; and why of that loam whereto he was converted might they not stop a beer barrel?
Imperious[52] Caesar, dead and turned to clay,
Might stop a hole to keep the wind away.
35 O, that that earth which kept the world in awe
Should patch a wall t' expel the winter's flaw! [53]

But soft, but soft awhile! Here comes the king—

(*Enter* KING, QUEEN, LAERTES, *and the* CORSE [*with* LORDS *attendant and a* DOCTOR OF DIVINITY *as* PRIEST])

The queen, the courtiers. Who is this they follow?
5   And with such maimèd rites? This doth betoken
The corse they follow did with desp'rate hand
Fordo[54] it[55] own life. 'Twas of some estate.[56]
Couch[57] we awhile, and mark.

(*Retires with* HORATIO)

10 LAERTES   What ceremony else?
    HAMLET   That is Laertes,
    A very noble youth. Mark.
    LAERTES   What ceremony else?
    DOCTOR   Her obsequies have been as far enlarged
15 As we have warranty. Her death was doubtful,
    And, but that great command o'ersways the order,
    She should in ground unsanctified have lodged
    Till the last trumpet. For charitable prayers,
    Shards,[58] flints, and pebbles should be thrown on her.
20 Yet here she is allowed her virgin crants,[59]
    Her maiden strewments,[60] and the bringing home[61]
    Of bell and burial.
    LAERTES   Must there no more be done?
    DOCTOR   No more be done.
25 We should profane the service of the dead
    To sing a requiem and such rest to her
    As to peace-parted souls.
    LAERTES   Lay her i' th' earth,
    And from her fair and unpolluted flesh
30 May violets spring! I tell thee, churlish priest,
    A minist'ring angel shall my sister be
    When thou liest howling.
    HAMLET   What, the fair Ophelia?
    QUEEN   Sweets to the sweet! Farewell.

35   (*Scatters flowers*)

    I hoped thou shouldst have been my Hamlet's wife.

---

54 *Fordo* destroy   55 *it* its   56 *estate* rank   57 *Couch* hide   58 *Shards* broken pieces of pottery   59 *crants* garland   60 *strewments* strewings of the grave with flowers   61 *bringing home* laying to rest

I thought thy bride-bed to have decked, sweet maid,
And not have strewed thy grave.
LAERTES   O, treble woe
Fall ten times treble on that cursèd head
5   Whose wicked deed thy most ingenious[62] sense
Deprived thee of! Hold off the earth awhile,
Till I have caught her once more in mine arms.

(Leaps in the grave)

Now pile your dust upon the quick and dead
10 Till of this flat a mountain you have made
T' o'ertop old Pelion[63] or the skyish head
Of blue Olympus.
HAMLET *(coming forward)*   What is he whose grief
Bears such an emphasis? whose phrase of sorrow
15 Conjures[64] the wand'ring stars,[65] and makes them stand
Like wonder-wounded hearers? This is I,
Hamlet the Dane.

(Leaps in after LAERTES*)*

LAERTES   The devil take thy soul!

20 *(Grapples with him)*

HAMLET   Thou pray'st not well.
I prithee take thy fingers from my throat,
For, though I am not splenitive[66] and rash,
Yet have I in me something dangerous,
25 Which let thy wisdom fear. Hold off thy hand.
KING   Pluck them asunder.
QUEEN   Hamlet, Hamlet!
ALL   Gentlemen!
HORATIO   Good my lord, be quiet.

30 *(*ATTENDANTS *part them, and they come out of the grave)*

HAMLET   Why, I will fight with him upon this theme
Until my eyelids will no longer wag.
QUEEN   O my son, what theme?

---

[62] *most ingenious* of quickest apprehension   [63] *Pelion* a mountain in Thessaly,
like Olympus and also Ossa (the allusion being to the war in which the Titans
fought the gods and attempted to heap Ossa and Olympus on Pelion, or
Pelion and Ossa on Olympus, in order to scale heaven)   [64] *Conjures* charms,
puts a spell upon   [65] *wand'ring stars* planets   [66] *splenitive* of fiery temper
(the spleen being considered the seat of anger)

HAMLET I loved Ophelia. Forty thousand brothers
Could not with all their quantity of love
Make up my sum. What wilt thou do for her?
KING O, he is mad, Laertes.
5 QUEEN For love of God, forbear him.
HAMLET 'Swounds, show me what thou't do.
Woo't [67] weep? woo't fight? woo't fast? woo't tear thyself?
Woo't drink up esill? [68] eat a crocodile?
I'll do't. Dost thou come here to whine?
10 To outface me with leaping in her grave?
Be buried quick[69] with her, and so will I.
And if thou prate of mountains, let them throw
Millions of acres on us, till our ground,
Singeing his pate against the burning zone,
15 Make Ossa like a wart! Nay, an thou'lt mouth,
I'll rant as well as thou.
QUEEN   This is mere[70] madness;
And thus a while the fit will work on him.
Anon, as patient as the female dove
20 When that her golden couplets[71] are disclosed,[72]
His silence will sit drooping.
HAMLET   Hear you, sir.
What is the reason that you use me thus?
I loved you ever. But it is no matter.
25 Let Hercules himself do what he may,
The cat will mew, and dog will have his day.
KING I pray thee, good Horatio, wait upon him.

(*Exit* HAMLET *and* HORATIO)

(*To* LAERTES)

30 Strengthen your patience in[73] our last night's speech.
We'll put the matter to the present push.[74]
Good Gertrude, set some watch over your son.—
This grave shall have a living monument.
An hour of quiet shortly shall we see;
35 Till then in patience our proceeding be.

(*Exeunt*)

---

[67] *Woo't* wilt (thou) [68] *esill* vinegar [69] *quick* alive [70] *mere* absolute
[71] *couplets* pair of fledglings [72] *disclosed* hatched [73] *in* by calling to mind
[74] *present push* immediate trial

Act V, Scene II

The hall of the castle

(*Enter* HAMLET *and* HORATIO)

HAMLET So much for this, sir; now shall you see the other.
5   You do remember all the circumstance?
HORATIO Remember it, my lord!
HAMLET Sir, in my heart there was a kind of fighting
That would not let me sleep. Methought I lay
Worse than the mutines[1] in the bilboes.[2] Rashly,
10 And praised be rashness for it—let us know,
Our indiscretion sometime serves us well
When our deep plots do pall,[3] and that should learn us
There's a divinity that shapes our ends,
Rough-hew[4] them how we will—
15 HORATIO   That is most certain.
HAMLET Up from my cabin,
My sea-gown scarfed about me, in the dark
Groped I to find out them, had my desire,
Fingered[5] their packet, and in fine[6] withdrew
20 To mine own room again, making so bold,
My fears forgetting manners, to unseal
Their grand commission; where I found, Horatio—
Ah, royal knavery!—an exact command,
Larded[7] with many several sorts of reasons,
25 Importing[8] Denmark's health, and England's too,
With, ho! such bugs[9] and goblins in my life,[10]
That on the supervise,[11] no leisure bated,[12]
No, not to stay the grinding of the axe,
My head should be struck off.
30 HORATIO   Is't possible?
HAMLET Here's the commission; read it at more leisure.
But wilt thou hear me how I did proceed?
HORATIO I beseech you.
HAMLET Being thus benetted round with villainies,
35 Or[13] I could make a prologue to my brains,
They had begun the play. I sat me down,

---

[1] *mutines* mutineers   [2] *bilboes* fetters   [3] *pall* fail   [4] *Rough-hew* shape roughly in trial form   [5] *Fingered* filched   [6] *in fine* finally   [7] *Larded* enriched   [8] *Importing* relating to   [9] *bugs* bugbears   [10] *in my life* to be encountered as dangers if I should be allowed to live   [11] *supervise* perusal   [12] *bated* deducted, allowed   [13] *Or* ere

Devised a new commission, wrote it fair.
I once did hold it, as our statists[14] do,
A baseness to write fair,[15] and labored much
How to forget that learning, but, sir, now
5   It did me yeoman's service.[16] Wilt thou know
Th' effect[17] of what I wrote?
HORATIO   Ay, good my lord.
HAMLET   An earnest conjuration from the king,
As England was his faithful tributary,
10   As love between them like the palm might flourish,
As peace should still her wheaten garland [18] wear
And stand a comma[19] 'tween their amities,
And many such-like as's of great charge,[20]
That on the view and knowing of these contents,
15   Without debatement further, more or less,
He should the bearers put to sudden death,
Not shriving time[21] allowed.
HORATIO   How was this sealed?
HAMLET   Why, even in that was heaven ordinant.[22]
20   I had my father's signet in my purse,
Which was the model [23] of that Danish seal,
Folded the writ up in the form of th' other,
Subscribed it, gave't th' impression,[24] placed it safely,
The changeling never known. Now, the next day
25   Was our sea-fight, and what to this was sequent[25]
Thou know'st already.
HORATIO   So Guildenstern and Rosencrantz go to't.
HAMLET   Why, man, they did make love to this employment.
They are not near my conscience; their defeat
30   Does by their own insinuation[26] grow.
'Tis dangerous when the baser nature comes
Between the pass[27] and fell [28] incensèd points
Of mighty opposites.

---

[14] *statists* statesmen   [15] *fair* with professional clarity (like a clerk or a scrivener, not like a gentleman)   [16] *yeoman's service* stout service such as yeomen
footsoldiers gave as archers   [17] *effect* purport   [18] *wheaten garland* adorn-
ment of fruitful agriculture   [19] *comma* connective (because it indicates con-
tinuity of thought in a sentence)   [20] *charge* burden (with a double meaning
to fit a play that makes *as's* into "asses"   [21] *shriving time* time for confession
and absolution   [22] *ordinant* controlling   [23] *model* counterpart   [24] *impression*
i.e. of the signet   [25] *sequent* subsequent   [26] *insinuation* intrusion   [27] *pass*
thrust   [28] *fell* fierce

HORATIO Why, what a king is this!

HAMLET Does it not, think thee, stand [29] me now upon—
He that hath killed my king, and whored my mother,
Popped in between th' election[30] and my hopes,

5 Thrown out his angle[31] for my proper[32] life,
And with such coz'nage[33]—is't not perfect conscience
To quit[34] him with this arm? And is't not to be damned
To let this canker[35] of our nature come
In further evil?

10 HORATIO It must be shortly known to him from England
What is the issue of the business there.

HAMLET It will be short; the interim is mine,
And a man's life 's no more than to say "one."
But I am very sorry, good Horatio,

15 That to Laertes I forgot myself,
For by the image of my cause I see
The portraiture of his. I'll court his favors.
But sure the bravery[36] of his grief did put me
Into a tow'ring passion.

20 HORATIO Peace, who comes here?

(*Enter* OSRIC, *a courtier*)

OSRIC Your lordship is right welcome back to Denmark.

HAMLET I humbly thank you, sir. (*aside to* HORATIO) Dost know
this waterfly?

25 HORATIO (*aside to* HAMLET) No, my good lord.

HAMLET (*aside to* HORATIO) Thy state is the more gracious, for
'tis a vice to know him. He hath much land, and fertile. Let a
beast be lord of beasts, and his crib shall stand at the king's
mess.[37] 'Tis a chough,[38] but, as I say, spacious in the possession

30 of dirt.

OSRIC Sweet lord, if your lordship were at leisure, I should impart
a thing to you from his majesty.

HAMLET I will receive it, sir, with all diligence of spirit. Put your
bonnet to his right use. 'Tis for the head.

35 OSRIC I thank your lordship, it is very hot.

HAMLET No, believe me, 'tis very cold; the wind is northerly.

OSRIC It is indifferent[39] cold, my lord, indeed.

---

[29] *stand* rest incumbent [30] *election* i.e. to the kingship (the Danish kingship
being elective) [31] *angle* fishing line [32] *proper* own [33] *coz'nage* cozenage,
trickery [34] *quit* repay [35] *canker* cancer, ulcer [36] *bravery* ostentatious display [37] *mess* table [38] *chough* jackdaw, chatterer [39] *indifferent* somewhat

HAMLET But yet methinks it is very sultry and hot for my complexion.[40]

OSRIC Exceedingly, my lord; it is very sultry, as 'twere—I cannot tell how. But, my lord, his majesty bade me signify to you that
5   'a has laid a great wager on your head. Sir, this is the matter—

HAMLET I beseech you remember.[41]

(HAMLET *moves him to put on his hat*)

OSRIC Nay, good my lord; for mine ease,[42] in good faith. Sir, here is newly come to court Laertes—believe me, an absolute gentle-
10   man, full of most excellent differences,[43] of very soft society[44] and great showing.[45] Indeed, to speak feelingly[46] of him, he is the card [47] or calendar[48] of gentry,[49] for you shall find in him the continent[50] of what part a gentleman would see.

HAMLET Sir, his definement[51] suffers no perdition[52] in you, though,
15   I know, to divide him inventorially would dozy[53] th' arithmetic of memory, and yet but yaw[54] neither[55] in respect of [56] his quick sail. But, in the verity of extolment, I take him to be a soul of great article,[57] and his infusion[58] of such dearth[59] and rareness as, to make true diction of him, his semblable[60] is his mirror, and
20   who else would trace[61] him, his umbrage,[62] nothing more.

OSRIC Your lordship speaks most infallibly of him.

HAMLET The concernancy,[63] sir? Why do we wrap the gentleman in our more rawer[64] breath?

OSRIC Sir?

25 HORATIO Is't not possible to understand in another tongue? You will to't,[65] sir, really.

HAMLET What imports the nomination[66] of this gentleman?

OSRIC Of Laertes?

---

[40] *complexion* temperament [41] *remember* i.e. remember you have done all that courtesy demands [42] *for mine ease* i.e. I keep my hat off just for comfort (a conventional polite phrase) [43] *differences* differentiating characteristics, special qualities [44] *soft society* gentle manners [45] *great showing* noble appearance [46] *feelingly* appropriately [47] *card* map [48] *calendar* guide [49] *gentry* gentlemanliness [50] *continent* all-containing embodiment (with an implication of geographical continent to go with *card*) [51] *definement* definition [52] *perdition* loss [53] *dozy* dizzy, stagger [54] *yaw* hold to a course unsteadily like a ship that steers wild [55] *neither* for all that [56] *in respect of* in comparison with [57] *article* scope, importance [58] *infusion* essence [59] *dearth* scarcity [60] *semblable* likeness (i.e. only true likeness) [61] *trace* follow [62] *umbrage* shadow [63] *concernancy* relevance [64] *rawer breath* cruder speech [65] *to't* i.e. get to an understanding [66] *nomination* mention

HORATIO (*aside to* HAMLET) His purse is empty already. All's golden words are spent.

HAMLET Of him, sir.

OSRIC I know you are not ignorant—

5 HAMLET I would you did, sir; yet, in faith, if you did, it would not much approve me.[67] Well, sir?

OSRIC You are not ignorant of what excellence Laertes is—

HAMLET I dare not confess that, lest I should compare[68] with him in excellence; but to know a man well were to know himself.

10 OSRIC I mean, sir, for his weapon; but in the imputation laid on him by them, in his meed [69] he's unfellowed.

HAMLET What's his weapon?

OSRIC Rapier and dagger.

HAMLET That's two of his weapons—but well.

15 OSRIC The king, sir, hath wagered with him six Barbary horses, against the which he has impawned,[70] as I take it, six French rapiers and poniards, with their assigns,[71] as girdle, hangers,[72] and so. Three of the carriages, in faith, are very dear to fancy,[73] very responsive[74] to the hilts, most delicate carriages, and of very

20 liberal conceit.[75]

HAMLET What call you the carriages?

HORATIO (*aside to* HAMLET) I knew you must be edified by the margent[76] ere you had done.

OSRIC The carriages, sir, are the hangers.

25 HAMLET The phrase would be more germane to the matter if we could carry a cannon by our sides. I would it might be hangers till then. But on! Six Barbary horses against six French swords, their assigns, and three liberal-conceited carriages—that's the French bet against the Danish. Why is this all impawned, as you

30 call it?

OSRIC The king, sir, hath laid, sir, that in a dozen passes between yourself and him he shall not exceed you three hits; he hath laid on twelve for nine, and it would come to immediate trial if your lordship would vouchsafe the answer.

35 HAMLET How if I answer no?

OSRIC I mean, my lord, the opposition of your person in trial.

---

[67] *approve me* be to my credit [68] *compare* compete [69] *meed* worth [70] *impawned* staked [71] *assigns* appurtenances [72] *hangers* straps by which the sword hangs from the belt [73] *dear to fancy* finely designed [74] *responsive* corresponding closely [75] *liberal conceit* tasteful design, refined conception [76] *margent* margin (i.e. explanatory notes there printed)

HAMLET Sir, I will walk here in the hall. If it please his majesty, it is the breathing time[77] of day with me. Let the foils be brought, the gentleman willing, and the king hold his purpose, I will win for him an[78] I can; if not, I will gain nothing but my shame and
5 the odd hits.

OSRIC Shall I redeliver you e'en so?

HAMLET To this effect, sir, after what flourish your nature will.

OSRIC I commend my duty to your lordship.

HAMLET Your, yours. (*Exit* OSRIC) He does well to commend it
10 himself; there are no tongues else for's turn.

HORATIO This lapwing[79] runs away with the shell on his head.

HAMLET 'A did comply,[80] sir, with his dug[81] before 'a sucked it. Thus has he, and many more of the same bevy[82] that I know the drossy[83] age dotes on, only got the tune of the time and, out of
15 an habit of encounter, a kind of yeasty collection, which carries them through and through the most fanned and winnowed [84] opinions; and do but blow them to their trial, the bubbles are out.

(*Enter a* LORD)

20 LORD My lord, his majesty commended him to you by young Osric, who brings back to him that you attend him in the hall. He sends to know if your pleasure hold to play with Laertes, or that you will take longer time.

HAMLET I am constant to my purposes; they follow the king's
25 pleasure. If his fitness speaks, mine is ready; now or whensoever, provided I be so able as now.

LORD The king and queen and all are coming down.

HAMLET In happy time.[85]

LORD The queen desires you to use some gentle entertainment[86] to
30 Laertes before you fall to play.

HAMLET She well instructs me.

(*Exit* LORD)

HORATIO You will lose this wager, my lord.

HAMLET I do not think so. Since he went into France I have been
35 in continual practice. I shall win at the odds. But thou wouldst not think how ill all's here about my heart. But it is no matter.

---

[77] *breathing time* exercise hour [78] *an* if [79] *lapwing* a bird reputed to be so precocious as to run as soon as hatched [80] *comply* observe formalities of courtesy [81] *dug* mother's nipple [82] *bevy* company [83] *drossy* frivolous [84] *fanned and winnowed* select and refined [85] *In happy time* I am happy (a polite response) [86] *entertainment* words of reception or greeting

HORATIO   Nay, good my lord—

HAMLET   It is but foolery, but it is such a kind of gaingiving[87] as would perhaps trouble a woman.

HORATIO   If your mind dislike anything, obey it. I will forestall
5   their repair hither and say you are not fit.

HAMLET   Not a whit, we defy augury. There is special providence in the fall of a sparrow. If it be now, 'tis not to come; if it be not to come, it will be now; if it be not now, yet it will come. The readiness is all.[88] Since no man of aught he leaves knows,
10   what is't to leave betimes? Let be.

A table prepared. Enter TRUMPETS, DRUMS, *and* OFFICERS *with cushions;* KING, QUEEN, OSRIC, *and all the* STATE, *with foils, daggers, and stoups of wine borne in; and* LAERTES

KING   Come, Hamlet, come, and take this hand from me.

15   (*The* KING *puts* LAERTES' *hand into* HAMLET'S)

HAMLET   Give me your pardon, sir. I have done you wrong,
But pardon't, as you are a gentleman.
This presence[89] knows, and you must needs have heard,
How I am punished with a sore distraction.
20   What I have done
That might your nature, honor, and exception[90]
Roughly awake, I here proclaim was madness.
Was't Hamlet wronged Laertes? Never Hamlet.
If Hamlet from himself be ta'en away,
25   And when he's not himself does wrong Laertes,
Then Hamlet does it not, Hamlet denies it.
Who does it then? His madness. If't be so,
Hamlet is of the faction[91] that is wronged;
His madness is poor Hamlet's enemy.
30   Sir, in this audience,
Let my disclaiming from a purposed evil
Free me so far in your most generous thoughts
That I have shot my arrow o'er the house
And hurt my brother.
35   LAERTES   I am satisfied in nature,[92]
Whose motive in this case should stir me most
To my revenge. But in my terms of honor[93]

---

[87] *gaingiving* misgiving   [88] *all* all that matters   [89] *presence* assembly   [90] *exception* disapproval   [91] *faction* body of persons taking a side in a contention   [92] *nature* natural feeling as a person   [93] *terms of honor* position as a man of honor

I stand aloof, and will no reconcilement
Till by some elder masters of known honor
I have a voice[94] and precedent of peace
To keep my name ungored.[95] But till that time
5   I do receive your offered love like love,
And will not wrong it.
   HAMLET   I embrace it freely,
And will this brother's wager frankly play.
Give us the foils. Come on.
10   LAERTES   Come, one for me.
   HAMLET   I'll be your foil,[96] Laertes. In mine ignorance
Your skill shall, like a star i' th' darkest night,
Stick fiery off [97] indeed.
   LAERTES   You mock me, sir.
15   HAMLET   No, by this hand.
   KING   Give them the foils, young Osric. Cousin Hamlet,
You know the wager?
   HAMLET   Very well, my lord.
Your grace has laid the odds o' the' weaker side.
20   KING   I do not fear it, I have seen you both;
But since he is bettered, we have therefore odds.
   LAERTES   This is too heavy; let me see another.
   HAMLET   This likes me well. These foils have all a length?

Prepare to play

25   OSRIC   Ay, my good lord.
   KING   Set me the stoups of wine upon that table.
If Hamlet give the first or second hit,
Or quit[98] in answer of the third exchange,
Let all the battlements their ordnance fire.
30   The king shall drink to Hamlet's better breath,
And in the cup an union[99] shall he throw
Richer than that which four successive kings
In Denmark's crown have worn. Give me the cups,
And let the kettle[100] to the trumpet speak,
35   The trumpet to the cannoneer without,
The cannons to the heavens, the heaven to earth,

---

[94] *voice* authoritative statement   [95] *ungored* uninjured   [96] *foil* setting that displays a jewel advantageously (with a play upon the meaning "weapon") [97] *Stick fiery off* show in brilliant relief   [98] *quit* repay by a hit   [99] *union* pearl   [100] *kettle* kettledrum

"Now the king drinks to Hamlet." Come, begin.

Trumpets the while

And you, the judges, bear a wary eye.
HAMLET   Come on, sir.
5   LAERTES   Come, my lord.

They play

HAMLET   One.
LAERTES   No.
HAMLET   Judgment?
10   OSRIC   A hit, a very palpable hit.

DRUM, TRUMPETS, *and* SHOT. *Flourish; a piece goes off*

LAERTES   Well, again.
KING   Stay, give me drink. Hamlet, this pearl is thine.
Here's to thy health. Give him the cup.
15   HAMLET   I'll play this bout first; set it by awhile.
Come. (*They play*) Another hit. What say you?
LAERTES   A touch, a touch; I do confess't.
KING   Our son shall win.
QUEEN   He's fat,[101] and scant of breath.
20   Here, Hamlet, take my napkin,[102] rub thy brows.
The queen carouses[103] to thy fortune, Hamlet.
HAMLET   Good madam!
KING   Gertrude, do not drink.
QUEEN   I will, my lord; I pray you pardon me.

25   *Drinks*

KING (*aside*)   It is the poisoned cup; it is too late.
HAMLET   I dare not drink yet, madam—by and by.
QUEEN   Come, let me wipe thy face.
LAERTES   My lord, I'll hit him now.
30   KING   I do not think't.
LAERTES (*aside*)   And yet it is almost against my conscience.
HAMLET   Come for the third, Laertes. You but dally.
I pray you pass with your best violence;
I am afeard you make a wanton[104] of me.

---

[101] *fat* not physically fit, out of training   [102] *napkin* handkerchief   [103] *ca-rouses* drinks a toast   [104] *wanton* pampered child

LAERTES   Say you so? Come on.

They play

OSRIC   Nothing neither way.
LAERTES   Have at you now!

5   *In scuffling they change rapiers, and both are wounded with the poisoned weapon*

KING   Part them. They are incensed.
HAMLET   Nay, come—again!

The QUEEN falls

10   OSRIC   Look to the queen there, ho!
HORATIO   They bleed on both sides. How is it, my lord?
OSRIC   How is't, Laertes?
LAERTES   Why, as a woodcock[105] to mine own springe,[106] Osric.
I am justly killed with mine own treachery.
15   HAMLET   How does the queen?
KING   She sounds[107] to see them bleed.
QUEEN   No, no, the drink, the drink! O my dear Hamlet!
The drink, the drink! I am poisoned.

Dies

20   HAMLET   O villainy! Ho! let the door be locked.
Treachery! Seek it out.

LAERTES falls

LAERTES   It is here, Hamlet. Hamlet, thou art slain;
No med'cine in the world can do thee good.
25   In thee there is not half an hour's life.
The treacherous instrument is in thy hand,
Unbated [108] and envenomed. The foul practice[109]
Hath turned itself on me. Lo, here I lie,
Never to rise again. Thy mother 's poisoned.
30   I can no more. The king, the king 's to blame.
HAMLET   The point envenomed too?
Then venom, to thy work.

Hurts the KING

ALL   Treason! treason!

---

105 *woodcock* a bird reputed to be stupid and easily trapped   106 *springe* trap
107 *sounds* swoons   108 *Unbated* unblunted   109 *practice* stratagem

KING   O, yet defend me, friends. I am but hurt.

HAMLET   Here, thou incestuous, murd'rous, damnèd Dane,
Drink off this potion. Is thy union here?
Follow my mother.

5   KING *dies*

LAERTES   He is justly served.
It is a poison tempered [110] by himself.
Exchange forgiveness with me, noble Hamlet.
Mine and my father's death come not upon thee,

10   Nor thine on me!

Dies

HAMLET   Heaven make thee free of it! I follow thee.
I am dead, Horatio. Wretched queen, adieu!
You that look pale and tremble at this chance,

15   That are but mutes[111] or audience to this act,
Had I but time—as this fell sergeant,[112] Death,
Is strict in his arrest—O, I could tell you—
But let it be. Horatio, I am dead;
Thou livest; report me and my cause aright   .

20   To the unsatisfied.

HORATIO   Never believe it.
I am more an antique Roman than a Dane.
Here's yet some liquor left.

HAMLET   As th' art a man,

25   Give me the cup. Let go. By heaven, I'll ha't!
O God, Horatio, what a wounded name,
Things standing thus unknown, shall live behind me!
If thou didst ever hold me in thy heart,
Absent thee from felicity awhile,

30   And in this harsh world draw thy breath in pain,
To tell my story.

A march afar off

               What warlike noise is this?

OSRIC   Young Fortinbras, with conquest come from Poland,

35   To the ambassadors of England gives
This warlike volley.

HAMLET   O, I die, Horatio!

---

[110] *tempered* mixed   [111] *mutes* actors in a play who speak no lines   [112] *sergeant* sheriff's officer

The potent poison quite o'ercrows[113] my spirit.
I cannot live to hear the news from England,
But I do prophesy th' election[114] lights
On Fortinbras. He has my dying voice.[115]
5   So tell him, with th' occurrents,[116] more and less,
Which have solicited [117]—the rest is silence.

Dies

HORATIO   Now cracks a noble heart. Good night, sweet prince,
And flights of angels sing thee to thy rest!

10   *March within*

Why does the drum come hither?

(*Enter* FORTINBRAS, *with the* AMBASSADORS [*and with his train of* DRUM,
COLORS, *and* ATTENDANTS])

FORTINBRAS   Where is this sight?
15   HORATIO   What is it you would see?
If aught of woe or wonder, cease your search.
FORTINBRAS   This quarry[118] cries on[119] havoc.[120] O proud Death,
What feast is toward [121] in thine eternal cell
That thou so many princes at a shot
20   So bloodily hast struck?
AMBASSADOR   The sight is dismal;
And our affairs from England come too late.
The ears are senseless that should give us hearing
To tell him his commandment is fulfilled,
25   That Rosencrantz and Guildenstern are dead.
Where should we have our thanks?
HORATIO   Not from his mouth,
Had it th' ability of life to thank you.
He never gave commandment for their death.
30   But since, so jump[122] upon this bloody question,
You from the Polack wars, and you from England,
Are here arrived, give order that these bodies
High on a stage[123] be placèd to the view,

---

113 *o'ercrows* triumphs over (like a victor in a cockfight)   114 *election* i.e. to
the throne 115 *voice* vote 116 *occurrents* occurrences 117 *solicited* incited,
provoked 118 *quarry* pile of dead (literally, of dead deer gathered after the
hunt) 119 *cries on* proclaims loudly 120 *havoc* indiscriminate killing and
destruction such as would follow the order "havoc," or "pillage," given to
an army 121 *toward* forthcoming 122 *jump* precisely 123 *stage* platform

And let me speak to th' yet unknowing world
How these things came about. So shall you hear
Of carnal, bloody, and unnatural acts,
Of accidental judgments,[124] casual [125] slaughters,
5   Of deaths put on[126] by cunning and forced cause,
And, in this upshot, purposes mistook
Fall'n on th' inventors' heads. All this can I
Truly deliver.
    FORTINBRAS   Let us haste to hear it,
10 And call the noblest to the audience.
For me, with sorrow I embrace my fortune.
I have some rights of memory[127] in this kingdom,
Which now to claim my vantage[128] doth invite me.
    HORATIO   Of that I shall have also cause to speak,
15 And from his mouth whose voice will draw on more.[129]
But let this same be presently[130] performed,
Even while men's minds are wild, lest more mischance
On[131] plots and errors happen.
    FORTINBRAS   Let four captains
20 Bear Hamlet like a soldier to the stage,
For he was likely, had he been put on,[132]
To have proved most royal; and for his passage[133]
The soldiers' music and the rites of war
Speak loudly for him.
25 Take up the bodies. Such a sight as this
Becomes the field, but here shows much amiss.
Go, bid the soldiers shoot.

(*Exeunt* [*marching; after the which a peal of ordinance are shot off*])

---

[124] *judgments* retributions   [125] *casual* not humanly planned (reinforcing *accidental*)   [126] *put on* instigated   [127] *of memory* traditional and kept in mind   [128] *vantage* advantageous opportunity   [129] *more* i.e. more voices, or votes, for the kingship   [130] *presently* immediately   [131] *On* on the basis of   [132] *put on* set to perform in office   [133] *passage* death

✒ THE MISANTHROPE
(1666)

MOLIÈRE (1622–1673)

Jean Baptiste Poquelin, better known as Molière, lived right in the middle of the century which saw the greatest achievements of the French neo-classic (new classic) revival. Molière, together with Pierre Corneille (1606–1684) and Jean Racine (1639–1699), created the greatest of the tragedies and comedies written during the French Renaissance. Although the modern appeal of the tragedies has never been strong outside France, the comedies of Molière seem to go on and on, as fresh and amusing as the day they were written. We have been fortunate in this country to have had the talents of Richard Wilbur as translator, for his rhymed couplet versions have retained the lilt of the original poetry and the spontaneous freshness and spirit which Molière injected into his very funny plays.

The structure, form, and style of the classics were regarded by the Renaissance as works of perfection, the imitation of which was obligatory if one were to create a "proper" tragedy. This included the application of the three "Unities," broadly adapted from Aristotle's *Poetics* as absolutes of dramatic law. The Unity of Time limited a play to one day; the Unity of Place, something Aristotle never mentions, held it to a single spot; the Unity of Action permitted a single story only, with no sub-plots of any kind. Subject matter was restricted to myths and legends, including the Bible. The overwhelming majority of French and Italian Renaissance tragedies, except for a few like Corneille's *The Cid* (1637) and Racine's *Phaedra* (1677), which present some effective and memorable dramatic characters, were insufferably boring and now rest in history's musty storerooms. Not so Molière.

The comedies of Molière may not at first seem "classic" in the sense of the tragedies, but as a comic dramatist he is in the best tradition of the "new" Greek comedies of Menander (343–291 B.C.), who gave the world the basic formula for the situation comedy as we know it today. The Renaissance became acquainted with the form through imitations of the Roman Plautus (254?–184? B.C.) and Terence (c. 190–159 B.C.). The endless struggles of young lovers to overcome the stupidities of ancient parents, particularly fathers, or husbands or guardians, the farcical intrigues, plots and counterplots and the impossibly happy endings are "classic" comedy situations. Molière knew how to handle them with great skill.

Molière, a highly versatile man of the theatre as actor, producer, and dramatist, was continually running into trouble with the church and the secular authorities for his frequently stinging satirical attacks against the "establishment" of seventeenth century France. His *Tartuffe,* concerning religious hypocrisy, was banned until King Louis XIV ordered it for presentation at court. But in *The Misanthrope* Molière is on comparatively safe ground as he presents the dilettantism and affected meaninglessness of the lives of those who occupy the higher levels of an indolent aristocratic society, dependent for diversion upon scandal, petty lawsuits, and seductive intrigues to revive flagging interests. *The Misanthrope* is fine high comedy, full of wit and sophisticated banter in its portrayal of a glittering human society without humanity, one which the straightforward Alceste insists on treating as it deserves. Opposed to him in their not altogether ineffective defense of their way of life are the more practical Philinte and the beautiful, talented, and intellectual Célimène. She is the personification of the kind of brittle brilliance the society of Molière's day could foster, living on her charm and her wit, aware of the artificial hothouse world in which she functions, but preferring it to the arid austerities of Alceste's desert island. *The Misanthrope* is a sparkling comedy of manners which can be performed today with considerable success.

The Misanthrope

MOLIÈRE

An English version by Richard Wilbur

CHARACTERS

ALCESTE, *in love with Célimène*
PHILINTE, *Alceste's friend*
ORONTE, *in love with Célimène*
CÉLIMÈNE, *Alceste's beloved*
ÉLIANTE, *Célimène's cousin*
ARSINOÉ, *a friend of Célimène's*
ACASTE ⎫
CLITANDRE ⎭ *Marquesses*
BASQUE, *Célimène's servant*
A GUARD *of the Marshalsea*
DUBOIS, *Alceste's valet*

The Scene throughout is in CÉLIMÈNE'S *house at Paris*

ACT I

Scene I (PHILINTE, ALCESTE)

PHILINTE   Now, what's got into you?
ALCESTE (*seated*)   Kindly leave me alone.
5   PHILINTE   Come, come, what is it? This lugubrious tone . . .
ALCESTE   Leave me, I said; you spoil my solitude.
PHILINTE   Oh, listen to me, now, and don't be rude.
ALCESTE   I choose to be rude, Sir, and to be hard of hearing.
PHILINTE   These ugly moods of yours are not endearing;
10   Friends though we are, I really must insist . . .
ALCESTE (*abruptly rising*)   Friends? Friends, you say? Well, cross
me off your list.
I've been your friend till now, as you well know;
But after what I saw a moment ago
15   I tell you flatly that our ways must part.
I wish no place in a dishonest heart.

PHILINTE   Why, what have I done, Alceste? Is this quite just?
ALCESTE   My God, you ought to die of self-disgust.
   I call your conduct inexcusable, Sir,
   And every man of honor will concur.
5   I see you almost hug a man to death,
   Exclaim for joy until you're out of breath,
   And supplement these loving demonstrations
   With endless offers, vows, and protestations;
   Then when I ask you "Who was that?" I find
10   That you can barely bring his name to mind!
   Once the man's back is turned, you cease to love him,
   And speak with absolute indifference of him!
   By God, I say it's base and scandalous
   To falsify the heart's affections thus;
15   If I caught myself behaving in such a way,
   I'd hang myself for shame, without delay.
PHILINTE   It hardly seems a hanging matter to me;
   I hope that you will take it graciously
   If I extend myself a slight reprieve,
20   And live a little longer, by your leave.
ALCESTE   How dare you joke about a crime so grave?
PHILINTE   What crime? How else are people to behave?
ALCESTE   I'd have them be sincere, and never part
   With any word that isn't from the heart.
25 PHILINTE   When someone greets us with a show of pleasure,
   It's but polite to give him equal measure,
   Return his love the best that we know how,
   And trade him offer for offer, vow for vow.
ALCESTE   No, no, this formula you'd have me follow,
30   However fashionable, is false and hollow,
   And I despise the frenzied operations
   Of all these barterers of protestations,
   These lavishers of meaningless embraces,
   These utterers of obliging commonplaces,
35   Who court and flatter everyone on earth
   And praise the fool no less than the man of worth.
   Should you rejoice that someone fondles you,
   Offers his love and service, swears to be true,
   And fills your ears with praises of your name,
40   When to the first damned fop he'll say the same?
   No, no: no self-respecting heart would dream
   Of prizing so promiscuous an esteem;
   However high the praise, there's nothing worse
   Than sharing honors with the universe.

Esteem is founded on comparison:
To honor all men is to honor none.
Since you embrace this indiscriminate vice,
Your friendship comes at far too cheap a price;
5   I spurn the easy tribute of a heart
Which will not set the worthy man apart:
I choose, Sir, to be chosen; and in fine,
The friend of mankind is no friend of mine.
    PHILINTE   But in polite society, custom decrees
10   That we show certain outward courtesies. . . .
    ALCESTE   Ah, no! we should condemn with all our force
Such false and artificial intercourse.
Let man behave like men; let them display
Their inmost hearts in everything they say;
15   Let the heart speak, and let our sentiments
Not mask themselves in silly compliments.
    PHILINTE   In certain cases it would be uncouth
And most absurd to speak the naked truth;
With all respect for your exalted notions,
20   It's often best to veil one's true emotions.
Wouldn't the social fabric come undone
If we were wholly frank with everyone?
Suppose you met with someone you couldn't bear;
Would you inform him of it then and there?
25   ALCESTE   Yes.
    PHILINTE   Then you'd tell old Emilie it's pathetic
The way she daubs her features with cosmetic
And plays the gay coquette at sixty-four?
    ALCESTE   I would.
30   PHILINTE   And you'd call Dorilas a bore,
And tell him every ear at court is lame
From hearing him brag about his noble name?
    ALCESTE   Precisely.
    PHILINTE   Ah, you're joking.
35   ALCESTE   *Au contraire:*
In this regard there's none I'd choose to spare.
All are corrupt; there's nothing to be seen
In court or town but aggravates my spleen.
I fall into deep gloom and melancholy
40   When I survey the scene of human folly,
Finding on every hand base flattery,
Injustice, fraud, self-interest, treachery. . . .
Ah, it's too much; mankind has grown so base,
I mean to break with the whole human race.

PHILINTE   This philosophic rage is a bit extreme;
 You've no idea how comical you seem;
 Indeed, we're like those brothers in the play
 Called *School for Husbands,* one of whom was prey . . .
5 ALCESTE   Enough, now! None of your stupid similes.
 PHILINTE   Then let's have no more tirades, if you please.
 The world won't change, whatever you say or do;
 And since plain speaking means so much to you,
 I'll tell you plainly that by being frank
10 You've earned the reputation of a crank,
 And that you're thought ridiculous when you rage
 And rant against the manners of the age.
 ALCESTE   So much the better; just what I wish to hear.
 No news could be more grateful to my ear.
15 All men are so detestable in my eyes,
 I should be sorry if they thought me wise.
 PHILINTE   Your hatred's very sweeping, is it not?
 ALCESTE   Quite right: I hate the whole degraded lot.
 PHILINTE   Must all poor human creatures be embraced,
20 Without distinction, by your vast distaste?
 Even in these bad times, there are surely a few . . .
 ALCESTE   No, I include all men in one dim view:
 Some men I hate for being rogues: the others
 I hate because they treat the rogues like brothers,
25 And, lacking a virtuous scorn for what is vile,
 Receive the villain with a complaisant smile.
 Notice how tolerant people choose to be
 Toward that bold rascal who's at law with me.
 His social polish can't conceal his nature;
30 One sees at once that he's a treacherous creature;
 No one could possibly be taken in
 By those soft speeches and that sugary grin.
 The whole world knows the shady means by which
 The low-brow's grown so powerful and rich,
35 And risen to a rank so bright and high
 That virtue can but blush, and merit sigh.
 Whenever his name comes up in conversation,
 None will defend his wretched reputation;
 Call him knave, liar, scoundrel, and all the rest,
40 Each head will nod, and no one will protest.
 And yet his smirk is seen in every house,
 He's greeted everywhere with smiles and bows,
 And when there's any honor that can be got

By pulling strings, he'll get it, like as not.
My God! It chills my heart to see the ways
Men come to terms with evil nowadays;
Sometimes, I swear, I'm moved to flee and find
5   Some desert land unfouled by humankind.
PHILINTE   Come, let's forget the follies of the times
And pardon mankind for its petty crimes;
Let's have an end of rantings and of railings,
And show some leniency toward human failings.
10   This world requires a pliant rectitude;
Too stern a virtue makes one stiff and rude;
Good sense views all extremes with detestation,
And bids us to be noble in moderation.
The rigid virtues of the ancient days
15   Are not for us; they jar with all our ways
And ask of us too lofty a perfection.
Wise men accept their times without objection,
And there's no greater folly, if you ask me,
Than trying to reform society.
20   Like you, I see each day a hundred and one
Unhandsome deeds that might be better done,
But still, for all the faults that meet my view,
I'm never known to storm and rave like you.
I take men as they are, or let them be,
25   And teach my soul to bear their frailty;
And whether in court or town, whatever the scene,
My phlegm's as philosophic as your spleen.
ALCESTE   This phlegm which you so eloquently commend,
Does nothing ever rile it up, my friend?
30   Suppose some man you trust should treacherously
Conspire to rob you of your property,
And do his best to wreck your reputation?
Wouldn't you feel a certain indignation?
PHILINTE   Why, no. These faults of which you so complain
35   Are part of human nature, I maintain,
And it's no more a matter for disgust
That men are knavish, selfish and unjust,
That that the vulture dines upon the dead,
And wolves are furious, and apes ill-bred.
40   ALCESTE   Shall I see myself betrayed, robbed, torn to bits,
And not . . . Oh, let's be still and rest our wits.
Enough of reasoning, now. I've had my fill.
PHILINTE   Indeed, you would do well, Sir, to be still.

Rage less at your opponent, and give some thought
To how you'll win this lawsuit that he's brought.
PHILINTE　I assure you I'll do nothing of the sort.
PHILINTE　Then who will plead your case before the court?
5　ALCESTE　Reason and right and justice will plead for me.
PHILINTE　Oh, Lord. What judges do you plan to see?
ALCESTE　Why, none. The justice of my cause is clear.
PHILINTE　Of course, man; but there's politics to fear....
ALCESTE　No, I refuse to lift a hand. That's flat.
10　I'm either right, or wrong.
PHILINTE　　　　　　　Don't count on that.
ALCESTE　No, I'll do nothing.
PHILINTE　　　　　　　Your enemy's influence
Is great, you know ...
15　ALCESTE　　　　　That makes no difference.
PHILINTE　It will; you'll see.
ALCESTE　　　　　　　Must honor bow to guile?
If so, I shall be proud to lose the trial.
PHILINTE　Oh, really ...
20　ALCESTE　　　　　　I'll discover by this case
Whether or not men are sufficiently base
And impudent and villainous and perverse
To do me wrong before the universe.
PHILINTE　What a man!
25　ALCESTE　　　　　Oh, I could wish, whatever the cost,
Just for the beauty of it, that my trial were lost.
PHILINTE　If people heard you talking so, Alceste,
They'd split their sides. Your name would be a jest.
ALCESTE　So much the worse for jesters.
30　PHILINTE　　　　　　　May I enquire
Whether this rectitude you so admire,
And these hard virtues you're enamored of
Are qualities of the lady whom you love?
It much surprises me that you, who seem
35　To view mankind with furious disesteem,
Have yet found something to enchant your eyes
Amidst a species which you so despise.
And what is more amazing, I'm afraid,
Is the most curious choice your heart has made.
40　The honest Éliante is fond of you,
Arsinoé, the prude, admires you too;
And yet your spirit's been perversely led
To choose the flighty Célimène instead,

Whose brittle malice and coquettish ways
So typify the manners of our days.
How is it that the traits you most abhor
Are bearable in this lady you adore?
5   Are you so blind with love that you can't find them?
Or do you contrive, in her case, not to mind them?
ALCESTE   My love for that young widow's not the kind
That can't perceive defects; no, I'm not blind.
I see her faults, despite my ardent love,
10   And all I see I fervently reprove.
And yet I'm weak; for all her falsity,
That woman knows the art of pleasing me,
And though I never cease complaining of her,
I swear I cannot manage not to love her.
15   Her charm outweighs her faults; I can but aim
To cleanse her spirit in my love's pure flame.
PHILINTE   That's no small task; I wish you all success.
You think then that she loves you?
ALCESTE   Heavens, yes!
20   I wouldn't love her did she not love me.
PHILINTE   Well, if her taste for you is plain to see,
Why do these rivals cause you such despair?
ALCESTE   True love, Sir, is possessive, and cannot bear
To share with all the world. I'm here today
25   To tell her she must send that mob away.
PHILINTE   If I were you, and had your choice to make,
Éliante, her cousin, would be the one I'd take;
That honest heart, which cares for you alone,
Would harmonize far better with your own.
30   ALCESTE   True, true: each day my reason tells me so;
But reason doesn't rule in love, you know.
PHILINTE   I fear some bitter sorrow is in store;
This love . . .

Scene II (ORONTE, ALCESTE, PHILINTE)

35   ORONTE (*to* ALCESTE)   The servants told me at the door
That Éliante and Célimène were out,
But when I heard, dear Sir, that you were about,
I came to say, without exaggeration,
That I hold you in the vastest admiration,
40   And that it's always been my dearest desire
To be the friend of one I so admire.
I hope to see my love of merit requited,

And you and I in friendship's bond united.
I'm sure you won't refuse—if I may be frank—
A friend of my devotedness—and rank.

5   *During this speech of* ORONTE'S, ALCESTE *is abstracted, and seems unaware that he is being spoken to. He only breaks off his reverie when* ORONTE *says:*

It was for you, if you please, that my words were intended.
ALCESTE   For me, Sir?
ORONTE   Yes, for you. You're not offended?
10   ALCESTE   By no means. But this much surprises me. . . .
    The honor comes most unexpectedly. . . .
ORONTE   My high regard should not astonish you;
    The whole world feels the same. It is your due.
ALCESTE   Sir . . .
15   ORONTE   Why, in all the State there isn't one
    Can match your merits; they shine, Sir, like the sun.
ALCESTE   Sir . . .
ORONTE   You are higher in my estimation
    Than all that's most illustrious in the nation.
20   ALCESTE   Sir . . .
ORONTE   If I lie, may heaven strike me dead!
    To show you that I mean what I have said,
    Permit me, Sir, to embrace you most sincerely,
    And swear that I will prize our friendship dearly.
25   Give me your hand. And now, Sir, if you choose,
    We'll make our vows.
ALCESTE   Sir . . .
ORONTE   What! You refuse?
ALCESTE   Sir, it's a very great honor you extend:
30   But friendship is a sacred thing, my friend;
    It would be profanation to bestow
    The name of friend on one you hardly know.
    All parts are better played when well-rehearsed;
    Let's put off friendship, and get acquainted first.
35   We may discover it would be unwise
    To try to make our natures harmonize.
ORONTE   By heaven! You're sagacious to the core;
    This speech has made me admire you even more.
    Let time, then, bring us closer day by day;
40   Meanwhile, I shall be yours in every way.
    If, for example, there should be anything
    You wish at court, I'll mention it to the King.

I have his ear, of course; it's quite well known
That I am much in favor with the throne.
In short, I am your servant. And now, dear friend,
Since you have such fine judgment, I intend
5   To please you, if I can, with a small sonnet
I wrote not long ago. Please comment on it,
And tell me whether I ought to publish it.
ALCESTE   You must excuse me, Sir; I'm hardly fit
To judge such matters.
10 ORONTE   Why not?
ALCESTE   I am, I fear,
Inclined to be unfashionably sincere.
ORONTE   Just what I ask; I'd take no satisfaction
In anything but your sincere reaction.
15 I beg you not to dream of being kind.
ALCESTE   Since you desire it, Sir, I'll speak my mind.
ORONTE   *Sonnet.* It's a sonnet.... *Hope* ... The poem's addressed
To a lady who wakened hopes within my breast.
Hope ... this is not the pompous sort of thing,
20 Just modest little verses, with a tender ring.
ALCESTE   Well, we shall see.
ORONTE   *Hope* ... I'm anxious to hear
Whether the style seems properly smooth and clear,
And whether the choice of words is good or bad.
25 ALCESTE   We'll see, we'll see.
ORONTE   Perhaps I ought to add
That it took me only a quarter-hour to write it.
ALCESTE   The time's irrelevant, Sir: kindly recite it.
ORONTE (*reading*)
30   *Hope comforts us awhile, 'tis true,*
           Lulling our cares with careless laughter,
           And yet such joy is full of rue,
           My Phyllis, if nothing follows after.
PHILINTE   I'm charmed by this already; the style's delightful.
35 ALCESTE (*sotto voce, to* PHILINTE)   How can you say that?
Why, the thing is frightful.
ORONTE   *Your fair face smiled on me awhile,*
           But was it kindness so to enchant me?
           'Twould have been fairer not to smile,
40   *If hope was all you meant to grant me.*
PHILINTE   What a clever thought! How handsomely you phrase it!
ALCESTE (*sotto voce, to* PHILINTE)   You know the thing is trash.
How dare you praise it?

ORONTE   *If it's to be my passion's fate*
Thus everlastingly to wait,
Then death will come to set me free:
For death is fairer than the fair;
5   *Phyllis, to hope is to despair*
When one must hope eternally.

PHILINTE   The close is exquisite—full of feeling and grace.

ALCESTE (*sotto voce, aside*)   Oh, blast the close; you'd better close your face
10   Before you send your lying soul to hell.

PHILINTE   I can't remember a poem I've liked so well.

ALCESTE (*sotto voce, aside*)   Good Lord!

ORONTE (*to* PHILINTE)   I fear you're flattering me a bit.

PHILINTE   Oh, no!

15   ALCESTE (*sotto voce, aside*)   What else d'you call it, you hypocrite?

ORONTE (*to* ALCESTE)   But you, Sir, keep your promise now: don't shrink
From telling me sincerely what you think.

ALCESTE   Sir, these are delicate matters; we all desire
20   To be told that we've the true poetic fire.
But once, to one whose name I shall not mention,
I said, regarding some verse of his invention,
That gentlemen should rigorously control
That itch to write which often afflicts the soul;
25   That one should curb the heady inclination
To publicize one's little avocation;
And that in showing off one's works of art
One often plays a very clownish part.

ORONTE   Are you suggesting in a devious way
30   That I ought not . . .

ALCESTE   Oh, that I do not say.
Further, I told him that no fault is worse
Than that of writing frigid, lifeless verse,
And that the merest whisper of such a shame
35   Suffices to destroy a man's good name.

ORONTE   D'you mean to say my sonnet's dull and trite?

ALCESTE   I don't say that. But I went on to cite
Numerous cases of once-respected men
Who came to grief by taking up the pen.

40   ORONTE   And am I like them? Do I write so poorly?

ALCESTE   I don't say that. But I told this person, "Surely
You're under no necessity to compose;
Why you should wish to publish, heaven knows.

There's no excuse for printing tedious rot
Unless one writes for bread, as you do not.
Resist temptation, then, I beg of you;
Conceal your pastimes from the public view;
5 And don't give up, on any provocation,
Your present high and courtly reputation,
To purchase at a greedy printer's shop
The name of silly author and scribbling fop."
These were the points I tried to make him see.
10 ORONTE   I sense that they are also aimed at me;
But now—about my sonnet—I'd like to be told . . .
ALCESTE   Frankly, that sonnet should be pigeonholed.
You've chosen the worst models to imitate.
The style's unnatural. Let me illustrate:
15 For example, *Your fair face smiled on me awhile,*
Followed by, *'Twould have been fairer not to smile!*
Or this: *such joy is full of rue;*
Or this: *For death is fairer than the fair;*
Or, *Phyllis, to hope is to despair*
20 *When one must hope eternally!*
This artificial style, that's all the fashion,
Has neither taste, nor honesty, nor passion;
It's nothing but a sort of wordy play,
And nature never spoke in such a way.
25 What, in this shallow age, is not debased?
Our fathers, though less refined, had better taste;
I'd barter all that men admire today
For one old love song I shall try to say:
If the King had given me for my own
30 *Paris, his citadel,*
And I for that must leave alone
Her whom I love so well,
I'd say then to the Crown,
Take back your glittering town;
35 *My darling is more fair, I swear,*
My darling is more fair.
The rhyme's not rich, the style is rough and old,
But don't you see that it's the purest gold
Beside the tinsel nonsense now preferred,
40 And that there's passion in its every word?
If the King had given me for my own
Paris, his citadel,
And I for that must leave alone

　　　　　Her whom I love so well,
　　　　　I'd say then to the Crown,
　　　　　Take back your glittering town;
　　　　　My darling is more fair, I swear,
5　　　　*My darling is more fair.*
There speaks a loving heart. (*To* PHILINTE.) You're laughing, eh?
Laugh on, my precious wit. Whatever you say,
I hold that song's worth all the bibelots
That people hail today with ah's and oh's.

10　ORONTE　And I maintain my sonnet's very good.

ALCESTE　It's not at all surprising that you should.
You have your reasons; permit me to have mine
For thinking that you cannot write a line.

ORONTE　Others have praised my sonnet to the skies.

15　ALCESTE　I lack their art of telling pleasant lies.

ORONTE　You seem to think you've got no end of wit.

ALCESTE　To praise your verse, I'd need still more of it.

ORONTE　I'm not in need of your approval, Sir.

ALCESTE　That's good; you couldn't have it if you were.

20　ORONTE　Come now, I'll lend you the subject of my sonnet;
I'd like to see you try to improve upon it.

ALCESTE　I might, by chance, write something just as shoddy;
But then I wouldn't show it to everybody.

ORONTE　You're most opinionated and conceited.

25　ALCESTE　Go find your flatterers, and be better treated.

ORONTE　Look here, my little fellow, pray watch your tone.

ALCESTE　My great big fellow, you'd better watch your own.

PHILINTE (*stepping between them*)　Oh, please, please, gentlemen!
This will never do.

30　ORONTE　The fault is mine, and I leave the field to you.
I am your servant, Sir, in every way.

ALCESTE　And I, Sir, am your most abject valet.

Scene III (PHILINTE, ALCESTE)

PHILINTE　Well, as you see, sincerity in excess
35　Can get you into a very pretty mess;
Oronte was hungry for appreciation....

ALCESTE　Don't speak to me.

PHILINTE　　　　　　　　What?

ALCESTE　　　　　　　　　　No more conversation.

40　PHILINTE　Really, now ...

ALCESTE　　　　　　　　Leave me alone.

PHILINTE　　　　　　　　　　If I ...

ALCESTE　　　　　　　　　　　　Out of my sight!

PHILINTE   But what . . .
ALCESTE   I won't listen.
PHILINTE   But . . .
ALCESTE   Silence!
5 PHILINTE   Now, is it polite . . .
ALCESTE   By heaven, I've had enough. Don't follow me.
PHILINTE   Ah, you're just joking. I'll keep you company.

ACT II

Scene I (ALCESTE, CÉLIMÈNE)

10 ALCESTE   Shall I speak plainly, Madam? I confess
Your conduct gives me infinite distress,
And my resentment's grown too hot to smother.
Soon, I foresee, we'll break with one another.
If I said otherwise, I should deceive you;
15 Sooner or later, I shall be forced to leave you,
And if I swore that we shall never part,
I should misread the omens of my heart.
CÉLIMÈNE   You kindly saw me home, it would appear,
So as to pour invectives in my ear.
20 ALCESTE   I've no desire to quarrel. But I deplore
Your inability to shut the door
On all these suitors who beset you so.
There's what annoys me, if you care to know.
CÉLIMÈNE   Is it my fault that all these men pursue me?
25 Am I to blame if they're attracted to me?
And when they gently beg an audience,
Ought I to take a stick and drive them hence?
ALCESTE   Madam, there's no necessity for a stick;
A less responsive heart would do the trick.
30 Of your attractiveness I don't complain;
But those your charms attract, you then detain
By a most melting and receptive manner,
And so enlist their hearts beneath your banner.
It's the agreeable hopes which you excite
35 That keep these lovers round you day and night;
Were they less liberally smiled upon,
That sighing troop would very soon be gone.
But tell me, Madam, why it is that lately
This man Clitandre interests you so greatly?
40 Because of what high merits do you deem
Him worthy of the honor of your esteem?

Is it that your admiring glances linger
On the splendidly long nail of his little finger?
Or do you share the general deep respect
For the blond wig he chooses to affect?
5   Are you in love with his embroidered hose?
Do you adore his ribbons and his bows?
Or is it that this paragon bewitches
Your tasteful eye with his vast German breeches?
Perhaps his giggle, or his falsetto voice,
10   Makes him the latest gallant of your choice?
CÉLIMÈNE   You're much mistaken to resent him so.
Why I put up with him you surely know:
My lawsuit's very shortly to be tried,
And I must have his influence on my side.
15   ALCESTE   Then lose your lawsuit, Madam, or let it drop;
Don't torture me by humoring such a fop.
CÉLIMÈNE   You're jealous of the whole world, Sir.
ALCESTE   That's true,
Since the whole world is well-received by you.
20   CÉLIMÈNE   That my good nature is so unconfined
Should serve to pacify your jealous mind;
Were I to smile on one, and scorn the rest,
Then you might have some cause to be distressed.
ALCESTE   Well, if I mustn't be jealous, tell me, then,
25   Just how I'm better treated than other men.
CÉLIMÈNE   You know you have my love. Will that not do?
ALCESTE   What proof have I that what you say is true?
CÉLIMÈNE   I would expect, Sir, that my having said it
Might give the statement a sufficient credit.
30   ALCESTE   But how can I be sure that you don't tell
The selfsame thing to other men as well?
CÉLIMÈNE   What a gallant speech! How flattering to me!
What a sweet creature you make me out to be!
Well then, to save you from the pangs of doubt,
35   All that I've said I hereby cancel out;
Now, none but yourself shall make a monkey of you:
Are you content?
ALCESTE   Why, why am I doomed to love you?
I swear that I shall bless the blissful hour
40   When this poor heart's no longer in your power!
I make no secret of it: I've done my best
To exorcise this passion from my breast;
But thus far all in vain; it will not go;
It's for my sins that I must love you so.

CÉLIMÈNE   Your love for me is matchless, Sir; that's clear.
ALCESTE   Indeed, in all the world it has no peer;
   Words can't describe the nature of my passion,
   And no man ever loved in such a fashion.
5 CÉLIMÈNE   Yes, it's a brand-new fashion, I agree:
   You show your love by castigating me,
   And all your speeches are enraged and rude.
   I've never been so furiously wooed.
ALCESTE   Yet you could calm that fury, if you chose.
10   Come, shall we bring our quarrels to a close?
   Let's speak with open hearts, then, and begin . . .

Scene II (CÉLIMÈNE, ALCESTE, BASQUE)

CÉLIMÈNE   What is it?
BASQUE   Acaste is here.
15 CÉLIMÈNE   Well, send him in.

Scene III (CÉLIMÈNE, ALCESTE)

ALCESTE   What! Shall we never be alone at all?
   You're always ready to receive a call,
   And you can't bear, for ten ticks of the clock,
20   Not to keep open house for all who knock.
CÉLIMÈNE   I couldn't refuse him: he'd be most put out.
ALCESTE   Surely that's not worth worrying about.
CÉLIMÈNE   Acaste would never forgive me if he guessed
   That I consider him a dreadful pest.
25 ALCESTE   If he's a pest, why bother with him then?
CÉLIMÈNE   Heavens! One can't antagonize such men;
   Why, they're the chartered gossips of the court,
   And have a say in things of every sort.
   One must receive them, and be full of charm;
30   They're no great help, but they can do you harm,
   And though your influence be ever so great,
   They're hardly the best people to alienate.
ALCESTE   I see, dear lady, that you could make a case
   For putting up with the whole human race;
35   These friendships that you calculate so nicely . . .

Scene IV (ALCESTE, CÉLIMÈNE, BASQUE)

BASQUE   Madam, Clitandre is here as well.
ALCESTE   Precisely.
CÉLIMÈNE   Where are you going?
40 ALCESTE   Elsewhere.
CÉLIMÈNE   Stay.

ALCESTE   No, no.
CÉLIMÈNE   Stay, Sir.
ALCESTE   I can't.
CÉLIMÈNE   I wish it.
5   ALCESTE   No, I must go.
I beg you, Madam, not to press the matter;
You know I have no taste for idle chatter.
CÉLIMÈNE   Stay. I command you.
ALCESTE   No, I cannot stay.
10   CÉLIMÈNE   Very well; you have my leave to go away.

Scene V (ÉLIANTE, PHILINTE, ACASTE, CLITANDRE, ALCESTE, CÉLIMÈNE, BASQUE)

ÉLIANTE (*to* CÉLIMÈNE)   The Marquesses have kindly come to call.
Were they announced?
15   CÉLIMÈNE   Yes. Basque, bring chairs for all.

BASQUE *provides the chairs, and exits.*

(*To* ALCESTE.) You haven't gone?
ALCESTE   No; and I shan't depart
Till you decide who's foremost in your heart.
20   CÉLIMÈNE   Oh, hush.
ALCESTE   It's time to choose; take them, or me.
CÉLIMÈNE   You're mad.
ALCESTE   I'm not, as you shall shortly see.
CÉLIMÈNE   Oh?
25   ALCESTE   You'll decide.
CÉLIMÈNE   You're joking now, dear friend.
ALCESTE   No, no; you'll choose; my patience is at an end.
CLITANDRE   Madam, I come from court, where poor Cléonte
Behaved like a perfect fool, as is his wont.
30   Has he no friend to counsel him, I wonder,
And teach him less unerringly to blunder?
CÉLIMÈNE   It's true, the man's a most accomplished dunce;
His gauche behavior charms the eye at once;
And every time one sees him, on my word,
35   His manner's grown a trifle more asburd.
ACASTE   Speaking of dunces, I've just now conversed
With old Damon, who's one of the very worst;
I stood a lifetime in the broiling sun.
Before his dreary monologue was done.
40   CÉLIMÈNE   Oh, he's a wondrous talker, and has the power
To tell you nothing hour after hour:

If, by mistake, he ever came to the point,
The shock would put his jawbone out of joint.
ÉLIANTE (*to* PHILINTE) The conversation takes its usual turn,
And all our dear friends' ears will shortly burn.
5 CLITANDRE Timante's a character, Madam.
CÉLIMÈNE   Isn't he, though?
A man of mystery from top to toe,
Who moves about in a romantic mist
On secret missions which do not exist.
10 His talk is full of eyebrows and grimaces;
How tired one gets of his momentous faces;
He's always whispering something confidential
Which turns out to be quite inconsequential;
Nothing's too slight for him to mystify;
15 He even whispers when he says "good-by."
ACASTE Tell us about Géralde.
CÉLIMÈNE   That tiresome ass.
He mixes only with the titled class,
And fawns on dukes and princes, and is bored
20 With anyone who's not at least a lord.
The man's obsessed with rank, and his discourses
Are all of hounds and carriages and horses;
He uses Christian names with all the great,
And the word Milord, with him, is out of date.
25 CLITANDRE He's very taken with Bélise, I hear.
CÉLIMÈNE She is the dreariest company, poor dear.
Whenever she comes to call, I grope about
To find some topic which will draw her out,
But, owing to her dry and faint replies,
30 The conversation wilts, and droops, and dies.
In vain one hopes to animate her face
By mentioning the ultimate commonplace;
But sun or shower, even hail or frost
Are matters she can instantly exhaust.
35 Meanwhile her visit, painful though it is,
Drags on and on through mute eternities,
And though you ask the time, and yawn, and yawn,
She sits there like a stone and won't be gone.
ACASTE Now for Adraste.
40 CÉLIMÉNE   Oh, that conceited elf
Has a gigantic passion for himself;
He rails against the court, and cannot bear it
That none will recognize his hidden merit;

All honors given to others give offense
To his imaginary excellence.
CLITANDRE   What about young Cléon? His house, they say,
Is full of the best society, night and day.
5   CÉLIMÈNE   His cook has made him popular, not he:
It's Cléon's table that people come to see.
ÉLIANTE   He gives a splendid dinner, you must admit.
CÉLIMÈNE   But must he serve himself along with it?
For my taste, he's a most insipid dish
10   Whose presence sours the wine and spoils the fish.
PHILINTE   Damis, his uncle, is admired no end.
What's your opinion, Madam?
CÉLIMÈNE   Why, he's my friend.
PHILINTE   He seems a decent fellow, and rather clever.
15   CÉLIMÈNE   He works too hard at cleverness, however.
I hate to see him sweat and struggle so
To fill his conversation with bons mots.
Since he's decided to become a wit
His taste's so pure that nothing pleases it;
20   He scolds at all the latest books and plays,
Thinking that wit must never stoop to praise,
That finding fault's a sign of intellect,
That all appreciation is abject,
And that by damning everything in sight
25   One shows oneself in a distinguished light.
He's scornful even of our conversations:
Their trivial nature sorely tries his patience;
He folds his arms, and stands above the battle,
And listens sadly to our childish prattle.
30   ACASTE   Wonderful, Madam! You've hit him off precisely.
CLITANDRE   No one can sketch a character so nicely.
ALCESTE   How bravely, Sirs, you cut and thrust at all
These absent fools, till one by one they fall:
But let one come in sight, and you'll at once
35   Embrace the man you lately called a dunce,
Telling him in a tone sincere and fervent
How proud you are to be his humble servant.
CLITANDRE   Why pick on us? *Madame's* been speaking, Sir.
And you should quarrel, if you must, with her.
40   ALCESTE   No, no, by God, the fault is yours, because
You lead her on with laughter and applause,
And make her think that she's the more delightful
The more her talk is scandalous and spiteful.
Oh, she would stoop to malice far, far less

If no such claque approved her cleverness.
It's flatterers like you whose foolish praise
Nourishes all the vices of these days.
PHILINTE   But why protest when someone ridicules
5   Those you'd condemn, yourself, as knaves or fools?
CÉLIMÈNE   Why, Sir? Because he loves to make a fuss.
You don't expect him to agree with us,
When there's an opportunity to express
His heaven-sent spirit of contrariness?
10   What other people think, he can't abide;
Whatever they say, he's on the other side;
He lives in deadly terror of agreeing;
'Twould make him seem an ordinary being.
Indeed, he's so in love with contradiction,
15   He'll turn against his most profound conviction
And with a furious eloquence deplore it,
If only someone else is speaking for it.
ALCESTE   Go on, dear lady, mock me as you please;
You have your audience in ecstasies.
20   PHILINTE   But what she says is true: you have a way
Of bridling at whatever people say;
Whether they praise or blame, your angry spirit
Is equally unsatisfied to hear it.
ALCESTE   Men, Sir, are always wrong, and that's the reason
25   That righteous anger's never out of season;
All that I hear in all their conversation
Is flattering praise or reckless condemnation.
CÉLIMÈNE   But . . .
ALCESTE   No, no, Madam, I am forced to state
30   That you have pleasures which I deprecate,
And that these others, here, are much to blame
For nourishing the faults which are your shame.
CLITANDRE   I shan't defend myself, Sir; but I vow
I'd thought this lady faultless until now.
35   ACASTE   I see her charms and graces, which are many;
But as for faults, I've never noticed any.
ALCESTE   I see them, Sir; and rather than ignore them,
I strenuously criticize her for them.
The more one loves, the more one should object
40   To every blemish, every least defect.
Were I this lady, I would soon get rid
Of lovers who approved of all I did,
And by their slack indulgence and applause
Endorsed my follies and excused my flaws.

CÉLIMÈNE   If all hearts beat according to your measure,
The dawn of love would be the end of pleasure;
And love would find its perfect consummation
In ecstasies of rage and reprobation.
5   ÉLIANTE   Love, as a rule, affects men otherwise,
And lovers rarely love to criticize.
They see their lady as a charming blur,
And find all things commendable in her.
If she has any blemish, fault, or shame,
10   They will redeem it by a pleasing name.
The pale-faced lady's lily-white, perforce;
The swarthy one's a sweet brunette, of course;
The spindly lady has a slender grace;
The fat one has a most majestic pace;
15   The plain one, with her dress in disarray,
They classify as *beauté négligée*;
The hulking one's a goddess in their eyes,
The dwarf, a concentrate of Paradise;
The haughty lady has a noble mind;
20   The mean one's witty, and the dull one's kind;
The chatterbox has liveliness and verve,
The mute one has a virtuous reserve.
So lovers manage, in their passion's cause,
To love their ladies even for their flaws.
25   ALCESTE   But I still say . . .
CÉLIMÈNE   I think it would be nice
To stroll around the gallery once or twice.
What! You're not going, Sirs?
CLITANDRE AND ACASTE   No, Madam, no.
30   ALCESTE   You seem to be in terror lest they go.
Do what you will, Sirs; leave, or linger on,
But I shan't go till after you are gone.
ACASTE   I'm free to linger, unless I should perceive
Madame is tired, and wishes me to leave.
35   CLITANDRE   And as for me, I needn't go today
Until the hour of the King's *coucher*.
CÉLIMÈNE (*to* ALCESTE)   You're joking, surely?
ALCESTE   Not in the least; we'll see
Whether you'd rather part with them, or me.

40   **Scene VI** (ALCESTE, CÉLIMÈNE, ÉLIANTE, ACASTE, PHILINTE,
CLITANDRE, BASQUE)

BASQUE (*to* ALCESTE)   Sir, there's a fellow here who bids me state
That he must see you, and that it can't wait.

ALCESTE   Tell him that I have no such pressing affairs.
BASQUE   It's a long tailcoat that this fellow wears,
With gold all over.
CÉLIMÈNE (*to* ALCESTE)   You'd best go down and see.
5   Or—have him enter.

Scene VII (ALCESTE, CÉLIMÈNE, ÉLIANTE, ACASTE, PHILINTE,
CLITANDRE, GUARD)

ALCESTE (*confronting the* GUARD)   Well, what do you want with
me?
10   Come in, Sir.
GUARD   I've a word, Sir, for your ear.
ALCESTE   Speak it aloud, Sir; I shall strive to hear.
GUARD   The Marshals have instructed me to say
You must report to them without delay.
15   ALCESTE   Who? Me, Sir?
GUARD   Yes, Sir; you.
ALCESTE   But what do they want?
PHILINTE (*to* ALCESTE)   To scotch your silly quarrel with Oronte.
CÉLIMÈNE (*to* PHILINTE)   What quarrel?
20   PHILINTE   Oronte and he have fallen out
Over some verse he spoke his mind about;
The Marshals wish to arbitrate the matter.
ALCESTE   Never shall I equivocate or flatter!
PHILINTE   You'd best obey their summons; come, let's go.
25   ALCESTE   How can they mend our quarrel, I'd like to know?
Am I to make a cowardly retraction,
And praise those jingles to his satisfaction?
I'll not recant; I've judged that sonnet rightly.
It's bad.
30   PHILINTE   But you might say so more politely. . . .
ALCESTE   I'll not back down; his verses make me sick.
PHILINTE   If only you could be more politic!
But come, let's go.
ALCESTE   I'll go, but I won't unsay
35   A single word.
PHILINTE   Well, let's be on our way.
ALCESTE   Till I am ordered by my lord the King
To praise that poem, I shall say the thing
Is scandalous, by God, and that the poet
40   Ought to be hanged for having the nerve to show it.
(*To* CLITANDRE and ACASTE, *who are laughing.*) By heaven, Sirs,
I really didn't know
That I was being humorous.

CÉLIMÈNE   Go, Sir, go;
  Settle your business.
ALCESTE   I shall, and when I'm through,
  I shall return to settle things with you.

5 ACT III

Scene I (CLITANDRE, ACASTE)

CLITANDRE   Dear Marquess, how contented you appear;
  All things delight you, nothing mars your cheer.
  Can you, in perfect honesty, declare
10 That you've a right to be so debonair?
ACASTE   By Jove, when I survey myself, I find
  No cause whatever for distress of mind.
  I'm young and rich; I can in modesty
  Lay claim to an exalted pedigree;
15 And owing to my name and my condition
  I shall not want for honors and position.
  Then as to courage, that most precious trait,
  I seem to have it, as was proved of late
  Upon the field of honor, where my bearing,
20 They say, was very cool and rather daring.
  I've wit, of course; and taste in such perfection
  That I can judge without the least reflection,
  And at the theater, which is my delight,
  Can make or break a play on opening night,
25 And lead the crowd in hisses or bravos,
  And generally be known as one who knows.
  I'm clever, handsome, gracefully polite;
  My waist is small, my teeth are strong and white;
  As for my dress, the world's astonished eyes
30 Assure me that I bear away the prize.
  I find myself in favor everywhere,
  Honored by men, and worshiped by the fair;
  And since these things are so, it seems to me
  I'm justified in my complacency.
35 CLITANDRE   Well, if so many ladies hold you dear,
  Why do you press a hopeless courtship here?
ACASTE   Hopeless, you say? I'm not the sort of fool
  That likes his ladies difficult and cool.
  Men who are awkward, shy, and peasantish

May pine for heartless beauties, if they wish,
Grovel before them, bear their cruelties,
Woo them with tears and sighs and bended knees,
And hope by dogged faithfulness to gain
5 What their poor merits never could obtain.
For men like me, however, it makes no sense
To love on trust, and foot the whole expense.
Whatever any lady's merits be,
I think, thank God, that I'm as choice as she;
10 That if my heart is kind enough to burn
For her, she owes me something in return;
And that in any proper love affair
The partners must invest an equal share.
CLITANDRE You think, then, that our hostess favors you?
15 ACASTE I've reason to believe that that is true.
CLITANDRE How did you come to such a mad conclusion?
You're blind, dear fellow. This is sheer delusion.
ACASTE All right, then: I'm deluded and I'm blind.
CLITANDRE Whatever put the notion in your mind?
20 ACASTE Delusion.
CLITANDRE What persuades you that you're right?
ACASTE I'm blind.
CLITANDRE But have you any proofs to cite?
ACASTE I tell you I'm deluded.
25 CLITANDRE Have you, then,
Received some secret pledge from Célimène?
ACASTE Oh, no: she scorns me.
CLITANDRE Tell me the truth, I beg.
ACASTE She just can't bear me.
30 CLITANDRE Ah, don't pull my leg.
Tell me what hope she's given you, I pray.
ACASTE I'm hopeless, and it's you who win the day.
She hates me thoroughly, and I'm so vexed
I mean to hang myself on Tuesday next.
35 CLITANDRE Dear Marquess, let us have an armistice
And make a treaty. What do you say to this?
If ever one of us can plainly prove
That Célimène encourages his love,
The other must abandon hope, and yield,
40 And leave him in possession of the field.
ACASTE Now, there's a bargain that appeals to me;
With all my heart, dear Marquess, I agree.
But hush.

Scene II (CÉLIMÈNE, ACASTE, CLITANDRE)

CÉLIMÈNE   Still here?

CLITANDRE   'Twas love that stayed our feet.

CÉLIMÈNE   I think I heard a carriage in the street.

5   Whose is it? D'you know?

Scene III (CÉLIMÈNE, ACASTE, CLITANDRE, BASQUE)

BASQUE   Arsinoé is here,
   Madame.

CÉLIMÈNE   Arsinoé, you say? Oh, dear.

10   BASQUE   Éliante is entertaining her below.

CÉLIMÈNE   What brings the creature here, I'd like to know?

ACASTE   They say she's dreadfully prudish, but in fact
   I think her piety . . .

CÉLIMÈNE   It's all an act.

15   At heart she's worldly, and her poor success
   In snaring men explains her prudishness.
   It breaks her heart to see the beaux and gallants
   Engrossed by other women's charms and talents,
   And so she's always in a jealous rage

20   Against the faulty standards of the age.
   She lets the world believe that she's a prude
   To justify her loveless solitude,
   And strives to put a brand of moral shame
   On all the graces that she cannot claim.

25   But still she'd love a lover; and Alceste
   Appears to be the one she'd love the best.
   His visits here are poison to her pride;
   She seems to think I've lured him from her side;
   And everywhere, at court or in the town,

30   The spiteful, envious woman runs me down.
   In short, she's just as stupid as can be,
   Vicious and arrogant in the last degree,
   And . . .

Scene IV (ARSINOÉ, CÉLIMÈNE, CLITANDRE, ACASTE)

3   CÉLIMÈNE   Ah! What happy chance has brought you here?
   I've thought about you ever so much, my dear.

ARSINOÉ   I've come to tell you something you should know.

CÉLIMÈNE   How good of you to think of doing so!

CLITANDRE *and* ACASTE *go out, laughing.*

Scene V (ARSINOÉ, CÉLIMÈNE)

ARSINOÉ   It's just as well those gentlemen didn't tarry.

CÉLIMÈNE   Shall we sit down?

ARSINOÉ   That won't be necessary.

5   Madam, the flame of friendship ought to burn
Brightest in matters of the most concern,
And as there's nothing which concerns us more
Than honor, I have hastened to your door
To bring you, as your friend, some information
10   About the status of your reputation.
I visited, last night, some virtuous folk,
And, quite by chance, it was of you they spoke;
There was, I fear, no tendency to praise
Your light behavior and your dashing ways.
15   The quantity of gentlemen you see
And your by now notorious coquetry
Were both so vehemently criticized
By everyone, that I was much surprised.
Of course, I needn't tell you where I stood;
20   I came to your defense as best I could,
Assured them you were harmless, and declared
Your soul was absolutely unimpaired.
But there are some things, you must realize,
One can't excuse, however hard one tries,
25   And I was forced at last into conceding
That your behavior, Madam, is misleading,
That it makes a bad impression, giving rise
To ugly gossip and obscene surmise,
And that if you were more *overtly* good,
30   You wouldn't be so much misunderstood.
Not that I think you've been unchaste—no! no!
The saints preserve me from a thought so low!
But mere good conscience never did suffice:
One must avoid the outward show of vice.
35   Madam, you're too intelligent, I'm sure,
To think my motives anything but pure
In offering you this counsel—which I do
Out of a zealous interest in you.

CÉLIMÈNE   Madam, I haven't taken you amiss;

40   I'm very much obliged to you for this;
And I'll at once discharge the obligation
By telling you about *your* reputation.
You've been so friendly as to let me know

What certain people say of me, and so
I mean to follow your benign example
By offering you a somewhat similar sample.
The other day, I went to an affair
5   And found some most distinguished people there
Discussing piety, both false and true.
The conversation soon came round to you.
Alas! Your prudery and bustling zeal
Appeared to have a very slight appeal.
10   Your affectation of a grave demeanor,
Your endless talk of virtue and of honor,
The aptitude of your suspicious mind
For finding sin where there is none to find,
Your towering self-esteem, that pitying face
15   With which you contemplate the human race,
Your sermonizings and your sharp aspersions
On people's pure and innocent diversions—
All these were mentioned, Madam, and, in fact,
Were roundly and concertedly attacked.
20   "What good," they said, "are all these outward shows,
When everything belies her pious pose?
She prays incessantly; but then, they say,
She beats her maids and cheats them of their pay;
She shows her zeal in every holy place,
25   But still she's vain enough to paint her face;
She holds that naked statues are immoral,
But with a naked *man* she'd have no quarrel."
Of course, I said to everybody there
That they were being viciously unfair;
30   But still they were disposed to criticize you,
And all agreed that someone should advise you
To leave the morals of the world alone,
And worry rather more about your own.
They felt that one's self-knowledge should be great
35   Before one thinks of setting others straight;
That one should learn the art of living well
Before one threatens other men with hell,
And that the Church is best equipped, no doubt,
To guide our souls and root our vices out.
40   Madam, you're too intelligent, I'm sure,
To think my motives anything but pure
In offering you this counsel—which I do
Out of a zealous interest in you.

ARSINOÉ   I dared not hope for gratitude, but I
Did not expect so acid a reply;
I judge, since you've been so extremely tart,
That my good counsel pierced you to the heart.
5   CÉLIMÈNE   Far from it, Madam. Indeed, it seems to me
We ought to trade advice more frequently.
One's vision of oneself is so defective
That it would be an excellent corrective.
If you are willing, Madam, let's arrange
10   Shortly to have another frank exchange
In which we'll tell each other, *entre nous,*
What you've heard tell of me, and I of you.
ARSINOÉ   Oh, people never censure you, my dear;
It's me they criticize. Or so I hear.
15   CÉLIMÈNE   Madam, I think we either blame or praise
According to our taste and length of days.
There is a time of life for coquetry,
And there's a season, too, for prudery.
When all one's charms are gone, it is, I'm sure,
20   Good strategy to be devout and pure:
It makes one seem a little less forsaken.
Some day, perhaps, I'll take the road you've taken:
Time brings all things. But I have time aplenty,
And see no cause to be a prude at twenty.
25   ARSINOÉ   You give your age in such a gloating tone
That one would think I was an ancient crone;
We're not so far apart, in sober truth,
That you can mock me with a boast of youth!
Madam, you baffle me. I wish I knew
30   What moves you to provoke me as you do.
CÉLIMÈNE   For my part, Madam, I should like to know
Why you abuse me everywhere you go.
Is it my fault, dear lady, that your hand
Is not, alas, in very great demand?
35   If men admire me, if they pay me court
And daily make me offers of the sort
You'd dearly love to have them make to you,
How can I help it? What would you have me do?
If what you want is lovers, please feel free
40   To take as many as you can from me.
ARSINOÉ   Oh, come. D'you think the world is losing sleep
Over the flock of lovers which you keep,
Or that we find it difficult to guess

What price you pay for their devotedness?
Surely you don't expect us to suppose
Mere merit could attract so many beaux?
It's not your virtue that they're dazzled by;
5   Nor is it virtuous love for which they sigh.
You're fooling no one, Madam; the world's not blind;
There's many a lady heaven has designed
To call men's noblest, tenderest feelings out,
Who has no lovers dogging her about;
10   From which it's plain that lovers nowadays
Must be acquired in bold and shameless ways,
And only pay one court for such reward
As modesty and virtue can't afford.
Then don't be quite so puffed up, if you please,
15   About your tawdry little victories;
Try, if you can, to be a shade less vain,
And treat the world with somewhat less disdain.
If one were envious of your amours,
One soon could have a following like yours;
20   Lovers are no great trouble to collect
If one prefers them to one's self-respect.
CÉLIMÈNE   Collect them then, my dear; I'd love to see
You demonstrate that charming theory;
Who knows, you might . . .
25   ARSINOÉ   Now, Madam, that will do;
It's time to end this trying interview.
My coach is late in coming to your door.
Or I'd have taken leave of you before.
CÉLIMÈNE   Oh, please don't feel that you must rush away;
30   I'd be delighted, Madam, if you'd stay.
However, lest my conversation bore you,
Let me provide some better company for you;
This gentleman, who comes most apropos,
Will please you more than I could do, I know.

35   **Scene VI** (ALCESTE, CÉLIMÈNE, ARSINOÉ)

CÉLIMÈNE   Alceste, I have a little note to write
Which simply must go out before tonight;
Please entertain *Madame;* I'm sure that she
Will overlook my incivility.

40   **Scene VII** (ALCESTE, ARSINOÉ)

ARSINOÉ   Well, Sir, our hostess graciously contrives
For us to chat until my coach arrives;

And I shall be forever in her debt
For granting me this little tête-à-tête.
We women very rightly give our hearts
To men of noble character and parts,
5   And your especial merits, dear Alceste,
Have roused the deepest sympathy in my breast.
Oh, how I wish they had sufficient sense
At court, to recognize your excellence!
They wrong you greatly, Sir. How it must hurt you
10   Never to be rewarded for your virtue!
    ALCESTE   Why, Madam, what cause have I to feel aggrieved?
What great and brilliant thing have I achieved?
What service have I rendered to the King
That I should look to him for anything?
15   ARSINOÉ   Not everyone who's honored by the State
Has done great services. A man must wait
Till time and fortune offer him the chance.
Your merit, Sir, is obvious at a glance,
And . . .
20   ALCESTE   Ah, forgot my merit; I am not neglected.
The court, I think, can hardly be expected
To mine men's souls for merit, and unearth
Our hidden virtues and our secret worth.
    ARSINOÉ   *Some* virtues, though, are far too bright to hide;
25   Yours are acknowledged, Sir, on every side.
Indeed, I've heard you warmly praised of late
By persons of considerable weight.
    ALCESTE   This fawning age has praise for everyone,
And all distinctions, Madam, are undone.
30   All things have equal honor nowadays,
And no one should be gratified by praise.
To be admired, one only need exist,
And every lackey's on the honors list.
    ARSINOÉ   I only wish, Sir, that you had your eye
35   On some position at court, however high;
You'd only have to hint at such a notion
For me to set the proper wheels in motion;
I've certain friendships I'd be glad to use
To get you any office you might choose.
40   ALCESTE   Madam, I fear that any such ambition
Is wholly foreign to my disposition.
The soul God gave me isn't of the sort
That prospers in the weather of a court.
It's all too obvious that I don't possess

The virtues necessary for success.
My only great talent is for speaking plain;
I've never learned to flatter or to feign;
And anyone so stupidly sincere
5   Had best not seek a courtier's career.
Outside the court, I know, one must dispense
With honors, privilege, and influence;
But still one gains the right, foregoing these,
Not to be tortured by the wish to please.
10   One needn't live in dread of snubs and slights,
Nor praise the verse that every idiot writes,
Nor humor silly Marquesses, nor bestow
Politic sighs on Madam So-and-So.
ARSINOÉ   Forget the court, then; let the matter rest.
15   But I've another cause to be distressed
About your present situation, Sir.
It's to your love affair that I refer.
She whom you love, and who pretends to love you,
Is, I regret to say, unworthy of you.
20   ALCESTE   Why, Madam? Can you seriously intend
To make so grave a charge against your friend?
ARSINOÉ   Alas, I must. I've stood aside too long
And let that lady do you grievous wrong;
But now my debt to conscience shall be paid:
25   I tell you that your love has been betrayed.
ALCESTE   I thank you, Madam; you're extremely kind.
Such words are soothing to a lover's mind.
ARSINOÉ   Yes, though she *is* my friend, I say again
You're very much too good for Célimène.
30   She's wantonly misled you from the start.
ALCESTE   You may be right; who knows another's heart?
But ask yourself if it's the part of charity
To shake my soul with doubts of her sincerity.
ARSINOÉ   Well, if you'd rather be a dupe than doubt her,
35   That's your affair. I'll say no more about her.
ALCESTE   Madam, you know that doubt and vague suspicion
Are painful to a man in my position;
It's most unkind to worry me this way
Unless you've some real proof of what you say.
40   ARSINOÉ   Sir, say no more: all doubts shall be removed,
And all that I've been saying shall be proved.
You've only to escort me home, and there
We'll look into the heart of this affair.
I've ocular evidence which will persuade you

Beyond a doubt, that Célimène's betrayed you.
Then, if you're saddened by that revelation,
Perhaps I can provide some consolation.

ACT IV

5 **Scene I** (ÉLIANTE, PHILINTE)

PHILINTE   Madam, he acted like a stubborn child;
I thought they never would be reconciled;
In vain we reasoned, threatened, and appealed;
He stood his ground and simply would not yield.
10   The Marshals, I feel sure, have never heard
An argument so splendidly absurd.
"No, gentlemen," said he, "I'll not retract.
His verse is bad: extremely bad, in fact.
Surely it does the man no harm to know it.
15   Does it disgrace him, not to be a poet?
A gentleman may be respected still,
Whether he writes a sonnet well or ill.
That I dislike his verse should not offend him;
In all that touches honor, I commend him;
20   He's noble, brave, and virtuous—but I fear
He can't in truth be called a sonneteer.
I'll gladly praise his wardrobe; I'll endorse
His dancing, or the way he sits a horse;
But, gentlemen, I cannot praise his rhyme.
25   In fact, it ought to be a capital crime
For anyone so sadly unendowed
To write a sonnet and read the thing aloud."
At length he fell into a gentler mood
And, striking a concessive attitude,
30   He paid Oronte the following courtesies:
"Sir, I regret that I'm so hard to please,
And I'm profoundly sorry that your lyric
Failed to provoke me to a panegyric."
After these curious words, the two embraced,
35   And then the hearing was adjourned—in haste.
ÉLIANTE   His conduct has been very singular lately;
Still, I confess that I respect him greatly.
The honesty in which he takes such pride
Has—to my mind—its noble, heroic side.
40   In this false age, such candor seems outrageous;
But I could wish that it were more contagious.

PHILINTE   What most intrigues me in our friend Alceste
Is the grand passion that rages in his breast.
The sullen humors he's compounded of
Should not, I think, dispose his heart to love;
5   But since they do, it puzzles me still more
That he should choose your cousin to adore.
ÉLIANTE   It does, indeed, belie the theory
That love is born of gentle sympathy,
And that the tender passion must be based
10   On sweet accords of temper and of taste.
PHILINTE   Does she return his love, do you suppose?
ÉLIANTE   Ah, that's a difficult question, Sir. Who knows?
How can we judge the truth of her devotion?
Her heart's a stranger to its own emotion.
15   Sometimes it thinks it loves, when no love's there;
At other times it loves quite unaware.
PHILINTE   I rather think Alceste is in for more
Distress and sorrow than he's bargained for;
Were he of my mind, Madam, his affection
20   Would turn in quite a different direction,
And we would see him more responsive to
The kind regard which he receives from you.
ÉLIANTE   Sir, I believe in frankness, and I'm inclined,
In matters of the heart, to speak my mind.
25   I don't oppose his love for her; indeed,
I hope with all my heart that he'll succeed,
And were it in my power, I'd rejoice
In giving him the lady of his choice.
But if, as happens frequently enough
30   In love affairs, he meets with a rebuff—
If Célimène should grant some rival's suit—
I'd gladly play the role of substitute;
Nor would his tender speeches please me less
Because they'd once been made without success.
35   PHILINTE   Well, Madam, as for me, I don't oppose
Your hopes in this affair; and heaven knows
That in my conversations with the man
I plead your cause as often as I can.
But if those two should marry, and so remove
40   All chance that he will offer you his love,
Then I'll declare my own, and hope to see
Your gracious favor pass from him to me.
In short, should you be cheated of Alceste,
I'd be most happy to be second best.

ÉLIANTE   Philinte, you're teasing.
PHILINTE   Ah, Madam, never fear;
No words of mine were ever so sincere,
And I shall live in fretful expectation
5   Till I can make a fuller declaration.

Scene II (ALCESTE, ÉLIANTE, PHILINTE)

ALCESTE   Avenge me, Madam! I must have satisfaction,
Or this great wrong will drive me to distraction!
ÉLIANTE   Why, what's the matter? What's upset you so?
10   ALCESTE   Madam, I've had a mortal, mortal blow.
If Chaos repossessed the universe,
I swear I'd not be shaken any worse.
I'm ruined. . . . I can say no more. . . . My soul . . .
ÉLIANTE   Do try, Sir, to regain your self-control.
15   ALCESTE   Just heaven! Why were so much beauty and grace
Bestowed on one so vicious and so base?
ÉLIANTE   Once more, Sir, tell us. . . .
ALCESTE   My world has gone to wrack;
I'm—I'm betrayed; she's stabbed me in the back:
20   Yes, Célimène (who would have thought it of her?)
Is false to me, and has another lover.
ÉLIANTE   Are you quite certain? Can you prove these things?
PHILINTE   Lovers are prey to wild imaginings
And jealous fancies. No doubt there's some mistake. . . .
25   ALCESTE   Mind your own business, Sir, for heaven's sake.
(*To* ÉLIANTE.) Madam, I have the proof that you demand
Here in my pocket, penned by her own hand.
Yes, all the shameful evidence one could want
Lies in this letter written to Oronte—
30   Oronte! whom I felt sure she couldn't love,
And hardly bothered to be jealous of.
PHILINTE   Still, in a letter, appearances may deceive;
This may not be so bad as you believe.
ALCESTE   Once more I beg you, Sir, to let me be;
35   Tend to your own affairs; leave mine to me.
ÉLIANTE   Compose yourself; this anguish that you feel . . .
ALCESTE   Is something, Madam, you alone can heal.
My outraged heart, beside itself with grief,
Appeals to you for comfort and relief.
40   Avenge me on your cousin, whose unjust
And faithless nature has deceived my trust;
Avenge a crime your pure soul must detest.
ÉLIANTE   But how, Sir?

ALCESTE   Madam, this heart within my breast
Is yours; pray take it; redeem my heart from her,
And so avenge me on my torturer.
Let her be punished by the fond emotion,
5   The ardent love, the bottomless devotion,
The faithful worship which this heart of mine
Will offer up to yours as to a shrine.
ÉLIANTE   You have my sympathy, Sir, in all you suffer;
Nor do I scorn the noble heart you offer;
10   But I suspect you'll soon be mollified,
And this desire for vengeance will subside.
When some belovèd hand has done us wrong
We thirst for retribution—but not for long;
However dark the deed that she's committed,
15   A lovely culprit's very soon acquitted.
Nothing's so stormy as an injured lover,
And yet no storm so quickly passes over.
ALCESTE   No, Madam, no—this is no lovers' spat;
I'll not forgive her; it's gone too far for that;
20   My mind's made up; I'll kill myself before
I waste my hopes upon her any more.
Ah, here she is. My wrath intensifies.
I shall confront her with her tricks and lies,
And crush her utterly, and bring you then
25   A heart no longer slave to Célimène.

Scene III (CÉLIMÈNE, ALCESTE)

ALCESTE (*aside*)   Sweet heaven, help me to control my passion.
CÉLIMÈNE (*aside*)   Oh, Lord.
(*To* ALCESTE.)   Why stand there staring in that fashion?
30   And what d'you mean by those dramatic sighs,
And that malignant glitter in your eyes?
ALCESTE   I mean that sins which cause the blood to freeze
Look innocent beside your treacheries;
That nothing Hell's or Heaven's wrath could do
35   Ever produced so bad a thing as you.
CÉLIMÈNE   Your compliments were always sweet and pretty.
ALCESTE   Madam, it's not the moment to be witty.
No, blush and hang your head; you've ample reason,
Since I've the fullest evidence of your treason.
40   Ah, this is what my sad heart prophesied;
Now all my anxious fears are verified;
My dark suspicion and my gloomy doubt

Divined the truth, and now the truth is out.
For all your trickery, I was not deceived;
It was my bitter stars that I believed.
But don't imagine that you'll go scot-free;
5   You shan't misuse me with impunity.
I know that love's irrational and blind;
I know the heart's not subject to the mind,
And can't be reasoned into beating faster;
I know each soul is free to choose its master;
10   Therefore had you but spoken from the heart,
Rejecting my attentions from the start,
I'd have no grievance, or at any rate
I could complain of nothing but my fate.
Ah, but so falsely to encourage me—
15   That was a treason and a treachery
For which you cannot suffer too severely,
And you shall pay for that behavior dearly.
Yes, now I have no pity, not a shred;
My temper's out of hand; I've lost my head;
20   Shocked by the knowledge of your double-dealings,
My reason can't restrain my savage feelings;
A righteous wrath deprives me of my senses,
And I won't answer for the consequences.
CÉLIMÈNE   What does this outburst mean? Will you please explain?
25   Have you, by any chance, gone quite insane?
ALCESTE   Yes, yes, I went insane the day I fell
A victim to your black and fatal spell,
Thinking to meet with some sincerity
Among the treacherous charms that beckoned me.
30   CÉLIMÈNE   Pooh. Of what treachery can you complain?
ALCESTE   How sly you are, how cleverly you feign!
But you'll not victimize me any more.
Look: here's a document you've seen before.
This evidence, which I acquired today,
35   Leaves you, I think, without a thing to say.
CÉLIMÈNE   Is this what sent you into such a fit?
ALCESTE   You should be blushing at the sight of it.
CÉLIMÈNE   Ought I to blush? I truly don't see why.
ALCESTE   Ah, now you're being bold as well as sly;
40   Since there's no signature, perhaps you'll claim . . .
CÉLIMÈNE   I wrote it, whether or not it bears my name.
ALCESTE   And you can view with equanimity
This proof of your disloyalty to me!

CÉLIMÈNE   Oh, don't be so outrageous and extreme.
ALCESTE   You take this matter lightly, it would seem.
Was it no wrong to me, no shame to you,
That you should send Oronte this billet-doux?
5   CÉLIMÈNTE   Oronte! Who said it was for him?
ALCESTE   Why, those
Who brought me this example of your prose.
But what's the difference? If you wrote the letter
To someone else, it pleases me no better.
10   My grievance and your guilt remain the same.
CÉLIMÈNE   But need you rage, and need I blush for shame,
If this was written to a *woman* friend?
ALCESTE   Ah! Most ingenious. I'm impressed no end;
And after that incredible evasion
15   Your guilt is clear. I need no more persuasion.
How dare you try so clumsy a deception?
D'you think I'm wholly wanting in perception?
Come, come, let's see how brazenly you'll try
To bolster up so palpable a lie:
20   Kindly construe this ardent closing section
As nothing more than sisterly affection!
Here, let me read it. Tell me, if you dare to,
That this is for a woman . . .
CÉLIMÈNE   I don't care to.
25   What right have you to badger and berate me,
And so highhandedly interrogate me?
ALCESTE   Now, don't be angry; all I ask of you
Is that you justify a phrase or two . . .
CÉLIMÈNE   No, I shall not. I utterly refuse,
30   And you may take those phrases as you choose.
ALCESTE   Just show me how this letter could be meant
For a woman's eyes, and I shall be content.
CÉLIMÈNE   No, no, it's for Oronte; you're perfectly right.
I welcome his attentions with delight,
35   I prize his character and his intellect,
And everything is just as you suspect.
Come, do your worst now; give your rage free rein;
But kindly cease to bicker and complain.
ALCESTE (*aside*)   Good God! Could anything be more inhuman?
40   Was ever a heart so mangled by a woman?
When I complain of how she has betrayed me,
She bridles, and commences to upbraid me!
She tries my tortured patience to the limit;
She won't deny her guilt; she glories in it!

And yet my heart's too faint and cowardly
To break these chains of passion, and be free,
To scorn her as it should, and rise above
This unrewarded, mad, and bitter love.
5   (*To* CÉLIMÈNE.)   Ah, traitress, in how confident a fashion
You take advantage of my helpless passion,
And use my weakness for your faithless charms
To make me once again throw down my arms!
But do at least deny this black transgression;
10   Take back that mocking and perverse confession;
Defend this letter and your innocence,
And I, poor fool, will aid in your defense.
Pretend, pretend, that you are just and true,
And I shall make myself believe in you.
15   CÉLIMÈNE   Oh, stop it. Don't be such a jealous dunce,
Or I shall leave off loving you at once.
Just why should I *pretend?* What could impel me
To stoop so low as that? And kindly tell me
Why, if I loved another, I shouldn't merely
20   Inform you of it, simply and sincerely!
I've told you where you stand, and that admission
Should altogether clear me of suspicion;
After so generous a guarantee,
What right have you to harbor doubts of me?
25   Since women are (from natural reticence)
Reluctant to declare their sentiments,
And since the honor of our sex requires
That we conceal our amorous desires,
Ought any man for whom such laws are broken
30   To question what the oracle has spoken?
Should he not rather feel an obligation
To trust that most obliging declaration?
Enough, now. Your suspicions quite disgust me;
Why should I love a man who doesn't trust me?
35   I cannot understand why I continue,
Fool that I am, to take an interest in you.
I ought to choose a man less prone to doubt,
And give you something to be vexed about.
     ALCESTE   Ah, what a poor enchanted fool I am;
40   These gentle words, no doubt, were all a sham,
But destiny requires me to entrust
My happiness to you, and so I must.
I'll love you to the bitter end, and see
How false and treacherous you dare to be.

CÉLIMÈNE   No, you don't really love me as you ought.
ALCESTE   I love you more than can be said or thought;
Indeed, I wish you were in such distress
That I might show my deep devotedness.
5   Yes, I could wish that you were wretchedly poor,
Unloved, uncherished, utterly obscure;
That fate had set you down upon the earth
Without possessions, rank, or gentle birth;
Then, by the offer of my heart, I might
10   Repair the great injustice of your plight;
I'd raise you from the dust, and proudly prove
The purity and vastness of my love.
CÉLIMÈNE   This is a strange benevolence indeed!
God grant that I may never be in need. . . .
15   Ah, here's Monsieur Dubois, in quaint disguise.

Scene IV (CÉLIMÈNE, ALCESTE, DUBOIS)

ALCESTE   Well, why this costume? Why those frightened eyes?
What ails you?
DUBOIS   Well, Sir, things are most mysterious.
20   ALCESTE   What do you mean?
DUBOIS   I fear they're very serious.
ALCESTE   What?
DUBOIS   Shall I speak more loudly?
ALCESTE   Yes; speak out.
25   DUBOIS   Isn't there someone here, Sir?
ALCESTE   Speak, you lout!
Stop wasting time.
DUBOIS   Sir, we must slip away.
ALCESTE   How's that?
30   DUBOIS   We must decamp without delay.
ALCESTE   Explain yourself.
DUBOIS   I tell you we must fly.
ALCESTE   What for?
DUBOIS   We mustn't pause to say good-by.
35   ALCESTE   Now what d'you mean by all of this, you clown?
DUBOIS   I mean, Sir, that we've got to leave this town.
ALCESTE   I'll tear you limb from limb and joint from joint
If you don't come more quickly to the point.
DUBOIS   Well, Sir, today a man in a black suit,
40   Who wore a black and ugly scowl to boot,
Left us a document scrawled in such a hand
As even Satan couldn't understand.

It bears upon your lawsuit, I don't doubt;
But all hell's devils couldn't make it out.
ALCESTE   Well, well, go on. What then? I fail to see
How this event obliges us to flee.
5   DUBOIS   Well, Sir, an hour later, hardly more,
A gentleman who's often called before
Came looking for you in an anxious way.
Not finding you, he asked me to convey
(Knowing I could be trusted with the same)
10   The following message. . . . Now, what *was* his name?
ALCESTE   Forget his name, you idiot. What did he say?
DUBOIS   Well, it was one of your friends, Sir, anyway.
He warned you to begone, and he suggested
That if you stay, you may well be arrested.
15   ALCESTE   What? Nothing more specific? Think, man, think!
DUBOIS   No, Sir. He had me bring him pen and ink,
And dashed you off a letter which, I'm sure,
Will render things distinctly less obscure.
ALCESTE   Well—let me have it!
20   CÉLIMÈNE   What *is* this all about?
ALCESTE   God knows; but I have hopes of finding out.
How long am I to wait, you blitherer?
DUBOIS   (*after a protracted search for the letter*)   I must have left
it on your table, Sir.
25   ALCESTE   I ought to . . .
CÉLIMÉNE   No, no, keep your self-control;
Go find out what's behind his rigmarole.
ALCESTE   It seems that fate, no matter what I do,
Has sworn that I may not converse with you;
30   But, Madam, pray permit your faithful lover
To try once more before the day is over.

ACT V

Scene I (ALCESTE, PHILINTE)

ALCESTE   No, it's too much. My mind's made up, I tell you.
35   PHILINTE   Why should this blow, however hard, compel you . . .
ALCESTE   No, no, don't waste your breath in argument;
Nothing you say will alter my intent;
This age is vile, and I've made up my mind
To have no further commerce with mankind.
40   Did not truth, honor, decency, and the laws

Oppose my enemy and approve my cause?
My claims were justified in all men's sight;
I put my trust in equity and right;
Yet, to my horror and the world's disgrace,
5   Justice is mocked, and I have lost my case!
A scoundrel whose dishonesty is notorious
Emerges from another lie victorious!
Honor and right condone his brazen fraud,
While rectitude and decency applaud!
10   Before his smirking face, the truth stands charmed,
And virtue conquered, and the law disarmed!
His crime is sanctioned by a court decree!
And not content with what he's done to me,
The dog now seeks to ruin me by stating
15   That I composed a book now circulating,
A book so wholly criminal and vicious
That even to speak its title is seditious!
Meanwhile Oronte, my rival, lends his credit
To the same libelous tale, and helps to spread it!
20   Oronte! a man of honor and of rank,
With whom I've been entirely fair and frank;
Who sought me out and forced me, willy nilly,
To judge some verse I found extremely silly;
And who, because I properly refused
25   To flatter him, or see the truth abused,
Abets my enemy in a rotten slander!
There's the reward of honesty and candor!
The man will hate me to the end of time
For failing to commend his wretched rhyme!
30   And not this man alone, but all humanity
Do what they do from interest and vanity;
They prate of honor, truth, and righteousness,
But lie, betray, and swindle nonetheless.
Come then: man's villainy is too much to bear;
35   Let's leave this jungle and this jackal's lair.
Yes! treacherous and savage race of men,
You shall not look upon my face again.
    PHILINTE   Oh, don't rush into exile prematurely;
Things aren't as dreadful as you make them, surely.
40   It's rather obvious, since you're still at large,
That people don't believe your enemy's charge.
Indeed, his tale's so patently untrue
That it may do more harm to him than you.

ALCESTE Nothing could do that scoundrel any harm:
His frank corruption is his greatest charm,
And, far from hurting him, a further shame
Would only serve to magnify his name.
5 PHILINTE In any case, his bald prevarication
Has done no injury to your reputation,
And you may feel secure in that regard.
As for your lawsuit, it should not be hard
To have the case reopened, and contest
10 This judgment . . .
ALCESTE No, no, let the verdict rest.
Whatever cruel penalty it may bring,
I wouldn't have it changed for anything.
It shows the times' injustice with such clarity
15 That I shall pass it down to our posterity
As a great proof and signal demonstration
Of the black wickedness of this generation.
It may cost twenty thousand francs; but I
Shall pay their twenty thousand, and gain thereby
20 The right to storm and rage at human evil,
And send the race of mankind to the devil.
PHILINTE Listen to me . . .
ALCESTE Why? What can you possibly say?
Don't argue, Sir; your labor's thrown away.
25 Do you propose to offer lame excuses
For men's behavior and the times' abuses?
PHILINTE No, all you say I'll readily concede:
This is a low, conniving age indeed;
Nothing but trickery prospers nowadays,
30 And people ought to mend their shabby ways.
Yes, man's a beastly creature; but must we then
Abandon the society of men?
Here in the world, each human frailty
Provides occasion for philosophy,
35 And that is virtue's noblest exercise;
If honesty shone forth from all men's eyes,
If every heart were frank and kind and just.
What could our virtues do but gather dust
(Since their employment is to help us bear
40 The villainies of men without despair)?
A heart well-armed with virtue can endure. . . .
ALCESTE Sir, you're a matchless reasoner, to be sure;
Your words are fine and full of cogency;

But don't waste time and eloquence on me.
My reason bids me go, for my own good.
My tongue won't lie and flatter as it should;
God knows what frankness it might next commit,
5   And what I'd suffer on account of it.
Pray let me wait for Célimène's return
In peace and quiet. I shall shortly learn,
By her response to what I have in view,
Whether her love for me is feigned or true.
10 PHILINTE   Till then, let's visit Éliante upstairs.
    ALCESTE   No, I am too weighed down with somber cares.
Go to her, do; and leave me with my gloom
Here in the darkened corner of this room.
    PHILINTE   Why, that's no sort of company, my friend;
15 I'll see if Éliante will not descend.

Scene II (CÉLIMÈNE, ORONTE, ALCESTE)

    ORONTE   Yes, Madam, if you wish me to remain
Your true and ardent lover, you must deign
To give me some more positive assurance.
20 All this suspense is quite beyond endurance.
If your heart shares the sweet desires of mine,
Show me as much by some convincing sign;
And here's the sign I urgently suggest:
That you no longer tolerate Alceste,
25 But sacrifice him to my love, and sever
All your relations with the man forever.
    CÉLIMÈNE   Why do you suddenly dislike him so?
You praised him to the skies not long ago.
    ORONTE   Madam, that's not the point. I'm here to find
30 Which way your tender feelings are inclined.
Choose, if you please, between Alceste and me,
And I shall stay or go accordingly.
    ALCESTE (*emerging from the corner*)   Yes, Madam, choose; this
    gentleman's demand
35 Is wholly just, and I support his stand.
I too am true and ardent; I too am here
To ask you that you make your feelings clear.
No more delays, now; no equivocation;
The time has come to make your declaration.
40 ORONTE   Sir, I've no wish in any way to be
An obstacle to your felicity.

ALCESTE   Sir, I've no wish to share her heart with you;
That may sound jealous, but at least it's true.
ORONTE   If, weighing us, she leans in your direction . . .
ALCESTE   If she regards you with the least affection . . .
5 ORONTE   I swear I'll yield her to you there and then.
ALCESTE   I swear I'll never see her face again.
ORONTE   Now, Madam, tell us what we've come to hear.
ALCESTE   Madam, speak openly and have no fear.
ORONTE   Just say which one is to remain your lover.
10 ALCESTE   Just name one name, and it will all be over.
ORONTE   What! Is it possible that you're undecided?
ALCESTE   What! Can your feelings possibly be divided?
CÉLIMÈNE   Enough: this inquisition's gone too far:
How utterly unreasonable you are!
15 Not that I couldn't make the choice with ease;
My heart has no conflicting sympathies;
I know full well which one of you I favor,
And you'd not see me hesitate or waver.
But how can you expect me to reveal
20 So cruelly and bluntly what I feel?
I think it altogether too unpleasant
To choose between two men when both are present;
One's heart has means more subtle and more kind
Of letting its affections be divined,
25 Nor need one be uncharitably plain
To let a lover know he loves in vain.
ORONTE   No, no, speak plainly; I for one can stand it.
I beg you to be frank.
ALCESTE   And I demand it.
30 The simple truth is what I wish to know,
And there's no need for softening the blow.
You've made an art of pleasing everyone,
But now your days of coquetry are done:
You have no choice now, Madam, but to choose,
35 For I'll know what to think if you refuse;
I'll take your silence for a clear admission
That I'm entitled to my worst suspicion.
ORONTE   I thank you for this ultimatum, Sir,
And I may say I heartily concur.
40 CÉLIMÈNE   Really, this foolishness is very wearing:
Must you be so unjust and overbearing?
Haven't I told you why I must demur?
Ah, here's Éliante; I'll put the case to her.

Scene III (ÉLIANTE, PHILINTE, CÉLIMÈNE, ORONTE, ALCESTE)

CÉLIMÈNE   Cousin, I'm being persecuted here
By these two persons, who, it would appear,
Will not be satisfied till I confess
5   Which one I love the more, and which the less,
And tell the latter to his face that he
Is henceforth banished from my company.
Tell me, has ever such a thing been done?
ÉLIANTE   You'd best not turn to me; I'm not the one
10   To back you in a matter of this kind:
I'm all for those who frankly speak their mind.
ORONTE   Madam, you'll search in vain for a defender.
ALCESTE   You're beaten, Madam, and may as well surrender.
ORONTE   Speak, speak, you must; and end this awful strain.
15   ALCESTE   Or don't, and your position will be plain.
ORONTE   A single word will close this painful scene.
ALCESTE   But if you're silent, I'll know what you mean.

Scene IV (ARSINOÉ, CÉLIMÈNE, ÉLIANTE, ALCESTE, PHILINTE,
ACASTE, CLITANDRE, ORONTE)

20   ACASTE (*to* CÉLIMÈNE)   Madam, with all due deference, we two
Have come to pick a little bone with you.
CLITANDRE (*to* ORONTE *and* ALCESTE)   I'm glad you're present,
Sirs, as you'll soon learn,
Our business here is also your concern.
25   ARSINOÉ (*to* CÉLIMÈNE)   Madam, I visit you so soon again
Only because of these two gentlemen,
Who came to me indignant and aggrieved
About a crime too base to be believed.
Knowing your virtue, having such confidence in it,
30   I couldn't think you guilty for a minute,
In spite of all their telling evidence;
And, rising above our little difference,
I've hastened here in friendship's name to see
You clear yourself of this great calumny.
35   ACASTE   Yes, Madam, let us see with what composure
You'll manage to respond to this disclosure.
You lately sent Clitandre this tender note.
CLITANDRE   And this one, for Acaste, you also wrote.
ACASTE (*to* ORONTE *and* ALCESTE)   You'll recognize this writing,
40   Sirs, I think;
The lady is so free with pen and ink

That you must know it all too well, I fear.
But listen: this is something you should hear.

5 "How absurd you are to condemn my lightheartedness in society, and to accuse me of being happiest in the company of others. Nothing could be more unjust; and if you do not come to me instantly and beg pardon for saying such a thing, I shall never forgive you as long as I live. Our big bumbling friend the Viscount . . ."

What a shame that he's not here.

10 "Our big bumbling friend the Viscount, whose name stands first in your complaint, is hardly a man to my taste; and ever since the day I watched him spend three-quarters of an hour spitting into a well, so as to make circles in the water, I have been unable to think highly of him. As for the little Mar-
15 quess . . ."

In all modesty, gentlemen, that is I.

"As for the little Marquess, who sat squeezing my hand for such a long while yesterday, I find him in all respects the most trifling creature alive; and the only things of value about him
20 are his cape and his sword. As for the man with the green ribbons . . ."

(*To* ALCESTE.) It's your turn now, Sir.

"As for the man with the green ribbons, he amuses me now and then with his bluntness and his bearish ill-humor; but
25 there are many times indeed when I think him the greatest bore in the world. And as for the sonneteer . . ."

(*To* ORONTE.) Here's your helping.

"And as for the sonneteer, who has taken it into his head to be witty, and insists on being an author in the teeth of opin-
30 ion, I simply cannot be bothered to listen to him, and his prose wearies me quite as much as his poetry. Be assured that I am not always so well-entertained as you suppose; that I long for your company, more than I dare to say, at all these entertainments to which people drag me; and that the pres-
35 ence of those one loves is the true and perfect seasoning to all one's pleasures."

CLITANDRE And now for me.

"Clitandre, whom you mention, and who so pesters me with his saccharine speeches, is the last man on earth for whom I could feel any affection. He is quite mad to suppose that I love him, and so are you, to doubt that you are loved. Do

5   come to your senses; exchange your suppositions for his; and visit me as often as possible, to help me bear the annoyance of his unwelcome attentions."

It's sweet character that these letters show,
And what to call it, Madam, you well know.

10 Enough. We're off to make the world acquainted
With this sublime self-portrait that you've painted.
ACASTE   Madam, I'll make you no farewell oration;
No, you're not worthy of my indignation.
Far choicer hearts than yours, as you'll discover,

15 Would like this little Marquess for a lover.

Scene V (CÉLIMÈNE, ÉLIANTE, ARSINOÉ, ALCESTE, ORONTE, PHILINTE)

ORONTE   So! After all those loving letters you wrote,
You turn on me like this, and cut my throat!

20 And your dissembling, faithless heart, I find,
Has pledged itself by turns to all mankind!
How blind I've been! But now I clearly see;
I thank you, Madam, for enlightening me.
My heart is mine once more, and I'm content;

25 The loss of it shall be your punishment.
(*To* ALCESTE)   Sir, she is yours; I'll seek no more to stand
Between your wishes and this lady's hand.

Scene VI (CÉLIMÈNE, ÉLIANTE, ARSINOÉ, ALCESTE, PHILINTE)

ARSINOÉ (*to* CÉLIMÈNE)   Madam, I'm forced to speak. I'm

30   far too stirred
To keep my counsel, after what I've heard.
I'm shocked and staggered by your want of morals.
It's not my way to mix in others' quarrels;
But really, when this fine and noble spirit,

35 This man of honor and surpassing merit,
Laid down the offering of his heart before you,
How *could* you . . .
ALCESTE   Madam, permit me, I implore you,
To represent myself in this debate.

40 Don't bother, please, to be my advocate.
My heart, in any case, could not afford
To give your services their due reward;

And if I chose, for consolation's sake,
Some other lady, 'twould not be you I'd take.
ARSINOÉ   What makes you think you could, Sir? And how dare you
Imply that I've been trying to ensnare you?
5   If you can for a moment entertain
Such flattering fancies, you're extremely vain.
I'm not so interested as you suppose
In Célimène's discarded gigolos.
Get rid of that absurd illusion, do.
10   Women like me are not for such as you.
Stay with this creature, to whom you're so attached;
I've never seen two people better matched.

Scene VII (CÉLIMÈNE, ÉLIANTE, ALCESTE, PHILINTE)
ALCESTE (*to* CÉLIMÈNE)   Well, I've been still throughout this
15   exposé,
Till everyone but me has said his say.
Come, have I shown sufficient self-restraint?
And may I now . . .
CÉLIMÈNE   Yes, make your just complaint.
20   Reproach me freely, call me what you will;
You've every right to say I've used you ill.
I've wronged you, I confess it; and in my shame
I'll make no effort to escape the blame.
The anger of those others I could despise;
25   My guilt toward you I sadly recognize.
Your wrath is wholly justified, I fear;
I know how culpable I must appear,
I know all things bespeak my treachery,
And that, in short, you've grounds for hating me.
30   Do so; I give you leave.
ALCESTE   Ah, traitress—how,
How should I cease to love you, even now?
Though mind and will were passionately bent
On hating you, my heart would not consent.
35   (*To* ÉLIANTE *and* PHILINTE.)   Be witness to my madness, both of
        you;
See what infatuation drives one to;
But wait; my folly's only just begun,
And I shall prove to you before I'm done
40   How strange the human heart is, and how far
From rational we sorry creatures are.
(*To* CÉLIMÈNE.)   Woman, I'm willing to forget your shame,
And clothe your treacheries in a sweeter name;

I'll call them youthful errors, instead of crimes,
And lay the blame on these corrupting times.
My one condition is that you agree
To share my chosen fate, and fly with me
5　To that wild, trackless, solitary place
In which I shall forget the human race.
Only by such a course can you atone
For those atrocious letters; by that alone
Can you remove my present horror of you,
10　And make it possible for me to love you.
CÉLIMÈNE　What! *I* renounce the world at my young age,
And die of boredom in some hermitage?
ALCESTE　Ah, if you really loved me as you ought,
You wouldn't give the world a moment's thought;
15　Must you have me, and all the world beside?
CÉLIMÈNE　Alas, at twenty one is terrified
Of solitude. I fear I lack the force
And depth of soul to take so stern a course.
But if my hand in marriage will content you,
20　Why, there's a plan which I might well consent to,
And . . .
ALCESTE　No, I detest you now. I could excuse
Everything else, but since you thus refuse
To love me wholly, as a wife should do,
25　And see the world in me, as I in you,
Go! I reject your hand, and disenthrall
My heart from your enchantments, once for all.

Scene VIII (ÉLIANTE, ALCESTE, PHILINTE)

ALCESTE (*to* ÉLIANTE)　Madam, your virtuous beauty has no peer;
30　Of all this world you only are sincere;
I've long esteemed you highly, as you know;
Permit me ever to esteem you so,
And if I do not now request your hand,
Forgive me, Madam, and try to understand.
35　I feel unworthy of it; I sense that fate
Does not intend me for the married state,
That I should do you wrong by offering you
My shattered heart's unhappy residue,
And that in short . . .
40　ÉLIANTE　　　　　Your argument's well taken:
Nor need you fear that I shall feel forsaken.
Were I to offer him this hand of mine,
Your friend Philinte, I think, would not decline.

PHILINTE   Ah, Madam, that's my heart's most cherished goal,
For which I'd gladly give my life and soul.
ALCESTE (*to* ÉLIANTE *and* PHILINTE)   May you be true to all
      you now profess,
5   And so deserve unending happiness.
Meanwhile, betrayed and wronged in everything,
I'll flee this bitter world where vice is king,
And seek some spot unpeopled and apart
Where I'll be free to have an honest heart.
10   PHILINTE   Come, Madam, let's do everything we can
To change the mind of this unhappy man.

THE WAY OF THE WORLD (1700)

WILLIAM CONGREVE (1670–1729)

With Charles II restored to the throne in 1660, the English theatre returned after suppression by Cromwell since 1642 in the form and style that has become known as Restoration drama. But it bore little resemblance to the broadly popular public entertainment that had thrived before the civil war. Moving into continental-style, artificially illuminated indoor theatres, and for the first time introducing women on stage, the theatre now became the playground of a privileged and indolent aristocratic society suddenly in control of things after years of repression under the dictatorship of the Commonwealth.

While tragedy was, of course, being written and performed, its slavish adherence to the neo-classic style of its French and Italian counterparts made it stilted and unimaginatively dull. Comedy was another matter.

The comedies written for this revived theatre bore notable similarities to the social satires of Molière. However, unlike Molière, who wrote his plays as the thorough stage professional, Restoration dramatists were mostly dilettantes who dabbled in the theatre by writing a play or two and then quitting. Nevertheless, the best of these Restoration comedies of manners remain among the finest examples of high comedy in any language. Their witty development of the recurring theme of sophisticated sex with its constant intrigues and dalliances places them in an exclusive niche of their own. Funny, bitingly satiric at times, often wryly cynical, sometimes scabrous and savagely brutal, they still entertain in their sparkling if frequently ribald exposés of the wicked ways of the world.

Congreve's play is the apogee of the Restoration style, unsurpassed in its dramatic brilliance. Though appearing when the open licentiousness of the era was waning fast, it is a stunning distillation of the behavior patterns exhibited by a society which existed mostly in fond memory. Its characters are memorable and exquisitely created. Mirabell represents the best of the Restoration "gallants," at one time known as "wild," but now more polished and less coarse. Dashingly handsome, sought by every woman, earnest in the pursuit of his lady love, in true Restoration manner he is not above gaining her by fraud, deceit, and cruel intrigue. Millamant is his perfect counterpart, sought by every man, an out-and-out flirt who dangles her suitors, especially the infatuated Mirabell, like puppets on a string. Lady Wishfort is a riotously funny parody of all those ladies who refuse to admit their age or acknowledge the decay of their beauty; and Witwoud and Petulant are two of the best portrayals of overdressed, oversexed, preposterously dim-witted fops in all comedy.

These glamorous characters live in a world of wealth and idleness, vitally concerned about *having* money but totally averse to *earning* it. They inherit wealth, marry it, if need be steal it, but heaven forbid that they ever lower themselves to work for it. Here is a universe where the Ten Commandments give way to the 10,000 commandments of social behavior. These people seduce and abandon at will; both male and female are ashamed if caught in the act, not because of their indiscretions, but because they have been found out, which is the real sin. They are neither moral nor immoral; they are *amoral*. They offer lip service to the traditional social values but proceed to ignore them without remorse.

Don't try to figure out all the intricacies of the plot; the effort is hardly worth it. In fact, the audience at the play's initial performance was unable to do so, and it was at first considered a resounding flop. Instead, listen to what everybody says to and about each other. Note the twisted logic of Mirabell's first-scene justification of his affair with Lady Wishfort; look at his callous explanation to the suffering, acquiescent Mrs. Fainall as to why she had to marry her rascal of a husband. Listen to what Mrs. Marwood and Mrs. Fainall have to say about the men in their lives and how they should be treated, both in and out of wedlock. Watch Millamant, who "loves to give pain," as she toys with the frustrated Mirabell. Follow the hilarious arguments of the famous proposal, or "proviso" scene, in which the lovers lay down their conditions of marriage in terms so preposterously unromantic yet eminently sensible. But last of all, don't ever believe that Mirabell and Millamant's life will be idyllically happy ever after. That's for fairy tales; it is emphatically not Congreve's *Way of the World*.

The Way of the World

WILLIAM CONGREVE

CHARACTERS[1]

FAINALL, *in love with Mrs. Marwood*

EDWARD MIRABELL, *in love with Mrs. Millamant*

ANTHONY WITWOUD, } *followers of*
PETULANT,   } *Mrs. Millamant*

SIR WILFULL WITWOUD, *half-brother to Witwoud, and nephew to Lady Wishfort*

LADY WISHFORT, *enemy to Mirabell, for having falsely pretended love to her*

MRS. MILLAMANT, *a fine lady, niece to Lady Wishfort, and loves Mirabell*

MRS. MARWOOD, *friend to Mr. Fainall, and likes Mirabell*

MRS. ARABELLA FAINALL, *daughter to Lady Wishfort, and wife to Fainall, formerly friend to Mirabell*

WAITWELL, *servant to Mirabell*

FOIBLE, *woman to Lady Wishfort*

MINCING, *woman to Mrs. Millamant*

BETTY, *servant in a chocolate-house*

PEG, *servant to Lady Wishfort*

DANCERS, FOOTMEN, and ATTENDANTS

SCENE. *London, the time equal to that of the presentation*[2]

---

[1] *Characters* note the use of "label names," so prevalent in Restoration comedy. *Witwoud* would be a "wit"; *Petulant* behaves with petulance; *Lady Wishfort* wishes "for it," i.e., sex; *Mrs. Marwood* is one who mars, or scratches, things as a cat on wood, intruding where she's not wanted. *Fainall* can be seen two ways: he would "fain have all," which he almost gets until the end, or he "feigns all," that is, pretends and dissembles. The names of *Mirabell* and *Millamant* reflect their "myriads, thousands" of lovers (belles, amours) because almost everybody in the play seems to be in love with one or the other[2] this stipulation is unique in any era, especially in plays written long before the advent of theatrical "realism" as we know it. Congreve actually conceived of the entire action of the play as taking place precisely within the elapsed time of the presentation itself. A careful check of the sequence of scenes will show how well he succeeded, with each following the other in chronological order within a single day.

PROLOGUE

Spoken by MR. FAINALL

Of those few fools, who with ill stars are curs'd,
Sure scribbling fools, call'd poets, fare the worst,
For they're a sort of fools which Fortune makes,
And, after she has made 'em fools, forsakes.
With Nature's oafs 'tis quite a diff'rent case,
For Fortune favours all her idiot race;
In her own nest the cuckoo-eggs[3] we find,
O'er which she broods to hatch the changeling[4] kind.
No portion for her own she has to spare,
So much she dotes on her adopted care.
   Poets are bubbles,[5] by the town drawn in,
Suffer'd at first some trifling stakes to win;
But what unequal hazards do they run! ⎫
Each time they write they venture all they've won; ⎬
The squire that's butter'd still is sure to be undone. ⎭
This author, heretofore, has found your favour,
But pleads no merit from his past behaviour.
To build on that might prove a vain presumption,
Should grants to poets made admit resumption;
And in Parnassus he must lose his seat
If that be found a forfeited estate.
   He owns, with toil he wrote the following scenes,
But if they're naught ne'er spare him for his pains.
Damn him the more: have no commiseration
For dulness on mature deliberation.
He swears he'll not resent one hissed-off scene, ⎫
Nor, like those peevish wits, his play maintain, ⎬
Who, to assert their sense, your taste arraign. ⎭
Some plot we think he has, and some new thought,
Some humour, too, no farce—but that's a fault.
Satire, he thinks, you ought not to expect:
For so reform'd a town[6] who dares correct?

---

[3] *Cuckoo-eggs* cuckoos often lay their eggs in other birds' nests   [4] *changeling* one child substituted for another; cuckoos will hatch and raise chicks of other birds   [5] *bubbles* dupes   [6] *So reformed a town* in 1698 the clergyman Jeremy Collier had attacked the licentiousness of Restoration theatre in a famous diatribe "A Short View of the Immorality and Profaneness of the English Stage." Though narrowly prejudiced and often irrational, the "Short View" stirred up a lively controversy and ultimately made itself felt in the "cleaning up" of the drama in the eighteenth century. Congreve, stung by Collier's singling out his three earlier plays, vigorously replied the same year in "Amendments of Mr. Collier's False and Imperfect Citation."

To please this time has been his sole pretence;
He'll not instruct, lest it should give offence.
Should he by chance a knave or fool expose,
That hurts none here; sure here are none of those.
In short, our play shall (with your leave to show it)
Give you one instance of a passive poet,
Who to your judgments yields all resignation:
So save or damn, after your own discretion.

ACT I

SCENE. *A chocolate-house*[1]
   MIRABELL *and* FAINALL, *rising from cards*
   BETTY *waiting*

MIRABELL   You are a fortunate man, Mr. Fainall.

FAINALL   Have we done?

MIRABELL   What you please. I'll play on to entertain you.

FAINALL   No, I'll give you your revenge another time, when you are not so indifferent; you are thinking of something else now, and play too negligently; the coldness of a losing gamester lessens the pleasure of the winner: I'd no more play with a man that slighted his ill fortune, than I'd make love to a woman who under-valued the loss of her reputation.

MIRABELL   You have a taste extremely delicate, and are for refining on your pleasures.

FAINALL   Prithee, why so reserved? Something has put you out of humor.

MIRABELL   Not at all: I happen to be grave today; and you are gay; that's all.

FAINALL   Confess, Millamant and you quarrelled last night, after I left you; my fair cousin has some humors that would tempt the patience of a Stoic. What! Some coxcomb[2] came in, and was well received by her, while you were by?

MIRABELL   Witwoud and Petulant; and what was worse, her aunt, your wife's mother, my evil genius; or to sum up all in her own name, my old Lady Wishfort came in.

---

[1] *A chocolate-house* chocolate and coffee houses were gathering places where gentlemen of leisure could while away their many idle hours in cards, conversation, and drinking of the rich exotic imported beverages, not to be confused with our common household varieties of cocoa and coffee, which were not household drinks at that time   [2] *coxcomb* another word for "fop," a generally vain, often obnoxious, always overdressed individual of which Witwoud and Petulant are two of the best examples in Restoration comedy. The term comes from the bright red wattles or comb of a cock.

FAINALL   Oh, there it is then! She has a lasting passion for you, and with reason. What! then my wife was there?

MIRABELL   Yes, and Mrs. Marwood and three or four more, whom I never saw before; seeing me, they all put on their grave faces, whispered to one another, then complained aloud of the vapors,[3] and after fell into a profound silence.

FAINALL   They had a mind to be rid of you.

MIRABELL   For which reason I resolved not to stir. At last the good old lady broke through her painful taciturnity, with an invective against long visits. I would not have understood her, but Millamant joining in the argument, I rose and with a constrained smile told her I thought nothing was so easy as to know when a visit began to be troublesome; she reddened and I withdrew, without expecting her reply.

FAINALL   You were to blame to resent what she spoke only in compliance with her aunt.

MIRABELL   She is more mistress of herself than to be under the necessity of such a resignation.

FAINALL   What? though half her fortune depends upon her marrying with my lady's approbation?

MIRABELL   I was then in such a humor, that I should have been better pleased if she had been less discreet.

FAINALL   Now I remember, I wonder not they were weary of you; last night was one of their cabal-nights;[4] they have 'em three times a week, and meet by turns, at one another's apartments, where they come together like the coroner's inquest, to sit upon the murdered reputations of the week. You and I are excluded; and it was once proposed that all the male sex should be excepted; but somebody moved that to avoid scandal there might be one man of the community; upon which motion Witwoud and Petulant were enrolled members.

MIRABELL   And who may have been the foundress of this sect? My Lady Wishfort, I warrant, who publishes her detestation of mankind; and full of the vigor of fifty-five, declared for a friend and ratafia;[5] and let posterity shift for itself, she'll breed no more.

FAINALL   The discovery of your sham addresses to her, to conceal your love to her niece, has provoked this separation: had you dissembled[6] better, things might have continued in the state of nature.

---

[3] *vapors* an attack of depression or nervous hysteria, to which ladies of the age seemed peculiarly prone, especially, as in this case, as a quick defense against an intrusive or offending male   [4] *cabal-night* a cabal was a group, often meeting in secret, to plot and plan intrigues   [5] *ratafia* a brandy-like fruit-flavored liqueur   [6] *dissembled* acted falsely, to conceal facts or real intentions

MIRABELL   I did as much as man could, with any reasonable conscience; I proceeded to the very last act of flattery with her, and was guilty of a song in her commendation. Nay, I got a friend to put her into a lampoon,[7] and compliment her with the imputation of an affair with a young fellow, which I carried so far, that I told her the malicious town took notice that she was grown fat of a sudden; and when she lay in of a dropsy,[8] persuaded her she was reported to be in labor. The devil's in't, if an old woman is to be flattered further, unless a man should endeavor downright personally to debauch her; and that my virtue forbade me. But for the discovery of that amour, I am indebted to your friend, or your wife's friend, Mrs. Marwood.

FAINALL   What should provoke her to be your enemy, without she has made you advances, which you have slighted? Women do not easily forgive omissions of that nature.

MIRABELL   She was always civil to me, till of late. I confess I am not one of those coxcombs who are apt to interpret a woman's good manners to her prejudice; and think that she who does not refuse 'em everything, can refuse 'em nothing.

FAINALL   You are a gallant man, Mirabell; and though you may have cruelty enough not to satisfy a lady's longing, you have too much generosity not to be tender of her honor. Yet you speak with an indifference which seems to be affected; and confesses you are conscious of a negligence.

MIRABELL   You pursue the argument with a distrust that seems to be unaffected, and confesses you are conscious of a concern for which the lady is more indebted to you than your wife.

FAINALL   Fie, fie, friend, if you grow censorious I must leave you. I'll look upon the gamesters in the next room.

MIRABELL   Who are they?

FAINALL   Petulant and Witwoud. (*To* BETTY.) Bring me some chocolate. (*Exit.*)

MIRABELL   Betty, what says your clock?

BETTY   Turned of the last canonical hour,[9] sir. (*Exit.*)

MIRABELL   How pertinently the jade answers me! Ha! almost one o'clock! (*Looking on his watch.*) Oh, y'are come—

(*Enter a* SERVANT.)

---

[7] *lampoon* a mocking, sometimes harsh satire directed against an individual, often performed in public. Because lampoons were normally aimed at persons of note in society, Lady Wishfort, a relative non-entity, would indeed have been flattered   [8] *dropsy* a not uncommon affliction of the era involving an abnormal accumulation of fluids and consequent bodily swelling   [9] *canonical hour* the last hour of the day when marriages could be legally performed within London was noon

Well, is the grand affair over? You have been something tedious.

SERVANT   Sir, there's such coupling at Pancras,[10] that they stand behind one another, as 'twere in a country dance. Ours was the last couple to lead up; and no hopes appearing of dispatch, besides, the parson growing hoarse, we were afraid his lungs would have failed before it came to our turn; so we drove around to Duke's Place;[11] and there they were riveted in a trice.

MIRABELL   So, so, you are sure they are married?

SERVANT   Married and bedded, sir: I am witness.

MIRABELL   Have you the certificate?

SERVANT   Here it is, sir.

MIRABELL   Has the tailor brought Waitwell's clothes home, and the new liveries?

SERVANT   Yes, sir.

MIRABELL   That's well. Do you go home again, d'ee hear, and adjourn the consummation till farther order; bid Waitwell shake his ears, and Dame Partlet[12] rustle up her feathers, and meet me at one o'clock by Rosamond's Pond;[13] that I may see her before she returns to her lady; and as you tender your ears be secret.

(*Exit* SERVANT. *Re-enter* FAINALL.)

FAINALL   Joy of your success, Mirabell; you look pleased.

MIRABELL   Ay; I have been engaged in a matter of some sort of mirth, which is not yet ripe for discovery. I am glad this is not a cabal-night. I wonder, Fainall, that you who are married, and of consequence should be discreet, will suffer your wife to be of such a party.

FAINALL   Faith, I am not jealous. Besides, most who are engaged are women and relations; and for the men, they are of a kind too contemptible to give scandal.

MIRABELL   I am of another opinion. The greater the coxcomb, always the more the scandal: for a woman who is not a fool can have but one reason for associating with a man that is.

FAINALL   Are you jealous as often as you see Witwoud entertained by Millamant?

MIRABELL   Of her understanding I am, if not of her person.

FAINALL   You do her wrong; for to give her her due, she has wit.

MIRABELL   She has beauty enough to make any man think so, and complaisance enough not to contradict him who shall tell her so.

---

[10] *Pancras* St. Pancras church, outside the city, where weddings could be performed quickly for a fee and without license   [11] *Duke's Place* St. James's Church in Duke's Place, similar to Pancras   [12] *Dame Partlet* the hen, Pertelote, from Chaucer's "Nun's Priest's Tale"   [13] *Rosamond's Pond* a pond in St. James's Park, a favorite trysting place

FAINALL   For a passionate lover, methinks you are a man somewhat too discerning in the failings of your mistress.

MIRABELL   And for a discerning man, somewhat too passionate a lover; for I like her with all her faults; nay, like her for her faults. Her follies are so natural, or so artful, that they become her; and those affectations which in another woman would be odious, serve but to make her more agreeable. I'll tell thee, Fainall, she once used me with that insolence, that in revenge I took her to pieces; sifted her and separated her failings; I studied 'em, and got 'em by rote. The catalogue was so large, that I was not without hopes, one day or other, to hate her heartily: to which end I so used myself to think of 'em, that at length, contrary to my design and expectation, they gave me every hour less and less disturbance; till in a few days it became habitual to me to remember 'em without being displeased. They are now grown as familiar to me as my own frailties; and in all probability in a little time longer I shall like 'em as well.

FAINALL   Marry her, marry her; be half as well acquainted with her charms as you are with her defects, and my life on't, you are your own man again.

MIRABELL   Say you so?

FAINALL   Ay, ay; I have experience: I have a wife, and so forth.

(*Enter* MESSENGER.)

MESSENGER   Is one Squire Witwoud here?

BETTY   Yes; what's your business?

MESSENGER   I have a letter for him, from his brother, Sir Wilfull, which I am charged to deliver into his own hands.

BETTY   He's in the next room, friend—that way.

(*Exit* MESSENGER.)

MIRABELL   What, is the chief of that noble family in town, Sir Wilfull Witwoud?

FAINALL   He is expected to-day. Do you know him?

MIRABELL   I have seen him; he promises to be an extraordinary person; I think you have the honor to be related to him.

FAINALL   Yes; he is half-brother to this Witwoud by a former wife, who was sister to my Lady Wishfort, my wife's mother. If you marry Millamant, you must call cousins too.

MIRABELL   I had rather be his relation than his acquaintance.

FAINALL   He comes to town in order to equip himself for travel.

MIRABELL   For travel! Why, the man that I mean is above forty.

FAINALL   No matter for that; 'tis for the honor of England, that all Europe should know we have blockheads of all ages.

MIRABELL   I wonder there is not an act of Parliament to save the credit of the nation, and prohibit the exportation of fools.

FAINALL   By no means, 'tis better as 'tis: 'tis better to trade with a little loss, than to be quite eaten up, with being overstocked.

MIRABELL   Pray, are the follies of this knight-errant, and those of the squire his brother, anything related?

FAINALL   Not at all; Witwoud grows by the knight, like a medlar grafted on a crab.[14] One will melt in your mouth, and t'other set your teeth on edge; one is all pulp, and the other all core.

MIRABELL   So one will be rotten before he be ripe, and the other will be rotten without ever being ripe at all.

FAINALL   Sir Wilfull is an odd mixture of bashfulness and obstinacy. But when he's drunk, he's as loving as the monster in *The Tempest*; and much after the same manner. To give the t'other his due, he has something of good nature, and does not always want wit.

MIRABELL   Not always; but as often as his memory fails him, and his commonplace of comparisons. He is a fool with a good memory, and some few scraps of other folks' wit. He is one whose conversation can never be approved, yet it is now and then to be endured. He has indeed one good quality, he is not exceptious;[15] for he so passionately affects the reputation of understanding raillery,[16] that he will construe an affront into a jest; and call downright rudeness and ill language, satire and fire.

FAINALL   If you have a mind to finish his picture, you have an opportunity to do it at full length. Behold the original.

(*Enter* WITWOUD.)

WITWOUD   Afford me your compassion, my dears; pity me, Fainall, Mirabell, pity me.

MIRABELL   I do from my soul.

FAINALL   Why, what's the matter?

WITWOUD   No letters for me, Betty?

BETTY   Did not the messenger bring you one but now, sir?

WITWOUD   Ay, but no other?

BETTY   No, sir.

WITWOUD   That's hard, that's very hard;—a messenger, a mule, a beast of burden: he has brought me a letter from the fool my brother, as heavy as a panegyric in a funeral sermon, or a copy of commendatory

---

[14] *medlar; crab* a soft pulpy pear; crabapple   [15] *exceptious* quarrelsome   [16] *raillery* in Restoration terms the art of jesting banter or verbal ridicule, mostly but not always good natured, especially affected by the likes of the foppish Witwoud, who obviously does not know its finer points as indicated by Mirabell's opinion of him

verses from one poet to another. And what's worse, 'tis as sure a forerunner of the author, as an epistle dedicatory.

MIRABELL   A fool, and your brother, Witwoud!

WITWOUD   Ay, ay, my half-brother. My half-brother he is, no nearer upon honor.

MIRABELL   Then 'tis possible he may be but half a fool.

WITWOUD   Good, good, Mirabell, *le drôle!* Good, good!—hang him, don't let's talk of him.—Fainall, how does your lady? Gad, I say anything in the world to get this fellow out of my head. I beg pardon that I should ask a man of pleasure, and the town, a question at once so foreign and domestic. But I talk like an old maid at a marriage, I don't know what I say: but she's the best woman in the world.

FAINALL   'Tis well you don't know what you say, or else your commendation would go near to make me either vain or jealous.

WITWOUD   No man in town lives well with a wife but Fainall. Your judgment, Mirabell.

MIRABELL   You had better step and ask his wife, if you would be credibly informed.

WITWOUD   Mirabell.

MIRABELL   Ay.

WITWOUD   My dear, I ask ten thousand pardons.—Gad. I have forgot what I was going to say to you.

MIRABELL   I thank you heartily, heartily.

WITWOUD   No, but prithee excuse me—my memory is such a memory.

MIRABELL   Have a care of such apologies, Witwoud; for I never knew a fool but he affected to complain, either of the spleen[17] or his memory.

FAINALL   What have you done with Petulant?

WITWOUD   He's reckoning his money—my money it was; I have no luck today.

FAINALL   You may allow him to win of you at play, for you are sure to be too hard for him at repartee: since you monopolize the wit that is between you, the fortune must be his of course.

MIRABELL   I don't find that Petulant confesses the superiority of wit to be your talent, Witwoud.

WITWOUD   Come, come, you are malicious now, and would breed debates. Petulant's my friend, and a very honest fellow, and a very pretty fellow, and has a smattering—faith and troth, a pretty deal of an odd sort of a small wit. Nay, I'll do him justice. I'm his friend, I

---

[17] *spleen* like the "vapors" a common affliction of the time, implying melancholy or even testiness and bad temper, derived from the internal organ which at one time was held to be the seat of emotions

won't wrong him, neither. And if he had but any judgment in the world, he would not be altogether contemptible. Come, come, don't detract from the merits of my friend.

FAINALL   You don't take your friend to be over-nicely bred.

WITWOUD   No, no, hang him, the rogue has no manners at all, that I must own—no more breeding than a bum-baily,[18] that I grant you. 'Tis pity, faith; the fellow has fire and life.

MIRABELL   What, courage?

WITWOUD   Hum, faith, I don't know as to that—I can't say as to that. Yes, faith, in a controversy he'll contradict anybody.

MIRABELL   Though 'twere a man whom he feared, or a woman whom he loved.

WITWOUD   Well, well, he does not always think before he speaks. We have all our failings; you're too hard upon him, you are, faith. Let me excuse him—I can defend most of his faults, except one or two; one he has, that's the truth on't, if he were my brother, I could not acquit him. That, indeed, I could wish were otherwise.

MIRABELL   Ay, marry, what's that, Witwoud?

WITWOUD   Oh, pardon me! Expose the infirmities of my friend? No, my dear, excuse me there.

FAINALL   What! I warrant, he's unsincere, or 'tis some such trifle.

WITWOUD   No, no, what if he be? 'Tis no matter for that, his wit will excuse that: a wit should no more be sincere, than a woman constant; one argues a decay of parts, as t'other of beauty.

MIRABELL   Maybe you think him too positive?

WITWOUD   No, no, his being positive is an incentive to argument, and keeps up conversation.

FAINALL   Too illiterate.

WITWOUD   That! that's his happiness. His want of learning gives him the more opportunities to show his natural parts.

MIRABELL   He wants words.

WITWOUD   Ay; but I like him for that now; for his want of words gives me the pleasure very often to explain his meaning.

FAINALL   He's impudent.

WITWOUD   No, that's not it.

MIRABELL   Vain.

WITWOUD   No.

MIRABELL   What, he speaks unseasonable truths sometimes, because he has not wit enough to invent an evasion!

WITWOUD   Truths! Ha, ha, ha! No, no, since you will have it—I mean, he never speaks truth at all—that's all. He will lie like a chambermaid, or a woman of quality's porter. Now that is a fault.

---

[18] *bum-baily* a low-ranking bailiff, or law officer

(*Enter* COACHMAN.)

COACHMAN   Is Master Petulant here, mistress?

BETTY   Yes.

COACHMAN   Three gentlewomen in the coach would speak with him.

FAINALL   O brave Petulant, three!

BETTY   I'll tell him.

COACHMAN   You must bring two dishes of chocolate and a glass of cinnamon-water.[19]

(*Exeunt* BETTY *and* COACHMAN.)

WITWOUD   That should be for two fasting strumpets, and a bawd troubled with wind. Now you may know what the three are.

MIRABELL   You are very free with your friend's acquaintance.

WITWOUD   Ay, ay, friendship with freedom is as dull as love without enjoyment, or wine without toasting; but to tell you a secret, these are trulls that he allows coach-hire, and something more by the week, to call on him once a day at public places.

MIRABELL   How!

WITWOUD   You shall see he won't go to 'em because there's no more company here to take notice of him. Why, this is nothing to what he used to do; before he found out this way, I have known him call for himself—

FAINALL   Call for himself? What dost thou mean?

WITWOUD   Mean?—why, he would slip you out of this chocolate-house, just when you had been talking to him. As soon as your back was turned—whip he was gone; then trip to his lodging, clap on a hood and scarf, and mask, slap into a hackney-coach, and drive hither to the door again in a trice; where he would send in for himself—that I mean—call for himself, wait for himself, nay and what's more, not finding himself, sometimes leave a letter for himself.

MIRABELL   I confess this is something extraordinary—I believe he waits for himself now, he is so long a-coming. Oh, I ask his pardon!

(*Enter* PETULANT *and* BETTY.)

BETTY   Sir, the coach stays. (*Exit.*)

PETULANT   Well, well; I come.—'Sbud,[20] a man had as good be a pro-

---

[19] *cinnamon-water* a strong mixture for dyspepsia, apparently afflicting one of the three "gentlewomen" and a good treatment for the "vapors"   [20] *'Sbud* corruption of "by God's blood," sometimes expressed as "'sblood" or "ods blood." Expletives of this nature were common as mild oaths during the Restoration and eighteenth century. You will encounter a variety of them in this play and elsewhere, such as "zooks," or "gadzooks," God's hooks, or nails, and "oons," "zoons," or "zounds," God's wounds—all alluding to the crucifixion. Others include "'slife," or "odslife," God's life; "'sheart," or "ods heart," God's heart; "'sdeath," or "ods death," God's death, and so on.

fessed midwife as a professed whoremaster, at this rate; to be knocked up and raised at all hours, and in all places! Pox[21] on 'em, I won't come.—D'ee hear, tell 'em I won't come. Let 'em snivel and cry their hearts out.

FAINALL   You are very cruel, Petulant.

PETULANT   All's one, let it pass—I have a humor to be cruel.

MIRABELL   I hope they are not persons of condition that you use at this rate.

PETULANT   Condition! condition's a dried fig, if I am not in humor. By this hand, if they were your—a—a—your what-d'ee-call-'ems themselves, they must wait or rub off, if I want appetite.

MIRABELL   What-d'ee-call-'ems! What are they, Witwoud?

WITWOUD   Empresses, my dear—by your what-d'ee-call-'ems he means sultana queens.

PETULANT   Ay, Roxolanas.[22]

MIRABELL   Cry you mercy.[23]

FAINALL   Witwoud says they are—

PETULANT   What does he say th'are?

WITWOUD   I—fine ladies, I say.

PETULANT   Pass on, Witwoud.—Hark'ee, by this light, his relations— two co-heiresses his cousins, and an old aunt, that loves catterwauling[24] better than a conventicle.[25]

WITWOUD   Ha, ha, ha! I had a mind to see how the rogue would come off. Ha, ha, ha! Gad, I can't be angry with him, if he said they were my mother and my sisters.

MIRABELL   No!

WITWOUD   No; the rogue's wit and readiness of invention charm me: dear Petulant.

(Re-enter BETTY.*)*

BETTY   They are gone, sir, in great anger.

PETULANT   Enough, let 'em trundle. Anger helps complexion, saves paint.

FAINALL   This continence is all dissembled; this is in order to have something to brag of the next time he makes court to Millamant, and swear he has abandoned the whole sex for her sake.

MIRABELL   Have you not left off your impudent pretensions there yet?

---

[21] *Pox* generally refers to syphilis, but could mean smallpox. A common oath directed as a mild curse against one's adversary   [22] *Empresses, sultana queens, Roxolanas* all cant terms for prostitute   [23] *Cry you mercy* a common expression meaning "beg pardon"   [24] *caterwauling* the cry of a cat, but here meaning a group of "cats," i.e., older women   [25] *conventicle* a meeting of "nonconformists," i.e., those not conforming to the state church and meeting outside the law

I shall cut your throat, sometime or other, Petulant, about that business.

PETULANT   Ay, ay, let that pass—there are other throats to be cut—

MIRABELL   Meaning mine, sir?

PETULANT   Not I—I mean nobody—I know nothing. But there are uncles and nephews in the world—and they may be rivals. What then? All's one for that—

MIRABELL   How! Hark'ee, Petulant, come hither. Explain, or I shall call your interpreter.

PETULANT   Explain! I know nothing. Why, you have an uncle, have you not, lately come to town, and lodges by my Lady Wishfort's?

MIRABELL   True.

PETULANT   Why, that's enough. You and he are not friends; and if he should marry and have a child, you may be disinherited, ha?

MIRABELL   Where hast thou stumbled upon all this truth?

PETULANT   All's one for that; why, then say I know something.

MIRABELL   Come, thou art an honest fellow, Petulant, and shalt make love to my mistress, thou shalt, faith. What hast thou heard of my uncle?

PETULANT   I? nothing I. If throats are to be cut, let swords clash; snug's the word, I shrug and am silent.

MIRABELL   A raillery, raillery. Come, I know thou art in the women's secrets. What, you're a cabalist; I know you stayed at Millamant's last night, after I went. Was there any mention made of my uncle, or me? Tell me; if thou hadst but good nature equal to thy wit, Petulant, Tony Witwoud, who is now thy competitor in fame, would show as dim by thee as a dead whiting's eye by a pearl of Orient; he would no more be seen by thee, than Mercury is by the sun. Come, I'm sure thou wo't tell me.

PETULANT   If I do, will you grant me common sense then, for the future?

MIRABELL   Faith, I'll do what I can for thee; and I'll pray that heaven may grant it thee in the meantime.

PETULANT   Well, hark'ee.

(They converse in dumb-show.)

FAINALL   Petulant and you both will find Mirabell as warm a rival as a lover.

WITWOUD   Pshaw, pshaw, that she laughs at Petulant is plain. And for my part—but that it is almost a fashion to admire her, I should—hark'ee—to tell you a secret, but let it go no further—between friends, I shall never break my heart for her.

FAINALL   How!

WITWOUD   She's handsome; but she's a sort of an uncertain woman.

FAINALL I thought you had died for her.

WITWOUD Umh—no—

FAINALL She has wit.

WITWOUD 'Tis what she will hardly allow anybody else. Now, demme,[26] I should hate that, if she were as handsome as Cleopatra. Mirabell is not so sure of her as he thinks for.

FAINALL Why do you think so?

WITWOUD We stayed pretty late there last night, and heard something of an uncle to Mirabell, who is lately come to town,—and is between him and the best part of his estate. Mirabell and he are at some distance, as my Lady Wishfort has been told; and you know she hates Mirabell, worse than a Quaker hates a parrot, or than a fishmonger hates a hard frost. Whether this uncle has seen Mrs. Millamant or not, I cannot say; but there were items of such a treaty being in embryo; and if it should come to life, poor Mirabell would be in some sort unfortunately fobbed[27] i'faith.

FAINALL 'Tis impossible Millamant should hearken to it.

WITWOUD Faith, my dear, I can't tell; she's a woman and a kind of a humorist.

MIRABELL (*conversing apart with* PETULANT) And this is the sum of what you could collect last night.

PETULANT The quintessence. Maybe Witwoud knows more, he stayed longer. Besides, they never mind him; they say anything before him.

MIRABELL I thought you had been the greatest favorite.

PETULANT Ay, *tête-à-tête*; but not in public, because I make remarks.

MIRABELL Do you?

PETULANT Ay, ay; pox, I'm malicious, man. Now, he's soft, you know; they are not in awe of him. The fellow's well bred, he's what you call a—what-d'ee-call-'em. A fine gentleman, but he's silly withal.

MIRABELL I thank you, I know as much as my curiosity requires.— Fainall, are you for the Mall?[28]

FAINALL Ay, I'll take a turn before dinner.

WITWOUD Ay, we'll all walk in the Park, the ladies talked of being there.

---

[26] *demme* damn me [27] *fobbed* tricked [28] *Mall* the tree-lined promenade in St. James's Park (the "Park" in Witwoud's next speech) where ladies and gentlemen of fashion went to be seen and where they spent a lot of their abundant idle time together or in pursuit of each other. The Mall, not to be confused with Pall Mall slightly to the north, still exists as a busy modern traffic way between Trafalgar Square and Buckingham Palace, neither of which existed in 1700. The Mall is today lined on its north side by beautiful eighteenth-century buildings. St. James's Park remains even now one of London's most attractive small parks.

MIRABELL   I thought you were obliged to watch for your brother Sir Wilfull's arrival.

WITWOUD   No, no, he comes to his aunt's, my Lady Wishfort; pox on him, I shall be troubled with him too; what shall I do with the fool?

PETULANT   Beg him for his estate, that I may beg you afterwards, and so have but one trouble with you both.

WITWOUD   O rare Petulant! thou art as quick as a fire in a frosty morning; thou shalt to the Mall with us, and we'll be very severe.[29]

PETULANT   Enough! I'm in a humor to be severe.

MIRABELL   Are you? Pray then walk by yourselves—let not us be accessory to your putting the ladies out of countenance[30] with your senseless ribaldry, which you roar out aloud as often as they pass by you; and when you have made a handsome woman blush, then you think you have been severe.

PETULANT   What, what? Then let 'em either show their innocence by not understanding what they hear, or else show their discretion by not hearing what they would not be thought to understand.

MIRABELL   But hast not thou then sense enough to know that thou ought'st to be most ashamed thyself, when thou hast put another out of countenance?

PETULANT   Not I, by this hand—I always take blushing either for a sign of guilt, or ill breeding.

MIRABELL   I confess you ought to think so. You are in the right, that you may plead the error of your judgment in defence of your practice.

>   Where modesty's ill manners, 'tis but fit
>   That impudence and malice pass for wit.

(*Exeunt.*)

ACT II

SCENE.   *St. James's Park*
   Enter MRS. FAINALL *and* MRS. MARWOOD

MRS. FAINALL   Ay, ay, dear Marwood, if we will be happy, we must find the means in ourselves, and among ourselves. Men are ever in ex-

---

[29] *severe* to be very serious in the matter of flirting. As usual, Witwoud and Petulant overdo it, and as Mirabell points out, they are consciously gross and harsh, inflicting distress through their embarrassing crudity in their execution of their "severity."
[30] *putting the ladies out of countenance* embarrassing them, causing them to blush excessively and be flustered. It is interesting to note that for all his own "dissembling" and, to us, bad manners, Mirabell is a true gentleman who refuses to associate himself with the open crudities of the two fops.

tremes; either doting or averse. While they are lovers, if they have fire and sense, their jealousies are insupportable: and when they cease to love, (we ought to think at least) they loathe; they look upon us with horror and distaste; they meet us like the ghosts of what we were, and as such, fly from us.

MRS. MARWOOD True, 'tis an unhappy circumstance of life, that love should ever die before us; and that the man so often should outlive the lover. But say what you will, 'tis better to be left, than never to have been loved. To pass our youth in dull indifference, to refuse the sweets of life because they once must leave us, is as preposterous as to wish to have been born old, because we one day must be old. For my part, my youth may wear and waste, but it shall never rust in my possession.

MRS. FAINALL Then it seems you dissemble an aversion to mankind, only in compliance with my mother's humor.

MRS. MARWOOD Certainly. To be free; I have no taste of those insipid dry discourses, with which our sex of force must entertain themselves, apart from men. We may affect endearments to each other, profess eternal friendships, and seem to dote like lovers; but 'tis not in our natures long to persevere. Love will resume his empire in our breasts, and every heart, or soon or late, receive and readmit him as its lawful tyrant.

MRS. FAINALL Bless me, how have I been deceived! Why, you profess a libertine.[1]

MRS. MARWOOD You see my friendship by my freedom. Come, be as sincere, acknowledge that your sentiments agree with mine.

MRS. FAINALL Never.

MRS. MARWOOD You hate mankind.

MRS. FAINALL Heartily, inveterately.

MRS. MARWOOD Your husband.

MRS. FAINALL Most transcendently; ay, though I say it, meritoriously.

MRS. MARWOOD Give me your hand upon it.

MRS. FAINALL There.

MRS. MARWOOD I join with you; what I have said has been to try you.

MRS. FAINALL Is it possible? Dost thou hate those vipers, men?

MRS. MARWOOD I have done hating 'em, and am now come to despise 'em; the next thing I have to do, is eternally to forget 'em.

MRS. FAINALL There spoke the spirit of an Amazon, a Penthesilea.[2]

---

[1] *profess a libertine* admit to being one who freely grants sexual favors [2] *Amazon, a Penthesilea* the Amazons were a mythical band of powerful female warriors who permitted no men to associate with them except to conceive. Penthesilea was one of their queens.

MRS. MARWOOD   And yet I am thinking sometimes to carry my aversion further.

MRS. FAINALL   How?

MRS. MARWOOD   Faith, by marrying; if I could but find one that loved me very well, and would be thoroughly sensible of ill usage, I think I should do myself the violence of undergoing the ceremony.

MRS. FAINALL   You would not make him a cuckold?[3]

MRS. MARWOOD   No; but I'd make him believe I did, and that's as bad.

MRS. FAINALL   Why, had not you as good do it?

MRS. MARWOOD   Oh, if he should ever discover it, he would then know the worst, and be out of his pain; but I would have him ever to continue upon the rack of fear and jealousy.

MRS. FAINALL   Ingenious mischief! Would thou wert married to Mirabell.

MRS. MARWOOD   Would I were.

MRS. FAINALL   You change color.

MRS. MARWOOD   Because I hate him.

MRS. FAINALL   So do I; but I can hear him named. But what reason have you to hate him in particular?

MRS. MARWOOD   I never loved him; he is, and always was, insufferably proud.

MRS. FAINALL   By the reason you give for your aversion, one would think it dissembled; for you have laid a fault to his charge, of which his enemies must acquit him.

MRS. MARWOOD   Oh, then it seems you are one of his favorable enemies. Methinks you look a little pale, and now you flush again.

MRS. FAINALL   Do I? I think I am a little sick o' the sudden.

MRS. MARWOOD   What ails you?

MRS. FAINALL   My husband. Don't you see him? He turned short upon me unawares, and has almost overcome me.

(*Enter* FAINALL *and* MIRABELL.)

MRS. MARWOOD   Ha, ha, ha! he comes opportunely for you.

MRS. FAINALL   For you, for he has brought Mirabell with him.

FAINALL   My dear.

MRS. FAINALL   My soul.

FAINALL   You don't look well today, child.

MRS. FAINALL   D'ee think so?

MIRABELL   He is the only man that does, madam.

MRS. FAINALL   The only man that would tell me so at least; and the only man from whom I could hear it without mortification.

---

[3] *cuckold* standard figure of ridicule as a man deceived by his wife, and who thereupon grew horns on his head

FAINALL O my dear, I am satisfied of your tenderness; I know you cannot resent anything from me; especially what is an effect of my concern.

MRS. FAINALL Mr. Mirabell, my mother interrupted you in a pleasant relation last night: I would fain hear it out.

MIRABELL The persons concerned in that affair have yet a tolerable reputation. I am afraid Mr. Fainall will be censorious.

MRS. FAINALL He has a humor more prevailing than his curiosity, and will willingly dispense with the hearing of one scandalous story, to avoid giving an occasion to make another by being seen to walk with his wife. This way, Mr. Mirabell, and I dare promise you will oblige us both.

(*Exeunt* MRS. FAINALL *and* MIRABELL.)

FAINALL Excellent creature! Well, sure if I should live to be rid of my wife, I should be a miserable man.

MRS. MARWOOD Ay!

FAINALL For having only that one hope, the accomplishment of it, of consequence, must put an end to all my hopes; and what a wretch is he who must survive his hopes! Nothing remains when that day comes, but to sit down and weep like Alexander, when he wanted other worlds to conquer.

MRS. MARWOOD Will you not follow 'em?

FAINALL Faith, I think not.

MRS. MARWOOD Pray let us; I have a reason.

FAINALL You are not jealous?

MRS. MARWOOD Of whom?

FAINALL Of Mirabell.

MRS. MARWOOD If I am, is it inconsistent with my love to you that I am tender of your honor?

FAINALL You would intimate, then, as if there were a fellow-feeling between my wife and him.

MRS. MARWOOD I think she does not hate him to that degree she would be thought.

FAINALL But he, I fear, is too insensible.

MRS. MARWOOD It may be you are deceived.

FAINALL It may be so. I do now begin to apprehend it.

MRS. MARWOOD What?

FAINALL That I have been deceived, madam, and you are false.

MRS. MARWOOD That I am false! What mean you?

FAINALL To let you know I see through all your little arts. Come, you both love him; and both have equally dissembled your aversion. Your mutual jealousies of one another have made you clash till you have both struck fire. I have seen the warm confession reddening on your cheeks, and sparkling from your eyes.

MRS. MARWOOD You do me wrong.

FAINALL I do not. 'Twas for my ease to oversee and wilfully neglect the gross advances made him by my wife, that by permitting her to be engaged, I might continue unsuspected in my pleasures, and take you oftener to my arms in full security. But could you think, because the nodding husband would not wake, that e'er the watchful lover slept?

MRS. MARWOOD And wherewithal can you reproach me?

FAINALL With infidelity, with loving of another, with love of Mirabell.

MRS. MARWOOD 'Tis false. I challenge you to show an instance that can confirm your groundless accusation. I hate him.

FAINALL And wherefore do you hate him? He is insensible, and your resentment follows his neglect. An instance? The injuries you have done him are a proof: your interposing in his love. What cause had you to make discoveries of his pretended passion? To undeceive the credulous aunt, and be the officious obstacle of his match with Millamant?

MRS. MARWOOD My obligations to my lady urged me: I had professed a friendship to her; and could not see her easy nature so abused by that dissembler.

FAINALL What, was it conscience then? Professed a friendship! Oh, the pious friendships of the female sex!

MRS. MARWOOD More tender, more sincere, and more enduring, than all the vain and empty vows of men, whether professing love to us, or mutual faith to one another.

FAINALL Ha, ha, ha! you are my wife's friend too.

MRS. MARWOOD Shame and ingratitude! Do you reproach me? You, you upbraid me! Have I been false to her, through strict fidelity to you, and sacrificed my friendship to keep my love inviolate? And have you the baseness to charge me with the guilt, unmindful of the merit! To you it should be meritorious that I have been vicious: and do you reflect that guilt upon me, which should lie buried in your bosom?

FAINALL You misinterpret my reproof. I meant but to remind you of the slight account you once could make of strictest ties, when set in competition with your love to me.

MRS. MARWOOD 'Tis false, you urged it with deliberate malice—'twas spoke in scorn, and I never will forgive it.

FAINALL Your guilt, not your resentment, begets your rage. If yet you loved, you could forgive a jealousy: but you are stung to find you are discovered.

MRS. MARWOOD It shall be all discovered. You too shall be discovered; be sure you shall. I can but be exposed. If I do it myself I shall prevent your baseness.

FAINALL Why, what will you do?

MRS. MARWOOD Disclose it to your wife; own what has passed between us.

FAINALL Frenzy!

MRS. MARWOOD By all my wrongs I'll do it!—I'll publish to the world the injuries you have done me, both in my fame and fortune. With both I trusted you, you bankrupt in honor, as indigent of wealth!

FAINALL Your fame I have preserved. Your fortune has been bestowed as the prodigality of your love would have it, in pleasures which we both have shared. Yet, had not you been false, I had e'er this repaid it. 'Tis true. Had you permitted Mirabell with Millamant to have stolen their marriage, my lady had been incensed beyond all means of reconcilement: Millamant had forfeited the moiety of her fortune, which then would have descended to my wife; and wherefore did I marry, but to make lawful prize of a rich widow's wealth, and squander it on love and you?

MRS. MARWOOD Deceit and frivolous pretence!

FAINALL Death, am I not married? What's pretence? Am I not imprisoned, fettered? Have I not a wife? Nay, a wife that was a widow, a young widow, a handsome widow; and would be again a widow, but that I have a heart of proof, and something of a constitution to bustle through the ways of wedlock and this world. Will you yet be reconciled to truth and me?

MRS. MARWOOD Impossible. Truth and you are inconsistent—I hate you, and shall forever.

FAINALL For loving you?

MRS. MARWOOD I loathe the name of love after such usage; and next to the guilt with which you would asperse me, I scorn you most. Farewell.

FAINALL Nay, we must not part thus.

MRS. MARWOOD Let me go.

FAINALL Come. I'm sorry.

MRS. MARWOOD I care not—let me go—break my hands, do—I'd leave 'em to get loose.

FAINALL I would not hurt you for the world. Have I no other hold to keep you here?

MRS. MARWOOD Well, I have deserved it all.

FAINALL You know I love you.

MRS. MARWOOD Poor dissembling!—Oh, that—well, it is not yet—

FAINALL What? What is it not? What is it not yet? It is not yet too late—

MRS. MARWOOD No, it is not yet too late—I have that comfort.

FAINALL It is, to love another.

MRS. MARWOOD But not to loathe, detest, abhor mankind, myself, and the whole treacherous world.

FAINALL Nay, this is extravagance. Come, I ask your pardon—no tears—I was to blame, I could not love you and be easy in my doubts. —Pray forbear—I believe you; I'm convinced I've done you wrong; and any way, every way will make amends; I'll hate my wife yet more, damn her, I'll part with her, rob her of all she's worth, and will retire somewhere, anywhere, to another world. I'll marry thee—be pacified.—'Sdeath, they come; hide your face, your tears. You have a mask,[4] wear it a moment. This way, this way, be persuaded.

(*Exeunt* FAINALL *and* MRS. MARWOOD. *Enter* MIRABELL *and* MRS. FAINALL.)

MRS. FAINALL   They are here yet.

MIRABELL   They are turning into the other walk.

MRS. FAINALL   While I only hated my husband, I could bear to see him; but since I have despised him, he's too offensive.

MIRABELL   Oh, you should hate with prudence.

MRS. FAINALL   Yes, for I have loved with indiscretion.

MIRABELL   You should have just so much disgust for your husband as may be sufficient to make you relish your lover.

MRS. FAINALL   You have been the cause that I have loved without bounds, and would you set limits to that aversion, of which you have been the occasion? Why did you make me marry this man?

MIRABELL   Why do we daily commit disagreeable and dangerous actions? To save that idol, reputation. If the familiarities of our loves had produced that consequence, of which you were apprehensive, where could you have fixed a father's name with credit, but on a husband? I knew Fainall to be a man lavish of his morals, an interested and professing friend, a false and designing lover; yet one whose wit and outward fair behavior have gained a reputation with the town, enough to make that woman stand excused, who has suffered herself to be won by his addresses. A better man ought not to have been sacrificed to the occasion; a worse had not answered to the purpose. When you are weary of him, you know your remedy.

MRS. FAINALL   I ought to stand in some degree of credit with you, Mirabell.

MIRABELL   In justice to you, I have made you privy to my whole design, and put it in your power to ruin or advance my fortune.

MRS. FAINALL   Whom have you instructed to represent your pretended uncle?

MIRABELL   Waitwell, my servant.

---

[4] *mask* the half-mask, or "domino," carried by ladies to hide their faces in public as needed to prevent identity. No self-respecting lady would walk recognized and unescorted in such a place as the Mall. The mask served as a veil or a hood on a cloak would serve for the same purpose.

MRS. FAINALL   He is an humble servant to Foible, my mother's woman, and may win her to your interest.

MIRABELL   Care is taken for that. She is won and worn by this time. They were married this morning.

MRS. FAINALL   Who?

MIRABELL   Waitwell and Foible. I would not tempt my servant to betray me by trusting him too far. If your mother, in hopes to ruin me, should consent to marry my pretended uncle, he might, like Mosca in *The Fox*,[5] stand upon terms; so I made him sure beforehand.

MRS. FAINALL   So, if my poor mother is caught in a contract, you will discover the imposture betimes, and release her by producing a certificate of her gallant's former marriage.

MIRABELL   Yes, upon condition she consent to my marriage with her niece, and surrender the moiety of her fortune in her possession.

MRS. FAINALL   She talked last night of endeavoring at a match between Millamant and your uncle.

MIRABELL   That was by Foible's direction, and my instruction, that she might seem to carry it more privately.

MRS. FAINALL   Well, I have an opinion of your success, for I believe my lady will do anything to get a husband; and when she has this, which you have provided for her, I suppose she will submit to anything to get rid of him.

MIRABELL   Yes, I think the good lady would marry anything that resembled a man, though 'twere no more than what a butler could pinch out of a napkin.

MRS. FAINALL   Female frailty! We must all come to it, if we live to be old, and feel the craving of a false appetite when the true is decayed.

MIRABELL   An old woman's appetite is depraved like that of a girl. 'Tis the green-sickness[6] of a second childhood; and like the faint offer of a latter spring, serves but to usher in the fall; and withers in an affected bloom.

MRS. FAINALL   Here's your mistress.

(*Enter* MRS. MILLAMANT, WITWOUD, *and* MINCING.)

MIRABELL   Here she comes, i'faith, full sail, with her fan spread and her streamers out, and a shoal of fools for tenders.—Ha, no, I cry her mercy!

MRS. FAINALL   I see but one poor empty sculler; and he tows her woman after him.

---

[5] *Mosca in The Fox* the scheming servant in Ben Jonson's comedy *Volpone, or the Fox*. Mirabell makes sure that Waitwell will not "stand upon terms," or blackmail him.

[6] *green-sickness* an affliction of young girls at puberty

MIRABELL You seem to be unattended, madam. You used to have the *beau monde* throng after you; and a flock of gay fine perukes[7] hovering round you.

WITWOUD Like moths about a candle.—I had like to have lost my comparison for want of breath.

MILLAMANT Oh, I have denied myself airs today. I have walked as fast through the crowd—

WITWOUD As a favorite in disgrace; and with as few followers.

MILLAMANT Dear Mr. Witwoud, truce with your similitudes: for I am sick of 'em—

WITWOUD As a physician of a good air.—I cannot help it, madam, though 'tis against myself.

MILLAMANT Yet again! Mincing, stand between me and his wit.

WITWOUD Do, Mrs. Mincing, like a screen before a great fire. I confess I do blaze today, I am too bright.

MRS. FAINALL But, dear Millamant, why were you so long?

MILLAMANT Long! Lord, have I not made violent haste? I have asked every living thing I met for you; I have enquired after you, as after a new fashion.

WITWOUD Madam, truce with your similitudes. No, you met her husband, and did not ask him for her.

MIRABELL By your leave, Witwood, that were like enquiring after an old fashion, to ask a husband for his wife.

WITWOUD Hum, a hit, a hit, a palpable hit, I confess it.

MRS. FAINALL You were dressed before I came abroad.

MILLAMANT Ay, that's true—oh, but then I had—Mincing, what had I? Why was I so long?

MINCING O mem, your la'ship stayed to peruse a pecquet[8] of letters.

MILLAMANT Oh, ay, letters—I had letters—I am persecuted with letters—I hate letters. Nobody knows how to write letters; and yet one has 'em, one does not know why. They serve one to pin up one's hair.

WITWOUD Is that the way? Pray, madam, do you pin up your hair with all your letters? I find I must keep copies.

MILLAMANT Only with those in verse, Mr. Witwoud. I never pin up my hair with prose. I fancy one's hair would not curl if it were pinned up with prose. I think I tried once, Mincing.

MINCING O mem, I shall never forget it.

MILLAMANT Ay, poor Mincing tift and tift all the morning.

MINCING Till I had the cremp in my fingers, I'll vow, mem. And all to

---

[7] *perukes* wigs. Mirabell means that Millamant normally is surrounded by bewigged suitors. [8] *pecquet* packet. Mincing has a habit of mispronunciation, as in "crips" on p. 324 for "crisp."

no purpose. But when your la'ship pins it up with poetry, it sits so pleasant the next day as anything, and is so pure and so crips.

WITWOUD Indeed, so "crips"?

MINCING You're such a critic, Mr. Witwoud.

MILLAMANT Mirabell, did you take exceptions last night? Oh, ay, and went away. Now I think on't I'm angry.—No, now I think on't I'm pleased—for I believe I gave you some pain.

MIRABELL Does that please you?

MILLAMANT Infinitely; I love to give pain.

MIRABELL You would affect a cruelty which is not in your nature; your true vanity is in the power of pleasing.

MILLAMANT Oh, I ask your pardon for that. One's cruelty is one's power, and when one parts with one's cruelty, one parts with one's power, and when one has parted with that, I fancy one's old and ugly.

MIRABELL Ay, ay, suffer your cruelty to ruin the object of your power, to destroy your lover—and then how vain, how lost a thing you'll be! Nay, 'tis true: you are no longer handsome when you've lost your lover; your beauty dies upon the instant: for beauty is the lover's gift; 'tis he bestows your charms—your glass is all a cheat. The ugly and the old, whom the looking-glass mortifies, yet after commendation can be flattered by it, and discover beauties in it: for that reflects our praises, rather than your face.

MILLAMANT Oh, the vanity of these men! Fainall, d'ee hear him? If they did not commend us, we were not handsome! Now you must know they could not commend one, if one was not handsome. Beauty the lover's gift—Lord, what is a lover, that it can give? Why, one makes lovers as fast as one pleases, and they live as long as one pleases, and they die as soon as one pleases: and then if one pleases, one makes more.

WITWOUD Very pretty. Why, you make no more of making of lovers, madam, than of making so many card-matches.[9]

MILLAMANT One no more owes one's beauty to a lover, than one's wit to an echo: they can but reflect what we look and say: vain empty things if we are silent or unseen, and want a being.

MIRABELL Yet, to those two vain empty things, you owe the two greatest pleasures of your life.

MILLAMANT How so?

MIRABELL To your lover you owe the pleasure of hearing yourselves praised; and to an echo the pleasure of hearing yourselves talk.

WITWOUD But I know a lady that loves talking so incessantly, she won't

---

9 *card-matches* crude cardboard and sulfur matches

give an echo fair play; she has that everlasting rotation of tongue, that an echo must wait till she dies, before it can catch her last words.

MILLAMANT Oh, fiction! Fainall, let us leave these men.

MIRABELL (*aside to* MRS. FAINALL) Draw off Witwoud.

MRS. FAINALL (*aside*) Immediately.—I have a word or two for Mr. Witwoud.

MIRABELL I would beg a little private audience too.

(*Exeunt* WITWOUD *and* MRS. FAINALL.)

You had the tyranny to deny me last night; though you knew I came to impart a secret to you that concerned my love.

MILLAMANT You saw I was engaged.

MIRABELL Unkind. You had the leisure to entertain a herd of fools; things who visit you from their excessive idleness; bestowing on your easiness that time, which is the incumbrance of their lives. How can you find delight in such society? It is impossible they should admire you, they are not capable: or if they were, it should be to you as a mortification; for sure to please a fool is some degree of folly.

MILLAMANT I please myself—besides, sometimes to converse with fools is for my health.

MIRABELL Your health! Is there a worse disease than the conversation of fools?

MILLAMANT Yes, the vapors; fools are physic[10] for it, next to asafœtida.[11]

MIRABELL You are not in a course of fools?

MILLAMANT Mirabell, if you persist in this offensive freedom, you'll displease me. I think I must resolve, after all, not to have you. We shan't agree.

MIRABELL Not in our physic, it may be.

MILLAMANT And yet our distemper in all likelihood will be the same; for we shall be sick of one another. I shan't endure to be reprimanded, nor instructed; 'tis so dull to act always by advice, and so tedious to be told of one's faults—I can't bear it. Well, I won't have you, Mirabell—I'm resolved—I think—you may go—ha, ha, ha! What would you give, that you could help loving me?

MIRABELL I would give something that you did not know I could not help it.

MILLAMANT Come, don't look grave then. Well, what do you say to me?

MIRABELL I say that a man may as soon make a friend by his wit, or a fortune by his honesty, as win a woman with plain dealing and sincerity.

---

[10] *physic* almost any medicine was termed a "physic"   [11] *asafœtida* a kind of smelling salts

MILLAMANT　Sententious Mirabell! Prithee, don't look with that violent and inflexible wise face, like Solomon at the dividing of the child in an old tapestry hanging.

MIRABELL　You are merry, madam, but I would persuade you for one moment to be serious.

MILLAMANT　What, with that face? No, if you keep your countenance, 'tis impossible I should hold mine. Well, after all, there is something very moving in a lovesick face. Ha, ha, ha!—well, I won't laugh, don't be peevish—heigho! Now I'll be melancholy, as melancholy as a watch-light. Well, Mirabell, if ever you will win me, woo me now.— Nay, if you are so tedious, fare you well; I see they are walking away.

MIRABELL　Can you not find in the variety of your disposition one moment—

MILLAMANT　To hear you tell me that Foible's married, and your plot like to speed? No.

MIRABELL　But how you came to know it—

MILLAMANT　Unless by the help of the devil, you can't imagine; unless she should tell me herself. Which of the two it may have been, I will leave you to consider; and when you have done thinking of that, think of me. (*Exit.*)

MIRABELL　I have something more—. Gone!—Think of you! To think of a whirlwind, though 'twere in a whirlwind, were a case of more steady contemplation; a very tranquillity of mind and mansion. A fellow that lives in a windmill, has not a more whimsical dwelling than the heart of a man that is lodged in a woman. There is no point of the compass to which they cannot turn, and by which they are not turned, and by one as well as another; for motion, not method, is their occupation. To know this, and yet continue to be in love, is to be made wise from the dictates of reason, and yet persevere to play the fool by the force of instinct. Oh, here come my pair of turtles![12]—What, billing so sweetly! Is not Valentine's Day over with you yet?

(*Enter* WAITWELL *and* FOIBLE.)

Sirrah Waitwell, why sure you think you were married for your own recreation, and not for my conveniency.

WAITWELL　Your pardon, sir. With submission, we have indeed been solacing in lawful delights; but still with an eye to business, sir. I have instructed her as well as I could. If she can take your directions as readily as my instructions, sir, your affairs are in a prosperous way.

MIRABELL　Give you joy, Mrs. Foible.

---

[12] *turtles* turtledoves, who bill and coo

FOIBLE   O 'las, sir, I'm so ashamed—I'm afraid my lady has been in a thousand inquietudes for me. But I protest, sir, I made as much haste as I could.

WAITWELL   That she did indeed, sir. It was my fault that she did not make more.

MIRABELL   That I believe.

FOIBLE   But I told my lady as you instructed me, sir. That I had a prospect of seeing Sir Rowland, your uncle; and that I would put her ladyship's picture in my pocket to show him; which I'll be sure to say has made him so enamored of her beauty, that he burns with impatience to lie at her ladyship's feet and worship the original.

MIRABELL   Excellent Foible! Matrimony has made you eloquent in love.

WAITWELL   I think she has profited, sir. I think so.

FOIBLE   You have seen Madam Millamant, sir?

MIRABELL   Yes.

FOIBLE   I told her, sir, because I did not know that you might find an opportunity; she had so much company last night.

MIRABELL   Your diligence will merit more. In the meantime—(MIRABELL *gives money to* FOIBLE.)

FOIBLE   O dear sir, your humble servant.

WAITWELL   Spouse!

MIRABELL   Stand off, sir, not a penny.—Go on and prosper, Foible. The lease shall be made good and the farm stocked, if we succeed.

FOIBLE   I don't question your generosity, sir: and you need not doubt of success. If you have no more commands, sir, I'll be gone; I'm sure my lady is at her toilet, and can't dress 'till I come.—Oh dear, I'm sure that (*looking out*) was Mrs. Marwood that went by in a mask; if she has seen me with you I'm sure she'll tell my lady. I'll make haste home and prevent her. Your servant, sir. B'w'y, Waitwell. (*Exit.*)

WAITWELL   Sir Rowland, if you please.—The jade's so pert upon her preferment she forgets herself.

MIRABELL   Come, sir, will you endeavor to forget yourself—and transform into Sir Rowland.

WAITWELL   Why, sir, it will be impossible I should remember myself— married, knighted and attended all in one day! 'Tis enough to make any man forget himself. The difficulty will be how to recover my acquaintance and familiarity with my former self; and fall from my transformation to a reformation into Waitwell. Nay, I shan't be quite the same Waitwell neither—for now I remember me, I am married, and can't be my own man again.

Ay, there's the grief; that's the sad change of life;
To lose my title, and yet keep my wife.

(*Exeunt.*)

ACT III

SCENE. *A room in* LADY WISHFORT'S *house*
        LADY WISHFORT *at her toilet,* PEG *waiting*

LADY WISHFORT   Merciful, no news of Foible yet?

PEG   No, madam.

LADY WISHFORT   I have no more patience. If I have not fretted myself till I am pale again, there's no veracity in me. Fetch me the red—the red, do you hear, sweetheart? An errant ash color, as I'm a person. Look you how this wench stirs! Why dost thou not fetch me a little red? Didst thou not hear me, mopus?

PEG   The red ratafia does your ladyship mean, or the cherry-brandy?

LADY WISHFORT   Ratafia, fool! No, fool. Not the ratafia, fool—grant me patience! I mean the Spanish paper,[1] idiot,—complexion, darling. Paint, paint, paint, dost thou understand that, changeling, dangling thy hands like bobbins before thee? Why dost thou not stir, puppet?— thou wooden thing upon wires!

PEG   Lord, madam, your ladyship is so impatient. I cannot come at the paint, madam; Mrs. Foible has locked it up, and carried the key with her.

LADY WISHFORT   A pox take you both! Fetch me the cherry-brandy then.

(Exit PEG.*)*

I'm as pale and as faint, I look like Mrs. Qualmsick the curate's wife, that's always breeding.—Wench, come, come, wench, what are thou doing, sipping? tasting? Save thee, dost thou not know the bottle?

PEG *(enters, with a bottle and china cup)*   Madam, I was looking for a cup.

LADY WISHFORT   A cup, save thee, and what a cup hast thou brought! Dost thou take me for a fairy, to drink out of an acorn? Why didst thou not bring thy thimble? Hast thou ne'er a brass thimble clinking in thy pocket with a bit of nutmeg? I warrant thee. Come, fill, fill.— So—again.

(One knocks.)

See who that is.—Set down the bottle first. Here, here, under the table. What, wouldst thou go with the bottle in thy hand like a tapster?[2]

(Exit PEG.*)*

As I'm a person, this wench has lived in an inn upon the road, before she came to me, like Maritornes the Asturian in *Don Quixote.*

---

[1] *Spanish paper* used to apply rouge   [2] *tapster* bartender

(*Re-enter* PEG.)

No Foible yet?

PEG   No, madam,—Mrs. Marwood.

LADY WISHFORT   Oh, Marwood! let her come in. Come in, good Marwood.

(*Enter* MRS. MARWOOD.)

MRS. MARWOOD   I'm surprised to find your ladyship in dishabille[3] at this time of day.

LADY WISHFORT   Foible's a lost thing; has been abroad since morning, and never heard of since.

MRS. MARWOOD   I saw her but now, as I came masked through the Park, in conference with Mirabell.

LADY WISHFORT   With Mirabell! You call my blood into my face, with mentioning that traitor. She durst not have the confidence. I sent her to negotiate an affair, in which if I'm detected I'm undone. If that wheedling villain has wrought upon Foible to detect me, I'm ruined. Oh, my dear friend, I'm a wretch of wretches if I'm detected.

MRS. MARWOOD   O madam, you cannot suspect Mrs. Foible's integrity.

LADY WISHFORT   Oh, he carries poison in his tongue that would corrupt integrity itself. If she has given him an opportunity, she has as good as put her integrity into his hands. Ah, dear Marwood, what's integrity to an opportunity?—Hark! I hear her. (*To* PEG.) Go, you thing, and send her in!

(*Exit* PEG.)

Dear friend, retire into my closet, that I may examine her with more freedom.—You'll pardon me, dear friend, I can make bold with you. —There are books over the chimney—Quarles and Prynne and *The Short View of the Stage*, with Bunyan's works,[4] to entertain you.

(*Exit* MARWOOD. *Enter* FOIBLE.)

O Foible, where hast thou been? What hast thou been doing?

FOIBLE   Madam, I have seen the party.

LADY WISHFORT   But what hast thou done?

FOIBLE   Nay, 'tis your ladyship has done, and are to do; I have only promised. But a man so enamored—so transported! Well, here it is, all that is left; all that is not kissed away. Well, if worshipping of pictures be a sin—poor Sir Rowland, I say.

---

[3] *dishabille* state of undress   [4] *Bunyan's works* Puritan writings by John Bunyan, the author of *Pilgrim's Progress*. Lady Wishfort seems to have quite a collection of these Puritan works in her "closet" (small anteroom) and the "Short View" is not without its ironies (see footnote 6, Prologue).

LADY WISHFORT   The miniature has been counted like—but hast thou not betrayed me, Foible? Hast thou not detected me to that faithless Mirabell? What hadst thou to do with him in the Park? Answer me, has he got nothing out of thee?

FOIBLE (*aside*)   So, the devil has been beforehand with me: what shall I say?—Alas, madam, could I help it, if I met that confident thing? Was I in fault? If you had heard how he used me, and all upon your ladyship's account, I'm sure you would not suspect my fidelity. Nay, if that had been the worst, I could have borne: but he had a fling at your ladyship too; and then I could not hold, but, i'faith, I gave him his own.

LADY WISHFORT   Me? What did the filthy fellow say?

FOIBLE   O madam, 'tis a shame to say what he said—with his taunts and his fleers, tossing up his nose. "Humh!" says he, "what, you are a hatching some plot," says he, "you are so early abroad, or catering," says he, "ferreting for some disbanded officer, I warrant—half pay is but thin subsistence," says he. "Well, what pension does your lady propose? Let me see," says he; "what, she must come down pretty deep now: she's superannuated,"[5] says he, "and—"

LADY WISHFORT   Ods my life, I'll have him—I'll have him murdered. I'll have him poisoned. Where does he eat? I'll marry a drawer[6] to have him poisoned in his wine. I'll send for Robin from Locket's[7] immediately.

FOIBLE   Poison him? Poisoning's too good for him. Starve him, madam, starve him; marry Sir Rowland and get him disinherited. Oh, you would bless yourself, to hear what he said.

LADY WISHFORT   A villain! "superannuated!"

FOIBLE   "Humh!" says he, "I hear you are laying designs against me, too," says he, "and Mrs. Millamant is to marry my uncle;"—(he does not suspect a word of our ladyship);—"but," says he, "I'll fit you for that, I warrant you," says he, "I'll hamper you for that," says he, "you and your old frippery,[8] too," says he, "I'll handle you—"

LADY WISHFORT   Audacious villain! handle me! would he durst!— "Frippery? old frippery?" Was there ever such a foul-mouthed fellow? I'll be married tomorrow, I'll be contracted tonight.

FOIBLE   The sooner the better, madam.

LADY WISHFORT   Will Sir Rowland be here, say'st thou? When, Foible?

FOIBLE   Incontinently, madam. No new sheriff's wife expects the return of her husband after knighthood, with that impatience in which Sir Rowland burns for the dear hour of kissing your ladyship's hands after dinner.

---

[5] *superannuated* obsolete, out of date, antiquated   [6] *drawer* tapster, bartender   [7] *Locket's* a well-known tavern   [8] *old frippery* old clothing

LADY WISHFORT   "Frippery, superannuated frippery!" I'll frippery the villain; I'll reduce him to frippery and rags. A tatterdemalion!—I hope to see him hung with tatters, like a Long Lane penthouse,[9] or a gibbet-thief.[10] A slander-mouthed railer: I warrant the spendthrift prodigal's in debt as much as the million lottery, or the whole court upon a birthday. I'll spoil his credit with his tailor. Yes, he shall have my niece with her fortune, he shall.

FOIBLE   He! I hope to see him lodge in Ludgate[11] first, and angle into Blackfriars for brass farthings, with an old mitten.

LADY WISHFORT   Ay, dear Foible; thank thee for that, dear Foible. He has put me out of all patience. I shall never recompose my features to receive Sir Rowland with any economy of face. This wretch has fretted me that I am absolutely decayed. Look, Foible.

FOIBLE   Your ladyship has frowned a little too rashly, indeed, madam. There are some cracks discernible in the white varnish.

LADY WISHFORT   Let me see the glass.—Cracks, say'st thou? Why, I am arrantly flayed. I look like an old peeled wall. Thou must repair me, Foible, before Sir Rowland comes; or I shall never keep up to my picture.

FOIBLE   I warrant you, madam; a little art once made your picture like you; and now a little of the same art must make you like your picture. Your picture must sit for you, madam.

LADY WISHFORT   But art thou sure Sir Rowland will not fail to come? Or will a' not fail when he does come? Will he be importunate, Foible, and push? For if he should not be importunate—I shall never break decorums—I shall die with confusion, if I am forced to advance—oh no, I can never advance—I shall swoon if he should expect advances. No, I hope Sir Rowland is better bred, than to put a lady to the necessity of breaking her forms. I won't be too coy neither. I won't give him despair—but a little disdain is not amiss; a little scorn is alluring.

FOIBLE   A little scorn becomes your ladyship.

LADY WISHFORT   Yes, but tenderness becomes me best—a sort of a dyingness.—You see that picture has a sort of a—ha, Foible? A swimminess in the eyes. Yes, I'll look so. My niece affects it; but she wants features. Is Sir Rowland handsome? Let my toilet be removed—I'll

---

[9] *Long Lane penthouse* a stall in an area of old clothing and furniture   [10] *gibbet-thief* criminals sentenced to the gibbet were hung in a cage until death, during which time their clothes rotted away   [11] *Ludgate* debtor's prison. Lady Wishfort would reduce Mirabell to abject beggary, seeking farthings (one-quarter of a penny) from passersby. The "million lottery" of which Lady Wishfort speaks was conducted by the government in 1694 in an attempt to raise a million pounds.

dress above. I'll receive Sir Rowland here. Is he handsome? Don't answer me. I won't know: I'll be surprised. I'll be taken by surprise.

FOIBLE By storm, madam. Sir Rowland's a brisk man.

LADY WISHFORT Is he! Oh, then he'll importune, if he's a brisk man. I shall save decorums if Sir Rowland importunes. I have a mortal terror at the apprehension of offending against decorums. Nothing but importunity can surmount decorums. Oh, I'm glad he's a brisk man! Let my things be removed, good Foible. (*Exit.*)

(*Enter* MRS. FAINALL.)

MRS. FAINALL O Foible, I have been in a fright, lest I should come too late. That devil, Marwood, saw you in the Park with Mirabell, and I'm afraid will discover it to my lady.

FOIBLE Discover what, madam?

MRS. FAINALL Nay, nay, put not on that strange face. I am privy to the whole design, and know that Waitwell, to whom thou wert this morning married, is to personate Mirabell's uncle, and as such, winning my lady, to involve her in those difficulties from which Mirabell only must release her, by his making his conditions to have my cousin and her fortune left to her own disposal.

FOIBLE O dear madam, I beg your pardon. It was not my confidence in your ladyship that was deficient; but I thought the former good correspondence between your ladyship and Mr. Mirabell might have hindered his communicating this secret.

MRS. FAINALL Dear Foible, forget that.

FOIBLE O dear madam, Mr. Mirabell is such a sweet winning gentleman—but your ladyship is the pattern of generosity. Sweet lady, to be so good! Mr. Mirabell cannot choose but be grateful. I find your ladyship has his heart still. Now, madam, I can safely tell your ladyship our success; Mrs. Marwood had told my lady, but I warrant I managed myself. I turned it all for the better. I told my lady that Mr. Mirabell railed at her. I laid horrid things to his charge, I'll vow; and my lady is so incensed, that she'll be contracted to Sir Rowland tonight, she says; I warrant I worked her up, that he may have her for asking for, as they say of a Welsh maidenhead.[12]

MRS. FAINALL O rare Foible!

FOIBLE Madam, I beg your ladyship to acquaint Mr. Mirabell of his success. I would be seen as little as possible to speak to him; besides, I believe Madam Marwood watches me. She has a month's mind; but I know Mr. Mirabell can't abide her.

(*Enter* Footman.)

---

[12] *Welsh maidenhead* apparently Welsh virgins were considered easily seduced

John, remove my lady's toilet. Madam, your servant. My lady is so impatient, I fear she'll come for me, if I stay.

MRS. FAINALL   I'll go with you up the back stairs, lest I should meet her.

(*Exeunt* MRS. FAINALL, FOIBLE, *and* Footman. *Enter* MRS. MARWOOD.)

MRS. MARWOOD   Indeed, Mrs. Engine, is it thus with you? Are you become a go-between of this importance? Yes, I shall watch you. Why, this wench is the *passe-partout*, a very master-key to everybody's strong box. My friend Fainall, have you carried it so swimmingly? I thought there was something in it; but it seems it's over with you. Your loathing is not from a want of appetite then, but from a surfeit. Else you could never be so cool to fall from a principal to be an assistant, to procure for him! A pattern of generosity, that I confess. Well, Mrs. Fainall, you have met with your match.—O man, man! Woman, woman! The devil's an ass: if I were a painter, I would draw him like an idiot, a driveler, with a bib and bells. Man should have his head and horns, and woman the rest of him. Poor simple fiend! "Madam Marwood has a month's mind,[13] but he can't abide her."— 'Twere better for him you had not been his confessor in that affair, without you could have kept his counsel closer. I shall not prove another pattern of generosity, and stalk for him, till he takes his stand to aim at a fortune; he has not obliged me to that with those excesses of himself; and now I'll have none of him. Here comes the good lady, panting ripe; with a heart full of hope, and a head full of care, like any chemist upon the day of projection.[14]

LADY WISHFORT (*enters*)   O dear Marwood, what shall I say for this rude forgetfulness? But my dear friend is all goodness.

MRS. MARWOOD   No apologies, dear madam. I have been very well entertained.

LADY WISHFORT   As I'm a person, I am in a very chaos to think I should so forget myself—but I have such an olio[15] of affairs, really I know not what to do.—(*calls*) Foible!—I expect my nephew Sir Wilfull every moment too.—Why, Foible!—He means to travel for improvement.

MRS. MARWOOD   Methinks Sir Wilfull should rather think of marrying than travelling at his years. I hear he is turned of forty.

LADY WISHFORT   Oh, he's in less danger of being spoiled by his travels. I am against my nephew's marrying too young. It will be time enough when he comes back, and has acquired discretion to choose for himself.

---

[13] *a month's mind* very strong inclination   [14] *day of projection* the moment when the alchemist hoped to convert lead into gold   [15] *olio* mix-up, mess

MRS. MARWOOD   Methinks Mrs. Millamant and he would make a very fit match. He may travel afterwards. 'Tis a thing very usual with young gentlemen.

LADY WISHFORT   I promise you I have thought on't—and since 'tis your judgment, I'll think on't again. I assure you I will; I value your judgment extremely. On my word, I'll propose it.

(*Enter* FOIBLE.)

Come, come Foible—I had forgot my nephew will be here before dinner. I must make haste.

FOIBLE   Mr. Witwoud and Mr. Petulant are come to dine with your ladyship.

LADY WISHFORT   Oh dear, I can't appear till I'm dressed. Dear Marwood, shall I be free with you again, and beg you to entertain 'em? I'll make all imaginable haste. Dear friend, excuse me.

(*Exeunt* LADY WISHFORT *and* FOIBLE. *Enter* MRS. MILLAMANT *and* MINCING.)

MILLAMANT   Sure never anything was so unbred as that odious man.—Marwood, your servant.

MRS. MARWOOD   You have a color; what's the matter?

MILLAMANT   That horrid fellow, Petulant, has provoked me into a flame. I have broke my fan.[16]—Mincing, lend me yours.—Is not all the powder out of my hair?

MRS. MARWOOD   No. What has he done?

MILLAMANT   Nay, he has done nothing; he has only talked. Nay, he has said nothing neither; but he has contradicted everything that has been said. For my part, I thought Witwoud and he would have quarrelled.

MINCING   I vow, mem, I thought once they would have fit.

MILLAMANT   Well, 'tis a lamentable thing, I'll swear, that one has not the liberty of choosing one's acquaintance as one does one's clothes.

MRS. MARWOOD   If we had the liberty, we should be as weary of one set of acquaintance, though never so good, as we are of one suit, though never so fine. A fool and a doily stuff would now and then find days of grace, and be worn for variety.

MILLAMANT   I could consent to wear 'em, if they would wear alike; but fools never wear out—they are such *drap-de-Berry*[17] things!—without one could give 'em to one's chambermaid after a day or two.

---

[16] *I have broke my fan* Millamant is indeed in a frenzy. The fan was an important female accessory, good for cooling one's countenance as in the case of an attack of the vapors, for hiding behind, coyly or otherwise, and, properly wielded, as an effective weapon against the face of some presumptuous male. To break this valued item shows a considerably violent reaction.   [17] *drap-de-Berry* coarse, long-wearing cloth

MRS. MARWOOD   'Twere better so indeed. Or what think you of the playhouse? A fine gay glossy fool should be given there, like a new masking habit, after the masquerade is over, and we have done with the disguise. For a fool's visit is always a disguise; and never admitted by a woman of wit, but to blind her affair with a lover of sense. If you would but appear barefaced now, and own Mirabell, you might as easily put off Petulant and Witwoud as your hood and scarf. And indeed 'tis time, for the town has found it: the secret is grown too big for the pretence. 'Tis like Mrs. Primly's great belly; she may lace it down before, but it burnishes on her hips. Indeed, Millamant, you can no more conceal it than my Lady Strammel can her face, that goodly face, which in defiance of her Rhenish-wine tea, will not be comprehended in a mask.

MILLAMANT   I'll take my death, Marwood, you are more censorious than a decayed beauty, or a discarded toast.—Mincing, tell the men they may come up. My aunt is not dressing.—Their folly is less provoking than your malice. 'The town has found it!'

(*Exit* MINCING.)

What has it found? That Mirabell loves me is no more a secret, than it is a secret that you discovered it to my aunt, or than the reason why you discovered it is a secret.

MRS. MARWOOD   You are nettled.

MILLAMANT   You're mistaken. Ridiculous!

MRS. MARWOOD   Indeed, my dear, you'll tear another fan, if you don't mitigate those violent airs.

MILLAMANT   O silly! Ha, ha, ha! I could laugh immoderately. Poor Mirabell! His constancy to me has quite destroyed his complaisance for all the world beside. I swear, I never enjoined it him, to be so coy. If I had the vanity to think he would obey me, I would command him to show more gallantry. 'Tis hardly well bred to be so particular on one hand, and so insensible on the other. But I despair to prevail, and so let him follow his own way. Ha, ha, ha! Pardon me, dear creature, I must laugh, ha, ha, ha!—though I grant you 'tis a little barbarous, ha, ha, ha!

MRS. MARWOOD   What pity 'tis, so much fine raillery, and delivered with so significant gesture, should be so unhappily directed to miscarry.

MILLAMANT   Heh? Dear creature, I ask your pardon—I swear I did not mind you.

MRS. MARWOOD   Mr. Mirabell and you both may think it a thing impossible, when I shall tell him by telling you—

MILLAMANT   O dear, what? for it is the same thing, if I hear it—ha, ha, ha!

MRS. MARWOOD   That I detest him, hate him, madam.

MILLAMANT   O madam, why so do I—and yet the creature loves me, ha, ha, ha! How can one forbear laughing to think of it? I am a sibyl if I am not amazed to think what he can see in me. I'll take my death, I think you are handsomer—and within a year or two as young. If you could but stay for me, I should overtake you—but that cannot be. Well, that thought makes me melancholy. Now I'll be sad.

MRS. MARWOOD   Your merry note may be changed sooner than you think.

MILLAMANT   D'ee say so? Then I'm resolved I'll have a song to keep up my spirits.

(*Enter* MINCING.)

MINCING   The gentlemen stay but to comb, madam, and will wait on you.

MILLAMANT   Desire Mrs. —— that is in the next room to sing the song I would have learnt yesterday. You shall hear it, madam—not that there's any great matter in it—but 'tis agreeable to my humor.

Song

(*Set by Mr. John Eccles, and sung by Mrs. Hodgson.*)[18]

I

Love's but the frailty of the mind,
   When 'tis not with ambition joined;
A sickly flame, which if not fed expires;
And feeding, wastes in self-consuming fires.

II

'Tis not to wound a wanton boy
   Or am'rous youth, that gives the joy;
But 'tis the glory to have pierced a swain,
For whom inferior beauties sighed in vain.

III

Then I alone the conquest prize,
   When I insult a rival's eyes:
If there's delight in love, 'tis when I see
That heart which others bleed for, bleed for me.

(*Enter* PETULANT *and* WITWOUD.)

MILLAMANT   Is your animosity composed, gentlemen?

WITWOUD   Raillery, raillery, madam; we have no animosity—we hit off

---

[18] *John Eccles, Mrs. Hodgson* Eccles apparently also wrote the play's incidental music, and Mrs. Hodgson was an "extra" who performed the singing.

a little wit now and then, but no animosity. The falling out of wits is like the falling out of lovers. We agree in the main, like treble and base. Ha, Petulant?

PETULANT   Ay, in the main. But when I have a humor to contradict—

WITWOUD   Ay, when he has a humor to contradict, then I contradict too. What, I know my cue. Then we contradict one another like two battledores;[19] for contradictions beget one another like Jews.

PETULANT   If he says black's black—if I have a humor to say 'tis blue— let that pass—all's one for that. If I have a humor to prove it, it must be granted.

WITWOUD   Not positively must—but it may—it may.

PETULANT   Yes, it positively must, upon proof positive.

WITWOUD   Ay, upon proof positive it must; but upon proof presumptive it only may. That's a logical distinction now, madam.

MRS. MARWOOD   I perceive your debates are of importance and very learnedly handled.

PETULANT   Importance is one thing, and learning's another; but a debate's a debate, that I assert.

WITWOUD   Petulant's an enemy to learning; he relies altogether on his parts.

PETULANT   No, I'm no enemy to learning; it hurts not me.

MRS. MARWOOD   That's a sign indeed it's no enemy to you.

PETULANT   No, no, it's no enemy to anybody, but them that have it.

MILLAMANT   Well, an illiterate man's my aversion. I wonder at the impudence of any illiterate man, to offer to make love.

WITWOUD   That I confess I wonder at too.

MILLAMANT   Ah! to marry an ignorant that can hardly read or write!

PETULANT   Why should a man be ever the further from being married though he can't read, any more than he is from being hanged? The ordinary's[20] paid for setting the psalm, and the parish-priest for reading the ceremony. And for the rest which is to follow in both cases, a man may do it without book—so all's one for that.

MILLAMANT   D'ee hear the creature? Lord, here's company, I'll be gone.

(*Exeunt* MILLAMANT *and* MINCING.)

WITWOUD   In the name of Bartlemew and his fair,[21] what have we here?

MRS. MARWOOD   'Tis your brother, I fancy. Don't you know him?

---

[19] *battledores* racquets, as in badminton   [20] *ordinary* clergyman ministering to the condemned   [21] *Bartlemew and his fair* Bartholomew's Fair was a popular country fair held in late summer in Smithfield. See Ben Jonson's comedy of the same name for a rowdy picture of the occasion.

WITWOUD Not I—yes, I think it is he—I've almost forgot him; I have not seen him since the Revolution.[22]

(*Enter* SIR WILFULL WITWOUD *in a country riding habit, and* Servant *to Lady Wishfort*.)

SERVANT Sir, my lady's dressing. Here's company, if you please to walk in, in the meantime.

SIR WILFULL Dressing! What, it's but morning here I warrant with you in London; we should count it towards afternoon in our parts, down in Shropshire. Why then belike my aunt han't dined yet—ha, friend?

SERVANT Your aunt, sir?

SIR WILFULL My aunt, sir, yes, my aunt, sir, and your lady, sir; your lady is my aunt, sir. Why, what, dost thou not know me, friend? Why then send somebody here that does. How long hast thou lived with my lady, fellow, ha?

SERVANT A week, sir; longer than anybody in the house, except my lady's woman.

SIR WILFULL Why then belike thou dost not know thy lady, if thou see'st her, ha, friend?

SERVANT Why truly, sir, I cannot safely swear to her face in a morning, before she is dressed. 'Tis like I may give a shrewd guess at her by this time.

SIR WILFULL Well, prithee try what thou canst do; if thou canst not guess, enquire her out, dost hear, fellow? And tell her, her nephew, Sir Wilfull Witwoud, is in the house.

SERVANT I shall, sir.

SIR WILFULL Hold ye, hear me, friend; a word with you in your ear; prithee who are these gallants?

SERVANT Really, sir, I can't tell; here come so many here, 'tis hard to know 'em all. (*Exit.*)

SIR WILFULL Oons, this fellow knows less than a starling; I don't think a' knows his own name.

MRS. MARWOOD Mr. Witwoud, your brother is not behindhand in forgetfulness—I fancy he has forgot you too.

WITWOUD I hope so—the devil take him that remembers first, I say.

SIR WILFULL Save you, gentlemen and lady.

MRS. MARWOOD For shame, Mr. Witwoud; why won't you speak to him? —And you, sir.

WITWOUD Petulant, speak.

PETULANT And you, sir.

SIR WILFULL No offence, I hope. (*Salutes* MARWOOD.)

MRS. MARWOOD No, sure, sir.

---

[22] *Revolution* the bloodless "Glorious Revolution" of 1688 which deposed the Catholic James II and brought William and Mary of Orange to the throne

WITWOUD This is a vile dog, I see that already. No offence! Ha, ha, ha! To him; to him, Petulant, smoke[23] him.

PETULANT It seems as if you had come a journey, sir; hem, hem. (*Surveying him round.*)

SIR WILFULL Very likely, sir, that it may seem so.

PETULANT No offence, I hope, sir.

WITWOUD Smoke the boots, the boots, Petulant, the boots; ha, ha, ha!

SIR WILFULL Maybe not, sir; thereafter as 'tis meant, sir.

PETULANT Sir, I presume upon the information of your boots.

SIR WILFULL Why, 'tis like you may, sir: if you are not satisfied with the information of my boots, sir, if you will step to the stable, you may enquire further of my horse, sir.

PETULANT Your horse, sir! Your horse is an ass, sir!

SIR WILFULL Do you speak by way of offence, sir?

MRS. MARWOOD The gentleman's merry, that's all, sir.—(*Aside.*) S'life, we shall have a quarrel betwixt an horse and an ass, before they find one another out.—(*Aloud.*) You must not take anything amiss from your friends, sir. You are among your friends here, though it may be you don't know it. If I am not mistaken, you are Sir Wilfull Witwoud.

SIR WILFULL Right, lady; I am Sir Wilfull Witwoud, so I write myself; no offence to anybody, I hope; and nephew to the Lady Wishfort of this mansion.

MRS. MARWOOD Don't you know this gentleman, sir?

SIR WILFULL Hum! What, sure 'tis not.—Yea, by'r Lady, but 'tis.— 'Sheart, I know not whether 'tis or no.—Yea, but 'tis, by the Wrekin.[24] Brother Anthony! What, Tony, i'faith! What, dost thou not know me? By'r Lady, nor I thee, thou are so becravatted, and so beperiwigged.—'Sheart, why dost not speak? Art thou o'erjoyed?

WITWOUD Odso, brother, is it you? Your servant, brother.

SIR WILFULL Your servant! Why yours, sir. Your servant again.— 'Sheart, and your friend and servant to that—and a—(*puff*) and a flap-dragon[25] for your service, sir, and a hare's foot, and a hare's scut[26] for your service, sir, and you be so cold and so courtly!

WITWOUD No offence, I hope, brother.

SIR WILFULL 'Sheart, sir, but there is, and much offence. A pox, is this your Inns o' Court[27] breeding, not to know your friends and your relations, your elders, and your betters?

---

[23] *smoke* an archaic verb meaning to ridicule, make fun of [24] *Wrekin* a hill in Shropshire [25] *flap-dragon* a raisin used in the game of snapdragon; also, a cant term for the pox (syphilis) [26] *scut* tail [27] *Inns o' Court* The Inns of Court were and still are the center of London's law offices and legal training. Young men (and women today) aspiring to the law received their legal apprenticeship here. Apparently Witwoud was once a clerk (the word is properly pronounced "clark") or student of the law, but as he indicates later to Petulant not very proud of it.

WITWOUD Why, brother Wilfull of Salop, you may be as short as a Shrewsbury cake, if you please. But I tell you 'tis not modish to know relations in town. You think you're in the country, where great lubberly brothers slabber and kiss one another when they meet, like a call of serjeants.[28] 'Tis not the fashion here; 'tis not indeed, dear brother.

SIR WILFULL The fashion's a fool; and you're a fop, dear brother. 'Sheart, I've suspected this. By'r Lady, I conjectured you were a fop, since you began to change the style of your letters, and write in a scrap of paper gilt round the edges, no broader than a *subpoena*. I might expect this when you left off "Honored Brother," and "hoping you are in good health," and so forth—to begin with a "Rat me,[29] knight, I'm so sick of a last night's debauch"—Od's heart, and then tell a familiar tale of a cock and a bull, and a whore and a bottle, and so conclude. You could write news before you were out of your time, when you lived with honest Pumple Nose, the attorney of Furnival's Inn.[30] You could intreat to be remembered then to your friends round the Wrekin. We could have gazettes then, and Dawks's Letter,[31] and the weekly bill,[32] 'till of late days.

PETULANT 'Slife, Witwoud, were you ever an attorney's clerk? Of the family of the Furnivals. Ha, ha, ha!

WITWOUD Ay, ay, but that was for a while. Not long, not long. Pshaw! I was not in my own power then. An orphan, and this fellow was my guardian; ay, ay, I was glad to consent to that man to come to London. He had the disposal of me then. If I had not agreed to that, I might have been bound prentice to a felt-maker in Shrewsbury; this fellow would have bound me to a maker of felts.

SIR WILFULL 'Sheart, and better than to be bound to a maker of fops; where, I suppose, you have served your time and now you may set up for yourself.

MRS. MARWOOD You intend to travel, sir, as I'm informed.

SIR WILFULL Belike I may, madam. I may chance to sail upon the salt seas, if my mind hold.

PETULANT And the wind serve.

SIR WILFULL Serve or not serve, I shan't ask license of you, sir; nor the weather-cock your companion. I direct my discourse to the lady, sir. 'Tis like my aunt may have told you, madam—yes, I have settled my concerns, I may say now, and am minded to see foreign parts. If an how that the peace[33] holds, whereby, that is, taxes abate.

---

[28] *call of serjeants* apparently a ritual when called to the Bar   [29] *rat me* a corruption of "may God rot me"   [30] *Furnival's Inn* one of the Inns of Court   [31] *Dawks's letter* a weekly newsletter   [32] *weekly bill* weekly list of deaths in London   [33] *the peace* England and France had stopped fighting by the Treaty of Ryswick in 1697

MRS. MARWOOD   I thought you had designed for France at all adventures.

SIR WILFULL   I can't tell that; 'tis like I may, and 'tis like I may not. I am somewhat dainty in making a resolution,—because when I make it I keep it. I don't stand shill I, shall I,[34] then; if I say't, I'll do't: but I have thoughts to tarry a small matter in town, to learn somewhat of your lingo first, before I cross the seas. I'd gladly have a spice of your French, as they say, whereby to hold discourse in foreign countries.

MRS. MARWOOD   Here is an academy in town for that use.

SIR WILFULL   There is? 'Tis like there may.

MRS. MARWOOD   No doubt you will return very much improved.

WITWOUD   Yes, refined, like a Dutch skipper from a whale-fishing.

(*Enter* LADY WISHFORT *and* FAINALL.)

LADY WISHFORT   Nephew, you are welcome.

SIR WILFULL   Aunt, your servant.

FAINALL   Sir Wilfull, your most faithful servant.

SIR WILFULL   Cousin Fainall, give me your hand.

LADY WISHFORT   Cousin Witwoud, your servant; Mr. Petulant, your servant.—Nephew, you are welcome again. Will you drink anything after your journey, nephew, before you eat? Dinner's almost ready.

SIR WILFULL   I'm very well, I thank you, aunt—however, I thank you for your courteous offer. 'Sheart, I was afraid you would have been in the fashion too, and have remembered to have forgot your relations. Here's your cousin Tony, belike, I mayn't call him brother for fear of offence.

LADY WISHFORT   Oh, he's a rallier,[35] nephew—my cousin's a wit; and your great wits always rally their best friends to choose. When you have been abroad, nephew, you'll understand raillery better.

(FAINALL *and* MRS. MARWOOD *talk apart.*)

SIR WILFULL   Why then let him hold his tongue in the meantime; and rail when that day comes.

(*Enter* MINCING.)

MINCING   Mem, I come to acquaint your la'ship that dinner is impatient.

SIR WILFULL   Impatient? Why then belike it won't stay till I pull off my boots. Sweetheart, can you help me to a pair of slippers? My man's with his horses, I warrant.

---

[34] *shill I, shall I* shillyshallying   [35] *rallier* one who likes to make fun of people. As Lady Wishfort explains in the next line, Witwoud will even make fun of his best friends.

LADY WISHFORT   Fie, fie, nephew, you would not pull off your boots here. Go down into the hall—dinner shall stay for you.—My nephew's a little unbred, you'll pardon him, madam.—Gentlemen, will you walk? Marwood—

MRS. MARWOOD   I'll follow you, madam, before Sir Wilfull is ready.

(*Manent*[36] MRS. MARWOOD *and* FAINALL.)

FAINALL   Why then Foible's a bawd, an arrant, rank, match-making bawd. And I, it seems, am a husband, a rank husband; and my wife a very arrant, rank wife—all in the way of the world. 'Sdeath, to be an anticipated cuckold, a cuckold in embryo! Sure I was born with budding antlers like a young satyr,[37] or a citizen's child.[38] 'Sdeath, to be outwitted, to be out-jilted—out-matrimonied! If I had kept my speed like a stag, 'twere somewhat, but to crawl after with my horns like a snail, and be outstripped by my wife—'tis scurvy wedlock.

MRS. MARWOOD   Then shake it off; you have often wished for an opportunity to part, and now you have it. But first prevent their plot—the half of Millamant's fortune is too considerable to be parted with, to a foe, to Mirabell.

FAINALL   Damn him, that had been mine, had you not made that fond discovery—that had been forfeited, had they been married. My wife had added lustre to my horns, by that increase of fortune; I could have worn 'em tipt with gold, though my forehead had been furnished like a deputy-lieutenant's hall.[39]

MRS. MARWOOD   They may prove a cap of maintenance[40] to you still, if you can away with your wife. And she's no worse than when you had her—I dare swear she had given up her game before she was married.

FAINALL   Hum! That may be.—She might throw up her cards; but I'll be hanged if she did not put Pam in her pocket.[41]

MRS. MARWOOD   You married her to keep you; and if you can contrive to have her keep you better than you expected, why should you not keep her longer than you intended?

FAINALL   The means, the means!

MRS. MARWOOD   Discover to my lady your wife's conduct; threaten to part with her. My lady loves her, and will come to any composition to save her reputation. Take the opportunity of breaking it, just upon

---

[36] *manent* remain   [37] *satyr* the half-man, half-goat figure of lechery in mythology   [38] *citizen's child* children of London "citizens" (merchants, etc.) apparently were likely to be cuckolded in later life by men of the upper class or nobility   [39] *furnished like a deputy-lieutenant's hall* as many horns as in a hunting trophy room or hall   [40] *cap of maintenance* a two-pointed cap in heraldry   [41] *Pam in her pocket* ace up her sleeve, that is, her relationship with Mirabell. Pam (Jack, or Knave of Clubs) was a high card in the popular game of loo.

the discovery of this imposture. My lady will be enraged beyond bounds, and sacrifice niece, and fortune, and all at that conjuncture. And let me alone to keep her warm; if she should flag in her part, I will not fail to prompt her.

FAINALL Faith, this has an appearance.

MRS. MARWOOD I'm sorry I hinted to my lady to endeavor a match between Millamant and Sir Wilfull; that may be an obstacle.

FAINALL Oh, for that matter leave me to manage him; I'll disable him for that; he will drink like a Dane: after dinner, I'll set his hand in.

MRS. MARWOOD Well, how do you stand affected towards your lady?

FAINALL Why, faith, I'm thinking of it.—Let me see—I am married already, so that's over;—my wife has played the jade with me—well, that's over too;—I never loved her, or if I had, why that would have been over too by this time.—Jealous of her I cannot be, for I am certain; so there's an end of jealousy. Weary of her, I am, and shall be—no, there's no end of that; no, no, that were too much to hope. Thus far concerning my repose. Now for my reputation—As to my own, I married not for it; so that's out of the question.—And as to my part in my wife's—why, she had parted with hers before; so bringing none to me, she can take none from me; 'tis against all rule of play, that I should lose to one who has not wherewithal to stake.

MRS. MARWOOD Besides, you forget, marriage is honorable.

FAINALL Hum! Faith, and that's well thought on; marriage is honorable, as you say; and if so, wherefore should cuckoldom be a discredit, being derived from so honorable a root?

MRS. MARWOOD Nay, I know not; if the root be honorable, why not the branches?

FAINALL So, so, why this point's clear. Well, how do we proceed?

MRS. MARWOOD I will contrive a letter which shall be delivered to my lady at the time when that rascal who is to act Sir Rowland is with her. It shall come as from an unknown hand—for the less I appear to know of the truth, the better I can play the incendiary. Besides, I would not have Foible provoked if I could help it,—because you know she knows some passages. Nay, I expect all will come out—but let the mine be sprung first, and then I care not if I'm discovered.

FAINALL If the worst come to the worst, I'll turn my wife to grass.—I have already a deed of settlement of the best part of her estate, which I wheedled out of her, and that you shall partake at least.

MRS. MARWOOD I hope you are convinced that I hate Mirabell; now you'll be no more jealous.

FAINALL Jealous, no!—by this kiss—let husbands be jealous, but let the lover still believe; or if he doubt, let it be only to endear his pleasure, and prepare the joy that follows, when he proves his mistress true; but let husbands' doubts convert to endless jealousy; or if they have belief, let it corrupt to superstition, and blind credulity. I am single, and will herd no more with 'em. True, I wear the badge, but I'll disown the order. And since I take my leave of 'em, I care not if I leave 'em a common motto to their common crest:

> All husbands must, or pain, or shame, endure;
> The wise too jealous are, fools too secure.

(*Exeunt.*)

ACT IV

Scene continues
Enter LADY WISHFORT *and* FOIBLE

LADY WISHFORT   Is Sir Rowland coming, say'st thou, Foible? and are things in order?

FOIBLE   Yes, madam. I have put waxlights in the sconces, and placed the footmen in a row in the hall, in their best liveries, with the coachman and postilion to fill up the equipage.

LADY WISHFORT   Have you pulvilled[1] the coachman and postilion, that they may not stink of the stable when Sir Rowland comes by?

FOIBLE   Yes, madam.

LADY WISHFORT   And are the dancers and the music ready, that he may be entertained in all points with correspondence to his passion?

FOIBLE   All is ready, madam.

LADY WISHFORT   And—well—and how do I look, Foible?

FOIBLE   Most killing well, madam.

LADY WISHFORT   Well, and how shall I receive him? In what figure shall I give his heart the first impression? There is a great deal in the first impression. Shall I sit?—No, I won't sit—I'll walk—ay, I'll walk from the door upon his entrance; and then turn full upon him.—No, that will be too sudden. I'll lie—ay, I'll lie down—I'll receive him in my little dressing-room; there's a couch—yes, yes, I'll give the first impression on a couch.—I won't lie neither, but loll and lean upon one elbow, with one foot a little dangling off, jogging in a thoughtful way—yes—and then as soon as he appears, start, ay, start and be surprised, and rise to meet him in a pretty disorder—yes—oh, nothing is more alluring than a levee from a couch in some confusion.—It shows the foot to advantage, and furnishes with blushes, and recomposing airs beyond comparison. Hark! There's a coach.

FOIBLE   'Tis he, madam.

---

[1] *pulvilled* powdered

LADY WISHFORT   Oh dear, has my nephew made his address to Millamant? I ordered him.

FOIBLE   Sir Wilfull is set in to drinking, madam, in the parlor.

LADY WISHFORT   Ods my life, I'll send him to her. Call her down, Foible; bring her hither. I'll send him as I go. When they are together, then come to me, Foible, that I may not be too long alone with Sir Rowland. (*Exit.*)

(*Enter* MRS. MILLAMANT *and* MRS. FAINALL.)

FOIBLE   Madam, I stayed here, to tell your ladyship that Mr. Mirabell has waited this half-hour for an opportunity to talk with you. Though my lady's orders were to leave you and Sir Wilfull together. Shall I tell Mr. Mirabell that you are at leisure?

MILLIMANT   No—what would the dear man have? I am thoughtful, and would amuse myself—bid him come another time. (*Repeating and walking about.*)

>   There never yet was woman made,
>   Nor shall, but to be curst.[2]

That's hard!

MRS. FAINALL   You are very fond of Sir John Suckling to-day, Millamant, and the poets.

MILLAMANT   Heh? Ay, and filthy verses—so I am.

FOIBLE   Sir Wilfull is coming, madam. Shall I send Mr. Mirabell away?

MILLAMANT   Ay, if you please, Foible, send him away,—or send him hither—just as you will, dear Foible.—I think I'll see him—Shall I? Ay, let the wretch come. (*Repeating.*)

>   Thyrsis, a youth of the inspired train.[3]

Dear Fainall, entertain Sir Wilfull—thou hast philosophy to undergo a fool; thou art married, and hast patience.—I would confer with my own thoughts.

MRS. FAINALL   I am obliged to you, that you would make me your proxy in this affair; but I have business of my own.

(*Enter* SIR WILFULL.)

—O Sir Wilfull, you are come at the critical instant. There's your mistress up to the ears in love and contemplation; pursue your point, now or never.

SIR WILFULL   Yes; my aunt would have it so,—I would gladly have been

---

[2] This and the next two couplets spoken by Millamant are from untitled works by Sir John Suckling, a Restoration poet favored by Millamant for his lyrics on love and faithless men   [3] from Edmund Waller's "Phoebus and Daphne"

encouraged with a bottle or two, because I'm somewhat wary at first, before I am acquainted.—

(*This while* MILLAMANT *walks about repeating to herself.*)

But I hope, after a time, I shall break my mind—that is, upon further acquaintance.—So for the present, cousin, I'll take my leave—if so be you'll be so kind to make my excuse, I'll return to my company—

MRS. FAINALL Oh, fie, Sir Wilfull! What, you must not be daunted.

SIR WILFULL Daunted! no, that's not it, it is not so much for that—for if so be that I set on't, I'll do't. But only for the present, 'tis sufficient till further acquaintance, that's all—your servant.

MRS. FAINALL Nay, I'll swear you shall never lose so favorable an opportunity, if I can help it. I'll leave you together, and lock the door. (*Exit.*)

SIR WILFULL Nay, nay, cousin,—I have forgot my gloves. What d'ee do?—'Sheart, a' has locked the door indeed, I think.—Nay, Cousin Fainall, open the door.—Pshaw, what a vixen trick is this?—Nay, now a' has seen me too.—Cousin, I made bold to pass through as it were— I think this door's inchanted—

MILLAMANT (*repeating*).

I prithee spare me, gentle boy.
Press me no more for that slight toy,—

SIR WILFULL Anan?[4] Cousin, your servant.

MILLAMANT (*repeating*).

That foolish trifle of a heart—

Sir Wilfull!

SIR WILFULL Yes—your servant. No offence, I hope, cousin.

MILLAMANT (*repeating*).

I swear it will not do its part,
Though thou dost thine, employ'st thy power and art.

Natural, easy Suckling!

SIR WILFULL Anan? Suckling? No such suckling neither, cousin, nor stripling: I thank heaven, I'm no minor.

MILLAMANT Ah, rustic, ruder than Gothic![5]

SIR WILFULL Well, well, I shall understand your lingo one of these days, cousin; in the meanwhile I must answer in plain English.

MILLAMANT Have you any business with me, Sir Wilfull?

SIR WILFULL Not at present, cousin.—Yes, I made bold to see, to come

---

[4] *Anan* how's that? [5] *Gothic* though a common term for much of medieval architecture, it was originally strongly derogatory, meaning "barbaric"

and know if that how you were disposed to fetch a walk this evening, if so be that I might not be troublesome, I would have sought a walk with you.

MILLAMANT   A walk? What then?

SIR WILFULL   Nay, nothing—only for the walk's sake, that's all—

MILLAMANT   I nauseate walking; 'tis a country diversion; I loathe the country and everything that relates to it.

SIR WILFULL   Indeed! Hah! Look ye, look ye, you do? Nay, 'tis like you may.—Here are choice of pastimes here in town, as plays and the like; that must be confessed indeed.

MILLAMANT   *Ah, l'étourdie!*[6] I hate the town too.

SIR WILFULL   Dear heart, that's much.—Hah! that you should hate 'em both! Hah! 'tis like you may; there are some can't relish the town, and others can't away with the country,—'tis like you may be one of those, cousin.

MILLAMANT   Ha, ha, ha! Yes, 'tis like I may.—You have nothing further to say to me?

SIR WILFULL   Not at present, cousin.—'Tis like when I have an opportunity to be more private,—I may break my mind in some measure.—I conjecture you partly guess.—However, that's as time shall try,—but spare to speak and spare to speed, as they say.

MILLAMANT   If it is of no great importance, Sir Wilfull, you will oblige me to leave me: I have just now a little business—

SIR WILFULL   Enough, enough, cousin: yes, yes, all a case.—When you're disposed, when you're disposed. Now's as well as another time; and another time as well as now. All's one for that,—yes, yes, if your concerns call you, there's no haste; it will keep cold as they say.—Cousin, your servant.—I think this door's locked.

MILLAMANT   You may go this way, sir.

SIR WILFULL   Your servant! then with your leave I'll return to my company. (*Exit.*)

MILLAMANT   Ay, ay; ha, ha, ha!

Like Phoebus sung the no less am'rous boy.[7]

---

[6] *Ah, l'étourdie* stupid, stuffy, etc. Millamant could be directing this toward Sir Wilfull, or at the town she hates.   [7] These lines exchanged by Mirabell and Millamant are from Waller's "Phoebus and Daphne." This extended exchange between the lovers, commonly known as the "proviso scene," is one of the most famous in Restoration comedy. It turns the traditional romantic proposal topsy-turvy into a brilliantly comic statement of the sophisticated and essentially equal relationship in marriage anticipated by this highly intelligent and witty couple. Unable to permit either to be dominated by the other in a more traditional union, they state their cases bluntly, and seriously, in the establishment of a working relationship to be free of sentimental intrusions. Each lays down some rather formidable conditions, which the other duly acknowledges as eminently "reasonable," but which probably neither one fully expects the other to abide by.

(*Enter* MIRABELL.)

MIRABELL

Like Daphne she, as lovely and as coy.

Do you lock yourself up from me, to make my search more curious? Or is this pretty artifice contrived, to signify that here the chase must end, and my pursuit be crowned, for you can fly no further?

MILLAMANT   Vanity! No—I'll fly and be followed to the last moment. Though I am upon the very verge of matrimony, I expect you should solicit me as much as if I were wavering at the grate of a monastery, with one foot over the threshold. I'll be solicited to the very last, nay, and afterwards.

MIRABELL   What, after the last?

MILLAMANT   Oh, I should think I was poor and had nothing to bestow, if I were reduced to an inglorious ease, and freed from the agreeable fatigues of solicitation.

MIRABELL   But do not you know, that when favors are conferred upon instant and tedious solicitation, that they diminish in their value, and that both the giver loses the grace, and the receiver lessens his pleasure?

MILLAMANT   It may be things of common application; but never sure in love. Oh, I hate a lover that can dare to think he draws a moment's air, independent on the bounty of his mistress. There is not so impudent a thing in nature, as the saucy look of an assured man, confident of success. The pedantic arrogance of a very husband has not so pragmatical an air. Ah! I'll never marry, unless I am first made sure of my will and pleasure.

MIRABELL   Would you have 'em both before marriage? Or will you be contented with the first now, and stay for the other till after grace?

MILLLAMANT   Ah, don't be impertinent.—My dear liberty, shall I leave thee? My faithful solitude, my darling contemplation, must I bid you then adieu? Ay-h, adieu—my morning thoughts, agreeable wakings, indolent slumbers, all ye *douceurs*, ye *sommeils du matin*,[8] adieu?—I can't do't, 'tis more than impossible. Positively, Mirabell, I'll lie abed in a morning as long as I please.

MIRABELL   Then I'll get up in a morning as early as I please.

MILLAMANT   Ah! Idle creature, get up when you will.—And d'ee hear, I won't be called names after I'm married; positively I won't be called names.

MIRABELL   Names!

---

[8] *douceurs, ye sommeils du matin* pleasant things, morning naps. Millamant is clearly a late riser.

MILLAMANT   Ay, as wife, spouse, my dear, joy, jewel, love, sweetheart, and the rest of that nauseous cant, in which men and their wives are so fulsomely familiar—I shall never bear that.—Good Mirabell, don't let us be familiar or fond, nor kiss before folks, like my Lady Fadler and Sir Francis: nor go to Hyde Park together the first Sunday in a new chariot, to provoke eyes and whispers; and then never to be seen there together again; as if we were proud of one another the first week, and ashamed of one another for ever after. Let us never visit together, nor go to a play together, but let us be very strange and well bred: let us be as strange as if we had been married a great while; and as well bred as if we were not married at all.

MIRABELL   Have you any more conditions to offer? Hitherto your demands are pretty reasonable.

MILLAMANT   Trifles,—as liberty to pay and receive visits to and from whom I please; to write and receive letters, without interrogatories or wry faces on your part. To wear what I please; and choose conversation with regard only to my own taste; to have no obligation upon me to converse with wits that I don't like, because they are your acquaintance; or to be intimate with fools, because they may be your relations. Come to dinner when I please, dine in my dressing-room when I'm out of humor, without giving a reason. To have my closet inviolate; to be sole empress of my tea-table, which you must never presume to approach without first asking leave. And lastly, wherever I am, you shall always knock at the door before you come in. These articles subscribed, if I continue to endure you a little longer, I may by degrees dwindle into a wife.

MIRABELL   Your bill of fare is something advanced in this latter account. Well, have I liberty to offer conditions—that when you are dwindled into a wife, I may not be beyond measure enlarged into a husband?

MILLAMANT   You have free leave; propose your utmost, speak and spare not.

MIRABELL   I thank you. *Imprimis*[9] then, I covenant that your acquaintance be general; that you admit no sworn confidante, or intimate of your own sex; no she-friend to screen her affairs under your countenance, and tempt you to make trial of a mutual secrecy. No decoy-duck to wheedle you a "fop-scrambling" to the play in a mask[10]—

---

[9] *Imprimis* the first thing. Mirabell uses this and other legal terms in proposing his "formal" contract.   [10] *No decoy-duck . . . in a mask* Mirabell's conditions are rather severe, as he seems to be trying to prevent Millamant from enjoying some primary Restoration pleasures with a "she-friend," that is, gossip, secrets, intrigues, and protecting each other in their sexual adventures. This particular passage is somewhat obscure and appears variously punctuated in different editions. As printed here it

then bring you home in a pretended fright, when you think you shall be found out—and rail at me for missing the play, and disappointing the frolic which you had, to pick me up and prove my constancy.

MILLAMANT   Detestable *imprimis!* I go to the play in a mask!

MIRABELL   *Item,* I article, that you continue to like your own face as long as I shall; and while it passes current with me, that you endeavor not to new-coin it. To which end, together with all vizards[11] for the day, I prohibit all masks for the night, made of oiled-skins and I know not what—hog's bones, hare's gall, pig-water, and the marrow of a roasted cat. In short, I forbid all commerce with the gentlewoman in What-d'ye-call-it Court. *Item,* I shut my doors against all bawds with baskets, and pennyworths of muslin, china, fans, atlases,[12] etc.—*Item,* when you shall be breeding—

MILLAMANT   Ah! name it not.

MIRABELL   Which may be presumed, with a blessing on our endeavors—

MILLAMANT   Odious endeavors!

MIRABELL   I denounce against all strait lacing, squeezing for a shape, till you mould my boy's head like a sugar-loaf; and instead of a man-child, make me the father to a crooked billet.[13] Lastly, to the dominion of the tea-table I submit,—but with proviso, that you exceed not in your province; but restrain yourself to native and simple tea-table drinks, as tea, chocolate, and coffee, as likewise to genuine and authorized tea-table talk—such as mending of fashions, spoiling reputations, railing at absent friends, and so forth—but that on no account you encroach upon the men's prerogative, and presume to drink healths, or toast fellows; for prevention of which I banish all foreign forces, all auxiliaries to the tea-table, as orange-brandy, all aniseed, cinnamon, citron, and Barbadoes waters, together with ratafia and the most noble spirit of clary[14]—but for cowslip-wine, poppy water,

---

seems to mean that Millamant could be enticed by her "decoy" friend to go "fop-scrambling" to the theatre, i.e., to go, properly masked of course to prevent identification, in order to flirt with the foppish dandies who generally occupied the pit (today's orchestra) beneath the boxes in which the ladies sat. Another reading, which is closer to early editions of the play, "to wheedle you a fop, scrambling to the play" renders a somewhat different meaning. This would assume the she-friend decoy could entice some fop to accompany them, so that they would have to "scramble" to the play surreptitiously and incognito. In either case, Millamant expresses shock that Mirabell even suggests that she as a respectable lady, married at that, would ever consider going to the play masked.   [11] *vizards* masks   [12] *atlases* rich far-Eastern satins   [13] *billet* stick   [14] *orange-brandy . . . clary* Mirabell would deny all alcoholic beverages, which these represent. Clary, or claret, seems to Mirabell to be "noble," or manly, therefore unfit for ladies. Mirabell is actually reflecting the male view as to what ladies should be permitted as he accepts the weak or non-alcoholic variety. Millamant again rejects his presumptions about her behavior as she rejects the "filthy strong waters."

and all dormitives, those I allow. These provisos admitted, in other things I may prove a tractable and complying husband.

MILLAMANT   Oh, horrid provisos! filthy strong waters! I toast fellows, odious men! I hate your odious provisos.

MIRABELL   Then we're agreed. Shall I kiss your hand upon the contract? And here comes one to be a witness to the sealing of the deed.

(*Enter* MRS. FAINALL.)

MILLAMANT   Fainall, what shall I do? Shall I have him? I think I must have him.

MRS. FAINALL   Ay, ay, take him, take him, what should you do?

MILLAMANT   Well then—I'll take my death, I'm in a horrid fright— Fainall, I shall never say it—well—I think—I'll endure you.

MRS. FAINALL   Fie, fie! have him, have him, and tell him so in plain terms: for I am sure you have a mind to him.

MILLAMANT   Are you? I think I have—and the horrid man looks as if he thought so too.—Well, you ridiculous thing you, I'll have you—I won't be kissed, nor I won't be thanked—here, kiss my hand though. —So, hold your tongue now, and don't say a word.

MRS. FAINALL   Mirabell, there's a necessity for your obedience!—you have neither time to talk nor stay. My mother is coming; and in my conscience, if she should see you, would fall into fits, and maybe not recover time enough to return to Sir Rowland, who, as Foible tells me, is in a fair way to succeed. Therefore spare your ecstasies for another occasion, and slip down the back stairs, where Foible waits to consult you.

MILLAMANT   Ay, go, go. In the meantime I suppose you have said something to please me.

MIRABELL   I am all obedience. (*Exit*.)

MRS. FAINALL   Yonder Sir Wilfull's drunk; and so noisy that my mother has been forced to leave Sir Rowland to appease him; but he answers her only with singing and drinking.—What they have done by this time I know not; but Petulant and he were upon quarrelling as I came by.

MILLAMANT   Well, if Mirabell should not make a good husband, I am a lost thing;—for I find I love him violently.

MRS. FAINALL   So it seems, when you mind not what's said to you.—If you doubt him, you had best take up with Sir Wilfull.

MILLAMANT   How can you name that superannuated lubber? foh!

(*Enter* WITWOUD *from drinking*.)

MRS. FAINALL   So, is the fray made up, that you have left 'em?

WITWOUD   Left 'em? I could stay no longer—I have laughed like ten christ'nings—I am tipsy with laughing.—If I had stayed any longer I should have burst.—I must have been let out and pieced in the sides like an unsized camlet[15]—Yes, yes, the fray is composed; my lady came in like a *nolle prosequi*[16] and stopped their proceedings.

MILLAMANT What was the dispute?

WITWOUD That's the jest; there was no dispute. They could neither of 'em speak for rage; and so fell a sputt'ring at one another like two roasting apples.

(*Enter* PETULANT *drunk.*)

WITWOUD Now, Petulant, all's over, all's well. Gad, my head begins to whim it about.—Why dost thou not speak? Thou art both as drunk and as mute as a fish.

PETULANT Look you, Mrs. Millamant—if you can love me, dear nymph—say it—and that's the conclusion—pass on, or pass off,— that's all.

WITWOUD Thou hast uttered volumes, folios, in less than *decimo sexto,*[17] my dear Lacedemonian.[18] Sirrah[19] Petulant, thou art an epitomizer of words.

PETULANT Witwoud—you are an annihilator of sense.

WITWOUD Thou art a retailer of phrases; and dost deal in remnants of remnants, like a maker of pincushions—thou art in truth (metaphorically speaking) a speaker of shorthand.

PETULANT Thou art (without a figure) just one half of an ass; and Baldwin yonder, thy half-brother, is the rest.—A gemini[20] of asses split, would make just four of you.

WITWOUD Thou dost bite, my dear mustard seed; kiss me for that.

PETULANT Stand off—I'll kiss no more males,—I have kissed your twin yonder in a humor of reconciliation, till he (*hiccup*) rises upon my stomach like a radish.

MILLAMANT Eh! filthy creature!—what was the quarrel?

PETULANT There was no quarrel—there might have been a quarrel.

WITWOUD If there had been words enow between 'em to have expressed provocation, they had gone together by the ears like a pair of castanets.

PETULANT You were the quarrel.

MILLAMANT Me!

PETULANT If I have a humor to quarrel, I can make less matters conclude premises. If you are not handsome, what then, if I have a

---

[15] *unsized camlet* an unstarched, or unstiffened, fabric   [16] *nolle prosequi* nothing follows. Witwoud remembers his law training with this legal term for ending a law case.
[17] *decimo sexto* publishing term for a small book   [18] *Lacedemonian* Spartan. The ancient Spartans were reputed to be persons of few words.   [19] *Sirrah* a derogatory form of Sir or Mr.   [20] *gemini* a pair of, or twins

humor to prove it?—If I shall have my reward, say so; if not, fight for your face the next time yourself.—I'll go sleep.

WITWOUD Do, wrap thyself up like a woodlouse, and dream revenge— and hear me, if thou canst learn to write by tomorrow morning, pen me a challenge—I'll carry it for thee.

PETULANT Carry your mistress's monkey a spider,—go flea dogs, and read romances!—I'll go to bed to my maid. (*Exit.*)

MRS. FAINALL He's horridly drunk.—How came you all in this pickle?

WITWOUD A plot, a plot, to get rid of the knight—your husband's advice; but he sneaked off.

(*Enter* LADY WISHFORT *and* SIR WILFULL, *drunk.*)

LADY WISHFORT Out upon't, out upon't, at years of discretion, and comport yourself at this rantipole[21] rate!

SIR WILFULL No offence, aunt.

LADY WISHFORT Offence? As I'm a person, I'm ashamed of you.— Fogh! how you stink of wine! D'ee think my niece will ever endure such a borachio! you're an absolute borachio.[22]

SIR WILFULL Borachio!

LADY WISHFORT At a time when you should commence an amour and put your best foot foremost—

SIR WILFULL 'Sheart, an you grutch[23] me your liquor, make a bill. Give me more drink, and take my purse. (*Sings.*)

> Prithee fill me the glass
> Till it laugh in my face,
> With ale that is potent and mellow;
> He that whines for a lass,
> Is an ignorant ass,
> For a bumper has not its fellow.

But if you would have me marry my cousin,—say the word, and I'll do't—Wilfull will do't, that's the word—Wilfull will do't, that's my crest!—my motto I have forgot.

LADY WISHFORT My nephew's a little overtaken, cousin—but 'tis with drinking your health.—O' my word you are obliged to him—

SIR WILFULL *In vino veritas,*[24] aunt.—If I drunk your health today, cousin—I am a borachio. But if you have a mind to be married, say the word, and send for the piper; Wilfull will do't. If not, dust it away, and let's have t'other round.—Tony, 'odsheart, where's Tony?— Tony's an honest fellow, but he spits after a bumper[25] and that's a fault. (*Sings.*)

---

[21] *rantipole* wild, quarrelsome [22] *borachio* a container for wine, hence, a drunkard [23] *grutch* grudge [24] *In vino veritas* in wine is truth [25] *bumper* a large cup or glass well-filled

We'll drink and we'll never ha' done, boys,
Put the glass then around with the sun, boys,
Let Apollo's example invite us;
For he's drunk every night,
And that makes him so bright,
That he's able next morning to light us.

The sun's a good pimple,[26] an honest soaker; he has a cellar at your Antipodes.[27] If I travel, aunt, I touch at your Antipodes.—Your Antipodes are a good rascally sort of topsy-turvy fellows. If I had a bumper, I'd stand upon my head and drink a health to 'em.—A match or no match, cousin with the hard name?—Aunt, Wilfull will do't. If she has her maidenhead, let her look to't; if she has not, let her keep her own counsel in the meantime, and cry out at the nine months' end.

MILLIMANT Your pardon, madam, I can stay no longer.—Sir Wilfull grows very powerful. Egh! how he smells! I shall be overcome if I stay. Come, cousin.

(*Exeunt* MILLAMANT *and* MRS. FAINALL.)

LADY WISHFORT Smells! he would poison a tallow-chandler[28] and his family. Beastly creature, I know not what to do with him.—Travel, quoth a; ay travel, travel, get thee gone, get thee but far enough, to the Saracens, or the Tartars, or the Turks—for thou art not fit to live in a Christian commonwealth, thou beastly pagan.

SIR WILFULL Turks, no; no Turks, aunt: your Turks are infidels, and believe not in the grape. Your Mahometan, your Mussulman, is a dry stinkard—no offence, aunt. My map says that your Turk is not so honest a man as our Christian—I cannot find by the map that your Mufti[29] is orthodox—whereby it is a plain case, that orthodox is a hard word, aunt and (*hiccup*) Greek for claret. (*Sings.*)

To drink is a Christian diversion,
Unknown to the Turk and the Persian:
Let Mahometan fools
Live by heathenish rules,
And be damned over tea-cups and coffee.
But let British lads sing,
Crown a health to the king,
And a fig for your Sultan and Sophy.[30]

---

[26] *pimple* friend [27] *Antipodes* opposite ends of the earth [28] *tallow-chandler* candles were made of tallow, or animal fat, and a candle maker would likely reek of his profession [29] *Mufti* a Muslim priest [30] *Sophy* Shah of Persia. Sir Wilfull's songs are apparently Congreve's creation.

Ah, Tony!

(*Enter* FOIBLE *and whispers* LADY WISHFORT.)

LADY WISHFORT Sir Rowland impatient? Good lack! what shall I do with this beastly tumbril?[31]—Go lie down and sleep, you sot—or as I'm a person, I'll have you bastinadoed[32] with broomsticks. Call up the wenches.

(*Exit* FOIBLE.)

SIR WILFULL Ahey! Wenches, where are the wenches?

LADY WISHFORT Dear Cousin Witwoud, get him away, and you will bind me to you inviolably. I have an affair of moment that invades me with some precipitation.—You will oblige me to all futurity.

WITWOUD Come, knight.—Pox on him, I don't know what to say to him.—Will you go to a cock-match?

SIR WILFULL With a wench, Tony? Is she a shakebag,[33] sirrah? Let me bite your cheek for that.

WITWOUD Horrible! He has a breath like a bagpipe.—Ay, ay; come, will you march, my Salopian?[34]

SIR WILFULL Lead on, little Tony—I'll follow thee, my Anthony, my Tantony.[35] Sirrah, thou sha't be my Tantony; and I'll be thy pig.

—And a fig for your Sultan and Sophy.

(SIR WILFULL *exits singing with* WITWOUD.)

LADY WISHFORT This will never do. It will never make a match. At least before he has been abroad.

(*Enter* WAITWELL, *disguised as for* SIR ROWLAND.)

Dear Sir Rowland, I am confounded with confusion at the retrospection of my own rudeness—I have more pardons to ask than the pope distributes in the year of jubilee. But I hope where there is likely to be so near an alliance, we may unbend the severity of decorum, and dispense with a little ceremony.

WAITWELL My impatience, madam, is the effect of my transport;—and till I have the possession of your adorable person, I am tantalized on a rack; and do but hang, madam, on the tenter of expectation.

LADY WISHFORT You have excess of gallantry, Sir Rowland; and press things to a conclusion, with a most prevailing vehemence.—But a day or two for decency of marriage—

---

[31] *tumbril* a cart often used to haul manure. Condemned prisoners were frequently hauled to the scaffold in a tumbril. [32] *bastinadoed* beaten, mainly on the soles of the feet [33] *shakebag* game cock [34] *Salopian* native of Shropshire [35] *Tantony* corruption of St. Anthony, patron saint of pig farmers

WAITWELL   For decency of funeral, madam. The delay will break my heart—or if that should fail, I shall be poisoned. My nephew will get an inkling of my designs, and poison me—and I would willingly starve him before I die—I would gladly go out of the world with that satisfaction. That would be some comfort to me, if I could but live so long as to be revenged on that unnatural viper.

LADY WISHFORT   Is he so unnatural, say you? Truly I would contribute much both to the saving of your life, and the accomplishment of your revenge. Not that I respect myself, though he has been a perfidious wretch to me.

WAITWELL   Perfidious to you!

LADY WISHFORT   O Sir Rowland, the hours that he has died away at my feet, the tears that he has shed, the oaths that he has sworn, the palpitations that he has felt, the trances, and the tremblings, the ardors and the ecstasies, the kneelings and the risings, the heart-heavings, and the hand-gripings, the pangs and the pathetic regards of his protesting eyes! Oh, no memory can register!

WAITWELL   What, my rival! is the rebel my rival? a' dies.

LADY WISHFORT   No, don't kill him at once, Sir Rowland; starve him gradually inch by inch.

WAITWELL   I'll do't. In three weeks he shall be barefoot; in a month out at knees with begging an alms;—he shall starve upward and upward, till he has nothing living but his head, and then go out in a stink like a candle's end upon a save-all.

LADY WISHFORT   Well, Sir Rowland, you have the way—you are no novice in the labyrinth of love—you have the clue.—But as I am a person, Sir Rowland, you must not attribute my yielding to any sinister appetite, or indigestion of widowhood; nor impute my complacency to any lethargy of continence. I hope you do not think me prone to any iteration of nuptials.—

WAITWELL   Far be it from me—

LADY WISHFORT   If you do, I protest I must recede—or think that I have made a prostitution of decorums, but in the vehemence of compassion, and to save the life of a person of so much importance—

WAITWELL   I esteem it so—

LADY WISHFORT   Or else you wrong my condescension—

WAITWELL   I do not, I do not—

LADY WISHFORT   Indeed you do.

WAITWELL   I do not, fair shrine of virtue.

LADY WISHFORT   If you think the least scruple of carnality was an ingredient—

WAITWELL   Dear madam, no. You are all camphire and frankincense, all chastity and odor.

LADY WISHFORT   Or that—

(*Enter* FOIBLE.)

FOIBLE Madam, the dancers are ready, and there's one with a letter, who must deliver it into your own hands.

LADY WISHFORT Sir Rowland, will you give me leave? Think favorably, judge candidly, and conclude you have found a person who would suffer racks in honor's cause, dear Sir Rowland, and will wait on you incessantly. (*Exit.*)

WAITWELL Fie, fie!—What a slavery have I undergone! Spouse, hast thou any cordial?—I want spirits.

FOIBLE What a washy rogue art thou, to pant thus for a quarter of an hour's lying and swearing to a fine lady!

WAITWELL Oh, she is the antidote to desire. Spouse, thou wilt fare the worse for't—I shall have no appetite to iteration of nuptials—this eight and forty hours:—by this hand I'd rather be a chairman in the dog-days[36]—than act Sir Rowland till this time tomorrow.

(*Enter* LADY WISHFORT *with a letter.*)

LADY WISHFORT Call in the dancers.—Sir Rowland, we'll sit, if you please, and see the entertainment.

(*Dance.*)

Now with your permission, Sir Rowland, I will peruse my letter—I would open it in your presence, because I would not make you uneasy. If it should make you uneasy I would burn it—speak if it does—but you may see by the superscription it is like a woman's hand.

FOIBLE (*to him*) By heaven! Mrs. Marwood's, I know it;—my heart aches—get it from her—

WAITWELL A woman's hand? No, madam, that's no woman's hand, I see that already. That's somebody whose throat must be cut.

LADY WISHFORT Nay, Sir Rowland, since you give me a proof of your passion by your jealousy, I promise you I'll make you a return, by a frank communication.—You shall see it—we'll open it together—look you here.

(*Reads.*) "Madam, though unknown to you,"—Look you there, 'tis from nobody that I know—"I have that honor for your character, that I think myself obliged to let you know you are abused. He who pretends to be Sir Rowland is a cheat and a rascal—" Oh heavens! what's this?

FOIBLE (*aside*) Unfortunate, all's ruined.

WAITWELL How, how, let me see, let me see! (*Reading.*) "A rascal, and

---

[36] *chairman in the dog-days* one who carried sedan chairs in the hottest days of summer

disguised and suborned for that imposture,"—O villainy! O villainy! —"by the contrivance of—"

LADY WISHFORT   I shall faint, I shall die, I shall die, oh!

FOIBLE (*to him*)   Say 'tis your nephew's hand.—Quickly, his plot, swear, swear it.

WAITWELL   Here's a villain! Madam, don't you perceive it, don't you see it?

LADY WISHFORT   Too well, too well. I have seen too much.

WAITWELL   I told you at first I knew the hand. A woman's hand? The rascal writes a sort of a large hand, your Roman hand. I saw there was a throat to be cut presently. If he were my son, as he is my nephew, I'd pistol him—

FOIBLE   O treachery! But you are sure, Sir Rowland, it is his writing?

WAITWELL   Sure? am I here? do I live? do I love this pearl of India? I have twenty letters in my pocket from him, in the same character.

LADY WISHFORT   How!

FOIBLE   Oh, what luck it is, Sir Rowland, that you were present at this juncture! This was the business that brought Mr. Mirabell disguised to Madam Millamant this afternoon. I thought something was contriving when he stole by me and would have hid his face.

LADY WISHFORT   How, how!—I heard the villain was in the house indeed, and now I remember, my niece went away abruptly, when Sir Wilfull was to have made his addresses.

FOIBLE   Then, then, madam, Mr. Mirabell waited for her in her chamber, but I would not tell your ladyship to discompose you when you were to receive Sir Rowland.

WAITWELL   Enough, his date is short.

FOIBLE   No, good Sir Rowland, don't incur the law.

WAITWELL   Law! I care not for law. I can die, and 'tis in a good cause— my lady shall be satisfied of my truth and innocence, though it cost me my life.

LADY WISHFORT   No, dear Sir Rowland, don't fight; if you should be killed I must never show my face; or hanged—oh, consider my reputation, Sir Rowland! No, you shan't fight. I'll go in and examine my niece; I'll make her confess. I conjure you, Sir Rowland, by all your love, not to fight.

WAITWELL   I am charmed, madam, I obey. But some proof you must let me give you;—I'll go for a black box, which contains the writings of my whole estate, and deliver that into your hands.

LADY WISHFORT   Ay, dear Sir Rowland, that will be some comfort; bring the black box.

WAITWELL   And may I presume to bring a contract to be signed this night? May I hope so far?

LADY WISHFORT   Bring what you will; but come alive, pray come alive. Oh, this is a happy discovery!

WAITWELL   Dead or alive I'll come—and married we will be in spite of treachery; ay, and get an heir that shall defeat the last remaining glimpse of hope in my abandoned nephew. Come, my buxom widow:

>Ere long you shall substantial proof receive
>That I'm an arrant knight—

FOIBLE (*aside*)   Or arrant knave.

(*Exeunt.*)

ACT V

Scene continues
LADY WISHFORT *and* FOIBLE

LADY WISHFORT   Out of my house, out of my house, thou viper, thou serpent, that I have fostered! thou bosom traitress, that I raised from nothing!—begone, begone, begone, go, go!—that I took from washing of old gauze and weaving of dead hair, with a bleak blue nose, over a chafing-dish of starved embers, and dining behind a traverse rag, in a shop no bigger than a bird-cage,[1]—go, go, starve again, do, do!

FOIBLE   Dear madam, I'll beg pardon on my knees.

LADY WISHFORT   Away, out, out, go set up for yourself again!—do, drive a trade, do, with your three-penny worth of small ware, flaunting upon a pack-thread, under a brandy-seller's bulk, or against a dead wall by a ballad-monger! Go, hang out an old Frisoneer[2] gorget, with a yard of yellow colberteen[3] again! do, an old gnawed mask, two rows of pins, and a child's fiddle; a glass necklace with the beads broken, and a quilted nightcap with one ear! Go, go, drive a trade!— These were your commodities, you treacherous trull, this was your merchandise you dealt in, when I took you into my house, placed you next myself, and made you governante of my whole family! You have forgot this, have you, now you have feathered your nest?

FOIBLE   No, no, dear madam. Do but hear me, have but a moment's patience—I'll confess all. Mr. Mirabell seduced me; I am not the first that he has wheedled with his dissembling tongue; your ladyship's own wisdom has been deluded by him—then how should I, a poor ignorant, defend myself? O madam, if you knew but what he promised me, and how he assured me your ladyship should come to no damage!—Or else the wealth of the Indies should not have bribed me

---

[1] Lady Wishfort apparently rescued Foible from a depressing life as a laundress, wig maker, and lowly assistant in a run-down shop   [2] *Frisoneer gorget* neckpiece worn over the bosom   [3] *colberteen* a coarse lace

to conspire against so good, so sweet, so kind a lady as you have been to me.

LADY WISHFORT   No damage? What, to betray me, to marry me to a cast servingman; to make me a receptacle, an hospital for a decayed pimp? No damage? O thou frontless[4] impudence, more than a big-bellied actress!

FOIBLE   Pray, do but hear me, madam; he could not marry your ladyship, madam.—No indeed, his marriage was to have been void in law; for he was married to me first, to secure your ladyship. He could not have bedded your ladyship; for if he had consummated with your ladyship, he must have run the risk of the law, and been put upon his clergy.[5]—Yes indeed, I enquired of the law in that case before I would meddle or make.

LADY WISHFORT   What, then I have been your property, have I? I have been convenient to you, it seems,—while you were catering for Mirabell, I have been broker for you? What, have you made a passive bawd of me?—This exceeds all precedent; I am brought to fine uses, to become a botcher[6] of second-hand marriages between Abigails and Andrews![7] I'll couple you! Yes, I'll baste you together, you and your Philander![8] I'll Duke's Place you, as I'm a person. Your turtle is in custody already; you shall coo in the same cage, if there be constable or warrant in the parish. (*Exit.*)

FOIBLE   Oh, that ever I was born! Oh, that I was ever married!—A bride, ay, I shall be a Bridewell-bride.[9] Oh!

(*Enter* MRS. FAINALL.)

MRS. FAINALL   Poor Foible, what's the matter?

FOIBLE   O madam, my lady's gone for a constable; I shall be had to a justice, and put to Bridewell to beat hemp! Poor Waitwell's gone to prison already.

MRS. FAINALL   Have a good heart, Foible; Mirabell's gone to give security for him. This is all Marwood's and my husband's doing.

FOIBLE   Yes, yes; I know it, madam; she was in my lady's closet, and overheard all that you said to me before dinner. She sent the letter to my lady; and that missing effect, Mr. Fainall laid this plot to arrest

---

[4] *frontless* shameless   [5] *put upon his clergy* if Waitwell had been caught and charged with bigamy, he could have escaped punishment by "benefit of clergy," which means proving that he could read and write, a legal "benefit" originally granted to clergymen   [6] *botcher* mender, as of old clothes   [7] *Abigails and Andrews* generic names for servants, such as calling all butlers James   [8] *Philander* love (philanderer)   [9] *Bridewell-bride* the women's prison, where poor Foible fears she may have to spend her honeymoon

Waitwell, when he pretended to go for the papers; and in the meantime Mrs. Marwood declared all to my lady.

MRS. FAINALL Was there no mention made of me in the letter?—My mother does not suspect my being in the confederacy? I fancy Marwood has not told her, though she has told my husband.

FOIBLE Yes, madam; but my lady did not see that part; we stifled the letter before she read so far. Has that mischievous devil told Mr. Fainall of your ladyship then?

MRS. FAINALL Ay, all's out, my affair with Mirabell, everything discovered. This is the last day of our living together, that's my comfort.

FOIBLE Indeed, madam, and so 'tis a comfort if you knew all—he has been even with your ladyship, which I could have told you long enough since, but I love to keep peace and quietness, by my good will: I had rather bring friends together than set 'em at distance. But Mrs. Marwood and he are nearer related than ever their parents thought for.

MRS. FAINALL Say'st thou so, Foible? Canst thou prove this?

FOIBLE I can take my oath of it, madam, so can Mrs. Mincing; we have had many a fair word from Madam Marwood, to conceal something that passed in our chamber one evening when you were at Hyde Park—and we were thought to have gone a-walking, but we went up unawares—though we were sworn to secrecy too. Madam Marwood took a book and swore us upon it; but it was but a book of verses and poems. So as long as it was not a Bible oath, we may break it with a safe conscience.

MRS. FAINALL This discovery is the most opportune thing I could wish.

(*Enter* MINCING.)

Now, Mincing?

MINCING My lady would speak with Mrs. Foible, mem. Mr. Mirabell is with her; he has set your spouse at liberty, Mrs. Foible, and would have you hide yourself in my lady's closet, till my old lady's anger is abated. Oh, my old lady is in a perilous passion at something Mr. Fainall has said; he swears, and my old lady cries. There's fearful hurricane, I vow. He says, mem, how that he'll have my lady's fortune made over to him, or he'll be divorced.

MRS. FAINALL Does your lady and Mirabell know that?

MINCING Yes, mem, they have sent me to see if Sir Wilfull be sober, and to bring him to them. My lady is resolved to have him, I think, rather than lose such a vast sum as six thousand pound. Oh, come, Mrs. Foible, I hear my old lady.

MRS. FAINALL Foible, you must tell Mincing that she must prepare to vouch when I call her.

FOIBLE Yes, yes, madam.

MINCING   Oh, yes, mem, I'll vouch anything for your ladyship's service, be what it will.

(*Exeunt* MINCING *and* FOIBLE. *Enter* LADY WISHFORT *and* MRS. MARWOOD.)

LADY WISHFORT   Oh, my dear friend, how can I enumerate the benefits that I have received from your goodness? To you I owe the timely discovery of the false vows of Mirabell; to you the detection of the impostor Sir Rowland. And now you are become an intercessor with my son-in-law, to save the honor of my house, and compound[10] for the frailties of my daughter. Well, friend, you are enough to reconcile me to the bad world, or else I would retire to deserts and solitudes; and feed harmless sheep by groves and purling streams. Dear Marwood, let us leave the world, and retire by ourselves and be shepherdesses.

MRS. MARWOOD   Let us first dispatch the affair in hand, madam. We shall have leisure to think of retirement afterwards.—Here is one who is concerned in the treaty.

LADY WISHFORT   O daughter, daughter, is it possible thou shouldst be my child, bone of my bone, and flesh of my flesh, and as I may say, another me, and yet transgress the most minute particle of severe virtue? Is it possible you should lean aside to iniquity, who have been cast in the direct mold of virtue? I have not only been a mold but a pattern for you, and a model for you, after you were brought into the world.

MRS. FAINALL   I don't understand your ladyship.

LADY WISHFORT   Not understand? Why, have you not been naught?[11] Have you not been sophisticated?[12] Not understand? Here I am ruined to compound for your caprices and your cuckoldoms. I must pawn my plate and my jewels, and ruin my niece, and all little enough—

MRS. FAINALL   I am wronged and abused, and so are you. 'Tis a false accusation, as false as hell, as false as your friend there, ay, or your friend's friend, my false husband.

MRS. MARWOOD   My friend, Mrs. Fainall? Your husband my friend! what do you mean?

MRS. FAINALL   I know what I mean, madam, and so do you; and so shall the world at a time convenient.

MRS. MARWOOD   I am sorry to see you so passionate, madam. More temper would look more like innocence. But I have done. I am sorry my zeal to serve your ladyship and family should admit of miscon-

---

[10] *compound* to make a financial settlement. Lady Wishfort is sure she will have to pay hush money to Fainall to protect her daughter from scandal.   [11] *naught* immoral (naughty)   [12] *sophisticated* corrupted

struction, or make me liable to affronts. You will pardon me, madam, if I meddle no more with an affair in which I am not personally concerned.

LADY WISHFORT   O dear friend, I am so ashamed that you should meet with such returns! (*To* MRS. FAINALL.) You ought to ask pardon on your knees, ungrateful creature! she deserves more from you, than all your life can accomplish. (*To* MRS. MARWOOD.) Oh, don't leave me destitute in this perplexity!—no, stick to me, my good genius.

MRS. FAINALL   I tell you, madam, you're abused.—Stick to you? ay, like a leech, to suck your best blood—she'll drop off when she's full. Madam, you sha' not pawn a bodkin,[13] not part with a brass counter in composition for me. I defy 'em all. Let 'em prove their aspersions: I know my own innocence, and dare stand by a trial. (*Exit.*)

LADY WISHFORT   Why, if she should be innocent, if she should be wronged after all, ha? I don't know what to think—and I promise you, her education has been unexceptionable[14]—I may say it; for I chiefly made it my own care to initiate her very infancy in the rudiments of virtue, and to impress upon her tender years a young odium and aversion to the very sight of men;—ay, friend, she would ha' shrieked if she had but seen a man, till she was in her teens. As I'm a person, 'tis true. She was never suffered to play with a male-child, though but in coats; nay, her very babies were of the feminine gender. Oh, she never looked a man in the face but her own father, or the chaplain, and him we made a shift to put upon her for a woman, by the help of his long garments, and his sleek face, till she was going in her fifteen.

MRS. MARWOOD   'Twas much she should be deceived so long.

LADY WISHFORT   I warrant you, or she would never have borne to have been catechised by him; and have heard his long lectures against singing and dancing, and such debaucheries; and going to filthy plays, and profane music-meetings, where the lewd trebles squeek nothing but bawdy, and the bases roar blasphemy. Oh, she would have swooned at the sight or name of an obscene play-book—and can I think, after all this, that my daughter can be naught? What, a whore? And thought it excommunication to set her foot within the door of a play-house! O my dear friend, I can't believe it, no, no! As she says, let him prove it, let him prove it!

MRS. MARWOOD   Prove it, madam? What, and have your name prostituted in a public court! yours and your daughter's reputation wor-

---

[13] *bodkin* in this case, a sharp needle or a hairpin; also a dagger   [14] *unexceptionable* Lady Wishfort really means "exceptional," or "exemplary," because she has, she thinks, done so well in keeping her daughter innocent

ried at the bar by a pack of bawling lawyers? To be ushered in with an "Oyez"[15] of scandal; and have your case opened by an old fumbling lecher in a quoif like a man midwife, to bring your daughter's infamy to light; to be a theme for legal punsters, and quibblers by the statute; and become a jest, against a rule of court, where there is no precedent for a jest in any record, not even in Doomsday Book;[16] to discompose the gravity of the bench, and provoke naughty interrogatories in more naughty law Latin; while the good judge, tickled with the proceeding, simpers under a grey beard, and fidges off and on his cushion as if he had swallowed cantharides, or sat upon cowitch![17]

LADY WISHFORT   Oh, 'tis very hard!

MRS. MARWOOD   And then to have my young revellers of the Temple[18] take notes, like 'prentices at a conventicle; and after, talk it all over again in Commons,[19] or before drawers[20] in an eating-house.

LADY WISHFORT   Worse and worse!

MRS. MARWOOD   Nay, this is nothing; if it would end here, 'twere well. But it must after this be consigned by the shorthand writers to the public press; and from thence be transferred to the hands, nay, into the throats and lungs of hawkers, with voices more licentious than the loud flounder-man's or the woman that cries grey-pease; and this you must hear till you are stunned; nay, you must hear nothing else for some days.

LADY WISHFORT   Oh, 'tis insupportable. No, no, dear friend, make it up, make it up; ay, ay, I'll compound. I'll give up all, myself and my all, my niece and her all—anything, everything for composition.

MRS. MARWOOD   Nay, madam, I advise nothing; I only lay before you, as a friend, the inconveniencies which perhaps you have overseen.[21] Here comes Mr. Fainall. If he will be satisfied to huddle up all in silence, I shall be glad. You must think I would rather congratulate than condole with you.

(*Enter* FAINALL.)

LADY WISHFORT   Ay, ay, I do not doubt it, dear Marwood; no, no, I do not doubt it.

FAINALL   Well, madam; I have suffered myself to be overcome by the importunity of this lady your friend; and am content you shall enjoy

---

[15] *Oyez* the cry by the bailiff or sergeant at arms in opening a session of court [16] *Doomsday Book* the land survey ordered by William I (The Conqueror) between 1085 and 1086 [17] *cantharides, cowitch* a diuretic and a plant with stiff irritating bristles, either of which would cause fidgeting [18] *revellers of the Temple* law students in one of the Inns of Court [19] *Commons* dining hall [20] *drawers* waiters, tapsters [21] *overseen* overlooked

your own proper estate during life, on condition you oblige yourself never to marry, under such penalty as I think convenient.

LADY WISHFORT   Never to marry?

FAINALL   No more Sir Rowlands;—the next imposture may not be so timely detected.

MRS. MARWOOD   That condition, I dare answer, my lady will consent to, without difficulty; she has already but too much experienced the perfidiousness of men. Besides, madam, when we retire to our pastoral solitude we shall bid adieu to all other thoughts.

LADY WISHFORT   Ay, that's true; but in case of necessity, as of health, or some such emergency—

FAINALL   Oh, if you are prescribed marriage, you shall be considered; I will only reserve to myself the power to choose for you. If your physic be wholesome, it matters not who is your apothecary. Next, my wife shall settle on me the remainder of her fortune, not made over already, and for her maintenance depend entirely on my discretion.

LADY WISHFORT   This is most inhumanly savage; exceeding the barbarity of a Muscovite husband.

FAINALL   I learned it from his Czarish majesty's retinue,[22] in a winter evening's conference over brandy and pepper, amongst other secrets of matrimony and policy, as they are at present practised in the northern hemisphere. But this must be agreed unto, and that positively. Lastly, I will be endowed, in right of my wife, with that six thousand pound, which is the moiety of Mrs. Millamant's fortune in your possession; and which she has forfeited (as will appear by the last will and testament of your deceased husband, Sir Jonathan Wishfort) by her disobedience in contracting herself against your consent or knowledge; and by refusing the offered match with Sir Wilfull Witwoud, which you, like a careful aunt, had provided for her.

LADY WISHFORT   My nephew was *non compos*,[23] and could not make his addresses.

FAINALL   I come to make demands—I'll hear no objections.

LADY WISHFORT   You will grant me time to consider?

FAINALL   Yes, while the instrument is drawing, to which you must set your hand till more sufficient deeds can be perfected: which I will take care shall be done with all possible speed. In the meanwhile, I will go for the sad instrument, and till my return you may balance this matter in your own discretion. (*Exit.*)

LADY WISHFORT   This insolence is beyond all precedent, all parallel; must I be subject to this merciless villain?

---

[22] *Czarish majesty's retinue* Peter the Great visited London in 1697   [23] *non compos* not responsible

MRS. MARWOOD   'Tis severe indeed, madam, that you should smart for your daughter's wantonness.

LADY WISHFORT   'Twas against my consent that she married this barbarian, but she would have him, though her year was not out[24]—Ah! her first husband, my son Languish, would not have carried it thus. Well, that was my choice, this is hers; she is matched now with a witness. I shall be mad, dear friend—is there no comfort for me? Must I live to be confiscated at this rebel-rate?—Here come two more of my Egyptian plagues, too.

(*Enter* MILLAMANT *and* SIR WILFULL.)

SIR WILFULL   Aunt, your servant.

LADY WISHFORT   Out, caterpillar, call not me aunt! I know thee not!

SIR WILFULL   I confess I have been a little in disguise as they say,— 'sheart! and I'm sorry for't. What would you have? I hope I committed no offence, aunt—and if I did I am willing to make satisfaction; and what can a man say fairer? If I have broke anything, I'll pay for't, an it cost a pound. And so let that content for what's past, and make no more words. For what's to come, to pleasure you I'm willing to marry my cousin. So pray let's all be friends; she and I are agreed upon the matter before a witness.

LADY WISHFORT   How's this, dear niece? Have I any comfort? Can this be true?

MILLAMANT   I am content to be a sacrifice to your repose, madam; and to convince you that I had no hand in the plot, as you were misinformed, I have laid my commands on Mirabell to come in person, and be a witness that I give my hand to this flower of knighthood; and for the contract that passed between Mirabell and me, I have obliged him to make a resignation of it in your ladyship's presence; he is without, and waits your leave for admittance.

LADY WISHFORT   Well, I'll swear I am something revived at this testimony of your obedience; but I cannot admit that traitor;—I fear I cannot fortify myself to support his appearance. He is as terrible to me as a Gorgon;[25] if I see him, I fear I shall turn to stone, petrify incessantly.

MILLAMANT   If you disoblige him, he may resent your refusal, and insist upon the contract still. Then, 'tis the last time he will be offensive to you.

LADY WISHFORT   Are you sure it will be the last time?—If I were sure of that—shall I never see him again?

---

[24] *her year was not out* she married again before a year of mourning as a widow had elapsed   [25] *Gorgon* the mythical beast whose sight turned people to stone

MILLAMANT   Sir Wilfull, you and he are to travel together, are you not?

SIR WILFULL   'Sheart, the gentleman's a civil gentleman, aunt, let him come in; why, we are sworn brothers and fellow-travellers. We are to be Pylades and Orestes,[26] he and I. He is to be my interpreter in foreign parts. He has been over-seas once already; and with proviso that I marry my cousin, will cross 'em once again, only to bear me company.—'Sheart, I'll call him in;—an I set on't once, he shall come in; and see who'll hinder him. (*Exit.*)

MRS. MARWOOD (*aside*)   This is precious fooling, if it would pass; but I'll know the bottom of it.

LADY WISHFORT   O dear Marwood, you are not going?

MRS. MARWOOD   Not far, madam; I'll return immediately. (*Exit.*)

(*Re-enter* SIR WILFULL *and* MIRABELL.)

SIR WILFULL   Look up man, I'll stand by you; 'sbud, an she do frown, she can't kill you;—besides—hark'ee, she dare not frown desperately, because her face is none of her own; 'sheart, and she should, her forehead would wrinkle like the coat of a cream-cheese; but mum for that, fellow-traveller.

MIRABELL   If a deep sense of the many injuries I have offered to so good a lady, with a sincere remorse, and a hearty contrition, can but obtain the least glance of compassion, I am too happy.—Ah, madam, there was a time—but let it be forgotten—I confess I have deservedly forfeited the high place I once held, of sighing at your feet; nay, kill me not, by turning from me in disdain—I come not to plead for favor—nay, not for pardon; I am a suppliant only for your pity—I am going where I never shall behold you more—

SIR WILFULL   How, fellow-traveller! You shall go by yourself then.

MIRABELL   Let me be pitied first; and afterwards forgotten—I ask no more.

SIR WILFULL   By'r Lady, a very reasonable request, and will cost you nothing, aunt. Come, come, forgive and forget, aunt; why you must, an you are a Christian.

MIRABELL   Consider, madam, in reality you could not receive much prejudice; it was an innocent device; though I confess it had a face of guiltiness, it was at most an artifice which love contrived—and errors which love produces have ever been accounted venial. At least think it is punishment enough, that I have lost what in my heart I hold most dear, that to your cruel indignation I have offered up this beauty,

---

[26] *Pylades and Orestes* close traveling companions. During his exile from Thebes, Orestes had traveled and returned with Pylades after the death of his father, King Agamemnon.

and with her my peace and quiet; nay, all my hopes of future comfort.

SIR WILFULL   An he does not move me, would I might never be o' the quorum!^{27}—an it were not as good a deed as to drink, to give her to him again, I would I might never take shipping!—Aunt, if you don't forgive quickly, I shall melt, I can tell you that. My contract went no further than a little mouth glue, and that's hardly dry—one doleful sigh more from my fellow-traveller and 'tis dissolved.

LADY WISHFORT   Well, nephew, upon your account.—Ah, he has a false insinuating tongue!—Well, sir, I will stifle my just resentment at my nephew's request. I will endeavor what I can to forget—but on proviso that you resign the contract with my niece immediately.

MIRABELL   It is in writing and with papers of concern; but I have sent my servant for it, and will deliver it to you, with all acknowledgments for your transcendent goodness.

LADY WISHFORT (*apart*)   Oh, he has witchcraft in his eyes and tongue! When I did not see him, I could have bribed a villain to his assassination; but his appearance rakes the embers which have so long lain smothered in my breast.

(*Enter* FAINALL *and* MRS. MARWOOD.)

FAINALL   Your date of deliberation, madam, is expired. Here is the instrument; are you prepared to sign?

LADY WISHFORT   If I were prepared, I am not impowered. My niece exerts a lawful claim, having matched herself by my direction to Sir Wilfull.

FAINALL   That sham is too gross to pass on me, though 'tis imposed on you, madam.

MILLAMANT   Sir, I have given my consent.

MIRABELL   And, sir, I have resigned my pretensions.

SIR WILFULL   And, sir, I assert my right; and will maintain it in defiance of you, sir, and of your instrument. 'Sheart, an you talk of an instrument, sir, I have an old fox by my thigh shall hack your instrument of ram vellum to shreds, sir! It shall not be sufficient for a mittimus^{28} or a tailor's measure; therefore, withdraw your instrument, sir, or by'r Lady I shall draw mine.

LADY WISHFORT   Hold, nephew, hold!

---

^{27} *be o' the quorum* quorum of justices of the peace. Sir Wilfull was a county justice. ^{28} the "old fox" of which Sir Wilfull speaks is his sword, with which he would cut Fainall's "instrument"—the "ram vellum" document—to shreds. He is also giving "instrument" a double meaning of "sword," which Fainall also carries. A "mittimus" is an arrest warrant.

MILLAMANT   Good Sir Wilfull, respite your valor!

FAINALL   Indeed? Are you provided of a guard, with your single beefeater[29] there? But I'm prepared for you; and insist upon my first proposal. You shall submit your own estate to my management, and absolutely make over my wife's to my sole use, as pursuant to the purport and tenor of this other covenant.—I suppose, madam, your consent is not requisite in this case; nor, Mr. Mirabell, your resignation; nor, Sir Wilfull, your right. You may draw your fox if you please, sir, and make a bear-garden[30] flourish somewhere else; for here it will not avail. This, my Lady Wishfort, must be subscribed, or your darling daughter's turned adrift, like a leaky hulk to sink or swim, as she and the current of this lewd town can agree.

LADY WISHFORT   Is there no means, no remedy, to stop my ruin? Ungrateful wretch! dost thou not owe thy being, thy subsistence, to my daughter's fortune?

FAINALL   I'll answer you when I have the rest of it in my possession.

MIRABELL   But that you would not accept of a remedy from my hands —I own I have not deserved you should owe any obligation to me; or else perhaps I could advise—

LADY WISHFORT   Oh, what? what? to save me and my child from ruin, from want, I'll forgive all that's past; nay, I'll consent to anything to come, to be delivered from this tyranny.

MIRABELL   Ay, madam; but that is too late, my reward is intercepted. You have disposed of her, who only could have made me a compensation for all my services;—but be it as it may, I am resolved I'll serve you—you shall not be wronged in this savage manner!

LADY WISHFORT   How! Dear Mr. Mirabell, can you be so generous at last! But it is not possible. Hark'ee, I'll break my nephew's match, you shall have my niece yet, and all her fortune, if you can but save me from this imminent danger.

MIRABELL   Will you? I take you at your word. I ask no more. I must have leave for two criminals to appear.

LADY WISHFORT   Ay, ay, anybody, anybody!

MIRABELL   Foible is one, and a penitent.

(*Enter* MRS. FAINALL, FOIBLE, *and* MINCING.)

MRS. MARWOOD (*to* FAINALL)   Oh, my shame! these corrupt things are bought and brought hither to expose me.

---

[29] *beefeater* common term for a uniformed guard, such as is still seen in such places as the Tower of London—as well as on familiar bottles of gin. [30] *bear-garden* an arena on the south side of the Thames where bears were baited (set upon) by dogs as a form of popular entertainment.

(MIRABELL *and* LADY WISHFORT *go to* MRS. FAINALL *and* FOIBLE.)

FAINALL   If it must all come out, why let 'em know it; 'tis but the *way of the world.* That shall not urge me to relinquish or abate one tittle of my terms; no, I will insist the more.

FOIBLE   Yes, indeed, madam, I'll take my Bible oath of it.

MINCING   And so will I, mem.—

LADY WISHFORT   O Marwood, Marwood, art thou false? my friend deceive me? Hast thou been a wicked accomplice with that profligate man?

MRS. MARWOOD   Have you so much ingratitude and injustice, to give credit against your friend, to the aspersions of two such mercenary trulls?

MINCING   Mercenary, mem? I scorn your words. 'Tis true we found you and Mr. Fainall in the blue garret; by the same token, you swore us to secrecy upon Messalina's poems.[31] Mercenary? No, if we would have been mercenary, we should have held our tongues; you would have bribed us sufficiently.

FAINALL   Go, you are an insignificant thing!—Well, what are you the better for this! Is this Mr. Mirabell's expedient? I'll be put off no longer.—You thing that was a wife, shall smart for this! I will not leave thee wherewithal to hide thy shame; your body shall be naked as your reputation.

MRS. FAINALL   I despise you, and defy your malice! You have aspersed me wrongfully—I have proved your falsehood. Go you and your treacherous—I will not name it—but starve together—perish!

FAINALL   Not while you are worth a groat, indeed, my dear. Madam, I'll be fooled no longer.

LADY WISHFORT   Ah, Mr. Mirabell, this is small comfort, the detection of this affair.

MIRABELL   Oh, in good time. Your leave for the other offender and penitent to appear, madam.

(*Enter* WAITWELL *with a box of writing.*)

LADY WISHFORT   O Sir Rowland!—Well, rascal!

WAITWELL   What your ladyship pleases. I have brought the black box at last, madam.

MIRABELL   Give it me. Madam, you remember your promise.

LADY WISHFORT   Ay, dear sir.

MIRABELL   Where are the gentlemen?

---

[31] *Messalina's poems* Mincing thinks the collection of poems, a "Miscellany," was written by a poet named "Messalina"

WAITWELL   At hand, sir, rubbing their eyes—just risen from sleep.

FAINALL   'Sdeath, what's this to me? I'll not wait your private concerns.

(*Enter* PETULANT *and* WITWOUD.)

PETULANT   How now? what's the matter? whose hand's out?

WITWOUD   Hey day! what, are you all got together, like players at the end of the last act?

MIRABELL   You may remember, gentlemen, I once requested your hands as witnesses to a certain parchment.

WITWOUD   Ay, I do, my hand I remember—Petulant set his mark.

MIRABELL   You wrong him, his name is fairly written, as shall appear. —You do not remember, gentlemen, anything of what that parchment contained? (*Undoing the box.*)

WITWOUD   No.

PETULANT   Not I. I writ, I read nothing.

MIRABELL   Very well, now you shall know.—Madam, your promise.

LADY WISHFORT   Ay, ay, sir, upon my honor.

MIRABELL   Mr. Fainall, it is now time that you should know that your lady, while she was at her own disposal, and before you had by your insinuations wheedled her out of a pretended settlement of the greatest part of her fortune—

FAINALL   Sir! pretended!

MIRABELL   Yes, sir. I say that this lady while a widow, having, it seems, received some cautions respecting your inconstancy and tyranny of temper, which from her own partial opinion and fondness of you she could never have suspected—she did, I say, by the wholesome advice of friends and of sages learned in the laws of this land, deliver this same as her act and deed to me in trust, and to the uses within mentioned. You may read if you please (*holding out the parchment*)— though perhaps what is inscribed on the back may serve your occasions.

FAINALL   Very likely, sir. What's here? Damnation! (*Reads.*) "A deed of conveyance of the whole estate real of Arabella Languish, widow, in trust to Edward Mirabell."—Confusion!

MIRABELL   Even so, sir: 'tis the *way of the world*, sir—of the widows of the world. I suppose this deed may bear an elder date than what you have obtained from your lady.

FAINALL   Perfidious fiend! then thus I'll be revenged.—(*Offers to run at*[32] MRS. FAINALL.)

---

[32] *to run at* Fainall, revealed as a true villain and now frustrated in his hopes to achieve his wife's fortune, would "run at" her in his anger, that is, strike at her with his sword. The gallant Sir Wilfull prevents him.

SIR WILFULL   Hold, sir! now you may make your bear-garden flourish somewhere else, sir.

FAINALL   Mirabell, you shall hear of this, sir, be sure you shall.—Let me pass, oaf. (*Exit.*)

MRS. FAINALL (*to* MRS. MARWOOD)   Madam, you seem to stifle your resentment. You had better give it vent.

MRS. MARWOOD   Yes, it shall have vent—and to your confusion, or I'll perish in the attempt. (*Exit.*)

LADY WISHFORT   O daughter, daughter! 'tis plain thou hast inherited thy mother's prudence.

MRS. FAINALL   Thank Mr. Mirabell, a cautious friend, to whose advice all is owing.

LADY WISHFORT   Well, Mr. Mirabell, you have kept your promise—and I must perform mine.—First, I pardon for your sake Sir Rowland there and Foible;—the next thing is to break the matter to my nephew—and how to do that—

MIRABELL   For that, madam, give yourself no trouble; let me have your consent. Sir Wilfull is my friend; he has had compassion upon lovers, and generously engaged a volunteer in this action, for our service, and now designs to prosecute his travels.

SIR WILFULL   'Sheart, aunt, I have no mind to marry. My cousin's a fine lady, and the gentleman loves her and she loves him, and they deserve one another; my resolution is to see foreign parts—I have set on't—and when I'm set on't, I must do't. And if these two gentlemen would travel too, I think they may be spared.

PETULANT   For my part, I say little—I think things are best off or on.

WITWOUD   I' gad, I understand nothing of the matter; I'm in a maze yet, like a dog in a dancing-school.

LADY WISHFORT   Well, sir, take her, and with her all the joy I can give you.

MILLAMANT   Why does not the man take me? Would you have me give myself to you over again?

MIRABELL   Ay, and over and over again; for I would have you as often as possibly I can. (*Kisses her hand.*) Well, heaven grant I love you not too well, that's all my fear.

SIR WILFULL   'Sheart, you'll have time enough to toy after you're married; or if you will toy now, let us have a dance in the mean time, that we who are not lovers may have some other employment besides looking on.

MIRABELL   With all my heart, dear Sir Wilfull. What shall we do for music?

FOIBLE   O sir, some that were provided for Sir Rowland's entertainment are yet within call. (*A dance.*)

LADY WISHFORT   As I am a person, I can hold out no longer; I have wasted my spirits so today already, that I am ready to sink under the fatigue; and I cannot but have some fears upon me yet, that my son Fainall will pursue some desperate course.

MIRABELL Madam, disquiet not yourself on that account; to my knowledge his circumstances are such, he must of force comply. For my part, I will contribute all that in me lies to a reunion; in the mean time, madam (*to* MRS. FAINALL), let me before these witnesses restore to you this deed of trust. It may be a means, well managed, to make you live easily together.

> From hence let those be warned, who mean to wed;
> Lest mutual falsehood stain the bridal-bed.
> For each deceiver to his cost may find,
> That marriage frauds too oft are paid in kind.

(*Exeunt omnes.*)

Epilogue

Spoken by MILLAMANT

After our epilogue this crowd dismisses
I'm thinking how this play'll be pulled to pieces.
But pray consider, ere you doom its fall,
How hard a thing 'twould be, to please you all.
There are some critics so with spleen diseased,
They scarcely come inclining to be pleased:
And sure he must have more than mortal skill,
Who pleases any one against his will.
Then, all bad poets we are sure are foes,
And how their number's swelled the town well knows:
In shoals, I've marked 'em judging in the pit;
Though they're on no pretence for judgment fit,
But that they have been damned for want of wit.
Since when, they by their own offences taught,
Set up for spies on plays and finding fault.
Others there are whose malice we'd prevent;
Such who watch plays with scurrilous intent
To mark out who by characters are meant.
And though no perfect likeness they can trace;
Yet each pretends to know the copied face.
These with false glosses feed their own ill-nature,
And turn to libel what was meant a satire.
May such malicious fops this fortune find,
To think themselves alone the fools designed:

If any are so arrogantly vain,
To think they singly can support a scene,
And furnish fool enough to entertain.
For well the learn'd and the judicious know,
That satire scorns to stoop so meanly low,
As any one abstracted fop to show.
For, as when painters form a matchless face,
They from each fair one catch some different grace,
And shining features in one portrait blend,
To which no single beauty must pretend;
So poets oft do in one piece expose
Whole *belles assemblées* of coquettes and beaux.

Curtain

✑ A DOLL'S HOUSE
(1879)

HENRIK IBSEN (1828–1906)

Henrik Ibsen is widely regarded as the "father" of modern drama because of his highly realistic plays devoted to the contemporary political and social problems of the 1870s and 1880s. He produced the dramatic shot heard round the world in *A Doll's House,* in which he sent the young wife, Nora, out into the Norwegian cold, slamming the door on home and children as she broke with the social forces that had kept her a plaything in her husband's house.

Ibsen has frequently been regarded as the first writer seriously to espouse the "liberation" of women. Both *A Doll's House* and *Hedda Gabler* (1890) could be so interpreted, as could certain others such as *Rosmersholm* (1886) and *The Master Builder* (1892), in which Ibsen presents fairly "liberated" feminine characters. He was not so much an advocate of "women's lib" in the general sense of the term today as he was a strong advocate of the right of individuals, irrespective of sex, to assert their own human dignity and integrity as persons, regardless of the forces that society brought to bear on them to hold their lives to the established patterns of morality.

Thus it would probably be a misinterpretation of *A Doll's House* to regard it as a polemic that advocates freeing women in general from the bonds of social deprivation and injustice, or of summarily releasing them from the confining restrictions of their domestic and conjugal obligations. It is, however, following the less-important *Pillars of Society* two years earlier, the first widely recognized and acclaimed "problem play," with which Ibsen was to be firmly identified during the rest of his career. Although a problem, or conflict (Aristotle's *agon*), has been acknowledged as essential to the development of any dramatic work, rather than acting as mere catalyst or motivating factor, the problem now becomes central, and its exploration and analysis within the framework of the existing society, though not necessarily its resolution, become the dramatist's primary consideration.

To be sure, Nora, at first, is unaware of her problem, and she accepts with apparent contentment her identity as "bustling squirrel," surreptitiously eating forbidden macaroons and twittering about, a "little songbird" whom her husband plainly regards as a featherhead. Her role as helpmate, charming little mother, and dainty dancing figure is expected by those around her and practiced to the full by Nora herself. True, she has, in the past, acted with indiscretion to save her husband's life, but then, should not any devoted spouse risk life and limb to preserve the well-being of the man she has sworn to love, honor, and, no doubt, obey?

Nora's ultimate realization of what she represents in an unthinking, male-dominated society brings into sharp focus the problem that she, and many like her, must face: how to establish one's own identity and live with self-respect intact when confronted with sinister threats from the outside and a totally uncomprehending, self-centered husband who cannot see beyond his own narrow personal concerns, blind to the sacrifices offered on his behalf.

Nora's decision to abandon home, husband, and children might be seen as a sudden and irresponsible act, but one cannot condemn her in the face of Helmer's almost incredibly stupid reaction to what she has done and to what she now confronts. Although the world, at the time, may have shuddered at the impact of that door slam, Nora's determination to cease playing her doll's role and to assert herself has long since vindicated her. Regardless of what she may have to endure outside the "comfort" of her toy house (Ibsen himself refused to speculate as to Nora's fate), we must admire and praise her for her final awareness of the impossibility of her predicament and to support her in her firm assertion that she has a right to be herself, notwithstanding the consequences that society may wish to force upon her.

A Doll's House

IBSEN

A new translation by Otto Reinert

CHARACTERS

TORVALD HELMER, *a lawyer*
NORA, *his wife*
DR. RANK
MRS. LINDE
KROGSTAD
THE HELMERS' THREE SMALL CHILDREN
ANNE-MARIE, *the children's nurse*
A HOUSEMAID
A PORTER

SCENE. *The Helmers' living room.*

ACT I

A pleasant, tastefully but not expensively furnished, living room. A door on the rear wall, right, leads to the front hall, another door, left, to HELMER'S *study. Between the two doors a piano. A third door in the middle of the left wall; further front a window. Near the window a round table and a small couch. Towards the rear of the right wall a fourth door; further front a tile stove with a rocking chair and a couple of armchairs in front of it. Between the stove and the door a small table. Copperplate etchings on the walls. A whatnot with porcelain figurines and other small objects. A small bookcase with de luxe editions. A rug on the floor; fire in the stove. Winter day.*

The doorbell rings, then the sound of the front door opening. NORA, *dressed for outdoors, enters, humming cheerfully. She carries several packages, which she puts down on the table, right. She leaves the door to the front hall open; there a* PORTER *is seen holding a Christmas tree and a basket. He gives them to the* MAID *who has let them in.*

NORA Be sure to hide the Christmas tree, Helene. The children mustn't see it before tonight when we've trimmed it. (*Opens her purse; to the* PORTER.) How much?

377

PORTER Fifty ore.

NORA Here's a crown. No, keep the change. (*The* PORTER *thanks her, leaves.* NORA *closes the door. She keeps laughing quietly to herself as she takes off her coat, etc. She takes a bag of macaroons from her pocket and eats a couple. She walks cautiously over to the door to the study and listens.*) Yes, he's home. (*Resumes her humming, walks over to the table, right.*)

HELMER (*in his study*) Is that my little lark twittering out there?

NORA (*opening some packages*) That's right.

HELMER My squirrel bustling about?

NORA Yes.

HELMER When did squirrel come home?

NORA Just now. (*Puts the bag of macaroons back in her pocket, wipes her mouth.*) Come out here, Torvald. I want to show you what I've bought.

HELMER I'm busy! (*After a little while he opens the door and looks in, pen in hand.*) Bought, eh? All that? So little wastrel has been throwing money around again?

NORA Oh but Torvald, this Christmas we can be a little extravagant, can't we? It's the first Christmas we don't have to scrimp.

HELMER I don't know about that. We certainly don't have money to waste.

NORA Yes, Torvald, we do. A little, anyway. Just a tiny little bit? Now that you're going to get that big salary and make lots and lots of money.

HELMER Starting at New Year's, yes. But payday isn't till the end of the quarter.

NORA That doesn't matter. We can always borrow.

HELMER Nora! (*Goes over to her and playfully pulls her ear.*) There you go being irresponsible again. Suppose I borrowed a thousand crowns today and you spent it all for Christmas and on New Year's Eve a tile hit me in the head and laid me out cold.

NORA (*putting her hand over his mouth*) I won't have you say such horrid things.

HELMER But suppose it happened. Then what?

NORA If it did, I wouldn't care whether we owed money or not.

HELMER But what about the people I had borrowed from?

NORA Who cares about them! They are strangers.

HELMER Nora, Nora, you *are* a woman! No, really! You know how I feel about that. No debts! A home in debt isn't a free home, and if it isn't free it isn't beautiful. We've managed nicely so far, you and I, and that's the way we'll go on. It won't be for much longer.

NORA (*walks over toward the stove*) All right, Torvald. Whatever you say.

HELMER (*follows her*) Come, come, my little songbird mustn't droop her wings. What's this? Can't have a pouty squirrel in the house, you know. (*Takes out his wallet.*) Nora, what do you think I have here?

NORA (*turns around quickly*) Money!

HELMER Here. (*Gives her some bills.*) Don't you think I know Christmas is expensive?

NORA (*counting*) Ten—twenty—thirty—forty. Thank you, thank you, Torvald. This helps a lot.

HELMER I certainly hope so.

NORA It does, it does. But I want to show you what I got. It was cheap, too. Look. New clothes for Ivar. And a sword. And a horse and trumpet for Bob. And a doll and a little bed for Emmy. It isn't any good, but it wouldn't last, anyway. And here's some dress material and scarves for the maids. I feel bad about old Anne-Marie, though. She really should be getting much more.

HELMER And what's in here?

NORA (*cries*) Not till tonight!

HELMER I see. But now what does my little prodigal have in mind for herself?

NORA Oh, nothing. I really don't care.

HELMER Of course you do. Tell me what you'd like. Within reason.

NORA Oh, I don't know. Really, I don't. The only thing—

HELMER Well?

NORA (*fiddling with his buttons, without looking at him*) If you really want to give me something, you might—you could—

HELMER All right, let's have it.

NORA (*quickly*) Some money, Torvald. Just as much as you think you can spare. Then I'll buy myself something one of these days.

HELMER No, really Nora—

NORA Oh yes, please, Torvald. Please? I'll wrap the money in pretty gold paper and hang it on the tree. Won't that be nice?

HELMER What's the name for little birds that are always spending money?

NORA Wastrels, I know. But please let's do it my way, Torvald. Then I'll have time to decide what I need most. Now that's sensible, isn't it?

HELMER (*smiling*) Oh, very sensible. That is, if you really bought yourself something you could use. But it all disappears in the household expenses or you buy things you don't need. And then you come back to me for more.

NORA Oh, but Torvald—

HELMER That's the truth, dear little Nora, and you know it. (*Puts his arm around her.*) My wastrel is a little sweetheart, but she *does* go through an awful lot of money awfully fast. You've no idea how expensive it is for a man to keep a wastrel.

NORA That's not fair, Torvald. I really save all I can.

HELMER (*laughs*) Oh, I believe that. All you can. Meaning, exactly nothing!

NORA (*hums, smiles mysteriously*) You don't know all the things we songbirds and squirrels need money for, Torvald.

HELMER You know, you're funny. Just like your father. You're always looking for ways to get money, but as soon as you do it runs through your fingers and you can never say what you spent it for. Well, I guess I'll just have to take you the way you are. It's in your blood. Yes, that sort of thing is hereditary, Nora.

NORA In that case, I wish I had inherited many of Daddy's qualities.

HELMER And I don't want you any different from just what you are—my own sweet little songbird. Hey!—I think I just noticed something. Aren't you looking—what's the word?—a little—sly—?

NORA I am?

HELMER You definitely are. Look at me.

NORA (*looks at him*) Well?

HELMER (*wagging a finger*) Little sweet-tooth hasn't by any chance been on a rampage today, has she?

NORA Of course not. Whatever makes you think that?

HELMER A little detour by the pastryshop maybe?

NORA No, I assure you, Torvald—

HELMER Nibbled a little jam?

NORA Certainly not!

HELMER Munched a macaroon or two?

NORA No, really, Torvald, I honestly—

HELMER All right. Of course I was only joking.

NORA (*walks toward the table, right*) You know I wouldn't do anything to displease you.

HELMER I know. And I have your promise. (*Over to her.*) All right, keep your little Christmas secrets to yourself, Nora darling. They'll all come out tonight, I suppose, when we light the tree.

NORA Did you remember to invite Rank?

HELMER No, but there's no need to. He knows he'll have dinner with us. Anyway, I'll see him later this morning. I'll ask him then. I did order some good wine. Oh Nora, you've no idea how much I'm looking forward to tonight!

NORA Me, too. And the children Torvald! They'll have such a good time!

HELMER   You know, it *is* nice to have a good, safe job and a comfortable income. Feels good just thinking about it. Don't you agree?

NORA   Oh, it's wonderful!

HELMER   Remember last Christmas? For three whole weeks you shut yourself up every evening till long after midnight making ornaments for the Christmas tree and I don't know what else. Some big surprise for all of us, anyway. I'll be damned if I've ever been so bored in my whole life!

NORA   I wasn't bored at all!

HELMER   (*smiling*)   But you've got to admit you didn't have much to show for it in the end.

NORA   Oh, don't tease me again about that! Could I help it that the cat got in and tore up everything?

HELMER   Of course you couldn't, my poor little Nora. You just wanted to please the rest of us, and that's the important thing. But I *am* glad the hard times are behind us. Aren't you?

NORA   Oh yes. I think it's just wonderful.

HELMER   This year, I won't be bored and lonely. And you won't have to strain your dear eyes and your delicate little hands—

NORA   (*claps her hands*)   No I won't, will I Torvald? Oh, how wonderful, how lovely, to hear you say that! (*Puts her arm under his.*) Let me tell you how I think we should arrange things, Torvald. Soon as Christmas is over—(*The doorbell rings.*) Someone's at the door. (*Straightens things up a bit.*) A caller, I suppose. Bother!

HELMER   Remember, I'm not home for visitors.

THE MAID   (*in the door to the front hall*)   Ma'am, there's a lady here—

NORA   All right. Ask her to come in.

THE MAID   (*to* HELMER)   And the Doctor just arrived.

HELMER   Is he in the study?

THE MAID   Yes, sir.

(HELMER *exits into his study.* THE MAID *shows* MRS. LINDE *in and closes the door behind her as she leaves.* MRS. LINDE *is in travel dress.*)

MRS. LINDE   (*timid and a little hesitant*)   Good morning, Nora.

NORA   (*uncertainly*)   Good morning.

MRS. LINDE   I don't believe you know who I am.

NORA   No—I'm not sure—Though I know I should—Of course! Kristine! It's you!

MRS. LINDE   Yes, it's me.

NORA   And I didn't even recognize you! I had no idea (*In a lower voice.*) You've changed, Kristine.

MRS. LINDE I'm sure I have. It's been nine or ten long years.

NORA Has it really been that long? Yes, you're right. I've been so happy these last eight years. And now you're here. Such a long trip in the middle of winter. How brave!

MRS. LINDE I got in on the steamer this morning.

NORA To have some fun over the holidays, of course. That's lovely. For we are going to have fun. But take off your coat! You aren't cold, are you? (*Helps her.*) There, now! Let's sit down here by the fire and just relax and talk. No, you sit there. I want the rocking chair. (*Takes her hands.*) And now you've got your old face back. It was just for a minute, right at first—Though you are a little more pale, Kristine. And maybe a little thinner.

MRS. LINDE And much, much older, Nora.

NORA Maybe a little older. Just a teeny-weeny bit, not much. (*Interrupts herself, serious.*) Oh, but how thoughtless of me, chatting away like this! Sweet, good Kristine, can you forgive me?

MRS. LINDE Forgive you what, Nora?

NORA (*in a low voice*) You poor dear, you lost your husband, didn't you?

MRS. LINDE Three years ago, yes.

NORA I know. I saw it in the paper. Oh please believe me, Kristine. I really meant to write you, but I never got around to it. Something was always coming up.

MRS. LINDE Of course, Nora. I understand.

NORA No, that wasn't very nice of me. You poor thing, all you must have been through. And he didn't leave you much, either, did he?

MRS. LINDE No.

NORA And no children?

MRS. LINDE No.

NORA Nothing at all, in other words?

MRS. LINDE Not so much as a sense of loss—a grief to live on—

NORA (*incredulous*) But Kristine, how can that *be*?

MRS. LINDE (*with a sad smile, strokes* NORA's *hair*) That's the way it sometimes is, Nora.

NORA All alone. How awful for you. I have three darling children. You can't see them right now, though; they're out with their nurse. But now you must tell me everything—

MRS. LINDE No, no; I'd rather listen to you.

NORA No, you begin. Today I won't be selfish. Today I'll think only of you. Except there's one thing I've just got to tell you first. Something marvelous that's happened to us just these last few days. You haven't heard, have you?

MRS. LINDE No; tell me.

NORA Just think. My husband's been made manager of the Mutual Bank.

MRS. LINDE Your husband—! Oh, I'm so glad!

NORA Yes, isn't that great? You see, private law practice is so uncertain, especially when you won't have anything to do with cases that aren't—you know—quite nice. And of course Torvald won't do that and I quite agree with him. Oh, you've no idea how delighted we are! He takes over at New Year's, and he'll be getting a big salary and all sorts of extras. From now on we'll be able to live in quite a different way—exactly as we like. Oh, Kristine! I feel so carefree and happy! It's lovely to have lots and lots of money and not have to worry about a thing! Don't you agree?

MRS. LINDE It would be nice to have enough at any rate.

NORA No, I don't mean just enough. I mean lots and lots!

MRS. LINDE (*smiles*) Nora, Nora, when are you going to be sensible? In school you spent a great deal of money.

NORA (*quietly laughing*) Yes, and Torvald says I still do. (*Raises her finger at* MRS. LINDE.) But "Nora, Nora" isn't so crazy as you all think. Believe me, we've had nothing to be extravagant with. We've both had to work.

MRS. LINDE You too?

NORA Yes. Oh, it's been little things, mostly—sewing, crocheting, embroidery—that sort of thing. (*Casually.*) And other things too. You know, of course, that Torvald left government service when we got married? There was no chance of promotion in his department, and of course he had to make more money than he had been making. So for the first few years he worked altogether too hard. He had to take jobs on the side and work night and day. It turned out to be too much for him. He became seriously ill. The doctors told him he needed to go south.

MRS. LINDE That's right; you spent a year in Italy, didn't you?

NORA Yes, we did. But you won't believe how hard it was to get away. Ivar had just been born. But of course we had to go. Oh, it was a wonderful trip. And it saved Torvald's life. But it took a lot of money, Kristine.

MRS. LINDE I'm sure it did.

NORA Twelve hundred specie dollars. Four thousand eight hundred crowns. That's a lot of money.

MRS. LINDE Yes. So it's lucky you have it when something like that happens.

NORA Well, actually we got the money from Daddy.

MRS. LINDE I see. That was about the time your father died, I believe.

NORA Yes, just about then. And I couldn't even go and take care of him. I was expecting little Ivar any day. And I had poor Torvald to look after, desperately sick and all. My dear, good Daddy! I never saw him again, Kristine. That's the saddest thing that's happened to me since I got married.

MRS. LINDE I know you were very fond of him. But then you went to Italy?

NORA Yes, for now we had the money, and the doctors urged us to go. So we left about a month later.

MRS. LINDE And when you came back your husband was well again?

NORA Healthy as a horse!

MRS. LINDE But—the doctor?

NORA What do you mean?

MRS. LINDE I thought the maid said it was the doctor, that gentleman who came the same time I did.

NORA Oh, that's Dr. Rank. He doesn't come as a doctor. He's our closest friend. He looks in at least once every day. No, Torvald hasn't been sick once since then. And the children are strong and healthy, too, and so am I. (*Jumps up and claps her hands.*) Oh God, Kristine! Isn't it wonderful to be alive and happy! Isn't it just lovely!—But now I'm being mean again, talking only about myself and my things. (*Sits down on a footstool close to* MRS. LINDE *and puts her arm on her lap.*) Please don't be angry with me! Tell me, is it really true that you didn't care for your husband? Then why did you marry him?

MRS. LINDE Mother was still alive then, but she was bedridden and helpless. And I had my two younger brothers to look after. I didn't think I had the right to turn him down.

NORA No, I suppose not. So he had money then?

MRS. LINDE He was quite well off, I think. But it was an uncertain business, Nora. When he died, the whole thing collapsed and there was nothing left.

NORA And then—?

MRS. LINDE Well, I had to manage as best I could. With a little store and a little school and anything else I could think of. The last three years have been one long work day for me, Nora, without any rest. But now it's over. My poor mother doesn't need me any more. She's passed away. And the boys are on their own too. They've both got jobs and support themselves.

NORA What a relief for you—

MRS. LINDE No, not relief. Just a great emptiness. Nobody to live for any more. (*Gets up restlessly.*) That's why I couldn't stand it any longer in that little hole. Here in town it has to be easier to find something to keep me busy and occupy my thoughts. With a little luck I should be able to find a permanent job, something in an office—

NORA Oh but Kristine, that's exhausting work, and you look worn out already. It would be much better for you to go to a resort.

MRS. LINDE (*walks over to the window*) I don't have a Daddy who can give me the money, Nora.

NORA (*getting up*) Oh, don't be angry with me.

MRS. LINDE (*over to her*) Dear Nora, don't *you* be angry with *me*. That's the worst thing about my kind of situation: you become so bitter. You've nobody to work for, and yet you have to look out for yourself, somehow. You've got to keep on living, and so you become selfish. Do you know—when you told me about your husband's new position I was delighted not so much for your sake as for my own.

NORA Why was that? Oh, I see. You think maybe Torvald can give you a job?

MRS. LINDE That's what I had in mind.

NORA And he will too, Kristine. Just leave it to me. I'll be ever so subtle about it. I'll think of something nice to tell him, something he'll like. Oh I so much want to help you.

MRS. LINDE That's very good of you, Nora—making an effort like that for me. Especially since you've known so little trouble and hardship in your own life.

NORA I—?—have known so little—?

MRS. LINDE (*smiling*) Oh well, a little sewing or whatever it was. You're still a child, Nora.

NORA (*with a toss of her head, walks away*) You shouldn't sound so superior.

MRS. LINDE I shouldn't?

NORA You're just like all the others. None of you think I'm good for anything really serious.

MRS. LINDE Well, now—

NORA That I've never been through anything difficult.

MRS. LINDE But Nora! You just told me all your troubles!

NORA That's nothing! (*Lowers her voice.*) I haven't told you about *it*.

MRS. LINDE It? What's that? What do you mean?

NORA You patronize me, Kristine, and that's not fair. You're proud that you worked so long and so hard for your mother.

MRS. LINDE I don't think I patronize anyone. But it *is* true that I'm both proud and happy that I could make mother's last years comparatively easy.

NORA And you're proud of all you did for your brothers.

MRS. LINDE   I think I have the right to be.

NORA   And so do I. But now I want to tell you something, Kristine. I have something to be proud and happy about too.

MRS. LINDE   I don't doubt that for a moment. But what exactly do you mean?

NORA   Not so loud! Torvald mustn't hear—not for anything in the world. Nobody must know about this, Kristine. Nobody but you.

MRS. LINDE   But what is it?

NORA   Come here. (*Pulls her down on the couch beside her.*) You see, I *do* have something to be proud and happy about. I've saved Torvald's life.

MRS. LINDE   Saved—? How do you mean—"saved"?

NORA   I told you about our trip to Italy. Torvald would have died if he hadn't gone.

MRS. LINDE   I understand that. And so your father gave you the money you needed.

NORA   (*smiles*)   Yes, that's what Torvald and all the others think. But—

MRS. LINDE   But what?

NORA   Daddy didn't give us a penny. *I* raised that money.

MRS. LINDE   *You* did? That whole big amount?

NORA   Twelve hundred specie dollars. Four thousand eight hundred crowns. *Now* what do you say?

MRS. LINDE   But Nora, how could you? Did you win in the state lottery?

NORA   (*contemptuously*)   State lottery! (*Snorts.*) What is so great about that?

MRS. LINDE   Where did it come from then?

NORA   (*humming and smiling, enjoying her secret*)   Hmmm. Tra-la-la-la-la!

MRS. LINDE   You certainly couldn't have borrowed it.

NORA   Oh? And why not?

MRS. LINDE   A wife can't borrow money without her husband's consent.

NORA   (*with a toss of her head*)   Oh, I don't know—take a wife with a little bit of a head for business—a wife who knows how to manage things—

MRS. LINDE   But Nora, I don't understand at all—

NORA   You don't have to. I didn't say I borrowed the money, did I? I could have gotten it some other way. (*Leans back.*) An admirer may have given it to me. When you're as tolerably good-looking as I am—

MRS. LINDE   Oh, you're crazy.

NORA   I think you're dying from curiosity, Kristine.

MRS. LINDE I'm beginning to think you've done something very foolish, Nora.

NORA (*sits up*) Is it foolish to save your husband's life?

MRS. LINDE I say it's foolish to act behind his back.

NORA But don't you see: he couldn't be told! You're missing the whole point, Kristine. We couldn't even let him know how seriously ill he was. The doctors came to *me* and told me his life was in danger, that nothing could save him but a stay in the south. Don't you think I tried to work on him? I told him how lovely it would be if I could go abroad like other young wives. I cried and begged. I said he'd better remember what condition I was in, that he had to be nice to me and do what I wanted. I even hinted he could borrow the money. But that almost made him angry with me. He told me I was being irresponsible and that it was his duty as my husband not to give in to my moods and whims—I think that's what he called it. All right, I said to myself, you've got to be saved somehow, and so I found a way—

MRS. LINDE And your husband never learned from your father that the money didn't come from him?

NORA Never. Daddy died that same week. I thought of telling him all about it and ask him not to say anything. But since he was so sick—It turned out I didn't have to—

MRS. LINDE And you've never told your husband?

NORA Of course not! Good heavens, how could I? He, with his strict principles! Besides, you know how men are. Torvald would find it embarrassing and humiliating to learn that he owed me anything. It would upset our whole relationship. Our happy, beautiful home would no longer be what it is.

MRS. LINDE Aren't you ever going to tell him?

NORA (*reflectively, half smiling*) Yes—one day, maybe. Many, many years from now, when I'm no longer young and pretty. Don't laugh! I mean when Torvald no longer feels about me the way he does now, when he no longer thinks it's fun when I dance for him and put on costumes and recite for him. Then it will be good to have something in reserve—(*Interrupts herself.*) Oh, I'm just being silly! That day will never come.—Well, now, Kristine, what do you think of my great secret? Don't you think I'm good for something too?—By the way, you wouldn't believe all the worry I've had because of it. It's been very hard to meet my obligations on schedule. You see, in business there's something called quarterly interest and something called installments on the principal, and those are terribly hard to come up with. I've had to save a little here and a little there, whenever I could. I couldn't use much of the housekeeping money, for Torvald has to eat well.

And I couldn't use what I got for clothes for the children. They have to look nice, and I didn't think it would be right to spend less than I got—the sweet little things!

MRS. LINDE   Poor Nora! So you had to take it from your own allowance!

NORA   Yes, of course. After all, it was my affair. Every time Torvald gave me money for a new dress and things like that, I never used more than half of it. I always bought the cheapest, simplest things for myself. Thank God, everything looks good on me, so Torvald never noticed. But it was hard many times, Kristine, for it's fun to have pretty clothes. Don't you think?

MRS. LINDE   Certainly.

NORA   Anyway, I had other ways of making money too. Last winter I was lucky enough to get some copying work. So I locked the door and sat up writing every night till quite late. God! I often got so tired—! But it was great fun, too, working and making money. It was almost like being a man.

MRS. LINDE   But how much have you been able to pay off this way?

NORA   I couldn't tell you exactly. You see, it's very difficult to keep track of business like that. All I know is I have been paying off as much as I've been able to scrape together. Many times I just didn't know what to do. (*Smiles.*) Then I used to imagine a rich old gentleman had fallen in love with me—

MRS. LINDE   What! What old gentleman?

NORA   Phooey! And now he was dead and they were reading his will, and there it said in big letters, "All my money is to be paid in cash immediately to the charming Mrs. Nora Helmer."

MRS. LINDE   But dearest Nora—who *was* this old gentleman?

NORA   For heaven's sake, Kristine, don't you see? There *was* no old gentleman. He was just somebody I made up when I couldn't think of any way to raise the money. But never mind him. The old bore can be anyone he likes to for all I care. I have no use for him or his last will, for now I don't have a single worry in the world. (*Jumps up.*) Dear God, what a lovely thought this is! To be able to play and have fun with the children, to have everything nice and pretty in the house, just the way Torvald likes it! Not a care! And soon spring will be here, and the air will be blue and high. Maybe we can travel again. Maybe I'll see the ocean again! Oh, yes, yes!—it's wonderful to be alive and happy!

The doorbell rings.

MRS. LINDE   (*getting up*) There's the doorbell. Maybe I better be going.

NORA   No, please stay. I'm sure it's just someone for Torvald—

THE MAID (*in the hall door*) Excuse me, ma'am. There's a gentleman here who'd like to see Mr. Helmer.

NORA You mean the bank manager.

THE MAID Sorry, ma'am; the bank manager. But I didn't know—since the Doctor is with him—

NORA Who is the gentleman?

KROGSTAD (*appearing in the door*) It's just me, Mrs. Helmer.

MRS. LINDE *starts, looks, turns away toward the window.*

NORA (*takes a step toward him, tense, in a low voice*) You? What do you want? What do you want with my husband?

KROGSTAD Bank business—in a way. I have a small job in the Mutual, and I understand your husband is going to be our new boss—

NORA So it's just—

KROGSTAD Just routine business, ma'am. Nothing else.

NORA All right. In that case, why don't you go through the door to the office.

Dismisses him casually as she closes the door. Walks over to the stove and tends the fire.

MRS. LINDE Nora—who was that man?

NORA His name's Krogstad. He's a lawyer.

MRS. LINDE So it *was* him.

NORA Do you know him?

MRS. LINDE I used to—many years ago. For a while he clerked in our part of the country.

NORA Right. He did.

MRS. LINDE He has changed a great deal.

NORA I believe he had a very unhappy marriage.

MRS. LINDE And now he's a widower, isn't he?

NORA With many children. There now; it's burning nicely again. (*Closes the stove and moves the rocking chair a little to the side.*)

MRS. LINDE They say he's into all sorts of business.

NORA Really? Maybe so. I wouldn't know. But let's not think about business. It's such a bore.

DR. RANK (*appears in the door to* HELMER'*s study.*) No. I don't want to be in the way. I'd rather talk to your wife a bit. (*Closes the door and notices* MRS. LINDE.) Oh, I beg your pardon. I believe I'm in the way here too.

NORA No, not at all. (*Introduces them.*) Dr. Rank. Mrs. Linde.

RANK Aha. A name often heard in this house. I believe I passed you on the stairs coming up.

MRS. LINDE Yes. I'm afraid I climb stairs very slowly. They aren't good for me.

RANK   I see. A slight case of inner decay, perhaps?

MRS. LINDE   Overwork, rather.

RANK   Oh, is that all? And now you've come to town to relax at all the parties?

MRS. LINDE   I have come to look for a job.

RANK   A proven cure for overwork, I take it?

MRS. LINDE   One has to live, Doctor.

RANK   Yes, that seems to be the common opinion.

NORA   Come on, Dr. Rank—you want to live just as much as the rest of us.

RANK   Of course I do. Miserable as I am, I prefer to go on being tortured as long as possible. All my patients feel the same way. And that's true of the moral invalids too. Helmer is talking with a specimen right this minute.

MRS. LINDE   (*in a low voice*)   Ah!

NORA   What do you mean?

RANK   Oh, this lawyer, Krogstad. You don't know him. The roots of his character are decayed. But even he began by saying something about having *to live*—as if it were a matter of the highest importance.

NORA   Oh? What did he want with Torvald?

RANK   I don't really know. All I heard was something about the bank.

NORA   I didn't know that Krog—that this Krogstad had anything to do with the Mutual Bank.

RANK   Yes, he seems to have some kind of job there. (*To* MRS. LINDE.) I don't know if you are familiar in your part of the country with the kind of person who is always running around trying to sniff out cases of moral decrepitude and as soon as he finds one puts the individual under observation in some excellent position or other. All the healthy ones are left out in the cold.

MRS. LINDE   I should think it's the sick who need looking after the most.

RANK   (*shrugs his shoulders*)   There we are. That's the attitude that turns society into a hospital.

(NORA, *absorbed in her own thoughts, suddenly starts giggling and clapping her hands.*)

RANK   What's so funny about that? Do you even know what society is?

NORA   What do I care about your stupid society! I laughed at something entirely different—something terribly amusing. Tell me, Dr. Rank—all the employees in the Mutual Bank, from now on they'll all be dependent on Torvald, right?

RANK   Is that what you find so enormously amusing?

NORA   (*smiles and hums*)   That's my business, that's my business! (*Walks around.*) Yes, I do think it's fun that we—that Torvald is going to have so much influence on so many people's lives. (*Brings out the bag of macaroons.*) Have a macaroon, Dr. Rank.

RANK   Well, well—macaroons. I thought they were banned around here.

NORA   Yes, but these were some that Kristine gave me.

MRS. LINDE   What! I?

NORA   That's all right. Don't look so scared. You couldn't know that Torvald won't let me have them. He's afraid they'll ruin my teeth. But who cares! Just once in a while—! Right, Dr. Rank? Have one! (*Puts a macaroon into his mouth.*) You too, Kristine. And one for me. A very small one. Or at most two. (*Walks around again.*) Yes, I really feel very, very happy. Now there's just one thing I'm dying to do.

RANK   Oh, And what's that?

NORA   Something I'm dying to say so Torvald could hear.

RANK   And why can't you?

NORA   I don't dare to, for it's not nice.

MRS. LINDE   Not nice?

RANK   In that case, I guess you'd better not. But surely to the two of us—? What is it you'd like to say for Helmer to hear?

NORA   I want to say, "Goddammit!"

RANK   Are you out of your mind!

MRS. LINDE   For heaven's sake, Nora!

RANK   Say it. Here he comes.

NORA   (*hiding the macaroons*).   Shhh!

(HELMER *enters from his study, carrying his hat and overcoat.*)

NORA   (*going to him*)   Well, dear, did you get rid of him?

HELMER   Yes, he just left.

NORA   Torvald, I want you to meet Kristine. She's just come to town.

HELMER   Kristine—? I'm sorry; I don't think—

NORA   Mrs. Linde, Torvald dear. Mrs. Kristine Linde.

HELMER   Ah, yes. A childhood friend of my wife's, I suppose.

MRS. LINDE   Yes, we've known each other for a long time.

NORA   Just think; she has come all this way just to see you.

HELMER   I'm not sure I understand—

MRS. LINDE   Well, not really—

NORA   You see, Kristine is an absolutely fantastic secretary, and she would so much like to work for a competent executive and learn more than she knows already—

HELMER   Very sensible, I'm sure, Mrs. Linde.

NORA   So when she heard about your appointment—there was a wire—she came here as fast as she could. How about it, Torvald? Couldn't you do something for Kristine? For my sake. Please?

HELMER   Quite possibly. I take it you're a widow, Mrs. Linde?

MRS. LINDE   Yes.

HELMER   And you've had office experience?

MRS. LINDE   Some—yes.

HELMER   In that case I think it's quite likely that I'll be able to find you a position.

NORA   (*claps her hands*)   I knew it! I knew it!

HELMER   You've arrived at a most opportune time, Mrs. Linde.

MRS. LINDE   Oh, how can I ever thank you—

HELMER   Not at all, not at all. (*Puts his coat on.*) But today you'll have to excuse me—

RANK   Wait a minute; I'll come with you. (*Gets his fur coat from the front hall, warms it by the stove.*)

NORA   Don't be long, Torvald.

HELMER   An hour or so; no more.

NORA   Are you leaving, too, Kristine?

MRS. LINDE   (*putting on her things*)   Yes, I'd better go and find a place to stay.

HELMER   Good. Then we'll be going the same way.

NORA   (*helping her*)   I'm sorry this place is so small, but I don't think we very well could—

MRS. LINDE   Of course! Don't be silly, Nora. Goodbye, and thank you for everything.

NORA   Goodbye. We'll see you soon. You'll be back this evening, of course. And you too, Dr. Rank; right? If you feel well enough? Of course you will. Just wrap yourself up.

(*General small talk as all exit into the hall. Children's voices are heard on the stairs.*)

NORA   There they are! There they are! (*She runs and opens the door. The nurse* ANNE-MARIE *enters with the children.*)

NORA   Come in! Come in! (*Bends over and kisses them.*) Oh, you sweet, sweet darlings! Look at them, Kristine! Aren't they beautiful?

RANK   No standing around in the draft!

HELMER   Come along, Mrs. Linde. This place isn't fit for anyone but mothers right now.

(DR. RANK, HELMER, *and* MRS. LINDE *go down the stairs. The* NURSE *enters the living room with the children.* NORA *follows, closing the door behind her.*)

NORA My, how nice you all look! Such red cheeks! Like apples and roses. (*The children all talk at the same time.*) You've had so much fun? I bet you have. Oh, isn't that nice! You pulled both Emmy and Bob on your sleigh? Both at the same time? That's very good, Ivar. Oh, let me hold her for a minute, Anne-Marie. My sweet little doll baby! (*Takes the smallest of the children from the* NURSE *and dances with her.*) Yes, yes, of course; Mama'll dance with you too, Bob. What? You threw snowballs? Oh, I wish I'd been there! No, no; *I* want to take their clothes off, Anne-Marie. Please let me; I think it's so much fun. You go on in. You look frozen. There's hot coffee on the stove.

(*The* NURSE *exits into the room to the left.* NORA *takes the children's wraps off and throws them all around. They all keep telling her things at the same time.*)

NORA Oh, really? A big dog ran after you? But it didn't bite you. Of course not. Dogs don't bite sweet little doll babies. Don't peek at the packages, Ivar! What's in them? Wouldn't you like to know! No, no; that's something terrible! Play? You want to play? What do you want to play? Okay, let's play hide-and-seek. Bob hides first. You want *me* to? All right. I'll go first.

(*Laughing and shouting,* NORA *and the children play in the living room and in the adjacent room, right. Finally,* NORA *hides herself under the table; the children rush in, look for her, can't find her. They hear her low giggle, run to the table, lift the rug that covers it, see her. General hilarity. She crawls out, pretends to scare them. New delight. In the meantime there has been a knock on the door between the living room and the front hall, but nobody has noticed. Now the door is opened half-way;* KROGSTAD *appears. He waits a little. The play goes on.*)

KROGSTAD Pardon me, Mrs. Helmer—
NORA (*with a muted cry turns around, jumps up*) Ah! What do you want?
KROGSTAD I'm sorry. The front door was open. Somebody must have forgotten to close it—
NORA (*standing up*) My husband isn't here, Mr. Krogstad.
KROGSTAD I know.
NORA So what do you want?
KROGSTAD I'd like a word with you.
NORA With—? (*To the children.*) Go in to Anne-Marie. What? No, the strange man won't do anything bad to Mama. When he's gone we'll play some more.

(*She takes the children into the room to the left and closes the door.*)

NORA (*tense, troubled*) You want to speak with me?
KROGSTAD Yes I do.

NORA   Today—? It isn't the first of the month yet.

KROGSTAD   No, it's Christmas Eve. It's up to you what kind of holiday you'll have.

NORA   What do you want? I can't possibly—

KROGSTAD   Let's not talk about that just yet. There's something else. You do have a few minutes, don't you?

NORA   Yes. Yes, of course. That is,—

KROGSTAD   Good. I was sitting in Olsen's restaurant when I saw your husband go by.

NORA   Yes—?

KROGSTAD   —with a lady.

NORA   What of it?

KROGSTAD   May I be so free as to ask: wasn't that lady Mrs. Linde?

NORA   Yes.

KROGSTAD   Just arrived in town?

NORA   Yes, today.

KROGSTAD   She's a good friend of yours, I understand?

NORA   Yes, she is. But I fail to see—

KROGSTAD   I used to know her myself.

NORA   I know that.

KROGSTAD   So you know about that. I thought as much. In that case, let me ask you a simple question. Is Mrs. Linde going to be employed in the bank?

NORA   What makes you think you have the right to cross-examine me like this, Mr. Krogstad—you, one of my husband's employees? But since you ask, I'll tell you. Yes, Mrs. Linde is going to be working in the bank. And it was I who recommended her, Mr. Krogstad. Now you know.

KROGSTAD   So I was right.

NORA   (*walks up and down*)   After all, one does have a little influence, you know. Just because you're a woman, it doesn't mean that—Really, Mr. Krogstad, people in a subordinate position should be careful not to offend someone who—oh well—

KROGSTAD   —has influence?

NORA   Exactly.

KROGSTAD   (*changing his tone*)   Mrs. Helmer, I must ask you to be good enough to use your influence on my behalf.

NORA   What do you mean?

KROGSTAD   I want you to make sure that I am going to keep my subordinate position in the bank.

NORA   I don't understand. Who is going to take your position away from you?

KROGSTAD   There's no point in playing ignorant with me, Mrs. Helmer. I can very well appreciate that your friend would find it unpleasant to run into me. So now I know who I can thank for my dismissal.

NORA But I assure you—

KROGSTAD Never mind. Just want to say you still have time. I advise you to use your influence to prevent it.

NORA But Mr. Krogstad, I don't have any influence—none at all.

KROGSTAD No? I thought you just said—

NORA Of course I didn't mean it that way. I! Whatever makes you think that I have any influence of that kind on my husband?

KROGSTAD I went to law school with your husband. I have no reason to think that the bank manager is less susceptible than other husbands.

NORA If you're going to insult my husband, I'll ask you to leave.

KROGSTAD You're brave, Mrs. Helmer.

NORA I'm not afraid of you any more. After New Year's I'll be out of this thing with you.

KROGSTAD (*more controlled*) Listen, Mrs. Helmer. If necessary I'll fight as for my life to keep my little job in the bank.

NORA So it seems.

KROGSTAD It isn't just the money; that's really the smallest part of it. There is something else—Well, I guess I might as well tell you. It's like this. I'm sure you know, like everybody else, that some years ago I committed—an impropriety.

NORA I believe I've heard it mentioned.

KROGSTAD The case never came to court, but from that moment all doors were closed to me. So I took up the kind of business you know about. I had to do something, and I think I can say about myself that I have not been among the worst. But now I want to get out of all that. My sons are growing up. For their sake I must get back as much of my good name as I can. This job in the bank was like the first rung on the ladder. And now your husband wants to kick me down and leave me back in the mud again.

NORA But I swear to you, Mr. Krogstad; it's not at all in my power to help you.

KROGSTAD That's because you don't want to. But I have the means to force you.

NORA You don't mean you're going to tell my husband I owe you money?

KROGSTAD And if I did?

NORA That would be a mean thing to do. (*Almost crying.*) That secret, which is my joy and my pride—for him to learn about it in such a coarse and ugly manner—to learn it from *you*—! It would be terribly unpleasant for me.

KROGSTAD Just unpleasant?

NORA (*heatedly*) But go ahead! Do it! It will be worse for you than for me. When my husband realizes what a bad person you are, you'll be sure to lose your job.

KROGSTAD I asked you if it was just domestic unpleasantness you were afraid of?

NORA When my husband finds out, of course he'll pay off the loan, and then we won't have anything more to do with you.

KROGSTAD (*stepping closer*) Listen, Mrs. Helmer—either you have a very bad memory, or you don't know much about business. I think I had better straighten you out on a few things.

NORA What do you mean?

KROGSTAD When your husband was ill, you came to me to borrow twelve hundred dollars.

NORA I knew nobody else.

KROGSTAD I promised to get you the money—

NORA And you did.

KROGSTAD I promised to get you the money on certain conditions. At the time you were so anxious about your husband's health and so set on getting him away that I doubt very much that you paid much attention to the details of our transaction. That's why I remind you of them now. Anyway, I promised to get you the money if you would sign an I.O.U., which I drafted.

NORA And which I signed.

KROGSTAD Good. But below your signature I added a few lines, making your father security for the loan. Your father was supposed to put his signature to those lines.

NORA Supposed to—? He did.

KROGSTAD I had left the date blank. That is, your father was to date his own signature. You recall that, don't you, Mrs. Helmer?

NORA I guess so—

KROGSTAD I gave the note to you. You were to mail it to your father. Am I correct?

NORA Yes.

KROGSTAD And of course you did so right away, for no more than five or six days later you brought the paper back to me, signed by your father. Then I paid you the money.

NORA Well? And haven't I been keeping up with the payments?

KROGSTAD Fairly well, yes. But to get back to what we were talking about—those were difficult days for you, weren't they, Mrs. Helmer?

NORA Yes, they were.

KROGSTAD Your father was quite ill, I believe.

NORA He was dying.

KROGSTAD And died shortly afterwards?

NORA That's right.

KROGSTAD Tell me, Mrs. Helmer; do you happen to remember the date of your father's death? I mean the exact day of the month?

NORA Daddy died on September 29.

KROGSTAD Quite correct. I have ascertained that fact. That's why there is something peculiar about this (*takes out a piece of paper*), which I can't account for.

NORA Peculiar? How? I don't understand—

KROGSTAD It seems very peculiar, Mrs. Helmer, that your father signed this promissory note three days after his death.

NORA How so? I don't see what—

KROGSTAD Your father died on September 29. Now look. He has dated his signature October 2. Isn't that odd?

(NORA *remains silent.*)

KROGSTAD Can you explain it?

(NORA *is still silent.*)

KROGSTAD I also find it striking that the date and the month and the year are not in your father's handwriting but in a hand I think I recognize. Well, that might be explained. Your father may have forgotten to date his signature and somebody else may have done it here, guessing at the date before he had learned of your father's death. That's all right. It's only the signature itself that matters. And that is genuine, isn't it, Mrs. Helmer? Your father *did* put his name to this note?

NORA (*after a brief silence tosses her head back and looks defiantly at him*) No, he didn't. *I* wrote Daddy's name.

KROGSTAD Mrs. Helmer—do you realize what a dangerous admission you just made?

NORA Why? You'll get your money soon.

KROGSTAD Let me ask you something. Why didn't you mail this note to your father?

NORA Because it was impossible. Daddy was sick—you know that. If I had asked him to sign it, I would have had to tell him what the money was for. But I couldn't tell him, as sick as he was, that my husband's life was in danger. That was impossible. Surely you can see that.

KROGSTAD Then it would have been better for you if you had given up your trip abroad.

NORA No, that was impossible! That trip was to save my husband's life. I couldn't give it up.

KROGSTAD   But didn't you realize that what you did amounted to fraud against me?

NORA   I couldn't let that make any difference. I didn't care about you at all. I hated the way you made all those difficulties for me, even though you knew the danger my husband was in. I thought you were cold and unfeeling.

KROGSTAD   Mrs. Helmer, obviously you have no clear idea of what you have done. Let me tell you that what I did that time was no more and no worse. And it ruined my name and reputation.

NORA   You! Are you trying to tell me that you did something brave once in order to save your wife's life?

KROGSTAD   The law doesn't ask about motives.

NORA   Then it's a bad law.

KROGSTAD   Bad or not—if I produce this note in court you'll be judged according to the law.

NORA   I refuse to believe you. A daughter shouldn't have the right to spare her dying old father worry and anxiety? A wife shouldn't have the right to save her husband's life? I don't know the laws very well, but I'm sure that somewhere they make allowance for cases like that. And you, a lawyer, don't know that? I think you must be a bad lawyer, Mr. Krogstad.

KROGSTAD   That may be. But business—the kind of business you and I have with one another—don't you think I know something about that? Very well. Do what you like. But let me tell you this: if I'm going to be kicked out again, you'll keep me company. (*He bows and exits through the front hall.*)

NORA   (*pauses thoughtfully; then, with a defiant toss of her head*) Oh, nonsense! Trying to scare me like that! I'm not all that silly. (*Starts picking up the children's clothes; soon stops.*) But—? No! That's impossible! I did it for love!

THE CHILDREN   (*in the door to the left*) Mama, the strange man just left. We saw him.

NORA   Yes, yes; I know. But don't tell anybody about the strange man. Do you hear? Not even Daddy.

THE CHILDREN   We won't. But now you'll play with us again, won't you, Mama?

NORA   No, not right now.

THE CHILDREN   But Mama—you promised.

NORA   I know, but I can't just now. Go to your own room. I've so much to do. Be nice now, my little darlings. Do as I say. (*She nudges them gently into the other room and closes the door. She sits down on the couch, picks up a piece of embroidery, makes a few stitches, then stops.*) No! (*Throws the embroidery down, goes to the hall door and calls out.*) Helene! Bring the Christmas tree in here, please! (*Goes to the table, left, opens the drawer, halts.*) No—that's impossible!

THE MAID (*with the Christmas tree*) Where do you want it, ma'am?

NORA There. The middle of the floor.

THE MAID You want anything else?

NORA No, thanks. I have everything I need. (THE MAID *goes out.* NORA *starts trimming the tree.*) I want candles—and flowers— That awful man! Oh, nonsense! There's nothing wrong. This will be a lovely tree. I'll do everything you want me to, Torvald. I'll sing for you—dance for you—

(*Helmer, a bundle of papers under his arm, enters from outside.*)

NORA Ah—you're back already?

HELMER Yes. Has anybody been here?

NORA Here? No.

HELMER That's funny. I saw Krogstad leaving just now.

NORA Oh? Oh yes, that's right. Krogstad was here for just a moment.

HELMER I can tell from your face that he came to ask you to put in a word for him.

NORA Yes.

HELMER And it was supposed to be your own idea, wasn't it? You were not to tell me he'd been here. He asked you that too, didn't he?

NORA Yes, Torvald, but—

HELMER Nora, Nora, how could you! Talk to a man like that and make him promises! And lying to me about it afterwards—!

NORA Lying—?

HELMER Didn't you say nobody had been here? (*Shakes his finger at her.*) My little songbird must never do that again. Songbirds are supposed to have clean beaks to chirp with—no false notes. (*Puts his arms around her waist.*) Isn't that so? Of course it is. (*Lets her go.*) And that's enough about that. (*Sits down in front of the fireplace.*) Ah, it's nice and warm in here. (*Begins to leaf through his papers.*)

NORA (*busy with the tree; after a brief pause*) Torvald.

HELMER Yes.

NORA I'm looking forward so much to the Stenborgs' costume party day after tomorrow.

HELMER And I can't wait to find out what you're going to surprise me with.

NORA Oh, that silly idea!

HELMER Oh?

NORA I can't think of anything. It all seems so foolish and pointless.

HELMER Ah, my little Nora admits that?

NORA (*behind his chair, her arms on the back of the chair*) Are you very busy, Torvald?

HELMER Well—

NORA What are all those papers?

HELMER Bank business.

NORA Already?

HELMER I've asked the board to give me the authority to make certain changes in organization and personnel. That's what I'll be doing over the holidays. I want it all settled before New Year's.

NORA So that's why this poor Krogstad—

HELMER Hm.

NORA (*leisurely playing with the hair on his neck*) If you weren't so busy, Torvald, I'd ask you for a great big favor.

HELMER Let's hear it, anyway.

NORA I don't know anyone with better taste than you, and I want so much to look nice at the party. Couldn't you sort of take charge of me, Torvald, and decide what I'll wear—Help me with my costume?

HELMER Aha! Little Lady Obstinate is looking for someone to rescue her?

NORA Yes, Torvald. I won't get anywhere without your help.

HELMER All right. I'll think about it. We'll come up with something.

NORA Oh, you *are* nice! (*Goes back to the Christmas tree. A pause.*) Those red flowers look so pretty.—Tell me, was it really all that bad what this Krogstad fellow did?

HELMER He forged signatures. Do you have any idea what that means?

NORA Couldn't it have been because he felt he had to?

HELMER Yes, or like so many others he may simply have been thoughtless. I'm not so heartless as to condemn a man absolutely because of a single imprudent act.

NORA Of course not, Torvald!

HELMER People like him can redeem themselves morally by openly confessing their crime and taking their punishment.

NORA Punishment—?

HELMER But that was not the way Krogstad chose. He got out of it with tricks and evasions. That's what has corrupted him.

NORA So you think that if—?

HELMER Can't you imagine how a guilty person like that has to lie and fake and dissemble wherever he goes—putting on a mask before everybody he's close to, even his own wife and children. It's this thing with the children that's the worst part of it, Nora.

NORA Why is that?

HELMER Because when a man lives inside such a circle of stinking lies he brings infection into his own home and contaminates his whole family. With every breath of air his children inhale the germs of something ugly.

NORA (*moving closer behind him*) Are you so sure of that?

HELMER Of course I am. I have seen enough examples of that in my work. Nearly all young criminals have had mothers who lied.

NORA Why mothers—particularly?

HELMER Most often mothers. But of course fathers tend to have the same influence. Every lawyer knows that. And yet, for years this Krogstad has been poisoning his own children in an atmosphere of lies and deceit. That's why I call him a lost soul morally. (*Reaches out for her hands.*) And that's why my sweet little Nora must promise me never to take his side again. Let's shake on that.—What? What's this? Give me your hand. There! Now that's settled. I assure you, I would find it impossible to work in the same room with that man. I feel literally sick when I'm around people like that.

NORA (*withdraws her hand and goes to the other side of the Christmas tree*) It's so hot in here. And I have so much to do.

HELMER (*gets up and collects his papers*) Yes, and I really should try to get some of this reading done before dinner. I must think about your costume too. And maybe just possibly I'll have something to wrap in gilt paper and hang on the Christmas tree. (*Puts his hand on her head.*) Oh my adorable little songbird! (*Enters his study and closes the door.*)

NORA (*after a pause, in a low voice*) It's all a lot of nonsense. It's not that way at all. It's impossible. It has to be impossible.

THE NURSE (*in the door, left*) The little ones are asking ever so nicely if they can't come in and be with their mama.

NORA No, no no! Don't let them in here! You stay with them, Anne-Marie.

THE NURSE If you say so, ma'am. (*Closes the door.*)

NORA (*pale with terror*) Corrupt my little children—! Poison my home—? (*Brief pause; she lifts her head.*) That's not true. Never. Never in a million years.

ACT II

The same room. The Christmas tree is in the corner by the piano, stripped, shabby-looking, with burnt-down candles. NORA's outside clothes are on the couch. NORA is alone. She walks around restlessly. She stops by the couch and picks up her coat.

NORA (*drops the coat again*) There's somebody now! (*Goes to the door, listens.*) No. Nobody. Of course not—not on Christmas. And not tomorrow either.[1]—But perhaps—(*Opens the door and looks.*) No, nothing in the mailbox. All empty. (*Comes forward.*) How silly I am! Of course he isn't serious. Nothing like that could happen. After all, I have three small children.

(*The NURSE enters from the room, left, carrying a big carton.*)

THE NURSE   Well, at last I found it—the box with your costume.

NORA   Thanks. Just put it on the table.

NURSE (*does so*) But it's all a big mess, I'm afraid.

NORA   Oh, I wish I could tear the whole thing to little pieces!

NURSE   Heavens! It's not as bad as all that. It can be fixed all right. All it takes is a little patience.

NORA   I'll go over and get Mrs. Linde to help me.

NURSE   Going out again? In this awful weather? You'll catch a cold.

NORA   That might not be such a bad thing. How are the children?

NURSE   The poor little dears are playing with their presents, but—

NORA   Do they keep asking for me?

NURSE   Well, you know, they're used to being with their mamma.

NORA   I know. But Anne-Marie, from now on I can't be with them as much as before.

NURSE   Oh well. Little children get used to everything.

NORA   You think so? Do you think they'll forget their mamma if I were gone altogether?

NURSE   Goodness me—gone altogether?

NORA   Listen, Anne-Marie—something I've wondered about. How could you bring yourself to leave your child with strangers?

NURSE   But I had to, if I were to nurse you.

NORA   Yes, but how could you *want* to?

NURSE   When I could get such a nice place? When something like that happens to a poor young girl, she'd better be grateful for whatever she gets. For *he* didn't do a thing for me—the louse!

NORA   But your daughter has forgotten all about you, hasn't she?

NURSE   Oh no! Not at all! She wrote to me both when she was confirmed and when she got married.

NORA (*putting her arms around her neck*) You dear old thing— you were a good mother to me when I was little.

NURSE   Poor little Nora had no one else, you know.

NORA   And if my little ones didn't, I know you'd—oh, I'm be-

---

[1] In Norway both December 25 and 26 are legal holidays.

ing silly! (*Opens the carton.*) Go in to them, please. I really should—. Tomorrow you'll see how pretty I'll be.

NURSE I know. There won't be anybody at that party half as pretty as you, ma'am. (*Goes out, left.*)

NORA (*begins to take clothes out of the carton; in a moment she throws it all down*) If only I dared to go out. If only I knew nobody would come. That nothing would happen while I was gone.—How silly! Nobody'll come. Just don't think about it. Brush the muff. Beautiful gloves. Beautiful gloves. Forget it. Forget it. One, two, three, four, five, six—(*Cries out.*) There they are! (*Moves toward the door, stops irresolutely.*)

(MRS. LINDE *enters from the hall. She has already taken off her coat.*)

NORA Oh, it's you, Kristine. There's no one else out there, is there? I'm so glad you're here.

MRS. LINDE They told me you'd asked for me.

NORA I just happened to walk by. I need your help with something—badly. Let's sit here on the couch. Look. Torvald and I are going to a costume party tomorrow night—at Consul Stenborg's upstairs—and Torvald wants me to go as a Neapolitan fisher girl and dance the tarantella. I learned it when we were on Capri.

MRS. LINDE Well, well! So you'll be putting on a whole show?

NORA Yes. Torvald thinks I should. Look, here's the costume. Torvald had it made for me while we were there. But it's all so torn and everything. I just don't know—

MRS. LINDE Oh, that can be fixed. It's not that much. The trimmings have come loose in a few places. Do you have needle and thread? Ah, here we are. All set.

NORA I really appreciate it, Kristine.

MRS. LINDE (*sewing*). So you'll be in disguise tomorrow night, eh? You know—I may come by for just a moment, just to look at you. —Oh dear. I haven't even thanked you for the nice evening last night.

NORA (*gets up, moves around*). Oh, I don't know. I don't think last night was as nice as it usually is.—You should have come to town a little earlier, Kristine.—Yes, Torvald knows how to make it nice and pretty around here.

MRS. LINDE You too, I should think. After all, you're your father's daughter. By the way, is Dr. Rank always as depressed as he was last night?

NORA No, last night was unusual. He's a very sick man, you know —very sick. Poor Rank, his spine is rotting away. Tuberculosis, I think. You see, his father was a nasty old man with mistresses and all that sort of thing. Rank has been sickly ever since he was a little boy.

MRS. LINDE (*dropping her sewing to her lap*) But dearest, Nora, where have you learned about things like that?

NORA (*still walking about*) Oh, you know—with three children you sometimes get to talk with—other wives. Some of them know quite a bit about medicine. So you pick up a few things.

MRS. LINDE (*resumes her sewing; after a brief pause*) Does Dr. Rank come here every day?

NORA Every single day. He's Torvald's oldest and best friend, after all. And my friend too, for that matter. He's part of the family, almost.

MRS. LINDE But tell me, is he quite sincere? I mean, isn't he the kind of man who likes to say nice things to people?

NORA No, not at all. Rather the opposite, in fact. What makes you say that?

MRS. LINDE When you introduced us yesterday, he told me he'd often heard my name mentioned in this house. But later on it was quite obvious that your husband really had no idea who I was. So how could Dr. Rank—?

NORA You're right, Kristine, but I can explain that. You see, Torvald loves me so very much that he wants me all to himself. That's what he says. When we were first married he got almost jealous when I as much as mentioned anybody from back home that I was fond of. So of course I soon stopped doing that. But with Dr. Rank I often talk about home. You see, he likes to listen to me.

MRS. LINDE Look here, Nora. In many ways you're still a child. After all, I'm quite a bit older than you and have had more experience. I want to give you a piece of advice. I think you should get out of this thing with Dr. Rank.

NORA Get out of what thing?

MRS. LINDE Several things in fact, if you want my opinion. Yesterday you said something about a rich admirer who was going to give you money—

NORA One who doesn't exist, unfortunately. What of it?

MRS. LINDE Does Dr. Rank have money?

NORA Yes, he does.

MRS. LINDE And no dependents?

NORA No. But—?

MRS. LINDE And he comes here every day?

NORA Yes, I told you that already.

MRS. LINDE But how can that sensitive man be so tactless?

NORA I haven't the slightest idea what you're talking about.

MRS. LINDE Don't play games with me, Nora. Don't you think I know who you borrowed the twelve hundred dollars from?

NORA Are you out of your mind! The very idea—! A friend of both of us who sees us every day—! What a dreadfully uncomfortable position that would be!

MRS. LINDE So it really isn't Dr. Rank?

NORA Most certainly not! I would never have dreamed of asking him—not for a moment. Anyway, he didn't have any money then. He inherited it afterwards.

MRS. LINDE Well, I still think it may have been lucky for you, Nora dear.

NORA The idea! It would never have occurred to me to ask Dr. Rank—. Though I'm sure that if I *did* ask him—

MRS. LINDE But of course you wouldn't.

NORA Of course not. I can't imagine that that would ever be necessary. But I am quite sure that if I told Dr. Rank—

MRS. LINDE Behind your husband's back?

NORA I must get out of—this other thing. That's also behind his back. I *must* get out of it.

MRS. LINDE That's what I told you yesterday. But—

NORA (*walking up and down*) A man manages these things so much better than a woman—

MRS. LINDE One's husband, yes.

NORA Silly, silly! (*Stops.*) When you've paid off all you owe, you get your I.O.U. back; right?

MRS. LINDE Yes, of course.

NORA And you can tear it into a hundred thousand little pieces and burn it—that dirty, filthy, paper!

MRS. LINDE (*looks hard at her, puts down her sewing, rises slowly*) Nora—you're hiding something from me.

NORA Can you tell?

MRS. LINDE Something's happened to you, Nora, since yesterday morning. What is it?

NORA (*going to her*) Kristine! (*Listens.*) Shhh. Torvald just came back. Listen. Why don't you go in to the children for a while. Torvald can't stand having sewing around. Get Anne-Marie to help you.

MRS. LINDE (*gathers some of the sewing things together*) All right, but I'm not leaving here till you and I have talked.

(*She goes out left, as* HELMER *enters from the front hall.*)

NORA (*towards him*) I have been waiting and waiting for you, Torvald.

HELMER Was that the dressmaker?

NORA No, it was Kristine. She's helping me with my costume. Oh Torvald, just wait till you see how nice I'll look!

HELMER I told you. Pretty good idea I had, wasn't it?

NORA Lovely! And wasn't it nice of me to go along with it?

HELMER (*his hands under her chin*) Nice? To do what your husband tells you? All right, you little rascal; I know you didn't mean it that way. But don't let me interrupt you. I suppose you want to try it on.

NORA And you'll be working?

HELMER Yes. (*Shows her a pile of papers.*) Look. I've been down to the bank. (*Is about to enter his study.*)

NORA Torvald.

HELMER (*halts*) Yes?

NORA What if your little squirrel asked you ever so nicely—

HELMER For what?

NORA Would you do it?

HELMER Depends on what it is.

NORA Squirrel would run around and do all sorts of fun tricks if you'd be nice and agreeable.

HELMER All right. What is it?

NORA Lark would chirp and twitter in all the rooms, up and down—

HELMER So what? Lark does that anyway.

NORA I'll be your elfmaid and dance for you in the moonlight, Torvald.

HELMER Nora, don't tell me it's the same thing you mentioned this morning?

NORA (*closer to him*) Yes, Torvald. I beg you!

HELMER You really have the nerve to bring that up again?

NORA Yes. You've just got to do as I say. You *must* let Krogstad keep his job.

HELMER My dear Nora. It's his job I intend to give to Mrs. Linde.

NORA I know. And that's ever so nice of you. But can't you just fire somebody else?

HELMER This is incredible! You just don't give up do you? Because you make some foolish promise, *I* am supposed to—!

NORA That's not the reason, Torvald. It's for your own sake. That man writes for the worst newspapers. You've said so yourself. There's no telling what he may do to you. I'm scared to death of him.

HELMER Ah, I understand. You're afraid because of what happened before.

NORA What do you mean?

HELMER You're thinking of your father, of course.

NORA Yes. Yes, you're right. Remember the awful things they wrote about Daddy in the newspapers. I really think they might have forced him to resign if the ministry hadn't sent you to look into the charges and if you hadn't been so helpful and understanding.

HELMER My dear little Nora, there is a world of difference between your father and me. Your father's official conduct was not above reproach. Mine is, and I intend for it to remain that way as long as I hold my position.

NORA Oh, but you don't know what vicious people like that may think of. Oh, Torvald! Now all of us could be so happy together here in our own home, peaceful and carefree. Such a good life, Torvald, for you and me and the children! That's why I implore you—

HELMER And it's exactly because you plead for him that you make it impossible for me to keep him. It's already common knowledge in the bank that I intend to let Krogstad go. If it gets out that the new manager has changed his mind because of his wife—

NORA Yes? What then?

HELMER No, of course, that wouldn't matter at all as long as little Mrs. Pighead here got her way! Do you want me to make myself look ridiculous before my whole staff—make people think I can be swayed by just anybody—by outsiders? Believe me, I would soon enough find out what the consequences would be! Besides, there's another thing that makes it absolutely impossible for Krogstad to stay on in the bank now that I'm in charge.

NORA What's that?

HELMER I suppose in a pinch I could overlook his moral shortcomings—

NORA Yes, you could; couldn't you, Torvald?

HELMER And I understand he's quite a good worker, too. But we've known each other for a long time. It's one of those imprudent relationships you get into when you're young that embarrass you for the rest of your life. I guess I might as well be frank with you: he and I are on a first name basis. And that tactless fellow never hides the fact even when other people are around. Rather, he seems to think it entitles him to be familiar with me. Every chance he gets he comes out with his damn "Torvald, Torvald." I'm telling you, I find it most awkward. He would make my position in the bank intolerable.

NORA You don't really mean any of this, Torvald.

HELMER Oh? I don't? And why not?

NORA No, for it's all so petty.

HELMER What! Petty? You think I'm being petty!

NORA No, I *don't* think you are petty, Torvald dear. That's exactly why I—

HELMER Never mind. You think my reasons are petty, so it follows that I must be petty too. Petty! Indeed! By God, I'll put an end to this right now! (*Opens the door to the front hall and calls out.*) Helene!

NORA What are you doing?

HELMER (*searching among his papers*) Making a decision. (THE MAID *enters.*) Here. Take this letter. Go out with it right away. Find somebody to deliver it. But quick. The address is on the envelope. Wait. Here's money.

THE MAID Very good sir. (*She takes the letter and goes out.*)

HELMER (*collecting his papers*) There now, little Mrs. Obstinate!

NORA (*breathless*) Torvald—what was that letter?

HELMER Krogstad's dismissal.

NORA Call it back, Torvald! There's still time! Oh Torvald, please —call it back! For my sake, for your own sake, for the sake of the children! Listen to me, Torvald! Do it! You don't know what you're doing to all of us!

HELMER Too late.

NORA Yes. Too late.

HELMER Dear Nora, I forgive you this fear you're in, although it really is an insult to me. Yes, it is! It's an insult to think that I am scared of a shabby scrivener's revenge. But I forgive you, for it's such a beautiful proof how much you love me. (*Takes her in his arms.*) And that's the way it should be, my sweet darling. Whatever happens, you'll see that when things get really rough I have both strength and courage. You'll find out that I am man enough to shoulder the whole burden.

NORA (*terrified*) What do you mean by that?

HELMER All of it, I tell you—

NORA (*composed*) You'll never have to do that.

HELMER Good. Then we'll share the burden, Nora—like husband and wife, the way it ought to be. (*Caresses her.*) Now are you satisfied? There, there, there. Not that look in your eyes—like a frightened dove. It's all your own foolish imagination.—Why don't you practice the tarantella—and your tambourine, too. I'll be in the inner office and close both doors, so I won't hear you. You can make as much noise as you like. (*Turning in the doorway.*) And when Rank comes, tell him where to find me. (*He nods to her, enters his study carrying his papers, and closes the door.*)

NORA (*transfixed by terror, whispers*) He would do it. He'll do it. He'll do it in spite of the whole world.—No, this mustn't happen.

Anything rather than that! There must be a way—! (*The door-bell rings.*) Dr. Rank! Anything rather than that! Anything—anything at all!

(*She passes her hand over her face, pulls herself together, and opens the door to the hall. DR. RANK is out there, hanging up his coat. Darkness begins to fall during the following scene.*)

NORA   Hello there, Dr. Rank. I recognized your ringing. Don't go in to Torvald yet. I think he's busy.

RANK   And you?

NORA   (*as he enters and she closes the door behind him*)   You know I always have time for you.

RANK   Thanks. I'll make use of that as long as I can.

NORA   What do you mean by that—As long as you can?

RANK   Does that frighten you?

NORA   Well, it's a funny expression. As if something was going to happen.

RANK   Something is going to happen that I've long been expecting. But I admit I hadn't thought it would come quite so soon.

NORA   (*seizes his arm*)   What is it you've found out? Dr. Rank—tell me!

RANK   (*sits down by the stove*)   I'm going downhill fast. There's nothing to do about that.

NORA   (*with audible relief*)   So it's *you*—

RANK   Who else? No point in lying to myself. I'm in worse shape than any of my other patients, Mrs. Helmer. These last few days I've been making up my inner status. Bankrupt. Chances are that within a month I'll be rotting up in the cemetery.

NORA   Shame on you! Talking that horrid way!

RANK   The thing itself is horrid—damn horrid. The worst of it, though, is all that other horror that comes first. There is only one more test I need to make. After that I'll have a pretty good idea when I'll start coming apart. There is something I want to say to you. Helmer's refined nature can't stand anything hideous. I don't want him in my sick room.

NORA   Oh, but Dr. Rank—

RANK   I don't want him there. Under no circumstances. I'll close my door to him. As soon as I have full certainty that the worst is about to begin I'll give you my card with a black cross on it. Then you'll know the last horror of destruction has started.

NORA   Today you're really quite impossible. And I had hoped you'd be in a particularly good mood.

RANK   With death on my hands? Paying for someone else's sins? Is there justice in that? And yet there isn't a single family that isn't ruled by the same law of ruthless retribution, in one way or another.

NORA (*puts her hands over her ears*) Poppycock! Be fun! Be fun!

RANK Well, yes. You may just as well laugh at the whole thing. My poor, innocent spine is suffering from my father's frolics as a young lieutenant.

NORA (*over by the table, left*) Right. He was addicted to asparagus and goose liver paté, wasn't he?

RANK And truffles.

NORA Of course. Truffles. And oysters too, I think.

RANK And oysters. Obviously.

NORA And all the port and champagne that go with it. It's really too bad that goodies like that ruin your backbone.

RANK Particularly an unfortunate backbone that never enjoyed any of it.

NORA Ah yes, that's the saddest part of it all.

RANK (*looks searchingly at her*) Hm—

NORA (*after a brief pause*) Why did you smile just then?

RANK No, it was you that laughed.

NORA No, it was you that smiled, Dr. Rank!

RANK (*gets up*) You're more of a mischief-maker than I thought.

NORA I feel in the mood for mischief today.

RANK So it seems.

NORA (*with both her hands on his shoulders*) Dear, dear Dr. Rank, don't you go and die and leave Torvald and me.

RANK Oh, you won't miss me for very long. Those who go away are soon forgotten.

NORA (*with an anxious look*) Do you believe that?

RANK You'll make new friends, and then—

NORA Who'll make new friends?

RANK Both you and Helmer, once I'm gone. You yourself seem to have made a good start already. What was this Mrs. Linde doing here last night?

NORA Aha—Don't tell me you're jealous of poor Kristine?

RANK Yes, I am. She'll be my successor in this house. As soon as I have made my excuses, that woman is likely to—

NORA Shh—not so loud. She's in there.

RANK Today too? There you are!

NORA She's mending my costume. My God, you really *are* unreasonable. (*Sits down on the couch*). Now be nice, Dr. Rank. Tomorrow you'll see how beautifully I'll dance, and then you are to pretend I'm dancing just for you—and for Torvald too, of course. (*Takes several items out of the carton.*) Sit down, Dr. Rank; I want to show you something.

RANK (*sitting down*) What?

NORA Look.

RANK Silk stockings.

NORA Flesh-colored. Aren't they lovely? Now it's getting dark in here, but tomorrow—No, no. You only get to see the foot. Oh well, you might as well see all of it.

RANK Hmm.

NORA Why do you look so critical? Don't you think they'll fit?

RANK That's something I can't possibly have a reasoned opinion about.

NORA (*looks at him for a moment*) Shame on you. (*Slaps his ear lightly with the stocking.*) That's what you get. (*Puts the things back in the carton.*)

RANK And what other treasures are you going to show me?

NORA Nothing at all, because you're naughty. (*She hums a little and rummages in the carton.*)

RANK (*after a brief silence*) When I sit here like this, talking confidently with you, I can't imagine—I can't possibly imagine what would have become of me if I hadn't had you and Helmer.

NORA (*smiles*) Well, yes—I do believe you like being with us.

RANK (*in a lower voice, lost in thought*) And then to have to go away from it all—

NORA Nonsense. You are not going anywhere.

RANK (*as before*) —and not to leave behind as much as a poor little token of gratitude, hardly a brief memory of someone missed, nothing but a vacant place that anyone can fill.

NORA And what if I were to ask you—? No—

RANK Ask me what?

NORA For a great proof of your friendship—

RANK Yes, yes—?

NORA No, I mean— for an enormous favor—

RANK Would you really for once make me as happy as all that?

NORA But you don't even know what it is.

RANK Well, then; tell me.

NORA Oh, but I can't, Dr. Rank. It's altogether too much to ask— It's advice and help and a favor—

RANK So much the better. I can't even begin to guess what it is you have in mind. So for heaven's sake tell me! Don't you trust me?

NORA Yes, I trust you more than anyone else I know. You are my best and most faithful friend. I know that. So I will tell you. All right, Dr. Rank. There is something you can help me prever You know how much Torvald loves me—beyond all words. N for a moment would he hesitate to give his life for me.

RANK (*leaning over to her*)   Nora—do you really think he's the only one—?

NORA (*with a slight start*)   Who—?

RANK   —would gladly give his life for you.

NORA (*heavily*)   I see.

RANK   I have sworn an oath to myself to tell you before I go. I'll never find a better occasion.—All right, Nora; now you know. And now you also know that you can confide in me more than in anyone else.

NORA (*gets up; in a calm, steady voice*)   Let me get by.

RANK (*makes room for her but remains seated*)   Nora—

NORA (*in the door to the front hall*)   Helene, bring the lamp in here, please. (*Walks over to the stove.*) Oh, dear Dr. Rank. That really wasn't very nice of you.

RANK (*gets up*)   That I have loved you as much as anybody—was that not nice?

NORA   No; not that. But that you told me. There was no need for that.

RANK   What do you mean? Have you known—?

(THE MAID *enters with the lamp, puts it on the table, and goes out.*)

RANK   Nora—Mrs. Helmer—I'm asking you: did you know?

NORA   Oh, how can I tell what I knew and didn't know! I really can't say—But that you could be so awkward, Dr. Rank! Just when everything was so comfortable.

RANK   Well, anyway, now you know that I'm at your service with my life and soul. And now you must speak.

NORA (*looks at him*)   After what just happened?

RANK   I beg of you—let me know what it is.

NORA   There is nothing I can tell you now.

RANK   Yes, yes. You mustn't punish me this way. Please let me do for you whatever anyone *can* do.

NORA   Now there is nothing you can do. Besides, I don't think I really need any help, anyway. It's probably just my imagination. Of course that's all it is. I'm sure of it! (*Sits down in the rocking chair, looks at him, smiles.*) Well, well, well, Dr. Rank! What a fine gentleman you turned out to be! Aren't you ashamed of yourself, now that we have light?

⌐ᴬɴᴋ   No, not really. But perhaps I ought to leave—and not come

t be silly; of course not! You'll come here exactly as you
ı doing. You know perfectly well that Torvald can't do
ɪou.

ɜ, but what about you?

NORA Oh, I always think it's perfectly delightful when you come.

RANK That's the very thing that misled me. You are a riddle to me. It has often seemed to me that you'd just as soon be with me as with Helmer.

NORA Well, you see, there are people you love, and then there are other people you'd almost rather be with.

RANK Yes, there is something in that.

NORA When I lived at home with Daddy, of course I loved him most. But I always thought it was so much fun to sneak off down to the maids' room, for they never gave me good advice and they always talked about such fun things.

RANK Aha! So it's *their* place I have taken.

NORA (*jumps up and goes over to him*) Oh dear, kind Dr. Rank, you know very well I didn't mean it that way. Can't you see that with Torvald it is the way it used to be with Daddy?

(THE MAID *enters from the front hall.*)

THE MAID Ma'am! (*Whispers to her and gives her a caller's card.*)

NORA (*glances at the card*) Ah! (*Puts it in her pocket*).

RANK Anything wrong?

NORA No, no; not at all. It's nothing—just my new costume—

RANK But your costume is lying right there!

NORA Oh yes, that one. But this is another one. I ordered it. Torvald mustn't know—

RANK Aha. So that's the great secret.

NORA That's it. Why don't you go in to him, please. He's in the inner office. And keep him there for a while—

RANK Don't worry. He won't get away. (*Enters* HELMER's *study.*)

NORA (*to* THE MAID) You say he's waiting in the kitchen?

THE MAID Yes. He came up the back stairs.

NORA But didn't you tell him there was somebody with me?

THE MAID Yes, but he wouldn't listen.

NORA He won't leave?

THE MAID No, not till he's had a word with you, ma'am.

NORA All right. But try not to make any noise. And, Helene— don't tell anyone he's here. It's supposed to be a surprise for my husband.

THE MAID I understand, ma'am—(*She leaves.*)

NORA The terrible is happening. It's happening, after all. No, no, no. It can't happen. It won't happen. (*She bolts the study door.*)

(THE MAID *opens the front hall door for* KROGSTAD *and closes the door behind him. He wears a fur coat for traveling, boots, and a fur hat.*)

NORA (*toward him*)   Keep your voice down. My husband's home.

KROGSTAD   That's all right.

NORA   What do you want?

KROGSTAD   To find out something.

NORA   Be quick, then. What is it?

KROGSTAD   I expect you know I've been fired.

NORA   I couldn't prevent it, Mr. Krogstad. I fought for you as long and as hard as I could but it didn't do any good.

KROGSTAD   Your husband doesn't love you any more than that? He knows what I can do to you, and yet he runs the risk—

NORA   Surely you didn't think I'd tell him?

KROGSTAD   No, I really didn't. It wouldn't be like Torvald Helmer to show that kind of guts—

NORA   Mr. Krogstad, I insist that you show respect for my husband.

KROGSTAD   By all means. All due respect. But since you're so anxious to keep this a secret, may I assume that you are a little better informed than yesterday about exactly what you have done?

NORA   Better than *you* could ever teach me.

KROGSTAD   Of course. Such a bad lawyer as I am—

NORA   What do you want of me?

KROGSTAD   I just wanted to find out how you are, Mrs. Helmer. I've been thinking about you all day. You see, even a bill collector, a pen pusher, a—anyway, someone like me—even he has a little of what they call a heart.

NORA   Then show it. Think of my little children.

KROGSTAD   Have you and your husband thought of mine? Never mind. All I want to tell you is that you don't need to take this business too seriously. I have no intention of bringing charges right away.

NORA   Oh no, you wouldn't; would you? I knew you wouldn't.

KROGSTAD   The whole thing can be settled quite amiably. Nobody else needs to know anything. It will be between the three of us.

NORA   My husband must never find out about this.

KROGSTAD   How are you going to prevent that? Maybe you can pay me the balance on the loan?

NORA   No, not right now.

KROGSTAD   Or do you have a way of raising the money one of these next few days?

NORA   None I intend to make use of.

KROGSTAD   It wouldn't do you any good, anyway. Even if you had the cash in your hand right this minute, I wouldn't give you your note back. It wouldn't make any difference *how* much money you offered me.

NORA   Then you'll have to tell me what you plan to use the note *for*.

KROGSTAD   Just keep it; that's all. Have it on hand, so to speak. I won't say a word to anybody else. So if you've been thinking about doing something desperate—

NORA   I have.

KROGSTAD   —like leaving house and home—

NORA   I have!

KROGSTAD   —or even something worse—

NORA   How did you know?

KROGSTAD   —then: don't.

NORA   How did you know I was thinking of *that*?

KROGSTAD   Most of us do, right at first. I did, too, but when it came down to it I didn't have the courage—

NORA   (*tonelessly*)   Nor do I.

KROGSTAD   (*relieved*)   See what I mean? I thought so. You don't either.

NORA   I don't. I don't.

KROGSTAD   Besides, it would be very silly of you. Once that first domestic blowup is behind you—. Here in my pocket is a letter for your husband.

NORA   Telling him everything?

KROGSTAD   As delicately as possible.

NORA   (*quickly*)   He mustn't get that letter. Tear it up. I'll get you the money somehow.

KROGSTAD   Excuse me, Mrs. Helmer, I thought I just told you—

NORA   I'm not talking about the money I owe you. Just let me know how much money you want from my husband, and I'll get it for you.

KROGSTAD   I want no money from your husband.

NORA   Then, what *do* you want?

KROGSTAD   I'll tell you, Mrs. Helmer. I want to rehabilitate myself; I want to get up in the world; and your husband is going to help me. For a year and a half I haven't done anything disreputable. All that time I have been struggling with the most miserable circumstances. I was content to work my way up step by step. Now I've been kicked out, and I'm no longer satisfied just getting my old job back. I want more than that; I want to get to the top. I'm being quite serious. I want the bank to take me back but in a higher position. I want your husband to create a new job for me—

NORA   He'll never do that!

KROGSTAD   He will. I know him. He won't dare not to. And once I'm back inside and he and I are working together, you'll see! Within a year I'll be the manager's right hand. It will be Nils

Krogstad and not Torvald Helmer who'll be running the Mutual Bank!

NORA You'll never see that happen!

KROGSTAD Are you thinking of—?

NORA Now I *do* have the courage.

KROGSTAD You can't scare me. A fine, spoiled lady like you—

NORA You'll see, you'll see!

KROGSTAD Under the ice, perhaps? Down into that cold, black water? Then spring comes, and you float up again—hideous, can't be identified, hair all gone—

NORA You don't frighten me.

KROGSTAD Nor you me. One doesn't do that sort of thing, Mrs. Helmer. Besides, what good would it do? He'd still be in my power.

NORA Afterwards? When I'm no longer—?

KROGSTAD Aren't you forgetting that your reputation would be in my hands?

(NORA *stares at him, speechless.*)

KROGSTAD All right; now I've told you what to expect. So don't do anything foolish. When Helmer gets my letter I expect to hear from him. And don't you forget that it's your husband himself who forces me to use such means again. That I'll never forgive him. Goodbye, Mrs. Helmer. (*Goes out through the hall.*)

NORA (*at the door, opens it a little, listens*) He's going. And no letter. Of course not! That would be impossible. (*Opens the door more.*) What's he doing? He's still there. Doesn't go down. Having second thoughts—? Will he—?

(*The sound of a letter dropping into the mailbox. Then* KROGSTAD'S *steps are heard going down the stairs, gradually dying away.*)

NORA (*with a muted cry runs forward to the table by the couch; brief pause*) In the mailbox. (*Tiptoes back to the door to the front hall.*) There it is. Torvald, Torvald—now we're lost!

MRS. LINDE (*enters from the left, carrying* NORA'S *Capri costume*) There now. I think it's all fixed. Why don't we try it on you—

NORA (*in a low, hoarse voice*) Kristine, come here.

MRS. LINDE What's wrong with you? You look quite beside yourself.

NORA Come over here. Do you see that letter? There, look— through the glass in the mailbox.

MRS. LINDE Yes, yes; I see it.

NORA That letter is from Krogstad.

MRS. LINDE Nora—it was Krogstad who lent you the money!

NORA Yes, and now Torvald will find out about it.

MRS. LINDE   Oh believe me, Nora. That's the best thing for both of you.

NORA   There's more to it than you know. I forged a signature—

MRS. LINDE   Oh my God—!

NORA   I just want to tell you this, Kristine, that you must be my witness.

MRS. LINDE   Witness? How? Witness to what?

NORA   If I lose my mind—and that could very well happen—

MRS. LINDE   Nora!

NORA   —or if something were to happen to me—something that made it impossible for me to be here—

MRS. LINDE   Nora, Nora! You're not yourself!

NORA   —and if someone were to take all the blame, assume the whole responsibility—Do you understand—?

MRS. LINDE   Yes, yes; but how can you think—!

NORA   Then you are to witness that that's not so, Kristine. I am not beside myself. I am perfectly rational, and what I'm telling you is that nobody else has known about this. I've done it all by myself, the whole thing. Just remember that.

MRS. LINDE   I will. But I don't understand any of it.

NORA   Oh, how could you! For it's the wonderful that's about to happen.

MRS. LINDE   The wonderful?

NORA   Yes, the wonderful. But it's so terrible, Kristine. It mustn't happen for anything in the whole world!

MRS. LINDE   I'm going over to talk to Krogstad right now.

NORA   No, don't. Don't go to him. He'll do something bad to you.

MRS. LINDE   There was a time when he would have done anything for me.

NORA   He!

MRS. LINDE   Where does he live?

NORA   Oh, I don't know—Yes, wait a minute—(*Reaches into her pocket.*)   here's his card.—But the letter, the letter—!

HELMER   (*in his study, knocks on the door*)   Nora!

NORA   (*cries out in fear*)   Oh, what is it? What do you want?

HELMER   That's all right. Nothing to be scared about. We're not coming in. For one thing, you've bolted the door, you know. Are you modeling your costume?

NORA   Yes, yes; I am. I'm going to be so pretty, Torvald.

MRS. LINDE   (*having looked at the card*)   He lives just around the corner.

NORA   Yes, but it's no use. Nothing can save us now. The letter is in the mailbox.

MRS. LINDE   And your husband has the key?

NORA Yes. He always keeps it with him.

MRS. LINDE Krogstad must ask for his letter back, unread. He's got to think up some pretext or other—

NORA But this is just the time of day when Torvald—

MRS. LINDE Delay him. Go in to him. I'll be back as soon as I can. (*She hurries out through the hall door.*)

NORA (*walks over to* HELMER's *door, opens it, and peeks in*) Torvald.

HELMER (*still offstage*) Well, well! So now one's allowed in one's own living room again. Come on, Rank. Now we'll see—(*In the doorway.*) But what's this?

NORA What, Torvald dear?

HELMER Rank prepared me for a splendid metamorphosis.

RANK (*in the doorway*) That's how I understood it. Evidently I was mistaken.

NORA Nobody gets to admire me in my costume before tomorrow.

HELMER But, dearest Nora—you look all done in. Have you been practicing too hard?

NORA No, I haven't practiced at all.

HELMER But you'll have to, you know.

NORA I know it, Torvald. I simply must. But I can't do a thing unless you help me. I have forgotten everything.

HELMER Oh it will all come back. We'll work on it.

NORA Oh yes, please, Torvald. You just have to help me. Promise? I am so nervous. That big party—. You mustn't do anything else tonight. Not a bit of business. Don't even touch a pen. Will you promise, Torvald?

HELMER I promise. Tonight I'll be entirely at your service—you helpless little thing.—Just a moment, though. First I want to— (*Goes to the door to the front hall.*)

NORA What are you doing out there?

HELMER Just looking to see if there's any mail.

NORA No, no! Don't, Torvald!

HELMER Why not?

NORA Torvald, I beg you. There is no mail.

HELMER Let me just look, anyway. (*Is about to go out.*)

(NORA *by the piano, plays the first bars of the tarantella dance.*)

HELMER (*halts at the door*) Aha!

NORA I won't be able to dance tomorrow if I don't get to practice with you.

HELMER (*goes to her*) Are you really all that scared, Nora dear?

NORA Yes, so terribly scared. Let's try it right now. There's still time before we eat. Oh please, sit down and play for me, Torvald. Teach me, coach me, the way you always do.

HELMER Of course I will, my darling, if that's what you want. (*Sits down at the piano.*)

(NORA *takes the tambourine out of the carton, as well as a long, many-colored shawl. She quickly drapes the shawl around herself, then leaps into the middle of the floor.*)

NORA Play for me! I want to dance!

(HELMER *plays and* NORA *dances.* DR. RANK *stands by the piano behind* HELMER *and watches.*)

HELMER (*playing*) Slow down, slow down!
NORA Can't!
HELMER Not so violent, Nora!
NORA It has to be this way.
HELMER (*stops playing*) No, no. This won't do at all.
NORA (*laughing, swinging her tambourine*) What did I tell you?
RANK Why don't you let me play?
HELMER (*getting up*) Good idea. Then I can direct her better.

(RANK *sits down at the piano and starts playing.* NORA *dances more and more wildly.* HELMER *stands over by the stove, repeatedly correcting her. She doesn't seem to hear. Her hair comes loose and falls down over her shoulders. She doesn't notice but keeps on dancing.* MRS. LINDE *enters.*)

MRS. LINDE (*stops by the door, dumbfounded*) Ah—!
NORA (*dancing*) We're having such fun, Kristine!
HELMER My dearest Nora, you're dancing as if it were a matter of life and death!
NORA It is! It is!
HELMER Rank, stop. This is sheer madness. Stop, I say!

(RANK *stops playing;* NORA *suddenly stops dancing.*)

HELMER (*goes over to her*) If I hadn't seen it I wouldn't have believed it. You've forgotten every single thing I ever taught you.
NORA (*tosses away the tambourine*) See? I told you.
HELMER Well! You certainly need coaching.
NORA Didn't I tell you I did? Now you've seen for yourself. I'll need your help till the very minute we're leaving for the party. Will you promise, Torvald?
HELMER You can count on it.
NORA You're not to think of anything except me—not tonight and

not tomorrow. You're not to read any letters—not to look in the mailbox—

HELMER Ah, I see. You're still afraid of that man.

NORA Yes—yes, that too.

HELMER Nora, I can tell from looking at you. There's a letter from him out there.

NORA I don't know. I think so. But you're not to read it now. I don't want anything ugly to come between us before it's all over.

RANK (*to* HELMER *in a low voice*) Better not argue with her.

HELMER (*throws his arm around her*) The child shall have her way. But tomorrow night, when you've done your dance—

NORA Then you'll be free.

THE MAID (*in the door, right*) Dinner can be served any time, ma'am.

NORA We want champagne, Helene.

THE MAID Very good, ma'am. (*Goes out.*)

HELMER Aha! Having a party, eh?

NORA Champagne from now till sunrise! (*Calls out.*) And some macaroons, Helene. Lots!—just this once.

HELMER (*taking her hands*) There, there—I don't like this wild—frenzy—Be my own sweet little lark again, the way you always are.

NORA Oh, I will. But you go on in. You too, Dr. Rank. Kristine, please help me put up my hair.

RANK (*in a low voice to* HELMER *as they go out*) You don't think she is—you know—expecting—?

HELMER Oh no. Nothing like that. It's just this childish fear I was telling you about. (*They go out, right.*)

NORA Well?

MRS. LINDE Left town.

NORA I saw it in your face.

MRS. LINDE He'll be back tomorrow night. I left him a note.

NORA You shouldn't have. I don't want you to try to stop anything. You see, it's a kind of ecstasy, too, this waiting for the wonderful.

MRS. LINDE But what is it you're waiting *for*?

NORA You wouldn't understand. Why don't you go in to the others. I'll be there in a minute.

(MRS. LINDE *enters the dining room, right.*)

NORA (*stands still for a little while, as if collecting herself; she looks at her watch*) Five o'clock. Seven hours till midnight. Twenty-four more hours till next midnight. Then the tarantella is over. Twenty-four plus seven—thirty-one more hours to live.

HELMER (*in the door, right*) What's happening to my little lark?

NORA (*to him, with open arms*) Here's your lark!

ACT III

The same room. The table by the couch and the chairs around it have been moved to the middle of the floor. A lighted lamp is on the table. The door to the front hall is open. Dance music is heard from upstairs.
MRS. LINDE *is seated by the table, idly leafing through the pages of a book. She tries to read but seems unable to concentrate. Once or twice she turns her head in the direction of the door, anxiously listening.)*

MRS. LINDE *(looks at her watch)* Not yet. It's almost too late. If only he hasn't—*(Listens again.)* Ah! There he is. *(She goes to the hall and opens the front door carefully. Quiet footsteps on the stairs. She whispers.)* Come in. There's nobody here.

KROGSTAD *(in the door)* I found your note when I got home. What's this all about?

MRS. LINDE I've got to talk to you.

KROGSTAD Oh? And it has to be here?

MRS. LINDE It couldn't be at my place. My room doesn't have a separate entrance. Come in. We're quite alone. The maid is asleep and the Helmers are at a party upstairs.

KROGSTAD *(entering)* Really? The Helmers are dancing tonight, are they?

MRS. LINDE And why not?

KROGSTAD You're right. Why not, indeed.

MRS. LINDE All right, Krogstad. Let's talk, you and I.

KROGSTAD I didn't know we had anything to talk about.

MRS. LINDE We have much to talk about.

KROGSTAD I didn't think so.

MRS. LINDE No, because you've never really understood me.

KROGSTAD What was there to understand? What happened was perfectly commonplace. A heartless woman jilts a man when she gets a more attractive offer.

MRS. LINDE Do you think I'm all that heartless? And do you think it was easy for me to break with you?

KROGSTAD No?

MRS. LINDE You really thought it was?

KROGSTAD If it wasn't, why did you write the way you did that time?

MRS. LINDE What else could I do? If I had to make a break, I also had the duty to destroy whatever feelings you had for me.

KROGSTAD *(clenching his hands)* So that's the way it was. And you did—*that*—just for money!

MRS. LINDE Don't forget I had a helpless mother and two small brothers. We couldn't wait for you, Krogstad. You know yourself how uncertain your prospects were then.

KROGSTAD All right. But you still didn't have the right to throw me over for somebody else.

MRS. LINDE I don't know. I have asked myself that question many times. Did I have that right?

KROGSTAD (*in a lower voice*) When I lost you I lost my footing. Look at me now. A shipwrecked man on a raft.

MRS. LINDE Rescue may be near.

KROGSTAD It *was* near. Then you came between.

MRS. LINDE I didn't know that, Krogstad. Only today did I find out it's your job I'm taking over in the bank.

KROGSTAD I believe you when you say so. But now that you *do* know, aren't you going to step aside?

MRS. LINDE No, for it wouldn't do you any good.

KROGSTAD Whether it would or not—*I* would do it.

MRS. LINDE I have learned common sense. Life and hard necessity have taught me that.

KROGSTAD And life has taught me not to believe in pretty speeches.

MRS. LINDE Then life has taught you a very sensible thing. But you do believe in actions, don't you?

KROGSTAD How do you mean?

MRS. LINDE You referred to yourself just now as a shipwrecked man.

KROGSTAD It seems to me I had every reason to do so.

MRS. LINDE And I am a shipwrecked woman. No one to grieve for, no one to care for.

KROGSTAD You made your choice.

MRS. LINDE I had no other choice that time.

KROGSTAD Let's say you didn't. What then?

MRS. LINDE Krogstad, how would it be if we two shipwrecked people got together?

KROGSTAD What's this!

MRS. LINDE Two on one wreck are better off than each on his own.

KROGSTAD Kristine!

MRS. LINDE Why do you think I came to town?

KROGSTAD Surely not because of me?

MRS. LINDE If I'm going to live at all I must work. All my life, for as long as I can remember, I have worked. That's been my one and only pleasure. But now that I'm all alone in the world I feel nothing but this terrible emptiness and desolation. There is no joy in working just for yourself. Krogstad—give me someone and something to work for.

KROGSTAD I don't believe this. Only hysterical females go in for that kind of high-minded self-sacrifice.

MRS. LINDE Did you ever know me to be hysterical?

KROGSTAD You really could do this? Listen—do you know about my past? All of it?

MRS. LINDE Yes, I do.

KROGSTAD Do you also know what people think of me around here?

MRS. LINDE A little while ago you sounded as if you thought that together with me you might have become a different person.

KROGSTAD I'm sure of it.

MRS. LINDE Couldn't that still be?

KROGSTAD Kristine—do you know what you are doing? Yes, I see you do. And you think you have the courage—?

MRS. LINDE I need someone to be a mother to, and your children need a mother. You and I need one another. Nils, I believe in you—in the real you. Together with you I dare to do anything.

KROGSTAD (*seizes her hands*) Thanks, thanks, Kristine—Now I know I'll raise myself in the eyes of others—Ah, but I forget—!

MRS. LINDE (*listening*) Shh!—there's the tarantella. You must go; hurry!

KROGSTAD Why? What is it?

MRS. LINDE Do you hear what they're playing up there? When that dance is over they'll be down.

KROGSTAD All right. I'm leaving. The whole thing is pointless, anyway. Of course you don't know what I'm doing to the Helmers.

MRS. LINDE Yes, Krogstad; I do know.

KROGSTAD Still, you're brave enough—?

MRS. LINDE I very well understand to what extremes despair can drive a man like you.

KROGSTAD If only it could be undone!

MRS. LINDE It could, for your letter is still out there in the mailbox.

KROGSTAD Are you sure?

MRS. LINDE Quite sure. But—

KROGSTAD (*looks searchingly at her*) Maybe I'm beginning to understand. You want to save your friend at any cost. Be honest with me. That's it, isn't it?

MRS. LINDE Krogstad, you may sell yourself once for somebody else's sake, but you don't do it twice.

KROGSTAD I'll demand my letter back.

MRS. LINDE No, no.

KROGSTAD Yes, of course. I'll wait here till Helmer comes down. Then I'll ask him for my letter. I'll tell him it's just about my dismissal—that he shouldn't read it.

MRS. LINDE No, Krogstad. You are not to ask for that letter back.

KROGSTAD But tell me—wasn't that the real reason you wanted to meet me here?

MRS. LINDE At first it was, because I was so frightened. But that was yesterday. Since then I have seen the most incredible things going on in this house. Helmer must learn the whole truth. This miserable secret must come out in the open; those two must come to a full understanding. They simply can't continue with all this concealment and evasion.

KROGSTAD All right; if you want to take that chance. But there is one thing I *can* do, and I'll do that right now.

MRS. LINDE (*listening*) But hurry! Go! The dance is over. We aren't safe another minute.

KROGSTAD I'll be waiting for you downstairs.

MRS. LINDE Yes, do. You must see me home.

KROGSTAD I've never been so happy in my whole life. (*He leaves through the front door. The door between the living room and the front hall remains open.*)

MRS. LINDE (*straightens up the room a little and gets her things ready*) What a change! Oh yes!—what a change! People to work for—to live for—a home to bring happiness to. I can't wait to get to work—! If only they'd come soon—(*Listens.*) Ah, there they are. Get my coat on—(*Puts on her coat and hat.*)

(HELMER's *and* NORA's *voices are heard outside. A key is turned in the lock, and* HELMER *almost forces* NORA *into the hall. She is dressed in her Italian costume, with a big black shawl over her shoulders. He is in evening dress under an open black cloak.*)

NORA (*in the door, still resisting*) No, no, no! I don't want to! I want to go back upstairs. I don't want to leave so early.

HELMER But dearest Nora—

NORA Oh please, Torvald—please! I'm asking you as nicely as I can—just another hour!

HELMER Not another minute, sweet. You know we agreed. There now. Get inside. You'll catch a cold out here. (*She still resists, but he guides her gently into the room.*)

MRS. LINDE Good evening.

NORA Kristine!

HELMER Ah, Mrs. Linde. Still here?

MRS. LINDE I know. I really should apologize, but I so much wanted to see Nora in her costume.

NORA You've been waiting up for me?

MRS. LINDE Yes, unfortunately I didn't get here in time. You were already upstairs, but I just didn't feel like leaving till I had seen you.

HELMER (*removing* NORA's *shawl*) Yes, do take a good look at her, Mrs. Linde. I think I may say she's worth looking at. Isn't she lovely?

MRS. LINDE   She certainly is—

HELMER   Isn't she a miracle of loveliness, though? That was the general opinion at the party, too. But dreadfully obstinate—that she is, the sweet little thing. What can we do about that? Will you believe it—I practically had to use force to get her away.

NORA   Oh Torvald, you're going to be sorry you didn't give me even half an hour more.

HELMER   See what I mean, Mrs. Linde? She dances the tarantella —she is a tremendous success—quite deservedly so, though perhaps her performance was a little too natural—I mean, more than could be reconciled with the rules of art. But all right! The point is: she's a success, a tremendous success. So should I let her stay after that? Weaken the effect? Of course not. So I take my lovely little Capri girl—I might say, my capricious little Capri girl— under my arm—a quick turn around the room—a graceful bow in all directions, and—as they say in the novels—the beautiful apparition is gone. A finale should always be done for effect, Mrs. Linde, but there doesn't seem to be any way of getting that into Nora's head. Poooh—! It's hot in here. (*Throws his cloak down on a chair and opens the door to his room.*) Why, it's dark in here! Of course. Excuse me—(*Goes inside and lights a couple of candles.*)

NORA   (*in a hurried, breathless whisper*)   Well?

MRS. LINDE   (*in a low voice*)   I have talked to him.

NORA   And—?

MRS. LINDE   Nora—you've got to tell your husband everything.

NORA   (*no expression in her voice*)   I knew it.

MRS. LINDE   You have nothing to fear from Krogstad. But you must speak.

NORA   I'll say nothing.

MRS. LINDE   Then the letter will.

NORA   Thank you, Kristine. Now I know what I have to do. Shh!

HELMER   (*returning*)   Well, Mrs. Linde, have you looked your fill?

MRS. LINDE   Yes. And now I'll say goodnight.

HELMER   So soon? Is that your knitting?

MRS. LINDE   (*takes it*)   Yes, thank you. I almost forgot.

HELMER   So you knit, do you?

MRS. LINDE   Oh yes.

HELMER   You know—you ought to take up embroidery instead.

MRS. LINDE   Oh? Why?

HELMER   Because it's so much more beautiful. Look. You hold the embroidery so—in your left hand. Then with your right you move the needle—like this—in an easy, elongated arc—you see?

MRS. LINDE   Maybe you're right—

HELMER   Knitting, on the other hand, can never be anything but ugly. Look here: arms pressed close to the sides—the needles going up and down—there's something Chinese about it somehow—. That really was an excellent champagne they served us tonight.

MRS. LINDE   Well, goodnight! Nora. And don't be obstinate any more.

HELMER   Well said, Mrs. Linde!

MRS. LINDE   Goodnight, sir.

HELMER   (*sees her to the front door*)   Goodnight, goodnight. I hope you'll get home all right? I'd be very glad to—but of course you don't have far to walk, do you? Goodnight, goodnight. (*She leaves. He closes the door behind her and returns to the living room.*) There! At last we got rid of her. She really is an incredible bore, that woman.

NORA   Aren't you very tired, Torvald?

HELMER   No, not in the least.

NORA   Not sleepy either?

HELMER   Not at all. Quite the opposite. I feel enormously—animated. How about you? Yes, you do look tired and sleepy.

NORA   Yes, I am very tired. Soon I'll be asleep.

HELMER   What did I tell you? I was right, wasn't I? Good thing I didn't let you stay any longer.

NORA   Everything you do is right.

HELMER   (*kissing her forehead*)   Now my little lark is talking like a human being. But did you notice what splended spirits Rank was in tonight?

NORA   Was he? I didn't notice. I didn't get to talk with him.

HELMER   Nor did I—hardly. But I haven't seen him in such a good mood for a long time. (*Looks at her, comes closer to her.*) Ah! It does feel good to be back in our own home again, to be quite alone with you—my young, lovely, ravishing woman!

NORA   Don't look at me like that, Torvald!

HELMER   Am I not to look at my most precious possession? All that loveliness that is mine, nobody's but mine, all of it mine.

NORA   (*walks to the other side of the table*)   I won't have you talk to me like that tonight.

HELMER   (*follows her*)   The Tarantella is still in your blood. I can tell. That only makes you all the more alluring. Listen! The guests are beginning to leave. (*Softly.*) Nora—soon the whole house will be quiet.

NORA   Yes, I hope so.

HELMER   Yes, don't you, my darling? Do you know—when I'm at a party with you, like tonight—do you know why I hardly ever talk to you, why I keep away from you, only look at you once in a while—a few stolen glances—do you know why I do that? It's because I pretend that you are my secret love, my young, secret bride-to-be, and nobody has the slightest suspicion that there is anything between us.

NORA Yes, I know. All your thoughts are with me.

HELMER Then when we're leaving and I lay your shawl around your delicate young shoulders—around that wonderful curve of your neck—then I imagine you're my young bride, that we're coming away from the wedding, that I am taking you to my home for the first time—that I am alone with you for the first time— quite alone with you, you young, trembling beauty! I have desired you all evening—there hasn't been a longing in me that hasn't been for you. When you were dancing the tarantella, chasing, inviting—my blood was on fire; I couldn't stand it any longer— that's why I brought you down so early—

NORA Leave me now, Torvald. Please! I don't want all this.

HELMER What do you mean? You're only playing your little teasing bird game with me; aren't you, Nora? Don't want to? I'm your husband, aren't I?

(There is a knock on the front door.)

NORA *(with a start)* Did you hear that—?

HELMER *(on his way to the hall)* Who is it?

RANK *(outside)* It's me. May I come in for a moment?

HELMER *(in a low voice, annoyed)* Oh, what does he want now? *(Aloud.)* Just a minute. *(Opens the door.)* Well! How good of you not to pass by our door.

RANK I thought I heard your voice, so I felt like saying hello. *(Looks around.)* Ah yes—this dear, familiar room. What a cozy, comfortable place you have here, you two.

HELMER Looked to me as if you were quite comfortable upstairs too.

RANK I certainly was. Why not? Why not enjoy all you can in this world? As much as you can for as long as you can, anyway. Excellent wine.

HELMER The champagne, particularly.

RANK You noticed that too? Incredible how much I managed to put away.

NORA Torvald drank a lot of champagne tonight, too.

RANK Did he?

NORA Yes, he did, and then he's always so much fun afterwards.

RANK Well, why not have some fun in the evening after a well spent day?

HELMER Well spent? I'm afraid I can't claim that.

RANK (*slapping him lightly on the shoulder*) But you see, I can!

NORA Dr. Rank, I believe you must have been conducting a scientific test today.

RANK Exactly.

HELMER What do you know—little Nora talking about scientific tests!

NORA May I congratulate you on the result?

RANK You may indeed.

NORA It was a good one?

RANK The best possible for both doctor and patient—certainty.

NORA (*a quick query*) Certainty?

RANK Absolute certainty. So why shouldn't I have myself an enjoyable evening afterwards?

NORA I quite agree with you, Dr. Rank. You should.

HELMER And so do I. If only you don't pay for it tomorrow.

RANK Oh well—you get nothing for nothing in this world.

NORA Dr. Rank—you are fond of costume parties, aren't you?

RANK Yes, particularly when there is a reasonable number of amusing disguises.

NORA Listen—what are the two of us going to be the next time?

HELMER You frivolous little thing! Already thinking about the next party!

RANK You and I? That's easy. You'll be Fortune's Child.

HELMER Yes, but what is a fitting costume for that?

RANK Let your wife appear just the way she always is.

HELMER Beautiful. Very good indeed. But how about yourself? Don't you know what you'll go as?

RANK Yes, my friend. I know precisely what I'll be.

HELMER Yes?

RANK At the next masquerade I'll be invisible.

HELMER That's a funny idea.

RANK There's a certain black hat—you've heard about the hat that makes you invisible, haven't you? You put that on, and nobody can see you.

HELMER (*suppressing a smile*) I guess that's right.

RANK But I'm forgetting what I came for. Helmer, give me a cigar —one of your dark Havanas.

HELMER With the greatest pleasure. (*Offers him his case.*)

RANK (*takes one and cuts off the tip*) Thanks.

NORA (*striking a match*) Let me give you a light.

RANK Thanks. (*She holds the match; he lights his cigar.*) And now goodbye!

HELMER Goodbye, goodbye, my friend.

NORA Sleep well, Dr. Rank.

RANK   I thank you.

NORA   Wish me the same.

RANK   You? Well, if you really want me to—. Sleep well. And thanks for the light. (*He nods to both of them and goes out.*)

HELMER (*in a low voice*)   He had had quite a bit to drink.

NORA (*absently*)   Maybe so.

(HELMER *takes out his keys and goes out into the hall.*)

NORA   Torvald—what are you doing out there?

HELMER   Emptying the mailbox. It is quite full. There wouldn't be room for the newspapers in the morning—

NORA   Are you going to work tonight?

HELMER   You know very well I won't.—Say! What's this? Somebody's been at the lock.

NORA   The lock—?

HELMER   Yes. Why, I wonder. I hate to think that any of the maids—. Here's a broken hairpin. It's one of yours. Nora.

NORA (*quickly*)   Then it must be one of the children.

HELMER   You better make damn sure they stop that. Hm, hm.— There! I got it open, finally. (*Gathers up the mail, calls out to the kitchen.*) Helene?—Oh Helene—turn out the light here in the hall, will you? (*He comes back into the living room and closes the door.*) Look how it's been piling up. (*Shows her the bundle of letters. Starts leafing through it.*) What's this?

NORA (*by the window*)   The letter! Oh no, no, Torvald!

HELMER   Two calling cards—from Rank.

NORA   From Dr. Rank?

HELMER (*looking at them*)   "Doctor medicinae Rank." They were on top. He must have put them there when he left just now.

NORA   Anything written on them?

HELMER   A black cross above the name. What a macabre idea. Like announcing his own death.

NORA   That's what it is.

HELMER   Hm? You know about this? Has he said anything to you?

NORA   That card means he has said goodbye to us. He'll lock himself up to die.

HELMER   My poor friend. I knew of course he wouldn't be with me very long. But so soon—. And hiding himself away like a wounded animal—

NORA   When it has to be, it's better it happens without words. Don't you think so, Torvald?

HELMER (*walking up and down*)   He'd grown so close to us. I find it hard to think of him as gone. With his suffering and loneliness he was like a clouded background for our happy sunshine.

Well, it may be better this way. For him, at any rate. (*Stops.*) And perhaps for us, too, Nora. For now we have nobody but each other. (*Embraces her.*) Oh you—my beloved wife! I feel I just can't hold you close enough. Do you know, Nora—many times I have wished some great danger threatened you, so I could risk my life and blood and everything—everything, for your sake.

NORA (*frees herself and says in a strong and firm voice*) I think you should go and read your letters now, Torvald.

HELMER No, no—not tonight. I want to be with you, my darling.

NORA With the thought of your dying friend—?

HELMER You are right. This has shaken both of us. Something not beautiful has come between us. Thoughts of death and dissolution. We must try to get over it—out of it. Till then—we'll each go to our own room.

NORA (*her arms around his neck*) Torvald—goodnight! Goodnight!

HELMER (*kisses her forehead*) Goodnight, my little songbird. Sleep well, Nora. Now I'll read my letters. (*He goes into his room, carrying the mail. Closes the door.*)

NORA (*her eyes desperate, her hands groping, finds Helmer's black cloak and throws it around her; she whispers, quickly, brokenly, hoarsely*) Never see him again. Never. Never. Never. (*Puts her shawl over her head.*) And never see the children again, either. Never; never.—The black, icy water—fathomless—this—! If only it was all over.—Now he has it. Now he's reading it. No, no; not yet. Torvald—goodbye—you—the children—

(*She is about to hurry through the hall, when* HELMER *flings open the door to his room and stands there with an open letter in his hand.*)

HELMER Nora!

NORA (*cries out*) Ah—!

HELMER What is it? You know what's in this letter?

NORA Yes, I do! Let me go! Let me out!

HELMER (*holds her back*). Where do you think you're going?

NORA (*trying to tear herself loose from him*) I won't let you save me, Torvald!

HELMER (*tumbles back*). True! Is it true what he writes? Oh my God! No, no—this can't possibly be true.

NORA It is true. I have loved you more than anything else in the whole world.

HELMER Oh, don't give me any silly excuses.

NORA (*taking a step towards him*) Torvald—!

HELMER You wretch! What have you done!

NORA Let me go. You are not to sacrifice yourself for me. You are not to take the blame.

HELMER No more playacting. (*Locks the door to the front hall.*) You'll stay here and answer me. Do you understand what you have done? Answer me! Do you understand?

NORA (*gazes steadily at him with an increasingly frozen expression*) Yes. Now I'm beginning to understand.

HELMER (*walking up and down*) What a dreadful awakening. All these years—all these eight years—she, my pride and my joy—a hypocrite, a liar—oh worse! worse!—a criminal! Oh, the bottomless ugliness in all this! Damn! Damn! Damn!

(NORA, *silent, keeps gazing at him.*)

HELMER (*stops in front of her*) I ought to have guessed that something like this would happen. I should have expected it. All your father's loose principles—Silence! You have inherited every one of your father's loose principles. No religion, no morals, no sense of duty—. Now I am being punished for my leniency with him. I did it for your sake, and this is how you pay me back.

NORA Yes. This is how.

HELMER You have ruined all my happiness. My whole future— that's what you have destroyed. Oh, it's terrible to think about. I am at the mercy of an unscrupulous man. He can do with me whatever he likes, demand anything of me, command me and dispose of me just as he pleases—I dare not say a word! To go down so miserably, to be destroyed—all because of an irresponsible woman!

NORA When I am gone from the world, you'll be free.

HELMER No noble gestures, please. Your father was always full of such phrases too. What good would it do me if you were gone from the world, as you put it? Not the slightest good at all. He could still make the whole thing public, and if he did, people would be likely to think I had been your accomplice. They might even think it was my idea—that it was I who urged you to do it! And for all this I have you to thank—you, whom I've borne on my hands through all the years of our marriage. *Now* do you understand what you've done to me?

NORA (*with cold calm*) Yes.

HELMER I just can't get it into my head that this is happening; it's all so incredible. But we have to come to terms with it somehow. Take your shawl off. Take it off, I say! I have to satisfy him one way or another. The whole affair must be kept quiet at whatever cost.—And as far as you and I are concerned, nothing must seem to have changed. I'm talking about appearances, of course. You'll go on living here; that goes without saying. But I won't let you bring up the children; I dare not trust you with them. —Oh! Having to say this to one I have loved so much, and whom I still—! But all that is past. It's not a question of happiness any more but of hanging on to what can be salvaged—pieces, appearances—(*The doorbell rings.*)

HELMER (*jumps*) What's that? So late. Is the worst—? Has he—! Hide, Nora! Say you're sick.

NORA *doesn't move.* HELMER *opens the door to the hall.*

THE MAID (*half dressed, out in the hall*) A letter for your wife, sir.

HELMER Give it to me. (*Takes the letter and closes the door.*) Yes, it's from him. But I won't let you have it. I'll read it myself.

NORA Yes—you read it.

HELMER (*by the lamp*) I hardly dare. Perhaps we're lost, both you and I. No; I've got to know. (*Tears the letter open, glances through it, looks at an enclosure; a cry of joy.*) Nora!

(NORA *looks at him with a question in her eyes.*)

HELMER Nora!—No, I must read it again.—Yes, yes; it is so! I'm saved! Nora, I'm saved!

NORA And I?

HELMER You too, of course; we're both saved, both you and I. Look! He's returning your note. He writes that he's sorry, he regrets, a happy turn in his life—oh, it doesn't matter what he writes. We're saved, Nora! Nobody can do anything to you now. Oh Nora, Nora—. No, I want to get rid of this disgusting thing first. Let me see—(*Looks at the signature.*) No, I don't want to see it. I don't want it to be more than a bad dream, the whole thing. (*Tears up the note and both letters, throws the pieces in the stove, and watches them burn.*) There! Now it's gone.—He wrote that ever since Christmas Eve—. Good God, Nora, these must have been three terrible days for you.

NORA I have fought a hard fight these last three days.

HELMER And been in agony and seen no other way out than—. No, we won't think of all that ugliness. We'll just rejoice and tell ourselves it's over, it's all over! Oh, listen to me, Nora. You don't seem to understand. It's over. What *is* it? Why do you look like that—that frozen expression on your face? Oh my poor little Nora, don't you think I know what it is? You can't make yourself believe that I have forgiven you. But I have, Nora; I swear to you, I have forgiven you for everything. Of course I know that what you did was for love of me.

NORA That is true.

HELMER You have loved me the way a wife ought to love her husband. You just didn't have the wisdom to judge the means. But do you think I love you any less because you don't know how to act on your own? Of course not. Just lean on me. I'll advise you; I'll guide you. I wouldn't be a man if I didn't find you twice as attractive because of your womanly helplessness. You mustn't pay any attention to the hard words I said to you right at first. It was just that first shock when I thought everything was collapsing all around me. I have forgiven you, Nora. I swear to you—I really have forgiven you.

NORA I thank you for your forgiveness. (*She goes out through the door, right.*)

HELMER No, stay—(*Looks into the room she entered.*) What are you doing in there?

NORA (*within*) Getting out of my costume.

HELMER (*by the open door*) Good, good. Try to calm down and compose yourself, my poor little frightened songbird. Rest safely; I have broad wings to cover you with. (*Walks around near the door.*) What a nice and cozy home we have, Nora. Here's shelter for you. Here I'll keep you safe like a hunted dove I have rescued from the hawk's talons. Believe me: I'll know how to quiet your beating heart. It will happen by and by, Nora; you'll see. Why, tomorrow you'll look at all this in quite a different light. And soon everything will be just the way it was before. I won't need to keep reassuring you that I have forgiven you; you'll feel it yourself. Did you really think I could have abandoned you, or even reproached you? Oh, you don't know a real man's heart, Nora. There is something unspeakably sweet and satisfactory for a man to know deep in himself that he has forgiven his wife—forgiven her in all the fullness of his honest heart. You see, that way she becomes his very own all over again—in a double sense, you might say. He has, so to speak, given her a second birth; it is as if she had become his wife and his child, both. From now on that's what you'll be to me, you lost and helpless creature. Don't worry about a thing, Nora. Only be frank with me, and I'll be your will and your conscience.—What's this? You're not in bed? You've changed your dress—!

NORA (*in an everyday dress*) Yes, Torvald. I have changed my dress.

HELMER But why—now—this late—?

NORA I'm not going to sleep tonight.

HELMER But my dear Nora—

NORA (*looks at her watch*) It isn't all that late. Sit down here with me, Torvald. You and I have much to talk about. (*Sits down at the table.*)

HELMER   Nora—what is this all about? That rigid face—

NORA   Sit down. This will take a while. I have much to say to you.

HELMER (*sits down, facing her across the table*)   You worry me, Nora. I don't understand you.

NORA   No, that's just it. You don't understand me. And I have never understood you—not till tonight. No, don't interrupt me. Just listen to what I have to say.—This is a settling of accounts, Torvald.

HELMER   What do you mean by that?

NORA (*after a brief silence*)   Doesn't one thing strike you, now that we are sitting together like this?

HELMER   What would that be?

NORA   We have been married for eight years. Doesn't it occur to you that this is the first time that you and I, husband and wife, are having a serious talk?

HELMER   Well—serious—. What do you mean by that?

NORA   For eight whole years—longer, in fact—ever since we first met, we have never talked seriously to each other about a single serious thing.

HELMER   You mean I should forever have been telling you about worries you couldn't have helped me with anyway?

NORA   I am not talking about worries. I'm saying we have never tried seriously to get to the bottom of anything together.

HELMER   But dearest Nora, I hardly think that would have been something *you*—

NORA   That's the whole point. You have never understood me. Great wrong has been done to me, Torvald. First by Daddy and then by you.

HELMER   What! By us two? We who have loved you more deeply than anyone else?

NORA (*shakes her head*)   You never loved me—neither Daddy nor you. You only thought it was fun to be in love with me.

HELMER   But, Nora—what an expression to use!

NORA   That's the way it has been, Torvald. When I was home with Daddy, he told me all his opinions, and so they became my opinions too. If I disagreed with him I kept it to myself, for he wouldn't have liked that. He called me his little doll baby, and he played with me the way I played with my dolls. Then I came to your house—

HELMER   What a way to talk about our marriage!

NORA (*imperturbably*)   I mean that I passed from Daddy's hands into yours. You arranged everything according to your taste, and so I came to share it—or I pretended to; I'm not sure which. I think it was a little of both, now one and now the other. When I look back on it now, it seems to me I've been living here like a pauper—just a hand-to-mouth kind of existence. I have earned my keep by doing tricks for you, Torvald. But that's the way you wanted it. You have great sins against me to answer for, Daddy and you. It's your fault that nothing has become of me.

HELMER Nora, you're being both unreasonable and ungrateful. Haven't you been happy here?

NORA No, never. I thought I was, but I wasn't.

HELMER Not—not happy!

NORA No; just having fun. And you have always been very good to me. But our home has never been more than a playroom. I have been your doll wife here, just the way I used to be Daddy's doll child. And the children have been my dolls. I thought it was fun when you played with me, just as they thought it was fun when I played with them. That's been our marriage, Torvald.

HELMER There is something in what you are saying—exaggerated and hysterical though it is. But from now on things will be different. Playtime is over; it's time for growing up.

NORA Whose growing up—mine or the children's?

HELMER Both yours and the children's, Nora darling.

NORA Oh Torvald, you're not the man to bring me up to be the right kind of wife for you.

HELMER How can you say that?

NORA And I—? What qualifications do I have for bringing up the children?

HELMER Nora!

NORA You said so yourself a minute ago—that you didn't dare to trust me with them.

HELMER In the first flush of anger, yes. Surely, you're not going to count that.

NORA But you were quite right. I am *not* qualified. Something else has to come first. Somehow I have to grow up myself. And you are not the man to help me do that. That's a job I have to do by myself. And that's why I'm leaving you.

HELMER (*jumps up*) What did you say!

NORA I have to be by myself if I am to find out about myself and about all the other things too. So I can't stay here with you any longer.

HELMER Nora, Nora!

NORA I'm leaving now. I'm sure Kristine will put me up for tonight.

HELMER You're out of your mind! I won't let you! I forbid you!

NORA   You can't forbid me anything any more; it won't do any good. I'm taking my own things with me. I won't accept anything from you, either now or later.

HELMER   But this is madness!

NORA   Tomorrow I'm going home—I mean back to my old home town. It will be easier for me to find some kind of job there.

HELMER   Oh, you blind, inexperienced creature—!

NORA   I must see to it that I get experience, Torvald.

HELMER   Leaving your home, your husband, your children! Not a thought of what people will say!

NORA   I can't worry about that. All I know is that I have to leave.

HELMER   Oh, this is shocking! Betraying your most sacred duties like this!

NORA   And what do you consider my most sacred duties?

HELMER   Do I need to tell you that? They are your duties to your husband and your children.

NORA   I have other duties equally sacred.

HELMER   You do not. What duties would they be?

NORA   My duties to myself.

HELMER   You are a wife and a mother before you are anything else.

NORA   I don't believe that any more. I believe I am first of all a human being, just as much as you—or at any rate that I must try to become one. Oh, I know very well that most people agree with you, Torvald, and that it says something like that in all the books. But what people say and what the books say is no longer enough for me. I have to think about these things myself and see if I can't find the answers.

HELMER   You mean to tell me you don't know what your proper place in your own home is? Don't you have a reliable guide in such matters? Don't you have religion?

NORA   Oh but Torvald—I don't really know what religion is.

HELMER   What are you saying!

NORA   All I know is what the Reverend Hansen told me when he prepared me for confirmation. He said that religion was *this* and it was *that.* When I get by myself, away from here, I'll have to look into that, too. I have to decide if what the Reverend Hansen said was right, or anyway if it is right for *me.*

HELMER   Oh, this is unheard of in a young woman! If religion can't guide you, let me appeal to your conscience. For surely you have moral feelings? Or—answer me—maybe you don't?

NORA   Well, you see, Torvald, I don't really know what to say. I just don't know. I am confused about these things. All I know is that my ideas are quite different from yours. I have just found out that the laws are different from what I thought they were, but in no way can I get it into my head that those laws are right. A woman shouldn't have the right to spare her dying old father or save her husband's life! I just can't believe that.

HELMER   You speak like a child. You don't understand the society you live in.

NORA   No, I don't. But I want to find out about it. I have to make up my mind who is right, society or I.

HELMER   You are sick, Nora; you have a fever. I really don't think you are in your right mind.

NORA   I have never felt so clearheaded and sure of myself as I do tonight.

HELMER   And clearheaded and sure of yourself you're leaving your husband and children?

NORA   Yes.

HELMER   Then there is only one possible explanation.

NORA   What?

HELMER   You don't love me any more.

NORA   No, that's just it.

HELMER   Nora! Can you say that?

NORA   I am sorry, Torvald, for you have always been so good to me. But I can't help it. I don't love you any more.

HELMER   (*with forced composure*)   And this too is a clear and sure conviction?

NORA   Completely clear and sure. That's why I don't want to stay here any more.

HELMER   And are you ready to explain to me how I came to forfeit your love?

NORA   Certainly I am. It was tonight, when the wonderful didn't happen. That was when I realized you were not the man I thought you were.

HELMER   You have to explain. I don't understand.

NORA   I have waited patiently for eight years, for I wasn't such a fool that I thought the wonderful is something that happens any old day. Then this—thing—came crashing in on me, and then there wasn't a doubt in my mind that now—now comes the wonderful. When Krogstad's letter was in that mailbox, never for a moment did it even occur to me that you would submit to his conditions. I was so absolutely certain that you would say to him: make the whole thing public—tell everybody. And when that had happened—

HELMER   Yes, then what? When I had surrendered my wife to shame and disgrace—!

NORA   When that had happened, I was absolutely certain that you would stand up and take the blame and say, "I'm the guilty one. '

HELMER Nora!

NORA You mean I never would have accepted such a sacrifice from you? Of course not. But what would my protests have counted against yours. *That* was the wonderful I was hoping for in terror. And to prevent that I was going to kill myself.

HELMER I'd gladly work nights and days for you, Nora—endure sorrow and want for your sake. But nobody sacrifices his *honor* for his love.

NORA A hundred thousand women have done so.

HELMER Oh, you think and talk like a silly child.

NORA All right. But you don't think and talk like the man I can live with. When you had gotten over your fright—not because of what threatened *me* but because of the risk to *you*—and the whole danger was past, then you acted as if nothing at all had happened. Once again I was your little songbird, your doll, just as before, only now you had to handle her even more carefully, because she was so frail and weak. (*Rises.*) Torvald—that moment I realized that I had been living here for eight years with a stranger and had borne him three children—Oh, I can't stand thinking about it! I feel like tearing myself to pieces!

HELMER (*heavily*) I see it, I see it. An abyss has opened up between us.—Oh but Nora—surely it can be filled?

NORA The way I am now I am no wife for you.

HELMER I have it in me to change.

NORA Perhaps—if your doll is taken from you.

HELMER To part—to part from you! No, no, Nora! I can't grasp that thought!

NORA (*goes out, right*) All the more reason why it has to be. (*She returns with her outdoor clothes and a small bag, which she sets down on the chair by the table.*)

HELMER Nora, Nora! Not now! Wait till tomorrow.

NORA (*putting on her coat*) I can't spend the night in a stranger's rooms.

HELMER But couldn't we live here together like brother and sister—?

NORA (*tying on her hat*) You know very well that wouldn't last long—. (*Wraps her shawl around her.*) Goodbye, Torvald. I don't want to see the children. I know I leave them in better hands than mine. The way I am now I can't be anything to them.

HELMER But some day, Nora—some day—?

NORA How can I tell? I have no idea what's going to become of me.

HELMER But you're still my wife, both as you are now and as you will be.

NORA Listen, Torvald—when a wife leaves her husband's house, the way I am doing now, I have heard he has no more legal responsibilities for her. At any rate, I now release you from all responsibility. You are not to feel yourself obliged to me for anything, and I have no obligations to you. There has to be full freedom on both sides. Here is your ring back. Now give me mine.

HELMER Even this?

NORA Even this.

HELMER Here it is.

NORA There. So now it's over. I'm putting the keys here. The maids know everything about the house—better than I. Tomorrow, after I'm gone, Kristine will come over and pack my things from home. I want them sent after me.

HELMER Over! It's all over! Nora, will you never think of me?

NORA I'm sure I'll often think of you and the children and this house.

HELMER May I write to you, Nora?

NORA No—never. I won't have that.

HELMER But send you things—? You must let me.

NORA Nothing, nothing.

HELMER —help you, when you need help—?

NORA I told you, no; I won't have it. I'll accept nothing from strangers.

HELMER Nora—can I never again be more to you than a stranger?

NORA (*picks up her bag*) Oh Torvald—then the most wonderful of all would have to happen—

HELMER Tell me what that would be—!

NORA For that to happen, both you and I would have to change so that—Oh Torvald, I no longer believe in the wonderful.

HELMER But I *will* believe. Tell me! Change, so that—?

NORA So that our living together would become a true marriage. Goodbye. (*She goes out through the hall.*)

HELMER (*sinks down on a chair near the door and covers his face with his hands*) Nora! Nora! (*Looks around him and gets up.*) All empty. She's gone. (*With sudden hope.*) The most wonderful—?!

(*From downstairs comes the sound of a heavy door slamming shut.*)

✒ MISS JULIE (1888)

AUGUST STRINDBERG (1849–1912)

In 1887 Strindberg wrote one of the great naturalistic plays, *The Father*. In this jungle battle of the sexes, husband and wife are pitted against each other in a death struggle, the winner of which is the predatory emasculating female. Belittled by his spouse, the father, a retired cavalry officer, finds his scientific experiments degraded and his paternity questioned so that in the end there is total victory for the exultant wife and a straightjacket for her raving husband.

One of the earliest exponents of expressionism in his *Dream Play* (1902) and *The Spook* (or *Ghost*) *Sonata* (1907), Strindberg created highly stylized interpretations of the nightmare world of life in extremely complex and difficult plays almost impossible to produce. But of equal, if not greater, importance is Strindberg's portrayal of one of the great emotional struggles of his own life—sex and marriage—in at least three almost unbearably intense dramas, *The Father, The Dance of Death* (1901), and *Miss Julie*. The young Eugene O'Neill in the United States was fascinated by Strindberg and publicly acknowledged the strong influence which the Swedish dramatist had on his own development. The detailed dissection of the human soul, the baring of raw flesh, and the animal snarling and tearing that goes on in Strindberg's marital battlefield, and which the young O'Neill often closely copied, are among the best examples that we have of the techniques of the dramatic naturalist.

Miss Julie is in many ways a terrifying play as it exhibits the conscious degradation of the protagonist who seeks to destroy what she cannot have and is simultaneously destroyed in turn in a kind of reversal from the usual Strindbergian female triumphant. Amidst

441

the eroticisms of the festivities of Midsummer Eve, the long day-night of the Scandinavian summer season, the nightmare of Julie's own depravity takes place. She is out of her element, which is "above stairs," but she must lower herself, having been rejected by her more "proper" lover's refusal to leap at her command, to establish her own female prowess. This time she orders her social inferior, her father's valet, to perform as she bids. The risks are great; the ultimate destruction complete.

Miss Julie is an excellent example of the spine-chilling effect which the naturalistic writer can weave when he chooses to delve into the elements of the inner soul and expose them piece by piece before an audience. The bloody execution of the bird, for no really legitimate reason, parallels the execution of the grovelling Julie, butchered first symbolically by the violation of her body in the self-induced seduction, and then by the razor in the barn, again self-administered, paralleling the sexual "violation" of her aristocratic purity. The natural strength of the more earthy sexual prowess of Jean has triumphed, but only at the "order" of the victim; the artificial strength of Julie's snobbery and spoiled rottenness, the result of her "higher" birth, has been conquered. There is nothing left but death.

Julie almost becomes in the inevitability of her catastrophe a tragic protagonist. She is a product of what nature and society have made her, a kind of hybrid monster, unable to control her fundamental natural sensuous urges. Ready to lower herself to become the wife of an innkeeper, obviously incapable of surviving under such conditions, she finally recognizes what she is and she sees the doom from which there is no escape. She must encounter it alone. Whether or not she rises to sufficient stature as a tragic protagonist may be a question, but there is a size, a certain larger-than-life quality about her, which makes her one of modern drama's most hypnotically fascinating naturalistic heroines.

Miss Julie

STRINDBERG

Translated by Elizabeth Sprigge

CHARACTERS

MISS JULIE, *aged 25*
JEAN, *the valet, aged 30*
KRISTIN, *the cook, aged 35*

SCENE: *The large kitchen of a Swedish manor house in a country district in the eighties.*
Midsummer eve.
The kitchen has three doors, two small ones into JEAN's *and* KRISTIN's *bedrooms, and a large, glass-fronted double one, opening on to a courtyard. This is the only way to the rest of the house.*
Through these glass doors can be seen part of a fountain with a cupid, lilac bushes in flower and the tops of some Lombardy poplars. On one wall are shelves edged with scalloped paper on which are kitchen utensils of copper, iron and tin.
To the left is the corner of a large tiled range and part of its chimney-hood, to the right the end of the servants' dinner table with chairs beside it.
The stove is decorated with birch boughs, the floor strewn with twigs of juniper. On the end of the table is a large Japanese spice jar full of lilac.
There are also an ice-box, a scullery table and a sink. Above the double door hangs a big old-fashioned bell; near it is a speaking-tube.
A fiddle can be heard from the dance in the barn near-by. KRISTIN *is standing at the stove, frying something in a pan. She wears a light-coloured cotton dress and a big apron.*
JEAN *enters, wearing livery and carrying a pair of large riding-boots with spurs, which he puts in a conspicuous place.*

JEAN   Miss Julie's crazy again to-night, absolutely crazy.
KRISTIN   Oh, so you're back, are you?
JEAN   When I'd taken the Count to the station, I came back and dropped in at the Barn for a dance. And who did I see there but our young lady leading off with the gamekeeper. But the moment she sets eyes on me, up she rushes and invites me to waltz with

443

her. And how she waltzed—I've never seen anything like it! She's crazy.

KRISTIN Always has been, but never so bad as this last fortnight since the engagement was broken off.

JEAN Yes, that was a pretty business, to be sure. He's a decent enough chap, too, even if he isn't rich. Oh, but they're choosy! (*Sits down at the end of the table.*) In any case, it's a bit odd that our young—er—lady would rather stay at home with the yokels than go with her father to visit her relations.

KRISTIN Perhaps she feels a bit awkward, after that bust-up with her fiancé.

JEAN Maybe. That chap had some guts, though. Do you know the sort of thing that was going on, Kristin? I saw it with my own eyes, though I didn't let on I had.

KRISTIN You saw them . . . ?

JEAN Didn't I just! Came across the pair of them one evening in the stableyard. Miss Julie was doing what she called "training" him. Know what that was? Making him jump over her riding-whip—the way you teach a dog. He did it twice and got a cut each time for his pains, but when it came to the third go, he snatched the whip out of her hand and broke it into simthereens. And then he cleared off.

KRISTIN What goings on! I never did!

JEAN Well, that's how it was with that little affair . . . Now, what have you got for me, Kristin? Something tasty?

KRISTIN (*serving from the pan to his plate*) Well, it's just a little bit of kidney I cut off their joint.

JEAN (*smelling it*) Fine! That's my special delice. (*Feels the plate.*) But you might have warmed the plate.

KRISTIN When you choose to be finicky you're worse than the Count himself. (*Pulls his hair affectionately.*)

JEAN (*crossly*) Stop pulling my hair. You know how sensitive I am.

KRISTIN There, there! It's only love, you know.

(JEAN *eats.* KRISTIN *brings a bottle of beer.*)

JEAN Beer on Midsummer Eve? No thanks! I've got something better than that. (*From a drawer in the table brings out a bottle of red wine with a yellow seal.*) Yellow seal, see! Now get me a glass. You use a glass with a stem, of course, when you're drinking it straight.

KRISTIN (*giving him a wine-glass*) Lord help the woman who gets you for a husband, you old fusser! (*She puts the beer in the ice-box and sets a small sauce-pan on the stove.*)

JEAN Nonsense! You'll be glad enough to get a fellow as smart as me. And I don't think it's done you any harm people calling me your fiancé. (*Tastes the wine.*) Good. Very good indeed. But not quite warmed enough. (*Warms the glass in his hand.*) We bought this in Dijon. Four francs the litre without the bottle, and duty on top of that. What are you cooking now? It stinks.

KRISTIN Some bloody muck Miss Julie wants for Diana.

JEAN You should be more refined in your speech, Kristin. But why should you spend a holiday cooking for that bitch? Is she sick or what?

KRISTIN Yes, she's sick. She sneaked out with the pug at the lodge and got in the usual mess. And that, you know, Miss Julie won't have.

JEAN Miss Julie's too high-and-mighty in some respects, and not enough in others, just like her mother before her. The Countess was more at home in the kitchen and cowsheds than anywhere else, but would she ever go driving with only one horse? She went round with her cuffs filthy, but she had to have the coronet on the cuff-links. Our young lady—to come back to her—hasn't any proper respect for herself or her position. I mean she isn't refined. In the Barn just now she dragged the gamekeeper away from Anna and made him dance with her—no waiting to be asked. We wouldn't do a thing like that. But that's what happens when the gentry try to behave like the common people—they become common . . . Still, she's a fine girl. Smashing! What shoulders! And what—er etcetera!

KRISTIN Oh come off it! I know what Clara says, and she dresses her.

JEAN Clara? Pooh, you're all jealous! But I've been out riding with her . . . and as for her dancing!

KRISTIN Listen, Jean. You will dance with me, won't you, as soon as I'm through?

JEAN Of course I will.

KRISTIN Promise?

JEAN Promise? When I say I'll do a thing I do it. Well, thanks for the supper. It was a real treat. (*Corks the bottle.*)

(JULIE *appears in the doorway, speaking to someone outside.*)

JULIE I'll be back in a moment. Don't wait.

(JEAN *slips the bottle into the drawer and rises respectfully.* JULIE *enters and joins* KRISTIN *at the stove.*)

Well, have you made it? (KRISTIN *signs that* JEAN *is near them.*)

JEAN (*gallantly*) Have you ladies got some secret?

JULIE (*flipping his face with her handkerchief*) You're very inquisitive.

JEAN What a delicious smell! Violets.

JULIE (*coquettishly*) Impertinence! Are you an expert of scent too? I must say you know how to dance. Now don't look. Go away. (*The music of a schottische begins.*)

JEAN (*with impudent politeness*) Is it some witches' brew you're cooking on Midsummer Eve? Something to tell your stars by, so you can see your future?

JULIE (*sharply*) If you could see that you'd have good eyes. (*To* KRISTIN.) Put it in a bottle and cork it tight. Come and dance this schottische with me, Jean.

JEAN (*hesitating*) I don't want to be rude, but I've promised to dance this one with Kristin.

JULIE Well, she can have another, can't you, Kristin? You'll lend me Jean, won't you?

KRISTIN (*bottling*) It's nothing to do with me. When you're so condescending, Miss, it's not his place to say no. Go on, Jean, and thank Miss Julie for the honour.

JEAN Frankly speaking, Miss, and no offence meant, I wonder if it's wise for you to dance twice running with the same partner, specially as those people are so ready to jump to conclusions.

JULIE (*flaring up*) What did you say? What sort of conclusions? What do you mean?

JEAN (*meekly*) As you choose not to understand, Miss Julie, I'll have to speak more plainly. It looks bad to show a preference for one of your retainers when they're all hoping for the same unusual favour.

JULIE Show a preference! The very idea! I'm surprised at you. I'm doing the people an honour by attending their ball when I'm mistress of the house, but if I'm really going to dance, I mean to have a partner who can lead and doesn't make me look ridiculous.

JEAN If those are your orders, Miss, I'm at your service.

JULIE (*gently*) Don't take it as an order. To-night we're all just people enjoying a party. There's no question of class. So now give me your arm. Don't worry, Kristin. I shan't steal your sweetheart.

(JEAN *gives* JULIE *his arm and leads her out.*)

Left alone, KRISTIN *plays her scene in an unhurried, natural way, humming to the tune of the schottische, played on a distant violin. She clears* JEAN's *place, washes up and puts things away, then takes off her apron, brings out a small mirror from a drawer, props it against the jar of lilac, lights a candle, warms a small pair of tongs and curls her fringe. She goes to the door and listens, then turning back to the table finds* MISS JULIE's *forgotten handkerchief. She smells it, then meditatively smooths it out and folds it.*

(Enter JEAN.*)*

JEAN   She really *is* crazy. What a way to dance! With people standing grinning at her too from behind the doors. What's got into her, Kristin?

KRISTIN   Oh, it's just her time coming on. She's always queer then. Are you going to dance with me now?

JEAN   Then you're not wild with me for cutting that one?

KRISTIN   You know I'm not—for a little thing like that. Besides, I know my place.

JEAN   *(putting his arm around her waist)*   You're a sensible girl, Kristin, and you'll make a very good wife . . .

(Enter JULIE, *unpleasantly surprised.)*

JULIE   *(with forced gaiety)*   You're a fine beau—running away from your partner.

JEAN   Not away, Miss Julie, but as you see, back to the one I deserted.

JULIE   *(changing her tone)*   You really can dance, you know. But why are you wearing your livery on a holiday? Take it off at once.

JEAN   Then I must ask you to go away for a moment, Miss. My black coat's here. *(Indicates it hanging on the door to his room.)*

JULIE   Are you so shy of me—just over changing a coat? Go into your room then—or stay here and I'll turn my back.

JEAN   Excuse me then, Miss. *(He goes to his room and is partly visible as he changes his coat.)*

JULIE   Tell me, Kristin, is Jean your fiancé? You seem very intimate.

KRISTIN   My fiancé? Yes, if you like. We call it that.

JULIE   Call it?

KRISTIN   Well, you've had a fiancé yourself, Miss, and . . .

JULIE   But we really were engaged.

KRISTIN   All the same it didn't come to anything.

*(*JEAN *returns in his black coat.)*

JULIE   Très gentil, Monsieur Jean. Très gentil.

JEAN   Vous voulez plaisanter, Madame.

JULIE   Et vous voulez parler français. Where did you learn it?

JEAN   In Switzerland, when I was sommelier at one of the biggest hotels in Lucerne.

JULIE   You look quite the gentleman in that get-up. Charming. (*Sits at the table.*)

JEAN   Oh, you're just flattering me!

JULIE (*annoyed*)   Flattering you?

JEAN   I'm too modest to believe you would pay real compliments to a man like me, so I must take it you are exaggerating—that this is what's known as flattery.

JULIE   Where on earth did you learn to make speeches like that? Perhaps you've been to the theatre a lot.

JEAN   That's right. And travelled a lot too.

JULIE   But you come from this neighbourhood, don't you?

JEAN   Yes, my father was a labourer on the next estate—the District Attorney's place. I often used to see you, Miss Julie, when you were little, though you never noticed me.

JULIE   Did you really?

JEAN   Yes. One time specially I remember . . . but I can't tell you about that.

JULIE   Oh do! Why not? This is just the time.

JEAN   No, I really can't now. Another time, perhaps.

JULIE   Another time means never. What harm in now?

JEAN   No harm, but I'd rather not.

(*Points to* KRISTIN, *now fast asleep.*)

Look at her.

JULIE   She'll make a charming wife, won't she? I wonder if she snores.

JEAN   No, she doesn't, but she talks in her sleep.

JULIE (*cynically*)   How do you know she talks in her sleep?

JEAN (*brazenly*)   I've heard her.

(*Pause. They look at one another.*)

JULIE   Why don't you sit down?

JEAN   I can't take such a liberty in your presence.

JULIE   Supposing I order you to.

JEAN   I'll obey.

JULIE   Then sit down. No, wait a minute. Will you get me a drink first?

JEAN   I don't know what's in the ice-box. Only beer, I expect.

JULIE   There's no only about it. My taste is so simple I prefer it to wine.

(JEAN *takes a bottle from the ice-box, fetches a glass and plate and serves the beer.*)

JEAN   At your service.

JULIE Thank you. Won't you have some yourself?

JEAN I'm not really a beer-drinker, but if it's an order . . .

JULIE Order? I should have thought it was ordinary manners to keep your partner company.

JEAN That's a good way of putting it.

(He opens another bottle and fetches a glass.)

JULIE Now, drink my health. *(He hesitates.)* I believe the man really is shy.

*(*JEAN *kneels and raises his glass with mock ceremony.)*

JEAN To the health of my lady!

JULIE Bravo! Now kiss my shoe and everything will be perfect. *(He hesitates, then boldly takes hold of her foot and lightly kisses it.)* Splendid. You ought to have been an actor.

JEAN *(rising)* We can't go on like this, Miss Julie. Someone might come in and see us.

JULIE Why would that matter?

JEAN For the simple reason that they'd talk, and if you knew the way their tongues were wagging out there just now, you . . .

JULIE What were they saying? Tell me. Sit down.

JEAN *(sitting)* No offence meant, Miss, but . . . well, their language wasn't nice, and they were hinting . . . oh, you know quite well what. You're not a child, and if a lady's seen drinking alone at night with a man—and a servant at that—then . . .

JULIE Then what? Besides, we're not alone. Kristin's here.

JEAN Yes, asleep.

JULIE I'll wake her up. *(Rises.)* Kristin, are you asleep? (KRISTIN *mumbles in her sleep.)* Kristin! Goodness, how she sleeps!

KRISTIN *(in her sleep)* The Count's boots are cleaned—put the coffee on—yes, yes, at once . . . *(Mumbles incoherently.)*

JULIE *(tweaking her nose)* Wake up, can't you!

JEAN *(sharply)* Let her sleep.

JULIE What?

JEAN When you've been standing at the stove all day you're likely to be tired at night. And sleep should be respected.

JULIE *(changing her tone)* What a nice idea. It does you credit. Thank you for it. *(Holds out her hand to him.)* Now come out and pick some lilac for me.

(During the following, KRISTIN *goes sleepily into her bedroom.)*

JEAN Out with you, Miss Julie?

JULIE Yes.

JEAN It wouldn't do. It really wouldn't.

JULIE I don't know what you mean. You can't possibly imagine that . . .

JEAN I don't, but others do.

JULIE What? That I'm in love with the valet?

JEAN I'm not a conceited man, but such a thing's been known to happen, and to these rustics nothing's sacred.

JULIE You, I take it, are an aristocrat.

JEAN Yes, I am.

JULIE And I am coming down in the world.

JEAN Don't come down, Miss Julie. Take my advice. No one will believe you came down of your own accord. They'll all say you fell.

JULIE I have a higher opinion of our people than you. Come and put it to the test. Come on. (*Gazes into his eyes.*)

JEAN You're very strange, you know.

JULIE Perhaps I am, but so are you. For that matter everything is strange. Life, human beings, everything, just scum drifting about on the water until it sinks—down and down. That reminds me of a dream I sometimes have, in which I'm on top of a pillar and can't see any way of getting down. When I look down I'm dizzy; I have to get down but I haven't the courage to jump. I can't stay there and I long to fall, but I don't fall. There's no respite. There can't be any peace at all for me until I'm down, right down on the ground. And if I did get to the ground I'd want to be under the ground . . . Have you ever felt like that?

JEAN No. In my dream I'm lying under a great tree in a dark wood. I want to get up, up to the top of it, and look out over the bright landscape where the sun is shining and rob that high nest of its golden eggs. And I climb and climb, but the trunk is so thick and smooth and it's so far to the first branch. But I know if I can once reach that first branch I'll go to the top just as if I'm on a ladder. I haven't reached it yet, but I shall get there, even if only in my dreams.

JULIE Here I am chattering about dreams with you. Come on. Only into the park. (*She takes his arm and they go towards the door.*)

JEAN We must sleep on nine midsummer flowers tonight; then our dreams will come true, Miss Julie.

(*They turn at the door. He has a hand to his eye.*)

JULIE Have you got something in your eye? Let me see.

JEAN Oh, it's nothing. Just a speck of dust. It'll be gone in a minute.

JULIE My sleeve must have rubbed against you. Sit down and let me see to it. (*Takes him by the arm and makes him sit down, bends his head back and tries to get the speck out with the corner of her handkerchief.*) Keep still now, quite still. (*Slaps his hand.*) Do as I tell you. Why, I believe you're trembling, big, strong man though you are! (*Feels his biceps.*) What muscles!

JEAN (*warning*) Miss Julie!

JULIE Yes, Monsieur Jean?

JEAN Attention. Je ne suis qu'un homme.

JULIE Will you stay still! There now. It's out. Kiss my hand and say thank you.

JEAN (*rising*) Miss Julie, listen. Kristin's gone to bed now. Will you listen?

JULIE Kiss my hand first.

JEAN Very well, but you'll have only yourself to blame.

JULIE For what?

JEAN For what! Are you still a child at twenty-five? Don't you know it's dangerous to play with fire?

JULIE Not for me. I'm insured.

JEAN (*bluntly*) No, you're not. And even if you are, there's still stuff here to kindle a flame.

JULIE Meaning yourself?

JEAN Yes. Not because I'm me, but because I'm a man and young and . . .

JULIE And good-looking? What incredible conceit! A Don Juan perhaps? Or a Joseph? Good Lord, I do believe you are a Joseph!

JEAN Do you?

JULIE I'm rather afraid so.

(JEAN *goes boldly up and tries to put his arms round her and kiss her. She boxes his ears.*)

How dare you!

JEAN Was that in earnest or a joke?

JULIE In earnest.

JEAN Then what went before was in earnest too. You take your games too seriously and that's dangerous. Anyhow, I'm tired of playing now and beg leave to return to my work. The Count will want his boots first thing and it's past midnight now.

JULIE Put those boots down.

JEAN No. This is my work, which it's my duty to do. But I never undertook to be your playfellow and I never will be. I consider myself too good for that.

JULIE You're proud.

JEAN   In some ways—not all.

JULIE   Have you ever been in love?

JEAN   We don't put it that way, but I've been gone on quite a few girls. And once I went sick because I couldn't have the one I wanted. Sick, I mean, like those princes in the Arabian Nights who couldn't eat or drink for love.

JULIE   Who was she? (*No answer.*) Who was she?

JEAN   You can't force me to tell you that.

JULIE   If I ask as an equal, ask as a—friend? Who was she?

JEAN   You.

JULIE (*sitting*)   How absurd!

JEAN   Yes, ludicrous, if you like. That's the story I wouldn't tell you before, see, but now I will . . . Do you know what the world looks like from below? No, you don't. No more than the hawks and falcons do whose backs one hardly ever sees because they're always soaring up aloft. I lived in a labourer's hovel with seven other children and a pig, out in the grey fields where there isn't a single tree. But from the window I could see the wall round the Count's park with apple-trees above it. That was the Garden of Eden, guarded by many terrible angels with flaming swords. All the same I and the other boys managed to get to the tree of life. Does all this make you despise me?

JULIE   Goodness, all boys steal apples!

JEAN   You say that now, but all the same you do despise me. However, one time I went into the Garden of Eden with my mother to weed the onion beds. Close to the kitchen garden there was a Turkish pavilion hung all over with jasmine and honeysuckle. I hadn't any idea what it was used for, but I'd never seen such a beautiful building. People used to go in and then come out again, and one day the door was left open. I crept up and saw the walls covered with pictures of kings and emperors, and the windows had red curtains with fringes—you know now what the place was, don't you? I . . . (*Breaks off a piece of lilac and holds it for* JULIE *to smell. As he talks, she takes it from him.*) I had never been inside the manor, never seen anything but the church, and this was more beautiful. No matter where my thoughts went, they always came back—to that place. The longing went on growing in me to enjoy it fully, just once. Enfin, I sneaked in, gazed and admired. Then I heard someone coming. There was only one way out for the gentry, but for me there was another and I had no choice but to take it. (JULIE *drops the lilac on the table.*) Then I took to my heels, plunged through the raspberry canes, dashed across the strawberry beds and found myself on the rose terrace. There I saw a pink dress and a pair of white stockings—it was you. I crawled into a weed pile and lay there right under it among prickly thistles and damp rank earth. I watched you walking among the roses and said to myself: "If its true that a thief can get to heaven and be with the angels, it's pretty strange that a labourer's child here on God's earth mayn't come in the park and play with the Count's daughter."

JULIE (*sentimentally*) Do you think all poor children feel the way you did?

JEAN (*taken aback, then rallying*) *All* poor children?...Yes, of course they do. Of course.

JULIE It must be terrible to be poor.

JEAN (*with exaggerated distress*) Oh yes, Miss Julie, yes. A dog may lie on the Countess's sofa, a horse may have his nose stroked by a young lady, but a servant... (*change of tone*) well, yes, now and then you meet one with guts enough to rise in the world, but how often? Anyhow, do you know what I did? Jumped in the millstream with my clothes on, was pulled out and got a hiding. But the next Sunday, when Father and all the rest went to Granny's, I managed to get left behind. Then I washed with soap and hot water, put my best clothes on and went to church so as to see you. I did see you and went home determined to die. But I wanted to die beautifully and peacefully, without any pain. Then I remembered it was dangerous to sleep under an elder bush. We had a big one in full bloom, so I stripped it and climbed into the oats-bin with the flowers. Have you ever noticed how smooth oats are? Soft to touch as human skin... Well, I closed the lid and shut my eyes, fell asleep, and when they woke me I was very ill. But I didn't die, as you see. What I meant by all that, I don't know. There was no hope of winning you—you were simply a symbol of the hopelessness of ever getting out of the class I was born in.

JULIE You put things very well, you know. Did you go to school?

JEAN For a while. But I've read a lot of novels and been to the theatre. Besides, I've heard educated folk talking—that's what's taught me most.

JULIE Do you stand round listening to what we're saying?

JEAN Yes, of course. And I've heard quite a bit too! On the carriage box or rowing the boat. Once I heard you, Miss Julie, and one of your young lady friends...

JULIE Oh! Whatever did you hear?

JEAN Well, it wouldn't be nice to repeat it. And I must say I was pretty startled. I couldn't think where you had learnt such words. Perhaps, at bottom, there isn't as much difference between people as one's led to believe.

JULIE   How dare you! We don't behave as you do when we're engaged.

JEAN   (*looking hard at her*)   Are you sure? It's no use making out so innocent to me.

JULIE   The man I gave my love to was a rotter.

JEAN   That's what you always say—afterwards.

JULIE   Always?

JEAN   I think it must be always. I've heard the expression several times in similar circumstances.

JULIE   What circumstances?

JEAN   Like those in question. The last time . . .

JULIE   (*rising*)   Stop. I don't want to hear any more.

JEAN   Nor did *she*—curiously enough. May I go to bed now, please?

JULIE   (*gently*)   Go to bed on Midsummer Eve?

JEAN   Yes. Dancing with that crowd doesn't really amuse me.

JULIE   Get the key of the boathouse and row me out on the lake. I want to see the sun rise.

JEAN   Would that be wise?

JULIE   You sound as though you're frightened for your reputation.

JEAN   Why not? I don't want to be made a fool of, nor to be sent packing without a character when I'm trying to better myself. Besides, I have Kristin to consider.

JULIE   So now it's Kristin.

JEAN   Yes, but it's you I'm thinking about too. Take my advice and go to bed.

JULIE   Am I to take orders from you?

JEAN   Just this once, for your own sake. Please. It's very late and sleepiness goes to one's head and makes one rash. Go to bed. What's more, if my ears don't deceive me, I hear people coming this way. They'll be looking for me, and if they find us here, you're done for.

(*The* CHORUS *approaches, singing. During the following dialogue the song is heard in snatches, and in full when the peasants enter.*)

Out of the wood two women came,
Tridiri-ralla, tridiri-ra.
The feet of one were bare and cold,
Tridiri-ralla-la.

The other talked of bags of gold,
Tridiri-ralla, tridiri-ra.
But neither had a sou to her name,
Tridiri-ralla-la.

The bridal wreath I give to you,
Tridiri-ralla, tridiri-ra.
But to another I'll be true,
Tridiri-ralla-la.

JULIE   I know our people and I love them, just as they do me. Let them come. You'll see.

JEAN   No, Miss Julie, they don't love you. They take your food, then spit at it. You must believe me. Listen to them, just listen to what they're singing . . . No, don't listen.

JULIE *(listening)*   What are they singing?

JEAN   They're mocking—you and me.

JULIE   Oh no! How horrible! What cowards!

JEAN   A pack like that's always cowardly. But against such odds there's nothing we can do but run away.

JULIE   Run away? Where to? We can't get out and we can't go into Kristin's room.

JEAN   Into mine, then. Necessity knows no rules. And you can trust me. I really am your true and devoted friend.

JULIE   But supposing . . . supposing they were to look for you in there?

JEAN   I'll bolt the door, and if they try to break in I'll shoot. Come on. *(Pleading.)* Please come.

JULIE *(tensely)*   Do you promise . . . ?

JEAN   I swear!

(JULIE *goes quickly into his room and he excitedly follows her.*)

Led by the fiddler, the peasants enter in the festive attire with flowers in their hats. They put a barrel of beer and a keg of spirits, garlanded with leaves, on the table, fetch glasses and begin to carouse. The scene becomes a ballet. They form a ring and dance and sing and mime: "Out of the wood two women came." Finally they go out, still singing.

(JULIE *comes in alone. She looks at the havoc in the kitchen, wrings her hands, then takes out her powder puff and powders her face.*)

(JEAN *enters in high spirits.*)

JEAN   Now you see! And you heard, didn't you? Do you still think it's possible for us to stay here?

JULIE   No, I don't. But what can we do?

JEAN   Run away. Far away. Take a journey.

JULIE   Journey? But where to?

JEAN   Switzerland. The Italian lakes. Ever been there?

JULIE   No. Is it nice?

JEAN   Ah! Eternal summer, oranges, evergreens . . . ah!

JULIE   But what would we do there?

JEAN   I'll start a hotel. First-class accommodation and first-class customers.

JULIE   Hotel?

JEAN   There's life for you. New faces all the time, new languages —no time for nerves or worries, no need to look for something to do—work rolling up of its own accord. Bells ringing night and day, trains whistling, buses coming and going, and all the time gold pieces rolling on to the counter. There's life for you!

JULIE   For *you*. And I?

JEAN   Mistress of the house, ornament of the firm. With your looks, and your style . . . oh, it's bound to be a success! Terrific! You'll sit like a queen in the office and set your slaves in motion by pressing an electric button. The guests will file past your throne and nervously lay their treasure on your table. You've no idea the way people tremble when they get their bills. I'll salt the bills and you'll sugar them with your sweetest smiles. Ah, let's get away from here! (*Produces a time-table.*) At once, by the next train. We shall be at Malmö at six-thirty, Hamburg eight-forty next morning, Frankfurt-Basle the following day, and Como by the St. Gothard pass in—let's see—three days. Three days!

JULIE   That's all very well. But Jean, you must give me courage. Tell me you love me. Come and take me in your arms.

JEAN   (*reluctantly*)   I'd like to, but I daren't. Not again in this house. I love you—that goes without saying. You can't doubt that, Miss Julie, can you?

JULIE   (*shyly, very feminine*)   Miss? Call me Julie. There aren't any barriers between us now. Call me Julie.

JEAN   (*uneasily*)   I can't. As long as we're in this house, there *are* barriers between us. There's the past and there's the Count. I've never been so servile to anyone as I am to him. I've only got to see his gloves on a chair to feel small. I've only to hear his bell and I shy like a horse. Even now, when I look at his boots, standing there so proud and stiff, I feel my back beginning to bend. (*Kicks the boots.*) It's those old, narrow-minded notions drummed into us as children . . . but they can soon be forgotten. You've only got to get to another country, a republic, and people will bend themselves double before my porter's livery. Yes, double they'll bend themselves, but I shan't. I wasn't born to bend. I've got guts, I've got character, and one I reach that first branch, you'll watch me climb. Today I'm valet, next year I'll be proprietor, in ten years I'll have made a fortune, and then I'll go to Roumania, get myself decorated and I may, I only say *may*, mind you, end up as a Count.

JULIE (*sadly*) That would be very nice.

JEAN You see in Roumania one can buy a title, and then you'll be a Countess after all. My Countess.

JULIE What do I care about all that? I'm putting those things behind me. Tell me you love me, because if you don't . . . if you don't, what am I?

JEAN I'll tell you a thousand times over—later. But not here. No sentimentality now or everything will be lost. We must consider this thing calmly like reasonable people. (*Takes a cigar, cuts and lights it.*) You sit down there and I'll sit here and we'll talk as if nothing has happened.

JULIE My God, have you no feelings at all?

JEAN Nobody has more. But I know how to control them.

JULIE A short time ago you were kissing my shoe. And now . . .

JEAN (*harshly*) Yes, that was then. Now, we have something else to think about.

JULIE Don't speak to me so brutally.

JEAN I'm not. Just sensibly. One folly's been committed, don't let's have more. The Count will be back at any moment and we've got to settle our future before that. Now, what do you think of my plans? Do you approve?

JULIE It seems a very good idea—but just one thing. Such a big undertaking would need a lot of capital. Have you got any?

JEAN (*chewing his cigar*) I certainly have. I've got my professional skill, my wide experience and my knowledge of foreign languages. That's capital worth having, it seems to me.

JULIE But it won't buy even one railway ticket.

JEAN Quite true. That's why I need a backer to advance some ready cash.

JULIE How could you get that at a moment's notice?

JEAN You must get it, if you want to be my partner.

JULIE I can't. I haven't any money of my own. (*Pause.*)

JEAN Then the whole thing's off.

JULIE And . . . ?

JEAN We go on as we are.

JULIE Do you think I'm going to stay under this roof as your mistress? With everyone pointing at me? Do you think I can face my father after this? No. Take me away from here, away from this shame, this humiliation. Oh my God, what have I done? My God, my God! (*Weeps.*)

JEAN So that's the tune now, is it? What have you done? Same as many before you.

JULIE (*hysterically*) And now you despise me. I'm falling, I'm falling.

JEAN Fall as far as me and I'll lift you up again.

JULIE Why was I so terribly attracted to you? The weak to the strong, the falling to the rising? Or was it love? Is that love? Do you know what love is?

JEAN Do I? You bet I do. Do you think I never had a girl before?

JULIE The things you say, the things you think!

JEAN That's what life's taught me, and that's what I am. It's no good getting hysterical or giving yourself airs. We're both in the same boat now. Here, my dear girl, let me give you a glass of something special.

(*Opens the drawer, takes out the bottle of wine and fills two used glasses.*)

JULIE Where did you get that wine?

JEAN From the cellar.

JULIE My father's burgundy.

JEAN Why not, for his son-in-law?

JULIE And I drink beer.

JEAN That only shows your taste's not so good as mine.

JULIE Thief!

JEAN Are you going to tell on me?

JULIE Oh God! The accomplice of a petty thief! Was I blind drunk? Have I dreamt this whole night? Midsummer Eve, the night for innocent merrymaking.

JEAN Innocent, eh?

JULIE Is anyone on earth as wretched as I am now?

JEAN Why should *you* be? After such a conquest. What about Kristin in there? Don't you think she has any feelings?

JULIE I did think so, but I don't any longer. No. A menial is a menial . . .

JEAN And a whore is a whore.

JULIE (*falling to her knees, her hands clasped*) O God in heaven, put an end to my miserable life! Lift me out of this filth in which I'm sinking. Save me! Save me!

JEAN I must admit I'm sorry for you. When I was in the onion bed and saw you up there among the roses, I . . . yes, I'll tell you now . . . I had the same dirty thoughts as all boys.

JULIE You, who wanted to die because of me?

JEAN In the oats-bin? That was just talk.

JULIE Lies, you mean.

JEAN (*getting sleepy*) More or less. I think I read a story in some paper about a chimney-sweep who shut himself up in a chest full of lilac because he'd been summonsed for not supporting some brat . . .

JULIE So this is what you're like.

JEAN I had to think up something. It's always the fancy stuff that catches the women.

JULIE Beast!

JEAN Merde!

JULIE Now you have seen the falcon's back.

JEAN Not exactly its *back*.

JULIE I was to be the first branch.

JEAN But the branch was rotten.

JULIE I was to be a hotel sign.

JEAN And I the hotel.

JULIE Sit at your counter, attract your clients and cook their accounts.

JEAN I'd have done that myself.

JULIE That any human being can be so steeped in filth!

JEAN Clean it up, then.

JULIE Menial! Lackey! Stand up when I speak to you.

JEAN Menial's whore, lackey's harlot, shut your mouth and get out of here! Are you the one to lecture me for being coarse? Nobody of my kind would ever be as coarse as you were tonight. Do you think any servant girl would throw herself at a man that way? Have you ever seen a girl of my class asking for it like that? I haven't. Only animals and prostitutes.

JULIE (*broken*) Go on. Hit me, trample on me—it's all I deserve. I'm rotten. But help me! If there's any way out at all, help me.

JEAN (*more gently*) I'm not denying myself a share in the honour of seducing you, but do you think anybody in my place would have dared look in your direction if you yourself hadn't asked for it? I'm still amazed . . .

JULIE And proud.

JEAN Why not? Though I must admit the victory was too easy to make me lose my head.

JULIE Go on hitting me.

JEAN (*rising*) No. On the contrary, I apologise for what I've said. I don't hit a person who's down—least of all a woman. I can't deny there's a certain satisfaction in finding that what dazzled one below was just moonshine, that that falcon's back is grey after all, that there's powder on the lovely cheek, that polished nails can have black tips, that the handkerchief is dirty although it smells of scent. On the other hand, it hurts to find that what I was struggling to reach wasn't high and isn't real. It hurts to see you fallen so low you're far lower than your own cook. Hurts like when you see the last flowers of summer lashed to pieces by rain and turned to mud.

JULIE   You're talking as if you're already my superior.

JEAN   I am. I might make you a Countess, but you could never make me a Count, you know.

JULIE   But I am the child of a Count, and you could never be that.

JEAN   True, but I might be the father of Counts if . . .

JULIE   You're a thief. I'm not.

JEAN   There are worse things than being a thief—much lower. Besides, when I'm in a place I regard myself as a member of the family to some extent, as one of the children. You don't call it stealing when children pinch a berry from overladen bushes. (*His passion is roused again.*) Miss Julie, you're a glorious woman, far too good for a man like me. You were carried away by some kind of madness, and now you're trying to cover up your mistake by persuading yourself you're in love with me. You're not, although you may find me physically attractive, which means your love's no better than mine. But I wouldn't be satisfied with being nothing but an animal for you, and I could never make you love me.

JULIE   Are you sure?

JEAN   You think there's a chance? Of my loving you, yes, of course. You're beautiful, refined (*takes her hand*) educated, and you can be nice when you want to be. The fire you kindle in a man isn't likely to go out. (*Puts his arm round her.*) You're like mulled wine, full of spices, and your kisses . . . (*He tries to pull her to him, but she breaks away.*)

JULIE   Let go of me! You won't win me that way.

JEAN   Not that way, how then? Not by kisses and fine speeches, not by planning the future and saving you from shame? How then?

JULIE   How? I don't know. There isn't any way. I loathe you—loathe you as I loathe rats, but I can't escape from you.

JEAN   Escape with me.

JULIE   (*pulling herself together*)   Escape? Yes, we must escape. But I'm so tired. Give me a glass of wine. (*He pours it out. She looks at her watch.*) First we must talk. We still have a little time. (*Empties the glass and holds it out for more.*)

JEAN   Don't drink like that. You'll get tipsy.

JULIE   What's that matter?

JEAN   What's it matter? It's vulgar to get drunk. Well, what have you got to say?

JULIE   We've got to run away, but we must talk first—or rather, I must, for so far you've done all the talking. You've told me about your life, now I want to tell you about mine, so that we really know each other before we begin this journey together.

JEAN   Wait. Excuse my saying so, but don't you think you may be sorry afterwards if you give away your secrets to me?

JULIE   Aren't you my friend?

JEAN   On the whole. But don't rely on me.

JULIE   You can't mean that. But anyway, everyone knows my secrets. Listen. My mother wasn't well-born; she came of quite humble people, and was brought up with all those new ideas of sex-equality and women's rights and so on. She thought marriage was quite wrong. So when my father proposed to her, she said she would never become his *wife* . . . but in the end she did. I came into the world, as far as I can make out, against my mother's will, and I was left to run wild, but I had to do all the things a boy does—to prove women are as good as men. I had to wear boys' clothes; I was taught to handle horses—and I wasn't allowed in the dairy. She made me groom and harness and go out hunting; I even had to try to plough. All the men on the estate were given the women's jobs, and the women the men's, until the whole place went to rack and ruin and we were the laughing-stock of the neighbourhood. At last my father seems to have come to his senses and rebelled. He changed everything and ran the place his own way. My mother got ill—I don't know what was the matter with her, but she used to have strange attacks and hide herself in the attic or the garden. Sometimes she stayed out all night. Then came the great fire which you have heard people talking about. The house and the stables and the barns—the whole place burnt to the ground. In very suspicious circumstances. Because the accident happened the very day the insurance had to be renewed, and my father had sent the new premium, but through some carelessness of the messenger it arrived too late.

(Refills her glass and drinks.)

JEAN   Don't drink any more.

JULIE   Oh, what does it matter? We were destitute and had to sleep in the carriages. My father didn't know how to get money to rebuild, and then my mother suggested he should borrow from an old friend of hers, a local brick manufacturer. My father got the loan and, to his surprise, without having to pay interest. So the place was rebuilt. *(Drinks.)* Do you know who set fire to it?

JEAN   Your lady mother.

JULIE   Do you know who the brick manufacturer was?

JEAN   Your mother's lover?

JULIE   Do you know whose the money was?

JEAN   Wait . . . no, I don't know that.

JULIE   It was my mother's.

JEAN   In other words, the Count's, unless there was a settlement.

JULIE   There wasn't any settlement. My mother had a little money of her own which she didn't want my father to control, so she invested it with her—friend.

JEAN   Who grabbed it.

JULIE   Exactly. He appropriated it. My father came to know all this. He couldn't bring an action, couldn't pay his wife's lover, nor prove it was his wife's money. That was my mother's revenge because he made himself master in his own house. He nearly shot himself then—at least there's a rumour he tried and didn't bring it off. So he went on living, and my mother had to pay dearly for what she'd done. Imagine what those five years were like for me. My natural sympathies were with my father, yet I took my mother's side, because I didn't know the facts. I'd learnt from her to hate and distrust men—you know how she loathed the whole male sex. And I swore to her I'd never become the slave of any man.

JEAN   And so you got engaged to that attorney.

JULIE   So that he should be my slave.

JEAN   But he wouldn't be.

JULIE   Oh yes, he wanted to be, but he didn't have the chance. I got bored with him.

JEAN   Is that what I saw—in the stable-yard?

JULIE   What did you see?

JEAN   What I saw was him breaking off the engagement.

JULIE   That's a lie. It was I who broke it off. Did he say it was him? The cad.

JEAN   He's not a cad. Do you hate men, Miss Julie?

JULIE   Yes . . . most of the time. But when that weakness comes, oh . . . the shame!

JEAN   Then, do you hate me?

JULIE   Beyond words. I'd gladly have you killed like an animal.

JEAN   Quick as you'd shoot a mad dog, eh?

JULIE   Yes.

JEAN   But there's nothing here to shoot with—and there isn't a dog. So what do we do now?

JULIE   Go abroad.

JEAN   To make each other miserable for the rest of our lives?

JULIE   No, to enjoy ourselves for a day or two, for a week, for as long as enjoyment lasts, and then—to die . . .

JEAN   Die? How silly! I think it would be far better to start a hotel.

JULIE   (*without listening*)   . . . die on the shores of Lake Como, where the sun always shines and at Christmas time there are green trees and glowing oranges.

JEAN Lake Como's a rainy hole and I didn't see any oranges outside the shops. But it's a good place for tourists. Plenty of villas to be rented by—er—honeymoon couples. Profitable business, that. Know why? Because they all sign a lease for six months and all leave after three weeks.

JULIE (*naïvely*) After three weeks? Why?

JEAN They quarrel, of course. But the rent has to be paid just the same. And then it's let again. So it goes on and on, for there's plenty of love although it doesn't last long.

JULIE You don't want to die with me?

JEAN I don't want to die at all. For one thing I like living and for another I consider suicide's a sin against the Creator who gave us life.

JULIE You believe in God—*you?*

JEAN Yes, of course. And I go to church every Sunday. Look here, I'm tired of all this. I'm going to bed.

JULIE Indeed! And do you think I'm going to leave things like this? Don't you know what you owe the woman you've ruined?

JEAN (*taking out his purse and throwing a silver coin on the table*) There you are. I don't want to be in anybody's debt.

JULIE (*pretending not to notice the insult*) Don't you know what the law is?

JEAN There's no law unfortunately that punishes a woman for seducing a man.

JULIE But can you see anything for it but to go abroad, get married and then divorce?

JEAN What if I refuse this mésalliance?

JULIE Mésalliance?

JEAN Yes, for me. I'm better bred than you, see! Nobody in my family committed arson.

JULIE How do you know?

JEAN Well, you can't prove otherwise, because we haven't any family records outside the Registrar's office. But I've seen your family tree in that book on the drawing-room table. Do you know who the founder of your family was? A miller who let his wife sleep with the King one night during the Danish war. I haven't any ancestors at all, but I might become one.

JULIE This is what I get for confiding in someone so low, for sacrificing my family honour . . .

JEAN Dishonour! Well, I told you so. One shouldn't drink, because then one talks. And one shouldn't talk.

JULIE Oh, how ashamed I am, how bitterly ashamed! If at least you loved me!

JEAN Look here—for the last time—what do you want? Am I to burst into tears? Am I to jump over your riding whip? Shall I kiss you and carry you off to Lake Como for three weeks, after which... What am I to do? What do you want? This is getting unbearable, but that's what comes of playing around with women. Miss Julie, I can see how miserable you are; I know you're going through hell, but I don't understand you. We don't have scenes like this; we don't go in for hating each other. We make love for fun in our spare time, but we haven't all day and all night for it like you. I think you must be ill. I'm sure you're ill.

JULIE Then you must be kind to me. You sound almost human now.

JEAN Well, be human yourself. You spit at me, then won't let me wipe it off—on you.

JULIE Help me, help me! Tell me what to do, where to go.

JEAN Jesus, as if I knew!

JULIE I've been mad, raving mad, but there must be a way out.

JEAN Stay here and keep quiet. Nobody knows anything.

JULIE I can't. People do know. Kristin knows.

JEAN They don't know and they wouldn't believe such a thing.

JULIE (*hesitating*) But—it might happen again.

JEAN That's true.

JULIE And there might be—consequences.

JEAN (*in panic*) Consequences! Fool that I am I never thought of that. Yes, there's nothing for it but to go. At once. I can't come with you. That would be a complete giveaway. You must go alone—abroad—anywhere.

JULIE Alone? Where to? I can't.

JEAN You must. And before the Count gets back. If you stay, we know what will happen. Once you've sinned you feel you might as well go on, as the harm's done. Then you get more and more reckless and in the end you're found out. No. You must go abroad. Then write to the Count and tell him everything, except that it was me. He'll never guess that—and I don't think he'll want to.

JULIE I'll go if you come with me.

JEAN Are you crazy, woman? "Miss Julie elopes with valet." Next day it would be in the headlines, and the Count would never live it down.

JULIE I can't go. I can't stay. I'm so tired, so completely worn out. Give me orders. Set me going. I can't think any more, can't act...

JEAN You see what weaklings you are. Why do you give yourselves airs and turn up your noses as if you're the lords of creation? Very well, I'll give you your orders. Go upstairs and dress. Get money for the journey and come down here again.

JULIE (*softly*) Come up with me.

JEAN To your room? Now you've gone crazy again. (*Hesitates a moment.*) No! Go along at once. (*Takes her hand and pulls her to the door.*)

JULIE (*as she goes*) Speak kindly to me, Jean.

JEAN Orders always sound unkind. Now you know. Now you know.

(*Left alone, JEAN sighs with relief, sits down at the table, takes out a notebook and pencil and adds up figures, now and then aloud. Dawn begins to break. KRISTIN enters dressed for church, carrying his white dickey and tie.*)

KRISTIN Lord Jesus, look at the state the place is in! What have you been up to?

(*Turns out the lamp.*)

JEAN Oh, Miss Julie invited the crowd in. Did you sleep through it? Didn't you hear anything?

KRISTIN I slept like a log.

JEAN And dressed for church already.

KRISTIN Yes, you promised to come to Communion with me today.

JEAN Why, so I did. And you've got my bib and tucker, I see. Come on then. (*Sits. KRISTIN begins to put his things on. Pause. Sleepily.*) What's the lesson today?

KRISTIN It's about the beheading of John the Baptist, I think.

JEAN That's sure to be horribly long. Hi, you're choking me! Oh Lord, I'm so sleepy, so sleepy!

KRISTIN Yes, what have you been doing up all night? You look absolutely green.

JEAN Just sitting here talking with Miss Julie.

KRISTIN She doesn't know what's proper, that one. (*Pause.*)

JEAN I say, Kristin.

KRISTIN What?

JEAN It's queer really, isn't it, when you come to think of it? Her.

KRISTIN What's queer?

JEAN The whole thing. (*Pause.*)

KRISTIN (*looking at the half-filled glasses on the table*) Have you been drinking together too?

JEAN Yes.

KRISTIN More shame you. Look me straight in the face.

JEAN Yes.

KRISTIN Is it possible? Is it possible?

JEAN (*after a moment*) Yes, it is.

KRISTIN Oh! This I would never have believed. How low!

JEAN You're not jealous of her, surely?

KRISTIN No, I'm not. If it had been Clara or Sophie I'd have scratched your eyes out. But not of her. I don't know why; that's how it is, though. But it's disgusting.

JEAN You're angry with her, then.

KRISTIN No. With you. It was wicked of you, very very wicked. Poor girl. And, mark my words, I won't stay here any longer now —in a place where one can't respect one's employers.

JEAN Why should one respect them?

KRISTIN You should know since you're so smart. But you don't want to stay in the service of people who aren't respectable, do you? I wouldn't demean myself.

JEAN But it's rather a comfort to find out they're no better than us.

KRISTIN I don't think so. If they're no better there's nothing for us to live up to. Oh and think of the Count! Think of him. He's been through so much already. No, I won't stay in the place any longer. A fellow like you too! If it had been that attorney, now, or somebody of her own class . . .

JEAN Why, what's wrong with . . .

KRISTIN Oh, you're all right in your own way, but when all's said and done there is a difference between one class and another. No, this is something I'll never be able to stomach. That our young lady who was so proud and so down on men you'd never believe she'd let one come near her should go and give herself to one like you. She who wanted to have poor Diana shot for running after the lodge-keeper's pug. No, I must say . . . ! Well, I won't stay here any longer. On the twenty-fourth of October I quit.

JEAN And then?

KRISTIN Well, since you mention it, it's about time you began to look around, if we're ever going to get married.

JEAN But what am I to look for? I shan't get a place like this when I'm married.

KRISTIN I know you won't. But you might get a job as porter or caretaker in some public institution. Government rations are small but sure, and there's a pension for the widow and children.

JEAN That's all very fine, but it's not in my line to start thinking at once about dying for my wife and children. I must say I had rather bigger ideas.

KRISTIN You and your ideas! You've got obligations too, and you'd better start thinking about them.

JEAN Don't *you* start pestering me about obligations. I've had enough of that. (*Listens to a sound upstairs.*) Anyway, we've plenty of time to work things out. Go and get ready, now, and we'll be off to church.

KRISTIN Who's that walking about upstairs?

JEAN Don't know—unless it's Clara.

KRISTIN (*going*) You don't think the Count could have come back without our hearing him?

JEAN (*scared*) The Count? No, he can't have. He'd have rung for me.

KRISTIN God help us! I've never known such goings on

(*Exit.*)

(*The sun has now risen and is shining on the treetops. The light gradually changes until it slants in through the windows.* JEAN *goes to the door and beckons.* JULIE *enters in travelling clothes, carrying a small bird-cage covered with a cloth which she puts on a chair.*)

JULIE I'm ready.

JEAN Hush! Kristin's up.

JULIE (*in a very nervous state*) Does she suspect anything?

JEAN Not a thing. But, my God, what a sight you are!

JULIE Sight? What do you mean?

JEAN You're white as a corpse and—pardon me—your face is dirty.

JULIE Let me wash, then. (*Goes to the sink and washes her face and hands.*) There. Give me a towel. Oh! The sun is rising!

JEAN And that breaks the spell.

JULIE Yes. The spell of Midsummer Eve . . . But listen, Jean. Come with me. I've got the money.

JEAN (*skeptically*) Enough?

JULIE Enough to start with. Come with me. I can't travel alone today. It's Midsummer Day, remember. I'd be packed into a suffocating train among crowds of people who'd all stare at me. And it would stop at every station while I yearned for wings. No, I can't do that, I simply can't. There will be memories too; memories of Midsummer Days when I was little. The leafy church—birch and lilac—the gaily spread dinner table, relatives, friends—evening in the park—dancing and music and flowers and fun. Oh, however far you run away—there'll always be memories in the baggage car—and remorse and guilt.

JEAN   I will come with you, but quickly now then, before it's too late. At once.

JULIE   Put on your things. (*Picks up the cage.*)

JEAN   No luggage, mind. That would give us away.

JULIE   No, only what we can take with us in the carriage.

JEAN   (*fetching his hat*)   What on earth have you got there? What is it?

JULIE   Only my greenfinch. I don't want to leave it behind.

JEAN   Well, I'll be damned! We're to take a bird-cage along, are we? You're crazy. Put that cage down.

JULIE   It's the only thing I'm taking from my home. The only living creature who cares for me since Diana went off like that. Don't be cruel. Let me take it.

JEAN   Put that cage down, I tell you—and don't talk so loud. Kristin will hear.

JULIE   No, I won't leave it in strange hands. I'd rather you killed it.

JEAN   Give the little beast here, then, and I'll wring its neck.

JULIE   But don't hurt it, don't . . . no, I can't.

JEAN   Give it here. I *can*.

JULIE   (*taking the bird out of the cage and kissing it*)   Dear little Serena, must you die and leave your mistress?

JEAN   Please don't make a scene. It's *your* life and future we're worrying about. Come on, quick now!

(*He snatches the bird from her, puts it on a board and picks up a chopper.* JULIE *turns away.*)

You should have learnt how to kill chickens instead of target-shooting. Then you wouldn't faint at a drop of blood.

JULIE   (*screaming*)   Kill me too! Kill me! You who can butcher an innocent creature without a quiver. Oh, how I hate you, how I loathe you! There is blood between us now. I curse the hour I first saw you. I curse the hour I was conceived in my mother's womb.

JEAN   What's the use of cursing? Let's go.

JULIE   (*going to the chopping-block as if drawn against her will*) No, I won't go yet. I can't . . . I must look. Listen! There's a carriage. (*Listens without taking her eyes off the board and chopper.*) You don't think I can bear the sight of blood. You think I'm so weak. Oh, how I should like to see your blood and your brains on a chopping-block! I'd like to see the whole of your sex swimming like that in a sea of blood. I think I could drink out of your skull, bathe my feet in your broken breast and eat your heart roasted whole. You think I'm weak. You think I love you, that my womb yearned for your seed and I want to carry your off-spring under my heart and nourish it with my blood. You think I want to bear your child and take your name. By the way, what is your name? I've never heard your surname. I don't suppose you've got one. I should be "Mrs. Hovel" or "Madam Dunghill." You dog wearing my collar, you lackey with my crest on your buttons! I share you with my cook; I'm my own servant's rival! Oh! Oh! Oh! . . . You think I'm a coward and will run away. No, now I'm going to stay—and let the storm break. My father will come back . . . find his desk broken open . . . his money gone. Then he'll ring that bell—twice for the valet—and then he'll send for the police . . . and I shall tell everything. Everything. Oh how wonderful to make an end of it all—a real end! He has a stroke and dies and that's the end of all of us. Just peace and quietness . . . eternal rest. The coat of arms broken on the coffin and the Count's line extinct . . . But the valet's line goes on in an orphanage, wins laurels in the gutter and ends in jail.

JEAN   There speaks the noble blood! Bravo, Miss Julie. But now, don't let the cat out of the bag.

(KRISTIN *enters dressed for church, carrying a prayer-book.* JULIE *rushes to her and flings herself into her arms for protection.*)

JULIE   Help me, Kristin! Protect me from this man!

KRISTIN   (*unmoved and cold*)   What goings-on for a feast day morning! (*Sees the board.*) And what a filthy mess. What's it all about? Why are you screaming and carrying on so?

JULIE   Kristin, you're a woman and my friend. Beware of that scoundrel!

JEAN   (*embarrassed*)   While you ladies are talking things over, I'll go and shave. (*Slips into his room.*)

JULIE   You must understand. You must listen to me.

KRISTIN   I certainly don't understand such loose ways. Where are you off to in those travelling clothes? And he had his hat on, didn't he, eh?

JULIE   Listen, Kristin. Listen, I'll tell you everything.

KRISTIN   I don't wan't to know anything.

JULIE   You must listen.

KRISTIN   What to? Your nonsense with Jean? I don't care a rap about that; it's nothing to do with me. But if you're thinking of getting him to run off with you, we'll soon put a stop to that.

JULIE   (*very nervously*)   Please try to be calm, Kristin, and listen. I can't stay here, nor can Jean—so we must go abroad.

KRISTIN   Hm, hm!

JULIE   (*brightening*)   But you see, I've had an idea. Supposing we

all three go—abroad—to Switzerland and start a hotel together
... I've got some money, you see ... and Jean and I could run
the whole thing—and I thought you would take charge of the
kitchen. Wouldn't that be splendid? Say yes, do. If you come
with us everything will be fine. Oh do say yes! (*Puts her arms
round* KRISTIN.)

KRISTIN (*coolly thinking*)   Hm, hm.

JULIE (*presto tempo*) You've never travelled, Kristin. You should
go abroad and see the world. You've no idea how nice it is travelling by train—new faces all the time and new countries. On our
way through Hamburg well go to the zoo—you'll love that—and
we'll go to the theatre and the opera too ... and when we get to
Munich there'll be the museums, dear, and pictures by Rubens
and Raphael—the great painters, you know ... You've heard of
Munich, haven't you? Where King Ludwig lived—you know, the
king who went mad.... We'll see his castles—some of his castles
are still just like in fairy-tales ... and from there it's not far to
Switzerland—and the Alps. Think of the Alps, Kristin dear, covered with snow in the middle of summer ... and there are oranges
there and trees that are green the whole year round ...

(JEAN *is seen in the door of his room, sharpening his razor on a strop
which he holds with his teeth and his left hand. He listens to the talk with
satisfaction and now and then nods approval.* JULIE *continues, tempo
prestissimo.*)

And then we'll get a hotel ... and I'll sit at the desk, while Jean
receives the guests and goes out marketing and writes letters ...
There's life for you! Trains whistling, buses driving up, bells ringing upstairs and downstairs ... and I shall make out the bills—
and I shall cook them too ... you've no idea how nervous trav-
ellers are when it comes to paying their bills. And you—you'll sit
like a queen in the kitchen ... of course there won't be any standing at the stove for you. You'll always have to be nicely dressed
and ready to be seen, and with your looks—no, I'm not flattering
you—one fine day you'll catch yourself a husband ... some rich
Englishman, I shouldn't wonder—they're the ones who are easy
(*slowing down*) to catch ... and then we'll get rich and build
ourselves a villa on Lake Como ... of course it rains there a little
now and then—but—(*dully*)—the sun must shine there too sometimes—even though it seems gloomy—and if not—then we can
come home again—come back—(*pause*)—here—or somewhere
else ...

KRISTIN   Look here, Miss Julie, do you believe all that yourself?

JULIE (*exhausted*)   Do I believe it?

KRISTIN Yes.

JULIE (*wearily*) I don't know. I don't believe anything any more. (*Sinks down on the bench; her head in her arms on the table.*) Nothing. Nothing at all.

KRISTIN (*turning to* JEAN) So you meant to beat it, did you?

JEAN (*disconcerted, putting the razor on the table*) Beat it? What are you talking about? You've heard Miss Julie's plan, and though she's tired now with being up all night, it's a perfectly sound plan.

KRISTIN Oh, is it? If you thought I'd work for that . . .

JEAN (*interrupting*) Kindly use decent language in front of your mistress. Do you hear?

KRISTIN Mistress?

JEAN Yes.

KRISTIN Well, well, just listen to that!

JEAN Yes, it would be a good thing if you did listen and talked less. Miss Julie is your mistress and what's made you lose your respect for her now ought to make you feel the same about yourself.

KRISTIN I've always had enough self-respect——

JEAN To despise other people.

KRISTIN —not to go below my own station. Has the Count's cook ever gone with the groom or the swineherd? Tell me that.

JEAN No, you were lucky enough to have a high-class chap for your beau.

KRISTIN High-class all right—selling the oats out of the Count's stable.

JEAN You're a fine one to talk—taking a commission on the groceries and bribes from the butcher.

KRISTIN What the devil . . . ?

JEAN And now you can't feel any respect for your employers. You, you!

KRISTIN Are you coming to church with me? I should think you need a good sermon after your fine deeds.

JEAN No, I'm not going to church today. You can go alone and confess your own sins.

KRISTIN Yes, I'll do that and bring back enough forgiveness to cover yours too. The Saviour suffered and died on the cross for all our sins, and if we go to Him with faith and a penitent heart, He takes all our sins upon Himself.

JEAN Even grocery thefts?

JULIE Do you believe that, Kristin?

KRISTIN That is my living faith, as sure as I stand here. The faith I learnt as a child and have kept ever since, Miss Julie. "But where sin abounded, grace did much more abound."

JULIE Oh, if I had your faith! Oh, if . . .

KRISTIN But you see you can't have it without God's special grace, and it's not given to all to have that.

JULIE Who is it given to then?

KRISTIN That's the great secret of the workings of grace, Miss Julie. God is no respecter of persons, and with Him the last shall be first . . .

JULIE Then I suppose He does respect the last.

KRISTIN (*continuing*) . . . and it is easier for a camel to go through the eye of a needle than for a rich man to enter into the kingdom of God. That's how it is, Miss Julie. Now I'm going—alone, and on my way I shall tell the groom not to let any of the horses out, in case anyone should want to leave before the Count gets back. Goodbye.

(*Exit.*)

JEAN What a devil! And all on account of a greenfinch.

JULIE (*wearily*) Never mind the greenfinch. Do you see any way out of this, any end to it?

JEAN (*pondering*) No.

JULIE If you were in my place, what would you do?

JEAN In your place? Wait a bit. If I was a woman—a lady of rank who had—fallen. I don't know. Yes, I do know now.

JULIE (*picking up the razor and making a gesture*) This?

JEAN Yes. But *I* wouldn't do it, you know. There's a difference between us.

JULIE Because you're a man and I'm a woman? What is the difference?

JEAN The usual difference—between man and woman.

JULIE (*holding the razor*) I'd like to. But I can't. My father couldn't either, that time he wanted to.

JEAN No, he didn't want to. He had to be revenged first.

JULIE And now my mother is revenged again, through me.

JEAN Didn't you ever love your father, Miss Julie?

JULIE Deeply, but I must have hated him too—unconsciously. And he let me be brought up to despise my own sex, to be half woman, half man. Whose fault is what's happened? My father's, my mother's or my own? My own? I haven't anything that's my own. I haven't one single thought that I didn't get from my father, one emotion that didn't come from my mother, and as for this last idea—about all people being equal—I got that from him, my fiancé—that's why I call him a cad. How can it be my fault? Push the responsibility on to Jesus, like Kristin does? No, I'm too proud and—thanks to my father's teaching—too intelligent. As for all that about a rich person not being able to get into heaven, it's just a lie, but Kristin, who has money in the savings-bank, will certainly not get in. Whose fault is it? What does it matter whose fault it is? In any case I must take the blame and bear the consequences.

JEAN   Yes, but... (*There are two sharp rings on the bell.* JULIE *jumps to her feet.* JEAN *changes into his livery.*) The Count is back. Supposing Kristin... (*Goes to the speaking-tube, presses it and listens.*)

JULIE   Has he been to his desk yet?

JEAN   This is Jean, sir. (*Listens.*) Yes, sir. (*Listens.*) Yes, sir, very good, sir. (*Listens.*) At once, sir? (*Listens.*) Very good, sir. In half an hour.

JULIE (*in panic*)   What did he say? My God, what did he say?

JEAN   He ordered his boots and his coffee in half an hour.

JULIE   Then there's half an hour... Oh, I'm so tired! I can't do anything. Can't be sorry, can't run away, can't stay, can't live— can't die. Help me. Order me, and I'll obey like a dog. Do me this last service—save my honour, save his name. You know what I ought to do, but haven't the strength to do. Use your strength and order me to do it.

JEAN   I don't know why—I can't now—I don't understand... It's just as if this coat made me—I can't give you orders—and now that the Count has spoken to me—I can't quite explain, but... well, that devil of a lackey is bending my back again. I believe if the Count came down now and ordered me to cut my throat, I'd do it on the spot.

JULIE   Then pretend you're him and I'm you. You did some fine acting before, when you knelt to me and played the aristocrat. Or... Have you ever seen a hypnotist at the theatre? (*He nods.*) He says to the person "Take the broom," and he takes it. He says "Sweep," and he sweeps...

JEAN   But the person has to be asleep.

JULIE (*as if in a trance*)   I am asleep already... the whole room has turned to smoke—and you look like a stove—a stove like a man in black with a tall hat—your eyes are glowing like coals when the fire is low—and your face is a white patch like ashes. (*The sunlight has now reached the floor and lights up* JEAN.) How nice and warm it is! (*She holds out her hands as though warming them at a fire.*) And so light—and so peaceful.

JEAN (*putting the razor in her hand*)   Here is the broom. Go now while its light—out to the barn—and... (*Whispers in her ear.*)

JULIE (*waking*)   Thank you. I am going now—to rest. But just tell me that even the first can receive the gift of grace.

JEAN   The first? No, I can't tell you that. But wait... Miss Julie,

I've got it! You aren't one of the first any longer. You're one of the last.

JULIE   That's true. I'm one of the very last. I *am* the last. Oh! ... But now I can't go. Tell me again to go.

JEAN   No, I can't now, either. I can't.

JULIE   And the first shall be last.

JEAN   Don't think, don't think. You're taking my strength away too and making me a coward. What's that? I thought I saw the bell move ... To be so frightened of a bell! Yes, but it's not just a bell. There's somebody behind it—a hand moving it—and something else moving the hand—and if you stop your ears—if you stop your ears—yes, then it rings louder than ever. Rings and rings until you answer—and then its too late. Then the police come and ... and ... (*The bell rings twice loudly.* JEAN *flinches, then straightens himself up.*) It's horrible. But there's no other way to end it ... Go!

(JULIE *walks firmly out through the door.*)

Curtain

THE CHERRY ORCHARD (1904)

ANTON CHEKHOV (1860–1904)

The good, gentle physician, Dr. Chekhov, doomed to die of consumption at a distressingly early age, wrote four plays, *The Seagull* (1896), *Uncle Vanya* (1899), *The Three Sisters* (1901), and *The Cherry Orchard*, uniformly regarded as among our finest pieces of dramatic realism. It is a very special kind of realism, and it makes unusual demands upon the actors who perform and the audience who watches. At first encounter, these dramas strike one as virtually plotless discussions of unrequited love and frustrated careers among a group of self-centered directionless human beings existing in genteel poverty who do nothing but sit around decaying country estates, attempting, mostly without success, to entertain or make love to each other, and drinking endless glasses of tea. Their creator regarded them as comedies.

What Chekhov has written, in fact, *are* some of the best examples of the realistic comedy of sensibility. With great sensitivity and sympathy, he portrays a modestly high level of Russian society whose members are caught amidst rapid social change that will soon see the end of their calm and indolent world. They are pitiful people, distressed in their inability to figure out what is happening while remaining resentfully incapable of adjusting. They are ultimately doomed, but they are charming refined people whose mundane daily existences the dramatist transforms into effective and highly literate drama. Their encounters may be far removed from our own, but their emotional reactions are not, and Chekhov is able to convey their humdrum, surfacy, existence through a downbeat but universally appealing portrayal of the human experience. He shows us his characters for what they are, mostly ordinary and second-rate, essentially comic, but very human personalities.

The task that is put upon the actor in Chekhov, plainly evident in *The Cherry Orchard,* is the ability to rise above the almost total lack of action in the story itself and to demonstrate the surging force of the drama that exists beneath each individual surface. The actor in Chekhov must portray, for instance, a Madame Ranevskaya who is not actually a simpleton in her wasteful extravagances and her inability to recognize that her fortune is gone, but one who is a thoroughly sympathetic woman whose foolishness we may not condone but we at least comprehend. Gayeff and his incessant billiards must come across as confused, charmingly absentminded, but certainly not crazy. Lopahin, confused as all the rest, must evoke sympathy, not antagonism, for he is far from being a villain. He may lack taste and "good breeding" but his search for security and social status as the son of a serf is legitimate. All of the characters are a touching lot, intrinsically comic, without being particularly funny. Yet it is impossible not to laugh at them. We are both amused and bemused. Emotionally we identify, while we seeth in frustration at their disturbing reality. And that's the problem in watching Chekhov. As an audience we yearn for action, for something to happen. If we remain disciplined in our observance, however, we recognize the storm and stress that make for genuinely effective drama.

Chekhov's plays support no stars. They demand something entirely new to the theatre of their time: carefully controlled *ensemble* acting. There is no leading part, no single major character. The group is the collective protagonist, and the actor who performs Chekhov must surrender any artistic ego to that group. At the same time, he must maintain the individual characterization needed to set himself apart from all the others. The performer must recognize how Chekhov loves the people he has created, refusing to criticize, but realizing their quiet desperation. He offers them for what they are, ordinary people, unimportant to the world around them, desperately important to themselves, while those among whom they exist continually look the other way.

The Cherry Orchard

CHEKHOV

Translated by Stark Young

CHARACTERS

YERMOLAY ALEXEEVICH LOPAHIN, *a merchant*
DUNYASHA, *a maid*
SEMYON PANTELEEVICH EPIHODOFF, *a clerk*
FIERS, *a valet, an old man of eighty-seven*
LYUBOFF ANDREEVNA RANEVSKAYA, *a landowner*
ANYA, *her daughter, seventeen years old*
CHARLOTTA IVANOVNA, *a governess*
VARYA, *Madam Ranevskaya's adopted daughter, twenty-four
    years old*
LEONID ANDREEVICH GAYEFF, *brother of Madam Ranevskaya*
BORIS BORISOVICH SEMYONOFF-PISHTCHIK, *a landowner*
YASHA, *a young valet*
PYOTR SERGEEVICH TROFIMOFF, *a student*
A STRANGER WHO PASSES BY
THE STATION-MASTER
A POST-OFFICE CLERK
VISITORS
SERVANTS

ACT I

A room that is still called the nursery. One of the doors leads into ANYA's *room. Dawn, the sun will soon be rising. It is May, the cherry trees are in blossom but in the orchard it is cold, with a morning frost. The windows in the room are closed.* DUNYASHA *enters with a candle and* LOPAHIN *with a book in his hand.*

LOPAHIN   The train got in, thank God! What time is it?
DUNYASHA   It's nearly two. (*Blows out his candle.*) It's already
    daylight.
LOPAHIN   But how late was the train? Two hours at least. (*Yawning and stretching.*) I'm a fine one, I am, look what a fool thing

477

I did! I drove here on purpose just to meet them at the station, and then all of a sudden I'd overslept myself! Fell asleep in my chair. How provoking!—You could have waked me up.

DUNYASHA I thought you had gone. (*Listening.*) Listen, I think they are coming now.

LOPAHIN (*listening*) No—No, there's the luggage and one thing and another. (*A pause.*) Lyuboff Andreevna has been living abroad five years. I don't know what she is like now—She is a good woman. An easy-going, simple woman. I remember when I was a boy about fifteen, my father, who is at rest—in those days he ran a shop here in the village—hit me in the face with his fist, my nose was bleeding—We'd come to the yard together for something or other, and he was a little drunk. Lyuboff Andreevna, I can see her now, still so young, so slim, led me to the washbasin here in this very room, in the nursery. "Don't cry," she says, "little peasant, it will be well in time for your wedding"— (*A pause.*) Yes, little peasant—My father was a peasant truly, and here I am in a white waistcoat and yellow shoes. Like a pig rooting in a pastry shop—I've got this rich, lots of money, but if you really stop and think of it, I'm just a peasant— (*Turning the pages of a book.*) Here I was reading a book and didn't get a thing out of it. Reading and went to sleep. (*A pause.*)

DUNYASHA And all night long the dogs were not asleep, they know their masters are coming.

LOPAHIN What is it, Dunyasha, you're so—

DUNYASHA My hands are shaking. I'm going to faint.

LOPAHIN You're just so delicate, Dunyasha. And all dressed up like a lady, and your hair all done up! Mustn't do that. Must know your place.

(EPIHODOFF *enters, with a bouquet: he wears a jacket and highly polished boots with a loud squeak. As he enters he drops the bouquet.*)

EPIHODOFF (*picking up the bouquet*) Look, the gardener sent these, he says to put them in the dining room.

(*Giving the bouquet to* DUNYASHA.)

LOPAHIN And bring me some kvass.

DUNYASHA Yes, sir.

(*Goes out.*)

EPIHODOFF There is a morning frost now, three degrees of frost (*sighing*) and the cherries all in bloom. I cannot approve of our climate—I cannot. Our climate can never quite rise to the occasion. Listen, Yermolay Alexeevich, allow me to subtend, I bought myself, day before yesterday, some boots and they, I venture to assure you, squeak so that it is impossible. What could I grease them with?

LOPAHIN   Go on. You annoy me.

EPIHODOFF   Every day some misfortune happens to me. But I don't complain, I am used to it and I even smile.

(DUNYASHA *enters, serves* LOPAHIN *the kvass.*)

EPIHODOFF   I'm going. (*Stumbling over a chair and upsetting it.*) There (*as if triumphant*), there, you see, pardon the expression, a circumstance like that, among others—It is simply quite remarkable.

(*Goes out.*)

DUNYASHA   And I must tell you, Yermolay Alexeevich, that Epihodoff has proposed to me.

LOPAHIN   Ah!

DUNYASHA   I don't know really what to—He is a quiet man but sometimes when he starts talking, you can't understand a thing he means. It's all very nice, and full of feeling, but just doesn't make any sense. I sort of like him. He loves me madly. He's a man that's unfortunate, every day there's something or other. They tease him around here, call him twenty-two misfortunes—

LOPAHIN (*cocking his ear*)   Listen, I think they are coming—

DUNYASHA   They are coming! But what's the matter with me— I'm cold all over.

LOPAHIN   They're really coming. Let's go meet them. Will she recognize me? It's five years we haven't seen each other.

DUNYASHA (*excitedly*)   I'm going to faint this very minute. Ah, I'm going to faint!

Two carriages can be heard driving up to the house. LOPAHIN *and* DUNYASHA *hurry out. The stage is empty. In the adjoining rooms a noise begins.* FIERS *hurries across the stage, leaning on a stick; he has been to meet* LYUBOFF ANDREEVNA, *and wears an old-fashioned livery and a high hat; he mutters something to himself, but you cannot understand a word of it. The noise offstage gets louder and louder. A voice: "Look! Let's go through here—"* LYUBOFF ANDREEVNA, ANYA *and* CHARLOTTA IVANOVNA, *with a little dog on a chain, all of them dressed for traveling,* VARYA, *in a coat and kerchief,* GAYEFF, SEMYONOFF-PISHTCHIK, LOPAHIN, DUNYASHA, *with a bundle and an umbrella, servants with pieces of luggage—all pass through the room.*

ANYA   Let's go through here. Mama, do you remember what room this is?

LYUBOFF ANDREEVNA (*happily, through her tears*)   The nursery!

VARYA How cold it is, my hands are stiff. (*To* LYUBOFF ANDRE-EVNA.) Your rooms, the white one and the violet, are just the same as ever, Mama.

LYUBOFF ANDREEVNA The nursery, my dear beautiful room—I slept here when I was little—(*Crying.*) And now I am like a child— (*Kisses her brother and* VARYA, *then her brother again.*) And Varya is just the same as ever, looks like a nun. And I knew Dunyasha— (*Kisses* DUNYASHA.)

GAYEFF The train was two hours late. How's that? How's that for good management?

CHARLOTTA (*to* PISHTCHIK) My dog he eats nuts too.

PISHTCHIK (*astonished*) Think of that!

(*Everybody goes out except* ANYA *and* DUNYASHA.)

DUNYASHA We waited so long—(*Taking off* ANYA's *coat and hat.*)

ANYA I didn't sleep all four nights on the way. And now I feel so chilly.

DUNYASHA It was Lent when you left, there was some snow then, there was frost, and now? My darling (*laughing and kissing her*), I waited so long for you, my joy, my life—I'm telling you now, I can't keep from it another minute.

ANYA (*wearily*) There we go again—

DUNYASHA The clerk Epihodoff, proposed to me after Holy Week.

ANYA You're always talking about the same thing— (*Arranging her hair.*) I've lost all my hairpins— (*She is tired to the point of staggering.*)

DUNYASHA I just don't know what to think. He loves me, loves me so!

ANYA (*looks in through her door, tenderly*) My room, my windows, its just as if I had never been away. I'm home! Tomorrow morning I'll get up, I'll run into the orchard—Oh, if I only could go to sleep! I haven't slept all the way, I was tormented by anxiety.

DUNYASHA Day before yesterday, Pyotr Sergeevich arrived.

ANYA (*joyfully*) Petya!

DUNYASHA He's asleep in the bathhouse, he lives there. I am afraid, he says, of being in the way. (*Taking her watch from her pocket and looking at it.*) Somebody ought to wake him up. It's only that Varvara Mikhailovna told us not to. Don't you wake him up, she said.

(VARYA *enters with a bunch of keys at her belt.*)

VARYA Dunyasha, coffee, quick—Mama is asking for coffee.

DUNYASHA This minute.

(*Goes out.*)

VARYA Well, thank goodness, you've come back. You are home again. (*Caressingly.*) My darling is back! My precious is back!

ANYA I've had such a time.

VARYA I can imagine!

ANYA I left during Holy Week, it was cold then. Charlotta talked all the way and did her tricks. Why did you fasten Charlotta on to me—?

VARYA But you couldn't have traveled alone, darling; not at seventeen!

ANYA We arrived in Paris, it was cold there and snowing. I speak terrible French. Mama lived on the fifth floor; I went to see her; there were some French people in her room, ladies, an old priest with his prayer book, and the place was full of tobacco smoke— very dreary. Suddenly I began to feel sorry for Mama, so sorry, I drew her to me, held her close and couldn't let her go. Then Mama kept hugging me, crying—yes—

VARYA (*tearfully*) Don't—oh, don't—

ANYA Her villa near Mentone she had already sold, she had nothing left, nothing. And I didn't have a kopeck left. It was all we could do to get here. And Mama doesn't understand! We sit down to dinner at a station and she orders, insists on the most expensive things and gives the waiters rouble tips. Charlotta does the same. Yasha too demands his share; it's simply dreadful. Mama has her butler, Yasha, we've brought him here—

VARYA I saw the wretch.

ANYA Well, how are things? Has the interest on the mortgage been paid?

VARYA How could we?

ANYA Oh, my God, my God—!

VARYA In August the estate is to be sold—

ANYA My God—!

LOPAHIN (*looking in through the door and mooing like a cow*) Moo-o-o— (*Goes away.*)

VARYA (*tearfully*) I'd land him one like that— (*Shaking her fist.*)

ANYA (*embracing* VARYA *gently*) Varya, has he proposed? (VARYA *shakes her head.*) But he loves you—Why don't you have it out with him, what are you waiting for?

VARYA I don't think anything will come of it for us. He is very busy, he hasn't any time for me—And doesn't notice me. God knows, it's painful for me to see him—Everybody talks about our marriage, everybody congratulates us, and the truth is, there's nothing to it—it's all like a dream— (*In a different tone.*) You have a brooch looks like a bee.

ANYA (*sadly*) Mama bought it. (*Going toward her room, speaking gaily, like a child.*) And in Paris I went up in a balloon!

VARYA My darling is back! My precious is back! (DUNYASHA *has returned with the coffee pot and is making coffee.* VARYA *is standing by the door.*) Darling, I'm busy all day long with the house and I go around thinking things. If only you could be married to a rich man, I'd be more at peace too, I would go all by myself to a hermitage—then to Kiev—to Moscow, and I'd keep going like that from one holy place to another—I would go on and on. Heavenly!

ANYA The birds are singing in the orchard. What time is it now?

VARYA It must be after two. It's time you were asleep, darling. (*Going into* ANYA's *room.*) Heavenly!

(YASHA *enters with a lap robe and a traveling bag.*)

YASHA (*crossing the stage airily*) May I go through here?

DUNYASHA We'd hardly recognize you, Yasha; you've changed so abroad!

YASHA Hm—And who are you?

DUNYASHA When you left here, I was like that— (*Her hand so high from the floor.*) I'm Dunyasha, Fyodor Kozoyedoff's daughter. You don't remember!

YASHA Hm—You little peach!

Looking around before he embraces her; she shrieks and drops a saucer; YASHA *hurries out.*

VARYA (*at the door, in a vexed tone*) And what's going on here?

DUNYASHA (*tearfully*) I broke a saucer—

VARYA That's good luck.

ANYA (*emerging from her room*) We ought to tell Mama beforehand: Petya is here—

VARYA I told them not to wake him up.

ANYA (*pensively*) Six years ago our father died, a month later our brother Grisha was drowned in the river, such a pretty little boy, just seven. Mama couldn't bear it, she went away, went away without ever looking back— (*Shuddering.*) How I understand her, if she only knew I did. (*A pause.*) And Petya Trofimoff was Grisha's tutor, he might remind—

(FIERS *enters; he is in a jacket and white waistcoat.*)

FIERS (*going to the coffee urn, busy with it*) The mistress will

have her breakfast here— (*Putting on white gloves.*) Is the coffee ready? (*To* DUNYASHA, *sternly.*) You! What about the cream?
DUNYASHA Oh, my God—

(*Hurrying out.*)

FIERS (*busy at the coffee urn*) Oh, you good-for-nothing—! (*Muttering to himself.*) Come back from Paris—And the master used to go to Paris by coach— (*Laughing.*)
VARYA Fiers, what are you—?
FIERS At your service. (*Joyfully.*) My mistress is back! It's what I've been waiting for! Now I'm ready to die— (*Crying for joy.*)

(LYUBOFF ANDREEVNA, GAYEFF *and* SEMYONOFF-PISHTCHIK *enter;* SEMYONOFF-PISHTCHIK *is in a podyovka[1] of fine cloth and sharovary.[2] GAYEFF enters; he makes gestures with his hands and body as if he were playing billiards.*)

LYUBOFF ANDREEVNA How is it? Let me remember—Yellow into the corner! Duplicate in the middle!
GAYEFF I cut into the corner. Sister, you and I slept here in this very room once, and now I am fifty-one years old, strange as that may seem—
LOPAHIN Yes, time passes.
GAYEFF What?
LOPAHIN Time, I say, passes.
GAYEFF And it smells like patchouli here.
ANYA I'm going to bed. Good night, Mama. (*Kissing her mother.*)
LYUBOFF ANDREEVNA My sweet little child. (*Kissing her hands.*) You're glad you are home? I still can't get myself together.
ANYA Good-by, Uncle.
GAYEFF (*kissing her face and hands*) God be with you. How like your mother you are! (*To his sister.*) Lyuba, at her age you were exactly like her.

(ANYA *shakes hands with* LOPAHIN *and* PISHTCHIK, *goes out and closes the door behind her.*)

LYUBOFF ANDREEVNA She's very tired.
PISHTCHIK It is a long trip, I imagine.
VARYA (*to* LOPAHIN *and* PISHTCHIK) Well, then, sirs? It's going on three o'clock, time for gentlemen to be going.
LYUBOFF ANDREEVNA (*laughing*) The same old Varya. (*Drawing

---

[1] *podyovka* short tunic worn under a coat or jacket
[2] *sharovary* loose, bloused trousers, the legs of which are tied at the ankle or tucked into the boots

her to her and kissing her.) There, I'll drink my coffee, then we'll all go. (FIERS *puts a small cushion under her feet.*) Thank you, my dear. I am used to coffee. Drink it day and night. Thank you, my dear old soul. (*Kissing* FIERS.)

VARYA   I'll go see if all the things have come.

(*Goes out.*)

LYUBOFF ANDREEVNA   Is it really me sitting here? (*Laughing.*) I'd like to jump around and wave my arms. (*Covering her face with her hands.*) But I may be dreaming! God knows I love my country, love it deeply, I couldn't look out of the car window, I just kept crying. (*Tearfully.*) However, I must drink my coffee. Thank you, Fiers, thank you, my dear old friend. I'm so glad you're still alive.

FIERS   Day before yesterday.

GAYEFF   He doesn't hear well.

LOPAHIN   And I must leave right now. It's nearly five o'clock in the morning, for Kharkov. What a nuisance! I wanted to look at you—talk—You are as beautiful as ever.

PISHTCHIK   (*breathing heavily*)   Even more beautiful—In your Paris clothes—It's a feast for the eyes—

LOPAHIN   Your brother, Leonid Andreevich here, says I'm a boor, a peasant money grubber, but that's all the same to me, absolutely. Let him say it. All I wish is you'd trust me as you used to, and your wonderful, touching eyes would look at me as they did. Merciful God! My father was a serf; belonged to your grandfather and your father; but you, your own self, you did so much for me once that I've forgotten all that and love you like my own kin—more than my kin.

LYUBOFF ANDREEVNA   I can't sit still—I can't. (*Jumping up and walking about in great excitement.*) I'll never live through this happiness—Laugh at me, I'm silly—My own little bookcase—! (*Kissing the bookcase.*) My little table!

GAYEFF   And in your absence the nurse here died.

LYUBOFF ANDREEVNA   (*sitting down and drinking coffee*)   Yes, may she rest in Heaven! They wrote me.

GAYEFF   And Anastasy died. Cross-eyed Petrushka left me and lives in town now at the police officer's. (*Taking out of his pocket a box of hard candy and sucking a piece.*)

PISHTCHIK   My daughter, Dashenka—sends you her greetings—

LOPAHIN   I want to tell you something very pleasant, cheerful. (*Glancing at his watch.*) I'm going right away. There's no time for talking. Well, I'll make it two or three words. As you know, your cherry orchard is to be sold for your debts; the auction is set for August 22nd, but don't you worry, my dear, you just sleep in peace, there's a way out of it. Here's my plan. Please listen to me. Your estate is only thirteen miles from town. They've run the railroad by it. Now if the cherry orchard and the land along the river were cut up into building lots and leased for summer cottages, you'd have at the very lowest twenty-five thousand roubles per year income.

GAYEFF Excuse me, what rot!

LYUBOFF ANDREEVNA I don't quite understand you, Yermolay Alexeevich.

LOPAHIN At the very least you will get from the summer residents twenty-five roubles per year for a two-and-a-half acre lot and if you post a notice right off, I'll bet you anything that by autumn you won't have a single patch of land free, everything will be taken. In a word, my congratulations, you are saved. The location is wonderful, the river's so deep. Except, of course, it all needs to be tidied up, cleared—For instance, let's say, tear all the old buildings down and this house, which is no good any more, and cut down the old cherry orchard—

LYUBOFF ANDREEVNA Cut down? My dear, forgive me, you don't understand at all. If there's one thing in the whole province that's interesting—not to say remarkable—it's our cherry orchard.

LOPAHIN The only remarkable thing about this cherry orchard is that it's very big. There's a crop of cherries once every two years and even that's hard to get rid of. Nobody buys them.

GAYEFF This orchard is even mentioned in the encyclopedia.

LOPAHIN (*glancing at his watch*) If we don't cook up something and don't get somewhere, the cherry orchard and the entire estate will be sold at auction on the twenty-second of August. Do get it settled then! I swear there is no other way out. Not a one!

FIERS There was a time, forty-fifty years ago when the cherries were dried, soaked, pickled, cooked into jam and it used to be—

GAYEFF Keep quiet, Fiers.

FIERS And it used to be that the dried cherries were shipped by the wagon-load to Moscow and to Kharkov. And the money there was! And the dried cherries were soft then, juicy, sweet, fragrant—They had a way of treating them then—

LYUBOFF ANDREEVNA And where is that way now?

FIERS They have forgotten it. Nobody remembers it.

PISHTCHIK (*to* LYUBOFF ANDREEVNA) What's happening in Paris? How is everything? Did you eat frogs?

LYUBOFF ANDREEVNA I ate crocodiles.

PISHTCHIK Think of it—!

LOPAHIN Up to now in the country there have been only the gentry and the peasants, but now in summer the villa people too are coming in. All the towns, even the least big ones, are surrounded with cottages. In about twenty years very likely the summer resident will multiply enormously. He merely drinks tea on the porch now, but it might well happen that on this two-and-a-half acre lot of his, he'll go in for farming, and then your cherry orchard would be happy, rich, splendid—

GAYEFF (*getting hot*) What rot!

(VARYA *and* YASHA *enter.*)

VARYA Here, Mama. Two telegrams for you. (*Choosing a key and opening the old bookcase noisily.*) Here they are.

LYUBOFF ANDREEVNA From Paris. (*Tearing up the telegrams without reading them.*) Paris, that's all over—

GAYEFF Do you know how old this bookcase is, Lyuba? A week ago I pulled out the bottom drawer and looked, and there the figures were burned on it. The bookcase was made exactly a hundred years ago. How's that? Eh? You might celebrate its jubilee. It's an inanimate object, but all the same, be that as it may, it's a bookcase.

PISHTCHIK (*in astonishment*) A hundred years—! Think of it—!

GAYEFF Yes—quite something— (*Shaking the bookcase.*) Dear, honored bookcase! I saluted your existence, which for more than a hundred years has been directed toward the clear ideals of goodness and justice; your silent appeal to fruitful endeavor has not flagged in all the course of a hundred years, sustaining (*tearfully.*) through the generations of our family, our courage and our faith in a better future and nurturing in us ideals of goodness and of a social consciousness.

(*A pause.*)

LOPAHIN Yes.

LYUBOFF ANDREEVNA You're the same as ever, Lenya.

GAYEFF (*slightly embarrassed*) Carom to the right into the corner pocket. I cut into the side pocket!

LOPAHIN (*glancing at his watch*) Well, it's time for me to go.

YASHA (*handing medicine to* LYUBOFF ANDREEVNA) Perhaps you'll take the pills now—

PISHTCHIK You should never take medicaments, dear madam— They do neither harm nor good—Hand them here, dearest lady. (*He takes the pillbox, shakes the pills out into his palm, blows on them, puts them in his mouth and washes them down with kvass.*) There! Now!

LYUBOFF ANDREEVNA (*startled*) Why, you've lost your mind!

PISHTCHIK   I took all the pills.

LOPAHIN   Such a glutton! (*Everyone laughs.*)

FIERS   The gentleman stayed with us during Holy Week, he ate half a bucket of pickles— (*Muttering.*)

LYUBOFF ANDREEVNA   What is he muttering about?

VARYA   He's been muttering like that for three years. We're used to it.

YASHA   In his dotage.

(CHARLOTTA IVANOVNA *in a white dress—she is very thin, her corset laced very tight—with a lorgnette at her belt, crosses the stage.*)

LOPAHIN   Excuse me, Charlotta Ivanovna, I haven't had a chance yet to welcome you. (*Trying to kiss her hand.*)

CHARLOTTA (*drawing her hand away*)   If I let you kiss my hand, 'twould be my elbow next, then my shoulder—

LOPAHIN   No luck for me today. (*Everyone laughs.*) Charlotta Ivanovna, show us a trick!

CHARLOTTA   No. I want to go to bed.

(*She goes out.*)

LOPAHIN   In three weeks we shall see each other. (*Kissing* LYUBOFF ANDREEVNA'S *hand.*) Till then, good-by. It's time. (*To* GAYEFF.) See you soon. (*Kissing* PISHTCHIK.) See you soon. (*Shaking* VARYA'S *hand, then* FIER'S *and* YASHA'S.) I don't feel like going. (*To* LYUBOFF ANDREEVNA.) If you think it over and make up your mind about the summer cottages, let me know and I'll arrange a loan of something like fifty thousand roubles. Think it over seriously.

VARYA (*angrily*)   Do go on, anyhow, will you!

LOPAHIN   I'm going, I'm going—

(*He goes out.*)

GAYEFF   Boor. However, pardon—Varya is going to marry him, it's Varya's little fiancé.

VARYA   Don't talk too much, Uncle.

LYUBOFF ANDREEVNA   Well, Varya, I should be very glad. He's a good man.

PISHTCHIK   A man, one must say truthfully—A most worthy— And my Dashenka—says also that—she says all sorts of things— (*Snoring but immediately waking up.*) Nevertheless, dearest lady, oblige me—With a loan of two hundred and forty roubles—Tomorrow the interest on my mortgage has got to be paid—

VARYA (*startled*)   There's not any money, none at all.

LYUBOFF ANDREEVNA   Really, I haven't got anything.

PISHTCHIK I'll find it, somehow. (*Laughing.*) I never give up hope. There, I think to myself, all is lost, I am ruined and lo and behold—a railroad is put through my land and—they paid me. And then, just watch, something else will turn up—if not today, then tomorrow—Dashenka will win two hundred thousand—She has a ticket.

LYUBOFF ANDREEVNA We've finished the coffee, now we can go to bed.

FIERS (*brushing* GAYEFF's *clothes, reprovingly*) You put on the wrong trousers again. What am I going to do with you!

VARYA (*softly*) Anya is asleep. (*Opening the window softly.*) Already the sun's rising—it's not cold. Look, Mama! What beautiful trees! My Lord, what air! The starlings are singing!

GAYEFF (*opening another window*) The orchard is all white. You haven't forgotten, Lyuba? That long lane there runs straight—as a strap stretched out. It glistens on moonlight nights. Do you remember? You haven't forgotten it?

LYUBOFF ANDREEVNA (*looking out of the window on to the orchard*) Oh, my childhood, my innocence! I slept in this nursery and looked out on the orchard from here, every morning happiness awoke with me, it was just as it is now, then, nothing has changed. (*Laughing with joy.*) All, all white! Oh, my orchard! After a dark, rainy autumn and cold winter, you are young again and full of happiness. The heavenly angels have not deserted you—If I only could lift the weight from my breast, from my shoulders, if I could only forget my past!

GAYEFF Yes, and the orchard will be sold for debt, strange as that may seem.

LYUBOFF ANDREEVNA Look, our dear mother is walking through the orchard—In a white dress! (*Laughing happily.*) It's she.

GAYEFF Where?

VARYA God be with you, Mama!

LYUBOFF ANDREEVNA There's not anybody, it only seemed so. To the right, as you turn to the summerhouse, a little white tree is leaning there, looks like a woman— (TROFIMOFF *enters, in a student's uniform, well worn, and glasses.*) What a wonderful orchard! The white masses of blossoms, the sky all blue.

TROFIMOFF Lyuboff Andreevna! (*She looks around at him.*) I will just greet you and go immediately. (*Kissing her hand warmly.*) I was told to wait until morning, but I hadn't the patience—

(LYUBOFF ANDREEVNA *looks at him puzzled.*)

VARYA (*tearfully*) This is Petya Trofimoff—

TROFIMOFF   Petya Trofimoff, the former tutor of your Grisha—
Have I really changed so?

(LYUBOFF ANDREEVNA *embraces him, crying quietly.*)

GAYEFF (*embarrassed*)   There, there, Lyuba.

VARYA (*crying*)   I told you, Petya, to wait till tomorrow.

LYUBOFF ANDREEVNA   My Grisha—My boy—Grisha—Son—

VARYA   What can we do, Mama? It's God's will.

TROFIMOFF (*in a low voice tearfully*)   There, there—

LYUBOFF ANDREEVNA (*weeping softly*)   My boy was lost, drowned—
Why? Why, my friend? (*More quietly.*) Anya is asleep there, and
I am talking so loud—Making so much noise—But why, Petya?
Why have you lost your looks? Why do you look so much older?

TROFIMOFF   A peasant woman on the train called me a mangy-
looking gentleman.

LYUBOFF ANDREEVNA   You were a mere boy then, a charming
young student, and now your hair's not very thick any more and
you wear glasses. Are you really a student still? (*Going to the
door.*)

TROFIMOFF   Very likely I'll be a perennial student.

LYUBOFF ANDREEVNA (*kissing her brother, then* VARYA)   Well, go
to bed—You've grown older too, Leonid.

PISHTCHIK (*following her*)   So that's it, we are going to bed now.
Oh, my gout! I'm staying here—I'd like, Lyuboff Andreevna, my
soul, tomorrow morning—Two hundred and forty roubles—

GAYEFF   He's still at it.

PISHTCHIK   Two hundred and forty roubles—To pay interest on
the mortgage.

LYUBOFF ANDREEVNA   I haven't any money, my dove.

PISHTCHIK   I'll pay it back, my dear—It's a trifling sum—

LYUBOFF ANDREEVNA   Oh, very well, Leonid will give—You give it
to him, Leonid.

GAYEFF   Oh, certainly, I'll give it to him. Hold out your pockets.

LYUBOFF ANDREEVNA   What can we do, give it, he needs it—He'll
pay it back.

(LYUBOFF ANDREEVNA, TROFIMOFF, PISHTCHIK *and* FIERS *go out.*
GAYEFF, VARYA *and* YASHA *remain.*)

GAYEFF   My sister hasn't yet lost her habit of throwing money away.
(*To* YASHA.) Get away, my good fellow, you smell like hens.

YASHA (*with a grin*)   And you are just the same as you used to be,
Leonid Andreevich.

GAYEFF   What? (*To* VARYA.) What did he say?

VARYA (*to* YASHA) Your mother has come from the village, she's been sitting in the servants' hall ever since yesterday, she wants to see you—

YASHA The devil take her!

VARYA Ach, shameless creature!

YASHA A lot I need her! She might have come tomorrow.

(*Goes out.*)

VARYA Mama is just the same as she was, she hasn't changed at all. If she could, she'd give away everything she has.

GAYEFF Yes—If many remedies are prescribed for an illness, you may know the illness is incurable. I keep thinking, I wrack my brains, I have many remedies, a great many, and that means, really, I haven't any at all. It would be fine to inherit a fortune from somebody, it would be fine to marry off our Anya to a very rich man, it would be fine to go to Yaroslavl and try our luck with our old aunt, the Countess. Auntie is very, very rich.

VARYA (*crying*) If God would only help us!

GAYEFF Don't bawl! Auntie is very rich but she doesn't like us. To begin with, Sister married a lawyer, not a nobleman— (ANYA *appears at the door.*) Married not a nobleman and behaved herself, you could say, not very virtuously. She is good, kind, nice, I love her very much, but no matter how much you allow for the extenuating circumstances, you must admit she's a depraved woman. You feel it in her slightest movement.

VARYA (*whispering*) Anya is standing in the door there.

GAYEFF What? (*A pause.*) It's amazing, something got in my right eye. I am beginning to see poorly. And on Thursday, when I was in the District Court—

(ANYA *enters.*)

VARYA But why aren't you asleep, Anya?

ANYA I don't feel like sleeping. I can't.

GAYEFF My little girl— (*Kissing* ANYA's *face and hands.*) My child— (*Tearfully.*) You are not my niece, you are my angel, you are everything to me. Believe me, believe—

ANYA I believe you, Uncle. Everybody loves you, respects you— But dear Uncle, you must keep quiet, just keep quiet—What were you saying, just now, about my mother, about your own sister? What did you say that for?

GAYEFF Yes, yes— (*Putting her hand up over his face.*) Really, it's terrible! My God! Oh, God, save me! And today I made a speech to the bookcase—So silly! And it was only when I finished it that I could see it was silly.

VARYA It's true, Uncle, you ought to keep quiet. Just keep quiet. That's all.

ANYA If you kept quiet, you'd have more peace.

GAYEFF I'll keep quiet. (*Kissing* ANYA's *and* VARYA's *hands.*) I'll keep quiet. Only this, it's about business. On Thursday I was in the District Court; well, a few of us gathered around and a conversation began about this and that, about lots of things; apparently it will be possible to arrange a loan on a promissory note to pay the bank the interest due.

VARYA If the Lord would only help us!

GAYEFF Tuesday I shall go and talk it over again. (*To* VARYA.) Don't bawl! (*To* ANYA.) Your mother will talk to Lopahin; of course, he won't refuse her ... And as soon as you rest up, you will go to Yaroslavl to your great-aunt, the Countess. There, that's how we will move from three directions, and the business is in the bag. We'll pay the interest. I am convinced of that— (*Putting a hard candy in his mouth.*) On my honor I'll swear, by anything you like, that the estate shall not be sold! (*Excitedly.*) By my happiness, I swear! Here's my hand, call me a worthless, dishonorable man, if I allow it to come up for auction! With all my soul I swear it!

ANYA (*A quieter mood returns to her; she is happy*) How good you are, Uncle, how clever! (*Embracing her uncle.*) I feel easy now! I feel easy! I'm happy!

FIERS (*enters, reproachfully*) Leonid Andreevich, have you no fear of God! When are you going to bed?

GAYEFF Right away, right away. You may go, Fiers. For this once I'll undress myself. Well, children, beddy bye—More details tomorrow, and now, go to bed (*kissing* ANYA *and* VARYA). I am a man of the eighties—It is a period that's not admired, but I can say, nevertheless, that I've suffered no little for my convictions in the course of my life. It is not for nothing that the peasant loves me. One must know the peasant! One must know from what—

ANYA Again, Uncle!

VARYA You, Uncle dear, keep quiet.

FIERS (*angrily*) Leonid Andreevich!

GAYEFF I'm coming, I'm coming—Go to bed. A double bank into the side pocket! A clean shot—

(*Goes out,* FIERS *hobbling after him.*)

ANYA I feel easy now. I don't feel like going to Yaroslavl; I don't like Great-aunt, but still I feel easy. Thanks to Uncle. (*Sits down.*)

VARYA I must get to sleep. I'm going. And there was unpleasantness here during your absence. In the old servants' quarters, as you know, live only the old servants: Yephemushka, Polya, Yevstignay, well, and Karp. They began to let every sort of creature spend the night with them—I didn't say anything. But then I hear they've spread the rumor that I'd given orders to feed them nothing but beans. Out of stinginess, you see—And all that from Yevstignay—Very well, I think to myself. If that's the way it is, I think to myself, then you just wait. I call in Yevstignay— (*Yawning.*) He comes—How is it, I say, that you, Yevstignay— You're such a fool— (*Glancing at* ANYA.) Anitchka!— (*A pause.*) Asleep! (*Takes* ANYA *by her arm.*) Let's go to bed—Come on!— (*Leading her.*) My little darling fell asleep! Come on— (*They go. Far away beyond the orchard a shepherd is playing on a pipe.* TROFIMOFF *walks across the stage and, seeing* VARYA *and* ANYA, *stops.*) Shh—She is asleep—asleep—Let's go, dear.

ANYA (*softly, half dreaming*)   I'm so tired—All the bells!—Uncle —dear—And Mama and Uncle—Varya.

VARYA   Come on, my dear, come on. (*They go into* ANYA's *room.*)

TROFIMOFF (*tenderly*)   My little sun! My spring!

ACT II

A field. An old chapel, long abandoned, with crooked walls, near it a well, big stones that apparently were once tombstones, and an old bench. A road to the estate of GAYEFF *can be seen. On one side poplars rise, casting their shadows, the cherry orchard begins there. In the distance a row of telegraph poles; and far, far away, faintly traced on the horizon, is a large town, visible only in the clearest weather. The sun will soon be down.* CHARLOTTA, YASHA *and* DUNYASHA *are sitting on the bench;* EPIHODOFF *is standing near and playing the guitar; everyone sits lost in thought.* CHARLOTTA *wears an old peak cap [fourrage];[1] she has taken a rifle from off her shoulders and is adjusting the buckle on the strap.*

CHARLOTTA (*pensively*)   I have no proper passport, I don't know how old I am—it always seems to me I'm very young. When I was a little girl, my father and mother traveled from fair to fair and gave performances, very good ones. And I did *salto mortale*[2] and different tricks. And when Papa and Mama died, a German lady took me to live with her and began teaching me. Good. I grew up. And became a governess. But where I came from and who I am I don't know—Who my parents were, perhaps they weren't even married—I don't know. (*Taking a cucumber out of her pocket and beginning to eat it.*) I don't know a thing. (*A*

---

[1] *fourrage* for hunting
[2] *salto mortale* leap of death

pause.) I'd like so much to talk but there's not anybody. I haven't anybody.

EPIHODOFF (*playing the guitar and singing*) "What care I for the noisy world, what care I for friends and foes."—How pleasant it is to play the mandolin!

DUNYASHA That's a guitar, not a mandolin. (*Looking into a little mirror and powdering her face.*)

EPIHODOFF For a madman who is in love this is a mandolin— (*Singing.*) "If only my heart were warm with the fire of requited love." (*Yasha sings with him.*)

CHARLOTTA How dreadfully these people sing—Phooey! Like jackals.

DUNYASHA (*to* YASHA) All the same what happiness to have been abroad.

YASHA Yes, of course. I cannot disagree with you. (*Yawning and then lighting a cigar.*)

EPIHODOFF That's easily understood. Abroad everything long since attained its complete development.

YASHA That's obvious.

EPIHODOFF I am a cultured man. I read all kinds of remarkable books, but the trouble is I cannot discover my own inclinations, whether to live or to shoot myself, but nevertheless, I always carry a revolver on me. Here it is— (*Showing a revolver.*)

CHARLOTTA That's done. Now I am going. (*Slinging the rifle over her shoulder.*) You are a very clever man, Epihodoff, and a very terrible one; the women must love you madly. Brrrr-r-r-r! (*Going.*) These clever people are all so silly, I haven't anybody to talk with. I'm always alone, alone, I have nobody and—Who I am, why I am, is unknown—

(*Goes out without hurrying.*)

EPIHODOFF Strictly speaking, not touching on other subjects, I must state about myself, in passing, that fate treats me mercilessly, as a storm does a small ship. If, let us suppose, I am mistaken, then why, to mention one instance, do I wake up this morning, look and there on my chest is a spider of terrific size— There, like that. (*Showing the size with both hands.*) And also I take some kvass to drink and in it I find something in the highest degree indecent, such as a cockroach. (*A pause.*) Have you read Buckle? [1] (*A pause.*) I desire to trouble you, Avdotya Feodorovna, with a couple of words.

---

[1] *Buckle* Henry Thomas Buckle (1821–1862), English historian who proposed a scientific method for writing history

DUNYASHA   Speak.

EPIHODOFF   I have a desire to speak with you alone— (*Sighing.*)

DUNYASHA (*embarrassed*)   Very well—But bring me my cape first —by the cupboard—It's rather damp here—

EPIHODOFF   Very well—I'll fetch it—Now I know what I should do with my revolver— (*Takes the guitar and goes out playing.*)

YASHA   Twenty-two misfortunes! Between us he's a stupid man, it must be said. (*Yawning.*)

DUNYASHA   God forbid he should shoot himself. (*A pause.*) I've grown so uneasy, I'm always fretting. I was only a girl when I was taken into the master's house, and now I've lost the habit of simple living—and here are my hands white, white as a lady's. I've become so delicate, fragile, ladylike, afraid of everything— Frightfully so. And, Yasha, if you deceive me, I don't know what will happen to my nerves.

YASHA (*kissing her*)   You little cucumber! Of course every girl must behave properly. What I dislike above everything is for a girl to conduct herself badly.

DUNYASHA   I have come to love you passionately, you are educated, you can discuss anything. (*A pause.*)

YASHA (*yawning*)   Yes, sir—To my mind it is like this: If a girl loves someone, it means she is immoral. (*A pause.*) It is pleasant to smoke a cigar in the clear air— (*Listening.*) They are coming here—It is the ladies and gentlemen— (DUNYASHA *impulsively embraces him.*)

YASHA   Go to the house, as though you had been to bathe in the river, go by this path, otherwise, they might meet you and suspect me of making a rendezvous with you. That I cannot tolerate.

DUNYASHA (*with a little cough*)   Your cigar has given me the headache.

(*Goes out.*)

(YASHA *remains, sitting near the chapel.* LYUBOFF ANDREEVNA, GAYEFF *and* LOPAHIN *enter.*)

LOPAHIN   We must decide definitely, time doesn't wait. Why, the matter's quite simple. Are you willing to lease your land for summer cottages or are you not? Answer in one word, yes or no? Just one word!

LYUBOFF ANDREEVNA   Who is it smokes those disgusting cigars out here—? (*Sitting down.*)

GAYEFF   The railroad running so near is a great convenience. (*Sitting down.*) We made a trip to town and lunched there—Yellow in the side pocket! Perhaps I should go in the house first and play one game—

LYUBOFF ANDREEVNA You'll have time.

LOPAHIN Just one word! (*Imploringly.*) Do give me your answer!

GAYEFF (*yawning*) What?

LYUBOFF ANDREEVNA (*looking in her purse*) Yesterday there was lots of money in it. Today there's very little. My poor Varya! For the sake of economy she feeds everybody milk soup, and in the kitchen the old people get nothing but beans, and here I spend money—senselessly— (*Dropping her purse and scattering gold coins.*) There they go scattering! (*She is vexed.*)

YASHA Allow me, I'll pick them up in a second. (*Picking up the coins.*)

LYUBOFF ANDREEVNA If you will, Yasha. And why did I go in town for lunch—? Your restaurant with its music is trashy, the tablecloths smell of soap—Why drink so much, Lyonya? Why eat so much? Why talk so much? Today in the restaurant you were talking a lot again, and all of it beside the point. About the seventies, about the decadents. And to whom? Talking to waiters about the decadents!

LOPAHIN Yes.

GAYEFF (*waving his hand*) I am incorrigible, that's evident— (*To* YASHA *irritably.*) What is it?—You are forever swirling around in front of us!

YASHA (*laughing*) I cannot hear your voice without laughing.

GAYEFF (*to his sister*) Either I or he—

LYUBOFF ANDREEVNA Go away, Yasha. Go on—

YASHA (*giving* LYUBOFF ANDREEVNA *her purse*) I am going right away. (*Barely suppressing his laughter.*) This minute.

(*Goes out.*)

LOPAHIN The rich Deriganoff intends to buy your estate. They say he is coming personally to the auction.

LYUBOFF ANDREEVNA And where did you hear that?

LOPAHIN In town they are saying it.

GAYEFF Our Yaroslavl aunt promised to send us something, but when and how much she will send, nobody knows—

LOPAHIN How much will she send? A hundred thousand? Two hundred?

LYUBOFF ANDREEVNA Well—maybe ten, fifteen thousand—we'd be thankful for that.

LOPAHIN Excuse me, but such light-minded people as you are, such odd, unbusinesslike people, I never saw. You are told in plain Russian that your estate is being sold up and you just don't seem to take it in.

LYUBOFF ANDREEVNA But what are we to do? Tell us what?

LOPAHIN   I tell you every day. Every day I tell you the same thing. Both the cherry orchard and the land have got to be leased for summer cottages, it has to be done right now, quick—The auction is right under your noses. Do understand! Once you finally decide that there are to be summer cottages, you will get all the money you want, and then you'll be saved.

LYUBOFF ANDREEVNA   Summer cottages and summer residents—it is so trivial, excuse me.

GAYEFF   I absolutely agree with you.

LOPAHIN   I'll either burst out crying, or scream, or faint. I can't bear it! You are torturing me! (*To* GAYEFF.) You're a perfect old woman!

GAYEFF   What?

LOPAHIN   A perfect old woman! (*About to go.*)

LYUBOFF ANDREEVNA   (*alarmed*)   No, don't go, stay, my lamb, I beg you. Perhaps we will think of something!

LOPAHIN   What is there to think about?

LYUBOFF ANDREEVNA   Don't go, I beg you. With you here it is more cheerful anyhow— (*A pause.*) I keep waiting for something, as if the house were about to tumble down on our heads.

GAYEFF   (*deep in thought*)   Double into the corner pocket—Bank into the wide pocket—

LYUBOFF ANDREEVNA   We have sinned so much—

LOPAHIN   What sins have you—?

GAYEFF   (*puts a hard candy into his mouth*)   They say I've eaten my fortune up in hard candies— (*Laughing.*)

LYUBOFF ANDREEVNA   Oh, my sins—I've always thrown money around like mad, recklessly, and I married a man who accumulated nothing but debts. My husband died from champagne—he drank fearfully—and to my misfortune I fell in love with another man. I lived with him, and just at that time—it was my first punishment—a blow over the head: right here in the river my boy was drowned and I went abroad—went away for good, never to return, never to see this river again—I shut my eyes, ran away, beside myself, and he after me—mercilessly, brutally. I bought a villa near Mentone, because he fell ill there, and for three years I knew no rest day or night, the sick man exhausted me, my soul dried up. And last year when the villa was sold for debts, I went to Paris and there he robbed me of everything, threw me over, took up with another woman; I tried to poison myself—so stupid, so shameful—And suddenly I was seized with longing for Russia, for my own country, for my little girl— (*Wiping away her tears.*) Lord, Lord, have mercy, forgive me my sins! Don't punish me any more! (*Getting a telegram out of her pocket.*) I got this today from Paris, he asks forgiveness, begs me to return— (*Tears up the telegram.*) That sounds like music somewhere.

(*Listening.*)

GAYEFF It is our famous Jewish orchestra. You remember, four violins, a flute and double bass.

LYUBOFF ANDREEVNA Does it still exist? We ought to get hold of it sometime and give a party.

LOPAHIN (*listening*) Can't hear it— (*Singing softly.*) "And for money the Germans will frenchify a Russian." (*Laughing.*) What a play I saw yesterday at the theatre, very funny!

LYUBOFF ANDREEVNA And most likely there was nothing funny about it. You shouldn't look at plays, but look oftener at yourselves. How gray all your lives are, what a lot of idle things you say!

LOPAHIN That's true. It must be said frankly this life of ours is idiotic— (*A pause.*) My father was a peasant, an idiot, he understood nothing, he taught me nothing, he just beat me in his drunken fits and always with a stick. At bottom I am just as big a dolt and idiot as he was. I wasn't taught anything, my handwriting is vile, I write like a pig—I am ashamed for people to see it.

LYUBOFF ANDREEVNA You ought to get married, my friend.

LOPAHIN Yes—That's true.

LYUBOFF ANDREEVNA To our Varya, perhaps. She is a good girl.

LOPAHIN Yes.

LYUBOFF ANDREEVNA She comes from simple people, and she works all day long, but the main thing is she loves you. And you, too, have liked her a long time.

LOPAHIN Why not? I am not against it—She's a good girl. (*A pause.*)

GAYEFF They are offering me a position in a bank. Six thousand a year—Have you heard that?

LYUBOFF ANDREEVNA Not you! You stay where you are—

(FIERS *enters, bringing an overcoat.*)

FIERS (*to* GAYEFF) Pray, Sir, put this on, it's damp.

GAYEFF (*putting on the overcoat*) You're a pest, old man.

FIERS That's all right—This morning you went off without letting me know. (*Looking him over.*)

LYUBOFF ANDREEVNA How old you've grown, Fiers!

FIERS At your service.

LOPAHIN   She says you've grown very old!

FIERS   I've lived a long time. They were planning to marry me off before your papa was born. (*Laughing.*) And at the time the serfs were freed I was already the head footman. I didn't want to be freed then, I stayed with the masters— (*A pause.*) And I remember, everybody was happy, but what they were happy about they didn't know themselves.

LOPAHIN   In the old days it was fine. At least they flogged.

FIERS (*not hearing*)   But, of course. The peasants stuck to the masters, the masters stuck to the peasants, and now everything is all smashed up, you can't tell about anything.

GAYEFF   Keep still, Fiers. Tomorrow I must go to town. They have promised to introduce me to a certain general who might make us a loan.

LOPAHIN   Nothing will come of it. And you can rest assured you won't pay the interest.

LYUBOFF ANDREEVNA   He's just raving on. There aren't any such generals.

(TROFIMOFF, ANYA *and* VARYA *enter.*)

GAYEFF   Here they come.

ANYA   There is Mama sitting there.

LYUBOFF ANDREEVNA (*tenderly*)   Come, come—My darlings— (*Embracing* ANYA *and* VARYA.) If you only knew how I love you both! Come sit by me—there—like that.

(*Everybody sits down.*)

LOPAHIN   Our perennial student is always strolling with the young ladies.

TROFIMOFF   It's none of your business.

LOPAHIN   He will soon be fifty and he's still a student.

TROFIMOFF   Stop your stupid jokes.

LOPAHIN   But why are you so peevish, you queer duck?

TROFIMOFF   Don't you pester me.

LOPAHIN (*laughing*)   Permit me to ask you, what do you make of me?

TROFIMOFF   Yermolay Alexeevich, I make this of you: you are a rich man, you'll soon be a millionaire. Just as it is in the metabolism of nature, a wild beast is needed to eat up everything that comes his way; so you, too, are needed.

(*Everyone laughs.*)

VARYA   Petya, you'd better tell us about the planets.

LYUBOFF ANDREEVNA   No, let's go on with yesterday's conversation.

TROFIMOFF   What was it about?

GAYEFF   About the proud man.

TROFIMOFF   We talked a long time yesterday, but didn't get any-where. In a proud man, in your sense of the word, there is some-thing mystical. Maybe you are right, from your standpoint, but if we are to discuss it in simple terms, without whimsy, then what pride can there be, is there any sense in it, if man physiologically is poorly constructed, if in the great majority he is crude, unintel-ligent, profoundly miserable. One must stop admiring oneself. One must only work.

GAYEFF   All the same, you will die.

TROFIMOFF   Who knows? And what does it mean—you will die? Man may have a hundred senses, and when he dies only the five that are known to us may perish, and the remaining ninety-five go on living.

LYUBOFF ANDREEVNA   How clever you are, Petya!

LOPAHIN (*ironically*)   Terribly!

TROFIMOFF   Humanity goes forward, perfecting its powers. Every-thing that's unattainable now will some day become familiar, un-derstandable; it is only that one must work and must help with all one's might those who seek the truth. With us in Russia so far only a very few work. The great majority of the intelligentsia that I know are looking for nothing, doing nothing, and as yet have no capacity for work. They call themselves intelligentsia, are free and easy with the servants, treat the peasants like animals, edu-cate themselves poorly, read nothing seriously, do absolutely noth-ing; about science they just talk and about art they understand very little. Every one of them is serious, all have stern faces; they all talk of nothing but important things, philosophize, and all the time everybody can see that the workmen eat abominably, sleep without any pillows, thirty or forty to a room, and everywhere there are bedbugs, stench, dampness, moral uncleanness—And apparently with us, all the fine talk is only to divert the attention of ourselves and of others. Show me where we have the day nurseries they are always talking so much about, where are the reading rooms? They only write of these in novels, for the truth is there are not any at all. There is only filth, vulgarity, orien-talism—I am afraid of very serious faces and dislike them. I'm afraid of serious conversations. Rather than that let's just keep still.

LOPAHIN   You know I get up before five o'clock in the morning and work from morning till night. Well, I always have money, my own and other people's, on hand, and I see what the people around me are. One has only to start doing something to find out how few honest and decent people there are. At times when I can't go to sleep, I think: Lord, thou gavest us immense forests, unbounded fields and the widest horizons, and living in the midst of them we should indeed be giants—

LYUBOFF ANDREEVNA You feel the need for giants—They are good only in fairly tales, anywhere else they only frighten us.

(*At the back of the stage* EPIHODOFF *passes by, playing the guitar.*)

LYUBOFF ANDREEVNA (*lost in thought*) Epihodoff is coming—
ANYA (*lost in thought*) Epihodoff is coming.
GAYEFF The sun has set, ladies and gentlemen.
TROFIMOFF Yes.
GAYEFF (*not loud and as if he were declaiming*) Oh, Nature, wonderful, you gleam with eternal radiance, beautiful and indifferent, you, whom we call Mother, combine in yourself both life and death, you give life and you take it away.
VARYA (*beseechingly*) Uncle!
ANYA Uncle, you're doing it again!
TROFIMOFF You'd better bank the yellow into the side pocket.
GAYEFF I'll be quiet, quiet.

(*All sit absorbed in their thoughts. There is only the silence.* FIERS *is heard muttering to himself softly. Suddenly a distant sound is heard, as if from the sky, like the sound of a snapped string, dying away, mournful.*)

LYUBOFF ANDREEVNA What's that?
LOPAHIN I don't know. Somewhere far off in a mine shaft a bucket fell. But somewhere very far off.
GAYEFF And it may be some bird—like a heron.
TROFIMOFF Or an owl—
LYUBOFF ANDREEVNA (*shivering*) It's unpleasant, somehow. (*A pause.*)
FIERS Before the disaster it was like that. The owl hooted and the samovar hummed without stopping, both.
GAYEFF Before what disaster?
FIERS Before the emancipation.

(*A pause.*)

LYUBOFF ANDREEVNA You know, my friends, let's go. Twilight is falling. (*To* ANYA.) You have tears in your eyes—What is it, my dear little girl? (*Embracing her.*)
ANYA It's just that, Mama. It's nothing.
TROFIMOFF Somebody is coming.

(*A stranger appears in a shabby white cap, and an overcoat; he is a little drunk.*)

THE STRANGER Allow me to ask you, can I go straight through here to the station?

GAYEFF You can. Go by that road.

THE STRANGER I am heartily grateful to you. (*Coughing.*) The weather is splendid— (*Declaiming.*) Brother of mine, suffering brother—Go out to the Volga, whose moans— (*To* VARYA.) Mademoiselle, grant a hungry Russian man some thirty kopecks— (VARYA *is frightened and gives a shriek.*)

LOPAHIN (*angrily*) There's a limit to everything.

LYUBOFF ANDREEVNA (*flustered*) Take this—Here's this for you— (*Searching in her purse.*) No silver—It's all the same, here's a gold piece for you—

THE STRANGER I am heartily grateful to you.

(*Goes out.*)

(*Laughter.*)

VARYA (*frightened*) I'm going—I'm going—Oh, Mama, you poor little Mama! There's nothing in the house for people to eat, and you gave him a gold piece.

LYUBOFF ANDREEVNA What is to be done with me, so silly? I shall give you all I have in the house. Yermolay Alexeevich, you will lend me some this once more!—

LOPAHIN Agreed.

LYUBOFF ANDREEVNA Let's go, ladies and gentlemen, it's time. And here, Varya, we have definitely made a match for you, I congratulate you.

VARYA (*through her tears*) Mama, that's not something to joke about.

LOPAHIN Achmelia, get thee to a nunnery.[1]

GAYEFF And my hands are trembling; it is a long time since I have played billiards.

LOPAHIN Achmelia, Oh nymph, in thine orisons be all my sins remember'd—[2]

LYUBOFF ANDREEVNA Let's go, my dear friends, it will soon be suppertime.

VARYA He frightened me. My heart is thumping so!

---

[1] *Achmelia . . . nunnery* Shakespeare, *Hamlet,* III.i.
[2] *Achmelia . . . remember'd Hamlet,* III.i.

LOPAHIN   I remind you, ladies and gentlemen: August 22nd the cherry orchard will be auctioned off. Think about that!— Think!—

(*All go out except* TROFIMOFF *and* ANYA.)

ANYA (*laughing*)   My thanks to the stranger, he frightened Varya, now we are alone.

TROFIMOFF   Varya is afraid we might begin to love each other and all day long she won't leave us to ourselves. With her narrow mind she cannot understand that we are above love. To sidestep the petty and illusory, which prevent our being free and happy, that is the aim and meaning of our life. Forward! We march on irresistibly toward the bright star that burns there in the distance. Forward! Do not fall behind, friends!

ANYA (*extending her arms upward*)   How well you talk! (*A pause.*) It's wonderful here today!

TROFIMOFF   Yes, the weather is marvelous.

ANYA   What have you done to me, Petya, why don't I love the cherry orchard any longer the way I used to? I loved it so tenderly, it seemed to me there was not a better place on earth than our orchard.

TROFIMOFF   All Russia is our orchard. The earth is immense and beautiful, and on it are many wonderful places. (*A pause.*) Just think, Anya: your grandfather, great-grandfather and all your ancestors were slave owners, in possession of living souls, and can you doubt that from every cherry in the orchard, from every leaf, from every trunk, human beings are looking at you, can it be that you don't hear their voices? To possess living souls, well, that depraved all of you who lived before and who are living now, so that your mother and you, and your uncle no longer notice that you live by debt, at somebody else's expense, at the expense of those very people whom you wouldn't let past your front door— We are at least two hundred years behind the times, we have as yet absolutely nothing, we have no definite attitude toward the past, we only philosophize, complain of our sadness or drink vodka. Why, it is quite clear that to begin to live in the present we must first atone for our past, must be done with it; and we can atone for it only through suffering, only through uncommon, incessant labor. Understand that, Anya.

ANYA   The house we live in ceased to be ours long ago, and I'll go away, I give you my word.

TROFIMOFF   If you have the household keys, throw them in the well and go away. Be free as the wind.

ANYA (*transported*)   How well you said that!

TROFIMOFF   Believe me, Anya, believe me! I am not thirty yet, I am young, I am still a student, but I have already borne so much! Every winter I am hungry, sick, anxious, poor as a beggar, and— where has destiny not chased me, where haven't I been! And yet, my soul has always, every minute, day and night, been full of inexplicable premonitions. I have a premonition of happiness, Anya, I see it already—

ANYA (*pensively*)   The moon is rising.

(EPIHODOFF *is heard playing on the guitar, always the same sad song. The moon rises. Somewhere near the poplars* VARYA *is looking for* ANYA *and calling:* "ANYA! *Where are you?*")

TROFIMOFF   Yes, the moon is rising. (*A pause.*) Here is happiness, here it comes, comes always nearer and nearer, I hear its foot-steps now. And if we shall not see it, shall not come to know it, what does that matter? Others will see it!

VARYA (*off*)   Anya! Where are you?

TROFIMOFF   Again, that Varya! (*Angrily.*) It's scandalous!

ANYA   Well, let's go to the river. It's lovely there.

TROFIMOFF   Let's go. (*They go out.*)

VARYA (*off*)   Anya! Anya!

ACT III

The drawing room, separated by an arch from the ballroom. A chandelier is lighted. A Jewish orchestra is playing—the same that was mentioned in Act II. Evening. In the ballroom they are dancing grand rond.[1] The voice of SEMYONOFF-PISHTCHIK: *"Promenade à une paire!"[2] They enter the drawing room; in the first couple are* PISHTCHIK *and* CHARLOTTA IVA-NOVNA; *in the second,* TROFIMOFF *and* LYUBOFF ANDREEVNA; *in the third,* ANYA *with the* POST-OFFICE CLERK; *in the fourth,* VARYA *with the* STA-TION-MASTER, *et cetera—*VARYA *is crying softly and wipes away her tears while she is dancing.* DUNYASHA *is in the last couple through the drawing room.* PISHTCHIK *shouts: "Grand rond, balancez!"[3] and "Les Cavaliers à genoux et remerciez vos dames!"[4]*

(FIERS *in a frock coat goes by with seltzer water on a tray.* PISHTCHIK *and* TROFIMOFF *come into the drawing room.*)

PISHTCHIK   I am full-blooded, I have had two strokes already, and dancing is hard for me, but as they say, if you are in a pack

[1] *grand rond* great circle, a dance
[2] *promenade . . . paire* promenade by single couple
[3] *balancez* a technical dance movement
[4] *Les . . . dames* "Gentlemen, kneel and thank your ladies"

of dogs, you may bark and bark, but you must still wag your tail. At that, I have the health of a horse. My dear father—he was a great joker—may he dwell in Heaven—used to talk as if our ancient line, the Semyonoff-Pishtchiks, were descended from the very horse that Caligula made a Senator— (*Sitting down.*) But here's my trouble: I haven't any money. A hungry dog believes in nothing but meat— (*Snoring but waking at once.*) And the same way with me—I can't talk about anything but money.

TROFIMOFF   Well, to tell you the truth, there is something of a horse about your figure.

PISHTCHIK   Well—a horse is a fine animal—You can sell a horse—

(*The sound of playing billiards comes from the next room.* VARYA *appears under the arch to the ballroom.*)

TROFIMOFF (*teasing*)   Madam Lopahin! Madam Lopahin!

VARYA (*angrily*)   A mangy-looking gentleman!

TROFIMOFF   Yes, I am a mangy-looking gentleman, and proud of it!

VARYA (*in bitter thought*)   Here we have gone and hired musicians and what are we going to pay them with?

(*Goes out.*)

TROFIMOFF (*to* PISHTCHIK)   If the energy you have wasted in the course of your life trying to find money to pay the interest had gone into something else, you could very likely have turned the world upside down before you were done with it.

PISHTCHIK   Nietzsche—the philosopher—the greatest—the most celebrated—a man of tremendous mind—says in his works that one may make counterfeit money.

TROFIMOFF   And have you read Nietzsche?

PISHTCHIK   Well—Dashenka told me. And I'm in such a state now that I could make counterfeit money myself— Day after tomorrow three hundred and ten roubles must be paid—one hundred and thirty I've on hand— (*Feeling in his pockets, alarmed.*) The money is gone! I have lost the money! (*Tearfully.*) Where is the money? (*Joyfully.*) Here it is, inside the lining—I was in quite a sweat—

(LYUBOFF ANDREEVNA *and* CHARLOTTA IVANOVNA *come in.*)

LYUBOFF ANDREEVNA (*humming lazginka, a Georgian dance*)   Why does Leonid take so long? What's he doing in town? (*To* DUN-YASHA.) Dunyasha, offer the musicians some tea—

TROFIMOFF   In all probability the auction did not take place.

LYUBOFF ANDREEVNA   And the musicians came at an unfortunate moment and we planned the ball at an unfortunate moment— Well, it doesn't matter. (*Sitting down and singing softly.*)

CHARLOTTA (*gives* PISHTCHIK *a deck of cards*) Here is a deck of cards for you, think of some one card.

PISHTCHIK I have thought of one.

CHARLOTTA Now, shuffle the deck. Very good. Hand it here; oh, my dear Monsieur Pishtchik. *Ein, zwei, drei!* Now look for it, it's in your coat pocket—

PISHTCHIK (*getting a card out of his coat pocket*) The eight of spades, that's absolutely right! (*Amazed.*) Fancy that!

CHARLOTTA (*holding a deck of cards in her palm; to* TROFIMOFF) Tell me quick now, which card is on top?

TROFIMOFF What is it? Well—the Queen of Spades.

CHARLOTTA Right! (*To* PISHTCHIK.) Well? Which card's on top?

PISHTCHIK The Ace of Hearts.

CHARLOTTA Right! (*Strikes the deck against her palm; the deck of cards disappears.*) And what beautiful weather we are having today!

(*A mysterious feminine voice answers her, as if from under the floor: "Oh, yes. The weather is splendid, madame." "You are so nice, you're my ideal—" The voice: "Madame, you too please me greatly."*)

THE STATIONMASTER (*applauding*) Madam Ventriloquist, bravo!

PISHTCHIK (*amazed*) Fancy that! Most charming Charlotta Ivanovna—I am simply in love with you.

CHARLOTTA In love? (*Shrugging her shoulders.*) Is it possible that you can love? *Guter Mensch aber schlechter Musikant.*[1]

TROFIMOFF (*slapping* PISHTCHIK *on the shoulder*) You horse, you—

CHARLOTTA I beg your attention, one more trick. (*Taking a lap robe from the chair.*) Here is a very fine lap robe—I want to sell it— (*Shaking it out.*) Wouldn't somebody like to buy it?

PISHTCHIK (*amazed*) Fancy that!

CHARLOTTA *Ein, zwei, drei!*

(*She quickly raises the lowered robe, behind it stands* ANYA, *who curtseys, runs to her mother, embraces her and runs back into the ballroom amid the general delight.*)

LYUBOFF ANDREEVNA (*applauding*) Bravo, bravo—!

CHARLOTTA Now again! *Ein, zwei, drei!*

(*Lifting the robe: behind it stands* VARYA, *she bows.*)

---

[1] *Guter . . . Musikant* "A good man, but a sloppy musician"

PISHTCHIK (*amazed*) Fancy that!

CHARLOTTA That's all. (*Throwing the robe at* PISHTCHIK, *curtseying and running into the ballroom.*)

PISHTCHIK (*hurrying after her*) You little rascal—What a girl! What a girl!

(*Goes out.*)

LYUBOFF ANDREEVNA And Leonid is not here yet. What he's doing in town so long, I don't understand! Everything is finished there, either the estate is sold by now, or the auction didn't take place. Why keep it from us so long?

VARYA (*trying to comfort her*) Uncle has bought it, I am sure of that.

TROFIMOFF (*mockingly*) Yes.

VARYA Great-aunt sent him power of attorney to buy it in her name and transfer the debt. She did this for Anya. And I feel certain, God willing, that Uncle will buy it.

LYUBOFF ANDREEVNA Our Yaroslavl great-aunt has sent fifteen thousand to buy the estate in her name—She doesn't trust us, but that wouldn't be enough to pay the interest even— (*Covering her face with her hands.*) Today my fate will be decided, my fate—

TROFIMOFF (*teasing* VARYA) Madam Lopahin!

VARYA (*angrily*) Perennial student! You have already been expelled from the University twice.

LYUBOFF ANDREEVNA But why are you angry, Varya? He teases you about Lopahin, what of it? Marry Lopahin if you want to, he is a good man, interesting. If you don't want to, don't marry him; darling, nobody is making you do it.

VARYA I look at this matter seriously, Mama, one must speak straight out. He's a good man, I like him.

LYUBOFF ANDREEVNA Then marry him. What there is to wait for I don't understand!

VARYA But I can't propose to him myself, Mama. It's two years now; everyone has been talking to me about him, everyone talks, and he either remains silent or jokes. I understand. He's getting rich, he's busy with his own affairs, and has no time for me. If there were money, ever so little, even a hundred roubles, I would drop everything, and go far away. I'd go to a nunnery.

TROFIMOFF How saintly!

VARYA (*to* TROFIMOFF) A student should be intelligent! (*In a low voice, tearfully.*) How homely you have grown, Petya, how old you've got. (*To* LYUBOFF ANDREEVNA, *no longer crying.*) It is just that I can't live without working, Mama. I must be doing something every minute.

YASHA (*enters, barely restraining his laughter*) Epihodoff has broken a billiard cue!—

(*Goes out.*)

VARYA But why is Epihodoff here? Who allowed him to play billiards? I don't understand these people—

(*Goes out.*)

LYUBOFF ANDREEVNA Don't tease her, Petya; you can see she has troubles enough without that.

TROFIMOFF She is just too zealous. Sticking her nose into things that are none of her business. All summer she gave us no peace, neither me nor Anya; she was afraid a romance would spring up between us. What business is that of hers? And besides I haven't shown any signs of it. I am so remote from triviality. We are above love!

LYUBOFF ANDREEVNA Well, then, I must be beneath love. (*Very anxiously.*) Why isn't Leonid here? Just to tell us whether the estate is sold or not? Calamity seems to me so incredible that I don't know what to think, I'm lost—I could scream this minute— I could do something insane. Save me, Petya. Say something, do say. . . .

TROFIMOFF Whether the estate is sold today or is not sold—is it not the same? There is no turning back, the path is all grown over. Calm yourself, my dear, all that was over long ago. One mustn't deceive oneself, one must for once at least in one's life look truth straight in the eye.

LYUBOFF ANDREEVNA What truth? You see where the truth is and where the untruth is, but as for me, it's as if I had lost my sight, I see nothing. You boldly decide all important questions, but tell me, my dear boy, isn't that because you are young and haven't had time yet to suffer through any one of your problems? You look boldly ahead, and isn't that because you don't see and don't expect anything terrible, since life is still hidden from your young eyes? You are braver, more honest, more profound than we are, but stop and think, be magnanimous, have a little mercy on me, just a little. Why, I was born here. My father and mother lived here and my grandfather. I love this house, I can't imagine my life without the cherry orchard and if it is very necessary to sell it, then sell me along with the orchard— (*Embracing* TROFIMOFF *and kissing him on the forehead.*) Why, my son was drowned here— (*Crying.*) Have mercy on me, good, kind man.

TROFIMOFF You know I sympathize with you from the bottom of my heart.

LYUBOFF ANDREEVNA But that should be said differently, differently— (*Taking out her handkerchief; a telegram falls on the floor.*) My heart is heavy today, you can't imagine how heavy. It is too noisy for me here, my soul trembles at every sound, I tremble all over and yet I can't go off to myself, when I am alone the silence frightens me. Don't blame me, Petya—I love you as one of my own. I should gladly have given you Anya's hand, I assure you, only, my dear, you must study and finish your course. You do nothing. Fate simply flings you about from place to place, and that's so strange—Isn't that so? Yes? And you must do something about your beard, to make it grow somehow— (*Laughing.*) You look funny!

TROFIMOFF (*picking up the telegram*) I do not desire to be beautiful.

LYUBOFF ANDREEVNA This telegram is from Paris. I get one every day. Yesterday and today too. That wild man has fallen ill again, something is wrong again with him—He asks forgiveness, begs me to come, and really I ought to make a trip to Paris and stay awhile near him. Your face looks stern, Petya, but what is there to do, my dear, what am I to do, he is ill, he is alone, unhappy, and who will look after him there, who will keep him from doing the wrong thing, who will give him his medicine on time? And what is there to hide or keep still about? I love him, that's plain. I love him, love him—It's a stone about my neck, I'm sinking to the bottom with it, but I love that stone and live without it I cannot. (*Pressing* TROFIMOFF's *hand.*) Don't think harshly of me, Petya, don't say anything to me, don't—

TROFIMOFF (*tearfully*) Forgive my frankness, for God's sake! Why, he picked your bones.

LYUBOFF ANDREEVNA No, no, no, you must not talk like that. (*Stopping her ears.*)

TROFIMOFF But he is a scoundrel, only you, you are the only one that doesn't know it. He is a petty scoundrel, a nonentity—

LYUBOFF ANDREEVNA (*angry but controlling herself*) You are twenty-six years old or twenty-seven, but you are still a schoolboy in the second grade!

TROFIMOFF Very well!

LYUBOFF ANDREEVNA You should be a man—at your age you should understand people who love. And you yourself should love someone—you should fall in love! (*Angrily.*) Yes, yes! And there is no purity in you; you are simply smug, a ridiculous crank, a freak—

TROFIMOFF (*horrified*) What is she saying!

LYUBOFF ANDREEVNA "I am above love!" You are not above love, Petya, you are, as our Fiers would say, just a good-for-nothing. Imagine, at your age, not having a mistress—!

TROFIMOFF (*horrified*) This is terrible! What is she saying! (*Goes quickly into the ballroom, clutching his head.*) This is horrible— I can't bear it, I am going— (*Goes out but immediately returns.*) All is over between us. (*Goes out into the hall.*)

LYUBOFF ANDREEVNA (*shouting after him*) Petya, wait! You funny creature, I was joking! Petya! (*In the hall someone can be heard running up the stairs and suddenly falling back down with a crash. ANYA and VARYA scream but immediately begin laughing.*) What's that?

ANYA (*runs in, laughing*) Petya fell down the stairs! (*Runs out.*)

LYUBOFF ANDREEVNA What a funny boy that Petya is—! (*The STATION-MASTER stops in the center of the ballroom and begins to recite "The Sinner" by A. Tolstoi. They listen to him but he has recited only a few lines when the strains of a waltz are heard from the hall and the recitation is broken off. They all dance. TROFIMOFF, ANYA, VARYA and LYUBOFF ANDREEVNA come in from the hall.*) But, Petya—but, dear soul—I beg your forgiveness—Let's go dance.

(*She dances with TROFIMOFF. ANYA and VARYA dance. FIERS enters, leaving his stick by the side door. YASHA also comes into the drawing room and watches the dancers.*)

YASHA What is it, Grandpa?

FIERS I don't feel very well. In the old days there were generals, barons, admirals dancing at our parties, and now we send for the post-office clerk and the stationmaster, and even they are none too anxious to come. Somehow I've grown feeble. The old master, the grandfather, treated everybody with sealing-wax for all sicknesses. I take sealing-wax every day, have done so for twenty-odd years or more; it may be due to that that I'm alive.

YASHA You are tiresome, Grandpa. (*Yawning.*) Why don't you go off and die?

FIERS Aw, you—good-for-nothing!— (*Muttering.*)

(*TROFIMOFF and LYUBOFF ANDREEVNA dance in the ballroom and then in the drawing room.*)

LYUBOFF ANDREEVNA *Merci.* I'll sit down awhile— (*Sitting down.*) I'm tired.

ANYA (*enters, agitated*) And just now in the kitchen some man was saying that the cherry orchard had been sold today.

LYUBOFF ANDREEVNA Sold to whom?

ANYA He didn't say who to. He's gone.

(*Dancing with* TROFIMOFF, *they pass into the ballroom.*)

YASHA It was some old man babbling there. A stranger.

FIERS And Leonid Andreevich is still not here, he has not arrived. The overcoat he has on is light, mid-season—let's hope he won't catch cold. Ach, these young things!

LYUBOFF ANDREEVNA I shall die this minute. Go, Yasha, find out who it was sold to.

YASHA But he's been gone a long time, the old fellow. (*Laughing.*)

LYUBOFF ANDREEVNA (*with some annoyance*) Well, what are you laughing at? What are you so amused at?

YASHA Epihodoff is just too funny. An empty-headed man. Twenty-two misfortunes!

LYUBOFF ANDREEVNA Fiers, if the estate is sold, where will you go?

FIERS Wherever you say, there I'll go.

LYUBOFF ANDREEVNA Why do you look like that? Aren't you well? You know you ought to go to bed—

FIERS Yes— (*With a sneer.*) I go to bed and without me who's going to serve, who'll take care of things? I'm the only one in the whole house.

YASHA (*to* LYUBOFF ANDREEVNA) Lyuboff Andreevna, let me ask a favor of you, do be so kind! If you ever go back to Paris, take me with you, please do! It's impossible for me to stay here. (*Looking around him, and speaking in a low voice.*) Why talk about it? You can see for yourself it's an uncivilized country, an immoral people and not only that, there's the boredom of it. The food they give us in that kitchen is abominable and there's that Fiers, too, walking about and muttering all kinds of words that are out of place. Take me with you, be so kind!

PISHTCHIK (*enters*) Allow me to ask you—for a little waltz, most beautiful lady— (LYUBOFF ANDREEVNA *goes with him.*) Charming lady, I must borrow a hundred and eighty roubles from you —will borrow— (*dancing*) a hundred and eighty roubles— (*They pass into the ballroom.*)

YASHA (*singing low*) "Wilt thou know the unrest in my soul!"

(*In the ballroom a figure in a gray top hat and checked trousers waves both hands and jumps about; there are shouts of "Bravo,* CHARLOTTA IVANOVNA!"*)

DUNYASHA (*stopping to powder her face*) The young lady orders me to dance—there are a lot of gentlemen and very few ladies— but dancing makes my head swim and my heart thump. Fiers,

Nikolaevich, the post-office clerk said something to me just now that took my breath away.

(*The music plays more softly.*)

FIERS   What did he say to you?

DUNYASHA   You are like a flower, he says.

YASHA (*yawning*)   What ignorance—!

(*Goes out.*)

DUNYASHA   Like a flower—I am such a sensitive girl, I love tender words awfully.

FIERS   You'll be getting your head turned.

(EPIHODOFF *enters.*)

EPIHODOFF   Avdotya Feodorovna, you don't want to see me—It's as if I were some sort of insect. (*Sighing.*) Ach, life!

DUNYASHA   What do you want?

EPIHODOFF   Undoubtedly you may be right. (*Sighing.*) But of course, if one considers it from a given point of view, then you, I will allow myself so to express it, forgive my frankness, absolutely led me into a state of mind. I know my fate, every day some misfortune happens to me, but I have long since become accustomed to that, and so I look on my misfortunes with a smile. You gave me your word and, although I—

DUNYASHA   I beg you, we'll talk later on, but leave me now in peace. I'm in a dream now. (*Playing with her fan.*)

EPIHODOFF   I have something wrong happen every day—I will allow myself so to express it—I just smile, I even laugh.

VARYA (*enters from the ballroom*)   You are not gone yet, Semyon? What a really disrespectful man you are! (*To* DUNYASHA.) Get out of here, Dunyasha. (*To* EPIHODOFF.) You either play billiards and break a cue or you walk about the drawing room like a guest.

EPIHODOFF   Allow me to tell you, you cannot make any demands on me.

VARYA   I'm not making any demands on you, I'm talking to you. All you know is to walk from place to place but not do any work. We keep a clerk, but what for, nobody knows.

EPIHODOFF (*offended*)   Whether I work, whether I walk, whether I eat, or whether I play billiards are matters to be discussed only by people of understanding and my seniors.

VARYA   You dare to say that to me! (*Flying into a temper.*) You dare? So I don't understand anything? Get out of here! This minute!

EPIHODOFF (*alarmed*) I beg you to express yourself in a delicate manner.

VARYA (*beside herself*) This very minute, get out of here! Get out! (*He goes to the door; she follows him.*) Twenty-two misfortunes! Don't you dare breathe in here! Don't let me set eyes on you! (EPIHODOFF *has gone out, but his voice comes from outside the door: "I shall complain about you."*) Ah, you are coming back? (*Grabbing the stick that* FIERS *put by the door.*) Come on, come —come on, I'll show you—Ah, you are coming? You are coming? Take that then—!

She swings the stick, at the very moment when LOPAHIN *is coming in.*

LOPAHIN Most humbly, I thank you.

VARYA (*angrily and ironically*) I beg your pardon!

LOPAHIN It's nothing at all. I humbly thank you for the pleasant treat.

VARYA It isn't worth your thanks. (*Moving away, then looking back and asking gently.*) I haven't hurt you?

LOPAHIN No, it's nothing. There's a great bump coming though.

*Voices in the ballroom: "*LOPAHIN *has come back." "*YERMOLAY ALEXEE-VICH!"*

PISHTCHIK (*enters*) See what we see, hear what we hear—! (*He and* LOPAHIN *kiss one another.*) You smell slightly of cognac, my dear, my good old chap. And we are amusing ourselves here too.

LYUBOFF ANDREEVNA (*enters*) Is that you, Yermolay Alexeevich? Why were you so long? Where is Leonid?

LOPAHIN Leonid Andreevich got back when I did, he's coming.

LYUBOFF ANDREEVNA (*agitated*) Well, what? Was there an auction? Do speak!

LOPAHIN (*embarrassed, afraid of showing the joy he feels*) The auction was over by four o'clock—We were late for the train, had to wait till half-past nine. (*Sighing heavily.*) Ugh, my head's swimming a bit!

(GAYEFF *enters; with his right hand he carries his purchases, with his left he wipes away his tears.*)

LYUBOFF ANDREEVNA Lyona, what? Lyona, eh? (*Impatiently, with tears in her eyes.*) Quick, for God's sake—

GAYEFF (*not answering her, merely waving his hand; to* FIERS, *crying*) Here, take it—There are anchovies, some Kertch herrings —I haven't eaten anything all day—What I have suffered! (*The door into the billiard room is open; you hear the balls clicking and* YASHA's *voice: "Seven and eighteen!"* GAYEFF's *expression changes, he is no longer crying.*) I'm terribly tired. You help me change, Fiers.

(*Goes to his room through the ballroom,* FIERS *behind him.*)

PISHTCHIK   What happened at the auction? Go on, tell us!

LYUBOFF ANDREEVNA   Is the cherry orchard sold?

LOPAHIN   It's sold.

LYUBOFF ANDREEVNA   Who bought it?

LOPAHIN   I bought it. (*A pause.* LYUBOFF ANDREEVNA *is overcome. She would have fallen had she not been standing near the chair and table.* VARYA *takes the keys from her belt, throws them on the floor in the middle of the drawing room and goes out.*) I bought it. Kindly wait a moment, ladies and gentlemen, everything is muddled up in my head, I can't speak— (*Laughing.*) We arrived at the auction, Deriganoff was already there. Leonid Andreevich had only fifteen thousand and Deriganoff right off bids thirty over and above indebtedness. I see how things are, I match him with forty thousand. He forty-five. I fifty-five. That is to say he raises it by fives, I by tens.—So it ended. Over and above the indebtedness, I bid up to ninety thousand, it was knocked down to me. The cherry orchard is mine now. Mine! (*Guffawing.*) My God, Lord, the cherry orchard is mine! Tell me I'm drunk, out of my head, that I'm imagining all this— (*Stamps his feet.*) Don't laugh at me! If only my father and grandfather could rise from their graves and see this whole business, see how their Yermolay, beaten, half-illiterate Yermolay, who used to run around barefoot in winter, how that very Yermolay has bought an estate that nothing in the world can beat. I bought the estate where grandfather and father were slaves, where you wouldn't even let me in the kitchen. I am asleep, it's only some dream of mine, it only seems so to me—That's nothing but the fruit of your imagination, covered with the darkness of the unknown— (*Picking up the keys, with a gentle smile.*) She threw down the keys, wants to show she is not mistress any more— (*Jingling the keys.*) Well, it's all the same. (*The orchestra is heard tuning up.*) Hey, musicians, play, I want to hear you! Come on, everybody, and see how Yermolay Lopahin will swing the ax in the cherry orchard, how the trees will fall to the ground! We are going to build villas and our grandsons and great-grandsons will see a new life here— Music, play! (*The music is playing.* LYUBOFF ANDREEVNA *has sunk into a chair, crying bitterly.* LOPAHIN *reproachfully.*) Why, then, didn't you listen to me? My poor dear, it can't be undone now. (*With tears.*) Oh, if this could all be over soon, if somehow our awkward, unhappy life would be changed!

PISHTCHIK (*taking him by the arm, in a low voice*) She is crying. Come on in the ballroom, let her be by herself—Come on—

(*Taking him by the arm and leading him into the ballroom.*)

LOPAHIN What's the matter? Music, there, play up! (*Sarcastically.*) Everything is to be as I want it! Here comes the new squire, the owner of the cherry orchard. (*Quite accidentally, he bumps into the little table, and very nearly upsets the candelabra.*) I can pay for everything!

(*Goes out with* PISHTCHIK. *There is nobody left either in the ballroom or the drawing room but* LYUBOFF ANDREEVNA, *who sits all huddled up and crying bitterly. The music plays softly.* ANYA *and* TROFIMOFF *enter hurriedly.* ANYA *comes up to her mother and kneels in front of her.* TROFIMOFF *remains at the ballroom door.*)

ANYA Mama—! Mama, you are crying? My dear, kind, good Mama, my beautiful, I love you—I bless you. The cherry orchard is sold, it's not ours any more, that's true, true; but don't cry, Mama, you've your life still left you, you've your good, pure heart ahead of you—Come with me, come on, darling, away from here, come on—We will plant a new orchard, finer than this one, you'll see it, you'll understand; and joy, quiet, deep joy will sink into your heart, like the sun at evening, and you'll smile, Mama! Come, darling, come on!

ACT IV

The same setting as in Act I. There are neither curtains on the windows nor are there any pictures on the walls. Only a little furniture remains piled up in one corner as if for sale. A sense of emptiness is felt. Near the outer door, at the rear of the stage, is a pile of suitcases, traveling bags, and so on. The door on the left is open, and through it VARYA's *and* ANYA's *voices are heard.* LOPAHIN *is standing waiting.* YASHA *is holding a tray with glasses of champagne. In the hall* EPIHODOFF *is tying up a box. Offstage at the rear there is a hum. It is the peasants who have come to say good-by.* GAYEFF's *voice: "Thanks, brothers, thank you."*

YASHA The simple folk have come to say good-by. I am of the opinion, Yermolay Alexeevich, that the people are kind enough but don't understand anything.

(*The hum subsides.* LYUBOFF ANDREEVNA *enters through the hall with* GAYEFF; *she is not crying, but is pale, her face quivers, she is not able to speak.*)

GAYEFF You gave them your purse, Lyuba. Mustn't do that! Mustn't do that!

LYUBOFF ANDREEVNA I couldn't help it! I couldn't help it!

(*Both go out.*)

LOPAHIN (*calling through the door after them*) Please, I humbly beg you! A little glass at parting. I didn't think to bring some from town, and at the station I found just one bottle. Please! (*A pause.*) Well, then, ladies and gentlemen! You don't want it? (*Moving away from the door.*) If I'd known that, I wouldn't have bought it. Well, then I won't drink any either. (YASHA *carefully sets the tray down on a chair.*) At least, you have some, Yasha.

YASHA To those who are departing! Pleasant days to those who stay behind! (*Drinking.*) This champagne is not the real stuff, I can assure you.

LOPAHIN Eight roubles a bottle. (*A pause.*) It's devilish cold in here.

YASHA They didn't heat up today, we are leaving anyway. (*Laughing.*)

LOPAHIN What are you laughing about?

YASHA For joy.

LOPAHIN Outside it's October, but it's sunny and still, like summer. Good for building. (*Looking at his watch, then through the door.*) Ladies and gentlemen, bear in mind we have forty-six minutes in all till train time! Which means you have to go to the station in twenty minutes. Hurry up a little.

TROFIMOFF (*in an overcoat, entering from outside*) Seems to me it is time to go. The carriages are ready. The devil knows where my rubbers are. They've disappeared. (*In the door.*) Anya, my rubbers are not here! I can't find them.

LOPAHIN And I have to go to Kharkov. I'm going on the same train with you. I'm going to live in Kharkov all winter. I've been dilly-dallying along with you, I'm tired of doing nothing. I can't be without work, look, I don't know what to do with my hands here, see, they are dangling somehow, as if they didn't belong to me.

TROFIMOFF We are leaving right away, and you'll set about your useful labors again.

LOPAHIN Here, drink a glass.

TROFIMOFF I shan't.

LOPAHIN It's to Moscow now?

TROFIMOFF Yes. I'll see them off to town, and tomorrow to Moscow.

LOPAHIN Yes—Maybe the professors are not giving their lectures. I imagine they are waiting till you arrive.

TROFIMOFF   That's none of your business.

LOPAHIN   How many years is it you've been studying at the University?

TROFIMOFF   Think of something newer. This is old and flat. (*Looking for his rubbers.*) You know, perhaps, we shall not see each other again; therefore, permit me to give you one piece of advice at parting! Don't wave your arms! Cure yourself of that habit— of arm waving. And also of building summer cottages, figuring that the summer residents will in time become individual landowners; figuring like that is arm waving too—Just the same, however, I like you. You have delicate soft fingers like an artist, you have a delicate soft heart—

LOPAHIN   (*embracing him*)   Good-by, my dear boy. Thanks for everything. If you need it, take some money from me for the trip.

TROFIMOFF   Why should I? There's no need for it.

LOPAHIN   But you haven't any!

TROFIMOFF   I have. Thank you. I got some for a translation. Here it is in my pocket. (*Anxiously.*) But my rubbers are gone.

VARYA   (*from another room*)   Take your nasty things!

(*Throws a pair of rubbers on to the stage.*)

TROFIMOFF   But what are you angry about, Varya? Hm—Why, these are not my rubbers.

LOPAHIN   In the spring I planted twenty-seven hundred acres of poppies and now I've made forty thousand clear. And when my poppies were in bloom, what a picture it was! So look, as I say, I've made forty thousand, which means I'm offering you a loan because I can afford to. Why turn up your nose? I'm a peasant— I speak straight out.

TROFIMOFF   Your father was a peasant, mine—an apothecary— and from that absolutely nothing follows. (LOPAHIN *takes out his wallet.*) Leave it alone, leave it alone—If you gave me two hundred thousand even, I wouldn't take it. I am a free man. And everything that you all value so highly and dearly, both rich man and beggars, has not the slightest power over me, it's like a mere feather floating in the air. I can get along without you, I can pass you by, I am strong and proud. Humanity is moving toward the loftiest truth, toward the loftiest happiness that is possible on earth and I am in the front ranks.

LOPAHIN   Will you get there?

TROFIMOFF   I'll get there. (*A pause.*) I'll get there, or I'll show the others the way to get there.

(*In the distance is heard the sound of an ax on a tree.*)

LOPAHIN Well, good-by, my dear boy. It's time to go. We turn up our noses at one another, but life keeps on passing. When I work a long time without stopping, my thoughts are clearer, and it seems as if I, too, know what I exist for, and, brother, how many people are there in Russia who exist, nobody knows for what! Well, all the same, it's not that that keeps things circulating. Leonid Andreevich, they say, has accepted a position—he'll be in a bank, six thousand a year—the only thing is he won't stay there, he's very lazy—

ANYA (*in the doorway*) Mama begs of you until she's gone, not to cut down the orchard.

TROFIMOFF Honestly, haven't you enough tact to—

(*Goes out through the hall.*)

LOPAHIN Right away, right away—What people, really!

(*Goes out after him.*)

ANYA Has Fiers been sent to the hospital?

YASHA I told them to this morning. They must have sent him.

ANYA (*to* EPIHODOFF, *who is passing through the room*) Semyon Panteleevich, please inquire whether or not they have taken Fiers to the hospital.

YASHA (*huffily*) This morning, I told Igor. Why ask ten times over!

EPIHODOFF The venerable Fiers, according to my conclusive opinion, is not worth mending, he ought to join his forefathers. And I can only envy him. (*Putting a suitcase on a hatbox and crushing it.*) Well, there you are, of course. I knew it.

(*Goes out.*)

YASHA (*mockingly*) Twenty-two misfortunes—

VARYA (*on the other side of the door*) Have they taken Fiers to the hospital?

ANYA They have.

VARYA Then why didn't they take the letter to the doctor?

ANYA We must send it on after them—

(*Goes out.*)

VARYA (*from the next room*) Where is Yasha? Tell him his mother has come, she wants to say good-by to him.

YASHA (*waving his hand*) They merely try my patience.

(DUNYASHA *has been busying herself with the luggage; now when* YASHA *is left alone, she goes up to him.*)

DUNYASHA If you'd only look at me once, Yasha. You are going away—leaving me— (*Crying and throwing herself on his neck.*)

YASHA Why are you crying? (*Drinking champagne.*) In six days I'll be in Paris again. Tomorrow we will board the express train and dash off out of sight; somehow, I can't believe it. *Vive la France!* It doesn't suit me here—I can't live here—Can't help that. I've seen enough ignorance—enough for me. (*Drinking champagne.*) Why do you cry? Behave yourself properly, then you won't be crying.

DUNYASHA (*powdering her face, looking into a small mirror*) Send me a letter from Paris. I loved you, Yasha, you know, loved you so! I am a tender creature, Yasha!

YASHA They are coming here. (*Bustling about near the suitcases, humming low.*)

(LYUBOFF ANDREEVNA, GAYEFF, ANYA *and* CHARLOTTA IVANOVNA *enter.*)

GAYEFF We should be going. There is very little time left. (*Looking at* YASHA.) Who is it smells like herring!

LYUBOFF ANDREEVNA In about ten minutes let's be in the carriage— (*Glancing around the room.*) Good-by, dear house, old Grandfather. Winter will pass; spring will be here, but you won't be here any longer, they'll tear you down. How much these walls have seen! (*Kissing her daughter warmly.*) My treasure, you are beaming, your eyes are dancing like two diamonds. Are you happy? Very?

ANYA Very! It's the beginning of a new life, Mama!

GAYEFF (*gaily*) Yes, indeed, everything is fine now. Before the sale of the cherry orchard, we all were troubled, distressed, and then when the question was settled definitely, irrevocably, we all calmed down and were even cheerful—I'm a bank official. I am a financier now—Yellow ball into the side pocket, anyway, Lyuba, you look better, no doubt about that.

LYUBOFF ANDREEVNA Yes. My nerves are better, that's true. (*They hand her her hat and coat.*) I sleep well. Carry out my things, Yasha. It's time. (*To* ANYA.) My little girl, we shall see each other again soon—I am going to Paris, I shall live there on the money your Yaroslavl great-aunt sent for the purchase of the estate— long live Great-aunt! But that money won't last long.

ANYA Mama, you'll come back soon, soon—Isn't that so? I'll prepare myself, pass the examination at high school, and then I'll work, I will help you. We'll read all sorts of books together. Mama, isn't that so? (*Kissing her mother's hands.*) We'll read in the autumn evenings, read lots of books, and a new, wonderful world will open up before us— (*daydreaming*) Mama, do come—

LYUBOFF ANDREEVNA I'll come, my precious. (*Embracing her daughter.*)

(LOPAHIN *enters with* CHARLOTTA *who is softly humming a song.*)

GAYEFF Lucky Charlotta: she's singing!

CHARLOTTA (*taking a bundle that looks like a baby wrapped up*) My baby, bye, bye— (*A baby's cry is heard: Ooah, ooah—!*) Hush, my darling, my dear little boy. (*Ooah, ooah—!*) I am so sorry for you! (*Throwing the bundle back.*) Will you please find me a position? I cannot go on like this.

LOPAHIN We will find something, Charlotta Ivanovna, don't worry.

GAYEFF Everybody is dropping us, Varya is going away.—All of a sudden we are not needed.

CHARLOTTA I have no place in town to live. I must go away. (*Humming.*) It's all the same—

(PISHTCHIK *enters.*)

LOPAHIN The freak of nature—!

PISHTCHIK (*out of breath*) Ugh, let me catch my breath—I'm exhausted—My honored friends—Give me some water—

GAYEFF After money, I suppose? This humble servant will flee from sin!

(*Goes out.*)

PISHTCHIK It's a long time since I was here—Most beautiful lady— (*To* LOPAHIN) You here—? Glad to see you—a man of the greatest intellect—Here—Take it— (*Giving* LOPAHIN *some money.*) Four hundred roubles—That leaves eight hundred and forty I still owe you—

LOPAHIN (*with astonishment, shrugging his shoulders*) I must be dreaming. But where did you get it?

PISHTCHIK Wait—I'm hot—Most extraordinary event. Some Englishmen came and found on my land some kind of white clay— (*To* LYUBOFF ANDREEVNA.) And four hundred for you—Beautiful lady—Wonderful lady— (*Handing over the money.*) The rest later. (*Taking a drink of water.*) Just now a young man was saying on the train that some great philosopher recommends jumping off roofs—"Jump!" he says, and "therein lies the whole problem." (*With astonishment.*) You don't say! Water!

LOPAHIN And what Englishmen were they?

PISHTCHIK I leased them the parcel of land with the clay for twenty-four years—And now, excuse me, I haven't time—I must run along—I'm going to Znoykoff's—To Kardamonoff's—I owe everybody— (*Drinking.*) I wish you well—I'll drop in on Thursday—

LYUBOFF ANDREEVNA　We are moving to town right away, and tomorrow I'm going abroad—

PISHTCHIK　What? (*Alarmed.*) Why to town? That's why I see furniture—Suitcases—Well, no matter— (*Tearfully.*) No matter —Men of the greatest minds—those Englishmen—No matter— Good luck! God will help you—No matter—Everything in this world comes to an end— (*Kissing* LYUBOFF ANDREEVNA's *hand.*) And should the report reach you that my end has come, think of that well-known horse and say: "There was once on earth a so and so—Semyonoff Pishtchik—The kingdom of Heaven be his." Most remarkable weather—yes— (*Going out greatly disconcerted, but immediately returning and speaking from the door.*) Dashenka sends her greetings!

(*Goes out.*)

LYUBOFF ANDREEVNA　And now we can go. I am leaving with two worries. First, that Fiers is sick. (*Glancing at her watch.*) We still have five minutes—

ANYA　Mama, Fiers has already been sent to the hospital. Yasha sent him off this morning.

LYUBOFF ANDREEVNA　My second worry—is Varya. She is used to getting up early and working, and now without any work she is like a fish out of water. She has grown thin, pale and cries all the time, poor thing— (*A pause.*) You know this, Yermolay Alexeevich: I dreamed—of marrying her to you. And there was every sign of your getting married. (*Whispering to* ANYA, *who beckons to* CHARLOTTA; *both go out.*) She loves you, you are fond of her, and I don't know, don't know why it is you seem to avoid each other—I don't understand it!

LOPAHIN　I don't understand it either, I must confess. It's all strange somehow—If there's still time, I am ready right now even—Let's finish it up—and *basta*,[1] but without you I feel I won't propose.

LYUBOFF ANDREEVNA　But that's excellent. Surely it takes only a minute. I'll call her at once.

LOPAHIN　And to fit the occasion there's the champagne. (*Looking at the glasses.*) Empty, somebody has already drunk them. (YASHA *coughs.*) That's what's called lapping it up—

---

[1] *basta* be done with it

LYUBOFF ANDREEVNA (*vivaciously*) Splendid! We'll go out—Yasha, *allez!*[1] I'll call her— (*Through the door.*) Varya, drop everything and come here. Come on! (*Goes out with* YASHA.)

LOPAHIN (*looking at his watch*) Yes—

(*A pause. Behind the door you hear smothered laughter, whispering, finally* VARYA *enters.*)

VARYA (*looking at the luggage a long time*) That's strange, I just can't find it—

LOPAHIN What are you looking for?

VARYA I packed it myself and don't remember where.

(*A pause.*)

LOPAHIN Where do you expect to go now, Varvara Mikhailovna?

VARYA I? To Regulin's. I agreed to go there to look after the house —As a sort of housekeeper.

LOPAHIN That's in Yashnevo? It's nigh on to seventy miles. (*A pause.*) And here ends life in this house—

VARYA (*examining the luggage*) But where is it? Either I put it in the trunk, perhaps—Yes, life in this house is ended—it won't be any more—

LOPAHIN And I am going to Kharkov now—By the next train. I've a lot to do. And I am leaving Epihodoff—on the ground here—I've hired him.

VARYA Well!

LOPAHIN Last year at this time it had already been snowing, if you remember, and now it's quiet, it's sunny. It's only that it's cold, about three degrees of frost.

VARYA I haven't noticed. (*A pause.*) And besides our thermometer is broken— (*A pause. A voice from the yard through the door.*) Yermolay Alexeevich—

LOPAHIN (*as if he had been expecting this call for a long time*) This minute!

(*Goes out quickly.*)

(VARYA, *sitting on the floor, putting her head on a bundle of clothes, sobs quietly. The door opens,* LYUBOFF ANDREEVNA *enters cautiously.*)

VARYA (*She is not crying any longer, and has wiped her eyes.*) Yes, it's time, Mama. I can get to Regulin's today, if we are just not too late for the train— (*Through the door.*) Anya, put your

―――――――
[1] *allez* go

things on! (ANYA, *then* GAYEFF *and* CHARLOTTA IVANOVNA *enter.* GAYEFF *has on a warm overcoat, with a hood. The servants gather, also the drivers.* EPIHODOFF *busies himself with the luggage.*) Now we can be on our way.

ANYA (*joyfully*) On our way!

GAYEFF My friends, my dear, kind friends! Leaving this house forever, can I remain silent, can I restrain myself from expressing, as we say, farewell, those feelings that fill now my whole being—

ANYA (*beseechingly*) Uncle!

VARYA Dear Uncle, don't!

GAYEFF (*dejectedly*) Bank the yellow into the side pocket—I am silent—

(TROFIMOFF *and then* LOPAHIN *enter.*)

TROFIMOFF Well, ladies and gentlemen, it's time to go!

LOPAHIN Epihodoff, my coat!

LYUBOFF ANDREEVNA I'll sit here just a minute more. It's as if I had never seen before what the walls in this house are like, what kind of ceilings, and now I look at them greedily, with such tender love—

GAYEFF I remember when I was six years old, on Trinity Day, I sat in this window and watched my father going to Church—

LYUBOFF ANDREEVNA Are all the things taken out?

LOPAHIN Everything, I think. (*Putting on his overcoat. To* EPIHODOFF.) Epihodoff, you see that everything is in order.

EPIHODOFF (*talking in a hoarse voice*) Don't worry, Yermolay Alexeevich!

LOPAHIN Why is your voice like that?

EPIHODOFF Just drank some water, swallowed something.

YASHA (*with contempt*) The ignorance—

LYUBOFF ANDREEVNA We are going and there won't be a soul left here—

LOPAHIN Till spring.

VARYA (*pulls an umbrella out from a bundle, it looks as if she were going to hit someone;* LOPAHIN *pretends to be frightened*) What do you, what do you—I never thought of it.

TROFIMOFF Ladies and gentlemen, let's get in the carriages—It's time! The train is coming any minute.

VARYA Petya, here they are, your rubbers, by the suitcase. (*Tearfully.*) And how dirty yours are, how old—!

TROFIMOFF (*putting on the rubbers*) Let's go, ladies and gentlemen!

GAYEFF (*greatly embarrassed, afraid he will cry*) The train—The station—Cross into the side, combination off the white into the corner—

LYUBOFF ANDREEVNA   Let's go!

LOPAHIN   Everybody here? Nobody there? (*Locking the side door on the left.*) Things are stored here, it must be locked up, let's go!

ANYA   Good-by, house! Good-by, the old life!

TROFIMOFF   Long live the new life!

(*Goes out with* ANYA. VARYA *casts a glance around the room and, without hurrying, goes out.* YASHA *and* CHARLOTTA, *with her dog, go out.*)

LOPAHIN   And so, till spring. Out, ladies and gentlemen—Till we meet.

(*Goes out.*)

(LYUBOFF ANDREEVNA *and* GAYEFF *are left alone. As if they had been waiting for this, they throw themselves on one another's necks sobbing, but smothering their sobs as if afraid of being heard.*)

GAYEFF (*in despair*)   Oh, Sister, Sister—

LYUBOFF ANDREEVNA   Oh, my dear, my lovely, beautiful orchard! My life, my youth, my happiness, good-by!

ANYA (ANYA's *voice, gaily, appealingly*)   Mama—!

TROFIMOFF (*gaily, excitedly*)   Aaooch!

LYUBOFF ANDREEVNA   For the last time, just to look at the walls, at the window—My dear mother used to love to walk around in this room—

GAYEFF   Oh, Sister, Sister—!

ANYA (*from outside*)   Mama—!

TROFIMOFF (*from outside*)   Aaooch—!

LYUBOFF ANDREEVNA   We are coming!

(*They go out.*)

(*The stage is empty. One hears the keys locking all the doors, then the carriages driving off. It grows quiet. In the silence the dull thud of an ax on a tree, a lonely, mournful sound. Footsteps are heard. From the door on the right* FIERS *appears. He is dressed as usual, in a jacket and a white waistcoat, slippers on his feet. He is sick.*)

FIERS (*going to the door and trying the knob*)   Locked. They've gone. (*Sitting down on the sofa.*) They forgot about me—No matter—I'll sit here awhile—And Leonid Andreevich, for sure, didn't put on his fur coat, he went off with his topcoat— (*Sighing anxiously.*) And I didn't see to it—The young saplings! (*He mutters something that cannot be understood.*) Life has gone by, as if I hadn't lived at all— (*Lying down.*) I'll lie down awhile— You haven't got any strength, nothing is left, nothing—Ach, you —good-for-nothing— (*He lies still.*)

(*There is a far-off sound as if out of the sky, the sound of a snapped string, dying away, sad. A stillness falls, and there is only the thud of an ax on a tree, far away in the orchard.*)

✑ MAJOR BARBARA
(1905)

BERNARD SHAW (1856–1950)

It once seemed that George Bernard Shaw might live forever. He had begun his career as a music and drama critic and as a sometime writer of fiction. He was 36 before his own first play, *Widower's Houses,* was written in 1892, and his greatest plays were done between his forties and seventies. He was still writing acceptable works into his eighties. Opinionated, garrulous, supremely egotistical, considering himself an expert on any given social or political problem, he was, as well, a true theatrical genius in the creation of some of the most superb comedies in the English language.

As a public figure on the lecture platform, in his outpouring of critical essays, and in his voluminous correspondence (virtually anyone writing him would get a prompt and often acerbic reply by postcard) Shaw was a born performer. It was next to impossible to determine the "real" Shaw, if, indeed, there ever was one, since he behaved continually as if he were on stage. He could at one moment be the bearded Irish pixie and the next the goading, irascible, devilish socialist. In the production of his plays he could command actors, directors, and audiences to do his bidding even across oceans.

Early in his life Shaw joined the Fabian Society in England and was a longtime advocate of state socialism, even, at times when it was dangerously unpopular to do so, supporting Russian Communism. He strongly espoused Ibsen's abandonment of the conventional attitude toward the "womanly woman," i.e., the traditional female who performed at the command of her husband and male-oriented society, imprisoned by the strictures of an unbending and arbitrary morality. He saw strength in the "life force," including that of natural sexuality, as a positive, driving element in the world, while assigning his romantic couples to virtually passionless, albeit wholly charming, affairs. Shaw himself advocated celibacy to the point of having endured, so far as is known, a totally abstinent marriage, while carrying on a kind of public, if Platonic, love affair of his own with the beautiful actress Mrs. Patrick Campbell, for whom he created *Pygmalion* in 1913, forever with us in *My Fair Lady.* One of the most "liberated" of women appears in his high comedy masterpiece, *Candida,* in 1895. His most magnificent feminine creation, at once a near-tragic and a delightfully comic figure, is in *Saint Joan* of 1923, Shaw's own personal view of one of history's freest and most captive women.

Above all, Shaw regarded poverty as an out-and-out crime. In *Major Barbara* he has written an effective exposé of human hypocrisy in the way society insists on handling its poor, but in a typical tongue-in-cheek Shavian twist, this ardent socialist has assigned his Utopian state, the perfect benevolent society, to the supercapitalist munitions lord. Against the diabolic reasoning of Undershaft, though it is based on the powderkeg of a cannon foundry, the classical scholarly mind of Adolphus ultimately loses, or at least seems to lose, in order to win the hand of the thoroughly do-good Barbara. She, disillusioned in her faith, surrenders as well to the powers of darkness as she sadly discovers that anyone in the world can be bought if the right amount of hard cash comes along. The fortuitous discovery of Adolphus's illegitimacy as a foundling, eligible for the Undershaft fortune, is not without its ironies.

Shaw is at his best in stringing us along, as he does so well in *Major Barbara,* but what fun there is in following him! Who has really been "had" in all of this? the Army? Bill? Barbara and Dolly? All of us and none of us? Whatever the socialist "thinker" that Shaw makes himself out to be, beneath everything is a dramatist who knows his theatre, for which he creates incident and action at their keenest levels, with charmingly attractive characters and brilliantly sophisticated comedy.

The Preface

Shaw's extensive non-dramatic writings range from religion and the arts to politics, economics, and philosophy, all, of course, delivered with a strongly personal Shavian didacticism. His *The Quintessence of Ibsenism,* first published in 1891, is one of the earliest significant endorsements of the Norwegian's dramatic realism, written at a time when Ibsen was being roundly condemned as perverse and obscene. In its subsequent revisions, Shaw's staunch support remains among the best critical studies of the playwright.

But with Shaw's popular reputation resting exclusively on his plays, most of his other works remain unread. The major exception, however, is the dramatic prefaces, considered by many to place Shaw among the masters of English prose. Purporting to introduce the plays, these lengthy and discursive essays, sometimes nearly as long as the plays themselves, while centering on the plays' individual themes, often digress far afield. In the aggregate, they espouse Shaw's philosophy on just about everything.

The Preface to *Major Barbara* is an excellent example. It is a brilliant argument in its support of the importance of money and its denunciation of the "crime" of poverty, attacking along the way the hypocrisies of religion and the outrages of modern social practices. He is, of course, quite right. His well-established points are based on solid evidence, and they are persuasively argued. His superb rationale for the behavior of his characters removes nearly all objections that they are merely talkative mouthpieces for Shaw's own eccentric ideas. His analysis of the Barbara-Bill relationship is exceptionally lucid and convincing, and his explanation of the seeming paradox of the Army's acceptance of tainted money is difficult to deny. His support of Undershaft's "gospel" is remarkably persuasive.

However, let the reader beware!

Shaw seldom, if ever, entertained the possibility of a viable counterargument. Things were to be seen as he saw them, since his own opinion of himself conceived of no other authority. After all, he does assert that he stands on the shoulders of Euripides, Voltaire, Marx, Molière, Goethe, Tolstoy, and Jesus, among others. The end result can be dangerous. The susceptible reader can easily be led down Shaw's garden path by the sheer verbal power displayed, failing to recognize that despite the seeming rightness of the cause and the mesmerizing persuasive logic, there are opposing and equally valid views. Moreover, since the "real" world refuses to behave in Shavian fashion, as Shaw thinks it should, his solutions to society's ills emerge as oversimplified and impossibly idealistic. Shaw is so good in presenting his side that it becomes disarmingly easy to be wholly convinced. There are, after all, modulations that Shaw refuses to recognize, even though the foundation he builds upon is firmly grounded.

Written in 1906, in the year following the opening of the play, the Preface to *Major Barbara* is as startingly pertinent at the end of the century as it was at the beginning. Shaw was no fool, and certainly no charlatan. He knew well of what he wrote and spoke, and in the manner of all creative artistic geniuses, his basic ideas transcend time and become universal in their recognition of humankind's often deadly foolishness. The problems raised—senseless buildup of armaments, terrorism on an international scale, the vacuities of established religion, and the inanities of social practices—remain frighteningly with us today. One may scoff at Shaw and ridicule his egocentricities, but one simply cannot ignore him. He may be wildly wrong in his narrow-minded attack on medical practices as expressed in his Preface to *The Doctor's Dilemma;* he may not be able to recognize that his insistence that Eliza and Higgins cannot possibly come together at the end of *Pygmalion* is plainly in error, when all the world knows they will since that's clearly the direction the play is written. (Shaw grudgingly acknowledged the popular will and added the present "happy" ending to the film version of *Pygmalion,* also included in *My Fair Lady.* But all definitive texts of the original play omit it.) But even at his most outrageous, Shaw still commands attention.

And finally, regardless of what he says in his prefaces, regardless of their sometimes overbearing philosophical involvements, which suggest that the plays under discussion can only emerge as deadly bores, what Shaw does is what really matters. His expansive philosophical discourse to the contrary, he has succeeded in creating delightfully entertaining pieces of theatre, thoroughly enjoyable on their own merits, without any necessity at all to know a single word of what has gone before.

Preface to Major Barbara

First Aid to Critics

Before dealing with the deeper aspects of Major Barbara, let me, for the credit of English literature, make a protest against an unpatriotic habit into which many of my critics have fallen. Whenever my view strikes them as being at all outside the range of, say, an ordinary suburban churchwarden, they conclude that I am echoing *Schopenhauer, Nietzsche, Ibsen, Strindberg, Tolstoy,* or some other heresiarch in northern or eastern Europe.

I confess there is something flattering in this simple faith in my accomplishment as a linguist and my erudition as a philosopher. But I cannot countenance the assumption that life and literature are so poor in these islands that we must go abroad for all dramatic material that is not common and all ideas that are not superficial. I therefore venture to put my critics in possession of certain facts concerning my contact with modern ideas.

About half a century ago, an Irish novelist, Charles Lever, wrote a story entitled A Day's Ride: A Life's Romance. It was published by Charles Dickens in Household Words, and proved so strange to the public taste that Dickens pressed Lever to make short work of it. I read scraps of this novel when I was a child; and it made an enduring impression on me. The hero was a very romantic hero, trying to live bravely, chivalrously, and powerfully by dint of mere romance-fed imagination, without courage, without means, without knowledge, without skill, without anything real except his bodily appetites. Even in my childhood I found in this poor devil's unsuccessful encounters with the facts of life, a poignant quality that romantic fiction lacked. The book, in spite of its first failure, is not dead: I saw its title the other day in the catalogue of Tauchnitz.

Now why is it that when I also deal in the tragi-comic irony of the conflict between real life and the romantic imagination, critics never affiliate me to my countryman and immediate forerunner, Charles Lever, whilst they confidently derive me from a Norwegian author of whose language I do not know three words, and of whom I knew nothing until years after the Shavian *Anschauung* was already unequivocally declared in books full of what came, ten years later, to be perfunctorily labelled Ibsenism? I was not Ibsenist even at second hand; for Lever, though he may have read Henri Beyle, *alias* Stendhal, certainly never read Ibsen. Of the books that made Lever popular, such as Charles O'Malley and Harry Lorrequer, I know nothing but the names and some of the illustrations. But the story of the day's ride and life's romance of Potts (claiming alliance with Pozzo di Borgo) caught me and fascinated me as something strange and significant, though I already knew all about Alnaschar and Don Quixote and Simon Tappertit and many another romantic hero mocked by reality. From the plays of Aristophanes to the tales of Stevenson that mockery has been made familiar to all who are properly saturated with letters.

Where, then, was the novelty in Lever's tale? Partly, I think, in a new seriousness in dealing with Potts's disease. Formerly, the contrast between madness and sanity was deemed comic: Hogarth shows us how fashionable people went in parties to Bedlam[1] to laugh at the lunatics. I myself have had a village idiot exhibited to me as something irresistibly funny. On the stage the madman was once a regular comic figure: that was how Hamlet got his opportunity before Shakespear touched him. The originality of Shakespear's version lay in his taking the lunatic sympathetically and seriously, and thereby making an advance towards the eastern consciousness of the fact that lunacy may be inspiration in disguise, since a man who has more brains than his fellows necessarily appears as mad to them as one who has less. But Shakespear did not do for Pistol and Parolles what he did for Hamlet. The particular sort of madman they represented, the romantic make-believer, lay outside the pale of sympathy in literature: he was pitilessly despised and ridiculed here as he was in the east under the name of Alnaschar, and was doomed to be, centuries later, under the name of Simon Tappertit. When Cervantes relented over Don Quixote, and Dickens relented over Pickwick, they did not become impartial: they simply changed sides, and became friends and apologists where they had formerly been mockers.

In Lever's story there is a real change of attitude. There is no relenting towards Potts: he never gains our affections like Don Quixote and Pickwick: he has not even the infatuate courage of Tappertit. But we dare not laugh at him, because, somehow, we recognize ourselves in Potts. We may, some of us, have enough nerve, enough muscle, enough luck, enough tact or skill or address or knowledge to carry things off better than he did; to impose on the people who saw through him; to fascinate Katinka (who cut Potts so ruthlessly at the end of the story); but for all that, we know that Potts plays an enormous part in ourselves and in the world, and that the social problem is not a problem of storybook heroes of the older pattern, but a problem of Pottses, and of how to make men of them. To fall back on my old phrase, we have the feeling—one that Alnaschar, Pistol, Parolles, and Tappertit never gave

---

[1] *Bedlam* corruption of Bethlehem, the name of the London insane asylum. Hogarth was the artist engraver who portrayed many vivid scenes of the age.

us—that Potts is a piece of really scientific natural history as distinguished from funny story telling. His author is not throwing a stone at a creature of another and inferior order, but making a confession, with the effect that the stone hits each of us full in the conscience and causes our self-esteem to smart very sorely. Hence the failure of Lever's book to please the readers of Household Words. That pain in the self-esteem nowadays causes critics to raise a cry of Ibsenism. I therefore assure them that the sensation first came to me from Lever and may have come to him from Beyle, or at least out of the Stendhalian atmosphere. I exclude the hypothesis of complete originality on Lever's part, because a man can no more be completely original in that sense than a tree can grow out of air.

Another mistake as to my literary ancestry is made whenever I violate the romantic convention that all women are angels when they are not devils; that they are better looking than men; that their part in courtship is entirely passive; and that the human female form is the most beautiful object in nature. Schopenhauer wrote a splenetic essay which, as it is neither polite nor profound, was probably intended to knock this nonsense violently on the head. A sentence denouncing the idolized form as ugly has been largely quoted. The English critics have read that sentence; and I must here affirm, with as much gentleness as the implication will bear, that it has yet to be proved that they have dipped any deeper. At all events, whenever an English playwright represents a young and marriageable woman as being anything but a romantic heroine, he is disposed of without further thought as an echo of Schopenhauer. My own case is a specially hard one, because, when I implore the critics who are obsessed with the Schopenhauerian formula to remember that playwrights, like sculptors, study their figures from life, and not from philosophic essays, they reply passionately that I am not a playwright and that my stage figures do not live. But even so, I may and do ask them why, if they must give the credit of my plays to a philosopher, they do not give it to an English philosopher? Long before I ever read a word by Schopenhauer, or even knew whether he was a philosopher or a chemist, the Socialist revival of the eighteen-eighties brought me into contact, both literary and personal, with Ernest Belfort Bax, an English Socialist and philosophic essayist, whose handling of modern feminism would provoke romantic protests from Schopenhauer himself, or even Strindberg. As a matter of fact I hardly noticed Schopenhauer's disparagements of women when they came under my notice later on, so thoroughly had Bax familiarized me with the homoist attitude, and forced me to recognize the extent to which public opinion, and consequently legislation and jurisprudence, is corrupted by feminist sentiment.

Belfort Bax's essays were not confined to the Feminist question. He was a ruthless critic of current morality. Other writers have gained sympathy for dramatic criminals by eliciting the alleged "soul of goodness in things evil"; but Bax would propound some quite undramatic and apparently shabby violation of our commercial law and morality, and not merely defend it with the most disconcerting ingenuity, but actually prove it to be a positive duty that nothing but the certainty of police persecution should prevent every right-minded man from at once doing on principle. The Socialists were naturally shocked, being for the most part morbidly moral people; but at all events they were saved later on from the delusion that nobody but Nietzsche had ever challenged our mercanto-Christian morality. I first heard the name of Nietzsche from a German mathematician, Miss Borchardt, who had read my Quintessence of Ibsenism, and told me that she saw what I had been reading: namely, Nietzsche's Jenseits von Gut und Böse. Which I protest I had never seen, and could not have read with any comfort, for want of the necessary German, if I had seen it.

Nietzsche, like Schopenhauer, is the victim in England of a single much quoted sentence containing the phrase "big blonde beast." On the strength of this alliteration it is assumed that Nietzsche gained his European reputation by a senseless glorification of selfish bullying as the rule of life, just as it is assumed, on the strength of the single word Superman (Übermensch) borrowed by me from Nietzsche, that I look for the salvation of society to the despotism of a single Napoleonic Superman, in spite of my careful demonstration of the folly of that outworn infatuation. But even the less recklessly superficial critics seem to believe that the modern objection to Christianity as a pernicious slave-morality was first put forward by Nietzsche. It was familiar to me before I ever heard of Nietzsche. The late Captain Wilson, author of several queer pamphlets, propagandist of a metaphysical system called Comprehensionism, and inventor of the term "Crosstianity" to distinguish the retrograde element in Christendom, was wont thirty years ago, in the discussions of the Dialectical Society, to protest earnestly against the beatitudes of the Sermon on the Mount as excuses for cowardice and servility, as destructive of our will, and consequently of our honour and manhood. Now it is true that Captain Wilson's moral criticism of Christianity was not a historical theory of it, like Nietzsche's; but this objection cannot be made to Stuart-Glennie, the successor of Buckle as a philosophic historian, who devoted his life to the elaboration and propagation of his theory that Christianity is part of an epoch (or rather an aberration, since it began as recently as 6000 B.C. and is already collapsing) produced by the necessity in which the numerically inferior white races found themselves to impose their domination on the colored races by priestcraft, making a virtue and a popular religion of drudgery and submissiveness in this world not only as a means of achieving saintliness of character but of securing a reward in heaven. Here was the slave-morality view formulated by a Scotch philosopher of my acquaintance long before we all began chattering about Nietzsche.

As Stuart-Glennie traced the evolution of society to the conflict of races, his theory made some sensation among Socialists—that is, among the only people who were seriously thinking about historical evolution at all—by its collision with the class-conflict theory of Karl Marx. Nietzsche, as I gather, regarded the slave-morality as having been invented and imposed on the world by slaves making a virtue of necessity and a religion of their servitude. Stuart-Glennie regarded the slave-morality as an invention of the superior white race to subjugate the minds of the inferior races whom they wished to exploit, and who would have destroyed them by force of numbers if their minds had not been subjugated. As this process is in operation still, and can be studied at first hand not only in our Church schools and in the struggle between our modern proprietary classes and the proletariat, but in the part played by Christian missionaries in reconciling the black races of Africa to their subjugation by European Capitalism, we can judge for ourselves whether the initiative came from above or below. My object here is not to argue the historical point, but simply to make our theatre critics ashamed of their habit of treating Britain as an intellectual void, and assuming that every philosophical idea, every historic theory, every criticism of our moral, religious and juridical institutions, must necessarily be either a foreign import, or else a fantastic sally (in rather questionable taste) totally unrelated to the existing body of thought. I urge them to remember that this body of thought is the slowest of growths and the rarest of blossomings, and that if there be such a thing on the philosophic plane as a matter of course, it is that no individual can make more than a minute contribution to it. In fact, their conception of clever persons parthenogenetically bringing forth complete original cosmogonies by dint of sheer "brilliancy" is part of that ignorant credulity which is the despair of the honest philosopher, and the opportunity of the religious impostor.

The Gospel of St Andrew Undershaft

It is this credulity that drives me to help my critics out with Major Barbara by telling them what to say about it. In the millionaire Undershaft I have represented a man who has become intellectually and spiritually as well as practically conscious of the irresistible natural truth which we all abhor and repudiate: to wit, that the greatest of our evils, and the worst of our crimes is poverty, and that our first duty, to which every other consideration should be sacrificed, is not to be poor. "Poor but honest," "the respectable poor," and such phrases are as intolerable and as immoral as "drunken but amiable," "fraudulent but a good after-dinner speaker," "splendidly criminal," or the like. Security, the chief pretence of civilization, cannot exist where the worst of dangers, the danger of poverty, hangs over everyone's head, and where the alleged protection of our persons from violence is only an accidental result of the existence of a police force whose real business is to force the poor man to see his children starve whilst idle people overfeed pet dogs with money that might feed and clothe them.

It is exceedingly difficult to make people realize that an evil is an evil. For instance, we seize a man and deliberately do him a malicious injury: say, imprison him for years. One would not suppose that it needed any exceptional clearness of wit to recognize in this an act of diabolical cruelty. But in England such a recognition provokes a stare of surprise, followed by an explanation that the outrage is punishment or justice or something else that is all right, or perhaps by a heated attempt to argue that we should all be robbed and murdered in our beds if such stupid villainies as sentences of imprisonment were not committed daily. It is useless to argue that even if this were true, which it is not, the alternative to adding crimes of our own to the crimes from which we suffer is not helpless submission. Chickenpox is an evil; but if I were to declare that we must either submit to it or else repress it sternly by seizing everyone who suffers from it and punishing them by inoculation with smallpox, I should be laughed at; for though nobody could deny that the result would be to prevent chickenpox to some extent by making people avoid it much more carefully, and to effect a further apparent prevention by making them conceal it very anxiously, yet people would have sense enough to see that the deliberate propagation of smallpox was a creation of evil, and must therefore be ruled out in favor of purely humane and hygienic measures. Yet in the precisely parallel case of a man breaking into my house and stealing my wife's diamonds I am expected as a matter of course to steal ten years of his life, torturing him all the time. If he tries to defeat that monstrous retaliation by shooting me, my survivors hang him. The net result suggested by the police statistics is that we inflict atrocious injuries on the burglars we catch in order to make the rest take effectual precautions against detection; so that instead of saving our wives' diamonds from burglary we only greatly decrease our chances of ever getting them back, and increase our chances of being shot by the robber if we are unlucky enough to disturb him at his work.

But the thoughtless wickedness with which we scatter sentences of imprisonment, torture in the solitary cell and on the plank bed, and flogging, on moral invalids and energetic rebels, is as nothing compared to the silly levity with which we tolerate poverty as if it were either a wholesome tonic for lazy people or else a virtue to be embraced as St

Francis embraced it. If a man is indolent, let him be poor. If he is drunken, let him be poor. If he is not a gentleman, let him be poor. If he is addicted to the fine arts or to pure science instead of to trade and finance, let him be poor. If he chooses to spend his urban eighteen shillings a week or his agricultural thirteen shillings a week on his beer and his family instead of saving it up for his old age, let him be poor. Let nothing be done for "the undeserving": let him be poor. Serve him right! Also—somewhat inconsistently—blessed are the poor!

Now what does this Let Him Be Poor mean? It means let him be weak. Let him be ignorant. Let him become a nucleus of disease. Let him be a standing exhibition and example of ugliness and dirt. Let him have rickety children. Let him be cheap, and drag his fellows down to his own price by selling himself to do their work. Let his habitations turn our cities into poisonous congeries of slums. Let his daughters infect our young men with the diseases of the streets, and his sons revenge him by turning the nation's manhood into scrofula, cowardice, cruelty, hypocrisy, political imbecility, and all the other fruits of oppression and malnutrition. Let the undeserving become still less deserving; and let the deserving lay up for himself, not treasures in heaven, but horrors in hell upon earth. This being so, is it really wise to let him be poor? Would he not do ten times less harm as a prosperous burglar, incendiary, ravisher or murderer, to the utmost limits of humanity's comparatively negligible impulses in these directions? Suppose we were to abolish all penalties for such activities, and decide that poverty is the one thing we will not tolerate—that every adult with less than, say, £365 a year, shall be painlessly but inexorably killed, and every hungry half naked child forcibly fattened and clothed, would not that be an enormous improvement on our existing system, which has already destroyed so many civilizations, and is visibly destroying ours in the same way?

Is there any radicle of such legislation in our parliamentary system? Well, there are two measures just sprouting in the political soil, which may conceivably grow to something valuable. One is the institution of a Legal Minimum Wage. The other, Old Age Pensions. But there is a better plan than either of these. Some time ago I mentioned the subject of Universal Old Age Pensions to my fellow Socialist Cobden-Sanderson, famous as an artist-craftsman in bookbinding and printing. "Why not Universal Pensions for Life?" said Cobden-Sanderson. In saying this, he solved the industrial problem at a stroke. At present we say callously to each citizen "If you want money, earn it" as if his having or not having it were a matter that concerned himself alone. We do not even secure for him the opportunity of earning it: on the contrary, we allow our industry to be organized in open dependence on the maintenance of "a reserve army of unemployed" for the sake of "elasticity."

The sensible course would be Cobden-Sanderson's: that is, to give every man enough to live well on, so as to guarantee the community against the possibility of a case of the malignant disease of poverty, and then (necessarily) to see that he earned it.

Undershaft, the hero of Major Barbara, is simply a man who, having grasped the fact that poverty is a crime, knows that when society offered him the alternative of poverty or a lucrative trade in death and destruction, it offered him, not a choice between opulent villainy and humble virtue, but between energetic enterprise and cowardly infamy. His conduct stands the Kantian test, which Peter Shirley's does not. Peter Shirley is what we call the honest poor man. Undershaft is what we call the wicked rich one: Shirley is Lazarus, Undershaft Dives.[2] Well, the misery of the world is due to the fact that the great mass of men act and believe as Peter Shirley acts and believes. If they acted and believed as Undershaft acts and believes, the immediate result would be a revolution of incalculable beneficence. To be wealthy, says Undershaft, is with me a point of honor for which I am prepared to kill at the risk of my own life. This preparedness is, as he says, the final test of sincerity. Like Froissart's medieval hero, who saw that "to rob and pill was a good life" he is not the dupe of that public sentiment against killing which is propagated and endowed by people who would otherwise be killed themselves, or of the mouth-honour paid to poverty and obedience by rich and insubordinate do-nothings who want to rob the poor without courage and command them without superiority. Froissart's knight, in placing the achievement of a good life before all the other duties—which indeed are not duties at all when they conflict with it, but plain wickedness—behaved bravely, admirably, and, in the final analysis, public-spiritedly. Medieval society, on the other hand, behaved very badly indeed in organizing itself so stupidly that a good life could be achieved by robbing and pilling. If the knight's contemporaries had been all as resolute as he, robbing and pilling would have been the shortest way to the gallows, just as, if we were all as resolute and clearsighted as Undershaft, an attempt to live by means of what is called "an independent income" would be the shortest way to the lethal chamber. But as, thanks to our political imbecility and personal cowardice (fruits of poverty, both), the best imitation of a good life now procurable is life on an independent income, all sensible people aim at securing such an income, and are, of course, careful to legalize and moralize both it and all the actions and sentiments which lead to it and support it as an institution. What else can they do? They know, of course, that they are rich because others are poor. But they cannot help that: it is for the

---

[2] *Lazarus* was the diseased beggar in Jesus' parable, and *Dives* was the rich man.

poor to repudiate poverty when they have had enough of it. The thing can be done easily enough: the demonstrations to the contrary made by the economists, jurists, moralists and sentimentalists hired by the rich to defend them, or even doing the work gratuitously out of sheer folly and abjectness, impose only on those who want to be imposed on.

The reason why the independent income-tax payers are not solid in defence of their position is that since we are not medieval rovers through a sparsely populated country, the poverty of those we rob prevents our having the good life for which we sacrifice them. Rich men or aristocrats with a developed sense of life—men like Ruskin and William Morris and Kropotkin—have enormous social appetites and very fastidious personal ones. They are not content with handsome houses: they want handsome cities. They are not content with be-diamonded wives and blooming daughters: they complain because the charwoman is badly dressed, because the laundress smells of gin, because the sempstress is anemic, because every man they meet is not a friend and every woman not a romance. They turn up their noses at their neighbor's drains, and are made ill by the architecture of their neighbor's houses. Trade patterns made to suit vulgar people do not please them (and they can get nothing else): they cannot sleep nor sit at ease upon "slaughtered" cabinet makers' furniture. The very air is not good enough for them: there is too much factory smoke in it. They even demand abstract conditions: justice, honor, a noble moral atmosphere, a mystic nexus to replace the cash nexus. Finally they declare that though to rob and pill with your own hand on horseback and in steel coat may have been a good life, to rob and pill by the hands of the policeman, the bailiff, and the soldier, and to underpay them meanly for doing it, is not a good life, but rather fatal to all possibility of even a tolerable one. They call on the poor to revolt, and, finding the poor shocked at their ungentlemanliness, despairingly revile the proletariat for its "damned wantlessness" (*verdammte Bedürfnislosigkeit*).

So far, however, their attack on society has lacked simplicity. The poor do not share their tastes nor understand their art-criticisms. They do not want the simple life, nor the esthetic life; on the contrary, they want very much to wallow in all the costly vulgarities from which the elect souls among the rich turn away with loathing. It is by surfeit and not by abstinence that they will be cured of their hankering after unwholesome sweets. What they do dislike and despise and are ashamed of is poverty. To ask them to fight for the difference between the Christmas number of the Illustrated London News and the Kelmscott Chaucer is silly: they prefer the News. The difference between a stock-broker's cheap and dirty starched white shirt and collar and the comparatively costly and carefully dyed blue shirt of William Morris is a difference so disgraceful to Morris in their eyes that if they fought on the subject at all, they would fight in defence of the starch. "Cease to be slaves, in order that you may become cranks" is not a very inspiring call to arms; nor is it really improved by substituting saints for cranks. Both terms denote men of genius; and the common man does not want to live the life of a man of genius: he would much rather live the life of a pet collie if that were the only alternative. But he does want more money. Whatever else he may be vague about, he is clear about that. He may or may not prefer Major Barbara to the Drury Lane pantomime;[3] but he always prefers five hundred pounds to five hundred shillings.

Now to deplore this preference as sordid, and teach children that it is sinful to desire money, is to strain towards the extreme possible limit of impudence in lying and corruption in hypocrisy. The universal regard for money is the one hopeful fact in our civilization, the one sound spot in our social conscience. Money is the most important thing in the world. It represents health, strength, honor, generosity and beauty as conspicuously and undeniably as the want of it represents illness, weakness, disgrace, meanness and ugliness. Not the least of its virtues is that it destroys base people as certainly as it fortifies and dignifies noble people. It is only when it is cheapened to worthlessness for some and made impossibly dear to others, that it becomes a curse. In short, it is a curse only in such foolish social conditions that life itself is a curse. For the two things are inseparable: money is the counter that enables life to be distributed socially: it *is* life as truly as sovereigns and bank notes are money. The first duty of every citizen is to insist on having money on reasonable terms; and this demand is not complied with by giving four men three shillings each for ten or twelve hours' drudgery and one man a thousand pounds for nothing. The crying need of the nation is not for better morals, cheaper bread, temperance, liberty, culture, redemption of fallen sisters and erring brothers, nor the grace, love and fellowship of the Trinity, but simply for enough money. And the evil to be attacked is not sin, suffering, greed, priestcraft, kingcraft, demagogy, monopoly, ignorance, drink, war, pestilence, nor any other of the scapegoats which reformers sacrifice, but simply poverty.

Once take your eyes from the ends of the earth and fix them on this truth just under your nose; and Andrew Undershaft's views will not perplex you in the least. Unless indeed his constant sense that he is only the instrument of a Will or Life Force which uses him for purposes wider than his own, may puzzle you. If so, that is because you are walking either in artificial Darwinian darkness, or in mere stupidity. All

---

[3] *Drury Lane pantomime* Drury Lane is a large London theatre. At Christmas time many London theatres present "pantomimes," which are ludicrously, often hilariously, embellished musical versions of well-known fairy tales performed by some of the best English actors. They have always been favorites at holiday time with children and adults alike.

genuinely religious people have that consciousness. To them Undershaft the Mystic will be quite intelligible, and his perfect comprehension of his daughter the Salvationist and her lover the Euripidean republican natural and inevitable. That, however, is not new, even on the stage. What is new, as far as I know, is that article in Undershaft's religion which recognizes in Money the first need and in poverty the vilest sin of man and society.

This dramatic conception has not, of course, been attained *per saltum*. Nor has it been borrowed from Nietzsche or from any man born beyond the Channel. The late Samuel Butler, in his own department the greatest English writer of the latter half of the XIX century, steadily inculcated the necessity and morality of a conscientious Laodiceanism in religion and of an earnest and constant sense of the importance of money. It drives one almost to despair of English literature when one sees so extraordinary a study of English life as Butler's posthumous Way of All Flesh making so little impression that when, some years later, I produce plays in which Butler's extraordinarily fresh, free and future-piercing suggestions have an obvious share, I am met with nothing but vague cacklings about Ibsen and Nietzsche, and am only too thankful that they are not about Alfred de Musset and Georges Sand. Really, the English do not deserve to have great men. They allowed Butler to die practically unknown, whilst I, a comparatively insignificant Irish journalist, was leading them by the nose into an advertisement of me which has made my own life a burden. In Sicily there is a Via Samuele Butler. When an English tourist sees it, he either asks "Who the devil was Samuele Butler?" or wonders why the Sicilians should perpetuate the memory of the author of Hudibras.

Well, it cannot be denied that the English are only too anxious to recognize a man of genius if somebody will kindly point him out to them. Having pointed myself out in this manner with some success, I now point out Samuel Butler, and trust that in consequence I shall hear a little less in future of the novelty and foreign origin of the ideas which are now making their way into the English theatre through plays written by Socialists. There are living men whose originality and power are as obvious as Butler's and when they die that fact will be discovered. Meanwhile I recommend them to insist on their own merits as an important part of their own business.

The Salvation Army

When Major Barbara was produced in London, the second act was reported in an important northern newspaper as a withering attack on the Salvation Army, and the despairing ejaculation of Barbara deplored by a London daily as a tasteless blasphemy. And they were set right, not by the professed critics of the theatre, but by religious and philosophical publicists like Sir Oliver Lodge and Dr Stanton Coit, and strenuous Nonconformist journalists like William Stead, who not only understood the act as well as the Salvationists themselves, but also saw it in its relation to the religious life of the nation, a life which seems to lie not only outside the sympathy of many of our theatre critics, but actually outside their knowledge of society. Indeed nothing could be more ironically curious than the confrontation Major Barbara effected of the theatre enthusiasts with the religious enthusiasts. On the one hand was the playgoer, always seeking pleasure, paying exorbitantly for it, suffering unbearable discomforts for it, and hardly ever getting it. On the other hand was the Salvationist, repudiating gaiety and courting effort and sacrifice, yet always in the wildest spirits, laughing, joking, singing, rejoicing, drumming, and tambourining: his life flying by in a flash of excitement, and his death arriving as a climax of triumph. And, if you please, the playgoer despising the Salvationist as a joyless person, shut out from the heaven of the theatre, self-condemned to a life of hideous gloom; and the Salvationist mourning over the playgoer as over a prodigal with vine leaves in his hair, careening outrageously to hell amid the popping of champagne corks and the ribald laughter of sirens! Could misunderstanding be more complete, or sympathy worse misplaced?

Fortunately, the Salvationists are more accessible to the religious character of the drama than the playgoers to the gay energy and artistic fertility of religion. They can see, when it is pointed out to them, that a theatre, as a place where two or three are gathered together, takes from that divine presence an inalienable sanctity of which the grossest and profanest farce can no more deprive it than a hypocritical sermon by a snobbish bishop can desecrate Westminster Abbey. But in our professional playgoers this indispensable preliminary conception of sanctity seems wanting. They talk of actors as mimes and mummers, and, I fear, think of dramatic authors as liars and pandars, whose main business is the voluptuous soothing of the tired city speculator when what he calls the serious business of the day is over. Passion, the life of drama, means nothing to them but primitive sexual excitement: such phrases as "impassioned poetry" or "passionate love of truth" have fallen quite out of their vocabulary and been replaced by "passional crime" and the like. They assume, as far as I can gather, that people in whom passion has a larger scope are passionless and therefore uninteresting. Consequently they come to think of religious people as people who are not interesting and not amusing. And so, when Barbara cuts the regular Salvation Army jokes, and snatches a kiss from her lover across his drum, the devotees of the theatre think they ought to appear shocked, and conclude that the whole play is an elaborate mockery of the Army. And then either hypocritically rebuke me for mocking, or foolishly take part in the supposed mockery!

Even the handful of mentally competent critics got into difficulties over my demonstration of the economic deadlock in which the Salvation Army finds itself. Some of them thought that the Army would not have taken money from a distiller and a cannon founder: others thought it should not have taken it: all assumed more or less definitely that it reduced itself to absurdity or hypocrisy by taking it. On the first point the reply of the Army itself was prompt and conclusive. As one of its officers said, they would take money from the devil himself and be only too glad to get it out of his hands and into God's. They gratefully acknowledged that publicans not only give them money but allow them to collect it in the bar—sometimes even when there is a Salvation meeting outside preaching teetotalism. In fact, they questioned the verisimilitude of the play, not because Mrs Baines took the money, but because Barbara refused it.

On the point that the Army ought not to take such money, its justification is obvious. It must take the money because it cannot exist without money, and there is no other money to be had. Practically all the spare money in the country consists of a mass of rent, interest, and profit, every penny of which is bound up with crime, drink, prostitution, disease, and all the evil fruits of poverty, as inextricably as with enterprise, wealth, commercial probity, and national prosperity. The notion that you can earmark certain coins as tainted is an unpractical individualist superstition. Nonetheless the fact that all our money is tainted gives a very severe shock to earnest young souls when some dramatic instance of the taint first makes them conscious of it. When an enthusiastic young clergyman of the Established Church first realizes that the Ecclesiastical Commissioners receive the rents of sporting public houses, brothels, and sweating dens; or that the most generous contributor at his last charity sermon was an employer trading in female labor cheapened by prostitution as unscrupulously as a hotel keeper trades in waiters' labor cheapened by tips, or commissionaires' labor cheapened by pensions; or that the only patron who can afford to rebuild his church or his schools or give his boys' brigade a gymnasium or a library is the son-in-law of a Chicago meat King, that young clergyman has, like Barbara, a very bad quarter hour. But he cannot help himself by refusing to accept money from anybody except sweet old ladies with independent incomes and gentle and lovely ways of life. He has only to follow up the income of the sweet ladies to its industrial source, and there he will find Mrs Warren's profession[4] and the poison-

---

[4] *Mrs Warren's profession* title of Shaw's early play (1893) which shocked audiences in England and America and on at least one occasion prompted the arrest of the performers. Its subject concerned the highly respectable Mrs. Warren who kept a string of brothels on the Continent. Her justification was that it was far better to have young girls employed in this manner rather than to have them die in factories such as the notorious watchmaking establishments which killed off the workers through radium poisoning in painting fluorescent dials.

ous canned meat and all the rest of it. His own stipend has the same root. He must either share the world's guilt or go to another planet. He must save the world's honour if he is to save his own. This is what all the Churches find just as the Salvation Army and Barbara find it in the play. Her discovery that she is her father's accomplice; that the Salvation Army is the accomplice of the distiller and the dynamite maker; that they can no more escape one another than they can escape the air they breathe; that there is no salvation for them through personal righteousness, but only through the redemption of the whole nation from its vicious, lazy, competitive anarchy: this discovery has been made by everyone except the Pharisees and (apparently) the professional playgoers, who still wear their Tom Hood shirts and underpay their washerwoman without the slightest misgiving as to the elevation of their private characters, the purity of their private atmospheres, and their right to repudiate as foreign to themselves the coarse depravity of the garret and the slum. Not that they mean any harm: they only desire to be, in their little private way, what they call gentlemen. They do not understand Barbara's lesson because they have not, like her, learnt it by taking their part in the larger life of the nation.

Barbara's Return to the Colors

Barbara's return to the colors may yet provide a subject for the dramatic historian of the future. To get back to the Salvation Army with the knowledge that even the Salvationists themselves are not saved yet: that poverty is not blessed, but a most damnable sin; and that when General Booth[5] chose Blood and Fire for the emblem of Salvation instead of the Cross, he was perhaps better inspired than he knew: such knowledge, for the daughter of Andrew Undershaft, will clearly lead to something hopefuller than distributing bread and treacle at the expense of Bodger.

It is a very significant thing, this instinctive choice of the military form of organization, this substitution of the drum for the organ, by the Salvation Army. Does it not suggest that the Salvationists divine that they must actually fight the devil instead of merely praying at him? At present, it is true, they have not quite ascertained his correct address. When they do, they may give a very rude shock to that sense of security which he has gained from his experience of the fact that hard words, even when uttered by eloquent essayists and lecturers, or carried unanimously at enthusiastic public meetings on the motion of eminent reformers, break no bones. It has been said that the French Revolution

---

[5] William Booth, founder of the Salvation Army, was its first General.

was the work of Voltaire, Rousseau and the Encyclopedists. It seems to me to have been the work of men who had observed that virtuous indignation, caustic criticism, conclusive argument and instructive pamphleteering, even when done by the most earnest and witty literary geniuses, were as useless as praying, things going steadily from bad to worse whilst the Social Contract and the pamphlets of Voltaire were at the height of their vogue. Eventually, as we know, perfectly respectable citizens and earnest philanthropists connived at the September massacres because hard experience had convinced them that if they contented themselves with appeals to humanity and patriotism, the aristocracy, though it would read their appeals with the greatest enjoyment and appreciation, flattering and admiring the writers, would none the less continue to conspire with foreign monarchists to undo the revolution and restore the old system with every circumstance of savage vengeance and ruthless repression of popular liberties.

The nineteenth century saw the same lesson repeated in England. It had its Utilitarians, its Christian Socialists, its Fabians (still extant): it had Bentham, Mill, Dickens, Ruskin, Carlyle, Butler, Henry George, and Morris. And the end of all their efforts is the Chicago described by Mr Upton Sinclair, and the London in which the people who pay to be amused by my dramatic representation of Peter Shirley turned out to starve at forty because there are younger slaves to be had for his wages, do not take, and have not the slightest intention of taking, any effective step to organize society in such a way as to make that everyday infamy impossible. I, who have preached and pamphleteered like any Encyclopedist, have to confess that my methods are no use, and would be no use if I were Voltaire, Rousseau, Bentham, Marx, Mill, Dickens, Carlyle, Ruskin, Butler, and Morris all rolled into one, with Euripides, More, Montaigne, Molière, Beaumarchais, Swift, Goethe, Ibsen, Tolstoy, Jesus and the prophets all thrown in (as indeed in some sort I actually am, standing as I do on all their shoulders). The problem being to make heroes out of cowards, we paper apostles and artist-magicians have succeeded only in giving cowards all the sensations of heroes whilst they tolerate every abomination, accept every plunder, and submit to every oppression. Christianity, in making a merit of such submission, has marked only that depth in the abyss at which the very sense of shame is lost. The Christian has been like Dickens' doctor in the debtor's prison, who tells the newcomer of its ineffable peace and security: no duns; no tyrannical collectors of rates, taxes, and rent; no importunate hopes nor exacting duties; nothing but the rest and safety of having no farther to fall.

Yet in the poorest corner of this soul-destroying Christendom vitality suddenly begins to germinate again. Joyousness, a sacred gift long dethroned by the hellish laughter of derision and obscenity, rises like a flood miraculously out of the fetid dust and mud of the slums; rousing marches and impetuous dithyrambs rise to the heavens from people among whom the depressing noise called "sacred music" is a standing joke; a flag with Blood and Fire on it is unfurled, not in murderous rancor, but because fire is beautiful and blood is vital and splendid red; Fear, which we flatter by calling Self, vanishes; and transfigured men and women carry their gospel through a transfigured world, calling their leader General, themselves captains and brigadiers, and their whole body an Army: praying, but praying only for refreshment, for strength to fight, and for needful MONEY (a notable sign, that); preaching, but not preaching submission; daring ill-usage and abuse, but not putting up with more of it than is inevitable; and practising what the world will let them practise, including soap and water, color and music. There is danger in such activity; and where there is danger there is hope. Our present security is nothing, and can be nothing, but evil made irresistible.

Weaknesses of the Salvation Army

For the present, however, it is not my business to flatter the Salvation Army. Rather must I point out to it that it has almost as many weaknesses as the Church of England itself. It is building up a business organization which will compel it eventually to see that its present staff of enthusiast-commanders shall be succeeded by a bureaucracy of men of business who will be no better than bishops, and perhaps a good deal more unscrupulous. That has always happened sooner or later to great orders founded by saints; and the order founded by St William Booth is not exempt from the same danger. It is even more dependent than the Church on rich people who would cut off supplies at once if it began to preach that indispensable revolt against poverty which must also be a revolt against riches. It is hampered by a heavy contingent of pious elders who are not really Salvationists at all, but Evangelicals of the old school. It still, as Commissioner Howard affirms, "sticks to Moses," which is flat nonsense at this time of day if the Commissioner means, as I am afraid he does, that the Book of Genesis contains a trustworthy scientific account of the origin of species, and that the god to whom Jephthah sacrificed his daughter is any less obviously a tribal idol than Dagon or Chemosh.

Further, there is still too much other-worldliness about the Army. Like Frederick's grenadier, the Salvationist wants to live for ever (the most monstrous way of crying for the moon); and though it is evident to anyone who has ever heard General Booth and his best officers that they would work as hard for human salvation as they do at present if they believed that death would be the end of them individually, they and their followers have a bad habit of talking as if the Salvationists were heroically enduring a very bad time on earth as an investment which will bring them in dividends later on in the form, not of a better life to come for the whole world, but of an eternity spent by themselves personally in a sort of bliss which would bore any active person to a second death. Surely the truth is that the Salvationists are unusually happy people. And is it not the very diagnostic of true salvation that it shall overcome the fear of death? Now the man who has come to believe that there is no such thing as death, the change so called being merely the transition to an exquisitely happy and utterly careless life, has not overcome the fear of death at all: on the contrary, it has overcome him so completely that he refuses to die on any terms whatever. I do not call a Salvationist really saved until he is ready to lie down cheerfully on the scrap heap, having paid scot and lot and something over, and let his eternal life pass on to renew its youth in the battalions of the future.

Then there is the nasty lying habit called confession, which the Army encourages because it lends itself to dramatic oratory, with plenty of thrilling incident. For my part, when I hear a convert relating the violences and oaths and blasphemies he was guilty of before he was saved, making out that he was a very terrible fellow then and is the most contrite and chastened of Christians now, I believe him no more than I believe the millionaire who says he came up to London or Chicago as a boy with only three halfpence in his pocket. Salvationists have said to me that Barbara in my play would never have been taken in by so transparent a humbug as Snobby Price; and certainly I do not think Snobby could have taken in any experienced Salvationist on a point on which the Salvationist did not wish to be taken in. But on the point of conversion all Salvationists wish to be taken in; for the more obvious the sinner the more obvious the miracle of his conversion. When you advertize a converted burglar or reclaimed drunkard as one of the attractions at an experience meeting, your burglar can hardly have been too burglarious or your drunkard too drunken. As long as such attractions are relied on, you will have your Snobbies claiming to have beaten their mothers when they were as a matter of prosaic fact habitually beaten by them, and your Rummies of the tamest respectability pretending to a past of reckless and dazzling vice. Even when confessions are sincerely autobiographic we should beware of assuming that the impulse to make them was pious or that the interest of the hearers is wholesome. As well might we assume that the poor people who insist on shewing disgusting ulcers to district visitors are convinced hygienists, or that the curiosity which sometimes welcomes such exhibitions is a pleasant and creditable one. One is often tempted to suggest that those who pester our police superintendents with confessions of murder might very wisely be taken at their word and executed, except in the few cases in which a real murderer is seeking to be relieved of his guilt by confession and expiation. For though I am not, I hope, an unmerciful person, I do not think that the inexorability of the deed once done should be disguised by any ritual, whether in the confessional or on the scaffold.

And here my disagreement with the Salvation Army, and with all propagandists of the Cross (which I loathe as I loathe all gibbets) becomes deep indeed. Forgiveness, absolution, atonement, are figments: punishment is only a pretence of canceling one crime by another; and you can no more have forgiveness without vindictiveness than you can have a cure without a disease. You will never get a high morality from people who conceive that their misdeeds are revocable and pardonable, or in a society where absolution and expiation are officially provided for us all. The demand may be very real; but the supply is spurious. Thus Bill Walker, in my play, having assaulted the Salvation Lass, presently finds himself overwhelmed with an intolerable conviction of sin under the skilled treatment of Barbara. Straightway he begins to try to unassault the lass and deruffianize his deed, first by getting punished for it in kind, and, when that relief is denied him, by fining himself a pound to compensate the girl. He is foiled both ways. He finds the Salvation Army is inexorable as fact itself. It will not punish him: it will not take his money. It will not tolerate a redeemed ruffian: it leaves him no means of salvation except ceasing to be a ruffian. In doing this, the Salvation Army instinctively grasps the central truth of Christianity and discards its central superstition: that central truth being the vanity of revenge and punishment, and that central superstition the salvation of the world by the gibbet.

For, be it noted, Bill has assaulted an old and starving woman also; and for this worse offence he feels no remorse whatever, because she makes it clear that her malice is as great as his own. "Let her have the law of me, as she said she would," says Bill: "what I done to her is no more on what you might call my conscience than sticking a pig." This shews a perfectly natural and wholesome state of mind on his part. The old woman, like the law she threatens him with, is perfectly ready to play the game of retaliation with him: to rob him if he steals, to flog him if he strikes, to murder him if he kills. By example and precept the law and public opinion teach him to impose his will on others by anger, violence, and cruelty, and to wipe off the moral score by punishment. That is sound Crosstianity. But this Crosstianity has got entangled with something which Barbara calls Christianity, and which unexpectedly causes her to refuse to play the hangman's game of Satan casting out Satan. She refuses to prosecute a drunken ruffian; she converses on equal terms with a blackguard to whom no lady should be seen speaking in the public street: in short, she imitates Christ. Bill's conscience reacts to this just as naturally as it does to the old woman's threats. He is placed in a position of unbearable moral inferiority, and strives by every means in his power to escape from it, whilst he is still quite ready to meet the abuse of the old woman by attempting to smash a mug on her face. And that is the triumphant justification of Barbara's Christianity as against our system of judicial punishment and the vindictive villain-thrashings and "poetic justice" of the romantic stage.

For the credit of literature it must be pointed out that the situation is only partly novel. Victor Hugo long ago gave us the epic of the convict and the bishop's candlesticks, of the Crosstian policeman annihilated by his encounter with the Christian Valjean. But Bill Walker is not, like Valjean, romantically changed from a demon into an angel. There are millions of Bill Walkers in all classes of society today; and the point which I, as a professor of natural psychology, desire to demonstrate, is that Bill, without any change in his character or circumstances whatsoever, will react one way to one sort of treatment and another way to another.

In proof I might point to the sensational object lesson provided by our commercial millionaires today. They begin as brigands: merciless, unscrupulous, dealing out ruin and death and slavery to their competitors and employees, and facing desperately the worst that their competitors can do to them. The history of the English factories, the American Trusts, the exploitation of African gold, diamonds, ivory and rubber, outdoes in villainy the worst that has ever been imagined of the buccaneers of the Spanish Main. Captain Kidd would have marooned a modern Trust magnate for conduct unworthy of a gentleman of fortune. The law every day seizes on unsuccessful scoundrels of this type and punishes them with a cruelty worse than their own, with the result that they come out of the torture house more dangerous than they went in, and renew their evil doing (nobody will employ them at anything else) until they are again seized, again tormented, and again let loose, with the same result.

But the successful scoundrel is dealt with very differently, and very Christianly. He is not only forgiven: he is idolized, respected, made much of, all but worshipped. Society returns him good for evil in the most extravagant overmeasure. And with what result? He begins to idolize himself, to respect himself, to live up to the treatment he receives. He preaches sermons; he writes books of the most edifying advice to young men, and actually persuades himself that he got on by taking his own advice; he endows educational institutions; he supports charities; he dies finally in the odor of sanctity, leaving a will which is a monument of public spirit and bounty. And all this without any change in his character. The spots of the leopard and the stripes of the tiger are as brilliant as ever, but the conduct of the world towards him has changed; and his conduct has changed accordingly. You have only to reverse your attitude towards him—to lay hands on his property, revile him, assault him, and he will be a brigand again in a moment, as ready to crush you as you are to crush him, and quite as full of pretentious moral reasons for doing it.

In short, when Major Barbara says that there are no scoundrels, she is right: there are no absolute scoundrels, though there are impracticable people of whom I shall treat presently. Every reasonable man (and woman) is a potential scoundrel and a potential good citizen. What a man is depends on his character; but what he does and what we think of what he does, depends on his circumstances. The characteristics that ruin a man in one class make him eminent in another. The characters that behave differently in different circumstances behave alike in similar circumstances. Take a common English character like that of Bill Walker. We meet Bill everywhere: on the judicial bench, on the episcopal bench, in the Privy Council, at the War Office and Admiralty, as well as in the Old Bailey dock or in the ranks of casual unskilled labor. And the morality of Bill's characteristics varies with these various circumstances. The faults of the burglar are the qualities of the financier: the manners and habits of a duke would cost a city clerk his situation. In short, though character is independent of circumstances, conduct is not; and our moral judgments of character are not: both are circumstantial. Take any condition of life in which the circumstances are for a mass of men practically alike: felony, the House of Lords, the factory, the stables, the gipsy encampment or where you please! In spite of diversity of character and temperament, the conduct and morals of the individuals in each group are as predictable and as alike in the main as if they were a flock of sheep, morals being mostly only social habits and circumstantial necessities. Strong people know this and count upon it. In nothing have the master-minds of the world been distinguished from the ordinary suburban season-ticket holder more than in their straightforward perception of the fact that mankind is practically a single species, and not a menagerie of gentlemen and bounders, villains and heroes, cowards and daredevils, peers and peasants, grocers and aristocrats, artisans and laborers, washerwomen and duchesses, in which all the grades of income and caste represent distinct animals who must not be introduced to one another or intermarry. Napoleon constructing a galaxy of generals and courtiers, and even of monarchs, out of his collection of social nobodies; Julius Caesar appointing as governor of Egypt the son of a freedman—one who but a short time before would have been legally disqualified for the post even of a private soldier in the Roman army; Louis XI making his barber his privy councillor: all these had in their different ways a firm hold of the scientific fact of human equality, expressed by Barbara in the Christian formula that all men are children of one father. A man who believes that men are naturally divided into upper and lower and middle classes morally is making exactly the same mistake as the man who believes that they are naturally divided in the same way socially. And just as our persistent attempts to found political institutions on a basis of social inequality have always produced long periods of destructive friction relieved from time to time by violent explosions of revolution; so the attempt—will Americans please note—to found moral institutions on a basis of moral inequality can lead to nothing but unnatural Reigns of the Saints relieved by licentious Restorations; to Americans who have made divorce a public institution turning the face of Europe into one huge sardonic smile by refusing to stay in the same hotel with a Russian man of genius who has changed wives without the sanction of South Dakota; to grotesque hypocrisy, cruel persecution, and final utter confusion of conventions and compliances with benevolence and respectability. It is quite useless to declare that all men are born free if you deny that they are born good. Guarantee a man's goodness and his liberty will take care of itself. To guarantee his freedom on condition that you approve of his moral character is formally to abolish all freedom whatsoever, as every man's liberty is at the mercy of a moral indictment which any fool can trump up against everyone who violates custom, whether as a prophet or as a rascal. This is the lesson Democracy has to learn before it can become anything but the most oppressive of all the priesthoods.

Let us now return to Bill Walker and his case of conscience against the Salvation Army. Major Barbara, not being a modern Tetzel, or the treasurer of a hospital, refuses to sell absolution to Bill for a sovereign. Unfortunately, what the Army can afford to refuse in the case of Bill Walker, it cannot refuse in the case of Bodger. Bodger is master of the situation because he holds the purse strings. "Strive as you will," says Bodger, in effect: "me you cannot do without. You cannot save Bill Walker without my money." And the Army answers, quite rightly under the circumstances, "We will take money from the devil himself sooner than abandon the work of Salvation." So Bodger pays his conscience-money and gets the absolution that is refused to Bill. In real life Bill would perhaps never know this. But I, the dramatist whose business it is to shew the connexion between things that seem apart and unrelated in the haphazard order of events in real life, have contrived to make it known to Bill, with the result that the Salvation Army loses its hold of him at once.

But Bill may not be lost, for all that. He is still in the grip of the facts and of his own conscience, and may find his taste for blackguardism permanently spoiled. Still, I cannot guarantee that happy ending. Walk through the poorer quarters of our cities on Sunday when the men are not working, but resting and chewing the cud of their reflections. You will find one expression common to every mature face: the expression of cynicism. The discovery made by Bill Walker about the Salvation Army has been made by everyone there. They have found that every man has his price; and they have been foolishly or corruptly taught to mistrust and despise him for that necessary and salutary condition of social existence. When they learn that General Booth, too, has his price, they do not admire him because it is a high one, and admit the need of organizing society so that he shall get it in an honorable way: they conclude that his character is unsound and that all religious men are hypocrites and allies of their sweaters and oppressors. They know that the large subscriptions which help to support the Army are endowments, not of religion, but of the wicked doctrine of docility in poverty and humility under oppression; and they are rent by the most agonizing of all the doubts of the soul, the doubt whether their true salvation must not come from their most abhorrent passions, from murder, envy, greed, stubbornness, rage, and terrorism, rather than from public spirit, reasonableness, humanity, generosity, tenderness, delicacy, pity and kindness. The confirmation of that doubt, at which our newspapers have been working so hard for years past, is the morality of militarism; and the justification of militarism is that circumstances may at any time make it the true morality of the moment. It is by producing such moments that we produce violent and sanguinary revolutions, such as the one now in progress in Russia and the one which Capitalism in England and America is daily and diligently provoking.

At such moments it becomes the duty of the Churches to evoke all the powers of destruction against the existing order. But if they do this, the existing order must forcibly suppress them. Churches are suffered to exist only on condition that they preach submission to the State as at present capitalistically organized. The Church of England itself is compelled to add to the thirty-six articles in which it formulates its religious tenets, three more in which it apologetically protests that the moment any of these articles comes in conflict with the State it is to be entirely renounced, abjured, violated, abrogated and abhorred, the policeman being a much more important person than any of the Persons of the Trinity. And this is why no tolerated Church nor Salvation Army can ever win the entire confidence of the poor. It must be on the side of the police and the military, no matter what it believes or disbelieves; and as the police and the military are the instruments by which the rich rob and oppress the poor (on legal and moral principles made for the purpose), it is not possible to be on the side of the poor and of the police at the same time. Indeed the religious bodies, as the almoners of the rich, become a sort of auxiliary police, taking off the insurrectionary edge of poverty with coals and blankets, bread and treacle, and soothing and cheering the victims with hopes of immense and inexpensive happiness in another world when the process of working them to premature death in the service of the rich is complete in this.

Christianity and Anarchism

Such is the false position from which neither the Salvation Army nor the Church of England nor any other religious organization whatever can escape except through a reconstitution of society. Nor can they merely endure the State passively, washing their hands of its sins. The State is constantly forcing the consciences of men by violence and cruelty. Not content with exacting money from us for the maintenance of its soldiers and policemen, its gaolers and executioners, it forces us to take an active personal part in its proceedings on pain of becoming ourselves the victims of its violence. As I write these lines, a sensational example is given to the world. A royal marriage has been celebrated, first by sacrament in a cathedral, and then by a bullfight having for its main amusement the spectacle of horses gored and disembowelled by the bull, after which, when the bull is so exhausted as to be no longer dangerous, he is killed by a cautious matador. But the ironic contrast between the bullfight and the sacrament of marriage does not move anyone. Another contrast—that between the splendor, the happiness, the atmosphere of kindly admiration surrounding the young couple, and the price paid for it under our abominable social arrangements in the misery, squalor and degradation of millions of other young couples—is drawn at the same moment by a novelist, Mr Upton Sinclair, who chips a corner of the veneering from the huge meat packing industries of Chicago, and shews it to us as a sample of what is going on all over the world underneath the top layer of prosperous plutocracy. One man is sufficiently moved by that contrast to pay his own life as the price of one terrible blow at the responsible parties. His poverty has left him ignorant enough to be duped by the pretence that the innocent young bride and bridegroom, put forth and crowned by plutocracy as the heads of a State in which they have less personal power than any policeman, and less influence than any Chairman of a Trust, are responsible. At them accordingly he launches his sixpennorth of fulminate, missing his mark, but scattering the bowels of as many horses as any bull in the arena, and slaying twenty-three persons, besides wounding ninety-nine. And of all these, the horses alone are innocent of the guilt he is avenging: had he blown all Madrid to atoms with every adult person in it, not one could have escaped the charge of being an accessory, before, at, and after the fact, to poverty and prostitution, to such wholesale massacre of infants as Herod never dreamt of, to plague, pestilence and famine, battle, murder and lingering death—perhaps not one who had not helped, through example, precept, connivance, and even clamor, to teach the dynamiter his well-learnt gospel of hatred and vengeance, by approving every day of sentences of years of imprisonment so infernal in their unnatural stupidity and panic-stricken cruelty, that their advocates can disavow neither the dagger nor the bomb without stripping the mask of justice and humanity from themselves also.

Be it noted that at this very moment there appears the biography of one of our dukes, who, being a Scot, could argue about politics, and therefore stood out as a great brain among our aristocrats. And what, if you please, was his grace's favorite historical episode, which he declared he never read without intense satisfaction? Why, the young General Bonapart's pounding of the Paris mob to pieces in 1795, called in playful approval by our respectable classes "the whiff of grapeshot," though Napoleon, to do him justice, took a deeper view of it, and would fain have had it forgotten. And since the Duke of Argyll was not a demon, but a man of like passions with ourselves, by no means rancorous or cruel as men go, who can doubt that all over the world proletarians of the ducal kidney are now revelling in "the whiff of dynamite" (the flavor of the joke seems to evaporate a little, does it not?) because it was aimed at the class they hate even as our argute duke hated what he called the mob.

In such an atmosphere there can be only one sequel to the Madrid explosion. All Europe burns to emulate it. Vengeance! More blood! Tear "the Anarchist beast" to shreds. Drag him to the scaffold. Imprison him for life. Let all civilized States band together to drive his like off the face of the earth; and if any State refuses to join, make war on it. This time the leading London newspaper, anti-Liberal and therefore anti-Russian in politics, does not say "Serve you right" to the victims, as it did, in effect, when Bobrikoff, and De Plehve, and Grand Duke Sergius, were in the same manner unofficially fulminated into fragments. No: fulminate our rivals in Asia by all means, ye brave Russian revolutionaries; but to aim at an English princess! monstrous! hideous! hound down the wretch to his doom; and observe, please, that we are a civilized and merciful people, and, however much we may regret it, must not treat him as Ravaillac and Damiens were treated. And meanwhile, since we have not yet caught him, let us soothe our quivering nerves with the bullfight, and comment in a courtly way on the unfailing tact and good taste of the ladies of our royal houses, who, though presumably of full normal natural tenderness, have been so effectually broken in to fashionable routine that they can be taken to see the horses slaughtered as helplessly as they could no doubt be taken to a gladiator show, if that happened to be the mode just now.

Strangely enough, in the midst of this raging fire of malice, the one man who still has faith in the kindness and intelligence of human nature is the fulminator, now a hunted wretch, with nothing, apparently, to secure his triumph over all the prisons and scaffolds of infuriate Europe except the revolver in his pocket and his readiness to discharge it at a moment's notice into his own or any other head. Think of him setting out to find a gentleman and a Christian in the multitude of human wolves howling for his blood. Think also of this: that at the very first essay he finds what he seeks, a veritable grandee of Spain, a noble, high-thinking, unterrified, malice-void soul, in the guise—of all masquerades in the world!—of a modern editor. The Anarchist wolf, flying from the wolves of plutocracy, throws himself on the honor of the man. The man, not being a wolf (nor a London editor), and therefore not having enough sympathy with his exploit to be made bloodthirsty by it, does not throw him back to the pursuing wolves—gives him, instead, what help he can to escape, and sends him off acquainted at last with a force that goes deeper than dynamite, though you cannot buy so much of it for sixpence. That righteous and honorable high human deed is not wasted on Europe, let us hope, though it benefits the fugitive wolf only for a moment. The plutocratic wolves presently smell him out. The fugitive shoots the unlucky wolf whose nose is nearest; shoots himself; and then convinces the world, by his photograph, that he was no monstrous freak of reversion to the tiger, but a good looking young man with nothing abnormal about him except his appalling courage and resolution (that is why the terrified shriek Coward at him): one to whom murdering a happy young couple on their wedding morning would have been an unthinkably unnatural abomination under rational and kindly human circumstances.

Then comes the climax of irony and blind stupidity. The wolves, balked of their meal of fellowwolf, turn on the man, and proceed to torture him, after their manner, by imprisonment, for refusing to fasten his teeth in the throat of the dynamiter and hold him down until they came to finish him.

Thus, you see, a man may not be a gentleman nowadays even if he wishes to. As to being a Christian, he is allowed some latitude in that matter, because, I repeat, Christianity has two faces. Popular Christianity has for its emblem a gibbet, for its chief sensation a sanguinary execution after torture, for its central mystery an insane vengeance bought off by a trumpery expiation. But there is a nobler and profounder Christianity which affirms the sacred mystery of Equality, and forbids the glaring futility and folly of vengeance, often politely called punishment or justice. The gibbet part of Christianity is tolerated. The other is criminal felony. Connoisseurs in irony are well aware of the fact that the only editor in England who denounces punishment as radically wrong, also repudiates Christianity; calls his paper The Freethinker; and has been imprisoned for "bad taste" under the law against blasphemy.

Sane Conclusions

And now I must ask the excited reader not to lose his head on one side or the other, but to draw a sane moral from these grim absurdities. It is not good sense to propose that laws against crime should apply to principals only and not to accessories whose consent, counsel, or silence may secure impunity to the principal. If you institute punishment as part of the law, you must punish people for refusing to punish. If you have a police, part of its duty must be to compel everybody to assist the police. No doubt if your laws are unjust, and your policemen agents of oppression, the result will be an unbearable violation of the private consciences of citizens. But that cannot be helped: the remedy is, not to license everybody to thwart the law if they please, but to make laws that will command the public assent, and not to deal cruelly and stupidly with law-breakers. Everybody disapproves of burglars; but the modern burglar, when caught and overpowered by a householder, usually appeals, and often, let us hope, with success, to his captor not to deliver him over to the useless horrors of penal servitude. In other cases the law-breaker escapes because those who could give him up do not consider his breach of the law a guilty action. Sometimes, even, private tribunals are formed in opposition to the official tribunals; and these private tribunals employ assassins as executioners, as was done, for example, by Mahomet before he had established his power officially, and by the Ribbon lodges of Ireland in their long struggle with the landlords. Under such circumstances, the assassin goes free although everybody in the district knows who he is and what he has done. They do not betray him, partly because they justify him exactly as the regular Government justifies its official executioner, and partly because they would themselves be assassinated if they betrayed him: another method learnt from the official government. Given a tribunal, employing a slayer who has no personal quarrel with the slain; and there is clearly no moral difference between official and unofficial killing.

In short, all men are anarchists with regard to laws which are against their consciences, either in the preamble or in the penalty. In London our worst anarchists are the magistrates, because many of them are so old and ignorant that when they are called upon to administer any law that is based on ideas or knowledge less than half a century old, they disagree with it, and being mere ordinary homebred private Englishmen without any respect for law in the abstract, naively set the example of violating it. In this instance the man lags behind the law; but when the law lags behind the man, he becomes equally an anarchist. When some huge change in social conditions, such as the industrial revolution of the eighteenth and nineteenth centuries, throws our legal and industrial institutions out of date, Anarchism becomes almost a religion. The whole force of the most energetic geniuses of the time in philosophy, economics, and art, concentrates itself on demonstrations and reminders that morality and law are only conventions, fallible and continually obsolescing. Tragedies in which the heroes are bandits, and comedies in which law-abiding and conventionally moral folk are compelled to satirize themselves by outraging the conscience of the spectators every time they do their duty, appear simultaneously with economic treatises entitled "What is Property? Theft!" and with histories of "The Conflict between Religion and Science."

Now this is not a healthy state of things. The advantages of living in society are proportionate, not to the freedom of the individual from a code, but to the complexity and subtlety of the code he is prepared not only to accept but to uphold as a matter of such vital importance that a lawbreaker at large is hardly to be tolerated on any plea. Such an attitude becomes impossible when the only men who can make themselves heard and remembered throughout the world spend all their energy in raising our gorge against current law, current morality, current respectability, and legal property. The ordinary man, uneducated in social theory even when he is schooled in Latin verse, cannot be set against all the laws of his country and yet persuaded to regard law in the abstract as vitally necessary to society. Once he is brought to repudiate the laws and institutions he knows, he will repudiate the very conception of law and the very groundwork of institutions, ridiculing human rights, extolling brainless methods as "historical," and tolerating nothing except pure empiricism in conduct, with dynamite as the basis of politics and vivisection as the basis of science. That is hideous; but what is to be done? Here am I, for instance, by class a respectable man, by common sense a hater of waste and disorder, by intellectual constitution legally minded to the verge of pedantry, and by temperament apprehensive and economically disposed to the limit of oldmaidishness; yet I am, and have always been, and shall now always be, a revolutionary writer, because our laws make law impossible; our liberties destroy all freedom; our property is organized robbery; our morality is an impudent hypocrisy; our wisdom is administered by inexperienced or malexperienced dupes, our power wielded by cowards and weaklings, and our honor false in all its points. I am an enemy of the existing order for good reasons; but that does not make my attacks any less encouraging or helpful to people who are its enemies for bad reasons. The existing order may shriek that if I tell the truth about it, some foolish person may drive it to become still worse by trying to assassinate it. I cannot help that, even if I could see what worse it could do than it is already doing. And the disadvantage of that worst even from its own point of view is that society, with all its prisons and bayonets and whips and ostracisms and starvations, is powerless in the face of the Anarchist who is prepared to sacrifice his own life in the battle with it. Our natural safety from the cheap and devastating explosives which every Russian student can make, and every Russian grenadier has learnt to handle in Manchuria, lies in the fact that brave and resolute men, when they are rascals, will not risk their skins for the good of humanity, and, when they are not, are sympathetic enough to care for humanity, abhorring murder, and never committing it until their consciences are outraged beyond endurance. The remedy is, then, simply not to outrage their consciences.

Do not be afraid that they will not make allowances. All men make very large allowances indeed before they stake their own lives in a war to the death with society. Nobody demands or expects the millennium. But there are two things that must be set right, or we shall perish, like Rome, of soul atrophy disguised as empire.

The first is that the daily ceremony of dividing the wealth of the country among its inhabitants shall be so conducted that no crumb shall, save as a criminal's ration, go to any able-bodied adults who are not producing by their personal exertions not only a full equivalent for what they take, but a surplus sufficient to provide for their superannuation and pay back the debt due for their nurture.

The second is that the deliberate infliction of malicious injuries which now goes on under the name of punishment be abandoned; so that the thief, the ruffian, the gambler, and the beggar, may without inhumanity be handed over to the law, and made to understand that a State which is too humane to punish will also be too thrifty to waste the life of honest men in watching or restraining dishonest ones. That is why we do not imprison dogs. We even take our chance of their first bite. But if a dog delights to bark and bite, it goes to the lethal chamber. That seems to me sensible. To allow the dog to expiate his bite by a period of torment, and then let him loose in a much more savage condition (for the chain makes a dog savage) to bite again and expiate again, having meanwhile spent a great deal of human life and happiness in the task of chaining and feeding and tormenting him, seems to me idiotic and superstitious. Yet that is what we do to men who bark and bite and steal. It would be far more sensible to put up with their vices, as we put up with their illnesses, until they give more trouble than they are worth, at which point we should, with many apologies and expressions of sympathy, and some generosity in complying with their last wishes, place them in the lethal chamber and get rid of them. Under no circumstances should they be allowed to expiate their misdeeds by a manufactured penalty, to subscribe to a charity, or to compensate the victims. If there is to be no punishment there can be no forgiveness. We shall never have real moral responsibility until everyone knows that his deeds are irrevocable, and that his life depends on his usefulness. Hitherto, alas! humanity has never dared face these hard facts. We frantically scatter conscience money and invent systems of conscience banking, with expiatory penalties, atonements, redemptions, salvations, hospital subscription lists and what not, to enable us to contract-out of the moral code. Not content with the old scapegoat and sacrificial lamb, we deify human saviors, and pray to miraculous virgin intercessors. We attribute mercy to the inexorable; soothe our consciences after committing murder by throwing ourselves on the bosom of divine love; and shrink even from our own gallows because we are forced to admit that it, at least, is irrevocable—as if one hour of imprisonment were not as irrevocable as any execution!

If a man cannot look evil in the face without illusion, he will never know what it really is, or combat it effectually. The few men who have been able (relatively) to do this have been called cynics, and have sometimes had an abnormal share of evil in themselves, corresponding to the abnormal strength of their minds; but they have never done mischief unless they intended to do it. That is why great scoundrels have been beneficent rulers whilst amiable and privately harmless monarchs have ruined their countries by trusting to the hocus-pocus of innocence and guilt, reward and punishment, virtuous indignation and pardon, instead of standing up to the facts without either malice or mercy. Major Barbara stands up to Bill Walker in that way, with the result that the ruffian who cannot get hated, has to hate himself. To relieve this agony he tries to get punished; but the Salvationist whom he tries to provoke is as merciless as Barbara, and only prays for him. Then he tries to pay, but can get nobody to take his money. His doom is the doom of Cain, who, failing to find either a savior, a policeman, or an almoner to help him to pretend that his brother's blood no longer cried from the ground, had to live and die a murderer. Cain took care not to commit another murder, unlike our railway shareholders (I am one) who kill and maim shunters by hundreds to save the cost of automatic couplings, and make atonement by annual subscriptions to deserving charities. Had Cain been allowed to pay off his score, he might possibly have killed Adam and Eve for the mere sake of a second luxurious reconciliation with God afterwards. Bodger, you may depend on it, will go on to the end of his life poisoning people with bad whisky, because he can always depend on the Salvation Army or the Church of England to negotiate a redemption for him in consideration of a trifling percentage of his profits.

There is a third condition too, which must be fulfilled before the great teachers of the world will cease to scoff at its religions. Creeds must become intellectually honest. At present there is not a single credible established religion in the world. That is perhaps the most stupendous fact in the whole world-situation. This play of mine, Major Barbara, is, I hope, both true and inspired; but whoever says that it all happened, and that faith in it and understanding of it consist in believing that it is a record of an actual occurrence, is, to speak according to Scripture, a fool and a liar, and is hereby solemnly denounced and cursed as such by me, the author, to all posterity.

London, June 1906

Major Barbara

ACT I

It is after dinner in January 1906, in the library in LADY BRITOMART UNDERSHAFT'S *house in Wilton Crescent. A large and comfortable settee is in the middle of the room, upholstered in dark leather. A person sitting on it (it is vacant at present) would have, on his right,* LADY BRITOMART'S *writing table, with the lady herself busy at it; a smaller writing table behind him on his left; the door behind him on* LADY BRITOMART'S *side; and a window with a window seat directly on his left. Near the window is an armchair.*

LADY BRITOMART *is a woman of fifty or thereabouts, well dressed and yet careless of her dress, well bred and quite reckless of her breeding, well mannered and yet appallingly outspoken and indifferent to the opinion of her interlocutors, amiable and yet peremptory, arbitrary, and hightempered to the last bearable degree, and withal a very typical managing matron of the upper class, treated as a naughty child until she grew into a scolding mother, and finally settling down with plenty of practical ability and worldly experience, limited in the oddest way with domestic and class limitations, conceiving the universe exactly as if it were a large house in Wilton Crescent, though handling her corner of it very effectively on that assumption, and being quite enlightened and liberal as to the books in the library, the pictures on the walls, the music in the portfolios, and the articles in the papers.*

Her son, STEPHEN, *comes in. He is a gravely correct young man under 25, taking himself very seriously, but still in some awe of his mother, from childish habit and bachelor shyness rather than from any weakness of character.*

STEPHEN Whats the matter?

LADY BRITOMART Presently, Stephen.

STEPHEN *submissively walks to the settee and sits down. He takes up a Liberal weekly called The Speaker.*

LADY BRITOMART Dont begin to read, Stephen. I shall require all your attention.

STEPHEN It was only while I was waiting—

LADY BRITOMART Dont make excuses, Stephen. (*He puts down The Speaker.*) Now! (*She finishes her writing; rises; and comes to the settee.*) I have not kept you waiting very long, I think.

STEPHEN Not at all, mother.

LADY BRITOMART Bring me my cushion. (*He takes the cushion from the chair at the desk and arranges it for her as she sits down on the settee.*) Sit down. (*He sits down and fingers his tie nervously.*) Dont fiddle with your tie, Stephen: there is nothing the matter with it.

STEPHEN I beg your pardon. (*He fiddles with his watch chain instead.*)

LADY BRITOMART Now are you attending to me, Stephen?

STEPHEN Of course, mother.

LADY BRITOMART No: it's not of course. I want something much more than your everyday matter-of-course attention. I am going to speak to you very seriously, Stephen. I wish you would let that chain alone.

STEPHEN (*hastily relinquishing the chain*) Have I done anything to annoy you, mother? If so, it was quite unintentional.

LADY BRITOMART (*astonished*) Nonsense! (*With some remorse.*) My poor boy, did you think I was angry with you?

STEPHEN What is it, then, mother? You are making me very uneasy.

LADY BRITOMART (*squaring herself at him rather aggressively*) Stephen: may I ask how soon you intend to realize that you are a grown-up man, and that I am only a woman?

STEPHEN (*amazed*) Only a—

LADY BRITOMART Dont repeat my words, please: it is a most aggravating habit. You must learn to face life seriously, Stephen. I really cannot bear the whole burden of our family affairs any longer. You must advise me: you must assume the responsibility.

STEPHEN I!

LADY BRITOMART Yes, you, of course. You were 24 last June. Youve been at Harrow and Cambridge. Youve been to India and Japan. You must know a lot of things, now; unless you have wasted your time most scandalously. Well, advise me.

STEPHEN (*much perplexed*) You know I have never interfered in the household—

LADY BRITOMART No: I should think not. I dont want you to order the dinner.

STEPHEN I mean in our family affairs.

LADY BRITOMART Well, you must interfere now for they are getting quite beyond me.

STEPHEN (*troubled*) I have thought sometimes that perhaps I ought; but really, mother, I know so little about them; and what I do know is so painful! it is so impossible to mention some things to you—(*he stops, ashamed*).

LADY BRITOMART   I suppose you mean your father.

STEPHEN (*almost inaudibly*)   Yes.

LADY BRITOMART   My dear: we cant go on all our lives not mentioning him. Of course you were quite right not to open the subject until I asked you to; but you are old enough now to be taken into my confidence, and to help me to deal with him about the girls.

STEPHEN   But the girls are all right. They are engaged.

LADY BRITOMART (*complacently*)   Yes: I have made a very good match for Sarah. Charles Lomax will be a millionaire at 35. But that is ten years ahead; and in the meantime his trustees cannot under the terms of his father's will allow him more than £800 a year.

STEPHEN   But the will says also that if he increases his income by his own exertions, they may double the increase.

LADY BRITOMART   Charles Lomax's exertions are much more likely to decrease his income than to increase it. Sarah will have to find at least another £800 a year for the next ten years; and even then they will be as poor as church mice. And what about Barbara? I thought Barbara was going to make the most brilliant career of all of you. And what does she do? Joins the Salvation Army; discharges her maid; lives on a pound a week and walks in one evening with a professor of Greek whom she has picked up in the street, and who pretends to be a Salvationist, and actually plays the big drum for her in public because he has fallen head over ears in love with her.

STEPHEN   I was certainly rather taken aback when I heard they were engaged. Cusins is a very nice fellow, certainly: nobody would ever guess that he was born in Australia; but—

LADY BRITOMART   Oh, Adolphus Cusins will make a very good husband. After all, nobody can say a word against Greek: it stamps a man at once as an educated gentleman. And my family, thank Heaven, is not a pig-headed Tory one. We are Whigs, and believe in liberty. Let snobbish people say what they please: Barbara shall marry, not the man they like, but the man *I* like.

STEPHEN   Of course I was thinking only of his income. However, he is not likely to be extravagant.

LADY BRITOMART   Dont be too sure of that, Stephen. I know your quiet, simple, refined, poetic people like Adolphus: quite content with the best of everything! They cost more than your extravagant people, who are always as mean as they are second rate. No: Barbara will need at least £2000 a year. You see it means two additional households. Besides, my dear, you must marry soon. I dont approve of the present fashion of philandering bachelors and late marriages; and I am trying to arrange something for you.

STEPHEN It's very good of you, mother; but perhaps I had better arrange that for myself.

LADY BRITOMART Nonsense! you are much too young to begin matchmaking: you would be taken in by some pretty little nobody. Of course I dont mean that you are not to be consulted: you know that as well as I do. (STEPHEN *closes his lips and is silent.*) Now dont sulk, Stephen.

STEPHEN I am not sulking, mother. What has all this got to do with—with—with my father?

LADY BRITOMART My dear Stephen: where is the money to come from? It is easy enough for you and the other children to live on my income as long as we are in the same house; but I cant keep four families in four separate houses. You know how poor my father is: he has barely seven thousand a year now; and really, if he were not the Earl of Stevenage, he would have to give up society. He can do nothing for us. He says, naturally enough, that it is absurd that he should be asked to provide for the children of a man who is rolling in money. You see, Stephen, your father must be fabulously wealthy, because there is always a war going on somewhere.

STEPHEN You need not remind me of that, mother. I have hardly ever opened a newspaper in my life without seeing our name in it. The Undershaft torpedo! The Undershaft quick firers! The Undershaft ten inch! the Undershaft disappearing rampart gun! the Undershaft submarine! and now the Undershaft aerial battleship! At Harrow they called me the Woolwich Infant. At Cambridge it was the same. A little brute at King's who was always trying to get up revivals, spoilt my Bible—your first birthday present to me—by writing under my name, "Son and heir to Undershaft and Lazarus, Death and Destruction Dealers: address Christendom and Judea." But that was not so bad as the way I was kowtowed to everywhere because my father was making millions by selling cannons.

LADY BRITOMART It is not only the cannons, but the war loans that Lazarus arranges under cover of giving credit for the cannons. You know, Stephen, it's perfectly scandalous. Those two men, Andrew Undershaft and Lazarus, positively have Europe under their thumbs. That is why your father is able to behave as he does. He is above the law. Do you think Bismarck or Gladstone or Disraeli could have openly defied every social and moral obligation all their lives as your father has? They simply wouldnt have dared. I asked Gladstone to take it up. I asked The Times to take it up. I asked the Lord Chamberlain to take it up. But it was just like asking them to declare war on the Sultan. They wouldnt. They said they couldnt touch him. I believe they were afraid.

STEPHEN   What could they do? He does not actually break the law.

LADY BRITOMART   Not break the law! He is always breaking the law. He broke the law when he was born: his parents were not married.

STEPHEN   Mother! Is that true?

LADY BRITOMART   Of course it's true: that was why we separated.

STEPHEN   He married without letting you know that!

LADY BRITOMART (*rather taken aback by this inference*)   Oh no. To do Andrew justice, that was not the sort of thing he did. Besides, you know the Undershaft motto: Unashamed. Everybody knew.

STEPHEN   But you said that was why you separated.

LADY BRITOMART   Yes, because he was not content with being a foundling himself: he wanted to disinherit you for another foundling. That was what I couldnt stand.

STEPHEN (*ashamed*)   Do you mean for—for—for—

LADY BRITOMART   Dont stammer, Stephen. Speak distinctly.

STEPHEN   But this is so frightful to me, mother. To have to speak to you about such things!

LADY BRITOMART   It's not pleasant for me, either, especially if you are still so childish that you must make it worse by a display of embarrassment. It is only in the middle classes, Stephen, that people get into a state of dumb helpless horror when they find that there are wicked people in the world. In our class, we have to decide what is to be done with wicked people; and nothing should disturb our self-possession. Now ask your question properly.

STEPHEN   Mother: have you no consideration for me? For Heaven's sake either treat me as a child, as you always do, and tell me nothing at all or tell me everything and let me take it as best I can.

LADY BRITOMART   Treat you as a child! What do you mean? It is most unkind and ungrateful of you to say such a thing. You know I have never treated any of you as children. I have always made you my companions and friends, and allowed you perfect freedom to do and say whatever you like, so long as you liked what I could approve of.

STEPHEN (*desperately*)   I daresay we have been the very imperfect children of a very perfect mother; but I do beg you to let me alone for once, and tell me about this horrible business of my father wanting to set me aside for another son.

LADY BRITOMART *(amazed)* Another son! I never said anything of the kind. I never dreamt of such a thing. This is what comes of interrupting me.

STEPHEN But you said—

LADY BRITOMART *(cutting him short)* Now be a good boy, Stephen, and listen to me patiently. The Undershafts are descended from a foundling in the parish of St Andrew Undershaft in the city. That was long ago, in the reign of James the First. Well, this foundling was adopted by an armorer and gun-maker. In the course of time the foundling succeeded to the business; and from some notion of gratitude, or some vow or something, he adopted another foundling, and left the business to him. And that foundling did the same. Ever since that, the cannon business has always been left to an adopted foundling named Andrew Undershaft.

STEPHEN But did they never marry? Were there no legitimate sons?

LADY BRITOMART Oh yes: they married just as your father did; and they were rich enough to buy land for their own children and leave them well provided for. But they always adopted and trained some foundling to succeed them in the business; and of course they always quarrelled with their wives furiously over it. Your father was adopted in that way and he pretends to consider himself bound to keep up the tradition and adopt somebody to leave the business to. Of course I was not going to stand that. There may have been some reason for it when the Undershafts could only marry women in their own class, whose sons were not fit to govern great estates. But there could be no excuse for passing over my son.

STEPHEN *(dubiously)* I am afraid I should make a poor hand of managing a cannon foundry.

LADY BRITOMART Nonsense! you could easily get a manager and pay him a salary.

STEPHEN My father evidently had no great opinion of my capacity.

LADY BRITOMART Stuff, child! you were only a baby: it had nothing to do with your capacity. Andrew did it on principle, just as he did every perverse and wicked thing on principle. When my father remonstrated, Andrew actually told him to his face that history tells us of only two successful institutions: one the Undershaft firm, and the other the Roman Empire under the Antonines.

That was because the Antonine emperors all adopted their successors. Such rubbish! The Stevenages are as good as the Antonines, I hope: and you are a Stevenage. But that was Andrew all over. There you have the man! Always clever and unanswerable when he was defending nonsense and wickedness: always awkward and sullen when he had to behave sensibly and decently!

STEPHEN Then it was on my account that your home life was broken up, mother. I am sorry.

LADY BRITOMART Well, dear, there were other differences. I really cannot bear an immoral man. I am not a Pharisee, I hope; and I should not have minded his merely doing wrong things: we are none of us perfect. But your father didnt exactly do wrong things: he said them and thought them: that was what was so dreadful. He really had a sort of religion of wrongness. Just as one doesnt mind men practising immorality so long as they own that they are in the wrong by preaching morality; so I couldnt forgive Andrew for preaching immorality while he practised morality. You would all have grown up without principles, without any knowledge of right and wrong, if he had been in the house. You know, my dear, your father was a very attractive man in some ways. Children did not dislike him; and he took advantage of it to put the wickedest ideas into their heads, and make them quite unmanageable. I did not dislike him myself: very far from it; but nothing can bridge over moral disagreement.

STEPHEN All this simply bewilders me, mother. People may differ about matters of opinion, or even about religion; but how can they differ about right and wrong? Right is right; and wrong is wrong; and if a man cannot distinguish them properly, he is either a fool or a rascal: thats all.

LADY BRITOMART (*touched*) Thats my own boy (*she pats his cheek*)! Your father never could answer that: he used to laugh and get out of it under cover of some affectionate nonsense. And now that you understand the situation, what do you advise me to do?

STEPHEN Well, what can you do?

LADY BRITOMART I must get the money somehow.

STEPHEN We cannot take money from him. I had rather go and live in some cheap place like Bedford Square or even Hampstead than take a farthing of his money.

LADY BRITOMART But after all, Stephen, our present income comes from Andrew.

STEPHEN (*shocked*) I never knew that.

LADY BRITOMART Well, you surely didnt suppose your grandfather had anything to give me. The Stevenages could not do everything for you. We gave you social position. Andrew had to contribute something. He had a very good bargain, I think.

STEPHEN (*bitterly*) We are utterly dependent on him and his cannons, then?

LADY BRITOMART Certainly not: the money is settled. But he provided it. So you see it is not a question of taking money from him or not: it is simply a question of how much. I dont want any more for myself.

STEPHEN Nor do I.

LADY BRITOMART But Sarah does; and Barbara does. That is, Charles Lomax and Adolphus Cusins will cost them more. So I must put my pride in my pocket and ask for it, I suppose. That is your advice, Stephen, is it not?

STEPHEN No.

LADY BRITOMART (*sharply*) Stephen!

STEPHEN Of course if you are determined—

LADY BRITOMART I am not determined: I ask your advice; and I am waiting for it. I will not have all the responsibility thrown on my shoulders.

STEPHEN (*obstinately*) I would die sooner than ask him for another penny.

LADY BRITOMART (*resignedly*) You mean that *I* must ask him. Very well, Stephen: it shall be as you wish. You will be glad to know that your grandfather concurs. But he thinks I ought to ask Andrew to come here and see the girls. After all, he must have some natural affection for them.

STEPHEN Ask him here!!!

LADY BRITOMART Do not repeat my words, Stephen. Where else can I ask him?

STEPHEN I never expected you to ask him at all.

LADY BRITOMART Now dont tease, Stephen. Come! you see that it is necessary that he should pay us a visit, dont you?

STEPHEN (*reluctantly*) I suppose so, if the girls cannot do without his money.

LADY BRITOMART Thank you, Stephen: I knew you would give me the right advice when it was properly explained to you. I have asked your father to come this evening. (STEPHEN *bounds from his seat.*) Dont jump, Stephen: it fidgets me.

STEPHEN (*in utter consternation*) Do you mean to say that my father is coming here tonight—that he may be here at any moment?

LADY BRITOMART (*looking at her watch*) I said nine. (*He gasps. She rises.*) Ring the bell, please. (STEPHEN *goes to the smaller writing table; presses a button on it; and sits at it with his elbows on the table and his head in his hands, outwitted and overwhelmed.*) It is ten minutes to nine yet; and I have to prepare the girls. I asked Charles Lomax and Adolphus to dinner on purpose that they might be here. Andrew had better see them in case he should cherish any delusion as to their being capable of supporting their wives. (*The butler enters:* LADY BRITOMART *goes behind the settee to speak to him.*) Morrison: go up to the drawing room and tell everybody to come down here at once. (MORRISON *withdraws.* LADY BRITOMART *turns to* STEPHEN.) Now remember, Stephen: I shall need all your countenance and authority. (*He rises and tries to recover some vestige of these attributes.*) Give me a chair, dear. (*He pushes a chair forward from the wall to where she stands, near the smaller writing table. She sits down; and he goes to the armchair, into which he throws himself.*) I dont know how Barbara will take it. Ever since they made her a major in the Salvation Army she has developed a propensity to have her own way and order people about which quite cows me sometimes. It's not ladylike: I'm sure I dont know where she picked it up. Anyhow, Barbara shant bully me but still it's just as well that your father should be here before she has time to refuse to meet him or make a fuss. Dont look nervous, Stephen: it will only encourage Barbara to make difficulties. *I* am nervous enough, goodness knows; but I dont shew it.

SARAH *and* BARBARA *come in with their respective young men,* CHARLES LOMAX *and* ADOLPHUS CUSINS. SARAH *is slender, bored, and mundane.* BARBARA *is robuster, jollier, much more energetic.* SARAH *is fashionably dressed:* BARBARA *is in Salvation Army uniform.* LOMAX, *a young man about town, is like many other young men about town. He is afflicted with a frivolous sense of humor which plunges him at the most inopportune moments into paroxysms of imperfectly suppressed laughter.* CUSINS *is a spectacled student, slight, thin haired, and sweet voiced, a more complex form of* LOMAX's *complaint. His sense of humor is intellectual and subtle, and is complicated by an appalling temper. The lifelong struggle of a benevolent temperament and a high conscience against impulses of inhuman ridicule and fierce impatience has set up a chronic strain which has visibly wrecked his constitution. He is a most implacable, determined, tenacious, intolerant person who by mere force of character presents himself as—and indeed actually is—considerate, gentle, explanatory, even mild and apologetic, capable possibly of murder, but not of cruelty or coarseness. By the operation of some instinct which is not merciful enough to blind him with the illusions of love, he is obstinately bent on marrying* BARBARA. LOMAX *likes* SARAH *and thinks it will be rather a lark to marry her. Consequently he has not attempted to resist* LADY BRITOMART's *arrangements to that end.*

All four look as if they had been having a good deal of fun in the drawing room. The girls enter first, leaving the swains outside. SARAH *comes to the settee.* BARBARA *comes in after her and stops at the door.*

BARBARA   Are Cholly and Dolly to come in?

LADY BRITOMART *(forcibly)*   Barbara: I will not have Charles called Cholly: the vulgarity of it positively makes me ill.

BARBARA   It's all right, mother: Cholly is quite correct nowadays. Are they to come in?

LADY BRITOMART   Yes, if they will behave themselves.

BARBARA *(through the door)*   Come in, Dolly; and behave yourself.

BARBARA *comes to her mother's writing table.* CUSINS *enters smiling, and wanders towards* LADY BRITOMART.

SARAH *(calling)*   Come in, Cholly. (LOMAX *enters, controlling his features very imperfectly, and places himself vaguely between* SARAH *and* BARBARA.)

LADY BRITOMART *(peremptorily)*   Sit down, all of you. *(They sit.* CUSINS *crosses to the window and seats himself there.* LOMAX *takes a chair.* BARBARA *sits at the writing table and* SARAH *on the settee.)* I dont in the least know what you are laughing at, Adolphus. I am surprised at you, though I expected nothing better from Charles Lomax.

CUSINS *(in a remarkably gentle voice)*   Barbara has been trying to teach me the West Ham Salvation March.

LADY BRITOMART   I see nothing to laugh at in that; nor should you if you are really converted.

CUSINS *(sweetly)*   You were not present. It was really funny, I believe.

LOMAX   Ripping.

LADY BRITOMART   Be quiet, Charles. Now listen to me, children. Your father is coming here this evening.

General stupefaction. LOMAX, SARAH, *and* BARBARA *rise:* SARAH *scared, and* BARBARA *amused and expectant.*

LOMAX *(remonstrating)*   Oh I say!

LADY BRITOMART   You are not called on to say anything, Charles.

SARAH   Are you serious, mother?

LADY BRITOMART   Of course I am serious. It is on your account, Sarah, and also on Charles's. *(Silence,* SARAH *sits, with a shrug.* CHARLES *looks painfully unworthy.)* I hope you are not going to object, Barbara.

BARBARA   I! why should I? My father has a soul to be saved like everybody else. He's quite welcome as far as I am concerned. *(She sits on the table, and softly whistles "Onward, Christian Soldiers".*)

LOMAX (*still remonstrant*) But really, dont you know! Oh I say!

LADY BRITOMART (*frigidly*) What do you wish to convey, Charles?

LOMAX Well, you must admit that this is a bit thick.

LADY BRITOMART (*turning with ominous suavity to* CUSINS). Adolphus: you are a professor of Greek. Can you translate Charles Lomax's remarks into reputable English for us?

CUSINS (*cautiously*) If I may say so, Lady Brit, I think Charles has rather happily expressed what we feel. Homer, speaking of Autolycus, uses the same phrase. πυκινὸν δόμον ἐλθεῖν means a bit thick.

LOMAX (*handsomely*) Not that I mind, you know, if Sarah dont. (*He sits.*)

LADY BRITOMART (*crushingly*) Thank you. Have I your permission, Adolphus, to invite my own husband to my own house?

CUSINS (*gallantly*) You have my unhesitating support in everything you do.

LADY BRITOMART Tush! Sarah: have you nothing to say?

SARAH Do you mean that he is coming regularly to live here?

LADY BRITOMART Certainly not. The spare room is ready for him if he likes to stay for a day or two and see a little more of you; but there are limits.

SARAH Well, he cant eat us, I suppose. *I* dont mind.

LOMAX (*chuckling*) I wonder how the old man will take it.

LADY BRITOMART Much as the old woman will, no doubt, Charles.

LOMAX (*abashed*) I didnt mean—at least—

LADY BRITOMART You didnt think, Charles. You never do; and the result is, you never mean anything. And now please attend to me, children. Your father will be quite a stranger to us.

LOMAX I suppose he hasnt seen Sarah since she was a little kid.

LADY BRITOMART Not since she was a little kid, Charles, as you express it with that elegance of diction and refinement of thought that seem never to desert you. Accordingly—er—(*impatiently*) Now I have forgotten what I was going to say. That comes of your provoking me to be sarcastic, Charles. Adolphus: will you kindly tell me where I was.

CUSINS (*sweetly*) You were saying that as Mr Undershaft has not seen his children since they were babies, he will form his opinion of the way you have brought them up from their behavior tonight, and that therefore you wish us all to be particularly careful to conduct ourselves well, especially Charles.

LADY BRITOMART (*with emphatic approval*) Precisely.

LOMAX Look here, Dolly: Lady Brit didnt say that.

LADY BRITOMART (*vehemently*)   I did, Charles. Adolphus's recollection is perfectly correct. It is most important that you should be good; and I do beg you for once not to pair off into opposite corners and giggle and whisper while I am speaking to your father.

BARBARA   All right, mother. We'll do you credit. (*She comes off the table, and sits in her chair with ladylike elegance.*)

LADY BRITOMART   Remember, Charles, that Sarah will want to feel proud of you instead of ashamed of you.

LOMAX   Oh I say! theres nothing to be exactly proud of, dont you know.

LADY BRITOMART   Well, try and look as if there was.

MORRISON, *pale and dismayed, breaks into the room in unconcealed disorder.*

MORRISON   Might I speak a word to you, my lady?

LADY BRITOMART   Nonsense! Shew him up.

MORRISON   Yes, my lady. (*He goes.*)

LOMAX   Does Morrison know who it is?

LADY BRITOMART   Of course. Morrison has always been with us.

LOMAX   It must be a regular corker for him, dont you know.

LADY BRITOMART   Is this a moment to get on my nerves, Charles, with your outrageous expressions?

LOMAX   But this is something out of the ordinary, really—

MORRISON (*at the door*)   The—er—Mr Undershaft. (*He retreats in confusion.*)

ANDREW UNDERSHAFT *comes in. All rise.* LADY BRITOMART *meets him in the middle of the room behind the settee.*

ANDREW *is, on the surface, a stoutish, easygoing elderly man, with kindly patient manners, and an engaging simplicity of character. But he has a watchful, deliberate, waiting, listening face, and formidable reserves of power, both bodily and mental, in his capacious chest and long head. His gentleness is partly that of a strong man who has learnt by experience that his natural grip hurts ordinary people unless he handles them very carefully, and partly the mellowness of age and success. He is also a little shy in his present very delicate situation.*

LADY BRITOMART   Good evening, Andrew.

UNDERSHAFT   How d'ye do, my dear.

LADY BRITOMART   You look a good deal older.

UNDERSHAFT (*apologetically*)   I am somewhat older. (*Taking her hand with a touch of courtship.*) Time has stood still with you.

LADY BRITOMART (*throwing away his hand*)   Rubbish! This is your family.

UNDERSHAFT (*surprised*)   Is it so large? I am sorry to say my memory is failing very badly in some things. (*He offers his hand with paternal kindness to* LOMAX.)

LOMAX (*jerkily shaking his hand*)   Ahdedoo.

UNDERSHAFT   I can see you are my eldest. I am very glad to meet you again, my boy.

LOMAX (*remonstrating*)   No, but look here dont you know— (*Overcome.*) Oh I say!

LADY BRITOMART (*recovering from momentary speechlessness*)   Andrew: do you mean to say that you dont remember how many children you have?

UNDERSHAFT   Well, I am afraid I—. They have grown so much— er. Am I making any ridiculous mistake? I may as well confess: I recollect only one son. But so many things have happened since, of course—er—

LADY BRITOMART (*decisively*)   Andrew: you are talking nonsense. Of course you have only one son.

UNDERSHAFT   Perhaps you will be good enough to introduce me, my dear.

LADY BRITOMART   That is Charles Lomax, who is engaged to Sarah.

UNDERSHAFT   My dear sir, I beg your pardon.

LOMAX   Notatall. Delighted, I assure you.

LADY BRITOMART   This is Stephen.

UNDERSHAFT (*bowing*)   Happy to make your acquaintance, Mr Stephen. Then (*going to* CUSINS) you must be my son. (*Taking* CUSINS' *hands in his.*) How are you, my young friend? (*To* LADY BRITOMART.) He is very like you, my love.

CUSINS   You flatter me, Mr Undershaft. My name is Cusins: engaged to Barbara. (*Very explicitly.*) That is Major Barbara Undershaft, of the Salvation Army. This is Sarah, your second daughter. This is Stephen Undershaft, your son.

UNDERSHAFT   My dear Stephen, I beg your pardon.

STEPHEN   Not at all.

UNDERSHAFT   Mr. Cusins: I am much indebted to you for explaining so precisely. (*Turning to* SARAH.) Barbara, my dear—

SARAH (*prompting him*)   Sarah.

UNDERSHAFT   Sarah, of course. (*They shake hands. He goes over to* BARBARA.) Barbara—I am right this time, I hope?

BARBARA   Quite right. (*They shake hands.*)

LADY BRITOMART (*resuming command*)   Sit down, all of you. Sit down, Andrew. (*She comes forward and sits on the settee.* CUSINS *also brings his chair forward on her left.* BARBARA *and* STEPHEN *resume their seats.* LOMAX *gives his chair to* SARAH *and goes for another.*)

UNDERSHAFT   Thank you, my love.

LOMAX (*conversationally, as he brings a chair forward between the writing table and the settee, and offers it to* UNDERSHAFT) Takes you some time to find out exactly where you are, dont it?

UNDERSHAFT (*accepting the chair, but remaining standing*) That is not what embarrasses me, Mr Lomax. My difficulty is that if I play the part of a father, I shall produce the effect of an intrusive stranger; and if I play the part of a discreet stranger, I may appear a callous father.

LADY BRITOMART There is no need for you to play any part at all, Andrew. You had much better be sincere and natural.

UNDERSHAFT (*submissively*) Yes, my dear: I daresay that will be best. (*He sits down comfortably.*) Well, here I am. Now what can I do for you all?

LADY BRITOMART You need not do anything, Andrew. You are one of the family. You can sit with us and enjoy yourself.

A painfully conscious pause. BARBARA *makes a face at* LOMAX, *whose too long suppressed mirth immediately explodes in agonized neighings.*

LADY BRITOMART (*outraged*) Charles Lomax: if you can behave yourself, behave yourself. If not, leave the room.

LOMAX I'm awfully sorry, Lady Brit; but really you know, upon my soul! (*He sits on the settee between* LADY BRITOMART *and* UNDERSHAFT, *quite overcome.*)

BARBARA Why dont you laugh if you want to, Cholly? It's good for your inside.

LADY BRITOMART Barbara: you have had the education of a lady. Please let your father see that; and dont talk like a street girl.

UNDERSHAFT Never mind me, my dear. As you know, I am not a gentleman; and I was never educated.

LOMAX (*encouragingly*) Nobody'd know it, I assure you. You look all right, you know.

CUSINS Let me advise you to study Greek, Mr Undershaft. Greek scholars are privileged men. Few of them know Greek; and none of them know anything else; but their position is unchallengeable. Other languages are the qualifications of waiters and commercial travelers: Greek is to a man of position what the hallmark is to silver.

BARBARA Dolly: dont be insincere. Cholly: fetch your concertina and play something for us.

LOMAX (*jumps up eagerly, but checks himself to remark doubtfully to* UNDERSHAFT) Perhaps that sort of thing isnt in your line, eh?

UNDERSHAFT I am particularly fond of music.

LOMAX (*delighted*) Are you? Then I'll get it. (*He goes upstairs for the instrument.*)

UNDERSHAFT Do you play, Barbara?

BARBARA Only the tambourine. But Cholly's teaching me the concertina.

UNDERSHAFT Is Cholly also a member of the Salvation Army?

BARBARA No: he says it's bad form to be a dissenter. But I dont despair of Cholly. I made him come yesterday to a meeting at the dock gates, and take the collection in his hat.

UNDERSHAFT (*looks whimsically at his wife*)*!!*

LADY BRITOMART It is not my doing, Andrew. Barbara is old enough to take her own way. She has no father to advise her.

BARBARA Oh yes she has. There are no orphans in the Salvation Army.

UNDERSHAFT Your father there has a great many children and plenty of experience, eh?

BARBARA (*looking at him with quick interest and nodding*) Just so. How did you come to understand that? (LOMAX *is heard at the door trying the concertina.*)

LADY BRITOMART Come in, Charles. Play us something at once.

LOMAX Righto! (*He sits down in his former place, and preludes.*)

UNDERSHAFT One moment, Mr Lomax. I am rather interested in the Salvation Army. Its motto might be my own: Blood and Fire.

LOMAX (*shocked*) But not your sort of blood and fire, you know.

UNDERSHAFT My sort of blood cleanses: my sort of fire purifies.

BARBARA So do ours. Come down tomorrow to my shelter—the West Ham shelter—and see what we're doing. We're going to march to a great meeting in the Assembly Hall at Mile End. Come and see the shelter and then march with us: it will do you a lot of good. Can you play anything?

UNDERSHAFT In my youth I earned pennies, and even shillings occasionally, in the streets and in public house parlors by my natural talent for stepdancing. Later on, I became a member of the Undershaft orchestral society, and performed passably on the tenor trombone.

LOMAX (*scandalized—putting down the concertina*) Oh I say!

BARBARA Many a sinner has played himself into heaven on the trombone, thanks to the Army.

LOMAX (*to* BARBARA, *still rather shocked*) Yes, but what about the cannon business, dont you know? (*To* UNDERSHAFT.) Getting into heaven is not exactly in your line, is it?

LADY BRITOMART Charles!!!

LOMAX Well; but it stands to reason, dont it? The cannon business may be necessary and all that: we cant get on without cannons; but it isnt right, you know. On the other hand, there may be a certain amount of tosh about the Salvation Army—I belong to the Established Church myself—but still you cant deny that it's religion; and you cant go against religion, can you? At least unless youre downright immoral, dont you know.

UNDERSHAFT You hardly appreciate my position, Mr Lomax—

LOMAX (*hastily*) I'm not saying anything against you personally—

UNDERSHAFT Quite so, quite so. But consider for a moment. Here I am, a profiteer in mutilation and murder. I find myself in a specially amiable humor just now because, this morning, down at the foundry, we blew twenty-seven dummy soldiers into fragments with a gun which formerly destroyed only thirteen.

LOMAX (*leniently*) Well, the more destructive war becomes, the sooner it will be abolished, eh?

UNDERSHAFT Not at all. The more destructive war becomes the more fascinating we find it. No, Mr Lomax: I am obliged to you for making the usual excuse for my trade; but I am not ashamed of it. I am not one of those men who keep their morals and their business in watertight compartments. All the spare money my trade rivals spend on hospitals, cathedrals, and other receptacles for conscience money, I devote to experiments and researches in improved methods of destroying life and property. I have always done so; and I always shall. Therefore your Christmas card moralities of peace on earth and goodwill among men are of no use to me. Your Christianity, which enjoins you to resist not evil, and to turn the other cheek, would make me a bankrupt. My morality—my religion—must have a place for cannons and torpedoes in it.

STEPHEN (*coldly—almost sullenly*) You speak as if there were half a dozen moralities and religions to choose from, instead of one true morality and one true religion.

UNDERSHAFT For me there is only one true morality; but it might not fit you, as you do not manufacture aerial battleships. There is only one true morality for every man; but every man has not the same true morality.

LOMAX (*overtaxed*) Would you mind saying that again? I didnt quite follow it.

CUSINS It's quite simple. As Euripides says, one man's meat is another man's poison morally as well as physically.

UNDERSHAFT Precisely.

LOMAX Oh, that! Yes, yes, yes. True. True.

STEPHEN In other words, some men are honest and some are scoundrels.

BARBARA Bosh! There are no scoundrels.

UNDERSHAFT Indeed? Are there any good men?

BARBARA   No. Not one. There are neither good men nor scoundrels: there are just children of one Father; and the sooner they stop calling one another names the better. You neednt talk to me: I know them. Ive had scores of them through my hands: scoundrels, criminals, infidels, philanthropists, missionaries, county councillors, all sorts. Theyre all just the same sort of sinner; and theres the same salvation ready for them all.

UNDERSHAFT   May I ask have you ever saved a maker of cannons?

BARBARA   No. Will you let me try?

UNDERSHAFT   Well, I will make a bargain with you. If I go to see you tomorrow in your Salvation Shelter, will you come the day after to see me in my cannon works?

BARBARA   Take care. It may end in your giving up the cannons for the sake of the Salvation Army.

UNDERSHAFT   Are you sure it will not end in your giving up the Salvation Army for the sake of the cannons?

BARBARA   I will take my chance of that.

UNDERSHAFT   And I will take my chance of the other. (*They shake hands on it.*) Where is your shelter?

BARBARA   In West Ham. At the sign of the cross. Ask anybody in Canning Town. Where are your works?

UNDERSHAFT   In Perivale St Andrews. At the sign of the sword. Ask anybody in Europe.

LOMAX   Hadnt I better play something?

BARBARA   Yes. Give us Onward, Christian Soldiers.

LOMAX   Well, thats rather a strong order to begin with, dont you know. Suppose I sing Thourt passing hence, my brother. It's much the same tune.

BARBARA   It's too melancholy. You get saved, Cholly; and youll pass hence, my brother, without making such a fuss about it.

LADY BRITOMART   Really, Barbara, you go on as if religion were a pleasant subject. Do have some sense of propriety.

UNDERSHAFT   I do not find it an unpleasant subject, my dear. It is the only one that capable people really care for.

LADY BRITOMART (*looking at her watch*)   Well, if you are determined to have it, I insist on having it in a proper and respectable way. Charles: ring for prayers.

General amazement. STEPHEN *rises in dismay.*

LOMAX (*rising*)   Oh I say!

UNDERSHAFT (*rising*)   I am afraid I must be going.

LADY BRITOMART   You cannot go now, Andrew: it would be most improper. Sit down. What will the servants think?

UNDERSHAFT My dear: I have conscientious scruples. May I suggest a compromise? If Barbara will conduct a little service in the drawing room, with Mr Lomax as organist, I will attend it willingly. I will even take part, if a trombone can be procured.

LADY BRITOMART Dont mock, Andrew.

UNDERSHAFT (*shocked—to* BARBARA) You dont think I am mocking, my love, I hope.

BARBARA No, of course not; and it wouldnt matter if you were: half the Army came to their first meeting for a lark. (*Rising.*) Come along. (*She throws her arm round her father and sweeps him out, calling to the others from the threshold.*) Come, Dolly. Come, Cholly.

LADY BRITOMART I will not be disobeyed by everybody. Adolphus: sit down. (*He does not.*) Charles: you may go. You are not fit for prayers: you cannot keep your countenance.

LOMAX Oh I say! (*He goes out.*)

LADY BRITOMART (*continuing*) But you, Adolphus, can behave yourself if you choose to. I insist on your staying.

CUSINS My dear Lady Brit: there are things in the family prayer book that I couldnt bear to hear you say.

LADY BRITOMART What things, pray?

CUSINS Well, you would have to say before all the servants that we have done things we ought not to have done, and left undone things we ought to have done, and that there is no health in us. I cannot bear to hear you doing yourself such an injustice, and Barbara such an injustice. As for myself, I flatly deny it: I have done my best. I shouldnt dare to marry Barbara—I couldnt look you in the face—if it were true. So I must go to the drawing room.

LADY BRITOMART (*offended*) Well, go. (*He starts for the door.*) And remember this, Adolphus (*he turns to listen*): I have a very strong suspicion that you went to the Salvation Army to worship Barbara and nothing else. And I quite appreciate the very clever way in which you systematically humbug me. I have found you out. Take care Barbara doesnt. Thats all.

CUSINS (*with unruffled sweetness*) Dont tell on me. (*He steals out.*)

LADY BRITOMART Sarah: if you want to go, go. Anything's better than to sit there as if you wished you were a thousand miles away.

SARAH (*languidly*) Very well, mamma. (*She goes.*)

LADY BRITOMART, *with a sudden flounce, gives way to a little gust of tears.*

STEPHEN (*going to her*) Mother: whats the matter?

LADY BRITOMART (*swishing away her tears with her handkerchief*)

Nothing. Foolishness. You can go with him, too, if you like, and leave me with the servants.

STEPHEN   Oh, you mustnt think that, mother. I—I dont like him.

LADY BRITOMART   The others do. That is the injustice of a woman's lot. A woman has to bring up her children; and that means to restrain them, to deny them things they want, to set them tasks, to punish them when they do wrong, to do all the unpleasant things. And then the father, who has nothing to do but pet them and spoil them, comes in when all her work is done and steals their affection from her.

STEPHEN   He has not stolen our affection from you. It is only curiosity.

LADY BRITOMART   (*violently*)   I wont be consoled, Stephen. There is nothing the matter with me. (*She rises and goes towards the door.*)

STEPHEN   Where are you going, mother?

LADY BRITOMART   To the drawing room, of course. (*She goes out. Onward, Christian Soldiers, on the concertina, with tambourine accompaniment, is heard when the door opens.*) Are you coming, Stephen?

STEPHEN   No. Certainly not. (*She goes. He sits down on the settee, with compressed lips and an expression of strong dislike.*)

ACT II

The yard of the West Ham shelter of the Salvation Army is a cold place on a January morning. The building itself, an old warehouse, is newly whitewashed. Its gabled end projects into the yard in the middle, with a door on the ground floor, and another in the loft above it without any balcony or ladder, but with a pulley rigged over it for hoisting sacks. Those who come from this central gable end into the yard have the gateway leading to the street on their left, with a stone horse-trough just beyond it, and, on the right, a penthouse shielding a table from the weather. There are forms at the table; and on them are seated a man and a woman, both much down on their luck, finishing a meal of bread (one thick slice each, with margarine and golden syrup) and diluted milk.

The man, a workman out of employment, is young, agile, a talker, a poser, sharp enough to be capable of anything in reason except honesty or altruistic considerations of any kind. The woman is a commonplace old bundle of poverty and hard-worn humanity. She looks sixty and probably is forty-five. If they were rich people, gloved and muffed and well wrapped up in furs and overcoats, they would be numbed and miserable; for it is a grindingly cold raw January day; and a glance at the background of grimy warehouses and leaden sky visible over the whitewashed walls of the yard would drive any idle rich person straight to the Mediterranean. But these two, being no more troubled with visions of the Mediterranean than of the moon, and being compelled to keep more of their clothes in the pawnshop, and less on their persons, in winter than in summer, are not depressed by the cold: rather are they stung into vivacity, to which their meal has just now given an almost jolly turn. The man takes a pull at his mug, and then gets up and moves about the yard with his hands deep in his pockets, occasionally breaking into a stepdance.

THE WOMAN   Feel better arter your meal, sir?

THE MAN   No. Call that a meal! Good enough for you, praps, but wot is it to me, an intelligent workin man.

THE WOMAN   Workin man! Wot are you?

THE MAN   Painter.

THE WOMAN (*sceptically*)   Yus, I dessay.

THE MAN   Yus, you dessay! I know. Every loafer that cant do nothink calls isself a painter. Well, I'm a real painter: grainer, finisher, thirty-eight bob a week when I can get it.

THE WOMAN   Then why dont you go and get it?

THE MAN   I'll tell you why. Fust: I'm intelligent—fffff! it's rotten cold here (*he dances a step or two*)—yes: intelligent beyond the station o life into which it has pleased the capitalists to call me; and they dont like a man that sees through em. Second, an intelligent bein needs a doo share of appiness; so I drink somethink cruel when I get the chawnce. Third, I stand by my class and do as little as I can so's to leave arf the job for me fellow workers. Fourth, I'm fly enough to know wots inside the law and wots outside it; and inside it I do as the capitalists do: pinch wot I can lay me ands on. In a proper state of society I am sober, industrious and honest: in Rome, so to speak, I do as the Romans do. Wots the consequence? When trade is bad—and it's rotten bad just now—and the employers az to sack arf their men, they generally start on me.

THE WOMAN   Whats your name?

THE MAN   Price. Bronterre O'Brien Price. Usually called Snobby Price, for short.

THE WOMAN   Snobby's a carpenter, aint it? You said you was a painter.

PRICE   Not that kind of snob, but the genteel sort. I'm too uppish, owing to my intelligence, and my father being a Chartist and a reading, thinking man: a stationer, too. I'm none of your common hewers of wood and drawers of water; and dont you forget it. (*He returns to his seat at the table, and takes up his mug.*) Wots your name?

THE WOMAN   Rummy Mitchens, sir.

PRICE (*quaffing the remains of his milk to her*) Your elth, Miss Mitchens.

RUMMY (*correcting him*) Missis Mitchens.

PRICE Wot! Oh Rummy, Rummy! Respectable married woman, Rummy, gittin rescued by the Salvation Army by pretendin to be a bad un. Same old game!

RUMMY What am I to do? I cant starve. Them Salvation lasses is dear good girls; but the better you are, the worse they likes to think you were before they rescued you. Why shouldnt they av a bit o credit, poor loves? theyre worn to rags by their work. And where would they get the money to rescue us if we was to let on we're no worse than other people? You know what ladies and gentlemen are.

PRICE Thievin swine! Wish I ad their job, Rummy, all the same. Wot does Rummy stand for? Pet name praps?

RUMMY Short for Romola.

PRICE For wot!?

RUMMY Romola. It was out of a new book. Somebody me mother wanted me to grow up like.

PRICE We're companions in misfortune, Rummy. Both on us got names that nobody cawnt pronounce. Consequently I'm Snobby and youre Rummy because Bill and Sally wasnt good enough for our parents. Such is life!

RUMMY Who saved you, Mr Price? Was it Major Barbara?

PRICE No: I come here on my own. I'm going to be Bronterre O'Brien Price, the converted painter. I know wot they like. I'll tell em how I blasphemed and gambled and wopped my poor old mother—

RUMMY (*shocked*) Used you to beat your mother?

PRICE Not likely. She used to beat me. No matter: you come and listen to the converted painter, and youll hear how she was a pious woman that taught me me prayers at er knee, an how I used to come home drunk and drag her out o bed be er snow white airs, an lam into er with the poker.

RUMMY Thats whats so unfair to us women. Your confessions is just as big lies as ours: you dont tell what you really done no more than us; but you men can tell your lies right out at the meetins and be made much of for it, while the sort o confessions we az to make az to be whispered to one lady at a time. It aint right, spite of all their piety.

PRICE Right! Do you spose the Army'd be allowed if it went and did right? Not much. It combs our air and makes us good little blokes to be robbed and put upon. But I'll play the game as good as any of em. I'll see somebody struck by lightnin, or hear a voice sayin "Snobby Price: where will you spend eternity?" I'll av a time of it, I tell you.

RUMMY   You wont be let drink, though.

PRICE   I'll take it out in gorspellin, then. I dont want to drink if I can get fun enough any other way.

JENNY HILL, *a pale, overwrought, pretty Salvation lass of 18, comes in through the yard gate, leading* PETER SHIRLEY, *a half hardened, half worn-out elderly man, weak with hunger.*

JENNY (*supporting him*)   Come! pluck up. I'll get you something to eat. Youll be all right then.

PRICE (*rising and hurrying officiously to take the old man off* JENNY's *hands*)   Poor old man! Cheer up, brother: youll find rest and peace and appiness ere. Hurry up with the food, miss: e's fair done. (*Jenny hurries into the shelter.*) Ere, buck up, daddy! she's fetchin y'a thick slice of breadn treacle, an a mug o skyblue. (*He seats him at the corner of the table.*)

RUMMY (*gaily*)   Keep up your old art! Never say die!

SHIRLEY   I'm not an old man. I'm only 46. I'm as good as ever I was. The grey patch come in my hair before I was thirty. All it wants is three pennorth o hair dye: am I to be turned on the streets to starve for it? Holy God! I've worked ten to twelve hours a day since I was thirteen, and paid my way all through; and now am I to be thrown into the gutter and my job given to a young man that can do it no better than me because Ive black hair that goes white at the first change?

PRICE (*cheerfully*)   No good jawrin about it. Youre ony a jumped-up, jerked-off, orspittle-turned-out incurable of an ole workin man: who cares about you? Eh? Make the thievin swine give you a meal: theyve stole many a one from you. Get a bit o your own back. (JENNY *returns with the usual meal.*) There you are, brother. Awsk a blessin an tuck that into you.

SHIRLEY (*looking at it ravenously but not touching it, and crying like a child*)   I never took anything before.

JENNY (*petting him*)   Come, come! the Lord sends it to you: he wasn't above taking bread from his friends; and why should you be? Besides, when we find you a job you can pay us for it if you like.

SHIRLEY (*eagerly*)   Yes, yes: thats true. I can pay you back: it's only a loan. (*Shivering.*) Oh Lord! oh Lord! (*He turns to the table and attacks the meal ravenously.*)

JENNY   Well, Rummy, are you more comfortable now?

RUMMY   God bless you, lovey! youve fed my body and saved my soul, havent you? (JENNY, *touched, kisses her.*) Sit down and rest a bit: you must be ready to drop.

JENNY   Ive been going hard since morning. But theres more work than we can do. I mustnt stop.

RUMMY   Try a prayer for just two minutes. Youll work all the better after.

JENNY   (*her eyes lighting up*)   Oh isnt it wonderful how a few minutes prayer revives you! I was quite lightheaded at twelve o'clock, I was so tired; but Major Barbara just sent me to pray for five minutes; and I was able to go on as if I had only just begun. (*To* PRICE.) Did you have a piece of bread?

PRICE   (*with unction*)   Yes, miss; but Ive got the piece that I value more; and thats the peace that passeth hall hannerstennin.

RUMMY   (*fervently*)   Glory Hallelujah!

BILL WALKER, *a rough customer of about 25, appears at the yard gate and looks malevolently at* JENNY.

JENNY   That makes me so happy. When you say that, I feel wicked for loitering here. I must get to work again.

She is hurrying to the shelter, when the new-comer moves quickly up to the door and intercepts her. His manner is so threatening that she retreats as he comes at her truculently, driving her down the yard.

BILL   Aw knaow you. Youre the one that took awy maw girl. Youre the one that set er agen me. Well, I'm gowin to ev er aht. Not that Aw care a carse for er or you: see? Bat Aw'll let er knaow; and Aw'll let you knaow. Aw'm gowing to give her a doin thatll teach er to cat awy from me. Nah in wiv you and tell er to cam aht afore Aw cam in and kick er aht. Tell er Bill Walker wants er. She'll knaow wot thet means; and if she keeps me witin itll be worse. You stop to jawr beck at me: and Aw'll stawt on you: d'ye eah? Theres your wy. In you gow. (*He takes her by the arm and slings her towards the door of the shelter. She falls on her hand and knee.* RUMMY *helps her up again.*)

PRICE   (*rising, and venturing irresolutely towards* BILL)   Easy there, mate. She aint doin you no arm.

BILL   Oo are you callin mite? (*Standing over him threateningly.*) Youre gowin to stend ap for er, aw yer? Put ap your ends.

RUMMY   (*running indignantly to him to scold him*)   Oh, you great brute—(*He instantly swings his left hand back against her face. She screams and reels back to the trough, where she sits down, covering her bruised face with her hands and rocking herself and moaning with pain.*)

JENNY (*going to her*) Oh, God forgive you! How could you strike an old woman like that?

BILL (*seizing her by the hair so violently that she also screams, and tearing her away from the old woman*) You Gawd forgimme again an Aw'll Gawd forgive you one on the jawr thetll stop you pryin for a week. (*Holding her and turning fiercely on* PRICE.) Ev you ennything to sy agen it?

PRICE (*intimidated*) No, matey: she aint anything to do with me.

BILL Good job for you! Aw'd pat two meals into you and fawt you with one finger arter, you stawved cur. (*To* JENNY.) Nah are you gowin to fetch aht Mog Ebbijem; or em Aw to knock your fice off you and fetch her meself?

JENNY (*writhing in his grasp*) Oh please someone go in and tell Major Barbara—(*she screams again as he wrenches her head down; and* PRICE *and* RUMMY *flee into the shelter*).

BILL You want to gow in and tell your Mijor of me, do you?

JENNY Oh please dont drag my hair. Let me go.

BILL Do you or downt you? (*She stifles a scream.*) Yus or nao?

JENNY God give me strength—

BILL (*striking her with his fist in the face*) Gow an shaow her thet, and tell her if she wants one lawk it to cam and interfere with me. (JENNY, *crying with pain, goes into the shed. He goes to the form and addresses the old man.*) Eah: finish your mess; an git aht o mah wy.

SHIRLEY (*springing up and facing him fiercely, with the mug in his hand*) You take a liberty with me, and I'll smash you over the face with the mug and cut your eye out. Aint you satisfied— young whelps like you—with takin the bread out o the mouths of your elders that have brought you up and slaved for you, but you must come shovin and cheekin and bullyin in here, where the bread o charity is sickenin in our stummicks?

BILL (*contemptuously, but backing a little*) Wot good are you, you aold palsy mag? Wot good are you?

SHIRLEY As good as you and better. I'll do a day's work agen you or any fat young soaker of your age. Go and take my job at Horrockses, where I worked for ten year. They want young men there: they cant afford to keep men over forty-five. They're very sorry—give you a character and happy to help you to get anything suited to your years—sure a steady man wont be long out of a job. Well, let em try you. Theyll find the differ. What do you know? Not as much as how to beeyave yourself—layin your dirty fist across the mouth of a respectable woman!

BILL Downt provowk me to ly it acrost yours: d'ye eah?

SHIRLEY (*with blighting contempt*) Yes: you like an old man to hit, dont you, when youve finished with the women. I ain't seen you hit a young one yet.

BILL (*stung*) You loy, you aold soupkitchener, you. There was a yang menn eah. Did Aw offer to itt him or did Aw not?

SHIRLEY Was he starvin or was he not? Was he a man or only a crossed-eyed thief an a loafer? Would you hit my son-in-law's brother?

BILL Oo's ee?

SHIRLEY Todger Fairmile o Balls Pond. Him that won £20 off the Japanese wrastler at the music hall by standin out 17 minutes 4 seconds agen him.

BILL (*sullenly*) Aw'm nao music awl wrastler. Ken he box?

SHIRLEY Yes: an you cant.

BILL Wot! Aw cawnt, cawnt Aw? Wots thet you sy (*threatening him*)?

SHIRLEY (*not budging an inch*) Will you box Todger Fairmile if I put him on to you? Say the word.

BILL (*subsiding with a slouch*) Aw'll stend ap to enny menn alawv, if he was ten Todger Fairmawls. But Aw dont set ap to be a perfeshnal.

SHIRLEY (*looking down on him with unfathomable disdain*) You box! Slap an old woman with the back o your hand! You hadnt even the sense to hit her where the magistrate couldnt see the mark of it, you silly young lump of conceit and ignorance. Hit a girl in the jaw and ony make her cry! If Todger Fairmile's done it, she wouldnt a got up inside o ten minutes, no more than you would if he got on to you. Yah! I'd set about you myself if I had a week's feedin in me instead o two months' starvation. (*He turns his back on him and sits down moodily at the table.*)

BILL (*following him and stooping over him to drive the taunt in*) You loy! youve the bread and treacle in you that you cam eah to beg.

SHIRLEY (*bursting into tears*) Oh God! it's true: I'm only an old pauper on the scrap heap. (*Furiously.*) But youll come to it yourself; and then youll know. Youll come to it sooner than a teetotaller like me, fillin yourself with gin at this hour o the mornin!

BILL Aw'm nao gin drinker, you oald lawr; but wen Aw want to give my girl a bloomin good awdin Aw lawk to ev a bit o devil in me: see? An eah Aw emm, talkin to a rotten aold blawter like you sted o givin her wot for. (*Working himself into a rage.*) Aw'm gowin in there to fetch her aht. (*He makes vengefully for the shelter door.*)

SHIRLEY Youre goin to the station on a stretcher, more likely; and theyll take the gin and the devil out of you there when they get you inside. You mind what youre about: the major here is the Earl o Stevenage's granddaughter.

BILL (*checked*)   Garn!

SHIRLEY   Youll see.

BILL (*his resolution oozing*)   Well, Aw aint dan nathin to er.

SHIRLEY   Spose she said you did! who'd believe you?

BILL (*very uneasy, skulking back to the corner of the penthouse*) Gawd! theres no jastice in this cantry. To think wot them people can do! Aw'm as good as er.

SHIRLEY   Tell her so. It's just what a fool like you would do.

BARBARA, *brisk and businesslike, comes from the shelter with a note book, and addresses herself to* SHIRLEY. BILL, *cowed, sits down in the corner on a form, and turns his back on them.*

BARBARA   Good morning.

SHIRLEY (*standing up and taking off his hat*)   Good morning, miss.

BARBARA   Sit down: make yourself at home. (*He hesitates; but she puts a friendly hand on his shoulder and makes him obey.*) Now then! since youve made friends with us, we want to know all about you. Names and addresses and trades.

SHIRLEY   Peter Shirley. Fitter. Chucked out two months ago because I was too old.

BARBARA (*not at all surprised*)   Youd pass still. Why didnt you dye your hair?

SHIRLEY   I did. Me age come out at a coroner's inquest on me daughter.

BARBARA   Steady?

SHIRLEY   Teetotaller. Never out of a job before. Good worker. And sent to the knackers like an old horse!

BARBARA   No matter: if you did your part God will do his.

SHIRLEY (*suddenly stubborn*)   My religion's no concern of anybody but myself.

BARBARA (*guessing*)   I know. Secularist?

SHIRLEY (*hotly*)   Did I offer to deny it?

BARBARA   Why should you? My own father's a Secularist, I think. Our Father—yours and mine—fulfils himself in many ways; and I daresay he knew what he was about when he made a Secularist of you. So buck up, Peter! we can always find a job for a steady man like you. (SHIRLEY, *disarmed and a little bewildered, touches his hat. She turns from him to* BILL.) Whats your name?

BILL (*insolently*)   Wots thet to you?

BARBARA (*calmly making a note*)   Afraid to give his name. Any trade?

BILL   Oo's afride to give is nime? (*Doggedly, with a sense of heroically defying the House of Lords in the person of Lord Stevenage.*) If you want to bring a chawge agen me, bring it. (*She waits, unruffled.*) Moy nime's Bill Walker.

BARBARA (*as if the name were familiar: trying to remember how*) Bill Walker? (*Recollecting.*) Oh, I know: youre the man that Jenny Hill was praying for inside just now. (*She enters his name in her note book.*)

BILL   Oo's Jenny Ill? And wot call as she to pry for me?

BARBARA   I dont know. Perhaps it was you that cut her lip.

BILL (*defiantly*)   Yus, it was me that cat her lip. Aw aint afride o you.

BARBARA   How could you be, since youre not afraid of God? Youre a brave man, Mr Walker. It takes some pluck to do our work here; but none of us dare lift our hand against a girl like that, for fear of her father in heaven.

BILL (*sullenly*)   I want nan o your kentin jawr. I spowse you think Aw cam eah to beg from you, like this demmiged lot eah. Not me. Aw downt want your bread and scripe and ketlep. Aw dont belive in your Gawd, no more than you do yourself.

BARBARA (*sunnily apologetic and ladylike, as on a new footing with him*).   Oh, I beg your pardon for putting your name down, Mr Walker. I didn't understand. I'll strike it out.

BILL (*taking this as a slight, and deeply wounded by it*)   Eah! you let maw nime alown. Aint it good enaff to be in your book?

BARBARA (*considering*)   Well, you see, theres no use putting down your name unless I can do something for you, is there? Whats your trade?

BILL (*still smarting*)   Thets nao concern o yours.

BARBARA   Just so. (*Very businesslike.*) I'll put you down as (*writing*) the man who—struck—poor little Jenny Hill—in the mouth.

BILL (*rising threateningly*)   See eah. Awve ed enaff o this.

BARBARA (*quite sunny and fearless*)   What did you come to us for?

BILL   Aw cam for maw gel, see? Aw cam to tike her aht o this and to brike er jawr for er.

BARBARA (*complacently*)   You see I was right about your trade. (BILL, *on the point of retorting furiously, finds himself, to his great shame and terror, in danger of crying instead. He sits down again suddenly.*)   Whats her name?

BILL (*dogged*)   Er nime's Mog Ebbijem: thets wot her nime is.

BARBARA   Mog Habbijam! Oh, she's gone to Canning Town, to our barracks there.

BILL (*fortified by his resentment of* MOG's *perfidy*)   Is she? (*Vindictively*).   Then Aw'm gowin to Kennintahn arter her. (*He crosses to the gate; hesitates; finally comes back at* BARBARA.) Are you loyin to me to git shat o me?

BARBARA   I dont want to get shut of you. I want to keep you here and save your soul. Youd better stay: youre going to have a bad time today, Bill.

BILL   Oo's gowin to give it to me? You, preps?

BARBARA   Someone you dont believe in. But youll be glad afterwards.

BILL   (*slinking off*)   Aw'll gow to Kennintahn to be aht o reach o your tangue. (*Suddenly turning on her with intense malice.*) And if Aw downt fawnd Mog there, Aw'll cam beck and do two years for you, selp me Gawd if Aw downt!

BARBARA   (*a shade kindlier, if possible*)   It's no use, Bill. She's got another bloke.

BILL   Wot!

BARBARA   One of her own converts. He fell in love with her when he saw her with her soul saved, and her face clean, and her hair washed.

BILL   (*surprised*)   Wottud she wash it for, the carroty slat? It's red.

BARBARA   It's quite lovely now, because she wears a new look in her eyes with it. It's a pity youre too late. The new bloke has put your nose out of joint, Bill.

BILL   Aw'll put his nowse aht o joint for him. Not that Aw care a carse for er, mawnd thet. But Aw'll teach her to drop me as if Aw was dirt. And Aw'll teach him to meddle with maw Judy. Wots iz bleedin nime?

BARBARA   Sergeant Todger Fairmile.

SHIRLEY   (*rising with grim joy*)   I'll go with him, miss. I want to see them two meet. I'll take him to the infirmary when it's over.

BILL   (*to* SHIRLEY, *with undissembled misgiving*)   Is thet im you was speakin on?

SHIRLEY   Thats him.

BILL   Im that wrastled in the music awl?

SHIRLEY   The competitions at the National Sportin Club was worth nigh a hundred a year to him. He's gev em up now for religion; so he's a bit fresh for want of the exercise he was accustomed to. He'll be glad to see you. Come along.

BILL   Wots is wight?

SHIRLEY   Thirteen four. (BILL's *last hope expires.*)

BARBARA   Go and talk to him, Bill. He'll convert you.

SHIRLEY   He'll convert your head into a mashed potato.

BILL   (*sullenly*)   Aw aint afride of im. Aw aint afride of ennybody. Bat e can lick me. She's dan me. (*He sits down moodily on the edge of the horse trough.*)

SHIRLEY You aint going. I thought not. (*He resumes his seat.*)

BARBARA (*calling*) Jenny!

JENNY (*appearing at the shelter door with a plaster on the corner of her mouth*) Yes, Major.

BARBARA Send Rummy Mitchens out to clear away here.

JENNY I think she's afraid.

BARBARA (*her resemblance to her mother flashing out for a moment*) Nonsense! she must do as she's told.

JENNY (*calling into the shelter*) Rummy: the Major says you must come.

JENNY *comes to* BARBARA, *purposely keeping on the side next* BILL, *lest he should suppose that she shrank from him or bore malice.*

BARBARA Poor little Jenny! Are you tired? (*Looking at the wounded cheek.*) Does it hurt?

JENNY No: it's all right now. It was nothing.

BARBARA (*critically*) It was as hard as he could hit, I expect. Poor Bill! You dont feel angry with him, do you?

JENNY Oh no, no, no: indeed I dont, Major, bless his poor heart! (BARBARA *kisses her; and she runs away merrily into the shelter.* BILL *writhes with an agonizing return of his new and alarming symptoms, but says nothing.* RUMMY MITCHENS *comes from the shelter.*)

BARBARA (*going to meet* RUMMY) Now Rummy, bustle. Take in those mugs and plates to be washed; and throw the crumbs about for the birds.

RUMMY *takes the three plates and mugs; but* SHIRLEY *takes back his mug from her, as there is still some milk left in it.*

RUMMY There aint any crumbs. This aint a time to waste good bread on birds.

PRICE (*appearing at the shelter door*) Gentleman come to see the shelter, Major. Says he's your father.

BARBARA All right. Coming. (SNOBBY *goes back into the shelter, followed by* BARBARA.)

RUMMY (*stealing across to* BILL *and addressing him in a subdued voice, but with intense conviction*) I'd av the lor of you, you flat eared pignosed potwalloper, if she'd let me. Youre no gentleman, to hit a lady in the face. (BILL, *with greater things moving in him, takes no notice.*)

SHIRLEY (*following her*) Here! in with you and dont get yourself into more trouble by talking.

RUMMY (*with hauteur*) I aint ad the pleasure o being hintroduced to you, as I can remember. (*She goes into the shelter with the plates.*)

SHIRLEY Thats the—

BILL (*savagely*) Downt you talk to me, d'ye eah? You lea me alown, or Aw'll do you a mischief. Aw'm not dirt under your feet, ennywy.

SHIRLEY (*calmly*) Dont you be afeerd. You aint such prime company that you need expect to be sought after. (*He is about to go into the shelter when* BARBARA *comes out, with* UNDERSHAFT *on her right.*)

BARBARA Oh, there you are, Mr Shirley! (*Between them.*) This is my father: I told you he was a Secularist, didn't I? Perhaps youll be able to comfort one another.

UNDERSHAFT (*startled*) A Secularist! Not the least in the world: on the contrary, a confirmed mystic.

BARBARA Sorry, I'm sure. By the way, papa, what is your religion? in case I have to introduce you again.

UNDERSHAFT My religion? Well, my dear, I am a Millionaire. That is my religion.

BARBARA Then I'm afraid you and Mr Shirley wont be able to comfort one another after all. Youre not a Millionaire, are you, Peter?

SHIRLEY No; and proud of it.

UNDERSHAFT (*gravely*) Poverty, my friend, is not a thing to be proud of.

SHIRLEY (*angrily*) Who made your millions for you? Me and my like. Whats kep us poor? Keepin you rich. I wouldnt have your conscience, not for all your income.

UNDERSHAFT I wouldnt have your income, not for all your conscience, Mr Shirley. (*He goes to the penthouse and sits down on a form.*)

BARBARA (*stopping* SHIRLEY *adroitly as he is about to retort*) You wouldnt think he was my father, would you, Peter? Will you go into the shelter and lend the lasses a hand for a while: we're worked off our feet.

SHIRLEY (*bitterly*) Yes: I'm in their debt for a meal, aint I?

BARBARA Oh, not because youre in their debt, but for love of them, Peter, for love of them. (*He cannot understand, and is rather scandalized.*) There! dont stare at me. In with you; and give that conscience of yours a holiday (*bustling him into the shelter*).

SHIRLEY (*as he goes in*) Ah! it's a pity you never was trained to use your reason, miss. Youd have been a very taking lecturer on Secularism.

(BARBARA *turns to her father.*)

UNDERSHAFT   Never mind me, my dear. Go about your work; and let me watch it for a while.

BARBARA   All right.

UNDERSHAFT   For instance, whats the matter with that outpatient over there?

BARBARA   (*looking at* BILL, *whose attitude has never changed, and whose expression of brooding wrath has deepened*)   Oh, we shall cure him in no time. Just watch. (*She goes over to* BILL *and waits. He glances up at her and casts his eyes down again, uneasy, but grimmer than ever.*) It would be nice to just stamp on Mog Habbijam's face, wouldnt it, Bill?

BILL   (*starting up from the trough in consternation*)   It's a loy: Aw never said so. (*She shakes her head.*) Oo taold you wot was in moy mawnd?

BARBARA   Only your new friend.

BILL   Wot new friend?

BARBARA   The devil, Bill. When he gets round people they get miserable, just like you.

BILL   (*with a heartbreaking attempt at devil-may-care cheerfulness*)   Aw aint miserable. (*He sits down again, and stretches his legs in an attempt to seem indifferent.*)

BARBARA   Well, if youre happy, why dont you look happy, as we do?

BILL   (*his legs curling back in spite of him*)   Aw'm eppy enaff, Aw tell you. Woy cawnt you lea me alown? Wot ev I dan to you? Aw aint smashed your fice, ev Aw?

BARBARA   (*softly: wooing his soul*)   It's not me thats getting at you, Bill.

BILL   Oo else is it?

BARBARA   Somebody that doesnt intend you to smash women's faces, I suppose. Somebody or something that wants to make a man of you.

BILL   (*blustering*)   Mike a menn o me! Aint Aw a menn? eh? Oo sez Aw'm not a menn?

BARBARA   Theres a man in you somewhere, I suppose. But why did he let you hit poor little Jenny Hill? That wasnt very manly of him, was it?

BILL   (*tormented*)   Ev dan wiv it, Aw tell you. Chack it. Aw'm sick o your Jenny Ill and er silly little fice.

BARBARA   Then why do you keep thinking about it? Why does it keep coming up against you in your mind? Youre not getting converted, are you?

BILL (*with conviction*) Not ME. Not lawkly.

BARBARA Thats right, Bill. Hold out against it. Put out your strength. Dont lets get you cheap. Todger Fairmile said he wrestled for three nights against his salvation harder than he ever wrestled with the Jap at the music hall. He gave in to the Jap when his arm was going to break. But he didnt give in to his salvation until his heart was going to break. Perhaps youll escape that. You havnt any heart, have you?

BILL Wot d'ye mean? Woy aint Aw got a awt the sime as ennybody else?

BARBARA A man with a heart wouldnt have bashed poor little Jenny's face, would he?

BILL (*almost crying*) Ow, will you lea me alown? Ev Aw ever offered to meddle with you, that you cam neggin and provowkin me lawk this? (*He writhes convulsively from his eyes to his toes.*)

BARBARA (*with a steady soothing hand on his arm and a gentle voice that never lets him go*) It's your soul thats hurting you, Bill, and not me. Weve been through it all ourselves. Come with us, Bill. (*He looks wildly round.*) To brave manhood on earth and eternal glory in heaven. (*He is on the point of breaking down.*) Come. (*A drum is heard in the shelter; and* BILL, *with a gasp, escapes from the spell as* BARBARA *turns quickly.* ADOLPHUS *enters from the shelter with a big drum.*) Oh! there you are, Dolly. Let me introduce a new friend of mine, Mr Bill Walker. This is my bloke, Bill: Mr Cusins. (CUSINS *salutes with his drumstick.*)

BILL Gowin to merry im?

BARBARA Yes.

BILL (*fervently*) Gawd elp im! Gaw-aw-aw-awd elp im!

BARBARA Why? Do you think he wont be happy with me?

BILL Awve aony ed to stend it for a mawnin: e'll ev to stend it for a lawftawm.

CUSINS That is a frightful reflection, Mr Walker. But I cant tear myself away from her.

BILL Well, Aw ken. (*To* BARBARA.) Eah do you knaow where Aw'm gowin to, and wot Aw'm gowin to do?

BARBARA Yes: youre going to heaven; and youre coming back here before the week's out to tell me so.

BILL You loy. Aw'm gowin to Kennintahn, to spit in Todger Fairmawl's eye. Aw beshed Jenny Ill's fice; an nar Aw'll git me aown fice beshed and cam bec and shaow it to er. Ee'll itt me ardern Aw itt her. Thatll mike us square. (*To* ADOLPHUS.) Is thet fair or is it not? Youre a genlmn: you oughter knaow.

BARBARA Two black eyes wont make one white one, Bill.

BILL   Aw didnt awst you. Cawnt you never keep your mahth shat? Oy awst the genlmn.

CUSINS (*reflectively*)   Yes: I think youre right, Mr Walker. Yes: I should do it. It's curious: it's exactly what an ancient Greek would have done.

BARBARA   But what good will it do?

CUSINS   Well, it will give Mr Fairmile some exercise; and it will satisfy Mr Walker's soul.

BILL   Rot! there aint nao sach a thing as a saoul. Ah kin you tell wevver Awve a saoul or not? You never seen it.

BARBARA   Ive seen it hurting you when you went against it.

BILL (*with compressed aggravation*)   If you was maw gel and took the word awt o me mahth lawk thet, Aw'd give you sathink youd feel urtin, Aw would. (*To* ADOLPHUS.) You tike maw tip, mite. Stop er jawr or youll doy afoah your tawm (*With intense expression.*) Wore aht: thets wot youll be: wore aht. (*He goes away through the gate.*)

CUSINS (*looking after him*)   I wonder!

BARBARA   Dolly! (*indignant, in her mother's manner*).

CUSINS   Yes, my dear, it's very wearing to be in love with you. If it lasts, I quite think I shall die young.

BARBARA   Should you mind?

CUSINS   Not at all. (*He is suddenly softened, and kisses her over the drum, evidently not for the first time, as people cannot kiss over a big drum without practice.* UNDERSHAFT *coughs.*)

BARBARA   It's all right, papa, weve not forgotten you. Dolly: explain the place to papa: I havnt time. (*She goes busily into the shelter.*)

UNDERSHAFT *and* ADOLPHUS *now have the yard to themselves.* UNDERSHAFT, *seated on a form, and still keenly attentive, looks hard at* ADOLPHUS. ADOLPHUS *looks hard at him.*

UNDERSHAFT   I fancy you guess something of what is in my mind, Mr Cusins. (CUSINS *flourishes his drumsticks as if in the act of beating a lively rataplan, but makes no sound.*) Exactly so. But suppose Barbara finds you out!

CUSINS   You know, I do not admit that I am imposing on Barbara. I am quite genuinely interested in the views of the Salvation Army. The fact is, I am a sort of collector of religions; and the curious thing is that I find I can believe them all. By the way, have you any religion?

UNDERSHAFT   Yes.

CUSINS   Anything out of the common?

UNDERSHAFT   Only that there are two things necessary to Salvation.

CUSINS   *(disappointed, but polite)*   Ah, the Church Catechism. Charles Lomax also belongs to the Established Church.

UNDERSHAFT   The two things are—

CUSINS   Baptism and—

UNDERSHAFT   No. Money and gunpowder.

CUSINS   *(surprised, but interested)*   That is the general opinion of our governing classes. The novelty is in hearing any man confess it.

UNDERSHAFT   Just so.

CUSINS   Excuse me: is there any place in your religion for honor, justice, truth, love, mercy and so forth?

UNDERSHAFT   Yes: they are the graces and luxuries of a rich, strong, and safe life.

CUSINS   Suppose one is forced to choose between them and money or gunpowder?

UNDERSHAFT   Choose money and gunpowder; for without enough of both you cannot afford the others.

CUSINS   That is your religion?

UNDERSHAFT   Yes.

The cadence of this reply makes a full close in the conversation. CUSINS *twists his face dubiously and contemplates* UNDERSHAFT. UNDERSHAFT *contemplates him.*

CUSINS   Barbara wont stand that. You will have to choose between your religion and Barbara.

UNDERSHAFT   So will you, my friend. She will find out that that drum of yours is hollow.

CUSINS   Father Undershaft: you are mistaken: I am a sincere Salvationist. You do not understand the Salvation Army. It is the army of joy, of love, of courage: it has banished the fear and remorse and despair of the old hell-ridden evangelical sects: it marches to fight the devil with trumpet and drum, with music and dancing, with banner and palm, as becomes a sally from heaven by its happy garrison. It picks the waster out of the public house and makes a man of him: it finds a worm wriggling in a back kitchen, and lo! a woman! Men and woman of rank too, sons and daughters of the Highest. It takes the poor professor of Greek, the most artificial and self-suppressed of human creatures, from his meal of roots, and lets loose the rhapsodist in him; reveals the true worship of Dionysos to him; sends him down the public street drumming dithyrambs *(he plays a thundering flourish on the drum)*.

UNDERSHAFT   You will alarm the shelter.

CUSINS   Oh, they are accustomed to these sudden ecstasies. However, if the drum worries you—(*he pockets the drumsticks; unhooks the drum and stands it on the ground opposite the gateway*).

UNDERSHAFT   Thank you.

CUSINS   You remember what Euripides says about your money and gunpowder?

UNDERSHAFT   No.

CUSINS   (*declaiming*)

> One and another
> In money and guns may outpass his brother;
> And men in their millions float and flow
> And seethe with a million hopes as leaven;
> And they win their will; or they miss their will;
> And their hopes are dead or are pined for still;
> But who'er can know
> As the long days go
> That to live is happy, has found his heaven.

My translation: what do you think of it?

UNDERSHAFT   I think, my friend, that if you wish to know, as the long days go, that to live is happy, you must first acquire money enough for a decent life, and power enough to be your own master.

CUSINS   You are damnably discouraging. (*He resumes his declamation.*)

> Is it so hard a thing to see
> That the spirit of God—whate'er it be—
> The law that abides and changes not, ages long,
> The Eternal and Nature-born: these things be strong?
> What else is Wisdom? What of Man's endeavor,
> Of God's high grace so lovely and so great?
> To stand from fear set free? to breathe and wait?
> To hold a hand uplifted over Fate?
> And shall not Barbara be loved for ever?

UNDERSHAFT   Euripides mentions Barbara, does he?

CUSINS   It is a fair translation. The word means Loveliness.

UNDERSHAFT   May I ask—as Barbara's father—how much a year she is to be loved for ever on?

CUSINS   As for Barbara's father, that is more your affair than mine. I can feed her by teaching Greek: that is about all.

UNDERSHAFT   Do you consider it a good match for her?

CUSINS   (*with polite obstinacy*)   Mr Undershaft: I am in many ways a weak, timid, ineffectual person; and my health is far from satisfactory. But whenever I feel that I must have anything, I get it, sooner or later. I feel that way about Barbara. I dont like marriage: I feel intensely afraid of it; and I dont know what I shall do with Barbara or what she will do with me. But I feel that I and nobody else must marry her. Please regard that as settled.— Not that I wish to be arbitrary; but why should I waste your time in discussing what is inevitable?

UNDERSHAFT   You mean that you will stick at nothing: not even the conversion of the Salvation Army to the worship of Dionysos.

CUSINS   The business of the Salvation Army is to save, not to wrangle about the name of the pathfinder. Dionysos or another: what does it matter?

UNDERSHAFT (*rising and approaching him*)   Professor Cusins: you are a young man after my own heart.

CUSINS   Mr Undershaft: you are, as far as I am able to gather, a most infernal old rascal; but you appeal very strongly to my sense of ironic humor.

UNDERSHAFT *mutely offers his hand. They shake.*

UNDERSHAFT (*suddenly concentrating himself*)   And now to business.

CUSINS   Pardon me. We are discussing religion. Why go back to such an uninteresting and unimportant subject as business?

UNDERSHAFT   Religion is our business at present, because it is through religion alone that we can win Barbara.

CUSINS   Have you, too, fallen in love with Barbara?

UNDERSHAFT   Yes, with a father's love.

CUSINS   A father's love for a grown-up daughter is the most dangerous of all infatuations. I apologize for mentioning my own pale, coy, mistrustful fancy in the same breath with it.

UNDERSHAFT   Keep to the point. We have to win her; and we are neither of us Methodists.

CUSINS   That doesnt matter. The power Barbara wields here—the power that wields Barbara herself—is not Calvinism, not Presbyterianism, not Methodism—

UNDERSHAFT   Not Greek Paganism either, eh?

CUSINS   I admit that. Barbara is quite original in her religion.

UNDERSHAFT (*triumphantly*)   Aha! Barbara Undershaft would be. Her inspiration comes from within herself.

CUSINS   How do you suppose it got there?

UNDERSHAFT (*in towering excitement*)   It is the Undershaft inheritance. I shall hand on my torch to my daughter. She shall make my converts and preach my gospel—

CUSINS   What! Money and gunpowder!

UNDERSHAFT   Yes, money and gunpowder. Freedom and power. Command of life and command of death.

CUSINS   (*urbanely: trying to bring him down to earth*)   This is extremely interesting, Mr Undershaft. Of course you know that you are mad.

UNDERSHAFT   (*with redoubled force*)   And you?

CUSINS   Oh, mad as a hatter. You are welcome to my secret since I have discovered yours. But I am astonished. Can a madman make cannons?

UNDERSHAFT   Would anyone else than a madman make them? And now (*with surging energy*) question for question. Can a sane man translate Euripides?

CUSINS   No.

UNDERSHAFT   (*seizing him by the shoulder*)   Can a sane woman make a man of a waster or a woman of a worm?

CUSINS   (*reeling before the storm*)   Father Colossus—Mammoth Millionaire—

UNDERSHAFT   (*pressing him*)   Are there two mad people or three in this Salvation shelter today?

CUSINS   You mean Barbara is as mad as we are?

UNDERSHAFT   (*pushing him lightly off and resuming his equanimity suddenly and completely*)   Pooh, Professor! let us call things by their proper names. I am a millionaire; you are a poet: Barbara is a savior of souls. What have we three to do with the common mob of slaves and idolators? (*He sits down again with a shrug of contempt for the mob.*)

CUSINS   Take care! Barbara is in love with the common people. So am I. Have you never felt the romance of that love?

UNDERSHAFT   (*cold and sardonic*)   Have you ever been in love with Poverty, like St Francis? Have you ever been in love with Dirt, like St Simeon! Have you ever been in love with disease and suffering, like our nurses and philanthropists? Such passions are not virtues, but the most unnatural of all the vices. This love of the common people may please an earl's granddaughter and a university professor; but I have been a common man and a poor man; and it has no romance for me. Leave it to the poor to pretend that poverty is a blessing: leave it to the coward to make a religion of his cowardice by preaching humility: we know better than that. We three must stand together above the common people: how else can we help their children to climb up beside us? Barbara must belong to us, not to the Salvation Army.

CUSINS   Well, I can only say that if you think you will get her away from the Salvation Army by talking to her as you have been talking to me, you dont know Barbara.

UNDERSHAFT   My friend: I never ask for what I can buy.

CUSINS (*in a white fury*)   Do I understand you to imply that you can buy Barbara?

UNDERSHAFT   No; but I can buy the Salvation Army.

CUSINS   Quite impossible.

UNDERSHAFT   You shall see. All religious organizations exist by selling themselves to the rich.

CUSINS   Not the Army. That is the Church of the poor.

UNDERSHAFT   All the more reason for buying it.

CUSINS   I dont think you quite know what the Army does for the poor.

UNDERSHAFT   Oh yes I do. It draws their teeth: that is enough for me as a man of business.

CUSINS   Nonsense! It makes them sober—

UNDERSHAFT   I prefer sober workmen. The profits are larger.

CUSINS   —honest—

UNDERSHAFT   Honest workmen are the most economical.

CUSINS—attached to their homes—

UNDERSHAFT   So much the better: they will put up with anything sooner than change their shop.

CUSINS   —happy—

UNDERSHAFT   An invaluable safeguard against revolution.

CUSINS   —unselfish—

UNDERSHAFT   Indifferent to their own interests, which suits me exactly.

CUSINS   —with their thoughts on heavenly things—

UNDERSHAFT (*rising*)   And not on Trade Unionism nor Socialism. Excellent.

CUSINS (*revolted*)   You really are an infernal old rascal.

UNDERSHAFT (*indicating* PETER SHIRLEY, *who has just come from the shelter and strolled dejectedly down the yard between them*)   And this is an honest man!

SHIRLEY   Yes; and what av I got by it? (*He passes on bitterly and sits on the form, in the corner of the penthouse.*)

SNOBBY PRICE, *beaming sanctimoniously, and* JENNY HILL, *with a tambourine full of coppers, come from the shelter and go to the drum, on which* JENNY *begins to count the money.*

UNDERSHAFT (*replying to* SHIRLEY)   Oh, your employers must have got a good deal by it from first to last. (*He sits on the table, with one foot on the side form,* CUSINS, *overwhelmed, sits down on the same form nearer the shelter.* BARBARA *comes from the shelter to the middle of the yard. She is excited and a little overwrought.*)

BARBARA Weve just had a splendid experience meeting at the other gate in Cripps's lane. Ive hardly ever seen them so much moved as they were by your confession, Mr Price.

PRICE I could almost be glad of my past wickedness if I could believe that it would elp to keep hathers stright.

BARBARA So it will, Snobby. How much, Jenny?

JENNY Four and tenpence, Major.

BARBARA Oh Snobby, if you had given your poor mother just one more kick, we should have got the whole five shillings!

PRICE If she heard you say that, miss, she'd be sorry I didnt. But I'm glad. Oh what a joy it will be to her when she hears I'm saved!

UNDERSHAFT Shall I contribute the odd twopence, Barbara? The millionaire's mite, eh? (*He takes a couple of pennies from his pocket.*)

BARBARA How did you make that twopence?

UNDERSHAFT As usual. By selling cannons, torpedoes, submarines, and my new patent Grand Duke hand grenade.

BARBARA Put it back in your pocket. You cant buy your salvation here for twopence: you must work it out.

UNDERSHAFT Is twopence not enough? I can afford a little more, if you press me.

BARBARA Two million millions would not be enough. There is bad blood on your hands; and nothing but good blood can cleanse them. Money is no use. Take it away. (*She turns to* CUSINS.) Dolly: you must write another letter for me to the papers. (*He makes a wry face.*) Yes: I know you dont like it; but it must be done. The starvation this winter is beating us: everybody is unemployed. The General says we must close this shelter if we cant get more money. I force the collections at the meetings until I am ashamed: dont I, Snobby?

PRICE It's a fair treat to see you work it, miss. The way you got them up from three-and-six to four-and-ten with that hymn, penny by penny and verse by verse, was a caution. Not a Cheap Jack on Mile End Waste could touch you at it.

BARBARA Yes; but I wish we could do without it. I am getting at last to think more of the collection than of the people's souls. And what are those hatfuls of pence and halfpence? We want thousands! tens of thousands! hundreds of thousands! I want to convert people, not to be always begging for the Army in a way I'd die sooner than beg for myself.

UNDERSHAFT (*in profound irony*) Genuine unselfishness is capable of anything, my dear.

BARBARA (*unsuspectingly, as she turns away to take the money from the drum and put it in a cash bag she carries*) Yes, isnt it? (UNDERSHAFT *looks sardonically at* CUSINS.)

CUSINS (*aside to* UNDERSHAFT) Mephistopheles! Machiavelli!

BARBARA (*tears coming into her eyes as she ties the bag and pockets it*) How are we to feed them? I cant talk religion to a man with bodily hunger in his eyes. (*Almost breaking down.*) It's frightful.

JENNY (*running to her*) Major, dear—

BARBARA (*rebounding*) No: dont comfort me. It will be all right. We shall get the money.

UNDERSHAFT How?

JENNY By praying for it, of course. Mrs Baines says she prayed for it last night; and she has never prayed for it in vain: never once. (*She goes to the gate and looks out into the street.*)

BARBARA (*who has dried her eyes and regained her composure*) By the way, dad, Mrs Baines has come to march with us to our big meeting this afternoon and she is very anxious to meet you, for some reason or other. Perhaps she'll convert you.

UNDERSHAFT I shall be delighted, my dear.

JENNY (*at the gate: excitedly*) Major! Major! here's that man back again.

BARBARA What man?

JENNY The man that hit me. Oh, I hope he's coming back to join us.

BILL WALKER, *with frost on his jacket, comes through the gate, his hands deep in his pockets and his chin sunk between his shoulders, like a cleaned-out gambler. He halts between* BARBARA *and the drum.*

BARBARA Hullo, Bill! Back already!

BILL (*nagging at her*) Bin talkin ever sence, ev you?

BARBARA Pretty nearly. Well, has Todger paid you out for poor Jenny's jaw?

BILL Nao e aint.

BARBARA I thought your jacket looked a bit snowy.

BILL Sao it is snaowy. You want to knaow where the snaow cam from, downt you?

BARBARA Yes.

BILL Well, it cam from orf the grahnd in Pawkinses Corner in Kennintahn. It got rabbed orf be maw shaoulders: see?

BARBARA Pity you didnt rub some off with your knees, Bill! That would have done you a lot of good.

BILL (*with sour mirthless humor*) Aw was sivin anather menn's knees at the tawm. E was kneelin on moy ed, e was.

JENNY Who was kneeling on your head?

BILL Todger was. E was pryin for me: pryin camfortable wiv me as a cawpet. Sow was Mog. Sao was the aol bloomin meeting. Mog she sez "Ow Lawd brike is stabborn sperrit; bat downt urt is dear art." Thet was wot she said. "Downt urt is dear art"! An er blowk—thirteen stun four!—kneelin wiv all is wight on me. Fanny, aint it?

JENNY Oh no. We're so sorry, Mr Walker.

BARBARA (*enjoying it frankly*) Nonsense! of course it's funny. Served you right, Bill! You must have done something to him first.

BILL (*doggedly*) Aw did wot Aw said Aw'd do. Aw spit in is eye. E looks ap at the skoy and sez, "Ow that Aw should be fahnd worthy to be spit upon for the gospel's sike!" e sez; an Mog sez "Glaory Allelloolier!"; and then e called me Braddher, an dahned me as if Aw was a kid and he was me mather worshin me a Setterda nawt. Aw ednt jast nao shaow wiv im at all. Arf the street pryed; an the tather arf larfed fit to split theirselves. (*To* BARBARA.) There are you settisfawd nah?

BARBARA (*her eyes dancing*) Wish I'd been there, Bill.

BILL Yus: youd a got in a hextra bit o talk on me, wouldnt you?

JENNY I'm so sorry, Mr Walker.

BILL (*fiercely*) Downt you gow being sorry for me: youve no call. Listen eah. Aw browk your jawr.

JENNY No, it didnt hurt me: indeed it didnt, except for a moment. It was only that I was frightened.

BILL Aw downt want to be forgive be you, or be ennybody. Wot Aw did Aw'll py for. Aw trawd to gat me aown jawr browk to settisfaw you—

JENNY (*distressed*) Oh no—

BILL (*impatiently*) Tell y' Aw did: cawnt you listen to wots being taold you? All Aw got be it was being mide a sawt of in the pablic street for me pines. Well, if Aw cawnt settisfaw you one wy, Aw ken anather. Listen eah! Aw ed two quid sived agen the frost; an Awve a pahnd of it left. A mite o mawn last week ed words with the judy e's gowing to merry. E give er wot-for; an e's bin fawned fifteen bob. E ed a rawt to itt er cause they was gowin to be merrid; but Aw ednt nao rawt to itt you; sao put anather fawv bob on an call it a pahnd's worth. (*He produces a sovereign.*) Eahs the manney. Tike it, and lets ev no more o your forgivin an prying and your Mijor jawrin me. Let wot Aw dan be dan an pide for; and let there be a end of it.

JENNY Oh, I couldn't take it, Mr Walker. But if you would give a shilling or two to poor Rummy Mitchens! you really did hurt her; and she's old.

BILL (*contemptuously*)   Not lawkly. Aw'd give her anather as soon as look at er. Let her ev the lawr o me as she threatened! She aint forgiven me: not mach. Wot Aw dan to er is not on me mawnd—wot she (*indicating* BARBARA) mawt call on me conscience—no more than stickin a pig. It's this Christian gime o yours that Aw wownt ev plyed agen me: this bloomin forgivin an neggin an jawrin that mikes a menn thet sore that iz lawf's a burdn to im. Aw wownt ev it, Aw tell you; sao tike your manney and stop thraowin your silly beshed fice hap agen me.

JENNY   Major: may I take a little of it for the Army?

BARBARA   No: the Army is not to be bought. We want your soul, Bill; and we'll take nothing less.

BILL (*bitterly*)   Aw knaow. Me an maw few shillins is not good enaff for you. Youre a earl's grendorter, you are. Nathink less than a andered pahnd for you.

UNDERSHAFT   Come, Barbara! you could do a great deal of good with a hundred pounds. If you will set this gentleman's mind at ease by taking his pound, I will give the other ninety-nine.

BILL, *dazed by such opulence, instinctively touches his cap.*

BARBARA   Oh, youre too extravagant, papa. Bill offers twenty pieces of silver. All you need offer is the other ten. That will make the standard price to buy anybody who's for sale. I'm not; and the Army's not. (*To* BILL.) Youll never have another quiet moment, Bill, until you come around to us. You cant stand out against your salvation.

BILL (*sullenly*)   Aw cawnt stend aht agen music awl wrastlers and awtful tangued women. Awve offered to py. Aw can do no more. Tike it or leave it. There it is. (*He throws the sovereign on the drum, and sits down on the horse trough. The coin fascinates* SNOBBY PRICE, *who takes an early opportunity of dropping his cap on it.*)

MRS BAINES *comes from the shelter. She is dressed as a Salvation Army Commissioner. She is an earnest looking woman of about 40, with a caressing, urgent voice, and an appealing manner.*

BARBARA   This is my father, Mrs Baines. (UNDERSHAFT *comes from the table, taking his hat off with marked civility.*) Try what you can do with him. He wont listen to me, because he remembers what a fool I was when I was a baby. (*She leaves them together and chats with* JENNY.)

MRS BAINES   Have you been shewn over the shelter, Mr Undershaft? You know the work we're doing, of course.

UNDERSHAFT (*very civilly*)   The whole nation knows it, Mrs Baines.

MRS BAINES No, sir: the whole nation does not know it, or we should not be crippled as we are for want of money to carry our work through the length and breadth of the land. Let me tell you that there would have been rioting this winter in London but for us.

UNDERSHAFT You really think so?

MRS BAINES I know it. I remember 1886, when you rich gentlemen hardened your hearts against the cry of the poor. They broke the windows of your clubs in Pall Mall.

UNDERSHAFT (*gleaming with approval of their method*) And the Mansion House Fund went up next day from thirty thousand pounds to seventy-nine thousand! I remember quite well.

MRS BAINES Well, wont you help me to get at the people? They wont break windows then. Come here, Price. Let me shew you to this gentleman (PRICE *comes to be inspected*). Do you remember the window breaking?

PRICE My ole father thought it was the revolution, maam.

MRS BAINES Would you break windows now?

PRICE Oh no, maam. The windows of eaven av bin opened to me. I know now that the rich man is a sinner like myself.

RUMMY (*appearing above at the loft door*) Snobby Price!

SNOBBY Wot is it?

RUMMY Your mother's askin for you at the other gate in Cripps's Lane. She's heard about your confession (PRICE *turns pale.*)

MRS BAINES Go, Mr Price; and pray with her.

JENNY You can go through the shelter, Snobby.

PRICE (*to* MRS BAINES) I couldnt face her now, maam, with all the weight of my sins fresh on me. Tell her she'll find her son at ome, waitin for her in prayer. (*He skulks off through the gate, incidentally stealing the sovereign on his way out by picking up his cap from the drum.*)

MRS BAINES (*with swimming eyes*) You see how we take the anger and the bitterness against you out of their hearts, Mr Undershaft.

UNDERSHAFT It is certainly most convenient and gratifying to all large employers of labor, Mrs Baines.

MRS BAINES Barbara: Jenny: I have good news: most wonderful news. (JENNY *runs to her.*) My prayers have been answered. I told you they would, Jenny, didnt I?

JENNY Yes, yes.

BARBARA (*moving nearer to the drum*) Have we got money enough to keep the shelter open?

MRS BAINES I hope we shall have enough to keep all the shelters open. Lord Saxmundham has promised us five thousand pounds—

BARBARA Hooray!

JENNY Glory!

MRS BAINES   —if—

BARBARA   "If!" If what?

MRS BAINES   —if five other gentlemen will give a thousand each to make it up to ten thousand.

BARBARA   Who is Lord Saxmundham? I never heard of him.

UNDERSHAFT   (*who has pricked up his ears at the peer's name, and is now watching* BARBARA *curiously*)   A new creation, my dear. You have heard of Sir Horace Bodger?

BARBARA   Bodger! Do you mean the distiller? Bodger's whisky!

UNDERSHAFT   That is the man. He is one of the greatest of our public benefactors. He restored the cathedral at Hakington. They made him a baronet for that. He gave half a million to the funds of his party: they made him a baron for that.

SHIRLEY   What will they give him for the five thousand?

UNDERSHAFT   There is nothing left to give him. So the five thousand, I should think, is to save his soul.

MRS BAINES   Heaven grant it may! Oh Mr Undershaft, you have some very rich friends. Cant you help us towards the other five thousand? We are going to hold a great meeting this afternoon at the Assembly Hall in the Mile End Road. If I could only announce that one gentleman had come forward to support Lord Saxmundham, others would follow. Dont you know somebody? couldnt you? wouldnt you? (*her eyes fill with tears*) oh, think of those poor people, Mr Undershaft: think of how much it means to them, and how little to a great man like you.

UNDERSHAFT   (*sardonically gallant*)   Mrs Baines: you are irresistible. I cant disappoint you; and I cant deny myself the satisfaction of making Bodger pay up. You shall have your five thousand pounds.

MRS BAINES   Thank God!

UNDERSHAFT   You dont thank me?

MRS BAINES   Oh sir, dont try to be cynical: dont be ashamed of being a good man. The Lord will bless you abundantly; and our prayers will be like a strong fortification round you all the days of your life. (*With a touch of caution.*) You will let me have the cheque to shew at the meeting, wont you? Jenny: go in and fetch a pen and ink. (JENNY *runs to the shelter door.*)

UNDERSHAFT   Do not disturb Miss Hill: I have a fountain pen. (JENNY *halts. He sits at the table and writes the cheque.* CUSINS *rises to make room for him. They all watch him silently.*)

BILL   (*cynically, aside to* BARBARA, *his voice and accent horribly debased*)   Wot prawce selvytion nah?

BARBARA   Stop. (UNDERSHAFT *stops writing: they all turn to her in surprise.*) Mrs Baines: are you really going to take this money?

MRS BAINES   (*astonished*)   Why not, dear?

BARBARA Why not! Do you know what my father is? Have you forgotten that Lord Saxmundham is Bodger the whisky man? Do you remember how we implored the County Council to stop him from writing Bodger's Whisky in letters of fire against the sky; so that the poor drink-ruined creatures on the Embankment could not wake up from their snatches of sleep without being reminded of their deadly thirst by that wicked sky sign? Do you know that the worst thing I have had to fight here is not the devil, but Bodger, Bodger, Bodger, with his whisky, his distilleries, and his tied houses? Are you going to make our shelter another tied house for him, and ask me to keep it?

BILL Rotten dranken whisky it is too.

MRS BAINES Dear Barbara: Lord Saxmundham has a soul to be saved like any of us. If heaven had found the way to make a good use of his money, are we to set ourselves up against the answer to our prayers?

BARBARA I know he has a soul to be saved. Let him come down here; and I'll do my best to help him to his salvation. But he wants to send his cheque down to buy us, and go on being as wicked as ever.

UNDERSHAFT (*with a reasonableness which* CUSINS *alone perceives to be ironical*) My dear Barbara: alcohol is a very necessary article. It heals the sick—

BARBARA It does nothing of the sort.

UNDERSHAFT Well, it assists the doctor: that is perhaps a less questionable way of putting it. It makes life bearable to millions of people who could not endure their existence if they were quite sober. It enables Parliament to do things at eleven at night that no sane person would do at eleven in the morning. Is it Bodger's fault that this inestimable gift is deplorably abused by less than one per cent of the poor? (*He turns again to the table; signs the cheque; and crosses it.*)

MRS BAINES Barbara: will there be less drinking or more if all those poor souls we are saving come tomorrow and find the doors of our shelters shut in their faces? Lord Saxmundham gives us the money to stop drinking—to take his own business from him.

CUSINS (*impishly*) Pure self-sacrifice on Bodger's part, clearly! Bless dear Bodger! (BARBARA *almost breaks down as* ADOLPHUS, *too, fails her.*)

UNDERSHAFT (*tearing out the cheque and pocketing the book as he rises and goes past* CUSINS *to* MRS BAINES) I also, Mrs Baines, may claim a little disinterestedness. Think of my business! think of the widows and orphans! the men and lads torn to pieces with shrapnel and poisoned with lyddite! (MRS BAINES *shrinks; but he goes on remorselessly*) the oceans of blood, not one drop of which is shed in a really just cause! the ravaged crops! the peaceful peasants forced, women and men, to till their fields under the fire of opposing armies on pain of starvation! the bad blood of the fierce little cowards at home who egg on others to fight for the gratification of their national vanity! All this makes money for me: I am never richer, never busier than when the papers are full of it. Well, it is your work to preach peace on earth and good will to men. (MRS BAINES's *face lights up again.*) Every convert you make is a vote against war. (*Her lips move in prayer.*) Yet I give you this money to help you to hasten my own commercial ruin. (*He gives her the cheque.*)

CUSINS (*mounting the form in an ecstasy of mischief*) The millennium will be inaugurated by the unselfishness of Undershaft and Bodger. Oh be joyful! (*He takes the drumsticks from his pocket and flourishes them.*)

MRS BAINES (*taking the cheque*) The longer I live the more proof I see that there is an Infinite Goodness that turns everything to the work of salvation sooner or later. Who would have thought that any good could have come out of war and drink? And yet their profits are brought today to the feet of salvation to do its blessed work. (*She is affected to tears.*)

JENNY (*running to* MRS BAINES *and throwing her arms round her*) Oh dear! how blessed, how glorious it all is!

CUSINS (*in a convulsion of irony*) Let us seize this unspeakable moment. Let us march to the great meeting at once. Excuse me just an instant. (*He rushes into the shelter.* JENNY *takes her tambourine from the drum head.*)

MRS BAINES Mr Undershaft: have you ever seen a thousand people fall on their knees with one impulse and pray? Come with us to the meeting. Barbara shall tell them that the Army is saved, and saved through you.

CUSINS (*returning impetuously from the shelter with a flag and a trombone, and coming between* MRS BAINES *and* UNDERSHAFT) You shall carry the flag down the first street, Mrs Baines (*he gives her the flag*). Mr Undershaft is a gifted trombonist: he shall intone an Olympian diapason to the West Ham Salvation March. (*Aside to* UNDERSHAFT, *as he forces the trombone on him.*) Blow, Machiavelli, blow.

UNDERSHAFT (*aside to him, as he takes the trombone*) The Trumpet in Zion! (CUSINS *rushes to the drum, which he takes up and puts on.* UNDERSHAFT *continues, aloud.*) I will do my best. I could vamp a bass if I knew the tune.

CUSINS It is a wedding chorus from one of Donizetti's operas; but we have converted it. We convert everything to good here, includ-

ing Bodger. You remember the chorus. 'For thee immense rejoicing—immenso giubilo—immenso giubilo.' (*With drum obbligato.*)
Rum tum ti tum tum, tum tum ti ta—

BARBARA   Dolly: you are breaking my heart.

CUSINS   What is a broken heart more or less here? Dionysos Undershaft has descended. I am possessed.

MRS BAINES   Come, Barbara: I must have my dear Major to carry
the flag with me.

JENNY   Yes, yes, Major darling.

CUSINS (*snatches the tambourine out of* JENNY's *hand and mutely
offers it to* BARBARA.)

BARBARA (*coming forward a little as she puts the offer behind her
with a shudder, whilst* CUSINS *recklessly tosses the tambourine
back to* JENNY *and goes to the gate*)   I cant come.

JENNY   Not come!

MRS BAINES (*with tears in her eyes*)   Barbara: do you think I am
wrong to take the money?

BARBARA (*impulsively going to her and kissing her*)   No, no: God
help you, dear, you must: you are saving the Army. Go; and may
you have a great meeting!

JENNY   But arnt you coming?

BARBARA   No. (*She begins taking off the silver S brooch from her
collar.*)

MRS BAINES   Barbara: what are you doing?

JENNY   Why are you taking your badge off? You cant be going
to leave us, Major.

BARBARA (*quietly*)   Father: come here.

UNDERSHAFT (*coming to her*)   My dear! (*Seeing that she is going
to pin the badge on his collar, he retreats to the penthouse in
some alarm.*)

BARBARA (*following him*)   Don't be frightened. (*She pins the badge
on and steps back towards the table, shewing him to the others.*)
There! It's not much for £5000, is it?

MRS BAINES   Barbara: if you wont come and pray with us, promise
me you will pray for us.

BARBARA   I cant pray now. Perhaps I shall never pray again.

MRS BAINES   Barbara!

JENNY   Major!

BARBARA (*almost delirious*)   I cant bear any more. Quick march!

CUSINS (*calling to the procession in the street outside*)   Off we go.
Play up, there! Immenso giubilo. (*He gives the time with his
drum; and the band strikes up the march, which rapidly becomes
more distant as the procession moves briskly away.*)

MRS BAINES   I must go, dear. Youre overworked: you will be all right tomorrow. We'll never lose you. Now Jenny: step out with the old flag. Blood and Fire! (*She marches out through the gate with her flag.*)

JENNY   Glory Hallelujah! (*Flourishing her tambourine and marching.*)

UNDERSHAFT (*to* CUSINS, *as he marches out past him easing the slide of his trombone*)   "My ducats and my daughter"!

CUSINS (*following him out*)   Money and gunpowder!

BARBARA   Drunkenness and Murder! My God: why hast thou forsaken me?

She sinks on the form with her face buried in her hands. The march passes away into silence. BILL WALKER *steals across to her.*

BILL (*taunting*)   Wot prawce selvytion nah?

SHIRLEY   Don't you hit her when she's down.

BILL   She it me wen aw wiz dahn. Waw shouldnt Aw git a bit o me aown beck?

BARBARA (*raising her head*)   I didnt take your money, Bill. (*She crosses the yard to the gate and turns her back on the two men to hide her face from them.*)

BILL (*sneering after her*)   Naow, it warnt enaff for you. (*Turning to the drum, he misses the money.*)   Ellow! If you aint took it sammun else ez. Weres it gorn? Bly me if Jenny Ill didnt tike it arter all!

RUMMY (*screaming at him from the loft*)   You lie, you dirty blackguard! Snobby Price pinched it off the drum when he took up his cap. I was up here all the time an see im do it.

BILL   Wot! Stowl may manney! Waw didnt you call thief on him, you silly aold macker you?

RUMMY   To serve you aht for ittin me acrost the fice. It's cost y'pahnd, that az. (*Raising a pæn of squalid triumph.*)   I done you. I'm even with you. Uve ad it aht o y—(BILL *snatches up* SHIRLEY's *mug and hurls it at her. She slams the loft door and vanishes. The mug smashes against the door and falls in fragments.*)

BILL (*beginning to chuckle*)   Tell us, aol menn, wot o'clock this mawnin was it wen im as they call Snobby Prawce was sived?

BARBARA (*turning to him more composedly, and with unspoiled sweetness*)   About half past twelve, Bill. And he pinched your pound at a quarter to two. *I* know. Well, you cant afford to lose it. I'll send it to you.

BILL (*his voice and accent suddenly improving*)   Not if Aw wiz to stawve for it. Aw aint to be bought.

SHIRLEY Aint you? Youd sell yourself to the devil for a pint o beer; only there aint no devil to make the offer.

BILL (*unashamed*) Sao Aw would, mite, and often ev, cheerful. But she cawnt baw me. (*Approaching* BARBARA.) You wanted maw soul, did you? Well, you aint got it.

BARBARA I nearly got it, Bill. But weve sold it back to you for ten thousand pounds.

SHIRLEY And dear at the money!

BARBARA No, Peter: it was worth more than money.

BILL (*salvationproof*) It's nao good: you cawnt get rahnd me nah. Aw downt blieve in it; and Awve seen tody that Aw was rawt. (*Going.*) Sao long, aol soupkitchener! Ta, ta, Mijor Earl's Grendorter! (*Turning at the gate.*) Wot prawce selvytion nah? Snobby Prawce! Ha! ha!

BARBARA (*offering her hand*) Goodbye, Bill.

BILL (*taken aback, half plucks his cap off; then shoves it on again defiantly*) Get aht. (BARBARA *drops her hand, discouraged. He has a twinge of remorse.*) But thets aw rawt, you knaow. Nathink pasnl. Naow mellice. Sao long, Judy. (*He goes.*)

BARBARA No malice. So long, Bill.

SHIRLEY (*shaking his head*) You make too much of him, miss, in your innocence.

BARBARA (*going to him*) Peter: I'm like you now. Cleaned out, and lost my job.

SHIRLEY Youve youth an hope. Thats two better than me.

BARBARA I'll get you a job, Peter. Thats hope for you: the youth will have to be enough for me. (*She counts her money.*) I have just enough left for two teas at Lockharts, a Rowton doss for you, and my tram and bus home. (*He frowns and rises with offended pride. She takes his arm.*) Dont be proud, Peter: it's sharing between friends. And promise me youll talk to me and not let me cry. (*She draws him towards the gate.*)

SHIRLEY Well, I'm not accustomed to talk to the like of you—

BARBARA (*urgently*) Yes, yes: you must talk to me. Tell me about Tom Paine's books and Bradlaugh's lectures. Come along.

SHIRLEY Ah, if you would only read Tom Paine in the proper spirit, miss! (*They go out through the gate together.*)

ACT III

Next day after lunch LADY BRITOMART *is writing in the library in Wilton Crescent.* SARAH *is reading in the armchair near the window.* BARBARA, *in ordinary fashionable dress, pale and brooding, is on the settee.* CHARLES

LOMAX *enters. He starts on seeing* BARBARA *fashionably attired and in low spirits.*

LOMAX   Youve left off your uniform!

BARBARA *says nothing; but an expression of pain passes over her face.*

LADY BRITOMART (*warning him in low tones to be careful*)   Charles!

LOMAX (*much concerned, coming behind the settee and bending sympathetically over* BARBARA)   I'm awfully sorry, Barbara. You know I helped you all I could with the concertina and so forth. (*Momentously.*) Still, I have never shut my eyes to the fact that there is a certain amount of tosh about the Salvation Army. Now the claims of the Church of England—

LADY BRITOMART   Thats enough, Charles. Speak of something suited to your mental capacity.

LOMAX   But surely the Church of England is suited to all our capacities.

BARBARA (*pressing his hand*)   Thank you for your sympathy, Cholly. Now go and spoon with Sarah.

LOMAX (*dragging a chair from the writing table and seating himself affectionately by* SARAH'S *side*)   How is my ownest today?

SARAH   I wish you wouldnt tell Cholly to do things, Barbara. He always comes straight and does them. Cholly: we're going to the works this afternoon.

LOMAX   What works?

SARAH   The cannon works.

LOMAX   What? your governor's shop!

SARAH   Yes.

LOMAX   Oh I say!

CUSINS *enters in poor condition. He also starts visibly when he sees* BARBARA *without her uniform.*

BARBARA   I expected you this morning, Dolly. Didnt you guess that?

CUSINS (*sitting down beside her*)   I'm sorry. I have only just breakfasted.

SARAH   But weve just finished lunch.

BARBARA   Have you had one of your bad nights?

CUSINS   No: I had rather a good night: in fact, one of the most remarkable nights I have ever passed.

BARBARA   The meeting?

CUSINS   No: after the meeting.

LADY BRITOMART   You should have gone to bed after the meeting. What were you doing?

CUSINS   Drinking.

LADY BRITOMART ⎫ Adolphus!
SARAH ⎪ Dolly!
BARBARA ⎬ Dolly!
LOMAX ⎭ Oh I say!

LADY BRITOMART What were you drinking, may I ask?

CUSINS A most devilish kind of Spanish burgundy, warranted free from added alcohol: a Temperance burgundy in fact. Its richness in natural alcohol made any addition superfluous.

BARBARA Are you joking, Dolly?

CUSINS (*patiently*) No. I have been making a night of it with the nominal head of this household: that is all.

LADY BRITOMART Andrew made you drunk!

CUSINS No: he only provided the wine. I think it was Dionysos who made me drunk. (*To* BARBARA.) I told you I was possessed.

LADY BRITOMART Youre not sober yet. Go home to bed at once.

CUSINS I have never before ventured to reproach you, Lady Brit; but how could you marry the Prince of Darkness?

LADY BRITOMART It was much more excusable to marry him than to get drunk with him. That is a new accomplishment of Andrew's, by the way. He usent to drink.

CUSINS He doesnt now. He only sat there and completed the wreck of my moral basis, the rout of my convictions, the purchase of my soul. He cares for you, Barbara. That is what makes him so dangerous to me.

BARBARA That has nothing to do with it, Dolly. There are larger loves and diviner dreams than the fireside ones. You know that, dont you?

CUSINS Yes: that is our understanding. I know it. I hold to it. Unless he can win me on that holier ground he may amuse me for a while; but he can get no deeper hold, strong as he is.

BARBARA Keep to that; and the end will be right. Now tell me what happened at the meeting?

CUSINS It was an amazing meeting. Mrs Baines almost died of emotion. Jenny Hill simply gibbered with hysteria. The Prince of Darkness played his trombone like a madman: its brazen roarings were like the laughter of the damned. 117 conversions took place then and there. They prayed with the most touching sincerity and gratitude for Bodger, and for the anonymous donor of the £5000. Your father would not let his name be given.

LOMAX That was rather fine of the old man, you know. Most chaps would have wanted the advertisement.

CUSINS He said all the charitable institutions would be down on him like kites on a battle-field if he gave his name.

LADY BRITOMART Thats Andrew all over. He never does a proper thing without giving an improper reason for it.

CUSINS He convinced me that I have all my life been doing improper things for proper reasons.

LADY BRITOMART Adolphus: now that Barbara has left the Salvation Army, you had better leave it too. I will not have you playing that drum in the streets.

CUSINS Your orders are already obeyed, Lady Brit.

BARBARA Dolly: were you ever really in earnest about it? Would you have joined if you had never seen me?

CUSINS (*disingenuously*) Well—er—well, possibly, as a collector of religions—

LOMAX (*cunningly*) Not as a drummer, though, you know. You are a very clearheaded brainy chap, Dolly; and it must have been apparent to you that there is a certain amount of tosh about—

LADY BRITOMART Charles: if you must drivel, drivel like a grown-up man and not like a schoolboy.

LOMAX (*out of countenance*) Well, drivel is drivel, dont you know, whatever a man's age.

LADY BRITOMART In good society in England, Charles, men drivel at all ages by repeating silly formulas with an air of wisdom. Schoolboys make their own formulas out of slang, like you. When they reach your age, and get political private secretaryships and things of that sort, they drop slang and get their formulas out of the Spectator or The Times. You had better confine yourself to The Times. You will find that there is a certain amount of tosh about The Times; but at least its language is reputable.

LOMAX (*overwhelmed*) You are so awfully strong-minded, Lady Brit—

LADY BRITOMART Rubbish! (MORRISON *comes in.*) What is it?

MORRISON If you please, my lady, Mr Undershaft has just drove up to the door.

LADY BRITOMART Well, let him in (MORRISON *hesitates.*) Whats the matter with you?

MORRISON Shall I announce him, my lady; or is he at home here, so to speak, my lady?

LADY BRITOMART Announce him.

MORRISON Thank you, my lady. You wont mind my asking, I hope. The occasion is in a manner of speaking new to me.

LADY BRITOMART Quite right. Go and let him in.

MORRISON Thank you, my lady. (*He withdraws.*)

LADY BRITOMART Children: go and get ready. (SARAH *and* BARBARA *go upstairs for their out-of-door wraps.*) Charles: go and tell Stephen to come down here in five minutes: you will find him in

the drawing room. (CHARLES *goes.*) Adolphus: tell them to send round the carriage in about fifteen minutes. (ADOLPHUS *goes.*)
MORRISON (*at the door*) Mr Undershaft.

UNDERSHAFT *comes in.* MORRISON *goes out.*

UNDERSHAFT Alone! How fortunate!

LADY BRITOMART (*rising*) Dont be sentimental, Andrew. Sit down. (*She sits on the settee: he sits beside her, on her left. She comes to the point before he has time to breath.*) Sarah must have £800 a year until Charles Lomax comes into his property. Barbara will need more, and need it permanently, because Adolphus hasnt any property.

UNDERSHAFT (*resignedly*) Yes, my dear: I will see to it. Anything else? for yourself, for instance?

LADY BRITOMART I want to talk to you about Stephen.

UNDERSHAFT (*rather wearily*) Dont, my dear. Stephen doesnt interest me.

LADY BRITOMART He does interest me. He is our son.

UNDERSHAFT Do you really think so? He has induced us to bring him into the world; but he chose his parents very incongruously, I think. I see nothing of myself in him, and less of you.

LADY BRITOMART Andrew: Stephen is an excellent son, and a most steady, capable, highminded young man. You are simply trying to find an excuse for disinheriting him.

UNDERSHAFT My dear Biddy: the Undershaft tradition disinherits him. It would be dishonest of me to leave the cannon foundry to my son.

LADY BRITOMART It would be most unnatural and improper of you to leave it to anyone else, Andrew. Do you suppose this wicked and immoral tradition can be kept up for ever? Do you pretend that Stephen could not carry on the foundry just as well as all the other sons of the big business houses?

UNDERSHAFT Yes: he could learn the office routine without understanding the business, like all the other sons; and the firm would go by its own momentum until the real Undershaft—probably an Italian or a German—would invent a new method and cut him out.

LADY BRITOMART There is nothing that any Italian or German could do that Stephen could not do. And Stephen at least has breeding.

UNDERSHAFT The son of a foundling! Nonsense!

LADY BRITOMART My son, Andrew! And even you may have good blood in your veins for all you know.

UNDERSHAFT   True. Probably I have. That is another argument in favour of a foundling.

LADY BRITOMART   Andrew: dont be aggravating. And dont be wicked. At present you are both.

UNDERSHAFT   This conversation is part of the Undershaft tradition, Biddy. Every Undershaft's wife has treated him to it ever since the house was founded. It is mere waste of breath. If the tradition be ever broken it will be for an abler man than Stephen.

LADY BRITOMART (*pouting*)   Then go away.

UNDERSHAFT (*deprecatory*)   Go away!

LADY BRITOMART   Yes: go away. If you will do nothing for Stephen, you are not wanted here. Go to your foundling, whoever he is; and look after him.

UNDERSHAFT   The fact is, Biddy—

LADY BRITOMART   Dont call me Biddy. I dont call you Andy.

UNDERSHAFT   I will not call my wife Britomart: it is not good sense. Seriously, my love, the Undershaft tradition has landed me in a difficulty. I am getting on in years; and my partner Lazarus has at last made a stand and insisted that the succession must be settled one way or the other; and of course he is quite right. You see, I havent found a fit successor yet.

LADY BRITOMART (*obstinately*)   There is Stephen.

UNDERSHAFT   Thats just it: all the foundlings I can find are exactly like Stephen.

LADY BRITOMART   Andrew!!

UNDERSHAFT   I want a man with no relations and no schooling: that is, a man who would be out of the running altogether if he were not a strong man. And I cant find him. Every blessed foundling nowadays is snapped up in his infancy by Barnardo homes, or School Board officers, or Boards of Guardians; and if he shews the least ability he is fastened on by schoolmasters; trained to win scholarships like a racehorse; crammed with secondhand ideas; drilled and disciplined in docility and what they call good taste; and lamed for life so that he is fit for nothing but teaching. If you want to keep the foundry in the family, you had better find an eligible foundling and marry him to Barbara.

LADY BRITOMART   Ah! Barbara! Your Pet! You would sacrifice Stephen to Barbara.

UNDERSHAFT   Cheerfully. And you, my dear, would boil Barbara to make soup for Stephen.

LADY BRITOMART   Andrew: this is not a question of our likings and dislikings: it is a question of duty. It is your duty to make Stephen your successor.

UNDERSHAFT   Just as much as it is your duty to submit to your husband. Come, Biddy! these tricks of the governing class are of no use with me. I am one of the governing class myself; and it is waste of time giving tracts to a missionary. I have the power in this matter; and I am not to be hum-bugged into using it for your purposes.

LADY BRITOMART Andrew: you can talk my head off; but you cant change wrong into right. And your tie is all on one side. Put it straight.

UNDERSHAFT (*disconcerted*) It won't stay unless it's pinned (*he fumbles at it with childish grimaces*)—

STEPHEN *comes in.*

STEPHEN (*at the door*) I beg your pardon (*about to retire*).

LADY BRITOMART No: come in, Stephen. (*Stephen comes forward to his mother's writing table.*)

UNDERSHAFT (*not very cordially*) Good afternoon.

STEPHEN (*Coldly*) Good afternoon.

UNDERSHAFT (*to* LADY BRITOMART) He knows all about the tradition, I suppose?

LADY BRITOMART Yes. (*To* STEPHEN.) It is what I told you last night, Stephen.

UNDERSHAFT (*sulkily*) I understand you want to come into the cannon business.

STEPHEN *I* go into trade! Certainly not.

UNDERSHAFT (*opening his eyes, greatly eased in mind and manner*) Oh! in that case—

LADY BRITOMART Cannons are not trade, Stephen. They are enterprise.

STEPHEN I have no intention of becoming a man of business in any sense. I have no capacity for business and no taste for it. I intend to devote myself to politics.

UNDERSHAFT (*rising*) My dear boy: this is an immense relief to me. And I trust it may prove an equally good thing for the country. I was afraid you would consider yourself disparaged and slighted. (*He moves towards* STEPHEN *as if to shake hands with him.*)

LADY BRITOMART (*rising and interposing*) Stephen: I cannot allow you to throw away an enormous property like this.

STEPHEN (*stiffly*) Mother: there must be an end of treating me as a child, if you please. (LADY BRITOMART *recoils, deeply wounded by his tone.*) Until last night I did not take your attitude seriously, because I did not think you meant it seriously. But I find now that you left me in the dark as to matters which you should have explained to me years ago. I am extremely hurt and offended. Any further discussion of my intentions had better take place with my father, as between one man and another.

LADY BRITOMART Stephen! (*She sits down again, her eyes filling with tears.*)

UNDERSHAFT (*with grave compassion*) You see, my dear, it is only the big men who can be treated as children.

STEPHEN I am sorry, mother, that you have forced me—

UNDERSHAFT (*stopping him*) Yes, yes, yes, yes: thats all right, Stephen. She wont interfere with you any more: your independence is achieved: you have won your latchkey. Dont rub it in; and above all, dont apologize. (*He resumes his seat.*) Now what about your future, as between one man and another—I beg your pardon, Biddy: as between two men and a woman.

LADY BRITOMART (*who has pulled herself together strongly*) I quite understand, Stephen. By all means go your own way if you feel strong enough. (STEPHEN *sits down magisterially in the chair at the writing table with an air of affirming his majority.*)

UNDERSHAFT It is settled that you do not ask for the succession to the cannon business.

STEPHEN I hope it is settled that I repudiate the cannon business.

UNDERSHAFT Come, come! dont be so devilishly sulky: it's boyish. Freedom should be generous. Besides, I owe you a fair start in life in exchange for disinheriting you. You cant become prime minister all at once. Havent you a turn for something? What about literature, art, and so forth?

STEPHEN I have nothing of the artist about me, either in faculty or character, thank Heaven!

UNDERSHAFT A philosopher, perhaps? Eh?

STEPHEN I make no such ridiculous pretension.

UNDERSHAFT Just so. Well, there is the army, the navy, the Church, the Bar. The Bar requires some ability. What about the Bar?

STEPHEN I have not studied law. And I am afraid I have not the necessary push—I believe that is the name barristers give to their vulgarity—for success in pleading.

UNDERSHAFT Rather a difficult case, Stephen. Hardly anything left but the stage, is there? (STEPHEN *makes an impatient movement.*) Well, come! is there anything you know or care for?

STEPHEN (*rising and looking at him steadily*) I know the difference between right and wrong.

UNDERSHAFT (*hugely tickled*) You dont say so! What! no capacity for business, no knowledge of law, no sympathy with art, no pretension to philosophy; only a simple knowledge of the secret that has puzzled all the philosophers, baffled all the lawyers, muddled all the men of business, and ruined most of the artists: the secret of right and wrong. Why, man, youre a genius, a master of masters, a god! At twenty-four, too!

STEPHEN (*keeping his temper with difficulty*) You are pleased to be facetious. I pretend to nothing more than any honorable English gentleman claims as his birthright (*he sits down angrily*).

UNDERSHAFT Oh, thats everybody's birthright. Look at poor little Jenny Hill, the Salvation lassie! she would think you were laughing at her if you asked her to stand up in the street and teach grammar or geography or mathematics or even drawing room dancing; but it never occurs to her to doubt that she can teach morals and religion. You are all alike, you respectable people. You cant tell me the bursting strain of a ten-inch gun, which is a very simple matter; but you all think you can tell me the bursting strain of a man under temptation. You darent handle high explosives; but youre all ready to handle honesty and truth and justice and the whole duty of man, and kill one another at that game. What a country! What a world!

LADY BRITOMART (*uneasily*) What do you think he had better do, Andrew?

UNDERSHAFT Oh, just what he wants to do. He knows nothing and he thinks he knows everything. That points clearly to a political career. Get him a private secretaryship to someone who can get him an Under Secretaryship; and then leave him alone. He will find his natural and proper place in the end on the Treasury Bench.

STEPHEN (*springing up again*) I am sorry, sir, that you force me to forget the respect due to you as my father. I am an Englishman and I will not hear the Government of my country insulted. (*He thrusts his hands in his pockets, and walks angrily across to the window.*)

UNDERSHAFT (*with a touch of brutality*) The government of your country! *I* am the government of your country: I, and Lazarus. Do you suppose that you and half a dozen amateurs like you, sitting in a row in that foolish gabble shop, can govern Undershaft and Lazarus? No, my friend: you will do what pays us. You will make war when it suits us, and keep peace when it doesnt. You will find out that trade requires certain measures when we have decided on those measures. When I want anything to keep my dividends up, you will discover that my want is a national need. When other people want something to keep my dividends down, you will call out the police and military. And in return you shall have the support and applause of my newspapers, and the delight of imagining that you are a great statesman. Government of your country! Be off with you, my boy, and play with your caucuses and leading articles and historic parties and great leaders and burning questions and the rest of your toys. *I* am going back to my counting-house to pay the piper and call the tune.

STEPHEN (*actually smiling, and putting his hand on his father's shoulder with indulgent patronage*) Really, my dear father, it is impossible to be angry with you. You dont know how absurd all this sounds to me. You are very properly proud of having been industrious enough to make money; and it is greatly to your credit that you have made so much of it. But it has kept you in circles where you are valued for your money and deferred to for it, instead of in the doubtless very old-fashioned and behind-the-times public school and university where I formed my habits of mind. It is natural for you to think that money governs England; but you must allow me to think I know better.

UNDERSHAFT And what does govern England, pray?

STEPHEN Character, father, character.

UNDERSHAFT Whose character? Yours or mine?

STEPHEN Neither yours nor mine, father, but the best elements in the English national character.

UNDERSHAFT Stephen: Ive found your profession for you. Youre a born journalist. I'll start you with a high-toned weekly review. There!

Before STEPHEN *can reply* SARAH, BARBARA, LOMAX, *and* CUSINS *come in ready for walking.* BARBARA *crosses the room to the window and looks out.* CUSINS *drifts amiably to the armchair.* LOMAX *remains near the door, whilst* SARAH *comes to her mother.*

STEPHEN *goes to the smaller writing table and busies himself with his letters.*

SARAH Go and get ready, mamma: the carriage is waiting. (LADY BRITOMART *leaves the room.*)

UNDERSHAFT (*to* SARAH) Good day, my dear. Good afternoon, Mr Lomax.

LOMAX (*vaguely*) Ahdedoo.

UNDERSHAFT (*to* CUSINS) Quite well after last night, Euripides, eh?

CUSINS As well as can be expected.

UNDERSHAFT Thats right. (*To* BARBARA.) So you are coming to see my death and devastation factory, Barbara?

BARBARA (*at the window*) You came yesterday to see my salvation factory. I promised you a return visit.

LOMAX (*coming forward between* SARAH *and* UNDERSHAFT) Youll find it awfully interesting. Ive been through the Woolwich Arsenal and it gives you a ripping feeling of security, you know, to think of the lot of beggars we could kill if it came to fighting. (*To* UNDERSHAFT, *with sudden solemnity.*) Still, it must be rather an awful reflection for you, from the religious point of view as it were. Youre getting on, you know, and all that.

SARAH   You dont mind Cholly's imbecility, papa, do you?

LOMAX (*much taken aback*)   Oh I say!

UNDERSHAFT   Mr Lomax looks at the matter in a very proper spirit, my dear.

LOMAX   Just so. Thats all I meant, I assure you.

SARAH   Are you coming, Stephen?

STEPHEN   Well, I am rather busy—er—(*Magnanimously.*) Oh well, yes: I'll come. That is, if there is room for me.

UNDERSHAFT   I can take two with me in a little motor I am experimenting with for field use. You wont mind its being rather unfashionable. It's not painted yet; but it's bullet proof.

LOMAX (*appalled at the prospect of confronting Wilton Crescent in an unpainted motor*)   Oh I say!

SARAH   The carriage for me, thank you. Barbara doesnt mind what she's seen in.

LOMAX   I say, Dolly, old chap: do you really mind the car being a guy? Because of course if you do I'll go in it. Still—

CUSINS   I prefer it.

LOMAX   Thanks awfully, old man. Come, my ownest. (*He hurries out to secure his seat in the carriage.* SARAH *follows him.*)

CUSINS (*moodily walking across to* LADY BRITOMART's *writing table*)   Why are we two coming to this Works Department of Hell? that is what I ask myself.

BARBARA   I have always thought of it as a sort of pit where lost creatures with blackened faces stirred up smoky fires and were driven and tormented by my father. Is it like that, dad?

UNDERSHAFT (*scandalized*)   My dear! It is a spotlessly clean and beautiful hillside town.

CUSINS   With a Methodist chapel? Oh do say theres a Methodist chapel.

UNDERSHAFT   There are two: a Primitive one and a sophisticated one. There is even an Ethical Society; but it is not much patronized, as my men are all strongly religious. In the High Explosives Sheds they object to the presence of Agnostics as unsafe.

CUSINS   And yet they dont object to you!

BARBARA   Do they obey all your orders?

UNDERSHAFT   I never give them any orders. When I speak to one of them it is "Well, Jones, is the baby doing well? and has Mrs

Jones made a good recovery?" "Nicely, thank you, sir." And thats all.

CUSINS   But Jones has to be kept in order. How do you maintain discipline among your men?

UNDERSHAFT   I dont. They do. You see, the one thing Jones wont stand is any rebellion from the man under him, or any assertion of social equality between the wife of the man with 4 shillings a week less than himself, and Mrs Jones! Of course they all rebel against me, theoretically. Practically, every man of them keeps the man just below him in his place. I never meddle with them. I never bully them. I dont even bully Lazarus. I say that certain things are to be done; but I dont order anybody to do them. I dont say, mind you, that there is no ordering about and snubbing and even bullying. The men snub the boys and order them about; the carmen snub the sweepers; the artisans snub the unskilled laborers; the foremen drive and bully both the laborers and artisans; the assistant engineers find fault with the foremen; the chief engineers drop on the assistants; the departmental managers worry the chiefs; and the clerks have tall hats and hymnbooks and keep up the social tone by refusing to associate on equal terms with anybody. The result is a colossal profit, which comes to me.

CUSINS   (*revolted*)   You really are a—well, what I was saying yesterday.

BARBARA   What was he saying yesterday?

UNDERSHAFT   Never mind, my dear. He thinks I have made you unhappy. Have I?

BARBARA   Do you think I can be happy in this vulgar silly dress? I! who have worn the uniform. Do you understand what you have done to me? Yesterday I had a man's soul in my hand. I set him in the way of life with his face to salvation. But when we took your money he turned back to drunkenness and derision. (*With intense conviction.*) I will never forgive you that. If I had a child, and you destroyed its body with your explosives—if you murdered Dolly with your horrible guns—I could forgive you if my forgiveness would open the gates of heaven to you. But to take a human soul from me, and turn it into the soul of a wolf! that is worse than any murder.

UNDERSHAFT   Does my daughter despair so easily? Can you strike a man to the heart and leave no mark on him?

BARBARA   (*her face lighting up*)   Oh, you are right: he can never be lost now: where was my faith?

CUSINS   Oh, clever clever devil!

BARBARA   You may be a devil; but God speaks through you sometimes. (*She takes her father's hands and kisses them.*) You have given me back my happiness: I feel it deep down now, though my spirit is troubled.

UNDERSHAFT You have learnt something. That always feels at first as if you had lost something.

BARBARA Well, take me to the factory of death; and let me learn something more. There must be some truth or other behind all this frightful irony. Come, Dolly. (*She goes out.*)

CUSINS My guardian angel! (*To* UNDERSHAFT.) Avaunt! (*He follows* BARBARA.)

STEPHEN (*quietly, at the writing table*) You must not mind Cusins, father. He is a very amiable good fellow; but he is a Greek scholar and naturally a little eccentric.

UNDERSHAFT Ah, quite so. Thank you, Stephen. Thank you. (*He goes out.*)

STEPHEN *smiles patronizingly; buttons his coat responsibly; and crosses the room to the door.* LADY BRITOMART, *dressed for out-of-doors, opens it before he reaches it. She looks round for the others; looks at* STEPHEN *and turns to go without a word.*

STEPHEN (*embarrassed*) Mother—

LADY BRITOMART Dont be apologetic, Stephen. And dont forget that you have outgrown your mother. (*She goes out.*)

Perivale St Andrews lies between two Middlesex hills, half climbing the northern one. It is an almost smokeless town of white walls, roofs of narrow green slates or red tiles, tall trees, domes, campaniles, and slender chimney shafts, beautifully situated and beautiful in itself. The best view of it is obtained from the crest of a slope about half a mile to the east, where the high explosives are dealt with. The foundry lies hidden in the depths between, the tops of its chimneys sprouting like huge skittles into the middle distance. Across the crest runs an emplacement of concrete, with a firestep, and a parapet which suggests a fortification, because there is a huge cannon of the obsolete Woolwich Infant pattern peering across it at the town. The cannon is mounted on an experimental gun carriage: possibly the original model of the UNDERSHAFT *disappearing rampart gun alluded to by* STEPHEN. *The firestep, being a convenient place to sit, is furnished here and there with straw disc cushions; and at one place there is the additional luxury of a fur rug.*

BARBARA *is standing on the firestep, looking over the parapet towards the town. On her right is the cannon; on her left the end of a shed raised on piles, with a ladder of three or four steps up to the door, which opens outwards and has a little wooden landing at the threshold, with a fire bucket in the corner of the landing. Several dummy soldiers more or less mutilated, with straw protruding from their gashes, have been shoved out of the way under the landing. A few others are nearly upright against the shed; and one has fallen forward and lies, like a grotesque corpse, on the emplacement. The parapet stops short of the shed, leaving a gap which is the beginning of the path down the hill through the foundry to the town. The rug is on the firestep near this gap. Down on the emplacement behind the cannon is a trolley carrying a huge conical bombshell with a red band painted on it. Further to the right is the door of an office, which, like the sheds, is of the lightest possible construction.*

Cusins arrives by the path from the town.

BARBARA Well?

CUSINS Not a ray of hope. Everything perfect! wonderful! real! It only needs a cathedral to be a heavenly city instead of a hellish one.

BARBARA Have you found out whether they have done anything for old Peter Shirley?

CUSINS They have found him a job as gatekeeper and timekeeper. He's frightfully miserable. He calls the time-keeping brainwork, and says he isnt used to it; and his gate lodge is so splendid that he's ashamed to use the rooms, and skulks in the scullery.

BARBARA Poor Peter!

Stephen arrives from the town. He carries a fieldglass.

STEPHEN *(enthusiastically)* Have you two seen the place? Why did you leave us?

CUSINS I wanted to see everything I was not intended to see; and Barbara wanted to make the men talk.

STEPHEN Have you found anything discreditable?

CUSINS No. They call him Dandy Andy and are proud of his being a cunning old rascal; but it's all horribly, frightfully, immorally, unanswerably perfect.

Sarah arrives.

SARAH Heavens! what a place! *(She crosses to the trolley.)* Did you see the nursing home? *(She sits down on the shell.)*

STEPHEN Did you see the libraries and schools?

SARAH Did you see the ball room and the banqueting chamber in the Town Hall!?

STEPHEN Have you gone into the insurance fund, the pension fund, the building society, the various applications of cooperation!?

Undershaft comes from the office, with a sheaf of telegrams in his hand.

UNDERSHAFT Well, have you seen everything? I'm sorry I was called away. *(Indicating the telegrams.)* Good news from Manchuria.

STEPHEN   Another Japanese victory?

UNDERSHAFT   Oh, I dont know. Which side wins does not concern us here. No: the good news is that the aerial battleship is a tremendous success. At the first trial it has wiped out a fort with three hundred soldiers in it.

CUSINS (*from the platform*)   Dummy soldiers?

UNDERSHAFT (*striding across to* STEPHEN *and kicking the prostrate dummy brutally out of his way*)   No: the real thing.

CUSINS *and* BARBARA *exchange glances. Then* CUSINS *sits on the step and buries his face in his hands.* BARBARA *gravely lays her hand on his shoulder. He looks up at her in whimsical desperation.*

UNDERSHAFT   Well, Stephen, what do you think of the place?

STEPHEN   Oh, magnificent. A perfect triumph of modern industry. Frankly, my dear father, I have been a fool: I had no idea of what it all meant: of the wonderful forethought, the power of organization, the administrative capacity, the financial genius, the colossal capital it represents. I have been repeating to myself as I came through your streets "Peace hath her victories no less renowned than War." I have only one misgiving about it all.

UNDERSHAFT   Out with it.

STEPHEN   Well, I cannot help thinking that all this provision for every want of your workmen may sap their independence and weaken their sense of responsibility. And greatly as we enjoyed our tea at that splendid restaurant—how they gave us all that luxury and cake and jam and cream for threepence I really cannot imagine!—still you must remember that restaurants break up home life. Look at the continent, for instance! Are you sure so much pampering is really good for the men's characters?

UNDERSHAFT   Well you see, my dear boy, when you are organizing civilization you have to make up your mind whether trouble and anxiety are good things or not. If you decide that they are, then, I take it, you simply dont organize civilization; and there you are, with trouble and anxiety enough to make us all angels! But if you decide the other way, you may as well go through with it. However, Stephen, our characters are safe here. A sufficient dose of anxiety is always provided by the fact that we may be blown to smithereens at any moment.

SARAH   By the way, papa, where do you make the explosives?

UNDERSHAFT   In separate little sheds like that one. When one of them blows up, it costs very little, and only the people quite close to it are killed.

STEPHEN, *who is quite close to it, looks at it rather scaredly, and moves away quickly to the cannon. At the same moment the door of the shed is thrown abruptly open; and a foreman in overalls and list slippers comes out on the little landing and holds the door for* LOMAX, *who appears in the doorway.*

LOMAX (*with studied coolness*) My good fellow: you neednt get into a state of nerves. Nothing's going to happen to you; and I suppose it wouldnt be the end of the world if anything did. A little bit of British pluck is what you want, old chap. (*He descends and strolls across to* SARAH.)

UNDERSHAFT (*to the foreman*) Anything wrong, Bilton?

BILTON (*with ironic calm*) Gentleman walked into the high explosives shed and lit a cigaret, sir: thats all.

UNDERSHAFT Ah, quite so. (*Going over to* LOMAX.) Do you happen to remember what you did with the match?

LOMAX Oh come! I'm not a fool. I took jolly good care to blow it out before I chucked it away.

BILTON The top of it was red hot inside, sir.

LOMAX Well, suppose it was! I didnt chuck it into any of your messes.

UNDERSHAFT Think no more of it, Mr. Lomax. By the way, would you mind lending me your matches.

LOMAX (*offering his box*) Certainly.

UNDERSHAFT Thanks. (*He pockets the matches.*)

LOMAX (*lecturing to the company generally*) You know, these high explosives dont go off like gunpowder, except when theyre in a gun. When theyre spread loose, you can put a match to them without the least risk: they just burn quietly like a bit of paper. (*Warming to the scientific interest of the subject.*) Did you know that, Undershaft? Have you ever tried?

UNDERSHAFT Not on a large scale, Mr Lomax. Bilton will give you a sample of guncotton when you are leaving if you ask him. You can experiment with it at home. (BILTON *looks puzzled.*)

SARAH Bilton will do nothing of the sort, papa. I suppose it's your business to blow up the Russians and Japs; but you might really stop short of blowing up poor Cholly. (BILTON *gives it up and retires into the shed.*)

LOMAX My ownest, there is no danger. (*He sits beside her on the shell.*)

LADY BRITOMART *arrives from the town with a bouquet.*

LADY BRITOMART (*impetuously*) Andrew: you shouldnt have let me see this place.

UNDERSHAFT Why, my dear?

LADY BRITOMART   Never mind why: you shouldnt have: thats all. To think of all that (*indicating the town*) being yours! and that you have kept it to yourself all these years!

UNDERSHAFT   It does not belong to me. I belong to it. It is the Undershaft inheritance.

LADY BRITOMART   It is not. Your ridiculous cannons and that noisy banking foundry may be the Undershaft inheritance; but all that plate and linen, all that furniture and those houses and orchards and gardens belong to us. They belong to me: they are not a man's business. I wont give them up. You must be out of your senses to throw them all away; and if you persist in such folly, I will call in a doctor.

UNDERSHAFT   (*stooping to smell the bouquet*)   Where did you get the flowers, my dear?

LADY BRITOMART   Your men presented them to me in your William Morris Labor Church.

CUSINS   Oh! It needed only that. A Labor Church! (*He mounts the firestep distractedly, and leans with his elbows on the parapet, turning his back to them.*)

LADY BRITOMART   Yes, with Morris's words in mosaic letters ten feet high around the dome. NO MAN IS GOOD ENOUGH TO BE ANOTHER MAN'S MASTER. The cynicism of it!

UNDERSHAFT   It shocked the men at first, I am afraid. But now they take no more notice of it than of the ten commandments in church.

LADY BRITOMART   Andrew: you are trying to put me off the subject of the inheritance by profane jokes. Well, you shant. I dont ask it any longer for Stephen: he has inherited far too much of your perversity to be fit for it. But Barbara has rights as well as Stephen. Why should not Adolphus succeed to the inheritance? I could manage the town for him and he can look after the cannons, if they are really necessary.

UNDERSHAFT   I should ask nothing better if Adophus were a foundling. He is exactly the sort of new blood that is wanted in English business. But he's not a foundling; and theres an end of it. (*He makes for the office door.*)

CUSINS   (*turning to them*)   Not quite. (*They all turn and stare at him.*) I think—Mind! I am not committing myself in any way as to my future course—but I think the foundling difficulty can be got over. (*He jumps down to the emplacement.*)

UNDERSHAFT   (*coming back to him*)   What do you mean?

CUSINS   Well, I have something to say which is in the nature of a confession.

SARAH
LADY BRITOMART
BARBARA   } Confession!
STEPHEN

LOMAX Oh I say!

CUSINS Yes, a confession. Listen, all. Until I met Barbara I thought myself in the main an honorable, truthful man, because I wanted the approval of my conscience more than I wanted anything else. But the moment I saw Barbara, I wanted her far more than the approval of my conscience.

LADY BRITOMART Adolphus!

CUSINS It is true. You accused me yourself, Lady Brit, of joining the Army to worship Barbara; and so I did. She bought my soul like a flower at a street corner; but she bought it for herself.

UNDERSHAFT What! Not for Dionysos or another?

CUSINS Dionysos and all the others are in herself. I adored what was divine in her, and was therefore a true worshipper. But I was romantic about her too. I thought she was a woman of the people, and that a marriage with a professor of Greek would be far beyond the wildest social ambitions of her rank.

LADY BRITOMART Adolphus!!

LOMAX Oh I say!!!

CUSINS When I learnt the horrible truth—

LADY BRITOMART What do you mean by the horrible truth, pray?

CUSINS That she was enormously rich; that her grandfather was an earl; that her father was the Prince of Darkness—

UNDERSHAFT Chut!

CUSINS —and that I was only an adventurer trying to catch a rich wife, then I stooped to deceive her about my birth.

BARBARA (*rising*) Dolly!

LADY BRITOMART Your birth! Now Adolphus, dont dare to make up a wicked story for the sake of these wretched cannons. Remember: I have seen photographs of your parents; and the Agent General for South Western Australia knows them personally and has assured me that they are most respectable married people.

CUSINS So they are in Australia; but here they are outcasts. Their marriage is legal in Australia, but not in England. My mother is my father's deceased wife's sister; and in this island I am consequently a foundling. (*Sensation.*)

BARBARA Silly! (*She climbs to the cannon, and leans, listening, in the angle it makes with the parapet.*)

CUSINS Is the subterfuge good enough, Machiavelli?

UNDERSHAFT (*thoughtfully*) Biddy: this may be a way out of the difficulty.

LADY BRITOMART   Stuff! A man cant make cannons any the better for being his own cousin instead of his proper self (*she sits down on the rug with a bounce that expresses her downright contempt for their casuistry*).

UNDERSHAFT   (*to* CUSINS)   You are an educated man. That is against the tradition.

CUSINS   Once in ten thousand times it happens that the schoolboy is a born master of what they try to teach him. Greek has not destroyed my mind: it has nourished it. Besides, I did not learn it at an English public school.

UNDERSHAFT   Hm! Well, I cannot afford to be too particular: you have cornered the foundling market. Let it pass. You are eligible, Euripides: you are eligible.

BARBARA   Dolly: yesterday morning, when Stephen told us all about the tradition, you became very silent, and you have been strange and excited ever since. Were you thinking of your birth then?

CUSINS   When the finger of Destiny suddenly points at a man in the middle of his breakfast, it makes him thoughtful.

UNDERSHAFT   Aha! You have had your eye on the business, my young friend, have you?

CUSINS   Take care! There is an abyss of moral horror between me and your accursed aerial battleships.

UNDERSHAFT   Never mind the abyss for the present. Let us settle the practical details and leave your final decision open. You know that you will have to change your name. Do you object to that?

CUSINS   Would any man named Adolphus—any man called Dolly! —object to be called something else?

UNDERSHAFT   Good. Now, as to money! I propose to treat you handsomely from the beginning. You shall start at a thousand a year.

CUSINS   (*with sudden heat, his spectacles twinkling with mischief*) A thousand! You dare offer a miserable thousand to the son-in-law of a millionaire! No, by Heavens, Machiavelli! you shall not cheat me. You cannot do without me; and I can do without you. I must have two thousand five hundred a year for two years. At the end of that time, if I am a failure, I go. But if I am a success, and stay on, you must give me the other five thousand.

UNDERSHAFT   What other five thousand?

CUSINS   To make the two years up to five thousand a year. The two thousand five hundred is only half pay in case I should turn out a failure. The third year I must have ten per cent on the profits.

UNDERSHAFT   (*taken aback*)   Ten per cent! Why, man, do you know what my profits are?

CUSINS   Enormous, I hope: otherwise I shall require twenty-five per cent.

UNDERSHAFT   But, Mr Cusins, this is a serious matter of business. You are not bringing any capital into the concern.

CUSINS   What! no capital! Is my mastery of Greek no capital? Is my access to the subtlest thought, the loftiest poetry yet attained by humanity, no capital? My character! my intellect! my life! my career! what Barbara calls my soul! are these no capital? Say another word; and I double my salary.

UNDERSHAFT   Be reasonable—

CUSINS   (*peremptorily*)   Mr Undershaft: you have my terms. Take them or leave them.

UNDERSHAFT   (*recovering himself*)   Very well, I note your terms; and I offer you half.

CUSINS   (*disgusted*)   Half!

UNDERSHAFT   (*firmly*)   Half.

CUSINS   You call yourself a gentleman; and you offer me half!!

UNDERSHAFT   I do not call myself a gentleman; but I offer you half.

CUSINS   This to your future partner! your successor! your son-in-law!

BARBARA   You are selling your own soul, Dolly, not mine. Leave me out of the bargain, please.

UNDERSHAFT   Come! I will go a step further for Barbara's sake. I will give you three fifths; but that is my last word.

CUSINS   Done!

LOMAX   Done in the eye! Why, *I* get only eight hundred, you know.

CUSINS   By the way, Mac, I am a classical scholar not an arithmetical one. Is three fifths more than half or less?

UNDERSHAFT   More, of course.

CUSINS   I would have taken two hundred and fifty. How you can succeed in business when you are willing to pay all that money to a University don who is obviously not worth a junior clerk's wages!—well! What will Lazarus say?

UNDERSHAFT   Lazarus is a gentle romantic Jew who cares for nothing but string quartets and stalls at fashionable theatres. He will be blamed for your rapacity in money matters, poor fellow! as he has hitherto been blamed for mine. You are a shark of the first order, Euripides. So much the better for the firm!

BARBARA   Is the bargain closed, Dolly? Does your soul belong to him now?

CUSINS   No: the price is settled: that is all. The real tug of war is still to come. What about the moral question?

LADY BRITOMART   There is no moral question in the matter at all, Adolphus. You must simply sell cannons and weapons to people whose cause is right and just, and refuse them to foreigners and criminals.

UNDERSHAFT (*determinedly*) No: none of that. You must keep the true faith of an Armorer, or you dont come in here.

CUSINS What on earth is the true faith of an Armorer?

UNDERSHAFT To give arms to all men who offer an honest price for them, without respect of persons or principles: to aristocrat and republican, to Nihilist and Tsar, to Capitalist and Socialist, to Protestant and Catholic, to burglar and policeman, to black man, white man and yellow man, to all sorts and conditions, all nationalities, all faiths, all follies, all causes and all crimes. The first Undershaft wrote up in his shop IF GOD GAVE THE HAND, LET NOT MAN WITHHOLD THE SWORD. The second wrote up ALL HAVE THE RIGHT TO FIGHT: NONE HAVE THE RIGHT TO JUDGE. The third wrote up TO MAN THE WEAPON: TO HEAVEN THE VICTORY. The fourth had no literary turn; so he did not write up anything; but he sold cannons to Napoleon under the nose of George the Third. The fifth wrote up PEACE SHALL NOT PREVAIL SAVE WITH A SWORD IN HER HAND. The sixth, my master, was the best of all. He wrote up NOTHING IS EVER DONE IN THIS WORLD UNTIL MEN ARE PREPARED TO KILL ONE ANOTHER IF IT IS NOT DONE. After that, there was nothing left for the seventh to say. So he wrote up, simply, UNASHAMED.

CUSINS My good Machiavelli. I shall certainly write something up on the wall; only, as I shall write it in Greek, you wont be able to read it. But as to your Armorer's faith, if I take my neck out of the noose of my own morality I am not going to put it into the noose of yours. I shall sell cannons to whom I please and refuse them to whom I please. So there!

UNDERSHAFT From the moment when you become Andrew Undershaft, you will never do as you please again. Dont come here lusting for power, young man.

CUSINS If power were my aim I should not come here for it. You have no power.

UNDERSHAFT None of my own, certainly.

CUSINS I have more power than you, more will. You do not drive this place: it drives you. And what drives the place?

UNDERSHAFT (*enigmatically*) A will of which I am a part.

BARBARA (*startled*) Father! Do you know what you are saying; or are you laying a snare for my soul?

CUSINS Dont listen to his metaphysics, Barbara. The place is driven by the most rascally part of society, the money hunters, the pleasure hunters, the military promotion hunters; and he is their slave.

UNDERSHAFT Not necessarily. Remember the Armorer's Faith. I will take an order from a good man as cheerfully as from a bad one. If you good people prefer preaching and shirking to buying my weapons and fighting the rascals, dont blame me. I can make cannons: I cannot make courage and conviction. Bah! you tire me, Euripides, with your morality mongering. Ask Barbara: she understands. (*He suddenly reaches up and takes* BARBARA'*s hands, looking powerfully into her eyes.*) Tell him, my love, what power really means.

BARBARA (*hypnotized*) Before I joined the Salvation Army, I was in my own power and the consequence was that I never knew what to do with myself. When I joined it, I had not time enough for all the things I had to do.

UNDERSHAFT (*approvingly*) Just so. And why was that, do you suppose?

BARBARA Yesterday I should have said, because I was in the power of God. (*She resumes her self-possession, withdrawing her hands from his with a power equal to his own.*) But you came and shewed me that I was in the power of Bodger and Undershaft. Today I feel—oh! how can I put it into words? Sarah: do you remember the earthquake at Cannes, when we were little children?—how little the surprise of the first shock mattered compared to the dread and horror of waiting for the second? That is how I feel in this place today. I stood on the rock I thought eternal; and without a word of warning it reeled and crumbled under me. I was safe with an infinite wisdom watching me, an army marching to Salvation with me; and in a moment, at a stroke of your pen in a cheque book, I stood alone; and the heavens were empty. That was the first shock of the earthquake: I am waiting for the second.

UNDERSHAFT Come, come, my daughter! dont make too much of your little tinpot tragedy. What do we do here when we spend years of work and thought and thousands of pounds of solid cash on a new gun or an aerial battleship that turns out just a hairsbreadth wrong after all? Scrap it. Scrap it without wasting another hour or another pound on it. Well, you have made for yourself something that you call a morality or a religion or what not. It doesnt fit the facts. Well, scrap it. Scrap it and get one that does fit. That is what is wrong with the world at present. It scraps its obsolete steam engines and dynamos; but it wont scrap its old prejudices and its old moralities and its old religions and its old political constitutions. Whats the result? In machinery it does very well; but in morals and religion and politics it is working at a loss that brings it nearer bankruptcy every year. Dont persist in that folly. If your old religion broke down yesterday, get a newer and a better one for tomorrow.

BARBARA   Oh how gladly I would take a better one to my soul! But you offer me a worse one. (*Turning on him with sudden vehemence.*) Justify yourself: shew me some light through the darkness of this dreadful place, with its beautifully clean workshops, and respectable workmen, and model homes.

UNDERSHAFT   Cleanliness and respectability do not need justification, Barbara: they justify themselves. I see no darkness here, no dreadfulness. In your Salvation shelter I saw poverty, misery, cold and hunger. You gave them bread and treacle and dreams of heaven. I give from thirty shillings a week to twelve thousand a year. They find their own dreams but I look after the drainage.

BARBARA   And their souls?

UNDERSHAFT   I save their souls just as I saved yours.

BARBARA (*revolted*)   You saved my soul! What do you mean?

UNDERSHAFT   I fed you and clothed you and housed you. I took care that you should have money enough to live handsomely— more than enough; so that you could be wasteful, careless, generous. That saved your soul from the seven deadly sins.

BARBARA (*bewildered*)   The seven deadly sins!

UNDERSHAFT   Yes, the deadly seven. (*Counting on his fingers.*) Food, clothing, firing, rent, taxes, respectability and children. Nothing can lift those seven millstones from Man's neck but money and the spirit cannot soar until the millstones are lifted. I lifted them from your spirit. I enabled Barbara to become Major Barbara; and I saved her from the crime of poverty.

CUSINS   Do you call poverty a crime?

UNDERSHAFT   The worst of crimes. All the other crimes are virtues beside it: all the other dishonors are chivalry itself by comparison. Poverty blights whole cities; spreads horrible pestilences; strikes dead the very souls of all who come within sight, sound, or smell of it. What you call crime is nothing: a murder here and a theft there, a blow now and a curse then: what do they matter? they are only the accidents and illnesses of life: there are not fifty genuine professional criminals in London. But there are millions of poor people, abject people, dirty people, ill fed, ill clothed people. They poison us morally and physically: they kill the happiness of society: they force us to do away with our own liberties and to organize unnatural cruelties for fear they should rise against us and drag us down into their abyss. Only fools fear crime: we all fear poverty. Pah! (*turning on* BARBARA) you talk of your half-saved ruffian in West Ham: you accuse me of dragging his soul back to perdition. Well, bring him to me here; and

I will drag his soul back again to salvation for you. Not by words and dreams; but by thirty-eight shillings a week, a sound house in a handsome street and a permanent job. In three weeks he will have a fancy waistcoat; in three months a tall hat and a chapel sitting; before the end of the year he will shake hands with a duchess at a Primrose League meeting, and join the Conservative Party.

BARBARA   And will he be the better for that?

UNDERSHAFT   You know he will. Dont be a hypocrite, Barbara. He will be better fed, better housed, better clothed, better behaved; and his children will be pounds heavier and bigger. That will be better than an American cloth mattress in a shelter, chopping firewood, eating bread and treacle, and being forced to kneel down from time to time to thank heaven for it: knee drill, I think you call it. It is cheap work converting starving men with a Bible in one hand and a slice of bread in the other. I will undertake to convert West Ham to Mahometanism on the same terms. Try your hand on my men: their souls are hungry because their bodies are full.

BARBARA   And leave the east end to starve?

UNDERSHAFT   (*his energetic tone dropping into one of bitter and brooding remembrance*)   I was an east ender. I moralized and starved until one day I swore that I would be a full-fed free man at all costs; that nothing should stop me except a bullet, neither reason nor morals nor the lives of other men. I said "Thou shalt starve ere I starve"; and with that word I became free and great. I was a dangerous man until I had my will: now I am a useful, beneficent, kindly person. That is the history of most self-made millionaires, I fancy. When it is the history of every Englishman we shall have an England worth living in.

LADY BRITOMART   Stop making speeches, Andrew. This is not the place for them.

UNDERSHAFT   (*punctured*)   My dear: I have no other means of conveying my ideas.

LADY BRITOMART   Your ideas are nonsense. You got on because you were selfish and unscrupulous.

UNDERSHAFT   Not at all. I had the strongest scruples about poverty and starvation. Your moralists are quite unscrupulous about both: they make virtues of them. I had rather be a thief than a pauper. I had rather be a murderer than a slave. I dont want to be either; but if you force the alternative on me, then, by Heaven, I'll choose the braver and more moral one. I hate poverty and slavery worse than any other crimes whatsoever. And let me tell you this.

Poverty and slavery have stood up for centuries to your sermons and leading articles: they will not stand up to my machine guns. Dont preach at them: dont reason with them. Kill them.

BARBARA   Killing. Is that your remedy for everything?

UNDERSHAFT   It is the final test of conviction, the only lever strong enough to overturn a social system, the only way of saying Must. Let six hundred and seventy fools loose in the streets; and three policemen can scatter them. But huddle them together in a certain house in Westminster; and let them go through certain ceremonies and call themselves certain names until at last they get the courage to kill; and your six hundred and seventy fools become a government. Your pious mob fills up ballot papers and imagines it is governing its masters; but the ballot paper that really governs is the paper that has a bullet wrapped up in it.

CUSINS   That is perhaps why, like most intelligent people, I never vote.

UNDERSHAFT   Vote! Bah! When you vote, you only change the names of the cabinet. When you shoot, you pull down governments, inaugurate new epochs, abolish old orders and set up new. Is that historically true. Mr Learned Man, or is it not?

CUSINS   It is historically true. I loathe having to admit it. I repudiate your sentiments. I abhor your nature. I defy you in every possible way. Still, it is true. But it ought not to be true.

UNDERSHAFT   Ought! ought! ought! ought! ought! Are you going to spend your life saying ought, like the rest of our moralists? Turn your oughts into shalls, man. Come and make explosives with me. Whatever can blow men up can blow society up. The history of the world is the history of those who had courage enough to embrace this truth. Have you the courage to embrace it, Barbara?

LADY BRITOMART   Barbara: I positively forbid you to listen to your father's abominable wickedness. And you, Adolphus, ought to know better than to go about saying that wrong things are true. What does it matter whether they are true if they are wrong?

UNDERSHAFT   What does it matter whether they are wrong if they are true?

LADY BRITOMART (*rising*)   Children: come home instantly. Andrew: I am exceedingly sorry I allowed you to call on us. You are wickeder than ever. Come at once.

BARBARA (*shaking her head*)   It's no use running away from wicked people, mamma.

LADY BRITOMART   It is every use. It shews your disapprobation of them.

BARBARA   It does not save them.

LADY BRITOMART   I can see that you are going to disobey me. Sarah: are you coming home or are you not?

SARAH   I daresay it's very wicked of papa to make cannons; but I dont think I shall cut him on that account.

LOMAX (*pouring oil on the troubled waters*)   The fact is, you know, there is a certain amount of tosh about this notion of wickedness. It doesnt work. You must look at facts. Not that I would say a word in favor of anything wrong; but then, you see, all sorts of chaps are always doing all sorts of things; and we have to fit them in somehow, dont you know. What I mean is that you cant go cutting everybody; and thats about what it comes to. (*Their rapt attention to his eloquence makes him nervous.*) Perhaps I dont make myself clear.

LADY BRITOMART   You are lucidity itself, Charles. Because Andrew is successful and has plenty of money to give to Sarah, you will flatter him and encourage him in his wickedness.

LOMAX (*unruffled*)   Well, where the carcase is, there will the eagles be gathered, dont you know. (*To* UNDERSHAFT.) Eh? What?

UNDERSHAFT   Precisely. By the way, may I call you Charles?

LOMAX   Delighted. Cholly is the usual ticket.

UNDERSHAFT (*to* LADY BRITOMART)   Biddy—

LADY BRITOMART (*violently*)   Dont dare call me Biddy. Charles Lomax: you are a fool. Adolphus Cusins: you are a Jesuit. Stephen: you are a prig. Barbara: you are a lunatic. Andrew: you are a vulgar tradesman. Now you all know my opinion; and my conscience is clear, at all events (*she sits down with a vehemence that the rug fortunately softens*).

UNDERSHAFT   My dear: you are the incarnation of morality. (*She snorts.*) Your conscience is clear and your duty done when you have called everybody names. Come, Euripides! it is getting late; and we all want to get home. Make up your mind.

CUSINS   Understand this, you old demon—

LADY BRITOMART   Adolphus!

UNDERSHAFT   Let him alone, Biddy. Proceed, Euripides.

CUSINS   You have me in a horrible dilemma. I want Barbara.

UNDERSHAFT   Like all young men, you greatly exaggerate the difference between one young woman and another.

BARBARA   Quite true, Dolly.

CUSINS   I also want to avoid being a rascal.

UNDERSHAFT (*with biting contempt*)   You lust for personal righteousness, for self-approval, for what you call a good conscience, for what Barbara calls salvation, for what I call patronizing people who are not so lucky as yourself.

CUSINS   I do not: all the poet in me recoils from being a good man. But there are things in me that I must reckon with. Pity—

UNDERSHAFT   Pity! The scavenger of misery.

CUSINS   Well, love.

UNDERSHAFT   I know. You love the needy and the outcast: you love the oppressed races, the negro, the Indian ryot, the underdog everywhere. Do you love the Japanese? Do you love the French? Do you love the English?

CUSINS   No. Every true Englishman detests the English. We are the wickedest nation on earth; and our success is a moral horror.

UNDERSHAFT   That is what comes of your gospel of love, is it?

CUSINS   May I not love even my father-in-law?

UNDERSHAFT   Who wants your love, man? By what right do you take the liberty of offering it to me? I will have your due heed and respect, or I will kill you. But your love! Damn your impertinence!

CUSINS   (*grinning*)   I may not be able to control my affections, Mac.

UNDERSHAFT   You are fencing, Euripides. You are weakening: your grip is slipping. Come! try your last weapon. Pity and love have broken in your hand: forgiveness is still left.

CUSINS   No: forgiveness is a beggar's refuge. I am with you there: we must pay our debts.

UNDERSHAFT   Well said. Come! you will suit me. Remember the words of Plato.

CUSINS   (*starting*)   Plato! You dare quote Plato to me!

UNDERSHAFT   Plato says, my friend, that society cannot be saved until either the Professors of Greek take to making gunpowder, or else the makers of gunpowder become Professors of Greek.

CUSINS   Oh, tempter, cunning tempter!

UNDERSHAFT   Come! choose, man, choose.

CUSINS   But perhaps Barbara will not marry me if I make the wrong choice.

BARBARA   Perhaps not.

CUSINS   (*desperately perplexed*)   You hear!

BARBARA   Father: do you love nobody?

UNDERSHAFT   I love my best friend.

LADY BRITOMART   And who is that, pray?

UNDERSHAFT   My bravest enemy. That is the man who keeps me up to the mark.

CUSINS   You know, the creature is really a sort of poet in his way. Suppose he is a great man, after all!

UNDERSHAFT   Suppose you stop talking and make up your mind, my young friend.

CUSINS But you are driving me against my nature. I hate war.

UNDERSHAFT Hatred is the coward's revenge for being intimidated. Dare you make war on war? Here are the means: my friend Mr Lomax is sitting on them.

LOMAX (*springing up*) Oh I say! You dont mean that this thing is loaded, do you? My ownest: come off it.

SARAH (*sitting placidly on the shell*) If I am to be blown up, the more thoroughly it is done the better. Dont fuss, Cholly.

LOMAX (*to* UNDERSHAFT, *strongly remonstrant*) Your own daughter, you know!

UNDERSHAFT So I see. (*To* CUSINS.) Well, my friend, may we expect you here at six tomorrow morning?

CUSINS (*firmly*) Not on any account. I will see the whole establishment blown up with its own dynamite before I will get up at five. My hours are healthy, rational hours: eleven to five.

UNDERSHAFT Come when you please: before a week you will come at six and stay until I turn you out for the sake of your health. (*Calling.*) Bilton! (*He turns to* LADY BRITOMART, *who rises.*) My dear: let us leave these two young people to themselves for a moment. (BILTON *comes from the shed.*) I am going to take you through the guncotton shed.

BILTON (*barring the way*) You cant take anything explosive in here, sir.

LADY BRITOMART What do you mean? Are you alluding to me?

BILTON (*unmoved*) No, maam. Mr Undershaft has the other gentleman's matches in his pocket.

LADY BRITOMART (*abruptly*) Oh! I beg your pardon! (*She goes into the shed.*)

UNDERSHAFT Quite right, Bilton, quite right: here you are. (*He gives* BILTON *the box of matches.*) Come, Stephen. Come, Charles. Bring Sarah. (*He passes into the shed.*)

BILTON *opens the box and deliberately drops the matches into the fire-bucket.*

LOMAX Oh! I say. (BILTON *stolidly hands him the empty box.*) Infernal nonsense! Pure scientific ignorance! (*He goes in.*)

SARAH Am I all right, Bilton?

BILTON Youll have to put on list slippers, miss: thats all. Weve got em inside. (*She goes in.*)

STEPHEN (*very seriously to* CUSINS) Dolly, old fellow, think. Think before you decide. Do you feel that you are a sufficiently practical man? It is a huge undertaking, an enormous responsibility. All this mass of business will be Greek to you.

CUSINS Oh, I think it will be much less difficult than Greek.

STEPHEN Well, I just want to say this before I leave you to yourselves. Dont let anything I have said about right and wrong prejudice you against this great chance in life. I have satisfied myself that the business is one of the highest character and a credit to our country. (*Emotionally.*) I am very proud of my father. I— (*Unable to proceed, he presses* CUSINS' *hand and goes hastily into the shed, followed by* BILTON.)

BARBARA *and* CUSINS, *left alone together, look at one another silently.*

CUSINS Barbara: I am going to accept this offer.

BARBARA I thought you would.

CUSINS You understand, dont you, that I had to decide without consulting you. If I had thrown the burden of the choice on you, you would sooner or later have despised me for it.

BARBARA Yes: I did not want you to sell your soul for me any more than for this inheritance.

CUSINS It is not the sale of my soul that troubles me: I have sold it too often to care about that. I have sold it for a professorship. I have sold it for an income. I have sold it to escape being imprisoned for refusing to pay taxes for hangmen's ropes and unjust wars and things that I abhor. What is all human conduct but the daily and hourly sale of our souls for trifles? What I am now selling it for is neither money nor position nor comfort, but for reality and for power.

BARBARA You know that you will have no power, and that he has none.

CUSINS I know. It is not for myself alone. I want to make power for the world.

BARBARA I want to make power for the world too; but it must be spiritual power.

CUSINS I think all power is spiritual: these cannons will not go off by themselves. I have tried to make spiritual power by teaching Greek. But the world can never be really touched by a dead language and a dead civilization. The people must have power; and the people cannot have Greek. Now the power that is made here can be wielded by all men.

BARBARA Power to burn women's houses down and kill their sons and tear their husbands to pieces.

CUSINS You cannot have power for good without having power for evil too. Even mother's milk nourishes murderers as well as heroes. This power which only tears men's bodies to pieces has never been so horribly abused as the intellectual power, the imaginative power, the poetic, religious power that can enslave men's souls. As a teacher of Greek I gave the intellectual man weapons against the common man. I now want to give the common man weapons against the intellectual man. I love the common people. I want to arm them against the lawyers, the doctors, the priests, the literary men, the professors, the artists, and the politicians, who, once in authority, are more disastrous and tyrannical than all the fools, rascals, and impostors. I want a power simple enough for common men to use, yet strong enough to force the intellectual oligarchy to use its genius for the general good.

BARBARA Is there no higher power than that (*pointing to the shell*)?

CUSINS Yes; but that power can destroy the higher powers just as a tiger can destroy a man: therefore Man must master that power first. I admitted this when the Turks and Greeks were last at war. My best pupil went out to fight for Hellas. My parting gift to him was not a copy of Plato's Republic, but a revolver and a hundred Undershaft cartridges. The blood of every Turk he shot—if he shot any—is on my head as well as on Undershaft's. That act committed me to this place for ever. Your father's challenge has beaten me. Dare I make war on war? I must. I will. And now, is it all over between us?

BARBARA (*touched by his evident dread of her answer*) Silly baby Dolly! How could it be!

CUSINS (*overjoyed*) Then you—you—you—Oh for my drum! (*He flourishes imaginary drumsticks.*)

BARBARA (*angered by his levity*) Take care, Dolly, take care. Oh, if only I could get away from you and from father and from it all! if I could have the wings of a dove and fly away to heaven!

CUSINS And leave me!

BARBARA Yes, you, and all the other naughty mischievous children of men. But I cant. I was happy in the Salvation Army for a moment. I escaped from the world into a paradise of enthusiasm and prayer and soul saving; but the moment our money ran short, it all came back to Bodger: it was he who saved our people: he, and the Prince of Darkness, my papa. Undershaft and Bodger: their hands stretch everywhere: when we feed a starving fellow creature, it is with their bread, because there is no other bread; when we tend the sick, it is in the hospitals they endow; if we turn from the churches they build, we must kneel on the stones of the streets they pave. As long as that lasts, there is no getting away from them. Turning our backs on Bodger and Undershaft is turning our backs on life.

CUSINS I thought you were determined to turn your back on the wicked side of life.

BARBARA There is no wicked side: life is all one. And I never wanted to shirk my share in whatever evil must be endured, whether it be sin or suffering. I wish I could cure you of middle-class ideas, Dolly.

CUSINS (*gasping*) Middle cl—! A snub! A social snub to me from the daughter of a foundling!

BARBARA That is why I have no class, Dolly: I come straight out of the heart of the whole people. If I were middle-class I should turn my back on my father's business; and we should both live in an artistic drawing room, with you reading the reviews in one corner, and I in the other at the piano, playing Schumann: both very superior persons, and neither of us a bit of use. Sooner than that, I would sweep out the guncotton shed, or be one of Bodger's barmaids. Do you know what would have happened if you had refused papa's offer?

CUSINS I wonder!

BARBARA I should have given you up and married the man who accepted it. After all, my dear old mother has more sense than any of you. I felt like her when I saw this place—felt that I must have it—that never, never, never could I let it go; only she thought it was the houses and the kitchen ranges and the linen and china, when it was really all the human souls to be saved: not weak souls in starved bodies, sobbing with gratitude for a scrap of bread and treacle, but fullfed, quarrelsome, snobbish, uppish creatures, all standing on their little rights and dignities, and thinking that my father ought to be greatly obliged to them for making so much money for him—and so he ought. That is where salvation is really wanted. My father shall never throw it in my teeth again that my converts were bribed with bread. (*She is transfigured.*) I have got rid of the bribe of bread. I have got rid of the bribe of heaven. Let God's work be done for its own sake: the work he had to create us to do because it cannot be done except by living men and women. When I die, let him be in my debt, not I in his; and let me forgive him as becomes a woman of my rank.

CUSINS Then the way of life lies through the factory of death?

BARBARA Yes, through the raising of hell to heaven and of man to God, through the unveiling of an eternal light in the Valley of The Shadow. (*Seizing him with both hands.*) Oh, did you think my courage would never come back? did you believe that I was a deserter? that I, who have stood in the streets, and taken my people to my heart, and talked of the holiest and greatest things with them, could ever turn back and chatter foolishly to fashionable people about nothing in a drawing room? Never, never, never, never: Major Barbara will die with the colors. Oh! and

I have my dear little Dolly boy still; and he has found me my place and my work. Glory Hallelujah! (*She kisses him.*)

CUSINS My dearest: consider my delicate health. I cannot stand as much happiness as you can.

BARBARA Yes: it is not easy work being in love with me, is it? But it's good for you. (*She runs to the shed, and calls, childlike.*) Mamma! Mamma! (BILTON *comes out of the shed, followed by* UNDERSHAFT.) I want Mamma.

UNDERSHAFT She is taking off her list slippers, dear. (*He passes on to* CUSINS.) Well? What does she say?

CUSINS She has gone right up into the skies.

LADY BRITOMART (*coming from the shed and stopping on the steps, obstructing* SARAH, *who follows with* LOMAX. BARBARA *clutches like a baby at her mother's skirt*) Barbara: when will you learn to be independent and to act and think for yourself? I know, as well as possible what that cry of "Mamma, Mamma," means. Always running to me!

SARAH (*touching* LADY BRITOMART'S *ribs with her finger tips and imitating a bicycle horn*) Pip! pip!

LADY BRITOMART (*highly indignant*) How dare you say Pip! pip! to me, Sarah? You are both very naughty children. What do you want, Barbara?

BARBARA I want a house in the village to live in with Dolly. (*Dragging at the skirt.*) Come and tell me which one to take.

UNDERSHAFT (*to* CUSINS) Six o'clock tomorrow morning, Euripides.

✑ SIX CHARACTERS IN SEARCH OF AN AUTHOR (1921)

LUIGI PIRANDELLO (1867–1936)

If you like Chinese puzzles; if you find it fun to be tortured and left high and dry by philosophical dilemmas that cannot be resolved; if you find it exciting to be pulled in all directions at once down several roads to nowhere, then you will be absorbed by the works of Nobel Prize winner, Luigi Pirandello.

When you see a Pirandello play you must surrender yourself to some pure theatricality, but not in the sense of frenzied stage action or technical displays. You will be constantly teased by being asked to make choices between the illusion of what you are seeing and the reality, while being denied at the same time any possible ability of doing so. It is an off-again-on-again world, in which absolute facts disintegrate into thin air, and the truth, always hovering overhead, remains permanently, tantalizingly elusive.

Pirandello has sometimes been considered as the first of the "absurdists," those dramatists identified in the 1950s as the ones who saw life as a maze of contradictions, wrong turns, dead ends, making of existence itself an experience in ridiculous absurdity. Certainly this exceptional Italian dramatist broke some interesting ground which the absurdists eventually cultivated, for he raises fundamental questions in existential terms, common to the absurdists, about who and what we are and how we appear to ourselves and to others. Everything that Pirandello presents is frighteningly, convincingly real, even though it borders on fantasy. It is very often hilariously funny, but it is terrifying. It is, to be sure, monumentally absurd.

In *Six Characters* Pirandello puts us squarely into the make-believe of the theatre in his play within a play, choosing as home base for his story the one place that demands the surrender of our ability to rationalize, where we must absolutely suspend our disbelief. His illusion is set in a world designed for illusion, where "real" men and women play at being what they are not. But suppose, says Pirandello, that there is a further basic "reality" that is beyond "real" actors and "real" theatre. Suppose there is an absolute, unchanging, continuing reality that is art, the reality lived by the characters who have sprung from the mind of the artist, but who have achieved such immediate reality that they must be abandoned. And suppose they turn up in the world of make-believe that "real" men create for themselves in the theatre, where they find that their own version of "reality" is incapable of imitation and interpretation, existing in an absolute that is known only to themselves and incomprehensible to "real" men and women. What then?

By the time you have finished *Six Characters* you will hope to have found the answers to what constitutes illusion and what makes up reality, but you will be totally frustrated. "Reality" will have abandoned you, even as the author has abandoned his characters. You will encounter the problem of the simultaneity of time, watching the six characters exist in linear time, on the stage of the theatre where they have so pitifully, desperately, come for help, but you will recognize that they also exist in a continuous circle of time that is always beginning, never ending, circling back on itself constantly and instantly. The six are doomed to be what they are and nothing more, nothing less. They have no way out; they must act their scene unchanging and forever. They are, in reality, far more *real* than those of us who live in a world of our own illusions, our own perspectives always different from all others.

Who, then, is really alive? Who suffers and dies? The six characters do it, all at once, all the time. It is a desperate, finite, unalterable, and utterly absurd existence, but who dares deny it? Who dares complete the story? Who dares tell these characters that they are only figments of imagination? Whose imagination? Try to figure it out, says Pirandello. Just try.

Six Characters in Search of an Author

PIRANDELLO

An English version by Edward Storer

CHARACTERS
OF THE COMEDY IN THE MAKING:

THE FATHER
THE MOTHER
THE STEPDAUGHTER
THE SON

MADAME PACE
THE BOY ⎫
THE CHILD ⎭ *(These two do not speak)*

ACTORS
OF THE COMPANY:

THE MANAGER
LEADING LADY
LEADING MAN
SECOND LADY LEAD
L'INGÉNUE
JUVENILE LEAD

OTHER ACTORS AND ACTRESSES
PROPERTY MAN
PROMPTER
MACHINIST
MANAGER'S SECRETARY
DOORKEEPER
SCENE-SHIFTERS

DAYTIME: *The Stage of a Theatre.*

N.B. The Comedy is without acts or scenes. The performance is interrupted once, without the curtain being lowered, when THE MANAGER *and the chief characters withdraw to arrange the scenario. A second interruption of the action takes place when, by mistake, the stage hands let the curtain down.*

ACT I

The spectators will find the curtain raised and the stage as it usually is during the daytime. It will be half dark, and empty, so that from the beginning the public may have the impression of an impromptu performance.

PROMPTER's *box and a small table and chair for* THE MANAGER. *Two other small tables and several chairs scattered about as during rehearsals.*

The ACTORS *and* ACTRESSES *of the company enter from the back of the stage:*

First one, then another, then two together: nine or ten in all. They are about to rehearse a Pirandello play: Mixing It Up. *Some of the company move off towards their dressing rooms. The* PROMPTER, *who has the "book" under his arm, is waiting for* THE MANAGER *in order to begin the rehearsal.*

The ACTORS *and* ACTRESSES, *some standing, some sitting, chat and smoke. One perhaps reads a paper; another cons his part.*

Finally, THE MANAGER *enters and goes to the table prepared for him. His* SECRETARY *brings him his mail, through which he glances. The* PROMPTER *takes his seat, turns on a light, and opens the "book."*

THE MANAGER (*Throwing a letter down on the table*) I can't see. (*To* PROPERTY MAN) Let's have a little light, please!

PROPERTY MAN Yes sir, yes, at once. (*A light comes down on to the stage*)

THE MANAGER (*Clapping his hands*) Come along! Come along! Second act of *Mixing It Up.* (*Sits down*)

(*The* ACTORS *and* ACTRESSES *go from the front of the stage to the wings, all except the three who are to begin the rehearsal*)

PROMPTER (*Reading the "book"*) "Leo Gala's house. A curious room serving as dining-room and study."

THE MANAGER (*To* PROPERTY MAN) Fix up the old red room.

PROPERTY MAN (*Noting it down*) Red set. All right!

PROMPTER (*Continuing to read from the "book"*) "Table already laid and writing desk with books and papers. Bookshelves. Exit rear to Leo's bedroom. Exit left to kitchen. Principal exit to right."

THE MANAGER (*Energetically*) Well, you understand: The principal exit over there; here, the kitchen. (*Turning to* ACTOR *who is to play the part of Socrates*) You make your entrances and exits here. (*To* PROPERTY MAN) The baize doors at the rear, and curtains.

PROPERTY MAN (*Noting it down*) Right-o!

PROMPTER (*Reading as before*) "When the curtain rises, Leo Gala, dressed in cook's cap and apron is busy beating an egg in a cup. Philip, also dressed as a cook, is beating another egg. Guido Venanzi is seated and listening."

LEADING MAN (*To* MANAGER) Excuse me, but must I absolutely wear a cook's cap?

THE MANAGER (*Annoyed*) I imagine so. It says so there anyway. (*Pointing to the "book"*)
LEADING MAN But it's ridiculous!
THE MANAGER Ridiculous? Ridiculous? Is it my fault if France won't send us any more good comedies, and we are reduced to putting on Pirandello's works where nobody understands anything, and where the author plays the fool with us all? (*The* ACTORS *grin.* THE MANAGER *goes to* LEADING MAN *and shouts*) Yes sir, you put on the cook's cap and beat eggs. Do you suppose that with all this egg-beating business you are on an ordinary stage? Get that out of your head. You represent the shell of the eggs you are beating! (*Laughter and comments among the* ACTORS) Silence! and listen to my explanations, please! (*To* LEADING MAN) "The empty form of reason without the fullness of instinct, which is blind"—You stand for reason, your wife is instinct. It's a mixing up of the parts, according to which you who act your own part become the puppet of yourself. Do you understand?
LEADING MAN I'm hanged if I do.
THE MANAGER Neither do I. But let's get on with it. It's sure to be a glorious failure anyway. (*Confidentially*) But I say, please face three-quarters. Otherwise, what with the abstruseness of the dialogue, and the public that won't be able to hear you, the whole thing will go to hell. Come on! come on!
PROMPTER Pardon sir, may I get into my box? There's a bit of a draught.
THE MANAGER Yes, yes, of course!

At this point, the DOORKEEPER *has entered from the stage door and advances towards* THE MANAGER'*s table, taking off his braided cap. During this maneuver, the* SIX CHARACTERS *enter, and stop by the door at back of stage, so that when the* DOORKEEPER *is about to announce their coming to* THE MANAGER, *they are already on the stage. A tenuous light surrounds them, almost as if irradiated by them—the faint breath of their fantastic reality.*

This light will disappear when they come forward towards the ACTORS. *They preserve, however, something of the dream lightness in which they seem almost suspended; but this does not detract from the essential reality of their forms and expressions.*

He who is known as THE FATHER *is a man of about 50: hair, reddish in color, thin at the temples; he is not bald, however; thick moustaches, falling over his still fresh mouth, which often opens in an empty and uncertain smile. He is fattish, pale; with an especially wide forehead. He has blue, oval-shaped eyes, very clear and piercing. Wears light trousers and a dark jacket. He is alternatively mellifluous and violent in his manner.*

THE MOTHER *seems crushed and terrified as if by an intolerable weight of shame and abasement. She is dressed in modest black and wears a thick widow's veil of crêpe. When she lifts this, she reveals a wax-like face. She always keeps her eyes downcast.*

THE STEPDAUGHTER *is dashing, almost impudent, beautiful. She wears mourning too, but with great elegance. She shows contempt for the timid half-frightened manner of the wretched* BOY *(14 years old, and also dressed in black); on the other hand, she displays a lively tenderness for her little sister,* THE CHILD *(about four), who is dressed in white, with a black silk sash at the waist.*

THE SON *(22) tall, severe in his attitude of contempt for* THE FATHER, *supercilious and indifferent to* THE MOTHER. *He looks as if he had come on the stage against his will.*

DOORKEEPER *(Cap in hand)*   Excuse me, sir. . . .

THE MANAGER *(Rudely)*   Eh? What is it?

DOORKEEPER *(Timidly)*   These people are asking for you, sir.

THE MANAGER *(Furious)*   I am rehearsing, and you know perfectly well no one's allowed to come in during rehearsals! *(Turning to the* CHARACTERS)   Who are you, please? What do you want?

THE FATHER *(Coming forward a little, followed by the others, who seem embarrassed)*   As a matter of fact . . . we have come here in search of an author. . . .

THE MANAGER *(Half angry, half amazed)*   An author? What author?

THE FATHER   Any author, sir.

THE MANAGER   But there's no author here. We are not rehearsing a new piece.

THE STEPDAUGHTER *(Vivaciously)*   So much the better, so much the better! We can be your new piece.

AN ACTOR *(Coming forward from the others)*   Oh, do you hear that?

THE FATHER *(To* STEPDAUGHTER)   Yes, but if the author isn't here . . . *(To* MANAGER) . . . unless you would be willing. . . .

THE MANAGER   You are trying to be funny.

THE FATHER   No, for Heaven's sake, what are you saying? We bring you a drama, sir.

THE STEPDAUGHTER   We may be your fortune.

THE MANAGER   Will you oblige me by going away? We haven't time to waste with mad people.

THE FATHER *(Mellifluously)*   Oh sir, you know well that life is full of infinite absurdities, which, strangely enough, do not even need to appear plausible, since they are true.

THE MANAGER   What the devil is he talking about?

THE FATHER   I say that to reverse the ordinary process may well be considered a madness: that is, to create credible situations, in order that they may appear true. But permit me to observe that if this be madness, it is the sole *raison d'être* of your profession, gentlemen. (*The* ACTORS *look hurt and perplexed*)

THE MANAGER (*Getting up and looking at him*) So our profession seems to you one worthy of madmen then?

THE FATHER Well, to make seem true that which isn't true . . . without any need . . . for a joke as it were . . . Isn't that your mission, gentlemen: to give life to fantastic characters on the stage?

THE MANAGER (*Interpreting the rising anger of the* COMPANY) But I would beg you to believe, my dear sir, that the profession of the comedian is a noble one. If today, as things go, the playwrights give us stupid comedies to play and puppets to represent instead of men, remember we are proud to have given life to immortal works here on these very boards! (*The* ACTORS, *satisfied, applaud their* MANAGER)

THE FATHER (*Interrupting furiously*) Exactly, perfectly, to living beings more alive than those who breathe and wear clothes: being less real perhaps, but truer! I agree with you entirely. (*The* ACTORS *look at one another in amazement*)

THE MANAGER But what do you mean? Before, you said . . .

THE FATHER No, excuse me, I meant it for you, sir, who were crying out that you had no time to lose with madmen, while no one better than yourself knows that nature uses the instrument of human fantasy in order to pursue her high creative purpose.

THE MANAGER Very well—but where does all this take us?

THE FATHER Nowhere! It is merely to show you that one is born to life in many forms, in many shapes, as tree, or as stone, as water, as butterfly, or as woman. So one may also be born a character in a play.

THE MANAGER (*With feigned comic dismay*) So you and these other friends of yours have been born characters?

THE FATHER Exactly, and alive as you see! (MANAGER *and* ACTORS *burst out laughing*)

THE FATHER (*Hurt*) I am sorry you laugh, because we carry in us a drama, as you can guess from this woman here, veiled in black.

THE MANAGER (*Losing patience at last and almost indignant*) Oh, chuck it! Get away please! Clear out of here! (*To* PROPERTY MAN) For Heaven's sake, turn them out!

THE FATHER (*Resisting*) No, no, look here, we. . . .

THE MANAGER (*Roaring*) We come here to work, you know.

LEADING MAN One cannot let oneself be made such a fool of.

THE FATHER (*Determined, coming forward*) I marvel at your incredulity, gentlemen. Are you not accustomed to see the characters created by an author spring to life in yourselves and face each other? Just because there is no "book" (*Pointing to the* PROMPT-ER's *box*) which contains us, you refuse to believe. . . .

THE STEPDAUGHTER (*Advances towards* MANAGER, *smiling and co-quettish*) Believe me, we are really six most interesting characters, sir; side-tracked however.

THE FATHER Yes, that is the word! (*To* MANAGER *all at once*) In the sense, that is, that the author who created us alive no longer wished, or was no longer able, materially to put us into a work of art. And this was a real crime, sir; because he who has had the luck to be born a character can laugh even at death. He cannot die. The man, the writer, the instrument of the creation will die, but his creation does not die. And to live for ever, it does not need to have extraordinary gifts or to be able to work wonders. Who was Sancho Panza? Who was Don Abbondio? Yet they live eternally because—live germs as they were—they had the fortune to find a fecundating matrix, a fantasy which could raise and nourish them: make them live for ever!

THE MANAGER That is quite all right. But what do you want here, all of you?

THE FATHER We want to live.

THE MANAGER (*Ironically*) For Eternity?

THE FATHER No, sir, only for a moment . . . in you.

AN ACTOR Just listen to him!

LEADING LADY They want to live, in us! . . .

JUVENILE LEAD (*Pointing to the* STEPDAUGHTER) I've no objection, as far as that one is concerned!

THE FATHER Look here! Look here! The comedy has to be made. (*To the* MANAGER) But if you and your actors are willing, we can soon concert it among ourselves.

THE MANAGER (*Annoyed*) But what do you want to concert? We don't go in for concerts here. Here we play dramas and comedies!

THE FATHER Exactly! That is just why we have come to you.

THE MANAGER And where is the "book"?

THE FATHER. It is in us! (*The* ACTORS *laugh*) The drama is in us, and we are the drama. We are impatient to play it. Our inner passion drives us on to this.

THE STEPDAUGHTER (*Disdainful, alluring, treacherous, full of impudence*) My passion, sir! Ah, if you only knew! My passion for him! (*Points to the* FATHER *and makes a pretence of embracing him. Then she breaks out into a loud laugh*)

THE FATHER (*Angrily*) Behave yourself! And please don't laugh in that fashion.

THE STEPDAUGHTER   With your permission, gentlemen, I, who am a two months' orphan, will show you how I can dance and sing. (*Sings and then dances* Prenez garde à Tchou-Tchin-Tchou)

Les chinois sont un peuple malin,
De Shanghaî à Pékin,
Ils ont mis des écriteaux partout:
Prenez garde à Tchou-Tchin-Tchou.

ACTORS and ACTRESSES   Bravo! Well done! Tip-top!

THE MANAGER   Silence! This isn't a café concert, you know! (*Turning to the* FATHER *in consternation*) Is she mad?

THE FATHER   Mad? No, she's worse than mad.

THE STEPDAUGHTER (*To* MANAGER)   Worse? Worse? Listen! Stage this drama for us at once! Then you will see that at a certain moment I . . . when this little darling here . . . (*Takes the* CHILD *by the hand and leads her to the* MANAGER) Isn't she a dear? (*Takes her up and kisses her*) Darling! Darling! (*Puts her down again and adds feelingly*) Well, when God suddenly takes this dear little child away from that poor mother there; and this imbecile here (*seizing hold of the* BOY *roughly and pushing him forward*) does the stupidest things, like the fool he is, you will see me run away. Yes, gentlemen, I shall be off. But the moment hasn't arrived yet. After what has taken place between him and me (*indicates the* FATHER *with a horrible wink*) I can't remain any longer in this society, to have to witness the anguish of this mother here for that fool . . . (*Indicates the* SON) Look at him! Look at him! See how indifferent, how frigid he is, because he is the legitimate son. He despises me, despises him (*pointing to the* BOY), despises this baby here; because . . . we are bastards. (*Goes to the* MOTHER *and embraces her*) And he doesn't want to recognize her as his mother—she who is the common mother of us all. He looks down upon her as if she were only the mother of us three bastards. Wretch! (*She says all this very rapidly, excitedly. At the word "bastards" she raises her voice, and almost spits out the final "Wretch!"*)

THE MOTHER (*To the* MANAGER, *in anguish*)   In the name of these two little children, I beg you . . . (*She grows faint and is about to fall*) Oh God!

THE FATHER (*Coming forward to support her as do some of the* ACTORS)   Quick, a chair, a chair for this poor widow!

THE ACTORS   Is it true? Has she really fainted?

THE MANAGER   Quick, a chair! Here!

(*One of the* ACTORS *brings a chair, the others proffer assistance. The* MOTHER *tries to prevent the* FATHER *from lifting the veil which covers her face*)

THE FATHER   Look at her! Look at her!

THE MOTHER   No, stop; stop it please!

THE FATHER (*Raising her veil*)   Let them see you!

THE MOTHER (*Rising and covering her face with her hands, in desperation*)   I beg you, sir, to prevent this man from carrying out his plan which is loathsome to me.

THE MANAGER (*Dumbfounded*)   I don't understand at all. What is the situation? Is this lady your wife? (*To the* FATHER)

THE FATHER   Yes, gentlemen: my wife!

THE MANAGER   But how can she be a widow if you are alive? (*The* ACTORS *find relief for their astonishment in a loud laugh*)

THE FATHER   Don't laugh! Don't laugh like that, for Heaven's sake. Her drama lies just here in this: she has had a lover, a man who ought to be here.

THE MOTHER (*With a cry*)   No! No!

THE STEPDAUGHTER   Fortunately for her, he is dead. Two months ago as I said. We are mourning, as you see.

THE FATHER   He isn't here you see, not because he is dead. He isn't here—look at her a moment and you will understand—because her drama isn't a drama of the love of two men for whom she was incapable of feeling anything except possibly a little gratitude—gratitude not for me but for the other. She isn't a woman, she is a mother, and her drama—powerful, sir, I assure you—lies, as a matter of fact, all in these four children she has had by two men.

THE MOTHER   I had them? Have you got the courage to say that I wanted them? (*To the* COMPANY) It was his doing. It was he who gave me that other man, who forced me to go away with him.

THE STEPDAUGHTER   It isn't true.

THE MOTHER (*Startled*)   Not true, isn't it?

THE STEPDAUGHTER   No, it isn't true, it just isn't true.

THE MOTHER   And what can you know about it?

THE STEPDAUGHTER   It isn't true. Don't believe it. (*To* MANAGER) Do you know why she says so? For that fellow there. (*Indicates the* SON) She tortures herself, destroys herself on account of the neglect of that son there; and she wants him to believe that if she abandoned him when he was only two years old, it was because he (*indicates the* FATHER) made her do so.

THE MOTHER (*Vigorously*)   He forced me to it, and I call God to witness it. (*To the* MANAGER) Ask him (*indicates the* FATHER) if it isn't true. Let him speak. You (*to* DAUGHTER) are not in a position to know anything about it.

THE STEPDAUGHTER   I know you lived in peace and happiness with my father while he lived. Can you deny it?

THE MOTHER   No, I don't deny it . . .

THE STEPDAUGHTER   He was always full of affection and kindness for you. (*To the* BOY, *angrily*) It's true, isn't it? Tell them! Why don't you speak, you little fool?

THE MOTHER   Leave the poor boy alone. Why do you want to make me appear ungrateful, daughter? I don't want to offend your father. I have answered him that I didn't abandon my house and my son through any fault of mine, nor from any wilful passion.

THE FATHER   It is true. It was my doing.

LEADING MAN (*To the* COMPANY)   What a spectacle!

LEADING LADY   We are the audience this time.

JUVENILE LEAD   For once, in a way.

THE MANAGER (*Beginning to get really interested*)   Let's hear them out. Listen!

THE SON   Oh yes, you're going to hear a fine bit now. He will talk to you of the Demon of Experiment.

THE FATHER   You are a cynical imbecile. I've told you so already a hundred times. (*To the* MANAGER) He tries to make fun of me on account of this expression which I have found to excuse myself with.

THE SON (*With disgust*)   Yes, phrases! phrases!

THE FATHER   Phrases! Isn't everyone consoled when faced with a trouble or fact he doesn't understand, by a word, some simple word, which tells us nothing and yet calms us?

THE STEPDAUGHTER   Even in the case of remorse. In fact, especially then.

THE FATHER   Remorse? No, that isn't true. I've done more than use words to quieten the remorse in me.

THE STEPDAUGHTER   Yes, there was a bit of money too. Yes, yes, a bit of money. There were the hundred lire he was about to offer me in payment, gentlemen. . . . (*Sensation of horror among the* ACTORS)

THE SON (*To the* STEPDAUGHTER)   This is vile.

THE STEPDAUGHTER   Vile? There they were in a pale blue envelope on a little mahogany table in the back of Madame Pace's shop. You know Madame Pace—one of those ladies who attract poor girls of good family into their ateliers, under the pretext of their selling *robes et manteaux*.

THE SON   And he thinks he has bought the right to tyrannize over us all with those hundred lire he was going to pay; but which, fortunately—note this, gentlemen—he had no chance of paying.

THE STEPDAUGHTER   It was a near thing, though, you know! (*Laughs ironically*)

THE MOTHER (*Protesting*)   Shame, my daughter, shame!

THE STEPDAUGHTER   Shame indeed! This is my revenge! I am dying to live that scene.... The room ... I see it ... Here is the window with the mantles exposed, there the divan, the looking-glass, a screen, there in front of the window the little mahogany table with the blue envelope containing one hundred lire. I see it. I see it. I could take hold of it... But you, gentlemen, you ought to turn your backs now: I am almost nude, you know. But I don't blush: I leave that to him. (*Indicating* FATHER)

THE MANAGER   I don't understand this at all.

THE FATHER   Naturally enough. I would ask you, sir, to exercise your authority a little here, and let me speak before you believe all she is trying to blame me with. Let me explain.

THE STEPDAUGHTER   Ah yes, explain it in your own way.

THE FATHER   But don't you see that the whole trouble lies here. In words, words. Each one of us has within him a whole world of things, each man of us his own special world. And how can we ever come to an understanding if I put in the words I utter the sense and value of things as I see them; while you who listen to me must inevitably translate them according to the conception of things each one of you has within himself. We think we understand each other, but we never really do. Look here! This woman (*indicating the* MOTHER) takes all my pity for her as a specially ferocious form of cruelty.

THE MOTHER   But you drove me away.

THE FATHER   Do you hear her? I drove her away! She believes I really sent her away.

THE MOTHER   You know how to talk, and I don't; but, believe me sir (*To* MANAGER), after he had married me ... who knows why? ... I was a poor insignificant woman....

THE FATHER   But, good Heaven! it was just for your humility that I married you. I loved this simplicity in you. (*He stops when he sees she makes signs to contradict him, opens his arms wide in sign of desperation, seeing how hopeless it is to make himself understood*) You see she denies it. Her mental deafness, believe me, is phenomenal, the limit (*touches his forehead*): deaf, deaf, mentally deaf! She had plenty of feeling. Oh yes, a good heart for the children; but the brain—deaf, to the point of desperation—!

THE STEPDAUGHTER   Yes, but ask him how his intelligence has helped us.

THE FATHER   If we could see all the evil that may spring from good, what should we do? (*At this point the* LEADING LADY *who is biting her lips with rage at seeing the* LEADING MAN *flirting with the* STEPDAUGHTER, *comes forward and says to the* MANAGER)

LEADING LADY   Excuse me, but are we going to rehearse today?

MANAGER   Of course, of course; but let's hear them out.

JUVENILE LEAD   This is something quite new.

L'INGÉNUE   Most interesting!

LEADING LADY   Yes, for the people who like that kind of thing. (*Casts a glance at* LEADING MAN)

THE MANAGER   (*To* FATHER)   You must please explain yourself quite clearly. (*Sits down*)

THE FATHER   Very well then: listen! I had in my service a poor man, a clerk, a secretary of mine, full of devotion, who became friends with her. (*Indicating the* MOTHER) They understood one another, were kindred souls in fact, without, however, the least suspicion of any evil existing. They were incapable even of thinking of it.

THE STEPDAUGHTER   So he thought of it—for them!

THE FATHER   That's not true. I meant to do good to them—and to myself, I confess, at the same time. Things had come to the point that I could not say a word to either of them without their making a mute appeal, one to the other, with their eyes. I could see them silently asking each other how I was to be kept in countenance, how I was to be kept quiet. And this, believe me, was just about enough of itself to keep me in a constant rage, to exasperate me beyond measure.

THE MANAGER   And why didn't you send him away then—this secretary of yours?

THE FATHER   Precisely what I did, sir. And then I had to watch this poor woman drifting forlornly about the house like an animal without a master, like an animal one has taken in out of pity.

THE MOTHER   Ah, yes! . . .

THE FATHER   (*Suddenly turning to the* MOTHER)   It's true about the son anyway, isn't it?

THE MOTHER   He took my son away from me first of all.

THE FATHER   But not from cruelty. I did it so that he should grow up healthy and strong by living in the country.

THE STEPDAUGHTER   (*Pointing to him ironically*)   As one can see.

THE FATHER   (*Quickly*)   Is it my fault if he has grown up like this? I sent him to a wet nurse in the country, a peasant, as *she* did not seem to me strong enough, though she is of humble origin. That was, anyway, the reason I married her. Unpleasant all this may be, but how can it be helped? My mistake possibly, but there we are! All my life I have had these confounded aspirations towards a certain moral sanity. (*At this point the* STEP-DAUGHTER *bursts out into a noisy laugh*) Oh, stop it! Stop it! I can't stand it.

THE MANAGER Yes, please stop it, for Heaven's sake.

THE STEPDAUGHTER But imagine moral sanity from him, if you please—the client of certain ateliers like that of Madame Pace!

THE FATHER Fool! That is the proof that I am a man! This seeming contradiction, gentlemen, is the strongest proof that I stand here a live man before you. Why, it is just for this very incongruity in my nature that I have had to suffer what I have. I could not live by the side of that woman (*indicating the* MOTHER) any longer; but not so much for the boredom she inspired me with as for the pity I felt for her.

THE MOTHER And so he turned me out—.

THE FATHER —well provided for! Yes, I sent her to that man, gentlemen . . . to let her go free of me.

THE MOTHER And to free himself.

THE FATHER Yes, I admit it. It was also a liberation for me. But great evil has come of it. I meant well when I did it; and I did it more for her sake than mine. I swear it. (*Crosses his arms on his chest; then turns suddenly to the* MOTHER) Did I ever lose sight of you until that other man carried you off to another town, like the angry fool he was? And on account of my pure interest in you . . . my pure interest, I repeat, that had no base motive in it . . . I watched with the tenderest concern the new family that grew up around her. She can bear witness to this. (*Points to the* STEPDAUGHTER)

THE STEPDAUGHTER Oh yes, that's true enough. When I was a kiddie, so so high, you know, with plaits over my shoulders and knickers longer than my skirts, I used to see him waiting outside the school for me to come out. He came to see how I was growing up.

THE FATHER This is infamous, shameful!

THE STEPDAUGHTER No. Why?

THE FATHER Infamous! Infamous! (*Then excitedly to* MANAGER, *explaining*) After she (*indicating* MOTHER) went away, my house seemed suddenly empty. She was my incubus, but she filled my house. I was like a dazed fly alone in the empty rooms. This boy here (*indicating the* SON) was educated away from home, and when he came back, he seemed to me to be no more mine. With no mother to stand between him and me, he grew up entirely for himself, on his own, apart, with no tie of intellect or affection binding him to me. And then—strange but true—I was driven, by curiosity at first and then by some tender sentiment, towards her family, which had come into being through my will. The thought of her began gradually to fill up the emptiness I felt all around me. I wanted to know if she were happy in living out the simple daily duties of life. I wanted to think of her as fortunate and happy because far away from the complicated torments of my spirit. And so, to have proof of this, I used to watch that child coming out of school.

THE STEPDAUGHTER Yes, yes. True. He used to follow me in the street and smiled at me, waved his hand, like this. I would look at him with interest, wondering who he might be. I told my mother, who guessed at once. (*The* MOTHER *agrees with a nod*) Then she didn't want to send me to school for some days; and when I finally went back, there he was again—looking so ridiculous—with a paper parcel in his hands. He came close to me, caressed me, and drew out a fine straw hat from the parcel, with a bouquet of flowers—all for me!

THE MANAGER A bit discursive this, you know!

THE SON (*Contemptuously*) Literature! Literature!

THE FATHER Literature indeed! This is life, this is passion!

THE MANAGER It may be, but it won't act.

THE FATHER I agree. This is only the part leading up. I don't suggest this should be staged. She (*pointing to the* STEPDAUGHTER), as you see, is no longer the flapper with plaits down her back—.

THE STEPDAUGHTER —and the knickers showing below the skirt!

THE FATHER The drama is coming now, sir; something new, complex, most interesting.

THE STEPDAUGHTER As soon as my father died. . . .

THE FATHER —there was absolute misery for them. They came back here, unknown to me. Through her stupidity! (*Pointing to the* MOTHER) It is true she can barely write her own name; but she could anyhow have got her daughter to write to me that they were in need. . . .

THE MOTHER And how was I to divine all this sentiment in him?

THE FATHER That is exactly your mistake, never to have guessed any of my sentiments.

THE MOTHER After so many years apart, and all that had happened. . . .

THE FATHER Was it my fault if that fellow carried you away? It happened quite suddenly; for after he had obtained some job or other, I could find no trace of them; and so, not unnaturally, my interest in them dwindled. But the drama culminated unforeseen and violent on their return, when I was impelled by my miserable flesh that still lives.... Ah! what misery, what wretchedness is that of the man who is alone and disdains debasing *liaisons!* Not old enough to do without women, and not young enough to go and look for one without shame. Misery? It's worse than misery; it's a horror; for no woman can any longer give him love; and when a man feels this.... One ought to do without, you say? Yes, yes, I know. Each of us when he appears before his fellows is clothed in a certain dignity. But every man knows what unconfessable things pass within the secrecy of his own heart. One gives way to the temptation, only to rise from it again, afterwards, with a great eagerness to restablish one's dignity, as if it were a tombstone to place on the grave of one's shame, and a monument to hide and sign the memory of our weaknesses. Everybody's in the same case. Some folks haven't the courage to say certain things, that's all!

THE STEPDAUGHTER   All appear to have the courage to do them though.

THE FATHER   Yes, but in secret. Therefore, you want more courage to say these things. Let a man but speak these things out, and folks at once label him a cynic. But it isn't true. He is like all the others, better indeed, because he isn't afraid to reveal with the light of the intelligence the red shame of human bestiality on which most men close their eyes so as not to see it. Woman—for example, look at her case! She turns tantalizing inviting glances on you. You seize her. No sooner does she feel herself in your grasp than she closes her eyes. It is the sign of her mission, the sign by which she says to man: "Blind yourself, for I am blind."

THE STEPDAUGHTER   Sometimes she can close them no more: when she no longer feels the need of hiding her shame to herself, but dry-eyed and dispassionately, sees only that of the man who has blinded himself without love. Oh, all these intellectual complications make me sick, disgust me—all this philosophy that uncovers the beast in man, and then seeks to save him, excuse him ... I can't stand it, sir. When a man seeks to "simplify" life bestially, throwing aside every relic of humanity, every chaste aspiration, every pure feeling, all sense of ideality, duty, modesty, shame ... then nothing is more revolting and nauseous than a certain kind of remorse—crocodiles' tears, that's what it is.

THE MANAGER   Let's come to the point. This is only discussion.

THE FATHER   Very good, sir! But a fact is like a sack which won't stand up when it is empty. In order that it may stand up, one has to put into it the reason and sentiment which have caused it to exist. I couldn't possibly know that after the death of that man, they had decided to return here, that they were in misery, and that she (*pointing to the* MOTHER) had gone to work as a modiste, and at a shop of the type of that of Madame Pace.

THE STEPDAUGHTER A real high-class modiste, you must know, gentlemen. In appearance, she works for the leaders of the best society; but she arranges matters so that these elegant ladies serve her purpose . . . without prejudice to other ladies who are . . . well . . . only so so.

THE MOTHER You will believe me, gentlemen, that it never entered my mind that the old hag offered me work because she had her eye on my daughter.

THE STEPDAUGHTER Poor mamma! Do you know, sir, what that woman did when I brought her back the work my mother had finished? She would point out to me that I had torn one of my frocks, and she would give it back to my mother to mend. It was I who paid for it, always I; while this poor creature here believed she was sacrificing herself for me and these two children here, sitting up at night sewing Madame Pace's robes.

THE MANAGER And one day you met there. . . .

THE STEPDAUGHTER Him, him. Yes, sir, an old client. There's a scene for you to play! Superb!

THE FATHER She, the Mother arrived just then. . . .

THE STEPDAUGHTER (*Treacherously*) Almost in time!

THE FATHER (*Crying out*) No, in time! in time! Fortunately I recognized her . . . in time. And I took them back home with me to my house. You can imagine now her position and mine: she, as you see her; and I who cannot look her in the face.

THE STEPDAUGHTER Absurd! How can I possibly be expected—after that—to be a modest young miss, a fit person to go with his confounded aspirations for "a solid moral sanity"?

THE FATHER For the drama lies all in this—in the conscience that I have, that each one of us has. We believe this conscience to be a single thing, but it is many-sided. There is one for this person, and another for that. Diverse consciences. So we have this illusion of being one person for all, of having a personality that is unique in all our acts. But it isn't true. We perceive this when, tragically perhaps, in something we do, we are, as it were, suspended, caught up in the air on a kind of hook. Then we perceive that all of us was not in that act, and that it would be an atrocious injustice to judge us by that action alone, as if all our existence were summed up in that one deed. Now do you understand the perfidy of this girl? She surprised me in a place where she ought not to have known me, just as I could not exist for her; and she now seeks to attach to me a reality such as I could never suppose

I should have to assume for her in a shameful and fleeting moment of my life. I feel this above all else. And the drama, you will see, acquires a tremendous value from this point. Then there is the position of the others . . . his . . . (*Indicating the* SON)

THE SON (*Shrugging his shoulders scornfully*) Leave me alone! I don't come into this.

THE FATHER What? You don't come into this?

THE SON I've got nothing to do with it, and don't want to have; because you know well enough I wasn't made to be mixed up in all this with the rest of you.

THE STEPDAUGHTER We are only vulgar folk! He is the fine gentleman. You may have noticed, Mr. Manager, that I fix him now and again with a look of scorn while he lowers his eyes—for he knows the evil he has done me.

THE SON (*Scarcely looking at her*) I?

THE STEPDAUGHTER You! you! I owe my life on the streets to you. Did you or did you not deny us, with your behavior, I won't say the intimacy of home, but even that mere hospitality which makes guests feel at their ease? We were intruders who had come to disturb the kingdom of your legitimacy. I should like to have you witness, Mr. Manager, certain scenes between him and me. He says I have tyrannized over everyone. But it was just his behavior which made me insist on the reason for which I had come into the house—this reason he calls "vile"—into his house, with my mother, who is his mother too. And I came as mistress of the house.

THE SON It's easy for them to put me always in the wrong. But imagine, gentlemen, the position of a son, whose fate it is to see arrive one day at his home a young woman of impudent bearing, a young woman who inquires for his father, with whom who knows what business she has. This young man has then to witness her return bolder than ever, accompanied by that child there. He is obliged to watch her treat his father in an equivocal and confidential manner. She asks money of him in a way that lets one suppose he must give it her, *must,* do you understand, because he has every obligation to do so.

THE FATHER But I have, as a matter of fact, this obligation. I owe it to your mother.

THE SON How should I know? When had I ever seen or heard of her? One day there arrive with her (*indicating* STEPDAUGHTER) that lad and this baby here. I am told: "This is *your* mother too, you know." I divine from her manner (*indicating* STEPDAUGHTER *again*) why it is they have come home. I had rather not say what

I feel and think about it. I shouldn't even care to confess to myself. No action can therefore be hoped for from me in this affair. Believe me, Mr. Manager, I am an "unrealized" character, dramatically speaking; and I find myself not at all at ease in their company. Leave me out of it, I beg you.

THE FATHER   What? It is just because you are so that...

THE SON   How do you know what I am like? When did you ever bother your head about me?

THE FATHER   I admit it. I admit it. But isn't that a situation in itself? This aloofness of yours which is so cruel to me and to your mother, who returns home and sees you almost for the first time grown up, who doesn't recognize you but knows you are her son... (*Pointing out the* MOTHER *to the* MANAGER) See, she's crying!

THE STEPDAUGHTER (*Angrily, stamping her foot*)   Like a fool!

THE FATHER (*Indicating* STEPDAUGHTER)   She can't stand him, you know. (*Then referring again to the* SON)   He says he doesn't come into the affair, whereas he is really the hinge of the whole action. Look at that lad who is always clinging to his mother, frightened and humiliated. It is on account of this fellow here. Possibly his situation is the most painful of all. He feels himself a stranger more than the others. The poor little chap feels mortified, humiliated at being brought into a home out of charity as it were. (*In confidence*)— He is the image of his father. Hardly talks at all. Humble and quiet.

THE MANAGER   Oh, we'll cut him out. You've no notion what a nuisance boys are on the stage...

THE FATHER   He disappears soon, you know. And the baby too. She is the first to vanish from the scene. The drama consists finally in this: when that mother re-enters my house, her family born outside of it, and shall we say superimposed on the original, ends with the death of the little girl, the tragedy of the boy and the flight of the elder daughter. It cannot go on, because it is foreign to its surroundings. So after much torment, we three remain: I, the mother, that son. Then, owing to the disappearance of that extraneous family, we too find ourselves strange to one another. We find we are living in an atmosphere of mortal desolation which is the revenge, as he (*indicating* SON) scornfully said of the Demon of Experiment, that unfortunately hides in me. Thus, sir, you see when faith is lacking, it becomes impossible to create certain states of happiness, for we lack the necessary humility. Vaingloriously, we try to substitute ourselves for this faith, creating thus for the rest of the world a reality which we believe after their fashion, while, actually, it doesn't exist. For each one of us has his own reality to be respected before God, even when it is harmful to one's very self.

THE MANAGER There is something in what you say. I assure you all this interests me very much. I begin to think there's the stuff for a drama in all this, and not a bad drama either.

THE STEPDAUGHTER (*Coming forward*) When you've got a character like me.

THE FATHER (*Shutting her up, all excited to learn the decision of the* MANAGER) You be quiet!

THE MANAGER (*Reflecting, heedless of interruption*) It's new . . . hem . . . yes . . .

THE FATHER Absolutely new!

THE MANAGER You've got a nerve though, I must say, to come here and fling it at me like this . . .

THE FATHER You will understand, sir, born as we are for the stage . . .

THE MANAGER Are you amateur actors then?

THE FATHER No, I say born for the stage, because . . .

THE MANAGER Oh, nonsense. You're an old hand, you know.

THE FATHER No sir, no. We act that rôle for which we have been cast, that rôle which we are given in life. And in my own case, passion itself, as usually happens, becomes a trifle theatrical when it is exalted.

THE MANAGER Well, well, that will do. But you see, without an author . . . I could give you the address of an author if you like . . .

THE FATHER No, no. Look here! You must be the author.

THE MANAGER I? What are you talking about?

THE FATHER Yes, you, you! Why not?

THE MANAGER Because I have never been an author: that's why.

THE FATHER Then why not turn author now? Everybody does it. You don't want any special qualities. Your task is made much easier by the fact that we are all here alive before you . . .

THE MANAGER It won't do.

THE FATHER What? When you see us live our drama . . .

THE MANAGER Yes, that's all right. But you want someone to write it.

THE FATHER No, no. Someone to take it down, possibly, while we play it, scene by scene! It will be enough to sketch it out at first, and then try it over.

THE MANAGER Well . . . I am almost tempted. It's a bit of an idea. One might have a shot at it.

THE FATHER Of course. You'll see what scenes will come out of it. I can give you one, at once . . .

THE MANAGER By Jove, it tempts me. I'd like to have a go at it. Let's try it out. Come with me to my office. (*Turning to the* ACTORS) You are at liberty for a bit, but don't stop out of the theatre for long. In a quarter of an hour, twenty minutes, all back here again! (*To the* FATHER) We'll see what can be done. Who knows if we don't get something really extraordinary out of it?

THE FATHER There's no doubt about it. They (*indicating the* CHARACTERS) had better come with us too, hadn't they?

THE MANAGER Yes, yes. Come on! come on! (*Moves away and then turning to the* ACTORS) Be punctual, please! (MANAGER *and the* SIX CHARACTERS *cross the stage and go off. The other* ACTORS *remain, looking at one another in astonishment*)

LEADING MAN Is he serious? What the devil does he want to do?

JUVENILE LEAD This is rank madness.

THIRD ACTOR Does he expect to knock up a drama in five minutes?

JUVENILE LEAD Like the improvisers!

LEADING LADY If he thinks I'm going to take part in a joke like this . . .

JUVENILE LEAD I'm out of it anyway.

FOURTH ACTOR I should like to know who they are. (*Aludes to* CHARACTERS)

THIRD ACTOR What do you suppose? Madmen or rascals!

JUVENILE LEAD And he takes them seriously!

L'INGÉNUE Vanity! He fancies himself as an author now.

LEADING MAN It's absolutely unheard of. If the stage has come to this . . . well I'm . . .

FIFTH ACTOR It's rather a joke.

THIRD ACTOR Well, we'll see what's going to happen next.

(*Thus talking, the* ACTORS *leave the stage; some going out by the little door at the back; others retiring to their dressing-rooms.*
The curtan remains up.
The action of the play is suspended for twenty minutes)

ACT II

The stage call-bells ring to warn the company that the play is about to begin again.

THE STEPDAUGHTER *comes out of the* MANAGER's *office along with the* CHILD *and the* BOY. *As she comes out of the office, she cries:* Nonsense! Nonsense! Do it yourselves! I'm not going to mix myself up in this mess. (*Turning to the* CHILD *and coming quickly with her on to the stage*) Come on, Rosetta, let's run!

(*The* BOY *follows them slowly, remaining a little behind and seeming perplexed*)

THE STEPDAUGHTER (*Stops, bends over the* CHILD *and takes the latter's face between her hands*) My little darling! You're frightened, aren't you? You don't know where we are, do you? (*Pretending to reply to a question of the* CHILD) What is the stage? It's a place, baby, you know, where people play at being serious, a place where they act comedies. We've got to act a comedy now, dead serious, you know; and you're in it also, little one. (*Embraces her, pressing the little head to her breast, and rocking the* CHILD *for a moment*) Oh darling, darling, what a horrid comedy you've got to play! What a wretched part they've found for you! A garden . . . a fountain . . . look . . . just suppose, kiddie, it's here. Where, you say? Why, right here in the middle. It's all pretence you know. That's the trouble, my pet: it's all make-believe here. It's better to imagine it though, because if they fix it up for you, it'll only be painted cardboard, painted cardboard for the rockery, the water, the plants . . . Ah, but I think a baby like this one would sooner have a make-believe fountain than a real one, so she could play with it. What a joke it'll be for the others! But for you, alas! not quite such a joke: you who are real, baby dear, and really play by a real fountain that is big and green and beautiful, with ever so many bamboos around it that are reflected in the water, and a whole lot of little ducks swimming about . . . No, Rosetta, no, your mother doesn't bother about you on account of that wretch of a son there. I'm in the devil of a temper, and as for that lad . . . (*Seizes* BOY *by the arm to force him to take one of his hands out of his pockets*) What have you got there? What are you hiding? (*Pulls his hand out of his pocket, looks into it and catches the glint of a revolver*) Ah, where did you get this?

(*The* BOY, *very pale in the face, looks at her, but does not answer*)

Idiot! If I'd been in your place, instead of killing myself, I'd have shot one of those two, or both of them: father and son.

(*The* FATHER *enters from the office, all excited from his work. The* MANAGER *follows him*)

THE FATHER Come on, come on, dear! Come here for a minute! We've arranged everything. It's all fixed up.

THE MANAGER (*Also excited*) If you please, young lady, there are one or two points to settle still. Will you come along?

THE STEPDAUGHTER (*Following him towards the office*) Ouff! what's the good, if you've arranged everything.

(*The* FATHER, MANAGER *and* STEPDAUGHTER *go back into the office again* [*off*] *for a moment. At the same time, the* SON, *followed by the* MOTHER, *comes out*)

THE SON (*Looking at the three entering office*) Oh this is fine, fine! And to think I can't even get away!

(*The* MOTHER *attempts to look at him, but lowers her eyes immediately when he turns away from her. She then sits down. The* BOY *and the* CHILD *approach her. She casts a glance again at the* SON, *and speaks with humble tones, trying to draw him into conversation*)

THE MOTHER And isn't my punishment the worst of all? (*Then seeing from the* SON's *manner that he will not bother himself about her*) My God! Why are you so cruel? Isn't it enough for one person to support all this torment? Must you then insist on others seeing it also?

THE SON (*Half to himself, meaning the* MOTHER *to hear, however*) And they want to put it on the stage! If there was at least a reason for it! He thinks he has got at the meaning of it all. Just as if each one of us in every circumstance of life couldn't find his own explanation of it! (*Pauses*) He complains he was discovered in a place where he ought not to have been seen, in a moment of his life which ought to have remained hidden and kept out of the reach of that convention which he has to maintain for other people. And what about my case? Haven't I had to reveal what no son ought ever to reveal: how father and mother live and are man and wife for themselves quite apart from that idea of father and mother which we give them? When this idea is revealed, our life is then linked at one point only to that man and that woman; and as such it should shame them, shouldn't it?

(*The* MOTHER *hides her face in her hands. From the dressing-rooms and the little door at the back of the stage the* ACTORS *and* STAGE MANAGER *return, followed by the* PROPERTY MAN, *and the* PROMPTER. *At the same moment, the* MANAGER *comes out of his office, accompanied by the* FATHER *and the* STEPDAUGHTER)

THE MANAGER Come on, come on, ladies and gentlemen! Heh! you there, machinist!

MACHINIST Yes sir?

THE MANAGER Fix up the white parlor with the floral decorations. Two wings and a drop with a door will do. Hurry up!

(*The* MACHINIST *runs off at once to prepare the scene, and arranges it while the* MANAGER *talks with the* STAGE MANAGER, *the* PROPERTY MAN, *and the* PROMPTER *on matters of detail*)

THE MANAGER (*To* PROPERTY MAN) Just have a look, and see if there isn't a sofa or divan in the wardrobe . . .

PROPERTY MAN There's the green one.

THE STEPDAUGHTER No, no! Green won't do. It was yellow, ornamented with flowers—very large! and most comfortable!

PROPERTY MAN There isn't one like that.

THE MANAGER It doesn't matter. Use the one we've got.

THE STEPDAUGHTER Doesn't matter? It's most important!

THE MANAGER We're only trying it now. Please don't interfere. (*To* PROPERTY MAN) See if we've got a shop window—long and narrowish.

THE STEPDAUGHTER And the little table! The little mahogany table for the pale blue envelope!

PROPERTY MAN (*To* MANAGER) There's that little gilt one.

THE MANAGER That'll do fine.

THE FATHER A mirror.

THE STEPDAUGHTER And the screen! We must have a screen. Otherwise how can I manage?

PROPERTY MAN That's all right, Miss. We've got any amount of them.

THE MANAGER (*To the* STEPDAUGHTER) We want some clothes pegs too, don't we?

THE STEPDAUGHTER Yes, several, several!

THE MANAGER See how many we've got and bring them all.

PROPERTY MAN All right!

(*The* PROPERTY MAN *hurries off to obey his orders. While he is putting the things in their places, the* MANAGER *talks to the* PROMPTER *and then with the* CHARACTERS *and the* ACTORS)

THE MANAGER (*To* PROMPTER) Take your seat. Look here: this is the outline of the scenes, act by act. (*Hands him some sheets of paper*) And now I'm going to ask you to do something out of the ordinary.

PROMPTER Take it down in shorthand?

THE MANAGER (*Pleasantly surprised*) Exactly! Can you do shorthand?

PROMPTER Yes, a little.

THE MANAGER Good! (*Turning to a stage hand*) Go and get some paper from my office, plenty, as much as you can find.

(*The* STAGE HAND *goes off, and soon returns with a handful of paper which he gives to the* PROMPTER)

THE MANAGER (*To* PROMPTER) You follow the scenes as we play them, and try and get the points down, at any rate the most important ones. (*Then addressing the* ACTORS) Clear the stage, ladies and gentlemen! Come over here (*Pointing to the Left*) and listen attentively.

LEADING LADY   But, excuse me, we . . .

THE MANAGER (*Guessing her thought*)   Don't worry! You won't have to improvise.

LEADING MAN   What have we to do then?

THE MANAGER   Nothing. For the moment you just watch and listen. Everybody will get his part written out afterwards. At present we're going to try the thing as best we can. They're going to act now.

THE FATHER (*As if fallen from the clouds into the confusion of the stage*)   We? What do you mean, if you please, by a rehearsal?

THE MANAGER   A rehearsal for them. (*Points to the* ACTORS)

THE FATHER   But since we are the characters . . .

THE MANAGER   All right: "characters" then, if you insist on calling yourselves such. But here, my dear sir, the characters don't act. Here the actors do the acting. The characters are there, in the "book"—(*Pointing towards* PROMPTER's *box*) when there is a "book"!

THE FATHER   I won't contradict you; but excuse me, the actors aren't the characters. They want to be, they pretend to be, don't they? Now if these gentlemen here are fortunate enough to have us alive before them . . .

THE MANAGER   Oh this is grand! You want to come before the public yourselves then?

THE FATHER   As we are . . .

THE MANAGER   I can assure you it would be a magnificent spectacle!

LEADING MAN   What's the use of us here anyway then?

THE MANAGER   You're not going to pretend that you can act? It makes me laugh! (*The* ACTORS *laugh*) There, you see, they are laughing at the notion. But, by the way, I must cast the parts. That won't be difficult. They cast themselves. (*To the* SECOND LADY LEAD) You play the Mother. (*To the* FATHER) We must find her a name.

THE FATHER   Amalia, sir.

THE MANAGER   But that is the real name of your wife. We don't want to call her by her real name.

THE FATHER   Why ever not, if it is her name? . . . Still, perhaps, if that lady must . . . (*Makes a slight motion of the hand to indicate the* SECOND LADY LEAD) I see this woman here (*means the*

MOTHER) as Amalia. But do as you like. (*Gets more and more confused*) I don't know what to say to you. Already, I begin to hear my own words ring false, as if they had another sound . . .

THE MANAGER Don't you worry about it. It'll be our job to find the right tones. And as for her name, if you want her Amalia, Amalia it shall be; and if you don't like it, we'll find another! For the moment though, we'll call the characters in this way (*to* JUVENILE LEAD) You are the Son; (*to the* LEADING LADY) You naturally are the Stepdaughter . . .

THE STEPDAUGHTER (*Excitedly*) What? what? I, that woman there? (*Bursts out laughing*)

THE MANAGER (*Angry*) What is there to laugh at?

LEADING LADY (*Indignant*) Nobody has ever dared to laugh at me. I insist on being treated with respect; otherwise I go away.

THE STEPDAUGHTER No, no, excuse me . . . I am not laughing at you . . .

THE MANAGER (*To* STEPDAUGHTER) You ought to feel honored to be played by . . .

LEADING LADY (*At once, contemptuously*) "That woman there" . . .

THE STEPDAUGHTER But I wasn't speaking of you, you know. I was speaking of myself—whom I can't see at all in you! That is all. I don't know . . . but . . . you . . . aren't in the least like me . . .

THE FATHER True. Here's the point. Look here, sir, our temperaments, our souls. . .

THE MANAGER Temperament, soul, be hanged. Do you suppose the spirit of the piece is in you? Nothing of the kind!

THE FATHER What, haven't we our own temperaments, our own souls?

THE MANAGER Not at all. Your soul or whatever you like to call it takes shape here. The actors give body and form to it, voice and gesture. And my actors—I may tell you—have given expression to much more lofty material than this little drama of yours, which may or may not hold up on the stage. But if it does, the merit of it, believe me, will be due to my actors.

THE FATHER I don't dare contradict you, sir; but, believe me, it is a terrible suffering for us who are as we are, with these bodies of ours, these features to see . . .

THE MANAGER (*Cutting him short and out of patience*) Good heavens! The make-up will remedy all that, man, the make-up . . .

THE FATHER Maybe. But the voice, the gestures . . .

THE MANAGER Now, look here! On the stage, you as yourself, cannot exist. The actor here acts you, and that's an end to it!

THE FATHER I understand. And now I think I see why our author who conceived us as we are, all alive, didn't want to put us on the stage after all. I haven't the least desire to offend your actors. Far from it! But when I think that I am to be acted by ... I don't know by whom ...

LEADING MAN (*On his dignity*) By me, if you've no objection!

THE FATHER (*Humbly, mellifluously*) Honored, I assure you, sir. (*Bows*) Still, I must say that try as this gentleman may, with all his good will and wonderful art, to absorb me into himself ...

LEADING MAN Oh chuck it! "Wonderful art!" Withdraw that, please!

THE FATHER The performance he will give, even doing his best with make-up to look like me ...

LEADING MAN It will certainly be a bit difficult! (*The* ACTORS *laugh*)

THE FATHER Exactly! It will be difficult to act me as I really am. The effect will be rather—apart from the make-up—according as to how he supposes I am, as he senses me—if he does sense me —and not as I inside of myself feel myself to be. It seems to me then that account should be taken of this by everyone whose duty it may become to criticize us ...

THE MANAGER Heavens! The man's starting to think about the critics now! Let them say what they like. It's up to us to put on the play if we can. (*Looking around*) Come on! come on! Is the stage set? (*To the* ACTORS *and* CHARACTERS) Stand back—stand back! Let me see, and don't let's lose any more time! (*To the* STEPDAUGHTER) Is it all right as it is now?

THE STEPDAUGHTER Well, to tell the truth, I don't recognize the scene.

THE MANAGER My dear lady, you can't possibly suppose that we can construct that shop of Madame Pace piece by piece here? (*To the* FATHER) You said a white room with flowered wall paper, didn't you?

THE FATHER Yes.

THE MANAGER Well then. We've got the furniture right, more or less. Bring that little table a bit further forward. (*The* STAGE HANDS *obey the order. To* PROPERTY MAN) You go and find an envelope, if possible, a pale blue one; and give it to that gentleman. (*Indicates* FATHER)

PROPERTY MAN An ordinary envelope?

MANAGER *and* FATHER Yes, yes, an ordinary envelope.

PROPERTY MAN At once, sir. (*Exit*)

THE MANAGER Ready, everyone! First scene—the Young Lady. (*The* LEADING LADY *comes forward*) No, no, you must wait. I meant her. (*Indicating the* STEPDAUGHTER) You just watch—

THE STEPDAUGHTER (*Adding at once*) How I shall play it, how I shall live it! . . .

LEADING LADY (*Offended*) I shall live it also, you may be sure, as soon as I begin!

THE MANAGER (*With his hands to his head*) Ladies and gentlemen, if you please! No more useless discussions! Scene I: the young lady with Madame Pace: Oh! (*Looks around as if lost*) And this Madame Pace, where is she?

THE FATHER She isn't with us, sir.

THE MANAGER Then what the devil's to be done?

THE FATHER But she is alive too.

THE MANAGER Yes, but where is she?

THE FATHER One minute. Let me speak! (*Turning to the* AC-TRESSES) If these ladies would be so good as to give me their hats for a moment . . .

THE ACTRESSES (*Half surprised, half laughing, in chorus*) What? Why?

Our hats?

What does he say?

THE MANAGER What are you going to do with the ladies' hats? (*The* ACTORS *laugh*)

THE FATHER Oh nothing. I just want to put them on these pegs for a moment. And one of the ladies will be so kind as to take off her mantle . . .

THE ACTORS Oh, what d'you think of that? Only the mantle? He must be mad.

SOME ACTRESSES But why?

Mantles as well?

THE FATHER To hang them up here for a moment. Please be so kind, will you?

THE ACTRESSES (*Taking off their hats, one or two also their cloaks, and going to hang them on the racks*) After all, why not?

There you are!

This is really funny.

We've got to put them on show.

THE FATHER Exactly; just like that, on show.

THE MANAGER May we know why?

THE FATHER I'll tell you. Who knows if, by arranging the stage for her, she does not come here herself, attracted by the very articles of her trade? (*Inviting the* ACTORS *to look towards the exit at back of stage*) Look! Look!

(*The door at the back of stage opens and* MADAME PACE *enters and takes a few steps forward. She is a fat, oldish woman with puffy oxy-*

genated hair. She is rouged and powdered, dressed with a comical elegance in black silk. Round her waist is a long silver chain from which hangs a pair of scissors. The STEPDAUGHTER *runs over to her at once amid the stupor of the* ACTORS)

THE STEPDAUGHTER (*Turning towards her*) There she is! There she is!

THE FATHER (*Radiant*) It's she! I said so, didn't I? There she is!

THE MANAGER (*Conquering his surprise, and then becoming indignant*) What sort of a trick is this?

LEADING MAN (*Almost at the same time*) What's going to happen next?

JUVENILE LEAD Where does *she* come from?

L'INGÉNUE They've been holding her in reserve, I guess.

LEADING LADY A vulgar trick!

THE FATHER (*Dominating the protests*) Excuse me, all of you! Why are you so anxious to destroy in the name of a vulgar, commonplace sense of truth, this reality which comes to birth attracted and formed by the magic of the stage itself, which has indeed more right to live here than you, since it is much truer than you—if you don't mind my saying so? Which is the actress among you who is to play Madame Pace? Well, here is Madame Pace herself. And you will allow, I fancy, that the actress who acts her will be less true than this woman here, who is herself in person. You see my daughter recognized her and went over to her at once. Now you're going to witness the scene!

(*But the scene between the* STEPDAUGHTER *and* MADAME PACE *has already begun despite the protest of the* ACTORS *and the reply of the* FATHER. *It has begun quietly, naturally, in a manner impossible for the stage. So when the* ACTORS, *called to attention by the* FATHER, *turn round and see* MADAME PACE, *who has placed one hand under the* STEPDAUGHTER'S *chin to raise her head, they observe her at first with great attention, but hearing her speak in an unintelligible manner their interest begins to wane*)

THE MANAGER Well? well?

LEADING MAN What does she say?

LEADING LADY One can't hear a word.

JUVENILE LEAD Louder! Louder please!

THE STEPDAUGHTER (*Leaving* MADAME PACE, *who smiles a Sphinx-like smile, and advancing towards the* ACTORS) Louder? Louder? What are you talking about? These aren't matters which can be shouted at the top of one's voice. If I have spoken them out loud, it was to shame him and have my revenge. (*Indicates* FATHER) But for Madame it's quite a different matter.

THE MANAGER   Indeed? indeed? But here, you know, people have got to make themselves heard, my dear. Even we who are on the stage can't hear you. What will it be when the public's in the theater? And anyway, you can very well speak up now among yourselves, since we shan't be present to listen to you as we are now. You've got to pretend to be alone in a room at the back of a shop where no one can hear you.

(*The* STEPDAUGHTER *coquettishly and with a touch of malice makes a sign of disagreement two or three times with her finger*)

THE MANAGER   What do you mean by no?

THE STEPDAUGHTER   (*Sotto voce, mysteriously*)   There's someone who will hear us if she (*indicating* MADAME PACE) speaks out loud.

THE MANAGER   (*In consternation*)   What? Have you got someone else to spring on us now? (*The* ACTORS *burst out laughing*)

THE FATHER   No, no sir. She is alluding to me. I've got to be here —there behind that door, in waiting; and Madame Pace knows it. In fact, if you will allow me, I'll go there at once, so I can be quite ready. (*Moves away*)

THE MANAGER   (*Stopping him*)   No! wait! wait! We must observe the conventions of the theater. Before you are ready . . .

THE STEPDAUGHTER   (*Interrupting him*)   No, get on with it at once! I'm just dying, I tell you, to act this scene. If he's ready, I'm more than ready.

THE MANAGER   (*Shouting*)   But, my dear young lady, first of all, we must have the scene between you and this lady . . . (*Indicates* MADAME PACE) Do you understand? . . .

THE STEPDAUGHTER   Good Heavens! She's been telling me what you know already: that Mamma's work is badly done again, that the material's ruined; and that if I want her to continue to help us in our misery I must be patient . . .

MADAME PACE   (*Coming forward with an air of great importance*) Yes indeed, sir, I no wanta take advantage of her, I no wanta be hard . . .

(*Note:* MADAME PACE *is supposed to talk in a jargon half Italian, half English*)

THE MANAGER   (*Alarmed*)   What? What? she talks like that? (*The* ACTORS *burst out laughing again*)

THE STEPDAUGHTER   (*Also laughing*)   Yes, yes, that's the way she talks, half English, half Italian! Most comical it is!

MADAME PACE   Itta seem not verra polite gentlemen laugha atta me eef I trya best speaka English.

THE MANAGER *Diamine!* Of course! Of course! Let her talk like that! Just what we want. Talk just like that, Madame, if you please! The effect will be certain. Exactly what was wanted to put a little comic relief into the crudity of the situation. Of course she talks like that! Magnificent!

THE STEPDAUGHTER Magnificent? Certainly! When certain suggestions are made to one in language of that kind, the effect is certain, since it seems almost a joke. One feels inclined to laugh when one hears her talk about an "old signore" "who wanta talka nicely with you." Nice old signore, eh, Madame?

MADAME PACE Not so old, my dear, not so old! And even if you no lika him, he won't make any scandal!

THE MOTHER (*Jumping up amid the amazement and consternation of the* ACTORS *who had not been noticing her. They move to restrain her*) You old devil! You murderess!

THE STEPDAUGHTER (*Running over to calm her* MOTHER) Calm yourself, mother, calm yourself! Please don't . . .

THE FATHER (*Going to her also at the same time*) Calm yourself! Don't get excited! Sit down now!

THE MOTHER Well then, take that woman away out of my sight!

THE STEPDAUGHTER (*To* MANAGER) It is impossible for my mother to remain here.

THE FATHER (*To* MANAGER) They can't be here together. And for this reason, you see: that woman there was not with us when we came . . . If they are on together, the whole thing is given away inevitably, as you see.

THE MANAGER It doesn't matter. This is only a first rough sketch —just to get an idea of the various points of the scene, even confusedly . . . (*Turning to the* MOTHER *and leading her to her chair*) Come along, my dear lady, sit down now, and let's get on with the scene . . .

(*Meanwhile, the* STEPDAUGHTER, *coming forward again, turns to* MADAME PACE)

THE STEPDAUGHTER Come on, Madame, come on!

MADAME PACE (*Offended*) No, no, *grazie*. I not do anything witha your mother present.

THE STEPDAUGHTER Nonsense! Introduce this "old signore" who wants to talk nicely to me. (*Addressing the company imperiously*) We've got to do this scene one way or another, haven't we? Come on! (*To* MADAME PACE) You can go!

MADAME PACE Ah yes! I go'way! I go'way! Certainly! (*Exits furious*)

THE STEPDAUGHTER (*To the* FATHER) Now you make your entry.

No, you needn't go over there. Come here. Let's suppose you've already come in. Like that, yes! I'm here with bowed head, modest-like. Come on! Out with your voice! Say "Good morning, Miss" in that peculiar tone, that special tone . . .

THE MANAGER Excuse me, but are you the Manager, or am I? (*To the* FATHER, *who looks undecided and perplexed*) Get on with it, man! Go down there to the back of the stage. You needn't go off. Then come right forward here.

(*The* FATHER *does as he is told, looking troubled and perplexed at first. But as soon as he begins to move, the reality of the action affects him, and he begins to smile and to be more natural. The* ACTORS *watch intently*)

THE MANAGER (*Sotto voce, quickly to the* PROMPTER *in his box*) Ready! ready? Get ready to write now.

THE FATHER (*Coming forward and speaking in a different tone*) Good afternoon, Miss!

THE STEPDAUGHTER (*Head bowed down slightly, with restrained disgust*) Good afternoon!

THE FATHER (*Looks under her hat which partly covers her face. Perceiving she is very young, he makes an exclamation, partly of surprise, partly of fear lest he compromise himself in a risky adventure*) Ah . . . but . . . ah . . . I say . . . this is not the first time that you have come here, is it?

THE STEPDAUGHTER (*Modestly*) No sir.

THE FATHER You've been here before, eh? (*Then seeing her nod agreement*) More than once? (*Waits for her to answer, looks under her hat, smiles, and then says*) Well then, there's no need to be so shy, is there? May I take off your hat?

THE STEPDAUGHTER (*Anticipating him and with veiled disgust*) No sir . . . I'll do it myself. (*Takes it off quickly*)

(*The* MOTHER, *who watches the progress of the scene with the* SON *and the other two* CHILDREN *who cling to her, is on thorns; and follows with varying expressions of sorrow, indignation, anxiety, and horror the words and actions of the other two. From time to time she hides her face in her hands and sobs*)

THE MOTHER Oh, my God, my God!

THE FATHER (*Playing his part with a touch of gallantry*) Give it to me! I'll put it down. (*Takes hat from her hands*) But a dear little head like yours ought to have a smarter hat. Come and help me choose one from the stock, won't you?

L'INGÉNUE (*Interrupting*) I say . . . those are our hats, you know.

THE MANAGER (*Furious*)   Silence! silence! Don't try and be funny, if you please . . . We're playing the scene now, I'd have you notice. (*To the* STEPDAUGHTER) Begin again, please!

THE STEPDAUGHTER (*Continuing*)   No thank you, sir.

THE FATHER   Oh, come now. Don't talk like that. You must take it. I shall be upset if you don't. There are some lovely little hats here; and then—Madame will be pleased. She expects it, anyway, you know.

THE STEPDAUGHTER   No, no! I couldn't wear it!

THE FATHER   Oh, you're thinking about what they'd say at home if they saw you come in with a new hat? My dear girl, there's always a way round these little matters, you know.

THE STEPDAUGHTER (*All keyed up*)   No, it's not that. I couldn't wear it because I am . . . as you see . . . you might have noticed . . . (*Showing her black dress*)

THE FATHER   . . . in mourning! Of course: I beg your pardon: I'm frightfully sorry . . .

THE STEPDAUGHTER (*Forcing herself to conquer her indignation and nausea*)   Stop! Stop! It's I who must thank you. There's no need for you to feel mortified or specially sorry. Don't think any more of what I've said. (*Tries to smile*) I must forget that I am dressed so . . .

THE MANAGER (*Interrupting and turning to the* PROMPTER)   Stop a minute! Stop! Don't write that down. Cut out that last bit. (*Then to the* FATHER *and* STEPDAUGHTER) Fine! it's going fine! (*To the* FATHER *only*) And now you can go on as we arranged. (*To the* ACTORS) Pretty good that scene, where he offers her the hat, eh?

THE STEPDAUGHTER   The best's coming now. Why can't we go on?

THE MANAGER   Have a little patience! (*To the* ACTORS) Of course, it must be treated rather lightly.

LEADING MAN   Still, with a bit of go in it!

LEADING LADY   Of course! It's easy enough! (*To* LEADING MAN) Shall you and I try it now?

LEADING MAN   Why, yes! I'll prepare my entrance. (*Exit in order to make his entrance*)

THE MANAGER (*To* LEADING LADY)   See here! The scene between you and Madame Pace is finished. I'll have it written out properly after. You remain here . . . oh, where are you going?

LEADING LADY   One minute. I want to put my hat on again. (*Goes over to hatrack and puts her hat on her head*).

THE MANAGER   Good! You stay here with your head bowed down a bit.

THE STEPDAUGHTER But she isn't dressed in black.

LEADING LADY But I shall be, and much more effectively than you.

THE MANAGER (*To* STEPDAUGHTER) Be quiet please, and watch! You'll be able to learn something. (*Clapping his hands*) Come on! come on! Entrance, please!

(*The door at rear of stage opens, and the* LEADING MAN *enters with the lively manner of an old gallant. The rendering of the scene by the* ACTORS *from the very first words is seen to be quite a different thing, though it has not in any way the air of a parody. Naturally, the* STEP-DAUGHTER *and the* FATHER, *not being able to recognize themselves in the* LEADING LADY *and the* LEADING MAN, *who deliver their words in different tones and with a different psychology, express, sometimes with smiles, sometimes with gestures, the impression they receive*)

LEADING MAN Good afternoon, Miss . . .

THE FATHER (*At once unable to contain himself*) No! no!

(*The* STEPDAUGHTER, *noticing the way the* LEADING MAN *enters, bursts out laughing*)

THE MANAGER (*Furious*) Silence! And you, please, just stop that laughing. If we go on like this, we shall never finish.

THE STEPDAUGHTER Forgive me, sir, but it's natural enough. This lady (*indicating* LEADING LADY) stands there still; but if she is supposed to be me, I can assure you that if I heard anyone say "Good afternoon" in that manner and in that tone, I should burst out laughing as I did.

THE FATHER Yes, yes, the manner, the tone . . .

THE MANAGER Nonsense! Rubbish! Stand aside and let me see the action.

LEADING MAN If I've got to represent an old fellow who's coming into a house of an equivocal character . . .

THE MANAGER Don't listen to them, for Heaven's sake! Do it again! It goes fine. (*Waiting for the* ACTORS *to begin again*) Well?

LEADING MAN Good afternoon, Miss.

LEADING LADY Good afternoon.

LEADING MAN (*Imitating the gesture of the* FATHER *when he looked under the hat, and then expressing quite clearly first satisfaction and then fear*) Ah, but . . . I say . . . this is not the first time that you have come here, is it?

THE MANAGER Good, but not quite so heavily. Like this. (*Acts himself*) "This isn't the first time that you have come here" . . . (*To* LEADING LADY) And you say: "No, sir."

LEADING LADY No, sir.

LEADING MAN You've been here before, more than once.

THE MANAGER No, no, stop! Let her nod "yes" first. "You've been here before, eh?" (*The* LEADING LADY *lifts up her head slightly and closes her eyes as though in disgust. Then she inclines her head twice*)

THE STEPDAUGHTER (*Unable to contain herself*) Oh my God! (*Puts a hand to her mouth to prevent herself from laughing*)

THE MANAGER (*Turning round*) What's the matter?

THE STEPDAUGHTER Nothing, nothing!

THE MANAGER (*To* LEADING MAN) Go on!

LEADING MAN You've been here before, eh? Well then, there's no need to be so shy, is there? May I take off your hat?

(*The* LEADING MAN *says this last speech in such a tone and with such gestures that the* STEPDAUGHTER, *though she has her hand to her mouth, cannot keep from laughing*)

LEADING LADY (*Indignant*) I'm not going to stop here to be made a fool of by that woman there.

LEADING MAN Neither am I! I'm through with it!

THE MANAGER (*Shouting to* STEPDAUGHTER) Silence! for once and all, I tell you!

THE STEPDAUGHTER Forgive me! forgive me!

THE MANAGER You haven't any manners: that's what it is! You go too far.

THE FATHER (*Endeavoring to intervene*) Yes, it's true, but excuse her . . .

THE MANAGER Excuse what? It's absolutely disgusting.

THE FATHER Yes, sir, but believe me, it has such a strange effect when . . .

THE MANAGER Strange? Why strange? Where is it strange?

THE FATHER No, sir; I admire your actors—this gentleman here, this lady; but they are certainly not us!

THE MANAGER I should hope not. Evidently they cannot be you, if they are actors.

THE FATHER Just so: actors! Both of them act our parts exceedingly well. But, believe me, it produces quite a different effect on us. They want to be us, but they aren't, all the same.

THE MANAGER What is it then anyway?

THE FATHER Something that is . . . that is theirs—and no longer ours . . .

THE MANAGER But naturally, inevitably. I've told you so already.

THE FATHER Yes, I understand . . . I understand . . .

THE MANAGER Well then, let's have no more of it! (*Turning to the* ACTORS) We'll have the rehearsals by ourselves, afterwards, in the ordinary way. I never could stand rehearsing with the author present. He's never satisfied! (*Turning to* FATHER *and* STEP-DAUGHTER) Come on! Let's get on with it again; and try and see if you can't keep from laughing.

THE STEPDAUGHTER Oh, I shan't laugh any more. There's a nice little bit coming from me now: you'll see.

THE MANAGER Well then: when she says "Don't think any more of what I've said. I must forget, etc.," you (*addressing the* FATHER) come in sharp with "I understand, I understand"; and then you ask her . . .

THE STEPDAUGHTER (*Interrupting*) What?

THE MANAGER Why she is in mourning.

THE STEPDAUGHTER Not at all! See here: when I told him that it was useless for me to be thinking about my wearing mourning, do you know how he answered me? "Ah well," he said, "then let's take off this little frock."

THE MANAGER Great! Just what we want, to make a riot in the theater!

THE STEPDAUGHTER But its the truth!

THE MANAGER What does that matter? Acting is our business here. Truth up to a certain point, but no further.

THE STEPDAUGHTER What do you want to do then?

THE MANAGER You'll see, you'll see! Leave it to me.

THE STEPDAUGHTER No sir! What you want to do is to piece together a little romantic sentimental scene out of my disgust, out of all the reasons, each more cruel and viler than the other, why I am what I am. He is to ask me why I'm in mourning; and I'm to answer with tears in my eyes, that it is just two months since papa died. No sir, no! He's got to say to me; as he did say: "Well, let's take off this little dress at once." And I; with my two months' mourning in my heart, went there behind that screen, and with these fingers tingling with shame . . .

THE MANAGER (*Running his hands through his hair*) For Heaven's sake! What are you saying?

THE STEPDAUGHTER (*Crying out excitedly*) The truth! The truth!

THE MANAGER It may be. I don't deny it, and I can understand all your horror; but you must surely see that you can't have this kind of thing on the stage. It won't go.

THE STEPDAUGHTER Not possible, eh? Very well! I'm much obliged to you—but I'm off!

THE MANAGER Now be reasonable! Don't lose your temper!

THE STEPDAUGHTER I won't stop here! I won't! I can see you've fixed it all up with him in your office. All this talk about what is possible for the stage . . . I understand! He wants to get at his complicated "cerebral drama," to have his famous remorses and torments acted; but I want to act my part, *my part!*

THE MANAGER (*Annoyed, shaking his shoulders*) Ah! Just *your* part! But, if you will pardon me, there are other parts than yours: his (*indicating the* FATHER) and hers! (*Indicating the* MOTHER) On the stage you can't have a character becoming too prominent and overshadowing all the others. The thing is to pack them all into a neat little framework and then act what is actable. I am aware of the fact that everyone has his own interior life which he wants very much to put forward. But the difficulty lies in this fact: to set out just so much as is necessary for the stage, taking the other characters into consideration, and at the same time hint at the unrevealed interior life of each. I am willing to admit, my dear young lady, that from your point of view it would be a fine idea if each character could tell the public all his troubles in a nice monologue or a regular one-hour lecture. (*Good-humoredly*) You must restrain yourself, my dear, and in your own interest, too; because this fury of yours, this exaggerated disgust you show, may make a bad impression, you know. After you have confessed to me that there were others before him at Madame Pace's and more than once . . .

THE STEPDAUGHTER (*Bowing her head, impressed*) It's true. But remember those others mean him for me all the same.

THE MANAGER (*Not understanding*) What? The others? What do you mean?

THE STEPDAUGHTER For one who has gone wrong, sir, he who was responsible for the first fault is responsible for all that follow. He is responsible for my faults, was, even before I was born. Look at him, and see if it isn't true!

THE MANAGER Well, well! And does the weight of so much responsibility seem nothing to you? Give him a chance to act it, to get it over!

THE STEPDAUGHTER How? How can he act all his "noble remorses," all his "moral torments," if you want to spare him the horror of being discovered one day—after he had asked her what he did ask her—in the arms of her, that already fallen woman, that child, sir, that child he used to watch come out of school? (*She is moved*)

(*The* MOTHER *at this point is overcome with emotion, and breaks out into a fit of crying.*
All are touched. A long pause)

THE STEPDAUGHTER (*As soon as the* MOTHER *becomes a little quieter, adds resolutely and gravely*)   At present, we are unknown to the public. Tomorrow, you will act us as you wish, treating us in your own manner. But do you really want to see drama, do you want to see it flash out as it really did?

THE MANAGER   Of course! That's just what I do want, so I can use as much of it as is possible.

THE STEPDAUGHTER   Well then, ask that Mother there to leave us.

THE MOTHER (*Changing her low plaint into a sharp cry*)   No! No! Don't permit it, sir, don't permit it!

THE MANAGER   But it's only to try it.

THE MOTHER   I can't bear it. I can't.

THE MANAGER   But since it has happened already . . . I don't understand!

THE MOTHER   It's taking place now. It happens all the time. My torment isn't a pretended one. I live and feel every minute of my torture. Those two children there—have you heard them speak? They can't speak any more. They cling to me to keep my torment actual and vivid for me. But for themselves, they do not exist, they aren't any more. And she (*indicating* STEPDAUGHTER) has run away, she has left me, and is lost. If I now see her here before me, it is only to renew for me the tortures I have suffered for her too.

THE FATHER   The eternal moment! She (*indicating the* STEP-DAUGHTER) is here to catch me, fix me, and hold me eternally in the stocks for that one fleeting and shameful moment of my life. She can't give it up! And you sir, cannot either fairly spare me it.

THE MANAGER   I never said I didn't want to act it. It will form, as a matter of fact, the nucleus of the whole first act right up to her surprise. (*Indicating the* MOTHER)

THE FATHER   Just so! This is my punishment: the passion in all of us that must culminate in her final cry.

THE STEPDAUGHTER   I can hear it still in my ears. It's driven me mad, that cry—You can put me on as you like; it doesn't matter. Fully dressed, if you like—provided I have at least the arm bare; because, standing like this (*she goes close to the* FATHER *and leans her head on his breast*) with my head so, and my arms round his neck, I saw a vein pulsing in my arm here; and then, as if that live vein had awakened disgust in me, I closed my eyes like this, and let my head sink on his breast. (*Turning to the* MOTHER) Cry out, mother! Cry out! (*Buries head in* FATHER's *breast, and with her shoulders raised as if to prevent her hearing the cry, adds in tones of intense emotion*) Cry out as you did then!

THE MOTHER (*Coming forward to separate them*)   No! My daughter, my daughter! (*And after having pulled her away from him*)

You brute! you brute! She is my daughter! Don't you see she's my daughter?

THE MANAGER (*Walking backwards towards footlights*)   Fine! fine! Damned good! And then, of course—curtain!

THE FATHER (*Going towards him excitedly*)   Yes, of course, because that's the way it really happened.

THE MANAGER (*Convinced and pleased*)   Oh, yes, no doubt about it. Curtain here, curtain!

(*At the reiterated cry of the* MANAGER, *the* MACHINIST *lets the curtain down, leaving the* MANAGER *and the* FATHER *in front of it before the footlights*)

THE MANAGER   The darned idiot! I said "curtain" to show the act should end there, and he goes and lets it down in earnest. (*To the* FATHER, *while he pulls the curtain back to go onto the stage again*) Yes, yes, it's all right. Effect certain! That's the right ending. I'll guarantee the first act, at any rate.

ACT III

When the curtain goes up again, it is seen that the stage hands have shifted the bit of scenery used in the last part, and have rigged up instead at the back of the stage a drop, with some trees, and one or two wings. A portion of a fountain basin is visible. THE MOTHER *is sitting on the* Right *with the two children by her side.* THE SON *is on the same side, but away from the others. He seems bored, angry, and full of shame.* THE FATHER *and* THE STEPDAUGHTER *are also seated towards the* Right *front. On the other side* (Left) *are the* ACTORS, *much in the positions they occupied before the curtain was lowered. Only* THE MANAGER *is standing up in the middle of the stage, with his hand closed over his mouth, in the act of meditating.*

THE MANAGER (*Shaking his shoulders after a brief pause*)   Ah yes: the second act! Leave it to me, leave it all to me as we arranged, and you'll see! It'll go fine!

THE STEPDAUGHTER   Our entry into his house (*indicates* FATHER) in spite of him . . . (*indicates the* SON)

THE MANAGER (*Out of patience*)   Leave it to me, I tell you!

THE STEPDAUGHTER   Do let it be clear, at any rate, that it is in spite of my wishes.

THE MOTHER (*From her corner, shaking her head*)   For all the good that's come of it . . .

THE STEPDAUGHTER (*Turning towards her quickly*)   It doesn't matter. The more harm done us, the more remorse for him.

THE MANAGER (*Impatiently*) I understand! Good Heavens! I understand! I'm taking it into account.

THE MOTHER (*Supplicatingly*) I beg you, sir, to let it appear quite plain that for conscience' sake I did try in every way . . .

THE STEPDAUGHTER (*Interrupting indignantly and continuing for the* MOTHER). . . . to pacify me, to dissuade me from spiting him. (*To* MANAGER) Do as she wants: satisfy her, because it is true! I enjoy it immensely. Anyhow, as you can see, the meeker she is, the more she tries to get at his heart, the more distant and aloof does he become.

THE MANAGER Are we going to begin this second act or not?

THE STEPDAUGHTER I'm not going to talk any more now. But I must tell you this: you can't have the whole action take place in the garden, as you suggest. It isn't possible!

THE MANAGER Why not?

THE STEPDAUGHTER Because he (*indicates the* SON *again*) is always shut up alone in his room. And then there's all the part of that poor dazed-looking boy there which takes place indoors.

THE MANAGER Maybe! On the other hand, you will understand— we can't change scenes three or four times in one act.

LEADING MAN They used to once.

THE MANAGER Yes, when the public was up to the level of that child there.

LEADING LADY It makes the illusion easier.

THE FATHER (*Irritated*) The illusion! For Heaven's sake, don't say illusion. Please don't use that word, which is particularly painful for us.

THE MANAGER (*Astounded*) And why, if you please?

THE FATHER It's painful, cruel, really cruel; and you ought to understand that.

THE MANAGER But why? What ought we to say then? The illusion, I tell you, sir, which we've got to create for the audience . . .

LEADING MAN With our acting.

THE MANAGER The illusion of a reality.

THE FATHER I understand; but you, perhaps, do not understand us. Forgive me! You see . . . here for you and your actors, the thing is only—and rightly so . . . a kind of game . . .

LEADING LADY (*Interrupting indignantly*) A game! We're not children here, if you please! We are serious actors.

THE FATHER I don't deny it. What I mean is the game, or play, of your art, which has to give, as the gentleman says, a perfect illusion of reality.

THE MANAGER Precisely——!

THE FATHER   Now, if you consider the fact that we (*indicates himself and the other five* CHARACTERS), as we are, have no other reality outside of this illusion . . .

THE MANAGER (*Astonished, looking at his* ACTORS, *who are also amazed*)   And what does that mean?

THE FATHER (*After watching them for a moment with a wan smile*) As I say, sir, that which is a game of art for you is our sole reality. (*Brief pause. He goes a step or two nearer the* MANAGER *and adds*) But not only for us, you know, by the way. Just you think it over well. (*Looks him in the eyes*) Can you tell me who you are?

THE MANAGER (*Perplexed, half smiling*)   What? Who am I? I am myself.

THE FATHER   And if I were to tell you that that isn't true, because you are I? . . .

THE MANAGER   I should say you were mad——! (*The* ACTORS *laugh*)

THE FATHER   You're quite right to laugh: because we are all making believe here. (*To* MANAGER) And you can therefore object that it's only for a joke that that gentleman there (*indicates the* LEADING MAN), who naturally is himself, has to be me, who am on the contrary myself—this thing you see here. You see I've caught you in a trap! (*The* ACTORS *laugh*)

THE MANAGER (*Annoyed*)   But we've had all this over once before. Do you want to begin again?

THE FATHER   No, no! that wasn't my meaning! In fact, I should like to request you to abandon this game of art (*Looking at the* LEADING LADY *as if anticipating her*) which you are accustomed to play here with your actors, and to ask you seriously once again: who are you?

THE MANAGER (*Astonished and irritated, turning to his* ACTORS) If this fellow here hasn't got a nerve! A man who calls himself a character comes and asks me who I am!

THE FATHER (*With dignity, but not offended*)   A character, sir, may always ask a man who he is. Because a character has really a life of his own, marked with his especial characteristics; for which reason he is always "somebody." But a man—I'm not speaking of you now—may very well be "nobody."

THE MANAGER   Yes, but you are asking these questions of me, the boss, the manager! Do you understand?

THE FATHER   But only in order to know if you, as you really are now, see yourself as you once were with all the illusions that were yours then, with all the things both inside and outside of you as they seemed to you—as they were then indeed for you. Well, sir, if you think of all those illusions that mean nothing to you now, of all those things which don't even *seem* to you to exist any more, while once they *were* for you, don't you feel that—I won't say these boards—but the very earth under your feet is sinking away from you when you reflect that in the same way this *you* as you feel it today—all this present reality of yours—is fated to seem a mere illusion to you tomorrow?

THE MANAGER (*Without having understood much, but astonished by the specious argument*)   Well, well! And where does all this take us anyway?

THE FATHER   Oh, nowhere! It's only to show you that if we (*indicating the* CHARACTERS) have no other reality beyond illusion, you too must not count overmuch on your reality as you feel it today, since, like that of yesterday, it may prove an illusion for you tomorrow.

THE MANAGER (*Determining to make fun of him*)   Ah, excellent! Then you'll be saying next that you, with this comedy of yours that you brought here to act, are truer and more real than I am.

THE FATHER (*With the greatest seriousness*)   But of course; without doubt!

THE MANAGER   Ah, really?

THE FATHER   Why, I thought you'd understand that from the beginning.

THE MANAGER   More real than I?

THE FATHER   If your reality can change from one day to another . . .

THE MANAGER   But everyone knows it can change. It is always changing, the same as anyone else's.

THE FATHER (*With a cry*)   No, sir, not ours! Look here! That is the very difference! Our reality doesn't change: it can't change! It can't be other than what it is, because it is already fixed for ever. It's terrible. Ours is an immutable reality which should make you shudder when you approach us if you are really conscious of the fact that your reality is a mere transitory and fleeting illusion, taking this form today and that tomorrow, according to the conditions, according to your will, your sentiments, which in turn are controlled by an intellect that shows them to you today in one manner and tomorrow . . . who knows how? . . . Illusions of reality represented in this fatuous comedy of life that never ends, nor can ever end! Because if tomorrow it were to end . . . then why, all would be finished.

THE MANAGER   Oh for God's sake, will you *at least* finish with this philosophizing and let us try and shape this comedy which you yourself have brought me here? You argue and philosophize a bit too much, my dear sir. You know you seem to me almost, almost ... (*Stops and looks him over from head to foot*) Ah, by the way, I think you introduced yourself to me as a—what shall ... we say —a "character," created by an author who did not afterwards care to make a drama of his own creations.

THE FATHER   It is the simple truth, sir.

THE MANAGER   Nonsense! Cut that out, please! None of us believes it, because it isn't a thing, as you must recognize yourself, which one can believe seriously. If you want to know, it seems to me you are trying to imitate the manner of a certain author whom I heartily detest—I warn you—although I have unfortunately bound myself to put on one of his works. As a matter of fact, I was just starting to rehearse it, when you arrived. (*Turning to the* ACTORS) And this is what we've gained—out of the frying-pan into the fire!

THE FATHER   I don't know to what author you may be alluding, but believe me I feel what I think; and I seem to be philosophizing only for those who do not think what they feel, because they blind themselves with their own sentiment. I know that for many people this self-blinding seems much more "human"; but the contrary is really true. For man never reasons so much and becomes so introspective as when he suffers; since he is anxious to get at the cause of his sufferings, to learn who has produced them, and whether it is just or unjust that he should have to bear them. On the other hand, when he is happy, he takes his happiness as it comes and doesn't analyze it, just as if happiness were his right. The animals suffer without reasoning about their sufferings. But take the case of a man who suffers and begins to reason about it. Oh no! it can't be allowed! Let him suffer like an animal, and then—ah yes, he is "human!"

THE MANAGER   Look here! Look here! You're off again, philosophizing worse than ever.

THE FATHER   Because I suffer, sir! I'm not philosophizing: I'm crying aloud the reason of my sufferings.

THE MANAGER   (*Makes brusque movement as he is taken with a new idea*) I should like to know if anyone has ever heard of a character who gets right out of his part and perorates and speechifies as you do. Have you ever heard of a case? I haven't.

THE FATHER   You have never met such a case, sir, because authors, as a rule, hide the labor of their creations. When the characters are really alive before their author, the latter does nothing but follow them in their action, in their words, in the situations which they suggest to him; and he has to will them the way they will themselves—for there's trouble if he doesn't. When a character is born, he acquires at once such an independence, even of his own author, that he can be imagined by everybody even in many other situations where the author never dreamed of placing him; and so he acquires for himself a meaning which the author never thought of giving him.

THE MANAGER   Yes, yes, I know this.

THE FATHER   What is there then to marvel at in us? Imagine such a misfortune for characters as I have described to you: to be born of an author's fantasy, and be denied life by him; and then answer me if these characters left alive, and yet without life, weren't right in doing what they did do and are doing now, after they have attempted everything in their power to persuade him to give them their stage life. We've all tried him in turn, I, she (*indicating the* STEPDAUGHTER) and she. (*Indicating the* MOTHER)

THE STEPDAUGHTER   It's true. I too have sought to tempt him, many, many times, when he had been sitting at his writing table, feeling a bit melancholy, at the twilight hour. He would sit in his armchair too lazy to switch on the light, and all the shadows that crept into his room were full of our presence coming to tempt him. (*As if she saw herself still there by the writing table, and was annoyed by the presence of the* ACTORS) Oh, if you would only go away, go away and leave us alone—mother here with that son of hers—I with that Child—that Boy there always alone —and then I with him—(*just hints at the* FATHER)—and then I alone, alone . . . in those shadows! (*Makes a sudden movement as if in the vision she has of herself illuminating those shadows she wanted to seize hold of herself*) Ah! my life! my life! Oh, what scenes we proposed to him—and I tempted him more than any of the others!

THE FATHER   Maybe. But perhaps it was your fault that he refused to give us life: because you were too insistent, too troublesome.

THE STEPDAUGHTER   Nonsense! Didn't he make me so himself? (*Goes close to the* MANAGER *to tell him as if in confidence*) In my opinion he abandoned us in a fit of depression, of disgust for the ordinary theater as the public knows it and likes it.

THE SON   Exactly what it was, sir; exactly that!

THE FATHER   Not at all! Don't believe it for a minute. Listen to me! You'll be doing quite right to modify, as you suggest, the excesses both of this girl here, who wants to do too much, and of this young man, who won't do anything at all.

THE SON   No, nothing!

THE MANAGER   You too get over the mark occasionally, my dear sir, if I may say so.

THE FATHER   I? When? Where?

THE MANAGER   Always! Continuously! Then there's this insistence of yours in trying to make us believe you are a character. And then too, you must really argue and philosophize less, you know, much less.

THE FATHER   Well, if you want to take away from me the possibility of representing the torment of my spirit which never gives me peace, you will be suppressing me: that's all. Every true man, sir, who is a little above the level of the beasts and plants does not live for the sake of living, without knowing how to live; but he lives so as to give a meaning and a value of his own to life. For me this is *everything*. I cannot give up this, just to represent a mere fact as she (*indicating the* STEPDAUGHTER) wants. It's all very well for her, since her "vendetta" lies in the "fact." I'm not going to do it. It destroys my *raison d'être*.

THE MANAGER   Your *raison d'être*! Oh, we're going ahead fine! First she starts off, and then you jump in. At this rate, we'll never finish.

THE FATHER   Now, don't be offended! Have it your own way— provided, however, that within the limits of the parts you assign us each one's sacrifice isn't too great.

THE MANAGER   You've got to understand that you can't go on arguing at your own pleasure. Drama is action, sir, action and not confounded philosophy.

THE FATHER   All right. I'll do just as much arguing and philosophizing as everybody does when he is considering his own torments.

THE MANAGER   If the drama permits! But for Heaven's sake, man, let's get along and come to the scene.

THE STEPDAUGHTER   It seems to me we've got too much action with our coming into his house. (*Indicating* FATHER) You said, before, you couldn't change the scene every five minutes.

THE MANAGER   Of course not. What we've got to do is to combine and group up all the facts in one simultaneous, close-knit action. We can't have it as you want, with your little brother wandering like a ghost from room to room, hiding behind doors and meditating a project which—what did you say it did to him?

THE STEPDAUGHTER   Consumes him, sir, wastes him away!

THE MANAGER   Well, it may be. And then at the same time, you want the little girl there to be playing in the garden . . . one in the house, and the other in the garden: isn't that it?

THE STEPDAUGHTER   Yes, in the sun, in the sun! That is my only pleasure: to see her happy and careless in the garden after the misery and squalor of the horrible room where we all four slept together. And I had to sleep with her—I, do you understand?—

with my vile contaminated body next to hers; with her folding me fast in her loving little arms. In the garden, whenever she spied me, she would run to take me by the hand. She didn't care for the big flowers, only the little ones; and she loved to show me them and pet me.

THE MANAGER   Well then, we'll have it in the garden. Everything shall happen in the garden; and we'll group the other scenes there. (*Calls a* STAGE HAND) Here, a back-cloth with trees and something to do as a fountain basin. (*Turning round to look at the back of the stage*) Ah, you've fixed it up. Good! (*To* STEP-DAUGHTER) This is just to give an idea, of course. The Boy, instead of hiding behind the doors, will wander about here in the garden, hiding behind the trees. But it's going to be rather difficult to find a child to do that scene with you where she shows you the flowers. (*Turning to the* BOY) Come forward a little, will you please? Let's try it now! Come along! come along! (*Then seeing him come shyly forward, full of fear and looking lost*) It's a nice business, this lad here. What's the matter with him? We'll have to give him a word or two to say. (*Goes close to him, puts a hand on his shoulders, and leads him behind one of the trees*) Come on! come on! Let me see you a little! Hide here . . . yes, like that. Try and show your head just a little as if you were looking for someone . . . (*Goes back to observe the effect, when the* BOY *at once goes through the action*) Excellent! fine! (*Turning to* STEPDAUGHTER) Suppose the little girl there were to surprise him as he looks round, and run over to him, so we could give him a word or two to say?

THE STEPDAUGHTER   It's useless to hope he will speak, as long as that fellow there is here . . . (*Indicates the* SON) You must send him away first.

THE SON (*Jumping up*)   Delighted! delighted! I don't ask for anything better. (*Begins to move away*)

THE MANAGER (*At once stopping him*)   No! No! Where are you going? Wait a bit!

(*The* MOTHER *gets up, alarmed and terrified at the thought that he is really about to go away. Instinctively she lifts her arms to prevent him, without, however, leaving her seat*)

THE SON (*To* MANAGER, *who stops him*)   I've got nothing to do with this affair. Let me go please! Let me go!

THE MANAGER   What do you mean by saying you've got nothing to do with this?

THE STEPDAUGHTER (*Calmly, with irony*)   Don't bother to stop him: he won't go away.

THE FATHER   He has to act the terrible scene in the garden with his mother.

THE SON (*Suddenly resolute and with dignity*)   I shall act nothing at all. I've said so from the very beginning. (*To the* MANAGER) Let me go!

THE STEPDAUGHTER (*Going over to the* MANAGER) Allow me? (*Puts down the* MANAGER's *arm which is restraining the* SON) Well, go away then, if you want to! (*The* SON *looks at her with contempt and hatred. She laughs and says*) You see, he can't, he can't go away! He is obliged to stay here, indissolubly bound to the chain. If I, who fly off when that happens which has to happen, because I can't bear him—if I am still here and support that face and expression of his, you can well imagine that he is unable to move. He has to remain here, has to stop with that nice father of his, and that mother whose only son he is. (*Turning to the* MOTHER) Come on, mother, come along! (*Turning to* MANAGER *to indicate her*) You see, she was getting up to keep him back. (*To the* MOTHER, *beckoning her with her hand*) Come on! come on! (*Then to* MANAGER) You can imagine how little she wants to show these actors of yours what she really feels; but so eager is she to get near him that . . . There, you see? She is willing to act her part. (*And in fact, the* MOTHER *approaches him; and as soon as the* STEPDAUGHTER *has finished speaking, opens her arms to signify that she consents*)

THE SON (*Suddenly*)   No! No! If I can't go away, then I'll stop here; but I repeat: I act nothing!

THE FATHER (*To* MANAGER *excitedly*)   You can force him, sir.

THE SON   Nobody can force me.

THE FATHER   I can.

THE STEPDAUGHTER   Wait a minute, wait . . . First of all, the baby has to go to the fountain . . . (*Runs to take the* CHILD *and leads her to the fountain*)

THE MANAGER   Yes, yes of course; that's it. Both at the same time.

(*The* SECOND LADY LEAD *and the* JUVENILE LEAD *at this point separate themselves from the group of* ACTORS. *One watches the* MOTHER *attentively; the other moves about studying the movements and manner of the* SON *whom he will have to act*)

THE SON (*To* MANAGER)   What do you mean by both at the same time? It isn't right. There was no scene between me and her. (*Indicates the* MOTHER) Ask her how it was!

THE MOTHER   Yes, it's true. I had come into his room . . .

THE SON   Into my room, do you understand? Nothing to do with the garden.

THE MANAGER   It doesn't matter. Haven't I told you we've got to group the action?

THE SON (*Observing the* JUVENILE LEAD *studying him*)   What do you want?

JUVENILE LEAD   Nothing! I was just looking at you.

THE SON (*Turning towards the* SECOND LADY LEAD)   Ah! she's at it too: to re-act her part! (*Indicating the* MOTHER)

THE MANAGER   Exactly! And it seems to me that you ought to be grateful to them for their interest.

THE SON   Yes, but haven't you yet perceived that it isn't possible to live in front of a mirror which not only freezes us with the image of ourselves, but throws our likeness back at us with a horrible grimace?

THE FATHER   That is true, absolutely true. You must see that.

THE MANAGER (*To* SECOND LADY LEAD *and* JUVENILE LEAD)   He's right! Move away from them!

THE SON   Do as you like. I'm out of this!

THE MANAGER   Be quiet, you, will you? And let me hear your mother! (*To* MOTHER) You were saying you had entered . . .

THE MOTHER   Yes, into his room, because I couldn't stand it any longer. I went to empty my heart to him of all the anguish that tortures me . . . But as soon as he saw me come in . . .

THE SON   Nothing happened! There was no scene. I went away, that's all! I don't care for scenes!

THE MOTHER   It's true, true. That's how it was.

THE MANAGER   Well now, we've got to do this bit between you and him. It's indispensable.

THE MOTHER   I'm ready . . . when you are ready. If you could only find a chance for me to tell him what I feel here in my heart.

THE FATHER (*Going to* SON *in a great rage*)   You'll do this for your mother, for your mother, do you understand?

THE SON (*Quite determined*)   I do nothing!

THE FATHER (*Taking hold of him and shaking him*)   For God's sake, do as I tell you! Don't you hear your mother asking you for a favor? Haven't you even got the guts to be a son?

THE SON (*Taking hold of the* FATHER)   No! No! And for God's sake stop it, or else . . . (*General agitation. The* MOTHER, *frightened, tries to separate them*)

THE MOTHER (*Pleading*)   Please! please!

THE FATHER (*Not leaving hold of the* SON)   You've got to obey, do you hear?

THE SON (*Almost crying from rage*)   What does it mean, this madness you've got? (*They separate*) Have you no decency, that you insist on showing everyone our shame? I won't do it! I won't!

And I stand for the will of our author in this. He didn't want to put us on the stage, after all!

THE MANAGER   Man alive! You came here . . .

THE SON (*Indicating* FATHER)   *He* did! I didn't!

THE MANAGER   Aren't you here now?

THE SON   It was his wish, and he dragged us along with him. He's told you not only the things that did happen, but also things that have never happened at all.

THE MANAGER   Well, tell me then what did happen. You went out of your room without saying a word?

THE SON   Without a word, so as to avoid a scene!

THE MANAGER   And then what did you do?

THE SON   Nothing . . . walking in the garden . . . (*Hesitates for a moment with expression of gloom*)

THE MANAGER (*Coming closer to him, interested by his extraordinary reserve*)   Well, well . . . walking in the garden . . .

THE SON (*Exasperated*)   Why on earth do you insist? It's horrible! (*The* MOTHER *trembles, sobs, and looks towards the fountain*)

THE MANAGER (*Slowly observing the glance and turning towards the* SON *with increasing apprehension*)   The baby?

THE SON   There in the fountain . . .

THE FATHER (*Pointing with tender pity to the* MOTHER)   She was following him at the moment . . .

THE MANAGER (*To the* SON, *anxiously*)   And then you . . .

THE SON   I ran over to her; I was jumping in to drag her out when I saw something that froze my blood . . . the boy there, standing stock still, with eyes like a madman's, watching his little drowned sister, in the fountain! (*The* STEPDAUGHTER *bends over the fountain to hide the* CHILD. *She sobs*) Then . . . (*A revolver shot rings out behind the trees where the* BOY *is hidden*)

THE MOTHER (*With a cry of terror runs over in that direction together with several of the* ACTORS *amid general confusion*)   My son! My son! (*Then amid the cries and exclamations one hears her voice*) Help! Help!

THE MANAGER (*Pushing the* ACTORS *aside while they lift up the* BOY *and carry him off*)   Is he really wounded?

SOME ACTORS   He's dead, dead!

OTHER ACTORS   No, no, it's only make-believe, it's only pretence!

THE FATHER (*With a terrible cry*)   Pretence? Reality, sir, reality!

THE MANAGER   Pretence? Reality? To hell with it all! Never in my life has such a thing happened to me. I've lost a whole day over these people, a whole day!

Curtain

⚮ DESIRE UNDER THE ELMS (1924)

EUGENE O'NEILL (1888–1953)

Eugene O'Neill has survived as America's greatest dramatist, but it was not always certain he would do so. Hailed in the 1920s and 1930s as the hewer of new ways, he produced a body of astonishingly good and frightfully bad plays between the two great wars, demonstrating a theatrical talent of unequalled skill and intensity while also displaying some incredibly inept artistic talent. Both in quality of what he did and in his thematic and stylistic approach, O'Neill baffled, confused, and infuriated his public, but he always attracted them. Like Shaw, who called him a "banshee Shakespeare," O'Neill eventually attained the ability to make audiences and actors do his bidding in stupendous feats of endurance in the presentation of the multi-act five-hour and longer marathons which capped the first half of his career prior to his long "retirement" before and during the Second War.

Welcomed as America's first great realist, O'Neill became almost at once our first great expressionist. Seen as the improvisor who would alter the basic concepts of contemporary theatre, he endures as probably the greatest writer of modern naturalistic tragedy. When he lived, his plays were front-page news. Those who liked him would often turn ecstatic; those who did not were known to try to close down his plays as dangerous and immoral obscenities. When he died he had so completely disappeared from public awareness that his funeral passed all but unnoticed, his plays seldom staged. The posthumous production of his later works, now accepted as his best, have returned O'Neill as a dramatic artist of world importance and of permanently high artistic stature.

Very early in his career O'Neill affirmed that he was not interested in the relationship of man to man but of man to God. This did not assume any particular religion or creed, but it was truly a classic tragic concept. *Desire Under the Elms* is O'Neill's first tragedy in the classic sense, although an earlier tragedy, his first commercial success called *Beyond the Horizon* (1920), had shown his very serious artistic bent. *Desire* is not Greek in the literal sense of neo-classic imitation, even though it follows the outline of the classic myth of Queen Phaedra and her incestuous passion for her stepson, Hippolytus. The closer imitation of the Greek was to come later in O'Neill's adaptation of *The Oresteia* in *Mourning Becomes Electra* in 1931, transferring the legend to Civil War New England. *Desire Under the Elms* makes use not of the fates, but of the natural environment, and instead of gods imposing curses it uses elemental passions beyond control of the protagonists. There is a primitive force in evidence, seen in the rock-hard unyielding land under the control of an equally hard unyielding god. The characters are at the mercy of what they are—ignorant, earthy, unlettered, performing with animal lust in the satisfaction of natural urges. They are trapped by what they are as much as is Oedipus, and their escape is equally impossible.

There is great size and stature here. Old Cabot is a huge man, able to challenge his demanding god, yet remaining an absolute child of nature who can find solace among the dumb beasts in the barn. The attraction between Eben and Abbie, first calculated for personal gain, then out of control as a natural force, passes through the walls of the house to create a sinister atmosphere that even old Cabot senses but cannot understand. In the end, the realization of what they have done and the recognition of their fate, which must be shared, compel Eben and Abbie to face the inevitable catastrophe. Ephraim can return to his cows, but destruction is total for the adulterous semi-incestuous lovers who have succumbed to, but at the same time conquered, the elemental forces of their downfall.

Desire Under the Elms

O'NEILL

CHARACTERS

EPHRAIM CABOT
SIMEON ⎫
PETER ⎬ his sons
EBEN ⎭
ABBIE PUTNAM

YOUNG GIRL, TWO FARMERS, THE FIDDLER, THE SHERIFF, OTHER FOLK *from the neighboring farms*

The action of the entire play takes place in, and immediately outside of, the CABOT *farmhouse in New England, in the year 1850. The south end of the house faces front to a stone wall with a wooden gate at center opening on a country road. The house is in good condition but in need of paint. Its walls are a sickly grayish, the green of the shutters faded. Two enormous elms are on each side of the house. They bend their trailing branches down over the roof. They appear to protect and at the same time subdue. There is a sinister maternity in their aspect, a crushing, jealous absorption. They have developed from their intimate contact with the life of man in the house an appalling humaneness. They brood oppressively over the house. They are like exhausted women resting their sagging breasts and hands and hair on its roof, and when it rains their tears trickle down monotonously and rot on the shingles.*

There is a path running from the gate around the right corner of the house to the front door. A narrow porch is on this side. The end wall facing us has two windows in its upper story, two larger ones on the floor below. The two upper are those of the father's bedroom and that of the brothers. On the left, ground floor, is the kitchen—on the right, the parlor, the shades of which are always drawn down.

PART I

Scene 1

Exterior of the farmhouse. It is sunset of a day at the beginning of summer in the year 1850. There is no wind and everything is still. The sky above

691

the roof is suffused with deep colors, the green of the elms glows, but the house is in shadow, seeming pale and washed out by contrast.

A door opens and EBEN CABOT *comes to the end of the porch and stands looking down the road to the right. He has a large bell in his hand and this he swings mechanically, awakening a deafening clangor. Then he puts his hands on his hips and stares up at the sky. He sighs with a puzzled awe and blurts out with halting appreciation.*

EBEN God! Purty! (*His eyes fall and he stares about him frowningly. He is twenty-five, tall and sinewy. His face is well-formed, good-looking, but its expression is resentful and defensive. His defiant, dark eyes remind one of a wild animal's in captivity. Each day is a cage in which he finds himself trapped but inwardly unsubdued. There is a fierce repressed vitality about him. He has black hair, mustache, a thin curly trace of beard. He is dressed in rough farm clothes.*

He spits on the ground with intense disgust, turns and goes back into the house.

SIMEON *and* PETER *come in from their work in the fields. They are tall men, much older than their half-brother [*SIMEON *is thirty-nine and* PETER *thirty-seven], built on a squarer, simpler model, fleshier in body, more bovine and homelier in face, shrewder and more practical. Their shoulders stoop a bit from years of farm work. They clump heavily along in their clumsy thick-soled boots caked with earth. Their clothes, their faces, hands, bare arms and throats are earth-stained. They smell of earth. They stand together for a moment in front of the house and, as if with the one impulse, stare dumbly up at the sky, leaning on their hoes. Their faces have a compressed, unresigned expression. As they look upward, this softens.*)

SIMEON (*grudgingly*) Purty.

PETER Ay-eh.

SIMEON (*suddenly*) Eighteen year ago.

PETER What?

SIMEON Jenn. My woman. She died.

PETER I'd fergot.

SIMEON I rec'lect—now an' agin. Makes it lonesome. She'd hair long's a hoss' tail—an' yaller like gold!

PETER Waal—she's gone. (*This with indifferent finality—then after a pause*) They's gold in the West, Sim.

SIMEON (*still under the influence of sunset—vaguely*) In the sky?

PETER Waal—in a manner o' speakin'—thar's the promise. (*growing excited*) Gold in the sky—in the West—Golden Gate—Californi-a!—Goldest West!—fields o' gold!

SIMEON (*excited in his turn*) Fortunes layin' just atop o' the ground waitin' t' be picked! Solomon's mines, they says! (*For a moment they continue looking up at the sky—then their eyes drop.*)

PETER (*with sardonic bitterness*) Here—it's stones atop o' the ground—stones atop o' stones—makin' stone walls—year atop o' year—him 'n' yew 'n' me 'n' then Eben—makin' stone walls fur him to fence us in!

SIMEON We've wuked. Give our strength. Give our years. Plowed 'em under in the ground—(*he stamps rebelliously*)—rottin'—makin' soil for his crops! (*a pause*) Waal—the farm pays good for hereabouts.

PETER If we plowed in Californi-a, they'd be lumps o' gold in the furrow!

SIMEON Californi-a's t'other side o' earth, a'most. We got t' calc'-late—

PETER (*after a pause*) 'Twould be hard fur me, too, to give up what we've 'arned here by our sweat. (*A pause,* EBEN *sticks his head out of the dining-room window, listening.*)

SIMEON Ay-eh. (*a pause*) Mebbe—he'll die soon.

PETER (*doubtfully*) Mebbe.

SIMEON Mebbe—fur all we knows—he's dead now.

PETER Ye'd need proof.

SIMEON He's been gone two months—with no word.

PETER Left us in the fields an evenin' like this. Hitched up an' druv off into the West. That's plum onnateral. He hain't never been off this farm 'ceptin' t' the village in thirty year or more, not since he married Eben's maw. (*A pause. Shrewdly*) I calc'late we might git him declared crazy by the court.

SIMEON He skinnned 'em too slick. He got the best o' all on 'em. They'd never b'lieve him crazy. (*a pause*) We got t' wait—till he's under ground.

EBEN (*with a sardonic chuckle*) Honor thy father! (*They turn, startled, and stare at him. He grins, then scowls.*) I pray he's died. (*They stare at him. He continues matter-of-factly*) Supper's ready.

SIMEON and PETER (*together*) Ay-eh.

EBEN (*gazing up at the sky*) Sun's downin' purty.

SIMEON and PETER (*together*) Ay-eh. They's gold in the West.

EBEN Ay-eh. (*pointing*) Yonder atop o' the hill pasture, ye mean?

SIMEON and PETER (*together*) In Californi-a!

EBEN Hunh? (*Stares at them indifferently for a second, then drawls*) Waal—supper's gittin' cold. (*He turns back into kitchen.*)

SIMEON (*startled—smacks his lips*) I air hungry!

PETER (*sniffing*) I smells bacon!

SIMEON (*with hungry appreciation*) Bacon's good!

PETER (*in same tone*) Bacon's bacon! (*They turn, shouldering each other, their bodies bumping and rubbing together as they hurry clumsily to their food, like two friendly oxen toward their evening meal. They disappear around the right corner of house and can be heard entering the door.*)

Scene 2

The color fades from the sky. Twilight begins. The interior of the kitchen is now visible. A pine table is at center, a cookstove in the right rear corner, four rough wooden chairs, a tallow candle on the table. In the middle of the rear wall is fastened a big advertising poster with a ship in full sail and the word "California" in big letters. Kitchen utensils hang from nails. Everything is neat and in order but the atmosphere is of a men's camp kitchen rather than that of a home.

Places for three are laid. EBEN *takes boiled potatoes and bacon from the stove and puts them on the table, also a loaf of bread and a crock of water.* SIMEON *and* PETER *shoulder in, slump down in their chairs without a word.* EBEN *joins them. The three eat in silence for a moment, the two elder as naturally unrestrained as beasts of the field,* EBEN *picking at his food without appetite, glancing at them with a tolerant dislike.*

SIMEON (*suddenly turns to* EBEN) Looky here! Ye'd oughtn't t' said that, Eben.

PETER 'Twa'n't righteous.

EBEN What?

SIMEON Ye prayed he'd died.

EBEN Waal—don't yew pray it? (*a pause*)

PETER He's our Paw.

EBEN (*violently*) Not mine!

SIMEON (*dryly*) ·Ye'd not let no one else say that about yer Maw! Ha! (*He gives one abrupt sardonic guffaw.* PETER *grins.*)

EBEN (*very pale*) I meant—I hain't his'n—I hain't like him—he hain't me!

PETER (*dryly*) Wait till ye've growed his age!

EBEN (*intensely*) I'm Maw—every drop o' blood! (*A pause. They stare at him with indifferent curiosity.*)

PETER (*reminiscently*) She was good t' Sim 'n' me. A good step-maw's scurse.

SIMEON She was good t' everyone.

EBEN (*greatly moved, gets to his feet and makes an awkward bow to each of them—stammering*) I be thankful t' ye. I'm her—her heir. (*He sits down in confusion.*)

PETER (*after a pause—judicially*) She was good even t' him.

EBEN (*fiercely*) An' fur thanks he killed her!

SIMEON (*after a pause*) No one never kills nobody. It's allus somethin'. That's the murderer.

EBEN Didn't he slave Maw t' death?

PETER He's slaved himself t' death. He's slaved Sim 'n' me 'n' yew t' death—on'y none o' us hain't died—yit.

SIMEON It's somethin'—drivin' him—t' drive us!

EBEN (*vengefully*) Waal—I hold him t' jedgment! (*then scornfully*) Somethin'! What's somethin'?

SIMEON Dunno.

EBEN (*sardonically*) What's drivin' yew to Californi-a, mebbe? (*They look at him in surprise.*) Oh, I've heerd ye! (*then, after a pause*) But ye'll never go t' the gold fields!

PETER (*assertively*) Mebbe!

EBEN Whar'll ye git the money?

PETER We kin walk. It's an a'mighty ways—Californi-a—but if yew was t' put all the steps we've walked on this farm end t' end we'd be in the moon!

EBEN The Injuns'll skulp ye on the plains.

SIMEON (*with grim humor*) We'll mebbe make 'em pay a hair fur a hair!

EBEN (*decisively*) But t'ain't that. Ye won't never go because ye'll wait here fur yer share o' the farm, thinkin' allus he'll die soon.

SIMEON (*after a pause*) We've a right.

PETER Two-thirds belongs t'us.

EBEN (*jumping to his feet*) Ye've no right! She wa'n't yewr Maw! It was her farm! Didn't he steal it from her? She's dead. It's my farm.

SIMEON (*sardonically*) Tell that t' Paw—when he comes! I'll bet ye a dollar he'll laugh—fur once in his life. Ha! (*He laughs himself in one single mirthless bark.*)

PETER (*amused in turn, echoes his brother*) Ha!

SIMEON (*after a pause*) What've ye got held agin us, Eben? Year arter year it's skulked in yer eye—somethin'.

PETER Ay-eh.

EBEN Ay-eh. They's somethin'. (*suddenly exploding*) Why didn't ye never stand between him 'n' my Maw when he was slavin' her to her grave—t' pay her back fur the kindness she done t' yew? (*There is a long pause. They stare at him in surprise.*)

SIMEON Waal—the stock'd got t' be watered.

PETER 'R they was woodin' t' do.

SIMEON 'R plowin'.

PETER 'R hayin'.

SIMEON 'R spreadin' manure.

PETER 'R weedin'.

SIMEON 'R prunin'.

PETER 'R milkin'.

EBEN (*breaking in harshly*) An' makin' walls—stone atop o' stone —makin' walls till yer heart's a stone ye heft up out o' the way o' growth onto a stone wall t' wall in yer heart!

SIMEON (*matter-of-factly*) We never had no time t' meddle.

PETER (*to* EBEN) Yew was fifteen afore yer Maw died—an' big fur yer age. Why didn't ye never do nothin'?

EBEN (*harshly*) They was chores t' do, wa'n't they? (*a pause— then slowly*) It was on'y arter she died I come to think o' it. Me cookin'—doin' her work—that made me know her, suffer her sufferin'—she'd come back t' help—come back t' bile potatoes— come back t' fry bacon—come back t' bake biscuits—come back all cramped up t' shake the fire, an' carry ashes, her eyes weepin' an' bloody with smoke an' cinders same's they used t' be. She still comes back—stands by the stove thar in the evenin'—she can't find it nateral sleepin' an' restin' in peace. She can't git used t' bein' free—even in her grave.

SIMEON She never complained none.

EBEN She'd got too tired. She'd got too used t' being' too tired. That was what he done. (*with vengeful passion*) An' sooner'r later, I'll meddle. I'll say the thin's I didn't say then t' him! I'll yell 'em at the top o' my lungs. I'll see t' it my Maw gits some rest an' sleep in her grave! (*He sits down again, relapsing into a brooding silence. They look at him with a queer indifferent curiosity.*)

PETER (*after a pause*) Whar in tarnation d'ye s'pose he went, Sim?

SIMEON Dunno. He druv off in the buggy, all spick an' span, with the mare all breshed an' shiny, druv off clackin' his tongue an' wavin' his whip. I remember it right well. I was finishin' plowin', it was spring an' May an' sunset, an' gold in the West, an' he druv off into it. I yells "Whar ye goin', Paw?" an' he hauls up by the stone wall a jiffy. His old snake's eyes was glitterin' in the sun like he'd been drinkin' a jugful an' he says with a mule's grin: "Don't ye run away till I come back!"

PETER Wonder if he knowed we was wantin' fur Californi-a?

SIMEON Mebbe. I didn't say nothin' and he says, lookin' kinder queer an' sick: "I been hearin' the hens cluckin' an' the roosters crowin' all the durn day. I been listenin' t' the cows lowin' an' everythin' else kickin' up till I can't stand it no more. It's spring an' I'm feelin' damned," he says. "Damned like an old bare hickory tree fit on'y fur burnin'," he says. An' then I calc'late I must've looked a mite hopeful, fur he adds real spry and vicious:

"But don't git no fool idee I'm dead. I've sworn t' live a hundred an' I'll do it, if on'y t' spite yer sinful greed! An' now I'm ridin' out t' learn God's message t' me in the spring, like the prophets done. An' yew git back t' yer plowin'," he says. An' he druv off singin' a hymn. I thought he was drunk—'r I'd stopped him goin'.

EBEN (*scornfully*) No, ye wouldn't! Ye're scared o' him. He's stronger—inside—than both o' ye put together!

PETER (*sardonically*) An' yew—be yew Samson?

EBEN I'm gittin' stronger. I kin feel it growin' in me—growin' an' growin'—till it'll bust out—! (*He gets up and puts on his coat and a hat. They watch him, gradually breaking into grins. EBEN avoids their eyes sheepishly.*) I'm goin' out fur a spell—up the road.

PETER T' the village?

SIMEON T' see Minnie?

EBEN (*defiantly*) Ay-eh!

PETER (*jeeringly*) The Scarlet Woman!

SIMEON Lust—that's what's growin' in ye!

EBEN Waal—she's purty!

PETER She's been purty fur twenty year!

SIMEON A new coat o' paint'll make a heifer out of forty.

EBEN She hain't forty!

PETER If she hain't, she's teeterin' on the edge.

EBEN (*desperately*) What d'yew know—

PETER All they is . . . Sim knew her—an' then me arter—

SIMEON An' Paw kin tell yew somethin' too! He was fust!

EBEN D'ye mean t' say he . . . ?

SIMEON (*with a grin*) Ay-eh! We air his heirs in everythin'!

EBEN (*intensely*) That's more to it! That grows on it! It'll bust soon! (*then violently*) I'll go smash my fist in her face! (*He pulls open the door in rear violently.*)

SIMEON (*with a wink at* PETER—*drawlingly*) Mebbe—but the night's wa'm—purty—by the time ye git thar mebbe ye'll kiss her instead!

PETER Sart'n he will! (*They both roar with coarse laughter. EBEN rushes out and slams the door—then the outside front door— comes around the corner of the house and stands still by the gate, staring up at the sky.*)

SIMEON (*looking after him*) Like his Paw.

PETER Dead spit an' image!

SIMEON Dog'll eat dog!

PETER Ay-eh. (*Pause. With yearning*) Mebbe a year from now we'll be in Californi-a.

SIMEON   Ay-eh. (*A pause. Both yawn.*) Let's git t'bed. (*He blows out the candle. They go out door in rear.* EBEN *stretches his arms up to the sky—rebelliously.*)

EBEN   Waal—thar's a star, an' somewhar's they's him, an' here's me, an' thar's Min up the road—in the same night. What if I does kiss her? She's like t'night, she's soft 'n' wa'm, her eyes kin wink like a star, her mouth's wa'm, her arms're wa'm, she smells like a wa'm plowed field, she's purty . . . Ay-eh! By God A'mighty she's purty, an' I don't give a damn how many sins she's sinned afore mine or who she's sinned 'em with, my sin's as purty as any one on 'em! (*He strides off down the road to the left.*)

Scene 3

It is the pitch darkness just before dawn. EBEN *comes in from the left and goes around to the porch, feeling his way, chuckling bitterly and cursing half-aloud to himself.*

EBEN   The cussed old miser! (*He can be heard going in the front door. There is a pause as he goes upstairs, then a loud knock on the bedroom door of the brothers.*) Wake up!

SIMEON (*startedly*)   Who's thar?

EBEN (*pushing open the door and coming in, a lighted candle in his hand. The bedroom of the brothers is revealed. Its ceiling is the sloping roof. They can stand upright only close to the center dividing wall of the upstairs.* SIMEON *and* PETER *are in a double bed, front.* EBEN's *cot is to the rear.* EBEN *has a mixture of silly grin and vicious scowl on his face*) I be!

PETER (*angrily*)   What in hell's-fire . . . ?

EBEN   I got news fur ye! Ha! (*He gives one abrupt sardonic guffaw.*)

SIMEON (*angrily*)   Couldn't ye hold it 'til we'd got our sleep?

EBEN   It's nigh sunup. (*then explosively*) He's gone an' married agen!

SIMEON *and* PETER (*explosively*)   Paw?

EBEN   Got himself hitched to a female 'bout thirty-five—an' purty, they says . . .

SIMEON (*aghast*)   It's a durn lie!

PETER   Who says?

SIMEON   They been stringin' ye!

EBEN   Think I'm a dunce, do ye? The hull village says. The preacher from New Dover, he brung the news—told it t'our preacher—New Dover, that's whar the old loon got himself hitched—that's whar the woman lived—

PETER (*no longer doubting—stunned*)   Waal . . . !

SIMEON (*the same*) Waal...!

EBEN (*sitting down on a bed—with vicious hatred*) Ain't he a devil out o' hell? It's jest t' spite us—the damned old mule!

PETER (*after a pause*) Everythin'll go t' her now.

SIMEON Ay-eh. (*A pause—dully*) Waal—if it's done—

PETER It's done us. (*pause—then persuasively*) They's gold in the fields o' Californi-a, Sim. No good a-stayin' here now.

SIMEON Jest what I was a-thinkin'. (*then with decision*) S'well fust's last! Let's light out and git this mornin'.

PETER Suits me.

EBEN Ye must like walkin'.

SIMEON (*sardonically*) If ye'd grow wings on us we'd fly thar!

EBEN Ye'd like ridin' better—on a boat, wouldn't ye? (*Fumbles in his pocket and takes out a crumpled sheet of foolscap.*) Waal, if ye sign this ye kin ride on a boat. I've had it writ out an' ready in case ye'd ever go. It says fur three hundred dollars t' each ye agree yewr shares o' the farm is sold t' me. (*They look suspiciously at the paper. A pause.*)

SIMEON (*wonderingly*) But if he's hitched agen—

PETER An' whar'd yew git that sum o' money, anyways?

EBEN (*cunningly*) I know whar it's hid. I been waitin'—Maw told me. She knew whar it lay fur years, but she was waitin'... It's her'n—the money he hoarded from her farm an' hid from Maw. It's my money by rights now.

PETER Whar's it hid?

EBEN (*cunningly*) Whar yew won't never find it without me. Maw spied on him—'r she'd never knowed. (*A pause. They look at him suspiciously, and he at them.*) Waal, is it fa'r trade?

SIMEON Dunno.

PETER Dunno.

SIMEON (*looking at window*) Sky's grayin'.

PETER Ye better start the fire, Eben.

SIMEON An' fix some vittles.

EBEN Ay-eh. (*Then with a forced jocular heartiness*) I'll git ye a good one. If ye're startin' t' hoof it t' Californi-a ye'll need somethin' that'll stick t' yer ribs. (*He turns to the door, adding meaningly*) But ye kin ride on a boat if ye'll swap. (*He stops at the door and pauses. They stare at him.*)

SIMEON (*suspiciously*) Whar was ye all night?

EBEN (*defiantly*) Up t' Min's. (*then slowly*) Walkin' thar, fust I felt 's if I'd kiss her; then I got a-thinkin' on' what ye'd said o' him an' her an' I says, I'll bust her nose fur that! Then I got t' the village an' heerd the news an' I got madder'n hell an' run all the way t' Min's not knowin' what I'd do—(*He pauses—then sheepishly but more defiantly*) Waal—when I seen her, I didn't hit her—nor I didn't kiss her nuther—I begun t' beller like a calf an' cuss at the same time, I was so durn mad—an' she got scared —an' I jest grabbed holt an' tuk her! (*Proudly*) Yes, sirree! I tuk her. She may've been his'n—an' your'n, too—but she's mine now!

SIMEON (*dryly*) In love, air yew?

EBEN (*with lofty scorn*) Love! I don't take no stock in sech slop!

PETER (*winking at* SIMEON) Mebbe Eben's aimin' t' marry, too.

SIMEON Min'd make a true faithful he'pmeet! (*They snicker.*)

EBEN What do I care fur her—'ceptin' she's round an' wa'm? The p'int is she was his'n—an' now she belongs t' me! (*He goes to the door—then turns—rebelliously.*) An' Min hain't sech a bad un. They's worse'n Min in the world, I'll bet ye! Wait'll we see this cow the Old Man's hitched t'! She'll beat Min, I got a notion! (*He starts to go out.*)

SIMEON (*suddenly*) Mebbe ye'll try t' make her your'n, too?

PETER Ha! (*He gives a sardonic laugh of relish at this idea.*)

EBEN (*spitting with disgust*) Her—here—sleepin' with him— stealin' my Maw's farm! I'd as soon pet a skunk 'r kiss a snake! (*He goes out. The two stare after him suspiciously. A pause. They listen to his steps receding.*)

PETER He's startin' the fire.

SIMEON I'd like t' ride t' Californi-a—but—

PETER Min might o' put some scheme in his head.

SIMEON Mebbe it's all a lie 'bout Paw marryin'. We'd best wait an' see the bride.

PETER An' don't sign nothin' till we does!

SIMEON Nor till we've tested it's good money! (*then with a grin*) But if Paw's hitched we'd be sellin' Eben somethin' we'd never git nohow!

PETER We'll wait an' see. (*then with sudden vindictive anger*) An' till he comes, let's yew 'n' me not wuk a lick, let Eben tend to thin's if he's a mind t', let's us jest sleep an' eat an' drink likker, an' let the hull damned farm go t' blazes!

SIMEON (*excitedly*) By God, we've 'arned a rest! We'll play rich fur a change. I hain't a-going to stir outa bed till breakfast's ready.

PETER An' on the table!

SIMEON (*after a pause—thoughtfully*) What d'ye calc'late she'll be like—our new Maw? Like Eben thinks?

PETER More'n likely.

SIMEON (*vindictively*) Waal—I hope she's a she-devil that'll make him wish he was dead an' livin' in the pit o' hell fur comfort!

PETER (*fervently*) Amen!

SIMEON (*imitating his father's voice*) "I'm ridin' out t' learn God's message t' me in the spring like the prophets done," he says. I'll bet right then an' thar he knew plumb well he was goin' whorin', the stinkin' old hypocrite!

Scene 4

Same as SCENE 2—*shows the interior of the kitchen with a lighted candle on table. It is gray dawn outside.* SIMEON *and* PETER *are just finishing their breakfast.* EBEN *sits before his plate of untouched food, brooding frowningly.*

PETER (*glancing at him rather irritably*) Lookin' glum don't help none.

SIMEON (*sarcastically*) Sorrowin' over his lust o' the flesh!

PETER (*with a grin*) Was she yer fust?

EBEN (*angrily*) None o' yer business. (*a pause*) I was thinkin' o' him. I got a notion he's gittin' near—I kin feel him comin' on like yew kin feel malaria chill afore it takes ye.

PETER It's too early yet.

SIMEON Dunno. He'd like t' catch us nappin'—jest t' have somethin' t' hoss us 'round over.

PETER (*mechanically gets to his feet.* SIMEON *does the same*) Waal —let's git t' wuk. (*They both plod mechanically toward the door before they realize. Then they stop short.*)

SIMEON (*grinning*) Ye're a cussed fool, Pete—and I be wuss! Let him see we hain't wukin'! We don't give a durn!

PETER (*as they go back to the table*) Not a damned durn! It'll serve t' show him we're done with him. (*They sit down again.* EBEN *stares from one to the other with surprise.*)

SIMEON (*grins at him*) We're aimin' t' start bein' lilies o' the field.

PETER Nary a toil 'r spin 'r lick o' wuk do we put in!

SIMEON Ye're sole owner—till he comes—that's what ye wanted. Waal, ye got t' be sole hand, too.

PETER The cows air bellerin'. Ye better hustle at the milkin'.

EBEN (*with excited joy*) Ye mean ye'll sign the paper?

SIMEON (*dryly*) Mebbe.

PETER Mebbe.

SIMEON We're considerin'. (*peremptorily*) Ye better git t' wuk.

EBEN (*with queer excitement*) It's Maw's farm agen! It's my farm! Them's my cows! I'll milk my durn fingers off fur cows o' mine! (*He goes out door in rear, they stare after him indifferently.*)

SIMEON Like his Paw.

PETER Dead spit 'n' image!

SIMEON Waal—let dog eat dog! (EBEN *comes out of front door and around the corner of the house. The sky is beginning to grow flushed with sunrise. EBEN stops by the gate and stares around him with glowing, possessive eyes. He takes in the whole farm with his embracing glance of desire.*)

EBEN It's purty! It's damned purty! It's mine! (*He suddenly throws his head back boldly and glares with hard, defiant eyes at the sky.*) Mine, d'ye hear? Mine! (*He turns and walks quickly off left, rear, toward the barn. The two brothers light their pipes.*)

SIMEON (*putting his muddy boots up on the table, tilting back his chair, and puffing defiantly*) Waal—this air solid comfort—fur once.

PETER Ay-eh. (*He follows suit. A pause. Unconsciously they both sigh.*)

SIMEON (*suddenly*) He never was much o' a hand at milkin', Eben wa'n't.

PETER (*with a snort*) His hands air like hoofs! (*a pause*)

SIMEON Reach down the jug thar! Let's take a swaller. I'm feelin' kind o' low.

PETER Good idee! (*He does so—gets two glasses—they pour out drinks of whisky.*) Here's t' the gold in Californi-a!

SIMEON An' luck t' find it! (*They drink—puff resolutely—sigh— take their feet down from the table.*)

PETER Likker don't pear t' sot right.

SIMEON We hain't used t' it this early. (*A pause. They become very restless.*)

PETER Gittin' close in this kitchen.

SIMEON (*with immense relief*) Let's git a breath o' air. (*They arise briskly and go out rear—appear around house and stop by the gate. They stare up at the sky with a numbed appreciation.*)

PETER Purty!

SIMEON Ay-eh. Gold's t' the East now.

PETER Sun's startin' with us fur the Golden West.

SIMEON (*staring around the farm, his compressed face tightened, unable to conceal his emotion*) Waal—it's our last mornin'— mebbe.

PETER (*the same*) Ay-eh.

SIMEON (*stamps his foot on the earth and addresses it desperately*) Waal—ye've thirty year o' me buried in ye—spread out over ye —blood an' bone an' sweat—rotted away—fertilizin' ye—richin' yer soul—prime manure, by God, that's what I been t' ye!

PETER Ay-eh! An' me!

SIMEON An' yew, Peter. (*He sighs—then spits.*) Waal—no use'n cryin' over spilt milk.

PETER They's gold in the West—an' freedom, mebbe. We been slaves t' stone walls here.

SIMEON (*defiantly*) We hain't nobody's slaves from this out—nor nothin's slaves nuther. (*a pause—restlessly*) Speakin' o' milk, wonder how Eben's managin'?

PETER I s'pose he's managin'.

SIMEON Mebbe we'd ought t' help—this once.

PETER Mebbe. The cows knows us.

SIMEON An' likes us. They don't know him much.

PETER An' the hosses, an' pigs, an' chickens. They don't know him much.

SIMEON They knows us like brothers—an' likes us! (*proudly*) Hain't we raised 'em t' be fust-rate, number one prize stock?

PETER We hain't—not no more.

SIMEON (*dully*) I was fergittin'. (*then resignedly*) Waal, let's go help Eben a spell an' git waked up.

PETER Suits me. (*They are starting off down left, rear, for the barn when* EBEN *appears from there hurrying toward them, his face excited.*)

EBEN (*breathlessly*) Waal—har they be! The old mule an' the bride! I seen 'em from the barn down below at the turnin'.

PETER How could ye tell that far?

EBEN Hain't I as far-sight as he's near-sight? Don't I know the mare 'n' buggy, an' two people settin' in it? Who else...? An' I tell ye I kin feel 'em a-comin', too! (*He squirms as if he had the itch.*)

PETER (*beginning to be angry*) Waal—let him do his own unhitchin'!

SIMEON (*angry in his turn*) Let's hustle in an' git our bundles an' be a-goin' as he's a-comin'. I don't want never t' step inside the door agen arter he's back. (*They both start back around the corner of the house.* EBEN *follows them.*)

EBEN (*anxiously*) Will ye sign it afore ye go?

PETER Let's see the color o' the old skinflint's money an' we'll sign. (*They disappear left. The two brothers clump upstairs to get their bundles.* EBEN *appears in the kitchen, runs to the window, peers out, comes back and pulls up a strip of flooring in under stove, takes out a canvas bag and puts it on table, then sets the floorboard back in place. The two brothers appear a moment after. They carry old carpet bags.*)

EBEN (*puts his hand on bag guardingly*) Have ye signed?

SIMEON (*shows paper in his hand*) Ay-eh. (*greedily*) Be that the money?

EBEN (*opens bag and pours out pile of twenty-dollar gold pieces*)

Twenty-dollar pieces—thirty on 'em. Count 'em. (PETER *does so, arranging them in stacks of five, biting one or two to test them.*)

PETER Six hundred. (*He puts them in bag and puts it inside his shirt carefully.*)

SIMEON (*handing paper to* EBEN) Har ye be.

EBEN (*after a glance, folds it carefully and hides it under his shirt— gratefully*) Thank yew.

PETER Thank yew fur the ride.

SIMEON We'll send ye a lump o' gold fur Christmas.(*A pause.* EBEN *stares at them and they at him.*)

PETER (*awkwardly*) Waal—we're a-goin'.

SIMEON Comin' out t' the yard?

EBEN No. I'm waitin' in here a spell. (*Another silence. The brothers edge awkwardly to door in rear—then turn and stand.*)

SIMEON Waal—good-by.

PETER Good-by.

EBEN Good-by. (*They go out. He sits down at the table, faces the stove and pulls out the paper. He looks from it to the stove. His face, lighted up by the shaft of sunlight from the window, has an expression of trance. His lips move. The two brothers come out to the gate.*)

PETER (*looking off toward barn*) Thar he be—unhitchin'.

SIMEON (*with a chuckle*) I'll bet ye he's riled!

PETER An' thar she be.

SIMEON Let's wait 'n' see what our new Maw looks like.

PETER (*with a grin*) An' give him our partin' cuss!

SIMEON (*grinning*) I feel like raisin' fun. I feel light in my head an' feet.

PETER Me, too. I feel like laffin' till I'd split up the middle.

SIMEON Reckon it's the likker?

PETER No. My feet feel itchin' t' walk an' walk—an' jump high over thin's—an' . . . .

SIMEON Dance? (*a pause*)

PETER (*puzzled*) It's plumb onnateral.

SIMEON (*a light coming over his face*) I calc'late it's 'cause school's out. It's holiday. Fur once we're free!

PETER (*dazedly*) Free?

SIMEON The halter's broke—the harness is busted—the fence bars is down—the stone walls air crumblin' an' tumblin'! We'll be kickin' up an' tearin' away down the road!

PETER (*drawing a deep breath—oratorically*) Anybody that wants this stinkin' old rock-pile of a farm kin hev it. 'Tain't our'n, no sirree!

SIMEON (*takes the gate off its hinges and puts it under his arm*) We harby 'bolishes shet gates an' open gates, an' all gates, by thunder!

PETER We'll take it with us fur luck an' let 'er sail free down some river.

SIMEON (*as a sound of voices comes from left, rear*) Har they comes! (*The two brothers congeal into two stiff, grim-visaged statues. EPHRAIM CABOT and ABBIE PUTNAM come in. CABOT is seventy-five, tall and gaunt, with great, wiry, concentrated power, but stoop-shouldered from toil. His face is as hard as if it were hewn out of a boulder, yet there is a weakness in it, a pretty pride in its own narrow strength. His eyes are small, close together, and extremely near-sighted, blinking continually in the effort to focus on objects, their stare having a straining, ingrowing quality. He is dressed in his dismal black Sunday suit. ABBIE is thirty-five, buxom, full of vitality. Her round face is pretty but marred by its rather gross sensuality. There is strength and obstinacy in her jaw, a hard determination in her eyes, and about her whole personality the same unsettled, untamed, desperate quality which is so apparent in EBEN.*)

CABOT (*as they enter—a queer strangled emotion in his dry cracking voice*) Har we be t' hum, Abbie.

ABBIE (*with lust for the word*) Hum! (*Her eyes gloating on the house without seeming to see the two stiff figures at the gate.*) It's purty—purty! I can't b'lieve it's r'ally mine.

CABOT (*sharply*) Yewr'n? Mine! (*He stares at her penetratingly. She stares back. He adds relentingly.*) Our'n—mebbe! It was lonesome too long. I was growin' old in the spring. A hum's got t' hev a woman.

ABBIE (*her voice taking possession*) A woman's got t' hev a hum!

CABOT (*nodding uncertainly*) Ay-eh. (*then irritably*) Whar be they? Ain't thar nobody about—'r wukin'—'r nothin'?

ABBIE (*sees the brothers. She returns their stare of cold appraising contempt with interest—slowly*) Thar's two men loafin' at the gate an' starin' at me like a couple o' strayed hogs.

CABOT (*straining his eyes*) I kin see 'em—but I can't make out. . . .

SIMEON It's Simeon.

PETER It's Peter.

CABOT (*exploding*) Why hain't ye wukin'?

SIMEON (*dryly*) We're waitin' t' welcome ye hum—yew an' the bride!

CABOT (*confusedly*) Huh? Waal—this be yer new Maw, boys. (*She stares at them and they at her.*)

SIMEON (*turns away and spits contemptuously*) I see her!

PETER (*spits also*) An' I see her!

ABBIE (*with the conqueror's conscious superiority*) I'll go in an' look at *my* house. (*She goes slowly around to porch.*)

SIMEON (*with a snort*) *Her* house!

PETER (*calls after her*) Ye'll find Eben inside. Ye better not tell him it's *yewr* house.

ABBIE (*mouthing the name*) Eben. (*then quietly*) I'll tell Eben.

CABOT (*with a contemptuous sneer*) Ye needn't heed Eben. Eben's a dumb fool—like his Maw—soft an' simple!

SIMEON (*with his sardonic burst of laughter*) Ha! Eben's a chip o' yew—spit 'n' image—hard 'n' bitter's a hickory tree! Dog'll eat dog. He'll eat ye yet, old man!

CABOT (*commandingly*) Ye git t' wuk!

SIMEON (*as* ABBIE *disappears in house—winks at* PETER *and says tauntingly*) So that thar's our new Maw, be it? Whar in hell did ye dig her up? (*He and* PETER *laugh.*)

PETER Ha! Ye'd better turn her in the pen with the other sows. (*They laugh uproariously, slapping their thighs.*)

CABOT (*so amazed at their effrontery that he stutters in confusion*) Simeon! Peter! What's come over ye? Air ye drunk?

SIMEON We're free, old man—free o' yew an' the hull damned farm! (*They grow more and more hilarious and excited.*)

PETER An' we're startin' out fur the gold fields o' Californi-a!

SIMEON Ye kin take this place an' burn it!

PETER An' bury it—fur all we cares!

SIMEON We're free, old man! (*He cuts a caper.*)

PETER Free! (*He gives a kick in the air.*)

SIMEON (*in a frenzy*) Whoop!

PETER Whoop! (*They do an absurd Indian war dance about the old man who is petrified between rage and the fear that they are insane.*)

SIMEON We're free as Injuns! Lucky we don't sculp ye!

PETER An' burn yer barn an' kill the stock!

SIMEON An' rape yer new woman! Whoop! (*He and* PETER *stop their dance, holding their sides, rocking with wild laughter.*)

CABOT (*edging away*) Lust fur gold—fur the sinful, easy gold o' Californi-a! It's made ye mad!

SIMEON (*tauntingly*) Wouldn't ye like us to send ye back some sinful gold, ye old sinner?

PETER They's gold besides what's in Californi-a! (*He retreats back beyond the vision of the old man and takes the bag of money and flaunts it in the air above his head, laughing.*)

SIMEON And sinfuller, too!

PETER We'll be voyagin' on the sea! Whoop! (*He leaps up and down.*)

SIMEON Livin' free! Whoop! (*He leaps in turn.*)

CABOT (*suddenly roaring with rage*) My cuss on ye!

SIMEON Take our'n in trade fur it! Whoop!

CABOT I'll hev ye both chained up in the asylum!

PETER Ye old skinflint! Good-by!

SIMEON Ye old blood sucker! Good-by!

CABOT Go afore I ... !

PETER Whoop! (*He picks a stone from the road.* SIMEON *does the same.*)

SIMEON Maw'll be in the parlor.

PETER Ay-eh! One! Two!

CABOT (*frightened*) What air ye ... ?

PETER Three! (*They both throw, the stones hitting the parlor window with a crash of glass, tearing the shade.*)

SIMEON Whoop!

PETER Whoop!

CABOT (*in a fury now, rushing toward them*) If I kin lay hands on ye—I'll break yer bones fur ye! (*But they beat a capering retreat before him,* SIMEON *with the gate still under his arm.* CABOT *comes back, panting with impotent rage. Their voices as they go off take up the song of the gold-seekers to the old tune of "Oh, Susannah!"*)

> "I jumped aboard the Liza ship,
> And traveled on the sea,
> And every time I thought of home
> I wished it wasn't me!
> Oh! Californi-a,
> That's the land fur me!
> I'm off to Californi-a!
> With my wash bowl on my knee."

(*In the meantime, the window of the upper bedroom on right is raised and* ABBIE *sticks her head out. She looks down at* CABOT— *with a sigh of relief.*)

ABBIE Waal—that's the last o' them two, hain't it? (*He doesn't answer. Then in possessive tones*) This here's a nice bedroom, Ephraim. It's a r'al nice bed. Is it my room, Ephraim?

CABOT (*grimly—without looking up*) Our'n! (*She cannot control a grimace of aversion and pulls back her head slowly and shuts the window. A sudden horrible thought seems to enter* CABOT's *head.*) They been up to somethin'! Mebbe—mebbe they've pizened the stock—'r somethin'! (*He almost runs off down toward the barn. A moment later the kitchen door is slowly pushed open and* ABBIE *enters. For a moment she stands looking at* EBEN. *He does not notice her at first. Her eyes take him in penetratingly with a calculating appraisal of his strength as against hers. But under this her desire is dimly awakened by his youth and good looks. Suddenly he becomes conscious of her presence and looks up. Their eyes meet. He leaps to his feet, glowering at her speechlessly.*)

ABBIE (*in her most seductive tones which she uses all through this scene*) Be you—Eben? I'm Abbie—(*She laughs.*) I mean, I'm yer new Maw.

EBEN (*viciously*) No, damn ye!

ABBIE (*as if she hadn't heard—with a queer smile*) Yer Paw's spoke a lot o' yew. . . .

EBEN Ha!

ABBIE Ye mustn't mind him. He's an old man. (*A long pause. They stare at each other.*) I don't want t' pretend playin' Maw t' ye, Eben. (*admiringly*) Ye're too big an' too strong fur that. I want t' be frens with ye. Mebbe with me fur a fren ye'd find ye'd like livin' here better. I kin make it easy fur ye with him, mebbe. (*with a scornful sense of power*) I calc'late I kin git him t' do most anythin' fur me.

EBEN (*with bitter scorn*) Ha! (*They stare again,* EBEN *obscurely moved, physically attracted to her—in forced stilted tones*) Yew kin go t' the devil!

ABBIE (*calmly*) If cussin' me does ye good, cuss all ye've a mind t'. I'm all prepared t' have ye agin me—at fust. I don't blame ye nuther. I'd feel the same at any stranger comin' t' take my Maw's place. (*He shudders. She is watching him carefully.*) Yew must've cared a lot fur yewr Maw, didn't ye? My Maw died afore I'd growed. I don't remember her none. (*A pause.*) But yew won't hate me long, Eben. I'm not the wust in the world—an' yew an' me've got a lot in common. I kin tell that by lookin' at ye. Waal —I've had a hard life, too—oceans o' trouble an' nuthin' but wuk fur reward. I was a orphan early an' had t' wuk fur others in other folks' hums. Then I married an' he turned out a drunken spreer an' so he had to wuk fur others an' me too agen in other folks' hums, an' the baby died, an' my husband got sick an' died too, an' I was glad sayin' now I'm free fur once, on'y I diskivered right away all I was free fur was t' wuk agen in other folks' hums, doin' other folks' wuk till I'd most give up hope o' ever doin' my own wuk in my own hum, an' then your Paw come. . . . (CABOT *appears returning from the barn. He comes to the gate and looks down the road the brothers have gone. A faint strain of their retreating voices is heard: "Oh, Californi-a! That's the place for me." He stands glowering, his fist clenched, his face grim with rage.*)

EBEN (*fighting against his growing attraction and sympathy— harshly*) An' bought yew—like a harlot! (*She is stung and flushes angrily. She has been sincerely moved by the recital of her troubles. He adds furiously*) An' the price he's payin' ye—this farm —was my Maw's, damn ye!—an' mine now!

ABBIE (*with a cool laugh of confidence*) Yewr'n? We'll see 'bout that! (*then strongly*) Waal—what if I did need a hum? What else'd I marry an old man like him fur?

EBEN (*maliciously*) I'll tell him ye said that!

ABBIE (*smiling*) I'll say ye're lyin' a-purpose—an' he'll drive ye off the place!

EBEN Ye devil!

ABBIE (*defying him*) This be my farm—this be my hum—this be my kitchen—!

EBEN (*furiously, as if he were going to attack her*) Shut up, damn ye!

ABBIE (*walks up to him—a queer coarse expression of desire in her face and body—slowly*) An' upstairs—that be my bedroom— an' my bed! (*He stares into her eyes, terribly confused and torn. She adds softly*) I hain't bad nor mean—'ceptin' fur an enemy —but I got t' fight fur what's due me out o' life, if I ever 'spect t' git it. (*Then putting her hand on his arm—seductively*) Let's yew 'n' me be frens, Eben.

EBEN (*stupidly—as if hypnotized*) Ay-eh. (*Then furiously flinging off her arm*) No, ye durned old witch! I hate ye! (*He rushes out the door.*)

ABBIE (*looks after him smiling satisfiedly—then half to herself, mouthing the word*) Eben's nice. (*She looks at the table, proudly.*) I'll wash up *my* dishes now. (EBEN *appears outside, slamming the door behind him. He comes around corner, stops on seeing his father, and stands staring at him with hate.*)

CABOT (*raising his arms to heaven in the fury he can no longer control*) Lord God o' Hosts, smite the undutiful sons with Thy wust cuss!

EBEN (*breaking in violently*) Yew 'n' yewr God! Allus cussin' folks —allus naggin' 'em!

CABOT (*oblivious to him—summoningly*) God o' the old! God o' the lonesome!

EBEN (*mockingly*) Naggin' His sheep t' sin! T' hell with yewr God! (CABOT *turns. He and* EBEN *glower at each other.*)

CABOT (*harshly*)   So it's yew. I might've knowed it. (*shaking his finger threateningly at him*) Blasphemin' fool! (*then quickly*) Why hain't ye t' wuk?

EBEN   Why hain't yew? They've went. I can't wuk it all alone.

CABOT (*contemptuously*)   Nor noways! I'm wuth ten o' ye yit, old's I be! Ye'll never be more'n half a man! (*then, matter-of-factly*) Waal—let's git t' the barn. (*They go. A last faint note of the "Californi-a" song is heard from the distance. ABBIE is washing her dishes.*)

PART II

Scene 1

The exterior of the farmhouse, as in PART I—*a hot Sunday afternoon two months later.* ABBIE, *dressed in her best, is discovered sitting in a rocker at the end of the porch. She rocks listlessly, enervated by the heat, staring in front of her with bored, half-closed eyes.*

EBEN *sticks his head out of his bedroom window. He looks around furtively and tries to see—or hear—if anyone is on the porch, but although he has been careful to make no noise,* ABBIE *has sensed his movement. She stops rocking, her face grows animated and eager, she waits attentively.* EBEN *seems to feel her presence, he scowls back his thoughts of her and spits with exaggerated disdain—then withdraws back into the room.* ABBIE *waits, holding her breath as she listens with passionate eagerness for every sound within the house.*

EBEN *comes out. Their eyes meet. His falter, he is confused, he turns away and slams the door resentfully. At this gesture,* ABBIE *laughs tantalizingly, amused but at the same time piqued and irritated. He scowls, strides off the porch to the path and starts to walk past her to the road with a grand swagger of ignoring her existence. He is dressed in his store suit, spruced up, his face shines from soap and water.* ABBIE *leans forward on her chair, her eyes hard and angry now, and, as he passes her, gives a sneering, taunting chuckle.*

EBEN (*stung—turns on her furiously*)   What air yew cacklin' 'bout?

ABBIE (*triumphant*)   Yew!

EBEN   What about me?

ABBIE   Ye look all slicked up like a prize bull.

EBEN (*with a sneer*)   Waal—ye hain't so durned purty yerself, be ye? (*They stare into each other's eyes, his held by hers in spite of himself, hers glowingly possessive. Their physical attraction becomes a palpable force quivering in the hot air.*)

ABBIE (*softly*)   Ye don't mean that, Eben. Ye may think ye mean it, mebbe, but ye don't. Ye can't. It's agin nature, Eben. Ye been fightin' yer nature ever since the day I come—tryin' t' tell yerself I hain't purty t'ye. (*She laughs a low humid laugh without taking her eyes from his. A pause—her body squirms desirously —she murmurs languorously.*) Hain't the sun strong an' hot? Ye kin feel it burnin' into the earth—Nature—makin' thin's grow— bigger 'n' bigger—burnin' inside ye—makin' ye want t' grow— into somethin' else—till ye're jined with it—an' it's your'n—but it owns ye, too—an' makes ye grow bigger—like a tree—like them elums— (*She laughs again softly, holding his eyes. He takes a step toward her, compelled against his will.*) Nature'll beat ye, Eben. Ye might's well own up t' it fust 's last.

EBEN (*trying to break from her spell—confusedly*) If Paw'd hear ye goin' on. . . . (*resentfully*) But ye've made such a damned idjit out o' the old devil . . . ! (ABBIE *laughs.*)

ABBIE Waal—hain't it easier fur yew with him changed softer?

EBEN (*defiantly*) No. I'm fightin' him—fightin' yew—fightin' fur Maw's right t' her hum! (*This breaks her spell for him. He glowers at her.*) An' I'm onto ye. Ye hain't foolin' me a mite. Ye're aimin' t' swaller up everythin' an' make it your'n. Waal, you'll find I'm a heap sight bigger hunk nor yew kin chew! (*He turns from her with a sneer.*)

ABBIE (*trying to regain her ascendancy—seductively*) Eben!

EBEN Leave me be! (*He starts to walk away.*)

ABBIE (*more commandingly*) Eben!

EBEN (*stops—resentfully*) What d'ye want?

ABBIE (*trying to conceal a growing excitement*) Whar air ye goin'?

EBEN (*with malicious nonchalance*) Oh—up the road a spell.

ABBIE T' the village?

EBEN (*airly*) Mebbe.

ABBIE (*excitedly*) T' see that Min, I s'pose?

EBEN Mebbe.

ABBIE (*weakly*) What d'ye want t' waste time on her fur?

EBEN (*revenging himself now—grinning at her*) Ye can't beat Nature, didn't ye say? (*He laughs and again starts to walk away.*)

ABBIE (*bursting out*) An ugly old hake!

EBEN (*with a tantalizing sneer*) She's purtier'n yew be!

ABBIE That every wuthless drunk in the country has. . . .

EBEN (*tauntingly*) Mebbe—but she's better'n yew. She owns up fa'r 'n' squar' t' her doin's.

ABBIE (*furiously*) Don't ye dare compare. . . .

EBEN She don't go sneakin' an' stealin'—what's mine.

ABBIE (*savagely seizing on his weak point*) Your'n? Yew mean— my farm?

EBEN I mean the farm yew sold yerself fur like any other old whore—my farm!

ABBIE (*stung—fiercely*)   Ye'll never live t' see the day when even a stinkin' weed on it 'll belong t' ye! (*then in a scream*) Git out o' my sight! Go on t' yer slut—disgracin' yer Paw 'n' me! I'll git yer Paw t' horsewhip ye off the place if I want t'! Ye're only livin' here 'cause I tolerate ye! Git along! I hate the sight o' ye! (*She stops, panting and glaring at him.*)

EBEN (*returning her glance in kind*)   An' I hate the sight o' yew! (*He turns and strides off up the road. She follows his retreating figure with concentrated hate. Old* CABOT *appears coming up from the barn. The hard, grim expression of his face has changed. He seems in some queer way softened, mellowed. His eyes have taken on a strange, incongruous dreamy quality. Yet there is no hint of physical weakness about him—rather he looks more robust and younger.* ABBIE *sees him and turns away quickly with unconcealed aversion. He comes slowly up to her.*)

CABOT (*mildly*)   War yew an' Eben quarrelin' agen?

ABBIE (*shortly*)   No.

CABOT   Ye was talkin' a'mighty loud. (*He sits down on the edge of porch.*)

ABBIE (*snappishly*)   If ye heerd us they hain't no need askin' questions.

CABOT   I didn't hear what ye said.

ABBIE (*relieved*)   Waal—it wa'n't nothin' t' speak on.

CABOT (*after a pause*)   Eben's queer.

ABBIE (*bitterly*)   He's the dead spit 'n' image o' yew!

CABOT (*queerly interested*)   D'ye think so, Abbie? (*After a pause, ruminatingly*) Me 'n' Eben's allus fit 'n' fit. I never could b'ar him noways. He's so thunderin' soft—like his Maw.

ABBIE (*scornfully*)   Ay-eh! 'Bout as soft as yew be!

CABOT (*as if he hadn't heard*)   Mebbe I been too hard on him.

ABBIE (*jeeringly*)   Waal—ye're gittin' soft now—soft as slop! That's what Eben was sayin'.

CABOT (*his face instantly grim and ominous*)   Eben was sayin'? Waal, he'd best not do nothin' t' try me 'r he'll soon diskiver. . . . (*A pause. She keeps her face turned away. His gradually softens. He stares up at the sky.*) Purty, hain't it?

ABBIE (*crossly*)   I don't see nothin' purty.

CABOT   The sky. Feels like a wa'm field up thar.

ABBIE (*sarcastically*)   Air yew aimin' t' buy up over the farm too? (*She snickers contemptuously.*)

CABOT (*strangely*)   I'd like t' own my place up thar. (*a pause*) I'm gittin' old, Abbie. I'm gittin' ripe on the bough. (*A pause. She stares at him mystified. He goes on.*) It's allus lonesome cold in the house—even when it's bilin' hot outside. Hain't yew noticed?

ABBIE No.

CABOT It's wa'm down t' the barn—nice smellin' an' warm—with the cows. (*a pause*) Cows is queer.

ABBIE Like yew?

CABOT Like Eben. (*a pause*) I'm gittin' t' feel resigned t' Eben— jest as I got t' feel 'bout his Maw. I'm gittin' t' learn to b'ar his softness—jest like her'n. I calc'late I c'd a'most take t' him—if he wa'n't sech a dumb fool! (*a pause*) I s'pose it's old age a-creepin' in my bones.

ABBIE (*indifferently*) Waal—ye hain't dead yet.

CABOT (*roused*) No, I hain't, yew bet—not by a hell of a sight— I'm sound 'n' tough as hickory! (*then moodily*) But arter three score and ten the Lord warns ye t' prepare. (*a pause*) That's why Eben's come in my head. Now that his cussed sinful brothers is gone their path t' hell, they's no one left but Eben.

ABBIE (*resentfully*) They's me, hain't they? (*Agitatedly*) What's all this sudden likin' ye tuk to Eben? Why don't ye say nothin' 'bout me? Hain't I yer lawful wife?

CABOT (*simply*) Ay-eh. Ye be. (*A pause—he stares at her desirously—his eyes grow avid—then with a sudden movement he seizes her hands and squeezes them, declaiming in a queer camp meeting preacher's tempo*) Yew air my Rose o' Sharon! Behold, yew air fair; yer eyes air doves; yer lips air like scarlet; yer two breasts air like two fawns; yer navel be like a round goblet; yer belly be like a heap o' wheat.... (*He covers her hand with kisses. She does not seem to notice. She stares before her with hard angry eyes.*)

ABBIE (*jerking her hands away—harshly*) So ye're plannin' t' leave the farm t' Eben, air ye?

CABOT (*dazedly*) Leave...? (*then with resentful obstinacy*) I hain't a-givin' it t' no one!

ABBIE (*remorselessly*) Ye can't take it with ye.

CABOT (*thinks a moment—then reluctantly*) No, I calc'late not. (*after a pause—with a strange passion*) But if I could, I would, by the Etarnal! 'R if I could, in my dyin' hour, I'd set it afire an' watch it burn—this house an' every ear o' corn an' every tree down t' the last blade o' hay! I'd sit an' know it was all a-dying with me an' no one else'd ever own what was mine, what I'd made out o' nothin' with my own sweat 'n' blood! (*a pause— then he adds with a queer affection*) 'Ceptin' the cows. Them I'd turn free.

ABBIE (*harshly*) An' me?

CABOT (*with a queer smile*)   Ye'd be turned free, too.

ABBIE (*furiously*)   So that's the thanks I git fur marryin' ye—t' have ye change kind to Eben who hates ye, an' talk o' turnin' me out in the road.

CABOT (*hastily*)   Abbie! Ye know I wa'n't. . . .

ABBIE (*vengefully*)   Just let me tell ye a thing or two 'bout Eben! Whar's he gone? T' see that harlot, Min! I tried fur t' stop him. Disgracin' yew an' me—on the Sabbath, too!

CABOT (*rather guiltily*)   He's a sinner—nateral-born. It's lust eatin' his heart.

ABBIE (*enraged beyond endurance—wildly vindictive*)   An' his lust fur me! Kin ye find excuses fur that?

CABOT (*stares at her—after a dead pause*)   Lust—fur yew?

ABBIE (*defiantly*)   He was tryin' t' make love t' me—when ye heerd us quarrelin'.

CABOT (*stares at her—then a terrible expression of rage comes over his face—he springs to his feet shaking all over*)   By the A'mighty God—I'll end him!

ABBIE (*frightened now for* EBEN)   No! Don't ye!

CABOT (*violently*)   I'll git the shotgun an' blow his soft brains t' the top o' them elums!

ABBIE (*throwing her arms around him*)   No, Ephraim!

CABOT (*pushing her away violently*)   I will, by God!

ABBIE (*in a quieting tone*)   Listen, Ephraim. 'Twa'n't nothin' bad —on'y a boy's foolin'—'twa'n't meant serious—jest jokin' an' teasin'. . . .

CABOT   Then why did ye say—lust?

ABBIE   It must hev sounded wusser'n I meant. An' I was mad at thinkin'—ye'd leave him the farm.

CABOT (*quieter but still grim and cruel*)   Waal then, I'll horsewhip him off the place if that much'll content ye.

ABBIE (*reaching out and taking his hand*)   No. Don't think o' me! Ye mustn't drive him off. 'Tain't sensible. Who'll ye get to help ye on the farm? They's no one hereabouts.

CABOT (*considers this—then nodding his appreciation*)   Ye got a head on ye. (*then irritably*) Waal, let them stay. (*He sits down on the edge of the porch. She sits beside him. He murmurs contemptuously*) I oughtn't t' git riled so—at that 'ere fool calf. (*a pause*) But har's the p'int. What son o' mine'll keep on here t' the farm—when the Lord does call me? Simeon an' Peter air gone t' hell—an' Eben's follerin' 'em.

ABBIE   They's me.

CABOT   Ye're on'y a woman.

ABBIE   I'm yewr wife.

CABOT   That hain't me. A son is me—my blood—mine. Mine ought t' git mine. An' then it's still mine—even though I be six foot under. D'ye see?

ABBIE (*giving him a look of hatred*) Ay-eh. I see. (*She becomes very thoughtful, her face growing shrewd, her eyes studying* CABOT *craftily.*)

CABOT   I'm gittin' old—ripe on the bough. (*then with a sudden forced reassurance*) Not but what I hain't a hard nut t' crack even yet—an' fur many a year t' come! By the Etarnal, I kin break most o' the young fellers' backs at any kind o' work any day o' the year!

ABBIE (*suddenly*) Mebbe the Lord'll give *us* a son.

CABOT (*turns and stares at her eagerly*) Ye mean—a son—t' me 'n' yew?

ABBIE (*with a cajoling smile*) Ye're a strong man yet, hain't ye? 'Tain't noways impossible, be it? We know that. Why d'ye stare so? Hain't ye never thought o' that afore? I been thinkin' o' it all along. Ay-eh—an' I been prayin' it'd happen, too.

CABOT (*his face growing full of joyous pride and a sort of religious ecstasy*) Ye been prayin', Abbie?—fur a son?—t' us?

ABBIE   Ay-eh. (*with a grim resolution*) I want a son now.

CABOT (*excitedly clutching both of her hands in his*) It'd be the blessin' o' God, Abbie—the blessin' o' God A'mighty on me—in my old age—in my lonesomeness! They hain't nothin' I wouldn't do fur ye then, Abbie. Ye'd hev on'y ask it—anythin' ye'd a mind t'!

ABBIE (*interrupting*) Would ye will the farm t' me then—t' me an' it . . . ?

CABOT (*vehemently*) I'd do anythin' ye axed, I tell ye! I swar it! May I be everlastin' damned t' hell if I wouldn't! (*He sinks to his knees pulling her down with him. He trembles all over with the fervor of his hopes.*) Pray t' the Lord agen, Abbie. It's the Sabbath! I'll jine ye! Two prayers air better nor one. "An' God hearkened unto Rachel"! An' God hearkened unto Abbie! Pray, Abbie! Pray fur him to hearken! (*He bows his head, mumbling. She pretends to do likewise but gives him a side glance of scorn and triumph.*)

Scene 2

*About eight in the evening. The interior of the two bedrooms on the top floor is shown—*EBEN *is sitting on the side of his bed in the room on the left. On account of the heat he has taken off everything but his under-shirt and pants. His feet are bare. He faces front, brooding moodily, his chin propped on his hands, a desperate expression on his face.*

In the other room CABOT *and* ABBIE *are sitting side by side on the edge of their bed, an old four-poster with feather mattress. He is in his night shirt, she in her nightdress. He is still in the queer, excited mood into which the notion of a son has thrown him. Both rooms are lighted dimly and flickeringly by tallow candles.*

CABOT   The farm needs a son.

ABBIE   I need a son.

CABOT   Ay-eh. Sometimes ye air the farm an' sometimes the farm be yew. That's why I clove t' ye in my lonesomeness. (*A pause. He pounds his knee with his fist.*) Me an' the farm has got t' beget a son!

ABBIE   Ye'd best go t' sleep. Ye're gittin' thin's all mixed.

CABOT   (*with an impatient gesture*) No, I hain't. My mind's clear's a bell. Ye don't know me, that's it. (*He stares hopelessly at the floor.*)

ABBIE   (*indifferently*)   Mebbe. (*In the next room* EBEN *gets up and paces up and down distractedly.* ABBIE *hears him. Her eyes fasten on the intervening wall with concentrated attention.* EBEN *stops and stares. Their hot glances seem to meet through the wall. Unconsciously he stretches out his arms for her and she half rises. Then aware, he mutters a curse at himself and flings himself face downward on the bed, his clenched fists above his head, his face buried in the pillow.* ABBIE *relaxes with a faint sigh but her eyes remain fixed on the wall; she listens with all her attention for some movement from* EBEN.)

CABOT   (*suddenly raises his head and looks at her—scornfully*)   Will ye ever know me—'r will any man 'r woman? (*Shaking his head*) No. I calc'late 't wa'n't t' be. (*He turns away.* ABBIE *looks at the wall. Then, evidently unable to keep silent about his thoughts, without looking at his wife, he puts out his hand and clutches her knee. She starts violently, looks at him, sees he is not watching her, concentrates again on the wall and pays no attention to what he says.*) Listen, Abbie. When I come here fifty odd year ago—I was jest twenty an' the strongest an' hardest ye ever seen—ten times as strong an' fifty times as hard as Eben. Waal—this place was nothin' but fields o' stones. Folks laughed when I tuk it. They couldn't know what I knowed. When he kin make corn sprout out o' stones, God's livin' in yew! They wa'n't strong enuf fur that! They reckoned God was easy. They laughed. They don't laugh no more. Some died hereabouts. Some went West an' died. They're all under ground—fur follerin' arter an easy God. God hain't easy. (*He shakes his head slowly.*) An' I growed hard. Folks kept allus sayin' he's a hard man like 'twas sinful t' be hard, so's at last I said back at 'em: Waal then, by thunder, ye'll git me hard an' see how ye like it! (*Then suddenly*) But I give in t' weakness once. 'Twas arter I'd been here two year. I got weak—despairful—they was so many stones. They was a party leavin', givin' up, goin' West. I jined 'em. We tracked on 'n' on. We come t' broad medders, plains, whar the soil was black an' rich as gold. Nary a stone. Easy. Ye'd on'y to plow an' sow an' then set an' smoke yer pipe an' watch thin's grow. I could o' been a rich man—but somethin' in me fit me an' fit me—the voice o' God sayin': "This hain't wuth nothin' t' Me. Get ye back t' hum!" I got afeerd o' that voice an' I lit out back t' hum here, leavin' my claim an' crops t' whoever'd a mind t' take 'em. Ay-eh. I actolly give up what was rightful mine! God's hard, not easy! God's in the stones! Build my church on a rock—out o' stones an' I'll be in them! That's what He meant t' Peter! (*He sighs heavily —a pause*) Stones. I picked 'em up an' piled 'em into walls. Ye kin read the years o' my life in them walls, every day a hefted stone, climbin' over the hills up and down, fencin' in the fields that was mine, whar I'd made thin's grow out o' nothin'—like the will o' God, like the servant o' His hand. It wa'n't easy. It was hard an' He made me hard fur it. (*He pauses.*) All the time I kept gittin' lonesomer. I tuk a wife. She bore Simeon an' Peter. She was a good woman. She wuked hard. We was married twenty year. She never knowed me. She helped but she never knowed what she was helpin'. I was allus lonesome. She died. After that it wa'n't so lonesome fur a spell. (*a pause*) I lost count o' the years. I had no time t' fool away countin' 'em. Sim an' Peter helped. The farm growed. It was all mine! When I thought o' that I didn't feel lonesome. (*a pause*) But ye can't hitch yer mind t' one thin' day an' night. I tuk another wife—Eben's Maw. Her folks was contestin' me at law over my deeds t' the farm—my farm! That's why Eben keeps a'talkin' his fool talk o' this bein' his Maw's farm. She bore Eben. She was purty—but soft. She tried t' be hard. She couldn't. She never knowed me nor nothin'. It was lonesomer 'n hell with her. After a matter o' sixteen odd years, she died. (*a pause*) I lived with the boys. They hated me 'cause I was hard. I hated them 'cause they was soft. They coveted the farm without knowin' what it meant. It made me bitter 'n wormwood. It aged me—them coveting what I'd made fur mine. Then this spring the call come—the voice o' God cryin' in my wilderness, in my lonesomeness—t' go out an' seek an' find! (*Turning to her with strange passion*) I sought ye an' I found ye! Yew air my Rose o' Sharon! Yer eyes air like.... (*She has turned a blank face, resentful eyes to his. He stares at her for a moment—then harshly)* Air ye any the wiser fur all I've told ye?

ABBIE (*confusedly*) Mebbe.

CABOT (*pushing her away from him—angrily*) Ye don't know nothin'—nor never will. If ye don't hev a son t' redeem ye . . . (*this in a tone of cold threat*)

ABBIE (*resentfully*) I've prayed, hain't I?

CABOT (*bitterly*) Pray agen—fur understandin'!

ABBIE (*a veiled threat in her tone*) Ye'll have a son out o' me, I promise ye.

CABOT How kin ye promise?

ABBIE I got second-sight mebbe. I kin foretell. (*She gives a queer smile.*)

CABOT I believe ye have. Ye give me the chills sometimes. (*He shivers.*) It's cold in this house. It's oneasy. They's thin's pokin' about in the dark—in the corners. (*He pulls on his trousers, tucking in his night shirt, and pulls on his boots.*)

ABBIE (*surprised*) Whar air ye goin'?

CABOT (*queerly*) Down whar it's restful—whar it's warm—down t' the barn. (*bitterly*) I kin talk t' the cows. They know. They know the farm an' me. They'll give me peace. (*He turns to go out the door.*)

ABBIE (*a bit frightenedly*) Air ye ailin' tonight, Ephraim?

CABOT Growin'. Growin' ripe on the bough. (*He turns and goes, his boots clumping down the stairs. EBEN sits up with a start, listening. ABBIE is conscious of his movement and stares at the wall. CABOT comes out of the house around the corner and stands by the gate, blinking at the sky. He stretches up his hands in a tortured gesture*) God A'mighty, call from the dark! (*He listens as if expecting an answer. Then his arms drop, he shakes his head and plods off toward the barn. EBEN and ABBIE stare at each other through the wall. EBEN sighs heavily and ABBIE echoes it. Both become terribly nervous, uneasy. Finally ABBIE gets up and listens, her ear to the wall. He acts as if he saw every move she was making, he becomes resolutely still. She seems driven into a decision—goes out the door in rear determinedly. His eyes follow her. Then as the door of his room is opened softly, he turns away, waits in an attitude of strained fixity. ABBIE stands for a second staring at him, her eyes burning with desire. Then with a little cry she runs over and throws her arms about his neck, she pulls his head back and covers his mouth with kisses. At first, he submits dumbly; then he puts his arms about her neck and returns her kisses, but finally, suddenly aware of his hatred, he hurls her away from him, springing to his feet. They stand speechless and breathless, panting like two animals.*)

ABBIE (*at last—painfully*) Ye shouldn't, Eben—ye shouldn't—I'd make ye happy!

EBEN (*harshly*) I don't want t' be happy—from yew!

ABBIE (*helplessly*) Ye do, Eben! Ye do! Why d'ye lie?

EBEN (*viciously*) I don't take t'ye, I tell ye! I hate the sight o' ye!

ABBIE (*with an uncertain troubled laugh*) Waal, I kissed ye anyways—an' ye kissed back—yer lips was burnin'—ye can't lie 'bout that! (*intensely*) If ye don't care, why did ye kiss me back —why was yer lips burnin'?

EBEN (*wiping his mouth*) It was like pizen on 'em (*then tauntingly*) When I kissed ye back, mebbe I thought 'twas someone else.

ABBIE (*wildly*) Min?

EBEN Mebbe.

ABBIE (*torturedly*) Did ye go t' see her? Did ye r'ally go? I thought ye mightn't. Is that why ye throwed me off jest now?

EBEN (*sneeringly*) What if it be?

ABBIE (*raging*) Then ye're a dog, Eben Cabot!

EBEN (*threateningly*) Ye can't talk that way t' me!

ABBIE (*with a shrill laugh*) Can't I? Did ye think I was in love with ye—a weak thin' like yew? Not much! I on'y wanted ye fur a purpose o' my own—an' I'll hev ye fur it yet 'cause I'm stronger'n yew be!

EBEN (*resentfully*) I knowed well it was on'y part o' yer plan t' swaller everythin'!

ABBIE (*taughtingly*) Mebbe!

EBEN (*furious*) Git out o' my room!

ABBIE This air my room an' ye're on'y hired help!

EBEN (*threateningly*) Git out afore I murder ye!

ABBIE (*quite confident now*) I hain't a mite afeerd. Ye want me, don't ye? Yes, ye do! An' yer Paw's son'll never kill what he wants! Look at yer eyes! They's lust fur me in 'em, burnin' 'em up! Look at yer lips now! They're tremblin' an' longin' t' kiss me, an' yer teeth t'bite! (*He is watching her now with a horrible fascination. She laughs a crazy triumphant laugh.*) I'm a-goin' t' make all o' this hum my hum! They's one room hain't mine yet, but it's a-goin' t' be tonight. I'm a-goin' down now an' light up! (*She makes him a mocking bow.*) Won't ye come courtin' me in the best parlor, Mister Cabot?

EBEN (*staring at her—horribly confused—dully*) Don't ye dare! It hain't been opened since Maw died an' was laid out thar! Don't ye . . . ! (*But her eyes are fixed on his so burningly that his will seems to wither before hers. He stands swaying toward her helplessly.*)

ABBIE (*holding his eyes and putting all her will into her words as she backs out the door*) I'll expect ye afore long, Eben.

EBEN (*stares after her for a while, walking toward the door. A light appears in the parlor window. He murmurs*) In the parlor? (*This seems to arouse connotations for he comes back and puts on his white shirt, collar, half ties the tie mechanically, puts on coat, takes his hat, stands barefooted looking about him in bewilderment, mutters wonderingly*) Maw! Whar air yew? (*Then goes slowly toward the door in rear.*)

Scene 3

A few minutes later. The interior of the parlor is shown. A grim, repressed room like a tomb in which the family has been interred alive. ABBIE *sits on the edge of the horsehair sofa. She has lighted all the candles and the room is revealed in all its preserved ugliness. A change has come over the woman. She looks awed and frightened now, ready to run away.*

The door is opened and EBEN *appears. His face wears an expression of obsessed confusion. He stands staring at her, his arms hanging disjointedly from his shoulders, his feet bare, his hat in his hand.*

ABBIE (*after a pause—with a nervous, formal politeness*) Won't ye set?

EBEN (*dully*) Ay-eh. (*Mechanically he places his hat carefully on the floor near the door and sits stiffly beside her on the edge of the sofa. A pause. They both remain rigid, looking straight ahead with eyes full of fear.*)

ABBIE When I fust came in—in the dark—they seemed somethin' here.

EBEN (*simply*) Maw.

ABBIE I kin still feel—somethin'. . . .

EBEN It's Maw.

ABBIE At fust I was feered o' it. I wanted t' yell an' run. Now—since yew come—seems like it's growin' soft an' kind t' me. (*Addressing the air—queerly*) Thank yew.

EBEN Maw allus loved me.

ABBIE Mebbe it knows I love yew too. Mebbe that makes it kind t' me.

EBEN (*dully*) I dunno. I should think she'd hate ye.

ABBIE (*with certainty*) No. I kin feel it don't—not no more.

EBEN Hate yer fur stealin' her place—here in her hum—settin' in her parlor whar she was laid— (*He suddenly stops, staring stupidly before him.*)

ABBIE What is it, Eben?

EBEN (*in a whisper*) Seems like Maw didn't want me t' remind ye.

ABBIE (*excitedly*) I knowed, Eben! It's kind t' me! It don't b'ar me no grudges fur what I never knowed an' couldn't help!

EBEN Maw b'ars him a grudge.

ABBIE Waal, so does all o' us.

EBEN Ay-eh. (*with passion*) I does, by God!

ABBIE (*taking one of his hands in hers and patting it*) Thar! Don't git riled thinkin' o' him. Think o' yer Maw who's kind t' us. Tell me about yer Maw, Eben.

EBEN They hain't nothin' much. She was kind. She was good.

ABBIE (*putting one arm over his shoulder. He does not seem to notice—passionately*) I'll be kind an' good t' ye!

EBEN Sometimes she used t' sing fur me.

ABBIE I'll sing fur ye!

EBEN This was her hum. This was her farm.

ABBIE This is my hum! This is my farm!

EBEN He married her t' steal 'em. She was soft an' easy. He couldn't 'preciate her.

ABBIE He can't 'preciate me!

EBEN He murdered her with his hardness.

ABBIE He's murderin' me!

EBEN She died. (*a pause*) Sometimes she used to sing fur me. (*He bursts into a fit of sobbing.*)

ABBIE (*both arms around him—with wild passion*) I'll sing fur ye! I'll die fur ye! (*In spite of her overwhelming desire for him, there is a sincere maternal love in her manner and voice—a horribly frank mixture of lust and mother love.*) Don't cry, Eben! I'll take yer Maw's place! I'll be everythin' she was t' ye! Let me kiss ye, Eben! (*She pulls his head around. He makes a bewildered pretense of resistance. She is tender.*) Don't be afeered! I'll kiss ye pure, Eben—same 's if I was a Maw t' ye—an' ye kin kiss me back 's if yew was my son—my boy—sayin' goodnight t' me! Kiss me, Eben. (*They kiss in restrained fashion. Then suddenly wild passion overcomes her. She kisses him lustfully again and again and he flings his arms about her and returns her kisses. Suddenly, as in the bedroom, he frees himself from her violently and springs to his feet. He is trembling all over, in a strange state of terror. ABBIE strains her arms toward him with fierce pleading.*) Don't ye leave me, Eben! Can't ye see it hain't enuf—lovin' ye like a Maw —can't ye see it's got t' be that an' more—much more—a hundred times more—fur me t' be happy—fur yew t' be happy?

EBEN (*to the presence he feels in the room*) Maw! Maw! What d'ye want? What air ye tellin' me?

ABBIE She's tellin' ye t' love me. She knows I love ye an' I'll be good t' ye. Can't ye feel it? Don't ye know? She's tellin' ye t' love me, Eben!

EBEN Ah-eh. I feel—mebbe she—but—I can't figger out—why—when ye've stole her place—here in her hum—in the parlor whar she was—

ABBIE (*fiercely*) She knows I love ye!

EBEN (*his face suddenly lighting up with a fierce triumphant grin*) I see it! I sees why. It's her vengeance on him—so's she kin rest quiet in her grave!

ABBIE (*wildly*) Vengeance o' God on the hull o' us! What d'we give a durn? I love ye, Eben! God knows I love ye! (*She stretches out her arms for him.*)

EBEN (*throws himself on his knees beside the sofa and grabs her in his arms—releasing all his pent-up passion*) An' I love yew, Abbie!—now I kin say it! I been dyin' fur want o' ye—every hour since ye come! I love ye! (*Their lips meet in a fierce, bruising kiss.*)

Scene 4

Exterior of the farmhouse. It is just dawn. The front door at right is opened.

EBEN *comes out and walks around to the gate. He is dressed in his working clothes. He seems changed. His face wears a bold and confident expression, he is grinning to himself with evident satisfaction. As he gets near the gate, the window of the parlor is heard opening and the shutters are flung back and* ABBIE *sticks her head out. Her hair tumbles over her shoulders in disarray, her face is flushed, she looks at* EBEN *with tender, languorous eyes and calls softly.*

ABBIE Eben. (*As he turns—playfully*) Jest one more kiss afore ye go. I'm goin' to miss ye fearful all day.

EBEN An' me yew, ye kin bet! (*He goes to her. They kiss several times. He draws away, laughingly.*) Thar. That's enuf, hain't it? Ye won't hev none left fur next time.

ABBIE I got a million o' 'em left fur yew! (*then a bit anxiously*) D'ye r'ally love me, Eben?

EBEN (*emphatically*) I like ye better'n any gal I ever knowed! That's gospel!

ABBIE Likin' hain't lovin'.

EBEN Waal then—I love ye. Now air yew satisfied?

ABBIE Ay-eh, I be. (*She smiles at him adoringly.*)

EBEN I better git t' the barn. The old critter's liable t' suspicion an' come sneakin' up.

ABBIE (*with a confident laugh*) Let him! I kin allus pull the wool over his eyes. I'm goin' t' leave the shutters open and let in the sun 'n' air. This room's been dead long enuf. Now it's goin' t' be my room!

EBEN (*frowning*) Ay-eh.

ABBIE We made it our'n last night, didn't we? We give it life— our lovin' did. (*a pause*)

EBEN (*with a strange look*) Maw's gone back t' her grave. She kin sleep now.

ABBIE May she rest in peace! (*then tenderly rebuking*) Ye oughtn't t' talk o' sad thin's—this mornin'.

EBEN It jest come up in my mind o' itself.

ABBIE Don't let it. (*He doesn't answer. She yawns.*) Waal, I'm a-goin' t' steal a wink o' sleep. I'll tell the Old Man I hain't feelin' pert. Let him git his own vittles.

EBEN I see him comin' from the barn. Ye better look smart an' git upstairs.

ABBIE Ay-eh. Good-by. Don't fergit me. (*She throws him a kiss. He grins—then squares his shoulders and awaits his father confidently. CABOT walks slowly up from the left, staring up at the sky with a vague face.*)

EBEN (*jovially*) Mornin', Paw. Star-gazin' in daylight?

CABOT Purty, hain't it?

EBEN (*looking around him possessively*) It's a durned purty farm.

CABOT I mean the sky.

EBEN (*grinning*) How d'ye know? Them eyes o' your'n can't see that fur. (*This tickles his humor and he slaps his thigh and laughs.*) Ho-ho! That's a good un!

CABOT (*grimly sarcastic*) Ye're feelin' right chipper, hain't ye? Whar'd ye steal the likker?

EBEN (*good-naturedly*) 'Taint likker. Jest life. (*Suddenly holding out his hand—soberly*) Yew 'n' me is quits. Let's shake hands.

CABOT (*suspiciously*) What's come over ye?

EBEN Then don't. Mebbe it's jest as well. (*a moment's pause*) What's come over me? (*queerly*) Didn't ye feel her passin'— goin' back t' her grave?

CABOT (*dully*) Who?

EBEN Maw. She kin rest now an' sleep content. She's quit with ye.

CABOT (*confusedly*) I rested. I slept good—down with the cows. They know how t' sleep. They're teachin' me.

EBEN (*suddenly jovial again*) Good fur the cows! Waal—ye better git t' work.

CABOT (*grimly amused*) Air yew bossin' me, ye calf?

EBEN (*beginning to laugh*) Ah-eh! I'm bossin' yew! Ha-ha-ha! see how ye like it! Ha-ha-ha! I'm the prize rooster o' this roost. Ha-ha-ha! (*He goes off toward the barn laughing.*)

CABOT (*looks after him with scornful pity*) Soft-headed. Like his Maw. Dead spit 'n' image. No hope in him! (*He spits with contemptuous disgust.*) A born fool! (*Then matter-of-factly*) Waal —I'm gittin' peckish. (*He goes toward door.*)

PART III

Scene 1

A night in late spring the following year. The kitchen and the two bedrooms upstairs are shown. The two bedrooms are dimly lighted by a tallow candle in each. EBEN *is sitting on the side of the bed in his room, his chin propped on his fists, his face a study of the struggle he is making to understand his conflicting emotions. The noisy laughter and music from below where a kitchen dance is in progress annoy and distract him. He scowls at the floor. In the next room a cradle stands beside the double bed.*

In the kitchen all is festivity. The stove has been taken down to give more room to the dancers. The chairs, with wooden benches added, have been pushed back against the walls. On these are seated, squeezed in tight against one another, farmers and their wives and their young folks of both sexes from the neighboring farms. They are all chattering and laughing loudly. They evidently have some secret joke in common. There is no end of winking, of nudging, of meaning nods of the head toward CABOT *who, in a state of extreme hilarious excitement increased by the amount he has drunk, is standing near the rear door where there is a small keg of whisky and serving drinks to all the men. In the left corner, front, dividing the attention with her husband,* ABBIE *is sitting in a rocking chair, a shawl wrapped about her shoulders. She is very pale, her face is thin and drawn, her eyes are fixed anxiously on the open door in rear as if waiting for someone.*

The MUSICIAN *is tuning up his fiddle, seated in the far right corner. He is a lanky young fellow with a long, weak face. His pale eyes blink incessantly and he grins about him slyly with a greedy malice.*

ABBIE (*suddenly turning to a young girl on her right*) Whar's Eben?

YOUNG GIRL (*eying her scornfully*) I dunno, Mrs. Cabot. I hain't seen Eben in ages. (*meaningly*) Seems like he's spent most o' his time t' hum since yew come.

ABBIE (*vaguely*) I tuk his Maw's place.

YOUNG GIRL Ay-eh. So I've heerd. (*She turns away to retail this bit of gossip to her mother sitting next to her.* ABBIE *turns to her left to a big stoutish middle-aged man whose flushed face and staring eyes show the amount of "likker" he has consumed.*)

ABBIE   Ye hain't seen Eben, hev ye?

MAN   No, I hain't. (*then he adds with a wink*) If yew hain't, who would?

ABBIE   He's the best dancer in the county. He'd ought t' come an' dance.

MAN (*with a wink*)   Mebbe he's doin' the dutiful an' walkin' the kid t' sleep. It's a boy, hain't it?

ABBIE (*nodding vaguely*)   Ay-eh—born two weeks back—purty's a picter.

MAN   They all is—t' their Maws. (*then in a whisper, with a nudge and a leer*) Listen, Abbie—if ye ever git tired o' Eben, remember me! Don't fergit now! (*He looks at her uncomprehending face for a second—then grunts disgustedly.*) Waal—guess I'll likker agin. (*He goes over and joins* CABOT *who is arguing noisily with an old farmer over cows. They all drink.*)

ABBIE (*this time appealing to nobody in particular*)   Wonder what Eben's a-doin'? (*Her remark is repeated down the line with many a guffaw and titter until it reaches the fiddler. He fastens his blinking eyes on* ABBIE.)

FIDDLER (*raising his voice*)   Bet I kin tell ye, Abbie, what Eben's doin'! He's down t' the church offerin' up prayers o' thanksgivin'. (*They all titter expectantly.*)

MAN   What fur? (*Another titter.*)

FIDDLER   'Cause unto him a—(*He hesitates just long enough.*)— brother is born! (*A roar of laughter. They all look from* ABBIE *to* CABOT. *She is oblivious, staring at the door.* CABOT, *although he hasn't heard the words, is irritated by the laughter and steps forward, glaring about him. There is an immediate silence.*)

CABOT   What're ye all bleatin' about—like a flock o' goats? Why don't ye dance, damn ye? I axed ye here t' dance—t' eat, drink an' be merry—an' thar ye set cacklin' like a lot o' wet hens with the pip! Ye've swilled my likker an' guzzled my vittles like hogs, hain't ye? Then dance fur me, can't ye? That's fa'r an' squar', hain't it? (*A grumble of resentment goes around but they are all evidently in too much awe of him to express it openly.*)

FIDDLER (*slyly*)   We're waitin' fur Eben. (*a suppressed laugh*)

CABOT (*with a fierce exultation*)   T'hell with Eben! Eben's done fur now! I got a new son! (*his mood switching with drunken suddenness*) But ye needn't t' laugh at Eben, none o' ye! He's my blood, if he be a dumb fool. He's better nor any o' yew! He kin do a day's work a'most up t' what I kin—an' that'd put any o' yew pore critters t' shame!

FIDDLER   An' he kin do a good night's work, too! (*a roar of laughter*)

CABOT   Laugh, ye damn fools! Ye're right jist the same, Fiddler. He kin work day an' night too, like I kin, if need be!

OLD FARMER   (*from behind the keg where he is weaving drunkenly back and forth—with great simplicity*)   They hain't many t' touch ye, Ephraim—a son at seventy-six. That's a hard man fur ye! I be on'y sixty-eight an' I couldn't do it. (*a roar of laughter in which* CABOT *joins uproariously*)

CABOT   (*slapping him on the back*)   I'm sorry fur ye, Hi. I'd never suspicion sech weakness from a boy like yew!

OLD FARMER   An' I never reckoned yew had it in ye nuther, Ephraim. (*There is another laugh.*)

CABOT   (*suddenly grim*)   I got a lot in me—a hell of a lot—folks don't know on. (*turning to the* FIDDLER) Fiddle 'er up, durn ye! Give 'em somethin' t' dance t'! What air ye, an ornament? Hain't this a celebration? Then grease yer elbow an' go it!

FIDDLER   (*seizes a drink which the* OLD FARMER *holds out to him and downs it*)   Here goes! (*He starts to fiddle "Lady of the Lake." Four young fellows and four girls form in two lines and dance a square dance. The* FIDDLER *shouts directions for the different movements, keeping his words in the rhythm of the music and interspersing them with jocular personal remarks to the dancers themselves. The people seated along the walls stamp their feet and clap their hands in unison.* CABOT *is especially active in this respect. Only* ABBIE *remains apathetic, staring at the door as if she were alone in a silent room.*)

FIDDLER   Swing your partner t' the right! That's it, Jim! Give her a b'ar hug! Her Maw hain't lookin'. (*laughter*) Change partners! That suits ye, don't it, Essie, now ye got Reub afore ye? Look at her redden up, will ye! Waal, life is short an' so's love, as the feller says. (*laughter*)

CABOT   (*excitedly, stamping his foot*)   Go it, boys! Go it, gals!

FIDDLER   (*with a wink at the others*)   Ye're the spryest seventy-six ever I sees, Ephraim! Now if ye'd on'y good eye-sight . . . ! (*Suppressed laughter. He gives* CABOT *no chance to retort but roars*) Promenade! Ye're walkin' like a bride down the aisle, Sarah! Waal, while they's life they's allus hope, I've heerd tell. Swing your partner to the left! Gosh A'mighty, look at Johnny Cook high-steppin'! They hain't goin' t'be much strength left fur howin' in the corn lot t'morrow. (*laughter*)

CABOT   Go it! Go it! (*Then suddenly, unable to restrain himself any longer, he prances into the midst of the dancers, scattering them, waving his arms about wildly.*) Ye're all hoofs! Git out o' my road! Give me room! I'll show ye dancin'. Ye're all too soft!

(*He pushes them roughly away. They crowd back toward the walls, muttering, looking at him resentfully.*)

FIDDLER (*jeeringly*) Go it, Ephraim! Go it! (*He starts "Pop Goes the Weasel," increasing the tempo with every verse until at the end he is fiddling crazily as fast as he can go.*)

CABOT (*starts to dance, which he does very well and with tremendous vigor. Then he begins to improvise, cuts incredibly grotesque capers, leaping up and cracking his heels together, prancing around in a circle with body bent in an Indian war dance, then suddenly straightening up and kicking as high as he can with both legs. He is like a monkey on a string. And all the while he intersperses his antics with shouts and derisive comments*) Whoop! Here's dancin' fur ye! Whoop! See that! Seventy-six, if I'm a day! Hard as iron yet! Beatin' the young 'uns like I allus done! Look at me! I'd invite ye t' dance on my hundredth birthday on'y ye'll all be dead by then. Ye're a sickly generation! Yer hearts air pink, not red! Yer veins is full o' mud an' water! I be the on'y man in the county! Whoop! See that! I'm a Injun! I've killed Injuns in the West afore ye was born—an' skulped 'em too! They's a arrer wound on my backside I c'd show ye! The hull tribe chased me. I outrun 'em all—with the arrer stuck in me! An' I tuk vengeance on 'em. Ten eyes fur an eye, that was my motter! Whoop! Look at me! I kin kick the ceilin' off the room! Whoop!

FIDDLER (*stops playing—exhaustedly*) God A'mighty, I got enuf. Ye got the devil's strength in ye.

CABOT (*delightedly*) Did I beat yew, too? Wa'al, ye played smart. Hev a swig. (*He pours whisky for himself and* FIDDLER. *They drink. The others watch* CABOT *silently with cold, hostile eyes. There is a dead pause. The* FIDDLER *rests.* CABOT *leans against the keg, panting, glaring around him confusedly. In the room above,* EBEN *gets to his feet and tiptoes out the door in rear, appearing a moment later in the other bedroom. He moves silently, even frightenedly, toward the cradle and stands there looking down at the baby. His face is as vague as his reactions are confused, but there is a trace of tenderness, of interested discovery. At the same moment that he reaches the cradle,* ABBIE *seems to sense something. She gets up weakly and goes to* CABOT.)

ABBIE I'm goin' up t' the baby.

CABOT (*with real solicitude*) Air ye able fur the stairs? D'ye want me t' help ye, Abbie?

ABBIE No. I'm able. I'll be down agen soon.

CABOT Don't ye git wore out! He needs ye, remember—our son

does! (*He grins affectionately, patting her on the back. She shrinks from his touch.*)

ABBIE (*dully*) Don't—tech me. I'm goin'—up. (*She goes.* CABOT *looks after her. A whisper goes around the room.* CABOT *turns. It ceases. He wipes his forehead streaming with sweat. He is breathing pantingly.*)

CABOT I'm a-goin' out t' git fresh air. I'm feelin' a mite dizzy. Fiddle up thar! Dance, all o' ye! Here's likker fur them as wants it. Enjoy yerselves. I'll be back. (*He goes, closing the door behind him.*)

FIDDLER (*sarcastically*) Don't hurry none on our account! (*A suppressed laugh. He imitates* ABBIE.) Whar's Eben? (*more laughter*)

A WOMAN (*loudly*) What's happened in this house is plain as the nose on yer face! (ABBIE *appears in the doorway upstairs and stands looking in surprise and adoration at* EBEN *who does not see her.*)

A MAN Ssshh! He's li'ble t' be listenin' at the door. That'd be like him. (*Their voices die to an intensive whispering. Their faces are concentrated on this gossip. A noise as of dead leaves in the wind comes from the room.* CABOT *has come out from the porch and stands by the gate, leaning on it, staring at the sky blinkingly.* ABBIE *comes across the room silently.* EBEN *does not notice her until quite near.*)

EBEN (*starting*) Abbie!

ABBIE Ssshh! (*She throws her arms around him. They kiss—then bend over the cradle together.*) Ain't he purty?—dead spit 'n' image o' yew!

EBEN (*pleased*) Air he? I can't tell none.

ABBIE E-zactly like!

EBEN (*frowningly*) I don't like this. I don't like lettin' on what's mine's his'n. I been doin' that all my life. I'm gittin' t' the end o' b'arin' it!

ABBIE (*putting her finger on his lips*) We're doin' the best we kin. We got t' wait. Somethin's bound t' happen. (*She puts her arms around him.*) I got t' go back.

EBEN I'm goin' out. I can't b'ar it with the fiddle playin' an' the laughin'.

ABBIE Don't git feelin' low. I love ye, Eben. Kiss me. (*He kisses her. They remain in each other's arms.*)

CABOT (*at the gate, confusedly*) Even the music can't drive it out —somethin'. Ye kin feel it droppin' off the elums, climbin' up the roof, sneakin' down the chimney, pokin' in the corners! They's no peace in houses, they's no rest livin' with folks. Somethin's always livin' with ye. (*with a deep sigh*) I'll go t' the barn an' rest a spell. (*He goes wearily toward the barn.*)

FIDDLER (*tuning up*)   Let's celebrate the old skunk gittin' fooled! We kin have some fun now he's went. (*He starts to fiddle "Turkey in the Straw." There is real merriment now. The young folks get up to dance.*)

Scene 2

A half hour later—exterior.

EBEN *is standing by the gate looking up at the sky, an expression of dumb pain bewildered by itself on his face.* CABOT *appears, returning from the barn, walking wearily, his eyes on the ground. He sees* EBEN *and his whole mood immediately changes. He becomes excited, a cruel, triumphant grin comes to his lips, he strides up and slaps* EBEN *on the back. From within comes the whining of the fiddle and the noise of stamping feet and laughing voices.*

CABOT   So har ye be!

EBEN (*startled, stares at him with hatred for a moment—then dully*) Ay-eh.

CABOT (*surveying him jeeringly*)   Why hain't ye been in t' dance? They was all axin' fur ye.

EBEN   Let 'em ax!

CABOT   They's a hull pasel o' purty gals.

EBEN   T' hell with 'em!

CABOT   Ye'd ought t' be marryin' one o' 'em soon.

EBEN   I hain't marryin' no one.

CABOT   Ye might 'arn a share o' a farm that way.

EBEN (*with a sneer*)   Like yew did, ye mean? I hain't that kind.

CABOT (*stung*)   Ye lie! 'Twas yer Maw's folks aimed t' steal my farm from me.

EBEN   Other folks don't say so. (*after a pause—defiantly*) An' I got a farm, anyways!

CABOT (*derisively*)   Whar?

EBEN (*stamps a foot on the ground*)   Har!

CABOT (*throws his head back and laughs coarsely*)   Ho-ho! Ye hev, hev ye? Waal, that's a good un!

EBEN (*controlling himself—grimly*)   Ye'll see!

CABOT (*stares at him suspiciously, trying to make him out—a pause —then with scornful confidence*) Ay-eh. I'll see. So'll ye. It's ye that's blind—blind as a mole underground. (EBEN *suddenly laughs, one short sardonic bark: "Ha." A pause.* CABOT *peers at him with renewed suspicion.*) Whar air ye hawin' 'bout? (EBEN *turns away without answering.* CABOT *grows angry.*) God

A'mighty, yew air a dumb dunce! They's nothin' in that thick skull o' your'n but noise—like a empty keg it be! (EBEN *doesn't seem to hear*—CABOT's *rage grows.*) Yewr farm! God A'mighty! If ye wa'n't a born donkey ye'd know ye'll never own stick nor stone on it, specially now arter him bein' born. It's his'n, I tell ye —his'n arter I die—but I'll live a hundred jest t' fool ye all—an' he'll be growed then—yewr age a'most! (EBEN *laughs again his sardonic "Ha." This drives* CABOT *into a fury.*) Ha? Ye think ye kin git 'round that someways, do ye? Waal, it'll be her'n, too— Abbie's—ye won't git 'round her—she knows yer tricks—she'll be too much fur ye—she wants the farm her'n—she was afeerd o' ye—she told me ye was sneakin' 'round tryin' t' make love t' her t' git her on yer side . . . ye . . . ye mad fool, ye! (*He raises his clenched fists threateningly.*)

EBEN (*is confronting him choking with rage*)   Ye lie, ye old skunk! Abbie never said no sech thing!

CABOT (*suddenly triumphant when he sees how shaken* EBEN *is*) She did. An' I says, I'll blow his brains t' the top o' them elums— an' she says no, that hain't sense, who'll ye git t'help ye on the farm in his place—an' then she says yew'n me ought t' have a son—I know we kin, she says—an' I says, if we do, ye kin have anythin' I've got ye've a mind t'. An' she says, I wants Eben cut off so's this farm'll be mine when ye die! (*with terrible gloating*) An' that's what's happened, hain't it? An' the farm's her'n! An' the dust o' the road—that's you'rn! Ha! Now who's hawin'?

EBEN (*has been listening, petrified with grief and rage—suddenly laughs wildly and brokenly*)   Ha-ha-ha! So that's her sneakin' game—all along!—like I suspicioned at fust—t' swaller it all— an' me, too . . . ! (*madly*) I'll murder her! (*He springs toward the porch but* CABOT *is quicker and gets in between.*)

CABOT   No, ye don't!

EBEN   Git out o' my road! (*He tries to throw* CABOT *aside. They grapple in what becomes immediately a murderous struggle. The old man's concentrated strength is too much for* EBEN. CABOT *gets one hand on his throat and presses him back across the stone wall. At the same moment,* ABBIE *comes out on the porch. With a stifled cry she runs toward them.*)

ABBIE   Eben! Ephraim! (*She tugs at the hand on* EBEN's *throat.*) Let go, Ephraim! Ye're chokin' him!

CABOT (*removes his hand and flings* EBEN *sideways full length on the grass, gasping and choking. With a cry,* ABBIE *kneels beside him, trying to take his head on her lap, but he pushes her away.* CABOT *stands looking down with fierce triumph*) Ye needn't' t've fret, Abbie, I wa'n't aimin' t' kill him. He hain't wuth hangin' fur

—not by a hell of a sight! (*more and more triumphantly*) Seventy-six an' him not thirty yit—an' look whar he be fur thinkin' his Paw was easy! No, by God, I hain't easy! An' him upstairs, I'll raise him t' be like me! (*He turns to leave them.*) I'm goin' in an' dance!—sing an' celebrate! (*He walks to the porch—then turns with a great grin.*) I don't calc'late it's left in him, but if he gits pesky, Abbie, ye jest sing out. I'll come a-runnin' an' by the Etarnal, I'll put him across my knee an' birch him! Ha-ha-ha! (*He goes into the house laughing. A moment later his loud "whoop" is heard.*)

ABBIE (*tenderly*) Eben. Air ye hurt? (*She tries to kiss him but he pushes her violently away and struggles to a sitting position.*)

EBEN (*gaspingly*) T'hell—with ye!

ABBIE (*not believing her ears*) It's me, Eben—Abbie—don't ye know me?

EBEN (*glowering at her with hatred*) Ay-eh—I know ye—now! (*He suddenly breaks down, sobbing weakly.*)

ABBIE (*fearfully*) Eben—what's happened t' ye—why did ye look at me 's if ye hated me?

EBEN (*violently, between sobs and gasps*) I do hate ye! Ye're a whore—a damn trickin' whore!

ABBIE (*shrinking back horrified*) Eben! Ye don't know what ye're sayin'!

EBEN (*scrambling to his feet and following her—accusingly*) Ye're nothin' but a stinkin' passel o' lies! Ye've been lyin' t' me every word ye spoke, day an' night, since we fust—done it. Ye've kept sayin' ye loved me. . . .

ABBIE (*frantically*) I do love ye! (*She takes his hand but he flings hers away.*)

EBEN (*unheeding*) Ye've made a fool o' me—a sick, dumb fool—a-purpose! Ye've been on'y playin' yer sneakin', stealin' game all along—gittin' me t' lie with ye so's ye'd hev a son he'd think was his'n, an' makin' him promise he'd give ye the farm and let me eat dust, if ye did git him a son! (*staring at her with anguished, bewildered eyes*) They must be a devil livin' in ye! 'Tain't human t' be as bad as that be!

ABBIE (*stunned—dully*) He told yew . . . ?

EBEN Hain't it true? It hain't no good in yew lyin'.

ABBIE (*pleadingly*) Eben, listen—ye must listen—it was long ago —afore we done nothin'—yew was scornin' me—goin' t' see Min —when I was lovin' ye—an' I said it t' him t' git vengeance on ye!

EBEN (*unheedingly. With tortured passion*) I wish ye was dead! I wish I was dead along with ye afore this come! (*ragingly*) But

I'll git my vengeance too! I'll pray Maw t' come back t' help me
—t' put her cuss on yew an' him!

ABBIE (*brokenly*) Don't ye, Eben! Don't ye! (*She throws herself
on her knees before him, weeping.*) I didn't mean t' do bad t'ye!
Fergive me, won't ye?

EBEN (*not seeming to hear her—fiercely*) I'll git squar' with the
old skunk—an' yew! I'll tell him the truth 'bout the son he's so
proud o'! Then I'll leave ye here t' pizen each other—with Maw
comin' out o' her grave at nights—an' I'll go t' the gold fields
o' Californi-a whar Sim an' Peter be!

ABBIE (*terrified*) Ye won't—leave me? Ye can't!

EBEN (*with fierce determination*) I'm a-goin', I tell ye! I'll git
rich thar an' come back an' fight him fur the farm he stole—an'
I'll kick ye both out in the road—t' beg an' sleep in the woods—
an' yer son along with ye—t' starve an' die! (*He is hysterical at
the end.*)

ABBIE (*with a shudder—humbly*) He's yewr son, too, Eben.

EBEN (*torturedly*) I wish he never was born! I wish he'd die this
minit! I wish I'd never sot eyes on him! It's him—yew havin' him
—a-purpose t' steal—that's changed everythin'!

ABBIE (*gently*) Did ye believe I loved ye—afore he come?

EBEN Ay-eh—like a dumb ox!

ABBIE An' ye don't believe no more?

EBEN B'lieve a lyin' thief! Ha!

ABBIE (*shudders—then humbly*) An did ye r'ally love me afore?

EBEN (*brokenly*) Ay-eh—an' ye was trickin' me!

ABBIE An' ye don't love me now!

EBEN (*violently*) I hate ye, I tell ye!

ABBIE An' ye're truly goin' West—goin' t' leave me—all account o'
him being born?

EBEN I'm a-goin' in the mornin'—or may God strike me t' hell!

ABBIE (*after a pause—with a dreadful cold intensity—slowly*) If
that's what his comin's done t' me—killin' yewr love—takin' yew
away—my on'y joy—the on'y joy I've ever knowed—like heaven
t' me—purtier'n heaven—then I hate him, too, even if I be his
Maw!

EBEN (*bitterly*) Lies! Ye love him! He'll steal the farm fur ye!
(*brokenly*) But 'tain't the farm so much—not no more—it's yew
foolin' me—gittin' me t' love ye—lyin' yew loved me—jest t' git
a son t' steal!

ABBIE (*distractedly*) He won't steal! I'd kill him fust! I do love
ye! I'll prove t' ye ... !

EBEN (*harshly*) 'Tain't no use lyin' no more. I'm deaf t' ye! (*He
turns away.*) I hain't seein' ye agen. Good-by!

ABBIE (*pale with anguish*) Hain't ye even goin' t' kiss me—not once—arter all we loved?

EBEN (*in a hard voice*) I hain't wantin' t' kiss ye never agen! I'm wantin' t' forgit I ever sot eyes on ye!

ABBIE Eben!—ye mustn't—wait a spell—I want t' tell ye. . . .

EBEN I'm a-goin' in t' git drunk. I'm a-goin' t' dance.

ABBIE (*clinging to his arm—with passionate earnestness*) If I could make it—'s if he'd never come up between us—if I could prove t' ye I wa'n't schemin' t' steal from ye—so's everythin' could be jest the same with us, lovin' each other jest the same, kissin' an' happy the same's we've been happy afore he come— if I could do it—ye'd love me agen, wouldn't ye? Ye'd kiss me agen? Ye wouldn't never leave me, would ye?

EBEN (*moved*) I calc'late not. (*Then shaking her hand off his arm —with a bitter smile*) But ye hain't God, be ye?

ABBIE (*exultantly*) Remember ye've promised! (*Then with strange intensity*) Mebbe I kin take back one thin' God does!

EBEN (*peering at her*) Ye're gittin' cracked, hain't ye? (*Then going towards door*) I'm a-goin' t' dance.

ABBIE (*calls after him intensely*) I'll prove t' ye! I'll prove I love ye better'n. . . . (*He goes in the door, not seeming to hear. She remains standing where she is, looking after him—then she finishes desperately*) Better'n everythin' else in the world!

Scene 3

Just before dawn in the morning—shows the kitchen and CABOT's *bedroom.*

In the kitchen, by the light of a tallow candle on the table, EBEN *is sitting, his chin propped on his hands, his drawn face blank and expressionless. His carpetbag is on the floor beside him. In the bedroom, dimly lighted by a small whale-oil lamp,* CABOT *lies asleep.* ABBIE *is bending over the cradle, listening, her face full of terror yet with an undercurrent of desperate triumph. Suddenly, she breaks down and sobs, appears about to throw herself on her knees beside the cradle; but the old man turns restlessly, groaning in his sleep, and she controls herself, and shrinking away from the cradle with a gesture of horror, backs swiftly toward the door in rear and goes out. A moment later she comes into the kitchen and, running to* EBEN, *flings her arms about his neck and kisses him wildly. He hardens himself, he remains unmoved and cold, he keeps his eyes straight ahead.*

ABBIE (*hysterically*) I done it, Eben! I told ye I'd do it! I've proved I love ye—better'n everythin'—so's ye can't never doubt me no more!

EBEN (*dully*) Whatever ye done, it hain't no good now.

ABBIE (*wildly*) Don't ye say that! Kiss me, Eben, won't ye? I need ye t' kiss me arter what I done! I need ye t' say ye love me!

EBEN (*kisses her without emotion—dully*) That's fur good-by. I'm a-goin' soon.

ABBIE No! No! Ye won't go—not now!

EBEN (*going on with his own thoughts*) I been a-thinkin'—an' I hain't goin' t' tell Paw nothin'. I'll leave Maw t' take vengeance on ye. If I told him, the old skunk'd jest be stinkin' mean enuf to take it out on that baby. (*His voice showing emotion in spite of him*) An' I don't want nothin' bad t' happen t' him. He hain't t' blame fur yew. (*He adds with a certain queer pride*) An' he looks like me! An' by God, he's mine! An' some day I'll be a-comin' back an' . . . !

ABBIE (*too absorbed in her own thoughts to listen to him—pleadingly*) They's no cause fur ye t' go now—they's no sense—it's all the same's it was—they's nothin' come b'tween us now—arter what I done!

EBEN (*something in her voice arouses him. He stares at her a bit frightenedly*) Ye look mad, Abbie. What did ye do?

ABBIE I—I killed him, Eben.

EBEN (*amazed*) Ye killed him?

ABBIE (*dully*) Ay-eh.

EBEN (*recovering from his astonishment—savagely*) An' serves him right! But we got t' do somethin' quick t' make it look s'if the old skunk'd killed himself when he was drunk. We kin prove by 'em all how drunk he got.

ABBIE (*wildly*) No! No! Not him! (*Laughing distractedly*) But that's what I ought t' done, hain't it? I oughter killed him instead! Why didn't ye tell me?

EBEN (*appalled*) Instead? What d'ye mean?

ABBIE Not him.

EBEN (*his face grown ghastly*) Not—not that baby!

ABBIE (*dully*) Ay-eh!

EBEN (*falls to his knees as if he'd been struck—his voice trembling with horror*) Oh, God A'mighty! A'mighty God! Maw, whar was ye, why didn't ye stop her?

ABBIE (*simply*) She went back t' her grave that night we fust done it, remember? I hain't felt her about since. (*A pause.* EBEN *hides his head in his hands, trembling all over as if he had the ague. She goes on dully*) I left the piller over his little face. Then he killed himself. He stopped breathin'. (*She begins to weep softly.*)

EBEN (*rage beginning to mingle with grief*) He looked like me. He was mine, damn ye!

ABBIE (*slowly and brokenly*) I didn't want t' do it. I hated myself fur doin' it. I loved him. He was so purty—dead spit 'n' image o' yew. But I loved yew more—an' yew was goin' away—far off whar I'd never see ye agen, never kiss ye, never feel ye pressed agin me agen—an' ye said ye hated me fur havin' him—ye said ye hated him an' wished he was dead—ye said if it hadn't been fur him comin' it'd be the same's afore between us.

EBEN (*unable to endure this, springs to his feet in a fury, threatening her, his twitching fingers seeming to reach out for her throat*) Ye lie! I never said—I never dreamed ye'd—I'd cut off my head afore I'd hurt his finger!

ABBIE (*piteously, sinking on her knees*) Eben, don't ye look at me like that—hatin' me—not after what I done fur ye—fur us—so's we could be happy agen—

EBEN (*furiously now*) Shut up, or I'll kill ye! I see yer game now —the same old sneakin' trick—ye're aimin' t' blame me fur the murder ye done!

ABBIE (*moaning—putting her hands over her ears*) Don't ye, Eben! Don't ye! (*She grasps his legs.*)

EBEN (*his mood suddenly changing to horror, shrinks away from her*) Don't ye tech me! Ye're pizen! How could ye—t' murder a pore little critter— Ye must've swapped yer soul t' hell! (*suddenly raging*) Ha! I kin see why ye done it! Not the lies ye jest told—but 'cause ye wanted t' steal agen—steal the last thin' ye'd left me—my part o' him—no, the hull o' him—ye saw he looked like me—ye knowed he was all mine—an' ye couldn't b'ar it—I know ye! Ye killed him fur bein' mine! (*All this has driven him almost insane. He makes a rush past her for the door—then turns —shaking both fists at her, violently.*) But I'll take vengeance now! I'll git the Sheriff! I'll tell him everythin'! Then I'll sing "I'm off to Californi-a!" an' go—gold—Golden Gate—gold sun —fields o' gold in the West! (*This last he half shouts, half croons incoherently, suddenly breaking off passionately.*) I'm a-goin' fur the Sheriff t' come an' git ye! I want ye tuk away, locked up from me! I can't stand t'luk at ye! Murderer an' thief 'r not, ye still tempt me! I'll give ye up t' the Sheriff! (*He turns and runs out, around the corner of house, panting and sobbing, and breaks into a swerving sprint down the road.*)

ABBIE (*struggling to her feet, runs to the door, calling after him*) I love ye, Eben! I love ye! (*She stops at the door weakly, swaying, about to fall.*) I don't care what ye do—if ye'll on'y love me agen—(*She falls limply to the floor in a faint.*)

Scene 4

About an hour later. Same as SCENE 3. *Shows the kitchen and* CABOT's *bedroom. It is after dawn. The sky is brilliant with the sunrise.*

In the kitchen, ABBIE *sits at the table, her body limp and exhausted, her head bowed down over her arms, her face hidden. Upstairs,* CABOT *is still asleep but awakens with a start. He looks toward the window and gives a snort of surprise and irritation—throws back the covers and begins hurriedly pulling on his clothes. Without looking behind him, he begins talking to* ABBIE *whom he supposes beside him.*

CABOT   Thunder 'n' lightnin', Abbie! I hain't slept this late in fifty year! Looks 's if the sun was full riz a'most. Must've been the dancin' an' likker. Must be gittin' old. I hope Eben's t' wuk. Ye might've tuk the trouble t' rouse me, Abbie. (*He turns—sees no one there—surprised.*) Waal—whar air she? Gittin' vittles, I calc'late. (*He tiptoes to the cradle and peers down—proudly*) Mornin', sonny. Purty's a picter! Sleepin' sound. He don't beller all night like most o' 'em. (*He goes quietly out the door in rear —a few moments later enters kitchen—sees* ABBIE—*with satisfaction*) So thar ye be. Ye got any vittles cooked?

ABBIE (*without moving*)   No.

CABOT (*coming to her, almost sympathetically*)   Ye feelin' sick?

ABBIE   No.

CABOT (*pats her on shoulder. She shudders*)   Ye'd best lie down a spell. (*half jocularly*) Yer son'll be needin' ye soon. He'd ought t' wake up with a gnashin' appetite, the sound way he's sleepin'.

ABBIE (*shudders—then in a dead voice*)   He ain't never goin' to wake up.

CABOT (*jokingly*)   Takes after me this mornin'. I ain't slept so late in . . .

ABBIE   He's dead.

CABOT (*stares at her—bewilderedly*)   What . . .

ABBIE   I killed him.

CABOT (*stepping back from her—aghast*)   Air ye drunk—'r crazy —'r . . . !

ABBIE (*suddenly lifts her head and turns on him—wildly*)   I killed him, I tell ye! I smothered him. Go up an' see if ye don't b'lieve me! (CABOT *stares at her a second, then bolts out the rear door, can be heard bounding up the stairs, and rushes into the bedroom and over to the cradle.* ABBIE *has sunk back lifelessly into her former position.* CABOT *puts his hand down on the body in the crib. An expression of fear and horror comes over his face.*)

CABOT (*shrinking away—tremblingly*)   God A'mighty! God A'mighty. (*He stumbles out the door—in a short while returns to the kitchen—comes to* ABBIE, *the stunned expression still on his face—hoarsely*) Why did ye do it? Why? (*As she doesn't answer, he grabs her violently by the shoulder and shakes her.*) I ax ye why ye done it! Ye'd better tell me 'r . . . !

ABBIE (*gives him a furious push which sends him staggering back and springs to her feet—with wild rage and hatred*) Don't ye dare tech me! What right hev ye t' question me 'bout him? He wa'n't yewr son! Think I'd have a son by yew? I'd die fust! I hate the sight o' ye an' allus did! It's yew I should've murdered, if I'd had good sense! I hate ye! I love Eben. I did from the fust. An' he was Eben's son—mine an' Eben's—not your'n!

CABOT (*stands looking at her dazedly—a pause—finding his words with an effort—dully*) That was it—what I felt—pokin' round the corners—while ye lied—holdin' herself from me—sayin' ye'd a'ready conceived—(*He lapses into crushed silence—then with a strange emotion*) He's dead, sart'n. I felt his heart. Pore little critter! (*He blinks back one tear, wiping his sleeve across his nose.*)

ABBIE (*hysterically*) Don't ye! Don't ye! (*She sobs unrestrainedly.*)

CABOT (*with a concentrated effort that stiffens his body into a rigid line and hardens his face into a stony mask—through his teeth to himself*) I got t' be—like a stone—a rock o' jedgment! (*A pause. He gets complete control over himself—harshly*) If he was Eben's, I be glad he air gone! An' mebbe I suspicioned it all along. I felt they was somethin' onnateral—somewhars—the house got so lonesome—an' cold—drivin' me down t' the barn—t' the beasts o' the field. . . . Ay-eh. I must've suspicioned—somethin'. Ye didn't fool me—not altogether, leastways—I'm too old a bird —growin' ripe on the bough. . . . (*He becomes aware he is wandering, straightens again, looks at* ABBIE *with a cruel grin.*) So ye'd liked t' hev murdered me 'stead o' him, would ye? Waal, I'll live to a hundred! I'll live t' see ye hung! I'll deliver ye up t' the jedgment o' God an' the law! I'll git the Sheriff now. (*Starts for the door.*)

ABBIE (*dully*) Ye needn't. Eben's gone fur him.

CABOT (*amazed*) Eben—gone fur the Sheriff?

ABBIE Ay-eh.

CABOT T' inform agen ye?

ABBIE Ay-eh.

CABOT (*considers this—a pause—then in a hard voice*) Waal, I'm thankful fur him savin' me the trouble. I'll git t' wuk. (*He goes to the door—then turns—in a voice full of strange emotion*) He'd ought t' been my son, Abbie. Ye'd ought t' loved me. I'm a man. If ye'd loved me, I'd never told no Sheriff on ye no matter what ye did, if they was t' brile me alive!

ABBIE (*defensively*) They's more to it nor yew know, makes him tell.

CABOT (*dryly*) Fur yewr sake, I hope they be. (*He goes out—*

comes around to the gate—stares up at the sky. His control relaxes. For a moment he is old and weary. He murmurs despairingly) God A'mighty, I be lonesomer'n ever! (*He hears running footsteps from the left, immediately is himself again.* EBEN *runs in, panting exhaustedly, wild-eyed and mad looking. He lurches through the gate.* CABOT *grabs him by the shoulder.* EBEN *stares at him dumbly.*) Did ye tell the Sheriff?

EBEN (*nodding stupidly*)   Ay-eh.

CABOT (*gives him a push away that sends him sprawling—laughing with withering contempt*)   Good fur ye! A prime chip o' yer Maw ye be! (*He goes toward the barn, laughing harshly.* EBEN *scrambles to his feet. Suddenly* CABOT *turns—grimly threatening*) Git off this farm when the Sheriff takes her—or, by God, he'll have t' come back an' git me fur murder, too! (*He stalks off.* EBEN *does not appear to have heard him. He runs to the door and comes into the kitchen.* ABBIE *looks up with a cry of anguished joy.* EBEN *stumbles over and throws himself on his knees beside her—sobbing brokenly.*)

EBEN   Fergive me!

ABBIE (*happily*)   Eben! (*She kisses him and pulls his head over against her breast.*)

EBEN   I love ye! Fergive me!

ABBIE (*ecstatically*)   I'd fergive ye all the sins in hell fur sayin' that! (*She kisses his head, pressing it to her with a fierce passion of possession.*)

EBEN (*brokenly*)   But I told the Sheriff. He's comin' fur ye!

ABBIE   I kin b'ar what happens t' me—now!

EBEN   I woke him up. I told him. He says, wait 'til I git dressed. I was waiting. I got to thinkin' o' yew. I got to thinkin' how I'd loved ye. It hurt like somethin' was bustin' in my chest an' head. I got t' cryin'. I knowed sudden I loved ye yet, an' allus would love ye!

ABBIE (*caressing his hair—tenderly*)   My boy, hain't ye?

EBEN   I begun t' run back. I cut across the fields an' through the woods. I thought ye might have time t' run away—with me— an' . . .

ABBIE (*shaking her head*)   I got t' take my punishment—t' pay fur my sin.

EBEN   Then I want t' share it with ye.

ABBIE   Ye didn't do nothin'.

EBEN   I put it in yer head. I wisht he was dead! I as much as urged ye t' do it!

ABBIE   No. It was me alone!

EBEN   I'm as guilty as yew be! He was the child o' our sin.

ABBIE (*lifting her head as if defying God*)   I don't repent that sin! I hain't askin' God t' fergive that!

EBEN   Nor me—but it led up t' the other—an' the murder ye did, ye did 'count o' me—an' it's my murder, too, I'll tell the Sheriff —an' if ye deny it, I'll say we planned it t'gether—an' they'll all b'lieve me, fur they suspicion everythin' we've done, an' it'll seem likely an' true to 'em. An' it is true—way down. I did help ye— somehow.

ABBIE (*laying her head on his—sobbing*)   No! I don't want ye t' suffer!

EBEN   I got t' pay fur my part o' the sin! An' I'd suffer wuss leavin' ye, goin' West, thinkin' o' ye day an' night, bein' out when yew was in—(*lowering his voice*)—'r bein' alive when yew was dead. (*a pause*) I want t' share with ye, Abbie—prison 'r death 'r hell 'r anythin'! (*He looks into her eyes and forces a trembling smile.*) If I'm sharin' with ye, I won't feel lonesome, leastways.

ABBIE (*weakly*)   Eben! I won't let ye! I can't let ye!

EBEN (*kissing her—tenderly*)   Ye can't he'p yerself. I got ye beat fur once!

ABBIE (*forcing a smile—adoringly*)   I hain't beat—s'long's I got ye!

EBEN (*hears the sound of feet outside*)   Ssshh! Listen! They've come t' take us!

ABBIE   No, it's him. Don't give him no chance to fight ye, Eben. Don't say nothin'—no matter what he says. An' I won't neither. (*It is* CABOT. *He comes up from the barn in a great state of excitement and strides into the house and then into the kitchen.* EBEN *is kneeling beside* ABBIE, *his arm around her, hers around him. They stare straight ahead.*)

CABOT (*stares at them, his face hard. A long pause—vindictively*) Ye make a slick pair o' murderin' turtle doves! Ye'd ought t' be both hung on the same limb an' left thar t' swing in the breeze an' rot—a warnin' t' old fools like me t' b'ar their lonesomeness alone —an' fur young fools like ye t' hobble their lust. (*A pause. The excitement returns to his face, his eyes snap, he looks a bit crazy.*) I couldn't work today. I couldn't take no interest. T' hell with the farm! I'm leavin' it! I've turned the cows an' other stock loose! I've druv 'em into the woods whar they kin be free! By freein' 'em, I'm freein' myself! I'm quittin' here today! I'll set fire t' house an' barn an' watch 'em burn, an' I'll leave yer Maw t' haunt the ashes, an' I'll will the fields back t' God, so that nothin' human kin never touch 'em! I'll be a-goin' to Californi-a—t' jine Simeon an' Peter—true sons o' mine if they be dumb fools—an' the Cabots'll find Solomon's Mines t'gether! (*He suddenly cuts a mad caper.*) Whoop! What was the song they sung? "Oh, Californi-a! That's the land fur me." (*He sings this—then gets on his knees by the floorboard under which the money was hid.*) An' I'll sail thar on one o' the finest clippers I kin find! I've got the money! Pity ye didn't know whar this was hidden so's ye could steal... (*He has pulled up the board. He stares—feels—stares again. A pause of dead silence. He slowly turns, slumping into a sitting position on the floor, his eyes like those of a dead fish, his face the sickly green of an attack of nausea. He swallows painfully several times—forces a weak smile at last.*) So—ye did steal it!

EBEN (*emotionlessly*) I swapped it t' Sim an' Peter fur their share o' the farm—t' pay their passage t' Californi-a.

CABOT (*with one sardonic*) Ha! (*He begins to recover. Gets slowly to his feet—strangly*) I calc'late God give it to 'em—not yew! God's hard, not easy! Mebbe they's easy gold in the West but it hain't God's gold. It hain't fur me. I kin hear His voice warnin' me agen t' be hard an' stay on my farm. I kin see his hand usin' Eben t' steal t' keep me from weakness. I kin feel I be in the palm o' His hand, His fingers guidin' me. (*A pause—then he mutters sadly*) It's a-goin' t' be lonesomer now than ever it war afore—an' I'm gittin' old, Lord—ripe on the bough.... (*Then stiffening*) Waal—what d'ye want? God's lonesome, hain't He? God's hard an' lonesome! (*A pause. The* SHERIFF *with two men comes up the road from the left. They move cautiously to the door. The* SHERIFF *knocks on it with the butt of his pistol.*)

SHERIFF Open in the name o' the law! (*They start.*)

CABOT They've come fur ye. (*He goes to the rear door.*) Come in, Jim! (*The three men enter.* CABOT *meets them in doorway.*) Jest a minit, Jim. I got 'em safe here. (*The* SHERIFF *nods. He and his companions remain in the doorway.*)

EBEN (*suddenly calls*) I lied this mornin', Jim. I helped her to do it. Ye kin take me, too.

ABBIE (*brokenly*) No!

CABOT Take 'em both. (*He comes forward—stares at* EBEN *with a trace of grudging admiration*) Purty good—fur yew! Waal, I got t' round up the stock. Good-by.

EBEN Good-by.

ABBIE Good-by. (CABOT *turns and strides past the men—comes out and around the corner of the house, his shoulders squared, his face stony, and stalks grimly toward the barn. In the meantime the* SHERIFF *and men have come into the room.*)

SHERIFF (*embarrassedly*) Waal—we'd best start.

ABBIE Wait. (*Turns to* EBEN) I love ye, Eben.

EBEN I love ye, Abbie. (*They kiss. The three men grin and shuffle embarrassedly.* EBEN *takes* ABBIE's *hand. They go out the door in rear, the men following, and come from the house, walking hand in hand to the gate.* EBEN *stops there and points to the sunrise sky.*) Sun's a-rizin'. Purty, hain't it?

ABBIE Ay-eh. (*They both stand for a moment looking up raptly in attitudes strangely aloof and devout.*)

SHERIFF (*looking around at the farm enviously—to his companion*) It's a jim-dandy farm, no denyin'. Wished I owned it!

THE GOOD WOMAN OF SETZUAN
(1940)

BERTOLT BRECHT (1898–1956)

Through the concerted effort of a single admirer, Eric Bentley, whose translations of and critical essays about Bertolt Brecht form a large and important library, this fascinating German dramatist has gradually earned a place as one of the geniuses of modern Western theatre. At times, during his residence in this country at the height of McCarthy witchhunts, he was the subject of ignorant suspicion and fear as an avowed Communist. Then, as a resident of East Germany until his death, he did not receive wide recognition as a major theatre artist until the decade of the 1960s. Only the phenomenally successful *Threepenny Opera,* that raucous raunchy adaptation of John Gay's *The Beggar's Opera* of 1728, originally done in collaboration with musician Kurt Weill in 1928 but not produced in New York until the 1950s, kept his name alive.

Brecht made no bones about his political orientation. He consciously alienated people at all levels of society as well as government, and the theatre, which he envisioned and for which he fashioned his plays he defined as the "theatre of alienation," admitting to agitation along clearly political lines. His view was one of attack, more than winning his audiences to his side, and while doing so he made it clear that he was using every effort to remind the audience that it is in the theatre, witnessing a show. He dubbed his style "epic," and tried his best to keep his viewer from any form of empathic identification. He saw governments and society in general as run by exploitive camp followers and gangsters, or petty unscrupulous incompetents. He expressed this view by throwing at his audiences every technical device of the theatre in sound effects, slides, films, and all manner of jolting interruptions specifically designed to destroy illusion and to heighten the theatrical effect.

One of Brecht's main problems, however, as you will see from a study of *The Good Woman of Setzuan,* is that, for all his attempts to keep his audiences at a considerable aesthetic distance, he frequently succeeds in spite of himself in creating highly sympathetic dramatic figures. In *Mother Courage* (1939) the promiscuous, hardened title figure makes her living through the misery of others by peddling her canteen wares up and down the battlefields of the Thirty Years War, facing bankruptcy every time peace "breaks out." Yet, exploitive and calloused—even cruel—as she is, she becomes, through her doggedness in the face of mounting personal catastrophe, one of Brecht's most compassionate characters. In *The Caucasian Chalk Circle* (1945), Grusha, the scrupulously honest kitchen maid, desperately attempts at the risk of her own life to save the hapless infant son of the fatuous uncaring Governor, but she is surrounded by a violent and corrupt society that gives her scant credit for the magnanimity of her deeds.

In *The Good Woman*, rather than involving his characters in the more impersonal violence of war and revolution, Brecht presents a society equally despicable not in its physical brutality but in the display of greedy unthinking selfishness by its members, who continually violate the hospitality of the gentle, sharing Shen Te. Her position as a prostitute is in ironic contrast to the supposedly respectable nature of those upright citizens who succeed in destroying her.

Brecht's portrayal of the plight of the one good person amidst the leeches who prey upon her sharply outlines his continuing low opinion of society, which cannot seem to function on any level of decency. He raises questions as old as civilization but always renewed: Is there a place for the kindly compassionate individual in a grasping self-centered society? Can basic human goodness ever succeed against the overwhelming odds aimed at its destruction? Is there no reward for deep-felt love, which always seems to endure betrayal? and, Cannot religion bring some sort of earthly comfort?

The answer to all of these, at least as Brecht sees them in *The Good Woman*, is No. To survive at all Shen Te must become the enterprising Shui Ta, who works within the system. But even "he" in the end faces the wrath of the crowd, who condemn him on shaky circumstantial evidence. And religion provides no help whatever. The very shabby gods who reward goodness with cash and start the whole unfortunate cycle in motion offer only platitudes, providing no solace in the end except to tell the pleading, helpless Shen Te to keep the faith as they pompously ascend into heaven.

Less "epic" than many of Brecht's plays, less disconnectedly episodic and more straightforwardly lineal in telling its story, *The Good Woman* still relies on theatrical devices such as song, disguises, and rapidly changing scenes. Moreover, it is underlain by much comedy, evident not only in the gods and the water seller Wong, but in a variety of dramatic incidents. In the end, however, Brecht does succeed in alienating us by leaving the final question as to what happens to Shen Te unanswered.

The Good Woman of Setzuan

BERTOLT BRECHT

An English version by Eric Bentley

CHARACTERS

Wong, *a water seller*
Three Gods
Shen Te, *a prostitute, later a shopkeeper*
Mrs. Shin, *former owner of* shen te's *shop*
A Family of Eight (*husband, wife, brother, sister-in-law, grandfather, nephew, niece, boy*)
An Unemployed Man
A Carpenter
Mrs. Mi Tzu, Shen Te's *landlady*
Yang Sun, *an unemployed pilot, later a factory manager*
An Old Whore
A Policeman
An Old Man
An Old Woman, *his wife*
Mr. Shu Fu, *a barber*
Mrs. Yang, *mother of* yang sun
Gentlemen, Voices, Children (*three*), *etc.*

PROLOGUE

At the gates of the half-Westernized city of Setzuan.* Evening. Wong *the Water Seller introduces himself to the audience.*

wong   I sell water here in the city of Setzuan. It isn't easy. When water is scarce, I have long distances to go in search of it, and when it is plentiful, I have no income. But in our part of the world there is

---

* Thus the first MS of the play. Brecht later learned that Setzuan (Szechwan) is not a city but a province, and changed the script accordingly. But, as often, the solecism seems more appropriate than the fact. E. B.

nothing unusual about poverty. Many people think only the gods can save the situation. And I hear from a cattle merchant—who travels a lot—that some of the highest gods are on their way here at this very moment. Informed sources have it that heaven is quite disturbed at all the complaining. I've been coming out here to the city gates for three days now to bid these gods welcome. I want to be the first to greet them. What about those fellows over there? No, no, they *work*. And that one there has ink on his fingers, he's no god, he must be a clerk from the cement factory. *Those* two are another story. They look as though they'd like to beat you. But gods don't need to beat you, do they? (THREE GODS *appear*.) What about those three? Old-fashioned clothes—dust on their feet—they *must* be gods! (*He throws himself at their feet.*) Do with me what you will, illustrious ones!

FIRST GOD (*with an ear trumpet*) Ah! (*He is pleased.*) So we were expected?

WONG (*giving them water*) Oh, yes. And I *knew* you'd come.

FIRST GOD We need somewhere to stay the night. You know of a place?

WONG The whole town is at your service, illustrious ones! What sort of a place would you like?

The GODS *eye each other.*

FIRST GOD Just try the first house you come to, my son.

WONG That would be Mr. Fo's place.

FIRST GOD Mr. Fo.

WONG One moment! (*He knocks at the first house.*)

VOICE FROM MR. FO'S No!

WONG *returns a little nervously.*

WONG It's too bad. Mr. Fo isn't in. And his servants don't dare do a thing without his consent. He'll have a fit when he finds out who they turned away, won't he?

FIRST GOD (*smiling*) He will, won't he?

WONG One moment! The next house is Mr. Cheng's. Won't he be thrilled!

FIRST GOD Mr. Cheng.

WONG *knocks.*

VOICE FROM MR. CHENG'S Keep your gods. We have our own troubles!

WONG (*back with the* GODS) Mr. Cheng is very sorry, but he has a houseful of relations. I think some of them are a bad lot, and naturally, he wouldn't like you to see them.

THIRD GOD Are we so terrible?

WONG Well, only with bad people, of course. Everyone knows the province of Kwan is always having floods.

SECOND GOD   Really? How's that?

WONG   Why, because they're so irreligious.

SECOND GOD   Rubbish. It's because they neglected the dam.

FIRST GOD (*to* SECOND)   Sh! (*To* WONG:) You're still in hopes, aren't you, my son?

WONG   Certainly. All Setzuan is competing for the honor! What happened up to now is pure coincidence. I'll be back. (*He walks away, but then stands undecided.*)

SECOND GOD   What did I tell you?

THIRD GOD   It *could* be pure coincidence.

SECOND GOD   The same coincidence in Shun, Kwan, and Setzuan? People just aren't religious any more, let's face the fact. Our mission has failed!

FIRST GOD   Oh come, we might run into a good person any minute.

THIRD GOD   How did the resolution read? (*Unrolling a scroll and reading from it:*) "The world can stay as it is if enough people are found (*at the word "found" he unrolls it a little more:*) living lives worthy of human beings." Good people, that is. Well, what about this Water Seller himself? *He's* good, or I'm very much mistaken.

SECOND GOD   You're very much mistaken. When he gave us a drink, I had the impression there was something odd about the cup. Well, look! (*He shows the cup to the* FIRST GOD.)

FIRST GOD   A false bottom!

SECOND GOD   The man is a swindler.

FIRST GOD   Very well, count *him* out. That's one man among millions. And as a matter of fact, we only need one on *our* side. These atheists are saying, "The world must be changed because no one can *be* good and *stay* good." No one, eh? I say: let us find one—just one—and we have those fellows where we want them!

THIRD GOD (*to* WONG)   Water Seller, is it so hard to find a place to stay?

WONG   Nothing could be easier. It's just me. I don't go about it right.

THIRD GOD   Really?

He returns to the others. A GENTLEMAN *passes by.*

WONG   Oh dear, they're catching on. (*He accosts the* GENTLEMAN.) Excuse the intrusion, dear sir, but three gods have just turned up. Three of the very highest. They need a place for the night. Seize this rare opportunity—to have real gods as your guests!

GENTLEMAN (*laughing*)   A new way of finding free rooms for a gang of crooks. (*Exit* GENTLEMAN.)

WONG (*shouting at him*)   Godless rascal! Have you no religion, gentlemen of Setzuan? (*Pause.*) Patience, illustrious ones! (*Pause.*) There's only one person left. Shen Te, the prostitute. She *can't* say no. (*Calls up to a window:*) Shen Te!

SHEN TE *opens the shutters and looks out.*

WONG   Shen Te, it's Wong. *They're* here, and nobody wants them. Will you take them?

SHEN TE   Oh, no, Wong, I'm expecting a gentleman.

WONG   Can't you forget about him for tonight?

SHEN TE   The rent has to be paid by tomorrow or I'll be out on the street.

WONG   This is no time for calculation, Shen Te.

SHEN TE   Stomachs rumble even on the Emperor's birthday, Wong.

WONG   Setzuan is one big dung hill!

SHEN TE   Oh, very well! I'll hide till my gentleman has come and gone. Then I'll take them. (*She disappears.*)

WONG   They mustn't see her gentleman or they'll know what she is.

FIRST GOD (*who hasn't heard any of this*)   I think it's hopeless.

They approach WONG.

WONG (*jumping, as he finds them behind him*)   A room has been found, illustrious ones! (*He wipes sweat off his brow.*)

SECOND GOD   Oh, good.

THIRD GOD   Let's see it.

WONG (*nervously*)   Just a minute. It has to be tidied up a bit.

THIRD GOD   Then we'll sit down here and wait.

WONG (*still more nervous*)   No, no! (*Holding himself back:*) Too much traffic, you know.

THIRD GOD (*with a smile*)   Of course, if you *want* us to move.

They retire a little. They sit on a doorstep. WONG *sits on the ground.*

WONG (*after a deep breath*)   You'll be staying with a single girl—the finest human being in Setzuan!

THIRD GOD   That's nice.

WONG (*to the audience*)   They gave me such a look when I picked up my cup just now.

THIRD GOD   You're worn out, Wong.

WONG   A little, maybe.

FIRST GOD   Do people here have a hard time of it?

WONG   The good ones do.

FIRST GOD   What about yourself?

WONG   You mean I'm not good. That's true. And I don't have an easy time either!

During this dialogue, a GENTLEMAN *has turned up in front of* SHEN TE'S *house, and has whistled several times. Each time* WONG *has given a start.*

THIRD GOD (*to* WONG, *softly*)   Psst! I think he's gone now.

WONG (*confused and surprised*)   Ye-e-es.

The GENTLEMAN *has left now, and* SHEN TE *has come down to the street.*

SHEN TE (*softly*) Wong!

Getting no answer, she goes off down the street. WONG *arrives just too late, forgetting his carrying pole.*

WONG (*softly*) Shen Te! Shen Te! (*To himself:*) So she's gone off to earn the rent. Oh dear, I can't go to the gods *again* with no room to offer them. Having failed in the service of the gods, I shall run to my den in the sewer pipe down by the river and hide from their sight!

He rushes off. SHEN TE *returns, looking for him, but finding the* GODS. *She stops in confusion.*

SHEN TE You are the illustrious ones? My name is Shen Te. It would please me very much if my simple room could be of use to you.

THIRD GOD Where is the Water Seller, Miss . . . Shen Te?

SHEN TE I missed him, somehow.

FIRST GOD Oh, he probably thought you weren't coming, and was afraid of telling us.

THIRD GOD (*picking up the carrying pole*) We'll leave this with you. He'll be needing it.

Led by SHEN TE, *they go into the house. It grows dark, then light. Dawn. Again escorted by* SHEN TE, *who leads them through the half-light with a little lamp, the* GODS *take their leave.*

FIRST GOD Thank you, thank you, dear Shen Te, for your elegant hospitality! We shall not forget! And give our thanks to the Water Seller—he showed us a good human being.

SHEN TE Oh, *I'm* not good. Let me tell you something: when Wong asked me to put you up, I hesitated.

FIRST GOD It's all right to hesitate if you then go ahead! And in giving us that room you did much more than you knew. You proved that good people still exist, a point that has been disputed of late—even in heaven. Farewell!

SECOND GOD Farewell!

THIRD GOD Farewell!

SHEN TE Stop, illustrious ones! I'm not sure you're right. I'd like to be good, it's true, but there's the rent to pay. And that's not all: I sell myself for a living. Even so I can't make ends meet, there's too much competition. I'd like to honor my father and mother and speak nothing but the truth and not covet my neighbor's house. I should love to stay with one man. But how? How is it done? Even breaking a few of your commandments, I can hardly manage.

FIRST GOD (*clearing his throat*) These thoughts are but, um, the misgivings of an unusually good woman!

THIRD GOD   Good-bye, Shen Te! Give our regards to the Water Seller!

SECOND GOD   And above all: be good! Farewell!

FIRST GOD   Farewell!

THIRD GOD   Farewell!

They start to wave good-bye.

SHEN TE   But everything is so expensive, I don't feel sure I can do it!

SECOND GOD   That's not in our sphere. We never meddle with economics.

THIRD GOD   One moment. (*They stop.*) Isn't it true she might do better if she had more money?

SECOND GOD   Come, come! How could we ever account for it Up Above?

FIRST GOD   Oh, there are ways. (*They put their heads together and confer in dumb show. To* SHEN TE, *with embarrassment:*) As you say you can't pay your rent, well, um, we're not paupers, so of course we *insist* on paying for our room. (*Awkwardly thrusting money into her hands:*) There! (*Quickly:*) But don't tell anyone! The incident is open to misinterpretation.

SECOND GOD   It certainly is!

FIRST GOD (*defensively*)   But there's no law against it! It was never decreed that a god mustn't pay hotel bills!

The GODS *leave.*

1

A small tobacco shop. The shop is not as yet completely furnished and hasn't started doing business.

SHEN TE (*to the audience*)   It's three days now since the gods left. When they said they wanted to pay for the room, I looked down at my hand, and there was more than a thousand silver dollars! I bought a tobacco shop with the money, and moved in yesterday. I don't own the building, of course, but I can pay the rent, and I hope to do a lot of good here. Beginning with Mrs. Shin, who's just coming across the square with her pot. She had the shop before me, and yesterday she dropped in to ask for rice for her children. (*Enter* MRS. SHIN. *Both women bow.*) How do you do, Mrs. Shin.

MRS. SHIN   How do you do, Miss Shen Te. You like your new home?

SHEN TE   Indeed, yes. Did your children have a good night?

MRS. SHIN   In that hovel? The youngest is coughing already.

SHEN TE   Oh, dear!

MRS. SHIN   You're going to learn a thing or two in these slums.

SHEN TE   Slums? That's not what you said when you sold me the shop!

MRS. SHIN Now don't start nagging! Robbing me and my innocent children of their home and then calling it a slum! That's the limit! (*She weeps.*)

SHEN TE (*tactfully*) I'll get your rice.

MRS. SHIN And a little cash while you're at it.

SHEN TE I'm afraid I haven't sold anything yet.

MRS. SHIN (*screeching*) I've got to have it. Strip the clothes from my back and then cut my throat, will you? I know what I'll do: I'll dump my children on your doorstep! (*She snatches the pot out of* SHEN TE's *hands.*)

SHEN TE Please don't be angry. You'll spill the rice.

Enter an elderly HUSBAND *and* WIFE *with their shabbily dressed* NEPHEW.

WIFE Shen Te, dear! You've come into money, they tell me. And we haven't a roof over our heads! A tobacco shop. We had one too. But it's gone. Could we spend the night here, do you think?

NEPHEW (*appraising the shop*) Not bad!

WIFE He's our nephew. We're inseparable!

MRS. SHIN And who are these . . . ladies and gentleman?

SHEN TE They put me up when I first came in from the country. (*To the audience:*) Of course, when my small purse was empty, they put me out on the street, and they may be afraid I'll do the same to them. (*To the newcomers, kindly:*) Come in, and welcome, though I've only one little room for you—it's behind the shop.

HUSBAND That'll do. Don't worry.

WIFE (*bringing* SHEN TE *some tea*) We'll stay over here, so we won't be in your way. Did you make it a tobacco shop in memory of your first real home? We can certainly give you a hint or two! That's one reason we came.

MRS. SHIN (*to* SHEN TE) Very nice! As long as you have a few customers too!

HUSBAND Sh! A customer!

Enter an UNEMPLOYED MAN, *in rags.*

UNEMPLOYED MAN Excuse me. I'm unemployed.

MRS. SHIN *laughs.*

SHEN TE Can I help you?

UNEMPLOYED MAN Have you any damaged cigarettes? I thought there might be some damage when you're unpacking.

WIFE What nerve, begging for tobacco! (*Rhetorically:*) Why don't they ask for bread?

UNEMPLOYED MAN Bread is expensive. One cigarette butt and I'll be a new man.

SHEN TE (*giving him cigarettes*) That's very important—to be a new man. You'll be my first customer and bring me luck.

The UNEMPLOYED MAN *quickly lights a cigarette, inhales, and goes off, coughing.*

WIFE   Was that right, Shen Te, dear?

MRS. SHIN   If this is the opening of a shop, you can hold the closing at the end of the week.

HUSBAND   I bet he had money on him.

SHEN TE   Oh, no, he said he hadn't!

NEPHEW   How d'you know he wasn't lying?

SHEN TE (*angrily*)   How do you know he was?

WIFE (*wagging her head*)   You're too good, Shen Te, dear. If you're going to keep this shop, you'll have to learn to say no.

HUSBAND   Tell them the place isn't yours to dispose of. Belongs to . . . some relative who insists on all accounts being strictly in order . . .

MRS. SHIN   That's right! What do you think you are—a philanthropist?

SHEN TE (*laughing*)   Very well, suppose I ask you for my rice back, Mrs. Shin?

WIFE (*combatively, at* MRS. SHIN)   So that's *her* rice?

Enter the CARPENTER, *a small man.*

MRS. SHIN (*who, at the sight of him, starts to hurry away*)   See you tomorrow, Miss Shen Te! (*Exit* MRS. SHIN.)

CARPENTER   Mrs. Shin, it's you I want!

WIFE (*to* SHEN TE)   Has she some claim on you?

SHEN TE   She's hungry. That's a claim.

CARPENTER   Are you the new tenant? And filling up the shelves already? Well, they're not yours till they're paid for, ma'am. I'm the carpenter, so I should know.

SHEN TE   I took the shop "furnishings included."

CARPENTER   You're in league with that Mrs. Shin, of course. All right. I demand my hundred silver dollars.

SHEN TE   I'm afraid I haven't got a hundred silver dollars.

CARPENTER   Then you'll find it. Or I'll have you arrested.

WIFE (*whispering to* SHEN TE)   That relative: make it a cousin.

SHEN TE   Can't it wait till next month?

CARPENTER   No!

SHEN TE   Be a little patient, Mr. Carpenter, I can't settle all claims at once.

CARPENTER   Who's patient with me? (*He grabs a shelf from the wall.*) Pay up—or I take the shelves back!

WIFE   Shen Te! Dear! Why don't you let your . . . cousin settle this affair? (*To* CARPENTER:) Put your claim in writing. Shen Te's cousin will see you get paid.

CARPENTER (*derisively*)   Cousin, eh?

HUSBAND   Cousin, yes.

CARPENTER I know these cousins!

NEPHEW Don't be silly. He's a personal friend of mine.

HUSBAND What a man! Sharp as a razor!

CARPENTER All right. I'll put my claim in writing. (*Puts shelf on floor, sits on it, writes out bill.*)

WIFE (*to* SHEN TE) He'd tear the dress off your back to get his shelves. Never recognize a claim! That's my motto.

SHEN TE He's done a job, and wants something in return. It's shameful that I can't give it to him. What will the gods say?

HUSBAND You did your bit when you took *us* in.

Enter the BROTHER, *limping, and the* SISTER-IN-LAW, *pregnant.*

BROTHER (*to* HUSBAND *and* WIFE) So this is where you're hiding out! There's family feeling for you! Leaving us on the corner!

WIFE (*embarrassed, to* SHEN TE) It's my brother and his wife. (*To them:*) Now stop grumbling, and sit quietly in that corner. (*To* SHEN TE:) It can't be helped. She's in her fifth month.

SHEN TE Oh yes. Welcome!

WIFE (*to the couple*) Say thank you. (*They mutter something.*) The cups are there. (*To* SHEN TE:) Lucky you bought this shop when you did!

SHEN TE (*laughing and bringing tea*) Lucky indeed!

Enter MRS. MI TZU, *the landlady.*

MRS. MI TZU Miss Shen Te? I am Mrs. Mi Tzu, your landlady. I hope our relationship will be a happy one. I like to think I give my tenants modern, personalized service. Here is your lease. (*To the others, as* SHEN TE *reads the lease:*) There's nothing like the opening of a little shop, is there? A moment of true beauty! (*She is looking around.*) Not very much on the shelves, of course. But everything in the god's good time! Where are your references, Miss Shen Te?

SHEN TE Do I *have* to have references?

MRS. MI TZU After all, I haven't a notion who you are!

HUSBAND Oh, *we'd* be glad to vouch for Miss Shen Te! We'd go through fire for her!

MRS. MI TZU And who may *you* be?

HUSBAND (*stammering*) Ma Fu, tobacco dealer.

MRS. MI TZU Where is your shop, Mr. . . . Ma Fu?

HUSBAND Well, um, I haven't got a shop—I've just sold it.

MRS. MI TZU I see. (*To* SHEN TE:) Is there no one else that knows you?

WIFE (*whispering to* SHEN TE) Your cousin! Your cousin!

MRS. MI TZU This is a respectable house, Miss Shen Te. I never sign a lease without certain assurances.

SHEN TE (*slowly, her eyes downcast*) I have . . . a cousin.

MRS. MI TZU On the square? Let's go over and see him. What does he do?

SHEN TE (*as before*) He lives . . . in another city.

WIFE (*prompting*) Didn't you say he was in Shung?

SHEN TE That's right. Shung.

HUSBAND (*prompting*) I had his name on the tip of my tongue. Mr. . . .

SHEN TE (*with an effort*) Mr. . . . Shui . . . Ta.

HUSBAND That it! Tall, skinny fellow!

SHEN TE Shui Ta!

NEPHEW (*to* CARPENTER) *You* were in touch with him, weren't you? About the shelves?

CARPENTER (*surlily*) Give him this bill. (*He hands it over.*) I'll be back in the morning. (*Exit* CARPENTER.)

NEPHEW (*calling after him, but with his eyes on* MRS. MI TZU) Don't worry! Mr. Shui Ta pays on the nail!

MRS. MI TZU (*looking closely at* SHEN TE) I'll be happy to make his acquaintance, Miss Shen Te. (*Exit* MRS. MI TZU.)

Pause.

WIFE By tomorrow morning she'll know more about you than you do yourself.

SISTER-IN-LAW (*to* NEPHEW) This thing isn't built to last.

Enter GRANDFATHER.

WIFE It's Grandfather! (*To* SHEN TE:) Such a good old soul!

The BOY *enters.*

BOY (*over his shoulder*) Here they are!

WIFE And the boy, how he's grown! But he always could eat enough for ten.

Enter the NIECE.

WIFE (*to* SHEN TE) Our little niece from the country. There are more of us now than in your time. The less we had, the more there were of us; the more there were of us, the less we had. Give me the key. We must protect ourselves from unwanted guests. (*She takes the key and locks the door.*) Just make yourself at home. I'll light the little lamp.

NEPHEW (*a big joke*) I hope her cousin doesn't drop in tonight! The strict Mr. Shui Ta!

SISTER-IN-LAW *laughs.*

BROTHER (*reaching for a cigarette*) One cigarette more or less . . .

HUSBAND One cigarette more or less.

They pile into the cigarettes. The BROTHER *hands a jug of wine round.*

NEPHEW Mr. Shui Ta'll pay for it!

GRANDFATHER (*gravely, to* SHEN TE) How do you do?

SHEN TE, *a little taken aback by the belatedness of the greeting, bows. She has the* CARPENTER's *bill in one hand, the landlady's lease in the other.*

WIFE How about a bit of a song? To keep Shen Te's spirits up?
NEPHEW Good idea. Grandfather: you start!

Song of the Smoke

GRANDFATHER

I used to think (before old age beset me)
    That brains could fill the pantry of the poor.
But where did all my cerebration get me?
    I'm just as hungry as I was before.
        So what's the use?
            See the smoke float free
        Into ever colder coldness!
            It's the same with me.

HUSBAND

The straight and narrow path leads to disaster
    And so the crooked path I tried to tread.
That got me to disaster even faster
    (They say we shall be happy when we're dead.)
        So what's the use?
            See the smoke float free
        Into ever colder coldness!
            It's the same with me.

NIECE

You older people, full of expectation,
    At any moment now you'll walk the plank!
The future's for the younger generation!
    Yes, even if that future is a blank.
        So what's the use?
            See the smoke float free
        Into ever colder coldness!
            It's the same with me.

NEPHEW (*to the* BROTHER) Where'd you get that wine?
SISTER-IN-LAW (*answering for the* BROTHER) He pawned the sack of tobacco.
HUSBAND (*stepping in*) What? That tobacco was all we had to fall back on! You pig!
BROTHER *You'd* call a man a pig because your wife was frigid! Did you refuse to drink it?

They fight. The shelves fall over.

SHEN TE (*imploringly*)   Oh don't! Don't break everything! Take it, take it all, but don't destroy a gift from the gods!

WIFE (*disparagingly*)   This shop isn't big enough. I should never have mentioned it to Uncle and the others. When *they* arrive, it's going to be disgustingly overcrowded.

SISTER-IN-LAW   And did you hear our gracious hostess? She cools off quick!

Voices outside. Knocking at the door.

UNCLE'S VOICE   Open the door!

WIFE   Uncle? Is that you, Uncle?

UNCLE'S VOICE   Certainly, it's me. Auntie says to tell you she'll have the children here in ten minutes.

WIFE (*to* SHEN TE)   I'll have to let him in.

SHEN TE (*who scarcely hears her*):
The little lifeboat is swiftly sent down
Too many men too greedily
Hold on to it as they drown.

1a

WONG'S *den in a sewer pipe.*

WONG (*crouching there*)   All quiet! It's four days now since I left the city. The gods passed this way on the second day. I heard their steps on the bridge over there. They must be a long way off by this time, so I'm safe. (*Breathing a sigh of relief, he curls up and goes to sleep. In his dream the pipe becomes transparent, and the* GODS *appear. Raising an arm, as if in self-defense:*) I know, I know, illustrious ones! I found no one to give you a room—not in all Setzuan! There, it's out. Please continue on your way!

FIRST GOD (*mildly*)   But you did find someone. Someone who took us in for the night, watched over us in our sleep, and in the early morning lighted us down to the street with a lamp.

WONG   It was . . . Shen Te that took you in?

THIRD GOD   Who else?

WONG   And I ran away! "She isn't coming," I thought, "she just can't afford it."

GODS (*singing*)
O you feeble, well-intentioned, and yet feeble chap!
Where there's need the fellow thinks there is no goodness!
When there's danger he thinks courage starts to ebb away!
Some people only see the seamy side!
What hasty judgment! What premature desperation!

WONG   I'm *very* ashamed, illustrious ones.
FIRST GOD   Do us a favor, Water Seller. Go back to Setzuan. Find Shen Te, and give us a report on her. We hear that she's come into a little money. Show interest in her goodness—for no one can be good for long if goodness is not in demand. Meanwhile we shall continue the search, and find other good people. After which, the idle chatter about the impossibility of goodness will stop!

The GODS *vanish.*

2

A knocking.

WIFE   Shen Te! Someone at the door. Where is she anyway?
NEPHEW   She must be getting the breakfast. Mr. Shui Ta will pay for it.

The WIFE *laughs and shuffles to the door. Enter* MR. SHUI TA *and the* CARPENTER.

WIFE   Who is it?
SHUI TA   I am Miss Shen Te's cousin.
WIFE   What??
SHUI TA   My name is Shui Ta.
WIFE   Her cousin?
NEPHEW   Her cousin?
NIECE   But that was a joke. She hasn't got a cousin.
HUSBAND   So early in the morning?
BROTHER   What's all the noise?
SISTER-IN-LAW   This fellow says he's her cousin.
BROTHER   Tell him to prove it.
NEPHEW   Right. If you're Shen Te's cousin, prove it by getting the breakfast.
SHUI TA (*whose regime begins as he puts out the lamp to save oil; loudly, to all present, asleep or awake*)   Would you all please get dressed! Customers will be coming! I wish to open my shop!
HUSBAND   *Your* shop? Doesn't it belong to our good friend Shen Te?

SHUI TA *shakes his head.*

SISTER-IN-LAW   So we've been cheated. Where *is* the little liar?
SHUI TA   Miss Shen Te has been delayed. She wishes me to tell you there will be nothing she can do—now I am here.
WIFE (*bowled over*)   I thought she was good!
NEPHEW   Do you have to believe *him?*
HUSBAND   I don't.
NEPHEW   Then do something.
HUSBAND   Certainly! I'll send out a search party at once. You, you, you,

and you, go out and look for Shen Te. (*As the* GRANDFATHER *rises and makes for the door:*) Not you, Grandfather, you and I will hold the fort.

SHUI TA You won't find Miss Shen Te. She has suspended her hospitable activity for an unlimited period. There are too many of you. She asked me to say: this is a tobacco shop, not a gold mine.

HUSBAND Shen Te never said a thing like that. Boy, food! There's a bakery on the corner. Stuff your shirt full when they're not looking!

SISTER-IN-LAW Don't overlook the raspberry tarts.

HUSBAND And don't let the policeman see you.

The BOY *leaves.*

SHUI TA Don't you depend on this shop now? Then why give it a bad name by stealing from the bakery?

NEPHEW Don't listen to him. Let's find Shen Te. She'll give him a piece of her mind.

SISTER-IN-LAW Don't forget to leave us some breakfast.

BROTHER, SISTER-IN-LAW *and* NEPHEW *leave.*

SHUI TA (*to the* CARPENTER) You see, Mr. Carpenter, nothing has changed since the poet, eleven hundred years ago, penned these lines:
A governor was asked what was needed
To save the freezing people in the city.
He replied:
"A blanket ten thousand feet long
To cover the city and all its suburbs."

He starts to tidy up the shop.

CARPENTER Your cousin owes me money. I've got witnesses. For the shelves.

SHUI TA Yes, I have your bill. (*He takes it out of his pocket.*) Isn't a hundred silver dollars rather a lot?

CARPENTER No deductions! I have a wife and children.

SHUI TA How many children?

CARPENTER Three.

SHUI TA I'll make you an offer. Twenty silver dollars.

The HUSBAND *laughs.*

CARPENTER You're crazy. Those shelves are real walnut.

SHUI TA Very well. Take them away.

CARPENTER What?

SHUI TA They cost too much. Please take them away.

WIFE Not bad! (*And she, too, is laughing.*)

CARPENTER (*a little bewildered*) Call Shen Te, someone! (*To* SHUI TA:) She's *good!*

SHUI TA Certainly. She's ruined.

CARPENTER (*provoked into taking some of the shelves*) All right, you can keep your tobacco on the floor.

SHUI TA (*to the* HUSBAND) Help him with the shelves.

HUSBAND (*grins and carries one shelf over to the door where the* CARPENTER *now is*) Good-bye, shelves!

CARPENTER (*to the* HUSBAND) You dog! You want my family to starve?

SHUI TA I repeat my offer. I have no desire to keep my tobacco on the floor. Twenty silver dollars.

CARPENTER (*with desperate aggressiveness*) One hundred!

SHUI TA *shows indifference, looks through the window. The* HUSBAND *picks up several shelves.*

CARPENTER (*to* HUSBAND) You needn't smash them against the door-post, you idiot! (*To* SHUI TA:) These shelves were made to measure. They're no use anywhere else!

SHUI TA Precisely.

The WIFE *squeals with pleasure.*

CARPENTER (*giving up, sullenly*) Take the shelves. Pay what you want to pay.

SHUI TA (*smoothly*) Twenty silver dollars.

He places two large coins on the table. The CARPENTER *picks them up.*

HUSBAND (*brings the shelves back in*) And quite enough too!

CARPENTER (*slinking off*) Quite enough to get drunk on.

HUSBAND (*happily*) Well, we got rid of *him!*

WIFE (*weeping with fun, gives a rendition of the dialogue just spoken*) "Real walnut," says he. "Very well, take them away," says his lordship. "I have three children," says he. "Twenty silver dollars," says his lord-ship. "They're no use anywhere else," says he. "Pre-cisely," said his lordship! (*She dissolves into shrieks of merriment.*)

SHUI TA And now: go!

HUSBAND What's that?

SHUI TA You're thieves, parasites. I'm giving you this chance. Go!

HUSBAND (*summoning all his ancestral dignity*) That sort deserves no an-swer. Besides, one should never shout on an empty stomach.

WIFE Where's that boy?

SHUI TA Exactly. The boy. I want no stolen goods in this shop. (*Very loudly:*) I strongly advise you to leave! (*But they remain seated, noses in the air. Quietly:*) As you wish. (SHUI TA *goes to the door. A* POLICEMAN *appears.* SHUI TA *bows.*) I am addressing the officer in charge of this precinct?

POLICEMAN That's right, Mr., um, what was the name, sir?

SHUI TA Mr. Shui Ta.

POLICEMAN Yes, of course, sir.

They exchange a smile.

SHUI TA Nice weather we're having.

POLICEMAN A little on the warm side, sir.

SHUI TA Oh, a little on the warm side.

HUSBAND (*whispering to the* WIFE) If he keeps it up till the boy's back, we're done for. (*Tries to signal* SHUI TA.)

SHUI TA (*ignoring the signal*) Weather, of course, is one thing indoors, another out on the dusty street!

POLICEMAN Oh, quite another, sir!

WIFE (*to the* HUSBAND) It's all right as long as he's standing in the doorway—the boy will see him.

SHUI TA Step inside for a moment! It's quite cool indoors. My cousin and I have just opened the place. And we attach the greatest importance to being on good terms with the, um, authorities.

POLICEMAN (*entering*) Thank you, Mr. Shui Ta. It *is* cool!

HUSBAND (*whispering to the* WIFE) And now the boy *won't* see him.

SHUI TA (*showing* HUSBAND *and* WIFE *to the* POLICEMAN) Visitors, I think my cousin knows them. They were just leaving.

HUSBAND (*defeated*) Ye-e-es, we were . . . just leaving.

SHUI TA I'll tell my cousin you couldn't wait.

Noise from the street. Shouts of "Stop, Thief!"

POLICEMAN What's that?

The BOY *is in the doorway with cakes and buns and rolls spilling out of his shirt. The* WIFE *signals desperately to him to leave. He gets the idea.*

POLICEMAN No, you don't! (*He grabs the* BOY *by the collar.*) Where's all this from?

BOY (*vaguely pointing*) Down the street.

POLICEMAN (*grimly*) So that's it. (*Prepares to arrest the* BOY.)

WIFE (*stepping in*) And *we* knew nothing about it. (*To the* BOY:) Nasty little thief!

POLICEMAN (*dryly*) Can you clarify the situation, Mr. Shui Ta?

SHUI TA *is silent.*

POLICEMAN (*who understands silence*) Aha. You're all coming with me—to the station.

SHUI TA I can hardly say how sorry I am that *my* establishment . . .

THE WIFE Oh, he saw the boy leave not ten minutes ago!

SHUI TA And to conceal the theft asked a policeman in?

POLICEMAN Don't listen to her, Mr. Shui Ta, I'll be happy to relieve you of their presence one and all! (*To all three:*) Out!

(*He drives them before him.*)

GRANDFATHER (*leaving last, gravely*) Good morning!
POLICEMAN Good morning!

SHUI TA, *left alone, continues to tidy up.* MRS. MI TZU *breezes in.*

MRS. MI TZU *You're* her cousin, are you? Then have the goodness to explain what all this means—police dragging people from a respectable house! By what right does your Miss Shen Te turn my property into a house of assignation?—Well, as you see, I know all!
SHUI TA Yes. My cousin has the worst possible reputation: that of being poor.
MRS. MI TZU No sentimental rubbish, Mr. Shui Ta. Your cousin was a common. . . .
SHUI TA Pauper. Let's use the uglier word.
MRS. MI TZU I'm speaking of her conduct, not her earnings. But there must have *been* earnings, or how did she buy all this? Several elderly gentlemen took care of it, I suppose. I repeat: this is a respectable house! I have tenants who prefer not to live under the same roof with such a person.
SHUI TA (*quietly*) How much do you want?
MRS. MI TZU (*he is ahead of her now*) I beg your pardon.
SHUI TA To reassure yourself. To reassure your tenants. How much will it cost?
MRS. MI TZU You're a cool customer.
SHUI TA (*picking up the lease*) The rent is high. (*He reads on.*) I assume it's payable by the month?
MRS. MI TZU Not in her case.
SHUI TA (*looking up*) What?
MRS. MI TZU Six months' rent payable in advance. Two hundred silver dollars.
SHUI TA Six . . . ! Sheer usury! And where am I to find it?
MRS. MI TZU You should have thought of that before.
SHUI TA Have you no heart, Mrs. Mi Tzu? It's true Shen Te acted foolishly, being kind to all those people, but she'll improve with time. I'll see to it she does. She'll work her fingers to the bone to pay her rent, and all the time be as quiet as a mouse, as humble as a fly.
MRS. MI TZU Her social background . . .
SHUI TA Out of the depths! She came out of the depths! And before she'll go back there, she'll work, sacrifice, shrink from nothing. . . . Such a tenant is worth her weight in gold, Mrs. Mi Tzu.
MRS. MI TZU It's silver we were talking about, Mr. Shui Ta. Two hundred silver dollars or . . .

Enter the POLICEMAN.

POLICEMAN   Am I intruding, Mr. Shui Ta?

MRS. MI TZU   This tobacco shop is well-known to the police, I see.

POLICEMAN   Mr. Shui Ta has done us a service, Mrs. Mi Tzu. I am here to present our official felicitations!

MRS. MI TZU   That means less than nothing to me, sir. Mr. Shui Ta, all I can say is: I hope your cousin will find my terms acceptable. Good day, gentlemen. (*Exit.*)

SHUI TA   Good day, ma'am.

Pause.

POLICEMAN   Mrs. Mi Tzu a bit of a stumbling block, sir?

SHUI TA   She wants six months' rent in advance.

POLICEMAN   And you haven't got it, eh? (SHUI TA *is silent.*) But surely you can get it, sir? A man like you?

SHUI TA   What about a woman like Shen Te?

POLICEMAN   You're not staying, sir?

SHUI TA   No, and I won't be back. Do you smoke?

POLICEMAN (*taking two cigars, and placing them both in his pocket*)   Thank you, sir—I see your point. Miss Shen Te—let's mince no words— Miss Shen Te lived by selling herself. "What else could she have done?" you ask. "How else was she to pay the rent?" True. But the fact remains, Mr. Shui Ta, it is not respectable. Why not? A very deep question. But, in the first place, love—love isn't bought and sold like cigars, Mr. Shui Ta. In the second place, it isn't respectable to go waltzing off with someone that's paying his way, so to speak—it must be for love! Thirdly and lastly, as the proverb has it: not for a handful of rice but for love! (*Pause. He is thinking hard.*) "Well," you may say, "and what good is all this wisdom if the milk's already spilt?" Miss Shen Te is what she is. Is *where* she is. We have to face the fact that if she doesn't get hold of six months' rent pronto, she'll be back on the streets. The question then as I see it—everything in this world is a matter of opinion—the question as I see it is: *how* is she to get hold of this rent? How? Mr. Shui Ta: I don't know. (*Pause.*) I take that back, sir. It's just come to me. A husband. We must find her a husband!

Enter a little OLD WOMAN.

OLD WOMAN   A good cheap cigar for my husband, we'll have been married forty years tomorrow and we're having a little celebration.

SHUI TA   Forty years? And you still want to celebrate?

OLD WOMAN   As much as we can afford to. We have the carpet shop across the square. We'll be good neighbors, I hope?

SHUI TA   I hope so too.

POLICEMAN (*who keeps making discoveries*)   Mr. Shui Ta, you know what we need? We need capital. And how do we acquire capital? We get married.

SHUI TA (*to* OLD WOMAN) I'm afraid I've been pestering this gentleman with my personal worries.

POLICEMAN (*lyrically*) We can't pay six months' rent, so what do we do? We marry money.

SHUI TA That might not be easy.

POLICEMAN Oh, I don't know. She's a good match. Has a nice, growing business. (*To the* OLD WOMAN:) What do you think?

OLD WOMAN (*undecided*) Well—

POLICEMAN Should she put an ad in the paper?

OLD WOMAN (*not eager to commit herself*) Well, if *she* agrees—

POLICEMAN I'll write it for her. *You* lend us a hand, and *we* write an ad for you! (*He chuckles away to himself, takes out his notebook, wets the stump of a pencil between his lips, and writes away.*)

SHUI TA (*slowly*) Not a bad idea.

POLICEMAN "What . . . *respectable* . . . man . . . with small capital . . . widower . . . not excluded . . . desires . . . marriage . . . into flourishing . . . tobacco shop?" And now let's add: "Am . . . pretty . . ." No! . . . "Prepossessing appearance."

SHUI TA If you don't think that's an exaggeration?

OLD WOMAN Oh, not a bit. I've seen her.

The POLICEMAN *tears the page out of his notebook, and hands it over to* SHUI TA.

SHUI TA (*with horror in his voice*) How much luck we need to keep our heads above water! How many ideas! How many friends! (*To the* POLICEMAN:) Thank you, sir. I think I see my way clear.

3

Evening in the municipal park. Noise of a plane overhead. YANG SUN, *a young man in rags, is following the plane with his eyes: one can tell that the machine is describing a curve above the park.* YANG SUN *then takes a rope out of his pocket, looking anxiously about him as he does so. He moves toward a large willow. Enter two prostitutes, one old, the other the* NIECE *whom we have already met.*

NIECE Hello. Coming with me?

YANG SUN (*taken aback*) If you'd like to buy me a dinner.

OLD WHORE Buy you a dinner! (*To the* NIECE:) Oh, we know him—it's the unemployed pilot. Waste no time on him!

NIECE But he's the only man left in the park. And it's going to rain.

OLD WHORE Oh, how do you know?

And they pass by. YANG SUN *again looks about him, again takes his rope, and this time throws it round a branch of the willow tree. Again he is interrupted. It is the two prostitutes returning—and in such a hurry they don't notice him.*

NIECE It's going to pour!

Enter SHEN TE.

OLD WHORE There's that *gorgon* Shen Te! That *drove* your family out into the cold!

NIECE It wasn't her. It was that cousin of hers. She offered to pay for the cakes. I've nothing against her.

OLD WHORE I have, though. (*So that* SHEN TE *can hear:*) Now where could the little lady be off to? She may be rich now but that won't stop her snatching our young men, will it?

SHEN TE I'm going to the tearoom by the pond.

NIECE Is it true what they say? You're marrying a widower—with three children?

SHEN TE Yes. I'm just going to see him.

YANG SUN (*his patience at breaking point*) Move on there! This is a park, not a whorehouse!

OLD WHORE Shut your mouth!

But the two prostitutes leave.

YANG SUN Even in the farthest corner of the park, even when it's raining, you can't get rid of them! (*He spits.*)

SHEN TE (*overhearing this*) And what right have you to scold them? (*But at this point she sees the rope.*) Oh!

YANG SUN Well, what are you staring at?

SHEN TE That rope. What is it for?

YANG SUN Think! Think! I haven't a penny. Even if I had, I wouldn't spend it on you. I'd buy a drink of water.

The rain starts.

SHEN TE (*still looking at the rope*) What is the rope for? You mustn't!

YANG SUN What's it to you? Clear out!

SHEN TE (*irrelevantly*) It's raining.

YANG SUN Well, don't try to come under this tree.

SHEN TE Oh, no. (*She stays in the rain.*)

YANG SUN Now go away. (*Pause.*) For one thing, I don't like your looks, you're bowlegged.

SHEN TE (*indignantly*) That's not true!

YANG SUN Well, don't show 'em to me. Look, it's raining. You better come under this tree.

Slowly, she takes shelter under the tree.

SHEN TE Why did you want to do it?

YANG SUN You really want to know? (*Pause.*) To get rid of you! (*Pause.*) You know what a flyer is?

SHEN TE Oh yes, I've met a lot of pilots. At the tearoom.

YANG SUN You call *them* flyers? Think they know what a machine is? Just 'cause they have leather helmets? They gave the airfield director a bribe, that's the way *those* fellows got up in the air! Try one of them out sometime. "Go up to two thousand feet," tell him, "then let it fall, then pick it up again with a flick of the wrist at the last moment." Know what he'll say to that? "It's not in my contract." Then again, there's the landing problem. It's like landing on your own backside. It's no different, planes are human. Those fools don't understand. (*Pause.*) And I'm the biggest fool for reading the book on flying in the Peking school and skipping the page where it says: "We've got enough flyers and we don't need you." I'm a mail pilot with no mail. You understand that?

SHEN TE (*shyly*) Yes. I do.

YANG SUN No, you don't. You'd never understand that.

SHEN TE When we were little we had a crane with a broken wing. He made friends with us and was very good-natured about our jokes. He would strut along behind us and call out to stop us going too fast for him. But every spring and autumn when the cranes flew over the villages in great swarms, he got quite restless. (*Pause.*) I understand that. (*She bursts out crying.*)

YANG SUN Don't!

SHEN TE (*quieting down*) No.

YANG SUN It's bad for the complexion.

SHEN TE (*sniffing*) I've stopped.

She dries her tears on her big sleeve. Leaning against the tree, but not looking at her, he reaches for her face.

YANG SUN You can't even wipe your own face. (*He is wiping it for her with his handkerchief. Pause.*)

SHEN TE (*still sobbing*) I don't know *anything!*

YANG SUN You interrupted me! What for?

SHEN TE It's such a rainy day. You only wanted to do . . . *that* because it's such a rainy day.

To the audience:
In our country
The evenings should never be somber
High bridges over rivers
The grey hour between night and morning
And the long, long winter:
Such things are dangerous
For, with all the misery,
A very little is enough
And men throw away an unbearable life.

Pause.

YANG SUN Talk about yourself for a change.

SHEN TE What about me? I have a shop.

YANG SUN (*incredulous*) You have a shop, have you? Never thought of walking the streets?

SHEN TE   I did walk the streets. Now I have a shop.

YANG SUN (*ironically*)   A gift of the gods, I suppose!

SHEN TE   How did you know?

YANG SUN (*even more ironical*)   One fine evening the gods turned up saying: here's some money!

SHEN TE (*quickly*)   One fine morning.

YANG SUN (*fed up*)   This isn't much of an entertainment.

Pause.

SHEN TE   I can play the zither a little. (*Pause.*) And I can mimic men. (*Pause.*) I got the shop, so the first thing I did was to give my zither away. I can be as stupid as a fish now, I said to myself, and it won't matter.

I'm rich now, I said
I walk alone, I sleep alone
For a whole year, I said
I'll have nothing to do with a man.

YANG SUN   And now you're marrying one! The one at the tearoom by the pond?

SHEN TE *is silent.*

YANG SUN   What do you know about love?

SHEN TE   Everything

YANG SUN   Nothing. (*Pause.*) Or d'you just mean you enjoyed it?

SHEN TE   No.

YANG SUN (*again without turning to look at her, he strokes her cheek with his hand*)   You like that?

SHEN TE   Yes.

YANG SUN (*breaking off*)   You're easily satisfied, I must say. (*Pause.*) What a town!

SHEN TE   You have no friends?

YANG SUN (*defensively*)   Yes, I have! (*Change of tone.*) But they don't want to hear I'm still unemployed. "What?" they ask. "Is there still water in the sea?" You have friends?

SHEN TE (*hesitating*)   Just a . . . cousin.

YANG SUN   Watch him carefully.

SHEN TE   He only came once. Then he went away. He won't be back. (YANG SUN *is looking away.*) But to be without hope, they say, is to be without goodness!

Pause.

YANG SUN   Go on talking. A voice is a voice.

SHEN TE   Once, when I was a little girl, I fell, with a load of brushwood. An old man picked me up. He gave me a penny too. Isn't it funny how people who don't have very much like to give some of it away? They must like to show what they can do, and how could they show it better than by being kind? Being wicked is just like being clumsy. When we sing a song, or build a machine, or plant some rice, we're being kind. You're kind.

YANG SUN   You make it sound easy.

SHEN TE   Oh, no. (*Little pause.*) Oh! A drop of rain!

YANG SUN   Where'd you feel it?

SHEN TE   Between the eyes.

YANG SUN   Near the right eye? Or the left?

SHEN TE   Near the left eye.

YANG SUN   Oh, good. (*He is getting sleepy.*) So you're through with men, eh?

SHEN TE (*with a smile*)   But I'm not bowlegged.

YANG SUN   Perhaps not.

SHEN TE   Definitely not.

Pause.

YANG SUN (*leaning wearily against the willow*)   I haven't had a drop to drink all day, I haven't eaten anything for *two* days. I couldn't love you if I tried.

Pause.

SHEN TE   I like it in the rain.

Enter WONG *the Water Seller, singing.*

The Song of the Water Seller in the Rain

"Buy my water," I am yelling
And my fury restraining
For no water I'm selling
'Cause it's raining, 'cause it's raining!
  I keep yelling: "Buy my water!"
  But no one's buying
  Athirst and dying
  And drinking and paying!
  Buy water!
  Buy water, you dogs!

Nice to dream of lovely weather!
Think of all the consternation
Were there no precipitation
Half a dozen years together!

Can't you hear them shrieking: "Water!"
Pretending they adore me?
They all would go down on their knees before me!
Down on your knees!
Go down on your knees, you dogs!

What are lawns and hedges thinking?
What are fields and forests saying?
"At the cloud's breast we are drinking!
And we've no idea who's paying!"
   I keep yelling: "Buy my water!"
   But no one's buying
   Athirst and dying
   And drinking and paying!
   Buy water!
   Buy water, you dogs!

The rain has stopped now. SHEN TE *sees* WONG *and runs toward him.*

SHEN TE   Wong! You're back! Your carrying pole's at the shop.
WONG   Oh, thank you, Shen Te. And how is life treating *you?*
SHEN TE   I've just met a brave and clever man. And I want to buy him a
cup of your water.
WONG (*bitterly*)   Throw back your head and open your mouth and you'll
have all the water you need—
SHEN TE (*tenderly*)
I want *your* water, Wong
The water that has tired you so
The water that you carried all this way
The water that is hard to sell because it's been raining.

I need it for the young man over there—he's a flyer!

A flyer is a bold man:
Braving the storms
In company with the clouds
He crosses the heavens
And brings to friends in far-away lands
The friendly mail!

She pays WONG, *and runs over to* YANG SUN *with the cup. But* YANG SUN *is fast asleep.*

SHEN TE (*calling to* WONG, *with a laugh*)   He's fallen asleep! Despair and
rain and I have worn him out!

3a

WONG's *den. The sewer pipe is transparent, and the* GODS *again appear to* WONG *in a dream.*

WONG (*radiant*)   I've seen her, illustrious ones! And she hasn't changed!
FIRST GOD   That's good to hear.
WONG   She loves someone.
FIRST GOD   Let's hope the experience gives her the strength to stay good!
WONG   It does. She's doing good deeds all the time.
FIRST GOD   Ah? What sort? What sort of good deeds, Wong?
WONG   Well, she has a kind word for everybody.
FIRST GOD (*eagerly*)   And then?
WONG   Hardly anyone leaves her shop without tobacco in his pocket—even if he can't pay for it.
FIRST GOD   Not bad at all. Next?
WONG   She's putting up a family of eight.
FIRST GOD (*gleefully, to the* SECOND GOD)   Eight! (*To* WONG:) And that's not all, of course!
WONG   She bought a cup of water from me even though it was raining.
FIRST GOD   Yes, yes, yes, all these smaller good deeds!
WONG   Even they run into money. A little tobacco shop doesn't make so much.
FIRST GOD (*sententiously*)   A prudent gardener works miracles on the smallest plot.
WONG   She hands out rice every morning. That eats up half her earnings.
FIRST GOD (*a little disappointed*)   Well, as a beginning . . .
WONG   They call her the Angel of the Slums—whatever the Carpenter may say!
FIRST GOD   What's this? A carpenter speaks ill of her?
WONG   Oh, he only says her shelves weren't paid for in full.
SECOND GOD (*who has a bad cold and can't pronounce his n's and m's*)   What's this? Not paying a carpenter? Why was that?
WONG   I suppose she didn't have the money.
SECOND GOD (*severely*)   One pays what one owes, that's in our book rules! First the letter of the law, then the spirit!
WONG   But it wasn't Shen Te, illustrious ones, it was her cousin. She called *him* in to help.
SECOND GOD   Then her cousin must never darken her threshold again!
WONG   Very well, illustrious ones! But in fairness to Shen Te, let me say that her cousin is a businessman.
FIRST GOD   Perhaps we should enquire what is customary? I find busi-

ness quite unintelligible. But everybody's doing it. Business! Did the Seven Good Kings do business? Did Kung the Just sell fish?

SECOND GOD   In any case, such a thing must not occur again!

The GODS start to leave.

THIRD GOD   Forgive us for taking this tone with you, Wong, we haven't been getting enough sleep. The rich recommend us to the poor, and the poor tell us they haven't enough room.

SECOND GOD   Feeble, feeble, the best of them!

FIRST GOD   No great deeds! No heroic daring!

THIRD GOD   On such a *small* scale!

SECOND GOD   Sincere, yes, but what is actually *achieved*?

One can no longer hear them.

WONG (*calling after them*)   I've thought of something, illustrious ones: Perhaps you shouldn't ask—too—much—all—at—once!

4

The square in front of SHEN TE'S *tobacco shop. Besides* SHEN TE'S *place, two other shops are seen: the carpet shop and a barber's. Morning. Outside* SHEN TE'S *the* GRANDFATHER, *the* SISTER-IN-LAW, *the* UNEMPLOYED MAN, *and* MRS. SHIN *stand waiting.*

SISTER-IN-LAW   She's been out all night again.

MRS. SHIN   No sooner did we get rid of that crazy cousin of hers than Shen Te herself starts carrying on! Maybe she does give us an ounce of rice now and then, but can you depend on her? Can you depend on her?

Loud voices from the Barber's.

VOICE OF SHU FU   What are you doing in my shop? Get out—at once!

VOICE OF WONG   But sir. They all let me sell . . .

WONG *comes staggering out of the Barber's shop pursued by* MR. SHU FU, *the Barber, a fat man carrying a heavy curling iron.*

SHU FU   Get out, I said! Pestering my customers with your slimy old water! Get out! Take your cup!

He holds out the cup. WONG *reaches out for it.* MR. SHU FU *strikes his hand with the curling iron, which is hot.* WONG *howls.*

SHU FU   You had it coming, my man!

Puffing, he returns to his shop. The UNEMPLOYED MAN *picks up the cup and gives it to* WONG.

UNEMPLOYED MAN   You can report that to the police.
WONG   My hand! It's smashed up!
UNEMPLOYED MAN   Any bones broken?
WONG   I can't move my fingers.
UNEMPLOYED MAN   Sit down. I'll put some water on it.

WONG *sits.*

MRS. SHIN   The water won't cost you anything.
SISTER-IN-LAW   You might have got a bandage from Miss Shen Te till she took to staying out all night. It's a scandal.
MRS. SHIN (*despondently*)   If you ask me, she's forgotten we ever existed!

Enter SHEN TE *down the street, with a dish of rice.*

SHEN TE (*to the audience*)   How wonderful to see Setzuan in the early morning! I always used to stay in bed with my dirty blanket over my head afraid to wake up. This morning I saw the newspapers being delivered by little boys, the streets being washed by strong men, and fresh vegetables coming in from the country on ox carts. It's a long walk from where Yang Sun lives, but I feel lighter at every step. They say you walk on air when you're in love, but it's even better walking on the rough earth, on the hard cement. In the early morning, the old city looks like a great heap of rubbish! Nice, though, with all its little lights. And the sky, so pink, so transparent, before the dust comes and muddies it! What a lot you miss if you never see your city rising from its slumbers like an honest old craftsman pumping his lungs full of air and reaching for his tools, as the poet says! (*Cheerfully, to her waiting guests:*) Good morning, everyone, here's your rice! (*Distributing the rice, she comes upon* WONG:) Good morning, Wong, I'm quite lightheaded today. On my way over, I looked at myself in all the shop windows. I'd love to be beautiful.

She slips into the carpet shop. MR. SHU FU *has just emerged from his shop.*

SHU FU (*to the audience*)   It surprises me how beautiful Miss Shen Te is looking today! I never gave her a passing thought before. But now I've been gazing upon her comely form for exactly three minutes! I begin to suspect I am in love with her. She is overpoweringly attractive! (*Crossly, to* WONG:) Be off with you, rascal!

He returns to his shop. SHEN TE *comes back out of the carpet shop with the* OLD MAN, *its proprietor, and his wife—whom we have already met—the* OLD WOMAN. SHEN TE *is wearing a shawl. The* OLD MAN *is holding up a looking glass for her.*

OLD WOMAN   Isn't it lovely? We'll give you a reduction because there's a little hole in it.

SHEN TE (*looking at another shawl on the* OLD WOMAN's *arm*) The other one's nice too.

OLD WOMAN (*smiling*) Too bad there's no hole in that!

SHEN TE That's right. My shop doesn't make very much.

OLD WOMAN And your good deeds eat it all up! Be more careful, my dear. . . .

SHEN TE (*trying on the shawl with the hole*) Just now, I'm lightheaded! Does the color suit me?

OLD WOMAN You'd better ask a man.

SHEN TE (*to the* OLD MAN) Does the color suit me?

OLD MAN You'd better ask your young friend.

SHEN TE I'd like to have your opinion.

OLD MAN It suits you very well. But wear it this way: the dull side out.

SHEN TE *pays up.*

OLD WOMAN If you decide you don't like it, you can exchange it. (*She pulls* SHEN TE *to one side.*) Has he got money?

SHEN TE (*with a laugh*) Yang Sun? Oh, no.

OLD WOMAN Then how're you going to pay your rent?

SHEN TE I'd forgotten about that.

OLD WOMAN And next Monday is the first of the month! Miss Shen Te, I've got something to say to you. After we (*indicating her husband*) got to know you, we had our doubts about that marriage ad. We thought it would be better if you'd let *us* help you. Out of our savings. We reckon we could lend you two hundred silver dollars. We don't need anything in writing—you could pledge us your tobacco stock.

SHEN TE You're prepared to lend money to a person like me?

OLD WOMAN It's folks like you that need it. We'd think twice about lending anything to your cousin.

OLD MAN (*coming up*) All settled, my dear?

SHEN TE I wish the gods could have heard what your wife was just saying, Mr. Ma. They're looking for good people who're happy—and helping me makes you happy because you know it was love that got me into difficulties!

The OLD COUPLE *smile knowingly at each other.*

OLD MAN And here's the money, Miss Shen Te.

He hands her an envelope. SHEN TE *takes it. She bows. They bow back. They return to their shop.*

SHEN TE (*holding up her envelope*) Look, Wong, here's six months' rent! Don't you believe in miracles now? And how do you like my new shawl?

WONG For the young fellow I saw you with in the park?

SHEN TE *nods.*

MRS. SHIN Never mind all that. It's time you took a look at his hand!

SHEN TE Have you hurt your hand?

MRS. SHIN That barber smashed it with his hot curling iron. Right in front of our eyes.

SHEN TE (*shocked at herself*) And I never noticed! We must get you to a doctor this minute or who knows what will happen?

UNEMPLOYED MAN It's not a doctor he should see, it's a judge. He can ask for compensation. The barber's filthy rich.

WONG You think I have a chance?

MRS. SHIN (*with relish*) If it's really good and smashed. But is it?

WONG I think so. It's very swollen. Could I get a pension?

MRS. SHIN You'd need a witness.

WONG Well, you all saw it. You could all testify.

He looks round. The UNEMPLOYED MAN, *the* GRANDFATHER, *and the* SISTER-IN-LAW *are all sitting against the wall of the shop eating rice. Their concentration on eating is complete.*

SHEN TE (*to* MRS. SHIN) You saw it yourself.

MRS. SHIN I want nothing to do with the police. It's against my principles.

SHEN TE (*to* SISTER-IN-LAW) What about you?

SISTER-IN-LAW Me? I wasn't looking.

SHEN TE (*to the* GRANDFATHER, *coaxingly*) Grandfather, *you'll* testify, won't you?

SISTER-IN-LAW And a lot of good that will do. He's simple-minded.

SHEN TE (*to the* UNEMPLOYED MAN) You seem to be the only witness left.

UNEMPLOYED MAN My testimony would only hurt him. I've been picked up twice for begging.

SHEN TE

Your brother is assaulted, and you shut your eyes?

He is hit, cries out in pain, and you are silent?

The beast prowls, chooses and seizes his victim, and you say:

"Because we showed no displeasure, he has spared us."

If no one present will be a witness, I will. I'll say *I* saw it.

MRS. SHIN (*solemnly*) The name for that is perjury.

WONG I don't know if I can accept that. Though maybe I'll have to. (*Looking at his hand:*) Is it swollen enough, do you think? The swelling's not going down?

UNEMPLOYED MAN No, no, the swelling's holding up well.

WONG Yes. It's *more* swollen if anything. Maybe my wrist is broken after all. I'd better see a judge at once.

Holding his hand very carefully, and fixing his eyes on it, he runs off. MRS. SHIN *goes quickly into the Barber's shop.*

UNEMPLOYED MAN (*seeing her*) She is getting on the right side of Mr. Shu Fu.

SISTER-IN-LAW You and I can't change the world, Shen Te.

SHEN TE Go away! Go away all of you!

The UNEMPLOYED MAN, *the* SISTER-IN-LAW, *and the* GRANDFATHER *stalk off, eating and sulking.*

To the audience:

They've stopped answering
They stay put
They do as they're told
They don't care
Nothing can make them look up
But the smell of food.

Enter MRS. YANG, YANG SUN'S *mother, out of breath.*

MRS. YANG Miss Shen Te. My son has told me everything. I am Mrs. Yang, Sun's mother. Just think. He's got an offer. Of a job as a pilot. A letter has just come. From the director of the airfield in Peking!

SHEN TE So he can fly again? Isn't that wonderful!

MRS. YANG (*less breathlessly all the time*) They won't give him the job for nothing. They want five hundred silver dollars.

SHEN TE We can't let money stand in his way, Mrs. Yang!

MRS. YANG If only you could help him out!

SHEN TE I have the shop. I can try! (*She embraces* MRS. YANG.) I happen to have two hundred with me now. Take it. (*She gives her the* OLD COUPLE'S *money.*) It was a loan but they said I could repay it with my tobacco stock.

MRS. YANG And they were calling Sun the Dead Pilot of Setzuan! A friend in need!

SHEN TE We must find another three hundred.

MRS. YANG How?

SHEN TE Let me think. (*Slowly:*) I know someone who can help. I didn't want to call on his services again, he's hard and cunning. But a flyer must fly. And I'll make this the last time.

Distant sound of a plane.

MRS. YANG If the man you mentioned can do it. . . . Oh, look, there's the morning mail plane, heading for Peking!

SHEN TE The pilot can see us, let's wave!

They wave. The noise of the engine is louder.

MRS. YANG You know that pilot up there?

SHEN TE Wave, Mrs. Yang! I know the pilot who will be up there. He gave up hope. But he'll do it now. One man to raise himself above the misery, above us all.

To the audience:

Yang Sun, my lover:
Braving the storms
In company with the clouds
Crossing the heavens
And bringing to friends in far-away lands
The friendly mail!

4a

In front of the inner curtain. Enter SHEN TE, *carrying* SHUI TA'S *mask. She sings.*

The Song of Defenselessness

In our country
A useful man needs luck
Only if he finds strong backers
Can he prove himself useful.
The good can't defend themselves and
Even the gods are defenseless.

Oh, why don't the gods have their own ammunition
And launch against badness their own expedition
Enthroning the good and preventing sedition
And bringing the world to a peaceful condition?

Oh, why don't the gods do the buying and selling
Injustice forbidding, starvation dispelling
Give bread to each city and joy to each dwelling?
Oh, why don't the gods do the buying and selling?

She puts on SHUI TA'S *mask and sings in his voice.*

You can only help one of your luckless brothers
By trampling down a dozen others.

Why is it the gods do not feel indignation
And come down in fury to end exploitation
Defeat all defeat and forbid desperation
Refusing to tolerate such toleration?

Why is it?

5

SHEN TE'S *tobacco shop. Behind the counter,* MR. SHUI TA, *reading the paper.* MRS. SHIN *is cleaning up. She talks and he takes no notice.*

MRS. SHIN And when certain rumors get about, what *happens* to a little place like this? It goes to pot. *I* know. So, if you want my advice, Mr. Shui Ta, find out just what has been going on between Miss Shen Te and that Yang Sun from Yellow Street. And remember: a certain interest in Miss Shen Te has been expressed by the barber next door, a man with twelve houses and only one wife, who, for that matter, is likely to drop off at any time. A certain interest has been expressed. He was even enquiring about her means and, if *that* doesn't prove a man is getting serious, what would? (*Still getting no response, she leaves with her bucket.*)

YANG SUN'S VOICE Is that Miss Shen Te's tobacco shop?

MRS. SHIN'S VOICE Yes, it is, but it's Mr. Shui Ta who's here today.

SHUI TA *runs to the mirror with the short, light steps of* SHEN TE, *and is just about to start primping, when he realizes his mistake, and turns away, with a short laugh. Enter* YANG SUN. MRS. SHIN *enters behind him and slips into the back room to eavesdrop.*

YANG SUN I am Yang Sun. (SHUI TA *bows.*) Is Shen Te in?

SHUI TA No.

YANG SUN I guess you know our relationship? (*He is inspecting the stock.*) Quite a place! And I thought she was just talking big. I'll be flying again, all right. (*He takes a cigar, solicits and receives a light from* SHUI TA.) You think we can squeeze the other three hundred out of the tobacco stock?

SHUI TA May I ask if it is your intention to sell at once?

YANG SUN It was decent of her to come out with the two hundred but they aren't much use with the other three hundred still missing.

SHUI TA Shen Te was overhasty promising so much. She might have to sell the shop itself to raise it. Haste, they say, is the wind that blows the house down.

YANG SUN Oh, she isn't a girl to keep a man waiting. For one thing or the other, if you take my meaning.

SHUI TA I take your meaning.

YANG SUN (*leering*) Uh, huh.

SHUI TA Would you explain what the five hundred silver dollars are for?

YANG SUN Want to sound me out? Very well. The director of the Peking airfield is a friend of mine from flying school. I give him five hundred: he gets me the job.

SHUI TA The price is high.

YANG SUN   Not as these things go. He'll have to fire one of the present pilots—for negligence. Only the man he has in mind isn't negligent. Not easy, you understand. You needn't mention that part of it to Shen Te.

SHUI TA (*looking intently at* YANG SUN)   Mr. Yang Sun, you are asking my cousin to give up her possessions, leave her friends, and place her entire fate in your hands. I presume you intend to marry her?

YANG SUN   I'd be prepared to.

Slight pause.

SHUI TA   Those two hundred silver dollars would pay the rent here for six months. If you were Shen Te wouldn't you be tempted to continue in business?

YANG SUN   What? Can you imagine Yang Sun the Flyer behind a counter? (*In an oily voice:*) "A strong cigar or a mild one, worthy sir?" Not in this century!

SHUI TA   My cousin wishes to follow the promptings of her heart, and, from her own point of view, she may even have what is called the right to love. Accordingly, she has commissioned me to help you to this post. There is nothing here that I am not empowered to turn immediately into cash. Mrs. Mi Tzu, the landlady, will advise me about the sale.

Enter MRS. MI TZU.

MRS. MI TZU   Good morning, Mr. Shui Ta, you wish to see me about the rent? As you know it falls due the day after tomorrow.

SHUI TA   Circumstances have changed, Mrs. Mi Tzu: my cousin is getting married. Her future husband here, Mr. Yang Sun, will be taking her to Peking. I am interested in selling the tobacco stock.

MRS. MI TZU   How much are you asking, Mr. Shui Ta?

YANG SUN   Three hundred sil—

SHUI TA   Five hundred silver dollars.

MRS. MI TZU   How much did she pay for it, Mr. Shui Ta?

SHUI TA   A thousand. And very little has been sold.

MRS. MI TZU   She was robbed. But I'll make you a special offer if you'll promise to be out by the day after tomorrow. Three hundred silver dollars.

YANG SUN (*shrugging*)   Take it, man, take it.

SHUI TA   It is not enough.

YANG SUN   Why not? Why not? Certainly, it's enough.

SHUI TA   Five hundred silver dollars.

YANG SUN   But why? We only need three!

SHUI TA (*to* MRS. MI TZU)   Excuse me. (*Takes* YANG SUN *on one side.*) The tobacco stock is pledged to the old couple who gave my cousin the two hundred.

YANG SUN Is it in writing?

SHUI TA: No.

YANG SUN (*to* MRS. MI TZU) Three hundred will do.

MRS. MI TZU Of course, I need an assurance that Miss Shen Te is not in debt.

YANG SUN Mr. Shui Ta?

SHUI TA She is not in debt.

YANG SUN When can you let us have the money?

MRS. MI TZU The day after tomorrow. And remember: I'm doing this because I have a soft spot in my heart for young lovers!

(Exit.)

YANG SUN (*calling after her*) Boxes, jars and sacks—three hundred for the lot and the pain's over! (*To* SHUI TA:) Where else can we raise money by the day after tomorrow?

SHUI TA Nowhere. Haven't you enough for the trip and the first few weeks?

YANG SUN Oh, certainly.

SHUI TA How much, exactly.

YANG SUN Oh, I'll dig it up, even if I have to steal it.

SHUI TA I see.

YANG SUN Well, don't fall off the roof. I'll get to Peking somehow.

SHUI TA Two people can't travel for nothing.

YANG SUN (*not giving* SHUI TA *a chance to answer*) I'm leaving *her* behind. No millstones round *my* neck!

SHUI TA Oh.

YANG SUN Don't look at me like that!

SHUI TA How precisely is my cousin to live?

YANG SUN Oh, you'll think of something.

SHUI TA A small request, Mr. Yang Sun. Leave the two hundred silver dollars here until you can show me two tickets for Peking.

YANG SUN You learn to mind your own business, Mr. Shui Ta.

SHUI TA I'm afraid Miss Shen Te may not wish to sell the shop when she discovers that . . .

YANG SUN You don't know women. She'll want to. Even then.

SHUI TA (*a slight outburst*) She is a human being, sir! And not devoid of common sense!

YANG SUN Shen Te is a woman: she *is* devoid of common sense. I only have to lay my hand on her shoulder, and church bells ring.

SHUI TA (*with difficulty*) Mr. Yang Sun!

YANG SUN Mr. Shui Whatever-it-is!

SHUI TA My cousin is devoted to you . . . because . . .

YANG SUN   Because I have my hands on her breasts. Give me a cigar. (*He takes one for himself, stuffs a few more in his pocket, then changes his mind and takes the whole box.*) Tell her I'll marry her, then bring me the three hundred. Or let her bring it. One or the other. (*Exit.*)

MRS. SHIN (*sticking her head out of the back room*)   Well, he has your cousin under his thumb, and doesn't care if all Yellow Street knows it!

SHUI TA (*crying out*)   I've lost my shop! And he doesn't love me! (*He runs berserk through the room, repeating these lines incoherently. Then stops suddenly, and addresses* MRS. SHIN:) Mrs. Shin, you grew up in the gutter, like me. Are we lacking in hardness? I doubt it. If you steal a penny from me, I'll take you by the throat till you spit it out! You'd do the same to me. The times are bad, this city is hell, but we're like ants, we keep coming, up and up the walls, however smooth! Till bad luck comes. Being in love, for instance. One weakness is enough, and love is the deadliest.

MRS. SHIN (*emerging from the back room*)   You should have a little talk with Mr. Shu Fu the Barber. He's a real gentleman and just the thing for your cousin. (*She runs off.*)

SHUI TA

A caress becomes a stranglehold
A sigh of love turns to a cry of fear
Why are there vultures circling in the air?
A girl is going to meet her lover.

SHUI TA *sits down and* MR. SHU FU *enters with* MRS. SHIN.

SHUI TA   Mr. Shu Fu?

SHU FU   Mr. Shui Ta.

They both bow.

SHUI TA   I am told that you have expressed a certain interest in my cousin Shen Te. Let me set aside all propriety and confess: she is at this moment in grave danger.

SHU FU   Oh, dear!

SHUI TA   She has lost her shop, Mr. Shu Fu.

SHU FU   The charm of Miss Shen Te, Mr. Shui Ta, derives from the goodness, not of her shop, but of her heart. Men call her the Angel of the Slums.

SHUI TA   Yet her goodness has cost her two hundred silver dollars in a single day: we must put a stop to it.

SHU FU   Permit me to differ, Mr. Shui Ta. Let us, rather, open wide the gates to such goodness! Every morning, with pleasure tinged by affection, I watch her charitable ministrations. For they are hungry, and she giveth them to eat! Four of them, to be precise. Why only four? I ask. Why not four hundred? I hear she has been seeking shelter for the homeless. What about my humble cabins behind the cattle run? They are at her disposal. And so forth. And so on. Mr. Shui Ta, do you think Miss Shen Te could be persuaded to listen to certain ideas of mine? Ideas like these?

SHUI TA   Mr. Shu Fu, she would be honored.

Enter WONG *and the* POLICEMAN. MR. SHU FU *turns abruptly away and studies the shelves.*

WONG   Is Miss Shen Te here?

SHUI TA   No.

WONG   I am Wong the Water Seller. You are Mr. Shui Ta?

SHUI TA   I am.

WONG   I am a friend of Shen Te's.

SHUI TA   An intimate friend, I hear.

WONG (*to the* POLICEMAN)   You see? (*To* SHUI TA:) It's because of my hand.

POLICEMAN   He hurt his hand, sir, that's a fact.

SHUI TA (*quickly*)   You need a sling, I see. (*He takes a shawl from the back room, and throws it to* WONG.)

WONG   But that's her new shawl!

SHUI TA   She has no more use for it.

WONG   But she bought it to please someone!

SHUI TA   It happens to be no longer necessary.

WONG (*making the sling*)   She is my only witness.

POLICEMAN   Mr. Shui Ta, your cousin is supposed to have seen the Barber hit the Water Seller with a curling iron.

SHUI TA   I'm afraid my cousin was not present at the time.

WONG   But she was, sir! Just ask her! Isn't she in?

SHUI TA (*gravely*)   Mr. Wong, my cousin has her own troubles. You wouldn't wish her to add to them by committing perjury?

WONG   But it was she that told me to go to the judge!

SHUI TA   Was the judge supposed to heal your hand?

MR. SHU FU *turns quickly around.* SHUI TA *bows to* SHU FU, *and vice versa.*

WONG (*taking the sling off, and putting it back*)   I see how it is.

POLICEMAN   Well, I'll be on my way. (*To* WONG:) And you be careful. If Mr. Shu Fu wasn't a man who tempers justice with mercy, as the saying is, you'd be in jail for libel. Be off with you!

Exit WONG, *followed by* POLICEMAN.

SHUI TA   Profound apologies, Mr. Shu Fu.

SHU FU   Not at all, Mr. Shui Ta. (*Pointing to the shawl:*) The episode is over?

SHUI TA   It may take her time to recover. There are some fresh wounds.

SHU FU We shall be discreet. Delicate. A short vacation could be arranged. . . .

SHUI TA First of course, you and she would have to talk things over.

MR. SHU FU At a small supper in a small, but high-class, restaurant.

SHUI TA I'll go and find her. (*Exit into back room.*)

MRS. SHIN (*sticking her head in again*) Time for congratulations, Mr. Shu Fu?

SHU FU Ah, Mrs. Shin! Please inform Miss Shen Te's guests they may take shelter in the cabins behind the cattle run!

MRS. SHIN *nods, grinning.*

SHU FU (*to the audience*) Well? What do you think of me, ladies and gentlemen? What could a man do more? Could he be less selfish? More farsighted? A small supper in a small but . . . Does that bring rather vulgar and clumsy thoughts into your mind? Ts, ts, ts. Nothing of the sort will occur. She won't even be touched. Not even accidentally while passing the salt. An exchange of ideas only. Over the flowers on the table—white chrysanthemums, by the way (*he writes down a note of this*)—yes, over the white chrysanthemums, two young souls will . . . shall I say "find each other"? We shall NOT exploit the misfortune of others. Understanding? Yes. An offer of assistance? Certainly. But quietly. Almost inaudibly. Perhaps with single glance. A glance that could also—mean more.

MRS. SHIN (*coming forward*) Everything under control, Mr. Shu Fu?

SHU FU Oh, Mrs. Shin, what do you know about this worthless rascal Yang Sun?

MRS. SHIN Why, he's the most worthless rascal . . .

SHU FU Is he really? You're sure? (*As she opens her mouth:*) From now on, he doesn't exist! Can't be found anywhere!

Enter YANG SUN.

YANG SUN What's been going on here?

MRS. SHIN Shall I call Mr. Shui Ta, Mr. Shu Fu? He wouldn't want strangers in here!

SHU FU Mr. Shui Ta is in conference with Miss Shen Te. Not to be disturbed!

YANG SUN Shen Te here? I didn't see her come in. What kind of conference?

SHU FU (*not letting him enter the back room*) Patience, dear sir! And if by chance I have an inkling who you are, pray take note that Miss Shen Te and I are about to announce our engagement.

YANG SUN What?

MRS. SHIN You didn't expect that, did you?

YANG SUN *is trying to push past the barber into the back room when* SHEN TE *comes out.*

SHU FU My dear Shen Te, ten thousand apologies! Perhaps you . . .

YANG SUN What is it, Shen Te? Have you gone crazy?

SHEN TE (*breathless*) My cousin and Mr. Shu Fu have come to an understanding. They wish me to hear Mr. Shu Fu's plans for helping the poor.

YANG SUN Your cousin wants to part us.

SHEN TE Yes.

YANG SUN And you've agreed to it?

SHEN TE Yes.

YANG SUN They told you I was bad. (SHEN TE *is silent.*) And suppose I am. Does that make me need you less? I'm low, Shen Te, I have no money, I don't do the right thing but at least I put up a fight! (*He is near her now, and speaks in an undertone.*) Have you no eyes? Look at him. Have you forgotten already?

SHEN TE No.

YANG SUN How it was raining?

SHEN TE No.

YANG SUN How you cut me down from the willow tree? Bought me water? Promised me money to fly with?

SHEN TE (*shakily*) Yang Sun, what do you want?

YANG SUN I want you to come with me.

SHEN TE (*in a small voice*) Forgive me, Mr. Shu Fu, I want to go with Mr. Yang Sun.

YANG SUN We're lovers you know. Give me the key to the shop. (SHEN TE *takes the key from around her neck.* YANG SUN *puts it on the counter. To* MRS. SHIN:) Leave it under the mat when you're through. Let's go, Shen Te.

SHU FU But this is rape! Mr. Shui Ta!!

YANG SUN (*to* SHEN TE) Tell him not to shout.

SHEN TE Please don't shout for my cousin, Mr. Shu Fu. He doesn't agree with me, I know, but he's wrong.

To the audience:

I want to go with the man I love.
I don't want to count the cost
I don't want to consider if it's wise
I don't want to know if he loves me
I want to go with the man I love.

YANG SUN That's the spirit.

And the couple leave.

5a

In front of the inner curtain. SHEN TE *in her wedding clothes, on the way to her wedding.*

SHEN TE Something terrible has happened. As I left the shop with Yang Sun, I found the old carpet dealer's wife waiting on the street, trembling all over. She told me her husband had taken to his bed— sick with all the worry and excitement over the two hundred silver dollars they lent me. She said it would be best if I gave it back now. Of course, I had to say I would. She said she couldn't quite trust my cousin Shui Ta or even my fiancé Yang Sun. There were tears in her eyes. With my emotions in an uproar, I threw myself into Yang Sun's arms, I couldn't resist him. The things he'd said to Shui Ta had taught Shen Te nothing. Sinking into his arms, I said to myself:

> To let no one perish, not even oneself
> To fill everyone with happiness, even oneself
> Is so good

How could I have forgotten those two old people? Yang Sun swept me away like a small hurricane. But he's not a bad man, and he loves me. He'd rather work in the cement factory than owe his flying to a crime. Though, of course, flying *is* a great passion with Sun. Now, on the way to my wedding, I waver between fear and joy.

6

The "private dining room" on the upper floor of a cheap restaurant in a poor section of town. With SHEN TE: *the* GRANDFATHER, *the* SISTER-IN-LAW, *the* NIECE, MRS. SHIN, *the* UNEMPLOYED MAN. *In a corner, alone, a* PRIEST. *A* WAITER *pouring wine. Downstage,* YANG SUN *talking to his* MOTHER. *He wears a dinner jacket.*

YANG SUN Bad news, Mamma. She came right out and told me she can't sell the shop for me. Some idiot is bringing a claim because he lent her the two hundred she gave you.

MRS. YANG What did you say? Of course, you can't marry her now.

YANG SUN It's no use saying anything to *her.* I've sent for her cousin, Mr. Shui Ta. He said there was nothing in writing.

MRS. YANG Good idea. I'll go out and look for him. Keep an eye on things.

Exit MRS. YANG. SHEN TE *has been pouring wine.*

SHEN TE (*to the audience, pitcher in hand*) I wasn't mistaken in him. He's bearing up well. Though it must have been an awful blow—giving up flying. I do love him so. (*Calling across the room to him:*) Sun, you haven't drunk a toast with the bride!

YANG SUN　What do we drink to?

SHEN TE　Why, to the future!

YANG SUN　When the bridegroom's dinner jacket won't be a hired one!

SHEN TE　But when the bride's dress will still get rained on sometimes!

YANG SUN　To everything we ever wished for!

SHEN TE　May all our dreams come true!

They drink.

YANG SUN (*with loud conviviality*)　And now, friends, before the wedding gets under way, I have to ask the bride a few questions. I've no idea what kind of a wife she'll make, and it worries me. (*Wheeling on* SHEN TE:) For example. Can you make five cups of tea with three tea leaves?

SHEN TE　No.

YANG SUN　So I won't be getting very much tea. Can you sleep on a straw mattress the size of that book? (*He points to the large volume the* PRIEST *is reading.*)

SHEN TE　The two of us?

YANG SUN　The one of you.

SHEN TE　In that case, no.

YANG SUN　What a wife! I'm shocked!

While the audience is laughing, his MOTHER *returns. With a shrug of her shoulders, she tells* SUN *the expected guest hasn't arrived. The* PRIEST *shuts the book with a bang, and makes for the door.*

MRS. YANG　Where are *you* off to? It's only a matter of minutes.

PRIEST (*watch in hand*)　Time goes on, Mrs. Yang, and I've another wedding to attend to. Also a funeral.

MRS. YANG (*irately*)　D'you think we planned it this way? I was hoping to manage with one pitcher of wine, and we've run through two already. (*Points to empty pitcher. Loudly:*) My dear Shen Te, I don't know where your cousin can be keeping himself!

SHEN TE　My cousin?!

MRS. YANG　Certainly. I'm old-fashioned enough to think such a close relative should attend the wedding.

SHEN TE　Oh, Sun, is it the three hundred silver dollars?

YANG SUN (*not looking her in the eye*)　Are you deaf? Mother says she's old-fashioned. And I say I'm considerate. We'll wait another fifteen minutes.

HUSBAND　Another fifteen minutes.

MRS. YANG (*addressing the company*)　Now you all know, don't you, that my son is getting a job as a mail pilot?

SISTER-IN-LAW　In Peking, too, isn't it?

MRS. YANG　In Peking, too! The two of us are moving to Peking!

SHEN TE　Sun, tell your mother Peking is out of the question now.

YANG SUN   Your cousin'll tell her. If he agrees. I don't agree.

SHEN TE (*amazed, and dismayed*)   Sun!

YANG SUN   I hate this godforsaken Setzuan. What people! Know what they look like when I half close my eyes? Horses! Whinnying, fretting, stamping, screwing their necks up! (*Loudly:*) And what is it the thunder says? They are su-per-flu-ous! (*He hammers out the syllables.*) They've run their last race! They can go trample themselves to death! (*Pause.*) I've got to get out of here.

SHEN TE   But I've promised the money to the old couple.

YANG SUN   And since you always do the wrong thing, it's lucky your cousin's coming. Have another drink.

SHEN TE (*quietly*)   My cousin can't be coming.

YANG SUN   How d'you mean?

SHEN TE   My cousin can't be where I am.

YANG SUN   Quite a conundrum!

SHEN TE (*desperately*)   Sun, I'm the one that loves you. Not my cousin. He was thinking of the job in Peking when he promised you the old couple's money—

YANG SUN   Right. And that's why he's bringing the three hundred silver dollars. Here—to my wedding.

SHEN TE   He is not bringing the three hundred silver dollars.

YANG SUN   Huh? What makes you think that?

SHEN TE (*looking into his eyes*)   He says you only bought one ticket to Peking.

Short pause.

YANG SUN   That was yesterday. (*He pulls two tickets part way out of his inside pocket, making her look under his coat.*) Two tickets. I don't want Mother to know. She'll get left behind. I sold her furniture to buy these tickets, so you see . . .

SHEN TE   But what's to become of the old couple?

YANG SUN   What's to become of me? Have another drink. Or do you believe in moderation? If I drink, I fly again. And if you drink, you may learn to understand me.

SHEN TE   You want to fly. But I can't help you.

YANG SUN   "Here a plane, my darling—but it's only got one wing!"

The WAITER enters.

WAITER   Mrs. Yang!

MRS. YANG   Yes?

WAITER   Another pitcher of wine, ma'am?

MRS. YANG   We have enough, thanks. Drinking makes me sweat.

WAITER   Would you mind paying, ma'am?

MRS. YANG (*to everyone*)   Just be patient a few moments longer, everyone, Mr. Shui Ta is on his way over! (*To the* WAITER:) Don't be a spoilsport.

WAITER   I can't let you leave till you've paid your bill, ma'am.

MRS. YANG   But they know me here!

WAITER   That's just it.

PRIEST (*ponderously getting up*)   I humbly take my leave. (*And he does.*)

MRS. YANG (*to the others, desperately*)   Stay where you are, everybody! The priest says he'll be back in two minutes!

YANG SUN   It's no good, Mamma. Ladies and gentlemen, Mr. Shui Ta still hasn't arrived and the priest has gone home. We won't detain you any longer.

They are leaving now.

GRANDFATHER (*in the doorway, having forgotten to put his glass down*)   To the bride! (*He drinks, puts down the glass, and follows the others.*)

Pause.

SHEN TE   Shall I go too?

YANG SUN   You? Aren't you the bride? Isn't this your wedding? (*He drags her across the room, tearing her wedding dress.*) If we can wait, you can wait. Mother calls me her falcon. She wants to see me in the clouds. But I think it may be St. Nevercome's Day before she'll go to the door and see my plane thunder by. (*Pause. He pretends the guests are still present.*) Why such a lull in the conversation, ladies and gentlemen? Don't you like it here? The ceremony is only slightly postponed—because an important guest is expected at any moment. Also because the bride doesn't know what love is. While we're waiting, the bridegroom will sing a little song. (*He does so:*)

The Song of St. Nevercome's Day

On a certain day, as is generally known,
   One and all will be shouting: Hooray, hooray!
For the beggar maid's son has a solid-gold throne
   And the day is St. Nevercome's Day
On St. Nevercome's, Nevercome's, Nevercome's Day
   He'll sit on his solid-gold throne

Oh, hooray, hooray! That day goodness will pay!
   That day badness will cost you your head!
And merit and money will smile and be funny
   While exchanging salt and bread
On St. Nevercome's, Nevercome's, Nevercome's Day
   While exchanging salt and bread

And the grass, oh, the grass will look down at the sky
And the pebbles will roll up the stream
And all men will be good without batting an eye
They will make of our earth a dream
On St. Nevercome's, Nevercome's, Nevercome's Day
They will make of our earth a dream

And as for me, that's the day I shall be
A flyer and one of the best
Unemployed man, you will have work to do
Washerwoman, you'll get your rest
On St. Nevercome's, Nevercome's, Nevercome's Day
Washerwoman, you'll get your rest

MRS. YANG   It looks like he's not coming.

The three of them sit looking at the door.

6a

WONG'S *den. The sewer pipe is again transparent and again the* GODS *appear to* WONG *in a dream.*

WONG   I'm so glad you've come, illustrious ones. It's Shen Te. She's in great trouble from following the rule about loving thy neighbor. Perhaps she's *too* good for this world!

FIRST GOD   Nonsense! You are eaten up by lice and doubts!

WONG   Forgive me, illustrious one, I only meant you might deign to intervene.

FIRST GOD   Out of the question! My colleague here intervened in some squabble or other only yesterday. (*He points to the* THIRD GOD *who has a black eye.*) The results are before us!

WONG   She had to call on her cousin again. But not even he could help. I'm afraid the shop is done for.

THIRD GOD (*a little concerned*)   Perhaps we should help after all?

FIRST GOD   The gods help those that help themselves.

WONG   What is we *can't* help ourselves, illustrious ones?

Slight pause.

SECOND GOD   Try, anyway! Suffering ennobles!

FIRST GOD   Our faith in Shen Te is unshaken!

THIRD GOD   We certainly haven't found any *other* good people. You can see where we spent our nights from the straw on our clothes.

WONG   You might help her find her way by—

FIRST GOD   The good man finds his own way here below!

SECOND GOD   The good woman too.

FIRST GOD   The heavier the burden, the greater her strength!

THIRD GOD   We're only onlookers, you know.

FIRST GOD   And everything will be all right in the end, O ye of little faith!

They are gradually disappearing through these last lines.

7

The yard behind SHEN TE'S *shop. A few articles of furniture on a cart.* SHEN TE *and* MRS. SHIN *are taking the washing off the line.*

MRS. SHIN   If you ask me, you should fight tooth and nail to keep the shop.

SHEN TE   How can I? I have to sell the tobacco to pay back the two hundred silver dollars today.

MRS. SHIN   No husband, no tobacco, no house and home! What are you going to live on?

SHEN TE   I can work. I can sort tobacco.

MRS. SHIN   Hey, look, Mr. Shui Ta's trousers! He must have left here stark naked!

SHEN TE   Oh, he may have another pair, Mrs. Shin.

MRS. SHIN   But if he's gone for good as you say, why has he left his pants behind?

SHEN TE   Maybe he's thrown them away.

MRS. SHIN   Can I take them?

SHEN TE   Oh, no.

Enter MR. SHU FU, *running.*

SHU FU   Not a word! Total silence! I know all. You have sacrificed your own love and happiness so as not to hurt a dear old couple who had put their trust in you! Not in vain does this district—for all its malevolent tongues—call you the Angel of the Slums! That young man couldn't rise to your level, so you left him. And now, when I see you closing up the little shop, that veritable haven of rest for the multitude, well, I cannot, I cannot let it pass. Morning after morning I have stood watching in the doorway not unmoved—while you graciously handed out rice to the wretched. Is that never to happen again? Is the good woman of Setzuan to disappear? If only you would allow *me* to assist you! Now don't say anything! No assurances, no exclamations of gratitude! (*He has taken out his check book.*) Here! A blank check. (*He places it on the cart.*) Just my signature. Fill it out as you wish. Any sum in the world. I herewith retire from the scene, quietly, unobtrusively, making no claims, on tiptoe, full of veneration, absolutely selflessly . . . (*He has gone.*)

MRS. SHIN Well! You're saved. There's always some idiot of a man. . . . Now hurry! Put down a thousand silver dollars and let me fly to the bank before he comes to his senses.

SHEN TE I can pay you for the washing without any check.

MRS. SHIN What? You're not going to cash it just because you might have to marry him? Are you crazy? Men like him *want* to be led by the nose! Are you still thinking of that flyer? All Yellow Street knows how he treated you!

SHEN TE

When I heard his cunning laugh, I was afraid
But when I saw the holes in his shoes, I loved him dearly.

MRS. SHIN Defending that good-for-nothing after all that's happened!

SHEN TE (*staggering as she holds some of the washing*) Oh!

MRS. SHIN (*taking the washing from her, dryly*) So you feel dizzy when you stretch and bend? There couldn't be a little visitor on the way? If that's it, you can forget Mr. Shu Fu's blank check: it wasn't meant for a christening present!

She goes to the back with a basket. SHEN TE'S *eyes follow* MRS. SHIN *for a moment. Then she looks down at her own body, feels her stomach, and a great joy comes into her eyes.*

SHEN TE O joy! A new human being is on the way. The world awaits him. In the cities the people say: he's got to be reckoned with, this new human being! (*She imagines a little boy to be present, and introduces him to the audience.*) This is my son, the well-known flyer!
Say: Welcome
To the conqueror of unknown mountains and unreachable regions
Who brings us our mail across the impassable deserts!

She leads him up and down by the hand.

Take a look at the world, my son. That's a tree. Tree, yes. Say: "Hello, tree!" And bow. Like this. (*She bows.*) Now you know each other. And, look, here comes the Water Seller. He's a friend, give him your hand. A cup of fresh water for my little son, please. Yes, it *is* a warm day. (*Handing the cup.*) Oh dear, a policeman, we'll have to make a circle round *him*. Perhaps we can pick a few cherries over there in the rich Mr. Pung's garden. But we mustn't be seen. You want cherries? Just like children with fathers. No, no, you can't go straight at them like that. Don't pull. We must learn to be reasonable. Well, have it your own way. (*She has let him make for the cherries.*) Can you reach? Where to put them? Your mouth is the best place. (*She tries one herself.*) Mmm,

they're good. But the policeman, we must run! (*They run.*) Yes, back to the street. Calm now, so no one will notice us. (*Walking the street with her child, she sings:*)
Once a plum—'twas in Japan—
Made a conquest of a man
But the man's turn soon did come
For he gobbled up the plum

Enter WONG, *with a* CHILD *by the hand. He coughs.*

SHEN TE   Wong!

WONG   It's about the Carpenter, Shen Te. He's lost his shop, and he's been drinking. His children are on the streets. This is one. Can you help?

SHEN TE (*to the* CHILD)   Come here, little man. (*Takes him down to the footlights. To the audience:*)
You there! A man is asking you for shelter!
A man of tomorrow says: what about today?
His friend the conqueror, whom you know,
Is his advocate!
(*To* WONG:) He can live in Mr. Shu Fu's cabins. I may have to go there myself. I'm going to have a baby. That's a secret—don't tell Yang Sun—we'd only be in his way. Can you find the Carpenter for me?

WONG   I knew you'd think of something. (*To the* CHILD:) Goodbye, son, I'm going for your father.

SHEN TE   What about your hand, Wong? I wanted to help, but my cousin . . .

WONG   Oh, I can get along with one hand, don't worry. (*He shows how he can handle his pole with his left hand alone.*)

SHEN TE   But your right hand! Look, take this cart, sell everything that's on it, and go to the doctor with the money . . .

WONG   She's still good. But first I'll bring the Carpenter. I'll pick up the cart when I get back. (*Exit* WONG.)

SHEN TE (*To the* CHILD)   Sit down over here, son, till your father comes.

The CHILD *sits crosslegged on the ground. Enter the* HUSBAND *and* WIFE, *each dragging a large, full sack.*

WIFE (*furtively*)   You're alone, Shen Te, dear?

SHEN TE *nods.*
The WIFE *beckons to the* NEPHEW *off stage. He comes on with another sack.*

WIFE   Your cousin's away? (SHEN TE *nods.*) He's not coming back?

SHEN TE   No. I'm giving up the shop.

WIFE   That's why we're here. We want to know if we can leave these things in your new home. Will you do us this favor?

SHEN TE Why, yes, I'd be glad to.

HUSBAND (*cryptically*) And if anyone asks about them, say they're yours.

SHEN TE Would anyone ask?

WIFE (*with a glance back at her husband*) Oh, someone might. The police, for instance. They don't seem to like us. Where can we put it?

SHEN TE Well, I'd rather not get in any more trouble . . .

WIFE Listen to her! The good woman of Setzuan!

SHEN TE *is silent.*

HUSBAND There's enough tobacco in those sacks to give us a new start in life. We could have our own tobacco factory!

SHEN TE (*slowly*) You'll have to put them in the back room.

The sacks are taken offstage, while the CHILD *is left alone. Shyly glancing about him, he goes to the garbage can, starts playing with the contents, and eating some of the scraps. The others return.*

WIFE We're counting on you, Shen Te!

SHEN TE Yes. (*She sees the* CHILD *and is shocked.*)

HUSBAND We'll see you in Mr. Shu Fu's cabins.

NEPHEW The day after tomorrow.

SHEN TE Yes. Now, go. Go! I'm not feeling well.

Exeunt all three, virtually pushed off.

He is eating the refuse in the garbage can!
Only look at his little grey mouth!

Pause. Music.

As this is the world *my* son will enter
I will study to defend him.
To be good to you, my son,
I shall be a tigress to all others
If I have to.
And I shall have to.

She starts to go.

One more time, then. I hope really the last.

Exit SHEN TE, *taking* SHUI TA's *trousers.* MRS. SHIN *enters and watches her with marked interest. Enter the* SISTER-IN-LAW *and the* GRANDFATHER.

SISTER-IN-LAW So it's true, the shop has closed down. And the furniture's in the back yard. It's the end of the road!

MRS. SHIN (*pompously*) The fruit of high living, selfishness, and sensuality! Down the primrose path to Mr. Shu Fu's cabins—with you!

SISTER-IN-LAW   Cabins? Rat holes! He gave them to us because his soap supplies only went moldy there!

Enter the UNEMPLOYED MAN.

UNEMPLOYED MAN   Shen Te is moving?
SISTER-IN-LAW   Yes. She was sneaking away.
MRS. SHIN   She's ashamed of herself, and no wonder!
UNEMPLOYED MAN   Tell her to call Mr. Shui Ta or she's done for this time!
SISTER-IN-LAW   Tell her to call Mr. Shui Ta or *we're* done for this time!

Enter WONG *and the* CARPENTER, *the latter with a* CHILD *on each hand.*

CARPENTER   So we'll have a roof over our heads for a change!
MRS. SHIN   Roof? Whose roof?
CARPENTER   Mr. Shu Fu's cabins. And we have little Feng to thank for it. (*Feng, we find, is the name of the child already there; his father now takes him. To the other two:*) Bow to your little brother, you two!

The CARPENTER *and the* TWO NEW ARRIVALS *bow to* FENG. *Enter* SHUI TA.

UNEMPLOYED MAN   Sst! Mr. Shui Ta!

Pause.

SHUI TA   And what is this crowd here for, may I ask?
WONG   How do you do, Mr. Shui Ta. This is the Carpenter. Miss Shen Te promised him space in Mr. Shu Fu's cabins.
SHUI TA   That will not be possible.
CARPENTER   We can't go there after all?
SHUI TA   All the space is needed for other purposes.
SISTER-IN-LAW   You mean we have to get out? But we've got nowhere to go.
SHUI TA   Miss Shen Te finds it possible to provide employment. If the proposition interests you, you may stay in the cabins.
SISTER-IN-LAW (*with distaste*)   You mean *work?* Work for Miss Shen Te?
SHUI TA   Making tobacco, yes. There are three bales here already. Would you like to get them?
SISTER-IN-LAW (*trying to bluster*)   We have our own tobacco! We were in the tobacco business before you were born!
SHUI TA (*to the* CARPENTER *and the* UNEMPLOYED MAN)   You *don't* have your own tobacco. What about you?

The CARPENTER *and the* UNEMPLOYED MAN *get the point, and go for the sacks. Enter* MRS. MI TZU.

MRS. MI TZU   Mr. Shui Ta? I've brought you your three hundred silver dollars.
SHUI TA   I'll sign your lease instead. I've decided not to sell.

MRS. MI TZU What? You don't need the money for that flyer?

SHUI TA No.

MRS. MI TZU And you can pay six months' rent?

SHUI TA (*takes the Barber's blank check from the cart and fills it out*) Here is a check for ten thousand silver dollars. On Mr. Shu Fu's account. Look! (*He shows her the signature on the check.*) Your six months' rent will be in your hands by seven this evening. And now, if you'll excuse me.

MRS. MI TZU So it's Mr. Shu Fu now. The flyer has been given his walking papers. These modern girls! In my day they'd have said she was flighty. That poor, deserted Mr. Yang Sun!

Exit MRS. MI TZU. *The* CARPENTER *and the* UNEMPLOYED MAN *drag the three sacks back on the stage.*

CARPENTER (*to* SHUI TA) I don't know why I'm doing this for you.

SHUI TA Perhaps your children want to eat, Mr. Carpenter.

SISTER-IN-LAW (*catching sight of the sacks*) Was my brother-in-law here?

MRS. SHIN Yes, he was.

SISTER-IN-LAW I thought as much. I know those sacks! That's our tobacco!

SHUI TA Really? I thought it came from my back room! Shall we consult the police on the point?

SISTER-IN-LAW (*defeated*) No.

SHUI TA Perhaps you will show me the way to Mr. Shu Fu's cabins?

Taking FENG *by the hand,* SHUI TA *goes off, followed by the* CARPENTER *and his* TWO OLDER CHILDREN, *the* SISTER-IN-LAW, *the* GRANDFATHER, *and the* UNEMPLOYED MAN. *Each of the last three drags a sack.*
Enter OLD MAN *and* OLD WOMAN.

MRS. SHIN A pair of pants—missing from the clothes line one minute—and next minute on the honorable backside of Mr. Shui Ta.

OLD WOMAN We thought Miss Shen Te was here.

MRS. SHIN (*preoccupied*) Well, she's not.

OLD MAN There was something she was going to give us.

WONG She was going to help me too. (*Looking at his hand:*) It'll be too late soon. But she'll be back. This cousin has never stayed long.

MRS. SHIN (*approaching a conclusion*) No, he hasn't, has he?

7a

The Sewer Pipe: WONG *asleep. In his dream, he tells the* GODS *his fears. The* GODS *seem tired from all their travels. They stop for a moment and look over their shoulders at the Water Seller.*

WONG Illustrious ones. I've been having a bad dream. Our beloved Shen Te was in great distress in the rushes down by the river—the spot where the bodies of suicides are washed up. She kept staggering and holding her head down as if she was carrying something and it was dragging her down into the mud. When I called out to her, she said she had to take your Book of Rules to the other side, and not get it wet, or the ink would all come off. You had talked to her about the virtues, you know, the time she gave you shelter in Setzuan.

THIRD GOD   Well, but what do you suggest, my dear Wong?

WONG   Maybe a little relaxation of the rules, Benevolent One, in view of the bad times.

THIRD GOD   As for instance?

WONG   Well, um, good-will, for instance, might do instead of love?

THIRD GOD   I'm afraid that would create new problems.

WONG   Or, instead of justice, good sportsmanship?

THIRD GOD   That would only mean more work.

WONG   Instead of honor, outward propriety?

THIRD GOD   Still more work! No, no! The rules will have to stand, my dear Wong!

Wearily shaking their heads, all three journey on.

8

SHUI TA'S *tobacco factory in* SHU FU'S *cabins. Huddled together behind bars, several families, mostly women and children. Among these people the* SISTER-IN-LAW, *the* GRANDFATHER, *the* CARPENTER *and his* THREE CHILDREN. *Enter* MRS. YANG *followed by* YANG SUN.

MRS. YANG (*to the audience*)   There's something I just *have* to tell you: strength and wisdom are wonderful things. The strong and wise Mr. Shui Ta has transformed my son from a dissipated good-for-nothing into a model citizen. As you may have heard, Mr. Shui Ta opened a small tobacco factory near the cattle runs. It flourished. Three months ago—I shall never forget it—I asked for an appointment, and Mr. Shui Ta agreed to see us—me and my son. I can see him now as he came through the door to meet us. . . .

Enter SHUI TA, *from a door.*

SHUI TA   What can I do for you, Mrs. Yang?

MRS. YANG   This morning the police came to the house. We find you've brought an action for breach of promise of marriage. In the name of Shen Te. You also claim that Sun came by two hundred silver dollars by improper means.

SHUI TA   That is correct.

MRS. YANG   Mr. Shui Ta, the money's all gone. When the Peking job didn't materialize, he ran through it all in three days. I know he's a good-for-nothing. He sold my furniture. He was moving to Peking without me. Miss Shen Te thought highly of him at one time.

SHUI TA What do *you* say, Mr. Yang Sun?

YANG SUN The money's gone.

SHUI TA (*to* MRS. YANG) Mrs. Yang, in consideration of my cousin's incomprehensible weakness for your son, I am prepared to give him another chance. He can have a job—here. The two hundred silver dollars will be taken out of his wages.

YANG SUN So it's the factory or jail?

SHUI TA Take your choice.

YANG SUN May I speak with Shen Te?

SHUI TA You may not.

Pause.

YANG SUN (*sullenly*) Show me where to go.

MRS. YANG Mr. Shui Ta, you are kindness itself: the gods will reward you! (*To* YANG SUN:) And honest work will make a man of you, my boy. (YANG SUN *follows* SHUI TA *into the factory*. MRS. YANG *comes down again to the footlights*.) Actually, honest work didn't agree with him—at first. And he got no opportunity to distinguish himself till—in the third week—when the wages were being paid . . .

SHUI TA *has a bag of money. Standing next to his foreman—the former* UNEMPLOYED MAN—*he counts out the wages. It is* YANG SUN'S *turn.*

UNEMPLOYED MAN (*reading*) Carpenter, six silver dollars. Yang Sun, six silver dollars.

YANG SUN (*quietly*) Excuse me, sir. I don't think it can be more than five. May I see? (*He takes the foreman's list.*) It says six working days. But that's a mistake, sir. I took a day off for court business. And I won't take what I haven't earned, however miserable the pay is!

UNEMPLOYED MAN Yang Sun. Five silver dollars. (*To* SHUI TA:) A rare case, Mr. Shui Ta!

SHUI TA How is it the book says six when it should say five?

UNEMPLOYED MAN I must've made a mistake, Mr. Shui Ta. (*With a look at* YANG SUN:) It won't happen again.

SHUI TA (*taking* YANG SUN *aside*) You don't hold back, do you? You give your all to the firm. You're even honest. Do the foreman's mistakes always favor the workers?

YANG SUN He does have . . . friends.

SHUI TA Thank you. May I offer you any little recompense?

YANG SUN Give me a trial period of one week, and I'll prove my intelligence is worth more to you than my strength.

MRS. YANG (*still down at the footlights*) Fighting words, fighting words! That evening, I said to Sun: "If you're a flyer, then fly, my falcon!

Rise in the world!" And he got to be foreman. Yes, in Mr. Shui Ta's tobacco factory, he worked real miracles.

We see YANG SUN *with his legs apart standing behind the* WORKERS *who are handing along a basket of raw tobacco above their heads.*

YANG SUN Faster! Faster! You, there, d'you think you can just stand around, now you're not foreman any more? It'll be your job to lead us in song. Sing!

UNEMPLOYED MAN *starts singing. The others join in the refrain.*

Song of the Eighth Elephant

Chang had seven elephants—all much the same—
But then there was Little Brother
The seven, they were wild, Little Brother, he was tame
And to guard them Chang chose Little Brother
Run faster!
Mr. Chang has a forest park
Which must be cleared before tonight
And already it's growing dark!

When the seven elephants cleared that forest park
Mr. Chang rode high on Little Brother
While the seven toiled and moiled till dark
On his big behind sat Little Brother
Dig faster!
Mr. Chang has a forest park
Which must be cleared before tonight
And already it's growing dark!

And the seven elephants worked many an hour
Till none of them could work another
Old Chang, he looked sour, on the seven he did glower
But gave a pound of rice to Little Brother
What was that?
Mr. Chang has a forest park
Which must be cleared before tonight
And already it's growing dark!

And the seven elephants hadn't any tusks
The one that had the tusks was Little Brother
Seven are no match for one, if the one has a gun!
How old Chang did laugh at Little Brother!

Keep on digging!
Mr. Chang has a forest park
Which must be cleared before tonight
And already it's growing dark!

Smoking a cigar, SHUI TA *strolls by.* YANG SUN, *laughing, has joined in the refrain of the third stanza and speeded up the tempo of the last stanza by clapping his hands.*

MRS. YANG   And that's why I say: strength and wisdom are wonderful things. It took the strong and wise Mr. Shui Ta to bring out the best in Yang Sun. A real superior man is like a bell. If you ring it, it rings, and if you don't, it don't, as the saying is.

9

SHEN TE'S *shop, now an office with club chairs and fine carpets. It is raining.* SHUI TA, *now fat, is just dismissing the* OLD MAN *and* OLD WOMAN. MRS. SHIN, *in obviously new clothes, looks on, smirking.*

SHUI TA   No! I can NOT tell you when we expect her back.
OLD WOMAN   The two hundred silver dollars came today. In an envelope. There was no letter, but it must be from Shen Te. We want to write and thank her. May we have her address?
SHUI TA   I'm afraid I haven't got it.
OLD MAN (*pulling* OLD WOMAN'S *sleeve*)   Let's be going.
OLD WOMAN   She's got to come back some time!

They move off, uncertainly, worried. SHUI TA *bows.*

MRS. SHIN   They lost the carpet shop because they couldn't pay their taxes. The money arrived too late.
SHUI TA   They could have come to me.
MRS. SHIN   People don't like coming to you.
SHUI TA (*sits suddenly, one hand to his head*)   I'm dizzy.
MRS. SHIN   After all, you *are* in your seventh month. But old Mrs. Shin will be there in your hour of trial! (*She cackles feebly.*)
SHUI TA (*in a stifled voice*)   Can I count on that?
MRS. SHIN   We all have our price, and mine won't be too high for the great Mr. Shui Ta! (*She opens* SHUI TA'S *collar.*)
SHUI TA   It's for the child's sake. All of this.
MRS. SHIN   "All for the child," of course.
SHUI TA   I'm so fat. People must notice.
MRS. SHIN   Oh no, they think it's 'cause you're rich.
SHUI TA (*more feelingly*)   What will happen to the child?
MRS. SHIN   You ask that nine times a day. Why, it'll have the best that money can buy!

SHUI TA   He must never see Shui Ta.

MRS. SHIN   Oh, no. Always Shen Te.

SHUI TA   What about the neighbors? There are rumors, aren't there?

MRS. SHIN   As long as Mr. Shu Fu doesn't find out, there's nothing to worry about. Drink this.

Enter YANG SUN *in a smart business suit, and carrying a businessman's briefcase.* SHUI TA *is more or less in* MRS. SHIN'S *arms.*

YANG SUN (*surprised*)   I guess I'm in the way.

SHUI TA (*ignoring this, rises with an effort*)   Till tomorrow, Mrs. Shin.

MRS. SHIN *leaves with a smile, putting her new gloves on.*

YANG SUN   Gloves now! She couldn't be fleecing you? And since when did *you* have a private life? (*Taking a paper from the briefcase:*) You haven't been at your best lately, and things are getting out of hand. The police want to close us down. They say that at the most they can only permit twice the lawful number of workers.

SHUI TA (*evasively*)   The cabins are quite good enough.

YANG SUN   For the workers maybe, not for the tobacco. They're too damp. We must take over some of Mrs. Mi Tzu's buildings.

SHUI TA   Her price is double what I can pay.

YANG SUN   Not unconditionally. If she has me to stroke her knees she'll come down.

SHUI TA   I'll never agree to that.

YANG SUN   What's wrong? Is it the rain? You get so irritable whenever it rains.

SHUI TA   Never! I will never . . .

YANG SUN   Mrs. Mi Tzu'll be here in five minutes. *You* fix it. And Shu Fu will be with her. . . . What's all that noise?

During the above dialogue, WONG *is heard offstage, calling: "The good Shen Te, where is she? Which of you has seen Shen Te, good people? Where is Shen Te?" A knock. Enter* WONG.

WONG   Mr. Shui Ta, I've come to ask when Miss Shen Te will be back, it's six months now. . . . There are rumors. People say something's happened to her.

SHUI TA   I'm busy. Come back next week.

WONG (*excited*)   In the morning there was always rice on her doorstep— for the needy. It's been there again lately!

SHUI TA   And what do people conclude from this?

WONG   That Shen Te is still in Setzuan! She's been . . . (*He breaks off.*)

SHUI TA   She's been what? Mr. Wong, if you're Shen Te's friend, talk a little less about her, that's my advice to you.

WONG   I don't want your advice! Before she disappeared, Miss Shen Te told me something very important—she's pregnant!

YANG SUN   What? What was that?

SHUI TA (*quickly*)   The man is lying.

WONG   A good woman isn't so easily forgotten, Mr. Shui Ta.

He leaves. SHUI TA *goes quickly into the back room.*

YANG SUN (*to the audience*)   Shen Te pregnant? So that's why. Her cousin sent her away, so I wouldn't get wind of it. I have a son, a Yang appears on the scene, and what happens? Mother and child vanish into thin air! That scoundrel, that unspeakable . . . (*The sound of sobbing is heard from the back room.*) What was that? Someone sobbing? Who was it? Mr. Shui Ta the Tobacco King doesn't weep his heart out. And where does the rice come from that's on the doorstep in the morning? (SHUI TA *returns. He goes to the door and looks out into the rain.*) Where is she?

SHUI TA   Sh! It's nine o'clock. But the rain's so heavy, you can't hear a thing.

YANG SUN   What do you want to hear?

SHUI TA   The mail plane.

YANG SUN   What?!

SHUI TA   I've been told *you* wanted to fly at one time. Is that all forgotten?

YANG SUN   Flying mail is night work. I prefer the daytime. And the firm is very dear to me—after all it belongs to my ex-fiancée, even if she's not around. And she's not, is she?

SHUI TA   What do you mean by that?

YANG SUN   Oh, well, let's say I haven't altogether—lost interest.

SHUI TA   My cousin might like to know that.

YANG SUN   I might not be indifferent—if I found she was being kept under lock and key.

SHUI TA   By whom?

YANG SUN   By you.

SHUI TA   What could you do about it?

YANG SUN   I could submit for discussion—my position in the firm.

SHUI TA   You are now my Manager. In return for a more . . . appropriate position, you might agree to drop the enquiry into your ex-fiancée's whereabouts?

YANG SUN   I might.

SHUI TA   What position *would* be more appropriate?

YANG SUN   The one at the top.

SHUI TA   My own? (*Silence.*) And if I preferred to throw you out on your neck?

YANG SUN   I'd come back on my feet. With suitable escort.

SHUI TA   The police?

YANG SUN   The police.

SHUI TA   And when the police found no one?

YANG SUN   I might ask them not to overlook the back room. (*Ending the pretense:*) In short, Mr. Shui Ta, my interest in this young woman has not been officially terminated. I should like to see more of her. (*Into* SHUI TA's *face:*) Besides, she's pregnant and needs a friend. (*He moves to the door.*) I shall talk about it with the Water Seller.

Exit. SHUI TA *is rigid for a moment, then he quickly goes into the back room. He returns with* SHEN TE's *belongings: underwear, etc. He takes a long look at the shawl of the previous scene. He then wraps the things in a bundle, which upon hearing a noise, he hides under the table. Enter* MRS. MI TZU *and* MR. SHU FU. *They put away their umbrellas and galoshes.*

MRS. MI TZU   I thought your Manager was here, Mr. Shui Ta. He combines charm with business in a way that can only be to the advantage of all of us.

SHU FU   You sent for us, Mr. Shui Ta?

SHUI TA   The factory is in trouble.

SHU FU   It always is.

SHUI TA   The police are threatening to close us down unless I can show that the extension of our facilities is imminent.

SHU FU   Mr. Shui Ta, I'm sick and tired of your constantly expanding projects. I place cabins at your cousin's disposal; you make a factory of them. I hand your cousin a check; you present it. Your cousin disappears: you find the cabins too small and start talking of yet more—

SHUI TA   Mr. Shu Fu, I'm authorized to inform you that Miss Shen Te's return is now imminent.

SHU FU   Imminent? It's becoming his favorite word.

MRS. MI TZU   Yes, what does it mean?

SHUI TA   Mrs. Mi Tzu, I can pay you exactly half what you asked for your buildings. Are you ready to inform the police that I am taking them over?

MRS. MI TZU   Certainly, if I can take over your Manager.

SHU FU   What?

MRS. MI TZU   He's so efficient.

SHUI TA   I'm afraid I need Mr. Yang Sun.

MRS. MI TZU   So do I.

SHUI TA   He will call on you tomorrow.

SHU FU   So much the better. With Shen Te likely to turn up at any moment, the presence of that young man is hardly in good taste.

SHUI TA   So we have reached a settlement. In what was once the good Shen Te's little shop we are laying the foundations for the great Mr. Shui Ta's twelve magnificent super tobacco markets. You will bear in mind that though they call me the Tobacco King of Setzuan, it is my cousin's interests that have been served . . .

VOICES (*off*)   The police, the police! Going to the tobacco shop! Something must have happened!

Enter YANG SUN, WONG, *and the* POLICEMAN.

POLICEMAN   Quiet there, quiet, quiet! (*They quiet down.*) I'm sorry, Mr. Shui Ta, but there's a report that you've been depriving Miss Shen Te of her freedom. Not that I believe all I hear, but the whole city's in an uproar.

SHUI TA   That's a lie.

POLICEMAN   Mr. Yang Sun has testified that he heard someone sobbing in the back room.

SHU FU   Mrs. Mi Tzu and myself will testify that no one here has been sobbing.

MRS. MI TZU   We have been quietly smoking our cigars.

POLICEMAN   Mr. Shui Ta, I'm afraid I shall have to take a look at that room. (*He does so. The room is empty.*) No one there, of course, sir.

YANG SUN   But I heard sobbing. What's that? (*He finds the clothes.*)

WONG   Those are Shen Te's things. (*To crowd:*) Shen Te's clothes are here!

VOICES (*off, in sequence*)
Shen Te's clothes!
They've been found under the table!
Body of murdered girl still missing!
Tobacco King suspected!

POLICEMAN   Mr. Shui Ta, unless you can tell us where the girl is, I'll have to ask you to come along.

SHUI TA   I do not know.

POLICEMAN   I can't say how sorry I am, Mr. Shui Ta. (*He shows him the door.*)

MR. SHUI TA   Everything will be cleared up in no time. There are still judges in Setzuan.

YANG SUN   I heard sobbing!

9a

WONG'S *den. For the last time, the* GODS *appear to the Water Seller in his dream. They have changed and show signs of a long journey, extreme fatigue, and plenty of mishaps. The* FIRST *no longer has a hat; the* THIRD *has lost a leg; all three are barefoot.*

WONG   Illustrious ones, at last you're here. Shen Te's been gone for months and today her cousin's been arrested. They think he murdered her to get the shop. But I had a dream and in this dream Shen Te said her cousin was keeping her prisoner. You must find her for us, illustrious ones!

FIRST GOD We've found very few good people anywhere, and even they didn't keep it up. Shen Te is still the only one that stayed good.

SECOND GOD If she *has* stayed good.

WONG Certainly she has. But she's vanished.

FIRST GOD That's the last straw. All is lost!

SECOND GOD A little moderation, dear colleague!

FIRST GOD (*plaintively*) What's the good of moderation now? If she can't be found, we'll have to resign! The world is a terrible place! Nothing but misery, vulgarity, and waste! Even the countryside isn't what it used to be. The trees are getting their heads chopped off by telephone wires, and there's such a noise from all the gunfire, and I can't stand those heavy clouds of smoke, and—

THIRD GOD The place is absolutely unlivable! Good intentions bring people to the brink of the abyss, and good deeds push them over the edge. I'm afraid our book of rules is destined for the scrap heap—

SECOND GOD It's people! They're a worthless lot!

THIRD GOD The world is too cold!

SECOND GOD It's people! They're too weak!

FIRST GOD Dignity, dear colleagues, dignity! Never despair! As for this world, didn't we agree that we only have to find one human being who can stand the place? Well, we found her. True, we lost her again. We must find her again, that's all! And at once!

They disappear.

10

Courtroom. Groups: SHU FU *and* MRS. MI TZU; YANG SUN *and* MRS. YANG; WONG, *the* CARPENTER, *the* GRANDFATHER, *the* NIECE, *the* OLD MAN, *the* OLD WOMAN; MRS. SHIN, *the* POLICEMAN; *the* UNEMPLOYED MAN, *the* SISTER-IN-LAW.

OLD MAN So much power isn't good for one man.

UNEMPLOYED MAN And he's going to open twelve super tobacco markets!

WIFE One of the judges is a friend of Mr. Shu Fu's.

SISTER-IN-LAW Another one accepted a present from Mr. Shui Ta only last night. A great fat goose.

OLD WOMAN (*to* WONG) And Shen Te is nowhere to be found.

WONG Only the gods will ever know the truth.

POLICEMAN Order in the court! My lords the judges!

Enter the THREE GODS *in judges' robes. We overhear their conversation as they pass along the footlights to their bench.*

THIRD GOD We'll never get away with it, our certificates were so badly forged.

SECOND GOD   My predecessor's "sudden indigestion" will certainly cause comment.

FIRST GOD   But he *had* just eaten a whole goose.

UNEMPLOYED MAN   Look at that! *New* judges!

WONG   New judges. And what good ones!

The THIRD GOD *hears this, and turns to smile at* WONG. *The* GODS *sit. The* FIRST GOD *beats on the bench with his gavel. The* POLICEMAN *brings in* SHUI TA *who walks with lordly steps. He is whistled at.*

POLICEMAN (*to* SHUI TA)   Be prepared for a surprise. The judges have been changed.

SHUI TA *turns quickly round, looks at them, and staggers.*

NIECE   What's the matter now?

WIFE   The great Tobacco King nearly fainted.

HUSBAND   Yes, as soon as he saw the new judges.

WONG   Does *he* know who they are?

SHUI TA *picks himself up, and the proceedings open.*

FIRST GOD   Defendant Shui Ta, you are accused of doing away with your cousin Shen Te in order to take possession of her business. Do you plead guilty or not guilty?

SHUI TA   Not guilty, my lord.

FIRST GOD (*thumbing through the documents of the case*)   The first witness is the Policeman. I shall ask him to tell us something of the respective reputations of Miss Shen Te and Mr. Shui Ta.

POLICEMAN   Miss Shen Te was a young lady who aimed to please, my lord. She liked to live and let live, as the saying goes. Mr. Shui Ta, on the other hand, is a man of principle. Though the generosity of Miss Shen Te forced him at times to abandon half measures, unlike the girl he was always on the side of the law, my lord. One time, he even unmasked a gang of thieves to whom his too trustful cousin had given shelter. The evidence, in short, my lord, proves that Mr. Shui Ta was *incapable* of the crime of which he stands accused!

FIRST GOD   I see. And are there others who could testify along, shall we say, the same lines?

SHU FU *rises.*

POLICEMAN (*whispering to* GODS)   Mr. Shu Fu—a very important person.

FIRST GOD (*inviting him to speak*)   Mr. Shu Fu!

SHU FU   Mr. Shui Ta is a businessman, my lord. Need I say more?

FIRST GOD   Yes.

SHU FU   Very well, I will. He is Vice President of the Council of Commerce and is about to be elected a Justice of the Peace.

(He returns to his seat. MRS. MI TZU *rises.)*

WONG   Elected! *He* gave him the job!

With a gesture the FIRST GOD *asks who* MRS. MI TZU *is.*

POLICEMAN   Another very important person. Mrs. Mi Tzu.

FIRST GOD *(inviting her to speak)*   Mrs. Mi Tzu!

MRS. MI TZU   My lord, as Chairman of the Committee on Social Work, I wish to call attention to just a couple of eloquent facts: Mr. Shui Ta not only has erected a model factory with model housing in our city, he is a regular contributor to our home for the disabled. *(She returns to her seat.)*

POLICEMAN *(whispering)*   And she's a great friend of the judge that ate the goose!

FIRST GOD *(to the* POLICEMAN)   Oh, thank you. What next? *(To the Court, genially:)* Oh, yes. We should find out if any of the evidence is less favorable to the defendant.

WONG, *the* CARPENTER, *the* OLD MAN, *the* OLD WOMAN, *the* UNEMPLOYED MAN, *the* SISTER-IN-LAW, *and the* NIECE *come forward.*

POLICEMAN *(whispering)*   Just the riffraff, my lord.

FIRST GOD *(addressing the "riffraff")*   Well, um, riffraff—do you know anything of the defendant, Mr. Shui Ta?

WONG   Too much, my lord.

UNEMPLOYED MAN   What don't we know, my lord.

CARPENTER   He ruined us.

SISTER-IN-LAW   He's a cheat.

NIECE   Liar.

WIFE   Thief.

BOY   Blackmailer.

BROTHER   Murderer.

FIRST GOD   Thank you. We should now let the defendant state his point of view.

SHUI TA   I only came on the scene when Shen Te was in danger of losing what I had understood was a gift from the gods. Because I did the filthy jobs which someone had to do, they hate me. My activities were restricted to the minimum, my lord.

SISTER-IN-LAW   He had us arrested!

SHUI TA   Certainly. You stole from the bakery!

SISTER-IN-LAW   Such concern for the bakery! You didn't want the shop for yourself, I suppose!

SHUI TA   I didn't want the shop overrun with parasites.

SISTER-IN-LAW   We had nowhere else to go.

SHUI TA   There were too many of you.

WONG   What about this old couple: Were *they* parasites?

OLD MAN   We lost our shop because of you!

SISTER-IN-LAW   And we gave your cousin money!

SHUI TA   My cousin's fiancé was a flyer. The money had to go to *him.*

WONG   Did you care whether he flew or not? Did you care whether she married him or not? You wanted her to marry someone else! (*He points at* SHU FU.)

SHUI TA   The flyer unexpectedly turned out to be a scoundrel.

YANG SUN (*jumping up*)   Which was the reason you made him your Manager?

SHUI TA   Later on he improved.

WONG   And when he improved, you sold him to her? (*He points out* MRS. MI TZU.)

SHUI TA   She wouldn't let me have her premises unless she had him to stroke her knees!

MRS. MI TZU   What? The man's a pathological liar. (*To him:*) Don't mention my property to me as long as you live! Murderer! (*She rustles off, in high dudgeon.*)

YANG SUN (*pushing in*)   My lord, I wish to speak for the defendant.

SISTER-IN-LAW   Naturally. He's your employer.

UNEMPLOYED MAN   And the worst slave driver in the country.

MRS. YANG   That's a lie! My lord, Mr. Shui Ta is a great man. He . . .

YANG SUN   He's this and he's that, but he is not a murderer, my lord. Just fifteen minutes before his arrest I heard Shen Te's voice in his own back room.

FIRST GOD   Oh? Tell us more!

YANG SUN   I heard sobbing, my lord!

FIRST GOD   But lots of women sob, we've been finding.

YANG SUN   Could I fail to recognize her voice?

SHU FU   No, you made her sob so often yourself, young man!

YANG SUN   Yes. But I also made her happy. Till he (*pointing at* SHUI TA) decided to sell her to you!

SHUI TA   Because you didn't love her.

WONG   Oh, no: it was for the money, my lord!

SHUI TA   And what was the money for, my lord? For the poor! And for Shen Te so she could go on being good!

WONG   For the poor? That he sent to his sweatshops? And why didn't you let Shen Te be good when you signed the big check?

SHUI TA   For the child's sake, my lord.

CARPENTER   What about *my* children? What did he do about them?

SHUI TA *is silent.*

WONG   The shop was to be a fountain of goodness. That was the gods' idea. You came and spoiled it!

SHUI TA   If I hadn't, it would have run dry!

MRS. SHIN   There's a lot in that, my lord.

WONG   What have you done with the good Shen Te, bad man? She *was* good, my lords, she was, I swear it! (*He raises his hand in an oath.*)

THIRD GOD   What's happened to your hand, Water Seller?

WONG (*pointing to* SHUI TA)   It's all his fault, my lord, *she* was going to send me to a doctor—(*To* SHUI TA:) You were her worst enemy!

SHUI TA   I was her only friend!

WONG   Where is she then? Tell us where your good friend is!

The excitement of this exchange has run through the whole crowd.

ALL   Yes, where is she? Where is Shen Te? (*Etc.*)

SHUI TA   Shen Te . . . had to go.

WONG   Where? Where to?

SHUI TA   I cannot tell you! I cannot tell you!

ALL   Why? Why did she have to go away? (*Etc.*)

WONG (*into the din with the first words, but talking on beyond the others*)   Why not, why not? Why did she have to go away?

SHUI TA (*shouting*)   Because you'd all have torn her to shreds, that's why! My lords, I have a request. Clear the court! When only the judges remain, I will make a confession.

ALL (*except* WONG, *who is silent, struck by the new turn of events*)   So he's guilty? He's confessing! (*Etc.*)

FIRST GOD (*using the gavel*)   Clear the court!

POLICEMAN   Clear the court!

WONG   Mr. Shui Ta has met his match this time.

MRS. SHIN (*with a gesture toward the judges*)   You're in for a little surprise.

The court is cleared. Silence.

SHUI TA   Illustrious ones!

The GODS *look at each other, not quite believing their ears.*

SHUI TA   Yes, I recognize you!

SECOND GOD (*taking matters in hand, sternly*)   What have you done with our good woman of Setzuan?

SHUI TA   I have a terrible confession to make: I am she! (*He takes off his mask, and tears away his clothes.* SHEN TE *stands there.*)

SECOND GOD   Shen Te!

SHEN TE   Shen Te, yes. Shui Ta *and* Shen Te. Both.

Your injunction
To be good and yet to live
Was a thunderbolt:
It has torn me in two
I can't tell how it was

But to be good to others
And myself at the same time
I could not do it
Your world is not an easy one, illustrious ones!
When we extend our hand to a beggar, he tears it off for us
When we help the lost, we are lost ourselves
And so
Since not to eat is to die
Who can long refuse to be bad?
As I lay prostrate beneath the weight of good intentions
Ruin stared me in the face
It was when I was unjust that I ate good meat
And hobnobbed with the mighty
Why?
Why are bad deeds rewarded?
Good ones punished?
I enjoyed giving
I truly wished to be the Angel of the Slums
But washed by a foster-mother in the water of the gutter
I developed a sharp eye
The time came when pity was a thorn in my side
And, later, when kind words turned to ashes in my mouth
And anger took over
I became a wolf
Find me guilty, then, illustrious ones,
But know:
All that I have done I did
To help my neighbor
To love my lover
And to keep my little one from want
For your great, godly deeds, I was too poor, too small.

Pause.

FIRST GOD (*shocked*) Don't go on making yourself miserable, Shen Te!
We're overjoyed to have found you!

SHEN TE I'm telling you I'm the bad man who committed all those
crimes!

FIRST GOD (*using—or failing to use—his ear trumpet*) The good woman
who did all those good deeds?

SHEN TE Yes, but the bad man too!

FIRST GOD (*as if something had dawned*) Unfortunate coincidences!
Heartless neighbors!

THIRD GOD (*shouting in his ear*) But how is she to continue?

FIRST GOD   Continue? Well, she's a strong, healthy girl . . .

SECOND GOD   You didn't hear what she said!

FIRST GOD   I heard every word! She is confused, that's all! (*He begins to bluster:*) And what about this book of rules—we can't renounce our rules, can we? (*More quietly:*) Should the world be changed? How? By whom? The world should *not* be changed! (*At a sign from him, the lights turn pink, and music plays.*)
And now the hour of parting is at hand.
Dost thou behold, Shen Te, yon fleecy cloud?
It is our chariot. At a sign from me
'Twill come and take us back from whence we came
Above the azure vault and silver stars. . . .

SHEN TE   No! Don't go, illustrious ones!

FIRST GOD
Our cloud has landed now in yonder field
From whence it will transport us back to heaven.
Farewell, Shen Te, let not thy courage fail thee. . . .

Exeunt GODS.

SHEN TE   What about the old couple? They've lost their shop! What about the Water Seller and his hand? And I've got to defend myself against the Barber, because I don't love him! And against Sun, because I do love him! How? How?

SHEN TE'S *eyes follow the* GODS *as they are imagined to step into a cloud which rises and moves forward over the orchestra and up beyond the balcony.*

FIRST GOD (*from on high*)   We have faith in you, Shen Te!

SHEN TE   There'll be a child. And he'll have to be fed. I can't stay here. Where shall I go?

FIRST GOD   Continue to be good, good woman of Setzuan!

SHEN TE   I need my bad cousin!

FIRST GOD   But not very often!

SHEN TE   Once a week at least!

FIRST GOD   Once a month will be quite enough!

SHEN TE (*shrieking*)   No, no! Help!

But the cloud continues to recede as the GODS *sing:*

Valedictory Hymn

What rapture, oh, it is to know
   A good thing when you see it
And having seen a good thing, oh,
   What rapture 'tis to flee it

Be good, sweet maid of Setzuan
Let Shui Ta be clever
Departing, we forget the man
Remember your endeavor

Because through all the length of days
Her goodness faileth never
Sing hallelujah! Make Shen Te's
Good name live on forever!

SHEN TE   Help!

⌒ THE GLASS MENAGERIE (1944)

TENNESSEE WILLIAMS (1911–1983)

Thomas Lanier Williams, nicknamed "Tennessee" for reasons not altogether clear, drifter in and out of jobs, in and out of colleges, abysmally unsuccessful writer of an abysmally unsuccessful play called *Battle of Angels* almost literally driven out of Boston in 1940, shy, introverted, but determined to become a writer, broke sharply upon the scene in 1944 when the successful Chicago premiere of *The Glass Menagerie* was followed quickly by equal success and critical acclaim in New York. Four years later one of the great modern American dramatic masterpieces, *A Streetcar Named Desire*, made Marlon Brando an instant star and virtual household word, and raised Tennessee Williams to membership in an elite group of post-war American dramatic artists of international reputation. O'Neill, Arthur Miller, of late Edward Albee, and Tennessee Williams still remain the best we're ever had.

Williams' dramatic technique relies all too often on overworked themes of decadence in the South, particularly among women, strutting young studs, horribly violent deaths and mutilations, and a look at the world and its inhabitants as in one way or another depraved. An effective picture of this world is summarized in the almost purely expressionistic *Camino Real*, an artistic failure of 1953, now regarded as one of Williams' major works. Even at that, Williams has been able to compose a substantial body of superior dramatic literature which has rightfully earned his far-reaching artistic reputation. His first commercial success, the charmingly appealing *The Glass Menagerie*, remains among his best efforts.

The Glass Menagerie has the surface qualities of realistic drama with its petty little people and their struggle for meaning and dignity in a shoddy world, but Williams has actually written one of the few truly *impressionistic* plays. The style suggests the quality of a painting by Pizzaro, or Monet, or, in music, of Debussy. There is a tremendous amount of mood, a sense of viewing through a glass, perhaps darkly, certainly hazily, and hearing from afar a life experience from a single vantage point. The actions are meant to be seen in the memory of the storyteller who colors it as he sees fit, reveals it as he wishes, creating for us his deeply personal impression of the way it was. We watch the play in certain sequences through a theatrical gauze, and the filminess is thus further heightened. We listen to the chorus figure, Tom, as he steps in and out of his reminiscences at will. It is a prolonged impression, a lengthy look, full of nostalgia, resentment, some hate, certainly regrets, and a lot of love.

Is *The Glass Menagerie* a tragedy? Probably not. It is a drama of compassion, and tragic only in the most pathetic sense, often much too fragile—like Laura's tiny animals—to achieve the necessary strength. There is, of course, an inevitability and sense of unavoidable catastrophe, and there is no way out. These people possess their individual flaws, but we see them with too much conscious emotion for tragedy. The tears raised on Laura's behalf become too sentimental. Amanda may be understandable as the frantic mother seeking a modicum of gentility among the ruins, but she is too much the smothering monster stage mother. Tom is certainly no tragic protagonist in his detachment.

Still, *The Glass Menagerie* is a forceful play. Williams wants us to understand and to pity these three lost creatures, driven into themselves, each by the others, to a final disintegration of the spirit. In *The Glass Menagerie* all survive, yet all die, making the play, perhaps, simply a tragedy of life itself.

The Glass Menagerie WILLIAMS

CHARACTERS

AMANDA WINGFIELD, the mother.

A little woman of great but confused vitality clinging frantically to another time and place. Her characterization must be carefully created, not copied from type. She is not paranoiac, but her life is paranoia. There is much to admire in AMANDA, and as much to love and pity as there is to laugh at. Certainly she has endurance and a kind of heroism, and though her foolishness makes her unwittingly cruel at times, there is tenderness in her slight person.

LAURA WINGFIELD, her daughter.

AMANDA, having failed to establish contact with reality, continues to live vitally in her illusions, but LAURA'S situation is even graver. A childhood illness has left her crippled, one leg slightly shorter than the other, and held in a brace. This defect need not be more than suggested on the stage. Stemming from this, LAURA'S separation increases till she is like a piece of her own glass collection, too exquisitely fragile to move from the shelf.

TOM WINGFIELD, her son, and the narrator of the play.

A poet with a job in a warehouse. His nature is not remorseless, but to escape from a trap he has to act without pity.

JIM O'CONNOR, the gentleman caller.

A nice, ordinary, young man.

SCENE: An alley in St. Louis.
PART I: Preparation for a Gentleman Caller.
PART II: The Gentleman Calls.
TIME: Now and the Past.

SCENE I

The Wingfield apartment is in the rear of the building, one of those vast hive-like conglomerations of cellular living-units that flower as warty growths in overcrowded urban centers of lower middle-class population and are symptomatic of the impulse of this largest and fundamentally enslaved section of American society to avoid fluidity and differentiation and to exist and function as one interfused mass of automatism.

The apartment faces an alley and is entered by a fire-escape, a structure whose name is a touch of accidental poetic truth, for all of these huge buildings are always burning with the slow and implacable fires of human desperation. The fire-escape is included in the set—that is, the landing of it and steps descending from it.

The scene is memory and is therefore nonrealistic. Memory takes a lot of poetic license. It omits some details; others are exaggerated, according to the emotional value of the articles it touches, for memory is seated predominantly in the heart. The interior is therefore rather dim and poetic.

At the rise of the curtain, the audience is faced with the dark, grim rear wall of the Wingfield tenement. This building, which runs parallel to the footlights, is flanked on both sides by dark, narrow alleys which run into murky canyons of tangled clotheslines, garbage cans and the sinister lattice-work of neighboring fire-escapes. It is up and down these side alleys that exterior entrances and exits are made, during the play. At the end of TOM's *opening commentary, the dark tenement wall slowly reveals (by means of a transparency) the interior of the ground floor Wingfield apartment.*

Downstage is the living room, which also serves as a sleeping room for LAURA, *the sofa unfolding to make her bed. Upstage, center, and divided by a wide arch or second proscenium with transparent faded portieres (or second curtain), is the dining room. In an old-fashioned what-not in the living room are seen scores of transparent glass animals. A blown-up photograph of the father hangs on the wall of the living room, facing the audience, to the left of the archway. It is the face of a very handsome young man in a doughboy's First World War cap. He is gallantly smiling, ineluctably smiling, as if to say, "I will be smiling forever."*

The audience hears and sees the opening scene in the dining room through both the transparent fourth wall of the building and the transparent gauze portieres of the dining-room arch. It is during this revealing scene that the fourth wall slowly ascends, out of sight. This transparent exterior wall is not brought down again until the very end of the play, during TOM's *final speech.*

The narrator is an undisguised convention of the play. He takes whatever license with dramatic convention as is convenient to his purposes.

TOM *enters dressed as a merchant sailor from alley, stage left, and strolls across the front of the stage to the fire-escape. There he stops and lights a cigarette. He addresses the audience.*

TOM Yes, I have tricks in my pocket, I have things up my sleeve. But I am the opposite of a stage magician. He gives you illusion that has the appearance of truth. I give you truth in the pleasant disguise of illusion. To begin with, I turn back time. I reverse it to that quaint period, the thirties, when the huge middle class of America was matriculating in a school for the blind. Their eyes had failed them, or they had failed their eyes, and so they were having their fingers pressed forcibly down on the fiery Braille alphabet of a dissolving economy. In Spain there was revolution.

Here there was only shouting and confusion. In Spain there was Guernica. Here there were disturbances of labor, sometimes pretty violent, in otherwise peaceful cities such as Chicago, Cleveland, Saint Louis.... This is the social background of the play.

(MUSIC.)

The play is memory. Being a memory play, it is dimly lighted, it is sentimental, it is not realistic. In memory everything seems to happen to music. That explains the fiddle in the wings. I am the narrator of the play, and also a character in it. The other characters are my mother, Amanda, my sister, Laura, and a gentleman caller who appears in the final scenes. He is the most realistic character in the play, being an emissary from a world of reality that we were somehow set apart from. But since I have a poet's weakness for symbols, I am using this character also as a symbol; he is the long delayed but always expected something that we live for. There is a fifth character in the play who doesn't appear except in this larger-than-life photograph over the mantel. This is our father who left us a long time ago. He was a telephone man who fell in love with long distances; he gave up his job with the telephone company and skipped the light fantastic out of town ... The last we heard of him was a picture post-card from Mazatlan, on the Pacific coast of Mexico, containing a message of two words—"Hello—Goodbye!" and an address. I think the rest of the play will explain itself....

Amanda's voice becomes audible through the portieres.

(LEGEND ON SCREEN: "OÙ SONT LES NEIGES.")

He divides the portieres and enters the upstage area.
    AMANDA *and* LAURA *are seated at a drop-leaf table. Eating is indicated by gestures without food or utensils.* AMANDA *faces the audience.* TOM *and* LAURA *are seated in profile.*
    The interior has lit up softly and through the scrim we see AMANDA *and* LAURA *seated at the table in the upstage area.*

AMANDA *(calling)* Tom?
TOM Yes, Mother.
AMANDA We can't say grace until you come to the table!
TOM Coming, Mother. (*He bows slightly and withdraws, reappearing a few moments later in his place at the table.*)
AMANDA *(to her son)* Honey, don't *push* with your *fingers*. If you have to push with something, the thing to push with is a crust of bread. And chew—chew! Animals have sections in their stomachs which enable them to digest food without mastication, but human

beings are supposed to chew their food before they swallow it down. Eat food leisurely, son, and really enjoy it. A well-cooked meal has lots of delicate flavors that have to be held in the mouth for appreciation. So chew your food and give your salivary glands a chance to function!

TOM *deliberately lays his imaginary fork down and pushes his chair back from the table.*

TOM   I haven't enjoyed one bite of this dinner because of your constant directions on how to eat it. It's you that makes me rush through meals with your hawk-like attention to every bite I take. Sickening—spoils my appetite—all this discussion of animals' secretion—salivary glands—mastication!

AMANDA (*lightly*)   Temperament like a Metropolitan star! (*He rises and crosses downstage.*) You're not excused from the table.

TOM   I am getting a cigarette.

AMANDA   You smoke too much.

LAURA *rises.*

LAURA   I'll bring in the blanc mange.

He remains standing with his cigarette by the portieres during the following.

AMANDA (*rising*)   No, sister, no, sister—you be the lady this time and I'll be the darky.

LAURA   I'm already up.

AMANDA   Resume your seat, little sister—I want you to stay fresh and pretty—for gentlemen callers!

LAURA   I'm not expecting any gentlemen callers.

AMANDA (*crossing out to kitchenette. Airily*)   Sometimes they come when they are least expected! Why, I remember one Sunday afternoon in Blue Mountain—(*Enters kitchenette.*)

TOM   I know what's coming!

LAURA   Yes. But let her tell it.

TOM   Again?

LAURA   She loves to tell it.

AMANDA *returns with bowl of dessert.*

AMANDA   One Sunday afternoon in Blue Mountain—your mother received—*seventeen!*—gentlemen callers! Why, sometimes there weren't chairs enough to accommodate them all. We had to send the nigger over to bring in folding chairs from the parish house.

TOM (*remaining at portieres*)   How did you entertain those gentlemen callers?

AMANDA   I understood the art of conversation!

TOM   I bet you could talk.

AMANDA   Girls in those days *knew* how to talk, I can tell you.

TOM   Yes?

(IMAGE: AMANDA AS A GIRL ON A PORCH GREETING CALLERS.)

AMANDA   They knew how to entertain their gentlemen callers. It wasn't enough for a girl to be possessed of a pretty face and a graceful figure—although I wasn't slighted in either respect. She also needed to have a nimble wit and a tongue to meet all occasions.

TOM   What did you talk about?

AMANDA   Things of importance going on in the world! Never anything coarse or common or vulgar. (*She addresses* TOM *as though he were seated in the vacant chair at the table though he remains by portieres. He plays this scene as though he held the book.*) My callers were gentlemen—all! Among my callers were some of the most prominent young planters of the Mississippi Delta—planters and sons of planters!

TOM *motions for music and a spot of light on* AMANDA.
Her eyes lift, her face glows, her voice becomes rich and elegiac.

(SCREEN LEGEND: "OÙ SONT LES NEIGES.")

There was young Champ Laughlin who later became vice-president of the Delta Planters Bank. Hadley Stevenson who was drowned in Moon Lake and left his widow one hundred and fifty thousand in Government bonds. There were the Cutrere brothers, Wesley and Bates. Bates was one of my bright particular beaux! He got in a quarrel with that wild Wainright boy. They shot it out on the floor of Moon Lake Casino. Bates was shot through the stomach. Died in the ambulance on his way to Memphis. His widow was also well-provided for, came into eight or ten thousand acres, that's all. She married him on the rebound—never loved her—carried my picture on him the night he died! And there was that boy that every girl in the Delta had set her cap for! That beautiful, brilliant young Fitzhugh boy from Green County!

TOM   What did he leave his widow?

AMANDA   He never married! Gracious, you talk as though all of my old admirers had turned up their toes to the daisies!

TOM   Isn't this the first you mentioned that still survives?

AMANDA   That Fitzhugh boy went North and made a fortune— came to be known as the Wolf of Wall Street! He had the Midas touch, whatever he touched turned to gold! And I could have been Mrs. Duncan J. Fitzhugh, mind you! But—I picked your *father!*

LAURA (*rising*)   Mother, let me clear the table.

AMANDA   No, dear, you go in front and study your typewriter chart. Or practice your shorthand a little. Stay fresh and pretty—It's almost time for our gentlemen callers to start arriving. (*She flounces girlishly toward the kitchenette.*) How many do you suppose we're going to entertain this afternoon?

TOM *throws down the paper and jumps up with a groan.*

LAURA (*alone in the dining room*)   I don't believe we're going to receive any, Mother.

AMANDA (*reappearing, airily*)   What? No one—not one? You must be joking! (LAURA *nervously echoes her laugh. She slips in a fugitive manner through the half-open portieres and draws them gently behind her. A shaft of very clear light is thrown on her face against the faded tapestry of the curtains.* MUSIC: "THE GLASS MENAGERIE" UNDER FAINTLY. *Lightly.*) Not one gentleman caller? It can't be true! There must be a flood, there must have been a tornado!

LAURA   It isn't a flood, it's not a tornado, Mother. I'm just not popular like you were in Blue Mountain.... (TOM *utters another groan.* LAURA *glances at him with a faint, apologetic smile. Her voice catching a little.*) Mother's afraid I'm going to be an old maid.

(THE SCENE DIMS OUT WITH "GLASS MENAGERIE" MUSIC.)

SCENE II

"Laura, Haven't You Ever Liked Some Boy?"

On the dark stage the screen is lighted with the image of blue roses. Gradually LAURA'S *figure becomes apparent and the screen goes out. The music subsides.*

LAURA *is seated in the delicate ivory chair at the small clawfoot table. She wears a dress of soft violet material for a kimono—her hair tied back from her forehead with a ribbon.*

She is washing and polishing her collection of glass.

AMANDA *appears on the fire-escape steps. At the sound of her ascent,* LAURA *catches her breath, thrusts the bowl of ornaments away and seats herself stiffly before the diagram of the typewriter keyboard as though it held her spellbound. Something has happened to* AMANDA. *It is written in her face as she climbs to the landing: a look that is grim and hopeless and a little absurd.*

She has on one of those cheap or imitation velvety-looking cloth coats

with imitation fur collar. Her hat is five or six years old, one of those dreadful cloche hats that were worn in the late twenties and she is clasping an enormous black patent-leather pocket-book with nickel clasp and initials. This is her full-dress outfit, the one she usually wears to the D.A.R. Before entering she looks through the door.
She purses her lips, opens her eyes wide, rolls them upward, and shakes her head.
Then she slowly lets herself in the door. Seeing her mother's expression LAURA *touches her lips with a nervous gesture.*

LAURA   Hello, Mother, I was—(*She makes a nervous gesture toward the chart on the wall.* AMANDA *leans against the shut door and stares at* LAURA *with a martyred look.*)

AMANDA   Deception? Deception? (*She slowly removes her hat and gloves, continuing the swift suffering stare. She lets the hat and gloves fall on the floor—a bit of acting.*)

LAURA   (*shakily*)   How was the D.A.R. meeting? (AMANDA *slowly opens her purse and removes a dainty white handkerchief which she shakes out delicately and delicately touches to her lips and nostrils.*) Didn't you go to the D.A.R. meeting, Mother?

AMANDA   (*faintly, almost inaudibly*)   —No.—No. (*Then more forcibly.*) I did not have the strength—to go to the D.A.R. In fact, I did not have the courage! I wanted to find a hole in the ground and hide myself in it forever! (*She crosses slowly to the wall and removes the diagram of the typewriter keyboard. She holds it in front of her for a second, staring at it sweetly and sorrowfully—then bites her lips and tears it in two pieces.*)

LAURA   (*faintly*)   Why did you do that, Mother? (AMANDA *repeats the same procedure with the chart of the Gregg Alphabet.*) Why are you—

AMANDA   Why? Why? How old are you, Laura?

LAURA   Mother, you know my age.

AMANDA   I thought that you were an adult; it seems that I was mistaken. (*She crosses slowly to the sofa and sinks down and stares at* LAURA.)

LAURA   Please don't stare at me, Mother.

AMANDA *closes her eyes and lowers her head. Count ten.*

AMANDA   What are we going to do, what is going to become of us, what is the future?

Count ten.

LAURA   Has something happened, Mother? (AMANDA *draws a long breath and takes out the handkerchief again. Dabbing process.*) Mother, has—something happened?

AMANDA   I'll be all right in a minute. I'm just bewildered—(*Count five.*)—by life. . . .

LAURA   Mother, I wish that you would tell me what's happened.

AMANDA   As you know, I was supposed to be inducted into my office at the D.A.R. this afternoon. (IMAGE: A SWARM OF TYPEWRITERS.) But I stopped off at Rubicam's Business College to speak to your teachers about your having a cold and ask them what progress they thought you were making down there.

LAURA   Oh. . . .

AMANDA   I went to the typing instructor and introduced myself as your mother. She didn't know who you were. Wingfield, she said. We don't have any such student enrolled at the school! I assured her she did, that you had been going to classes since early in January. "I wonder," she said, "if you could be talking about that terribly shy little girl who dropped out of school after only a few days' attendance?" "No," I said, "Laura, my daughter, has been going to school every day for the past six weeks!" "Excuse me," she said. She took the attendance book out and there was your name, unmistakably printed, and all the dates you were absent until they decided that you had dropped out of school. I still said, "No, there must have been some mistake! There must have been some mix-up in the records!" And she said, "No—I remember her perfectly now. Her hand shook so that she couldn't hit the right keys! The first time we gave a speed-test, she broke down completely—was sick at the stomach and almost had to be carried into the wash-room! After that morning she never showed up any more. We phoned the house but never got any answer—while I was working at Famous and Barr, I suppose, demonstrating those —Oh!" I felt so weak I could barely keep on my feet! I had to sit down while they got me a glass of water! Fifty dollars' tuition, all of our plans—my hopes and ambitions for you—just gone up the spout, just gone up the spout like that. (LAURA *draws a long breath and gets awkwardly to her feet. She crosses to the victrola and winds it up.*) What are you doing?

LAURA   Oh! (*She releases the handle and returns to her seat.*)

AMANDA   Laura, where have you been going when you've gone out pretending that you were going to business college?

LAURA   I've just been going out walking.

AMANDA   That's not true.

LAURA   It is. I just went walking.

AMANDA   Walking? Walking? In winter? Deliberately courting pneumonia in that light coat? Where did you walk to, Laura?

LAURA   All sorts of places—mostly in the park.

AMANDA   Even after you'd started catching that cold?

LAURA It was the lesser of two evils, Mother. (IMAGE: WINTER SCENE IN PARK.) I couldn't go back up. I—threw up—on the floor!

AMANDA From half past seven till after five every day you mean to tell me you walked around in the park, because you wanted to make me think that you were still going to Rubicam's Business College?

LAURA It wasn't as bad as it sounds. I went inside places to get warmed up.

AMANDA Inside where?

LAURA I went in the art museum and the bird-houses at the Zoo. I visited the penguins every day! Sometimes I did without lunch and went to the movies. Lately I've been spending most of my afternoons in the Jewel-box, that big glass house where they raise the tropical flowers.

AMANDA You did all this to deceive me, just for the deception? (LAURA *looks down.*) Why?

LAURA Mother, when you're disappointed, you get that awful suffering look on your face, like the picture of Jesus' mother in the museum!

AMANDA Hush!

LAURA I couldn't face it.

Pause. A whisper of strings.

(LEGEND: "THE CRUST OF HUMILITY.")

AMANDA (*hopelessly fingering the huge pocketbook*) So what are we going to do the rest of our lives? Stay home and watch the parades go by? Amuse ourselves with the glass menagerie, darling? Eternally play those worn-out phonograph records your father left as a painful reminder of him? We won't have a business career—we've given that up because it gave us nervous indigestion! (*Laughs wearily.*) What is there left but dependency all our lives? I know so well what becomes of unmarried women who aren't prepared to occupy a position. I've seen such pitiful cases in the South—barely tolerated spinsters living upon the grudging patronage of sister's husband or brother's wife!—stuck away in some little mouse-trap of a room—encouraged by one in-law to visit another—little birdlike women without any nest—eating the crust of humility all their life! Is that the future that we've mapped out for ourselves? I swear it's the only alternative I can think of! It isn't a very pleasant alternative, is it? Of course—some girls *do marry.* (LAURA *twists her hands nervously.*) Haven't you ever liked some boy?

LAURA   Yes. I liked one once. (*Rises.*) I came across his picture a while ago.

AMANDA (*with some interest*)   He gave you his picture?

LAURA   No, it's in the year-book.

AMANDA (*disappointed*)   Oh—a high-school boy.

(SCREEN IMAGE: JIM AS A HIGH-SCHOOL HERO BEARING A SILVER CUP.)

LAURA   Yes. His name was Jim. (LAURA *lifts the heavy annual from the claw-foot table.*) Here he is in *The Pirates of Penzance.*

AMANDA (*absently*)   The what?

LAURA   The operetta the senior class put on. He had a wonderful voice and we sat across the aisle from each other Mondays, Wednesdays and Fridays in the Aud. Here he is with the silver cup for debating! See his grin?

AMANDA (*absently*)   He must have had a jolly disposition.

LAURA   He used to call me—Blue Roses.

(IMAGE: BLUE ROSES.)

AMANDA   Why did he call you such a name as that?

LAURA   When I had that attack of pleurosis—he asked me what was the matter when I came back. I said pleurosis—he thought that I said Blue Roses! So that's what he always called me after that. Whenever he saw me, he'd holler, "Hello, Blue Roses!" I didn't care for the girl that he went out with. Emily Meisenbach. Emily was the best-dressed girl at Soldan. She never struck me, though, as being sincere . . . It says in the Personal Section—they're engaged. That's—six years ago! They must be married by now.

AMANDA   Girls that aren't cut out for business careers usually wind up married to some nice man. (*Gets up with a spark of revival.*) Sister, that's what you'll do!

LAURA *utters a startled, doubtful laugh. She reaches quickly for a piece of glass.*

LAURA   But, Mother—

AMANDA   Yes? (*Crossing to photograph.*)

LAURA (*in a tone of frightened apology*)   I'm—crippled!

(IMAGE: SCREEN.)

AMANDA   Nonsense! Laura, I've told you never, never to use that word. Why, you're not crippled, you just have a little defect—hardly noticeable, even! When people have some slight disadvantage like that, they cultivate other things to make up for it—develop charm—and vivacity—and—*charm!* That's all you have to do! (*She turns again to the photograph.*) One thing your father had *plenty of*—was *charm!*

TOM *motions to the fiddle in the wings.*

(THE SCENE FADES OUT WITH MUSIC.)

SCENE III

(LEGEND ON SCREEN: "AFTER THE FIASCO—")

TOM *speaks from the fire-escape landing.*

TOM After the fiasco at Rubicam's Business College, the idea of getting a gentleman caller for Laura began to play a more important part in Mother's calculations. It became an obsession. Like some archetype of the universal unconscious, the image of the gentleman caller haunted our small apartment.... (IMAGE: YOUNG MAN AT DOOR WITH FLOWERS.) An evening at home rarely passed without some allusion to this image, this spectre, this hope.... Even when he wasn't mentioned, his presence hung in Mother's preoccupied look and in my sister's frightened, apologetic manner—hung like a sentence passed upon the Wingfields! Mother was a woman of action as well as words. She began to take logical steps in the planned direction. Late that winter and in the early spring—realizing that extra money would be needed to properly feather the nest and plume the bird—she conducted a vigorous campaign on the telephone, roping in subscribers to one of those magazines for matrons called *The Home-maker's Companion,* the type of journal that features the serialized sublimations of ladies of letters who think in terms of delicate cup-like breasts, slim, tapering waists, rich, creamy thighs, eyes like woodsmoke in autumn, fingers that soothe and caress like strains of music, bodies as powerful as Etruscan sculpture.

(SCREEN IMAGE: GLAMOR MAGAZINE COVER.)

AMANDA *enters with phone on long extension cord. She is spotted in the dim stage.*

AMANDA Ida Scott? This is Amanda Wingfield! We *missed* you at the D.A.R. last Monday! I said to myself: She's probably suffering with that sinus condition! How is that sinus condition? Horrors! Heaven have mercy!—You're a Christian martyr, yes, that's what you are, a Christian martyr! Well, I just now happened to notice that your subscription to the *Companion's* about to expire!

Yes, it expires with the next issue, honey!—just when that wonderful new serial by Bessie Mae Hopper is getting off to such an exciting start. Oh, honey, it's something that you can't miss! You remember how *Gone With the Wind* took everybody by storm? You simply couldn't go out if you hadn't read it. All everybody *talked* was Scarlett O'Hara. Well, this is a book that critics already compare to *Gone With the Wind*. It's the *Gone With the Wind* of the post-World War generation!—What?—Burning?— Oh, honey, don't let them burn, go take a look in the oven and I'll hold the wire! Heavens—I think she's hung up!

(DIM OUT.)

(LEGEND ON SCREEN: "YOU THINK I'M IN LOVE WITH CONTINENTAL SHOEMAKERS?")

Before the stage is lighted, the violent voices of TOM *and* AMANDA *are heard.*

They are quarreling behind the portieres. In front of them stands LAURA *with clenched hands and panicky expression.*

A clear pool of light on her figure throughout this scene.

TOM　What in Christ's name am I—

AMANDA (*shrilly*)　Don't you use that—

TOM　Supposed to do!

AMANDA　Expression! Not in my—

TOM　Ohhh!

AMANDA　Presence! Have you gone out of your senses?

TOM　I have, that's true, *driven* out!

AMANDA　What is the matter with you, you—big—big—IDIOT!

TOM　Look—I've got *no thing,* no single thing—

AMANDA　Lower your voice!

TOM　In my life here that I can call my OWN! Everything is—

AMANDA　Stop that shouting!

TOM　Yesterday you confiscated my books! You had the nerve to—

AMANDA　I took that horrible novel back to the library—yes! That hideous book by that insane Mr. Lawrence. (TOM *laughs wildly.*) I cannot control the output of diseased minds or people who cater to them—(TOM *laughs still more wildly.*) BUT I WON'T ALLOW SUCH FILTH BROUGHT INTO MY HOUSE! No, no, no, no, no!

TOM　House, house! Who pays rent on it, who makes a slave of himself to—

AMANDA (*fairly screeching*)　Don't you DARE to—

TOM　No, no, *I* mustn't say things! *I've* got to just—

AMANDA　Let me tell you—

TOM I don't want to hear any more! (*He tears the portieres open. The upstage area is lit with a turgid smoky red glow.*)

AMANDA'*s hair is in metal curlers and she wears a very old bathrobe, much too large for her slight figure, a relic of the faithless Mr. Wingfield. An upright typewriter and a wild disarray of manuscripts is on the dropleaf table. The quarrel was probably precipitated by* AMANDA'*s interruption of his creative labor. A chair lying overthrown on the floor. Their gesticulating shadows are cast on the ceiling by the fiery glow.*

AMANDA You *will* hear more, you—

TOM No, I won't hear more, I'm going out!

AMANDA You come right back in—

TOM Out, out out! Because I'm—

AMANDA Come back here, Tom Wingfield! I'm not through talking to you!

TOM Oh, go—

LAURA (*desperately*) —Tom!

AMANDA You're going to listen, and no more insolence from you! I'm at the end of my patience! (*He comes back toward her.*)

TOM What do you think I'm at? Aren't I supposed to have any patience to reach the end of, Mother? I know, I know. It seems unimportant to you, what I'm *doing*—what I *want* to do—having a little *difference* between them! You don't think that—

AMANDA I think you've been doing things that you're ashamed of. That's why you act like this. I don't believe that you go every night to the movies. Nobody goes to the movies night after night. Nobody in their right minds goes to the movies as often as you pretend to. People don't go to the movies at nearly midnight, and movies don't let out at two A.M. Come in stumbling. Muttering to yourself like a maniac! You get three hours sleep and then go to work. Oh, I can picture the way you're doing down there. Moping, doping, because you're in no condition.

TOM (*wildly*) No, I'm in no condition!

AMANDA What right have you got to jeopardize your job? Jeopardize the security of us all? How do you think we'd manage if you were—

TOM Listen! You think I'm crazy *about* the *warehouse?* (*He bends fiercely toward her slight figure.*) You think I'm in love with the Continental Shoemakers? You think I want to spend fifty-five *years* down there in that—*celotex interior!* with—*fluorescent— tubes!* Look! I'd rather somebody picked up a crowbar and battered out my brains—than go back mornings! I *go!* Every time you come in yelling that God damn *"Rise and Shine!" "Rise and*

Shine!" I say to myself "How *lucky dead* people are!" But I get up. I *go!* For sixty-five dollars a month I give up all that I dream of doing and being *ever!* And you say self—*self's* all I ever think of. Why, listen, if self is what I thought of, Mother, I'd be where he is—GONE! (*Pointing to father's picture.*) As far as the system of transportation reaches! (*He starts past her. She grabs his arm.*) Don't grab me, Mother!

AMANDA   Where are you going?

TOM   I'm going to the *movies!*

AMANDA   I don't believe that lie!

TOM (*crouching toward her, overtowering her tiny figure. She backs away, gasping*)   I'm going to opium dens! Yes, opium dens, dens of vice and criminals' hang-outs, Mother. I've joined the Hogan gang, I'm a hired assassin, I carry a tommy-gun in a violin case! I run a string of cat-houses in the Valley! They call me Killer, Killer Wingfield, I'm leading a double-life, a simple, honest warehouse worker by day, by night, a dynamic *czar* of the *underworld, Mother.* I go to gambling casinos, I spin away fortunes on the roulette table! I wear a patch over one eye and a false mustache, sometimes I put on green whiskers. On those occasions they call me—*El Diablo!* Oh, I could tell you things to make you sleepless! My enemies plan to dynamite this place. They're going to blow us all sky-high some night! I'll be glad, very happy, and so will you! You'll go up, up on a broomstick, over Blue Mountain with seventeen gentlemen callers! You ugly—babbling old—*witch....* (*He goes through a series of violent, clumsy movements, seizing his overcoat, lunging to the door, pulling it fiercely open. The women watch him, aghast. His arm catches in the sleeve of the coat as he struggles to pull it on. For a moment he is pinioned by the bulky garment. With an outraged groan he tears the coat off again, splitting the shoulders of it, and hurls it across the room. It strikes against the shelf of* LAURA's *glass collection, there is a tinkle of shattering glass.* LAURA *cries out as if wounded.*)

(MUSIC LEGEND: "THE GLASS MENAGERIE.")

LAURA (*shrilly*)   *My glass!*—menagerie.... (*She covers her face and turns away.*)

But AMANDA *is still stunned and stupefied by the "ugly witch" so that she barely notices this occurrence. Now she recovers her speech.*

AMANDA (*in an awful voice*)   I won't speak to you—until you apologize! (*She crosses through portieres and draws them together behind her.* TOM *is left with* LAURA. LAURA *clings weakly to the mantel with her face averted.* TOM *stares at her stupidly for a moment. Then he crosses to shelf. Drops awkwardly to his knees to collect the fallen glass, glancing at* LAURA *as if he would speak but couldn't.*

"The Glass Menagerie" steals in as

(THE SCENE DIMS OUT.)

SCENE IV

The interior is dark. Faint light in the alley.
A deep-voiced bell in a church is tolling the hour of five as the scene commences.
TOM *appears at the top of the alley. After each solemn boom of the bell in the tower, he shakes a little noise-maker or rattle as if to express the tiny spasm of man in contrast to the sustained power and dignity of the Almighty. This and the unsteadiness of his advance make it evident that he has been drinking.*
As he climbs the few steps to the fire-escape landing light steals up inside. LAURA *appears in night-dress, observing* TOM's *empty bed in the front room.*
TOM *fishes in his pockets for the door-key, removing a motley assortment of articles in the search, including a perfect shower of movie-ticket stubs and an empty bottle. At last he finds the key, but just as he is about to insert it, it slips from his fingers. He strikes a match and crouches below the door.*

TOM (*bitterly*) One crack—and it falls through!

LAURA *opens the door.*

LAURA Tom! Tom, what are you doing?
TOM Looking for a door-key.
LAURA Where have you been all this time?
TOM I have been to the movies.
LAURA All this time at the movies?
TOM There was a very long program. There was a Garbo picture and a Mickey Mouse and a travelogue and a newsreel and a preview of coming attractions. And there was an organ solo and a collection for the milk-fund—simultaneously—which ended up in a terrible fight between a fat lady and an usher!
LAURA (*innocently*) Did you have to stay through everything?
TOM Of course! And, oh, I forgot! There was a big stage show! The headliner on this stage show was Malvolio the Magician. He performed wonderful tricks, many of them, such as pouring water back and forth between pitchers. First it turned to wine and then

it turned to beer and then it turned to whiskey. I know it was whiskey it finally turned into because he needed somebody to come up out of the audience to help him, and I came up—both shows! It was Kentucky Straight Bourbon. A very generous fellow, he gave souvenirs. (*He pulls from his back pocket a shimmering rainbow-colored scarf.*) He gave me this. This is his magic scarf. You can have it, Laura. You wave it over a canary cage and you get a bowl of gold-fish. You wave it over the gold-fish bowl and they fly away canaries. . . . But the wonderfullest trick of all was the coffin trick. We nailed him into a coffin and he got out of the coffin without removing one nail. (*He has come inside.*) There is a trick that would come in handy for me—get me out of this 2 by 4 situation! (*Flops onto bed and starts removing shoes.*)

LAURA   Tom—Shhh!

TOM   What you shushing me for?

LAURA   You'll wake up Mother.

TOM   Goody, goody! Pay 'er back for all those "Rise an' Shines." (*Lies down, groaning.*) You know it don't take much intelligence to get yourself into a nailed-up coffin, Laura. But who in hell ever got himself out of one without removing one nail?

As if in answer, the father's grinning photograph lights up.

(SCENE DIMS OUT.)

Immediately following: The church bell is heard striking six. At the sixth stroke the alarm clock goes off in AMANDA's *room, and after a few moments we hear her calling: "Rise and Shine! Rise and Shine! Laura, go tell your brother to rise and shine!"*

TOM   (*Sitting up slowly*)   I'll rise—but I won't shine.

The light increases.

AMANDA   Laura, tell your brother his coffee is ready.

LAURA *slips into front room.*

LAURA   Tom! it's nearly seven. Don't make Mother nervous. (*He stares at her stupidly. Beseechingly.*) Tom, speak to Mother this morning. Make up with her, apologize, speak to her!

TOM   She won't to me. It's her that started not speaking.

LAURA   If you just say you're sorry she'll start speaking.

TOM   Her not speaking—is that such a tragedy?

LAURA   Please—please!

AMANDA   (*calling from kitchenette*)   Laura, are you going to do what I asked you to do, or do I have to get dressed and go out myself?

LAURA Going, going—soon as I get on my coat! (*She pulls on a shapeless felt hat with nervous, jerky movement, pleadingly glancing at* TOM. *Rushes awkwardly for coat. The coat is one of* AMANDA'S, *inaccurately made-over, the sleeves too short for* LAURA.) Butter and what else?

AMANDA (*entering upstage*) Just butter. Tell them to charge it.

LAURA Mother, they make such faces when I do that.

AMANDA Sticks and stones may break my bones, but the expression on Mr. Garfinkel's face won't harm us! Tell your brother his coffee is getting cold.

LAURA (*at door*) Do what I asked you, will you, will you, Tom?

He looks sullenly away.

AMANDA Laura, go now or just don't go at all!

LAURA (*rushing out*) Going—going! (*A second later she cries out.* TOM *springs up and crosses to the door.* AMANDA *rushes anxiously in.* TOM *opens the door.*)

TOM Laura?

LAURA I'm all right. I slipped, but I'm all right.

AMANDA (*peering anxiously after her*) If anyone breaks a leg on those fire-escape steps, the landlord ought to be sued for every cent he possesses! (*She shuts door. Remembers she isn't speaking and returns to other room.*)

As TOM *enters listlessly for his coffee, she turns her back to him and stands rigidly facing the window on the gloomy gray vault of the areaway. Its light on her face with its aged but childish features is cruelly sharp, satirical as a Daumier print.*

(MUSIC UNDER: "AVE MARIA.")

TOM *glances sheepishly but sullenly at her averted figure and slumps at the table. The coffee is scalding hot; he sips it and gasps and spits it back in the cup. At his gasp,* AMANDA *catches her breath and half turns. Then catches herself and turns back to window.*

TOM *blows on his coffee, glancing sidewise at his mother. She clears her throat.* TOM *clears his. He starts to rise. Sinks back down again, scratches his head, clears his throat again.* AMANDA *coughs.* TOM *raises his cup in both hands to blow on it, his eyes staring over the rim of it at his mother for several moments. Then he slowly sets the cup down and awkwardly and hesitantly rises from the chair.*

TOM (*hoarsely*) Mother. I—I apologize. Mother. (AMANDA *draws a quick, shuddering breath. Her face works grotesquely. She breaks into childlike tears.*) I'm sorry for what I said, for everything that I said, I didn't mean it.

AMANDA (*sobbingly*) My devotion has made me a witch and so I make myself hateful to my children!

TOM No, you *don't*.

AMANDA I worry so much, don't sleep, it makes me nervous!

TOM (*gently*) I understand that.

AMANDA I've had to put up a solitary battle all these years. But you're my right-hand bower! Don't fall down, don't fail!

TOM (*gently*) I try, Mother.

AMANDA (*with great enthusiasm*) Try and you will SUCCEED! (*The notion makes her breathless.*) Why, you—you're just *full* of natural endowments! Both of my children—they're *unusual* children! Don't you think I know it? I'm so—*proud!* Happy and—feel I've —so much to be thankful for but—Promise me one thing, son!

TOM What, Mother?

AMANDA Promise, son, you'll—never be a drunkard!

TOM (*turns to her grinning*) I will never be a drunkard, Mother.

AMANDA That's what frightened me so, that you'd be drinking! Eat a bowl of Purina!

TOM Just coffee, Mother.

AMANDA Shredded wheat biscuit?

TOM No. No, Mother, just coffee.

AMANDA You can't put in a day's work on an empty stomach. You've got ten minutes—don't gulp! Drinking too-hot liquids makes cancer of the stomach. . . . Put cream in.

TOM No, thank you.

AMANDA To cool it.

TOM No! No, thank you, I want it black.

AMANDA I know, but it's not good for you. We have to do all that we can to build ourselves up. In these trying times we live in, all that we have to cling to is—each other. . . . That's why it's so important to—Tom, I—I sent out your sister so I could discuss something with you. If you hadn't spoken I would have spoken to you. (*Sits down.*)

TOM (*gently*) What is it, Mother, that you want to discuss?

AMANDA Laura!

TOM *puts his cup down slowly.*

(LEGEND ON SCREEN: "LAURA.")

(MUSIC: "THE GLASS MENAGERIE.")

TOM —Oh.—Laura . . .

AMANDA (*touching his sleeve*) You know how Laura is. So quiet but—still water runs deep! She notices things and I think she—

broods about them. (TOM *looks up*.) A few days ago I came in and she was crying.

TOM What about?

AMANDA You.

TOM Me?

AMANDA She has an idea that you're not happy here.

TOM What gave her that idea?

AMANDA What gives her any idea? However, you do act strangely. I—I'm not criticizing, understand *that!* I know your ambitions do not lie in the warehouse, that like everybody in the whole wide world—you've had to—make sacrifices, but—Tom—Tom —life's not easy, it calls for—Spartan endurance! There's so many things in my heart that I cannot describe to you! I've never told you but I—*loved* your father. . . .

TOM (*gently*) I know that, Mother.

AMANDA And you—when I see you taking after his ways! Staying out late—and—well, you *had* been drinking the night you were in that—terrifying condition! Laura says that you hate the apartment and that you go out nights to get away from it! Is that true, Tom?

TOM No. You say there's so much in your heart that you can't describe to me. That's true of me, too. There's so much in my heart that I can't describe to *you!* So let's respect each other's—

AMANDA But, why—*why*, Tom—are you always so *restless?* Where do you go to, nights?

TOM I—go to the movies.

AMANDA Why do you go to the movies so much, Tom?

TOM I go to the movies because—I like adventure. Adventure is something I don't have much of at work, so I go to the movies.

AMANDA But, Tom, you go to the movies *entirely* too *much!*

TOM I like a lot of adventure.

AMANDA *looks baffled, then hurt. As the familiar inquisition resumes he becomes hard and impatient again.* AMANDA *slips back into her querulous attitude toward him.*

(IMAGE ON SCREEN: SAILING VESSEL WITH JOLLY ROGER.)

AMANDA Most young men find adventure in their careers.

TOM Then most young men are not employed in a warehouse.

AMANDA The world is full of young men employed in warehouses and offices and factories.

TOM Do all of them find adventure in their careers?

AMANDA They do or they do without it! Not everybody has a craze for adventure.

TOM   Man is by instinct a lover, a hunter, a fighter, and none of those instincts are given much play at the warehouse!

AMANDA   Man is by instinct! Don't quote instinct to me! Instinct is something that people have got away from! It belongs to animals! Christian adults don't want it!

TOM   What do Christian adults want, then, Mother?

AMANDA   Superior things! Thinks of the mind and the spirit! Only animals have to satisfy instincts! Surely your aims are somewhat higher than theirs! Than monkeys—pigs—

TOM   I reckon they're not.

AMANDA   You're joking. However, that isn't what I wanted to discuss.

TOM   (*rising*)   I haven't much time.

AMANDA   (*pushing his shoulders*)   Sit down.

TOM   You want me to punch in red at the warehouse, Mother?

AMANDA   You have five minutes. I want to talk about Laura.

(LEGEND: "PLANS AND PROVISIONS.")

TOM   All right! What about Laura?

AMANDA   We have to be making plans and provisions for her. She's older than you, two years, and nothing has happened. She just drifts along doing nothing. It frightens me terribly how she just drifts along.

TOM   I guess she's the type that people call home girls.

AMANDA   There's no such type, and if there is, it's a pity! That is unless the home is hers, with a husband!

TOM   What?

AMANDA   Oh, I can see the handwriting on the wall as plain as I see the nose in front of my face! It's terrifying! More and more you remind me of your father! He was out all hours without explanation—Then *left! Goodbye!* And me with a bag to hold. I saw that letter you got from the Merchant Marine. I know what you're dreaming of. I'm not standing here blindfolded. Very well, then. Then *do* it! But not till there's somebody to take your place.

TOM   What do you mean?

AMANDA   I mean that as soon as Laura has got somebody to take care of her, married, a home of her own, independent—why, then you'll be free to go wherever you please, on land, on sea, whichever way the wind blows! But until that time you've got to look out for your sister. I don't say me because I'm old and don't matter! I say for your sister because she's young and dependent. I put her in business college—a dismal failure! Frightened her so it made her sick to her stomach. I took her over to the Young People's League at the church. Another fiasco. She spoke to nobody,

nobody spoke to her. Now all she does is fool with those pieces of glass and play those worn-out records. What kind of a life is that for a girl to lead?

TOM   What can I do about it?

AMANDA   Overcome selfishness! Self, self, self is all that you ever think of! (TOM *springs up and crosses to get his coat. It is ugly and bulky. He pulls on a cap with earmuffs.*) Where is your muffler? Put your wool muffler on! (*He snatches it angrily from the closet and tosses it around his neck and pulls both ends tight.*) Tom! I haven't said what I had in mind to ask you.

TOM   I'm too late to—

AMANDA   (*catching his arm—very importunately. Then shyly*). Down at the warehouse, aren't there some—nice young men?

TOM   No!

AMANDA   There *must* be—*some* . . .

TOM   Mother—

Gesture.

AMANDA   Find out one that's clean-living—doesn't drink and—ask him out for sister!

TOM   What?

AMANDA   For *sister!* To *meet!* Get *acquainted!*

TOM   (*stamping to door*)   Oh, my go-osh!

AMANDA   Will you? (*He opens door. Imploringly.*) Will you? (*He starts down.*) Will you? *Will* you, dear?

TOM   (*calling back*)   YES!

AMANDA *closes the door hesitantly and with a troubled but faintly hopeful expression.*

(SCREEN IMAGE: GLAMOR MAGAZINE COVER.)

Spot AMANDA *at phone.*

AMANDA   Ella Cartwright? This is Amanda Wingfield! How are you, honey? How is that kidney condition? (*Count five.*) *Horrors!* (*Count five.*) You're a Christian martyr, yes, honey, that's what you are, a Christian martyr! Well, I just happened to notice in my little red book that your subscription to the *Companion* has just run out! I knew that you wouldn't want to miss out on the wonderful serial starting in this new issue. It's by Bessie Mae Hopper, the first thing she's written since *Honeymoon for Three.* Wasn't that a strange and interesting story? Well, this one is even lovelier, I believe. It has a sophisticated society background. It's all about the horsey set on Long Island!

(FADE OUT.)

SCENE V

(LEGEND ON SCREEN: "ANNUNCIATION.")

Fade with music.

It is early dusk of a spring evening. Supper has just been finished in the Wingfield apartment. AMANDA *and* LAURA *in light colored dresses are removing dishes from the table, in the upstage area, which is shadowy, their movements formalized almost as a dance or ritual, their moving forms as pale and silent as moths.*

Tom, in white shirt and trousers, rises from the table and crosses toward the fire-escape.

AMANDA (*as he passes her*) Son, will you do me a favor?

TOM What?

AMANDA Comb your hair! You look so pretty when your hair is combed! (TOM *slouches on sofa with evening paper. Enormous caption "Franco Triumphs."*) There is only one respect in which I would like you to emulate your father.

TOM What respect is that?

AMANDA The care he always took of his appearance. He never allowed himself to look untidy. (*He throws down the paper and crosses to fire-escape.*) Where are you going?

TOM I'm going out to smoke.

AMANDA You smoke too much. A pack a day at fifteen cents a pack. How much would that amount to in a month? Thirty times fifteen is how much, Tom? Figure it out and you will be astounded at what you could save. Enough to give you a night-school course in accounting at Washington U! Just think what a wonderful thing that would be for you, son!

TOM *is unmoved by the thought.*

TOM I'd rather smoke. (*He steps out on landing, letting the screen door slam.*)

AMANDA (*sharply*) I know! That's the tragedy of it.... (*Alone, she turns to look at her husband's picture.*)

(DANCE MUSIC: "ALL THE WORLD IS WAITING FOR THE SUNRISE!")

TOM (*to the audience*) Across the alley from us was the Paradise Dance Hall. On evenings in spring the windows and doors were open and the music came outdoors. Sometimes the lights were turned out except for a large glass sphere that hung from the ceiling. It would turn slowly about and filter the dusk with delicate rainbow colors. Then the orchestra played a waltz or a tango, something that had a slow and sensuous rhythm. Couples would come outside, to the relative privacy of the alley. You could see them kissing behind ash-pits and telephone poles. This was the compensation for lives that passed like mine, without any change or adventure. Adventure and change were imminent in this year. They were waiting around the corner for all these kids. Suspended in the mist over Berchtesgaden, caught in the folds of Chamberlain's umbrella—In Spain there was Guernica! But here there was only hot swing music and liquor, dance halls, bars, and movies, and sex that hung in the gloom like a chandelier and flooded the world with brief, deceptive rainbows. . . . All the world was waiting for bombardments!

AMANDA *turns from the picture and comes outside.*

AMANDA (*sighing*) A fire-escape landing's a poor excuse for a porch. (*She spreads a newspaper on a step and sits down, gracefully and demurely as if she were settling into a swing on a Mississippi veranda.*) What are you looking at?

TOM The moon.

AMANDA Is there a moon this evening?

TOM It's rising over Garfinkel's Delicatessen.

AMANDA So it is! A little silver slipper of a moon. Have you made a wish on it yet?

TOM Um-hum.

AMANDA What did you wish for?

TOM That's a secret.

AMANDA A secret, huh? Well, I won't tell mine either. I will be just as mysterious as you.

TOM I bet I can guess what yours is.

AMANDA Is my head so transparent?

TOM You're not a sphinx.

AMANDA No, I don't have secrets. I'll tell you what I wished for on the moon. Success and happiness for my precious children! I wish for that whenever there's a moon, and when there isn't a moon, I wish for it, too.

TOM I thought perhaps you wished for a gentleman caller.

AMANDA Why do you say that?

TOM Don't you remember asking me to fetch one?

AMANDA I remember suggesting that it would be nice for your sister if you brought home some nice young man from the warehouse. I think I've made that suggestion more than once.

TOM Yes, you have made it repeatedly.

AMANDA Well?

TOM   We are going to have one.

AMANDA   *What?*

TOM   A gentleman caller!

(THE ANNUNCIATION IS CELEBRATED WITH MUSIC.)

AMANDA *rises.*

(IMAGE ON SCREEN: CALLER WITH BOUQUET.)

AMANDA   You mean you have asked some nice young man to come over?

TOM   Yep. I've asked him to dinner.

AMANDA   You really did?

TOM   I did!

AMANDA   You did, and did he—*accept?*

TOM   He did!

AMANDA   Well, well—well, well! That's—lovely!

TOM   I thought that you would be pleased.

AMANDA   It's definite, then?

TOM   Very definite.

AMANDA   Soon?

TOM   Very soon.

AMANDA   For heaven's sake, stop putting on and tell me some things, will you?

TOM   What things do you want me to tell you?

AMANDA   *Naturally* I would like to know when he's *coming!*

TOM   He's coming tomorrow.

AMANDA   *Tomorrow?*

TOM   Yep. Tomorrow.

AMANDA   But, Tom!

TOM   Yes, Mother?

AMANDA   Tomorrow gives me no time!

TOM   Time for what?

AMANDA   Preparations! Why didn't you phone me at once, as soon as you asked him, the minute that he accepted? Then, don't you see, I could have been getting ready!

TOM   You don't have to make any fuss.

AMANDA   Oh, Tom, Tom, Tom, of course I have to make a fuss! I want things nice, not sloppy! Not thrown together. I'll certainly have to do some fast thinking, won't I?

TOM   I don't see why you have to think at all.

AMANDA   You just don't know. We can't have a gentleman caller in a pig-sty! All my wedding silver has to be polished, the mono-grammed table linen ought to be laundered! The windows have to be washed and fresh curtains put up. And how about clothes? We have to *wear* something, don't we?

TOM   Mother, this boy is no one to make a fuss over!

AMANDA   Do you realize he's the first young man we've introduced to your sister? It's terrible, dreadful, disgraceful that poor little sister has never received a single gentleman caller! Tom, come inside! (*She opens the screen door.*)

TOM   What for?

AMANDA   I want to ask you some things.

TOM   If you're going to make such a fuss, I'll call it off, I'll tell him not to come.

AMANDA   You certainly won't do anything of the kind. Nothing offends people worse than broken engagements. It simply means I'll have to work like a Turk! We won't be brilliant, but we'll pass inspection. Come on inside. (TOM *follows, groaning.*) Sit down.

TOM   Any particular place you would like me to sit?

AMANDA   Thank heavens I've got that new sofa! I'm also making payments on a floor lamp I'll have sent out! And put the chintz covers on, they'll brighten things up! Of course I'd hoped to have these walls re-papered. . . . What is the young man's name?

TOM   His name is O'Connor.

AMANDA   That, of course, means fish—tomorrow is Friday! I'll have that salmon loaf—with Durkee's dressing! What does he do? He works at the warehouse?

TOM   Of course! How else would I—

AMANDA   Tom, he—doesn't drink?

TOM   Why do you ask me that?

AMANDA   Your father *did!*

TOM   Don't get started on that!

AMANDA   He *does* drink, then?

TOM   Not that I know of!

AMANDA   Make sure, be certain! The last thing I want for my daughter's a boy who drinks!

TOM   Aren't you being a little premature? Mr. O'Connor has not yet appeared on the scene!

AMANDA   But will tomorrow. To meet your sister, and what do I know about his character? Nothing! Old maids are better off than wives of drunkards!

TOM   Oh, my God!

AMANDA   Be still!

TOM   (*leaning forward to whisper*)   Lots of fellows meet girls whom they don't marry!

AMANDA   Oh, talk sensibly, Tom—and don't be sarcastic! (*She has gotten a hairbrush.*)

TOM   What are you doing?

AMANDA   I'm brushing that cow-lick down! What is this young man's position at the warehouse?

TOM (*submitting grimly to the brush and the interrogation*)   This young man's position is that of a shipping clerk, Mother.

AMANDA   Sounds to me like a fairly responsible job, the sort of a job *you* would be in if you just had more *get-up*. What is his salary? Have you got any idea?

TOM   I would judge it to be approximately eighty-five dollars a month.

AMANDA   Well—not princely, but—

TOM   Twenty more than I make.

AMANDA   Yes, how well I know! But for a family man, eighty-five dollars a month is not much more than you can just get by on. . . .

TOM   Yes, but Mr. O'Connor is not a family man.

AMANDA   He might be, mightn't he? Some time in the future?

TOM   I see. Plans and provisions.

AMANDA   You are the only young man that I know of who ignores the fact that the future becomes the present, the present the past, and the past turns into everlasting regret if you don't plan for it!

TOM   I will think that over and see what I can make of it.

AMANDA   Don't be supercilious with your mother! Tell me some more about this—what do you call him?

TOM   James D. O'Connor. The D. is for Delaney.

AMANDA   Irish on *both* sides! *Gracious!* And doesn't drink?

TOM   Shall I call him up and ask him right this minute?

AMANDA   The only way to find out about those things is to make discreet inquiries at the proper moment. When I was a girl in Blue Mountain and it was suspected that a young man drank, the girl whose attentions he had been receiving, if any girl *was,* would sometimes speak to the minister of his church, or rather her father would if her father was living, and sort of feel him out on the young man's character. That is the way such things are discreetly handled to keep a young woman from making a tragic mistake!

TOM   Then how did you happen to make a tragic mistake?

AMANDA   That innocent look of your father's had everyone fooled! He *smiled*—the world was *enchanted!* No girl can do worse than put herself at the mercy of a handsome appearance! I hope that Mr. O'Connor is not too good-looking.

TOM   No, he's not too good-looking. He's covered with freckles and hasn't too much of a nose.

AMANDA   He's not right-down homely, though?

TOM Not right-down homely. Just medium homely. I'd say.

AMANDA Character's what to look for in a man.

TOM That's what I've always said, Mother.

AMANDA You've never said anything of the kind and I suspect you would never give it a thought.

TOM Don't be suspicious of me.

AMANDA At least I hope he's the type that's up and coming.

TOM I think he really goes in for self-improvement.

AMANDA What reason have you to think so?

TOM He goes to night school.

AMANDA (*beaming*) Splendid! What does he do, I mean study?

TOM Radio engineering and public speaking!

AMANDA Then he has visions of being advanced in the world! Any young man who studies public speaking is aiming to have an executive job some day! And radio engineering? A thing for the future! Both of these facts are very illuminating. Those are the sort of things that a mother should know concerning any young man who comes to call on her daughter. Seriously or—not.

TOM One little warning. He doesn't know about Laura. I didn't let on that we had dark ulterior motives. I just said, why don't you come have dinner with us? He said okay and that was the whole conversation.

AMANDA I bet it was! You're eloquent as an oyster. However, he'll know about Laura when he gets here. When he sees how lovely and sweet and pretty she is, he'll thank his lucky stars he was asked to dinner.

TOM Mother, you mustn't expect too much of Laura.

AMANDA What do you mean?

TOM Laura seems all those things to you and me because she's ours and we love her. We don't even notice she's crippled any more.

AMANDA Don't say crippled! You know that I never allow that word to be used!

TOM But face facts, Mother. She is and—that's not all—

AMANDA What do you mean "not all"?

TOM Laura is very different from other girls.

AMANDA I think the difference is all to her advantage.

TOM Not quite all—in the eyes of others—strangers—she's terribly shy and lives in a world of her own and those things make her seem a little peculiar to people outside the house.

AMANDA Don't say peculiar.

TOM Face the facts. She is.

(THE DANCE-HALL MUSIC CHANGES TO A TANGO THAT HAS A MINOR AND SOMEWHAT OMINOUS TONE.)

AMANDA   In what way is she peculiar—may I ask?

TOM   (*gently*)   She lives in a world of her own—a world of—little glass ornaments, Mother.... (*Gets up.* AMANDA *remains holding brush, looking at him, troubled.*) She plays old phonograph records and—that's about all—(*He glances at himself in the mirror and crosses to door.*)

AMANDA   (*sharply*)   Where are you going?

TOM   I'm going to the movies. (*Out screen door.*)

AMANDA   Not to the movies, every night to the movies! (*Follows quickly to screen door.*) I don't believe you always go to the movies! (*He is gone.* AMANDA *looks worriedly after him for a moment. Then vitality and optimism return and she turns from the door. Crossing to portieres.*) Laura! Laura! (LAURA *answers from kitchenette.*)

LAURA   Yes, Mother.

AMANDA   Let those dishes go and come in front! (LAURA *appears with dish towel. Gaily.*) Laura, come here and make a wish on the moon!

LAURA   (*entering*)   Moon—moon?

AMANDA   A little silver slipper of a moon. Look over your left shoulder, Laura, and make a wish! (LAURA *looks faintly puzzled as if called out of sleep.* AMANDA *seizes her shoulders and turns her at an angle by the door.*) No! Now, darling, *wish!*

LAURA   What shall I wish for, Mother?

AMANDA   (*her voice trembling and her eyes suddenly filling with tears*)   Happiness! Good Fortune!

The violin rises and the stage dims out.

SCENE VI

(IMAGE: HIGH SCHOOL HERO.)

TOM   And so the following evening I brought Jim home to dinner. I had known Jim slightly in high school. In high school Jim was a hero. He had tremendous Irish good nature and vitality with the scrubbed and polished look of white chinaware. He seemed to move in a continual spotlight. He was a star in basketball, captain of the debating club, president of the senior class and the glee club and he sang the male lead in the annual light operas. He was always running or bounding, never just walking. He seemed always at the point of defeating the law of gravity. He was shooting with such velocity through his adolescence that you would logically expect him to arrive at nothing short of the White House by the time he was thirty. But Jim apparently ran into more interference after his graduation from Soldan. His speed had definitely slowed. Six years after he left high school he was holding a job that wasn't much better than mine.

(IMAGE: CLERK.)

He was the only one at the warehouse with whom I was on friendly terms. I was valuable to him as someone who could remember his former glory, who had seen him win basketball games and the silver cup in debating. He knew of my secret practice of retiring to a cabinet of the washroom to work on poems when business was slack in the warehouse. He called me Shakespeare. And while the other boys in the warehouse regarded me with suspicious hostility, Jim took a humorous attitude toward me. Gradually his attitude affected the others, their hostility wore off and they also began to smile at me as people smile at an oddly fashioned dog who trots across their path at some distance.

I knew that Jim and Laura had known each other at Soldan, and I had heard Laura speak admiringly of his voice. I didn't know if Jim remembered her or not. In high school Laura had been as unobtrusive as Jim had been astonishing. If he did remember Laura, it was not as my sister, for when I asked him to dinner, he grinned and said, "You know, Shakespeare, I never thought of you as having folks!"

He was about to discover that I did. . . .

(LIGHT UP STAGE.)

(LEGEND ON SCREEN: "THE ACCENT OF A COMING FOOT.")

Friday evening. It is about five o'clock of a late spring evening which comes "scattering poems in the sky."

A delicate lemony light is in the Wingfield apartment.

AMANDA *has worked like a Turk in preparation for the gentleman caller. The results are astonishing. The new floor lamp with its rose-silk shade is in place, a colored paper lantern conceals the broken light fixture in the ceiling, new billowing white curtains are at the windows, chintz covers are on chairs and sofa, a pair of new sofa pillows make their initial appearance.*

Open boxes and tissue paper are scattered on the floor.

LAURA *stands in the middle with lifted arms while* AMANDA *crouches before her, adjusting the hem of the new dress, devout and ritualistic. The dress is colored and designed by memory. The arrangement of* LAURA'S *hair is changed; it is softer and more becoming. A fragile, unearthly prettiness has come out in* LAURA: *she is like a piece of translucent glass touched by light, given a momentary radiance, not actual, not lasting.*

AMANDA (*impatiently*) Why are you trembling?

LAURA Mother, you've made me so nervous!

AMANDA How have I made you nervous?

LAURA By all this fuss! You make it seem so important!

AMANDA I don't understand you, Laura. You couldn't be satisfied with just sitting home, and yet whenever I try to arrange something for you, you seem to resist it. (*She gets up.*) Now take a look at yourself. No, wait! Wait just a moment—I have an idea!

LAURA What is it now?

AMANDA *produces two powder puffs which she wraps in handkerchiefs and stuffs in* LAURA'*s bosom.*

LAURA Mother, what are you doing?

AMANDA They call them "Gay Deceivers"!

LAURA I won't wear them!

AMANDA You will!

LAURA Why should I?

AMANDA Because, to be painfully honest, your chest is flat.

LAURA You make it seem like we were setting a trap.

AMANDA All pretty girls are a trap, a pretty trap, and men expect them to be. (LEGEND: "A PRETTY TRAP.") Now look at yourself, young lady. This is the prettiest you will ever be! I've got to fix myself now! You're going to be surprised by your mother's appearance! (*She crosses through portieres, humming gaily.*)

LAURA *moves slowly to the long mirror and stares solemnly at herself.*
A wind blows the white curtains inward in a slow, graceful motion and with a faint, sorrowful sighing.

AMANDA (*off stage*) It isn't dark enough yet. (*She turns slowly before the mirror with a troubled look.*)

(LEGEND ON SCREEN: "THIS IS MY SISTER: CELEBRATE HER WITH STRINGS!" MUSIC.)

AMANDA (*laughing, off*) I'm going to show you something. I'm going to make a spectacular appearance!

LAURA What is it, mother?

AMANDA Possess your soul in patience—you will see! Something I've resurrected from that old trunk! Styles haven't changed so terribly much after all.... (*She parts the portieres.*) Now just look at your mother! (*She wears a girlish frock of yellowed voile with a blue silk sash. She carries a bunch of jonquils—the legend of her youth is nearly revived. Feverishly.*) This is the dress in which I led the cotillion. Won the cakewalk twice at Sunset Hill, wore one spring to the Governor's ball in Jackson! See how I sashayed around the ballroom, Laura? (*She raises her skirt and does a mincing step around the room.*) I wore it on Sundays for my gentlemen callers! I had it on the day I met your father—I had malaria fever all that spring. The change of climate from East Tennessee to the Delta—weakened resistance—I had a little temperature all the time—not enough to be serious—just enough to make me restless and giddy! Invitations poured in—parties all over the Delta!—"Stay in bed," said Mother, "you have fever!" —but I just wouldn't.—I took quinine but kept on going, going! —Evenings, dances!—Afternoons, long, long rides! Picnics— lovely!—So lovely, that country in May.—All lacy with dogwood, literally flooded with jonquils!—That was the spring I had the craze for jonquils. Jonquils became an absolute obsession. Mother said, "Honey, there's no more room for jonquils." And still I kept bringing in more jonquils. Whenever, wherever I saw them, I'd say, "Stop! Stop! I see jonquils!" I made the young men help me gather the jonquils! It was a joke, Amanda and her jonquils! Finally there were no more vases to hold them, every available space was filled with jonquils. No vases to hold them? All right, I'll hold them myself! And then I—(*She stops in front of the picture.* MUSIC.) met your father! Malaria fever and jonquils and then—this—boy. . . . (*She switches on the rose-colored lamp.*) I hope they get here before it starts to rain. (*She crosses upstage and places the jonquils in bowl on table.*) I gave your brother a little extra change so he and Mr. O'Connor could take the service car home.

LAURA (*with altered look*) What did you say his name was?
AMANDA O'Connor.
LAURA What is his first name?
AMANDA I don't remember. Oh, yes, I do. It was—Jim!

LAURA *sways slightly and catches hold of a chair.*

(LEGEND ON SCREEN: "NOT JIM!")

LAURA (*faintly*) Not—Jim!
AMANDA Yes, that was it, it was Jim! I've never known a Jim that wasn't nice!

(MUSIC: OMINOUS.)

LAURA Are you sure his name is Jim O'Connor?
AMANDA Yes. Why?
LAURA Is he the one that Tom used to know in high school?
AMANDA He didn't say so. I think he just got to know him at the warehouse.
LAURA There was a Jim O'Connor we both knew in high school—

(*Then, with effort.*) If that is the one that Tom is bringing to dinner—you'll have to excuse me, I won't come to the table.

AMANDA What sort of nonsense is this?

LAURA You asked me once if I'd ever liked a boy. Don't you remember I showed you this boy's picture?

AMANDA You mean the boy you showed me in the year book?

LAURA Yes, that boy.

AMANDA Laura, Laura, were you in love with that boy?

LAURA I don't know, Mother. All I know is I couldn't sit at the table if it was him!

AMANDA It won't be him! It isn't the least bit likely. But whether it is or not, you will come to the table. You will not be excused.

LAURA I'll have to be, Mother.

AMANDA I don't intend to humor your silliness, Laura. I've had too much from you and your brother, both! So just sit down and compose yourself till they come. Tom has forgotten his key so you'll have to let them in, when they arrive.

LAURA (*panicky*) Oh, Mother—*you* answer the door!

AMANDA (*lightly*) I'll be in the kitchen—busy!

LAURA Oh, Mother, please answer the door, don't make me do it!

AMANDA (*crossing into kitchenette*) I've got to fixe the dressing for the salmon. Fuss, fuss—silliness!—over a gentleman caller!

Door swings shut. LAURA *is left alone.*

(LEGEND: "TERROR!")

She utters a low moan and turns off the lamp—sits stiffly on the edge of the sofa, knotting her fingers together.

(LEGEND ON SCREEN: "THE OPENING OF A DOOR!")

TOM *and* JIM *appear on the fire-escape steps and climb to landing. Hearing their approach,* LAURA *rises with a panicky gesture. She retreats to the portieres.*

The doorbell. LAURA *catches her breath and touches her throat. Low drums.*

AMANDA (*calling*) Laura, sweetheart! The door!

LAURA *stares at it without moving.*

JIM I think we just beat the rain.

TOM Uh-huh. (*He rings again, nervously.* JIM *whistles and fishes for a cigarette.*)

AMANDA (*very, very gaily*) Laura, that is your brother and Mr. O'Connor! Will you let them in, darling?

LAURA *crosses toward kitchenette door.*

LAURA (*breathlessly*)   Mother—you go to the door!

AMANDA *steps out of kitchenette and stares furiously at* LAURA. *She points imperiously at the door.*

LAURA   Please, please!

AMANDA (*in a fierce whisper*)   What is the matter with you, you silly thing?

LAURA (*desperately*)   Please, you answer it, *please!*

AMANDA   I told you I wasn't going to humor you, Laura. Why have you chosen this moment to lose your mind?

LAURA   Please, please, please, you go!

AMANDA   You'll have to go to the door because I can't!

LAURA (*despairingly*)   I can't either!

AMANDA   Why?

LAURA   I'm *sick!*

AMANDA   I'm sick, too—of your nonsense! Why can't you and your brother be normal people? Fantastic whims and behavior! (TOM *gives a long ring.*) Preposterous goings on! Can you give me one reason—(*Calls out lyrically.*) COMING! JUST ONE SECOND!—why should you be afraid to open a door? Now you answer it, Laura!

LAURA   Oh, oh, oh . . . (*She returns through the portieres. Darts to the victrola and winds it frantically and turns it on.*)

AMANDA   Laura Wingfield, you march right to that door!

LAURA   Yes—yes, Mother!

A faraway, scratchy rendition of "Dardanella" softens the air and gives her strength to move through it. She slips to the door and draws it cautiously open.

   TOM *enters with the caller,* JIM O'CONNOR.

TOM   Laura, this is Jim. Jim, this is my sister, Laura.

JIM (*stepping inside*)   I didn't know that Shakespeare had a sister!

LAURA (*retreating stiff and trembling from the door*)   How—how do you do?

JIM (*heartily extending his hand*)   Okay!

LAURA *touches it hesitantly with hers.*

JIM   Your hand's *cold,* Laura!

LAURA   Yes, well—I've been playing the victrola. . . .

JIM   Must have been playing classical music on it! You ought to play a little hot swing music to warm you up!

LAURA   Excuse me—I haven't finished playing the victrola. . . .

She turns awkwardly and hurries into the front room. She pauses a second by the victrola. Then catches her breath and darts through the portieres like a frightened deer.

JIM (*grinning*)   What was the matter?

TOM   Oh—with Laura? Laura is—terribly shy.

JIM   Shy, huh? It's unusual to meet a shy girl nowadays. I don't believe you ever mentioned you had a sister.

TOM   Well, now you know. I have one. Here is the *Post Dispatch.* You want a piece of it?

JIM   Uh-huh.

TOM   What piece? The comics?

JIM   Sports! (*Glances at it.*) Ole Dizzy Dean is on his bad behavior.

TOM (*disinterest*)   Yeah? (*Lights cigarette and crosses back to fire-escape door.*)

JIM   Where are *you* going?

TOM   I'm going out on the terrace.

JIM (*goes after him*)   You know, Shakespeare—I'm going to sell you a bill of goods!

TOM   What goods?

JIM   A course I'm taking.

TOM   Huh?

JIM   In public speaking! You and me, we're not the warehouse type.

TOM   Thanks—that's good news. But what has public speaking got to do with it?

JIM   It fits you for—executive positions!

TOM   Awww.

JIM   I tell you it's done a helluva lot for me.

(IMAGE: EXECUTIVE AT DESK.)

TOM   In what respect?

JIM   In every! Ask yourself what is the difference between you an' me and men in the office down front? Brains?—No!—Ability?—No! Then what? Just one little thing—

TOM   What is that one little thing?

JIM   Primarily it amounts to—social poise! Being able to square up to people and hold your own on any social level!

AMANDA (*off stage*)   Tom?

TOM   Yes, Mother?

AMANDA   Is that you and Mr. O'Connor?

TOM   Yes, Mother.

AMANDA   Well, you just make yourselves comfortable in there.

TOM   Yes, Mother.

AMANDA   Ask Mr. O'Connor if he would like to wash his hands.

JIM   Aw—no—no—thank you—I took care of that at the warehouse. Tom—

TOM   Yes?

JIM   Mr. Mendoza was speaking to me about you.

TOM   Favorably?

JIM   What do you think?

TOM   Well—

JIM   You're going to be out of a job if you don't wake up.

TOM   I am waking up—

JIM   You show no signs.

TOM   The signs are interior.

(IMAGE ON SCREEN: THE SAILING VESSEL WITH JOLLY ROGER AGAIN.)

TOM   I'm planning to change. (*He leans over the rail speaking with quiet exhilaration. The incandescent marquees and signs of the first-run movie houses light his face from across the alley. He looks like a voyager.*) I'm right at the point of committing myself to a future that doesn't include the warehouse and Mr. Mendoza or even a night-school course in public speaking.

JIM   What are you gassing about?

TOM   I'm tired of the movies.

JIM   Movies!

TOM   Yes, movies! Look at them—(*A wave toward the marvels of Grand Avenue.*) All of those glamorous people—having adventures—hogging it all, gobbling the whole thing up! You know what happens? People go to the *movies* instead of *moving!* Hollywood characters are supposed to have all the adventures for everybody in America, while everybody in America sits in a dark room and watches them have them! Yes, until there's a war. That's when adventure becomes available to the masses! *Everyone's* dish, not only Gable's! Then the people in the dark room come out of the dark room to have some adventures themselves— Goody, goody!—It's our turn now, to go to the South Sea Island —to make a safari—to be exotic, far-off!—But I'm not patient. I don't want to wait till then. I'm tired of the *movies* and I am *about* to *move!*

JIM   (*incredulously*)   Move?

TOM   Yes.

JIM   When?

TOM   Soon!

JIM   Where? Where?

(THEME THREE MUSIC SEEMS TO ANSWER THE QUESTION, WHILE TOM THINKS IT OVER. HE SEARCHES AMONG HIS POCKETS.)

TOM   I'm starting to boil inside. I know I seem dreamy, but inside —well, I'm boiling! Whenever I pick up a shoe, I shudder a little thinking how short life is and what I am doing!—Whatever that means. I know it doesn't mean shoes—except as something to wear on a traveler's feet! (*Finds paper.*) Look—

JIM   What?

TOM   I'm a member.

JIM (*reading*)   The Union of Merchant Seamen.

TOM   I paid my dues this month, instead of the light bill.

JIM   You will regret it when they turn the lights off.

TOM   I won't be here.

JIM   How about your mother?

TOM   I'm like my father. The bastard son of a bastard! See how he grins? And he's been absent going on sixteen years!

JIM   You're just talking, you drip. How does your mother feel about it?

TOM   Shhh!—Here comes Mother! Mother is not acquainted with my plans!

AMANDA (*enters portieres*)   Where are you all?

TOM   On the terrace, Mother.

They start inside. She advances to them. TOM *is distinctly shocked at her appearance. Even* JIM *blinks a little. He is making his first contact with girlish Southern vivacity and in spite of the night-school course in public speaking is somewhat thrown off the beam by the unexpected outlay of social charm.*

Certain responses are attempted by JIM *but are swept aside by* AMANDA's *gay laughter and chatter.* TOM *is embarrassed but after the first shock* JIM *reacts very warmly. Grins and chuckles, is altogether won over.*

(IMAGE: AMANDA AS A GIRL.)

AMANDA (*coyly smiling, shaking her girlish ringlets*)   Well, well, well, so this is Mr. O'Connor. Introductions entirely unnecessary. I've heard so much about you from my boy. I finally said to him, Tom—good gracious!—why don't you bring this paragon to supper? I'd like to meet this nice young man at the warehouse!— Instead of just hearing him sing your praises so much! I don't know why my son is so stand-offish—that's not Southern behavior! Let's sit down and—I think we could stand a little more air in here! Tom, leave the door open. I felt a nice fresh breeze a moment ago. Where has it gone? Mmm, so warm already! And not quite summer, even. We're going to burn up when summer really gets started. However, we're having—we're having a very light supper. I think light things are better fo' this time of year. The same as light clothes are. Light clothes an' light food are what warm weather calls fo'. You know our blood gets so thick during th' winter—it takes a while fo' us to *adjust* ou'selves!—

when the season changes . . . It's come so quick this year. I wasn't prepared. All of a sudden—heavens! Already summer!—I ran to the trunk an' pulled out this light dress—Terribly old! Historical almost! But feels so good—so good an' co-ol, y'know. . . .

TOM Mother—

AMANDA Yes, honey?

TOM How about—supper?

AMANDA Honey, you go ask Sister if supper is ready! You know that Sister is in full charge of supper! Tell her you hungry boys are waiting for it. (*To* JIM.) Have you met Laura?

JIM She—

AMANDA Let you in? Oh, good, you've met already! It's rare for a girl as sweet an' pretty as Laura to be domestic! But Laura is, thank heavens, not only pretty but also very domestic. I'm not at all. I never was a bit. I never could make a thing but angel-food cake. Well, in the South we had so many servants. Gone, gone, gone. All vestige of gracious living! Gone completely! I wasn't prepared for what the future brought me. All of my gentlemen callers were sons of planters and so of course I assumed that I would be married to one and raise my family on a large piece of land with plenty of servants. But man proposes—and woman accepts the proposal!—To vary that old, old saying a little bit—I married no planter! I married a man who worked for the telephone company!—That gallantly smiling gentleman over there! (*Points to the picture.*) A telephone man who—fell in love with long-distance!—Now he travels and I don't even know where!— But what am I going on for about my—tribulations? Tell me yours—I hope you don't have any! Tom?

TOM (*returning*) Yes, Mother?

AMANDA Is supper nearly ready?

TOM It looks to me like supper is on the table.

AMANDA Let me look—(*She rises prettily and looks through portieres.*) Oh, lovely!—But where is Sister?

TOM Laura is not feeling well and she says that she thinks she'd better not come to the table.

AMANDA What?—Nonsense!—Laura? Oh, Laura!

LAURA (*off stage, faintly*) Yes, Mother.

AMANDA You really must come to the table. We won't be seated until you come to the table! Come in, Mr. O'Connor. You sit over there and I'll—Laura? Laura Wingfield! You're keeping us waiting, honey! We can't say grace until you come to the table!

The back door is pushed weakly open and LAURA *comes in. She is obviously quite faint, her lips trembling, her eyes wide and staring. She moves unsteadily toward the table.*

(LEGEND: "TERROR!")

Outside a summer storm is coming abruptly. The white curtains billow inward at the windows and there is a sorrowful murmur and deep blue dusk.

LAURA *suddenly stumbles—she catches at a chair with a faint moan.*

TOM Laura!

AMANDA Laura! (*There is a clap of thunder.*) (LEGEND: "AH!")
(*Despairingly.*) Why, Laura, you *are* sick, darling! Tom, help your sister into the living room, dear! Sit in the living room, Laura —rest on the sofa. Well! (*To the gentleman caller.*) Standing over the hot stove made her ill!—I told her that it was just too warm this evening, but—(TOM *comes back in.* LAURA *is on the sofa.*) Is Laura all right now?

TOM Yes.

AMANDA What *is* that? Rain? A nice cool rain has come up! (*She gives the gentleman caller a frightened look.*) I think we may— have grace—now ... (TOM *looks at her stupidly.*) Tom, honey— you say grace!

TOM Oh ... "For these and all thy mercies—" (*They bow their heads,* AMANDA *stealing a nervous glance at* JIM. *In the living room* LAURA, *stretched on the sofa, clenches her hand to her lips, to hold back a shuddering sob.*) God's Holy Name be praised—

(THE SCENE DIMS OUT.)

SCENE VII

(LEGEND: "A SOUVENIR.")

Half an hour later. Dinner is just being finished in the upstage area which is concealed by the drawn portieres.

As the curtain rises LAURA *is still huddled upon the sofa, her feet drawn under her, her head resting on a pale blue pillow, her eyes wide and mysteriously watchful. The new floor lamp with its shade of rose-colored silk gives a soft, becoming light to her face, bringing out the fragile, unearthly prettiness which usually escapes attention. There is a steady murmur of rain, but it is slackening and stops soon after the scene begins; the air outside becomes pale and luminous as the moon breaks out.*

A moment after the curtain rises, the lights in both rooms flicker and go out.

JIM Hey, there, Mr. Light Bulb!

AMANDA *laughs nervously.*

(LEGEND: "SUSPENSION OF A PUBLIC SERVICE.")

AMANDA Where was Moses when the lights went out? Ha-ha. Do you know the answer to that one, Mr. O'Connor?

JIM No, Ma'am, what's the answer?

AMANDA In the dark! (JIM *laughs appreciably*.) Everybody sit still. I'll light the candles. Isn't it lucky we have them on the table? Where's a match? Which of you gentlemen can provide a match?

JIM Here.

AMANDA Thank you, sir.

JIM Not at all, Ma'am!

AMANDA I guess the fuse has burnt out. Mr. O'Connor, can you tell a burnt-out fuse? I know I can't and Tom is a total loss when it comes to mechanics. (SOUND: GETTING UP: VOICES RECEDE A LITTLE TO KITCHENETTE.) Oh, be careful you don't bump into something. We don't want our gentleman caller to break his neck. Now wouldn't that be a fine howdy-do?

JIM Ha-ha! Where is the fuse-box?

AMANDA Right here next to the stove. Can you see anything?

JIM Just a minute.

AMANDA Isn't electricity a mysterious thing? Wasn't it Benjamin Franklin who tied a key to a kite? We live in such a mysterious universe, don't we? Some people say that science clears up all the mysteries for us. In my opinion it only creates more! Have you found it yet?

JIM No, Ma'am. All these fuses look okay to me.

AMANDA Tom!

TOM Yes, Mother?

AMANDA That light bill I gave you several days ago. The one I told you we got the notices about?

TOM Oh.—Yeah.

(LEGEND: "HA!")

AMANDA You didn't neglect to pay it by any chance?

TOM Why, I—

AMANDA Didn't! I might have known it!

JIM Shakespeare probably wrote a poem on that light bill, Mrs. Wingfield.

AMANDA I might have known better than to trust him with it! There's such a high price for negligence in this world!

JIM Maybe the poem will win a ten-dollar prize.

AMANDA We'll just have to spend the remainder of the evening in the nineteenth century, before Mr. Edison made the Mazda lamp!

JIM Candlelight is my favorite kind of light.

AMANDA That shows you're romantic! But that's no excuse for

Tom. Well, we got through dinner. Very considerate of them to let us get through dinner before they plunged us into everlasting darkness, wasn't it, Mr. O'Connor?

JIM Ha-ha!

AMANDA Tom, as a penalty for your carelessness you can help me with the dishes.

JIM Let me give you a hand.

AMANDA Indeed you will not!

JIM I ought to be good for something.

AMANDA Good for something? (*Her tone is rhapsodic.*) *You?* Why, Mr. O'Connor, nobody, *nobody's* given me this much entertainment in years—as you have!

JIM Aw, now, Mrs. Wingfield!

AMANDA I'm not exaggerating, not one bit! But Sister is all by her lonesome. You go keep her company in the parlor! I'll give you this lovely old candelabrum that used to be on the altar at the church of the Heavenly Rest. It was melted a little out of shape when the church burnt down. Lightning struck it one spring. Gypsy Jones was holding a revival at the time and he intimated that the church was destroyed because the Episcopalians gave card parties.

JIM Ha-ha.

AMANDA And how about coaxing Sister to drink a little wine? I think it would be good for her! Can you carry both at once?

JIM Sure. I'm Superman!

AMANDA Now, Thomas, get into this apron!

The door of kitchenette swings closed on AMANDA'S *gay laughter; the flickering light approaches the portieres.*

LAURA *sits up nervously as he enters. Her speech at first is low and breathless from the almost intolerable strain of being alone with a stranger.*

(THE LEGEND: "I DON'T SUPPOSE YOU REMEMBER ME AT ALL!")

In her first speeches in this scene, before JIM'S *warmth overcomes her paralyzing shyness,* LAURA'S *voice is thin and breathless as though she has just run up a steep flight of stairs.*

JIM'S *attitude is gently humorous. In playing this scene it should be stressed that while the incident is apparently unimportant, it is to* LAURA *the climax of her secret life.*

JIM Hello, there, Laura.

LAURA (*faintly*) Hello (*She clears her throat.*)

JIM How are you feeling now? Better?

LAURA Yes. Yes, thank you.

JIM This is for you. A little dandelion wine. (*He extends it toward her with extravagant gallantry.*)

LAURA   Thank you.

JIM   Drink it—but don't get drunk! (*He laughs heartily.* LAURA *takes the glass uncertainly; laughs shyly.*) Where shall I set the candles?

LAURA   Oh—oh, anywhere . . .

JIM   How about here on the floor? Any objections?

LAURA   No.

JIM   I'll spread a newspaper under to catch the drippings. I like to sit on the floor. Mind if I do?

LAURA   Oh, no.

JIM   Give me a pillow?

LAURA   What?

JIM   A pillow!

LAURA   Oh . . . (*Hands him one quickly.*)

JIM   How about you? Don't you like to sit on the floor?

LAURA   Oh—yes.

JIM   Why don't you, then?

LAURA   I—will.

JIM   Take a pillow! (LAURA *does. Sits on the other side of the candelabrum.* JIM *crosses his legs and smiles engagingly at her.*) I can't hardly see you sitting way over there.

LAURA   I can—see you.

JIM   I know, but that's not fair, I'm in the limelight. (LAURA *moves her pillow closer.*) Good! Now I can see you! Comfortable?

LAURA   Yes.

JIM   So am I. Comfortable as a cow. Will you have some gum?

LAURA   No, thank you.

JIM   I think that I will indulge, with your permission. (*Musingly unwraps it and holds it up.*) Think of the fortune made by the guy that invented the first piece of chewing gum. Amazing, huh? The Wrigley Building is one of the sights of Chicago.—I saw it summer before last when I went up to the Century of Progress. Did you take in the Century of Progress?

LAURA   No, I didn't.

JIM   Well, it was quite a wonderful exposition. What impressed me most was the Hall of Science. Gives you an idea of what the future will be in America, even more wonderful than the present time is! (*Pause. Smiling at her.*) Your brother tells me you're shy. Is that right, Laura?

LAURA   I—don't know.

JIM   I judge you to be an old-fashioned type of girl. Well, I think that's a pretty good type to be. Hope you don't think I'm being too personal—do you?

LAURA   (*hastily, out of embarrassment*)   I believe I *will* take a piece of gum, if you—don't mind. (*Clearing her throat.*) Mr. O'Connor, have you—kept up with your singing?

JIM   Singing? Me?

LAURA   Yes. I remember what a beautiful voice you had.

JIM   When did you hear me sing?

(VOICE OFF STAGE IN THE PAUSE.)

VOICE (*off stage*)

> O blow, ye winds, heigh-ho,
> A-roving I will go!
> I'm off to my love
> With a boxing glove—
> Ten thousand miles away!

JIM   You say you've heard me sing?

LAURA   Oh, yes! Yes, very often . . . I—don't suppose you remember me—at all?

JIM (*smiling doubtfully*)   You know I have an idea I've seen you before. I had that idea soon as you opened the door. It seemed almost like I was about to remember your name. But the name that I started to call you—wasn't a name! And so I stopped myself before I said it.

LAURA   Wasn't it—Blue Roses?

JIM (*springs up, grinning*)   Blue Roses! My gosh, yes—Blue Roses! That's what I had on my tongue when you opened the door! Isn't it funny what tricks your memory plays? I didn't connect you with the high school somehow or other. But that's where it was; it was high school. I didn't even know you were Shakespeare's sister! Gosh, I'm sorry.

LAURA   I didn't expect you to. You—barely knew me!

JIM   But we did have a speaking acquaintance, huh?

LAURA   Yes, we—spoke to each other.

JIM   When did you recognize me?

LAURA   Oh, right away!

JIM   Soon as I came in the door?

LAURA   When I heard your name I thought it was probably you. I knew that Tom used to know you a little in high school. So when you came in the door—Well, then I was—sure.

JIM   Why didn't you *say* something, then?

LAURA (*breathlessly*)   I didn't know what to say, I was—too surprised!

JIM   For goodness' sakes! You know, this sure is funny!

LAURA   Yes! Yes, isn't it, though . . .

JIM   Didn't we have a class in something together?

LAURA Yes, we did.

JIM What class was that?

LAURA It was—singing—Chorus!

JIM Aw!

LAURA I sat across the aisle from you in the Aud.

JIM Aw.

LAURA Mondays, Wednesdays and Fridays.

JIM Now I remember—you always came in late.

LAURA Yes, it was so hard for me, getting upstairs. I had that brace on my leg—it clumped so loud!

JIM I never heard any clumping.

LAURA (*wincing at the recollection*) To me it sounded like—thunder!

JIM Well, well, well. I never even noticed.

LAURA And everybody was seated before I came in. I had to walk in front of all those people. My seat was in the back row. I had to go clumping all the way up the aisle with everyone watching!

JIM You shouldn't have been self-conscious.

LAURA I know, but I was. It was always such a relief when the singing started.

JIM Aw, yes. I've placed you now! I used to call you Blue Roses. How was it that I got started calling you that?

LAURA I was out of school a little while with pleurosis. When I came back you asked me what was the matter. I said I had pleurosis—you thought I said Blue Roses. That's what you always called me after that!

JIM I hope you didn't mind.

LAURA Oh, no—I liked it. You see, I wasn't acquainted with many —people. . . .

JIM As I remember you sort of stuck by yourself.

LAURA I—I—never had much luck at—making friends.

JIM I don't see why you wouldn't.

LAURA Well, I—started out badly.

JIM You mean being—

LAURA Yes, it sort of—stood between me—

JIM You shouldn't have let it!

LAURA I know, but it did, and—

JIM You were shy with people!

LAURA I tried not to be but never could—

JIM Overcome it?

LAURA No, I—I never could!

JIM I guess being shy is something you have to work out of kind of gradually.

LAURA (*sorrowfully*) Yes—I guess it—

JIM Takes time!

LAURA Yes—

JIM People are not so dreadful when you know them. That's what you have to remember! And everybody has problems, not just you, but practically everybody has got some problems. You think of yourself as having the only problems, as being the only one who is disappointed. But just look around you and you will see lots of people as disappointed as you are. For instance, I hoped when I was going to high school that I would be further along at this time, six years later, than I am now—You remember that wonderful write-up I had in *The Torch?*

LAURA Yes! (*She rises and crosses to table.*)

JIM It said I was bound to succeed in anything I went into! (LAURA *returns with the annual.*) Holy Jeez! *The Torch!* (*He accepts it reverently. They smile across it with mutual wonder.* LAURA *crouches beside him and they begin to turn through it.* LAURA's *shyness is dissolving in his warmth.*)

LAURA Here you are in *Pirates of Penzance!*

JIM (*wistfully*) I sang the baritone lead in that operetta.

LAURA (*rapidly*) So—*beautifully!*

JIM (*protesting*) Aw—

LAURA Yes, yes—beautifully—beautifully!

JIM You heard me?

LAURA All three times!

JIM No!

LAURA Yes!

JIM All three performances?

LAURA (*looking down*) Yes.

JIM Why?

LAURA I—wanted to ask you to—autograph my program.

JIM Why didn't you ask me to.

LAURA You were always surrounded by your own friends so much that I never had a chance to.

JIM You should have just—

LAURA Well, I—thought you might think I was—

JIM Thought I might think you was—what?

LAURA Oh—

JIM (*with reflective relish*) I was beleaguered by females in those days.

LAURA You were terribly popular!

JIM Yeah—

LAURA You had such a—friendly way—

JIM I was spoiled in high school.

LAURA Everybody—liked you!

JIM   Including you?

LAURA   I—yes, I—I did, too—(*She gently closes the book in her lap.*)

JIM   Well, well, well!—Give me that program, Laura. (*She hands it to him. He signs it with a flourish.*) There you are—better late than never!

LAURA   Oh, I—what a—surprise!

JIM   My signature isn't worth very much right now. But some day —maybe—it will increase in value! Being disappointed is one thing and being discouraged is something else. I am disappointed but I am not discouraged. I'm twenty-three years old. How old are you?

LAURA   I'll be twenty-four in June.

JIM   That's not old age!

LAURA   No, but—

JIM   You finished high school?

LAURA   (*with difficulty*)   I didn't go back.

JIM   You mean you dropped out?

LAURA   I made bad grades in my final examinations. (*She rises and replaces the book and the program. Her voice strained.*) How is—Emily Meisenbach getting along?

JIM   Oh, that kraut-head!

LAURA   Why do you call her that?

JIM   That's what she was.

LAURA   You're not still—going with her?

JIM   I never see her.

LAURA   It said in the Personal Section that you were—engaged!

JIM   I know, but I wasn't impressed by that—propaganda!

LAURA   It wasn't—the truth?

JIM   Only in Emily's optimistic opinion!

LAURA   Oh—

(LEGEND: "WHAT HAVE YOU DONE SINCE HIGH SCHOOL?")

JIM *lights a cigarette and leans indolently back on his elbows smiling at* LAURA *with a warmth and charm which lights her inwardly with altar candles. She remains by the table and turns in her hands a piece of glass to cover her tumult.*

JIM   (*after several reflective puffs on a cigarette*)   What have you done since high school? (*She seems not to hear him.*) Huh? (LAURA *looks up.*) I said what have you done since high school, Laura?

LAURA   Nothing much.

JIM   You must have been doing something these six long years.

LAURA   Yes.

JIM   Well, then, such as what?

LAURA   I took a business course at business college—

JIM   How did that work out?

LAURA   Well, not very—well—I had to drop out, it gave me—indigestion—

JIM *laughs gently.*

JIM   What are you doing now?

LAURA   I don't do anything—much. Oh, please don't think I sit around doing nothing! My glass collection takes up a good deal of my time. Glass is something you have to take good care of.

JIM   What did you say—about glass?

LAURA   Collection I said—I have one—(*She clears her throat and turns away again, acutely shy.*)

JIM   (*abruptly*)   You know what I judge to be the trouble with you? Inferiority complex! Know what that is? That's what they call it when someone low-rates himself! I understand it because I had it, too. Although my case was not so aggravated as yours seems to be. I had it until I took up public speaking, developed my voice, and learned that I had an aptitude for science. Before that time I never thought of myself as being outstanding in any way whatsoever! Now I've never made a regular study of it, but I have a friend who says I can analyze people better than doctors that make a profession of it. I don't claim that to be necessarily true, but I can sure guess a person's psychology, Laura! (*Takes out his gum.*) Excuse me, Laura. I always take it out when the flavor is gone. I'll use this scrap of paper to wrap it in. I know how it is to get it stuck on a shoe. Yep—that's what I judge to be your principal trouble. A lack of confidence in yourself as a person. You don't have the proper amount of faith in yourself. I'm basing that fact on a number of your remarks and also on certain observations I've made. For instance that clumping you thought was so awful in high school. You say that you even dreaded to walk into class. You see what you did? You dropped out of school, you gave up an education because of a clump, which as far as I know was practically non-existent! A little physical defect is what you have. Hardly noticeable even! Magnified thousands of times by imagination! You know what my strong advice to you is? Think of yourself as *superior* in some way!

LAURA   In what way would I think?

JIM   Why, man alive, Laura! Just look about you a little. What do you see? A world full of common people! All of 'em born and all of 'em going to die! Which of them has one-tenth of your good points! Or mine! Or anyone else's, as far as that goes—Gosh!

Everybody excels in some one thing. Some in many! (*Unconsciously glances at himself in the mirror.*) All you've got to do is discover in *what!* Take me, for instance. (*He adjusts his tie at the mirror.*) My interest happens to lie in electro-dynamics. I'm taking a course in radio engineering at night school, Laura, on top of a fairly responsible job at the warehouse. I'm taking that course and studying public speaking.

LAURA Ohhhh.

JIM Because I believe in the future of television! (*Turning back to her.*) I wish to be ready to go up right along with it. Therefore I'm planning to get in on the ground floor. In fact, I've already made the right connections and all that remains is for the industry itself to get under way! Full steam—(*His eyes are starry.*) *Knowledge*—Zzzzzp! *Money*—Zzzzzzp!—*Power!* That's the cycle democracy is built on! (*His attitude is convincingly dynamic.* LAURA *stares at him, even her shyness eclipsed in her absolute wonder. He suddenly grins.*) I guess you think I think a lot of myself!

LAURA No—o-o-o, I—

JIM Now how about you? Isn't there something you take more interest in than anything else?

LAURA Well, I do—as I said—have my—glass collection—

A peal of girlish laughter from the kitchen.

JIM I'm not right sure I know what you're talking about. What kind of glass is it?

LAURA Little articles of it, they're ornaments mostly! Most of them are little animals made out of glass, the tiniest little animals in the world. Mother calls them a glass menagerie! Here's an example of one, if you'd like to see it! This one is one of the oldest. It's nearly thirteen. (*He stretches out his hand.*) (MUSIC: "THE GLASS MENAGERIE.") Oh, be careful—if you breathe, it breaks!

JIM I'd better not take it. I'm pretty clumsy with things.

LAURA Go on, I trust you with him! (*Places it in his palm.*) There now—you're holding him gently! Hold him over the light, he loves the light! You see how the light shines through him?

JIM It sure does shine!

LAURA I shouldn't be partial, but he is my favorite one.

JIM What kind of a thing is this one supposed to be?

LAURA Haven't you noticed the single horn on his forehead?

JIM A unicorn, huh?

LAURA Mmm-hmmm!

JIM Unicorns, aren't they extinct in the modern world?

LAURA I know!

JIM   Poor little fellow, he must feel sort of lonesome.

LAURA (*smiling*)   Well, if he does he doesn't complain about it. He stays on a shelf with some horses that don't have horns and all of them seem to get along nicely together.

JIM   How do you know?

LAURA (*lightly*)   I haven't heard any arguments among them!

JIM (*grinning*)   No arguments, huh? Well, that's a pretty good sign! Where shall I set him?

LAURA   Put him on the table. They all like a change of scenery once in a while!

JIM (*stretching*)   Well, well, well, well—Look how big my shadow is when I stretch!

LAURA   Oh, oh, yes—it stretches across the ceiling!

JIM (*crossing to door*)   I think it's stopped raining. (*Opens fire-escape door.*) Where does the music come from?

LAURA   From the Paradise Dance Hall across the alley.

JIM   How about cutting the rug a little, Miss Wingfield?

LAURA   Oh, I—

JIM   Or is your program filled up? Let me have a look at it. *Grasps imaginary card.*) Why, every dance is taken! I'll just have to scratch some out. (WALTZ MUSIC: "LA GOLONDRINA.") Ahhh, a waltz! (*He executes some sweeping turns by himself, then holds his arms toward* LAURA.)

LAURA (*breathlessly*)   I—can't dance!

JIM   There you go, that inferiority stuff!

LAURA   I've never danced in my life!

JIM   Come on, try!

LAURA   Oh, but I'd step on you!

JIM   I'm not made out of glass.

LAURA   How—how—how do we start?

JIM   Just leave it to me. You hold your arms out a little.

LAURA   Like this?

JIM   A little bit higher. Right. Now don't tighten up, that's the main thing about it—relax.

LAURA (*laughing breathlessly*)   It's hard not to.

JIM   Okay.

LAURA   I'm afraid you can't budge me.

JIM   What do you bet I can't? (*He swings her into motion.*)

LAURA   Goodness, yes, you can!

JIM   Let yourself go, now, Laura, just let yourself go.

LAURA   I'm—

JIM   Come on!

LAURA   Trying!

JIM   Not so stiff—Easy does it!

LAURA I know but I'm—

JIM Loosen th' backbone! There now, that's a lot better.

LAURA Am I?

JIM Lots, lots better! (*He moves her about the room in a clumsy waltz.*)

LAURA Oh, my!

JIM Ha-ha!

LAURA Goodness, yes you can!

JIM Ha-ha-ha! (*They suddenly bump into the table.* JIM *stops.*) What did we hit on?

LAURA Table.

JIM Did something fall off it? I think—

LAURA Yes.

JIM I hope that it wasn't the little glass horse with the horn!

LAURA Yes.

JIM Aw, aw, aw. Is it broken?

LAURA Now it is just like all the other horses.

JIM It's lost its—

LAURA Horn! It doesn't matter. Maybe it's a blessing in disguise.

JIM You'll never forgive me. I bet that that was your favorite piece of glass.

LAURA I don't have favorites much. It's no tragedy, Freckles. Glass breaks so easily. No matter how careful you are. The traffic jars the shelves and things fall off them.

JIM Still I'm awfully sorry that I was the cause.

LAURA (*smiling*) I'll just imagine he had an operation. The horn was removed to make him feel less—freakish! (*They both laugh.*) Now he will feel more at home with the other horses, the ones that don't have horns . . .

JIM Ha-ha, that's very funny! (*Suddenly serious.*) I'm glad to see that you have a sense of humor. You know—you're—well—very different! Surprisingly different from anyone else I know! (*His voice becomes soft and hesitant with a genuine feeling.*) Do you mind me telling you that? (LAURA *is abashed beyond speech.*) You make me feel sort of—I don't know how to put it! I'm usually pretty good at expressing things, but—This is something that I don't know how to say! (LAURA *touches her throat and clears it—turns the broken unicorn in her hands.*) (*Even softer.*) Has anyone ever told you that you were pretty? (PAUSE: MUSIC.) (LAURA *looks up slowly, with wonder, and shakes her head.*) Well, you are! In a very different way from anyone else. And all the nicer because of the difference, too. (*His voice becomes low and husky.* LAURA *turns away, nearly faint with the novelty of her emotions.*) I wish that you were my sister. I'd teach you to have some confidence in yourself. The different people are not like other people, but being different is nothing to be ashamed of. Because other people are not such wonderful people. They're one hundred times one thousand. You're one times one! They walk all over the earth. You just stay here. They're common as—weeds, but—you—well, you're—*Blue Roses!*

(IMAGE ON SCREEN: BLUE ROSES.)

(MUSIC CHANGES.)

LAURA   But blue is wrong for—roses . . .

JIM   It's right for you—You're—pretty!

LAURA   In what respect am I pretty?

JIM   In all respects—believe me! Your eyes—your hair—are pretty! Your hands are pretty! (*He catches hold of her hand.*) You think I'm making this up because I'm invited to dinner and have to be nice. Oh, I could do that! I could put on an act for you, Laura, and say lots of things without being very sincere. But this time I am. I'm talking to you sincerely. I happened to notice you had this inferiority complex that keeps you from feeling comfortable with people. Somebody needs to build your confidence up and make you proud instead of shy and turning away and—blushing —Somebody ought to—Ought to—*kiss* you, Laura! (*His hand slips slowly up her arm to her shoulder.*) (MUSIC SWELLS TU-MULTUOUSLY.) (*He suddenly turns her about and kisses her on the lips. When he releases her* LAURA *sinks on the sofa with a bright, dazed look.* JIM *backs away and fishes in his pocket for a cigarette.*) (LEGEND ON SCREEN: "SOUVENIR.") Stumble-john! (*He lights the cigarette, avoiding her look. There is a peal of girlish laughter from* AMANDA *in the kitchen.* LAURA *slowly raises and opens her hand. It still contains the little broken glass animal. She looks at it with a tender, bewildered expression.*) Stumble-john! I shouldn't have done that—That was way off the beam. You don't smoke, do you? (*She looks up, smiling, not hearing the question. He sits beside her a little gingerly. She looks at him speechlessly —waiting. He coughs decorously and moves a little farther aside as he considers the situation and senses her feelings, dimly, with perturbation. Gently.*) Would you—care for a—mint? (*She doesn't seem to hear him but her look grows brighter even.*) Peppermint—Life Saver? My pocket's a regular drug store—wherever I go . . . (*He pops a mint in his mouth. Then gulps and decides to make a clean breast of it. He speaks slowly and gingerly.*) Laura, you know, if I had a sister like you, I'd do the same thing as Tom. I'd bring out fellows—introduce her to them. The right type of boys of a type to—appreciate her. Only—well—he made a mistake about me. Maybe I've got no call to be saying this. That may not have been the idea in having me over. But what if it was? There's nothing wrong about that. The only trouble is that in my case—I'm not in a situation to—do the right thing. I can't take down your number and say I'll phone. I can't call up next week and—ask for a date. I thought I had better explain the situation in case you misunderstood it and—hurt your feelings. . . . (*Pause. Slowly, very slowly,* LAURA'S *look changes, her eyes returning slowly from his to the ornament in her palm.*)

AMANDA *utters another gay laugh in the kitchen.*

LAURA (*faintly*) You—won't—call again?

JIM No, Laura, I can't. (*He rises from the sofa.*) As I was just explaining, I've—got strings on me, Laura, I've—been going steady! I go out all the time with a girl named Betty. She's a home-girl like you, and Catholic, and Irish, and in a great many ways we—get along fine. I met her last summer on a moonlight boat trip up the river to Alton, on the *Majestic*. Well—right away from the start it was—love! (LEGEND: LOVE!) (LAURA *sways slightly forward and grips the arm of the sofa. He fails to notice, now enrapt in his own comfortable being.*) Being in love has made a new man of me! (*Leaning stiffly forward, clutching the arm of the sofa,* LAURA *struggles visibly with her storm. But* JIM *is oblivious, she is a long way off.*) The power of love is really pretty tremendous! Love is something that—changes the whole world, Laura! (*The storm abates a little and* LAURA *leans back. He notices her again.*) It happened that Betty's aunt took sick, she got a wire and had to go to Centralia. So Tom—when he asked me to dinner—I naturally just accepted the invitation, not knowing that you—that he—that I—(*He stops awkwardly.*) Huh—I'm a stumble-john! (*He flops back on the sofa. The holy candles in the altar of* LAURA'S *face have been snuffed out! There is a look of almost infinite desolation.* JIM *glances at her uneasily.*) I wish that you would—say something. (*She bites her lip which was trembling and then bravely smiles. She opens her hand again on the broken glass ornament. Then she gently takes his hand and raises it level with her own. She carefully places the unicorn in the palm of his hand, then pushes his fingers closed upon it.*) What are you—doing that for? You want me to have him?—Laura? (*She nods.*) What for?

LAURA A—souvenir . . .

She rises unsteadily and crouches beside the victrola to wind it up.

(LEGEND ON SCREEN: "THINGS HAVE A WAY OF TURNING OUT SO BADLY.")

(OR IMAGE: "GENTLEMAN CALLER WAVING GOODBYE!—GAILY.")

At this moment AMANDA *rushes brightly back in the front room. She bears a pitcher of fruit punch in an old-fashioned cut-glass pitcher and a plate of macaroons. The plate has a gold border and poppies painted on it.*

AMANDA Well, well, well! Isn't the air delightful after the shower? I've made you children a little liquid refreshment. (*Turns gaily to the gentleman caller.*) Jim, do you know that song about lemonade?

"Lemonade, lemonade
Made in the shade and stirred with a spade—
Good enough for any old maid!"

JIM (*uneasily*) Ha-ha! No—I never heard it.
AMANDA Why, Laura! You look so serious!
JIM We were having a serious conversation.
AMANDA Good! Now you're better acquainted!
JIM (*uncertainly*) Ha-ha! Yes.
AMANDA You modern young people are much more serious-minded than my generation. I was so gay as a girl!
JIM You haven't changed, Mrs. Wingfield.
AMANDA Tonight I'm rejuvenated! The gaiety of the occasion, Mr. O'Connor! (*She tosses her head with a peal of laughter. Spills lemonade.*) Oooo! I'm baptizing myself!
JIM Here—let me—
AMANDA (*setting the pitcher down*) There now. I discovered we had some maraschino cherries. I dumped them in, juice and all!
JIM You shouldn't have gone to that trouble, Mrs. Wingfield.
AMANDA Trouble, trouble? Why it was loads of fun! Didn't you hear me cutting up in the kitchen? I bet your ears were burning! I told Tom how outdone with him I was for keeping you to himself so long a time! He should have brought you over much, much sooner! Well, now that you've found your way, I want you to be a very frequent caller! Not just occasional but all the time. Oh, we're going to have a lot of gay times together! I see them coming! Mmm, just breathe that air! So fresh, and the moon's so pretty! I'll skip back out—I know where my place is when young folks are having a—serious conversation!
JIM Oh, don't go out, Mrs. Wingfield. The fact of the matter is I've got to be going.

AMANDA Going, now? You're joking! Why, it's only the shank of the evening, Mr. O'Connor!

JIM Well, you know how it is.

AMANDA You mean you're a young workingman and have to keep workingmen's hours. We'll let you off early tonight. But only on the condition that next time you stay later. What's the best night for you? Isn't Saturday night the best night for you workingmen?

JIM I have a couple of time-clocks to punch, Mrs. Wingfield. One at morning, another one at night!

AMANDA My, but you *are* ambitious! You work at night, too?

JIM No, Ma'am, not work but—Betty! (*He crosses deliberately to pick up his hat. The band at the Paradise Dance Hall goes into a tender waltz.*)

AMANDA Betty? Betty? Who's—Betty! (*There is an ominous cracking sound in the sky.*)

JIM Oh, just a girl. The girl I go steady with! (*He smiles charmingly. The sky falls.*)

(LEGEND: "THE SKY FALLS.")

AMANDA (*a long-drawn exhalation*) Ohhhh . . . Is it a serious romance, Mr. O'Connor?

JIM We're going to be married the second Sunday in June.

AMANDA Ohhhh—how nice! Tom didn't mention that you were engaged to be married.

JIM The cat's not out of the bag at the warehouse yet. You know how they are. They call you Romeo and stuff like that. (*He stops at the oval mirror to put on his hat. He carefully shapes the brim and the crown to give a discreetly dashing effect.*) It's been a wonderful evening, Mrs. Wingfield. I guess this is what they mean by Southern hospitality.

AMANDA It really wasn't anything at all.

JIM I hope it don't seem like I'm rushing off. But I promised Betty I'd pick her up at the Wabash depot, an' by the time I get my jalopy down there her train'll be in. Some women are pretty upset if you keep 'em waiting.

AMANDA Yes, I know—The tyranny of women! (*Extends her hand.*) Goodbye, Mr. O'Connor. I wish you luck—and happiness —and success! All three of them, and so does Laura!—Don't you, Laura?

LAURA Yes!

JIM (*taking her hand*) Good-bye, Laura. I'm certainly going to treasure that souvenir. And don't you forget the good advice I gave you. (*Raises his voice to a cheery shout.*) So long, Shakespeare! Thanks again, ladies—Good night!

He grins and ducks jauntily out.
Still bravely grimacing, AMANDA *closes the door on the gentleman caller.*
Then she turns back to the room with a puzzled expression. She and LAURA
don't dare to face each other. LAURA *crouches beside the victrola to wind it.*

AMANDA *(faintly)* Things have a way of turning out so badly. I
don't believe that I would play the victrola. Well, well—well—
Our gentleman caller was engaged to be married! Tom!

TOM *(from back)* Yes, Mother?

AMANDA Come in here a minute. I want to tell you something awfully funny.

TOM *(enters with a macaroon and a glass of the lemonade)* Has
the gentleman caller gotten away already?

AMANDA The gentleman caller has made an early departure. What
a wonderful joke you played on us!

TOM How do you mean?

AMANDA You didn't mention that he was engaged to be married.

TOM Jim? Engaged?

AMANDA That's what he just informed us.

TOM I'll be jiggered! I didn't know about that.

AMANDA That seems very peculiar.

TOM What's peculiar about it?

AMANDA Didn't you call him your best friend down at the warehouse?

TOM He is, but how did I know?

AMANDA It seems extremely peculiar that you wouldn't know your
best friend was going to be married!

TOM The warehouse is where I work, not where I know things
about people!

AMANDA You don't know things anywhere! You live in a dream;
you manufacture illusions! *(He crosses to door.)* Where are you
going?

TOM I'm going to the movies.

AMANDA That's right, now that you've had us make such fools of
ourselves. The effort, the preparations, all the expense! The new
floor lamp, the rug, the clothes for Laura! All for what? To entertain some other girl's fiancé! Go to the movies, go! Don't think
about us, a mother deserted, an unmarried sister who's crippled
and has no job! Don't let anything interfere with your selfish
pleasure! Just go, go, go—to the movies!

TOM All right, I will! The more you shout about my selfishness to
me the quicker I'll go, and I won't go to the movies!

AMANDA Go, then! Then go to the moon—you selfish dreamer!

TOM *smashes his glass on the floor. He plunges out on the fire-escape, slamming the door,* LAURA *screams—cut off by the door.*

Dance-hall music up. TOM *goes to the rail and grips it desperately, lifting his face in the chill white moonlight penetrating the narrow abyss of the alley.*

(LEGEND ON SCREEN: "AND SO GOOD-BYE . . .")

TOM'S *closing speech is timed with the interior pantomime. The interior scene is played as though viewed through soundproof glass.* AMANDA *appears to be making a comforting speech to* LAURA *who is huddled upon the sofa. Now that we cannot hear the mother's speech, her silliness is gone and she has dignity and tragic beauty.* LAURA'S *dark hair hides her face until at the end of the speech she lifts it to smile at her mother.* AMANDA'S *gestures are slow and graceful, almost dancelike, as she comforts the daughter. At the end of her speech she glances a moment at the father's picture—then withdraws through the portieres. At close of* TOM'S *speech,* LAURA *blows out the candles, ending the play.*

TOM   I didn't go to the moon, I went much further—for time is the longest distance between two places—Not long after that I was fired for writing a poem on the lid of a shoe-box. I left Saint Louis. I descended the steps of this fire-escape for a last time and followed, from then on, in my father's footsteps, attempting to find in motion what was lost in space—I traveled around a great deal. The cities swept about me like dead leaves, leaves that were brightly colored but torn away from the branches. I would have stopped, but I was pursued by something. It always came upon me unawares, taking me altogether by surprise. Perhaps it was a familiar bit of music. Perhaps it was only a piece of transparent glass—Perhaps I am walking along a street at night, in some strange city, before I have found companions. I pass the lighted window of a shop where perfume is sold. The window is filled with pieces of colored glass, tiny transparent bottles in delicate colors, like bits of a shattered rainbow. Then all at once my sister touches my shoulder. I turn around and look into her eyes . . . Oh, Laura, Laura, I tried to leave you behind me, but I am more faithful than I intended to be! I reach for a cigarette, I cross the street, I run into the movies or a bar, I buy a drink, I speak to the nearest stranger—anything that can blow your candles out! (LAURA *bends over the candles.*)—for nowadays the world is lit by lightning! Blow out your candles, Laura—and so good-bye. . . .

She blows the candles out.

(THE SCENE DISSOLVES.)

ᴄ⌇ DEATH OF A SALESMAN (1949)

ARTHUR MILLER (1915–   )

If, among the four great modern American dramatists, the final reputation of Eugene O'Neill rests upon *Long Day's Journey Into Night,* produced posthumously in 1955, of Tennessee Williams upon *A Streetcar Named Desire,* and of Edward Albee upon *Who's Afraid of Virginia Woolf* (1962), so will the ultimate judgment of Arthur Miller probably rest upon *Death of a Salesman.*

Death of a Salesman was the theatre sensation of the immediate post-Second War years. *All My Sons* (1947) and *The Crucible* (1953) could well have earned Arthur Miller a distinguished place in American drama, but *Salesman* clearly surpasses them in its portrait of the broken drummer, Willy Loman. If O'Neill was the dramatic artist pursuing the relationship of man to God, Miller is certainly the one who devotes his full energies to exploring the relationship of man to man, particularly father to son, most explicitly and devastatingly in Willy and his family. The father-son love-hate combat predominates in *All My Sons, A View from the Bridge* (1955) and *The Price* (1968), but *Salesman* gives it its most powerful thrust.

Because Willy has quite rightfully been viewed as a kind of universal figure from American business folklore, his play has too often been regarded as the great *American* tragedy, a brutal indictment of "the system," which makes and breaks the best it has, chews it up, spits it out, and leaves it helpless without a sign of appreciation. It builds giant cities that suffocate and drown the little men in their cottages in shadows that prevent the flowering of the fruits of the earth. It turns good men into burned-out shells. There, but for the Grace of God, go all of us, and God Help Willy Loman.

Death of a Salesman is not, however, a modern tragedy. Society has not destroyed Willy Loman. Willy Loman has destroyed himself. More precisely, he has destroyed an image of himself in his own imagination of what society is and what the business world expects of him. Nowhere are we permitted to see Willy Loman except through his own eyes. He says he was a great salesman. There is not a shred of evidence. Why has the old refrigerator had to last so many years, the old car so many miles? Willy insists that there are great rewards for what he does and he seems at one time to have reaped them. But we see nothing of substance to support his claims. Willy is a sham, through and through, living on what he thinks he is and what he thinks is right, while all along the young Bernard next door gives the lie to Willy's theories of how to raise a family and how to perform in society. The fact that Bernard can argue before the Supreme Court is incomprehensible to the Willy who could see no purpose in the scholarly bookishness of his next door neighbor's son. And Willy never really sees that Charlie is the one who has succeeded, and who has the money to keep Willy alive. How come Willy doesn't have it?

Brother Ben is shown only as Willy sees him. Was he the whiz-kid that Willy makes him out? Or was he as false as Willy? To the very end Willy never realizes what he has done. All that he has discovered is that, despite his shabby sleaziness and the ruin he has brought, Biff loves him. Indeed!

Willy's suicide is not the positive act of tragedy. It is the act of one who still thinks in terms of self-redemption, of being able to "make it up" to those he has done wrong. True, Willy is a man, and maybe he should have some attention paid. But Willy is a very little man in all ways, and while we weep for him and may be deeply moved, he remains with feet of very sticky clay, firmly fastened to the ground, far from the heights demanded of tragedy.

Death of a Salesman

MILLER

Certain Private Conversations in Two Acts and a Requiem

CHARACTERS

WILLY LOMAN
LINDA
BIFF
HAPPY
BERNARD
THE WOMAN
CHARLEY
UNCLE BEN
HOWARD WAGNER
JENNY
STANLEY
MISS FORSYTHE
LETTA

The action takes place in WILLY LOMAN's *house and yard and in various places he visits in the New York and Boston of today.*

Throughout the play, in the stage directions, left and right mean stage left and stage right.

ACT ONE

An Overture

A melody is heard, played upon a flute. It is small and fine, telling of grass and trees and the horizon. The curtain rises.

Before us is the Salesman's house. We are aware of towering, angular shapes behind it, surrounding it on all sides. Only the blue light of the sky falls upon the house and forestage; the surrounding area shows an angry glow of orange. As more light appears, we see a solid vault of apartment houses around the small, fragile-seeming home. An air of the dream clings to the place, a dream rising out of reality. The kitchen at center seems actual enough, for there is a kitchen table with three chairs, and a refrig-

erator. But no other fixtures are seen. At the back of the kitchen there is a draped entrance, which leads to the living room. To the right of the kitchen, on a level raised two feet, is a bedroom furnished only with a brass bedstead and a straight chair. On a shelf over the bed a silver athletic trophy stands. A window opens onto the apartment house at the side.

Behind the kitchen, on a level raised six and a half feet, is the boys' bedroom, at present barely visible. Two beds are dimly seen, and at the back of the room a dormer window. (This bedroom is above the unseen living room.) At the left a stairway curves up to it from the kitchen.

The entire setting is wholly or, in some places, partially transparent. The roof-line of the house is one-dimensional; under and over it we see the apartment buildings. Before the house lies an apron, curving beyond the forestage into the orchestra. This forward area serves as the back yard as well as the locale of all WILLY'S *imaginings and of his city scenes. Whenever the action is in the present the actors observe the imaginary wall-lines, entering the house only through its door at the left. But in the scenes of the past these boundaries are broken, and characters enter or leave a room by stepping "through" a wall onto the forestage.*

From the right, WILLY LOMAN, *the Salesman, enters, carrying two large sample cases. The flute plays on. He hears but is not aware of it. He is past sixty years of age, dressed quietly. Even as he crosses the stage to the doorway of the house, his exhaustion is apparent. He unlocks the door, comes into the kitchen, and thankfully lets his burden down, feeling the soreness of his palms. A word-sigh escapes his lips—it might be "Oh, boy, oh, boy." He closes the door, then carries his cases out into the living room, through the draped kitchen doorway.*

LINDA, his wife, has stirred in her bed at the right. She gets out and puts on a robe, listening. Most often jovial, she has developed an iron repression of her exceptions to WILLY'S *behavior—she more than loves him, she admires him, as though his mercurial nature, his temper, his massive dreams and little cruelties, served her only as sharp reminders of the turbulent longings within him, longings which she shares but lacks the temperament to utter and follow to their end.*

LINDA (*hearing* WILLY *outside the bedroom, calls with some trepidation*) Willy!

WILLY It's all right. I came back.

LINDA Why? What happened? (*Slight pause*) Did something happen, Willy?

WILLY No, nothing happened.

LINDA You didn't smash the car, did you?

WILLY (*with casual irritation*) I said nothing happened. Didn't you hear me?

LINDA Don't you feel well?

WILLY I'm tired to the death. (*The flute has faded away. He sits on the bed beside her, a little numb*) I couldn't make it. I just couldn't make it, Linda.

LINDA (*very carefully, delicately*) Where were you all day? You look terrible.

WILLY I got as far as a little above Yonkers. I stopped for a cup of coffee. Maybe it was the coffee.

LINDA What?

WILLY (*after a pause*) I suddenly couldn't drive any more. The car kept going off onto the shoulder, y'know?

LINDA (*helpfully*) Oh. Maybe it was the steering again. I don't think Angelo knows the Studebaker.

WILLY No, it's me, it's me. Suddenly I realize I'm goin' sixty miles an hour and I don't remember the last five minutes. I'm—I can't seem to—keep my mind to it.

LINDA Maybe it's your glasses. You never went for your new glasses.

WILLY No, I see everything. I came back ten miles an hour. It took me nearly four hours from Yonkers.

LINDA (*resigned*) Well, you'll just have to take a rest, Willy, you can't continue this way.

WILLY I just got back from Florida.

LINDA But you didn't rest your mind. Your mind is overactive, and the mind is what counts, dear.

WILLY I'll start out in the morning. Maybe I'll feel better in the morning. (*She is taking off his shoes*) These goddam arch supports are killing me.

LINDA Take an aspirin. Should I get you an aspirin? It'll soothe you.

WILLY (*with wonder*) I was driving along, you understand? And I was fine. I was even observing the scenery. You can imagine, me looking at scenery, on the road every week of my life. But it's so beautiful up there, Linda, the trees are so thick, and the sun is warm. I opened the windshield and just let the warm air bathe over me. And then all of a sudden I'm goin' off the road! I'm tellin' ya, I absolutely forgot I was driving. If I'd've gone the other way over the white line I might've killed somebody. So I went on again—and five minutes later I'm dreamin' again, and I nearly—(*He presses two fingers against his eyes*) I have such thoughts, I have such strange thoughts.

LINDA Willy, dear. Talk to them again. There's no reason why you can't work in New York.

WILLY They don't need me in New York. I'm the New England man. I'm vital in New England.

LINDA But you're sixty years old. They can't expect you to keep traveling every week.

WILLY I'll have to send a wire to Portland. I'm supposed to see

Brown and Morrison tomorrow morning at ten o'clock to show the line. Goddammit, I could sell them! (*He starts putting on his jacket*)

LINDA (*taking the jacket from him*) Why don't you go down to the place tomorrow and tell Howard you've simply got to work in New York? You're too accommodating, dear.

WILLY If old man Wagner was alive I'd a been in charge of New York now! That man was a prince, he was a masterful man. But that boy of his, that Howard, he don't appreciate. When I went north the first time, the Wagner Company didn't know where New England was!

LINDA Why don't you tell those things to Howard, dear?

WILLY (*encouraged*) I will, I definitely will. Is there any cheese?

LINDA I'll make you a sandwich.

WILLY No, go to sleep. I'll take some milk. I'll be up right away. The boys in?

LINDA They're sleeping. Happy took Biff on a date tonight.

WILLY (*interested*) That so?

LINDA It was so nice to see them shaving together, one behind the other, in the bathroom. And going out together. You notice? The whole house smells of shaving lotion.

WILLY Figure it out. Work a lifetime to pay off a house. You finally own it, and there's nobody to live in it.

LINDA Well, dear, life is a casting off. It's always that way.

WILLY No, no, some people—some people accomplish something. Did Biff say anything after I went this morning?

LINDA You shouldn't have criticized him, Willy, especially after he just got off the train. You mustn't lose your temper with him.

WILLY When the hell did I lose my temper? I simply asked him if he was making any money. Is that a criticism?

LINDA But, dear, how could he make any money?

WILLY (*worried and angered*) There's such an undercurrent in him. He became a moody man. Did he apologize when I left this morning?

LINDA He was crestfallen, Willy. You know how he admires you. I think if he finds himself, then you'll both be happier and not fight any more.

WILLY How can he find himself on a farm? Is that a life? A farm-hand? In the beginning, when he was young, I thought, well, a young man, it's good for him to tramp around, take a lot of different jobs. But it's more than ten years now and he has yet to make thirty-five dollars a week!

LINDA He's finding himself, Willy.

WILLY Not finding yourself at the age of thirty-four is a disgrace!

LINDA   Shh!

WILLY   The trouble is he's lazy, goddammit!

LINDA   Willy, please!

WILLY   Biff is a lazy bum!

LINDA   They're sleeping. Get something to eat. Go on down.

WILLY   Why did he come home? I would like to know what brought him home.

LINDA   I don't know. I think he's still lost, Willy. I think he's very lost.

WILLY   Biff Loman is lost. In the greatest country in the world a young man with such—personal attractiveness, gets lost. And such a hard worker. There's one thing about Biff—he's not lazy.

LINDA   Never.

WILLY   (*with pity and resolve*)   I'll see him in the morning; I'll have a nice talk with him. I'll get him a job selling. He could be big in no time. My God! Remember how they used to follow him around in high school? When he smiled at one of them their faces lit up. When he walked down the street . . . (*He loses himself in reminiscences*)

LINDA   (*trying to bring him out of it*)   Willy, dear, I got a new kind of American-type cheese today. It's whipped.

WILLY   Why do you get American when I like Swiss?

LINDA   I just thought you'd like a change—

WILLY   I don't want a change! I want Swiss cheese. Why am I always being contradicted?

LINDA   (*with a covering laugh*)   I thought it would be a surprise.

WILLY   Why don't you open a window in here, for God's sake?

LINDA   (*with infinite patience*)   They're all open, dear.

WILLY   The way they boxed us in here. Bricks and windows, windows and bricks.

LINDA   We should've bought the land next door.

WILLY   The street is lined with cars. There's not a breath of fresh air in the neighborhood. The grass don't grow any more, you can't raise a carrot in the back yard. They should've had a law against apartment houses. Remember those two beautiful elm trees out there? When I and Biff hung the swing between them?

LINDA   Yeah, like being a million miles from the city.

WILLY   They should've arrested the builder for cutting those down. They massacred the neighborhood. (*Lost*) More and more I think of those days, Linda. This time of year it was lilac and wisteria. And then the peonies would come out, and the daffodils. What fragrance in this room!

LINDA   Well, after all, people had to move somewhere.

WILLY   No, there's more people now.

LINDA I don't think there's more people. I think—

WILLY There's more people! That's what's ruining this country! Population is getting out of control. The competition is maddening! Smell the stink from that apartment house! And another one on the other side . . . How can they whip cheese?

On WILLY's *last line,* BIFF *and* HAPPY *raise themselves up in their beds, listening.*

LINDA Go down, try it. And be quiet.

WILLY (*turning to* LINDA, *guiltily*) You're not worried about me, are you, sweetheart?

BIFF What's the matter?

HAPPY Listen!

LINDA You've got too much on the ball to worry about.

WILLY You're my foundation and my support, Linda.

LINDA Just try to relax, dear. You make mountains out of molehills.

WILLY I won't fight with him any more. If he wants to go back to Texas, let him go.

LINDA He'll find his way.

WILLY Sure. Certain men just don't get started till later in life. Like Thomas Edison, I think. Or B. F. Goodrich. One of them was deaf. (*He starts for the bedroom doorway*) I'll put my money on Biff.

LINDA And Willy—if it's warm Sunday we'll drive in the country. And we'll open the windshield, and take lunch.

WILLY No, the windshields don't open on the new cars.

LINDA But you opened it today.

WILLY Me? I didn't. (*He stops*) Now isn't that peculiar! Isn't that a remarkable—(*He breaks off in amazement and fright as the flute is heard distantly*)

LINDA What, darling?

WILLY That is the most remarkable thing.

LINDA What, dear?

WILLY I was thinking of the Chevvy. (*Slight pause*) Nineteen twenty-eight . . . when I had that red Chevvy—(*Breaks off*) That funny? I coulda sworn I was driving that Chevvy today.

LINDA Well, that's nothing. Something must've reminded you.

WILLY Remarkable. Ts. Remember those days? The way Biff used to simonize that car? The dealer refused to believe there was eighty thousand miles on it. (*He shakes his head*) Heh! (*To* LINDA) Close your eyes, I'll be right up. (*He walks out of the bedroom*)

HAPPY (*to* BIFF) Jesus, maybe he smashed up the car again!

LINDA (*calling after* WILLY) Be careful on the stairs, dear! The cheese is on the middle shelf! (*She turns, goes over to the bed, takes his jacket, and goes out of the bedroom*)

Light has risen on the boys' room. Unseen, WILLY *is heard talking to himself, "Eighty thousand miles," and a little laugh.* BIFF *gets out of bed, comes downstage a bit, and stands attentively.* BIFF *is two years older than his brother* HAPPY, *well built, but in these days bears a worn air and seems less self-assured. He has succeeded less, and his dreams are stronger and less acceptable than* HAPPY's. HAPPY *is tall, powerfully made. Sexuality is like a visible color on him, or a scent that many women have discovered. He, like his brother, is lost, but in a different way, for he has never allowed himself to turn his face toward defeat and is thus more confused and hard-skinned, although seemingly more content.*

HAPPY (*getting out of bed*) He's going to get his license taken away if he keeps that up. I'm getting nervous about him, y'know, Biff?

BIFF His eyes are going.

HAPPY No, I've driven with him. He sees all right. He just doesn't keep his mind on it. I drove into the city with him last week. He stops at a green light and then it turns red and he goes. (*He laughs*)

BIFF Maybe he's color-blind.

HAPPY Pop? Why he's got the finest eye for color in the business. You know that.

BIFF (*sitting down on his bed*) I'm going to sleep.

HAPPY You're not still sour on Dad, are you, Biff?

BIFF He's all right, I guess.

WILLY (*underneath them, in the living-room*) Yes, sir, eighty thousand miles—eighty-two thousand!

BIFF You smoking?

HAPPY (*holding out a pack of cigarettes*) Want one?

BIFF (*taking a cigarette*) I can never sleep when I smell it.

WILLY What a simonizing job, heh!

HAPPY (*with deep sentiment*) Funny, Biff, y'now? Us sleeping in here again? The old beds. (*He pats his bed affectionately*) All the talk that went across those two beds, huh? Our whole lives.

BIFF Yeah. Lotta dreams and plans.

HAPPY (*with a deep and masculine laugh*) About five hundred women would like to know what was said in this room.

They share a soft laugh.

BIFF Remember that big Betsy something—what the hell was her name—over on Bushwick Avenue?

HAPPY (*combing his hair*) With the collie dog!

BIFF That's the one. I got you in there, remember?

HAPPY Yeah, that was my first time—I think. Boy, there was a pig! (*They laugh, almost crudely*) You taught me everything I know about women. Don't forget that.

BIFF I bet you forgot how bashful you used to be. Especially with girls.

HAPPY Oh, I still am, Biff.

BIFF Oh, go on.

HAPPY I just control it, that's all. I think I got less bashful and you got more so. What happened, Biff? Where's the old humor, the old confidence? (*He shakes* BIFF's *knee.* BIFF *gets up and moves restlessly about the room*) What's the matter?

BIFF Why does Dad mock me all the time?

HAPPY He's not mocking you, he—

BIFF Everything I say there's a twist of mockery on his face. I can't get near him.

HAPPY He just wants you to make good, that's all. I wanted to talk to you about Dad for a long time, Biff. Something's—happening to him. He—talks to himself.

BIFF I noticed that this morning. But he always mumbled.

HAPPY But not so noticeable. It got so embarrassing I sent him to Florida. And you know something? Most of the time he's talking to you.

BIFF What's he say about me?

HAPPY I can't make it out.

BIFF What's he say about me?

HAPPY I think the fact that you're not settled, that you're still kind of up in the air . . .

BIFF There's one or two other things depressing him, Happy.

HAPPY What do you mean?

BIFF Never mind. Just don't lay it all to me.

HAPPY But I think if you just got started—I mean—is there any future for you out there?

BIFF I tell ya, Hap, I don't know what the future is. I don't know —what I'm supposed to want.

HAPPY What do you mean?

BIFF Well, I spent six or seven years after high school trying to work myself up. Shipping clerk, salesman, business of one kind or another. And it's a measly manner of existence. To get on that subway on the hot mornings in summer. To devote your whole life to keeping stock, or making phone calls, or selling or buying. To suffer fifty weeks of the year for the sake of a two-week vacation, when all you really desire is to be outdoors, with your shirt off. And always to have to get ahead of the next fella. And still—that's how you build a future.

HAPPY   Well, you really enjoy it on a farm? Are you content out there?

BIFF (*with rising agitation*)   Hap, I've had twenty or thirty different kinds of jobs since I left home before the war, and it always turns out the same. I just realized it lately. In Nebraska when I herded cattle, and the Dakotas, and Arizona, and now in Texas. It's why I came home now, I guess, because I realized it. This farm I work on, it's spring there now, see? And they've got about fifteen new colts. There's nothing more inspiring or—beautiful than the sight of a mare and a new colt. And it's cool there now, see? Texas is cool now, and it's spring. And whenever spring comes to where I am, I suddenly get the feeling, my God, I'm not gettin' anywhere! What the hell am I doing, playing around with horses, twenty-eight dollars a week! I'm thirty-four years old, I oughta be makin' my future. That's when I come running home. And now, I get here, and I don't know what to do with myself. (*After a pause*) I've always made a point of not wasting my life, and everytime I come back here I know that all I've done is to waste my life.

HAPPY   You're a poet, you know that, Biff? You're a—you're an idealist!

BIFF   No, I'm mixed up very bad. Maybe I oughta get married. Maybe I oughta get stuck into something. Maybe that's my trouble. I'm like a boy. I'm not married, I'm not in business, I just —I'm like a boy. Are you content, Hap? You're a success, aren't you? Are you content?

HAPPY   Hell, no!

BIFF   Why? You're making money, aren't you?

HAPPY (*moving about with energy, expressiveness*)   All I can do now is wait for the merchandise manager to die. And suppose I get to be merchandise manager? He's a good friend of mine, and he just built a terrific estate on Long Island. And he lived there about two months and sold it, and now he's building another one. He can't enjoy it once it's finished. And I know that's just what I would do. I don't know what the hell I'm workin' for. Sometimes I sit in my apartment—all alone. And I think of the rent I'm paying. And it's crazy. But then, it's what I always wanted. My own apartment, a car, and plenty of women. And still, goddammit. I'm lonely.

BIFF (*with enthusiasm*)   Listen, why don't you come out West with me?

HAPPY You and I, heh?

BIFF Sure, maybe we could buy a ranch. Raise cattle, use our muscles. Men built like we are should be working out in the open.

HAPPY (*avidly*) The Loman Brothers, heh?

BIFF (*with vast affection*) Sure, we'd be known all over the counties!

HAPPY (*enthralled*) That's what I dream about, Biff. Sometimes I want to just rip my clothes off in the middle of the store and outbox that goddam merchandise manager. I mean I can outbox, outrun, and outlift anybody in that store, and I have to take orders from those common, petty sons-of-bitches till I can't stand it any more.

BIFF I'm tellin' you, kid, if you were with me I'd be happy out there.

HAPPY (*enthused*) See, Biff, everybody around me is so false that I'm constantly lowering my ideals . . .

BIFF Baby, together we'd stand up for one another, we'd have someone to trust.

HAPPY If I were around you—

BIFF Hap, the trouble is we weren't brought up to grub for money. I don't know how to do it.

HAPPY Neither can I!

BIFF Then let's go!

HAPPY The only thing is—what can you make out there?

BIFF But look at your friend. Builds an estate and then hasn't the peace of mind to live in it.

HAPPY Yeah, but when he walks into the store the waves part in front of him. That's fifty-two thousand dollars a year coming through the revolving door, and I got more in my pinky finger than he's got in his head.

BIFF Yeah, but you just said—

HAPPY I gotta show some of those pompous, self-important executives over there that Hap Loman can make the grade. I want to walk into the store the way he walks in. Then I'll go with you, Biff. We'll be together yet, I swear. But take those two we had tonight. Now weren't they gorgeous creatures?

BIFF Yeah, yeah, most gorgeous I've had in years.

HAPPY I get that any time I want, Biff. Whenever I feel disgusted. The only trouble is, it gets like bowling or something. I just keep knockin' them over and it doesn't mean anything. You still run around a lot?

BIFF Naa. I'd like to find a girl—steady, somebody with substance.

HAPPY That's what I long for.

BIFF   Go on! You'd never come home.

HAPPY   I would! Somebody with character, with resistance! Like Mom, y'know? You're gonna call me a bastard when I tell you this. That girl Charlotte I was with tonight is engaged to be married in five weeks. (*He tries on his new hat*)

BIFF   No kiddin'!

HAPPY   Sure, the guy's in line for the vice-presidency of the store. I don't know what gets into me, maybe I just have an over-developed sense of competition or something, but I went and ruined her, and furthermore I can't get rid of her. And he's the third executive I've done that to. Isn't that a crummy characteristic? And to top it all, I go to their weddings! (*Indignantly, but laughing*) Like I'm not supposed to take bribes. Manufacturers offer me a hundred-dollar bill now and then to throw an order their way. You know how honest I am, but it's like this girl, see. I hate myself for it. Because I don't want the girl, and, still, I take it and—I love it!

BIFF   Let's go to sleep.

HAPPY   I guess we didn't settle anything, heh?

BIFF   I just got one idea that I think I'm going to try.

HAPPY   What's that?

BIFF   Remember Bill Oliver?

HAPPY   Sure, Oliver is very big now. You want to work for him again?

BIFF   No, but when I quit he said something to me. He put his arm on my shoulder, and he said, "Biff, if you ever need anything, come to me."

HAPPY   I remember that. That sounds good.

BIFF   I think I'll go to see him. If I could get ten thousand or even seven or eight thousand dollars I could buy a beautiful ranch.

HAPPY   I bet he'd back you. 'Cause he thought highly of you, Biff. I mean, they all do. You're well liked, Biff. That's why I say to come back here, and we both have the apartment. And I'm tellin' you, Biff, any babe you want . . .

BIFF   No, with a ranch I could do the work I like and still be something. I just wonder though. I wonder if Oliver still thinks I stole that carton of basketballs.

HAPPY   Oh, he probably forgot that long ago. It's almost ten years. You're too sensitive. Anyway, he didn't really fire you.

BIFF   Well, I think he was going to. I think that's why I quit. I was never sure whether he knew or not. I know he thought the world of me, though. I was the only one he'd let lock up the place.

WILLY (*below*) You gonna wash the engine, Biff?
HAPPY Shh!

BIFF *looks at* HAPPY, *who is gazing down, listening.* WILLY *is mumbling in the parlor.*

HAPPY You hear that?

They listen. WILLY *laughs warmly.*

BIFF (*growing angry*) Doesn't he know Mom can hear that?
WILLY Don't get your sweater dirty, Biff!

A look of pain crosses BIFF's *face.*

HAPPY Isn't that terrible? Don't leave again, will you? You'll find a job here. You gotta stick around. I don't know what to do about him, it's getting embarrassing.
WILLY What a simonizing job!
BIFF Mom's hearing that!
WILLY No kiddin', Biff, you got a date? Wonderful!
HAPPY Go on to sleep. But talk to him in the morning, will you?
BIFF (*reluctantly getting into bed*) With her in the house. Brother!
HAPPY (*getting into bed*) I wish you'd have a good talk with him.

The light on their room begins to fade.

BIFF (*to himself in bed*) That selfish, stupid . . .
HAPPY Sh . . . Sleep, Biff.

Their light is out. Well before they have finished speaking, WILLY's *form is dimly seen below in the darkened kitchen. He opens the refrigerator, searches in there, and takes out a bottle of milk. The apartment houses are fading out, and the entire house and surroundings become covered with leaves. Music insinuates itself as the leaves appear.*

WILLY Just wanna be careful with those girls, Biff, that's all. Don't make any promises. No promises of any kind. Because a girl, y'know, they always believe what you tell 'em, and you're very young, Biff, you're too young to be talking seriously to girls.

Light rises on the kitchen. WILLY, *talking, shuts the refrigerator door and comes downstage to the kitchen table. He pours milk into a glass. He is totally immersed in himself, smiling faintly.*

WILLY Too young entirely, Biff. You want to watch your schooling first. Then when you're all set, there'll be plenty of girls for a boy like you. (*He smiles broadly at a kitchen chair*) That so? The girls pay for you? (*He laughs*) Boy, you must really be makin' a hit.

WILLY *is gradually addressing—physically—a point offstage, speaking through the wall of the kitchen, and his voice has been rising in volume to that of a normal conversation.*

WILLY   I been wondering why you polish the car so careful. Ha! Don't leave the hubcabs, boys. Get the chamois to the hubcaps. Happy, use newspaper on the windows, it's the easiest thing. Show him how to do it, Biff! You see, Happy? Pad it up, use it like a pad. That's it, that's it, good work. You're doin' all right, Hap. (*He pauses, then nods in approbation for a few seconds, then looks upward*) Biff, first thing we gotta do when we get time is clip that big branch over the house. Afraid it's gonna fall in a storm and hit the roof. Tell you what. We get a rope and sling her around, and then we climb up there with a couple of saws and take her down. Soon as you finish the car, boys, I wanna see ya. I got a surprise for you, boys.

BIFF (*offstage*)   Whatta ya got, Dad?

WILLY   No, you finish first. Never leave a job till you're finished— remember that. (*Looking toward the "big trees"*) Biff, up in Albany I saw a beautiful hammock. I think I'll buy it next trip, and we'll hang it right between those two elms. Wouldn't that be something? Just swingin' there under those branches. Boy, that would be . . .

Young BIFF *and Young* HAPPY *appear from the direction* WILLY *was addressing.* HAPPY *carries rags and a pail of water.* BIFF, *wearing a sweater with a block "S," carries a football.*

BIFF (*pointing in the direction of the car offstage*)   How's that, Pop, professional?

WILLY   Terrific. Terrific job, boys. Good work, Biff.

HAPPY   Where's the surprise, Pop?

WILLY   In the back seat of the car.

HAPPY   Boy! (*He runs off*)

BIFF   What is it, Dad? Tell me, what'd you buy?

WILLY (*laughing, cuffs him*)   Never mind, something I want you to have.

BIFF (*turns and starts off*)   What is it, Hap?

HAPPY (*offstage*)   It's a punching bag!

BIFF   Oh, Pop!

WILLY   It's got Gene Tunney's signature on it!

HAPPY *runs onstage with a punching bag.*

BIFF   Gee, how'd you know we wanted a punching bag?

WILLY   Well, it's the finest thing for the timing.

HAPPY (*lies down on his back and pedals with his feet*) I'm losing weight, you notice, Pop?

WILLY (*to* HAPPY) Jumping rope is good too.

BIFF Did you see the new football I got?

WILLY (*examining the ball*) Where'd you get a new ball?

BIFF The coach told me to practice my passing.

WILLY That so? And he gave you the ball, heh?

BIFF Well, I borrowed it from the locker room. (*He laughs confidentially*)

WILLY (*laughing with him at the theft*) I want you to return that.

HAPPY I told you he wouldn't like it!

BIFF (*angrily*) Well, I'm bringing it back!

WILLY (*stopping the incipient argument, to* HAPPY) Sure, he's gotta practice with a regulation ball, doesn't he? (*To* BIFF) Coach'll probably congratulate you on your initiative!

BIFF Oh, he keeps congratulating my initiative all the time, Pop.

WILLY That's because he likes you. If somebody else took that ball there'd be an uproar. So what's the report, boys, what's the report?

BIFF Where'd you go this time, Dad? Gee we were lonesome for you.

WILLY (*pleased, puts an arm around each boy and they come down to the apron*) Lonesome, heh?

BIFF Missed you every minute.

WILLY Don't say? Tell you a secret, boys. Don't breathe it to a soul. Someday I'll have my own business, and I'll never have to leave home any more.

HAPPY Like Uncle Charley, heh?

WILLY Bigger than Uncle Charley! Because Charley is not—liked. He's liked, but he's not—well liked.

BIFF Where'd you go this time, Dad?

WILLY Well, I got on the road, and I went north to Providence. Met the Mayor.

BIFF The Mayor of Providence!

WILLY He was sitting in the hotel lobby.

BIFF What'd he say?

WILLY He said, "Morning!" And I said, "You got a fine city here, Mayor." And then he had coffee with me. And then I went to Waterbury. Waterbury is a fine city. Big clock city, the famous Waterbury clock. Sold a nice bill there. And then Boston—Boston is the cradle of the Revolution. A fine city. And a couple of other towns in Mass., and on to Portland and Bangor and straight home!

BIFF Gee, I'd love to go with you sometime, Dad.

WILLY Soon as summer comes.

HAPPY Promise?

WILLY You and Hap and I, and I'll show you all the towns. America is full of beautiful towns and fine, upstanding people. And they know me, boys, they know me up and down New England. The finest people. And when I bring you fellas up, there'll be open sesame for all of us, 'cause one thing, boys: I have friends. I can park my car in any street in New England, and the cops protect it like their own. This summer, heh?

BIFF and HAPPY (*together*) Yeah! You bet!

WILLY We'll take our bathing suits.

HAPPY We'll carry your bags, Pop!

WILLY Oh, won't that be something! Me comin' into the Boston stores with you boys carryin' my bags. What a sensation!

BIFF *is prancing around, practicing passing the ball.*

WILLY You nervous, Biff, about the game?

BIFF Not if you're gonna be there.

WILLY What do they say about you in school, now that they made you captain?

HAPPY There's a crowd of girls behind him everytime the classes change.

BIFF (*taking* WILLY's *hand*) This Saturday, Pop, this Saturday— just for you, I'm going to break through for a touchdown.

HAPPY You're supposed to pass.

BIFF I'm takin' one play for Pop. You watch me, Pop, and when I take off my helmet, that means I'm breakin' out. Then you watch me crash through that line!

WILLY (*kisses* BIFF) Oh, wait'll I tell this in Boston!

BERNARD *enters in knickers. He is younger than* BIFF, *earnest and loyal, a worried boy.*

BERNARD Biff, where are you? You're supposed to study with me today.

WILLY Hey, looka Bernard. What're you lookin' so anemic about, Bernard?

BERNARD He's gotta study, Uncle Willy. He's got Regents next week.

HAPPY (*tauntingly, spinning* BERNARD *around*) Let's box, Bernard!

BERNARD Biff! (*He gets away from* HAPPY) Listen, Biff, I heard Mr. Birnbaum say that if you don't start studyin' math he's gonna flunk you, and you won't graduate. I heard him!

WILLY You better study with him, Biff. Go ahead now.

BERNARD I heard him!

BIFF Oh, Pop, you didn't see my sneakers! (*He holds up a foot for* WILLY *to look at*)

WILLY Hey, that's a beautiful job of printing!

BERNARD (*wiping his glasses*) Just because he printed University of Virginia on his sneakers doesn't mean they've got to graduate him, Uncle Willy!

WILLY (*angrily*) What're you talking about? With scholarships to three universities they're gonna flunk him?

BERNARD But I heard Mr. Birnbaum say—

WILLY Don't be a pest, Bernard! (*To his boys*) What an anemic!

BERNARD Okay, I'm waiting for you in my house, Biff.

BERNARD *goes off. The* LOMANS *laugh.*

WILLY Bernard is not well liked, is he?

BIFF He's liked, but he's not well liked.

HAPPY That's right, Pop.

WILLY That's just what I mean. Bernard can get the best marks in school, y'understand, but when he gets out in the business world, y'understand, you are going to be five times ahead of him. That's why I thank Almighty God you're both built like Adonises. Because the man who makes an appearance in the business world, the man who creates personal interest, is the man who gets ahead. Be liked and you will never want. You take me, for instance. I never have to wait in line to see a buyer. "Willy Loman is here!" That's all they have to know, and I go right through.

BIFF Did you knock them dead, Pop?

WILLY Knocked 'em cold in Providence, slaughtered 'em in Boston.

HAPPY (*on his back, pedaling again*) I'm losing weight, you notice, Pop?

LINDA *enters, as of old, a ribbon in her hair, carrying a basket of washing.*

LINDA (*with youthful energy*) Hello, dear!

WILLY Sweetheart!

LINDA How'd the Chevvy run?

WILLY Chevrolet, Linda, is the greatest car ever built. (*To the boys*) Since when do you let your mother carry wash up the stairs?

BIFF Grab hold there, boy!

HAPPY Where to, Mom?

LINDA Hang them up on the line. And you better go down to your friends, Biff. The cellar is full of boys. They don't know what to do with themselves.

BIFF   Ah, when Pop comes home they can wait!

WILLY   (*laughs appreciatively*)   You better go down and tell them what to do, Biff.

BIFF   I think I'll have them sweep out the furnace room.

WILLY   Good work, Biff.

BIFF   (*goes through wall-line of kitchen to doorway at back and calls down*)   Fellas! Everybody sweep out the furnace room! I'll be right down!

VOICES   All right! Okay, Biff.

BIFF   George and Sam and Frank, come out back! We're hangin' up the wash! Come on, Hap, on the double! (*He and* HAPPY *carry out the basket*)

LINDA   The way they obey him!

WILLY   Well, that's training, the training. I'm tellin' you, I was sellin' thousands and thousands, but I had to come home.

LINDA   Oh, the whole block'll be at that game. Did you sell anything?

WILLY   I did five hundred gross in Providence and seven hundred gross in Boston.

LINDA   No! Wait a minute, I've got a pencil. (*She pulls pencil and paper out of her apron pocket*) That makes your commission . . . Two hundred—my God! Two hundred and twelve dollars!

WILLY   Well, I didn't figure it yet, but . . .

LINDA   How much did you do?

WILLY   Well, I—I did—about a hundred and eighty gross in Providence. Well, no—it came to—roughly two hundred gross on the whole trip.

LINDA   (*without hesitation*)   Two hundred gross. That's . . . (*She figures*)

WILLY   The trouble was that three of the stores were half closed for inventory in Boston. Otherwise I woulda broke records.

LINDA   Well, it makes seventy dollars and some pennies. That's very good.

WILLY   What do we owe?

LINDA   Well, on the first there's sixteen dollars on the refrigerator—

WILLY   Why sixteen?

LINDA   Well, the fan belt broke, so it was a dollar eighty.

WILLY   But it's brand new.

LINDA   Well, the man said that's the way it is. Till they work themselves in, y'know.

They move through the wall-line into the kitchen.

WILLY   I hope we didn't get stuck on that machine.

LINDA   They got the biggest ads of any of them!

WILLY I know, it's a fine machine. What else?

LINDA Well, there's nine-sixty for the washing machine. And for the vacuum cleaner there's three and a half due on the fifteenth. Then the roof, you got twenty-one dollars remaining.

WILLY It don't leak, does it?

LINDA No, they did a wonderful job. Then you owe Frank for the carburetor.

WILLY I'm not going to pay that man! That goddam Chevrolet, they ought to prohibit the manufacture of that car!

LINDA Well, you owe him three and a half. And odds and ends, comes to around a hundred and twenty dollars by the fifteenth.

WILLY A hundred and twenty dollars! My God, if business don't pick up I don't know what I'm gonna do!

LINDA Well, next week you'll do better.

WILLY Oh, I'll knock 'em dead next week. I'll go to Hartford. I'm very well liked in Hartford. You know, the trouble is, Linda, people don't seem to take to me.

They move onto the forestage.

LINDA Oh, don't be foolish.

WILLY I know it when I walk in. They seem to laugh at me.

LINDA Why? Why would they laugh at you? Don't talk that way, Willy.

WILLY *moves to the edge of the stage.* LINDA *goes into the kitchen and starts to darn stockings.*

WILLY I don't know the reason for it, but they just pass me by. I'm not noticed.

LINDA But you're doing wonderful, dear. You're making seventy to a hundred dollars a week.

WILLY But I gotta be at it ten, twelve hours a day. Other men— I don't know—they do it easier. I don't know why—I can't stop myself—I talk too much. A man oughta come in with a few words. One thing about Charley. He's a man of few words, and they respect him.

LINDA You don't talk too much, you're just lively.

WILLY *(smiling)* Well, I figure, what the hell, life is short, a couple of jokes. *(To himself)* I joke too much! *(The smile goes)*

LINDA Why? You're—

WILLY I'm fat. I'm very—foolish to look at, Linda. I didn't tell you, but Christmas time I happened to be calling on F. H. Stewarts, and a salesman I know, as I was going in to see the buyer I heard him say something about—walrus. And I—I cracked him right across the face. I won't take that. I simply will not take that. But they do laugh at me. I know that.

LINDA Darling . . .

WILLY I gotta overcome it. I know I gotta overcome it. I'm not dressing to advantage, maybe.

LINDA Willy, darling, you're the handsomest man in the world—

WILLY Oh, no, Linda.

LINDA To me you are. (*Slight pause*) The handsomest.

From the darkness is heard the laughter of a woman. WILLY *doesn't turn to it, but it continues through* LINDA's *lines.*

LINDA And the boys, Willy. Few men are idolized by their children the way you are.

Music is heard as behind a scrim, to the left of the house. THE WOMAN, *dimly seen, is dressing.*

WILLY (*with great feeling*) You're the best there is, Linda, you're a pal, you know that? On the road—on the road I want to grab you sometimes and just kiss the life outa you.

The laughter is loud now, and he moves into a brightening area at the left, where THE WOMAN *has come from behind the scrim and is standing, putting on her hat, looking into a "mirror" and laughing.*

WILLY 'Cause I get so lonely—especially when business is bad and there's nobody to talk to. I get the feeling that I'll never sell anything again, that I won't make a living for you, or a business, a business for the boys. (*He talks through* THE WOMAN's *subsiding laughter;* THE WOMAN *primps at the "mirror."*) There's so much I want to make for—

THE WOMAN Me? You didn't make me, Willy. I picked you.

WILLY (*pleased*) You picked me?

THE WOMAN (*who is quite proper-looking,* WILLY's *age*) I did. I've been sitting at that desk watching all the salesmen go by, day in, day out. But you've got such a sense of humor, and we do have such a good time together, don't we?

WILLY Sure, sure. (*He takes her in his arms*) Why do you have to go now?

THE WOMAN It's two o'clock . . .

WILLY No, come on in! (*He pulls her*)

THE WOMAN . . . my sisters'll be scandalized. When'll you be back?

WILLY Oh, two weeks about. Will you come up again?

THE WOMAN Sure thing. You do make me laugh. It's good for me. (*She squeezes his arm, kisses him*) And I think you're a wonderful man.

WILLY   You picked me, heh?

THE WOMAN   Sure. Because you're so sweet. And such a kidder.

WILLY   Well, I'll see you next time I'm in Boston.

THE WOMAN   I'll put you right through to the buyers.

WILLY (*slapping her bottom*)   Right. Well, bottoms up!

THE WOMAN (*slaps him gently and laughs*)   You just kill me, Willy. (*He suddenly grabs her and kisses her roughly*) You kill me. And thanks for the stockings. I love a lot of stockings. Well, good night.

WILLY   Good night. And keep your pores open!

THE WOMAN   Oh, Willy!

THE WOMAN *bursts out laughing, and* LINDA's *laughter blends in.* THE WOMAN *disappears into the dark. Now the area at the kitchen table brightens.* LINDA *is sitting where she was at the kitchen table, but now is mending a pair of her silk stockings.*

LINDA   You are, Willy. The handsomest man. You've got no reason to feel that—

WILLY (*coming out of* THE WOMAN's *dimming area and going over to* LINDA)   I'll make it all up to you, Linda, I'll—

LINDA   There's nothing to make up, dear. You're doing fine, better than—

WILLY (*noticing her mending*)   What's that?

LINDA   Just mending my stockings. They're so expensive—

WILLY (*angrily, taking them from her*)   I won't have you mending stockings in this house! Now throw them out!

LINDA *puts the stockings in her pocket.*

BERNARD (*entering on the run*)   Where is he? If he doesn't study!

WILLY (*moving to the forestage, with great agitation*)   You'll give him the answers!

BERNARD   I do, but I can't on a Regents! That's a state exam! They're liable to arrest me!

WILLY   Where is he? I'll whip him, I'll whip him!

LINDA   And he'd better give back that football, Willy, it's not nice.

WILLY   Biff! Where is he? Why is he taking everything?

LINDA   He's too rough with the girls, Willy. All the mothers are afraid of him!

WILLY   I'll whip him!

BERNARD   He's driving the car without a license!

THE WOMAN's *laugh is heard.*

WILLY   Shut up!

LINDA   All the mothers—

WILLY   Shut up!

BERNARD (*backing quietly away and out*) Mr. Birnbaum says he's stuck up.

WILLY Get outa here!

BERNARD If he doesn't buckle down he'll flunk math! (*He goes off*)

LINDA He's right, Willy, you've gotta—

WILLY (*exploding at her*) There's nothing the matter with him! You want him to be a worm like Bernard? He's got spirit, personality . . .

As he speaks, LINDA, *almost in tears, exits into the living room.* WILLY *is alone in the kitchen, wilting and staring. The leaves are gone. It is night again, and the apartment houses look down from behind.*

WILLY Loaded with it. Loaded! What is he stealing? He's giving it back, isn't he? Why is he stealing? What did I tell him? I never in my life told him anything but decent things.

HAPPY *in pajamas has come down the stairs;* WILLY *suddenly becomes aware of* HAPPY's *presence.*

HAPPY Let's go now, come on.

WILLY (*sitting down at the kitchen table*) Huh! Why did she have to wax the floors herself? Everytime she waxes the floors she keels over. She knows that!

HAPPY Shh! Take it easy. What brought you back tonight?

WILLY I got an awful scare. Nearly hit a kid in Yonkers. God! Why didn't I go to Alaska with my brother Ben that time! Ben! That man was a genius, that man was success incarnate! What a mistake! He begged me to go.

HAPPY Well, there's no use in—

WILLY You guys! There was a man started with the clothes on his back and ended up with diamond mines!

HAPPY Boy, someday I'd like to know how he did it.

WILLY What's the mystery? The man knew what he wanted and went out and got it! Walked into a jungle, and comes out, the age of twenty-one, and he's rich! The world is an oyster, but you don't crack it open on a mattress!

HAPPY Pop, I told you I'm gonna retire you for life.

WILLY You'll retire me for life on seventy goddam dollars a week? And your women and your car and your apartment, and you'll retire me for life! Christ's sake, I couldn't get past Yonkers today! Where are you guys, where are you? The woods are burning! I can't drive a car!

CHARLEY *has appeared in the doorway. He is a large man, slow of speech, laconic, immovable. In all he says, despite what he says, there is pity, and, now, trepidation. He has a robe over pajamas, slippers on his feet. He enters the kitchen.*

CHARLEY   Everything all right?

HAPPY   Yeah, Charley, everything's . . .

WILLY   What's the matter?

CHARLEY   I heard some noise. I thought something happened. Can't we do something about the walls? You sneeze in here, and in my house hats blow off.

HAPPY   Let's go to bed, Dad. Come on.

CHARLEY *signals to* HAPPY *to go.*

WILLY   You go ahead, I'm not tired at the moment.

HAPPY   (*to* WILLY)   Take it easy, huh? (*He exits*)

WILLY   What're you doin' up?

CHARLEY   (*sitting down at the kitchen table opposite* WILLY) Couldn't sleep good. I had a heartburn.

WILLY   Well, you don't know how to eat.

CHARLEY   I eat with my mouth.

WILLY   No, you're ignorant. You gotta know about vitamins and things like that.

CHARLEY   Come on, let's shoot. Tire you out a little.

WILLY   (*hesitantly*)   All right. You got cards?

CHARLEY   (*taking a deck from his pocket*)   Yeah, I got them. Some-place. What is it with those vitamins?

WILLY   (*dealing*)   They build up your bones. Chemistry.

CHARLEY   Yeah, but there's no bones in a heartburn.

WILLY   What are you talkin' about? Do you know the first thing about it?

CHARLEY   Don't get insulted.

WILLY   Don't talk about something you don't know anything about.

They are playing. Pause.

CHARLEY   What're you doin' home?

WILLY   A little trouble with the car.

CHARLEY   Oh. (*Pause*) I'd like to take a trip to California.

WILLY   Don't say.

CHARLEY   You want a job?

WILLY   I got a job, I told you that. (*After a slight pause*) What the hell are you offering me a job for?

CHARLEY   Don't get insulted.

WILLY   Don't insult me.

CHARLEY   I don't see no sense in it. You don't have to go on this way.

WILLY   I got a good job. (*Slight pause*) What do you keep comin' in here for?

CHARLEY   You want me to go?

WILLY (*after a pause, withering*)   I can't understand it. He's going back to Texas again. What the hell is that?

CHARLEY   Let him go.

WILLY   I got nothin' to give him, Charley. I'm clean, I'm clean.

CHARLEY   He won't starve. None a them starve. Forget about him.

WILLY   Then what have I got to remember?

CHARLEY   You take it too hard. To hell with it. When a deposit bottle is broken you don't get your nickel back.

WILLY   That's easy enough for you to say.

CHARLEY   That ain't easy for me to say.

WILLY   Did you see the ceiling I put up in the living-room?

CHARLEY   Yeah, that's a piece of work. To put up a ceiling is a mystery to me. How do you do it?

WILLY   What's the difference?

CHARLEY   Well, talk about it.

WILLY   You gonna put up a ceiling?

CHARLEY   How could I put up a ceiling?

WILLY   Then what the hell are you bothering me for?

CHARLEY   You're insulted again.

WILLY   A man who can't handle tools is not a man. You're disgusting.

CHARLEY   Don't call me disgusting, Willy.

UNCLE BEN, *carrying a valise and an umbrella, enters the forestage from around the right corner of the house. He is a stolid man, in his sixties, with a mustache and an authoritative air. He is utterly certain of his destiny, and there is an aura of far places about him. He enters exactly as* WILLY *speaks.*

WILLY   I'm getting awfully tired, Ben.

BEN's *music is heard.* BEN *looks around at everything.*

CHARLEY   Good, keep playing; you'll sleep better. Did you call me Ben?

BEN *looks at his watch.*

WILLY   That's funny. For a second there you reminded me of my brother Ben.

BEN   I only have a few minutes. (*He strolls, inspecting the place.* WILLY *and* CHARLEY *continue playing*)

CHARLEY   You never heard from him again, heh? Since that time?

WILLY   Didn't Linda tell you? Couple of weeks ago we got a letter from his wife in Africa. He died.

CHARLEY That so.

BEN (*chuckling*) So this is Brooklyn, eh?

CHARLEY Maybe you're in for some of his money.

WILLY Naa, he had seven sons. There's just one opportunity I had with that man . . .

BEN I must make a train, William. There are several properties I'm looking at in Alaska.

WILLY Sure, sure! If I'd gone with him to Alaska that time, everything would've been totally different.

CHARLEY Go on, you'd froze to death up there.

WILLY What're you talking about?

BEN Opportunity is tremendous in Alaska, William. Surprised you're not up there.

WILLY Sure, tremendous.

CHARLEY Heh?

WILLY There was the only man I ever met who knew the answers.

CHARLEY Who?

BEN How are you all?

WILLY (*taking a pot, smiling*) Fine, fine.

CHARLEY Pretty sharp tonight.

BEN Is Mother living with you?

WILLY No, she died a long time ago.

CHARLEY Who?

BEN That's too bad. Fine specimen of a lady, Mother.

WILLY (*to* CHARLEY) Heh?

BEN I'd hoped to see the old girl.

CHARLEY Who died?

BEN Heard anything from Father, have you?

WILLY (*unnerved*) What do you mean, who died?

CHARLEY (*taking a pot*) What're you talkin' about?

BEN (*looking at his watch*) William, it's half-past eight!

WILLY (*as though to dispel his confusion he angrily stops* CHARLEY'S *hand*) That's my build!

CHARLEY I put the ace—

WILLY If you don't know how to play the game I'm not gonna throw my money away on you!

CHARLEY (*rising*) It was my ace, for God's sake!

WILLY I'm through, I'm through!

BEN When did Mother die?

WILLY Long ago. Since the beginning you never knew how to play cards.

CHARLEY (*picks up the cards and goes to the door*) All right! Next time I'll bring a deck with five aces.

WILLY   I don't play that kind of game!

CHARLEY   (*turning to him*)   You ought to be ashamed of yourself!

WILLY   Yeah?

CHARLEY   Yeah! (*He goes out*)

WILLY   (*slamming the door after him*)   Ignoramus!

BEN   (*as* WILLY *comes toward him through the wall-line of the kitchen*)   So you're William.

WILLY   (*shaking* BEN's *hand*)   Ben! I've been waiting for you so long! What's the answer? How did you do it?

BEN   Oh, there's a story in that.

LINDA *enters the forestage, as of old, carrying the wash basket.*

LINDA   Is this Ben?

BEN   (*gallantly*)   How do you do, my dear.

LINDA   Where've you been all these years? Willy's always wondered why you—

WILLY   (*pulling* BEN *away from her impatiently*)   Where is Dad? Didn't you follow him? How did you get started?

BEN   Well, I don't know how much you remember.

WILLY   Well, I was just a baby, of course, only three or four years old—

BEN   Three years and eleven months.

WILLY   What a memory, Ben!

BEN   I have many enterprises, William, and I have never kept books.

WILLY   I remember I was sitting under the wagon in—was it Nebraska?

BEN   It was South Dakota, and I gave you a bunch of wild flowers.

WILLY   I remember you walking away down some open road.

BEN   (*laughing*)   I was going to find Father in Alaska.

WILLY   Where is he?

BEN   At that age I had a very faulty view of geography, William. I discovered after a few days that I was heading due south, so instead of Alaska, I ended up in Africa.

LINDA   Africa!

WILLY   The Gold Coast!

BEN   Principally diamond mines.

LINDA   Diamond mines!

BEN   Yes, my dear. But I've only a few minutes—

WILLY   No! Boys! Boys! (*Young* BIFF *and* HAPPY *appear*)   Listen to this. This is your Uncle Ben, a great man! Tell my boys, Ben!

BEN   Why, boys, when I was seventeen I walked into the jungle, and when I was twenty-one I walked out. (*He laughs*) And by God I was rich.

WILLY (*to the boys*)   You see what I been talking about? The greatest things can happen!

BEN (*glancing at his watch*)   I have an appointment in Ketchikan Tuesday week.

WILLY   No, Ben! Please tell about Dad. I want my boys to hear. I want them to know the kind of stock they spring from. All I remember is a man with a big beard, and I was in Mamma's lap, sitting around a fire, and some kind of high music.

BEN   His flute. He played the flute.

WILLY   Sure, the flute, that's right!

New music is heard, a high, rollicking tune.

BEN   Father was a very great and a very wild-hearted man. We would start in Boston, and he'd toss the whole family into the wagon, and then he'd drive the team right across the country; through Ohio, and Indiana, Michigan, Illinois, and all the Western states. And we'd stop in the towns and sell the flutes that he'd made on the way. Great inventor, Father. With one gadget he made more in a week than a man like you could make in a lifetime.

WILLY   That's just the way I'm bringing them up, Ben—rugged, well liked, all-around.

BEN   Yeah? (*To* BIFF)   Hit that, boy—hard as you can. (*He pounds his stomach*)

BIFF   Oh, no, sir!

BEN (*taking boxing stance*)   Come on, get to me! (*He laughs*)

WILLY   Go to it, Biff! Go ahead, show him!

BIFF   Okay! (*He cocks his fists and starts in*)

LINDA (*to* WILLY)   Why must he fight, dear?

BEN (*sparring with* BIFF)   Good boy! Good boy!

WILLY   How's that, Ben, heh?

HAPPY   Give him the left, Biff!

LINDA   Why are you fighting?

BEN   Good boy! (*Suddenly comes in, trips* BIFF, *and stands over him, the point of his umbrella poised over* BIFF's *eye*)

LINDA   Look out, Biff!

BIFF   Gee!

BEN (*patting* BIFF's *knee*)   Never fight fair with a stranger, boy. You'll never get out of the jungle that way. (*Taking* LINDA's *hand and bowing*)   It was an honor and a pleasure to meet you, Linda.

LINDA (*withdrawing her hand coldly, frightened*)   Have a nice—trip.

BEN (*to* WILLY)   And good luck with your—what do you do?

WILLY Selling.

BEN Yes. Well ... (*He raises his hand in farewell to all*)

WILLY No, Ben, I don't want you to think ... (*He takes* BEN's *arm to show him*) It's Brooklyn, I know, but we hunt too.

BEN Really, now.

WILLY Oh, sure, there's snakes and rabbits and—that's why I moved out here. Why, Biff can fell any one of these trees in no time! Boys! Go right over to where they're building the apartment house and get some sand. We're gonna rebuild the entire front stoop right now! Watch this, Ben!

BIFF Yes, sir! On the double, Hap!

HAPPY (*as he and* BIFF *run off*) I lost weight, Pop, you notice?

CHARLEY *enters in knickers, even before the boys are gone.*

CHARLEY Listen, if they steal any more from that building the watchman'll put the cops on them!

LINDA (*to* WILLY) Don't let Biff ...

BEN *laughs lustily.*

WILLY You shoulda seen the lumber they brought home last week. At least a dozen six-by-tens worth all kinds a money.

CHARLEY Listen, if that watchman—

WILLY I gave them hell, understand. But I got a couple of fearless characters there.

CHARLEY Willy, the jails are full of fearless characters.

BEN (*clapping* WILLY *on the back, with a laugh at* CHARLEY) And the stock exchange, friend!

WILLY (*joining in* BEN's *laughter*) Where are the rest of your pants?

CHARLEY My wife bought them.

WILLY Now all you need is a golf club and you can go upstairs and go to sleep. (*To* BEN) Great athlete! Between him and his son Bernard they can't hammer a nail!

BERNARD (*rushing in*) The watchman's chasing Biff!

WILLY (*angrily*) Shut up! He's not stealing anything!

LINDA (*alarmed, hurrying off left*) Where is he? Biff, dear! (*She exits*)

WILLY (*moving toward the left, away from* BEN) There's nothing wrong. What's the matter with you?

BEN Nervy boy. Good!

WILLY (*laughing*) Oh, nerves of iron, that Biff!

CHARLEY Don't know what it is. My New England man comes back and he's bleedin', they murdered him up there.

WILLY It's contacts, Charley, I got important contacts!

CHARLEY (*sarcastically*) Glad to hear it, Willy. Come in later, we'll shoot a little casino. I'll take some of your Portland money. (*He laughs at* WILLY *and exits*)

WILLY (*turning to* BEN) Business is bad, it's murderous. But not for me, of course.

BEN I'll stop by on my way back to Africa.

WILLY (*longingly*) Can't you stay a few days? You're just what I need, Ben, because I—I have a fine position here, but I—well, Dad left when I was such a baby and I never had a chance to talk to him and I still feel—kind of temporary about myself.

BEN I'll be late for my train.

They are at opposite ends of the stage.

WILLY Ben, my boys—can't we talk? They'd go into the jaws of hell for me, see, but I—

BEN William, you're being first-rate with your boys. Outstanding, manly chaps!

WILLY (*hanging on to his words*) Oh, Ben, that's good to hear! Because sometimes I'm afraid that I'm not teaching them the right kind of— Ben, how should I teach them?

BEN (*giving great weight to each word, and with a certain vicious audacity*) William, when I walked into the jungle, I was seventeen. When I walked out I was twenty-one. And, by God, I was rich! (*He goes off into darkness around the right corner of the house*)

WILLY ...was rich! That's just the spirit I want to imbue them with! To walk into a jungle! I was right! I was right! I was right!

BEN *is gone, but* WILLY *is still speaking to him as* LINDA, *in nightgown and robe, enters the kitchen, glances around for* WILLY, *then goes to the door of the house, looks out and sees him. Comes down to his left. He looks at her.*

LINDA Willy, dear? Willy?

WILLY I was right!

LINDA Did you have some cheese? (*He can't answer*) It's very late, darling. Come to bed, heh?

WILLY (*looking straight up*) Gotta break your neck to see a star in this yard.

LINDA You coming in?

WILLY Whatever happened to that diamond watch fob? Remember? When Ben came from Africa that time? Didn't he give me a watch fob with a diamond in it?

LINDA You pawned it, dear. Twelve, thirteen years ago. For Biff's radio correspondence course.

WILLY Gee, that was a beautiful thing. I'll take a walk.

LINDA But you're in your slippers.

WILLY (*starting to go around the house at the left*) I was right! I was! (*Half to* LINDA, *as he goes, shaking his head*) What a man! There was a man worth talking to I was right!

LINDA (*calling after* WILLY) But in your slippers, Willy!

WILLY *is almost gone when* BIFF, *in his pajamas, comes down the stairs and enters the kitchen.*

BIFF What is he doing out there?

LINDA Sh!

BIFF God Almighty, Mom, how long has he been doing this?

LINDA Don't, he'll hear you.

BIFF What the hell is the matter with him?

LINDA It'll pass by morning.

BIFF Shouldn't we do anything?

LINDA Oh, my dear, you should do a lot of things, but there's nothing to do, so go to sleep.

HAPPY *comes down the stairs and sits on the steps.*

HAPPY I never heard him so loud, Mom.

LINDA Well, come around more often; you'll hear him. (*She sits down at the table and mends the lining of* WILLY's *jacket*)

BIFF Why didn't you ever write me about this, Mom?

LINDA How would I write to you? For over three months you had no address.

BIFF I was on the move. But you know I thought of you all the time. You know that, don't you, pal?

LINDA I know, dear, I know. But he likes to have a letter. Just to know that there's still a possibility for better things.

BIFF He's not like this all the time, is he?

LINDA It's when you come home he's always the worst.

BIFF When I come home?

LINDA When you write you're coming, he's all smiles, and talks about the future, and—he's just wonderful. And then the closer you seem to come, the more shaky he gets, and then, by the time you get here, he's arguing, and he seems angry at you. I think it's just that maybe he can't bring himself to—to open up to you. Why are you so hateful to each other? Why is that?

BIFF (*evasively*) I'm not hateful, Mom.

LINDA But you no sooner come in the door than you're fighting!

BIFF I don't know why. I mean to change. I'm tryin', Mom, you understand?

LINDA Are you home to stay now?

BIFF I don't know. I want to look around, see what's doin'.

LINDA Biff, you can't look around all your life, can you?

BIFF I just can't take hold, Mom. I can't take hold of some kind of a life.

LINDA Biff, a man is not a bird, to come and go with the springtime.

BIFF Your hair... (*He touches her hair*) Your hair got so gray.

LINDA Oh, it's been gray since you were in high school. I just stopped dyeing it, that's all.

BIFF Dye it again, will ya? I don't want my pal looking old. (*He smiles*)

LINDA You're such a boy! You think you can go away for a year and... You've got to get it into your head now that one day you'll knock on this door and there'll be strange people here—

BIFF What are you talking about? You're not even sixty, Mom.

LINDA But what about your father?

BIFF (*lamely*) Well, I meant him too.

HAPPY He admires Pop.

LINDA Biff, dear, if you don't have any feeling for him, then you can't have any feeling for me.

BIFF Sure I can, Mom.

LINDA No. You can't just come to see me, because I love him. (*With a threat, but only a threat, of tears*) He's the dearest man in the world to me, and I won't have anyone making him feel unwanted and low and blue. You've got to make up your mind now, darling, there's no leeway any more. Either he's your father and you pay him that respect, or else you're not to come here. I know he's not easy to get along with—nobody knows that better than me—but...

WILLY (*from the left, with a laugh*) Hey, hey, Biffo!

BIFF (*starting to go out after* WILLY) What the hell is the matter with him? (HAPPY *stops him*)

LINDA Don't—don't go near him!

BIFF Stop making excuses for him! He always, always wiped the floor with you. Never had an ounce of respect for you.

HAPPY He's always had respect for—

BIFF What the hell do you know about it?

HAPPY (*surlily*) Just don't call him crazy!

BIFF He's got no character—Charley wouldn't do this. Not in his own house—spewing out that vomit from his mind.

HAPPY Charley never had to cope with what he's got to.

BIFF People are worse off than Willy Loman. Believe me, I've seen them!

LINDA Then make Charley your father, Biff. You can't do that, can you? I don't say he's a great man. Willy Loman never made a lot of money. His name was never in the paper. He's not the finest character that ever lived. But he's a human being, and a terrible thing is happening to him. So attention must be paid. He's not to be allowed to fall into his grave like an old dog. Attention, attention must be finally paid to such a person. You called him crazy—

BIFF I didn't mean—

LINDA No, a lot of people think he's lost his—balance. But you don't have to be very smart to know what his trouble is. The man is exhausted.

HAPPY Sure!

LINDA A small man can be just as exhausted as a great man. He works for a company thirty-six years this March, opens up unheard-of territories to their trademark, and now in his old age they take his salary away.

HAPPY (*indignantly*) I didn't know that, Mom.

LINDA You never asked, my dear! Now that you get your spending money someplace else you don't trouble your mind with him.

HAPPY But I gave you money last—

LINDA Christmas time, fifty dollars! To fix the hot water it cost ninety-seven fifty! For five weeks he's been on straight commission, like a beginner, an unknown!

BIFF Those ungrateful bastards!

LINDA Are they any worse than his sons? When he brought them business, when he was young, they were glad to see him. But now his old friends, the old buyers that loved him so and always found some order to hand him in a pinch—they're all dead, retired. He used to be able to make six, seven calls a day in Boston. Now he takes his valises out of the car and puts them back and takes them out again and he's exhausted. Instead of walking he talks now. He drives seven hundred miles, and when he gets there no one knows him any more, no one welcomes him. And what goes through a man's mind, driving seven hundred miles home without having earned a cent? Why shouldn't he talk to himself? Why? When he has to go to Charley and borrow fifty dollars a week and pretend to me that it's his pay? How long can that go on? How long? You see what I'm sitting here and waiting for? And you tell me he has no character? The man who never worked a day but for your benefit? When does he get the medal for that? Is this his reward—to turn around at the age of sixty-three and find his sons, who he loved better than his life, one a philandering bum—

HAPPY Mom!

LINDA That's all you are, my baby! (*To* BIFF) And you! What happened to the love you had for him? You were such pals! How you used to talk to him on the phone every night! How lonely he was till he could come home to you!

BIFF All right, Mom. I'll live here in my room, and I'll get a job. I'll keep away from him, that's all.

LINDA No, Biff. You can't stay here and fight all the time.

BIFF He threw me out of this house, remember that.

LINDA Why did he do that? I never knew why.

BIFF Because I know he's a fake and he doesn't like anybody around who knows!

LINDA Why a fake? In what way? What do you mean?

BIFF Just don't lay it all at my feet. It's between me and him— that's all I have to say. I'll chip in from now on. He'll settle for half my pay check. He'll be all right. I'm going to bed. (*He starts for the stairs*)

LINDA He won't be all right.

BIFF (*turning on the stairs, furiously*) I hate this city and I'll stay here. Now what do you want?

LINDA He's dying, Biff.

HAPPY *turns quickly to her, shocked.*

BIFF (*after a pause*) Why is he dying?

LINDA He's been trying to kill himself.

BIFF (*with great horror*) How?

LINDA I live from day to day.

BIFF What're you talking about?

LINDA Remember I wrote you that he smashed up the car again? In February?

BIFF Well?

LINDA The insurance inspector came. He said that they have evidence. That all these accidents in the last year—weren't—weren't —accidents.

HAPPY How can they tell that? That's a lie.

LINDA It seems there's a woman ... (*She takes a breath as* ...)

⎧ BIFF (*sharply but contained*) What woman?

⎩ LINDA (*simultaneously*) ... and this woman ...

LINDA What?

BIFF Nothing. Go ahead.

LINDA What did you say?

BIFF   Nothing. I just said what woman?

HAPPY   What about her?

LINDA   Well, it seems she was walking down the road and saw his car. She says that he wasn't driving fast at all, and that he didn't skid. She says he came to that little bridge, and then deliberately smashed into the railing, and it was only the shallowness of the water that saved him.

BIFF   Oh, no, he probably just fell asleep again.

LINDA   I don't think he fell asleep.

BIFF   Why not?

LINDA   Last month . . . (*With great difficulty*) Oh, boys, it's so hard to say a thing like this! He's just a big stupid man to you, but I tell you there's more good in him than in many other people. (*She chokes, wipes her eyes*) I was looking for a fuse. The lights blew out, and I went down the cellar. And behind the fuse box —it happened to fall out—was length of rubber pipe—just short.

HAPPY   No kidding?

LINDA   There's a little attachment on the end of it. I knew right away. And sure enough, on the bottom of the water heater there's a new little nipple on the gas pipe.

HAPPY   (*angrily*)   That—jerk.

BIFF   Did you have it taken off?

LINDA   I'm—I'm ashamed to. How can I mention it to him? Every day I go down and take away that little rubber pipe. But, when he comes home, I put it back where it was. How can I insult him that way? I don't know what to do. I live from day to day, boys. I tell you, I know every thought in his mind. It sounds so old-fashioned and silly, but I tell you he put his whole life into you and you've turned your backs on him. (*She is bent over in the chair, weeping, her face in her hands*) Biff, I swear to God! Biff, his life is in your hands!

HAPPY   (*to* BIFF)   How do you like that damned fool!

BIFF   (*kissing her*)   All right, pal, all right. It's all settled now. I've been remiss. I know that, Mom. But now I'll stay, and I swear to you, I'll apply myself. (*Kneeling in front of her, in a fever of self-reproach*) It's just—you see, Mom, I don't fit in business. Not that I won't try. I'll try, and I'll make good.

HAPPY   Sure you will. The trouble with you in business was you never tried to please people.

BIFF   I know, I—

HAPPY   Like when you worked for Harrison's. Bob Harrison said you were tops, and then you go and do some damn fool thing like whistling whole songs in the elevator like a comedian.

BIFF (*against* HAPPY) So what? I like to whistle sometimes.

HAPPY You don't raise a guy to a responsible job who whistles in the elevator!

LINDA Well, don't argue about it now.

HAPPY Like when you'd go off and swim in the middle of the day instead of taking the line around.

BIFF (*his resentment rising*) Well, don't you run off? You take off sometimes, don't you? On a nice summer day?

HAPPY Yeah, but I cover myself!

LINDA Boys!

HAPPY If I'm going to take a fade the boss can call any number where I'm supposed to be and they'll swear to him that I just left. I'll tell you something that I hate to say, Biff, but in the business world some of them think you're crazy.

BIFF (*angered*) Screw the business world!

HAPPY All right, screw it! Great, but cover yourself!

LINDA Hap, Hap!

BIFF I don't care what they think! They've laughed at Dad for years, and you know why? Because we don't belong in this nuthouse of a city! We should be mixing cement on some open plain, or—or carpenters. A carpenter is allowed to whistle!

WILLY *walks in from the entrance of the house, at left.*

WILLY Even your grandfather was better than a carpenter. (*Pause. They watch him*) You never grew up. Bernard does not whistle in the elevator, I assure you.

BIFF (*as though to laugh* WILLY *out of it*) Yeah, but you do, Pop.

WILLY I never in my life whistled in an elevator! And who in the business world thinks I'm crazy?

BIFF I didn't mean it like that, Pop. Now don't make a whole thing out of it, will ya?

WILLY Go back to the West! Be a carpenter, a cowboy, enjoy yourself!

LINDA Willy, he was just saying—

WILLY I heard what he said!

HAPPY (*trying to quiet* WILLY) Hey, Pop, come on now . . .

WILLY (*continuing over* HAPPY's *line*) They laugh at me, heh? Go to Filene's, go to the Hub, go to Slattery's, Boston. Call out the name Willy Loman and see what happens! Big shot!

BIFF All right, Pop.

WILLY Big!

BIFF All right!

WILLY Why do you always insult me?

BIFF I didn't say a word. (*To* LINDA) Did I say a word?

LINDA He didn't say anything, Willy.

WILLY (*going to the doorway of the living-room*) All right, good night, good night.

LINDA Willy, dear, he just decided ...

WILLY (*to* BIFF) If you get tired hanging around tomorrow, paint the ceiling I put up in the living-room.

BIFF I'm leaving early tomorrow.

HAPPY He's going to see Bill Oliver, Pop.

WILLY (*interestedly*) Oliver? For what?

BIFF (*with reserve, but trying, trying*) He always said he'd stake me. I'd like to go into business, so maybe I can take him up on it.

LINDA Isn't that wonderful?

WILLY Don't interrupt. What's wonderful about it? There's fifty men in the City of New York who'd stake him. (*To* BIFF) Sporting goods?

BIFF I guess so. I know something about it and—

WILLY He knows something about it! You know sporting goods better than Spalding, for God's sake! How much is he giving you?

BIFF I don't know, I didn't even see him yet, but—

WILLY Then what're you talkin' about?

BIFF (*getting angry*) Well, all I said was I'm gonna see him, that's all!

WILLY (*turning away*) Ah, you're counting your chickens again.

BIFF (*starting left for the stairs*) Oh, Jesus, I'm going to sleep!

WILLY (*calling after him*) Don't curse in this house!

BIFF (*turning*) Since when did you get so clean?

HAPPY (*trying to stop them*) Wait a ...

WILLY Don't use that language to me! I won't have it!

HAPPY (*grabbing* BIFF, *shouts*) Wait a minute! I got an idea. I got a feasible idea. Come here, Biff, let's talk this over now, let's talk some sense here. When I was down in Florida last time, I thought of a great idea to sell sporting goods. It just came back to me. You and I, Biff—we have a line, the Loman Line. We train a couple of weeks, and put on a couple of exhibitions, see?

WILLY That's an idea!

HAPPY Wait! We form two basketball teams, see? Two water-polo teams. We play each other. It's a million dollars' worth of publicity. Two brothers, see? The Loman Brothers. Displays in the Royal Palms—all the hotels. And banners over the ring and the basketball court: "Loman Brothers." Baby, we could sell sporting goods!

WILLY That is a one-million-dollar idea!

LINDA Marvelous!

BIFF I'm in great shape as far as that's concerned.

HAPPY And the beauty of it is, Biff, it wouldn't be like a business. We'd be out playin' ball again . . .

BIFF (*enthused*) Yeah, that's . . .

WILLY Million-dollar . . .

HAPPY And you wouldn't get fed up with it, Biff. It'd be the family again. There'd be the old honor, and comradeship, and if you wanted to go off for a swim or somethin'—well, you'd do it! Without some smart cooky gettin' up ahead of you!

WILLY Lick the world! You guys together could absolutely lick the civilized world.

BIFF I'll see Oliver tomorrow. Hap, if we could work that out . . .

LINDA Maybe things are beginning to—

WILLY (*wildly enthused, to* LINDA) Stop interrupting! (*To* BIFF) But don't wear sport jacket and slacks when you see Oliver.

BIFF No, I'll—

WILLY A business suit, and talk as little as possible, and don't crack any jokes.

BIFF He did like me. Always liked me.

LINDA He loved you!

WILLY (*to* LINDA) Will you stop! (*To* BIFF) Walk in very serious. You are not applying for a boy's job. Money is to pass. Be quiet, fine, and serious. Everybody likes a kidder, but nobody lends him money.

HAPPY I'll try to get some myself, Biff. I'm sure I can.

WILLY I see great things for you kids, I think your troubles are over. But remember, start big and you'll end big. Ask for fifteen. How much you gonna ask for?

BIFF Gee, I don't know—

WILLY And don't say "Gee." "Gee" is a boy's word. A man walking in for fifteen thousand dollars does not say "Gee!"

BIFF Ten, I think, would be top though.

WILLY Don't be so modest. You always started too low. Walk in with a big laugh. Don't look worried. Start off with a couple of your good stories to lighten things up. It's not what you say, it's how you say it—because personality always wins the day.

LINDA Oliver always thought the highest of him—

WILLY Will you let me talk?

BIFF Don't yell at her, Pop, will ya?

WILLY (*angrily*) I was talking, wasn't I?

BIFF I don't like you yelling at her all the time, and I'm tellin' you, that's all.

WILLY What're you, takin' over this house?

LINDA Willy—

WILLY (*turning on her*) Don't take his side all the time, goddammit!

BIFF (*furiously*) Stop yelling at her!

WILLY (*suddenly pulling on his cheek, beaten down, guilt ridden*) Give my best to Bill Oliver—he may remember me. (*He exits through the living-room doorway*)

LINDA (*her voice subdued*) What'd you have to start that for? (BIFF *turns away*) You see how sweet he was as soon as you talked hopefully? (*She goes over to* BIFF) Come up and say good night to him. Don't let him go to bed that way.

HAPPY Come on, Biff, let's buck him up.

LINDA Please, dear. Just say good night. It takes so little to make him happy. Come. (*She goes through the living-room doorway, calling upstairs from within the living-room*) Your pajamas are hanging in the bathroom, Willy!

HAPPY (*looking toward where* LINDA *went out*) What a woman! They broke the mold when they made her. You know that, Biff?

BIFF He's off salary. My God, working on commission!

HAPPY Well, let's face it: he's no hot-shot selling man. Except that sometimes, you have to admit, he's a sweet personality.

BIFF (*deciding*) Lend me ten bucks, will ya? I want to buy some new ties.

HAPPY I'll take you to a place I know. Beautiful stuff. Wear one of my striped shirts tomorrow.

BIFF She got gray. Mom got awful old. Gee, I'm gonna go in to Oliver tomorrow and knock him for a—

HAPPY Come on up. Tell that to Dad. Let's give him a whirl. Come on.

BIFF (*steamed up*) You know, with ten thousand bucks, boy!

HAPPY (*as they go into the living-room*) That's the talk, Biff, that's the first time I've heard the old confidence out of you! (*From within the living-room, fading off*) You're gonna live with me, kid, and any babe you want just say the word . . .

The last lines are hardly heard. They are mounting the stairs to their parents' bedroom.

LINDA (*entering her bedroom and addressing* WILLY, *who is in the bathroom. She is straightening the bed for him*) Can you do anything about the shower? It drips.

WILLY (*from the bathroom*) All of a sudden everything falls to pieces! Goddam plumbing, oughta be sued, those people. I hardly finished putting it in and the thing . . .(*His words rumble off*)

LINDA I'm just wondering if Oliver will remember him. You think he might?

WILLY (*coming out of the bathroom in his pajamas*) Remember him? What's the matter with you, you crazy? If he'd've stayed with Oliver he'd be on top by now! Wait'll Oliver gets a look at him. You don't know the average caliber any more. The average young man today—(*he is getting into bed*)—is got a caliber of zero. Greatest thing in the world for him was to bum around.

BIFF and HAPPY *enter the bedroom. Slight pause.*

WILLY (*stops short, looking at* BIFF) Glad to hear it, boy.

HAPPY He wanted to say good night to you, sport.

WILLY (*to* BIFF) Yeah. Knock him dead, boy. What'd you want to tell me?

BIFF Just take it easy, Pop. Good night. (*He turns to go*)

WILLY (*unable to resist*) And if anything falls off the desk while you're talking to him—like a package or something—don't you pick it up. They have office boys for that.

LINDA I'll make a big breakfast—

WILLY Will you let me finish? (*To* BIFF) Tell him you were in the business in the West. Not farm work.

BIFF All right, Dad.

LINDA I think everything—

WILLY (*going right through her speech*) And don't undersell yourself. No less than fifteen thousand dollars.

BIFF (*unable to bear him*) Okay. Good night, Mom. (*He starts moving*)

WILLY Because you got a greatness in you, Biff, remember that. You got all kinds a greatness ... (*He lies back, exhausted.* BIFF *walks out*)

LINDA (*calling after* BIFF) Sleep well, darling!

HAPPY I'm gonna get married, Mom. I wanted to tell you.

LINDA Go to sleep, dear.

HAPPY (*going*) I just wanted to tell you.

WILLY Keep up the good work. (HAPPY *exits*) God ... remember that Ebbets Field game? The championship of the city?

LINDA Just rest. Should I sing to you?

WILLY Yeah. Sing to me. (LINDA *hums a soft lullaby*) When that team came out—he was the tallest, remember?

LINDA Oh, yes. And in gold.

BIFF *enters the darkened kitchen, takes a cigarette, and leaves the house. He comes downstage into a golden pool of light. He smokes, staring at the night.*

WILLY Like a young god. Hercules—something like that. And the sun, the sun all around him. Remember how he waved to me?

Right up from the field, with the representatives of three colleges standing by? And the buyers I brought, and the cheers when he came out—Loman, Loman, Loman! God almighty, he'll be great yet. A star like that, magnificent, can never really fade away!

The light on WILLY *is fading. The gas heater begins to glow through the kitchen wall, near the stairs, a blue flame beneath red coils.*

LINDA (*timidly*) Willy dear, what has he got against you?
WILLY I'm so tired. Don't talk any more.

BIFF *slowly returns to the kitchen. He stops, stares toward the heater.*

LINDA Will you ask Howard to let you work in New York?
WILLY First thing in the morning. Everything'll be all right.

BIFF *reaches behind the heater and draws out a length of rubber tubing. He is horrified and turns his head toward* WILLY'S *room, still dimly lit, from which the strains of* LINDA'S *desperate but monotonous humming rise.*

WILLY (*staring through the window into the moonlight*) Gee, look at the moon moving between the buildings!

BIFF *wraps the tubing around his hand and quickly goes up the stairs.*

Curtain

ACT TWO

Music is heard, gay and bright. The curtain rises as the music fades away. WILLY, *in shirt sleeves, is sitting at the kitchen table, sipping coffee, his hat in his lap.* LINDA *is filling his cup when she can.*

WILLY Wonderful coffee. Meal in itself.
LINDA Can I make you some eggs?
WILLY No. Take a breath.
LINDA You look so rested, dear.
WILLY I slept like a dead one. First time in months. Imagine, sleeping till ten on a Tuesday morning. Boys left nice and early, heh?
LINDA They were out of here by eight o'clock.
WILLY Good work!
LINDA It was so thrilling to see them leaving together. I can't get over the shaving lotion in this house!
WILLY (*smiling*) Mmm—
LINDA Biff was very changed this morning. His whole attitude seemed to be hopeful. He couldn't wait to get downtown to see Oliver.

WILLY He's heading for a change. There's no question, there simply are certain men that take longer to get—solidified. How did he dress?

LINDA His blue suit. He's so handsome in that suit. He could be a—anything in that suit!

WILLY *gets up from the table.* LINDA *holds his jacket for him.*

WILLY There's no question, no question at all. Gee, on the way home tonight I'd like to buy some seeds.

LINDA (*laughing*) That'd be wonderful. But not enough sun gets back there. Nothing'll grow any more.

WILLY You wait, kid, before it's all over we're gonna get a little place out in the country, and I'll raise some vegetables, a couple of chickens . . .

LINDA You'll do it yet, dear.

WILLY *walks out of his jacket.* LINDA *follows him.*

WILLY And they'll get married, and come for a weekend. I'd build a little guest house. 'Cause I got so many fine tools, all I'd need would be a little lumber and some peace of mind.

LINDA (*joyfully*) I sewed the lining . . .

WILLY I could build two guest houses, so they'd both come. Did he decide how much he's going to ask Oliver for?

LINDA (*getting him into the jacket*) He didn't mention it, but I imagine ten or fifteen thousand. You going to talk to Howard today?

WILLY Yeah. I'll put it to him straight and simple. He'll just have to take me off the road.

LINDA And Willy, don't forget to ask for a little advance, because we've got the insurance premium. It's the grace period now.

WILLY That's a hundred . . . ?

LINDA A hundred and eight, sixty-eight. Because we're a little short again.

WILLY Why are we short?

LINDA Well, you had the motor job on the car . . .

WILLY That goddam Studebaker!

LINDA And you got one more payment on the refrigerator . . .

WILLY But it just broke again!

LINDA Well, it's old, dear.

WILLY I told you we should've bought a well-advertised machine. Charley bought a General Electric and it's twenty years old and it's still good, that son-of-a-bitch.

LINDA But, Willy—

WILLY Whoever heard of a Hastings refrigerator? Once in my life I would like to own something outright before it's broken! I'm always in a race with the junkyard! I just finished paying for the car and it's on its last legs. The refrigerator consumes belts like a goddam maniac. They time those things. They time them so when you finally paid for them, they're used up.

LINDA (*buttoning up his jacket as he unbuttons it*) All told, about two hundred dollars would carry us, dear. But that includes the last payment on the mortgage. After this payment, Willy, the house belongs to us.

WILLY It's twenty-five years!

LINDA Biff was nine years old when we bought it.

WILLY Well, that's a great thing. To weather a twenty-five year mortgage is—

LINDA It's an accomplishment.

WILLY All the cement, the lumber, the reconstruction I put in this house! There ain't a crack to be found in it any more.

LINDA Well, it served its purpose.

WILLY What purpose? Some stranger'll come along, move in, and that's that. If only Biff would take this house, and raise a family . . . (*He starts to go*) Good-by, I'm late.

LINDA (*suddenly remembering*) Oh, I forgot! You're supposed to meet them for dinner.

WILLY Me?

LINDA At Frank's Chop House on Forty-eighth near Sixth Avenue.

WILLY Is that so! How about you?

LINDA No, just the three of you. They're gonna blow you to a big meal!

WILLY Don't say! Who thought of that?

LINDA Biff came to me this morning, Willy, and he said, "Tell Dad, we want to blow him to a big meal." Be there six o'clock. You and your two boys are going to have dinner.

WILLY Gee whiz! That's really somethin'. I'm gonna knock Howard for a loop, kid. I'll get an advance, and I'll come home with a New York job. Goddammit, now I'm gonna do it!

LINDA Oh, that's the spirit, Willy!

WILLY I will never get behind a wheel the rest of my life!

LINDA It's changing, Willy, I can feel it changing!

WILLY Beyond a question. G'by, I'm late. (*He starts to go again*)

LINDA (*calling after him as she runs to the kitchen table for a handkerchief*) You got your glasses?

WILLY (*feels for them, then comes back in*) Yeah, yeah, got my glasses.

LINDA (*giving him the handkerchief*)   And a handkerchief.

WILLY   Yeah, handkerchief.

LINDA   And your saccharine?

WILLY   Yeah, my saccharine.

LINDA   Be careful on the subway stairs.

She kisses him, and a silk stocking is seen hanging from her hand. WILLY *notices it.*

WILLY   Will you stop mending stockings? At least while I'm in the house. It gets me nervous. I can't tell you. Please.

LINDA *hides the stocking in her hand as she follows* WILLY *across the fore-stage in front of the house.*

LINDA   Remember, Frank's Chop House.

WILLY (*passing the apron*)   Maybe beets would grow out there.

LINDA (*laughing*)   But you tried so many times.

WILLY   Yeah. Well, don't work hard today. (*He disappears around the right corner of the house*)

LINDA   Be careful!

As WILLY *vanishes,* LINDA *waves to him. Suddenly the phone rings. She runs across the stage and into the kitchen and lifts it.*

LINDA   Hello? Oh, Biff! I'm so glad you called, I just . . . Yes, sure, I just told him. Yes, he'll be there for dinner at six o'clock, I didn't forget. Listen, I was just dying to tell you. You know that little rubber pipe I told you about? That he connected to the gas heater? I finally decided to go down the cellar this morning and take it away and destroy it. But it's gone! Imagine? He took it away himself, it isn't there! (*She listens*) When? Oh, then you took it. Oh—nothing, it's just that I'd hoped he'd taken it away himself. Oh, I'm not worried, darling, because this morning he left in such high spirits, it was like the old days! I'm not afraid any more. Did Mr. Oliver see you? . . . Well, you wait there then. And make a nice impression on him, darling. Just don't perspire too much before you see him. And have a nice time with Dad. He may have big news too! . . . That's right, a New York job. And be sweet to him tonight, dear. Be loving to him. Because he's only a little boat looking for a harbor. (*She is trembling with sorrow and joy*) Oh, that's wonderful, Biff, you'll save his life. Thanks, darling. Just put your arm around him when he comes into the restaurant. Give him a smile. That's the boy . . . Good-by, dear. . . . You got your comb? . . . That's fine. Good-by, Biff dear.

In the middle of her speech, HOWARD WAGNER, *thirty-six, wheels on a small typewriter table on which is a wire-recording machine and proceeds to plug it in. This is on the left forestage. Light slowly fades on* LINDA *as it rises on* HOWARD. HOWARD *is intent on threading the machine and only glances over his shoulder as* WILLY *appears.*

WILLY   Pst! Pst!

HOWARD   Hello, Willy, come in.

WILLY   Like to have a little talk with you, Howard.

HOWARD   Sorry to keep you waiting. I'll be with you in a minute.

WILLY   What's that, Howard?

HOWARD   Didn't you ever see one of these? Wire recorder.

WILLY   Oh. Can we talk a minute?

HOWARD   Records things. Just got delivery yesterday. Been driving me crazy, the most terrific machine I ever saw in my life. I was up all night with it.

WILLY   What do you do with it?

HOWARD   I bought it for dictation, but you can do anything with it. Listen to this. I had it home last night. Listen to what I picked up. The first one is my daughter. Get this. (*He flicks the switch and "Roll out the Barrel" is heard being whistled*) Listen to that kid whistle.

WILLY   That is lifelike, isn't it?

HOWARD   Seven years old. Get that tone.

WILLY   Ts, ts. Like to ask a little favor if you . . .

The whistling breaks off, and the voice of HOWARD's *daughter is heard.*

HIS DAUGHTER   "Now you, Daddy."

HOWARD   She's crazy for me! (*Again the same song is whistled*) That's me! Ha! (*He winks*)

WILLY   You're very good!

The whistling breaks off again. The machine runs silent for a moment.

HOWARD   Sh! Get this now, this is my son.

HIS SON   "The capital of Alabama is Montgomery; the capital of Arizona is Phoenix; the capital of Arkansas is Little Rock; the capital of California is Sacramento . . ." (*and on, and on*)

HOWARD   (*holding up five fingers*)   Five years old, Willy!

WILLY   He'll make an announcer some day!

HIS SON (*continuing*)   "The capital . . ."

HOWARD   Get that—alphabetical order! (*The machine breaks off suddenly*) Wait a minute. The maid kicked the plug out.

WILLY   It certainly is a—

HOWARD   Sh, for God's sake!

HIS SON   "It's nine o'clock, Bulova watch time. So I have to go to sleep."

WILLY That really is—

HOWARD Wait a minute! The next is my wife.

They wait.

HOWARD'S VOICE "Go on, say something." (*Pause*) "Well, you gonna talk?"

HIS WIFE "I can't think of anything."

HOWARD'S VOICE "Well, talk—it's turning."

HIS WIFE (*shyly, beaten*) "Hello." (*Silence*) "Oh, Howard, I can't talk into this . . ."

HOWARD (*snapping the machine off*) That was my wife.

WILLY That is a wonderful machine. Can we—

HOWARD I tell you, Willy, I'm gonna take my camera, and my bandsaw, and all my hobbies, and out they go. This is the most fascinating relaxation I ever found.

WILLY I think I'll get one myself.

HOWARD Sure, they're only a hundred and a half. You can't do without it. Supposing you wanna hear Jack Benny, see? But you can't be at home at that hour. So you tell the maid to turn the radio on when Jack Benny comes on, and this automatically goes on with the radio . . .

WILLY And when you come home you . . .

HOWARD You can come home twelve o'clock, one o'clock, any time you like, and you get yourself a Coke and sit yourself down, throw the switch, and there's Jack Benny's program in the middle of the night!

WILLY I'm definitely going to get one. Because lots of time I'm on the road, and I think to myself, what I must be missing on the radio!

HOWARD Don't you have a radio in the car?

WILLY Well, yeah, but who ever thinks of turning it on?

HOWARD Say, aren't you supposed to be in Boston?

WILLY That's what I want to talk to you about, Howard. You got a minute? (*He draws a chair in from the wing*)

HOWARD What happened? What're you doing here?

WILLY Well . . .

HOWARD You didn't crack up again, did you?

WILLY Oh, no. No . . .

HOWARD Geez, you had me worried there for a minute. What's the trouble?

WILLY Well, tell you the truth, Howard. I've come to the decision that I'd rather not travel any more.

HOWARD Not travel! Well, what'll you do?

WILLY Remember, Christmas time, when you had the party here? You said you'd try to think of some spot for me here in town.

HOWARD With us?

WILLY Well, sure.

HOWARD Oh, yeah, yeah. I remember. Well, I couldn't think of anything for you, Willy.

WILLY I tell ya, Howard. The kids are all grown up, y'know. I don't need much any more. If I could take home—well, sixty-five dollars a week, I could swing it.

HOWARD Yeah, but Willy, see I—

WILLY I tell ya why, Howard. Speaking frankly and between the two of us, y'know—I'm just a little tired.

HOWARD Oh, I could understand that, Willy. But you're a road man, Willy, and we do a road business. We've only got a half-dozen salesmen on the floor here.

WILLY God knows, Howard, I never asked a favor of any man. But I was with the firm when your father used to carry you in here in his arms.

HOWARD I know that, Willy, but—

WILLY Your father came to me the day you were born and asked me what I thought of the name of Howard, may he rest in peace.

HOWARD I appreciate that, Willy, but there just is no spot here for you. If I had a spot I'd slam you right in, but I just don't have a single solitary spot.

He looks for his lighter. WILLY *has picked it up and gives it to him. Pause.*

WILLY (*with increasing anger*) Howard, all I need to set my table is fifty dollars a week.

HOWARD But where am I going to put you, kid?

WILLY Look, it isn't a question of whether I can sell merchandise, is it?

HOWARD No, but it's a business, kid, and everybody's gotta pull his own weight.

WILLY (*desperately*) Just let me tell you a story, Howard—

HOWARD 'Cause you gotta admit, business is business.

WILLY (*angrily*) Business is definitely business, but just listen for a minute. You don't understand this. When I was a boy—eighteen, nineteen—I was already on the road. And there was a question in my mind as to whether selling had a future for me. Because in those days I had a yearning to go to Alaska. See, there were three gold strikes in one month in Alaska, and I felt like going out. Just for the ride, you might say.

HOWARD (*barely interested*) Don't say.

WILLY Oh, yeah, my father lived many years in Alaska. He was an adventurous man. We've got quite a little streak of self-reliance in our family. I thought I'd go out with my older brother and try to locate him, and maybe settle in the North with the old man. And I was almost decided to go, when I met a salesman in the Parker House. His name was Dave Singleman. And he was eighty-four years old, and he'd drummed merchandise in thirty-one states. And old Dave, he'd go up to his room, y'understand, put on his green velvet slippers—I'll never forget—and pick up his phone and call the buyers, and without ever leaving his room, at the age of eighty-four, he made his living. And when I saw that, I realized that selling was the greatest career a man could want. 'Cause what could be more satisfying than to be able to go, at the age of eighty-four, into twenty or thirty different cities, and pick up a phone, and be remembered and loved and helped by so many different people? Do you know? when he died —and by the way he died the death of a salesman, in his green velvet slippers in the smoker of the New York, New Haven and Hartford, going into Boston—when he died, hundreds of salesmen and buyers were at his funeral. Things were sad on a lotta trains for months after that. (*He stands up.* HOWARD *has not looked at him*) In those days there was personality in it, Howard. There was respect, and comradeship, and gratitude in it. Today, it's all cut and dried, and there's no chance for bringing friendship to bear—or personality. You see what I mean? They don't know me any more.

HOWARD (*moving away, to the right*) That's just the thing, Willy.

WILLY If I had forty dollars a week—that's all I'd need. Forty dollars, Howard.

HOWARD Kid, I can't take blood from a stone, I—

WILLY (*desperation is on him now*) Howard, the year Al Smith was nominated, your father came to me and—

HOWARD (*starting to go off*) I've got to see some people, kid.

WILLY (*stopping him*) I'm talking about your father! There were promises made across this desk! You mustn't tell me you've got people to see—I put thirty-four years into this firm, Howard, and now I can't pay my insurance! You can't eat the orange and throw the peel away—a man is not a piece of fruit! (*After a pause*) Now pay attention. Your father—in 1928 I had a big year. I averaged a hundred and seventy dollars a week in commissions.

HOWARD (*impatiently*) Now, Willy, you never averaged—

WILLY (*banging his hand on the desk*) I averaged a hundred and seventy dollars a week in the year of 1928! And your father came to me—or rather, I was in the office here—it was right over this desk—and he put his hand on my shoulder—

HOWARD (*getting up*) You'll have to excuse me, Willy, I gotta see some people. Pull yourself together. (*Going out*) I'll be back in a little while.

On HOWARD's *exit, the light on his chair grows very bright and strange.*

WILLY Pull myself together! What the hell did I say to him? My God, I was yelling at him! How could I! (WILLY *breaks off, staring at the light, which occupies the chair, animating it. He approaches this chair, standing across the desk from it*) Frank, Frank, don't you remember what you told me that time? How you put your hand on my shoulder, and Frank . . .

He leans on the desk and as he speaks the dead man's name he accidentally switches on the recorder, and instantly

HOWARD'S SON " . . . of New York is Albany. The capital of Ohio is Cincinnati, the capital of Rhode Island is . . ." (*The recitation continues*)

WILLY (*leaping away with fright, shouting*) Ha! Howard! Howard! Howard!

HOWARD (*rushing in*) What happened?

WILLY (*pointing at the machine, which continues nasally, childishly, with the capital cities*) Shut it off! Shut it off!

HOWARD (*pulling the plug out*) Look, Willy . . .

WILLY (*pressing his hands to his eyes*) I gotta get myself some coffee. I'll get some coffee . . .

WILLY *starts to walk out.* HOWARD *stops him.*

HOWARD (*rolling up the cord*) Willy, look . . .

WILLY I'll go to Boston.

HOWARD Willy, you can't go to Boston for us.

WILLY Why can't I go?

HOWARD I don't want you to represent us. I've been meaning to tell you for a long time now.

WILLY Howard, are you firing me?

HOWARD I think you need a good long rest, Willy.

WILLY Howard—

HOWARD And when you feel better, come back, and we'll see if we can work something out.

WILLY But I gotta earn money, Howard. I'm in no position to—

HOWARD Where are your sons? Why don't your sons give you a hand?

WILLY They're working on a very big deal.

HOWARD   This is no time for false pride, Willy. You go to your sons and you tell them that you're tired. You've got two great boys, haven't you?

WILLY   Oh, no question, no question, but in the meantime . . .

HOWARD   Then that's that, heh?

WILLY   All right, I'll go to Boston tomorrow.

HOWARD   No, no.

WILLY   I can't throw myself on my sons. I'm not a cripple!

HOWARD   Look, kid, I'm busy this morning.

WILLY   (*grasping* HOWARD'S *arm*)   Howard, you've got to let me go to Boston!

HOWARD   (*hard, keeping himself under control*)   I've got a line of people to see this morning. Sit down, take five minutes, and pull yourself together, and then go home, will ya? I need the office, Willy. (*He starts to go, turns, remembering the recorder, starts to push off the table holding the recorder*) Oh, yeah. Whenever you can this week, stop by and drop off the samples. You'll feel better, Willy, and then come back and we'll talk. Pull yourself together, kid, there's people outside.

HOWARD *exits, pushing the table off left.* WILLY *stares into space, exhausted. Now the music is heard—*BEN'S *music—first distantly, then closer, closer. As* WILLY *speaks,* BEN *enters from the right. He carries valise and umbrella.*

WILLY   Oh, Ben, how did you do it? What is the answer? Did you wind up the Alaska deal already?

BEN   Doesn't take much time if you know what you're doing. Just a short business trip. Boarding ship in an hour. Wanted to say good-by.

WILLY   Ben, I've got to talk to you.

BEN   (*glancing at his watch*)   Haven't the time, William.

WILLY   (*crossing the apron to* BEN)   Ben, nothing's working out. I don't know what to do.

BEN   Now, look here, William. I've bought timberland in Alaska and I need a man to look after things for me.

WILLY   God, timberland! Me and my boys in those grand outdoors!

BEN   You've a new continent at your doorstep, William. Get out of these cities, they're full of talk and time payments and courts of law. Screw on your fists and you can fight for a fortune up there.

WILLY   Yes, yes! Linda, Linda!

LINDA *enters as of old, with the wash.*

LINDA Oh, you're back?

BEN I haven't much time.

WILLY No, wait! Linda, he's got a proposition for me in Alaska.

LINDA But you've got—(*To* BEN) He's got a beautiful job here.

WILLY But in Alaska, kid, I could—

LINDA You're doing well enough, Willy!

BEN (*to* LINDA) Enough for what, my dear?

LINDA (*frightened of* BEN *and angry at him*) Don't say those things to him! Enough to be happy right here, right now. (*To* WILLY, *while* BEN *laughs*) Why must everybody conquer the world? You're well liked, and the boys love you, and someday— (*to* BEN)—why, old man Wagner told him just the other day that if he keeps it up he'll be a member of the firm, didn't he, Willy?

WILLY Sure, sure. I am building something with this firm, Ben, and if a man is building something he must be on the right track, mustn't he?

BEN What are you building? Lay your hand on it. Where is it?

WILLY (*hesitantly*) That's true, Linda, there's nothing.

LINDA Why? (*To* BEN) There's a man eighty-four years old—

WILLY That's right, Ben, that's right. When I look at that man I say, what is there to worry about?

BEN Bah!

WILLY It's true, Ben. All he has to do is go into any city, pick up the phone, and he's making his living and you know why?

BEN (*picking up his valise*) I've got to go.

WILLY (*holding* BEN *back*) Look at this boy!

BIFF, *in his high school sweater, enters carrying suitcase.* HAPPY *carries* BIFF's *shoulder guards, gold helmet, and football pants.*

WILLY Without a penny to his name, three great universities are begging for him, and from there the sky's the limit, because it's not what you do, Ben. It's who you know and the smile on your face! It's contacts, Ben, contacts! The whole wealth of Alaska passes over the lunch table at the Commodore Hotel, and that's the wonder, the wonder of this country, that a man can end with diamonds here on the basis of being liked! (*He turns to* BIFF) And that's why when you get out on that field today it's important. Because thousands of people will be rooting for you and loving you. (*To* BEN, *who has again begun to leave*) And Ben! when he walks into a business office his name will sound out like a bell and all the doors will open to him! I've seen it, Ben, I've seen it a thousand times! You can't feel it with your hand like timber, but it's there!

BEN Good-by, William.

WILLY Ben, am I right? Don't you think I'm right? I value your advice.

BEN There's a new continent at your doorstep, William. You could walk out rich. Rich! (*He is gone*)

WILLY We'll do it here, Ben! You hear me? We're gonna do it here!

Young BERNARD *rushes in. The gay music of the Boys is heard.*

BERNARD Oh, gee, I was afraid you left already!

WILLY Why? What time is it?

BERNARD It's half-past one!

WILLY Well, come on, everybody! Ebbets Field next stop! Where's the pennants? (*He rushes through the wall-line of the kitchen and out into the living-room*)

LINDA (*to* BIFF) Did you pack fresh underwear?

BIFF (*who has been limbering up*) I want to go!

BERNARD Biff, I'm carrying your helmet, ain't I?

HAPPY No, I'm carrying the helmet.

BERNARD Oh, Biff, you promised me.

HAPPY I'm carrying the helmet.

BERNARD How am I going to get in the locker room?

LINDA Let him carry the shoulder guards. (*She puts her coat and hat on in the kitchen*)

BERNARD Can I, Biff? 'Cause I told everybody I'm going to be in the locker room.

HAPPY In Ebbets Field it's the clubhouse.

BERNARD I meant the clubhouse. Biff!

HAPPY Biff!

BIFF (*grandly, after a slight pause*) Let him carry the shoulder guards.

HAPPY (*as he gives* BERNARD *the shoulder guards*) Stay close to us now.

WILLY *rushes in with the pennants.*

WILLY (*handing them out*) Everybody wave when Biff comes out on the field. (HAPPY *and* BERNARD *run off*) You set now, boy?

The music has died away.

BIFF Ready to go, Pop. Every muscle is ready.

WILLY (*at the edge of the apron*) You realize what this means?

BIFF That's right, Pop.

WILLY (*feeling* BIFF's *muscles*) You're comin' home this afternoon captain of the All-Scholastic Championship Team of the City of New York.

BIFF   I got it, Pop. And remember, pal, when I take off my helmet, that touchdown is for you.

WILLY   Let's go! (*He is starting out, with his arm around* BIFF, *when* CHARLEY *enters, as of old, in knickers*) I got no room for you, Charley.

CHARLEY   Room? For what?

WILLY   In the car.

CHARLEY   You goin' for a ride? I wanted to shoot some casino.

WILLY   (*furiously*) Casino! (*Incredulously*) Don't you realize what today is?

LINDA   Oh, he knows, Willy. He's just kidding you.

WILLY   That's nothing to kid about!

CHARLEY   No, Linda, what's goin' on?

LINDA   He's playing in Ebbets Field.

CHARLEY   Baseball in this weather?

WILLY   Don't talk to him. Come on, come on! (*He is pushing them out*)

CHARLEY   Wait a minute, didn't you hear the news?

WILLY   What?

CHARLEY   Don't you listen to the radio? Ebbets Field just blew up.

WILLY   You go to hell! (CHARLEY *laughs*) (*Pushing them out*) Come on, come on! We're late.

CHARLEY   (*as they go*) Knock a homer, Biff, knock a homer!

WILLY   (*the last to leave, turning to* CHARLEY) I don't think that was funny, Charley. This is the greatest day of his life.

CHARLEY   Willy, when are you going to grow up?

WILLY   Yeah, heh? When this game is over, Charley, you'll be laughing out of the other side of your face. They'll be calling him another Red Grange. Twenty-five thousand a year.

CHARLEY   (*kidding*) Is that so?

WILLY   Yeah, that's so.

CHARLEY   Well, then, I'm sorry. Willy. But tell me something.

WILLY   What?

CHARLEY   Who is Red Grange?

WILLY   Put up your hands. Goddam you, put up your hands!

CHARLEY, *chuckling, shakes his head and walks away, around the left corner of the stage.* WILLY *follows him. The music rises to a mocking frenzy.*

WILLY   Who the hell do you think you are, better than everybody else? You don't know everything, you big, ignorant, stupid . . . Put up your hands!

Light rises, on the right side of the forestage, on a small table in the reception room of CHARLEY's *office. Traffic sounds are heard.* BERNARD, *now mature, sits whistling to himself. A pair of tennis rackets and an overnight bag are on the floor beside him.*

WILLY (*offstage*) What are you walking away for? Don't walk away! If you're going to say something say it to my face! I know you laugh at me behind my back. You'll laugh out of the other side of your goddam face after this game. Touchdown! Touchdown! Eighty thousand people! Touchdown! Right between the goal posts.

BERNARD *is a quiet, earnest, but self-assured young man.* WILLY's *voice is coming from right upstage now.* BERNARD *lowers his feet off the table and listens.* JENNY, *his father's secretary, enters.*

JENNY (*distressed*) Say, Bernard, will you go out in the hall?
BERNARD What is that noise? Who is it?
JENNY Mr. Loman. He just got off the elevator.
BERNARD (*getting up*) Who's he arguing with?
JENNY Nobody. There's nobody with him. I can't deal with him any more, and your father gets all upset everytime he comes. I've got a lot of typing to do, and your father's waiting to sign it. Will you see him?
WILLY (*entering*) Touchdown! Touch—(*He sees* JENNY) Jenny, Jenny, good to see you. How're ya? Working'? Or still honest?
JENNY Fine. How've you been feeling?
WILLY Not much any more, Jenny. Ha, ha! (*He is surprised to see the rackets*)
BERNARD Hello, Uncle Willy.
WILLY (*almost shocked*) Bernard! Well, look who's here! (*He comes quickly, guiltily, to* BERNARD *and warmly shakes his hand*)
BERNARD How are you? Good to see you.
WILLY What are you doing here?
BERNARD Oh, just stopped by to see Pop. Get off my feet till my train leaves. I'm going to Washington in a few minutes.
WILLY Is he in?
BERNARD Yes, he's in his office with the accountant. Sit down.
WILLY (*sitting down*) What're you going to do in Washington?
BERNARD Oh, just a case I've got there, Willy.
WILLY That so? (*Indicating the rackets*) You going to play tennis there?
BERNARD I'm staying with a friend who's got a court.
WILLY Don't say. His own tennis court. Must be fine people, I bet.
BERNARD They are, very nice. Dad tells me Biff's in town.
WILLY (*with a big smile*) Yeah, Biff's in. Working on a very big deal, Bernard.

BERNARD   What's Biff doing?

WILLY   Well, he's been doing very big things in the West. But he decided to establish himself here. Very big. We've having dinner. Did I hear your wife had a boy?

BERNARD   That's right. Our second.

WILLY   Two boys! What do you know!

BERNARD   What kind of a deal has Biff got?

WILLY   Well, Bill Oliver—very big sporting-goods man—he wants Biff very badly. Called him in from the West. Long distance, carte blanche, special deliveries. Your friends have their own private tennis court?

BERNARD   You still with the old firm, Willy?

WILLY   (*after a pause*)   I'm—I'm overjoyed to see how you made the grade, Bernard, overjoyed. It's an encouraging thing to see a young man really—really— Looks very good for Biff—very— (*He breaks off, then*) Bernard—(*He is so full of emotion, he breaks off again*)

BERNARD   What is it, Willy?

WILLY   (*small and alone*)   What—what's the secret?

BERNARD   What secret?

WILLY   How—how did you? Why didn't he ever catch on?

BERNARD   I wouldn't know that, Willy.

WILLY   (*confidentially, desperately*)   You were his friend, his boyhood friend. There's something I don't understand about it. His life ended after that Ebbets Field game. From the age of seventeen nothing good ever happened to him.

BERNARD   He never trained himself for anything.

WILLY   But he did, he did. After high school he took so many correspondence courses. Radio mechanics; television; God knows what, and never made the slightest mark.

BERNARD   (*taking off his glasses*)   Willy, do you want to talk candidly?

WILLY   (*rising, faces* BERNARD)   I regard you as a very brilliant man, Bernard. I value your advice.

BERNARD   Oh, the hell with the advice, Willy. I couldn't advise you. There's just one thing I've always wanted to ask you. When he was supposed to graduate, and the math teacher flunked him—

WILLY   Oh, that son-of-a-bitch ruined his life.

BERNARD   Yeah, but, Willy, all he had to do was go to summer school and make up that subject.

WILLY   That's right, that's right.

BERNARD   Did you tell him not to go to summer school?

WILLY   Me? I begged him to go. I ordered him to go!

BERNARD   Then why wouldn't he go?

WILLY   Why? Why! Bernard, that question has been trailing me like a ghost for the last fifteen years. He flunked the subject, and laid down and died like a hammer hit him!

BERNARD   Take it easy, kid.

WILLY   Let me talk to you—I got nobody to talk to. Bernard, Bernard, was it my fault? Y'see? It keeps going around in my mind, maybe I did something to him. I got nothing to give him.

BERNARD   Don't take it so hard.

WILLY   Why did he lay down? What is the story there? You were his friend!

BERNARD   Willy, I remember, it was June, and our grades came out. And he'd flunked math.

WILLY   That son-of-a-bitch!

BERNARD   No, it wasn't right then. Biff just got very angry, I remember, and he was ready to enroll in summer school.

WILLY   (*surprised*)   He was?

BERNARD   He wasn't beaten by it at all. But then, Willy, he disappeared from the block for almost a month. And I got the idea that he'd gone up to New England to see you. Did he have a talk with you then?

WILLY *stares in silence.*

BERNARD   Willy?

WILLY   (*with a strong edge of resentment in his voice*)   Yeah, he came to Boston. What about it?

BERNARD   Well, just that when he came back—I'll never forget this, it always mystifies me. Because I'd thought so well of Biff, even though he'd always taken advantage of me. I loved him, Willy, y'know? And he came back after that month and took his sneakers—remember those sneakers with "University of Virginia" printed on them? He was so proud of those, wore them every day. And he took them down in the cellar, and burned them up in the furnace. We had a fist fight. It lasted at least half an hour. Just the two of us, punching each other down the cellar, and crying right through it. I've often thought of how strange it was that I knew he'd given up his life. What happened in Boston, Willy?

WILLY *looks at him as at an intruder.*

BERNARD   I just bring it up because you asked me.

WILLY   (*angrily*)   Nothing. What do you mean, "What happened?" What's that got to do with anything?

BERNARD   Well, don't get sore.

WILLY What are you trying to do, blame it on me? If a boy lays down is that my fault?

BERNARD Now, Willy, don't get—

WILLY Well, don't—don't talk to me that way! What does that mean, "What happened?"

CHARLEY *enters. He is in his vest, and he carries a bottle of bourbon.*

CHARLEY Hey, you're going to miss that train. (*He waves the bottle*)

BERNARD Yeah, I'm going. (*He takes the bottle*) Thanks, Pop. (*He picks up his rackets and bag*) Good-by, Willy, and don't worry about it. You know, "If at first you don't succeed . . ."

WILLY Yes, I believe in that.

BERNARD But sometimes, Willy, it's better for a man just to walk away.

WILLY Walk away?

BERNARD That's right.

WILLY But if you can't walk away?

BERNARD (*after a slight pause*) I guess that's when it's tough. (*Extending his hand*) Good-by, Willy.

WILLY (*shaking* BERNARD's *hand*) Good-by, boy.

CHARLEY (*an arm on* BERNARD's *shoulder*) How do you like this kid? Gonna argue a case in front of the Supreme Court.

BERNARD (*protesting*) Pop!

WILLY (*genuinely shocked, pained, and happy*) No! The Supreme Court!

BERNARD I gotta run. 'By, Dad!

CHARLEY Knock 'em dead, Bernard!

BERNARD *goes off.*

WILLY (*as* CHARLEY *takes out his wallet*) The Supreme Court! And he didn't even mention it!

CHARLEY (*counting out money on the desk*) He don't have to— he's gonna do it.

WILLY And you never told him what to do, did you? You never took any interest in him.

CHARLEY My salvation is that I never took any interest in anything. There's some money—fifty dollars. I got an accountant inside.

WILLY Charley, look . . . (*With difficulty*) I got my insurance to pay. If you can manage it—I need a hundred and ten dollars.

CHARLEY *doesn't reply for a moment; merely stops moving.*

WILLY I'd draw it from my bank but Linda would know, and I ...

CHARLEY Sit down, Willy.

WILLY (*moving toward the chair*) I'm keeping an account of everything, remember. I'll pay every penny back. (*He sits*)

CHARLEY Now listen to me, Willy.

WILLY I want you to know I appreciate ...

CHARLEY (*sitting down on the table*) Willy, what're you doin'? What the hell is goin' on in your head?

WILLY Why? I'm simply ...

CHARLEY I offered you a job. You can make fifty dollars a week. And I won't send you on the road.

WILLY I've got a job.

CHARLEY Without pay? What kind of a job is a job without pay? (*He rises*) Now, look, kid, enough is enough. I'm no genius but I know when I'm being insulted.

WILLY Insulted!

CHARLEY Why don't you want to work for me?

WILLY What's the matter with you? I've got a job.

CHARLEY Then what're you walkin' in here every week for?

WILLY (*getting up*) Well, if you don't want me to walk in here—

CHARLEY I am offering you a job.

WILLY I don't want your goddam job!

CHARLEY When the hell are you going to grow up?

WILLY (*furiously*) You big ignoramus, if you say that to me again I'll rap you one! I don't care how big you are! (*He's ready to fight*)

Pause.

CHARLEY (*kindly, going to him*) How much do you need, Willy?

WILLY Charley, I'm strapped. I'm strapped. I don't know what to do. I was just fired.

CHARLEY Howard fired you?

WILLY That snotnose. Imagine that? I named him. I named him Howard.

CHARLEY Willy, when're you gonna realize that them things don't mean anything? You named him Howard, but you can't sell that. The only thing you got in this world is what you can sell. And the funny thing is that you're a salesman, and you don't know that.

WILLY I've always tried to think otherwise, I guess. I always felt that if a man was impressive, and well liked, that nothing—

CHARLEY Why must everybody like you? Who liked J. P. Morgan?

Was he impressive? In a Turkish bath he'd look like a butcher. But with his pockets on he was very well liked. Now listen, Willy, I know you don't like me, and nobody can say I'm in love with you, but I'll give you a job because—just for the hell of it, put it that way. Now what do you say?

WILLY   I—I just can't work for you, Charley.

CHARLEY   What're you, jealous of me?

WILLY   I can't work for you, that's all, don't ask me why.

CHARLEY   (*angered, takes out more bills*)   You been jealous of me all your life, you damned fool! Here, pay your insurance. (*He puts the money in* WILLY's *hand*)

WILLY   I'm keeping strict accounts.

CHARLEY   I've got some work to do. Take care of yourself. And pay your insurance.

WILLY   (*moving to the right*)   Funny, y'know? After all the highways, and the trains, and the appointments, and the years, you end up worth more dead than alive.

CHARLEY   Willy, nobody's worth nothin' dead. (*After a slight pause*) Did you hear what I said?

WILLY *stands still, dreaming.*

CHARLEY   Willy!

WILLY   Apologize to Bernard for me when you see him. I didn't mean to argue with him. He's a fine boy. They're all fine boys, and they'll end up big—all of them. Someday they'll all play tennis together. Wish me luck, Charley. He saw Bill Oliver today.

CHARLEY   Good luck.

WILLY   (*on the verge of tears*)   Charley, you're the only friend I got. Isn't that a remarkable thing? (*He goes out*)

CHARLEY   Jesus!

CHARLEY *stares after him a moment and follows. All light blacks out. Suddenly raucous music is heard, and a red glow rises behind the screen at right.* STANLEY, *a young waiter, appears, carrying a table, followed by* HAPPY, *who is carrying two chairs.*

STANLEY   (*putting the table down*)   That's all right, Mr. Loman, I can handle it myself. (*He turns and takes the chairs from* HAPPY *and places them at the table*)

HAPPY   (*glancing around*)   Oh, this is better.

STANLEY   Sure, in the front there you're in the middle of all kinds a noise. Whenever you got a party, Mr. Loman, you just tell me and I'll put you back here. Y'know, there's a lotta people they don't like it private, because when they go out they like to see a lotta action around them because they're sick and tired to stay in the house by theirself. But I know you, you ain't from Hackensack. You know what I mean?

HAPPY (*sitting down*)　So how's it coming, Stanley?

STANLEY　Ah, it's a dog's life. I only wish during the war they'd a took me in the Army. I coulda been dead by now.

HAPPY　My brother's back, Stanley.

STANLEY　Oh, he come back, heh? From the Far West.

HAPPY　Yeah, big cattle man, my brother, so treat him right. And my father's coming too.

STANLEY　Oh, your father too!

HAPPY　You got a couple of nice lobsters?

STANLEY　Hundred per cent, big.

HAPPY　I want them with the claws.

STANLEY　Don't worry, I don't give you no mice. (HAPPY *laughs*) How about some wine? It'll put a head on the meal.

HAPPY　No. You remember, Stanley, that recipe I brought you from overseas? With the champagne in it?

STANLEY　Oh, yeah, sure. I still got it tacked up yet in the kitchen. But that'll have to cost a buck apiece anyways.

HAPPY　That's all right.

STANLEY　What'd you, hit a number or somethin'?

HAPPY　No, it's a little celebration. My brother is—I think he pulled off a big deal today. I think we're going into business together.

STANLEY　Great! That's the best for you. Because a family business, you know what I mean?—that's the best.

HAPPY　That's what I think.

STANLEY　'Cause what's the difference? Somebody steals? It's in the family. Know what I mean? (*Sotto voce*) Like this bartender here. The boss is goin' crazy what kinda leak he's got in the cash register. You put it in but it don't come out.

HAPPY (*raising his head*)　Sh!

STANLEY　What?

HAPPY　You notice I wasn't lookin' right or left, was I?

STANLEY　No.

HAPPY　And my eyes are closed.

STANLEY　So what's the—?

HAPPY　Strudel's comin'.

STANLEY (*catching on, looks around*)　Ah, no, there's no—

He breaks off as a furred, lavishly dressed girl enters and sits at the next table. Both follow her with their eyes.

STANLEY Geez, how'd ya know?

HAPPY I got radar or something. (*Staring directly at her profile*) Oooooooo . . . Stanley.

STANLEY I think that's for you, Mr. Loman.

HAPPY Look at that mouth. Oh, God. And the binoculars.

STANLEY Geez, you got a life, Mr. Loman.

HAPPY Wait on her.

STANLEY (*going to the* GIRL's *table*) Would you like a menu, ma'am?

GIRL I'm expecting someone, but I'd like a—

HAPPY Why don't you bring her—excuse me, miss, do you mind? I sell champagne, and I'd like you to try my brand. Bring her a champagne, Stanley.

GIRL That's awfully nice of you.

HAPPY Don't mention it. It's all company money. (*He laughs*)

GIRL That's a charming product to be selling, isn't it?

HAPPY Oh, gets to be like everything else. Selling is selling, y'know.

GIRL I suppose.

HAPPY You don't happen to sell, do you?

GIRL No, I don't sell.

HAPPY Would you object to a compliment from a stranger? You ought to be on a magazine cover.

GIRL (*looking at him a little archly*) I have been.

STANLEY *comes in with a glass of champagne.*

HAPPY What'd I say before, Stanley? You see? She's a cover girl.

STANLEY Oh, I could see, I could see.

HAPPY (*to the* GIRL) What magazine?

GIRL Oh, a lot of them. (*She takes the drink*) Thank you.

HAPPY You know what they say in France, don't you? "Champagne is the drink of the complexion"—Hya, Biff!

BIFF *has entered and sits with* HAPPY.

BIFF Hello, kid. Sorry I'm late.

HAPPY I just got here. Uh, Miss—?

GIRL Forsythe.

HAPPY Miss Forsythe, this is my brother.

BIFF Is Dad here?

HAPPY His name is Biff. You might've heard of him. Great football player.

GIRL Really? What team?

HAPPY Are you familiar with football?

GIRL No, I'm afraid I'm not.

HAPPY   Biff is quarterback with the New York Giants.

GIRL   Well, that is nice, isn't it? (*She drinks*)

HAPPY   Good health.

GIRL   I'm happy to meet you.

HAPPY   That's my name. Hap. It's really Harold, but at West Point they called me Happy.

GIRL   (*now really impressed*)   Oh, I see. How do you do? (*She turns her profile*)

BIFF   Isn't Dad coming?

HAPPY   You want her?

BIFF   Oh, I could never make that.

HAPPY   I remember the time that idea would never come into your head. Where's the old confidence, Biff?

BIFF   I just saw Oliver—

HAPPY   Wait a minute. I've got to see that old confidence again. Do you want her? She's on call.

BIFF   Oh, no. (*He turns to look at the* GIRL)

HAPPY   I'm telling you. Watch this. (*Turning to the* GIRL) Honey? (*She turns to him*) Are you busy?

GIRL   Well, I am . . . but I could make a phone call.

HAPPY   Do that, will you, honey? And see if you can get a friend. We'll be here for a while. Biff is one of the greatest football players in the country.

GIRL   (*standing up*)   Well, I'm certainly happy to meet you.

HAPPY   Come back soon.

GIRL   I'll try.

HAPPY   Don't try, honey, try hard.

The GIRL *exits.* STANLEY *follows, shaking his head in bewildered admiration.*

HAPPY   Isn't that a shame now? A beautiful girl like that? That's why I can't get married. There's not a good woman in a thousand. New York is loaded with them, kid!

BIFF   Hap, look—

HAPPY   I told you she was on call!

BIFF   (*strangely unnerved*)   Cut it out, will ya? I want to say something to you.

HAPPY   Did you see Oliver?

BIFF   I saw him all right. Now look, I want to tell Dad a couple of things and I want you to help me.

HAPPY   What? Is he going to back you?

BIFF   Are you crazy? You're out of your goddam head, you know that?

HAPPY Why? What happened?

BIFF (*breathlessly*) I did a terrible thing today, Hap. It's been the strangest day I ever went through. I'm all numb, I swear.

HAPPY You mean he wouldn't see you?

BIFF Well, I waited six hours for him, see? All day. Kept sending my name in. Even tried to date his secretary so she'd get me to him, but no soap.

HAPPY Because you're not showin' the old confidence, Biff. He remembered you, didn't he?

BIFF (*stopping* HAPPY *with a gesture*) Finally, about five o'clock, he comes out. Didn't remember who I was or anything. I felt like such an idiot, Hap.

HAPPY Did you tell him my Florida idea?

BIFF He walked away. I saw him for one minute. I got so mad I could've torn the walls down! How the hell did I ever get the idea I was a salesman there? I even believed myself that I'd been a salesman for him! And then he gave one look and— I realized what a ridiculous lie my whole life has been! We've been talking in a dream of fifteen years. I was a shipping clerk.

HAPPY What'd you do?

BIFF (*with great tension and wonder*) Well, he left, see. And the secretary went out. I was all alone in the waiting-room. I don't know what came over me, Hap. The next thing I know I'm in his office—paneled walls, everything. I can't explain it. I—Hap, I took his fountain pen.

HAPPY Geez, did he catch you?

BIFF I ran out. I ran down all eleven flights. I ran and ran and ran.

HAPPY That was an awful dumb—what'd you do that for?

BIFF (*agonized*) I don't know, I just—wanted to take something, I don't know. You gotta help me, Hap. I'm gonna tell Pop.

HAPPY You crazy? What for?

BIFF Hap, he's got to understand that I'm not the man somebody lends that kind of money to. He thinks I've been spiting him all these years and it's eating him up.

HAPPY That's just it. You tell him something nice.

BIFF I can't.

HAPPY Say you got a lunch date with Oliver tomorrow.

BIFF So what do I do tomorrow?

HAPPY You leave the house tomorrow and come back at night and say Oliver is thinking it over. And he thinks it over for a couple of weeks, and gradually it fades away and nobody's the worse.

BIFF But it'll go on forever!

HAPPY Dad is never so happy as when he's looking forward to something!

WILLY *enters.*

HAPPY Hello, scout!

WILLY Gee, I haven't been here in years!

STANLEY *has followed* WILLY *in and sets a chair for him.* STANLEY *starts off but* HAPPY *stops him.*

HAPPY Stanley!

STANLEY *stands by, waiting for an order.*

BIFF (*going to* WILLY *with guilt, as to an invalid*) Sit down, Pop. You want a drink?

WILLY Sure, I don't mind.

BIFF Let's get a load on.

WILLY You look worried.

BIFF N-no. (*To* STANLEY) Scotch all around. Make it doubles.

STANLEY Doubles, right. (*He goes*)

WILLY You had a couple already, didn't you?

BIFF Just a couple, yeah.

WILLY Well, what happened, boy? (*Nodding affirmatively, with a smile*) Everything go all right?

BIFF (*takes a breath, then reaches out and grasps* WILLY's *hand*) Pal ... (*He is smiling bravely, and* WILLY *is smiling too*) I had an experience today.

HAPPY Terrific, Pop.

WILLY That so? What happened?

BIFF (*high, slightly alcoholic, above the earth*) I'm going to tell you everything from first to last. It's been a strange day. (*Silence. He looks around, composes himself as best he can, but his breath keeps breaking the rhythm of his voice*) I had to wait quite a while for him, and—

WILLY Oliver?

BIFF Yeah, Oliver. All day, as a matter of cold fact. And a lot of —instances—facts, Pop, facts about my life came back to me. Who was it, Pop? Who ever said I was a salesman with Oliver?

WILLY Well, you were.

BIFF No, Dad, I was a shipping clerk.

WILLY But you were practically—

BIFF (*with determination*) Dad, I don't know who said it first, but I was never a salesman for Bill Oliver.

WILLY What're you talking about?

BIFF   Let's hold on to the facts tonight, Pop. We're not going to get anywhere bullin' around. I was a shipping clerk.

WILLY (*angrily*)   All right, now listen to me—

BIFF   Why don't you let me finish?

WILLY   I'm not interested in stories about the past or any crap of that kind because the woods are burning, boys, you understand? There's a big blaze going on all around. I was fired today.

BIFF (*shocked*)   How could you be?

WILLY   I was fired, and I'm looking for a little good news to tell your mother, because the woman has waited and the woman has suffered. The gift of it is that I haven't got a story left in my head, Biff. So don't give me a lecture about facts and aspects. I am not interested. Now what've you got to say to me?

STANLEY *enters with three drinks. They wait until he leaves.*

WILLY   Did you see Oliver?

BIFF   Jesus, Dad!

WILLY   You mean you didn't go up there?

HAPPY   Sure he went up there.

BIFF   I did. I—saw him. How could they fire you?

WILLY (*on the edge of his chair*)   What kind of a welcome did he give you?

BIFF   He won't even let you work on commission?

WILLY   I'm out! (*Driving*)   So tell me, he gave you a warm welcome?

HAPPY   Sure, Pop, sure!

BIFF (*driven*)   Well, it was kind of—

WILLY   I was wondering if he'd remember you. (*To* HAPPY) Imagine, man doesn't see him for ten, twelve years and gives him that kind of a welcome!

HAPPY   Damn right!

BIFF (*trying to return to the offensive*)   Pop, look—

WILLY   You know why he remembered you, don't you? Because you impressed him in those days.

BIFF   Let's talk quietly and get this down to the facts, huh?

WILLY (*as though* BIFF *had been interrupting*)   Well, what happened? It's great news, Biff. Did he take you into his office or'd you talk in the waiting-room?

BIFF   Well, he came in, see, and—

WILLY (*with a big smile*)   What'd he say? Betcha he threw his arm around you.

BIFF   Well, he kinda—

WILLY   He's a fine man. (*To* HAPPY) Very hard man to see, y'know.

HAPPY (*agreeing*) Oh, I know.

WILLY (*to* BIFF) Is that where you had the drinks?

BIFF Yeah, he gave me a couple of—no, no!

HAPPY (*cutting in*) He told him my Florida idea.

WILLY Don't interrupt. (*To* BIFF) How'd he react to the Florida idea?

BIFF Dad, will you give me a minute to explain?

WILLY I've been waiting for you to explain since I sat down here! What happened? He took you into his office and what?

BIFF Well—I talked. And—and he listened, see.

WILLY Famous for the way he listens, y'know. What was his answer?

BIFF His answer was—(*He breaks off, suddenly angry*) Dad, you're not letting me tell you what I want to tell you!

WILLY (*accusing, angered*) You didn't see him, did you?

BIFF I did see him!

WILLY What'd you insult him or something? You insulted him, didn't you?

BIFF Listen, will you let me out of it, will you just let me out of it!

HAPPY What the hell!

WILLY Tell me what happened!

BIFF (*to* HAPPY) I can't talk to him!

A single trumpet note jars the ear. The light of green leaves stains the house, which holds the air of night and a dream. Young BERNARD *enters and knocks on the door of the house.*

YOUNG BERNARD (*frantically*) Mrs. Loman, Mrs. Loman!

HAPPY Tell him what happened!

BIFF (*to* HAPPY) Shut up and leave me alone!

WILLY No, no! You had to go and flunk math!

BIFF What math? What're you talking about?

YOUNG BERNARD Mrs. Loman, Mrs. Loman!

LINDA *appears in the house, as of old.*

WILLY (*wildly*) Math, math, math!

BIFF Take it easy, Pop!

YOUNG BERNARD Mrs. Loman!

WILLY (*furiously*) If you hadn't flunked you'd've been set by now!

BIFF Now, look, I'm gonna tell you what happened, and you're going to listen to me.

YOUNG BERNARD Mrs. Loman!

BIFF I waited six hours—

HAPPY What the hell are you saying?

BIFF I kept sending in my name but he wouldn't see me. So finally he ... (*He continues unheard as light fades low on the restaurant*)

YOUNG BERNARD Biff flunked math!

LINDA No!

YOUNG BERNARD Birnbaum flunked him! They won't graduate him!

LINDA But they have to. He's gotta go to the university. Where is he? Biff! Biff!

YOUNG BERNARD No, he left. He went to Grand Central.

LINDA Grand— You mean he went to Boston!

YOUNG BERNARD Is Uncle Willy in Boston?

LINDA Oh, maybe Willy can talk to the teacher. Oh, the poor, poor boy!

Light on house area snaps out.

BIFF (*at the table, now audible, holding up a gold fountain pen*) ... so I'm washed up with Oliver, you understand? Are you listening to me?

WILLY (*at a loss*) Yeah, sure. If you hadn't flunked—

BIFF Flunked what? What're you talking about?

WILLY Don't blame everything on me! I didn't flunk math—you did! What pen?

HAPPY That was awful dumb, Biff, a pen like that is worth—

WILLY (*seeing the pen for the first time*) You took Oliver's pen?

BIFF (*weakening*) Dad, I just explained it to you.

WILLY You stole Bill Oliver's fountain pen!

BIFF I didn't exactly steal it! That's just what I've been explaining to you!

HAPPY He had it in his hand and just then Oliver walked in, so he got nervous and stuck it in his pocket!

WILLY My God, Biff!

BIFF I never intended to do it, Dad!

OPERATOR'S VOICE Standish Arms, good evening!

WILLY (*shouting*) I'm not in my room!

BIFF (*frightened*) Dad, what's the matter? (*He and* HAPPY *stand up*)

OPERATOR Ringing Mr. Loman for you!

WILLY I'm not there, stop it!

BIFF (*horrified, gets down on one knee before* WILLY) Dad, I'll make good, I'll make good. (WILLY *tries to get to his feet.* BIFF *holds him down*) Sit down now.

WILLY　No, you're no good, you're no good for anything.

BIFF　I am, Dad, I'll find something else, you understand? Now don't worry about anything. (*He holds up* WILLY's *face*) Talk to me, Dad.

OPERATOR　Mr. Loman does not answer. Shall I page him?

WILLY　(*attempting to stand, as though to rush and silence the Operator*)　No, no, no!

HAPPY　He'll strike something, Pop.

WILLY　No, no . . .

BIFF　(*desperately, standing over* WILLY)　Pop, listen! Listen to me! I'm telling you something good. Oliver talked to his partner about the Florida idea. You listening? He—he talked to his partner, and he came to me . . . I'm going to be all right, you hear? Dad, listen to me, he said it was just a question of the amount!

WILLY　Then you . . . got it?

HAPPY　He's gonna be terrific, Pop!

WILLY　(*trying to stand*)　Then you got it, haven't you? You got it! You got it!

BIFF　(*agonized, holds* WILLY *down*)　No, no. Look, Pop. I'm supposed to have lunch with them tomorrow. I'm just telling you this so you'll know that I can still make an impression, Pop. And I'll make good somewhere, but I can't go tomorrow, see?

WILLY　Why not? You simply—

BIFF　But the pen, Pop!

WILLY　You give it to him and tell him it was an oversight!

HAPPY　Sure, have lunch tomorrow!

BIFF　I can't say that—

WILLY　You were doing a crossword puzzle and accidentally used his pen!

BIFF　Listen, kid, I took those balls years ago, now I walk in with his fountain pen? That clinches it, don't you see? I can't face him like that! I'll try elsewhere.

PAGE's VOICE　Paging Mr. Loman!

WILLY　Don't you want to be anything?

BIFF　Pop, how can I go back?

WILLY　You don't want to be anything, is that what's behind it?

BIFF　(*now angry at* WILLY *for not crediting his sympathy*)　Don't take it that way! You think it was easy walking into that office after what I'd done to him? A team of horses couldn't have dragged me back to Bill Oliver!

WILLY　Then why'd you go?

BIFF　Why did I go? Why did I go! Look at you! Look at what's become of you!

Off left, THE WOMAN *laughs.*

WILLY Biff, you're going to go to that lunch tomorrow, or—
BIFF I can't go. I've got no appointment!
HAPPY Biff, for . . .!
WILLY Are you spiting me?
BIFF Don't take it that way! Goddammit!
WILLY (*strikes* BIFF *and falters away from the table*) You rotten little louse! Are you spiting me?
THE WOMAN Someone's at the door, Willy!
BIFF I'm no good, can't you see what I am?
HAPPY (*separating them*) Hey, you're in a restaurant! Now cut it out, both of you! (*The girls enter*) Hello, girls, sit down.

THE WOMAN *laughs, off left.*

MISS FORSYTHE I guess we might as well. This is Letta.
THE WOMAN Willy, are you going to wake up?
BIFF (*ignoring* WILLY) How're ya, miss, sit down. What do you drink?
MISS FORSYTHE Letta might not be able to stay long.
LETTA I gotta get up very early tomorrow. I got jury duty. I'm so excited! Were you fellows ever on a jury?
BIFF No, but I been in front of them! (*The girls laugh*) This is my father.
LETTA Isn't he cute? Sit down with us, Pop.
HAPPY Sit him down, Biff!
BIFF (*going to him*) Come on, slugger, drink us under the table. To hell with it! Come on, sit down, pal.

On BIFF's *last insistence,* WILLY *is about to sit.*

THE WOMAN (*now urgently*) Willy, are you going to answer the door!

THE WOMAN's *call pulls* WILLY *back. He starts right, befuddled.*

BIFF Hey, where are you going?
WILLY Open the door.
BIFF The door?
WILLY The washroom . . . the door . . . where's the door?
BIFF (*leading* WILLY *to the left*) Just go straight down.

WILLY *moves left.*

THE WOMAN Willy, Willy, are you going to get up, get up, get up, get up?

WILLY *exits left.*

LETTA   I think it's sweet you bring your daddy along.

MISS FORSYTHE   Oh, he isn't really your father!

BIFF (*at left, turning to her resentfully*)   Miss Forsythe, you've just seen a prince walk by. A fine, troubled prince. A hard-working, unappreciated prince. A pal, you understand? A good companion. Always for his boys.

LETTA   That's so sweet.

HAPPY   Well, girls, what's the program? We're wasting time. Come on, Biff. Gather round. Where would you like to go?

BIFF   Why don't you do something for him?

HAPPY   Me!

BIFF   Don't you give a damn for him, Hap?

HAPPY   What're you talking about? I'm the one who—

BIFF   I sense it, you don't give a good goddam about him. (*He takes the rolled-up hose from his pocket and puts it on the table in front of* HAPPY) Look what I found in the cellar, for Christ's sake. How can you bear to let it go on?

HAPPY   Me? Who goes away? Who runs off and—

BIFF   Yeah, but he doesn't mean anything to you. You could help him—I can't! Don't you understand what I'm talking about? He's going to kill himself, don't you know that?

HAPPY   Don't I know it! Me!

BIFF   Hap, help him! Jesus . . . help him . . . Help me, help me, I can't bear to look at his face! (*Ready to weep, he hurries out, up right*)

HAPPY (*starting after him*)   Where are you going?

MISS FORSYTHE   What's he so mad about?

HAPPY   Come on, girls, we'll catch up with him.

MISS FORSYTHE (*as* HAPPY *pushes her out*)   Say, I don't like that temper of his!

HAPPY   He's just a little overstrung, he'll be all right!

WILLY (*off left, as* THE WOMAN *laughs*)   Don't answer! Don't answer!

LETTA   Don't you want to tell your father—

HAPPY   No, that's not my father. He's just a guy. Come on, we'll catch Biff, and, honey, we're going to paint this town! Stanley, where's the check! Hey, Stanley!

They exit. STANLEY *looks toward left.*

STANLEY (*calling to* HAPPY *indignantly*)   Mr. Loman! Mr. Loman!

STANLEY *picks up a chair and follows them off. Knocking is heard off left.*

THE WOMAN *enters, laughing.* WILLY *follows her. She is in a black slip; he is buttoning his shirt. Raw, sensuous music accompanies their speech.*

WILLY Will you stop laughing? Will you stop?

THE WOMAN Aren't you going to answer the door? He'll wake the whole hotel.

WILLY I'm not expecting anybody.

THE WOMAN Whyn't you have another drink, honey, and stop being so damn self-centered?

WILLY I'm so lonely.

THE WOMAN You know you ruined me, Willy? From now on, whenever you come to the office, I'll see that you go right through to the buyers. No waiting at my desk any more, Willy. You ruined me.

WILLY That's nice of you to say that.

THE WOMAN Gee, you are self-centered! Why so sad? You are the saddest, self-centeredest soul I ever did see-saw. (*She laughs. He kisses her*) Come on inside, drummer boy. It's silly to be dressing in the middle of the night. (*As knocking is heard*) Aren't you going to answer the door?

WILLY They're knocking on the wrong door.

THE WOMAN But I felt the knocking. And he heard us talking in here. Maybe the hotel's on fire!

WILLY (*his terror rising*) It's a mistake.

THE WOMAN Then tell him to go away!

WILLY There's nobody there.

THE WOMAN It's getting on my nerves, Willy. There's somebody standing out there and it's getting on my nerves!

WILLY (*pushing her away from him*) All right, stay in the bathroom here, and don't come out. I think there's a law in Massachusetts about it, so don't come out. It may be that new room clerk. He looked very mean. So don't come out. It's a mistake, there no fire.

The knocking is heard again. He takes a few steps away from her, and she vanishes into the wing. The light follows him, and now he is facing YOUNG BIFF, *who carries a suitcase.* BIFF *steps toward him. The music is gone.*

BIFF Why didn't you answer?

WILLY Biff! What are you doing in Boston?

BIFF Why didn't you answer? I've been knocking for five minutes, I called you on the phone—

WILLY I just heard you. I was in the bathroom and had the door shut. Did anything happen home?

BIFF   Dad—I let you down.

WILLY   What do you mean?

BIFF   Dad ...

WILLY   Biffo, what's this about? (*Putting his arm around* BIFF) Come on, let's go downstairs and get you a malted.

BIFF   Dad, I flunked math.

WILLY   Not for the term?

BIFF   The term. I haven't got enough credits to graduate.

WILLY   You mean to say Bernard wouldn't give you the answers?

BIFF   He did, he tried, but I only got a sixty-one.

WILLY   And they wouldn't give you four points?

BIFF   Birnbaum refused absolutely. I begged him, Pop, but he won't give me those points. You gotta talk to him before they close the school. Because if he saw the kind of man you are, and you just talked to him in your way, I'm sure he'd come through for me. The class came right before practice, see, and I didn't go enough. Would you talk to him? He'd like you, Pop. You know the way you could talk.

WILLY   You're on. We'll drive right back.

BIFF   Oh, Dad, good work! I'm sure he'll change it for you!

WILLY   Go downstairs and tell the clerk I'm checkin' out. Go right down.

BIFF   Yes, sir! See, the reason he hates me, Pop—one day he was late for class so I got up at the blackboard and imitated him. I crossed my eyes and talked with a lithp.

WILLY   (*laughing*)   You did? The kids like it?

BIFF   They nearly died laughing!

WILLY   Yeah? What'd you do?

BIFF   The thquare root of thixty twee is ... (WILLY *bursts out laughing;* BIFF *joins him*) And in the middle of it he walked in!

WILLY *laughs and* THE WOMAN *joins in offstage.*

WILLY   (*without hesitation*)   Hurry downstairs and—

BIFF   Somebody in there?

WILLY   No, that was next door.

THE WOMAN *laughs offstage.*

BIFF   Somebody got in your bathroom!

WILLY   No, it's the next room, there's a party—

THE WOMAN   (*enters, laughing. She lisps this*)   Can I come in? There's something in the bathtub, Willy, and it's moving!

WILLY *looks at* BIFF, *who is staring open-mouthed and horrified at* THE WOMAN.

WILLY Ah—you better go back to your room. They must be finished painting by now. They're painting her room so I let her take a shower here. Go back, go back ... (*He pushes her*)

THE WOMAN (*resisting*) But I've got to get dressed, Willy, I can't—

WILLY Get out of here! Go back, go back ... (*Suddenly striving for the ordinary*) This is Miss Francis, Biff, she's a buyer. They're painting her room. Go back, Miss Francis, go back ...

THE WOMAN But my clothes, I can't go out naked in the hall!

WILLY (*pushing her offstage*) Get outa here! Go back, go back!

BIFF *slowly sits down on his suitcase as the argument continues offstage.*

THE WOMAN Where's my stockings? You promised me stockings, Willy!

WILLY I have no stockings here!

THE WOMAN You had two boxes of size nine sheers for me, and I want them!

WILLY Here, for God's sake, will you get outa here!

THE WOMAN (*enters holding a box of stockings*) I just hope there's nobody in the hall. That's all I hope. (*To* BIFF) Are you football or baseball?

BIFF Football.

THE WOMAN (*angry, humiliated*) That's me too. G'night. (*She snatches her clothes from* WILLY, *and walks out*)

WILLY (*after a pause*) Well, better get going. I want to get to the school first thing in the morning. Get my suits out of the closet. I'll get my valise. (BIFF *doesn't move*) What's the matter? (BIFF *remains motionless, tears falling*) She's a buyer. Buys for J. H. Simmons. She lives down the hall—they're painting. You don't imagine—(*He breaks off. After a pause*) Now listen, pal, she's just a buyer. She sees merchandise in her room and they have to keep it looking just so ... (*Pause. Assuming command*) All right, get my suits. (BIFF *doesn't move*) Now stop crying and do as I say. I gave you an order. Biff, I gave you an order! Is that what you do when I give you an order? How dare you cry! (*Putting his arm around* BIFF) Now look, Biff, when you grow up you'll understand about these things. You mustn't—you mustn't overemphasize a thing like this. I'll see Birnbaum first thing in the morning.

BIFF Never mind.

WILLY (*getting down beside* BIFF) Never mind! He's going to give you those points. I'll see to it.

BIFF He wouldn't listen to you.

WILLY He certainly will listen to me. You need those points for the U. of Virginia.

BIFF I'm not going there.

WILLY Heh? If I can't get him to change that mark you'll make it up in summer school. You've got all summer to—

BIFF (*his weeping breaking from him*) Dad . . .

WILLY (*infected by it*) Oh, my boy . . .

BIFF Dad . . .

WILLY She's nothing to me, Biff. I was lonely, I was terribly lonely.

BIFF You—you gave her Mama's stockings! (*His tears break through and he rises to go*)

WILLY (*grabbing for* BIFF) I gave you an order!

BIFF Don't touch me, you—liar!

WILLY Apologize for that!

BIFF You fake! You phony little fake! You fake! (*Overcome, he turns quickly and weeping fully goes out with his suitcase.* WILLY *is left on the floor on his knees*)

WILLY I gave you an order! Biff, come back here or I'll beat you! Come back here! I'll whip you!

STANLEY *comes quickly in from the right and stands in front of* WILLY.

WILLY (*shouts at* STANLEY) I gave you an order . . .

STANLEY Hey, let's pick it up, pick it up, Mr. Loman. (*He helps* WILLY *to his feet*) Your boys left with the chippies. They said they'll see you home.

A second WAITER *watches some distance away.*

WILLY But we were supposed to have dinner together.

Music is heard, WILLY's *theme.*

STANLEY Can you make it?

WILLY I'll—sure, I can make it. (*Suddenly concerned about his clothes*) Do I—I look all right?

STANLEY Sure, you look all right. (*He flicks a speck off* WILLY's *lapel*)

WILLY Here—here's a dollar.

STANLEY Oh, your son paid me. It's all right.

WILLY (*putting it in* STANLEY's *hand*) No, take it. You're a good boy.

STANLEY Oh, no, you don't have to . . .

WILLY Here—here's some more, I don't need it any more. (*After a slight pause*) Tell me—is there a seed store in the neighborhood?

STANLEY   Seeds? You mean like to plant?

As WILLY *turns,* STANLEY *slips the money back into his jacket pocket.*

WILLY   Yes. Carrots, peas . . .

STANLEY   Well, there's hardware stores on Sixth Avenue, but it may be too late now.

WILLY (*anxiously*)   Oh, I'd better hurry. I've got to get some seeds. (*He starts off to the right*) I've got to get some seeds, right away. Nothing's planted. I don't have a thing in the ground.

WILLY *hurries out as the light goes down.* STANLEY *moves over to the right after him, watches him off. The other* WAITER *has been staring at* WILLY.

STANLEY (*to the* WAITER)   Well, whatta you looking at?

The WAITER *picks up the chairs and moves off right.* STANLEY *takes the table and follows him. The light fades on this area. There is a long pause, the sound of the flute coming over. The light gradually rises on the kitchen, which is empty.* HAPPY *appears at the door of the house, followed by* BIFF. HAPPY *is carrying a large bunch of long-stemmed roses. He enters the kitchen, looks around for* LINDA. *Not seeing her, he turns to* BIFF, *who is just outside the house door, and makes a gesture with his hands, indicating "Not here, I guess." He looks into the living-room and freezes. Inside,* LINDA, *unseen, is seated,* WILLY's *coat on her lap. She rises ominously and quietly and moves toward* HAPPY, *who backs up into the kitchen, afraid.*

HAPPY   Hey, what're you doing up? (LINDA *says nothing but moves toward him implacably*) Where's Pop? (*He keeps backing to the right, and now* LINDA *is in full view in the doorway to the living-room*) Is he sleeping?

LINDA   Where were you?

HAPPY (*trying to laugh it off*)   We met two girls, Mom, very fine types. Here, we brought you some flowers. (*Offering them to her*) Put them in your room, Ma.

She knocks them to the floor at BIFF's *feet. He has now come inside and closed the door behind him. She stares at* BIFF, *silent.*

HAPPY   Now what'd you do that for? Mom, I want you to have some flowers—

LINDA (*cutting* HAPPY *off, violently to* BIFF)   Don't you care whether he lives or dies?

HAPPY (*going to the stairs*)   Come upstairs, Biff.

BIFF (*with a flare of disgust, to* HAPPY)   Go away from me! (*To* LINDA) What do you mean, lives or dies? Nobody's dying around here, pal.

LINDA   Get out of my sight! Get out of here!

BIFF   I wanna see the boss.

LINDA   You're not going near him!

BIFF   Where is he? (*He moves into the living-room and* LINDA *follows*)

LINDA   (*shouting after* BIFF)   You invite him for dinner. He looks forward to it all day—(BIFF *appears in his parents' bedroom, looks around, and exits*)—and then you desert him there. There's no stranger you'd do that to!

HAPPY   Why? He had a swell time with us. Listen, when I— (LINDA *comes back into the kitchen*)—desert him I hope I don't outlive the day!

LINDA   Get out of here!

HAPPY   Now look, Mom . . .

LINDA   Did you have to go to women tonight? You and your lousy rotten whores!

BIFF *re-enters the kitchen.*

HAPPY   Mom, all we did was follow Biff around trying to cheer him up! (*To* BIFF) Boy, what a night you gave me!

LINDA   Get out of here, both of you, and don't come back! I don't want you tormenting him any more. Go on now, get your things together! (*To* BIFF) You can sleep in his apartment. (*She starts to pick up the flowers and stops herself*) Pick up this stuff, I'm not your maid any more. Pick it up, you bum, you!

HAPPY *turns his back to her in refusal.* BIFF *slowly moves over and gets down on his knees, picking up the flowers.*

LINDA   You're a pair of animals! Not one, not another living soul would have had the cruelty to walk out on that man in a restaurant!

BIFF   (*not looking at her*)   Is that what he said?

LINDA   He didn't have to say anything. He was so humiliated he nearly limped when he came in.

HAPPY   But, Mom, he had a great time with us—

BIFF   (*cutting him off violently*)   Shut up!

Without another word, HAPPY *goes upstairs.*

LINDA   You! You didn't even go in to see if he was all right!

BIFF   (*still on the floor in front of* LINDA, *the flowers in his hand; with self-loathing*)   No. Didn't. Didn't do a damned thing. How do you like that, heh? Left him babbling in a toilet.

LINDA   You louse. You . . .

BIFF Now you hit it on the nose! (*He gets up, throws the flowers in the wastebasket*) The scum of the earth, and you're looking at him!

LINDA Get out of here!

BIFF I gotta talk to the boss, Mom. Where is he?

LINDA You're not going near him. Get out of this house!

BIFF (*with absolute assurance, determination*) No. We're gonna have an abrupt conversation, him and me.

LINDA You're not talking to him!

Hammering is heard from outside the house, off right. BIFF *turns toward the noise.*

LINDA (*suddenly pleading*) Will you please leave him alone?

BIFF What's he doing out there?

LINDA He's planting the garden!

BIFF (*quietly*) Now? Oh, my God!

BIFF *moves outside,* LINDA *following. The light dies down on them and comes up on the center of the apron as* WILLY *walks into it. He is carrying a flashlight, a hoe, and a handful of seed packets. He raps the top of the hoe sharply to fix it firmly, and then moves to the left, measuring off the distance with his foot. He holds the flashlight to look at the seed packets, reading off the instructions. He is in the blue of night.*

WILLY Carrots ... quarter-inch apart. Rows ... one-foot rows. (*He measures it off*) One foot. (*He puts down a package and measures off*) Beets. (*He puts down another package and measures again*) Lettuce. (*He reads the package, puts it down*) One foot— (*He breaks off as* BEN *appears at the right and moves slowly down to him*) What a proposition, ts, ts. Terrific, terrific. 'Cause she's suffered, Ben, the woman has suffered. You understand me? A man can't go out the way he came in, Ben, a man has got to add up to something. You can't, you can't—(BEN *moves toward him as though to interrupt*) You gotta consider, now. Don't answer so quick. Remember, it's a guaranteed twenty-thousand-dollar proposition. Now look, Ben, I want you to go through the ins and outs of this thing with me. I've got nobody to talk to, Ben, and the woman has suffered, you hear me?

BEN (*standing still, considering*) What's the proposition?

WILLY It's twenty thousand dollars on the barrelhead. Guaranteed, gilt-edged, you understand?

BEN You don't want to make a fool of yourself. They might not honor the policy.

WILLY How can they dare refuse? Didn't I work like a coolie to meet every premium on the nose? And now they don't pay off? Impossible!

BEN It's called a cowardly thing, William.

WILLY Why? Does it take more guts to stand here the rest of my life ringing up a zero?

BEN (*yielding*) That's a point, William. (*He moves, thinking, turns*) And twenty thousand—that *is* something one can feel with the hand, it is there.

WILLY (*now assured, with rising power*) Oh, Ben, that's the whole beauty of it! I see it like a diamond, shining in the dark, hard and rough, that I can pick up and touch in my hand. Not like— like an appointment! This would not be another damned-fool appointment, Ben, and it changes all the aspects. Because he thinks I'm nothing, see, and so he spites me. But the funeral— (*Straightening up*) Ben, that funeral will be massive! They'll come from Maine, Massachusetts, Vermont, New Hampshire! All the old-timers with the strange license plates—that boy will be thunderstruck, Ben, because he never realized—I am known! Rhode Island, New York, New Jersey—I am known, Ben, and he'll see it with his eyes once and for all. He'll see what I am, Ben! He's in for a shock, that boy!

BEN (*coming down to the edge of the garden*) He'll call you a coward.

WILLY (*suddenly fearful*) No, that would be terrible.

BEN Yes. And a damned fool.

WILLY No, no, he mustn't, I won't have that! (*He is broken and desperate*)

BEN He'll hate you, William.

The gay music of the Boys is heard.

WILLY Oh, Ben, how do we get back to all the great times? Used to be so full of light, and comradeship, the sleigh-riding in winter, and the ruddiness on his cheeks. And always some kind of good news coming up, always something nice coming up ahead. And never even let me carry the valises in the house, and simonizing, simonizing that little red car! Why, why can't I give him something and not have him hate me?

BEN Let me think about it. (*He glances at his watch*) I still have a little time. Remarkable proposition, but you've got to be sure you're not making a fool of yourself.

BEN *drifts off upstage and goes out of sight.* BIFF *comes down from the left.*

WILLY (*suddenly conscious of* BIFF, *turns and looks up at him, then begins picking up the packages of seeds in confusion*) Where the hell is that seed? (*Indignantly*) You can't see nothing out here! They boxed in the whole goddam neighborhood!

BIFF   There are people all around here. Don't you realize that?

WILLY   I'm busy. Don't bother me.

BIFF   (*taking the hoe from* WILLY) I'm saying good-by to you, Pop. (WILLY *looks at him, silent, unable to move*) I'm not coming back any more.

WILLY   You're not going to see Oliver tomorrow?

BIFF   I've got no appointment, Dad.

WILLY   He put his arm around you, and you've got no appointment?

BIFF   Pop, get this now, will you? Everytime I've left it's been a fight that sent me out of here. Today I realized something about myself and I tried to explain it to you and I—I think I'm just not smart enough to make any sense out of it for you. To hell with whose fault it is or anything like that. (*He takes* WILLY's *arm*) Let's just wrap it up, heh? Come on in, we'll tell Mom. (*He gently tries to pull* WILLY *to left*)

WILLY   (*frozen, immobile, with guilt in his voice*) No, I don't want to see her.

BIFF   Come on! (*He pulls again, and* WILLY *tries to pull away*)

WILLY   (*highly nervous*) No, no, I don't want to see her.

BIFF   (*tries to look into* WILLY's *face, as if to find the answer there*) Why don't you want to see her?

WILLY   (*more harshly now*) Don't bother me, will you?

BIFF   What do you mean, you don't want to see her? You don't want them calling you yellow, do you? This isn't your fault; it's me, I'm a bum. Now come inside! (WILLY *strains to get away*) Did you hear what I said to you?

WILLY *pulls away and quickly goes by himself into the house.* BIFF *follows.*

LINDA   (*to* WILLY) Did you plant, dear?

BIFF   (*at the door, to* LINDA) All right, we had it out. I'm going and I'm not writing any more.

LINDA   (*going to* WILLY *in the kitchen*) I think that's the best way, dear. 'Cause there's no use drawing it out, you'll just never get along.

WILLY *doesn't respond.*

BIFF   People ask where I am and what I'm doing, you don't know, and you don't care. That way it'll be off your mind and you can start brightening up again. All right? That clears it, doesn't it?

(WILLY *is silent, and* BIFF *goes to him*) You gonna wish me luck, scout? (*He extends his hand*) What do you say?

LINDA   Shake his hand, Willy.

WILLY (*turning to her, seething with hurt*)   There's no necessity to mention the pen at all, y'know.

BIFF (*gently*)   I've got no appointment, Dad.

WILLY (*erupting fiercely*)   He put his arm around . . . ?

BIFF   Dad, you're never going to see what I am, so what's the use of arguing? If I strike oil I'll send you a check. Meantime forget I'm alive.

WILLY (*to* LINDA)   Spite, see?

BIFF   Shake hands, Dad.

WILLY   Not my hand.

BIFF   I was hoping not to go this way.

WILLY   Well, this is the way you're going. Good-by.

BIFF *looks at him a moment, then turns sharply and goes to the stairs.*

WILLY (*stops him with*)   May you rot in hell if you leave this house!

BIFF (*turning*)   Exactly what is it that you want from me?

WILLY   I want you to know, on the train, in the mountains, in the valleys, wherever you go, that you cut down your life for spite!

BIFF   No, no.

WILLY   Spite, spite, is the word of your undoing! And when you're down and out, remember what did it. When you're rotting somewhere beside the railroad tracks, remember, and don't you dare blame it on me!

BIFF   I'm not blaming it on you!

WILLY   I won't take the rap for this, you hear?

HAPPY *comes down the stairs and stands on the bottom step, watching.*

BIFF   That's just what I'm telling you!

WILLY (*sinking into a chair at the table, with full accusation*)   You're trying to put a knife in me—don't think I don't know what you're doing!

BIFF   All right, phony! Then let's lay it on the line. (*He whips the rubber tube out of his pocket and puts it on the table*)

HAPPY   You crazy—

LINDA   Biff! (*She moves to grab the hose, but* BIFF *holds it down with his hand*)

BIFF   Leave it there! Don't move it!

WILLY (*not looking at it*)   What is that?

BIFF   You know goddam well what that is.

WILLY (*caged, wanting to escape*)   I never saw that.

BIFF   You saw it. The mice didn't bring it into the cellar! What is this supposed to do, make a hero out of you? This supposed to make me sorry for you?

WILLY   Never heard of it.

BIFF   There'll be no pity for you, you hear it? No pity!

WILLY   (*to* LINDA)   You hear the spite!

BIFF   No, you're going to hear the truth—what you are and what I am!

LINDA   Stop it!

WILLY   Spite!

HAPPY   (*coming down toward* BIFF)   You cut it now!

BIFF   (*to* HAPPY)   The man don't know who we are! The man is gonna know! (*To* WILLY) We never told the truth for ten minutes in this house!

HAPPY   We always told the truth!

BIFF   (*turning on him*)   You big blow, are you the assistant buyer? You're one of the two assistants to the assistant, aren't you?

HAPPY   Well, I'm practically—

BIFF   You're practically full of it! We all are! And I'm through with it. (*To* WILLY) Now hear this, Willy, this is me.

WILLY   I know you!

BIFF   You know why I had no address for three months? I stole a suit in Kansas City and I was in jail. (*To* LINDA, *who is sobbing*) Stop crying. I'm through with it.

LINDA *turns away from them, her hands covering her face.*

WILLY   I suppose that's my fault!

BIFF   I stole myself out of every good job since high school!

WILLY   And whose fault is that?

BIFF   And I never got anywhere because you blew me so full of hot air I could never stand taking orders from anybody! That's whose fault it is!

WILLY   I hear that!

LINDA   Don't, Biff!

BIFF   It's goddam time you heard that! I had to be boss big shot in two weeks, and I'm through with it!

WILLY   Then hang yourself! For spite, hang yourself!

BIFF   No! Nobody's hanging himself, Willy! I ran down eleven flights with a pen in my hand today. And suddenly I stopped, you hear me? And in the middle of that office building, do you hear this? I stopped in the middle of that building and I saw—the sky. I saw the things that I love in this world. The work and the food and time to sit and smoke. And I looked at the pen and said to myself, what the hell am I grabbing this for? Why am I trying to become what I don't want to be? What am I doing in an office, making a contemptuous, begging fool of myself, when all I want is out there, waiting for me the minute I say I know who I am! Why can't I say that, Willy? (*He tries to make* WILLY *face him, but* WILLY *pulls away and moves to the left*)

WILLY (*with hatred, threateningly*) The door of your life is wide open!

BIFF Pop! I'm a dime a dozen, and so are you!

WILLY (*turning on him now in an uncontrolled outburst*) I am not a dime a dozen! I am Willy Loman, and you are Biff Loman!

BIFF *starts for* WILLY, *but is blocked by* HAPPY. *In his fury,* BIFF *seems on the verge of attacking his* FATHER.

BIFF I am not a leader of men, Willy, and neither are you. You were never anything but a hard-working drummer who landed in the ash can like all the rest of them! I'm one dollar an hour, Willy! I tried seven states and couldn't raise it. A buck an hour! Do you gather my meaning? I'm not bringing home any prizes any more, and you're going to stop waiting for me to bring them home!

WILLY (*directly to* BIFF) You vengeful, spiteful mut!

BIFF *breaks from* HAPPY. WILLY, *in fright, starts up the stairs.* BIFF *grabs him.*

BIFF (*at the peak of his fury*) Pop, I'm nothing! I'm nothing, Pop. Can't you understand that? There's no spite in it any more. I'm just what I am, that's all.

BIFF's *fury has spent itself, and he breaks down, sobbing, holding on to* WILLY, *who dumbly fumbles for* BIFF's *face.*

WILLY (*astonished*) What're you doing? What're you doing? (*To* LINDA) Why is he crying?

BIFF (*crying, broken*) Will you let me go, for Christ's sake? Will you take that phony dream and burn it before something happens? (*Struggling to contain himself, he pulls away and moves to the stairs*) I'll go in the morning. Put him—put him to bed. (*Exhausted,* BIFF *moves up the stairs to his room*)

WILLY (*after a long pause, astonished, elevated*) Isn't that—isn't that remarkable? Biff—he likes me!

LINDA He loves you, Willy!

HAPPY (*deeply moved*) Always did, Pop.

WILLY Oh, Biff! (*Staring wildly*) He cried! Cried to me. (*He is choking with his love, and now cries out his promise*) That boy —that boy is going to be magnificent!

BEN *appears in the light just outside the kitchen.*

BEN Yes, outstanding, with twenty thousand behind him.

LINDA (*sensing the racing of his mind, fearfully, carefully*) Now come to bed, Willy. It's all settled now.

WILLY (*finding it difficult not to rush out of the house*) Yes, we'll sleep. Come on. Go to sleep, Hap.

BEN And it does take a great kind of a man to crack the jungle.

In accents of dread, BEN'S *idyllic music starts up.*

HAPPY (*his arm around* LINDA) I'm getting married, Pop, don't forget it. I'm changing everything. I'm gonna run that department before the year is up. You'll see, Mom. (*He kisses her*)

BEN The jungle is dark but full of diamonds, Willy.

WILLY *turns, moves, listening to* BEN.

LINDA Be good. You're both good boys, just act that way, that's all.

HAPPY 'Night, Pop. (*He goes upstairs*)

LINDA (*to* WILLY) Come, dear.

BEN (*with greater force*) One must go in to fetch a diamond out.

WILLY (*to* LINDA, *as he moves slowly along the edge of the kitchen, toward the door*) I just want to get settled down, Linda. Let me sit alone for a little.

LINDA (*almost uttering her fear*) I want you upstairs.

WILLY (*taking her in his arms*) In a few minutes, Linda. I couldn't sleep right now. Go on, you look awful tired. (*He kisses her*)

BEN Not like an appointment at all. A diamond is rough and hard to the touch.

WILLY Go on now. I'll be right up.

LINDA I think this is the only way, Willy.

WILLY Sure, it's the best thing.

BEN Best thing!

WILLY The only way. Everything is gonna be—go on, kid, get to bed. You look so tired.

LINDA Come right up.

WILLY Two minutes.

LINDA *goes into the living-room, then reappears in her bedroom.* WILLY *moves just outside the kitchen door.*

WILLY Loves me. (*Wonderingly*) Always loved me. Isn't that a remarkable thing? Ben, he'll worship me for it!

BEN (*with promise*) It's dark there, but full of diamonds.

WILLY　Can you imagine that magnificence with twenty thousand dollars in his pocket?

LINDA　(*calling from her room*)　Willy! Come up!

WILLY　(*calling into the kitchen*)　Yes! Yes. Coming! It's very smart, you realize that, don't you, sweetheart? Even Ben sees it. I gotta go, baby. 'By! 'By! (*Going over to* BEN, *almost dancing*) Imagine? When the mail comes he'll be ahead of Bernard again!

BEN　A perfect proposition all around.

WILLY　Did you see how he cried to me? Oh, if I could kiss him, Ben!

BEN　Time, William, time!

WILLY　Oh, Ben, I always knew one way or another we were gonna make it, Biff and I!

BEN　(*looking at his watch*)　The boat. We'll be late. (*He moves slowly off into the darkness*)

WILLY　(*elegiacally, turning to the house*)　Now when you kick off, boy, I want a seventy-yard boot, and get right down the field under the ball, and when you hit, hit low and hit hard, because it's important, boy. (*He swings around and faces the audience*) There's all kinds of important people in the stands, and the first thing you know . . . (*Suddenly realizing he is alone*) Ben! Ben, where do I . . . ? (*He makes a sudden movement of search*) Ben, how do I . . . ?

LINDA　(*calling*)　Willy, you coming up?

WILLY　(*uttering a gasp of fear, whirling about as if to quiet her*) Sh! (*He turns around as if to find his way; sounds, faces, voices, seem to be swarming in upon him and he flicks at them, crying*) Sh! Sh! (*Suddenly music, faint and high, stops him. It rises in intensity, almost to an unbearable scream. He goes up and down on his toes, and rushes off around the house*) Shhh!

LINDA　Willy?

There is no answer. LINDA *waits.* BIFF *gets up off his bed. He is still in his clothes.* HAPPY *sits up.* BIFF *stands listening.*

LINDA　(*with real fear*)　Willy, answer me! Willy!

There is the sound of a car starting and moving away at full speed.

LINDA　No!

BIFF　(*rushing down the stairs*)　Pop!

As the car speeds off, the music crashes down in a frenzy of sound, which becomes the soft pulsation of a single cello string. BIFF *slowly returns to his bedroom. He and* HAPPY *gravely don their jackets.* LINDA *slowly walks out of her room. The music has developed into a dead march. The leaves of day are appearing over everything.* CHARLEY *and* BERNARD, *somberly dressed, appear and knock on the kitchen door.* BIFF *and* HAPPY *slowly descend the stairs to the kitchen as* CHARLEY *and* BERNARD *enter. All stop a moment when* LINDA, *in clothes of mourning, bearing a little bunch of roses, comes through the draped doorway into the kitchen. She goes to* CHARLEY *and takes his arm. Now all move toward the audience, through the wall-line of the kitchen. At the limit of the apron,* LINDA *lays down the flowers, kneels, and sits back on her heels. All stare down at the grave.*

REQUIEM

CHARLEY   It's getting dark, Linda.

LINDA *doesn't react. She stares at the grave.*

BIFF   How about it, Mom? Better get some rest, heh? They'll be closing the gate soon.

LINDA *makes no move. Pause.*

HAPPY *(deeply angered)*   He had no right to do that. There was no necessity for it. We would've helped him.

CHARLEY *(grunting)*   Hmmm.

BIFF   Come along, Mom.

LINDA   Why didn't anybody come?

CHARLEY   It was a very nice funeral.

LINDA   But where are all the people he knew? Maybe they blame him.

CHARLEY   Naa. It's a rough world, Linda. They wouldn't blame him.

LINDA   I can't understand it. At this time especially. First time in thirty-five years we were just about free and clear. He only needed a little salary. He was even finished with the dentist.

CHARLEY   No man only needs a little salary.

LINDA   I can't understand it.

BIFF   There were a lot of nice days. When he'd come home from a trip; or on Sundays, making the stoop; finishing the cellar; putting on the new porch; when he built the extra bathroom; and put up the garage. You know something, Charley, there's more of him in that front stoop than in all the sales he ever made.

CHARLEY   Yeah. He was a happy man with a batch of cement.

LINDA   He was so wonderful with his hands.

BIFF   He had the wrong dreams. All, all, wrong.

HAPPY *(almost ready to fight* BIFF)   Don't say that!

BIFF   He never knew who he was.

CHARLEY *(stopping* HAPPY's *movement and reply. To* BIFF)   Nobody dast blame this man. You don't understand: Willy was a salesman. And for a salesman, there is no rock bottom to the life. He don't put a bolt to a nut, he don't tell you the law or give you medicine. He's a man way out there in the blue, riding on a smile and a shoeshine. And when they start not smiling back—that's an earthquake. And then you get yourself a couple of spots on your hat, and you're finished. Nobody dast blame this man. A salesman is got to dream, boy. It comes with the territory.

BIFF   Charley, the man didn't know who he was.

HAPPY *(infuriated)*   Don't say that!

BIFF   Why don't you come with me, Happy?

HAPPY   I'm not licked that easily. I'm staying right in this city, and I'm gonna beat this racket! *(He looks at* BIFF, *his chin set)* The Loman Brothers!

BIFF   I know who I am, kid.

HAPPY   All right, boy. I'm gonna show you and everybody else that Willy Loman did not die in vain. He had a good dream. It's the only dream you can have—to come out number-one man. He fought it out here, and this is where I'm gonna win it for him.

BIFF *(with a hopeless glance at* HAPPY, *bends toward his mother)* Let's go, Mom.

LINDA   I'll be with you in a minute. Go on, Charley. *(He hesitates)* I want to, just for a minute. I never had a chance to say good-by.

CHARLEY *moves away, followed by* HAPPY. BIFF *remains a slight distance up and left of* LINDA. *She sits there, summoning herself. The flute begins, not far away, playing behind her speech.*

LINDA   Forgive me, dear. I can't cry. I don't know what it is, but I can't cry. I don't understand it. Why did you ever do that? Help me, Willy, I can't cry. It seems to me that you're just on another trip. I keep expecting you. Willy, dear, I can't cry. Why did you do it? I search and search and I search, and I can't understand it, Willy. I made the last payment on the house today. Today, dear. And there'll be nobody home. *(A sob rises in her throat)* We're free and clear. *(Sobbing more fully, released)* We're free. *(*BIFF *comes slowly toward her)* We're free . . . We're free . . .

BIFF *lifts her to her feet and moves out up right with her in his arms.* LINDA *sobs quietly.* BERNARD *and* CHARLEY *come together and follow them, followed by* HAPPY. *Only the music of the flute is left on the darkening stage as over the house the hard towers of the apartment buildings rise into sharp focus, and*

The Curtain Falls

A RAISIN IN THE SUN (1959)

LORRAINE HANSBERRY (1930–1965)

During her short lifetime of 34 years, Lorraine Hansberry contributed only two plays to the American theater: the first, *A Raisin in the Sun,* won the New York Drama Critics Circle Award and became an outstanding success both in the theatre and on the screen; the second, *The Sign in Sidney Brustein's Window* (1964), was a commercial failure. (Two other pieces, *Les Blancs,* patched together from an incomplete manuscript, and *To Be Young, Gifted and Black,* a collection of excerpts from other writings, were both posthumous.) Her reputation as a major American dramatist rests solely on these two plays, and almost exclusively on *Raisin.*

Hansberry's position in American drama is unique, for she was representative of two neglected minorities in American dramatic art: she was Black, and she was a woman. Yet without drawing attention to herself because of either of these situations, she wrote, in *A Raisin in the Sun,* one of the major plays of the 1950s and, indeed, of the modern American drama. It is a play about Blacks without being a "black" play; it is a well-made problem play centering on one of the most volatile problems of modern American society—social integration of blacks and whites—without making the problem overbearingly central; and it constantly borders on presenting stereotypical characters in a predictably melodramatic situation without actually descending either into stereotype or into overt melodrama.

There is certainly no question that the basic social problem of the 1950s, that of the driving desire of Blacks to pull themselves out of the stifling debilitation of second-class citizenry living in degrading slums, is the basic motivating factor of the play. Close behind are other problems: the suppressed human dignity of people working in menial positions as servants to The Man, with little or no opportunity for advancement; their frustration at being unable to acquire a good education, and so on, down the familiar line. And, of course, climaxing all of this is the crude attempt by the self-righteous residents of Clybourne Park to buy off these intruders into their lily-white WASP paradise.

Nevertheless, Hansberry has devised a very human and humane play based upon the universal problems of human aspirations and striving toward individual and collective dignity, which are exacerbated by the racial situation but which in no way are related *only* to that situation. One can, in fact, be almost colorblind in looking at *A Raisin in the Sun,* because many of the problems—personal, financial, or otherwise—are those faced by any close-knit family attempting to better themselves when the opportunity, in this case in the form of the $10,000 insurance check, presents itself.

It is clear that this family, despite its being led by the dominating matriarch Lena, was once headed by the absent Big Walter, whose hard work and devotion enabled him to provide a relatively decent home and to purchase a substantial and costly life-insurance policy. It is not a gratuitous gift from the gods, but well-earned, well-deserved. It can serve this family very well materially.

The use and misuse of the money, through Lena's determination to have a better home with sun, air, and flowers, and through Walter Lee's determination to become the man of the house, provide impetus for the development of the characters, but none of the action of the limited plot line centers primarily around blackness and social prejudice as such. It introduces Lindner's misguided efforts to thwart the move, but any violent or traumatic encounter resulting from the move is relegated to the future, off-stage, of no immediate concern.

A Raisin in the Sun is a touching, appealing drama about human beings who happen to be black, written by a dramatist who also happened to be black. But there is no cry to arms, no appeal to resist the white man's sinister prejudices. The Youngers choose to function, if permitted, within the world as it exists, making this move toward the comforts and conveniences that should be the privilege of all. Walter Lee has demonstrated that he *can* be a man, liquor store or not, and Lena has seen that her trust in her son, momentarily set back, is justified. The dream is no longer deferred, and we, admiring their determination, cheer the Youngers on, as we would *any* such family, regardless of their race, creed, or color.

A Raisin in the Sun

To Mama: in gratitude for the dream

CHARACTERS

RUTH YOUNGER
TRAVIS YOUNGER
WALTER LEE YOUNGER (*Brother*)
BENEATHA YOUNGER
LENA YOUNGER (*Mama*)
JOSEPH ASAGAI
GEORGE MURCHISON
KARL LINDNER
BOBO
MOVING MEN

The action of the play is set in Chicago's Southside, sometime between World War II and the present.

ACT I

Scene I.
Friday morning

Scene II.
The following morning

ACT II

Scene I.
Later, the same day

Scene II.
Friday night, a few weeks later

Scene III.
Saturday, moving day, one week later

ACT III

An hour later

What happens to a dream deferred?
Does it dry up
Like a raisin in the sun?
Or fester like a sore—

And then run?
Does it stink like rotten meat?
Or crust and sugar over—
Like a syrupy sweet?

Maybe it just sags
Like a heavy load.

Or does it explode?

Langston Hughes[1]

ACT I

Scene I

The YOUNGER *living room would be a comfortable and well-ordered room if it were not for a number of indestructible contradictions to this state of being. Its furnishings are typical and undistinguished and their primary feature now is that they have clearly had to accommodate the living of too many people for too many years—and they are tired. Still, we can see that at some time, a time probably no longer remembered by the family (except perhaps for* MAMA*), the furnishings of this room were actually selected with care and love and even hope—and brought to this apartment and arranged with taste and pride.*

That was a long time ago. Now the once loved pattern of the couch upholstery has to fight to show itself from under acres of crocheted doilies and couch covers which have themselves finally come to be more important than the upholstery. And here a table or a chair has been moved to disguise the worn places in the carpet; but the carpet has fought back by showing its weariness, with depressing uniformity, elsewhere on its surface.

Weariness has, in fact, won in this room. Everything has been polished, washed, sat on, used, scrubbed too often. All pretenses but living itself have long since vanished from the very atmosphere of this room.

Moreover, a section of this room, for it is not really a room unto itself, though the landlord's lease would make it seem so, slopes backward to provide a small kitchen area, where the family prepares the meals that are eaten in the living room proper, which must also serve as dining room. The single window that has been provided for these "two" rooms is located in this kitchen area. The sole natural light the family may enjoy in the course of a day is only that which fights its way through this little window.

At left, a door leads to a bedroom which is shared by MAMA *and her daughter,* BENEATHA. *At right, opposite, is a second room (which in the beginning of the life of this apartment was probably a breakfast room), which serves as a bedroom for* WALTER *and his wife,* RUTH.

Time: Sometime between World War II and the present.

Place: Chicago's Southside.

At rise: It is morning dark in the living room. TRAVIS *is asleep on the make-down bed at center. An alarm clock sounds from within the bedroom at right, and presently* RUTH *enters from that room and closes the door behind her. She crosses sleepily toward the window. As she passes her sleeping son she reaches down and shakes him a little. At the window she raises the shade and a dusky Southside morning light comes in feebly. She fills a pot with water and puts it on to boil. She calls to the boy, between yawns, in a slightly muffled voice.*

RUTH *is about thirty. We can see that she was a pretty girl, even exceptionally so, but now it is apparent that life has been little that she expected, and disappointment has already begun to hang in her face. In a few years, before thirty-five even, she will be known among her people as a "settled woman."*

She crosses to her son and gives him a good, final, rousing shake.

RUTH   Come on now, boy, it's seven thirty! (*Her son sits up at last, in a stupor of sleepiness.*) I say hurry up, Travis! You ain't the only person in the world got to use a bathroom! (*The child, a sturdy, handsome little boy of ten or eleven, drags himself out of the bed and almost blindly takes his towels and "today's clothes" from drawers and a closet and goes out to the bathroom, which is in an outside hall and which is shared by another family or families on the same floor.* RUTH *crosses to the bedroom door at right and opens it and calls in to her husband.*) Walter Lee! ... It's after seven thirty! Lemme see you do some waking up in there now! (*She waits.*) You better get up from there, man! It's after seven thirty I tell you. (*She waits again.*) All right, you just go ahead and lay there and next thing you know Travis be finished and Mr. Johnson'll be in there and you'll be fussing and cussing round here like a mad man! And be late too! (*She waits, at the end of patience.*) Walter Lee—it's time for you to get up!

(*She waits another second and then starts to go into the bedroom, but is apparently satisfied that her husband has begun to get up. She stops, pulls the door to, and returns to the kitchen area. She wipes her face with a moist cloth and runs her fingers through her sleep-disheveled hair in a vain effort and ties an apron around her housecoat. The bedroom door at right opens and her husband stands in the doorway in his pajamas, which are rumpled and mismated. He is a lean, intense young man in his middle thirties, inclined to quick nervous movements and erratic speech habits—and always in his voice there is a quality of indictment.)*

WALTER   Is he out yet?

RUTH   What you mean *out*? He ain't hardly got in there good yet.

WALTER   (*wandering in, still more oriented to sleep than to a new day*)   Well, what was you doing all that yelling for if I can't even get in there yet? (*Stopping and thinking*) Check coming today?

RUTH   They *said* Saturday and this is just Friday and I hopes to God you ain't going to get up here first thing this morning and start talking to me 'bout no money—'cause I 'bout don't want to hear it.

WALTER   Something the matter with you this morning?

RUTH   No—I'm just sleepy as the devil. What kind of eggs you want?

WALTER   Not scrambled. (RUTH *starts to scramble eggs.*) Paper come? (RUTH *points impatiently to the rolled up* Tribune *on the table, and he gets it and spreads it out and vaguely reads the front page.*) Set off another bomb yesterday.

RUTH (*maximum indifference*)   Did they?

WALTER (*looking up*)   What's the matter with you?

RUTH   Ain't nothing the matter with me. And don't keep asking me that this morning.

WALTER   Ain't nobody bothering you. (*Reading the news of the day absently again*) Say Colonel McCormick is sick.

RUTH (*affecting tea-party interest*)   Is he now? Poor thing.

WALTER (*sighing and looking at his watch*)   Oh, me. (*He waits.*) Now what is that boy doing in that bathroom all this time? He just going to have to start getting up earlier. I can't be being late to work on account of him fooling around in there.

RUTH (*turning on him*)   Oh, no he ain't going to be getting up no earlier no such thing! It ain't his fault that he can't get to bed no earlier nights 'cause he got a bunch of crazy good-for-nothing clowns sitting up running their mouths in what is supposed to be his bedroom after ten o'clock at night. . . .

WALTER   That's what you mad about, ain't it? The things I want to talk about with my friends just couldn't be important in your mind, could they?

He rises and finds a cigarette in her handbag on the table and crosses to the little window and looks out, smoking and deeply enjoying this first one.

RUTH (*almost matter of factly, a complaint too automatic to deserve emphasis*) Why you always got to smoke before you eat in the morning?

WALTER (*at the window*) Just look at 'em down there. . . . Running and racing to work . . . (*he turns and faces his wife and watches her a moment at the stove, and then, suddenly*) You look young this morning, baby.

RUTH (*indifferently*) Yeah?

WALTER Just for a second—stirring them eggs. It's gone now—just for a second it was—you looked real young again. (*Then, drily*) It's gone now—you look like yourself again.

RUTH Man, if you don't shut up and leave me alone.

WALTER (*looking out to the street again*) First thing a man ought to learn in life is not to make love to no colored woman first thing in the morning. You all some evil people at eight o'clock in the morning.

(TRAVIS *appears in the hall doorway, almost fully dressed and quite wide awake now, his towels and pajamas across his shoulders. He opens the door and signals for his father to make the bathroom in a hurry.*)

TRAVIS (*watching the bathroom*) Daddy, come on!

(WALTER *gets his bathroom utensils and flies out to the bathroom.*)

RUTH Sit down and have your breakfast, Travis.

TRAVIS Mama, this is Friday. (*Gleefully*) Check coming tomorrow, huh?

RUTH You get your mind off money and eat your breakfast.

TRAVIS (*eating*) This is the morning we supposed to bring the fifty cents to school.

RUTH Well, I ain't got no fifty cents this morning.

TRAVIS Teacher say we have to.

RUTH I don't care what teacher say. I ain't got it. Eat your breakfast, Travis.

TRAVIS I *am* eating.

RUTH Hush up now and just eat!

The boy gives her an exasperated look for her lack of understanding, and eats grudgingly.

TRAVIS You think Grandmama would have it?

RUTH No! And I want you to stop asking your grandmother for money, you hear me?

TRAVIS (*outraged*) Gaaaleee! I don't ask her, she just gimme it sometimes!

RUTH Travis Willard Younger—I got too much on me this morning to be—

TRAVIS Maybe Daddy—

RUTH *Travis!*

The boy hushes abruptly. They are both quiet and tense for several seconds.

TRAVIS (*presently*) Could I maybe go carry some groceries in front of the supermarket for a little while after school then?

RUTH Just hush, I said. (TRAVIS *jabs his spoon into his cereal bowl viciously, and rests his head in anger upon his fists.*) If you through eating, you can get over there and make up your bed.

(*The boy obeys stiffly and crosses the room, almost mechanically, to the bed and more or less carefully folds the covering. He carries the bedding into his mother's room and returns with his books and cap.*)

TRAVIS (*sulking and standing apart from her unnaturally*) I'm gone.

RUTH (*looking up from the stove to inspect him automatically*) Come *here.* (*He crosses to her and she studies his head.*) If you don't take this comb and fix this here head, you better! (TRAVIS *puts down his books with a great sigh of oppression, and crosses to the mirror. His mother mutters under her breath about his "slubbornness."*) 'Bout to march out of here with that head looking just like chickens slept in it! I just don't know where you get your slubborn ways. . . . And get your jacket, too. Looks chilly out this morning.

TRAVIS (*with conspicuously brushed hair and jacket*) I'm gone.

RUTH Get carfare and milk money—(*waving one finger*)—and not a single penny for no caps, you hear me?

TRAVIS (*with sullen politeness*) Yes'm.

He turns in outrage to leave. His mother watches after him as in his frustration he approaches the door almost comically. When she speaks to him her voice has become a very gentle tease.

RUTH (*mocking; as she thinks he would say it*) Oh, Mama makes me so mad sometimes, I don't know what to do! (*She waits and continues to his back as he stands stock-still in front of the door.*) I wouldn't kiss that woman good-bye for nothing in this world this morning! (*The boy finally turns around and rolls his eyes at her, knowing the mood has changed and he is vindicated; he does not, however, move toward her yet.*) Not for nothing in this world! (*She finally laughs aloud at him and holds out her arms to him and we see that it is a way between them, very old and practiced. He crosses to her and allows her to embrace him warmly but keeps his face fixed with masculine rigidity. She holds him back from her presently and looks at him and runs her fingers over the features of his face. With utter gentleness—)* Now— whose little old angry man are you?

TRAVIS *(the masculinity and gruffness start to fade at last)* Aw gaalee—Mama . . .

RUTH *(mimicking)* Aw—gaaaaalleeeee, Mama! *(She pushes him, with rough playfulness and finality, toward the door.)* Get on out of here or you going to be late.

TRAVIS *(in the face of love, new aggressiveness)* Mama, could I *please* go carry groceries?

RUTH Honey, it's starting to get so cold evenings.

WALTER *(coming in from the bathroom and drawing a make-believe gun from a make-believe holster and shooting at his son)* What is it he wants to do?

RUTH Go carry groceries after school at the supermarket.

WALTER Well, let him go . . .

TRAVIS *(quickly, to the ally)* I *have* to—she won't gimme the fifty cents. . . .

WALTER *(to his wife only)* Why not?

RUTH *(simply, and with flavor)* 'Cause we don't have it.

WALTER *(to* RUTH *only)* What you tell the boy things like that for? *(Reaching down into his pants with a rather important gesture)* Here, son—

He hands the boy the coin, but his eyes are directed to his wife's. TRAVIS *takes the money happily.*

TRAVIS Thanks, Daddy.

He starts out. RUTH *watches both of them with murder in her eyes.* WALTER *stands and stares back at her with defiance, and suddenly reaches into his pocket again on an afterthought.*

WALTER *(without even looking at his son, still staring hard at his wife)* In fact, here's another fifty cents. . . . Buy yourself some fruit today—or take a taxicab to school or something!

TRAVIS Whoopee—

He leaps up and clasps his father around the middle with his legs, and they face each other in mutual appreciation; slowly WALTER LEE *peeks around the boy to catch the violent rays from his wife's eyes and draws his head back as if shot.*

WALTER You better get down now—and get to school, man.

TRAVIS *(at the door)* O.K. Good-bye. *(He exits.)*

WALTER *(after him, pointing with pride)* That's *my* boy. *(She looks at him in disgust and turns back to her work.*) You know what I was thinking 'bout in the bathroom this morning?

RUTH   No.

WALTER   How come you always try to be so pleasant!

RUTH   What is there to be pleasant 'bout!

WALTER   You want to know what I was thinking 'bout in the bathroom or not!

RUTH   I know what you thinking 'bout.

WALTER   (*ignoring her*)   'Bout what me and Willy Harris was talking about last night.

RUTH   (*immediately—a refrain*)   Willy Harris is a good-for-nothing loud mouth.

WALTER   Anybody who talks to me has got to be a good-for-nothing loud mouth, ain't he? And what you know about who is just a good-for-nothing loud mouth? Charlie Atkins was just a "good-for-nothing loud mouth" too, wasn't he! When he wanted me to go in the dry-cleaning business with him. And now—he's grossing a hundred thousand a year. A hundred thousand dollars a year! You still call *him* a loud mouth!

RUTH   (*bitterly*)   Oh, Walter Lee.... (*She folds her head on her arms over the table.*)

WALTER   (*rising and coming to her and standing over her*)   You tired, ain't you? Tired of everything. Me, the boy, the way we live—this beat-up hole—everything. Ain't you? (*She doesn't look up, doesn't answer.*) So tired—moaning and groaning all the time, but you wouldn't do nothing to help, would you? You couldn't be on my side that long for nothing, could you?

RUTH   Walter, please leave me alone.

WALTER   A man needs for a woman to back him up....

RUTH   Walter—

WALTER   Mama would listen to you. You know she listen to you more than she do me and Bennie. She think more of you. All you have to do is just sit down with her when you drinking your coffee one morning and talking 'bout things like you do and—(*he sits down beside her and demonstrates graphically what he thinks her methods and tone should be*)—you just sip your coffee, see, and say easy like that you been thinking 'bout that deal Walter Lee is so interested in, 'bout the store and all, and sip some more coffee, like what you saying ain't really that important to you— And the next thing you know, she be listening good and asking you questions and when I come home—I can tell her the details. This ain't no fly-by-night proposition, baby. I mean we figured it out, me and Willy and Bobo.

RUTH   (*with a frown*)   Bobo?

WALTER Yeah. You see, this little liquor store we got in mind cost seventy-five thousand and we figured the initial investment on the place be 'bout thirty thousand, see. That be ten thousand each. Course, there's a couple of hundred you got to pay so's you don't spend your life just waiting for them clowns to let your license get approved—

RUTH You mean graft?

WALTER (*frowning impatiently*) Don't call it that. See there, that just goes to show you what women understand about the world. Baby, don't *nothing* happen for you in this world 'less you pay *somebody* off!

RUTH Walter, leave me alone! (*She raises her head and stares at him vigorously—then says, more quietly*) *Eat* your eggs, they gonna be cold.

WALTER (*straightening up from her and looking off*) That's it. There you are. Man say to his woman: I got me a dream. His woman say: Eat your eggs. (*Sadly, but gaining in power*) Man say: I got to take hold of this here world, baby! And a woman will say: Eat your eggs and go to work. (*Passionately now*) Man say: I got to change my life, I'm choking to death, baby! And his woman say—(*in utter anguish as he brings his fists down on his thighs*)—Your eggs is getting cold!

RUTH (*softly*) Walter, that ain't none of our money.

WALTER (*not listening at all or even looking at her*) This morning, I was lookin' in the mirror and thinking about it. . . . I'm thirty-five years old; I been married eleven years and I got a boy who sleeps in the living room—(*very, very quietly*)—and all I got to give him is stories about how rich white people live. . . .

RUTH Eat your eggs, Walter.

WALTER *Damn my eggs . . . damn all the eggs that ever was!*

RUTH Then go to work.

WALTER (*looking up at her*) See—I'm trying to talk to you 'bout myself—(*shaking his head with the repetition*)—and all you can say is eat them eggs and go to work.

RUTH (*wearily*) Honey, you never say nothing new. I listen to you every day, every night and every morning, and you never say nothing new. (*Shrugging.*) So you would rather *be* Mr. Arnold than be his chauffeur. So— I would *rather* be living in Buckingham Palace.

WALTER That is just what is wrong with the colored woman in this world. . . . Don't understand about building their men up and making 'em feel like they somebody. Like they can do something.

RUTH (*drily, but to hurt*) There *are* colored men who do things.

WALTER No thanks to the colored woman.

RUTH   Well, being a colored woman, I guess I can't help myself none.

She rises and gets the ironing board and sets it up and attacks a huge pile of rough-dried clothes, sprinkling them in preparation for the ironing and then rolling them into tight fat balls.

WALTER   (*mumbling*)   We one group of men tied to a race of women with small minds.

His sister BENEATHA *enters. She is about twenty, as slim and intense as her brother. She is not as pretty as her sister-in-law, but her lean, almost intellectual face has a handsomeness of its own. She wears a bright-red flannel nightie, and her thick hair stands wildly about her head. Her speech is a mixture of many things; it is different from the rest of the family's insofar as education has permeated her sense of English—and perhaps the Midwest rather than the South has finally—at last—won out in her inflection; but not altogether, because over all of it is a soft slurring and transformed use of vowels which is the decided influence of the Southside. She passes through the room without looking at either* RUTH *or* WALTER *and goes to the outside door and looks, a little blindly, out to the bathroom. She sees that it has been lost to the Johnsons. She closes the door with a sleepy vengeance and crosses to the table and sits down a little defeated.*

BENEATHA   I am going to start timing those people.

WALTER   You should get up earlier.

BENEATHA   (*her face in her hands; she is still fighting the urge to go back to bed*)   Really—would you suggest dawn? Where's the paper?

WALTER   (*pushing the paper across the table to her as he studies her almost clinically, as though he has never seen her before*)   You a horrible-looking chick at this hour.

BENEATHA   (*drily*)   Good morning, everybody.

WALTER   (*senselessly*)   How is school coming?

BENEATHA   (*in the same spirit*)   Lovely. Lovely. And you know, biology is the greatest. (*Looking up at him.*) I dissected something that looked just like you yesterday.

WALTER   I just wondered if you've made up your mind and everything.

BENEATHA   (*gaining in sharpness and impatience*)   And what did I answer yesterday morning—and the day before that?

RUTH   (*from the ironing board, like someone disinterested and old*)   Don't be so nasty, Bennie.

BENEATHA   (*still to her brother*)   And the day before that and the day before that!

WALTER (*defensively*) I'm interested in you. Something wrong with that? Ain't many girls who decide—

WALTER *and* BENEATHA (*in unison*) —"to be a doctor."

Silence.

WALTER Have we figured out yet just exactly how much medical school is going to cost?

RUTH Walter Lee, why don't you leave that girl alone and get out of here to work?

BENEATHA (*exits to the bathroom and bangs on the door*) Come on out of there, please! (*She comes back into the room.*)

WALTER (*looking at his sister intently*) You know the check is coming tomorrow.

BENEATHA (*turning on him with a sharpness all her own*) That money belongs to Mama, Walter, and it's for her to decide how she wants to use it. I don't care if she wants to buy a house or a rocket ship or just nail it up somewhere and look at it. It's hers. Not ours—*hers.*

WALTER (*bitterly*) Now ain't that fine! You just got your mother's interest at heart, ain't you, girl? You such a nice girl—but if Mama got that money she can always take a few thousand and help you through school too—can't she?

BENEATHA I have never asked anyone around here to do anything for me!

WALTER No! And the line between asking and just accepting when the time comes is big and wide—ain't it!

BENEATHA (*with fury*) What do you want from me, Brother—that I quit school or just drop dead, which!

WALTER I don't want nothing but for you to stop acting holy 'round here. Me and Ruth done made some sacrifices for you—why can't you do something for the family?

RUTH Walter, don't be dragging me in it.

WALTER You are in it—Don't you get up and go work in somebody's kitchen for the last three years to help put clothes on her back?

RUTH Oh, Walter—that's not fair. . . .

WALTER It ain't that nobody expects you to get on your knees and say thank you, Brother; thank you, Ruth; thank you, Mama—and thank you, Travis, for wearing the same pair of shoes for two semesters—

BENEATHA (*dropping to her knees*) Well—I *do*—all right?—thank everybody . . . and forgive me for ever wanting to be anything at all . . . forgive me, forgive me!

RUTH   Please stop it! Your mama'll hear you.

WALTER   Who the hell told you you had to be a doctor? If you so crazy 'bout messing 'round with sick people—then go be a nurse like other women—or just get married and be quiet. . . .

BENEATHA   Well—you finally got it said. . . . It took you three years but you finally got it said. Walter, give up; leave me alone—it's Mama's money.

WALTER   *He was my father, too!*

BENEATHA   So what? He was mine, too—and Travis' grandfather— but the insurance money belongs to Mama. Picking on me is not going to make her give it to you to invest in any liquor stores— (*underbreath, dropping into a chair*)—and I for one say, God bless Mama for that!

WALTER (*to* RUTH)   See—did you hear? Did you hear!

RUTH   Honey, please go to work.

WALTER   Nobody in this house is ever going to understand me.

BENEATHA   Because you're a nut.

WALTER   Who's a nut?

BENEATHA   You—you are a nut. Thee is mad, boy.

WALTER (*looking at his wife and his sister from the door, very sadly*) The world's most backward race of people, and that's a fact.

BENEATHA (*turning slowly in her chair*)   And then there are all those prophets who would lead us out of the wilderness—(WALTER *slams out of the house*)—into the swamps!

RUTH   Bennie, why you always gotta be pickin' on your brother? Can't you be a little sweeter sometimes?

(*Door opens.* WALTER *walks in.*)

WALTER (*to* RUTH)   I need some money for carfare.

RUTH (*looks at him, then warms; teasing, but tenderly*)   Fifty cents? (*She goes to her bag and gets money.*) Here, take a taxi.

(WALTER *exits.* MAMA *enters. She is a woman in her early sixties, full-bodied and strong. She is one of those women of a certain grace and beauty who wear it so unobtrusively that it takes a while to notice. Her dark-brown face is surrounded by the total whiteness of her hair, and, being a woman who has adjusted to many things in life and overcome many more, her face is full of strength. She has, we can see, wit and faith of a kind that keep her eyes lit and full of interest and expectancy. She is, in a word, a beautiful woman. Her bearing is perhaps most like the noble bearing of the women of the Hereros of Southwest Africa— rather as if she imagines that as she walks she still bears a basket or a vessel upon her head. Her speech, on the other hand, is as careless as her carriage is precise—she is inclined to slur everything—but her voice is perhaps not so much quiet as simply soft.*)

MAMA Who that 'round here slamming doors at this hour?

She crosses through the room, goes to the window, opens it, and brings in a feeble little plant growing doggedly in a small pot on the window sill. She feels the dirt and puts it back out.

RUTH That was Walter Lee. He and Bennie was at it again.

MAMA My children and they tempers. Lord, if this little old plant don't get more sun than it's been getting it ain't never going to see spring again. (*She turns from the window.*) What's the matter with you this morning, Ruth? You looks right peaked. You aiming to iron all them things? Leave some for me. I'll get to 'em this afternoon. Bennie honey, it's too drafty for you to be sitting 'round half dressed. Where's your robe?

BENEATHA In the cleaners.

MAMA Well, go get mine and put it on.

BENEATHA I'm not cold, Mama, honest.

MAMA I know—but you so thin. . . .

BENEATHA (*irritably*) Mama, I'm not cold.

MAMA (*seeing the make-down bed as* TRAVIS *has left it*) Lord have mercy, look at that poor bed. Bless his heart—he tries, don't he? (*She moves to the bed* TRAVIS *has sloppily made up.*)

RUTH No—he don't half try at all 'cause he knows you going to come along behind him and fix everything. That's just how come he don't know how to do nothing right now—you done spoiled that boy so.

MAMA Well—he's a little boy. Ain't supposed to know 'bout housekeeping. My baby, that's what he is. What you fix for his breakfast this morning?

RUTH (*angrily*) I feed my son, Lena!

MAMA I ain't meddling—(*underbreath; busy bodyish*)—I just noticed all last week he had cold cereal, and when it starts getting this chilly in the fall a child ought to have some hot grits or something when he goes out in the cold—

RUTH (*furious*) I gave him hot oats—is that all right!

MAMA I ain't meddling. (*Pause.*) Put a lot of nice butter on it? (RUTH *shoots her an angry look and does not reply.*) He likes lots of butter.

RUTH (*exasperated*) Lena—

MAMA (*to* BENEATHA; MAMA *is inclined to wander conversationally sometimes*) What was you and your brother fussing 'bout this morning?

BENEATHA It's not important, Mama.

(*She gets up and goes to look out at the bathroom, which is apparently free, and she picks up her towels and rushes out.*)

MAMA   What was they fighting about?

RUTH   Now you know as well as I do.

MAMA   (*shaking her head*)   Brother still worrying his self sick about that money?

RUTH   You know he is.

MAMA   You had breakfast?

RUTH   Some coffee.

MAMA   Girl, you better start eating and looking after yourself better. You almost thin as Travis.

RUTH   Lena—

MAMA   Un-hunh?

RUTH   What are you going to do with it?

MAMA   Now don't you start, child. It's too early in the morning to be talking about money. It ain't Christian.

RUTH   It's just that he got his heart set on that store—

MAMA   You mean that liquor store that Willy Harris want him to invest in?

RUTH   Yes—

MAMA   We ain't no business people, Ruth. We just plain working folks.

RUTH   Ain't nobody business people till they go into business. Walter Lee say colored people ain't never going to start getting ahead till they start gambling on some different kinds of things in the world—investments and things.

MAMA   What done got into you, girl? Walter Lee done finally sold you on investing.

RUTH   No. Mama, something is happening between Walter and me. I don't know what it is—but he needs something—something I can't give him any more. He needs this chance, Lena.

MAMA   (*frowning deeply*)   But liquor, honey—

RUTH   Well—like Walter say—I spec people going to always be drinking themselves some liquor.

MAMA   Well—whether they drinks it or not ain't none of my business. But whether I go into business selling it to 'em *is,* and I don't want that on my ledger this late in life. (*Stopping suddenly and studying her daughter-in-law*) Ruth Younger, what's the matter with you today? You look like you could fall over right there.

RUTH   I'm tired.

MAMA   Then you better stay home from work today.

RUTH   I can't stay home. She'd be calling up the agency and screaming at them, "My girl didn't come in today—send me somebody! My girl didn't come in!" Oh, she just have a fit. . . .

MAMA   Well, let her have it. I'll just call her up and say you got the flu—

RUTH (*laughing*)   Why the flu?

MAMA   'Cause it sounds respectable to 'em. Something white people get, too. They know 'bout the flu. Otherwise they think you been cut up or something when you tell 'em you sick.

RUTH   I got to go in. We need the money.

MAMA   Somebody would of thought my children done all but starved to death the way they talk about money here late. Child, we got a great big old check coming tomorrow.

RUTH (*sincerely, but also self-righteously*)   Now that's your money. It ain't got nothing to do with me. We all feel like that—Walter and Bennie and me—even Travis.

MAMA (*thoughtfully, and suddenly very far away*)   Ten thousand dollars—

RUTH   Sure is wonderful.

MAMA   Ten thousand dollars.

RUTH   You know what you should do, Miss Lena? You should take yourself a trip somewhere. To Europe or South America or someplace—

MAMA (*throwing up her hands at the thought*)   Oh, child!

RUTH   I'm serious. Just pack up and leave! Go on away and enjoy yourself some. Forget about the family and have yourself a ball for once in your life—

MAMA (*drily*)   You sound like I'm just about ready to die. Who'd go with me? What I look like wandering 'round Europe by myself?

RUTH   Shoot—these here rich white women do it all the time. They don't think nothing of packing up they suitcases and piling on one of them big steamships and—swoosh!—they gone, child.

MAMA   Something always told me I wasn't no rich white woman.

RUTH   Well—what are you going to do with it then?

MAMA   I ain't rightly decided. (*Thinking. She speaks now with emphasis.*) Some of it got to be put away for Beneatha and her schoolin'—and ain't nothing going to touch that part of it. Nothing. (*She waits several seconds, trying to make up her mind about something, and looks at* RUTH *a little tentatively before going on.*) Been thinking that we maybe could meet the notes on a little old two-story somewhere, with a yard where Travis could play in the summertime, if we use part of the insurance for a down payment and everybody kind of pitch in. I could maybe take on a little day work again, few days a week—

RUTH (*studying her mother-in-law furtively and concentrating on her ironing, anxious to encourage without seeming to*)   Well, Lord knows, we've put enough rent into this here rat trap to pay for four houses by now....

MAMA (*looking up at the words "rat trap" and then looking around and leaning back and sighing—in a suddenly reflective mood—)* "Rat trap"—yes, that's all it is. *(Smiling)* I remember just as well the day me and Big Walter moved in here. Hadn't been married but two weeks and wasn't planning on living here no more than a year. *(She shakes her head at the dissolved dream.)* We was going to set away, little by little, don't you know, and buy a little place out in Morgan Park. We had even picked out the house. *(Chuckling a little)* Looks right dumpy today. But Lord, child, you should know all the dreams I had 'bout buying that house and fixing it up and making me a little garden in the back— *(She waits and stops smiling.)* And didn't none of it happen. *(Dropping her hands in a futile gesture)*

RUTH *(keeps her head down, ironing)* Yes, life can be a barrel of disappointments, sometimes.

MAMA Honey, Big Walter would come in here some nights back then and slump down on that couch there and just look at the rug, and look at me and look at the rug and then back at me— and I'd know he was down then ... really down. *(After a second very long and thoughtful pause; she is seeing back to times that only she can see.)* And then, Lord, when I lost that baby—little Claude—I almost thought I was going to lose Big Walter too. Oh, that man grieved hisself! He was one man to love his children.

RUTH Ain't nothin' can tear at you like losin' your baby.

MAMA I guess that's how come that man finally worked hisself to death like he done. Like he was fighting his own war with this here world that took his baby from him.

RUTH He sure was a fine man, all right. I always liked Mr. Younger.

MAMA Crazy 'bout his children! God knows there was plenty wrong with Walter Younger—hard-headed, mean, kind of wild with women—plenty wrong with him. But he sure loved his children. Always wanted them to have something—be something. That's where Brother gets all these notions, I reckon. Big Walter used to say, he'd get right wet in the eyes sometimes, lean his head back with the water standing in his eyes and say, "Seem like God didn't see fit to give the black man nothing but dreams—but He did give us children to make them dreams seem worth while." *(She smiles.)* He could talk like that, don't you know.

RUTH Yes, he sure could. He was a good man, Mr. Younger.

MAMA Yes, a fine man—just couldn't never catch up with his dreams, that's all.

(BENEATHA comes in, brushing her hair and looking up to the ceiling, where the sound of a vacuum cleaner has started up.)

BENEATHA   What could be so dirty on that woman's rugs that she has to vacuum them every single day?

RUTH   I wish certain young women 'round here who I could name would take inspiration about certain rugs in a certain apartment I could also mention.

BENEATHA (*shrugging*)   How much cleaning can a house need, for Christ's sakes.

MAMA (*not liking the Lord's name used thus*)   Bennie!

RUTH   Just listen to her—just listen!

BENEATHA   Oh, God!

MAMA   If you use the Lord's name just one more time—

BENEATHA (*a bit of a whine*)   Oh, Mama—

RUTH   Fresh—just fresh as salt, this girl!

BENEATHA (*drily*)   Well—if the salt loses its savor—

MAMA   Now that will do. I just ain't going to have you 'round here reciting the scriptures in vain—you hear me?

BENEATHA   How did I manage to get on everybody's wrong side by just walking into a room?

RUTH   If you weren't so fresh—

BENEATHA   Ruth, I'm twenty years old.

MAMA   What time you be home from school today?

BENEATHA   Kind of late. (*With enthusiasm*) Madeline is going to start my guitar lessons today.

MAMA *and* RUTH *look up with the same expression.*

MAMA   Your *what* kind of lessons?

BENEATHA   Guitar.

RUTH   Oh, Father!

MAMA   How come you done taken it in your mind to learn to play the guitar?

BENEATHA   I just want to, that's all.

MAMA (*smiling*)   Lord, child, don't you know what to do with yourself? How long it going to be before you get tired of this now—like you got tired of that little play-acting group you joined last year? (*Looking at* RUTH) And what was it the year before that?

RUTH   The horseback-riding club for which she bought that fifty-five-dollar riding habit that's been hanging in the closet ever since!

MAMA (*to* BENEATHA)   Why you got to flit so from one thing to another, baby?

BENEATHA (*sharply*)   I just want to learn to play the guitar. Is there anything wrong with that?

MAMA   Ain't nobody trying to stop you. I just wonders sometimes why you has to flit so from one thing to another all the time. You ain't never done nothing with all that camera equipment you brought home—

BENEATHA I don't flit! I—I experiment with different forms of expression—

RUTH Like riding a horse?

BENEATHA —People have to express themselves one way or another.

MAMA What is it you want to express?

BENEATHA (*angrily*) Me! (MAMA *and* RUTH *look at each other and burst into raucous laughter.*) Don't worry—I don't expect you to understand.

MAMA (*to change the subject*) Who you going out with tomorrow night?

BENEATHA (*with displeasure*) George Murchison again.

MAMA (*pleased*) Oh—you getting a little sweet on him?

RUTH You ask me, this child ain't sweet on nobody but herself— (*Underbreath*) Express herself!

They laugh.

BENEATHA Oh—I like George all right, Mama. I mean I like him enough to go out with him and stuff, but—

RUTH (*for devilment*) What does *and stuff* mean?

BENEATHA Mind your own business.

MAMA Stop picking at her now, Ruth. (*A thoughtful pause, and then a suspicious sudden look at her daughter as she turns in her chair for emphasis*) What *does* it mean?

BENEATHA (*wearily*) Oh, I just mean I couldn't ever really be serious about George. He's—he's so shallow.

RUTH Shallow—what do you mean he's shallow? He's *rich!*

MAMA Hush, Ruth.

BENEATHA I know he's rich. He knows he's rich, too.

RUTH Well—what other qualities a man got to have to satisfy you, little girl?

BENEATHA You wouldn't even begin to understand. Anybody who married Walter could not possibly understand.

MAMA (*outraged*) What kind of way is that to talk about your brother?

BENEATHA Brother is a flip—let's face it.

MAMA (*to* RUTH, *helplessly*) What's a flip?

RUTH (*glad to add kindling*) She's saying he's crazy.

BENEATHA Not crazy. Brother isn't really crazy yet—he—he's an elaborate neurotic.

MAMA Hush your mouth!

BENEATHA As for George. Well. George looks good—he's got a beautiful car and he takes me to nice places and, as my sister-in-law says, he is probably the richest boy I will ever get to know and I even like him sometimes—but if the Youngers are sitting around waiting to see if their little Bennie is going to tie up the family with the Murchisons, they are wasting their time.

RUTH You mean you wouldn't marry George Murchison if he asked you someday? That pretty, rich thing? Honey, I knew you was odd—

BENEATHA No I would not marry him if all I felt for him was what I feel now. Besides, George's family wouldn't really like it.

MAMA Why not?

BENEATHA Oh, Mama—The Murchisons are honest-to-God-real-*live*-rich colored people, and the only people in the world who are more snobbish than rich white people are rich colored people. I thought everybody knew that. I've met Mrs. Murchison. She's a scene!

MAMA You must not dislike people 'cause they well off, honey.

BENEATHA Why not? It makes just as much sense as disliking people 'cause they are poor, and lots of people do that.

RUTH (*a wisdom-of-the-ages manner; to* MAMA) Well, she'll get over some of this—

BENEATHA Get over it? What are you talking about, Ruth? Listen, I'm going to be a doctor. I'm not worried about who I'm going to marry yet—if I ever get married.

MAMA *and* RUTH *If!*

MAMA Now, Bennie—

BENEATHA Oh, I probably will . . . but first I'm going to be a doctor, and George, for one, still think's that's pretty funny. I couldn't be bothered with that, I am going to be a doctor and everybody around here better understand that!

MAMA (*kindly*) 'Course you going to be a doctor, honey, God willing.

BENEATHA (*drily*) God hasn't got a thing to do with it.

MAMA Beneatha—that just wasn't necessary.

BENEATHA Well—neither is God. I get sick of hearing about God.

MAMA Beneatha!

BENEATHA I mean it! I'm just tired of hearing about God all the time. What has He got to do with anything? Does He pay tuition?

MAMA You 'bout to get your fresh little jaw slapped!

RUTH That's just what she needs, all right!

BENEATHA Why? Why can't I say what I want to around here, like everybody else?

MAMA It don't sound nice for a young girl to say things like that—you wasn't brought up that way. Me and your father went to trouble to get you and Brother to church every Sunday.

BENEATHA   Mama, you don't understand. It's all a matter of ideas, and God is just one idea I don't accept. It's not important, I am not going out and be immoral or commit crimes because I don't believe in God. I don't even think about it. It's just that I get tired of Him getting credit for all the things the human race achieves through its own stubborn effort. There simply is no blasted God—there is only man and it is he who makes miracles!

MAMA *absorbs this speech, studies her daughter and rises slowly and crosses to* BENEATHA *and slaps her powerfully across the face. After, there is only silence and the daughter drops her eyes from her mother's face, and* MAMA *is very tall before her.*

MAMA   Now—you say after me, in my mother's house there is still God. (*There is a long pause and* BENEATHA *stares at the floor wordlessly.* MAMA *repeats the phrase with precision and cool emotion.*) In my mother's house there is still God.

BENEATHA   In my mother's house there is still God.

A long pause.

MAMA (*walking away from* BENEATHA, *too disturbed for triumphant posture; stopping and turning back to her daughter*)   There are some ideas we ain't going to have in this house. Not long as I am at the head of this family.

BENEATHA   Yes, ma'am.

(MAMA *walks out of the room.*)

RUTH (*almost gently, with profound understanding*)   You think you a woman, Bennie—but you still a little girl. What you did was childish—so you got treated like a child.

BENEATHA   I see. (*Quietly*) I also see that everybody thinks it's all right for Mama to be a tyrant. But all the tyranny in the world will never put a God in the heavens! (*She picks up her books and goes out.*)

RUTH (*goes to* MAMA's *door*)   She said she was sorry.

MAMA (*coming out, going to her plant*)   They frightens me, Ruth. My children.

RUTH   You got good children, Lena. They just a little off sometimes—but they're good.

MAMA   No—there's something come down between me and them that don't let us understand each other and I don't know what it is. One done almost lost his mind thinking 'bout money all the time and the other done commence to talk about things I can't seem to understand in no form or fashion. What is it that's changing, Ruth?

RUTH (*soothingly, older than her years*) Now . . . you taking it all too seriously. You just got strong-willed children and it takes a strong woman like you to keep 'em in hand.

MAMA (*looking at her plant and sprinkling a little water on it*) They spirited all right, my children. Got to admit they got spirit— Bennie and Walter. Like this little old plant that ain't never had enough sunshine or nothing—and look at it. . . .

She has her back to RUTH, *who has had to stop ironing and lean against something and put the back of her hand to her forehead.*

RUTH (*trying to keep* MAMA *from noticing*) You . . . sure . . . loves that little old thing, don't you? . . .

MAMA Well, I always wanted me a garden like I used to see some-times at the back of the houses down home. This plant is close as I ever got to having one. (*She looks out of the window as she replaces the plant.*) Lord, ain't nothing as dreary as the view from this window on a dreary day, is there? Why ain't you singing this morning, Ruth? Sing that "No Ways Tired." That song always lifts me up so—(*She turns at last to see that* RUTH *has slipped quietly into a chair, in a state of semiconsciousness.*) Ruth! Ruth honey—what's the matter with you . . . Ruth!

Curtain

Scene II

It is the following morning; a Saturday morning, and house cleaning is in progress at the YOUNGERS. *Furniture has been shoved hither and yon and* MAMA *is giving the kitchen-area walls a washing down.* BENEATHA, *in dungarees, with a handkerchief tied around her face, is spraying insecticide into the cracks in the walls. As they work, the radio is on and a Southside disc-jockey program is inappropriately filling the house with a rather exotic saxophone blues.* TRAVIS, *the sole idle one, is leaning on his arms, looking out of the window.*

TRAVIS Grandmama, that stuff Bennie is using smells awful. Can I go downstairs, please?

MAMA Did you get all them chores done already? I ain't see you doing much.

TRAVIS Yes'm—finished early. Where did Mama go this morning?

MAMA (*looking at* BENEATHA) She had to go on a little errand.

TRAVIS Where?

MAMA To tend to her business.

TRAVIS Can I go outside then?

MAMA Oh, I guess so. You better stay right in front of the house, though . . . and keep a good lookout for the postman.

TRAVIS Yes'm. (*He starts out and decides to give his* AUNT BE-NEATHA *a good swat on the legs as he passes her.*) Leave them poor little old cockroaches alone, they ain't bothering you none.

(*He runs as she swings the spray gun at him both viciously and playfully.* WALTER *enters from the bedroom and goes to the phone.*)

MAMA Look out there, girl, before you be spilling some of that stuff on that child!

TRAVIS (*teasing*) That's right—look out now! (*He exits.*)

BENEATHA (*drily*) I can't imagine that it would hurt him—it has never hurt the roaches.

MAMA Well, little boys' hides ain't as tough as Southside roaches.

WALTER (*into phone*) Hello—Let me talk to Willy Harris.

MAMA You better get over there behind the bureau. I seen one marching out of there like Napoleon yesterday.

WALTER Hello. Willy? It ain't come yet. It'll be here in a few minutes. Did the lawyer give you the papers?

BENEATHA There's really only one way to get rid of them, Mama—

MAMA How?

BENEATHA Set fire to this building.

WALTER Good. Good. I'll be right over.

BENEATHA Where did Ruth go, Walter?

WALTER I don't know. (*He exits abruptly.*)

BENEATHA Mama, where did Ruth go?

MAMA (*looking at her with meaning*) To the doctor, I think.

BENEATHA The doctor? What's the matter? (*They exchange glances.*) You don't think—

MAMA (*with her sense of drama*) Now I ain't saying what I think. But I ain't never been wrong 'bout a woman neither.

The phone rings.

BENEATHA (*at the phone*) Hay-lo... (*Pause, and a moment of recognition*) Well—when did you get back!... And how was it? ... Of course I've missed you—in my way.... This morning? No... house cleaning and all that and Mama hates it if I let people come over when the house is like this.... You *have*? Well, that's different.... What is it— Oh, what the hell, come on over.... Right, see you then. (*She hangs up.*)

MAMA (*who has listened vigorously, as is her habit*) Who is that you inviting over here with this house looking like this? You ain't got the pride you was born with!

BENEATHA Asagai doesn't care how houses look, Mama—he's an intellectual.

MAMA *Who?*

BENEATHA Asagai—Joseph Asagai. He's an African boy I met on campus. He's been studying in Canada all summer.

MAMA What's his name?

BENEATHA Asagai, Joseph. Ah-sah-guy . . . He's from Nigeria.

MAMA Oh, that's the little country that was founded by slaves way back. . . .

BENEATHA No, Mama—that's Liberia.

MAMA I don't think I never met no African before.

BENEATHA Well, do me a favor and don't ask him a whole lot of ignorant questions about Africans. I mean, do they wear clothes and all that—

MAMA Well, now, I guess if you think we so ignorant 'round here maybe you shouldn't bring your friends here—

BENEATHA It's just that people ask such crazy things. All anyone seems to know about when it comes to Africa is Tarzan—

MAMA (*indignantly*) Why should I know anything about Africa?

BENEATHA Why do you give money at church for the missionary work?

MAMA Well, that's to help save people.

BENEATHA You mean to save them from *heathenism*—

MAMA (*innocently*) Yes.

BENEATHA I'm afraid they need more salvation from the British and the French.

(RUTH *comes in forlornly and pulls off her coat with dejection. They both turn to look at her.*)

RUTH (*dispiritedly*) Well, I guess from all the happy faces—everybody knows.

BENEATHA You pregnant?

MAMA Lord have mercy, I sure hope it's a little old girl. Travis ought to have a sister.

BENEATHA *and* RUTH *give her a hopeless look for this grandmotherly enthusiasm.*

BENEATHA How far along are you?

RUTH Two months.

BENEATHA Did you mean to? I mean did you plan it or was it an accident?

MAMA What do you know about planning or not planning?

BENEATHA Oh, Mama.

RUTH (*wearily*) She's twenty years old, Lena.

BENEATHA Did you plan it, Ruth?

RUTH Mind your own business.

BENEATHA It is my business—where is he going to live, on the *roof?*

(*There is silence following the remark as the three women react to the sense of it.*) Gee—I didn't mean that, Ruth, honest. Gee, I don't feel like that at all. I—I think it is wonderful.

RUTH (*dully*) Wonderful.

BENEATHA Yes—really.

MAMA (*looking at* RUTH, *worried*) Doctor say everything going to be all right?

RUTH (*far away*) Yes—she says everything is going to be fine. . . .

MAMA (*immediately suspicious*) "She"—What doctor you went to?

RUTH *folds over, near hysteria.*

MAMA (*worriedly hovering over* RUTH) Ruth honey—what's the matter with you—you sick?

RUTH *has her fists clenched on her thighs and is fighting hard to suppress a scream that seems to be rising in her.*

BENEATHA What's the matter with her, Mama?

MAMA (*working her fingers in* RUTH's *shoulder to relax her*) She be all right. Women gets right depressed sometimes when they get her way. (*Speaking softly, expertly, rapidly*) Now you just relax. That's right . . . just lean back, don't think 'bout nothing at all . . . nothing at all—

RUTH I'm all right. . . .

The glassy-eyed look melts and then she collapses into a fit of heavy sobbing. The bell rings.

BENEATHA Oh, my God—that must be Asagai.

MAMA (*to* RUTH) Come on now, honey. You need to lie down and rest awhile . . . then have some nice hot food.

(*They exit,* RUTH's *weight on her mother-in-law.* BENEATHA, *herself profoundly disturbed, opens the door to admit a rather dramatic-looking young man with a large package.*)

ASAGAI Hello, Alaiyo—

BENEATHA (*holding the door open and regarding him with pleasure*) Hello . . . (*Long pause*) Well—come in. And please excuse everything. My mother was very upset about my letting anyone come here with the place like this.

ASAGAI (*coming into the room*) You look disturbed too. . . . Is something wrong?

BENEATHA (*still at the door, absently*) Yes . . . we've all got acute ghetto-itus. (*She smiles and comes toward him, finding a cigarette and sitting.*) So—sit down! How was Canada?

ASAGAI (*a sophisticate*) Canadian.

BENEATHA (*looking at him*) I'm very glad you are back.

ASAGAI (*looking back at her in turn*) Are you really?

BENEATHA Yes—very.

ASAGAI Why—you were quite glad when I went away. What happened?

BENEATHA You went away.

ASAGAI Ahhhhhhhh.

BENEATHA Before—you wanted to be so serious before there was time.

ASAGAI How much time must there be before one knows what one feels?

BENEATHA (*stalling this particular conversation; her hands pressed together, in a deliberately childish gesture*) What did you bring me?

ASAGAI (*handing her the package*) Open it and see.

BENEATHA (*eagerly opening the package and drawing out some records and the colorful robes of a Nigerian woman*) Oh, Asagai! ... You got them for me! ... How beautiful ... and the records too! (*She lifts out the robes and runs to the mirror with them and holds the drapery up in front of herself.*)

ASAGAI (*coming to her at the mirror*) I shall have to teach you how to drape it properly. (*He flings the material about her for the moment and stands back to look at her.*) Ah—Oh-pay-gay-day, oh-gbah-mu-shay. (*A Yoruba exclamation for admiration*) You wear it well ... very well ... mutilated hair and all.

BENEATHA (*turning suddenly*) My hair—what's wrong with my hair?

ASAGAI (*shrugging*) Were you born with it like that?

BENEATHA (*reaching up to touch it*) No ... of course not. (*She looks back to the mirror, disturbed.*)

ASAGAI (*smiling*) How then?

BENEATHA You know perfectly well how ... as crinkly as yours ... that's how.

ASAGAI And it is ugly to you that way?

BENEATHA (*quickly*) Oh, no—not ugly ... (*More slowly, apologetically*) But it's so hard to manage when it's well—raw.

ASAGAI And so to accommodate that—you mutilate it every week?

BENEATHA It's not mutilation!

ASAGAI (*laughing aloud at her seriousness*) Oh ... please! I am only teasing you because you are so very serious about these things. (*He stands back from her and folds his arms across his chest as he watches her pulling at her hair and frowning in the mirror.*) Do you remember the first time you met me at school? ... (*He laughs.*) You came up to me and you said—and I thought you were the most serious little thing I had ever seen—you said: (*He imitates her.*) "Mr. Asagai—I want very much to talk with you. About Africa. You see, Mr. Asagai, I am looking for my *identity*!" (*He laughs.*)

BENEATHA (*turning to him, not laughing*)   Yes—(*Her face is quizzical, profoundly disturbed.*)

ASAGAI (*still teasing and reaching out and taking her face in his hands and turning her profile to him*)   Well ... it is true that this is not so much a profile of a Hollywood queen as perhaps a queen of the Nile—(*A mock dismissal of the importance of the question*) But what does it matter? Assimilationism is so popular in your country.

BENEATHA (*wheeling, passionately, sharply*)   I am not an assimilationist!

ASAGAI (*the protest hangs in the room for a moment and* ASAGAI *studies her, his laughter fading*)   Such a serious one. (*There is a pause.*) So—you like the robes? You must take excellent care of them—they are from my sister's personal wardrobe.

BENEATHA (*with incredulity*)   You—you sent all the way home—for me?

ASAGAI (*with charm*)   For you—I would do much more.... Well, that is what I came for. I must go.

BENEATHA   Will you call me Monday?

ASAGAI   Yes ... We have a great deal to talk about. I mean about identity and time and all that.

BENEATHA   Time?

ASAGAI   Yes. About how much time one needs to know what one feels.

BENEATHA   You never understood that there is more than one kind of feeling which can exist between a man and a woman—or, at least, there should be.

ASAGAI (*shaking his head negatively but gently*)   No. Between a man and a woman there need be only one kind of feeling. I have that for you.... Now even ... right this moment....

BENEATHA   I know—and by itself—it won't do. I can find that anywhere.

ASAGAI   For a woman it should be enough.

BENEATHA   I know—because that's what it says in all the novels that men write. But it isn't. Go ahead and laugh—but I'm not interested in being someone's little episode in America or—(*with feminine vengeance*)—one of them! (ASAGAI *has burst into laughter again.*) That's funny as hell, huh!

ASAGAI   It's just that every American girl I have known has said that to me. White—black—in this you are all the same. And the same speech, too!

BENEATHA (*angrily*) Yuk, yuk, yuk!

ASAGAI It's how you can be sure that the world's most liberated women are not liberated at all. You all talk about it too much!

(MAMA *enters and is immediately all social charm because of the presence of a guest.*)

BENEATHA Oh—Mama—this is Mr. Asagai.

MAMA How do you do?

ASAGAI (*total politeness to an elder*) How do you do, Mrs. Younger. Please forgive me for coming at such an outrageous hour on a Saturday.

MAMA Well, you are quite welcome. I just hope you understand that our house don't always look like this. (*Chatterish*) You must come again. I would love to hear all about—(*not sure of the name*)—your country. I think it's so sad the way our American Negroes don't know nothing about Africa 'cept Tarzan and all that. And all that money they pour into these churches when they ought to be helping you people over there drive out them French and Englishmen done taken away your land.

The mother flashes a slightly superior look at her daughter upon completion of the recitation.

ASAGAI (*taken aback by this sudden and acutely unrelated expression of sympathy*) Yes . . . yes. . . .

MAMA (*smiling at him suddenly and relaxing and looking him over*) How many miles is it from here to where you come from?

ASAGAI Many thousands.

MAMA (*looking at him as she would* WALTER) I bet you don't half look after yourself, being away from your mama either. I spec you better come 'round here from time to time and get yourself some decent home-cooked meals. . . .

ASAGAI (*moved*) Thank you. Thank you very much. (*They are all quiet, then—*) Well . . . I must go. I will call you Monday, Alaiyo.

MAMA What's that he call you?

ASAGAI Oh—"Alaiyo." I hope you don't mind. It is what you would call a nickname, I think. It is a Yoruba word. I am a Yoruba.

MAMA (*looking at* BENEATHA) I—I thought he was from—

ASAGAI (*understanding*) Nigeria is my country. Yoruba is my tribal origin—

BENEATHA You didn't tell us what Alaiyo means . . . for all I know, you might be calling me Little Idiot or something. . . .

ASAGAI Well . . . let me see . . . I do not know how just to explain it.

... The sense of a thing can be so different when it changes languages.

BENEATHA   You're evading.

ASAGAI   No—really it is difficult.... (*Thinking*) It means ... it means One for Whom Bread—Food—Is Not Enough. (*He looks at her.*) Is that all right?

BENEATHA (*understanding, softly*)   Thank you.

MAMA (*looking from one to the other and not understanding any of it*)   Well ... that's nice.... You must come see us again—Mr.—

ASAGAI   Ah-sah-guy ...

MAMA   Yes ... Do come again.

ASAGAI   Good-bye. (*He exits.*)

MAMA (*after him*)   Lord, that's a pretty thing just went out here! (*Insinuatingly, to her daughter*) Yes, I guess I see why we done commence to get so interested in Africa 'round here. Missionaries my aunt Jenny! (*She exits.*)

BENEATHA   Oh, Mama! ...

(*She picks up the Nigerian dress and holds it up to her in front of the mirror again. She sets the headdress on haphazardly and then notices her hair again and clutches at it and then replaces the headdress and frowns at herself. Then she starts to wriggle in front of the mirror as she thinks a Nigerian woman might.* TRAVIS *enters and regards her.*)

TRAVIS   You cracking up?

BENEATHA   Shut up.

She pulls the headdress off and looks at herself in the mirror and clutches at her hair again and squinches her eyes as if trying to imagine something. Then, suddenly, she gets her raincoat and kerchief and hurriedly prepares for going out.

MAMA (*coming back into the room*)   She's resting now. Travis, baby, run next door and ask Miss Johnson to please let me have a little kitchen cleanser. This here can is empty as Jacob's kettle.

TRAVIS   I just come in.

MAMA   Do as you told. (*He exits and she looks at her daughter.*) Where you going?

BENEATHA (*halting at the door*)   To become a queen of the Nile!

(*She exits in a breathless blaze of glory.* RUTH *appears in the bedroom doorway.*)

MAMA   Who told you to get up?

RUTH   Ain't nothing wrong with me to be lying in no bed for. Where did Bennie go?

MAMA (*drumming her fingers*)   Far as I could make out—to Egypt. (RUTH *just looks at her.*) What time is it getting to?

RUTH   Ten twenty. And the mailman going to ring that bell this morning just like he done every morning for the last umpteen years.

(TRAVIS *comes in with the cleanser can.*)

TRAVIS   She say to tell you that she don't have much.

MAMA (*angrily*)   Lord, some people I could name sure is tight-fisted! (*Directing her grandson*) Mark two cans of cleanser down on the list there. If she that hard up for kitchen cleanser, I sure don't want to forget to get her none!

RUTH   Lena—maybe the woman is just short on cleanser—

MAMA (*not listening*)   —Much baking powder as she done borrowed from me all these years, she could of done gone into the baking business!

The bell sounds suddenly and sharply and all three are stunned—serious and silent—mid-speech. In spite of all the other conversations and distractions of the morning, this is what they have been waiting for, even TRAVIS, *who looks helplessly from his mother to his grandmother.* RUTH *is the first to come to life again.*

RUTH (*to* TRAVIS)   *Get down them steps, boy!*

(TRAVIS *snaps to life and flies out to get the mail.*)

MAMA (*her eyes wide, her hand to her breast*)   You mean it done really come?

RUTH (*excitedly*)   Oh, Miss Lena!

MAMA (*collecting herself*)   Well . . . I don't know what we all so excited about 'round here for. We known it was coming for months.

RUTH   That's a whole lot different from having it come and being able to hold it in your hands . . . a piece of paper worth ten thousand dollars. . . . (TRAVIS *bursts back into the room. He holds the envelope high above his head, like a little dancer, his face is radiant and he is breathless. He moves to his grandmother with sudden slow ceremony and puts the envelope into her hands. She accepts it, and then merely holds it and looks at it.*) Come on! Open it . . . Lord have mercy, I wish Walter Lee was here!

TRAVIS   Open it, Grandmama!

MAMA (*staring at it*)   Now you all be quiet. It's just a check.

RUTH   *Open it. . . .*

MAMA (*still staring at it*)   Now don't act silly. . . . We ain't never been no people to act silly 'bout no money—

RUTH (*swiftly*)   We ain't never had none before—*open it!*

MAMA *finally makes a good strong tear and pulls out the thin blue slice of paper and inspects it closely. The boy and his mother study it raptly over* MAMA'S *shoulders.*

MAMA   *Travis! (She is counting off with doubt.)* Is that the right number of zeros.

TRAVIS   Yes'm . . . ten thousand dollars. Gaalee, Grandmama, you rich.

MAMA   *(She holds the check away from her, still looking at it. Slowly her face sobers into a mask of unhappiness)* Ten thousand dollars. *(She hands it to* RUTH.*)* Put it away somewhere, Ruth. *(She does not look at* RUTH; *her eyes seem to be seeing something somewhere very far off.)* Ten thousand dollars they give you. Ten thousand dollars.

TRAVIS   *(to his mother, sincerely)* What's the matter with Grandmama—don't she want to be rich?

RUTH   *(distractedly)* You go on out and play now, baby. *(*TRAVIS *exits.* MAMA *starts wiping dishes absently, humming intently to herself.* RUTH *turns to her, with kind exasperation.)* You're gone and got yourself upset.

MAMA   *(not looking at her)* I spec if it wasn't for you all . . . I would just put that money away or give it to the church or something.

RUTH   Now what kind of talk is that. Mr. Younger would just be plain mad if he could hear you talking foolish like that.

MAMA   *(stopping and staring off)* Yes . . . he sure would. *(Sighing)* We got enough to do with that money, all right. *(She halts then, and turns and looks at her daughter-in-law hard;* RUTH *avoids her eyes and* MAMA *wipes her hands with finality and starts to speak firmly to* RUTH.*)* Where did you go today, girl?

RUTH   To the doctor.

MAMA   *(impatiently)* Now, Ruth . . . you know better than that. Old Doctor Jones is strange enough in his way but there ain't nothing 'bout him make somebody slip and call him "she"—like you done this morning.

RUTH   Well, that's what happened—my tongue slipped.

MAMA   You went to see that woman, didn't you?

RUTH   *(defensively, giving herself away)* What woman you talking about?

MAMA   *(angrily)* That woman who—

*(*WALTER *enters in great excitement.)*

WALTER   Did it come?

MAMA   *(quietly)* Can't you give people a Christian greeting before you start asking about money?

WALTER (*to* RUTH) Did it come? (RUTH *unfolds the check and lays it quietly before him, watching him intently with thoughts of her own.* WALTER *sits down and grasps it close and counts off the zeros.*) Ten thousand dollars—(*He turns suddenly, frantically to his mother and draws some papers out of his breast pocket.*) Mama—look. Old Willy Harris put everything on paper—

MAMA Son—I think you ought to talk to your wife. . . . I'll go on out and leave you alone if you want—

WALTER I can talk to her later—Mama, look—

MAMA Son—

WALTER WILL SOMEBODY PLEASE LISTEN TO ME TO-DAY!

MAMA (*quietly*) I don't 'low no yellin' in this house, Walter Lee, and you know it—(WALTER *stares at them in frustration and starts to speak several times.*) And there ain't going to be no investing in no liquor stores. I don't aim to have to speak on that again.

A long pause.

WALTER Oh—so you don't aim to have to speak on that again? So *you* have decided. . . . (*Crumpling his papers*) Well, *you* tell that to my boy tonight when you put him to sleep on the living-room couch. . . . (*Turning to* MAMA *and speaking directly to her*) Yeah —and tell it to my wife, MAMA, tomorrow when she has to go out of here to look after somebody else's kids. And tell it to *me,* Mama, every time we need a new pair of curtains and I have to watch *you* go out and work in somebody's kitchen. Yeah, you tell me then!

(WALTER *starts out.*)

RUTH Where you going?

WALTER I'm going out!

RUTH Where?

WALTER Just out of this house somewhere—

RUTH (*getting her coat*) I'll come too.

WALTER I don't want you to come!

RUTH I got something to talk to you about, Walter.

WALTER That's too bad.

MAMA (*still quietly*) Walter Lee—(*She waits and he finally turns and looks at her.*) Sit down.

WALTER I'm a grown man, Mama.

MAMA Ain't nobody said you wasn't grown. But you still in my house and my presence. And as long as you are—you'll talk to your wife civil. Now sit down.

RUTH (*suddenly*) Oh, let him go on out and drink himself to death! He makes me sick to my stomach! (*She flings her coat against him.*)

WALTER (*violently*) And you turn mine too, baby! (RUTH *goes into their bedroom and slams the door behind her.*) That was my greatest mistake—

MAMA (*still quietly*) Walter, what is the matter with you?

WALTER Matter with me? Ain't nothing the matter with *me!*

MAMA Yes there is. Something eating you up like a crazy man. Something more than me not giving you this money. The past few years I been watching it happen to you. You get all nervous acting and kind of wild in the eyes—(WALTER *jumps up impatiently at her words.*) I said sit there now, I'm talking to you!

WALTER Mama—I don't need no nagging at me today.

MAMA Seem like you getting to a place where you always tied up in some kind of knot about something. But if anybody ask you 'bout it you just yell at 'em and bust out the house and go out and drink somewheres. Walter Lee, people can't live with that. Ruth's a good, patient girl in her way—but you getting to be too much. Boy, don't make the mistake of driving that girl away from you.

WALTER Why—what she do for me?

MAMA She loves you.

WALTER Mama—I'm going out. I want to go off somewhere and be by myself for a while.

MAMA I'm sorry 'bout your liquor store, son. It just wasn't the thing for us to do. That's what I want to tell you about—

WALTER I got to go out, Mama—(*He rises.*)

MAMA It's dangerous, son.

WALTER What's dangerous?

MAMA When a man goes outside his home to look for peace.

WALTER (*beseechingly*) Then why can't there never be no peace in this house then?

MAMA You done found it in some other house?

WALTER No—there ain't no woman! Why do women always think there's a woman somewhere when a man gets restless. (*Coming to her*) Mama—Mama—I want so many things. . . .

MAMA Yes, son—

WALTER I want so many things that they are driving me kind of crazy. . . . Mama—look at me.

MAMA I'm looking at you. You a good-looking boy. You got a job, a nice wife, a fine boy and—

WALTER A job. (*Looks at her*) Mama, a job? I open and close car doors all day long. I drive a man around in his limousine and I say, "Yes, sir; no, sir; very good, sir; shall I take the Drive, sir?" Mama, that ain't no kind of job . . . that ain't nothing at all. (*Very quietly*) Mama, I don't know if I can make you understand.

MAMA Understand what, baby?

WALTER (*quietly*) Sometimes it's like I can see the future stretched out in front of me—just plain as day. The future, Mama. Hanging over there at the edge of my days. Just waiting for me—a big, looming blank space—full of *nothing*. Just waiting for *me*. (*Pause*) Mama—sometimes when I'm downtown and I pass them cool, quiet-looking restaurants where them white boys are sitting back and talking 'bout things . . . sitting there turning deals worth millions of dollars . . . sometimes I see guys don't look much older than me—

MAMA Son—how come you talk so much 'bout money?

WALTER (*with immense passion*) Because it is life, Mama!

MAMA (*quietly*) Oh—(*Very quietly*) So now it's life. Money is life. Once upon a time freedom used to be life—now it's money. I guess the world really do change. . . .

WALTER No—it was always money, Mama. We just didn't know about it.

MAMA No . . . something has changed. (*She looks at him.*) You something new, boy. In my time we was worried about not being lynched and getting to the North if we could and how to stay alive and still have a pinch of dignity too. . . . Now here come you and Beneatha—talking 'bout things we ain't never even thought about hardly, me and your daddy. You ain't satisfied or proud of nothing we done. I mean that you had a home; that we kept you out of trouble till you was grown; that you don't have to ride to work on the back of nobody's streetcar—You my children—but how different we done become.

WALTER You just don't understand, Mama, you just don't understand.

MAMA Son—do you know your wife is expecting another baby? (WALTER *stands, stunned, and absorbs what his mother has said.*) That's what she wanted to talk to you about. (WALTER *sinks down into a chair.*) This ain't for me to be telling—but you ought to know. (*She waits.*) I think Ruth is thinking 'bout getting rid of that child.

WALTER (*slowly understanding*) No—no—Ruth wouldn't do that.

MAMA When the world gets ugly enough—a woman will do anything for her family. *The part that's already living.*

WALTER You don't know Ruth, Mama, if you think she would do that.

(RUTH *opens the bedroom door and stands there a little limp.*)

RUTH (*beaten*) Yes I would too, Walter. (*Pause*) I gave her a five-dollar down payment.

There is total silence as the man stares at his wife and the mother stares at her son.

MAMA (*presently*) Well—(*Tightly*) Well—son, I'm waiting to hear you say something. . . . I'm waiting to hear how you be your father's son. Be the man he was. . . . (*Pause*) Your wife say she going to destroy your child. And I'm waiting to hear you talk like him and say we a people who give children life, not who destroys them—(*She rises.*) I'm waiting to see you stand up and look like your daddy and say we done give up one baby to poverty and that we ain't going to give up nary another one. . . . I'm waiting.

WALTER Ruth—

MAMA If you a son of mine, tell her! (WALTER *turns, looks at her and can say nothing. She continues, bitterly.*) You . . . you are a disgrace to your father's memory. Somebody get me my hat.

Curtain

ACT II

Scene I

Time: Later the same day.
At rise: RUTH *is ironing again. She has the radio going. Presently* BE-NEATHA's *bedroom door opens and* RUTH's *mouth falls and she puts down the iron in fascination.*

RUTH What have we got on tonight!

BENEATHA (*emerging grandly from the doorway so that we can see her thoroughly robed in the costume* ASAGAI *brought*) You are looking at what a well-dressed Nigerian woman wears—(*She parades for* RUTH, *her hair completely hidden by the headdress; she is coquettishly fanning herself with an ornate oriental fan, mistakenly more like Butterfly than any Nigerian that ever was.*) Isn't it beautiful? (*She promenades to the radio and, with an arrogant flourish, turns off the good loud blues that is playing.*) Enough of this assimilationist junk! (RUTH *follows her with her eyes as she goes to the phonograph and puts on a record and turns and waits ceremoniously for the music to come up. Then, with a shout—*) OCOMOGOSIAY!

RUTH *jumps. The music comes up, a lovely Nigerian melody.* BENEATHA *listens, enraptured, her eyes far away—"back to the past." She begins to dance.* RUTH *is dumfounded.*

RUTH   What kind of dance is that?

BENEATHA   A folk dance.

RUTH   (*Pearl Bailey*)   What kind of folks do that, honey?

BENEATHA   It's from Nigeria. It's a dance of welcome.

RUTH   Who you welcoming?

BENEATHA   The men back to the village.

RUTH   Where they been?

BENEATHA   How should I know—out hunting or something. Anyway, they are coming back now. . . .

RUTH   Well, that's good.

BENEATHA   (*with the record*)

> Alundi, alundi
> Alundi alunya
> Jop pu a jeepua
> Ang gu soooooooooo
>
> Ai yai yae . . .
> Ayehaye—alundi . . .

(WALTER *comes in during this performance; he has obviously been drinking. He leans against the door heavily and watches his sister, at first with distaste. Then his eyes look off—"back to the past"—as he lifts both his fists to the roof, screaming.*)

WALTER   YEAH . . . AND ETHIOPIA STRETCH FORTH HER HANDS AGAIN! . . .

RUTH   (*drily, looking at him*)   Yes—and Africa sure is claiming her own tonight. (*She gives them both up and starts ironing again.*)

WALTER   (*all in a drunken, dramatic shout*)   Shut up! . . . I'm digging them drums . . . them drums move me! . . . (*He makes his weaving way to his wife's face and leans in close to her.*) In my heart of hearts—(*he thumps his chest*)—I am much warrior!

RUTH   (*without even looking up*)   In your heart of hearts you are much drunkard.

WALTER   (*coming away from her and starting to wander around the room, shouting*)   Me and Jomo . . . (*Intently, in his sister's face. She has stopped dancing to watch him in this unknown mood.*) That's my man, Kenyatta. (*Shouting and thumping his chest*) FLAMING SPEAR! HOT DAMN! (*He is suddenly in possession of an imaginary spear and actively spearing enemies all over the room.*) OCOMOGOSIAY . . . THE LION IS WAKING . . . . OWIMOWEH! (*He pulls his shirt open and leaps up on a table and gestures with his spear. The bell rings.* RUTH *goes to answer.*)

BENEATHA (*to encourage* WALTER, *thoroughly caught up with this side of him*) OCOMOGOSIAY, FLAMING SPEAR!

WALTER (*on the table, very far gone, his eyes pure glass sheets; he sees what we cannot, that he is a leader of his people, a great chief, a descendant of Chaka, and that the hour to march has come*) Listen, my black broth—ers—

BENEATHA OCOMOGOSIAY!

WALTER —Do you hear the waters rushing against the shores of the coastlands—

BENEATHA OCOMOGOSIAY!

WALTER —Do you hear the screeching of the cocks in yonder hills beyond where the chiefs meet in council for the coming of the mighty war—

BENEATHA OCOMOGOSIAY!

WALTER —Do you hear the beating of the wings of the birds flying low over the mountains and the low places of our land—

(RUTH *opens the door.* GEORGE MURCHISON *enters.*)

BENEATHA OCOMOGOSIAY!

WALTER —Do you hear the singing of the women, singing the war songs of our fathers to the babies in the great houses . . . singing the sweet war songs? OH, DO YOU HEAR, MY BLACK BROTHERS!

BENEATHA (*completely gone*) We hear you, Flaming Spear—

WALTER Telling us to prepare for the greatness of the time—(*To* GEORGE) Black Brother! (*He extends his hand for the fraternal clasp.*)

GEORGE Black Brother, hell!

RUTH (*having had enough, and embarrassed for the family*) Beneatha, you got company—what's the matter with you? Walter Lee Younger, get down off that table and stop acting like a fool. . . .

(WALTER *comes down off the table suddenly and makes a quick exit to the bathroom.*)

RUTH He's had a little to drink. . . . I don't know what her excuse is.

GEORGE (*to* BENEATHA) Look honey, we're going *to* the theater— we're not going to be *in* it . . . so go change, huh?

RUTH You expect this boy to go out with you looking like that?

BENEATHA (*looking at* GEORGE) That's up to George. If he's ashamed of his heritage—

GEORGE Oh, don't be so proud of yourself, Bennie—just because you look eccentric.

BENEATHA   How can something that's natural be eccentric?

GEORGE   That's what being eccentric means—being natural. Get dressed.

BENEATHA   I don't like that, George.

RUTH   Why must you and your brother make an argument out of everything people say?

BENEATHA   Because I hate assimilationist Negroes!

RUTH   Will somebody please tell me what assimila-whoever means!

GEORGE   Oh, it's just a college girl's way of calling people Uncle Toms—but that isn't what it means at all.

RUTH   Well, what does it mean?

BENEATHA   (*cutting* GEORGE *off and staring at him as she replies to* RUTH)   It means someone who is willing to give up his own culture and submerge himself completely in the dominant, and in this case, *oppressive* culture!

GEORGE   Oh, dear, dear, dear! Here we go! A lecture on the African past! On our Great West African Heritage! In one second we will hear all about the great Ashanti empires; the great Songhay civilizations; and the great sculpture of Bénin—and then some poetry in the Bantu—and the whole monologue will end with the word *heritage!* (*Nastily*) Let's face it, baby, your heritage is nothing but a bunch of raggedy-assed spirituals and some grass huts!

BENEATHA   *Grass huts!* (RUTH *crosses to her and forcibly pushes her toward the bedroom.*) See there ... you are standing there in your splendid ignorance talking about people who were the first to smelt iron on the face of the earth! (RUTH *is pushing her through the door.*) The Ashanti were performing surgical operations when the English—(RUTH *pulls the door to, with* BENEATHA *on the other side, and smiles graciously at* GEORGE. BENEATHA *opens the door and shouts the end of the sentence defiantly at* GEORGE)—were still tattooing themselves with blue dragons.... (*She goes back inside.*)

RUTH   Have a seat, George. (*They both sit.* RUTH *folds her hands rather primly on her lap, determined to demonstrate the civilization of the family.*) Warm, ain't it? I mean for September. (*Pause*) Just like they always say about Chicago weather: If it's too hot or cold for you, just wait a minute and it'll change. (*She smiles happily at this cliché of clichés.*) Everybody say it's got to do with them bombs and things they keep setting off. (*Pause*) Would you like a nice cold beer?

GEORGE   No, thank you. I don't care for beer. (*He looks at his watch.*) I hope she hurries up.

RUTH   What time is the show?

GEORGE   It's an eight-thirty curtain. That's just Chicago, though. In New York standard curtain time is eight forty. (*He is rather proud of this knowledge.*)

RUTH   (*properly appreciating it*)   You get to New York a lot?

GEORGE   (*offhand*)   Few times a year.

RUTH   Oh—that's nice. I've never been to New York.

(WALTER *enters. We feel he has relieved himself, but the edge of unreality is still with him.*)

WALTER   New York ain't got nothing Chicago ain't. Just a bunch of hustling people all squeezed up together—being "Eastern." (*He turns his face into a screw of displeasure.*)⁻

GEORGE   Oh—you've been?

WALTER   *Plenty* of times.

RUTH   (*shocked at the lie*)   Walter Lee Younger!

WALTER   (*staring her down*)   Plenty! (*Pause*) What we got to drink in this house? Why don't you offer this man some refreshment? (*To* GEORGE) They don't know how to entertain people in this house, man.

GEORGE   Thank you—I don't really care for anything.

WALTER   (*feeling his head; sobriety coming*)   Where's Mama?

RUTH   She ain't come back yet.

WALTER   (*looking* MURCHISON *over from head to toe, scrutinizing his carefully casual tweed sports jacket over cashmere V-neck sweater over soft eyelet shirt and tie, and soft slacks, finished off with white buckskin shoes*)   Why all you college boys wear them fairyish-looking white shoes?

RUTH   Walter Lee!

(GEORGE MURCHISON *ignores the remark.*)

WALTER   (*to* RUTH)   Well, they look crazy as hell—white shoes, cold as it is.

RUTH   (*crushed*)   You have to excuse him—

WALTER   No he don't! Excuse me for what? What you always excusing me for! I'll excuse myself when I needs to be excused! (*A pause*) They look as funny as them black knee socks Beneatha wears out of here all the time.

RUTH   It's the college *style,* Walter.

WALTER   Style, hell. She looks like she got burnt legs or something!

RUTH   Oh, Walter—

WALTER   (*an irritable mimic*)   Oh, Walter! Oh, Walter! (*To* MURCHISON) How's your old man making out? I understand you all going to buy that big hotel on the Drive? (*He finds a beer in the refrigerator, wanders over to* MURCHISON, *sipping and wiping his lips with the back of his hand, and straddling a chair back-*

wards to talk to the other man.) Shrewd move. Your old man is all right, man. (*Tapping his head and half winking for emphasis*) I mean he knows how to operate. I mean he thinks *big,* you know what I mean, I mean for a *home,* you know? But I think he's kind of running out of ideas now. I'd like to talk to him. Listen, man, I got some plans that could turn this city upside down. I mean I think like he does. *Big.* Invest big, gamble big, hell, lose *big* if you have to, you know what I mean. It's hard to find a man on this whole Southside who understands my kind of thinking—you dig? (*He scrutinizes* MURCHISON *again, drinks his beer, squints his eyes and leans in close, confidential, man to man.*) Me and you ought to sit down and talk sometimes, man. Man, I got me some ideas. . . .

MURCHISON (*with boredom*) Yeah—sometimes we'll have to do that, Walter.

WALTER (*understanding the indifference, and offended*) Yeah— well, when you get the time, man. I know you a busy little boy.

RUTH Walter, please—

WALTER (*bitterly, hurt*) I know ain't nothing in this world as busy as you colored college boys with your fraternity pins and white shoes. . . .

RUTH (*covering her face with humiliation*) Oh, Walter Lee—

WALTER I see you all all the time—with the books tucked under your arms—going to your (*British A—a mimic*) "clahsses." And for what! What the hell you learning over there? Filling up your heads—(*counting off on his fingers*)—with the sociology and the psychology—but they teaching you how to be a man? How to take over and run the world? They teaching you how to run a rubber plantation or a steel mill? Naw—just to talk proper and read books and wear white shoes. . . .

GEORGE (*looking at him with distaste, a little above it all*) You're all wacked up with bitterness, man.

WALTER (*intently, almost quietly, between the teeth, glaring at the boy*) And you—ain't you bitter, man? Ain't you just about had it yet? Don't you see no stars gleaming that you can't reach out and grab? You happy?—You contented son-of-a-bitch—you happy? You got it made? Bitter? Man, I'm a volcano. Bitter? Here I am a giant—surrounded by ants! Ants who can't even understand what it is the giant is talking about.

RUTH (*passionately and suddenly*) Oh, Walter—ain't you with nobody!

WALTER (*violently*) No! 'Cause ain't nobody with me! Not even my own mother!

RUTH Walter, that's a terrible thing to say!

(BENEATHA *enters, dressed for the evening in a cocktail dress and earrings.*)

GEORGE Well—hey, you look great.

BENEATHA Let's go, George. See you all later.

RUTH Have a nice time.

GEORGE Thanks. Good night. (*To* WALTER, *sarcastically*) Good night, *Prometheus.* (BENEATHA *and* GEORGE *exit.*)

WALTER (*to* RUTH) Who is Prometheus?

RUTH I don't know. Don't worry about it.

WALTER (*in fury, pointing after* GEORGE) See there—they get to a point where they can't insult you man to man—they got to talk about something ain't nobody never heard of!

RUTH How do you know it was an insult? (*To humor him*) Maybe Prometheus is a nice fellow.

WALTER Prometheus! I bet there ain't even no such thing! I bet that simple-minded clown—

RUTH Walter—(*She stops what she is doing and looks at him.*)

WALTER (*yelling*) Don't start!

RUTH Start what?

WALTER Your nagging! Where was I? Who was I with? How much money did I spend?

RUTH (*plaintively*) Walter Lee—why don't we just try to talk about it. . . .

WALTER (*not listening*) I been out talking with people who understand me. People who care about the things I got on my mind.

RUTH (*wearily*) I guess that means people like Willy Harris.

WALTER Yes, people like Willy Harris.

RUTH (*with a sudden flash of impatience*) Why don't you all just hurry up and go into the banking business and stop talking about it!

WALTER Why? You want to know why? 'Cause we all tied up in a race of people that don't know how to do nothing but moan, pray and have babies!

The line is too bitter even for him and he looks at her and sits down.

RUTH Oh, Walter . . . (*Softly*) Honey, why can't you stop fighting me?

WALTER (*without thinking*) Who's fighting you? Who even cares about you?

This line begins the retardation of his mood.

RUTH Well—(*She waits a long time, and then with resignation starts to put away her things.*) I guess I might as well go on to bed.... (*More or less to herself*) I don't know where we lost it...but we have.... (*Then, to him*) I—I'm sorry about this new baby, Walter. I guess maybe I better go on and do what I started... I guess I just didn't realize how bad things was with us... I guess I just didn't really realize—(*She starts out to the bedroom and stops.*) You want some hot milk?

WALTER Hot milk?

RUTH Yes—hot milk.

WALTER Why hot milk?

RUTH 'Cause after all that liquor you come home with you ought to have something hot in your stomach.

WALTER I don't want no milk.

RUTH You want some coffee then?

WALTER No, I don't want no coffee. I don't want nothing hot to drink. (*Almost plaintively*) Why you always trying to give me something to eat?

RUTH (*standing and looking at him helplessly*) What else can I give you, Walter Lee Younger?

She stands and looks at him and presently turns to go out again. He lifts his head and watches her going away from him in a new mood which began to emerge when he asked her "Who cares about you?"

WALTER It's been rough, ain't it, baby? (*She hears and stops but does not turn around and he continues to her back.*) I guess between two people there ain't never as much understood as folks generally thinks there is. I mean like between me and you— (*She turns to face him.*) How we gets to the place where we scared to talk softness to each other. (*He waits, thinking hard himself.*) Why you think it got to be like that? (*He is thoughtful, almost as a child would be.*) Ruth, what is it gets into people ought to be close?

RUTH I don't know, honey. I think about it a lot.

WALTER On account of you and me, you mean? The way things are with us. The way something done come down between us.

RUTH There ain't so much between us, Walter.... Not when you come to me and try to talk to me. Try to be with me...a little even.

WALTER (*total honesty*) Sometimes...sometimes...I don't even know how to try.

RUTH Walter—

WALTER Yes?

RUTH (*coming to him, gently and with misgiving, but coming to him*) Honey...life don't have to be like this. I mean sometimes people can do things so that things are better...

remember how we used to talk when Travis was born . . . about the way we were going to live . . . the kind of house . . . (*She is stroking his head.*) Well, it's all starting to slip away from us. . . .

(MAMA *enters, and* WALTER *jumps up and shouts at her.*)

WALTER   Mama, where have you been?

MAMA   My—them steps is longer than they used to be. Whew! (*She sits down and ignores him.*) How you feeling this evening, Ruth?

RUTH *shrugs, disturbed some at having been prematurely interrupted and watching her husband knowingly.*

WALTER   Mama, where have you been all day?

MAMA (*still ignoring him and leaning on the table and changing to more comfortable shoes*)   Where's Travis?

RUTH   I let him go out earlier and he ain't come back yet. Boy, is he going to get it!

WALTER   Mama!

MAMA (*as if she has heard him for the first time*)   Yes, son?

WALTER   Where did you go this afternoon?

MAMA   I went downtown to tend to some business that I had to tend to.

WALTER   What kind of business?

MAMA   You know better than to question me like a child, Brother.

WALTER (*rising and bending over the table*)   Where were you, Mama? (*Bringing his fists down and shouting*) Mama, you didn't go do something with that insurance money, something crazy?

(*The front door opens slowly, interrupting him, and* TRAVIS *peeks his head in, less than hopefully.*)

TRAVIS (*to his mother*)   Mama, I—

RUTH   "Mama I" nothing! You're going to get it, boy! Get on in that bedroom and get yourself ready!

TRAVIS   But I—

MAMA   Why don't you all never let the child explain hisself.

RUTH   Keep out of it now, Lena.

MAMA *clamps her lips together, and* RUTH *advances toward her son menacingly.*

TH   A thousand times I have told you not to go off like that—
A (*holding out her arms to her grandson*)   Well—at least let 'ell him something. I want him to be the first one to hear. . . . here, Travis. (*The boy obeys, gladly.*) Travis—(*she takes the shoulder and looks into his face*)—you know that got in the mail this morning?

TRAVIS Yes'm—

MAMA Well—what do you think your grandmama gone and done with that money?

TRAVIS I don't know, Grandmama.

MAMA (*putting her finger on his nose for emphasis*) She went out and she bought you a house! (*The explosion comes from* WALTER *at the end of the revelation and he jumps up and turns away from all of them in a fury.* MAMA *continues, to* TRAVIS) You glad about the house? It's going to be yours when you get to be a man.

TRAVIS Yeah—I always wanted to live in a house.

MAMA All right, gimme some sugar then—(TRAVIS *puts his arms around her neck as she watches her son over the boy's shoulder. Then, to* TRAVIS, *after the embrace*) Now when you say your prayers tonight, you thank God and your grandfather—'cause it was him who give you the house—in his way.

RUTH (*taking the boy from* MAMA *and pushing him toward the bedroom*) Now you get out of here and get ready for your beating.

TRAVIS Aw, Mama—

RUTH Get on in there—(*Closing the door behind him and turning radiantly to her mother-in-law*) So you went and did it!

MAMA (*quietly, looking at her son with pain*) Yes, I did.

RUTH (*raising both arms classically*) Praise God! (*Looks at* WALTER *a moment, who says nothing. She crosses rapidly to her husband.*) Please, honey—let me be glad . . . you be glad too. (*She has laid her hands on his shoulders, but he shakes himself free of her roughly, without turning to face her.*) Oh, Walter . . . a home . . . a home . . . a home. (*She comes back to* MAMA) Well—where is it? How big is it? How much it going to cost?

MAMA Well—

RUTH When we moving?

MAMA (*smiling at her*) First of the month.

RUTH (*throwing back her head with jubilance*) Praise God!

MAMA (*tentatively, still looking at her son's back turned against her and* RUTH) It's—it's a nice house too. . . . (*She cannot help speaking directly to him. An imploring quality in her voice, her manner, makes her almost like a girl now.*) Three bedrooms— nice big one for you and Ruth. . . . Me and Beneatha still have to share our room, but Travis have one of his own—and (*with difficulty*) I figure if the—new baby—is a boy, we could get one of them double-decker outfits. . . . And there's a yard with a little patch of dirt where I could maybe get to grow me a few flowers. . . . And a nice big basement. . . .

RUTH Walter honey, be glad—

MAMA (*still to his back, fingering things on the table*)

don't want to make it sound fancier than it is. . . . It's just a plain little old house—but it's made good and solid—and it will be *ours.* Walter Lee—it makes a difference in a man when he can walk on floors that belong to *him.* . . .

RUTH   Where is it?

MAMA (*frightened at this telling*)   Well—well—it's out there in Clybourne Park—

RUTH's *radiance fades abruptly, and* WALTER *finally turns slowly to face his mother with incredulity and hostility.*

RUTH   Where?

MAMA (*matter-of-factly*)   Four o six Clybourne Street, Clybourne Park.

RUTH   Clybourne Park? Mama, there ain't no colored people living in Clybourne Park.

MAMA (*almost idiotically*)   Well, I guess there's going to be some now.

WALTER (*bitterly*)   So that's the peace and comfort you went out and bought for us today!

MAMA (*raising her eyes to meet his finally*)   Son—I just tried to find the nicest place for the least amount of money for my family.

RUTH (*trying to recover from the shock*)   Well—well—'course I ain't one never been 'fraid of no crackers, mind you—but—well, wasn't there no other houses nowhere?

MAMA   Them houses they put up for colored in them areas way out all seem to cost twice as much as other houses. I did the best I could.

RUTH (*struck senseless with the news, in its various degrees of goodness and trouble, she sits a moment, her fists propping her chin in thought, and then she starts to rise, bringing her fists down with vigor, the radiance spreading from cheek to cheek again*) Well—well!—All I can say is—if this is my time in life—*my time* —to say goodbye—(*and she builds with momentum as she starts to circle the room with an exuberant, almost tearfully happy release*)—to these Goddamned cracking walls!—(*she pounds the walls*)—and these marching *roaches!*—(*she wipes at an imaginary ⸣ of marching roaches*)—and this cramped little closet which ⸣ow or never was no kitchen! . . . then I say it loud and good, ⸣iah! and good-bye misery. . . . I don't never want to see ⸣y face again! (She laughs joyously, having practically the apartment, and flings her arms up and lets them happily, slowly, reflectively, over her abdomen, aware time perhaps that the life therein pulses with happi- ⸣espair.) Lena?*

MAMA (*moved, watching her happiness*) Yes, honey?

RUTH (*looking off*) Is there—is there a whole lot of sunlight?

MAMA (*understanding*) Yes, child, there's a whole lot of sunlight.

Long pause.

RUTH (*collecting herself and going to the door of the room* TRAVIS *is in*) Well—I guess I better see 'bout Travis. (*To* MAMA) Lord, I sure don't feel like whipping nobody today! (*She exits.*)

MAMA (*the mother and son are left alone now and the mother waits a long time, considering deeply, before she speaks*) Son—you—you understand what I done, don't you? (WALTER *is silent and sullen.*) I—I just seen my family falling apart today . . . just falling to pieces in front of my eyes. . . . We couldn't of gone on like we was today. We was going backwards 'stead of forwards—talking 'bout killing babies and wishing each other was dead. . . . When it gets like that in life—you just got to do something different, push on out and do something bigger. . . . (*She waits.*) I wish you say something, son . . . I wish you'd say how deep inside you you think I done the right thing—

WALTER (*crossing slowly to his bedroom door and finally turning there and speaking measuredly*) What you need me to say you done right for? *You* the head of this family. You run our lives like you want to. It was your money and you did what you wanted with it. So what you need for me to say it was all right for? (*Bitterly, to hurt her as deeply as he knows is possible*) So you butchered up a dream of mine—you—who always talking 'bout your children's dreams. . . .

MAMA Walter Lee—

(*He just closes the door behind him.* MAMA *sits alone, thinking heavily.*)

Curtain

Scene II

Time: Friday night, a few weeks later.

At rise: Packing crates mark the intention of the family to move. BENEATHA *and* GEORGE *come in, presumably from an evening out again.*

GEORGE O.K. . . . O.K., whatever you say. . . . (*They both sit on the couch. He tries to kiss her. She moves away.*) Look, we've had a nice evening; let's not spoil it, huh? . . .

He again turns her head and tries to nuzzle in and she turns aw
him, not with distaste but with momentary lack of interest; ir
pursue what they were talking about.

BENEATHA   I'm *trying* to talk to you.

GEORGE   We always talk.

BENEATHA   Yes—and I love to talk.

GEORGE (*exasperated; rising*)   I know it and I don't mind it some-times . . . I want you to cut it out, see—The moody stuff. I mean. I don't like it. You're a nice-looking girl . . . all over. That's all you need, honey, forget the atmosphere. Guys aren't going to go for the atmosphere—they're going to go for what they see. Be glad for that. Drop the Garbo routine. It doesn't go with you. As for myself, I want a nice—(*groping*)—simple (*thoughtfully*)—sophisticated girl . . . not a poet—O.K.?

She rebuffs him again and he starts to leave.

BENEATHA   Why are you angry?

GEORGE   Because this is stupid! I don't go out with you to discuss the nature of "quiet desperation" or to hear all about your thoughts—because the world will go on thinking what it thinks regardless—

BENEATHA   Then why read books? Why go to school?

GEORGE (*with artificial patience, counting on his fingers*)   It's sim-ple. You read books—to learn facts—to get grades—to pass the course—to get a degree. That's all—it has nothing to do with thoughts.

A long pause.

BENEATHA   I see. (*A longer pause as she looks at him*) Good night, George.

GEORGE *looks at her a little oddly, and starts to exit. He meets* MAMA *coming in.*

GEORGE   Oh—hello, Mrs. Younger.

MAMA   Hello, George, how you feeling?

GEORGE   Fine—fine, how are you?

MAMA   Oh, a little tired. You know them steps can get you after a
d⁀ ⁀rk. You all have a nice time tonight?
          ⁀es—a fine time. Well, good night.
          d night. (*He exits.* MAMA *closes the door behind her.*)
          ⁀y. What you sitting like that for?
          n just sitting.
          ou have a nice time?

          t's the matter?
          , George is a fool—honest. (*She rises.*)

MAMA (*hustling around unloading the packages she has entered with; she stops*)   Is he, baby?
BENEATHA   Yes.

BENEATHA *makes up* TRAVIS' *bed as she talks.*

MAMA   You sure?
BENEATHA   Yes.
MAMA   Well—I guess you better not waste your time with no fools.

BENEATHA *looks up at her mother, watching her put groceries in the refrigerator. Finally she gathers up her things and starts into the bedroom. At the door she stops and looks back at her mother.*

BENEATHA   Mama—
MAMA   Yes, baby—
BENEATHA   Thank you.
MAMA   For what?
BENEATHA   For understanding me this time.

(*She exits quickly and the mother stands, smiling a little, looking at the place where* BENEATHA *just stood.* RUTH *enters.*)

RUTH   Now don't you fool with any of this stuff, Lena—
MAMA   Oh, I just thought I'd sort a few things out.

The phone rings. RUTH *answers.*

RUTH (*at the phone*)   Hello—Just a minute. (*Goes to the door*) Walter, it's Mrs. Arnold. (*Waits. Goes back to the phone. Tense*) Hello. Yes, this is his wife speaking . . . He's lying down now. Yes . . . well, he'll be in tomorrow. He's been very sick. Yes—I know we should have called, but we were so sure he'd be able to come in today. Yes—yes, I'm very sorry. Yes . . . Thank you very much. (*She hangs up.* WALTER *is standing in the doorway of the bedroom behind her.*) That was Mrs. Arnold.
WALTER (*indifferently*)   Was it?
RUTH   She said if you don't come in tomorrow that they are getting a new man. . . .
WALTER   Ain't that sad—ain't that crying sad.
RUTH   She said Mr. Arnold has had to take a cab for three days. . . . Walter, you ain't been to work for three days! (*This is a revelation to her.*) Where you been, Walter Lee Younger? (WALTER *looks at her and starts to laugh.*) You're going to lose your job.
WALTER   That's right . . .
RUTH   Oh, Walter, and with your mother working like a dog every day—
WALTER   That's sad too—Everything is sad.

MAMA   What you been doing for these three days, son?

WALTER   Mama—you don't know all the things a man what got leisure can find to do in this city.... What's this—Friday night? Well—Wednesday I borrowed Willy Harris' car and I went for a drive ... just me and myself and I drove and drove ... Way out ... way past South Chicago, and I parked the car and I sat and looked at the steel mills all day long. I just sat in the car and looked at them big black chimneys for hours. Then I drove back and I went to the Green Hat. (*Pause*) And Thursday— Thursday I borrowed the car again and I got in it and I pointed it the other way and I drove the other way—for hours—way, way up to Wisconsin, and I looked at the farms. I just drove and looked at the farms. Then I drove back and I went to the Green Hat. (*Pause*) And today—today I didn't get the car. Today I just walked. All over the South side. And I looked at the Negroes and they looked at me and finally I just sat down on the curb at Thirty-ninth and South Parkway and I just sat there and watched the Negroes go by. And then I went to the Green Hat. You all sad? You all depressed? And you know where I am going right now—

(RUTH *goes out quietly.*)

MAMA   Oh, Big Walter, is this the harvest of our days?

WALTER   You know what I like about the Green Hat? (*He turns the radio on and a steamy, deep blues pours into the room.*) I like this little cat they got there who blows a sax.... He blows. He talks to me. He ain't but 'bout five feet tall and he's got a conked head and his eyes is always closed and he's all music—

MAMA   (*rising and getting some papers out of her handbag*) Walter—

WALTER   And there's this other guy who plays the piano ... and they got a sound. I mean they can work on some music.... They got the best little combo in the world in the Green Hat.... You can just sit there and drink and listen to them three men play and you realize that don't nothing matter worth a damn, but just being there—

MAMA   I've helped do it to you, haven't I, son? Walter, I been wrong.

WALTER   Naw—you ain't never been wrong about nothing, Mama.

MAMA   Listen to me, now. I say I been wrong, son. That I been doing to you what the rest of the world been doing to you. (*She stops and he looks up slowly at her and she meets his eyes pleadingly.*) Walter—what you ain't never understood is that I ain't got nothing, don't own nothing, ain't never really wanted nothing that wasn't for you. There ain't nothing as precious to me. . . . There ain't nothing worth holding on to, money, dreams, nothing else—if it means—if it means it's going to destroy my boy. (*She puts her papers in front of him and he watches her without speaking or moving.*) I paid the man thirty-five hundred dollars down on the house. That leaves sixty-five hundred dollars. Monday morning I want you to take this money and take three thousand dollars and put it in a savings account for Beneatha's medical schooling. The rest you put in a checking account—with your name on it. And from now on any penny that come out of it or that go in it is for you to look after. For you to decide. (*She drops her hands a little helplessly.*) It ain't much, but it's all I got in the world and I'm putting it in your hands. I'm telling you to be the head of this family from now on like you supposed to be.

WALTER (*stares at the money*) You trust me like that, Mama?

MAMA I ain't never stop trusting you. Like I ain't never stop loving you.

(*She goes out, and* WALTER *sits looking at the money on the table as the music continues in its idiom, pulsing in the room. Finally, in a decisive gesture, he gets up, and, in mingled joy and desperation, picks up the money. At the same moment,* TRAVIS *enters for bed.*)

TRAVIS What's the matter, Daddy? You drunk?

WALTER (*sweetly, more sweetly than we have ever known him*) No, Daddy ain't drunk. Daddy ain't going to never be drunk again. . . .

TRAVIS Well, good night, Daddy.

The Father has come from behind the couch and leans over, embracing his son.

WALTER Son, I feel like talking to you tonight.

TRAVIS About what?

WALTER Oh, about a lot of things. About you and what kind of man you going to be when you grow up. . . . Son—son, what do you want to be when you grow up?

TRAVIS A bus driver.

WALTER (*laughing a little*) A what? Man, that ain't nothing to want to be!

TRAVIS Why not?

WALTER 'Cause, man—it ain't big enough—you know what I mean.

TRAVIS I don't know then. I can't make up my mind. Sometimes Mama asks me that too. And sometimes when I tell her I just want to be like you—she says she don't want me to be like that and sometimes she says she does. . . .

WALTER (*gathering him up in his arms*) You know what, Travis? In seven years you going to be seventeen years old. And things is going to be very different with us in seven years, Travis. . . . One day when you are seventeen I'll come home—home from my office downtown somewhere—

TRAVIS You don't work in no office, Daddy.

WALTER No—but after tonight. After what your daddy gonna do tonight, there's going to be offices—a whole lot of offices. . . .

TRAVIS What you gonna do tonight, Daddy?

WALTER You wouldn't understand yet, son, but your daddy's gonna make a transaction . . . a business transaction that's going to change our lives. . . . That's how come one day when you 'bout seventeen years old I'll come home and I'll be pretty tired, you know what I mean, after a day of conferences and secretaries getting things wrong the way they do . . . 'cause an executive's life is hell, man—(*The more he talks, the farther away he gets.*) And I'll pull the car up on the driveway . . . just a plain black Chrysler, I think, with white walls—no—black tires. More elegant. Rich people don't have to be flashy . . . though I'll have to get something a little sportier for Ruth—maybe a Cadillac convertible to do her shopping in. . . . And I'll come up the steps to the house and the gardener will be clipping away at the hedges and he'll say, "Good evening, Mr. Younger." And I'll say, "Hello, Jefferson, how are you this evening?" And I'll go inside and Ruth will come downstairs and meet me at the door and we'll kiss each other and she'll take my arm and we'll go up to your room to see you sitting on the floor with the catalogues of all the great schools in America around you. . . . All the great schools in the world! And—and I'll say, all right son—it's your seventeenth birthday, what is it you've decided? . . . Just tell me where you want to go to school and you'll *go*. Just tell me, what it is you want to be—and you'll *be* it. . . . Whatever you want to be— Yessir! (*He holds his arms open for* TRAVIS.) You just name it, son . . . (TRAVIS *leaps into them.*) and I hand you the world!

WALTER's *voice has risen in pitch and hysterical promise and on the last line he lifts* TRAVIS *high.*

Blackout

Scene III

Time: Saturday, moving day, one week later.

Before the curtain rises, RUTH's *voice, a strident, dramatic church alto cuts through the silence.*

It is, in the darkness a triumphant surge, a penetrating statement of ex-

pectation: "Oh, Lord, I don't feel no ways tired! Children, oh, glory halle-lujah!"

As the curtain rises we see that RUTH *is alone in the living room, finishing up the family's packing. It is moving day. She is nailing crates and tying cartons.* BENEATHA *enters, carrying a guitar case, and watches her exuberant sister-in-law.*

RUTH Hey!

BENEATHA (*putting away the case*) Hi.

RUTH (*pointing at a package*) Honey—look in that package there and see what I found on sale this morning at the South Center. (RUTH *gets up and moves to the package and draws out some curtains.*) Lookahere—hand-turned hems!

BENEATHA How do you know the window size out there?

RUTH (*who hadn't thought of that*) Oh—Well, they bound to fit something in the whole house. Anyhow, they was too good a bargain to pass up. (RUTH *slaps her head, suddenly remembering something.*) Oh, Bennie—I meant to put a special note on that carton over there. That's your mamma's good china and she wants 'em to be very careful with it.

BENEATHA I'll do it.

BENEATHA *finds a piece of paper and starts to draw large letters on it.*

RUTH You know what I'm going to do soon as I get in that new house?

BENEATHA What?

RUTH Honey—I'm going to run me a tub of water up to here. . . . (*With her fingers practically up to her nostrils*) And I'm going to get in it—and I am going to sit . . . and sit . . . and sit in that hot water and the first person who knocks to tell *me* to hurry up and come out—

BENEATHA Gets shot at sunrise.

RUTH (*laughing happily*) You said it, sister! (*Noticing how large* BENEATHA *is absent-mindedly making the note*) Honey, they ain't going to read that from no airplane.

BENEATHA (*laughing herself*) I guess I always think things have more emphasis if they are big, somehow.

RUTH (*looking up at her and smiling*) You and your brother seem to have that as a philosophy of life. Lord, that man—done changed so 'round here. You know—you know what we did last night? Me and Walter Lee?

BENEATHA What?

RUTH (*smiling to herself*) We went to the movies. (*Looking at* BENEATHA *to see if she understands*) We went to the movies. You know the last time me and Walter went to the movies together?

BENEATHA   No.

RUTH   Me neither. That's how long it been. (*Smiling again*) But we went last night. The picture wasn't much good, but that didn't seem to matter. We went—and we held hands.

BENEATHA   Oh, Lord!

RUTH   We held hands—and you know what?

BENEATHA   What?

RUTH   When we come out of the show it was late and dark and all the stores and things was closed up . . . and it was kind of chilly and there wasn't many people on the streets . . . and we was still holding hands, me and Walter.

BENEATHA   You're killing me.

(WALTER *enters with a large package. His happiness is deep in him; he cannot keep still with his new-found exuberance. He is singing and wiggling and snapping his fingers. He puts his package in a corner and puts a phonograph record, which he has brought in with him, on the record player. As the music comes up he dances over to* RUTH *and tries to get her to dance with him. She gives in at last to his raunchiness and in a fit of giggling allows herself to be drawn into his mood and together they deliberately burlesque an old social dance of their youth.*)

BENEATHA   (*regarding them a long time as they dance, then drawing in her breath for a deeply exaggerated comment which she does not particularly mean*)   Talk about—oldddddddddd-fashionedddddddd—Negroes!

WALTER   (*stopping momentarily*)   What kind of Negroes?

He says this in fun. He is not angry with her today, nor with anyone. He starts to dance with his wife again.

BENEATHA   Old-fashioned.

WALTER   (*as he dances with* RUTH)   You know, when these *New Negroes* have their convention—(*pointing at his sister*)—that is going to be the chairman of the Committee on Unending Agitation. (*He goes on dancing, then stops.*) Race, race, race! . . . Girl, I do believe you are the first person in the history of the entire human race to successfully brainwash yourself. (BENEATHA *breaks up and he goes on dancing. He stops again, enjoying his tease.*) Damn, even the N double A C P takes a holiday sometimes! (BENEATHA *and* RUTH *laugh. He dances with* RUTH *some more and starts to laugh and stops and pantomimes someone over an operating table.*) I can just see that chick someday looking down at some poor cat on an operating table before she starts to slice him, saying . . . (*pulling his sleeves back maliciously*) "By the way, what are your views on civil rights down there? . . ."

He laughs at her again and starts to dance happily. The bell sounds.

BENEATHA Sticks and stones may break my bones but . . . words will never hurt me!

(BENEATHA *goes to the door and opens it as* WALTER *and* RUTH *go on with the clowning.* BENEATHA *is somewhat surprised to see a quiet-looking middle-aged white man in a business suit holding his hat and a briefcase in his hand and consulting a small piece of paper.*)

MAN Uh—how do you do, miss. I am looking for a Mrs.—(*he looks at the slip of paper*) Mrs. Lena Younger?

BENEATHA (*smoothing her hair with slight embarrassment*) Oh—yes, that's my mother. Excuse me. (*She closes the door and turns to quiet the other two.*) Ruth! Brother! Somebody's here. (*Then she opens the door. The man casts a curious quick glance at all of them.*) Uh—come in please.

MAN (*coming in*) Thank you.

BENEATHA My mother isn't here just now. Is it business?

MAN Yes . . . well, of a sort.

WALTER (*freely, the Man of the House*) Have a seat. I'm Mrs. Younger's son. I look after most of her business matters.

RUTH *and* BENEATHA *exchange amused glances.*

MAN (*regarding* WALTER, *and sitting*) Well—my name is Karl Lindner . . .

WALTER (*stretching out his hand*) Walter Younger. This is my wife—(RUTH *nods politely*)—and my sister.

LINDNER How do you do.

WALTER (*amiably, as he sits himself easily on a chair, leaning with interest forward on his knees and looking expectantly into the newcomer's face*) What can we do for you, Mr. Lindner!

LINDNER (*some minor shuffling of the hat and briefcase on his knees*) Well—I am a representative of the Clybourne Park Improvement Association—

WALTER (*pointing*) Why don't you sit your things on the floor?

LINDNER Oh—yes. Thank you. (*He slides the briefcase and hat under the chair.*) And as I was saying—I am from the Clybourne Park Improvement Association and we have had it brought to our attention at the last meeting that you people—or at least your mother—has bought a piece of residential property at—(*he digs for the slip of paper again*)—four o six Clybourne Street. . . .

WALTER That's right. Care for something to drink? Ruth, get Mr. Lindner a beer.

LINDNER (*upset for some reason*) Oh—no, really. I mean thank you very much, but no thank you.

RUTH (*innocently*) Some coffee?

LINDNER Thank you, nothing at all.

BENEATHA *is watching the man carefully.*

LINDNER Well, I don't know how much you folks know about our organization. (*He is a gentle man; thoughtful and somewhat labored in his manner.*) It is one of those community organizations set up to look after—oh, you know, things like block upkeep and special projects and we also have what we call our New Neighbors Orientation Committee. . . .

BENEATHA (*drily*) Yes—and what do they do?

LINDNER (*turning a little to her and then returning the main force to* WALTER) Well—it's what you might call a sort of welcoming committee, I guess. I mean they, we, I'm the chairman of the committee—go around and see the new people who move into the neighborhood and sort of give them the lowdown on the way we do things out in Clybourne Park.

BENEATHA (*with appreciation of the two meanings, which escape* RUTH *and* WALTER) Uh-huh.

LINDNER And we also have the category of what the association calls—(*he looks elsewhere*)—uh—special community problems. . . .

BENEATHA Yes—and what are some of those?

WALTER Girl, let the man talk.

LINDNER (*with understated relief*) Thank you. I would sort of like to explain this thing in my own way. I mean I want to explain to you in a certain way.

WALTER Go ahead.

LINDNER Yes. Well. I'm going to try to get right to the point. I'm sure we'll all appreciate that in the long run.

BENEATHA Yes.

LINDNER Well—

WALTER Be still now!

LINDNER Well—

RUTH (*still innocently*) Would you like another chair—you don't look comfortable.

LINDNER (*more frustrated than annoyed*) No, thank you very much. Please. Well—to get right to the point I—(*a great breath, and he is off at last*) I am sure you people must be aware of some of the incidents which have happened in various parts of the city when colored people have moved into certain areas—(BENEATHA *exhales heavily and starts tossing a piece of fruit up and down in the air.*) Well—because we have what I think is going to be a unique type of organization in American community life —not only do we deplore that kind of thing—but we are trying to do something about it. (BENEATHA *stops tossing and turns with a new and quizzical interest to the man.*) We feel—(*gaining confidence in his mission because of the interest in the faces of the people he is talking to*)—we feel that most of the trouble in this world, when you come right down to it—(*he hits his knee for emphasis*)—most of the trouble exists because people just don't sit down and talk to each other.

RUTH (*nodding as she might in church, pleased with the remark*) You can say that again, mister.

LINDNER (*more encouraged by such affirmation*) That we don't try hard enough in this world to understand the other fellow's problem. The other guy's point of view.

RUTH Now that's right.

BENEATHA *and* WALTER *merely watch and listen with genuine interest.*

LINDNER Yes—that's the way we feel out in Clybourne Park. And that's why I was elected to come here this afternoon and talk to you people. Friendly like, you know, the way people should talk to each other and see if we couldn't find some way to work this thing out. As I say, the whole business is a matter of *caring* about the other fellow. Anybody can see that you are a nice family of folks, hard-working and honest I'm sure. (BENEATHA *frowns slightly, quizzically, her head tilted regarding him.*) Today everybody knows what it means to be on the outside of *something.* And of course, there is always somebody who is out to take the advantage of people who don't always understand.

WALTER What do you mean?

LINDNER Well—you see our community is made up of people who've worked hard as the dickens for years to build up that little community. They're not rich and fancy people; just hard-working, honest people who don't really have much but those little homes and a dream of the kind of community they want to raise their children in. Now, I don't say we are perfect and there is a lot wrong in some of the things they want. But you've got to admit that a man, right or wrong, has the right to want to have the neighborhood he lives in a certain kind of way. And at the moment the overwhelming majority of our people out there feel that people get along better, take more of a common interest in the life of the community, when they share a common background. I want you to believe me when I tell you that race prejudice simply doesn't enter into it. It is a matter of the people of Clybourne Park believing, rightly or wrongly, as I say, that for the happiness of all concerned that our Negro families are happier when they live in their *own* communities.

BENEATHA (*with a grand and bitter gesture*)　This, friends, is the Welcoming Committee!

WALTER (*dumbfounded, looking at* LINDNER)　Is this what you came marching all the way over here to tell us?

LINDNER　Well, now we've been having a fine conversation. I hope you'll hear me all the way through.

WALTER (*tightly*)　Go ahead, man.

LINDNER　You see—in the face of all things I have said, we are prepared to make your family a very generous offer. . . .

BENEATHA　Thirty pieces and not a coin less!

WALTER　Yeah?

LINDNER (*putting on his glasses and drawing a form out of the briefcase*)　Our association is prepared, through the collective effort of our people, to buy the house from you at a financial gain to your family.

RUTH　Lord have mercy, ain't this the living gall!

WALTER　All right, you through?

LINDNER　Well, I want to give you the exact terms of the financial arrangement—

WALTER　We don't want to hear no exact terms of no arrangements. I want to know if you got any more to tell us 'bout getting together?

LINDNER (*taking off his glasses*)　Well—I don't suppose that you feel. . . .

WALTER　Never mind how I feel—you got any more to say 'bout how people ought to sit down and talk to each other? . . . Get out of my house, man. (*He turns his back and walks to the door.*)

LINDNER (*looking around at the hostile faces and reaching and assembling his hat and briefcase*)　Well—I don't understand why you people are reacting this way. What do you think you are going to gain by moving into a neighborhood where you just aren't wanted and where some elements—well—people can get awful worked up when they feel that their whole way of life and everything they've ever worked for is threatened.

WALTER　Get out.

LINDNER (*at the door, holding a small card*)　Well—I'm sorry it went like this.

WALTER　Get out.

LINDNER (*almost sadly, regarding* WALTER)　You just can't force people to change their hearts, son.

(*He turns and puts his card on a table and exits.* WALTER *pushes the door to with stinging hatred, and stands looking at it.* RUTH *just sits and* BENEATHA *just stands. They say nothing.* MAMA *and* TRAVIS *enter.*)

MAMA Well—this all the packing got done since I left out of here this morning. I testify before God that my children got all the energy of the dead. What time the moving men due?

BENEATHA Four o'clock. You had a caller, Mama. (*She is smiling, teasingly.*)

MAMA Sure enough—who?

BENEATHA (*her arms folded saucily*) The Welcoming Committee.

WALTER *and* RUTH *giggle.*

MAMA (*innocently*) Who?

BENEATHA The Welcoming Committee. They said they're sure going to be glad to see you when you get there.

WALTER (*devilishly*) Yeah, they said they can't hardly wait to see your face.

Laughter.

MAMA (*sensing their facetiousness*) What's the matter with you all?

WALTER Ain't nothing the matter with us. We just telling you 'bout the gentleman who came to see you this afternoon. From the Clybourne Park Improvement Association.

MAMA What he want?

RUTH (*in the same mood as* BENEATHA *and* WALTER) To welcome you, honey.

WALTER He said they can't hardly wait. He said the one thing they don't have, that they just *dying* to have out there is a fine family of colored people! (*To* RUTH *and* BENEATHA) Ain't that right!

RUTH *and* BENEATHA (*mockingly*) Yeah! He left his card in case—

They indicate the card, and MAMA *picks it up and throws it on the floor —understanding and looking off as she draws her chair up to the table on which she has put her plant and some sticks and some cord.*

MAMA Father, give us strength. (*Knowingly—and without fun*) Did he threaten us?

BENEATHA Oh—Mama—they don't do it like that any more. He talked Brotherhood. He said everybody ought to learn how to sit down and hate each other with good Christian fellowship.

She and WALTER *shake hands to ridicule the remark.*

MAMA (*sadly*) Lord, protect us. . . .

RUTH You should hear the money those folks raised to buy the house from us. All we paid and then some.

BENEATHA What they think we going to do—eat 'em?

RUTH　No, honey, marry 'em.

MAMA (*shaking her head*)　Lord, Lord, Lord. . . .

RUTH　Well—that's the way the crackers crumble. Joke.

BENEATHA (*laughingly noticing what her mother is doing*)　Mama, what are you doing?

MAMA　Fixing my plant so it won't get hurt none on the way. . . .

BENEATHA　Mama, you going to take *that* to the new house?

MAMA　Uh-huh—

BENEATHA　That raggedy-looking old thing?

MAMA (*stopping and looking at her*)　It expresses *me.*

RUTH (*with delight, to* BENEATHA)　So there, Miss Thing!

WALTER *comes to* MAMA *suddenly and bends down behind her and squeezes her in his arms with all his strength. She is overwhelmed by the suddenness of it and, though delighted, her manner is like that of* RUTH *with* TRAVIS.

MAMA　Look out now, boy! You make me mess up my thing here!

WALTER (*his face lit, he slips down on his knees beside her, his arms still about her*)　Mama . . . you know what it means to climb up in the chariot?

MAMA (*gruffly, very happy*)　Get on away from me now. . . .

RUTH (*near the gift-wrapped package, trying to catch* WALTER's *eye*)　Psst—

WALTER　What the old song say, Mama. . . .

RUTH　Walter—Now? (*She is pointing at the package.*)

WALTER (*speaking the lines, sweetly, playfully, in his mother's face*)

I got wings . . . you got wings . . .
All God's children got wings . . .

MAMA　Boy—get out of my face and do some work. . . .

WALTER

When I get to heaven gonna put on my wings.
Gonna fly all over God's heaven . . .

BENEATHA (*teasingly, from across the room*)　Everybody talking 'bout heaven ain't going there!

WALTER (*to* RUTH, *who is carrying the box across to them*)　I don't know, you think we ought to give her that. . . . Seems to me she ain't been very appreciative around here.

MAMA (*eying the box, which is obviously a gift*)　What is that?

WALTER (*taking it from* RUTH *and putting it on the table in front of* MAMA)　Well—what you all think? Should we give it to her?

RUTH　Oh—she was pretty good today.

MAMA I'll good you—(*She turns her eyes to the box again.*)
BENEATHA Open it, Mama.

She stands up, looks at it, turns and looks at all of them, and then presses her hands together and does not open the package.

WALTER (*sweetly*) Open it, Mama. It's for you. (MAMA *looks in his eyes. It is the first present in her life without its being Christmas. Slowly she opens her package and lifts out, one by one, a brand-new sparkling set of gardening tools.* WALTER *continues, prodding*) Ruth made up the note— read it . . .
MAMA (*picking up the card and adjusting her glasses*) "To our own Mrs. Miniver—Love from Brother, Ruth and Beneatha." Ain't that lovely. . . .
TRAVIS (*tugging at his father's sleeve*) Daddy, can I give her mine now?
WALTER All right, son. (TRAVIS *flies to get his gift*) Travis didn't want to go in with the rest of us, Mama. He got his own. (*Somewhat amused*) We don't know what it is. . . .
TRAVIS (*racing back in the room with a large hatbox and putting it in front of his grandmother*) Here!
MAMA Lord have mercy, baby. You done gone and bought your grandmother a hat?
TRAVIS (*very proud*) Open it!

She does and lifts out an elaborate, but very elaborate, wide gardening hat, and all the adults break up at the sight of it.

RUTH Travis, honey, what is that?
TRAVIS (*who thinks it is beautiful and appropriate*) It's a gardening hat! Like the ladies always have on in the magazines when they work in their gardens.
BENEATHA (*giggling fiercely*) Travis—we were trying to make MAMA Mrs. Miniver—not Scarlett O'Hara!
MAMA (*indignantly*) What's the matter with you all! This here is a beautiful hat! (*Absurdly*) I always wanted me one just like it!

She pops it on her head to prove it to her grandson, and the hat is ludicrous and considerably oversized.

RUTH Hot dog! Go, Mama!
WALTER (*doubled over with laughter*) I'm sorry, Mama—but you look like you ready to go out and chop you some cotton sure enough!

They all laugh except MAMA, *out of deference to* TRAVIS' *feelings.*

MAMA (*gathering the boy up to her*) Bless your heart—this is the prettiest hat I ever owned—(WALTER, RUTH, *and* BENEATHA *chime in noisily, festively and insincerely congratulating* TRAVIS *on his gift.*) What are we all standing around here for? We ain't finished packin' yet. Bennie, you ain't packed one book.

The bell rings.

BENEATHA That couldn't be the movers . . . it's not hardly two good yet—

(BENEATHA *goes into her room.* MAMA *starts for door.*)

WALTER (*turning, stiffening*) Wait—wait—I'll get it. (*He stands and looks at the door.*)

MAMA You expecting company, son?

WALTER (*just looking at the door*) Yeah—yeah. . . .

MAMA *looks at* RUTH, *and they exchange innocent and unfrightened glances.*

MAMA (*not understanding*) Well, let them in, son.

BENEATHA (*from her room*) We need some more string.

MAMA Travis—you run to the hardware and get me some string cord.

(MAMA *goes out and* WALTER *turns and looks at* RUTH. TRAVIS *goes to a dish for money.*)

RUTH Why don't you answer the door, man?

WALTER (*suddenly bounding across the floor to her*) 'Cause sometimes it hard to let the future begin! (*Stooping down in her face*)

I got wings! You got wings!
All God's children got wings!

(*He crosses to the door and throws it open. Standing there is a very slight little man in a not too prosperous business suit and with haunted frightened eyes and a hat pulled down tightly, brim up, around his forehead.* TRAVIS *passes between the men and exits.* WALTER *leans deep in the man's face, still in his jubilance.*)

When I get to heaven gonna put on my wings.
Gonna fly all over God's heaven . . .

The little man just stares at him.

Heaven—

(*Suddenly he stops and looks past the little man into the empty hallway.*) Where's Willy, man?

BOBO He ain't with me.

WALTER (*not disturbed*) Oh—come on in. You know my wife.

BOBO (*dumbly, taking off his hat*) Yes—h'you, Miss Ruth.

RUTH (*quietly, a mood apart from her husband already, seeing* BOBO) Hello, Bobo.

WALTER You right on time today.... Right on time. That's the way! (*He slaps* BOBO *on his back.*) Sit down ... lemme hear.

RUTH *stands stiffly and quietly in back of them, as though somehow she senses death, her eyes fixed on her husband.*

BOBO (*his frightened eyes on the floor, his hat in his hands*) Could I please get a drink of water, before I tell you about it, Walter Lee?

WALTER *does not take his eyes off the man.* RUTH *goes blindly to the tap and gets a glass of water and brings it to* BOBO.

WALTER There ain't nothing wrong, is there?

BOBO Lemme tell you—

WALTER Man—didn't nothing go wrong?

BOBO Lemme tell you—Walter Lee. (*Looking at* RUTH *and talking to her more than to* WALTER) You know how it was. I got to tell you how it was. I mean first I got tell you how it was all the way ... I mean about the money I put in, Walter Lee....

WALTER (*with taut agitation*) What about the money you put in?

BOBO Well—it wasn't much as we told you—me and Willy—(*He stops.*) I'm sorry, Walter. I got a bad feeling about it. I got a real bad feeling about it....

WALTER Man, what you telling me about all this for? ... Tell me what happened in Springfield....

BOBO Springfield.

RUTH (*like a dead woman*) What was supposed to happen in Springfield?

BOBO (*to her*) This deal that me and Walter went into with Willy —Me and Willy was going to go down to Springfield and spread some money 'round so's we wouldn't have to wait so long for the liquor license.... That's what we were going to do. Everybody said that was the way you had to do, you understand, Miss Ruth?

WALTER Man—what happened down there?

BOBO (*a pitiful man, near tears*) I'm trying to tell you, Walter.

WALTER (*screaming at him suddenly*) THEN TELL ME, GOD-DAMMIT ... WHAT'S THE MATTER WITH YOU?

BOBO Man ... I didn't go to no Springfield, yesterday.

WALTER (*halted, life hanging in the moment*) Why not?

BOBO (*the long way, the hard way to tell*) 'Cause I didn't have no reasons to. . . .

WALTER Man, what are you talking about!

BOBO I'm talking about the fact that when I got to the train station yesterday morning—eight o'clock like we planned . . . Man—*Willy didn't never show up.*

WALTER Why . . . where was he . . . where is he?

BOBO That's what I'm trying to tell you . . . I don't know . . . I waited six hours . . . I called his house . . . and I waited . . . six hours . . . I waited in that train station six hours . . . (*Breaking into tears*) That was all the extra money I had in the world. . . . (*Looking up at* WALTER *with the tears running down his face*) Man, *Willy is gone.*

WALTER Gone, what you mean Willy is gone? Gone where? You mean he went by himself. You mean he went off to Springfield by himself—to take care of getting the license—(*Turns and looks anxiously at* RUTH) You mean maybe he didn't want too many people in on the business down there? (*Looks to* RUTH *again, as before*) You know Willy got his own ways. (*Looks back to* BOBO) Maybe you was late yesterday and he just went on down there without you. Maybe—maybe—he's been callin' you at home tryin' to tell you what happened or something. Maybe—maybe—he just got sick. He's somewhere—he's got to be somewhere. We just got to find him—me and you got to find him. (*Grabs* BOBO *senselessly by the collar and starts to shake him*) We got to!

BOBO (*in sudden angry, frightened agony*) What's the matter with you, Walter! *When a cat take off with your money he don't leave you no maps!*

WALTER (*turning madly, as though he is looking for* WILLY *in the very room*) Willy! . . . Willy . . . don't do it. . . . Please don't do it . . . Man, not with that money . . . Man, please not with that money . . . Oh, God . . . Don't let it be true. . . . (*He is wandering around, crying out for* WILLY *and looking for him or perhaps for help from God.*) Man . . . I trusted you . . . Man, I put my life in your hands. . . . (*He starts to crumple down on the floor as* RUTH *just covers her face in horror.* MAMA *opens the door and comes into the room, with* BENEATHA *behind her.*) Man . . . (*He starts to pound the floor with his fists, sobbing wildly.*) That money is made out of my father's flesh. . . .

BOBO (*standing over him helplessly*) I'm sorry, Walter. . . . (*Only* WALTER's *sobs reply.* BOBO *puts on his hat.*) I had my life staked on this deal, too. . . . (*He exits.*)

MAMA (*to* WALTER) Son—(*She goes to him, bends down to him, talks to his bent head.*) Son . . . Is it gone? Son, I gave you sixty-five hundred dollars. Is it gone? All of it? Beneatha's money too?

WALTER (*lifting his head slowly*) Mama...I never...went to the bank at all....

MAMA (*not wanting to believe him*) You mean...your sister's school money...you used that too...Walter?...

WALTER Yessss!...All of it....It's all gone....

There is total silence. RUTH *stands with her face covered with her hands;* BENEATHA *leans forlornly against a wall, fingering a piece of red ribbon from the mother's gift.* MAMA *stops and looks at her son without recognition and then, quite without thinking about it, starts to beat him senselessly in the face.* BENEATHA *goes to them and stops it.*

BENEATHA Mama!

MAMA *stops and looks at both of her children and rises slowly and wanders vaguely, aimlessly away from them.*

MAMA I seen...him...night after night...come in...and look at that rug...and then look at me...the red showing in his eyes...the veins moving in his head....I seen him grow thin and old before he was forty...working and working and working like somebody's old horse...killing himself...and you—you give it all away in a day....

BENEATHA Mama—

MAMA Oh, God....(*She looks up to Him.*) Look down here—and show me the strength.

BENEATHA Mama—

MAMA (*plaintively*) Strength....

BENEATHA (*plaintively*) Mama....

MAMA Strength!

Curtain

ACT III

An hour later.

At curtain, there is a sullen light of gloom in the living room, gray light not unlike that which began the first scene of Act I. At left we can see WALTER *within his room, alone with himself. He is stretched out on the bed, his shirt out and open, his arms under his head. He does not smoke, he does not cry out, he merely lies there, looking up at the ceiling, much as if he were alone in the world.*

In the living room BENEATHA *sits at the table, still surrounded by the now almost ominous packing crates. She sits looking off. We feel that this is a mood struck perhaps an hour before, and it lingers now, full of the empty sound of profound disappointment. We see on a line from her brother's bedroom the sameness of their attitudes. Presently the bell rings and* BENEATHA *rises without ambition or interest in answering. It is* ASAGAI, *smiling broadly, striding into the room with energy and happy expectation and conversation.*

ASAGAI I came over . . . I had some free time. I thought I might help with the packing. Ah, I like the look of packing crates! A household in preparation for a journey! It depresses some people . . . but for me . . . it is another feeling. Something full of the flow of life, do you understand? Movement, progress . . . It makes me think of Africa.

BENEATHA Africa!

ASAGAI What kind of a mood is this? Have I told you how deeply you move me?

BENEATHA He gave away the money, Asagai. . . .

ASAGAI Who gave away what money?

BENEATHA The insurance money. My brother gave it away.

ASAGAI Gave it away?

BENEATHA He made an investment! With a man even Travis wouldn't have trusted.

ASAGAI And it's gone?

BENEATHA Gone!

ASAGAI I'm very sorry. . . . And you, now?

BENEATHA Me? . . . Me? . . . Me I'm nothing. . . . Me. When I was very small . . . we used to take our sleds out in the wintertime and the only hills we had were the ice-covered stone steps of some houses down the street. And we used to fill them in with snow and make them smooth and slide down them all day . . . and it was very dangerous you know . . . far too steep . . . and sure enough one day a kid named Rufus came down too fast and hit the sidewalk . . . and we saw his face just split open right there in front of us. . . . And I remember standing there looking at his bloody open face thinking that was the end of Rufus. But the ambulance came and they took him to the hospital and they fixed the broken bones and they sewed it all up . . . and the next time I saw Rufus he just had a little line down the middle of his face. . . . I never got over that. . . .

WALTER *sits up, listening on the bed. Throughout this scene it is important that we feel his reaction at all times, that he visibly respond to the words of his sister and* ASAGAI.

ASAGAI What?

BENEATHA That was what one person could do for another, fix him up—sew up the problem, make him all right again. That was the most marvelous thing in the world. . . . I wanted to do that. I always thought it was the one concrete thing in the world that a human being could do. Fix up the sick, you know—and make them whole again. This was truly being God. . . .

ASAGAI You wanted to be God?

BENEATHA No—I wanted to cure. It used to be so important to me. I wanted to cure. It used to matter. I used to care. I mean about people and how their bodies hurt. . . .

ASAGAI And you've stopped caring?

BENEATHA Yes—I think so.

ASAGAI Why?

WALTER *rises, goes to the door of his room and is about to open it, then stops and stands listening, leaning on the door jamb.*

BENEATHA Because it doesn't seem deep enough, close enough to what ails mankind—I mean this thing of sewing up bodies or administering drugs. Don't you understand? It was a child's reaction to the world. I thought that doctors had the secret to all the hurts. . . . That's the way a child sees things—or an idealist.

ASAGAI Children see things very well sometimes—and idealists even better.

BENEATHA I know that's what you think. Because you are still where I left off—you still care. This is what you see for the world, for Africa. You with the dreams of the future will patch up all Africa—you are going to cure the Great Sore of colonialism with Independence—

ASAGAI Yes!

BENEATHA Yes—and you think that one word is the penicillin of the human spirit: "Independence!" But then what?

ASAGAI That will be the problem for another time. First we must get there.

BENEATHA And where does it end?

ASAGAI End? Who even spoke of an end? To life? To living?

BENEATHA An end to misery!

ASAGAI *(smiling)* You sound like a French intellectual.

BENEATHA No! I sound like a human being who just had her future taken right out of her hands! While I was sleeping in my bed in there, things were happening in this world that directly concerned me—and nobody asked me, consulted me—they just went out and did things—and changed my life. Don't you see there isn't any real progress, Asagai, there is only one large circle that we march in, around and around, each of us with our own little picture—in front of us—our own little mirage that we think is the future.

ASAGAI That is the mistake.

BENEATHA What?

ASAGAI What you just said—about the circle. It isn't a circle—it is simply a long line—as in geometry, you know, one that reaches into infinity. And because we cannot see the end—we also cannot see how it changes. And it is very odd but those who see the changes are called "idealists"—and those who cannot, or refuse to think, they are the "realists." It is very strange, and amusing too, I think.

BENEATHA You—you are almost religious.

ASAGAI Yes . . . I think I have the religion of doing what is necessary in the world—and of worshipping man—because he is so marvelous, you see.

BENEATHA Man is foul! And the human race deserves its misery!

ASAGAI You see: *you* have become the religious one in the old sense. Already, and after such a small defeat, you are worshipping despair.

BENEATHA From now on, I worship the truth—and the truth is that people are puny, small and selfish. . . .

ASAGAI Truth? Why is it that you despairing ones always think that only you have the truth? I never thought to see *you* like that. You! Your brother made a stupid, childish mistake—and you are grateful to him. So that now you can give up the ailing human race on account of it. You talk about what good is struggle; what good is anything? Where are we all going? And why are we bothering?

BENEATHA *And you cannot answer it!* All your talk and dreams about Africa and Independence. Independence and then what? What about all the crooks and petty thieves and just plain idiots who will come into power to steal and plunder the same as before —only now they will be black and do it in the name of the new Independence—You cannot answer that.

ASAGAI (*shouting over her*) *I live the answer!* (*Pause.*) In my village at home it is the exceptional man who can even read a newspaper . . . or who ever *sees* a book at all. I will go home and much of what I will have to say will seem strange to the people of my village. . . . But I will teach and work and things will happen, slowly and swiftly. At times it will seem that nothing changes at all . . . and then again . . . the sudden dramatic events which make history leap into the future. And then quiet again. Retrogression even. Guns, murder, revolution. And I even will have moments when I wonder if the quiet was not better than all that death and hatred. But I will look about my village at the illiteracy and disease and ignorance and I will not wonder long. And perhaps . . . perhaps I will be a great man. . . . I mean perhaps I will hold on to the substance of truth and find my way always with the right course . . . and perhaps for it I will be butchered in my bed some night by the servants of the empire. . . .

BENEATHA *The martyr!*

ASAGAI . . . or perhaps I shall live to be a very old man, respected and esteemed in my new nation. . . . And perhaps I shall hold office and this is what I'm trying to tell you, Alaiyo; perhaps the things I believe now for my country will be wrong and outmoded, and I will not understand and do terrible things to have things my way or merely to keep my power. Don't you see that there will be young men and women, not British soldiers then, but my own black countrymen . . . to step out of the shadows some evening and slit my then useless throat? Don't you see they have always been there . . . that they always will be. And that such a thing as my own death will be an advance? They who might kill me even . . . actually replenish me!

BENEATHA Oh, Asagai, I know all that.

ASAGAI Good! Then stop moaning and groaning and tell me what you plan to do.

BENEATHA Do?

ASAGAI I have a bit of a suggestion.

BENEATHA What?

ASAGAI (*rather quietly for him*) That when it is all over—that you come home with me—

BENEATHA (*slapping herself on the forehead with exasperation born of misunderstanding*) Oh—Asagai—at this moment you decide to be romantic!

ASAGAI (*quickly understanding and misunderstanding*) My dear, young creature of the New World—I do not mean across the city—I mean across the ocean; home—to Africa.

BENEATHA (*slowly understanding and turning to him with murmured amazement*) To—to Nigeria?

ASAGAI Yes! . . . (*Smiling and lifting his arms playfully*) Three hundred years later the African Prince rose up out of the seas and swept the maiden back across the middle passage over which her ancestors had come—

BENEATHA (*unable to play*) Nigeria?

ASAGAI Nigeria. Home. (*Coming to her with genuine romantic flippancy.*) I will show you our mountains and our stars; and give you cool drinks from gourds and teach you the old songs and the ways of our people—and, in time, we will pretend that—(*very softly*)—you have only been away for a day—

She turns her back to him, thinking. He swings her around and takes her full in his arms in a long embrace which proceeds to passion.

BENEATHA (*pulling away*)   You're getting me all mixed up—

ASAGAI   Why?

BENEATHA   Too many things—too many things have happened to-day. I must sit down and think. I don't know what I feel about anything right this minute. (*She promptly sits down and props her chin on her fist.*)

ASAGAI (*charmed*)   All right, I shall leave you. No—don't get up. (*Touching her, gently, sweetly*) Just sit awhile and think.... Never be afraid to sit awhile and think. (*He goes to door and looks at her.*) How often I have looked at you and said, "Ah—so this is what the New World hath finally wrought...."

(*He exits.* BENEATHA *sits on alone. Presently* WALTER *enters from his room and starts to rummage through things, feverishly looking for something. She looks up and turns in her seat.*)

BENEATHA (*hissingly*)   Yes—just look at what the New World hath wrought!... Just look! (*She gestures with bitter disgust.*) There he is! *Monsieur le petit bourgeois noir*—himself! There he is—Symbol of a Rising Class! Entrepreneur! Titan of the system! (WALTER *ignores her completely and continues frantically and destructively looking for something and hurling things to floor and tearing things out of their place in his search.* BENEATHA *ignores the eccentricity of his actions and goes on with the monologue of insult.*) Did you dream of yachts on Lake Michigan, Brother? Did you see yourself on that Great Day sitting down at the Conference Table, surrounded by all the mighty bald-headed men in America? All halted, waiting, breathless, waiting for your pronouncements on industry? Waiting for you—Chairman of the Board? (WALTER *finds what he is looking for—a small piece of white paper—and pushes it in his pocket and puts on his coat and rushes out without even having looked at her. She shouts after him.*) I look at you and I see the final triumph of stupidity in the world!

(*The door slams and she returns to just sitting again.* RUTH *comes quickly out of* MAMA'S *room.*)

RUTH   Who was that?

BENEATHA   Your husband.

RUTH   Where did he go?

BENEATHA   Who knows—maybe he has an appointment at U.S. Steel.

RUTH (*anxiously, with frightened eyes*)   You didn't say nothing bad to him, did you?

BENEATHA   Bad? Say anything bad to him? No—I told him he was a sweet boy and full of dreams and everything is strictly peachy keen, as the ofay kids say!

(MAMA *enters from her bedroom. She is lost, vague, trying to catch hold, to make some sense of her former command of the world, but it still eludes her. A sense of waste overwhelms her gait; a measure of apology rides on her shoulders. She goes to her plant, which has remained on the table, looks at it, picks it up and takes it to the window sill and sits it outside, and she stands and looks at it a long moment. Then she closes the window, straightens her body with effort and turns around to her children.*)

MAMA   Well—ain't it a mess in here, though? (*A false cheerfulness, a beginning of something*) I guess we all better stop moping around and get some work done. All this unpacking and everything we got to do. (RUTH *raises her head slowly in response to the sense of the line; and* BENEATHA *in similar manner turns very slowly to look at her mother.*) One of you all better call the moving people and tell 'em not to come.

RUTH   Tell 'em not to come?

MAMA   Of course, baby. Ain't no need in 'em coming all the way here and having to go back. They charges for that too. (*She sits down, fingers to her brow, thinking.*) Lord, ever since I was a little girl, I always remembers people saying, "Lena—Lena Eggleston, you aims too high all the time. You needs to slow down and see life a little more like it is. Just slow down some." That's what they always used to say down home—"Lord, that Lena Eggleston is a high-minded thing. She'll get her due one day!"

RUTH   No, Lena. . . .

MAMA   Me and Big Walter just didn't never learn right.

RUTH   Lena, no! We gotta go. Bennie—tell her. . . . (*She rises and crosses to* BENEATHA *with her arms outstretched.* BENEATHA *doesn't respond.*) Tell her we can still move . . . the notes ain't but a hundred and twenty-five a month. We got four grown people in this house—we can work. . . .

MAMA (*to herself*)   Just aimed too high all the time—

RUTH (*turning and going to* MAMA *fast—the words pouring out with urgency and desperation*)   Lena—I'll work. . . . I'll work twenty hours a day in all the kitchens in Chicago. . . . I'll strap my baby on my back if I have to and scrub all the floors in America and wash all the sheets in America if I have to—but we got to move. . . . We got to get out of here. . . .

MAMA *reaches out absently and pats* RUTH's *hand.*

MAMA   No—I see things differently now. Been thinking 'bout some of the things we could do to fix this place up some. I seen a second-hand bureau over on Maxwell Street just the other day that could fit right there. (*She points to where the new furniture might go.* RUTH *wanders away from her.*) Would need some new handles on it and then a little varnish and then it look like something brand-new. And—we can put up them new curtains in the kitchen.... Why this place be looking fine. Cheer us all up so that we forget trouble ever came.... (*To* RUTH) And you could get some nice screens to put up in your room round the baby's bassinet.... (*She looks at both of them, pleadingly.*) Sometimes you just got to know when to give up some things ... and hold on to what you got.

(WALTER *enters from the outside, looking spent and leaning against the door, his coat hanging from him.*)

MAMA   Where you been, son?

WALTER (*breathing hard*)   Made a call.

MAMA   To who, son?

WALTER   To The Man.

MAMA   What man, baby?

WALTER   The Man, Mama. Don't you know who The Man is?

RUTH   Walter Lee?

WALTER   *The Man*. Like the guys in the streets say—The Man. Captain Boss—Mistuh Charley ... Old Captain Please Mr. Bossman ...

BENEATHA (*suddenly*)   Lindner!

WALTER   That's right! That's good. I told him to come right over.

BENEATHA (*fiercely, understanding*)   For what? What do you want to see him for!

WALTER (*looking at his sister*)   We going to do business with him.

MAMA   What you talking 'bout, son?

WALTER   Talking 'bout life, Mama. You all always telling me to see life like it is. Well—I laid in there on my back today ... and I figured it out. Life just like it is. Who gets and who don't get. (*He sits down with his coat on and laughs.*) Mama, you know it's all divided up. Life is. Sure enough. Between the takers and the "tooken." (*He laughs.*)   I've figured it out finally. (*He looks around at them.*) Yeah. Some of us always getting "tooken." (*He laughs.*) People like Willy Harris, they don't never get "tooken." And you know why the rest of us do? 'Cause we all mixed up. Mixed up bad. We get to looking 'round for the right and the wrong; and we worry about it and cry about it and stay up nights trying to figure out 'bout the wrong and the right of things all the time. . . . And all the time, man, them takers is out there operating, just taking and taking. Willy Harris? Shoot—Willy Harris don't even count. He don't even count in the big scheme of things. But I'll say one thing for old Willy Harris . . . he's taught me something. He's taught me to keep my eye on what counts in this world. Yeah—(*shouting out a little*). Thanks, Willy!

RUTH   What did you call that man for, Walter Lee?

WALTER   Called him to tell him to come on over to the show. Gonna put on a show for the man. Just what he wants to see. You see, Mama, the man came here today and he told us that them people out there where you want us to move—well they so upset they willing to pay us not to move out there. (*He laughs again.*) And—and oh, Mama—you would of been proud of the way me and Ruth and Bennie acted. We told him to get out . . . Lord have mercy! We told the man to get out. Oh, we was some proud folks this afternoon, yeah. (*He lights a cigarette.*) We were still full of that old-time stuff. . . .

RUTH   (*coming toward him slowly*)   You talking 'bout taking them people's money to keep us from moving in that house?

WALTER   I ain't just talking 'bout it, baby—I'm telling you that's what's going to happen.

BENEATHA   Oh, God! Where is the bottom! Where is the real honest-to-God bottom so he can't go any farther!

WALTER   See—that's old stuff. You and that boy that was here today. You all want everybody to carry a flag and a spear and sing some marching songs, huh? You wanna spend your life looking into things and trying to find the right and the wrong part, huh? Yeah. You know what's going to happen to that boy someday—he'll find himself sitting in a dungeon, locked in forever—and the takers will have the key! Forget it, baby! There ain't no causes—there ain't nothing but taking in this world, and he who takes most is smartest—and it don't make a damn bit of difference *how*.

MAMA   You making something inside me cry, son. Some awful pain inside me.

WALTER   Don't cry, Mama. Understand. That white man is going to walk in that door able to write checks for more money than we ever had. It's important to him and I'm going to help him . . . I'm going to put on the show, Mama.

MAMA   Son—I come from five generations of people who was slaves and sharecroppers—but ain't nobody in my family never let nobody pay 'em no money that was a way of telling us we wasn't fit to walk the earth. We ain't never been that poor. (*Raising her eyes and looking at him*) We ain't never been that dead inside.

BENEATHA   Well—we are dead now. All the talk about dreams and sunlight that goes on in this house. All dead.

WALTER   What's the matter with you all! I didn't make this world! It was give to me this way! Hell, yes, I want me some yachts someday! Yes, I want to hang some real pearls 'round my wife's neck. Ain't she supposed to wear no pearls? Somebody tell me— tell me, who decides which women is suppose to wear pearls in this world. I tell you I am a *man*—and I think my wife should wear some pearls in this world!

This last line hangs a good while and WALTER *begins to move about the room. The word "Man" has penetrated his consciousness; he mumbles it to himself repeatedly between strange agitated pauses as he moves about.*

MAMA   Baby, how you going to feel on the inside?

WALTER   Fine! . . . Going to feel fine . . . a man. . . .

MAMA   You won't have nothing left then, Walter Lee.

WALTER   (*coming to her*)   I'm going to feel fine, Mama. I'm going to look that son-of-a-bitch in the eyes and say—(*he falters*)—and say, "All right, Mr. Lindner—(*he falters even more*)—that's your neighborhood out there. You got the right to keep it like you want. You got the right to have it like you want. Just write the check and—the house is yours." And, and I am going to say—(*His voice almost breaks.*) And you—you people just put the money in my hand and you won't have to live next to this bunch of stinking niggers! . . . (*He straightens up and moves away from his mother, walking around the room.*) Maybe—maybe I'll just get down on my black knees. . . . (*He does so;* RUTH *and* BENNIE *and* MAMA *watch him in frozen horror.*) Captain, Mistuh, Bossman. (*He starts crying.*) A-hee-hee-hee! (*Wringing his hands in profoundly anguished imitation*) Yassssssuh! Great White Father, just gi' ussen de money, fo' God's sake, and we's ain't gwine come out deh and dirty up yo' white folks neighborhood. . . .

(*He breaks down completely, then gets up and goes into the bedroom.*)

BENEATHA   That is not a man. That is nothing but a toothless rat.

MAMA   Yes—death done come in this here house. (*She is nodding, slowly, reflectively.*) Done come walking in my house. On the lips of my children. You what supposed to be my beginning again. You—what supposed to be my harvest. (*To* BENEATHA) You— you mourning your brother?

BENEATHA   He's no brother of mine.

MAMA   What you say?

BENEATHA   I said that that individual in that room is no brother of mine.

MAMA That's what I thought you said. You feeling like you better than he is today? (BENEATHA *does not answer.*) Yes? What you tell him a minute ago? That he wasn't a man? Yes? You give him up for me? You done wrote his epitaph too—like the rest of the world? Well, who give you the privilege?

BENEATHA Be on my side for once! You saw what he just did, Mama! You saw him—down on his knees. Wasn't it you who taught me—to despise any man who would do that. Do what he's going to do.

MAMA Yes—I taught you that. Me and your daddy. But I thought I taught you something else too . . . I thought I taught you to love him.

BENEATHA Love him? There is nothing left to love.

MAMA There is always something left to love. And if you ain't learned that, you ain't learned nothing. (*Looking at her*) Have you cried for that boy today? I don't mean for yourself and for the family 'cause we lost the money. I mean for him; what he been through and what it done to him. Child, when do you think is the time to love somebody the most; when they done good and made things easy for everybody? Well then, you ain't through learning—because that ain't the time at all. It's when he's at his lowest and can't believe in hisself 'cause the world done whipped him so. When you starts measuring somebody, measure him right, child, measure him right. Make sure you done taken into account what hills and valleys he come through before he got to wherever he is.

(TRAVIS *bursts into the room at the end of the speech, leaving the door open.*)

TRAVIS Grandmama—the moving men are downstairs! The truck just pulled up.

MAMA (*turning and looking at him*) Are they, baby? They downstairs?

(*She sighs and sits.* LINDNER *appears in the doorway. He peers in and knocks lightly, to gain attention, and comes in. All turn to look at him.*

LINDNER (*hat and briefcase in hand*) Uh—hello . . .

RUTH *crosses mechanically to the bedroom door and opens it and lets it swing open freely and slowly as the lights come up on* WALTER *within, still in his coat, sitting at the far corner of the room. He looks up and out through the room to* LINDNER.

RUTH He's here.

A long minute passes and WALTER *slowly gets up.*

LINDNER (*coming to the table with efficiency, putting his briefcase on the table and starting to unfold papers and unscrew fountain pens*) Well, I certainly was glad to hear from you people. (WALTER *has begun the trek out of the room, slowly and awkwardly, rather like a small boy, passing the back of his sleeve across his mouth from time to time.*) Life can really be so much simpler than people let it be most of the time. Well—with whom do I negotiate? You, Mrs. Younger, or your son here? (MAMA *sits with her hands folded on her lap and her eyes closed as* WALTER *advances.* TRAVIS *goes close to* LINDNER *and looks at the papers curiously.*) Just some official papers, sonny.

RUTH Travis, you go downstairs.

MAMA (*opening her eyes and looking into* WALTER'S) No. Travis, you stay right here. And you make him understand what you doing, Walter Lee. You teach him good. Like Willy Harris taught you. You show where our five generations done come to. Go ahead, son—

WALTER (*looks down into his boy's eyes;* TRAVIS *grins at him merrily and* WALTER *draws him beside him with his arm lightly around his shoulders*) Well, Mr. Lindner. (BENEATHA *turns away.*) We called you—(*there is a profound, simple groping quality in his speech*)—because, well, me and my family—(*He looks around and shifts from one foot to the other.*) Well—we are very plain people. . . .

LINDNER Yes—

WALTER I mean—I have worked as a chauffeur most of my life— and my wife here, she does domestic work in people's kitchens. So does my mother. I mean—we are plain people. . . .

LINDNER Yes, Mr. Younger—

WALTER (*really like a small boy, looking down at his shoes and then up at the man*) And—uh—well, my father, well, he was a laborer most of his life.

LINDNER (*absolutely confused*) Uh, yes—

WALTER (*looking down at his toes once again*) My father almost beat a man to death once because this man called him a bad name or something, you know what I mean?

LINDNER No, I'm afraid I don't.

WALTER (*finally straightening up*) Well, what I mean is that we come from people who had a lot of pride. I mean—we are very proud people. And that's my sister over there and she's going to be a doctor—and we are very proud—

LINDNER Well—I am sure that is very nice, but—

WALTER (*starting to cry and facing the man eye to eye*) What I am telling you is that we called you over here to tell you that we are very proud and that this is—this is my son, who makes the sixth generation of our family in this country, and that we have all thought about your offer and we have decided to move into our house because my father—my father—he earned it. (MAMA *has her eyes closed and is rocking back and forth as though she were in church, with her head nodding the amen yes.*) We don't want to make no trouble for nobody or fight no causes—but we will try to be good neighbors. That's all we got to say. (*He looks the man absolutely in the eyes.*) We don't want your money. (*He turns and walks away from the man.*)

LINDNER (*looking around at all of them*)   I take it then that you have decided to occupy.

BENEATHA   That's what the man said.

LINDNER (*to* MAMA *in her reverie*)   Then I would like to appeal to you, Mrs. Younger. You are older and wiser and understand things better I am sure . . .

MAMA (*rising*)   I am afraid you don't understand. My son said we was going to move and there ain't nothing left for me to say. (*Shaking her head with double meaning*) You know how these young folks is nowadays, mister. Can't do a thing with 'em. Good-bye.

LINDNER (*folding up his materials*)   Well—if you are that final about it. . . . There is nothing left for me to say. (*He finishes. He is almost ignored by the family, who are concentrating on* WALTER LEE. *At the door* LINDNER *halts and looks around.*) I sure hope you people know what you're doing. (*He shakes his head and exits.*)

RUTH (*looking around and coming to life*)   Well, for God's sake— if the moving men are here—LET'S GET THE HELL OUT OF HERE!

MAMA (*into action*)   Ain't it the truth! Look at all this here mess. Ruth, put Travis' good jacket on him. . . . Walter Lee, fix your tie and tuck your shirt in, you look just like somebody's hoodlum. Lord have mercy, where is my plant? (*She flies to get it amid the general bustling of the family, who are deliberately trying to ignore the nobility of the past moment.*) You all start on down. . . . Travis child, don't go empty-handed. . . . Ruth, where did I put that box with my skillets in it? I want to be in charge of it myself. . . . I'm going to make us the biggest dinner we ever ate tonight. . . . Beneatha, what's the matter with them stockings? Pull them things up, girl. . . .

(*The family starts to file out as two moving men appear and begin to carry out the heavier pieces of furniture, bumping into the family as they move about.*)

BENEATHA   Mama, Asagai—asked me to marry him today and go to Africa—

MAMA (*in the middle of her getting-ready activity*)   He did? You ain't old enough to marry nobody—(*Seeing the moving men lifting one of her chairs precariously*) Darling, that ain't no bale of cotton, please handle it so we can sit in it again. I had that chair twenty-five years. . . .

The movers sigh with exasperation and go on with their work.

BENEATHA (*girlishly and unreasonably trying to pursue the conversation*)   To go to Africa, Mama—be a doctor in Africa. . . .

MAMA (*distracted*)   Yes, baby—

WALTER   Africa! What he want you to go to Africa for?

BENEATHA   To practice there. . . .

WALTER   Girl, if you don't get all them silly ideas out your head! You better marry yourself a man with some loot. . . .

BENEATHA (*angrily, precisely as in the first scene of the play*)   What have you got to do with who I marry!

WALTER   Plenty. Now I think George Murchison—

(*He and* BENEATHA *go out yelling at each other vigorously;* BENEATHA *is heard saying that she would not marry* GEORGE MURCHISON *if he were Adam and she were Eve, etc. The anger is loud and real till their voices diminish.* RUTH *stands at the door and turns to* MAMA *and smiles knowingly.*)

MAMA (*fixing her hat at last*)   Yeah—they something all right, my children. . . .

RUTH   Yeah—they're something. Let's go, Lena.

MAMA (*stalling, starting to look around at the house*)   Yes—I'm coming. Ruth—

RUTH   Yes?

MAMA (*quietly, woman to woman*)   He finally come into his manhood today, didn't he? Kind of like a rainbow after the rain. . . .

RUTH (*biting her lip lest her own pride explode in front of* MAMA) Yes, Lena.

WALTER's *voice calls for them raucously.*

MAMA (*waving* RUTH *out vaguely*)   All right, honey—go on down. I be down directly.

(RUTH *hesitates, then exits.* MAMA *stands, at last alone in the living room, her plant on the table before her as the lights start to come down. She looks around at all the walls and ceilings and suddenly, despite herself, while the children call below, a great heaving thing rises in her and she puts her fist to her mouth, takes a final desperate look, pulls her coat about her, pats her hat and goes out. The lights dim down. The door opens and she comes back in, grabs her plant, and goes out for the last time.)*

Curtain

⌢ THE GAP
(1969)

EUGÈNE IONESCO (1912–   )

In his 1961 volume about contemporary drama British critic and theatrical producer Martin Esslin coined a new phrase in the title of his book which has stuck as a definition of a particular dramatic style, *The Theatre of the Absurd*. Esslin's lengthy discussions of Romanian Eugène Ionesco, Irish Samuel Beckett, French Jean Genet, American Edward Albee, and British Harold Pinter include a substantial body of plays under the "absurd" rubric, and ever since there has been debate as to precisely what the absurd is, and whether or not all of the major and minor writers assigned by Esslin to the genre really belong there.

Generally speaking the absurd assumes a fundamental ridiculousness in the fact of being alive. Man knows, above all other creatures, that he will die and that whatever he accomplishes in his instant of eternity is an exercise in futility. He waits endlessly for he knows not what; he hopes endlessly for something significant to happen, deprived of that hope, but never abandoning it. There are unseen and uncomprehended forces at work somewhere in the dim background, but nobody knows quite what they are or where they come from. It is a dark and dismal view, but it is often riotously funny. It looks at the maddening quirks of "nature" or whatever it is that rules mankind, and it shows the often idiotic bumblings of human creatures desperately trying to find out what is happening, but unable to do so. The world won't stand still; things grow and diminish not only in size, but in shape and numbers, without reason. A series of sounds called language is meant for communication, but all too often prevents any meaningful communication at all.

The plays of Eugène Ionesco are among the very best representatives of Esslin's genre. In a series of short plays and, notably, in the full-length *Rhinoceros* (1960), Ionesco has captured just about every nuance of Esslin's definition. In his first, *The Bald Soprano* (1950), prompted by the uninspired nonsense of most phrase-book texts used in the teaching of foreign languages, Ionesco creates a hilariously insane world in which husbands and wives have difficulty recognizing each other, everybody in one family, male and female, has the same name, clocks tell whatever time pleases them, firemen come searching for fires to put out, and language is reduced to absolute gibberish, with characters at the end of the play exchanging places and beginning the whole routine all over again. In *The Lesson* (1951), language becomes a kind of deadly weapon used by the teacher to reduce his defenseless pupil to blubbering ineptitude and eventually to death. In *Rhinoceros,* while rampaging and rapidly multiplying horned beasts ravage a town, the inhabitants calmly debate their origin and numbers of horns, while, in the end, literally becoming rhinoceroses themselves, so that even the single survivor who refuses to succumb stands isolated and alone, ashamed of his soft skin and human features. The world of Ionesco is one in which reason and rational behavior, both human and otherwise, do not exist. Yet under it all lies a frighteningly sane view of the world's inanities.

The Gap, one of Ionesco's briefer efforts, although conveyed to us in readily comprehensible language, touches several of the basic aspects of the "absurd," shown in a world in which the rules can change without notice and its inhabitants find that logic and meaning have somehow slipped out of their lives. A minor oversight, the "gap," in the Academician's educational record sets in motion a series of catastrophes far beyond rationality. What, indeed, is one's professional reputation based on—diplomas by the score, Nobel prizes in triplicate, honors uncounted—or a seemingly insignificant portion of a bachelor's program decades ago? Shame and disgrace, causing the utter collapse of a scholarly house of cards, follow hard upon the Academician's total inability to use the very language that has up to now served him so well. His brilliant mind has gone blank; the examination has been a nightmare of his inability even to respond to the right questions, let alone write intelligible answers. Like the student in *The Lesson* he is reduced to helplessness, finding his life without meaning as he rips the diplomas from the wall and stamps them into oblivion. Simultaneously funny and terrifying, the fate of the Academician does raise the unanswerable question for us as much as for the Academician himself: where is the sense of it all?

The Gap

IONESCO

Translated by Rosette Lamont

CHARACTERS

THE FRIEND
THE ACADEMICIAN
THE ACADEMICIAN's WIFE
THE MAID

SET. *A rich bourgeois living room with artistic pretensions. One or two sofas, a number of armchairs, among which, a green, Régence style one, right in the middle of the room. The walls are covered with framed diplomas. One can make out, written in heavy script at the top of a particularly large one, "Doctor Honoris causa." This is followed by an almost illegible Latin inscription. Another equally impressive diploma states: "Doctorat honoris causa," again followed by a long, illegible text. There is an abundance of smaller diplomas, each of which bears a clearly written "doctorate."*

A door to the right of the audience.

As the curtain rises, one can see THE ACADEMICIAN's WIFE *dressed in a rather crumpled robe. She has obviously just gotten out of bed, and has not had time to dress.* THE FRIEND *faces her. He is well dressed: hat, umbrella in hand, stiff collar, black jacket and striped trousers, shiny black shoes.*

THE WIFE Dear friend, tell me all.

THE FRIEND I don't know what to say.

THE WIFE I know.

THE FRIEND I heard the news last night. I did not want to call you. At the same time I couldn't wait any longer. Please forgive me for coming so early with such terrible news.

THE WIFE He didn't make it! How terrible! We were still hoping. . . .

THE FRIEND It's hard, I know. He still had a chance. Not much of one. We had to expect it.

THE WIFE I didn't expect it. He was always so successful. He could always manage somehow, at the last moment.

1037

THE FRIEND   In that state of exhaustion. You shouldn't have let him!

THE WIFE   What can we do, what can we do! . . . How awful!

THE FRIEND   Come on, dear friend, be brave. That's life.

THE WIFE   I feel faint: I'm going to faint. (*She falls in one of the armchairs.*)

THE FRIEND   (*holding her, gently slapping her cheeks and hands*) I shouldn't have blurted it out like that. I'm sorry.

THE WIFE   No, you were right to do so. I had to find out somehow or other.

THE FRIEND   I should have prepared you, carefully.

THE WIFE   I've got to be strong. I can't help thinking of him, the wretched man. I hope they won't put it in the papers. Can we count on the journalists' discretion?

THE FRIEND   Close your door. Don't answer the telephone. It will still get around. You could go to the country. In a couple of months, when you are better, you'll come back, you'll go on with your life. People forget such things.

THE WIFE   People won't forget so fast. That's all they were waiting for. Some friends will feel sorry, but the others, the others. . . . (*The Academician comes in, fully dressed: uniform, chest covered with decorations, his sword on his side.*)

THE ACADEMICIAN   Up so early, my dear? (*To* THE FRIEND.) You've come early too. What's happening? Do you have the final results?

THE WIFE   What a disgrace!

THE FRIEND   You mustn't crush him like this, dear friend. (*To* THE ACADEMICIAN.) You have failed.

THE ACADEMICIAN   Are you quite sure?

THE FRIEND   You should never have tried to pass the baccalaureate examination.

THE ACADEMICIAN   They failed me. The rats! How dare they do this to me!

THE FRIEND   The marks were posted late in the evening.

THE ACADEMICIAN   Perhaps it was difficult to make them out in the dark. How could you read them?

THE FRIEND   They had set up spotlights.

THE ACADEMICIAN   They're doing everything to ruin me.

THE FRIEND   I passed by in the morning; the marks were still up.

THE ACADEMICIAN   You could have bribed the concierge into pulling them down.

THE FRIEND   That's exactly what I did. Unfortunately the police were there. Your name heads the list of those who failed. Everyone's standing in line to get a look. There's an awful crush.

THE ACADEMICIAN   Who's there? The parents of the candidates?

THE FRIEND   Not only they.

THE WIFE   All your rivals, all your colleagues must be there. All those you attacked in the press for ignorance: your undergraduates, your graduate students, all those you failed when you were chairman of the board of examiners.

THE ACADEMICIAN   I am discredited! But I won't let them. There must be some mistake.

THE FRIEND   I saw the examiners. I spoke with them. They gave me your marks. Zero in mathematics.

THE ACADEMICIAN   I had no scientific training.

THE FRIEND   Zero in Greek, zero in Latin.

THE WIFE (*to her husband*)   You, a humanist, the spokesman for humanism, the author of that famous treatise "The Defense of Poesy and Humanism."

THE ACADEMICIAN   I beg your pardon, but my book concerns itself with twentieth century humanism. (*To* THE FRIEND.) What about composition? What grade did I get in composition?

THE FRIEND   Nine hundred. You have nine hundred points.

THE ACADEMICIAN   That's perfect. My average must be all the way up.

THE FRIEND   Unfortunately not. They're marking on the basis of two thousand. The passing grade is one thousand.

THE ACADEMICIAN   They must have changed the regulations.

THE WIFE   They didn't change them just for you. You have a frightful persecution complex.

THE ACADEMICIAN   I tell you they changed them.

THE FRIEND   They went back to the old ones, back to the time of Napoleon.

THE ACADEMICIAN   Utterly outmoded. Besides, when did they make those changes? It isn't legal. I'm chairman of the Baccalaureate Commission of the Ministry of Public Education. They didn't consult me, and they cannot make any changes without my approval. I'm going to expose them. I'm going to bring government charges against them.

THE WIFE   Darling, you don't know what you're doing. You're in your dotage. Don't you recall handing in your resignation just before taking the examination so that no one could doubt the complete objectivity of the board of examiners?

THE ACADEMICIAN   I'll take it back.

THE WIFE   You should never have taken that test. I warned you. After all, it's not as if you needed it. But you have to collect all the honors, don't you? You're never satisfied. What did you need this diploma for? Now all is lost. You have your Doctorate, your

Master's, your high school diploma, your elementary school certificate, and even the first part of the baccalaureate.

THE ACADEMICIAN   There was a gap.

THE WIFE   No one suspected it.

THE ACADEMICIAN   But *I* knew it. Others might have found out. I went to the office of the Registrar and asked for a transcript of my record. They said to me: "Certainly Professor, Mr. President, Your Excellency. . . ." Then they looked up my file, and the Chief Registrar came back looking embarrassed, most embarrassed indeed. He said: "There's something peculiar, very peculiar. You have your Master's, certainly, but it's no longer valid." I asked him why, of course. He answered: "There's a gap behind your Master's. I don't know how it happened. You must have registered and been accepted at the University without having passed the second part of the baccalaureate examination."

THE FRIEND   And then?

THE WIFE   Your Master's degree is no longer valid?

THE ACADEMICIAN   No, not quite. It's suspended. "The duplicate you are asking for will be delivered to you upon completion of the baccalaureate. Of course you will pass the examination with no trouble." That's what I was told, so you see now that I had to take it.

THE FRIEND   Your husband, dear friend, wanted to fill the gap. He's a conscientious person.

THE WIFE   It's clear you don't know him as I do. That's not it at all. He wants fame, honors. He never had enough. What does one diploma more or less matter? No one notices them anyway, but he sneaks in at night, on tiptoe, into the living room, just to look at them, and count them.

THE ACADEMICIAN   What else can I do when I have insomnia?

THE FRIEND   The questions asked at the baccalaureate are usually known in advance. You were admirably situated to get this particular information. You could also have sent in a replacement to take the test for you. One of your students, perhaps. Or if you wanted to take the test without people realizing that you already knew the questions, you could have sent your maid to the black market, where one can buy them.

THE ACADEMICIAN   I don't understand how I could have failed in my composition. I filled three sheets of paper, I treated the subject fully, taking into account the historical background. I interpreted the situation accurately . . . at least plausibly. I didn't deserve a bad grade.

THE FRIEND   Do you recall the subject?

THE ACADEMICIAN   Hum . . . let's see. . . .

THE FRIEND   He doesn't even remember what he discussed.

THE ACADEMICIAN   I do . . . wait . . . hum.

THE FRIEND   The subject to be treated was the following: "Discuss the influence of Renaissance painters on novelists of the Third Republic." I have here a photostatic copy of your examination paper. Here is what you wrote.

THE ACADEMICIAN   (*grabbing the photostat and reading*)   "The trial of Benjamin: After Benjamin was tried and acquitted, the assessors holding a different opinion from that of the President murdered him, and condemned Benjamin to the suspension of his civic rights, imposing on him a fine of nine hundred francs. . . ."

THE FRIEND   That's where the nine hundred points come from.

THE ACADEMICIAN   "Benjamin appealed his case . . . Benjamin appealed his case. . . ." I can't make out the rest. I've always had bad handwriting. I ought to have taken a typewriter along with me.

THE WIFE   Horrible handwriting, scribbling and crossing out; ink spots didn't help you much.

THE ACADEMICIAN   (*goes on with his reading after having retrieved the text his wife had pulled out of his hand*)   "Benjamin appealed his case. Flanked by policemen dressed in zouave uniforms . . . in zouave uniforms. . . ." It's getting dark. I can't see the rest. . . . I don't have my glasses.

THE WIFE   What you've written has nothing to do with the subject.

THE FRIEND   Your wife's quite right, friend. It has nothing to do with the subject.

THE ACADEMICIAN   Yes, it has. Indirectly.

THE FRIEND   Not even indirectly.

THE ACADEMICIAN   Perhaps I chose the second question.

THE FRIEND   There was only one.

THE ACADEMICIAN   Even if there was only that one, I treated another quite adequately. I went to the end of the story. I stressed the important points, explaining the motivations of the characters, highlighting their behavior. I explained the mystery, making it plain and clear. There was even a conclusion at the end. I can't make out the rest. (*To* THE FRIEND.) Can you read it?

THE FRIEND   It's illegible. I don't have my glasses either.

THE WIFE   (*taking the text*)   It's illegible and I have excellent eyes. You pretended to write. Mere scribbling.

THE ACADEMICIAN   That's not true. I've even provided a conclusion. It's clearly marked here in heavy print: "Conclusion or sanction . . . Conclusion or sanction. . . ." They can't get away with it. I'll have this examination rendered null and void.

THE WIFE   Since you treated the wrong subject, and treated it badly, setting down only titles, and writing nothing in between, the mark you received is justified. You'd lose your case.

THE FRIEND   You'd most certainly lose. Drop it. Take a vacation.

THE ACADEMICIAN   You're always on the side of the Others.

THE WIFE   After all, these professors know what they're doing. They haven't been granted their rank for nothing. They passed examinations, received serious training. They know the rules of composition.

THE ACADEMICIAN   Who was on the board of examiners?

THE FRIEND   For Mathematics, a movie star. For Greek, one of the Beatles. For Latin, the champion of the automobile race, and many others.

THE ACADEMICIAN   But these people aren't any more qualified than I am. And for composition?

THE FRIEND   A woman, a secretary in the editorial division of the review *Yesterday, the Day Before Yesterday, and Today.*

THE ACADEMICIAN   Now I know. This wretch gave me a poor grade out of spite because I never joined her political party. It's an act of vengeance. But I have ways and means of rendering the examination null and void. I'm going to call the President.

THE WIFE   Don't. You'll make yourself look even more ridiculous. (*To* THE FRIEND.) Please try to restrain him. He listens to you more than to me. (THE FRIEND *shrugs his shoulders, unable to cope with the situation.* THE WIFE *turns to her husband, who has just lifted the receiver off the hook.*) Don't call!

THE ACADEMICIAN (*on the telephone*)   Hello, John? It is I . . . What? . . . What did you say? . . . But, listen, my dear friend . . . but, listen to me . . Hello! Hello! (*Puts down the receiver.*)

THE FRIEND   What did he say?

THE ACADEMICIAN   He said. . . He said. . . . "I don't want to talk to you. My mummy won't let me make friends with boys at the bottom of the class." Then he hung up on me.

THE WIFE   You should have expected it. All is lost. How could you do this to me? How could you do this to me?

THE ACADEMICIAN   Think of it! I lectured at the Sorbonne, at Oxford, at American universities. Ten thousand theses have been written on my work; hundreds of critics have analyzed it. I hold an *honoris causa* doctorate from Amsterdam as well as a secret university Chair with the Duchy of Luxembourg. I received the Nobel Prize three times. The King of Sweden himself was amazed by my erudition. A doctorate *honoris causa, honoris causa* . . . and I failed the baccalaureate examination!

THE WIFE   Everyone will laugh at us!

THE ACADEMICIAN *takes off his sword and breaks it on his knee.*

THE FRIEND (*picking up the two pieces*)   I wish to preserve these in memory of our ancient glory.

THE ACADEMICIAN *meanwhile in a fit of rage is tearing down his decorations, throwing them on the floor, and stepping on them.*

THE WIFE (*trying to salvage the remains*)   Don't do this! Don't! That's all we've got left.

Curtain

SELECT BIBLIOGRAPHY

This is a highly selective bibliography designed to provide a list of basic critical and historical references pertinent to the study of dramatic literature. A number of these books are out of print, but they are standard works and most of them should be available in any college or university library. Many contain extensive bibliographies of their own.

Studies of individual dramatists are so numerous, what with research anthologies, books of interpretation, and collections of various essays, that to list any of them, however limited, would be impractical. Students are therefore urged to consult their library catalogues if further pursuit of any one author is desired. Outstanding in their publication of critical essays on a wide variety of dramatists and their works are the Prentice-Hall series, *Twentieth Century Views* and *Twentieth Century Interpretations*. The Twayne Authors Series is also good, but frequently uneven in quality.

General References

FREEDLEY, GEORGE, and JOHN A. REEVES. *A History of the Theatre.* New York, Crown, 1955.

GASSNER, JOHN. *Masters of the Drama,* 3d ed. New York, Dover, 1954.

LEECH, CLIFFORD, and T. W. CRAIK, gen. eds. *The Revels History of Drama in English,* 8 vols. London, Methuen, 1975 and following.

A compendium of extended essays by a variety of noted theatre and drama historians, covering the drama in English from its beginnings. See below for the volume on American drama.

MACGOWAN, KENNETH, and WILLIAM MELNITZ. *The Living Stage: A History of the World Theatre.* Englewood Cliffs, N.J., Prentice-Hall, 1955.

NICOLL, ALLARDYCE. *The Development of the Theatre.* New York, Harcourt Brace, 1967.

————. *World Drama.* New York, Harcourt Brace, 1950.

STEINER, GEORGE. *The Death of Tragedy.* New York, Knopf, 1961.

SYPHER, WYLIE. *Comedy.* New York, Doubleday, 1956.

Steiner's and Sypher's books are valuable studies in the concepts of tragedy and comedy throughout history. Steiner's first chapter is especially valuable. Sypher's volume is actually three separate studies: "An Essay on Comedy," by George Meredith, and "Laughter," by Henri Bergson, both of which are very famous studies, and the third study, Sypher's own essay, "The Meaning of Comedy."

Classical Drama

EPPS, PRESTON H. *The Poetics of Aristotle.* Chapel Hill, Univ. of N.C. Press, 1970.

There are many versions of *The Poetics.* This is a convenient and very readable one.

HAMILTON, EDITH. *The Greek Way.* New York, The New American Library, reprinted from Little, Brown edition, Boston, 1942.

————. *Mythology,* New York, The New American Library, 1953, reprinted from Little, Brown edition, Boston, 1942.

These are not about drama as such but are basic texts for the study of the

Greek view of themselves, the gods, and tragedy. They are also fascinating reading.

KITTO, H. D. F. *Greek Tragedy*. Garden City, N.Y., Doubleday, 1954.

KOTT, JAN. *The Eating of the Gods: An Interpretation of Greek Tragedy*. New York, Vintage Books, Random House, 1974.

NORWOOD, GILBERT. *Greek Comedy*. New York, Hill & Wang Dramabook, 1963.

————. *Greek Tragedy*. New York, Hill & Wang Dramabook, 1960.

Shakespeare

The books on Shakespeare are, of course, legion. The following works provide a variety of studies of Shakespeare and his theatre.

CHUTE, MARCHETTE. *Shakespeare of London*. New York, Dutton, 1949.

FLUCHERE, HENRI. *Shakespeare and the Elizabethans*. New York, Hill & Wang, 1956.

GRANVILLE-BARKER, HARLEY. *Prefaces to Shakespeare*, rev. ed. London, Batsford, 1972.
These are classic essays on individual plays. Especially recommended is the preface to *Hamlet*.

HARBAGE, ALFRED. *As They Liked It*. New York, Macmillan, 1947.

————. *Shakespeare's Audiences*, New York, Columbia Univ., 1941.

HODGES, C. WALTER. *The Globe Restored*. London, Benn, 1953.

JONES, ERNEST. *Hamlet and Oedipus*, New York, Doubleday, 1954.

SMITH, WARREN D. *Shakespeare's Playhouse Practice*. Hanover, N.H., Univ. Press of New England, 1973.

Seventeenth-Century French and English Restoration

KRUTCH, JOSEPH WOOD. *Comedy and Conscience after the Restoration*. New York, Columbia Univ., 1949.
The best single source of explanation and analysis of the British Restoration drama and its society.

LAWRENSON, T. E. *The French Stage of the 17th Century*. Manchester, Engl., Univ. of Manchester, 1957.

WILCOX, JOHN. *The Relation of Molière to Restoration Comedy*. New York, Columbia Univ., 1938.

WILSON, JOHN HAROLD. *All the King's Ladies*. Chicago, Univ. of Chicago, 1958.

The Modern Era

The following represent general histories and critical studies of the drama of Europe, England, and America, from the latter part of the nineteenth century until the present.

BIGSBY, C. W. E. *Confrontation and Commitment: A Study of Contemporary American Drama*. Columbia, Univ. of Missouri, 1968.

————. *A Critical Introduction to Twentieth Century American Drama*, 3 vols. Cambridge, Cambridge Univ., 1982, 1984, 1985.

BOGARD, TRAVIS, et al. *The Revels History of Drama in English*, vol. 8. London, Methuen, 1975.

BROCKETT, OSCAR G., and ROBERT R. FINDLAY. *Century of Innovation: A History of*

European and American Theatre and Drama Since 1870. Englewood Cliffs, N.J., Prentice-Hall, 1973.

BENTLEY, ERIC. *The Theory of the Modern Theatre.* New York, Penguin, 1979.

DRIVER, TOM F. *Romantic Quest and Modern Query: A History of the Modern Theatre.* New York, Dell, 1970.

ESSLIN, MARTIN. *The Theatre of the Absurd,* 3d rev. ed. London, Methuen, 1974. The book which contributed a new, and highly controversial, term to the study of modern drama.

KRUTCH, JOSEPH WOOD. *The American Drama Since 1918.* New York, George Braziller, 1957.

————. *Modernism in Modern Drama.* Ithaca, Cornell, 1953.

MOODY, RICHARD. *America Takes the Stage,* Bloomington, Univ. of Indiana, 1955.

SHAW, BERNARD. *The Quintessence of Ibsenism.* Toronto, Univ. of Toronto, 1959. Shaw's classic study of the Norwegian, reflecting, of course, many of Shaw's views beyond Ibsen alone.

VALENCY, MAURICE. *The Flower and the Castle: An Introduction to Modern Drama.* New York, Macmillan, 1963.

WILSON, GARFF B. *Three Hundred Years of American Drama and Theatre.* Englewood Cliffs, N.J., Prentice-Hall, 1973.

INDEX OF TERMS

INDEX OF AUTHORS

3 4 5 6 7 8 9 0